KATHERINE PARR

KATHERINE PARR

COMPLETE WORKS AND CORRESPONDENCE

EDITED BY JANEL MUELLER

THE UNIVERSITY OF CHICAGO PRESS
Chicago and London

The University of Chicago Press, Chicago 60637
The University of Chicago Press, Ltd., London

Paperback edition 2014
Printed in the United States of America

23 22 21 20 19 18 17 16 15 14 2 3 4 5 6

ISBN-13: 978-0-226-64724-1 (cloth)
ISBN-13: 978-0-226-21379-8 (paperback)
ISBN-13: 978-0-226-64726-5 (ebook)
10.7208/chicago/9780226647265.001.0001

The University of Chicago Press gratefully acknowledges the generous support of the Division of the Humanities at the University of Chicago, and the Andrew W. Mellon Foundation, toward the publication of this book.

Library of Congress Cataloging-in-Publication Data

Catharine Parr, Queen, consort of Henry VIII, King of England, 1512–1548. [Works. 2011]
Complete works and correspondence / Katherine Parr ; edited by Janel Mueller.
p. cm.
Includes index.
ISBN-13: 978-0-226-64724-1 (cloth : alk. paper)
ISBN-10: 0-226-64724-2 (cloth : alk. paper) 1. Catharine Parr, Queen, consort of Henry VIII, King of England, 1512–1548—Correspondence. 2. Catharine Parr, Queen, consort of Henry VIII, King of England, 1512–1548—Religion. I. Mueller, Janel M., 1938– II. Title.
DA333.P3A2 2011
942.05'2092—dc22
2010039369

♾ This paper meets the requirements of ANSI/NISO Z39.48-1992 (Permanence of Paper).

CONTENTS

PREFACE

❧

This edition is the fruit of two discontinuous periods of scholarly activity. In the early to mid 1990s I transcribed and provisionally annotated the bulk of Katherine Parr's correspondence as well as *Prayers or Meditations* and *The Lamentation of a Sinner*. After a detour (but who can call it such?) into coediting the works of Elizabeth I, the completion of those four volumes enabled me to resume and progress more quickly in 2008–10 with transcribing and annotating the two additional works attributable to Parr: *Psalms or Prayers* and my own discovery, her autograph personal prayerbook (British Library, Harley MS 2342). Due to the hiatus, I have two sets of people to acknowledge and thank for indispensable assistance as I have wended my prolonged way.

During summer sojourns in England in 1993 and 1996, I benefited from the generosity of several people in gaining access to various primary sources. Mr. Percy S. Duff, treasurer of Kendal Town Council, kindly arranged for me to transcribe the Kendal autograph fragment of *Prayers or Meditations*. Lady Elizabeth Ashcombe of Sudeley Castle graciously permitted me to examine and transcribe autograph materials in the hands of Parr, Henry VIII, and Thomas Seymour from books and papers in her collection. Robin Harcourt Williams, librarian and archivist of Hatfield House, made several autograph letters available to me. For access and permission to transcribe early editions of *Prayers or Meditations* and *The Lamentation of a Sinner* as well as various letters and documents, I am indebted to several Cambridge college librarians: Mrs. E. M. Coleman of The Pepys Library, Magdalene College; Rhiannon Jones of the Emmanuel College Library; and the librarians of Corpus Christi College and of Pembroke College, who modestly declined to give me their names. I am additionally indebted to Mr. R. C. Yorke, archivist, and Mrs. G. Cannell, librarian, of the College of Arms, London, for enabling me to transcribe the contemporary manuscript account of Katherine Parr's funeral. Beyond these individual kindnesses in this earlier period, warm gratitude is owed to the knowledgeable, helpful staff of the major manuscript collections in the British Library (then located in the British Museum) and the Public Record Office (then located in Chancery Lane, before its transformation into the National Archives at Kew). A high point of my earlier phase of work was an invitation to offer a Folger Shakespeare Library seminar in the fall semester of 1994 on the writings of Katherine Parr and Elizabeth I. Beyond the catalysts to my often tentative thoughts and hunches provided by the able, motivated enrollees in my seminar, I profited from the courtesies and assistance of the program's director, Dr. Kathleen Lynch, and of Folger's polymathic research librarian, Dr. Georgianna Ziegler. I remain most grateful.

The intervening stretch of years brought invigorating engagements with other scholars interested in Katherine Parr: Diarmaid Mac Cullough (he and I were guest copresenters in a Folger summer seminar), John N. King, Jeri McIntosh, Cathy Shrank, and Micheline White. Their perspectives, questions, and intuitions have been a valuable stimulus.

Resuming work in England on this edition a decade and more later, I again benefited from the generosity of several people in permitting access to various primary sources. The staff of the rare books and manuscripts reading room of Cambridge University Library facilitated my transcriptions of jottings in the book of hours owned by Sir Thomas Parr, Katherine's father. Juliet Chadwick, librarian of Exeter College, Oxford, enabled me to check a transcription I had made from a microfilm of *Psalms or Prayers* against the very rare copy preserved there. Lady Meredyth Proby of Elton Hall gave freely of her interest and hospitality when I visited its library and transcribed the inscriptions in the copies of *Psalms or Prayers* and Cranmer's Litany that are the subjects of my appendix 1. John Abbott of collection care at the National Archives afforded me special access to two documents then undergoing conservation: Cranmer's Latin license authorizing the marriage of Henry VIII and Katherine Parr, and Richard Watkins's account of the marriage proceedings. Again, too, the auspices of the manuscript reading room of the British Library provided indispensable assistance and access, in particular, to Harley MS 2342 (Parr's autograph personal prayerbook), Edward VI's epistolary copy book (Harley MS 5087), and several collections of letters and documents.

The Andrew W. Mellon Foundation advanced my vision and aspirations for this edition by generously underwriting research and publication expenses with the award of an emeritus fellowship in calendar 2008 and 2009. I owe a greater debt than I can readily express to Don Michael Randel, Harriet Zuckerman, and Joe Meisel for their trust, encouragement, and understanding. I am also grateful to administrators and staff at the University of Chicago for their roles in implementing the cooperation of the home institution with provisions of the Mellon grant: Dean Martha T. Roth, Simrit Dhesi, Jennie Myers, and Daniel Parisi.

In broader terms and in manifold ways, the University of Chicago has enlivened, channeled, and sustained the entire course of my academic career, not just the preparation of this edition. It is a pleasure to acknowledge the colleagueship of David Bevington, Bradin Cormack, Michael Murrin, Wendy Olmsted, Joshua Scodel, and Richard Strier, manifested most recently in vigorous discussion of my edition's general introduction at a meeting of the Renaissance Workshop in 2009. On that occasion I also profited from incisive questions raised by PhD student Billy Junker at the outset of discussion.

It gives me no less pleasure to acknowledge the combined rigor and nurture that my work has received over the years from the University of Chicago Press. At the crucial evaluation stage, the (then anonymous) referees Susan M. Felch and Anne Lake Prescott gave unstintingly of their acuity and knowledge in critiquing my manuscript and pinpointing needed improvements. Among Press personnel, I owe particular thanks to Alan Thomas, Randy Petilos, Ruth Goring, and Micah Fehrenbacher, as well as to Jill Shimabukuro, Renate Gokl, Maia Wright, and Joan Davies, who coped with the design and production challenges posed by this edition.

In the classroom and in discussions beyond, Katherine Parr's biography, correspondence, and works have held a special fascination for successive cohorts of my women students (in fact, the microfilm of *Psalms or Prayers* mentioned earlier was obtained for me by Meiling Hazelton when she was a Rhodes scholar). This edition of *Katherine Parr: Complete Works and Correspondence* is dedicated to the memory of two exceptionally capable and creative University of Chicago undergraduates, Meiling Hazelton (1973–2009) and Kathleen A. Kelly (1960–2009), whom I had the privilege to teach, to know, and to cherish.

Figure 1. Opening page of Kendal autograph fragment of Katherine Parr's Prayers or Meditations. *Photograph by Trevor Hughes. Copyright © Kendal Town Council.*

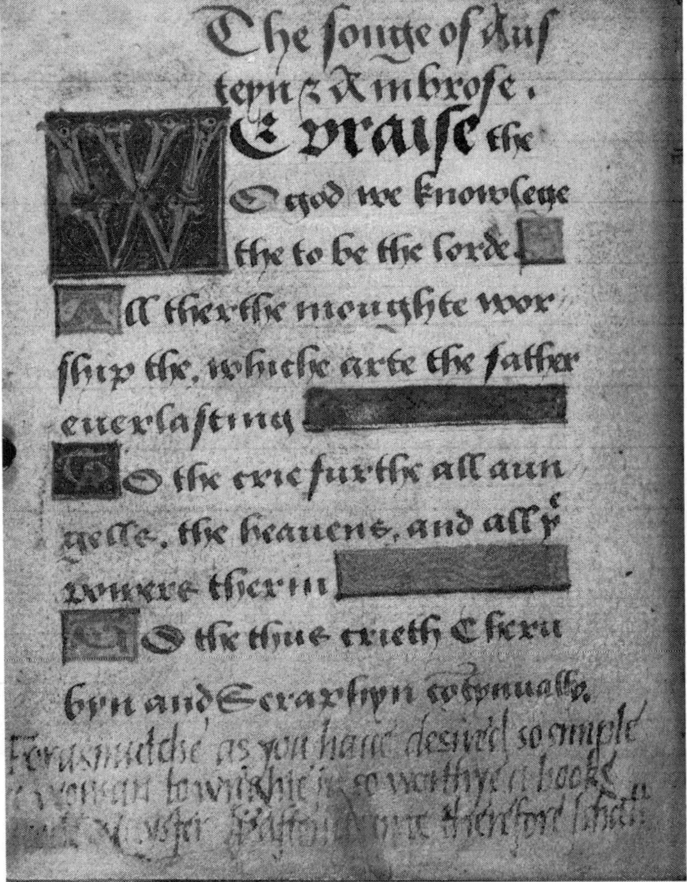

Figure 2. Illuminated page in British Library, Harley MS 2342 (fol. 74V). Copyright © The British Library Board.

GENERAL INTRODUCTION

The first woman to publish in print a work of her own under her own name, in England and in English, was Katherine Parr, King Henry VIII's last queen, who survived him into widowhood as a royal dowager.[1] The wording of the work's title seems implicitly to explain why Parr is identified as the author: *PRAYERS OR Medytacions . . . Collected out of holy woorkes by the most vertuous and graciouse Princesse Katherine quene of Englande, Fraunce, and Irelande. Anno domini 1545.*[2] Such public acknowledgment by name accrued to her, evidently, by virtue of her rank as queen. Biography looks like destiny in registering this first for Katherine Parr as a female author in English.

A presumptive link between royal status and the naming of a female in conjunction with a work's publication is borne out by the few facts pertaining to the

1. The popular mnemonic rhyme "Divorced, beheaded, died; / Divorced, beheaded, survived" serves to situate Katherine Parr last in the sequence of Henry's queens, after Catherine of Aragon, Anne Boleyn, Jane Seymour, Anne of Cleves, and Katherine Howard. Seemingly aware that a means of distinguishing her from Henry VIII's other Catherines could be useful to her and to others, Katherine Parr always appended the initials of her birth name to her royal signature: "Kateryn the Quene KP." Because she herself employed this abbreviation of her name, it is used in the notes to the present edition.

2. In fact, three editions of this work were published in 1545, all explicitly attributed to Katherine as queen. Two of these, identical except for differently worded main titles, appeared on June 2: *Prayers stirryng the mynd vnto heauenly medytacions* (STC 4818) and *Prayers or meditacions, wherin the mynde is styrred* (STC 4818.5); both of these editions append two prayers, the second possibly written by KP. Another edition, also titled *Prayers or Medytacions, wherein the mynd is stirred* (STC 4819), appeared on November 6; it is the first complete edition of this work, appending a full set of five prayers, four of which may be KP's compositions.

question for the first seventy-five years of print in England.[3] The earliest evidence comes from William Atkynson's composite English version of Thomas à Kempis's *De Imitatione Christi*, published in 1503–4. Atkynson translated the first three books of the *Imitatio* from the original Latin but printed the fourth book, as the heading within the text states, "at the commaundement of Margarete," Countess of Richmond and Derby, mother of King Henry VII, "and by the same prynces [princess] traunslated oute of frenche."[4] By contrast, around 1526, when Richard Hyrde saw through the press the English translation of Erasmus's *Precatio Dominica* made by Margaret More Roper, Sir Thomas More's superbly educated oldest daughter, its title page left her identity unspecified: *A deuout treatise vpon the Pater noster, made fyrst in latyn and tourned in to englisshe by a yong gentylwoman.*[5]

Again by contrast, when John Bale somehow obtained and published in 1548 at Marburg, Germany, the English prose translation of Marguerite de Navarre's poem *Le Miroir de l'âme pécheresse*, made as a gift for New Year's 1545 by Princess Elizabeth for her stepmother, Queen Katherine Parr, Bale proudly identified the young royal translator three times over. His prefatory letter to Elizabeth salutes her lineage; she appears crowned and kneeling at the feet of Christ in a woodcut on the title page and again on the last page; and she and her rank (as well as her virtue and learning) are prominently credited in the title that Bale gives to her work: *A Godly Medytacion of the christen sowle . . . compyled in frenche by Lady Margarete quene of Nauer, and aptely translated into Englysh by the ryght vertuouse lady Elyzabeth doughter to our late souerayne Kynge Henri the viij.*[6]

Rather than the special treatment accorded to exalted rank, however, the prolific body of recent scholarship on women's writing in early modern England has tended to emphasize a generic factor—the frequent choice of religious and devo-

3. The ensuing discussion bypasses, as an indecipherable enigma, the reference "Explicit Dam Julians Barnes in her boke of huntyng" in *The book of hawking, hunting and blasing of arms* (St. Albans, 1486) (STC 3308), sig. f3j r. See Julia Boffey, "Berners, Juliana," article 2255 in the online *Oxford Dictionary of National Biography* (2004).

4. STC 23954.7 and accompanying bibliographical information. Throughout the present edition the first citation of the title of a work is given in original spelling; subsequent citations are in modern spelling.

5. STC 10477 and accompanying bibliographical information. John A. Guy notes the applicable inhibitions: "Margaret didn't contemplate publishing under her own name. . . . Fully aware of the risk to her modesty, she meant to conform broadly to the expectations of her father and his society" (*A Daughter's Love: Thomas More and Margaret More* [London: Fourth Estate, 2008], 149). Guy also remarks on the disparate destinies of Margaret More's unpublished and now lost work on the Four Last Things and Thomas More's ultimately published work on the same subject; "her father sincerely protested [that Margaret's] was better than his" (ibid., 73–74).

6. STC 17320. For a reproduction of the woodcut image of the kneeling Princess Elizabeth, see Marc Shell, *Elizabeth's Glass* (Lincoln: University of Nebraska Press, 1993), 5; for her translated text, see *Elizabeth I: Translations, 1544–1589*, ed. Janel Mueller and Joshua Scodel (Chicago: University of Chicago Press, 2009), 25–125.

tional materials—by which women writers of whatever rank secured cultural validation for themselves and strengthened their incentive to write and publish.[7] No exceptions in this regard, the above-cited literary productions of Queen Katherine Parr, Lady Margaret Beaufort, Margaret More Roper, and Princess Elizabeth are conspicuous for their devotional cast. Devotion, moreover, remains the primary genre and referent for Parr's authorial output from first to last. Yet in proposing to account for Katherine Parr's authorship, an interpretive choice does not have to be made between devotion and royal rank. As she confides in a letter written to Henry VIII in the summer of 1544, a year after she became his wife and queen, she experiences God's grace and the king's graciousness to her as closely concurrent if not convergent sources of blessings:

> I make like account with your majesty as I do with God for His benefits and gifts heaped upon me daily, acknowledging myself always a great debtor unto Him . . . , not being able to recompense the least of His benefits: in which state I am certain and sure to die, but yet I hope in His gracious acceptation of my goodwill. And even such confidence I have in your majesty's gentleness, knowing myself never to have done my duty as was requisite and meet to such a noble and worthy prince, at whose hands I have found and received so much love and goodness, that with words I cannot express it.[8]

The preceding quotation sets the perspective for the present edition of Katherine Parr's correspondence and complete works. The fact that all her works are religious in nature compels recognition of the importance of devotion as an incentive for

7. Scholarship on this topic has grown extensive. Formative contributions include the essays in *Silent but for the Word: Tudor Women as Translators, Patrons, and Writers of Religious Works*, ed. Margaret P. Hannay (Kent, OH: Kent State University Press, 1985) and those in *Women and Literature in Britain, 1500–1700*, ed. Helen Wilcox (Cambridge: Cambridge University Press, 1996) as well as the primary texts and critical commentary in *The Renaissance Englishwoman in Print: Counterbalancing the Canon*, ed. Anne M. Haselkorn and Betty S. Travitsky (Amherst: University of Massachusetts Press, 1990) and *Half Humankind: Contexts and Texts of the Controversy about Women in England, 1540–1640*, ed. Katherine Usher Henderson and Barbara F. McManus (Urbana: University of Illinois Press, 1985). Margaret R. Sommerville sums up as follows: "It was a medieval platitude that the female sex was the more pious. . . . Renaissance theorists admitted to few areas where the whole female sex excelled the male but a number held that devotion, prayer, and church attendance was one. . . . Not all women were inferior to all males. . . . All women might comfort themselves with the belief that they could outdo males in piety" (*Sex and Subjection: Attitudes to Women in Early-Modern Society* [London: Arnold, 1995], 42–43).

8. The full text of this letter is no. 11 in part 2 of the correspondence. Spelling and punctuation are modernized here and in subsequent quotations.

female authorship in early modern England. In the latter sections of this edition, where Parr's complete works are presented in chronological order, devotion comes repeatedly to the fore. In the earlier sections, however, the sequencing and grouping of Parr's correspondence, broadly construed, aim to establish her biography as not only important but a sine qua non of her earliness as an English woman author.

To call biography a sine qua non is to gesture pointedly at the absence of any evidence of literary production (including correspondence) by Katherine Parr until she becomes Henry VIII's queen in July 1543; thereafter, the evidence in both categories is appreciable and increasingly self-assured. But if Parr's biography as the precondition of her authorship and its public expression turns crucially on her position as Henry VIII's queen, there are contributory factors from her earlier life to be reckoned with as well. Most prominent among these are her family's history of acquaintance with the court through her father's and her mother's careers of professional service, and the advantage of an educational preparation that, however irretrievable in its specifics, left decisive traces in Parr's capacity to recognize and capitalize on opportunities for authorship when they came her way.

The thorough biographical research provided by Susan E. James in *Kateryn Parr: The Making of a Queen* (1999) has been an invaluable resource in preparing the present edition of Katherine Parr's complete works and correspondence.[9] The correspondence, consisting of primary materials divided into five parts, is positioned as a contextual frame for the four literary works to follow. My use of the term *correspondence* revives its currently less prominent sense of "connection" to encompass letters to and from Katherine Parr; documents pertaining to her marriage to Henry VIII in 1543 and to her death after bearing a daughter to Lord Thomas Seymour in 1548; proclamations and instructions that she issued as regent of the realm during Henry's military campaign in France in 1544; dedications addressed to her as the commissioning patron of a project to translate and publish for open access in English churches the first five books of Erasmus's Latin *Paraphrases upon the New Testament*; and verses addressed to her or describing her and her intimates. Parr's complete works, positioned to follow the correspondence, include the two publications that appeared in her lifetime and bear her name as author, *Prayers or Meditations* (1545) and *The Lamentation of a Sinner* (1547), as well as *Psalms or Prayers* (1544), the anonymously published English translation of Bishop John Fisher's *Psalmi seu Precationes* (Cologne, ca. 1525; reprinted London, 1544), which on a variety of circumstantial grounds can plausibly be ascribed to Parr as queen.[10]

9. Although Anthony K. Martienssen's biography, *Queen Katherine Parr* (New York: McGraw-Hill, 1973), lacks scholarly pretensions and sometimes relies too heavily on conjecture, it offers many apt and sensitive insights. Some new information and insights grace the most recent biography, by Linda Porter, *Katherine the Queen: The Remarkable Life of Katherine Parr* (London: Macmillan, 2010).

10. For prior argument see Susan E. James, *Kateryn Parr: The Making of a Queen* (Aldershot, UK: Ashgate, 1999), 200–207.

Rounding out the category of "complete works" is British Library MS Harley 2342, the sizable compilation of devotional materials that I have identified as Katherine Parr's personal prayerbook, written entirely in her own hand and left unfinished in manuscript at her death in 1548. A separate introduction is provided for each of Queen Katherine's four works. To facilitate the reader's engagement with her correspondence, the remainder of this general introduction outlines significant aspects of her biography and concludes with a brief statement of editorial procedures.[11]

Katherine Parr's parents, Sir Thomas Parr (1478–1517) and Matilda or Maud Green Parr (1492–1531), were both in service at the court of Henry VIII, who came to the throne in 1509 at the age of eighteen. Despite Parr family roots and properties in Westmorland, Sir Thomas and Maud mainly resided in the south of England within convenient reach of the court. Sir Thomas was popular with Henry VIII, serving his sovereign variously as a member of several diplomatic missions to France and as master of the king's wards. Nonetheless, political advancement and financial success eluded Sir Thomas. Maud Parr served Queen Catherine of Aragon as a lady-in-waiting; over time the two women became close friends. Prior to Katherine's birth in the summer (probably August) of 1512, the Parrs purchased or leased a house in the Blackfriars quarter of London. Katherine may well have been born in this house, as was an elder brother who died in infancy and was buried in the churchyard of St. Anne's, Blackfriars. Two more Parr children followed in quick succession—a brother, William, in August 1513, and a sister, Anne, around 1515. In November 1517, Sir Thomas Parr died suddenly in his fortieth year, leaving his twenty-five-year-old widow, Maud, to raise their three small children.[12]

From all evidence, circumstantial and textual (some extant letters in her hand), Maud Parr was a resourceful, determined, intelligent woman who made the choice, unusual for her time, not to remarry. Instead, she divided herself between sustaining her service and familiarity with Queen Catherine and providing as a single parent for the education and future of Katherine, William, and Anne. The children's formative years were spent at Rye House in Hertfordshire, the family's more or less permanent home after Sir Thomas's death, until Maud Parr's own death in late 1531. Maud was advised on the education of her daughters and son by Cuthbert Tunstall, Bishop of London and, later, Bishop of Durham—a cousin of Sir Thomas's and one of the executors of his will. A single tutor educated the three Parr children under a program of study that included Latin, French, Italian, arithmetic, and even some

11. Portions of the following biographical summary have appeared in Janel Mueller, "Katherine Parr and Her Circle," in *The Oxford Handbook to Tudor Literature, 1485–1603*, ed. Mike Pincombe and Cathy Shrank (Oxford: Oxford University Press, 2009), 222–37.

12. James, *Kateryn Parr*, 9–14, 17; Porter, *Katherine the Queen*, 21–23. Katherine's likeliest alternative birthplace is Rye House in Hertfordshire.

basic medical lore.[13] As an adult, Anne Parr recalled that her mother had modeled her children's studies on those prescribed by Sir Thomas More for the children and wards of his household.[14]

From this formative educational period there is a sole material remnant, the deceased Sir Thomas's *Horae ad Usum Sarum*, a book of hours or primer of Salisbury use in Latin, with a few appended prayers in English. In light of the broad and varied familiarity with this type of devotional collection that Katherine Parr would show in compiling her personal prayerbook as queen, the survival of this particular volume is almost too neatly fortuitous. The inkblots, doodles, and recopied words found inside it attest its use in the Parr children's schoolroom.[15] At the bottoms of intermittent pages, there are inscriptions in English—one in Maud Parr's hand, two in young Katherine's hand, and one in young William's hand—which are reproduced as the first item in part 1 of the correspondence. The similarities to be observed between Maud's and Katherine's hybrid ("bastard") style of handwriting, a variant of the secretary hand, suggest that the mother taught her daughter—and presumably her other children—to write. Each of the inscriptions affectionately addresses the children's uncle, Sir William Parr of Horton, who acted as a father substitute for all three and continued this role into their adult lives.

Beyond ensuring the basics of a sound humanistic education for her children, Maud Parr extended to them the double agenda for advancement that she had set for herself. This consisted in cultivating court connections along a circuit of acquaintance and affiliation with well-born and well-placed persons, and in simultaneously seeking the financial means to enable such cultivation. The weight of Maud Parr's agenda made by far the heaviest personal demands on Katherine, her oldest child. In 1525 Sir William Parr contrived to launch his nephew William's future at the age of eleven by placing him in the household of Henry VIII's bastard son the Duke of Richmond; a marriage with an heiress, Lady Anne Bourchier, followed for William in 1527. Around 1531, at the age of fifteen or sixteen, Anne Parr entered court service as a maid-in-waiting and was subsequently attached to the households of Henry's successive queens—including, eventually, her sister Katherine's. Anne too would contract an advantageous marriage with the soldier-courtier William Herbert, later Earl of Pembroke, around 1538.[16] Yet well before these placements of William and Anne, Maud Parr was determined to marry off her elder

13. James, *Kateryn Parr*, 19, 24–30. Parr's knowledge of French can be inferred from Prince Edward's letter to her in that language; see no. 13 in part 3 of the correspondence. Parr's knowledge of Italian can be inferred from Princess Elizabeth's letter to her in that language; see no. 4 in part 3.

14. Dakota Lee Hamilton, "The Household of Queen Katherine Parr" (DPhil thesis, University of Oxford, 1992), 311–12, cited in James, *Kateryn Parr*, 27.

15. James, *Kateryn Parr*, 30–31; Porter, *Katherine the Queen*, 28.

16. James, *Kateryn Parr*, 40, 88, 96.

daughter as advantageously and promptly as she could contrive. She began her efforts before Katherine had reached her twelfth birthday.

Conducted in a letter exchange between the spring of 1523 and the spring of 1524, Maud's first set of negotiations, for a match with Henry Scrope, son and heir of Henry, Lord Scrope of Bolton, met with frustration. On the Scrope side, doubts about the desirability of the marriage grew, in light of the modest character of Katherine's dowry and lineage. The failure was fortunate, however, for young Henry Scrope died in 1525. If Katherine had married him, she would have been a widow before she turned thirteen.[17]

Maud Parr's second set of negotiations can be said to have succeeded in the sense of obtaining a marriage for Katherine, with Edward Borough, grandson of Edward, Lord Borough of Gainsborough, and son of Sir Thomas Borough, of an old and well-established gentry family in Lincolnshire. The marriage probably occurred in spring 1529, when Katherine was sixteen and her husband, Edward, in his early twenties. Sent to live in the North, a region wholly unknown to her, far from her mother and her siblings, Katherine would probably have had some difficulty in adjusting to her new life even if it had been pleasant. What she found at Gainsborough Old Hall was a young husband in frail health and "an overbearing father-in-law given to violent rages."[18] The young couple endured the vagaries of this multgenerational household for more than a year. When Maud Parr visited her daughter in summer 1530, she significantly chose to stay at her own manor of Maltby, some eighteen miles from Gainsborough Old Hall. Maud's perceptions and her presence seem to have worked to obtain a house for Edward and Katherine at Kirton-in-Lindsey, a property belonging to Edward's father, the irascible Sir Thomas Borough. There the pair maintained a separate household until Edward's death in his midtwenties in April 1533.

Whatever grief widowhood might have entailed for Katherine, she had already lost the first object of her love, her mother.[19] Like Sir Thomas Parr, Maud Parr died in her fortieth year, on December 1, 1531, leaving Katherine "a cross of diamonds with a pendant pearl, a cache of loose pearls, and, ironically or propheticallly, a

17. For observations on Lady Parr's sagacity and tenacity in her marriage negotiations with Lord Scrope, see Barbara Harris, "Women and Politics in Early Tudor England," *Historical Journal* 33 (1990): 262, 268; and James, *Kateryn Parr*, 52–55. The letter exchange regarding this proposed marriage has survived in the collection of Scrope family papers that is British Library Additional MS 24965.

18. James, *Kateryn Parr*, 60–61. Porter (*Katherine the Queen*, 53) has clarified that the newly wed KP did not endure the ravings of the family's demented grandfather, the elder Sir Edward Borough, who died in August 1528, more than six months before KP's marriage.

19. James remarks: "In learning, charity and responsibility for the welfare of her family, Maud was the pattern from which Kateryn constructed her own self-image and her loss was irreplaceable" (ibid., 64).

jewelled portrait of . . . Henry VIII."[20] A year and a half later, with the death of the frail Edward, Katherine Parr Borough found herself altogether alone, far from her brother and sister, with little money, no home, and no maintenance forthcoming from her late husband's family because she was childless. How the twenty-one-year-old widow felt or how or where she contrived to live remains uncertain. There is a tradition to the effect that Catherine Neville, dowager Lady Strickland, a relative of Katherine's by blood and by marriage, invited her to live for the time being at Sizergh Castle in Westmorland.

It is certain, however, that sometime during the summer of 1534 Katherine Parr married a second cousin of her father's, the forty-year-old John Neville, Lord Latimer, of Snape Castle in Yorkshire. Twice widowed himself, Lord Latimer had two children, John (born in 1520) and Margaret (born around 1525). In contracting this marriage for herself, Katherine advanced as her mother never had on the agenda for her and the other Parr children. Katherine now had "a home of her own at Snape Castle, a husband with position and influence in the north where her own family's lands lay, a ready-made family and a title."[21] Yet the information surviving from the period of this nine-year marriage centers on Lord Latimer's acute financial troubles, sums requisitioned by the king that he was unable to pay, and his no less acute political difficulties. Three of Lord Latimer's brothers incurred charges of treason in the 1530s for their overt unwillingness to support Henry VIII's wars with Scotland. During the so-called Pilgrimage of Grace (1536), when religiously conservative northeners took up arms to impress on Henry VIII their opposition to the dissolution of the monasteries and other religious reforms, as well as their aversion to Thomas Cromwell, chief minister and executor of these reforms, Lord Latimer attempted to mediate between the crown and his insurgent countrymen, whose cause had his sympathy short of committing him to treason. In his efforts to placate all parties, he failed to placate anyone. On the one side, Katherine's husband brought upon himself the king's distrust and Cromwell's settled animosity. On the other side, the suspicions of the northern nobility that Lord Latimer was betraying them and their cause drove an armed mob to storm Snape Castle in mid-January 1537, while he was en route to London to treat with the king. Katherine and the two Latimer children were taken hostage, and the castle was ransacked.[22] A summons went out to Lord Latimer to return to Yorkshire immediately or his family would be killed and his house burned to the ground. Returning in haste, he somehow persuaded the insurgents to release his family and vacate his house. But after royal

20. Ibid., 63.

21. Ibid., 64, 69.

22. Porter (*Katherine the Queen*, 76–109) gives an admirable account of Lord Latimer's predicament and the challenges it entailed for KP. For two other instances of gentlewomen who coped with grave physical danger in their husbands' absence during the Pilgrimage of Grace, see Harris, "Women and Politics in Early Tudor England," 270.

force, both military and judicial, put an end to the uprising, Latimer was unable to repair either his reputation or his fortunes.[23]

Lord and Lady Latimer moved south with the two children, first to Latimer's lands in Worcestershire, then to Northamptonshire, where he acquired the manor of Stowe as a likely favor to Katherine, whose uncle and aunt lived only a few miles away. Between 1538 and 1542, the Latimers divided their residence between their southern manors, two properties near York acquired in an exchange with the crown, and a leased house in London, probably in Blackfriars—the quarter where Katherine had lived as a small child. Latimer was kept relentlessly busy during this period with assignments to serve on royal commissions that continued to prosecute and execute rebels and other malefactors. Shuttling between York, London, and his southern manors, he conscientiously applied his energies to carrying out the king's and Cromwell's behests.

In August 1542, as hostilities with Scotland resumed, Lord Latimer was sent north with a thousand men to reinforce the king's troops in the borderlands. Fearing that he would die on this assignment, he made his will. One particularly interesting aspect of this document is its insistently generous provision for the childless Katherine, "whether of right she ought to have or not," "if she will be so contented and do so accept the same." Latimer bequeaths to his son and daughter a third each of his landed properties, and the same proportion of his movable possessions and valuables. Although she will inherit no landed property, Katherine will receive more than a third of his movable goods—not a portion necessarily to be anticipated by a wife who had not borne an heir. Latimer's concern for her well-being emerges in the details of his disposition: "I give and bequeath to Lady Katherine, my wife, the third part of all my goods and chattels, whether of right she ought to have or not. And I give her also, over and besides the said third part of my goods, all and every such goods of mine as is now within her lying chamber; and also two of my best gilt standing-cups with their covers, two gilt goblets with one cover, my best basin and ewer of silver, and my two silver flagons." Latimer further provides a life interest for Katherine in two properties, "the manor of Stowe with mine church and Little Stowe, with all and singular the appurtenances to the same belonging," and "the rent of threescore pounds at Bewdley in the county of Worcester in full satisfaction and recompense of her whole dower, over and besides her jointure."[24]

Katherine's continuing affection and care for Margaret Neville would be demonstrated by her retention of her stepdaughter in her own household until Margaret's untimely death at the age of nineteen in 1546. Katherine's affection for Lord Latimer, otherwise unrecorded, can be inferred from the particular personal ef-

23. James, *Kateryn Parr*, 78, 81–84.

24. Kew, Surrey: The National Archives, PROB 11/29 [1542], quire 17; text in a clerk's hand bearing an abbreviated marginal heading in Latin to the effect of "Testament of John Neville, Lord Latimer."

fect that she kept with her throughout her life as a remembrance: a New Testament inscribed with his name.[25] Despite his forebodings, Lord Latimer did not meet his death on a northern battlefield. Returning south to attend the Parliament convened in January 1543, he died in his bed in London in February 1543, in his fiftieth year. Katherine's skillful attentions as a herbalist and nurse in caring for her husband could not prevail against a sudden illness perhaps rendered fatal by the seven years of disheartenment and exhaustion that had followed his unfortunate self-involvement with the Pilgrimage of Grace.[26]

Finding herself a widow for the second time at the age of thirty, Katherine Parr Latimer again faced the question of her future. This new period of transition is almost as obscure as the year that intervened between the death of her first husband and her second marriage. But it is much briefer—a mere four months, when a year of mourning was customary for a widow—and the decision regarding Katherine Parr's third marriage would not be hers to make. It was made for her by her sovereign, Henry VIII. Our understanding of how this happened, however, rests more on likelihood than on known fact. It seems that Katherine undertook to follow the precedent of her mother and sister in seeking a place at court, specifically in Princess Mary's household. As Maud Parr had served Queen Catherine of Aragon—and in the process surely acquired some familiarity with Princess Mary—so too Anne Parr had been serving in the households of Henry's successive queens.[27]

The resumption by two adult women, Princess Mary and Katherine Parr, of a prior acquaintance contracted by way of their mothers' close relationship is evidently what triggered Henry VIII's sudden marital interest in the newly widowed Katherine. A court observer noted in mid-February that the king was visiting Mary and her ladies in their apartments two or three times a day. Also in mid-February, Thomas Arundel, a keeper of the king's accounts who would later serve Katherine in the same capacity, signed a bill for the costs of fashionable mourning attire for "Lady Latimer" and her stepdaughter, Margaret Neville. This curious expenditure must have been made on Henry's instructions.[28] Facing Lord Latimer's demise without an inherited share of his landed estate, Katherine seems to have sought to secure her future at court as an attendant to the king's elder daughter. What she

25. See appendix 2, n40, below.

26. James, *Kateryn Parr*, 85–86, 89–90.

27. Ibid., 95.

28. See David Loades, *Mary Tudor: A Life* (Oxford: Basil Blackwell, 1989), 114, for the observer's comment. Dated February 16, 1543, headed "My Lady Latimer," and containing a marginal note "for your daughter" opposite the entry "Item For making a kirtle, black taffeta ii s.," the clothing bill from a tailor lists seventy-four lengths of various fabrics at various prices. Gowns, petticoats, sleeves, hoods, tippets, and other items of apparel are specified; the only color named is black. This document is preserved as State Papers 1/177, fols. 107–9, in The National Archives. The different construal offered by James, *Kateryn Parr*, 90, fails to account satisfactorily for the "your daughter" reference and also fails to note the significance of the black garments.

secured instead was a future at court as the primary object of the king's affections. An improvised set of verses titled "Respect," scrawled by Henry in a book belonging to Katherine, casts a brief sidelight on his imperious interest in her.[29] Another sidelight is provided by the reverse side of the leaf on which Henry wrote his poetic verses. There Katherine inscribed a series of sententious Bible verses, signed by her as queen. Although undated, these verses read like maxims to guide the conduct of a prudent queenship. They have accordingly been placed in part 1 of the correspondence to highlight the contrast between the king's goal-directed levity in a wooing mode and Katherine's circumspect piety.

Cutting short her period of mourning, Henry VIII made Katherine Parr Latimer his sixth wife on July 12, 1543, in the presence of a small company of friends and intimates in the private oratory of the Queen's Closet at Hampton Court. The new queen's profile was that of a cultivated, twice-widowed, childless woman nearing her thirty-first birthday who presented, to all appearances, a traditionalist orientation in religion and politics. The choice of the cleric to officiate at the wedding—Stephen Gardiner, Bishop of Winchester, the most powerful conservative of the day—caps a consistent sequence of political and religious associations including Maud Parr's service to Catherine of Aragon and Katherine's own affiliations with Lord Latimer, with Princess Mary, and with Henry himself. Katherine Parr trails a distinct aura of conservatism as she steps onto the mainstage of Tudor history. It is now that her political and religious positioning begins to be observable, and the dynamics of her spiritual and literary activity become traceable for the first time.

The household that was the matrix of Katherine's spiritual and literary activity typified that of English royalty of the sixteenth century; its four interrelated groups included members of her family and close affinity, servants from her earlier households, appointees who had been given places as favors to friends and relatives, and professional civil servants who had served in the households of Henry's former queens.[30] As already noted with regard to Maud Parr and Anne Parr, some

29. Henry's verses are no. 2 in part 1.

30. See John N. King's pioneering study "The Patronage and Piety of Catherine Parr," in *Silent but for the Word*, ed. Hannay, 43–60. For advances in social theory that have promoted the conception of the royal (and noble) household as a dynamic means to female agency and influence, and for the specific significance of letter exchanges, see Barbara Stephenson, *The Power and Patronage of Marguerite de Navarre* (Aldershot, UK: Ashgate, 2004), chaps. 1–2. On the importance of household religious activities to women's self-definition and self-expression in the sixteenth century, see Diane Willen, "Women and Religion in Early Modern England," in *Women in Reformation and Counter-Reformation Europe*, ed. Sherrin Marshall (Bloomington: Indiana University Press, 1989), 140–65. The Tudor categorization of Queen Katherine's household in 1545 in terms of who had what meal privileges ("bouch of court") is detailed in *Letters and Papers, Foreign and Domestic, of the Reign of Henry VIII*, arr. James Gairdner and R. H. Brodie, 20.2 (London: Mackie. for HMSO, 1907), appendix 2, sec. 2, 549–50. In April 2009 Gairdner and Brodie's compilation became available electronically through Medieval and Early Modern Sources Online (MEMSO) from Tanner Ritchie Publishing.

of these relationships overlapped significantly. Two new appointments in Queen Katherine's household, her distant cousins Sir Robert Tyrwhit and his wife Elizabeth, would come to figure among her friends. Robert became master of her horse and, later, her comptroller, while Elizabeth gained Queen Katherine's recognition as a kindred spirit among her ladies.[31]

Probably in early 1544, Francis Goldsmith, who joined Queen Katherine's household as her attorney, saluted her in a Latin letter praising the atmosphere she was creating at court. "The most good and most great God set your mind toward piety. . . . He formed it to . . . pious studies . . . of Christ alone and His Word. . . . Days that were seldom such [are] truly Sundays now." Goldsmith proceeds to credit "the great labor of our most serene and most invincible Prince," Henry VIII, for "Christ brought in," but directly returns to Katherine in her "holy household where Christ is daily celebrated." "By your example, . . . O noblest among women surrendered to Christ," enthuses Goldsmith, "your company . . . will be able to understand how much and in what way . . . it will have been advantageous . . . to have brought Christ in."[32] Goldsmith's florid Latin assumes and affirms Katherine's learning while characterizing her "pious studies" as Christ-centered devotions in a traditional yet contemporary vein—"brought in" under Henry "a long while since" but vitalized anew in her household.

The "pious studies" that Goldsmith observed to be occupying Katherine can be traced by way of another member of her new household: George Day, Bishop of Chichester, the Queen's almoner (alms-distributor), who became her first religious and literary mentor. Day was one of a group of fellows of St. John's College, Cambridge, whose spiritual and intellectual formation had been shaped by the university's chancellor John Fisher, later Bishop of Rochester. Younger members of the St. John's group under Fisher's influence included Roger Ascham, one of Day's protégés. Day's name figures prominently in a book bill of May 12, 1544, submitted to William Harper, clerk of Queen Katherine's closet, by Thomas Berthelet, the king's printer. The bill records the delivery of twenty copies of "the Psalm prayers for the Queen's grace."[33] These "Psalm prayers" are the otherwise unattributed *Psalmes or Prayers taken out of holye scripture*, published by Berthelet in 1544 with a colophon dated April 25; this English work, in turn, is a translation of John Fisher's Latin Psalms, first published circa 1525 and republished in London by Berthelet in 1544 as *Psalmi seu precationes ex variis scripturae locis collectae*, with a colophon dated April 18. The early eighteenth-century church historian John Strype affirmed the English *Psalms or Prayers* to be Queen Katherine's work. Susan James has strengthened Queen Katherine's connection with the translation of Fisher's Latin original

31. James, *Kateryn Parr*, 145–46.

32. A translation of Goldsmith's letter and its Latin original are no. 1 in part 3.

33. F. Rose-Troup, "Two Book Bills of Katherine Parr," *The Library*, 3rd ser. 2 (1911): 40–48, quotation at 41.

by noting its inclusion of two prayers, "A prayer for the King" and "A prayer for men to say entering into battle."[34] These two prayers were reprinted a year later in *Prayers or Meditations*, the first work to explicitly bear her name.

Among the likely recipients of the fourteen presentation copies of *Psalms or Prayers* Henry himself surely had pride of place. His regard for the work may have prompted the informal title "The King's Prayers" that it acquired in later printings.[35] Other likely recipients of copies of *Psalms or Prayers* include the group of ladies who attended Henry and Katherine's wedding: Princesses Mary and Elizabeth; Henry's niece Margaret Douglas; Katherine's sister, Anne; Katherine's stepdaughter, Margaret Neville; Jane Guildford, Duchess of Northumberland; Katherine Willoughby Brandon, Duchess of Suffolk, the daughter of a lady-in-waiting who had served with Maud Parr; and Anne Stanhope Seymour, Countess of Hertford (she and her husband, Edward Seymour, Earl of Hertford, older brother of Queen Jane Seymour, owed their positions in royal service to that kinship relation).

All of these ladies already were or soon would become members of Queen Katherine's inner circle.[36] A letter dated June 3, 1544, six weeks after *Psalms or Prayers* was published, offers a charming glimpse of the queen and Princess Mary sharing a single sheet of paper to write to Lady Hertford.[37] Further likely recipients of Katherine's volume include her cousin and close friend from childhood Maud, Lady Lane; another more distant cousin and developing friend, Elizabeth Tyrwhit; and Mary Wotton, Lady Carew, who also had served with Maud Parr as a lady-in-waiting; they, together with Katherine Brandon and Anne Parr Herbert, rounded out the queen's most intimate circle.[38] Besides these ladies, other likely recipients include Francis Mallet, her personal chaplain, a Cambridge graduate who had formerly served Cranmer and Henry VIII in that capacity; Walter Bucler, her personal secretary; and Anthony Cope, her chamberlain.

A compact volume (about five by seven inches), *Psalms or Prayers* made a designedly local impact in Katherine's royal household. Its format, that of a hand-

34. John Strype, *Ecclesiastical Memorials relating chiefly to Religion, and to the Reformation of it . . . under King Henry VIII, King Edward VI, and Queen Mary I* (London: John Wyat, 1721; rpt. Oxford: Clarendon, 1822), 2.1: 204–5; James, *Kateryn Parr*, 205.

35. Unfortunately lacking its sumptuous original binding, Henry VIII's copy of *Psalms or Prayers* is preserved in the library of Elton Hall. Henry made two reader's jottings in its margins and penned an affectionate couplet to Katherine Parr at the bottom of a page. See appendix 1.

36. On the composition of Queen Katherine's household, see Harris, "Women and Politics in Early Tudor England," 274.

37. See no. 2 in part 3 of the correspondence. Another conjoint initiative by Queen KP and Princess Mary was their successful suit in 1545 to have Richard Baldwin, one of Mary's chaplains, appointed a prebend of Newark College in Leicester. Their letter is described and calendared in *Letters and Papers . . . of the Reign of Henry VIII*, arr. Gairdner and Brodie, 20.2, no. 418, item 18.

38. James, *Kateryn Parr*, 153–54.

book, suggests that the queen intended it for personal use as occasion might arise, as an adjunct to the household prayers at which Mallet officiated as chaplain.[39] Yet a distinctly public implication arises as well from its concluding prayers for the king and for men to say entering into battle. The stately cadences of the latter prayer call on God to grant victory and unity to the English: "Our cause now being just, and being enforced to enter into war and battle, we most humbly beseech Thee, O Lord God of hosts, . . . that with small effusion of blood, and to the little hurt and damage of innocents, we may to Thy glory obtain victory: and that the wars being soon ended, we may all with one heart and mind, . . . laud and praise Thee, which livest and reignest, world without end."[40]

Such phrasing sounded highly seasonable notes. On May 27, Archbishop Thomas Cranmer published the first service book in English for public use: the alternating intercessions and responses spoken by priest and people and known as the *Litany*.[41] Henry VIII authorized its publication because he was persuaded that praying the *Litany* in English would unite his subjects in support of his impending invasion of France in summer 1544. The queen's two prayers and the archbishop's innovation of a royally sanctioned vernacular service book reveal a shared objective of enlarging the people's role in worship. Katherine's conjoining with Cranmer in this literary initiative is the first sign of a developing shift in her religious orientation, from conservative traditionalism to the promotion of Reformation objectives.

In other respects, Katherine was making heady discoveries regarding the extent of her influence with Henry. She is credited with bringing his children together for a family Christmas celebration in 1543, and with advocating the restoration of Mary and Elizabeth in the line of succession, officially decreed by king and Parliament on January 14, 1544. Katherine is also credited with proposing the appointments of two Cambridge scholars, Richard Cox and John Cheke (the latter another of Day's protégés), as tutors to Prince Edward in his newly instituted household, created by the king and Privy Council on July 7, 1544. Providing for the prince's household and education was one part of Henry's larger purpose in arranging for the interim exer-

39. That *Psalms or Prayers* had some such purpose and use in the queen's household seems likely in view of the later compilation published by Elizabeth Tyrwhit. Tyrwhit's *Morning and euening prayers, with diuers psalmes himnes and meditations* provides a rich surround of private devotions to complement Morning Prayer and Evening Prayer in the *Book of Common Prayer*. The volume was registered for publication in 1569–70, and a single copy with an abbreviated text was printed in a girdle prayerbook format in 1574 (STC 24477.5). Thomas Bentley published a fuller version of Tyrwhit's text in Lamp 2 of *The Monument of Matrones* (1582) (STC 1892). On the biographical context and the compositional genesis of this work, see Susan M. Felch's edition of *Elizabeth Tyrwhit's Morning and Evening Prayers* (Aldershot, UK: Ashgate, 2008).

40. *Psalms or Prayers*, sig. Mi r–v. See below, p. 364.

41. This is *An exhortation vnto prayer . . . to be read in euery church afore processyons. Also a letanie with suffrages* (T. Berthelet, 1544) (STC 10620–10621.5). Enjoined by Henry's authority for use throughout his realm, this volume went through several printings in its initial year.

cise of royal authority while he was absent on his military campaign in France. Another part was his appointment of Queen Katherine as Regent General of England on July 11. Henry divided his Privy Council, assigning half its core members to accompany him, half to remain in England to advise Katherine. Cranmer was the principal councillor among those assigned to the queen; he was to attend her daily, as was the king's secretary, Sir William Petre. Lord Chancellor Thomas Wriothesley and Prince Edward's elder uncle, the Earl of Hertford (later Duke of Somerset), were to attend as often as their other responsibilities permitted.[42]

Katherine acted in Henry's stead as regent general for two and a half months, from mid-July to late September 1544.[43] This exercise of sovereign authority in daily consultation with Cranmer was to prove catalytic for recent tendencies in her spiritual and literary activity. While Katherine gained confidence in her powers and potential, the princesses Mary and Elizabeth had the opportunity to observe the kingdom in a queen's charge. The correspondence from Katherine's regency has been given its separate section, as part 2 of the correspondence; it includes four proclamations that she issued exercising Henry's authority.

During her regency, moreover, Katherine apparently came to regard the translation of spiritually valuable works as an activity that she would no longer undertake personally but instead would promote. The earliest ramifications of this decision appear within the queen's inner circle: as a gift for her at New Year's 1545, Elizabeth translated Marguerite of Navarre's *Le Miroir de l'âme pécheresse* into English under the title *The Glasse of the Synnefull Soule*. Like Katherine's translation of Fisher, Elizabeth's translation of Marguerite closely tracks the spirituality of a prominent contemporary.[44]

In and after her regency, Katherine presided over an ambitious project: the preparation of English versions of Erasmus's Latin paraphrases of the four Gospels and Acts in *Paraphrases in Novum Testamentum*, first published by Frobenius at Basel in 1524.[45] This project's conception sheds light on the queen's own spiri-

42. Martienssen, *Queen Katherine Parr*, 164–65, 172–74, 179–80; James, *Kateryn Parr*, 131–5, 138–39, 141–44, 167; Porter, *Katherine the Queen*, 170–80; Diarmaid MacCullough, *Thomas Cranmer: A Life* (New Haven, CT: Yale University Press, 1996), 318.

43. A proclamation dated October 6, 1544, refers to "the King's majesty, being (thanks be to Almighty God) in his most royal person safely returned into this his realm of England" (Paul L. Hughes and James F. Larkin, eds., *Tudor Royal Proclamations*, vol. 1, *The Early Tudors, 1485–1553* (New Haven, CT: Yale University Press, 1964), 340, no. 239). "Thanks be to God" is a recurrent phrase of KP's.

44. See Anne Lake Prescott, "The Pearl of the Valois and Elizabeth I," in *Silent but for the Word*, ed. Hannay, 61–76; *Elizabeth's Glass*, ed. Shell; and *Elizabeth I: Translations, 1544–1589*, ed. Mueller and Scodel, 40–125.

45. The standard account is E. J. Devereux, "The Publication of the English *Paraphrases* of Erasmus," *Bulletin of the John Rylands Library* 51 (1968–69): 348–67, recently reprised by Gregory D. Dodds, *Exploiting Erasmus: The Erasmian Legacy and Religious Change in Early Modern England* (Toronto: University of Toronto Press, 2009), 3–26.

tual and literary proclivities in 1544–45—her attraction to artfully composed works with a markedly Biblical tenor, written by eminent contemporaries, that mingle Christ-centered piety with moral urgency—but it also attests her new concerns and her new sense of a public role that bespeak Cranmer's influence. As patron of the English *Paraphrases* Katherine committed herself to advancing the people's understanding of Scripture and, with it, their capacity to nurture and answer for the state of their own souls—thus exercising, by indirect means, functions analogous to those of a pastor.

This notable extension on her prior activity was not lost on Nicholas Udall, whom the queen commissioned to serve as general editor and to translate Erasmus's paraphrases of Luke and Acts. His lengthy letter to her dated September 30, 1545, hails Katherine's progression from "Psalms and contemplative meditations, on which your highness, in the lieu and place of vain courtly pastimes and gaming, doth bestow your night-and-day's study," to her commissioning of translations of specified paraphrases. Udall addresses her as an energetic and effective promoter of the Reformation in England. He commends the queen's "most earnest zeal" in "sustaining the burden" and procuring "other workmen" at "your exceeding great costs and charges." "By this means," proclaims Udall, "doth your highness right well declare that all your delight, all your study, and all your endeavor is by all possible means employed to the public commodity of all good English people, the King's most loving and obedient subjects, to be nuzzled and trained in the reading of God's Word, and in the meditation of His most holy Gospel."[46]

To realize her godly objectives, Queen Katherine turned to her household for further help with the *Paraphrases* project. Thomas Caius, an Oxford scholar who became one of her chaplains, explained in his prefatory letter to Katherine that he had been "moved" by George Owen, one of the royal physicians, to volunteer to translate the paraphrase of Mark, "trusting rather upon the benign acceptation of your gracious goodness than upon the slenderness of my wit and learning."[47] Help from a less predictable quarter is described in Udall's letter to Katherine prefacing the paraphrase of John, which praises "the most studious" Princess Mary, "for taking such great study and travail in translating this paraphrase . . . at your highness' special contemplation." Udall commends Mary for persisting through "a grievous and long sickness" until finally compelled to consign the John paraphrase to the queen's chaplain, Francis Mallet, for completion. Mary's participation in this project is confirmed by a Latin letter to her from Katherine that survives as a copy in Elizabeth's italic handwriting—probably because the queen thought it more suitable than her own hybrid secretary hand for transmitting a composition of hers in Latin. Katherine asks after Mary's health and probes her wishes regarding public credit for her efforts. The sinuous phrases mingle frankness with fondness:

46. This letter is no. 10 in part 3.

47. Caius's letter is no. 11 in part 3.

> I pray you to . . . signify whether you wish it [Mary's translation of the John paraphrase] to go out most happily into the light under your name, or whether rather by an unknown author. To which work really, in my opinion, you will be seen to do an injury, if you refuse the book to be transmitted to posterity on the authority of your name: for the most accurate translating of which you have undertaken so many labors for the highest good of the commonwealth: and more than these (as is well enough known) you would have undertaken, if the health of your body had permitted. Since no one does not know the amount of sweat that you have laboriously put into this work, I do not see why you should reject the praise that all confer on you deservedly. However I leave this whole matter to your prudence, so that whatever position you wish to take, I will esteem it most greatly to be approved.[48]

The preface to the Luke paraphrase, which Udall addressed to Katherine and dated September 30, 1545, bears further witness to her motivating concerns as patron of the project: on the one hand, a deepening realization of the nature of the Gospel message; on the other, a heightened awareness of what deviated from Scripture in the church and society of her day. Udall enthuses over the queen's assignment of the Luke paraphrase to him. Of all the Gospels, Luke is the one with the firmest theological grounding—in Udall's words, "most earnest and full in the justification of faith, and most pithy against the justification of works"—and therefore the one most effective in exposing the "Romish abomination" of "all things . . . contrary to Christ." A colorful catalog counterposes New Testament truth with the papal "traditions" and "fond ceremonies" then in process of reformation in England: "Instead of pure faith such as Christ requireth, a faith lapped in a cloak of beggarly works . . . , building of chantries in place of relieving and maintaining the lively temple and image of God in the poor, incensing of images instead of the pure sacrifice of an innocent life; . . . instead of heaven, a purgatory consisting of material fire, and the same to be redeemed with money . . . instead of declaring our free redemption in Christ, and by Christ sealed with His most precious blood." Udall's emphases in this letter to Katherine tally with Cranmer's known convictions at this date. The archbishop's influence with the queen was being reinforced from other quarters.[49]

In the event, it would not be Katherine's persuasions that would ensure Henry's authorization of the English paraphrases of the Gospels and Acts, as Udall imag-

48. KP's Latin letter and an English translation are no. 9 in part 3.

49. On the centrality of justification by faith and the careful articulation of the relation of faith, salvation, and good works in Cranmer's theology through the mid-1540s, see MacCullough, *Thomas Cranmer*, 209–12, 229, 309, 313, 342–43.

ined. Publication, occurring in Edward's reign, would reveal a project falling short of its anticipated homiletic benefits, as English readers revealed their preference for the plain vernacular New Testament over Erasmus's copious rephrasings.[50] Yet Katherine Parr's reputation as a leading advocate of making Scripture—and aids for understanding it—publicly available in English was assured by her patronage of the *Paraphrases* project.

If she no longer viewed translation as a literary and spiritual role for her, Queen Katherine took up the redacting functions that Fisher had performed in his *Psalmi seu Precationes* and Cranmer in his *Litany*: the selecting, adapting, and free recombining of source materials that yields a transformative synthesis, a creation that qualifies as authorship. The queen affirms her authorship of *Prayers or Meditations* (1545) by publishing it under her own name and reprinting the two concluding prayers from *Psalms or Prayers* while adding three more that quite likely are her own compositions.

After Henry returned from France in late September 1544, the effects of exercising the regency continued to work on Queen Katherine. Daily consultations with Cranmer had fostered Reformed tendencies in her spiritual and literary activity, and the wielding of royal authority had bolstered her self-confidence about this activity, which she now refocused mainly within the compass of her household. It is probable that by this time Katherine had begun to compile an English prayerbook for herself.[51] This diminutive volume, entirely written in her hand and illuminated in red, blue, and gilt, comprises a sequence of prayers, meditations, and portions of Scripture taken from books of devotion issued, in large part, by English Lutheran translators, redactors, and printers. These include George Joye's *Ortulus anime* (*Garden of the Soul*) and *The psalter of Dauid in Englishe* (both 1530), Thomas Godfray's *Fountayne or well of life* (1534?), William Marshall's *A prymer in Englyshe* (1534) and *A goodly prymer in Englyshe* (1535), Robert Redman's *Prayers of the Byble* (1535?), John Gough's *This prymer of Salysbery vse, bothe in Englyshe and in Laten* (1536), and Richard Taverner's *An epitome of the psalmes* (1539).[52] But Queen Katherine's manuscript prayerbook also contains several prayers composed by two illustrious Catholic contemporaries, Bishop John Fisher and Sir Thomas More, while they were awaiting execution in the Tower of London in 1535 for refusing to swear to Henry VIII's headship of the Church of England. Notable for its

50. Devereux remarks on the paucity of influence suggested by the absence of reprints of the *Paraphrases* after 1552 and the relinquishing of copyright altogether in 1583 ("English *Paraphrases* of Erasmus," 367).

51. British Library, Harley MS 2342, has hitherto been known as "Lady Jane Grey's Prayerbook," which it did become, almost certainly as a deathbed gift from Katherine to Jane in early September 1548.

52. See Charles C. Butterworth, *The English Primers (1529–1545)* (Philadelphia: University of Pennsylvania Press, 1953), 11–199. Marshall's *Primer* was one source for Cranmer's *Litany* (MacCullough, *Thomas Cranmer*, 328).

Erasmian spirit of inclusiveness in compiling Christian devotions, this very quality of her prayerbook may have prompted Henry's last queen to keep this work of hers personal in the sense of confidential—out of the public eye of a contentious and censorious age.

Again figuring as a nurturing stepmother, Katherine sustained a lively interest in the developing capacities of Elizabeth and Edward, partly by fostering in them her own Reformed inclinations. The incentive to translate probably provided by Katherine continued in the New Year's gifts presented by Elizabeth in 1546: for the queen, an English translation of the first chapter of the first French version of Calvin's *Institution de la religion chrestienne* (1541), with its author prudently left unidentified; for the king, a trilingual (Latin, French, Italian) translation of Katherine's *Prayers or Meditations*.[53] A series of Latin letters from Prince Edward to Queen Katherine, written between May 1546 and January 1547, convey the nine-year-old's eagerness to please his stepmother with his progress in his studies while also expressing his and his tutor Cox's delight in the queen's recent mastery of italic handwriting (*romanis literis*) and his thanks for a joint portrait of her and King Henry which she had sent as a gift. Katherine's draft of a response in Latin to Edward's thanks for the joint portrait is written in her newly acquired italic handwriting on the back of one of his letters to her; it urges him "to keep the depicted image . . . of your most distinguished father . . . before your eyes: to whose rare virtues attentively beheld and observed, as long as you direct your mind and make them visible, . . . you will distinguish both yourself and this commonwealth."[54]

The further reaches of Katherine's interests in education in the aftermath of her regency brought more adherents of a Reformed bent within the scope of her patronage. On November 14, 1544, she wrote administrative instructions to Matthew Parker, a future archbishop of Canterbury, then dean of the college of canons at Stoke in Suffolk—a property that was part of the jointure conferred on her by Henry VIII.[55] After transferring Francis Mallet to serve as Princess Mary's chaplain and collaborator in translating the John paraphrase, Katherine appointed as her new chaplain John Parkhurst, a graduate of Magdalen College, Oxford, who had written a Latin epigram that subtly hailed her skillful conduct as regent of the realm, pronouncing her virtues greater than those of Ulysses's Penelope.[56] In 1544–

53. For original-spelling and modern-spelling transcriptions, introductions, and notes to these two texts, see *Elizabeth I: Translations, 1544–1589*, ed. Mueller and Scodel, 129–287.

54. Edward's Latin letters with English translations are nos. 16–18, 20–21, 23 in part 3 of the correspondence; KP's Latin draft with an English translation is no. 24.

55. James, *Kateryn Parr*, 137; the letter is no. 5 in part 3 of the correspondence. Further sidelights on Matthew Parker's careful provision for godly education for children as well as alms and hospitality at the queen's college of Stoke emerge in his 1546 report to KP's council, as calendared in *Letters and Papers . . . of the Reign of Henry VIII*, arr. Gairdner and Brodie, 20.2, no. 968.

56. This epigram is no. 21 in part 2 of the correspondence.

45 Parkhurst held the position of chaplain to Charles Brandon, Duke of Suffolk, and Katherine Willoughby Brandon, Duchess of Suffolk. This "other Katherine" (as Parkhurst would style her) was one of the queen's inner circle of intimates; they encouraged each other in seeking channels of expression for their shared religious sympathies.[57]

In late fall 1545, Reformation and Realpolitik steered a convergent course as Parliament sought to relieve the severely depleted royal finances resulting from Henry VIII's campaign in France. Acts passed on November 23 and 24 directed the further dissolution of specified religious foundations—including chantries and colleges—and the transfer of their assets to the crown. The rationale alleged was the lack of need to train priests to offer masses for souls of the dead in purgatory; but where colleges served genuine needs for preaching and other forms of pastoral care, exemptions were to be made. In the wake of these acts, alarm set in at Cambridge University. Roger Ascham, writing for the university as its orator, and Dr. Thomas Smith, former university vice chancellor and current clerk of the Privy Council, signaled the public recognition of the leadership Queen Katherine had demonstrated in the regency of the realm as well as the reputation she had gained as sponsor of the *Paraphrases* project. Ascham and Smith appealed to her to exercise her influence with King Henry in behalf of the Cambridge colleges. Smith probably pleaded the cause in person; Ascham's appeal was lodged in a letter that evidently does not survive. The queen couches her candid, confident response to the university in a letter dated February 26, 1546:

> You . . . move me diversely, showing how agreeable it is . . . not only for mine own part to be studious, but also a maintainer and cherisher of the learned state. . . . And forasmuch as I do well understand, all kind of learning doth flourish amongst you in this age, as it did amongst the Greeks at Athens long ago, I require and desire you all not so to hunger for the exquisite knowledge of profane learning, that it may be thought the Greeks' university was but transposed or now in England again revived, forgetting our Christianity, since their excellency only did attain to moral and natural things. But, rather, I gently exhort you to study and apply those doctrines as means and apt degrees, to the attaining and setting forth the better, Christ's reverent and most sacred doctrine. . . . For this Latin lesson I am taught to say of St. Paul, *Non me pudet evangelii.*[58] . . . I trust universally in all your vocations and ministries

57. Parkhurst's epigram on the two Katherines is no. 12 in part 3 of the correspondence.

58. *Non . . . evangelii*: "I am not ashamed of the gospel" (Romans 1:16). This is not the Vulgate rendering but, significantly, that of Desiderius Erasmus in his *Annotationes in Epistolam ad Romanos*. See *Erasmus's Annotations on the New Testament: Acts—Romans—I and II Cor-*

> you will apply and conform your sundry gifts, arts, and studies, to such end and sort that Cambridge may be accounted rather an university of divine philosophy than of natural or moral, as Athens was. Upon the confidence of which your accomplishment to my expectation, zeal, and request, I according to your desire attempted my lord, the King's majesty, for the stay of your possessions: in which, notwithstanding his majesty's property and interest . . . , his highness being such a patron to good learning . . . will rather advance and erect now occasion therefor than confound these your colleges.[59]

Katherine's letter to Cambridge University makes revealing disclosures. Her words resonate with the concern for propagating the Gospel that spurred her *Paraphrases* project. But the queen sounds distinctly imperious notes as well. She declares, as a condition to be met, her desire that Cambridge become "rather an university of divine philosophy than of natural or moral"—"divine philosophy" being Erasmus's frequent form of reference to Christ's teachings and example in the *Paraphrases* and other works. To ensure the university's compliance with her desire, she serves notice that, on the strength of her persuasions, the king has resolved not to dissolve the colleges and confiscate their properties but instead to erect and endow a new college (Henry VIII duly founded Trinity College, Cambridge, in 1546). In effect, the queen puts herself forward as an instrument of royal authority for advancing the highest knowledge, which she equates with the religion of Christ and St. Paul.

As before, her religious and literary initiatives in the spring and summer of 1546 registered and reverberated in her household. John Foxe's second edition of *Acts and Monuments* (1570) recounts, manifestly on information from a firsthand observer, "The story of Q. Katherine Parre . . . Wherein appeareth in what daunger she was for the Gospell."[60] The story begins by describing how the queen "was very

inthians; Facsimile of the Final Latin Text with All Earlier Variants, ed. Anne Reeve and M. A. Screech (Leiden: E. J. Brill, 1990), 145. The final version of the *Annotationes in Novum Testamentum* was published by Frobenius at Basel in 1535.

59. This letter is no. 14 in part 3 of the correspondence.

60. Some scholars have questioned the veracity of this episode on the grounds that it did not appear in the first (1563) edition of *Acts and Monuments*; see, most recently, John N. King, "Fiction and Fact in Foxe's *Book of Martyrs*," in *John Foxe and the English Reformation*, ed. David Loades (Aldershot, UK: Scolar, 1997), 31–33. Two factors should be borne in mind, however—first, that this is a story of "what might have happened but did not" that could have eluded Foxe in his initial English compilation of salient events that did happen. Second is the problem of identifying Foxe's informant. The two obvious prospects, named by Foxe as having accompanied KP to her crucial meeting with Henry, had died: Anne Parr Herbert in February 1552, Maud Parr Lane in 1557 or 1558. It could have taken a while for some other intimate of KP's household (possibly John Parkhurst) to come forward to Foxe with the story.

much given to the reading and study of the holy Scriptures" and quickly shifts to the Lenten season of 1546, in which, every afternoon for an hour, one of her chaplains preached to her and the ladies of her privy chamber and others disposed to hear, frequently addressing abuses current in the church. One likely participant was the new household chaplain, Parkhurst. As for the content of these special Lenten sermons, the catalog cited earlier from Udall's letter of September 1545 can be taken as indicative.[61] These exercises in interpreting and applying Scripture emboldened the queen, "being indeed become very zealous toward the Gospel and the professors thereof, frankly to debate with the king touching religion, and therein flatly to discover herself." She was observed "ofttimes wishing, exhorting, and persuading the King, that as he had, to the glory of God, and his eternal fame, begun a good and godly work in banishing that monstrous idol of Rome, so he would thoroughly perfect and finish the same, cleansing and purging his church of England clean from the dregs thereof."[62]

According to Foxe, such was Henry's affection for Katherine that he bore her importunities for a time, refraining "his accustomed manner . . . that of few he could be content to be taught, but worst of all to be contended withal by argument." Two religously conservative members of his privy chamber and Privy Council, Bishop Gardiner and Lord Chancellor Wriothesley, took note of Henry's smoldering irritation, which increased with worsening pain in his phlebitic leg. Both men had grown hostile to the queen and her recent religious tendencies. After another visit in which Katherine urged him "zealously to proceed in the reformation of the church," Henry's sarcastic remark reached the ears of the courtiers attending him. " 'A good hearing,' quoth he, 'it is, when women become such clerks; and a thing much to my comfort, to come in mine old days to be taught of my wife.' " Gardiner seized the opportunity to deplore what he represented as the queen's insubordinate, disrespectful, and dangerous behavior. He characterized her religion as a mixture of treason and heresy that "did not only disallow and dissolve the policy and politic government of princes, but also taught the people that all things ought to be in common."[63] Henry gave Gardiner permission to collect evidence and draw up for-

61. See p. 17 above. A contemporary sidelight on the evangelical intensity of Queen Katherine's household at this time is provided by the will of Margaret Neville, her stepdaughter from her previous marriage, who died suddenly in March 1546. Margaret professes to die solely "trusting unto His [God's] mercy that He through the mercies of my Saviour and only Mediator Jesus Christ will now perform His promise unto me that death may have no power over me." She also entrusts the disposition of her earthly goods and estate to Queen Katherine. For the full text of the will, see James, *Kateryn Parr*, 417–18.

62. John Foxe, *The first (second) volume of the ecclesiasticall history contaynyng the Actes and monuments . . . Newly recognised and inlarged* (J. Daye, 1570) (STC 11223), fol. 1422a (Early English Books Online image 742), among entries for the year 1546. Spelling in quotations modernized.

63. Foxe, fols. 1422b–1423a (EEBO image 742).

mal charges against Katherine, thus making his sixth queen the centerpiece of an all too familiar royal game of checkmate.

Gardiner pursued a dual strategy. He attempted, with the aid of Wriothesley and Sir Richard Rich, another member of Henry's Privy Council, to wring testimony from a gentlewoman, Anne Askew, who was then undergoing prosecution on heresy charges for a second time. The premise on which the three men worked was to ferret out connections linking several of the queen's intimates—her sister, Anne, and her cousins Lady Lane and Lady Tyrwhit—with Askew and her forthright denial of transubstantiation, the doctrine that the priest's consecration transforms the substance of the bread and wine of the Eucharist into Christ's body and blood. If the torture applied personally (and therefore illegally) by Wriothesley and Rich had succeeded, Askew would have incriminated the queen as well as her ladies, But she held firm in denying any dealings with them and courageously endured her death at the stake in mid-July 1546.[64]

Gardiner's other attempt aimed directly at the queen: a secret search was made of her chamber for heretical books and writings. Since nothing was found, loyal members of her household, perhaps her ladies or her uncle Sir William Parr, then serving as her chamberlain, must have removed the incriminating volumes—among them, the Lutheran primers being used by Katherine to compile her personal prayerbook[65]—in the nick of time. No evidence, however, did not mean no danger; because Henry had consented to the drawing up of charges, it would be only a matter of time before Katherine's enemies found a way to bring her down. She, meanwhile, was unaware of Gardiner and Wriostheley's lethal machinations, learning of them only when Henry was moved, after one of her irritating visits, to divulge "the whole practice unto one of his physicians, either Dr. Wendy, or else Owen, . . . pretending unto him, as though he intended not any longer to be troubled with such a doctress as she was."

The queen was immediately informed of her great danger by this physician—whom it is tempting to identify as George Owen, the man who persuaded Thomas Caius to translate Erasmus's paraphrase on Mark. The news completely unnerved Katherine, who collapsed into bed, where Henry visited her and listened to her for an hour as she "uttered her grief, fearing lest his majesty (she said) had taken displeasure with her, and had utterly forsaken her; he, like a loving husband, with sweet and comfortable words . . . refreshed and appeased her careful mind." Afterward, alone with her thoughts, Katherine realized the rightness of what the physician had urged her to do: "somewhat to frame and conform herself unto the King's mind, . . . and show her humble submission to him." There could be no question, however, of admitting any guilt or expressing contrition; this would seal this

64. Askew wrote her own accounts of her experiences and beliefs. See *The Examinations of Anne Askew*, ed. Elaine V. Beilin (New York: Oxford University Press, 1996).

65. See the introduction to KP's personal prayerbook, pp. 496, 500.

queen's doom with Henry, as it had sealed Anne Boleyn's and Katherine Howard's. The next evening, "waited upon only by the Lady Herbert her sister, and the Lady Lane," Katherine "went unto the King's bedchamber, whom she found sitting and talking with certain gentlemen of his chamber." Henry welcomed Katherine "very courteously," ended the conversation in which he had been engaged, and "began of himself, contrary to his manner before accustomed, to enter into talk of religion, seeming as it were desirous to be resolved by the Queen, of certain doubts which he propounded."[66]

Queen Katherine did not rise to this bait of the king's. Instead she discoursed on the "great imperfection and weakness" of women and the superior resemblance of men to the "shape and likeness" of God, who "appointed such a natural difference between man and woman" that, in her case, she as "a silly poor woman, so much inferior in all respects of nature" could and would do nothing but "refer my judgment in this, and in all other cases, to your majesty's wisdom, as my only anchor, supreme head and governor here in earth, next under God, to lean unto."

Henry contradicted her bluntly: "Not so, by St. Mary; you are become a doctor, Kate, to instruct us (as we take it) and not to be instructed or directed by us."

Now it was Katherine's turn to contradict. "'If your majesty take it so,' quoth the Queen, 'then hath your majesty very much mistaken me.'" She declared how "unseemly, and preposterous" she thought it "for the woman to take upon her the office of an instructor or teacher to her lord and husband." She had "been bold" to draw out his opinions and the differences in their two judgments for two reasons: first, to distract him from the pain in his leg, and second, to improve and advance her own understanding from "hearing your majesty's learned discourse."

Henry took this bait of the queen's. "'And is it even so, sweetheart?' quoth the King, 'and tended your arguments to no worse end? Then perfect friends we are now again, as ever at any time heretofore.' And . . . he sat in his chair, embracing her in his arms, and kissing her."[67] In the epilogue to this story, when Wriostheley arrived the next day with an armed guard to arrest Katherine and take her to the Tower, Henry angrily dismissed them and told her not to try to excuse the lord chancellor, for he had meant her much harm. The religious conservatives headed by Gardiner would remain out of Henry's favor for the last six months of his life and reign.

Despite overt signs (such as lavish new jewels) indicating that the king had restored the queen to favor in the late summer of 1546, things would not be "again, as ever at any time heretofore."[68] Katherine had zealously used her special position to promote what she regarded as the prime imperative of God's will, the further

66. Foxe, fols. 1424a–b (EEBO image 743).

67. Foxe, fols. 1424b–1425a (EEBO image 743).

68. Among grants made by the king in July 1546, there is one to two Parisian jewelers, John Lange and his son Giles, to import a range of jewels and wrought gold "for the pleasure of us, our derest wief the Quene, our nobles, gentlemen, and other" (*Letters and Papers . . . of the*

reformation of the Church of England. The result was the fearsome alienation of Henry, and a Tudor near-death experience that she had escaped only by prevaricating about her beliefs. In the voice of a generic Christian soul with immediate access to Christ and with personal accountability for that soul's state, her *Prayers or Meditations* had projected gender equality.[69] Her *Paraphrases* project and her letter to Cambridge University had borne witness to the priority she placed on the knowing of Christ—faith in salvation through Him, familiarity with His teachings and example—that would animate the people of England to genuinely Christlike living. But Katherine had pretended to Henry that her deepest convictions were mere thought experiments or pretexts for diverting conversation.[70] Setting the record straight by setting out what she truly believed must have been a dominant preoccupation in the later summer and fall of 1546, the period in which Queen Katherine probably composed the three-part sequence of reflections that constitute her wholly original work, *The Lamentation of a Sinner*.[71] This work remained in manuscript, unpublished, until nine months after Henry's death.

As the king's health declined in December 1546, he was even more not "friends as before" when the queen had nursed him. Katherine probably saw Henry for the last time shortly before Christmas.[72] Thereafter he sequestered himself with his Privy Council and excluded all female companionship. The male dominance to which Katherine had paid lip service in Henry's presence became hard political fact in the weeks leading up to his death on January 28, 1547, and the three days thereafter when Henry's death was kept secret. During this time Edward Seymour engineered control of the government as the newly elevated Duke of Somerset and lord protector of his nephew, now the boy-king Edward VI. Other powerful councillors negotiated major appointments in the new, energetically Protestant regime. No place was made for the queen. With Henry's death, Katherine's status became that of a royal dowager excluded from formal political agency.[73] She was denied

---

Reign of Henry VIII, arr. Gairdner and Brodie, 20.2, no. 1383, item 96). This jewelry may signal KP's restoration to Henry's good graces.

69. Deriving ultimately from St. Paul, KP's Reformation conviction of the equality of all souls before God may have prompted Gardiner to misconstrue the queen as teaching "that all things ought to be in common." But a simpler explanation is sheer enmity on his part, kindled by their now overt religious differences.

70. Early Reformers disparaged covert acceptance of their teachings as "Nicodemism," an allusion to the Pharisee Nicodemus who visited Jesus by night to learn of Him in secret (John 3:1–9; 7:50; 19:39).

71. This dating to the latter half of 1546 corrects my conjecture of a date one year earlier, proposed in my "A Tudor Queen Finds Voice: Katherine Parr's *Lamentation of a Sinner*," in *The Historical Renaissance: New Essays*, ed. Heather Dubrow and Richard Strier (Chicago: University of Chicago Press, 1988), 28, which James has convincingly challenged (*Kateryn Parr*, 242n).

72. James, *Kateryn Parr*, 286; Porter, *Katherine the Queen*, 269–72.

73. Porter (*Katherine the Queen*, 175–83) deftly evokes the sidelining of KP after Henry's death.

regular contact with Edward, and later any contact at all, although Elizabeth was permitted to reside with her during intervals in 1547–48. The change reduced Katherine's full royal complement of ladies-in-waiting and other attendants but would not have been expected to affect her core group of retainers or her circle of intimate friends. She was an extremely wealthy noblewoman of exalted standing who would retain the use and the income of extensive crown holdings for the duration of her life.[74]

As in February 1543 when Lord Latimer died, the cataclysmic change that befell dowager Queen Katherine in February 1547 involved a new husband. This time her response was not self-schooled acquiescence to a king's irresistible will but abandonment to a long-deferred sexual passion for the boy-king's younger uncle, Thomas Seymour, whom Katherine had intended to marry when Henry decided to make her his wife.[75] A full recounting of her infatuation with this adventurous, physically attractive, socially charming, and madly ambitious nobleman four years her senior, and her consequent indulgence of his frequently poor judgment, is beyond the scope of present discussion.[76] It must suffice to say that the secret affair quickly begun by the pair flouted the decorum of the queen's expected period of mourning and its tacit testimony that her womb was not carrying an heir to the throne. The affair did not escape the notice of (among others) Katherine's sister Anne, who put Thomas Seymour candidly on notice regarding his dangerous maneuverings when she informed him that she knew that he and Katherine had married secretly, probably sometime in May 1547.[77] A letter exchange between Katherine and Thomas in the spring and summer of 1547 intermittently discloses the mutual intensity of the lovers' attraction—as in Thomas's subscription at the end of one letter, "From the body of him whose heart ye have," and Katherine's request in a subsequent letter, "I pray you let me have knowledge near night at what hour ye will come, that your porteress may wait at the gate to the fields for you."

The dangers of the secret marriage of dowager Queen Katherine to Lord Admiral Thomas Seymour were manifold, and all of them were realized in the course of time—some later, some sooner. Under Henry, it had been made treason to contract marriage with any person having a potential claim to the throne without the express permission of the king and the Privy Council. In the nine-month period following Henry's death, Katherine (who could have been carrying a child by him) was such a person. Although no move was then made against Thomas Seymour,

74. For a listing of the numerous manors and properties in which KP received a life interest as her jointure when she married Henry, see *Letters and Papers . . . of the Reign of Henry VIII*, arr. Gairdner and Brodie, 19.1, no. 1036.

75. See the autograph letter from KP to Thomas Seymour that is no. 2 in part 4 of the corresondence.

76. James gives a lively circumstantial account in *Kateryn Parr*, chap. 15.

77. Thomas Seymour recounts the incident to KP in a letter that is no. 5 in part 4 of the correspondence.

his failure to obtain this requisite permission worked against him in the winter and spring of 1548–49, when, as a widower, he was suspected of making similar advances toward Princess Elizabeth, compounding the case being built against him and rendering more likely his eventual arrest on a bill of attainder and his execution as a traitor.[78]

Another danger of this secret marriage was the possibility of alienating Katherine from her special place in the affections of Henry's children, by manipulating and deceiving their trust. A letter from Princess Mary to Thomas Seymour conveys her distaste at what she saw as the sordid dealings of his affair with Katherine, and her refusal to play a part in persuading Edward to favor a marriage that had already taken place; another letter from Edward to Katherine, urging her to marry Thomas Seymour, reveals that the impressionable boy-king had been duped by some other go-between.[79] Katherine's previously close friendship with Mary also seemed to be at an end. Yet another danger of this marriage was to involve Katherine in the bitter rivalry between Edward Seymour and Thomas Seymour for the guardianship of their nephew, young King Edward. An immediate casualty of this struggle was the previously close relation between Katherine and her former lady-in-waiting Anne Stanhope Seymour. The new Duchess of Somerset, wife of the lord protector, constantly challenged the dowager queen's right of precedence in ceremonies and court protocol. Rancor seethed between the two women.

Yet in the aftermath of her fourth and final marriage, Katherine Parr maintained the domestic focus of her spiritual and literary activities. Against the backdrop of the ostentatious Protestantism of the Seymours and their allies, who now controlled the government and the court, she had more latitude than ever to continue the daily devotions and Bible study that were the mainstays of her household. Anthony Cope, one of its members, paid her tribute in dedicating to her the twenty Psalm paraphrases that he published in 1547: "I long imagined . . . what thing I might best offer unto your grace . . . wherein I might in some part declare my loyal and obedient heart. . . . At the last, when I considered your gracious intent and godly purpose in the reading and study of Holy Scripture, and the advancement of the true Word of God: I thought . . . to make an exposition of certain Psalms."[80] Her extended roles as patron of the *Paraphrases* project and advocate for the Cambridge colleges also received some fresh confirmation in this period.

In November 1547, when colleges again faced possible crown confiscation of

78. See no. 18 of part 4 of the correspondence section for a Latin admonition in Elizabeth's hand on the reverse of a letter written by KP to Thomas Seymour. Also see Janel Mueller with Linda Shenk and Carole Levin, "Elizabeth Tudor: Maidenhood in Crisis," in *Elizabeth I and the Sovereign Arts*, ed. Carole Levin, Donald Stump, and Linda Shenk (Tempe: Arizona Center for Medieval and Renaissance Studies, 2011).

79. Princess Mary's and King Edward's letters are nos. 10 and 11 in part 4 of the correspondence.

80. Cope's letter is no. 22 in part 3 of the correspondence.

their properties, this time menaced by the zeal of the lord protector, Roger Ascham addressed Katherine in Latin with a new appeal, hailing her possession of "the glory of learning . . . to be shared with only one, the divine Elizabeth," and imploring her to exert what influence she could on behalf of Cambridge University during the Parliament then in session. Ascham also touched with some asperity on her strain of unworldliness: "Spurn not this repute of learning, most prudent Queen, for it is a glory of your diligence and your gifts of mind, greater than all the ornaments of your state. But what of your state? . . . you attribute to Christ alone all that you have received."[81] Ascham seems to allude to the intensity of the Christ-centered, first-person expression in Katherine's last work. On November 5, 1547, the day that Parliament convened, her *Lamentation of a Sinner* appeared in print.

The fuller title states that the work was *set furth and put in print at the instaunt desire of the righte gracious ladie, Caterin, Duchesse of Suffolke, and the earnest requeste of the right honourable Lord, William Parre, Marquess of North Hampton*—Katherine's most steadfast friend in her post-Henry years, and her own brother, newly advanced in rank and prestige. The decision to publish the *Lamentation* must have been difficult: on the one hand, it was Katherine's most complete and forthright statement of her spiritual state and beliefs; on the other, it opened with a ruthlessly degrading self-study of her soul in sin. Nothing at all similar to her self-abasement as a queen and Christian had thus far been presented to English readers.[82] Sir William Cecil, then serving as the lord protector's master of requests and soon to become his secretary, wrote a prefatory letter for the *Lamentation*, defending Katherine's frankness and honesty as necessary means to making a powerful reformist impact on her readers: "This good lady thought no shame to detect her sin, to obtain remission; no vileness, to become nothing, to be a member of Him, which is all things in all; no folly to forget the wisdom of the world, to learn the simplicity of the Gospel; at the last, no displeasantness to submit herself to the school of the cross, the learning of the crucifix, the book of our redemption, the very absolute library of God's mercy and wisdom." Cecil exhorts the readers of Katherine's *Lamentation* to study and emulate her: "These great mysteries and graces be not well perceived, except they be surely studied; neither be they perfectly studied, except they be diligently practiced; neither profitably practiced, without amendment. See and learn hereby what she hath done; then mayst thou practice, and amend . . . with profit, having a zeal."[83]

Yet little imagination is required to project what different reactions readers might have had to this dowager queen who, having newly buried Henry VIII,

81. Ascham's letter with a translation is no. 13 in part 4 of the correspondence.

82. Within a year, however, John Bale would make Marguerite de Navarre's extremes of self-denigration accessible to English readers in his edition of Elizabeth's translation of the *Miroir: A Godly Medytacyon of the christen sowle* (1548). See nn6, 44 above.

83. For the complete text of Cecil's prefatory letter, see pp. 443–46 below.

rushed into the arms of Edward VI's younger uncle and now publicly confessed herself a great sinner. Roger Ascham's Latin letter to William Cecil on January 5, 1548, barely takes note of the *Lamentation* itself while lavishing praise on Cecil's preface: "We have read the most holy confessions of our Queen, with your most eloquent letter. Would that you would wish to devote some of your time to cultivating the English language, so that men might know that our language easily admits all the elements of eloquence."[84]

The end of the same month saw the publication of the first volume of the English *Paraphrases on the New Testament* with a colophon dated January 31, 1548. Udall's new letters prefacing the volume sustain his earlier praise of Katherine, but his phrasing is notably retrospective. He refers in the perfect tense to her commissioning of the several portions of the translation, as actions now completed and belonging to the past: "Ye have therein, most gracious lady, right well declared both how much ye tender God's honor, and also how earnestly ye mind the benefit of your country." Likewise, Udall's prefatory letters to John and Acts respectively affirm her reputation among other learned ladies of England and, now, as the third-ranking "public benefactor," after King Edward and the lord protector. To document Katherine's standing as "chief patroness . . . next unto these two," Udall instances "divers most godly Psalms and meditations of your own penning and setting forth," but he makes no mention of her *Lamentation*.[85]

Judging from Cecil's exculpatory letter and Ascham's and Udall's carefully couched addresses, dowager Queen Katherine's power and influence had become both disputable and diminished since her marriage to Thomas Seymour. Repercussions could be felt even near at hand. When Princess Elizabeth's tutor, William Grindal, died in January 1548, Katherine seconded by Thomas Seymour urged that Francis Goldsmith be appointed in his place. Elizabeth, however, held out for Roger Ascham, and she prevailed.[86]

By January 1548, Katherine knew that she was pregnant—a development not known to have occurred in any of her previous marriages—and the confines of her household gradually delimited the range of her activity. Her friendship with Katherine Brandon, Duchess of Suffolk, deepened as the two supported each other's advancing reformist convictions. Probably at the duchess's suggestion, Katherine appointed Miles Coverdale as her almoner on his return from Germany in March 1548. For his part, Thomas Seymour seems to have taken little or no interest in the godly household cultivated by Katherine. This, at least, is what Hugh Latimer would

84. Roger Ascham, *Whole Works*, ed. Rev. Dr. Giles (London: J. R. Smith, 1864–65), 1:1, 157–58. My translation.

85. The letter prefacing Acts is no. 16 in part 4 of the correspondence.

86. Ascham angled for this appointment in fulsomely complimentary Latin letters to Elizabeth and to Sir John Cheke, Edward's tutor, whose advice Elizabeth sought in the matter (*Whole Works*, 1:1, 280–86).

assert in a sermon preached before the king and court in Lent 1549, after Katherine had died and Seymour had been executed as a traitor: "I have heard say when that good Queen that is gone had ordained in her house daily prayer both before noon and after noon, the Admiral gets him out of the way, like a mole digging in the earth."[87] In the spring of 1548, however, the quotient of godliness in Katherine's household was bolstered by Seymour's political ambition. He secured the wardship of the ardently reformist Lady Jane Grey from her father, the Marquess of Dorset, promising that he would arrange Jane's marriage to Edward VI.

In mid-June 1548 Thomas Seymour escorted his wife, now six months pregnant, and his young ward Jane to his newly acquired property, Sudeley Castle in Gloucestershire, where the baby would be born safely distant from plague-ridden London. Katherine was attended by her friend and doctor, Robert Huick; her almoner, Coverdale; her chaplain, Parkhurst; and close attendants such as Elizabeth Tyrwhit. Despite his duties as lord admiral, Seymour seems to have spent much of the summer with Katherine; the expected male child excited fresh hopes for the dynastic struggle with the lord protector. One unexpected happiness was a letter of August 9 from Princess Mary, conveying her well-wishes to her stepmother. In the event, Katherine gave birth to a daughter, Mary, on August 30 but lay dead of puerperal fever on September 5. Elizabeth Tyrwhit later recorded her observations of Katherine's fevered delirium and Seymour's attempts to soothe her.[88] The extremity of his grief must explain his absence from Katherine's funeral, held in the chapel at Sudeley.

Lady Jane took the role of chief mourner, her newest possession Katherine's personal prayerbook. Coverdale's funeral sermon included a Reformer's account of the candles around the bier: they had been lit in the dead queen's honor, not as accessories to prayers for the fate of her soul (which went unsaid).[89] Parkhurst composed and later published a Latin epitaph: "In this urn lies Katherine: / Lately Queen of England, / Women's greatest glory. / She died in giving birth. / After bringing forth an infant girl, / Lo, at daylight's seventh shining, / She breathed her spirit forth."[90] The dowager queen's orbit precipitously contracts to the bed in which she gave birth and died one week later, then to the urn enclosing her remains.

So sudden had Katherine's death been that there was no opportunity to take leave of her sister, Anne, or her brother, William, whose conditions of life had spectacularly improved after Katherine married Henry VIII. Why, after Thomas Seymour's execution, neither of them received their infant niece, Mary Seymour,

87. "The Seventh Sermon before King Edward VI, April 19, 1549," in *Selected Sermons of Hugh Latimer*, ed. Allan G. Chester (Charlottesville: University of Virginia Press for Folger Shakespeare Library, 1968), 127–28.

88. This document is no. 1 in part 5 of the correspondence.

89. James, *Kateryn Parr*, 331–33, and references given there.

90. Parkhurst's Latin epitaph with translation is no. 5 in part 5.

into their household is not adequately explained—and surely not justified—by the motive of avoiding any political taint associated with the child's father.[91] As one of his last requests, Thomas Seymour asked that his baby be transferred to the Duchess of Suffolk's care.[92] With that arrangement, the circle of Katherine Parr seemed to dissolve into the oblivion of history. What became of Mary Seymour was long a mystery; the series of legal and financial documents relating to her ends in September 1550, shortly after her second birthday.[93]

In a final demonstration of the spiritual and literary activity generated by and around Katherine Parr in the circle of her household, Parkhurst composed and published a set of short-lined Latin verses in which, appropriately enough for an orphan, the baby daughter pronounces her own epitaph: "With what great travail, / And at her life's expense, / My mother, the Queen, gave birth. / A wayfarer, I, her infant girl, / Sleep beneath this marble stone. / If cruel death had given me / A longer while to live, / Those virtues of that best of mothers— / Propriety, modesty, strength, / Both heavenly and manly— / Would have lived again as my own nature. / Now, whoever you are, farewell; / And because I say no more, you / Will excuse this by my infancy."[94] Parkhurst's puns on the meanings of Latin "infans" (infant, one unable to speak) evoke a very young daughter on the threshold of speech, who crosses it briefly, inspired by her dead mother's surpassing virtues to extol them, and then lapses into the speechlessness of death.

The rest is not silence, however. A richly expressive legacy survives in the spiritual and literary works left by Katherine Parr, the first Englishwoman to publish under her name, and by members of her circle who were inspired by her example.[95]

The presentation of my transcriptions of original-spelling manuscripts by Katherine Parr and her correspondents adheres to the procedures followed in *Elizabeth I: Autograph Compositions and Foreign Language Originals* (ed. Mueller and Marcus)

91. KP's brother, William Parr, who had shared the Duke of Somerset's animosity toward his brother, was actively conspiring in the summer of 1550 with supporters of John Dudley, Earl of Warwick, to replace Somerset with Warwick as lord protector (James, *Kateryn Parr*, 353–54). The Duchess of Suffolk reports on her care of baby Mary Seymour in nos. 6 and 7 of part 5.

92. On the unusually full surviving documentation of the Duchess of Suffolk's subsequent court affiliations and activities, see Harris, "Women and Politics in Early Tudor England," 278–80.

93. James, *Kateryn Parr*, 339.

94. Parkhurst's Latin epitaph with translation is no. 8 in part 5 of the correspondence.

95. The spiritual and literary legacy of Katherine Parr and her circle was acknowledged though not explicitly signaled by Thomas Bentley in *The Monument of Matrons* (1582). His Lamp 2 contains, in this order, Elizabeth's translation of Marguerite's *Miroir*; KP's *Lamentation*, preceded by Cecil's letter; KP's *Prayers or Meditations*; Lady Jane Grey's *Prayers* and *Exhorta-*

and in *Elizabeth I: Translations, 1544–1589* and *Elizabeth I: Translations, 1592–1598* (ed. Mueller and Scodel). Translations of Latin texts are mine. I do not provide original-spelling transcriptions of manuscripts that survive in scribal copies, nor do I reproduce the typography and punctuation of sixteenth-century printed texts. I offer typographical reproductions only of texts that survive in the handwriting of Katherine Parr and her contemporary correspondents, retaining spellings, capitalization, punctuation, and paragraphing while expanding conventional contractions (e.g., &, ~, -er, -es, y^{e}, y^{ou}, y^{t}, w^{ch}, w^{t}) and indicating additions, deletions, and other corrections.

It should be remarked in general that Queen Katherine's handwriting presents virtually no reading difficulties, not even in its recourse to currently utilized contractions. The one modest difficulty is the recurrent indistinguishability of *-es* from *-ce* at the ends of several words. In transcribing I have chosen the easier-to-construe alternative—for example, "miseries" rather than "miserice," "tymes" rather than "tymce." Where the text is short, its typographical reproduction is appended in an early footnote; where the text is long—notably in the cases of Queen Katherine's incomplete autograph version of *Prayers or Meditations* and her personal prayerbook, Harley 2342—the original-spelling version precedes the modern-spelling version.

For a handful of texts whose originals have been destroyed or whose present whereabouts are unknown, I have had recourse to later transcriptions that have acquired a reputation for reliability. These include Roger Ascham, *Familiarium Epistolarum Libri Tres* (London, 1578); Bodleian Library, MS Smith 42 (late seventeenth century); John Strype, *Ecclesiastical Memorials relating chiefly to Religion and the Reformation of it, . . . under King Henry VIII, King Edward VI, and Queen Mary I* (London, 1721); Thomas Hearne's *Sylloge Epistularum* appended to his *Titi Livii Foro-Juliensis Vita Henrici Quinti, Regis Angliae* (Oxford, 1726); and Samuel Haynes, *A Collection of State Papers, Relating to Affairs . . . From the Year 1542 to 1570, Transcribed from Original Letters and other Authentick Memorials, Never before Publish'd, Left by William Cecill Lord Burghley, and Now remaining at Hatfield House, in the Library of the Right Honourable the present Earl of Salisbury* (London, 1740).

Unless otherwise identified, Biblical citations in the notes are taken from the

---

tion; and Elizabeth Tyrwhit's *Morning and Evening Prayers*. Additionally an unsignaled abridgment of KP's *Prayers or Meditations* forms part of the contents of *Christian Prayers and Meditations in English, French, Italian, Spanish, Greeke, and Latine. Imprinted at London, by Iohn Daye. Anno 1569* (STC 6428), sigs. Liiii r–Nii r. This volume contains a frontispiece depicting Queen Elizabeth at prayer in her private chapel, as well as expatiating English adaptations of two of her Latin prayers from *Precationes priuatae. Regiae E. R.* (1563) (STC 7576.7). The Latin originals are nos. 7 and 9 in *Elizabeth I: Autograph Compositions and Foreign Language Originals*, ed. Janel Mueller and Leah S. Marcus (Chicago: University of Chicago Press, 2003), 119–21, 122–23; the expatiating English versions are respectively found in *Christian Prayers and Meditations* on sigs. Kii v–Lii v and sigs. pii v–piiii v.

so-called Great Bible of 1538–39, the first to be authorized by Henry VIII for use in the Church of England and made available for public access in the churches of the realm.

Modernized punctuation and spelling in the present edition conform to the guidelines set out in *Elizabeth I: Collected Works* (ed. Marcus, Mueller, and Rose) and *Elizabeth I: Translations, 1544–1589* and *Elizabeth I: Translations, 1592–1598* (ed. Mueller and Scodel). I have inserted apostrophes as markers of possessive constructions where the original lacks an *-s*. When the spelling of a word is close to its form in modern English, I have silently modernized its spelling. I have modernized no longer current verb forms, changing, for example, "astonied" to "astonished," "constrain" to "constrained," "hable" to "able," "lese" to "lose." I have modernized names of persons and places as well as noun forms that are no longer current, changing "burthen" to "burden," "ensaumple" to "example," "huisshers" to "ushers," "middest" to "midst," "party" to "part." Modernized adjectives include the changing of "christen" to "Christian" and "rightwise" to "righteous." Modernized adverbs and conjunctions include the changing of "furth" to "forth," "mo" to "more," "no thing" to "nothing," "other . . . or" to "either . . . or," "syth" to "since," and "thorough" to "through." I additionally distinguish between "aught" and "ought," "other" and "utter," "then" and "than," "whether" and "whither," as Tudor writers did not. Depending on the context, I have modernized "the" as "thee" or "they"; "ne" as "not," "neither," or "nor"; "off" as "of" (or the inverse).

Notes in the five-part presentation of the correspondence aim at supplementing this introduction's summary account of Katherine Parr's biography with locally specific information to assist understanding and enhance appreciation. These are also the aims of the notes to her complete works. A separate introduction to each of the four texts describes the source or sources on which Katherine Parr drew, significant features of her handling of source materials, and the most telling aspects of her literary and spiritual achievement in *Psalms or Prayers*, *Prayers or Meditations*, *The Lamentation of a Sinner*, and British Library, Harley MS 2342, to which I have given the title "Katherine Parr's Personal Prayerbook."

Correspondence

LETTERS AND OTHER TEXTS

BY, FOR, OR ABOUT

KATHERINE PARR

PART 1

Prologue to Queenship

before July 1543

NO. 1 INSCRIPTIONS BY PARR FAMILY MEMBERS IN A BOOK OF HOURS BELONGING TO SIR THOMAS PARR, KATHERINE'S DECEASED FATHER, BEFORE BECOMING THE PROPERTY OF HER UNCLE, SIR WILLIAM PARR OF HORTON, WRITTEN CIRCA 1520[1]

[In Maud Parr's hand][2]

Brother, it is an old saying
That, out of sight, out of mind.

1. Source: Cambridge University Library, Inc. 4.J.1.2 (3570), a *Horum ad Usum Sarum* lacking all front matter up to sig. aii r, which a CUL bibliographer identifies as a "Hoskins 7," that is, no. 7 in "A Handlist of Horae or Primers" in Edgar Hoskins, *Horae Beatae Mariae Virginis or Sarum & York Primers with Kindred Books & Primers of the Reformed and Roman Use* (London: Longmans, Green, 1901); no. 7 is an imprint without title page issued by Wynkyn de Worde's Westminster press in 1494; the edition is STC 15875, although the Cambridge copy is not recorded there. This book of hours came into the possession of Sir William Parr of Horton at some point after the death of his brother, Sir Thomas, on November 12, 1517. The poignancy of the inscription entered by Maud Parr, widowed mother of three young children, Katherine (aged five when her father died), William (aged four), and Anne (aged about two), and the elementary capacity to write demonstrated by Katherine's and William's inscriptions suggest that these entries were made about 1520, when the loss of Sir Thomas as head of this family was still keenly felt. In no event can the inscriptions be later than mid-1524, when Parr of Horton presented this book of hours to Thomas Howard, Earl of Surrey, a ranking military commander under Henry VIII. Parr of Horton inscribed several Latin distichs addressed to Surrey, offering the book as a gift in token of his affection and gratitude (sigs. jviii r, kvii r; lvi r; piiii r; pviii r).

2. CUL, Inc. 4.J.1.2 (3570), sig. piiii v, in Maud Parr's hybrid secretary hand, under a full-page woodcut of the crucifixion of Jesus between two thieves, with His mother Mary fainting in the

But, I trust, in you
I shall not find it true. Maud Parr

[First inscription in Katherine Parr's hand][3]
We, humble and hearty, pray you to remember us, your loving niece and her little Parrs. Katherine Parr

[Second inscription in Katherine Parr's hand][4]
Uncle, when you do on this look,
I pray you, remember who wrote this in your book.
Your loving niece, Katherine Parr

[In William Parr's hand][5]
Uncle, when you on this book do look, I pray you remember your loving nephew. William Parr

---

disciple John's arms and the caption "Psalmi de passione Christi" (Psalms of Christ's Passion). The original reads: "brother et es anolld sayeng / that owt of syt owt of mynd / but I troste in yow / I shall not fynd et treu mawd parre."

3. CUL, Inc. 4.J.1.2 (3570), sig. ciii v, in Katherine's hand, closely resembling her mother's, faintly scratched with a too-dry pen. The original reads: "We vmbel and harty pray yow to remember vs your loueng ness and her lytell parrs Kathren Parr."

4. CUL, Inc. 4.J.1.2 (3570), sig. ciiii r, in KP's hand, at the foot of a page immediately preceded by a rubric and prayer to St. Catherine of Alexandria, KP's name saint, which reads "Virgo sancta katherina grecie gemma vrbe alexandria costi regis erat filia. Ora pro nobis beata katherina ut digni efficeamur promissionibus christi" (St. Katherine, virgin, jewel of the Greek city Alexandria, was the daughter of King Kostos. Pray for us, blessed Katherine, that we may be made worthy of Christ's promises). KP's original inscription reads: "oncle Wan you do on thys loke / I pray you remember Wo Wrete thys in your bo[ke] / your louuynge nys Kathren Parr." Square brackets enclose restored letters lost at the worn page edge.

5. CUL, Inc. 4.J.1.2 (3570), sig. ciiii v, in William Parr's hand, also closely resembling that of his mother and sister, on the overleaf of KP's second inscription. The page contains woodcuts of St. Catherine of Alexandria and St. Margaret, with capsule accounts of their holy lives. William's original reads: "Oncle wen yow on this boke do loke I pray yow r[e]member yowr louynge nevew William Parr."

NO. 2 VERSES WRITTEN BY KING HENRY VIII IN A VOLUME CONTAINING A SERMON BY ST. JOHN CHRYSOSTOM, BELONGING TO KATHERINE PARR, RECENT WIDOW OF JOHN NEVILLE, LORD LATIMER, BETWEEN FEBRUARY AND JULY 1543[6]

Respect[7]

Blush not, fair nymphs; they[8] are of noble blood,
I fain avouch it, and of manners good;
Spotless in life, of mind sincere and sound;
In whom a world of virtues doth abound.
And since, besides, ye license give withal,
Set doubts aside, and to some sporting fall.
Therefore, Suspicion,[9] I do banish thee

6. Source: Sudeley Castle, Gloucestershire, KP's copy of *A sermon of saint chrysostome, wherein . . . he wonderfully proueth, that No man is hurted but of hym selfe*, trans. Thomas Lupset (London: T. Berthelet, 1534) (edition not listed in STC), recto of flyleaf preceding the title page. There is a photographic reproduction of this autograph inscription in R. G. Siemens, "'Respect': Verses Attributed to Henry VIII in a Prayer Book Owned by Katherine Parr," *Notes and Queries*, n.s. 46, no. 2 (1999): 187. Susan E. James's attribution of these verses to Thomas Seymour in 1547 (*Kateryn Parr: The Making of a Queen* [Aldershot, UK: Ashgate, 1999], 413) cannot be sustained on the evidence of several secretary letter forms; the *I*'s, *p*'s, *r*'s, and the ampersand, which are distinctly unlike TS's practice. While the hand here is dashed and scrawling, much less regular than the specimen of Henry's writing in a postscript to KP in a 1544 letter (BL, Cotton MS Caligula, E.IV, fol. 56v), the traditional ascription of these verses to the king is independently supported by the mention of "Jove" in the final line, which reads as a self-reference by the sovereign, manifestly in a courting mood. Henry's original, with phrasal and clausal units marked by virgules, reads as follows:

Respect

blush not fayer nimphes / thei are of nobell blod
I fane avowtch it & of maners ‸ ^{good} /
spottles in ƒ lif of mynd sencere / & sound /
in whom a world of verteus / doth abowend:
& sith besyds ye / lysenc giu with alll
set doughtes asyed and to som / sporting fall
therfoor suspisyon I do / / banysh thee /
that casles thou theyse nimphes / dost traise
on / yon wilbe ^{C}le^{vp} oon Ioues suspysion

7. **Respect** regard, relationship. Both meanings are in play.

8. **nymphs . . . they nymphs** ladies of the court, possibly in an implied context of a mythological masque or festivity, but equally possibly a complimentary reference to Princess Mary's female attendants. **they** King Henry's male courtiers.

9. **Suspicion** a personification of the negative connotations of this word, "expectation or surmise of something evil."

That, causeless, thou these nymphs dost traise:[10]
One, yon,
Will be clepe on
Jovë's suspiciön.[11]

NO. 3 ARCHBISHOP THOMAS CRANMER'S LICENSE FOR THE MARRIAGE OF KING HENRY VIII AND KATHERINE PARR LATIMER, INCLUDING DISPENSATION OF THE REQUIRED PROCLAMATION OF BANNS, JULY 10, 1543[12]

To the most excellent and most invincible prince on a throne, and our supreme lord Henry VIII, by the grace of God King of England, France, and Ireland, Defender of the Faith, and on earth Supreme Head, under Christ, of the Churches of England and Ireland: Thomas, by divine compassion Archbishop of Canterbury, Primate of all England, and Metropolitan, duly and lawfully invested therein by the subscribed authority of the Parliament of England:

Health and perpetual happiness, with honor.

Since by your most excellent royal majesty it has been considered worthy to lead into matrimony the noble and distinguished woman Lady Katherine Latimer, lately the wife of the distinguished and powerful man, Lord Latimer, during his natural life, now deceased, she being favored by the most good and most great God and by your initiatives:

Therefore, that marriage between your most excellent kingly majesty and the said noblewoman, Lady Katherine, in whatever church, chapel, or oratory or wherever else your kingly majesty may wish to choose, without any proclamation of banns, may be solemnized by any bishop or priest whatsoever; and that you may be empowered and enabled to act, freely and licitly and for legitimate reasons, exempt from actual constraints,

We and our soul, moved in this regard duly and legitimately by the honor of your estate and concerned for the benefit of the whole realm of England, with the authority established by these presents, do dispense with constitutions and ordinances propounded to the contrary, nothing whatsoever standing in the way.

Given at our manor of Lambeth, under our seal for enactments, the tenth day

10. **traise** betray—an obsolete verb whose stem shows kinship with the noun "treason."

11. **One . . . suspiciön** Henry caps his series of four rhymed couplets with a refrainlike turn—a triple rhyme on three short lines. **One** The "nymph" Katherine Parr. **yon** over there—an abbreviation of "yonder." **clepe** called, summoned, bidden to come. **suspiciön** expectation of some future occurrence—here, a positive term anticipating marital happiness with "Jove" (Henry himself).

12. Source: Kew, Surrey: The National Archives, E 30/1472(6). A formulaic Latin writ in the engrossing hand of Richard Lyell, Cranmer's clerk for enactments, sealed with the archbishop's outsized seal.

of the month of July, the year of our Lord one thousand five hundred forty-three; and of your majesty's most happy and most illustrious reign, the thirty-fifth; and of our consecration, the eleventh year.

[Witnessed by]
Nicholas Wotton, Commissioner
Richard Lyell, Clerk for enactments by the said very Reverend [Lord Archbishop]

NO. 4 NOTARIAL INSTRUMENT WITNESSING THE MARRIAGE OF HENRY VIII AND KATHERINE PARR LATIMER, JULY 12, 1543[13]

In the name of God, Amen. By this public instrument, let it manifestly appear and be noted by all:

That in the year of Our Lord one thousand five hundred forty-three; and of the reign of the most illustrious and most serene Prince, our lord Henry VIII, by the grace of God King of England, France, and Ireland, Defender of the Faith, and on earth, immediately under Christ, Supreme Head of the Church of England and also of Ireland, the thirty-fifth year;

On the twelfth day of the month of July, in that upstairs oratory called in English "the Queen's privy closet" within the royal honor of Hampton Court, situated in the diocese known as Westminster:

In the presence of nobility and of eminent persons named as witnesses in this instrument by me, Richard Watkins, prothonotary[14] of our lord the King, there present, then attending the said most illustrious lord, our King Henry, as well as the most serene and most distinguished woman, Lady Katherine Latimer, alias Parr, to be brought and joined in matrimony, solemnized by grace and by the intent of those then assembled:

The reverend father in Christ and spiritual lord, Stephen, by divine permission Bishop of Winchester,[15] and by pontifical appointment, of Westminster, garbed and vested, presided at the aforesaid gathering and spoke the following words in English, to this effect:[16]

13. Source: The National Archives, E 3/.1472 (5). A formal attestation of the described words and actions, in Latin, on an outsized parchment sheet measuring 20 by 22 inches. The document is the creation of Richard Watkins, the king's prothonotary, and is written in his compact hand with many contracted word forms. The text contains intermittent passages in English, usually indicated as such by Watkins, whose cues I reproduce.

14. **prothonotary** (or protonotary) a principal notary, chief clerk or recorder of a court.

15. **Stephen . . . Winchester** Stephen Gardiner, leader of the religiously conservative faction at court.

16. **to . . . effect** Watkins continues in Latin to give the "effect" of Gardiner's words in English.

"Lo, we persons assemble here for honoring, in the presence of God and His angels and all saints, the joining together of two bodies, namely, that of the most illustrious prince, our lord Henry VIII, King by the grace of God, and that of the most serene woman, Lady Katherine, here present in person" (whom he then and there beheld with due reverence) "so that, from other, they may be made one body in the faith and law of God, and that their souls at the same time may be advanced by the Lord to eternal life. Wherefore I admonish you, all and singly, present here, by the Father and the Son and the Holy Spirit, that if any among you there be who may know some lawful impediment to exist between these most distinguished persons, that they may not be able to be joined together in lawful matrimony and may not prosper thereafter in continuing therein, let it now be openly and frankly declared and shown.[17]

"Let the license be displayed forthwith, of the sort for solemnizing matrimony, exempted from proclamation of banns, between the aforesaid most illustrious lord, our King, and the aforenamed most serene Lady Katherine, redacted in writing, with the seal of the reverend father in God and spiritual lord, Thomas, by divine permission Archbishop, Primate of all England, and Metropolitan, sealed in red-colored wax, with the last and first names of Nicholas Wotton, commissioner, and Richard Lyell, clerk of the enactments of the said court, undersigned below. Dated the tenth day of the month of July, in the year of Our Lord one thousand five hundred forty-three; and of the reign of the said lord our King, the thirty-fifth; and of the consecration of the Primate, the eleventh year."

When the license had been brought in, and nobody objected to contracting and solemnizing matrimony in this way or to doing the same then, it was announced that nothing, either, had been objected against them that they might not be able to be conjoined in lawful matrimony, and that they might cause the same to be solemnized between them. Wherefore, when all the interested parties together besought, with great accord, joyful spirit, and applause, this happy and holy and auspicious conjoining in matrimony, the aforesaid reverend father, the Bishop of Winchester, with due reverence asked the said most illustrious lord, our King, before all the

17. **Lo . . . shown** Bishop Gardiner's words follow, with some modifications, "De modo solemnizandi sponsalia" (Ordo Sponsalium), the rite for the solemnization of marriage in the missal according to Salisbury use, *Missale ad Usum insignis et praeclarae Ecclesiae Sarum*. I have consulted STC 16212, an edition (Paris: François Regnault, 1532) prepared for English use as shown by the English words in this service and the title-page images of Henry VIII's coat of arms borne aloft by two angels and of a crowned Tudor rose. The "Ordo Sponsalium" appears on fols. xxxviii v–xxxix v. Gardiner's modifications include the more honorific references to Henry and Katherine (rather than simple specifications of "this man" and "this woman") and a more emphatic exhortation that any person who may know of an impediment to this marriage should disclose it.

hearers then present, in this form and substance of words in our English language,[18] as follows:

"Most illustrious lord, our King Henry, will you have this woman most serene of aspect, the said Lady Katherine," (the same then and there present) "for your wife and spouse, and love and honor her as a spouse and husband ought to love and honor his wife? And put away all other women besides her, and cleave to her alone, as long as you both shall live?"

To which questioning the said most illustrious lord, our King, with a joyful countenance, answered affirmatively in English as follows: "Yea!" This means, "I am willing."[19]

Then the aforementioned reverend father asked the said Lady Katherine both questions: if she would have the said most illustrious lord, our King Henry, for her spouse and husband; and if she would obey him and serve him in sickness and in health, care for him and bind herself to be used as a spouse and wife, to obey, serve, and sustain her spouse and husband, and to forsake and put away all men besides him, and cleave to him only, as long as they both should live. To him the most serene Lady Katherine then returned her word, the same. Yes, she was willing to do all these things.

And then when the same most illustrious lord, our King Henry, brought and joined his right hand with the right hand of the said Lady Katherine,[20] the aforesaid Reverend, presiding without pausing, told him to say the following words in English to the most serene Lady Katherine. Then he said the same, and declared as follows, thus: "I, Henry, take thee, Katherine, to my wedded wife, to have and to hold, from this day forward: for better, for worse, for richer, for poorer, in sickness and in health, till death us do part. And thereto I plight unto thee my troth."[21]

Then, hands unclasped, and again joining, the said reverend bishop, solemnly

18. **in . . . language** Here Watkins continues in Latin, reproducing the questions put to the bridegroom and bride on their respective willingness to plight their troths as well as the shift to English for the plighting itself. These are specifications of the "Ordo Sponsalium" in the missal according to Salisbury use.

19. **Yea! . . . willing** **Yea!** The word is in English. **This . . . willing** Watkins's explanation of the obvious betrays his anxiety that everything in this narrative be taken as validly performed. Since the "Ordo Sponsalium" specifies the bridegroom's response as "Volo" (I am willing), Watkins wants it known that Henry gave an equivalent response. KP's correct response as the bride follows in indirect discourse.

20. **And . . . Katherine** Because KP is a widow, the ceremonial raising of the bride's veil is omitted. Gardiner proceeds directly to the blessing and bestowing of the wedding ring, eliminating two prescribed prayers and the sprinkling of the ring with holy water.

21. **I, Henry . . . troth** This vow, known as *in praesentis*, is given in English in the document. Both Henry's vow and KP's deviate significantly from the English of the "Ordo Sponsalium" in omitting the phrase "yf holy chyrche wol it ordeyne" that follows "tyll deth vs departe." The omission signals the independence of the English church from the Roman papacy.

presiding, gave the aforesaid Lady Katherine the following words to say in English to the said most illustrious lord, our King, thus: "I, Katherine, take thee, Henry, to my wedded husband: to have and to hold, from this day forward: for better, for worse, for richer, for poorer, in sickness and in health, to be bonaire and buxom[22] in bed and at board, till death us do part. And thereto I plight unto thee my troth."

And they unclasped their hands accordingly. And then, as the custom is, the most illustrious lord, our King, displayed a gold wedding ring as well as gold and silver.[23] He presented and conveyed the gold and silver to the said Lady Katherine, his spouse. And after the said wedding ring had been blessed by the said lord bishop, who said, "Henry, take the right hand of the most serene Lady Katherine," then the most illustrious lord, our King, taking it, and holding out the ring to the said Lady Katherine, spoke the following words in English:

"With this ring I thee wed; and this gold and silver I thee give. And with my body I thee worship; and with all my worldly goods I thee honor."

And putting the wedding ring first on the said Lady Katherine's thumb, he[24] said the following words: "In the name of the Father," (he spoke, moving the ring to her index finger) "and of the Son," (he intoned, now touching her middle finger) "and of the Holy Spirit." In this manner also the man put the ring on her fourth finger. And releasing the same, he said, "Amen."

When they had been married thus, the aforementioned reverend father, the Bishop of Winchester, uttered solemnizings of matrimony and prayers. He solemnly blessed the most illustrious lord, our King Henry, and the most serene Lady Katherine, espoused in this manner. And immediately after their vows, the said reverend bishop celebrated the mass of the Trinity for espousals and marriages, performing all the solemnities and ceremonies to be done in their behalf, and he dispatched these customary proceedings.

Concerning which proceedings, all and singly, the aforesaid most illustrious lord, our King, commanded me, his appointed prothonotary, to prepare for him one or more public instruments in writing, and he asked me therewith to compile a list of witnesses to subscribe to a deposition of witnessing. These actions, all and singly, were verified and read out in the year of Our Lord and of the King's reign, in the month, day, and place aforesaid.

22. **bonaire . . . buxom** **bonaire** gentle, courteous. **buxom** obedient, compliant.

23. **as . . . custom** The "Ordo Sponsalium" states that the bridegroom's gift of precious metals to the bride "represents the inward love that ought always to be had between them" ("designatur interna dilectio: que inter eos semper debet esse retens"). The "Ordo" also stipulates that the bridegroom should place the gold and silver "super scutum vel librum" (on top of a shield or a book).

24. **he** King Henry. The "Ordo Sponsalium" specifies that the bridegroom is to move the wedding ring stepwise from the bride's thumb to her fingers while invoking the Persons of the Trinity.

Present, then, were the honorable and steadfast John Russell, Lord Russell, distinguished knight of the Order of the Garter, keeper of the king's seal; and the noble man Anthony Browne, knight of the aforesaid order, prefect of the royal pensioners. Also, Sirs Thomas Henage, Edward Seymour, Henry Knyvet, Richard Long, Thomas Darcy, Edward Boynton, and Thomas Speke, knights, as well as Sirs Anthony Denny and William Herbert,[25] bearers of coats of arms. And in addition, the most distinguished women, Lady Mary and Lady Elizabeth, our King's near relations, and the most noble woman, Lady Margaret Douglas, daughter of the sister of our lord and King. Also, among the noblewomen and ladies, Katherine, Duchess of Suffolk; Anne, Countess of Hertford; and Joan Dudley, Lady Dudley; and the eminent Anne Herbert,[26] as witnesses and approvers of the makings of vows.

[In a separate block of text, at the bottom right of the outsized parchment sheet]

And I, Richard Watkins, baccalaureate of laws, prothonotary of the said most illustrious and most mighty lord, our King: because it had been determined that such actions would proceed in the year of Our Lord and the year of the said lord our King's reign, in the month, the day, and the place aforesaid, they were performed and done then, together with the witness of the prothonotary, present in person:

Such are the things I have seen and heard done, and I have provided this account for these purposes: first, a public instrument faithfully written with my own hand; next in order, I have made a public instrument, and have drawn it up in this public and authentic form with my sign and my name, in the usual and customary fashion. I have signed and subscribed in good faith to the witnessings and vows, all and severally, as I was commanded to do above.

[Facing this block of text, at the bottom left of the sheet, Watkins has drawn a pedestal mounting for a cross with curvilinear arms, ringed at their joining by an intertwined circular band. This emblem is evidently his "sign." Underneath, he has written in Latin]

I bear witness of the truth.

25. **William Herbert** husband of Anne Parr Herbert, KP's sister. William Parr, KP's brother, was not in attendance. He was commanding the English forces safeguarding the border with Scotland, as the address to him in no. 5 below indicates.

26. **Katherine . . . Herbert** **Katherine . . . Suffolk** the woman who would become KP's closest associate in her subsequent embrace of Reformed beliefs. **Anne . . . Hertford** Anne Stanhope Seymour, wife of Edward Seymour, Earl of Hertford, Prince Edward's elder uncle. **Anne Herbert** née Parr; KP's sister.

NO. 5 QUEEN KATHERINE PARR TO HER BROTHER, LORD WILLIAM PARR, JULY 20, 1543[27]

[Addressed] To our right dear and entirely beloved brother, the Lord Parr, Lord Warden of the Marches[28]

Right dear and well-beloved brother, we greet you well. Letting you wit that when it hath pleased almighty God of His goodness to incline the King's majesty in such wise towards me, as it hath pleased his highness to take me of all others, most unworthy, to his wife, which is, as of reason it ought to be, the greatest joy and comfort that could happen to me in this world:

To the intent, you being my natural brother, may rejoice with me in the goodness of God and of his majesty,[29] as the person who by nature hath most cause of the same, I thought meet to give you this advertisement. And to require you to let me sometime hear of your health as friendly as you would have done, if God and his majesty had not called me to this honor: which, I assure you, shall be much to my comfort. Given at my lord's manor of Oatlands, the twentieth of July, the thirty-fifth year of his majesty's most noble reign.

Katherine the Queen

27. Source: Transcription in *The Huth Library: A Catalogue of the Printed Books, Manuscripts, Autograph Letters and Engravings, Collected by Henry Huth, with Collations and Bibliographical Descriptions* (London: Ellis and White, 1880), 5:1695–96. In the earlier twentieth century the Huth Library collection was broken into several lots and auctioned; the present whereabouts of this letter are not traceable. The catalog transcribes the letter as follows:

> *[Addressed]* To our right der and entirely beloved Brother the Lord Parre Lord Warden of the Marches.
>
> Ryght der and welbiloued brother we grete youe wel. Lating youe wit that when it hath pleased Almighty god of his goodnes to inclyne the Kings Maiestie in suche wise towards me as it hath pleased his highnes to take me of all others most unworthie to his wief whiche is as of reason it ought to be the greatest Joye and comfort that could happen to me in this world. To thintent you being my natural brother may reioyse with me in the goodnes of god and of his Maiestie as the person who by nature hath most cause of the same I thought mete to give you this advertisement and to require you to let me som tyme here of your healthe as freendly as ye wold have doon if god and his Maiestie had not called me to this honor, which I assure you shal be moch to my comfort. Given at my lords manor of Otelands the xxth of July the xxxvth year of his Maiesties most noble reign.
>
> Kateryn the quene

28. **Lord . . . Marches** William received this appointment from Henry VIII in April 1543 (James, *Kateryn Parr*, 102).

29. **the goodness . . . majesty** This is KP's earliest expression of her sense of close conjunction between God's grace and the king's graciousness to her, as remarked in the general introduction, p. 3.

NO. 7 BIBLICAL VERSES INSCRIBED BY QUEEN KATHERINE IN HER VOLUME CONTAINING A SERMON OF ST. JOHN CHRYSOSTOM, PERHAPS AROUND THE TIME OF HER MARRIAGE TO KING HENRY[30]

Delight not in the multitude of ungodly men, and have no pleasure in them: for they fear not God.[31]
Trust not in wicked riches, for they shall not help in the day of punishment and wrath.[32]
Be not carried away with every wind, and walk not in every path: for so doth the sinner that hath a double tongue.[33]

30. Source: Sudeley Castle, Gloucestershire. KP's copy of *A sermon of saint chrysostome, wherein . . . he wonderfully proueth, that No man is hurted but of hym selfe*, verso of flyleaf preceding the title page. These verses in KP's hand are found on the same flyleaf on which Henry wrote "Respect" (no. 2 above). He wrote on the recto of the flyleaf, she on its verso. Her signature as queen is found at the bottom of the facing title page. Because of the close physical proximity of the two entries in the same volume, I conjecturally assign KP's verses to the summer of 1543, shortly after her marriage to Henry. I also conjecture that she may have assembled these verses, all taken from Ecclesiasticus in the Great Bible rendering, to serve as maxims that would guide her queenship. This is probably the first and certainly the briefest result of her characteristic practice of selecting and combining Biblical verses into new wholes; the last and longest result is her personal prayerbook. The inscriptions read:

> delite not y[n] the multytude of vngodly men, and haue no pleasur in th[em] for they feare not god.
> trust not in wycked ryches, for they shal not helpe in the day of punyschement and wrathe.
> Be not caryd awaye with every wynd and walke not in every pathe: for so dothe the synner that hathe a double tonge.
> Be gentyll to heare the worde of god, that thu mayst vnderstande it, and make a true answere wythe wysdome.
> Be swyfte to heare and slowe in gevynge answere.
> Be not a preuy acusor as long as thou lyvest, and vse no sla[u]nder with thy tong.
> Se that thow iustyfie small and grete alyke.
> Refuse not the prayer of one that ys in troble, and turne not away thy face from the nedye.
>
> Kateryn the Quene KP

31. **Delight . . . God** This and the following verses are taken with slight or no alterations from Ecclesiasticus in the Great Bible authorized by Henry VIII and printed as *The byble in Englyshe* (1540) (STC 2069), fols. lxxxii r–v, lxxxvi r. Verses in this edition are unnumbered; here square brackets enclose the numbers later inserted in English Bibles. This verse is a close citation of Ecclesiasticus 16[:1]. **not in** "not thou in." **men** "chyldren." **for** "yf."

32. **Trust . . . wrath** A verbatim citation of Ecclesiasticus 5[:10].

33. **Be . . . tongue** A close citation of Ecclesiasticus 5[:11]. **away with** "about to." **walk not in** "go not into."

Be gentle to hear the word of God, that thou mayest understand it; and make a true answer with wisdom.
Be swift to hear, and slow in giving answer.[34]
Be not a privy accuser as long as thou livest, and use no slander with thy tongue.[35]
See that thou justify small and great alike.[36]
Refuse not the prayer of one that is in trouble, and turn not away thy face from the needy.[37]

[Signed with swags and underscoring at the bottom of the facing page]
Katherine the Queen KP

34. **Be gentle . . . answer** A close citation of Ecclesiasticus 5[:13]. **and slow** "but slowe and pacyent."

35. **Be . . . tongue** A verbatim citation of Ecclesiasticus 5[:16].

36. **See . . . alike** A close citation of Ecclesiasticus 5[:18]. **justify small** "justify the small."

37. **Refuse . . . needy** A close citation of Ecclesiasticus 4[:4]. **and turn** "turn."

PART 2

Katherine as Regent of England

July to September 1544[1]

NO. 1 RESOLUTIONS TAKEN BY HENRY VIII AND HIS PRIVY COUNCIL, JULY 7, 1544, BEFORE THE KING'S DEPARTURE[2]

[Endorsed] Things ordered at home.
[Headed] At Westminster, the 7th of July, in the 36th year of our King Henry VIII.

First, touching the Queen's highness and my lord Prince, the King's majesty hath resolved that the Queen's highness shall be Regent in his grace's absence, and that his highness's process shall pass and bear *teste* in his name,[3] as in like cases heretofore hath been accustomed. And that a commission shall be made for this purpose, to be delivered unto her before his grace's departure. Wherein shall be expressed that, for her aid and the better administration of his affairs, she shall in her proceedings use the advice and counsel of the Archbishop of Canterbury; of the Lord

1. **Part 2 . . . 1544** For relevant documents in parts 2–4, after the source reference, I append the assigned number in James Gairdner and R. H. Brodie, *Letters and Papers, Foreign and Domestic, of the Reign of Henry VIII* (London: Mackie for HMSO, 1903), preceded by "G&B" and the series or supplement volume and part numbers. Electronic access to *Letters and Papers* is available through Medieval and Early Modern Sources Online (MEMSO).

2. Source: Kew, Surrey, The National Archives, State Papers 1/189, fols. 184r–186r; G&B 19.1:864. Minutes of the meeting in a clerk's secretary hand. Here and hereafter in part 2, italicized phrases have been translated from Latin.

3. **process . . . name** course of action shall be authorized by the affixing of the king's seal to a writ or proclamation. Bearing *teste* in Henry's name becomes one of KP's prominent functions as regent—see, e.g., no. 3.

Wriothesley, Lord Chancellor of England; the Earl of Hertford, the Bishop of Westminster;[4] and Sir William Petre, secretary.

Item: His majesty will that my lord Prince[5] shall on Wednesday next remove to Hampton Court, and that the lord chancellor and the Earl of Hertford shall repair thither on Thursday, and there discharge all the ladies and gentlewomen out of the house. And next admit and swear Sir Richard Page chamberlain[6] to my lord Prince, Mr. Sidney to be advanced to the office of steward,[7] Jasper Horsey[8] to be chief gentleman of his privy chamber, and Mr. Cox to be his almoner, and he, that [is] now almoner, to be dean.[9] And Mr. Cheke as a supplement to Mr. Cox, both for the better instruction of the Prince, and the diligent teaching of such children as be appointed to attend upon him.[10]

Item: For the number of his majesty's council and their order, his majesty hath appointed to be of his Privy Council, in his absence,[11] the Archbishop of Canterbury; the Lord Wriostheley, Lord Chancellor of England; the Earl of Hertford, the

4. **Lord Wriothesley . . . Westminster Lord Wriostheley . . . England** Sir Thomas Wriostheley, first Earl of Southampton, Lord Chancellor of England. **earl . . . Hertford** Sir Edward Seymour, elder uncle of Prince Edward. **Bishop . . . Westminster** Stephen Gardiner held this office by pontifical appointment (see part 1, no. 4); he was ordinarily identified by his other appointment as Bishop of Winchester.

5. **lord Prince** eight-year-old Edward, heir to the throne.

6. **Sir . . . chamberlain** Sir Richard Page (d. 1548), a gentleman of Henry VIII's privy chamber who outlasted suspicion of disloyal dealings with Queen Anne Boleyn to become lieutenant of the king's gentlemen pensioners in 1540, to render service in fortifying Hull during the king's northern expedition of 1542, and to attain the coveted appointment of chamberlain in Prince Edward's newly constituted household in 1544. **chamberlain** an official in the royal household charged with supervising the service and servants of the table and with regulating household expenditures.

7. **Mr. . . steward** Sir William Sidney (1482?–1554), a trusted courtier whom Henry VIII had sent on several embassies to France. Sir William would establish the Sidney family in its seat at Penshurst, a property granted to him by Edward VI in April 1552. **steward** an officer charged with the management of the private chambers of a sovereign or nobleman.

8. **Jasper Horsey** Previously appointed steward to Anne of Cleves in July 1540 and commissioner of the peace for Surrey in October 1542 (G&B 15:937; 17:1012 [45]).

9. **almoner . . . dean** The somewhat garbled syntax suggests that Dr. Richard Cox is to fill both posts, almoner and dean, in the reorganized household, no longer the nursery, of Prince Edward. See James Kelsey McConica, "The Role of Catherine Parr," in *English Humanists and Reformation Politics under Henry VIII and Edward VI* (Oxford: Oxford University Press, 1965), 215–17. **almoner** alms-distributor. **dean** senior supervisor of the conduct and studies of junior students—a post originating in Oxford and Cambridge colleges.

10. **Mr. Cheke . . . him** The detailed specifications for the education of the heir to the throne, under the provisions of the regency when the king would be absent from the realm, suggest KP's advisory input.

11. **his Privy . . . absence** Henry VIII divided the Privy Council, leaving half its members as "the Council with the Queen" and taking the other half of its members on his campaign in France as "the Council with the King."

Bishop of Westminster; and Sir William Petre, secretary.[12] And his pleasure is that either the said chancellor or the said Earl of Hertford, or both, shall ever be attendant upon her person, and resident in her grace's court. And if, by occasion of business or other impediment, neither of them can conveniently be there, then the said archbishop for the time to remain with her grace,[13] with the said Sir William Petre. And when they may conveniently, all five to be attendant upon her.

Item: His majesty is pleased that the Lord Parr of Horton[14] shall be used in counsel with them, for all such matters as concern the realm.

Item: For a lieutenant-in-case,[15] and who shall be of counsel with him, his majesty is pleased that my lord of Hertford shall be his lieutenant-in-case. And to take his commission for that purpose, with all things requisite, by the authority of the Queen Regent, with the advice of the council aforesaid, if need so require.

Item: For musters, and the appointment of certain in every shire, to have the principal cure[16] of the same, and for commissioners for the bulwarks, his majesty is content that the council take advice in these matters at their discretions.

Item: For ordnance and munition, both to serve in time of need and for the furniture of the Tower,[17] the state whereof would be declared, and for a master of the ordnance, his majesty is pleased that the council shall order these things at discretion, being ordnance, etc. sufficient left for all purposes; and Mr. Walsingham,[18] in case, to be commissioner with the lieutenant in the Tower.

12. **Sir . . . secretary** Sir William Petre (1505?–72) entered court service through his connections with the Boleyn family. He served as an emissary to France, as a clerk in chancery, and as a deputy for Thomas Cromwell, the king's vicegerent for spirituals, in the dissolution of the monasteries. Having served on various ecclesiastical commissions under Henry, he was knighted and appointed secretary of state in 1543. After serving KP as regent by helping to raise supplies for the king's expedition against Boulogne, he successively became an ambassador to Emperor Charles V, a member of the Privy Council, and an executor of Henry VIII's will.

13. **his pleasure . . . her grace** A key stipulation for KP's exercise of the regency was that she consult daily with the members of the Privy Council whom Henry instructed to attend on her, to the extent that their other responsibilities permitted. Cranmer and Petre, the secretary, were to be the staple figures in attendance. See the general introduction, p. 15.

14. **Lord Parr . . . Horton** KP's now aged uncle, who had played the role of stepfather to her and her brother and sister after their father died in November 1517.

15. **a . . . case** a subordinate to fill a civil or military office in place of the king, if need arose. During Henry's absence, need would constantly arise for KP to take counsel and frame correspondence, and for Edward Seymour, Earl of Hertford, to act as lieutenant-in-case to deal with the alternating hostilities and negotiations with rival Scottish factions in the borderlands.

16. **cure** responsibility.

17. **furniture . . . Tower** armor, weapons, and munitions for the Tower of London, the city's ancient stronghold.

18. **Mr. Walsingham** Sir Edmund Walsingham (1490?–1550). After early military service, he was appointed lieutenant of the Tower of London in 1525—a post he held for twenty-two years, overseeing the treatment of important political prisoners (including the executions of certain of them) during Henry VIII's reign.

Item: Who shall be in commission for passing of all warrants for payment of money. The stamp to remain, and things to be passed by that warrant.

Item: To know the King's majesty's pleasure for horsemen to be retained here at home, and for requiring of certain footmen. It is not thought necessary.

Item: For his majesty's license to such his officers and feedmen[19] as be not appointed to wait in this journey. A commission to be made to the lord chancellor, the Earl of Hertford, the Bishop of Westminster, and Mr. Secretary Petre to license such as are sure to remain at home, agreeing reasonably for it.

Warrants for the denizens, the Mint, Yarmouth, the Ports,[20] the lord chancellor's warrants for the commissioners to my lord of Norfolk, my lord privy seal,[21] etc. His majesty is pleased to sign all these bills, with all the commissioners and things necessary, when they shall be prepared.

A commission to the Queen and [the lords][22] of the Privy Council, to make warrants for money.

NO. 2 HENRY VIII'S COMMISSION FOR PAYMENT OF MONIES BY QUEEN KATHERINE AS REGENT, JULY 11, 1544[23]

[Endorsed] Copy of the commission for payment of money.

To all, etc.

Henry VIII, etc. Know ye that whereas, taking our voyage at this present over the seas to invade the realm of France, we have in our absence ordained our most dear-

19. **feedmen** soldiers serving for pay.

20. **denizens . . . Ports** **denizens** inhabitants, a term that could apply to both citizens and authorized resident aliens. In this context, the latter group is probably meant; see no. 3, n27 below. **Ports** originally "Cinque Ports" (Five Ports), an ancient defensive system comprising a string of harbors along the southeast coast of England, with jurisdiction from Seaford in Sussex to Birchington near Margate.

21. **my . . . seal** John, Lord Russell, first Earl of Bedford (1486?–1555), a gentleman of the privy chamber under Henry VII and Henry VIII and a trusted principal emissary of Henry VIII in dealings with France and with the pope. He was appointed a privy councillor in 1538, lord high admiral and lord privy seal in 1542, and commander of the vanguard of Henry VIII's troops during the invasion of France in summer 1544.

22. **[the lords]** There is a ten-character blank in the document at this point. The term supplied in square brackets is taken from KP's reiterated phrasing in the letter to Henry VIII that is no. 7 below.

23. Source: The National Archives, State Papers 1/189, fol. 218; G&B 19.1:889. Draft in the secretary hand of Sir William Petre—apparently, to judge from frequent abbreviations and recurrently omitted and struck-through words, a text taken down by dictation from the king.

est and most entirely beloved wife, Queen Katherine, to be Regent General of this our realm, in such sort as is expressed in our letters patents of everything made under our great seal of England in that behalf, having also in the said commission appointed and named certain lords and others of our Privy Council to be her assistants in the same:

Forasmuch as there may fortune, in the time of our said absence, divers occasions to defray sundry sums of money, as for posting, victualing, rewards, and manifold other payments that must instantly be made for our affairs, as matters shall then, for the time, occur:

We be pleased and contented that our said most dearest wife, with the advice of, at the least, our said Privy Council named in our said commission of regency, shall and may address from time to time, as occasion shall require, a warrant or warrants in writing, signed with her hand and subscribed with the hands of the said [lords][24] of our said Privy Council, to all and sundry our treasurer and treasurers, receiver and receivers, and to all and sundry other our officer and officers, having charge or custody of any our treasure or money, to deliver and make payment of such sums of money to such assigns or their heirs and successors, and for such matter or matters, as to the discretion of her and of the said [lords] of our said Privy Council shall be thought convenient; and that all such warrants as they shall address forth, signed with her hand and subscribed with the hands of the said [lords][25] of our said Privy Council, shall be a sufficient warrant, and discharge us and our heirs and successors to all and sundry such our officer and officers as shall pay or deliver any sums of money being in their charge or custody. By virtue of such warrants to and made by our said most dearest wife's exercise as aforesaid, willing and commanding as well all and singular of our treasurers, receivers, and other our officers, having charge of any our treasure or money, to serve and execute all such warrants as shall be addressed unto them in form aforesaid; as also charging all and singular our auditors, comptrollers and other our officers having charge to take accounts, to admit and allow in their audits the foresaid warrants for the discharge of all such as pay by money, by witness of the same.

24. **[lords]** Here and at junctures similarly indicated below, there is an 8-character blank in the text.

25. **[lords]** At this point, "councillors," partly written, has been struck through, thus: "~~cou-~~," but no replacement was inserted.

NO. 3 THE QUEEN REGENT'S PROCLAMATION REQUIRING ALL FRENCH RESIDENTS OF ENGLAND TO ASCERTAIN IF THEY HAVE BEEN GRANTED THE STATUS OF DENIZENS AND TO OBTAIN THE LETTERS PATENT FOR IT, JULY 19, 1544[26]

[Headed] The 36th year of Henry VIII, 1544.

A proclamation commanding all Frenchmen whose names were entered before the lord chancellor to be made denizens, speedily to repair to the lord chancellor's house, to know if they be in the roll[27] signed with the King's hand to be made denizens. And that such as were in the roll procure their patents to be sealed with the great seal before the first of September next. And that all Frenchmen in the roll, not having their patents sealed by that date, and all other Frenchmen, not denizens, shall avoid the realm, according to the King's former proclamation.[28]

The King to the mayor, aldermen, and citizens of London, greetings. We charge you that, as soon as these patents are known to you,

Where the King's most royal majesty hath of late published and declared by his proclamation that all Frenchmen not being denizens, which hath entered their names before the Lord Chancellor of England to the intent to be made denizens, should remain, dwell, and abide within this his highness's realm, without any punishment, danger, or forfeiture[29] to them, or any of them, or to any man keeping them in his house or company, unto such time as his grace's determinate pleasure were further known and declared in that behalf.

Forasmuch as, at this present, his majesty hath now determined his pleasure how many of the said Frenchmen so entered shall be made denizens, and signed a roll with his most gracious hand containing the names of the same: his highness

26. Source: British Library, Harley MS 442, fol. 161; G&B 19.1:936; H&L 1, no. 234. A copy in a clerk's secretary hand, bound in a volume titled *Proclamations*. I have cross-referenced the four proclamations issued by KP as queen regent with their numbers in Paul L. Hughes and James F. Larkin, eds., *Tudor Royal Proclamations*, vol. 1, *The Early Tudors, 1485–1553* (New Haven, CT: Yale University Press, 1964), abbreviated "H&L" and followed by the volume and document number.

27. **denizens . . . roll** **denizens** under English law, aliens admitted to citizenship by royal letters patent but barred from inheriting or holding any public office. **roll** a piece of parchment or paper inscribed with some formal or official record, a document or instrument of this form.

28. **patents . . . proclamation** **patents** (or letters patents) open letters or documents, usually from a sovereign or person in authority, issued for various purposes, e.g., to confer some privilege. **avoid** depart, withdraw from. **King's . . . proclamation** This proclamation is H&L 1, no. 227, dated May 16, 1544.

29. **without . . . forfeiture** These stipulations evoke the hostile relations between the two countries as Henry VIII embarked on his campaign to recapture former English territories repossessed by France.

therefore straitly chargeth and commandeth, by this his present proclamation, that all Frenchmen and others, whose names be entered before the said Lord Chancellor of England to be made denizens as is aforesaid, eftsoons[30] repair to the house of the said lord chancellor, there to know whether they be in the said roll or no. And that all such as his highness is pleased shall be denizens, and be in the said roll signed as aforesaid, shall procure and sue out their letters patents for the same, in due form to be made under his majesty's great seal, before the first day of September next coming.

And all those Frenchmen and others that be not in the roll aforesaid, signed with his majesty's hand for this purpose, and all such, being in the same, as shall not procure or sue out their letters patents of denizen as before specified before the said first day of September next coming, shall forthwith avoid this his highness's realm according to his highness's former proclamation, upon the pains and penalties contained and expressed in the same.

And of this, under the applicable legal penalty, let you omit nothing at all. Witness: Katherine Queen of England, and General Regent of the same. From Westminster, the nineteenth day of July, the thirty-sixth of our reign.[31]

NO. 4 QUEEN KATHERINE'S LETTER TO SIR RALPH EVERS, JULY [22,] 1544[32]

[Endorsed] A minute from the Queen to Sir Ralph Evers,[33] July 1544.
[Headed] By the Queen Regent.

Trusty and right well-beloved, we greet you well. And having perceived by such letters as you lately addressed to our right trusty and right well-beloved cousin and councillor, the Earl of Shrewsbury,[34] the King's majesty my lord's lieutenant general in those parts, the good success and victory you lately had upon my said lord's enemies in Scotland,

30. **eftsoons** soon afterward.

31. ***And . . . reign*** In the formulaic language of the royal proclamations issued by KP as regent, she declares as if in the king's own person until the final clause of the text. There her agency and authority are delineated: she "witnesses" (or bears *teste*) as queen and regent to the contents, and their proclaiming is "by" her.

32. Source: BL, Additional MS 32655, fols. 127r–128r; G&B 19.1:962, a "minute"—i.e., digest—of a letter from KP, in Sir William Petre's hand. The sent letter was enclosed with the sent text of no. 5 below.

33. **Sir . . . Evers** the otherwise unknown commander of the English army in the border wars with Scotland.

34. **the Earl . . . Shrewsbury** Francis Talbot, fifth Earl of Shrewsbury (1500–1560), spent most of his career on the borders with Scotland, first as lieutenant general of the North, later as president of the council of the North.

Like as, upon knowledge heretofore of your good service ministered divers times unto his highness, the same hath been much to our rejoice and good contentation, so forasmuch as it hath pleased my said lord to appoint me Regent of this his grace's realm in his highness's absence,

It is not a little to our comfort to perceive the towardness of service in such ministers as his majesty hath left behind him in place of trust and service. And have thought meet therefore, by these our special letters, not only to give unto you our right hearty thanks, but also to require you to do the semblable, on our behalf, to all such gentlemen and others as, by the commendation of your letters, have served his highness in the late journey in Scotland: assuring you that, as occasion shall serve, we shall not fail to retain the same in our good remembrance, and endeavor ourself to administer it to all your comforts accordingly.

NO. 5 LETTER OF THE COUNCIL WITH THE QUEEN TO THE EARL OF SHREWSBURY, ENCLOSING THE QUEEN'S LETTER [NO. 4], JULY 22, 1544[35]

[Endorsed] Minute to the Earl of Shrewsbury 22nd July 1544.

After our most hearty commendations unto your good lordship, the Queen's highness, understanding by such letters as you addressed unto her grace at this present, sent unto you by Sir Ralph Evers, of the good service done by him and others against the King's majesty's enemies; and taking the same in very good and thankful part hath, of her gracious disposition, written letters of thanks unto the said Sir Ralph, requiring him also to do the semblable, in her majesty's name, to such other gentlemen as served in the said exploit: which letters being late sent unto you, we pray your lordship to see delivered accordingly.

And where by your said letters you desire to know her highness's pleasure whether you shall stay there the Scottish herald and open his letters, and after advertise[36] her grace, or else dispatch him without opening his letters, etc., you shall understand that, forasmuch as the King's majesty, answering such letters as the herald brought before, signified his gracious pleasure upon what conditions his majesty would grant safe conduct for the ambassadors, and what things his highness required to be done by them in that behalf: unto which his majesty's resolution, your lordship was also made privy,

The Queen's highness, minding in all things to ensure that resolution, hath willed us to write unto your lordship, praying you to detain the said herald at his

35. Source: BL, Additional MS 32655, fol. 106r; G&B 19.1:963; a digest of a letter in Sir William Petre's hand. **Council . . . Queen** See n11 above.

36. **Scottish . . . advertise** **Scottish herald** a certain Rothesey. **advertise** inform.

arrival there. And so, opening his letters, and knowing of him such credence as he shall have to be further declared, your lordship shall with diligence advertise her grace of the same: upon knowledge whereof, such further answer shall be made unto you as shall appertain. And that not doubting, but your lordship will take order for the sure keeping of the Laird of Fernihurst and his son[37] in such sort and place in the land as shall appertain, we bid you most heartily farewell from Hampton Court the twenty-second of July, anno 1544.

Your good lordship's assured loving friends.

NO. 6 QUEEN KATHERINE'S LETTER TO AN UNKNOWN ADDRESSEE, JULY 23, 1544[38]

[Signed] Katherine the Queen Regent KP

By the Queen.

Right trusty and well-beloved, we greet you well. And forasmuch as we are informed by credible report, at the time of the surrender taken of the nunnery of Holywell,[39] my lord the King majesty's will and pleasure was that our trusty and well-beloved servant, Henry Webb, gentleman usher of our Privy Chamber, should have the preferment of the house and demesnes of the same. Albeit after that, means were found to defeat him, that he had but only the house, chambers, and certain gardens lying within the precinct of the same, amounting to the rent of six pounds yearly, as by his indenture[40] more plainly it doth appear. Since that time he hath been in suit for the purchase of the whole, and hath had the particulars long time in his custom:[41] wherefore, in consideration that our said servant never obtained the whole benefit of his first grant, but that the best part of the said demesne was holden from him, and so continually is like to be,

We shall heartily desire and pray you to be so favorable to him, at this our earnest request, as that he may, for his money, have the purchase, of your hands, of the said six pounds whereof he hath the indenture. And in declaring your kind

37. **the Laird . . . son** Sir Thomas Ker and his heir, two prominent persons in the anti-English faction of the Scottish nobility.

38. Source: BL, Cotton MS Vespasian, F.III, art. 36, fol. 38. Letter in a secretary's hand, boldly signed by KP with her sign manual (official signature) in the upper left corner: "Kateryn the Quene Regent KP."

39. **Holywell** a convent located in Flintshire, northeast Wales, at the site of St. Winifred's Well, the reputed place of her martyrdom circa 634 and a place of Catholic pilgrimage until Henry VIII's dissolution of the religious houses in 1536.

40. **indenture** a deed or sealed agreement or contract between two or more parties.

41. **had . . . custom** This assertion has the approximate force of "use is nine-tenths of possession."

and loving friendship towards him effectuously at the contemplation of these two letters: we shall gratefully accept it and also thankfully remember it, whensoever occasion shall serve us to do you pleasure. Given under our signet, at my lord the King's majesty's honor[42] of Hampton Court, the twenty-third of July, the thirty-sixth year of his highness's most noble reign.

NO. 7 QUEEN KATHERINE'S LETTER TO KING HENRY AT CALAIS, JULY 25, 1544[43]

[Endorsed by a secretary] The Queen's grace to the King's majesty, 25th July 1544.
[Addressed] To the King's most excellent majesty.

Pleaseth your majesty to be advertised that, by such letters as I have received from the lords of your highness's Council dated at Calais the twenty-third of this present, I am fully informed as well of your majesty's good health as also of the prosperous beginning in your highness's affairs and proceedings against your enemies. Both which are so joyful news unto me that, giving unto almighty God upon my knees most humble thanks, I assuredly trust that it shall please Him, by whose only goodness this good commencement and beginning hath taken good effect, to grant such an end and perfection in all your majesty's most noble enterprises, as shall redound to His glory, to the common benefit of Christendom, and especially of your majesty's realms and dominions, to the singular comforts of me and all your faithful subjects, who daily make our prayers and intercessions for preservation and continuance of the same.

My lords of your majesty's Council attendant here have taken order that the sum of forty thousand pounds shall be, on Monday next, conveyed towards your highness by Clement Higham, appointed for that purpose by the high treasurer of your grace's wars, for the sure wafting[44] whereof to Calais. It may please your maj-

42. **honor** a seigniory of several manors held by a baron or lord.

43. Source: TNA, State Papers 1/190, fol. 155r; G&B 19.1:979. In a clerk's secretary hand, with an addition, subscription, and signature by KP, which read:

> I can do no lesse but advertissethe your maieste of the good dyligence of your conseilours here Who taketh muche payne in the settyng forthe of your hiegnis affayres accordyng to ther moost bounde duties not doutyng but all thynges schall be acomplyssched to your graces wyll and plesur.
>
> your graces moost obedyent
> ~~and~~ loving Wyfe and servant
> Kateryn the Quene KP

44. **Clement . . . wafting Clement Higham** a soldier from Suffolk serving in the vanguard of the king's army against France (G&B 19.1:274 [p. 151]). **wafting** transporting.

esty to command order to be taken there, as we shall for our parts do the semblable here, to the best of our powers. And, even so, with no less diligence shall travail to advance unto your majesty, against the beginning of the next month, such and as great a mass of treasure to be employed upon your affairs there, as we may possibly. And of our proceeding therein, and all other affairs here (which, thanks be to almighty God, are in very good order) advertise your majesty from time to time, according to our most bounden duties.

And where, by my said lords' letters, your majesty's pleasure was signified unto me, to have the number of four thousand men more to be put in such a readiness, as the same might set forwards upon one hour's warning, to serve in such sort as your majesty shall further appoint: It may like your highness to understand that my lords of your majesty's Council, having taken order before the arrival of these letters, according to your grace's commandment for the general musters in all parts of your highness's realm, have now eftsoons written again unto the commissioners in such parts, near the seaside, as are most meet to have men transported from, for the speedy hasting of their certificates.[45] Upon the receipt whereof, order shall be taken for the said number, according to your majesty's commandment in that behalf, for the speedy expedition whereof we shall earnestly call on. And of our further proceedings therein, and in all other your majesty's affairs, not fail to advertise your highness with diligence.

My lord Prince and the rest of your majesty's children are all (thanks be to God) in very good health. And thus with my most humble commendations unto your majesty, I pray almighty God have the same in His most blessed keeping, and send you the accomplishments of your most noble heart. From your majesty's honor of Hampton Court the twenty-fifth of July, the thirty-sixth year of your most noble reign.

[Addition in KP's hand]
I can do no less, but advertiseth your majesty of the good diligence of your councillors here: who taketh much pain in the setting forth of your highness's affairs according to their most bound duties, not doubting but all things shall be accomplished to your grace's will and pleasure.

Your grace's most obedient and loving wife and servant,
Katherine the Queen KP

45. **certificates** documents assuring the commissioners' capacity to exercise a particular function—here, to dispatch mustered men to fight in the English army in France.

NO. 8 QUEEN KATHERINE'S LETTER TO THE COUNCIL WITH THE KING AT CALAIS, JULY 25, 1544[46]

[Addressed] To our right trusty and well-beloved, the Council attending upon my lord the King's majesty's most noble person.
[Signed] Katherine the Queen KP

Right trusty and right well-beloved cousins, and trusty and right well-beloved, we greet you well. Letting you wit that, having received your letters of the twenty-third of this present, we have by the same had singular comfort: as well to perceive thereby the state of health my lord, the King's majesty, was in at that present, as also for the good beginning of success of his great affairs there. For your joyful news whereof, we give unto you our right hearty thanks. And forasmuch as, touching the other contents of your said letters, we have presently written at length unto my said lord, the King's majesty, we forbear to repeat the same unto you, not doubting that his highness will communicate the same unto you accordingly. Given under our signet at my said lord the King's majesty's honor of Hampton Court the twenty-fifth day of July, the thirty-sixth year of his majesty's most noble reign.

NO. 9 THE QUEEN REGENT'S MANDATE FOR PAYMENT OF A DEBT, JULY 25, 1544[47]

[Addressed] To the heirs of the Lord Sandes, farmer of the herbage[48] of the great part of Stratfield Mortimer in the county Berkshire
[Signed] Katherine the Queen Regent

By the Queen.[49]

Whereas you are indebted unto us in the sum of twenty-five pounds seven shillings, our pleasure and commandment is that, immediately upon the receipt hereof, you

46. Source: TNA, State Papers 1/190, fol. 156; G&B 19.1:980. In a secretary's hand, with KP's sign manual in the upper left corner.

47. Source: TNA, State Papers 1/191, fol. 201; G&B 19.2:165 mistakenly records a total of twenty-one documents in this set, rather than thirteen. In a clerk's secretary hand, with KP's sign manual in the upper left corner, underscored with looped scrolls. Her signature reads: "Kateryn the Quene Regente."

48. **farmer . . . herbage** **farmer** one who rents or has a lease on a property. **herbage** the pasture of any land as a species of property distinct from the land itself.

49. **By . . . Queen** This mandate is the first of a total of thirteen requiring payment of a debt due, all formerly sealed with KP's signet (now visible as a red stain on the paper). The other mandates, however, are not written as this one is, in the first person but by the signatories Sir Thomas Arundel, Robert Tyrwhit, and Walter Bucler, on the queen's behalf. Their formulaic language varies accordingly; for example, they read "indebted unto the Queen's highness,"

content[50] and pay the same unto our right trusty and well-beloved councillor Wymond Carew, esquire, our treasurer. Or else forthwith to appear before our Council attendant upon our person, wheresoever we shall be, to make answer. Wherefore you ought not, so to do, not failing this to do, as you tender[51] to avoid our high displeasure.

Given under our signet at my lord the King's majesty's honor of Hampton Court the twenty-fifth day of July, the thirty-sixth year of my said lord's the King's highness's reign.

NO. 10 QUEEN KATHERINE'S LETTER TO KING HENRY IN FRANCE, JULY 31, 1544[52]

Pleaseth it your majesty to be advertised: this afternoon were brought unto me letters from your majesty's lieutenant of the North,[53] declaring the apprehension of a Scottish ship by certain fishermen of Rye; and, in the same, certain Frenchmen and Scots, being sent with diverse letters and credence towards the French king[54] and others in France.

And because I thought this taking of them, with the interception of the said letters, to be of much importance for the advancement of your majesty's affairs, ordained (I doubt not) of God, as well to the intent your highness might thereby certainly understand the crafty dealing and juggling of that nation, as also meet with the same after such sort as to your high wisdom shall be thought most convenient, I have presently sent such of the said letters as, upon the view of the same, appeared of most importance unto your majesty. There are a great number of other letters to the French king and others, both from the dowager[55] and others. But they are either of the same effect that these be which I have sent unto your majesty, or general letters only, for credence.

My lords of your majesty's Council have sent to have certain of the chief, both

---

"her highness's pleasure is that," "to appear forthwith before her councillors attendant upon her highness's person," "avoid her grace's high displeasure, And fare you well from the King's majesty's honor of Hampton Court."

50. **content** satisfy.

51. **tender** have respect.

52. Source: TNA, State Papers 1/190, fol. 220; G&B 19.1:1019. In a clerk's secretary hand, with KP's subscription and signature.

53. **lieutenant . . . North** Francis Talbot, fifth Earl of Shrewsbury; see n34 above.

54. **credence . . . king** **credence** a document recommending its bearer as trustworthy. **French king** François I (1494–1547), son of Charles de Valois and Louise of Savoy.

55. **the dowager** Mary of Guise.

of the Scots and Frenchmen, sent up: upon whose examination your majesty shall be further advertised with diligence.

My lord Prince and the rest of your majesty's children are all, thanks be to God, in very good health. And thus, with my most humble commendations unto your majesty, I pray almighty God have the same in His most blessed keeping. From your majesty's honor of Hampton Court, the last day of July, the thirty-sixth year of your majesty's most noble reign.

Your grace's most humble, loving wife and servant,
Katherine the Queen KP[56]

NO. 11 QUEEN KATHERINE'S SECOND LETTER OF THIS DATE TO KING HENRY IN FRANCE, [JULY 31,] 1544[57]

[Endorsed in two other hands] Queen Katherine's letter. 1544. To King Henry, being gone in an expedition to France.

56. **Your . . . KP** The subscription in KP's hand reads as follows, with an underscoring of looped flourishes: "youre graces most humble loving Wiffe and Servant Kateryn the Quene KP."

57. Source: BL, Lansdowne MS 1236, art. 7. fol. 9r; G&B 19.1:1029, whose dating I adopt. In KP's hand. Her original reads:

> Although the dyscourse of tyme and accompte of dayes nether ~~be~~ ys long nor many of your maiesties absens, yett the [wante of] your presens so muche beloved and desired of me, ~~the wante therof~~ maketh me [that] I can [not] quyetly pleasur in any thynge, vntyll I here from your maiestye: the tyme ther for Semeth to me very long, wythe agrett desire to knowe how youre hyeghnes hathe done Syns your departyng hense, whose prosperyte and helthe I prefer and desyre more than myne owne. And wher as I knowe your maiesties absens ys never wythe out grett respectes of thynges moost convenyent and necessary, yett love and affection compelleth me to desyre your presens: And agayne the Same zele and love forces me also to be best content wythe that ‸ [whyche] ys your wyll and pleasure: And thus love maketh me in all thynges to Sett apart myne owne comody[te] and pleasure, and to enbrase moost Ioyfully hys wyll and pleasur, whom I love. God the knower of Secretes can Iuge these wordes not to be only wrytten wythe ynke, but moost truely impressed in the hart, muche more I omytte, lest I Schuld Seme to go aboute to prayse my self, or crave a thanke, whyche thynge to do I mynde nothyng lesse, but aplayne Symple relacyon of my zele and love towarde your maiestye procedying ‸ [from] the abundance of the herte, wheryn I must nedes confesse I deserve no ~~co~~ worthye comendation, havyng Suche Iuste occasion to do the Same. I make lyke acompte wythe your maiestye, as I do wythe God for hys benefytes and gyftes heped apon me dayly, knowlegyng my self all wayes a grette detter vnto hym in that I do omytt my dutye towarde hym, nott being able to recompense the

Although the discourse[58] of time and account of days neither is long nor many, of your majesty's absence, yet the want of your presence, so much beloved and desired of me, maketh me that I cannot quietly pleasure in anything, until I hear from your majesty. The time, therefore, seemeth to me very long, with a great desire to know how your highness hath done since your departing hence: whose prosperity and health I prefer and desire more than mine own. And whereas I know your majesty's absence is never without great respects of things most convenient and necessary, yet love and affection compelleth me to desire your presence. And, again, the same zeal and love forces me also to be best content with that which is your will and pleasure. And thus, love maketh me in all things to set apart mine own commodity[59] and pleasure, and to embrace most joyfully his will and pleasure, whom I love.

God, the knower of secrets, can judge these words not to be only written with ink, but most truly impressed in the heart. Much more I omit, lest I should seem to go about to praise myself or crave a thank. Which thing to do, I mind nothing less, but a plain, simple relation of my zeal and love toward your majesty, proceeding from the abundance of the heart. Wherein, I must needs confess, I deserve no worthy commendation, having such just occasion to do the same.

I make like account with your majesty as I do with God for His benefits and gifts heaped upon me daily, knowledging[60] myself always a great debtor unto Him in that I do omit my duty toward Him, not being able to recompense the least of His benefits: in which state I am certain and sure to die, but yet I hope in His gracious acceptation of my goodwill. And even such confidence I have in your majesty's gentleness, knowing myself never to have done my duty as was requisite and meet to such a noble and worthy prince. At whose hands I have found and received so much love and goodness, that with words I cannot express it.

Lest I should be too tedious unto your majesty, I finish this my scribbled letter, committing you into the governance of the Lord, with long life and prosperous fe-

---

leste of hys benefytes, in wyche state I am certeyne and Sure to dye, but yett I hope in [hys] gracyous acceptation of my good wyll. And even Suche confydence I have in your maiestyes gentyllnes, knowyng my self never to have done my dutye as was requysite and mete to Suche anoble and worthy prynce, at whose handes I have founde and receyved So muche love and Goodnes, ~~which~~ [that] wythe wordes I can not expresse yt, lest I Schuld be to tedyouse vnto your maiestye, I fynyssche thys my scrybeled letter, comyttyng you in to the gouernance of the lorde with long lyf and prossperous felycite here, and after this lyf to enioy the kyngdome of hys electe. from grenewyche

by your maiesties humble obedyent lovyng Wyfe and Servant

Kateryn the Quene KP

58. **discourse** succession, onward movement—a former variant of "course."

59. **commodity** desired condition of things.

60. **knowledging** acknowledging.

licity here, and, after this life, to enjoy the kingdom of His elect. From Greenwich, by your majesty's humble, obedient, loving wife and servant,

Katherine the Queen KP

NO. 12 QUEEN KATHERINE'S LETTER TO THE COUNCIL WITH THE KING IN FRANCE, AUGUST 6, 1544[61]

[Addressed] To our right trusty and right well-beloved, and to our trusty and right well-beloved, the lords and others of the King's majesty's my lord's Privy Council, attendant upon his most royal person
[Signed] Katherine the Queen KP

Right trusty and right well-beloved cousins, and trusty and right well-beloved, we greet you well. And having seen your letters of the fourth of this instant, addressed unto us, containing in one part thereof the good health and prosperous success of my lord the King's majesty, which we doubt not, in the goodness of God, whose almighty hand directeth and preserveth his highness, shall long continue and increase more and more: like as the same being to our most singular comfort, we account ourself to have good cause to give unto you our most hearty thanks, so we do you to understand that we have communicated them to my lords and others of the King's majesty my lord's Council.

By whose advice Sir Robert Tyrwhit[62] is sent to London to take order for the sending unto you, with all diligence, the proportion of ordnance mentioned in your said letters, with the shot according, and also for two thousand shovels, spades, and mattocks, if so many may possibly be gotten:[63] which we doubt not shall be conveyed unto you with as much diligence as may [be]. And where, by your said letters, appeareth that the master of the hoys can by no means be induced to transport the lead, but only for the number of thirteen hoys, which also will go only to the ports of Lynn, Boston, and Newcastle, and yet not thither without wafting: for the which course you would have order taken here, for the transporting of the said lead by so many crayers and other English vessels as shall be meet for that purpose.[64]

61. Source: TNA, State Papers 1/191, fol 53; G&B 19.2:39. In a secretary's hand, with KP's sign manual in the upper left corner.

62. **Sir Robert Tyrwhit** a distant cousin of KP's, who first served in her royal household as her master of the horse and later as her comptroller.

63. **mattocks** tools for digging and grubbing that combine features of axes and picks. **if . . . gotten** A July 23, 1544 letter from the Council with the King in France to the Council with the Queen had requisitioned two thousand shovels and spades for trenching and fortifying.

64. **appeareth . . . wafting** The Council with the King has reported difficulties in securing transport for lead needed by the English army, and the English navy does not appear up to the job. Its **master of the hoys** will risk loading only thirteen **hoys** (small vessels rigged as sloops to carry passengers and goods for short distances along the seacoast) with such a heavy cargo.

You shall understand that my lords of the Council, with as good diligence as they may, will take order to have crayers and ships for this purpose. And yet, considering of the other side, that if we shall send the said lead without wafters, there may follow that loss which we would be most sorry to hear of, we have thought good to advertise you thereof: to the intent either some order may be taken there, my lord admiral[65] now being with you, or, at the least, your good advices sent unto us, what you shall think most meet in this case. Wherein my said lords in the meantime will travail, and, your good advices had, bring the same to full effect with diligence accordingly: thinking for the meantime that it is better, the said lead should remain here, than be with danger sent forth without more surety of wafters than can here be provided with such speed as the thing requireth.

Finally, we have thought good also to send unto you certain letters which were sent unto my lords of the Council: whereby appeared that a vain rumor began to spread, of the landing of certain Frenchmen. And because they, upon the first hearing of the same, casting the worst, feared rather the same to have been done by some seditious person minding, that way, to have raised the countries for some seditious purpose than otherwise (for of the landing of Frenchmen about Gloucester was no likelihood), we dispatched in post, immediately,[66] to the justices of peace of the countries adjoining: as well for the stay of the countries in both events, as also to have further knowledge of the truth therein. And shortly after, received other letters that the thing was begun upon no ground, and that all things, thanks be to God, be very well.

They supposed, at the first, the cause of this rumor to have commenced upon the departing of the navy from Bristol for the conveyance of my lord of Lennox,[67]

The Council with the Queen seeks other craft suitable for **wafting** (transporting), such as **crayers** (small trading vessels), to convey the lead across the English Channel. In the absence of a standing army or an adequate navy, the challenge of securing voluntary cooperation for military maneuvers would continue to bedevil later Tudors.

65. **my lord admiral** John Dudley, Viscount Lisle, and Baron of Malpas, later Duke of Northumberland.

66. **we . . . immediately** Armed with information and interpretation provided by her attendant privy councillors, KP moves quickly as regent. She bolsters defenses against any possibility that the French might invade England on behalf of the Scots while Henry is campaigning in France. She also stifles rumors that the possibility of a French invasion has already become fact. Her anxiety that Henry not take alarm and judge badly of the state of affairs in England bespeaks the danger as well as the burden of the responsibility that her sovereign and husband has entrusted to her.

67. **the conveyance . . . Lennox** Shortly before Henry embarked for France, Matthew Stewart, Earl of Lennox, had married Henry VIII's niece, Lady Margaret Douglas, and had been promised the governorship of Scotland when, as Henry expected, that kingdom would fall into his hands. This political alliance and Henry's attendant promise aimed at consolidating a pro-English faction in Scotland. The opposite conclusion was drawn in the west country, where war hysteria caused Lennox's sailing for Scotland to be construed as a move in a Scottish-French offensive against England.

which they judged to have departed thence. As we thought good to advertise you of the same, lest any other vain report, passing over, might have caused the King's majesty to have conceived other opinion of the state of things than (thanks be unto God) cause is for (praise be to Him). All things here are in very good quiet and order. My lord Prince and the rest of the King's majesty's my lord's children are all in health.

Given under our signet at my lord the King's majesty's honor of Hampton Court, the seventh of August, the thirty-sixth year of his majesty's most noble reign.

NO. 13 QUEEN KATHERINE'S LETTER TO KING HENRY AT BOULOGNE, AUGUST 9, 1544[68]

[Headed] The Queen, Katherine Parr, to King Henry VIII, he being then at the siege of Boulogne.

Pleaseth it your majesty to be advertised, this day I received certain advertisements from my lord of Lennox which, being first showed to my lords of your majesty's Council, I thought it my bounden duty to address unto your majesty with all diligence: having a firm trust and confidence in almighty God, who, of His only goodness, prospereth your affairs in the parties of Scotland to peace;[69] and that, very shortly, much better success of your highness's most noble doings in France. For the good achievement whereof, I and all others, your majesty's loving subjects, do make our daily and continual prayers to almighty God.

My lord Prince and the rest of your majesty's children are all, thanks be to God, in very good health. And thus, with my most humble commendations unto your majesty, I pray almighty God to send the same continuance of health. From your majesty's honor of Hampton Court, the ninth of August, the thirty-sixth year of your majesty's most noble reign.

[Addition][70]
I promise your majesty: I do impute the goodspeed of my lord of Lennox's friends at this time, even because he hath given himself to serve such a master,[71] whom

68. Source: BL, Additional MS 27402, fols. 39v-40r; G&B 19.2:58, describing this as "a modern copy from a MS of Sir Thomas Hanmer." Another copy in BL, Additional MS 39288, fol. 5, reads identically except for one word that does not affect meaning.

69. **prospereth . . . peace** KP expresses the short-lived hopes that Lennox would consolidate a pro-English faction in Scotland; see n67.

70. ***[Addition]*** The copy in Additional MS 27402 describes this as a "Post script in the Queens own hand."

71. **goodspeed . . . master goodspeed . . . time** KP refers to Lennox's early success (goodspeed) in cultivating pro-English affiliates in Scotland. With time, however, Lennox would

God doth aid and support in all things. He might have served the French king, his old master, many years and not attained such a victory of his enemies.

Your majesty's most humble, loving wife and servant,
Katherine the Queen KP

NO. 14 THE QUEEN REGENT'S PROCLAMATION AGAINST EXCESSIVE PRICING OF VARIOUS MILITARY OUTFITTINGS, AUGUST 18, 1544[72]

[Headed] The thirty-sixth year of Henry VIII. 1544.

A proclamation against the excessive price of harness, and commanding all persons having any Almain-rivets[73] to sell, shall show them openly in their shops and outward houses, that such as want them may know where to buy them. And that none sell the best pair of Almain-rivets and all the furniture[74] thereof above the price of nine shillings six pence, on pain of imprisonment, and forfeiture of five pounds per every pair sold above that price.

The King to the mayor and aldermen of London, greetings. We charge you that

Forasmuch as the King's most royal majesty hath of late sent forth his several commissions of musters into all parts of this his realm of England for mustering and levying of his loving, faithful, and obedient subjects, a great number whereof be charged, by virtue of the same, to provide them harness for the defense of themselves and of the realm, at days by the commissioners for that purpose appointed:

His highness understanding that harness hath, of late days, been sold at unreasonable and excessive prices, and minding to have now such a certain price set upon the same as shall be reasonable for all his good subjects, as well the buyers as the sellers of the same, hath therefore ordained and determined, by this his highness's present proclamation made by the advice and consent of his grace's most honorable Council:

That no manner of person or persons, having any Almain-rivets to sell, shall sell any pair of the same, of the best sort with all the furniture thereof, above the price of nine shillings six pence of the lawful money of England, upon pain of im-

---

prove ineffectual in furthering Henry's objective of uniting the two kingdoms. **such . . . master** Henry himself—a characteristically fulsome turn of phrase from KP.

72. Source: BL, Harley MS 442, fol. 162; not calendared in G&B; H&L, 1: no. 235. Copy in a clerk's secretary hand.

73. **harness . . . Almain-rivets harness** military gear, either the defensive or body armor of a foot soldier or all the defensive equipment of an armed horseman. **Almain-rivets** a type of light armor first used in Germany; its overlapping plates joined by rivets, short nails, or bolts provided great flexibility. **Almain** German—an adjective derived from Allemagne (French for "Germany").

74. **furniture** armor, weapons, munitions of war.

prisonment without bail or mainprize,[75] and to lose and forfeit five pounds sterling for every pair sold contrary to this his highness's proclamation.

And his highness further straitly chargeth and commandeth that every person and persons, having any such Almain-rivets to sell, shall make some show of the same outward in their shops and outward houses, that such of his said subjects as will buy the same may thereby know where to be served thereof, for the price aforesaid, upon the pains and penalties above expressed.

And also his highness straitly chargeth and commandeth, all and singular, mayors, sheriffs, justices of peace, bailiffs, constables, and other his officers and ministers that they and every of them, from time to time as often as the case shall require, see this his present proclamation to be put in due execution, as they will avoid his most high displeasure and indignation, and will answer to the contrary at their uttermost perils.

And of this let you omit nothing at all, under the applicable legal penalty. Witness: Katherine, Queen of England, and General Regent thereof. From Hampton Court the eighteenth day of August, the thirty-sixth year of our reign.

NO. 15 QUEEN KATHERINE'S LETTER TO KING HENRY IN FRANCE, AUGUST 25, 1544[76]

[Endorsed] The Queen's grace to the King's majesty, 25 August 1544.
[Addressed] To the King's most excellent majesty.

Pleaseth it your majesty to be advertised: albeit I had at this present none occurrences of importance to be signified unto your highness, your realm being, thanks to almighty God, in very good order and quiet: yet, forasmuch as Richard Higham[77] is at this time dispatched hence unto your majesty with a mass of twenty thousand pounds, I thought it my duty to advertise your majesty of the sending of the same, praying almighty God to send your majesty continuance of health and most prosperous success in all your highness's most noble enterprises.

My lord Prince and the rest of your majesty's children be in very good health.

75. **mainprize** release from detention obtained by finding someone else to take the legal responsibility for one's appearance in court at a specified time.

76. Source: TNA, State Papers 1/191, fol. 166; G&B 19.2:136. In a clerk's secretary hand, with KP's subscription and signature. They read as follows, with an underscoring of looped flourishes: "youre graces moost humble loving Wiffe and Servant Kateryn the Quene KP."

77. **Richard Higham** a soldier from Essex serving in the vanguard of the king's army against France. In his later capacity as under-steward of Waltham, he received an annuity from the king's treasurer of augmentations in November 1544 (G&B 19.1:273 [p. 150], 274 [p. 159], 368 [f. 47]).

And thus, with my most humble commendations unto your majesty, I pray almighty God have the same in His most blessed keeping. From your majesty's honor of Hampton Court, the twenty-fifth of August, the thirty-sixth year of your majesty's most noble reign.

Your grace's most humble, loving wife and servant,

Katherine the Queen KP

NO. 16 QUEEN KATHERINE'S LETTER TO SIR RALPH EVERS AND SIR THOMAS WHARTON, SEPTEMBER 2, 1544[78]

[Endorsed] Minute to the Lords of the East and West marches[79] from the Queen, September 2, 1544.

Right trusty and worshipful, we greet you well. Letting you weet that being by the goodness of my lord the King's majesty appointed Regent of this his grace's realm during his highness's absence, and understanding by sundry advertisements of our right trusty and right well-beloved cousin, the Earl of Shrewsbury, the good and diligent service which hath been and is daily done by you within the office committed unto you, as well for the defense and safeguard of the country and borders there, as also for the chastising of my said lord the King's majesty's enemies, as time and occasion may serve: we have thought good both to give unto you, by these our letters, our right hearty thanks for the same. And also to pray and require you to give the like, in our name, to such captains and gentlemen as have served you within the limits of your commission.[80]

We assure you, by this party, that we neither have failed to report nor shall fail to declare the same to my lord the King's majesty, to yourself, and these councillors, requiring you to continue your accustomed diligence in this behalf accordingly, especially now in the time of the harvest, so as their corn may be wasted as much as may be.[81] My duty remembered, it may like your good lordship to be advertised that this bearer, my lord of Fife, this afternoon with other such warrant . . . [text breaks off]

78. Source: BL, Additional MS 32655, fol. 168; G&B 19.2:172; a heavily revised summary in Sir William Petre's hand. On Sir Ralph Evers, see n33. Sir Thomas Wharton was deputy warden of the western marches (Susan E. James, *Kateryn Parr: The Making of a Queen* [Aldershot, UK: Ashgate, 1999], 102, 184).

79. **marches** areas of England bordering on Scotland and Wales—in this context, those bordering on the Scottish lowlands to the east and the west.

80. **commission** Petre mistakenly left undeleted the immediately following phrase, "assuring you that our," after the "We assure you" clause had been substituted for it.

81. **especially . . . be** KP's formulaic commendations for past services give way jarringly to her present order that Evers and Wharton, Henry's military commanders in the border-

NO. 17 KING HENRY'S ADDENDUM, IN HIS OWN HAND, TO A LETTER TO QUEEN KATHERINE, SEPTEMBER 8, 1544[82]

. . . the closing up of these our letters, the . . . the castle aforenamed, with the dike, is at our commandment and not like to be recovered by the Frenchmen again, as we trust, not doubting, with God's grace, but that the castle and town shall shortly follow the same trade. For as this day, which is the eighth day of September, we began three batteries and have three mines[83] going beside: one which hath done his execution, in shaking and tearing off one of their greatest bulwarks.

No more to you at this time, sweetheart, both for lack of time and great occupation of business, saving we pray you to give, in our name, our hearty blessings to all our children, and recommendations to our cousin Margaret[84] and the rest of the ladies and gentlewomen, and to our Council also. Written with the hand of your loving husband,

Henry R[85]

---

land with Scotland, see to the destruction of as much of the Scots' harvest (and future food supply) as they can. Her severity indicates the recent sharp deterioration in English-Scottish relations (see nn 67, 69, 71) and contrasts markedly with instructions she had given on July 20. The Council with the Queen asked her how to deal with Scottish prisoners in jails in northern England, many of whom could not pay for their own food. KP instructed that those prisoners who "be able to bear their own charges" should do so, and that indigent prisoners should be given some modest relief "if extreme necessity shall so require," until the king's pleasure should be known. This report, in Petre's hand, signed by Cranmer and four other councillors, is calendared as G&B 19.1:943; also see Porter, *Katherine the Queen*, 216.

82. Source: BL, Cotton MS Caligula, E.IV, fol. 56v. Henry's letter, reporting circumstantially to KP on the course of the French campaign, is in a secretary's hand. The letter was damaged during the 1742 fire in Sir Robert Cotton's library. I transcribe what survives, with considerable charring of the edges of the addendum, in Henry's large, blockish "bastard" hand. Prior to the damage, this letter was printed in Edward Rymer's *Foedera, conventiones, literae et cuiusconque generis acta publica* (London, 1703–35), 15:50.

83. **mines** land mines.

84. **Margaret** Margaret Douglas, Countess of Lennox; see n67.

85. **the closing . . . Henry R** In its original spelling, this damaged autograph addendum reads as follows:

> the closyng upp off thes our letters the . . . the castell affore namyd with the Dike is att our commandment and nott lyke to be recovert by the frence men agayne as we trust not dwghtyng with gods grace but that the castell and towne shall shortly folow the same trade for as thys day whyche is the viiith day of september We begone thre bateryse and have iii mynys goyng bysyd won whych hath done hys execution in scakyng and teryng off woon off theyre grettest bulwarkes / nomore to yow att thys tyme swethart both for lacke off tyme and grett occupation off bysynes savyng we pray yow to gyff in our name our hartie blessynges to all our chyldren and recommendations to our cousin margett and the rest off the

NO. 18 THE QUEEN REGENT'S PROCLAMATION REGARDING DESERTERS FROM THE KING'S ARMY WHO HAVE RETURNED FROM FRANCE, SEPTEMBER 10, 1544[86]

[Headed] The thirty-sixth year of Henry VIII. 1544.

A proclamation for the examination of all such persons as left the King and his army in France, and returned into England. And for the attachment and imprisonment of such of them as had not sufficient passport[87] to return, signed with the King's hand, or with the hand of some of the King's lieutenants, or at least with the hand of such, under whom they were appointed to serve.

King Henry VIII to the mayor and aldermen and citizens of London, greetings. We charge you that, as soon as these presents are known to you,

Forasmuch as it is come to the present knowledge and understanding of the King's most royal majesty that divers and sundry persons, being retained to serve his highness in his wars beyond the seas, be returned into England in great numbers and companies, without any manner of safe conduct, passport, or license from his majesty, or any of his grace's lieutenants, or any of the captains of his highness's army, leaving his majesty (being there in his own most royal person) unfurnished of his prescribed and determined force and company, to the great peril and danger of the same, and of all his nobility and the rest of his good subjects attending upon him:

His highness, therefore, by the advice of his most honorable Council, straitly[88] chargeth and commandeth, all and singular, his justices of peace, mayors, sheriffs, bailiffs, constables, and all other his officers and ministers to whom it shall appertain, to examine all such persons as shall come from the army. And if they shall not be able to show sufficient passport and license for their return, signed with his majesty's hand or with the hand of some of his highness's lieutenants, or at the least with the hand of the captain or head officer under whom they were pressed and appointed to do service in the said army, they shall forthwith attach the bodies of the same persons, and that[89] him or them commit to prison, there to remain and

ladies and gentyll women and to our consell allsoo / wryttyn with the hand off your lovyng howsbonde Henry R.

R Abbreviation of "Rex"—Latin for "King."

86. Source: BL, Harley MS 442, fol. 163; copy in a clerk's secretary hand (G&B 19.2:210). H&L 1, no. 236, transcribes a manuscript copy in the Society of Antiquaries library, London, 2, 139.

87. **attachment . . . passport** **attachment** the action of apprehending a person and placing him under the control of a court of law. **passport** a letter or document authorizing a person to pass from a port and leave a country.

88. **straitly** strictly, rigorously.

89. **pressed . . . that** **pressed** (or impressed) compelled to perform military service. **that** the same—the reading in both the BL copy and the Society of Antiquaries copy.

abide, without bail or mainprize, unto such time as they shall be tried according to his laws provided in that behalf.

And of this, let nothing at all be omitted. By Katherine, Queen and General Regent of England. From Westminster the tenth day of September, the thirty-sixth year of our reign.

NO. 19 THE QUEEN REGENT'S PROCLAMATION THAT NO PERSON EXPOSED TO THE PLAGUE MAY COME TO COURT, SEPTEMBER 18, 1544[90]

[Headed] The 36th year of Henry VIII. 1544.

A proclamation that no person, in whose house the infection of the plague doth reign, shall repair to the court.

King Henry VIII to the mayor, alderman, and citizens of London, greetings. We charge you that

Forasmuch as the Queen's highness,[91] General Regent of the realm in the King's majesty's absence, hath been credibly informed that the infection of the plague reigneth in sundry parts within these the cities of London and Westminster, whereby great danger might ensue to her grace's person, the Prince's grace, and other the King's majesty's children, in case any of the inhabitants of the said cities, who have had the infection in their houses, or have resorted to any infected persons, or dwell near any place where the infection is or lately hath been, should repair to court or permit any of those which attend in the court to enter their houses:

Her highness straitly chargeth and commandeth that no manner of person or persons, in whose houses the plague is or hath been, or have resorted to any other infected persons, or dwell near any place where the infection is or lately hath been, do from henceforth repair to the court, or do suffer any of the attendants of the said court to enter their houses where the infection hath been, upon pain of her grace's indignation, and further punishment at her highness's pleasure.

And of this, under the applicable legal penalty, let nothing at all be omitted. By Katherine, Queen of England, and its General Regent. From Oking,[92] the eighteenth day of September, the thirty-sixth year of our reign.

90. Source: BL, Harley MS 442, fol. 164r; copy in a clerk's secretary hand; G&B 19.2:246; H&L, 1, no. 237.

91. **Queen's highness** Between the opening and closing formulas in the king's name, this proclamation originates from KP as regent, as repeatedly documented by the perspective from which concerns are expressed in the body of the text.

92. **Oking** a royal manor in Surrey, where KP and the king's children were distancing themselves from the plague in London and Westminster.

NO. 20 THE QUEEN REGENT'S PROCLAMATION THAT UNDENIZENED FRENCHMEN MAY REMAIN IN ENGLAND DESPITE THE KING'S EARLIER PROHIBITION OF THIS, SEPTEMBER 30, 1544[93]

[Headed] The 36th year of Henry VIII. 1544.

A proclamation that all Frenchmen being no denizens may dwell and remain in England, notwithstanding the King's former proclamation to the contrary.

The King to the mayor and aldermen and citizens, greetings. We charge you, as soon as you know these presents, that in the separate wards, parishes, and other places within the aforesaid city, and within its suburbs as well as its outlying liberties, you will see to it, amply to expound a public proclamation from us, and you will cause it to be done in these words,

Where the King's most royal majesty hath of late published and declared by his proclamation,[94] that all Frenchmen, and others whose names were entered before the Lord Chancellor of England, should repair to the house of the said lord chancellor, there to know whether they were in the roll signed with his most gracious grace or not; and that all such, as his highness was pleased should be made denizens, should procure and sue out their letters patents for the same, in due form to be made under his majesty's great seal, before the first day of September now last past; and all those Frenchmen that were not in the roll aforesaid, signed with his majesty's hand for that purpose, should forthwith avoid this his highness's realm, according to his highness's former proclamation in that behalf, made upon the pains and penalties contained and expressed in the same, as by the same proclamation more plainly appeareth:

His majesty, upon a merciful disposition, and for certain respects and considerations his highness thereunto moving,[95] hath resolved, and is contented and pleased, that all Frenchmen which be not yet denizens nor have not entered their names before the said Chancellor of England shall, by his gracious toleration, re-

93. Source: BL, Harley MS 442, fol. 165; copy. G&B 19.2:332; H&L 1, no. 238. **undenizened** living in a country without a formally accorded right of residence or other rights.

94. **his proclamation** This is no. 3 above, dated July 19, 1544.

95. **certain . . . moving** One of the considerations inhibiting Henry from severity to French subjects residing in England was the disappointing course of his two-front war in France and along the Scottish border. An isolated success for the English army was the siege of Boulogne. The town and castle surrendered on September 14, and KP's brother-in-law Sir William Herbert brought her the news on September 18. Immediately recognizing the value of this news for bolstering the morale of English soldiers and residents along the Scottish border, KP directed her council to inform the English commander, the Earl of Shrewsbury, that "Boulogne is in the King's heads without effusion of blood." Shrewsbury "shall cause thanks to be given to God" by "devout and general processions" in all the towns and villages of the north, and also signify to the wardens of the marches "this great benefit which God hath heaped upon us." The text of these instructions, signed by Cranmer and three other councillors, is dated September 19 and calendared as G&B 19.2:251; also see Porter, *Katherine the Queen*, 219–20.

main, dwell, and abide within this his highness's realm without punishment, danger, or forfeiture to them, or any of them, or to any man keeping them in his house or company, unto such time as his grace, by his proclamation, shall determine his further pleasure in that behalf.

And of this, under the applicable legal penalty, let nothing at all be omitted. By Katherine, Queen of England, and General Regent thereof. From Eltham[96] *the thirtieth day of September, the thirty-sixth year of our reign.*

NO. 21 JOHN PARKHURST'S EPIGRAM ON QUEEN KATHERINE PARR, PROBABLY COMPOSED IN OR SHORTLY AFTER SEPTEMBER 1544[97]

To the incomparable woman, Katherine, Queen of England

If the old Latin and Greek[98] poets had known of you,
Would they have adorned Penelope[99] with such praises?
Surely they would not, for in virtues you excel
Penelope, and her of Argos,[100] by many paces.

96. **Eltham** a royal manor in Kent, at a distance from the plague in the capital.

97. Source: John Parkhurst, *Ludicra siue epigrammata iuuenilia* (1573) (STC 19299), fols. 10–11. An Oxford graduate and accomplished Latin epigrammatist, Parkhurst prepared verses in Latin to welcome King Henry and Queen Katherine to Oxford in 1543, but the visit was cancelled and the verses went unpresented. This epigram on KP is undated, but it can plausibly be assigned to the period of her regency—when the comparison of her to Penelope, who skillfully managed her royal household in the absence of her husband, Odysseus, would have been singularly pertinent. Parkhurst's original reads:

Ad incomparabilem faeminam Catherinam Reginam Angliae

Si te nouissent Latij vatesquè Pelasgi,
Ornassent tantae laudéne Penelopen?
Non certè ornassent: nam tu virtuibus anteis
Penelopen multis passibus Argolicam.

Parkhurst's note in the left margin reads "Hac Regina post paucos annos me in suam familiam ascinit" (After a few years, this Queen received me into her household). Parkhurst became KP's chaplain in or after 1545.

98. **old . . . Greek** Parkhurst employs two adjectives referring respectively to the most ancient inhabitants of Italy and Greece ("Latij," "Pelasgi").

99. **Penelope** Parkhurst's hyperbole compares KP's two and a half months as regent with the mythic Penelope's twenty years of caretaking while Odysseus went to fight in the Trojan War and struggled to return home.

100. **her of Argos** Possibly Electra, who pinned all her loyalty on her father, Agamemnon, when her mother Clytemnestra murdered him to avenge his religious sacrifice of their daughter Iphigenia. Electra incited her brother Orestes to the revenge killing of their mother.

PART 3

Queen Katherine and Her Correspondents

January 1544 to January 1547

NO. 1 FRANCIS GOLDSMITH'S LATIN LETTER TO QUEEN KATHERINE [EARLY JANUARY 1544][1]

[Endorsed in William Cecil's hand, partly cut away] . . . Goldsmith's letter to Queen Katherine. Latin.

1. Source: BL, Lansdowne MS 97, fol. 43. G&B 18.2:531, date this letter to 1543, but Goldsmith's description of KP's pious conduct of her household could refer to any phase of her queenship. KP appointed Goldsmith as her attorney (James, *Kateryn Parr*, 140); in this letter, however, he raises the possibility of serving as her chaplain. His additional mention of a prospective gift of money from her may indicate that he was writing in the New Year's season, and I have conjectured the date accordingly. The original Latin reads as follows, with letters obliterated by tears in the paper restored in square brackets:

> Katerinae Angliae uerè serenissimae reginae, ac dominae suae munificentissimae, Franciscus Goldsmyth salutem optat perpetuam ac honorem nunquam interiturum.
>
> Si regina Austri quae suis finibus excita, iter perquam laboriosum in se suscipere non quaerita est, ut Solomonis sapientiam hauriret, facti sui praeconium sonum iustissimum, Scripturarum resonante tuba, perpetuò consequuta est, Si Hester regina pientissima, zoelo domus dei absorpta, atque eius gloriae quod studiosissime nihil prius aut antiquius ~~haberis~~ habuit, quam populum Israeliticum dura seruitute (qua subinde premebatur) liberatum iri nunquam sui nominis gloriam apud sanctos presertim, deletam patientur; Quanto magis Tuae Excellentiae (Regina nobilissima) nomen, ea post se suimet dabit uestigia quae nec curiosa aetar, (qua una solent omnia ferè intercidere) nec vlla hominum ingrata plerumque obliuio obscurare, aut abluere poterint. Quanto enim christus Solomone maior, quanto huius prae illius sapientia uberior, quanto doctrina firmior ac quanto satius est, populum dei à Diaboli tyrannide asserendum obnixe studere,

[Endorsed in a later hand] Francis Goldsmith, Queen Katherine's chaplain, to her, praising her piety in the profession of the Gospel. XLVII.[2]

To Katherine of England,
truly its most serene Queen and most munificent mistress,
Francis Goldsmith wishes perpetual health, and honor that will never perish.

If the Queen of the South,[3] who, drawn to her borders, had not sought earnestly within herself to undertake an exceedingly laborious journey so that she might drink in the wisdom of Solomon, but if, on the contrary, had been ever urged to

---

atque elaborare, quod à praessura quàm in carne patiuntur, tanto tua laus in regno dei potiores parteis haud dubie habitura est. Ita etenim Deus optimus Maximus tuam ad pietatem mentem instituit, ita prorsus ad pia studia formauit, ut omnia tibi iam prae uno christo, ac eius uerbo uilescere coeperint. Hoc tua rarissima bonitas diebus quibusque, nunc uerè dominicis, è suggestu tibi, tuisque pientissimis famulis resonandum (quod nunquam ante hac in ulla regali praesertim domo factum intelligimus) instituit, cura uitae. Nimis enim raró (prob[a] dolor) christus in regalia palatia admittitur. Tua uero pietas Christum iam diu ab hinc optimis auspicijs ac non sine magno labore Serenissimi a[t]que inuictissimi nostri principis in aulam introductum. Sic excoluit fouitque atque in dies magis ac magis ea liberalitate excipit, ut me[a] auidem spes animum meum habeat, illum non aliquando hospitium quod s[uum] utar in animum posse introducere. Quod uero tua singularis Beneficentia, (quae cum omnibus obuia expromptaque sit, mihi tame[n] praecipue ac impensissime) me licet indignissimum, in tam sanctum tuum famulitium, ubi quotidie Christus celebratur, admittere dignata sit, uerbum sane explicare, imò ne mentis quidem cogitatione ulla dignem satis concipere, quantum tibi pro tanta munificentia, atque pietate debeatur nequeo. Vnde nihil in notis magis habere cogor, quam Deum patrem optimum indefessis praecibus sollicitare, ut tuam sublimitatem perpetuò saluam esse uelit, sic animam tuam sacro coelestis sui uerbi cibo pascat, ut in dies auctior, ac uegetior in illo (per quem sunt omnia) efficiaris. mihi porro, ut Gratiae suae thesauri longe opulentissimum uel minimum assimile impartire dignetur, unde tuae Celcitudin[ae] aliqua ex parte dignum, seruitium, praestare possim. Denique ut tuo exemplo omnibus omnium gentium Nobilissimis mulieribus ad Christum traductis, tandem tecum intelligere possint, quanto quamque certo illo ornamento fuerit, Christum ex a[euum] sibimet induisse. Deus Optimus Maximus tuam Celcitudinem diutissime regnare, ac florere, perpetuòque sibi incollumen esse uelit.

Tuus, tibi magis quam effari possit, addictissimus seruus,
Franciscus Goldsmythus

2. **XLVII** This numeral written in a later hand presumably means "1547," but it is impossible to situate KP in a "royal palace" at any point after Henry VIII's death on January 28, 1547. Perhaps the *V* is a mistake for *I*, and the intended date XLIII (1543), a year that in old-style dating concluded in March 1544 (new style).

3. **Queen . . . South** Goldsmith alludes to the Biblical narrative of the Queen of Sheba, who, hearing of the wisdom of King Solomon, visited him "to prove him with hard questions." His

the deed by a resounding and most righteous public crier with the reechoing trumpet of the Scriptures:

If the most pious Queen Esther,[4] consumed by zeal of the house of God and His glory, will never suffer the glory of her name to be blotted out, especially among the saints, because she ever most eagerly cherished nothing more important or illustrious than that the Israelite people, hard pressed by the harsh servitude under which they had been put, should go free:

By how much more the name of your excellency, most noble Queen, will leave its traces, so that neither a prying age (by which one thing almost all things are wont to go to ruin) nor the ingratitude of many men will be able to darken it with oblivion or wash it away. By as much as Christ is greater than Solomon; by as much as the wisdom of the former abounds over that of the latter; by how much more steadfast and more sufficient learning is, freeing the people of God from the tyranny of the devil to strive with all their might and exert themselves; by how much they suffer in the flesh toward the things to come; by so much more your praise in the kingdom of God will doubtless be sustained by the mightier fruits that you bring forth.

For thus the most good and most great God set your mind toward piety. He thus formed it aright to pious studies, all else now becoming worthless in comparison with Christ alone and His Word. Your most rare goodness has made days that were seldom such, truly Sundays now. Your most pious service and your carefulness of life have redounded from your most exalted station as things that we perceive never to have been done before, in a royal house especially. Exceedingly seldom (affliction is the proof)[5] is Christ admitted into royal palaces.

Your piety cherishes the Christ brought in, a long while since, under the best auspices and not without the great labor of our most serene and most invincible Prince.[6] Your piety so cultivates, fosters, and expands in liberality daily more and

answers satisfied her fully as to his wisdom, for which she blessed God and then presented Solomon with lavish gifts, before returning to her own country (1 Kings 10:1–13; 2 Chronicles 9:1–12).

4. **Queen Esther** How Esther, wife of King Ahasuerus (Artaxerxes) of Persia, rescues her people, the Jews, from the destruction plotted against them by Haman, the king's chief minister, is narrated in Esther 2–8.

5. **(affliction . . . proof)** In the prefatory epistle to his *Obedience of a Christian Man* (1528), William Tyndale assures his reader that "persecution" is "an evident token . . . that it is the true word of God; which word is ever hated of the world, neither was ever without persecution, as thou seest in all the stories of the Bible" (*Doctrinal Treatises and Introductions to Different Portions of the Holy Scriptures, by William Tyndale*, ed. Henry Walker, Parker Society 42 [Cambridge: Cambridge University Press, 1848], 131).

6. **brought in . . . Prince** Goldsmith does not clarify how he considers Henry VIII to have reestablished true Chrstianity in England, but the formal break with papal authority in Rome in April 1533 is a probable referent.

more that hope possesses my eager soul, which otherwise could not be brought to entertain what I feel within it. What in fact your singular kindness may permit (which in all things is ready and easy of access, yet to me extraordinary and most profusely expended) insofar as your holy household where Christ is daily celebrated, may it think proper to admit me, most unworthy, to expound the Word soundly.[7] But I am not worthy to conceive in any thought of my mind how much is owing to you for so much generosity and piety, for I am not able.

Nothing known to me more greatly urges me to entreat the best Father, God, with unwearied prayers that He will keep your highness perpetually safe and sound, that your soul may be fed with the holy food of His heavenly Word, so that every day you will attain to more abundant and more plenteous life, in Him by whom all things are. Henceforth, when I am in your presence, it may be thought proper by your grace to impart to me the smallest share from your very rich treasure: whenceforth I may be able to distinguish myself as worthy in some degree of your highness, in the condition of a servant. Finally, by your example to all of every nation, O noblest among women surrendered to Christ, they who are in your company will be able to understand, by this assured honoring, how much and in what way it will have been advantageous, after a very long time, to have brought Christ in. May the most good and most great God will your highness to reign and flourish, perpetually safe and sound with Him.

Your (more than can be uttered to you) very devoted servant,
Francis Goldsmith

NO. 2 PRINCESS MARY'S AND QUEEN KATHERINE'S JOINT LETTER TO ANNE SEYMOUR, COUNTESS OF HERTFORD, JUNE 3, [1544][8]

[Endorsed by two later hands] Princess Mary and Queen Katherine. To the lady Hertford.
[Addressed in the hand of Princess Mary's secretary] To my lady of Hertford[9]

Madam, after my most hearty commendations, this shall be to advertise you that I have received your letters; and I heartily thank you for your kind remembrance, and the desire ye have of my health. I have been nothing well as yet, these holi-

7. **What . . . soundly** Goldsmith obliquely expresses his desire that KP appoint him one of her chaplains.

8. Source: Hatfield House, Cecil Papers 147/6; G&B 19.1:620. Princess Mary's portion of the letter is in a secretary's hand, subscribed and signed by Mary at the foot of the sheet; KP's portion is entirely in her hand. The assignment of the year is explained in n11.

9. **To . . . Hertford** Anne Stanhope Seymour was the wife of Edward Seymour, first Earl of Hertford, Prince Edward's elder uncle and a member of the Privy Council.

days,[10] wherefore I pray you hold me excused that I write not this to you with my hand. I have delivered your letters unto the Queen's grace, who accepted the same very well.[11] And thus, good Madam, I bid you most heartily well to fare. At Saint James[12] the third day of June.

[Midpage insert in Queen Katherine's hand]
Madam,

My lord your husband's coming hither is not altered. For he shall come home before the King's majesty take his journey over the seas, as it pleaseth his majesty to declare to me of late.[13] You may be right well assured: I would not have forgotten my promise to you in a matter of less effect than this, and so I pray you most heartily to think. And thus, with my very hearty commendations to you, I end, wishing you so well to fare as I would myself.

Your assured friend,
Katherine the Queen KP[14]

[Subscription at page bottom in Princess Mary's hand]
Your assured friend to my power during my life,
Mary[15]

10. **these holidays** Ascension Day followed by Whitsunday (Pentecost), seven weeks after Easter.

11. **your letters . . . well** As becomes clear in KP's text below, Anne Seymour had entreated her, by way of Princess Mary, to persuade Henry to recall her husband from military duty at Newcastle, where his assignment was to secure the border with Scotland. The recall took effect June 10, 1544—one of a series of successes with Henry privately scored by KP.

12. **Saint James** The royal palace now incorporated within the grounds of London's Kensington Gardens.

13. **of late** This allusion identifies 1544 as the year of the letter. Henry's resolutions for the regency are dated July 7 (see No. 1 in Part 2), and he took ship with his army for France on July 12.

14. **Madam . . . KP** KP's message reads as follows in original spelling:

> madam my lord youre husbandes comyng hyther is not altered for he schall come home before the kynges maiegstye take hys journey over the sees as it pleasyth hys maiegstye to declare to me of late You may be ryght well asseuryd I wold not have forgotten my promyse to you in amater of lesse effect than thys and so I pray you moost hartely to thynke. And thus with my very harty commendations to you I ende wyssing you so well to fare as I wold myself
>
> your asseuryd frend
> Kateryn the Quene KP

15. **Your . . . Mary** The princess's subscription and signature read as follows in original spelling: "your assured frend to my power duryng my lyef Marye."

NO. 3 QUEEN KATHERINE'S LETTER OF CONDOLENCE TO LADY JANE WRIOTHESLEY, WIFE OF SIR THOMAS, ON THE DEATH OF A YOUNG SON [SUMMER 1544][16]

[Endorsed in another hand] A letter consolatory to the Lady Wriothesley for the death of her son.

Good my lady Wriothesley,

Understanding it hath pleased God, of late, to disinherit your son of this world, of intent he should become partner and chosen heir of the everlasting inheritance (which calling and happy vocation ye may rejoice), yet when I consider you are a mother by flesh and nature, doubting how you can give place quietly to the same, inasmuch as Christ's mother, endued with all godly virtues, did utter a sorrowful, natural passion of her Son's death, whereby we have all obtained everlastingly to live: therefore, amongst other discreet and godly consolations given unto you as well by my lord your husband as other your wise friends, I have thought with mine own hand to recommend unto you my simple counsel and advice, desiring you not

16. Source: BL, Lansdowne MS 76, art. 81, fol. 182r. An undated text in KP's hand, perhaps the sent letter, perhaps a draft. Births of Wriothesley children occurred in the springs of three successive years from 1543 to 1545, but no record survives of their sexes or names (James, *Kateryn Parr*, 196n). While the phrase "his years . . . so young" could refer to the death of a child older than an infant, I follow James in conjecturally assigning this letter to 1544. Outside the compass of KP's prose works, this letter contains the most developed expression of her conviction that a true Christian must submit to the dictates of God's will without repining or resistance. The original letter reads:

> Good my lady Wreseley Vnderstandynge yt hathe pleasyd god of late to dysinheryte your sonne of thys world ~~for the~~ [of] intent he schuld become partener and chosen heyre of the ever lastynge inherytance wyche callyng and happy vocation ye may reyoise yett when I consyder ~~hym~~ [you] are amother by flessch and nature ~~doubte~~ [doubtyng] how you can geve place quyetly to the same in as muche as chrystes mother indued wythe all godly virtues dyd vtter asorowfull naturall passyon of her sonnes dethe wherby we have all obtayned everlastyngly to lyve therfor amongeste other dyscrete and godlye consolatyons gyven vnto you as wel ~~by~~ by my lord your husband as other your wyse frendes I have thought with myne one hand to recom[m]ende vnto you my sympell counsell and advyse desyri[n]g you not so to vtter your naturall affectyon by inordynate sorowe that ~~o~~ god have cause to take you as amurrer ageynst hys apoyntementes and ordynaunces for what is exessyfe sorow but apleyne evydens ageynst you that your inward mynde dothe repyne ageynste godes doynges and adeclaratyon that you are [not] contented ~~bycause~~ that god hathe put ~~put~~ your sonne by nature but hys by adoptyon in possesyon of the hevenly kyndome Suche as have doubtyd of the everlastyng lyf to ~~come~~ come ~~of~~ dothe sorowe and bewayle the departure hense but those wyche be perswadyd that to dy here ys lyf ageyne do rather honger for deathe and counte ytt ~~ytt~~ afolysche thyng to bewayll yt as an vtter dystinatyon. how muche madam ar you to be co[w]nted

so to utter your natural affection by inordinate sorrow that God have cause to take you as a m[urm]urer against His appointments and ordinances.

For what is excessive sorrow but a plain evidence against you, that your inward mind doth repine against God's doings, and a declaration that you are not contented that God hath put your son—by nature, but His by adoption—in possession of the heavenly kingdom? Such as have doubted of the everlasting life to come doth sorrow and bewail the departure hence. But those which be persuaded that, to die here, is life again, do rather hunger for death, and count it a foolish thing to bewail it as an utter destination. How much, Madam, are you to be counted godly wise that will and can prevent, through your godly wisdom, knowledge, and humble submission, that thing that time would at length finish? If you lament your son's death, you do him great wrong and show yourself to sorrow for the happiest thing there ever came to him, being in the hands of his best Father. If you be sorry for your own commodity, you show yourself to live to yourself.

And, as of his towardness you could but only hope (his years were so young, which could perform nothing), it seemeth that he was, now, a meet and pleasant sacrifice for Christ. Wherefore, good my lady Wriothesley, put away all immoderate and unjust heaviness: requiring you with thanksgiving to frame your heart, that the Father in heaven may think you are most glad and best contented to make Him a present of His spiritual and your only natural son, glorifying Him more in that it hath pleased His majesty to accept and able him to His kingdom than that it first pleased Him to comfort you with such a gift. Who can, at His pleasure, recompense your loss with such a rich jewel, if gladly and quietly ye submit, and refer all to His pleasure.

---

godly wyse that woll and can prevente thowrowghe your godly wysdome knowledge and humble submyssyon that ~~that~~ thynge that tyme wold at lenght fynysche. yf you lament your son^{n}es deathe you do hym grett ~~w~~ wronge and schewe your self to sorowe for the happyest thynge ther ever cam to hym. ~~yf~~ beyng in the handes of hys ~~f~~ best father yf you be sory for your one comodyte you schewe your self to lyve to your self. And as of hys towardnes you could but only hope hys yeares wer so yong wyche could perfourme nothyng yt semythe that he was now a mete and pleasant Sacryfyce for chryst Wherfor good my lady wreseley put awaye all immoderate and vniuste hevynes requyry^{n}g yow with thankes gyving to frame your hart that the father in heven may thynke you are ~~best conte~~ moast glad and best contentyd to make hym apresent of hys spryrytuall and your only ~~spir~~ naturall sonne gloryfyng hym more in that yt hathe pleased hys mayeste to accepte and able hym to hys kyngdome then that yt ^{fyrst} pleased hym to comfort~~he~~ you wythe suche agyfte. who can at hys pleasur reco^{m}pe^{n}se your losse with suche aryche Iuell yf gladly and quyetly ye submyte and refferre all to hys pleasur [The text ends in midline, just above the bottom of the present page edge, which appears to have been cropped of its subscription and signature.]

NO. 4 PRINCESS ELIZABETH'S ITALIAN LETTER TO QUEEN KATHERINE, JULY 31, 1544[17]

Inimical Fortune, envious of all good, she who revolves things human, has deprived me for a whole year of your most illustrious presence, and still not being content with that, has robbed me once again of the same good: the which would be intolerable to me if I did not think to enjoy it soon. And in this my exile I know surely that your highness's clemency has had as much care and solicitude for my health[18] as the King's majesty would have had. For which I am not only bound to serve you but also to revere you with daughterly love, since I understand that your most illustrious highness has not forgotten me every time that you have written to the King's majesty, which would have been for me to do. However, heretofore I have not dared to write to him, for which at present I humbly entreat your most excellent highness that in writing to his majesty you will deign to recommend me to him, entreating ever his sweet benediction and likewise entreating the Lord God to send him best success in gaining victory over his enemies,[19] so that your highness, and I together with you, may rejoice the sooner at his happy return. I entreat nothing else from God but that He may preserve your most illustrious highness, to whose grace, humbly kissing your hands, I offer and commend myself. From Saint James on the thirty-first of July.

Your most obedient daughter and most faithful servant,
Elizabeth

17. Source: *Elizabeth I: Collected Works*, ed. Leah S. Marcus, Janel Mueller, and Mary Beth Rose (Chicago: University of Chicago Press, 2000), 5–6, a modern translation of BL, MS Cotton Otho C.X, fol. 235r. For the text of the princess's Italian original, see *Elizabeth I: Autograph Compositions and Foreign Language Originals*, ed. Janel Mueller and Leah S. Marcus (Chicago: University of Chicago Press, 2003), 5–6. This letter is material evidence that KP could read Italian. One of her prized possessions was an edition of Petrarch's *Canzoniere e Trionfi* (Venice, 1544) in a binding embroidered with her initials and coat of arms (James P. Carley, *The Books of King Henry VIII and His Wives* [London: British Library, 2004], 139).

18. **I know . . . health** During Henry's absence in France, KP's letters repeatedly assured him of the health of all of his children. See nos. 7, 10, 12, 13, and 15 in part 2.

19. **entreating . . . enemies** Elizabeth had a precedent for such an appeal in KP's translation of John Fisher's "A prayer for the King," the first of two that conclude her *Psalms or Prayers* (1544), and her *Prayers or Meditations* (1545).

NO. 5 QUEEN KATHERINE'S INSTRUCTION TO DR. MATTHEW PARKER, DEAN OF THE COLLEGE OF CANONS AT STOKE, SUFFOLK, NOVEMBER 14, 1544[20]

[Signed] Katherine the Queen KP

By the Queen.

Trusty and well-beloved, we greet you well. And whereas by credible report we are informed that the bailiwick of our college of Stoke[21] is now void, to dispose as you and certain other there shall think it meet and convenient: we therefore heartily desire you, at the contemplation of these our letters, to give the same office unto our well-beloved Randall Radcliff,[22] the bearer hereof, who hath already the goodwill of three of them that have interest in the granting of it. So that there rest no farther travail for him, your goodwill once obtained: the which, at this our earnest request, we doubt not but that you will show and declare effectuously, confirmably[23] to our desire in this behalf, accordingly to the expectation that we have hitherto conceived in you. Given under [our] signet, at my lord the King's majesty's palace of Westminster, the fourteenth of November, the thirty-sixth year of his majesty's most noble reign.

NO. 6 QUEEN KATHERINE'S WARRANT FOR PAYMENTS TO HER MASTER OF HAWKS FOR TWO FALCONERS, DECEMBER 8, 1544[24]

[Addressed] To our right trusty and well-beloved councillor, Wymond Carew, esquire, our treasurer and receiver general. And to our treasurer and receiver general hereafter, for the time being.

20. Source: Corpus Christi College, Cambridge, MS 114A, fol. 7r; G&B 20.1:613. In a secretary's hand, with KP's sign manual in the upper left corner.

21. **bailiwick . . . Stoke** **bailiwick** the office or jurisdiction of a bailie or bailiff, specifically, one who manages the estates of a landholder. **our . . . Stoke** This institution was part of KP's marriage jointure as queen and had previously been in the grant of Queen Anne Boleyn (Retha Warnicke, *The Rise and Fall of Anne Boleyn: Family Politics at the Court of Henry VIII* [Cambridge: Cambridge University Press, 1989], 155). Matthew Parker, a future archbishop of Canterbury under Elizabeth, had been serving for more than a decade as its master. KP, recognizing his capacities, continued his appointment (James, *Kateryn Parr*, 137).

22. **Randall Radcliff** Nothing seems to be known of this man beyond his name.

23. **confirmably** KP's word choice springs a rhetorical surprise. She says that her desire will be confirmable by Parker's action rather than, more conventionally, that his action will be conformable to her desire.

24. Source: Kew, Surrey, The National Archives, State Papers 1/244, art. 248; G&B appendix, no. 1664. In a secretary's hand, with KP's sign manual in the upper left corner.

[Signed] Katherine the Queen KP

By the Queen.

Right trusty and well-beloved, we greet you well. And where, for sundry considerations us moving, we have given and granted unto our right trusty and well-beloved servant Anthony Cope,[25] esquire, master of our hawks, the allowance for two falconers to keep our hawks, to either of them sixpence the day: we will and command you to content and pay unto the said master of our hawks, yearly from time to time, the said sums, and discharge in that behalf. Given under our signet at my lord the King's majesty's palace of Westminster, the eighth day of December in the thirty-sixth year of my said lord's reign.

NO. 7 PRINCESS ELIZABETH'S LETTER TO QUEEN KATHERINE, PREFACING HER ENGLISH TRANSLATION OF MARGUERITE OF NAVARRE'S *MIROIR DE L'ÂME PÉCHERESSE*, DECEMBER 31, 1544[26]

To our most noble and virtuous Queen Katherine, Elizabeth, her humble daughter, wisheth perpetual felicity and everlasting joy.

Not only knowing the affectuous[27] will and fervent zeal the which your highness hath towards all godly learning, as also my duty towards you, most gracious and sovereign princess; but knowing also that pusillanimity and idleness are most repugnant unto a reasonable creature and that, as the philosopher[28] saith, even as an instrument of iron or of other metal waxeth soon rusty unless it be continually occupied, even so shall the wit of a man or woman wax dull and unapt to do or understand any thing perfectly unless it be always occupied upon some manner of study. Which things considered hath moved so small a portion as God hath lent me to prove[29] what I could do. And therefore have I (as for assay[30] or beginning, following the right notable saying of the proverb aforesaid) translated this little book

25. **Anthony Cope** a longtime friend of the Parr family, appointed to serve in Queen Katherine's household. He dedicated to her his publication *A godly meditacion vpon .XX. select and chosen Psalmes of the prophet Dauid* (STC 5717) as a New Year's gift in 1547 (see James, *Kateryn Parr*, 148, 201, and the general introduction, p. 27). Also see no. 22 below.

26. Source: *Elizabeth I: Collected Works*, ed. Marcus, Mueller, and Rose, 6–7, a modern-spelling transcription of the original in the princess's hand that is University of Oxford, Bodleian Library, Cherry MS 36, fols. 2–4. For the original-spelling text, see *Elizabeth I: Autograph Compositions and Foreign Language Originals*, ed. Mueller and Marcus, 6–7.

27. **affectuous** earnest, ardent.

28. **the philosopher** a standard form of reference to Aristotle.

29. **portion . . . prove portion . . . me** an allusion to the parable of the talents (Matthew 25:14-30). **prove** try, put to the test.

30. **assay** attempt, trial.

out of French rhyme into English prose, joining the sentences together as well as the capacity of my simple wit and small learning could extend themselves. The which book is entitled or named *The Mirror or Glass of the Sinful Soul*, wherein is contained how she (beholding and contempling[31] what she is) doth perceive how of herself and of her own strength she can do nothing that good is or prevaileth for her salvation, unless it be through the grace of God, whose mother, daughter, sister, and wife by the Scriptures she proveth herself to be. Trusting also that through His incomprehensible love, grace, and mercy she, being called from sin to repentance, doth faithfully hope to be saved.[32]

And although I know that, as for my part which I have wrought in it (as well spiritual as manual) there is nothing done as it should be, nor else worthy to come in your grace's hands, but rather all unperfect and uncorrect; yet do I trust also that, howbeit it is like a work which is but new begun and shapen, that the file of your excellent wit and godly learning in the reading of it, if so it vouchsafe your highness[33] to do, shall rub out, polish, and mend (or else cause to mend) the words or, rather, the order of my writing, the which I know in many places to be rude and nothing done as it should be. But I hope that after to have been in your grace's hands, there shall be nothing in it worthy of reprehension, and that in the meanwhile no other, but your highness only, shall read it or see it, les[t][34] my faults be known of many. Then shall they be better excused (as my confidence is in your grace's accustomed benevolence) than if I should bestow a whole year in writing or inventing ways for to excuse them. Praying God almighty, the Maker and Creator of all things, to grant unto your highness the same New Year's Day a lucky and a prosperous year, with prosperous issue,[35] and continuance of many years in good health and continual joy, and all to His honor, praise, and glory. From Ashridge[36] the last day of the year of our Lord God, 1544.

31. **contempling** contemplating.

32. **doth . . . saved** Elizabeth expresses an identifiably Reformed emphasis on the soul's incapacity to cooperate in its own salvation. KP's embrace of the Reformed faith—markedly aligned, in her case, with Lutheranism—is most plausibly dated to her regency in July–September 1544, when she consulted daily with Archbishop Cranmer, under the absent Henry's directive (no. 1 in part 2; also see the general introduction, pp. 14–15).

33. **if so . . . highness** if your highness so vouchsafe (grant).

34. **les[t]** Elizabeth wrote "less"— a penslip.

35. **with . . . issue** This phrasing can be read as intimating a wish that KP will bear Henry a child in 1545, but it is not necessary to do so.

36. **Ashridge** one of the crown manors, located in Buckinghamshire.

NO. 8 PRINCE EDWARD'S LETTER TO QUEEN KATHERINE, [JUNE 18, 1545][37]

Most honorable and entirely beloved mother, I have me most humbly recommended unto your grace with like thanks, both for that your grace did accept so gently my simple and rude letters, and also that it pleased your grace so gently to vouchsafe to direct unto me your loving and tender letters. Which do give me much comfort and encouragement to go forward in such things wherein your grace beareth me on hand[38] that I am already entered. I pray God I may be able in part to satisfy the good expectation of the King's majesty, my father, and your grace: whom God have ever in His most blessed keeping.

Your loving son,
E. Prince

NO. 9 QUEEN KATHERINE'S LATIN LETTER TO PRINCESS MARY, SEPTEMBER 20, [1545][39]

While the reasons are many, most noble and most beloved lady, that readily invite me at this time to writing, still nothing quite so much moves me as care for your

37. Source: BL, Cotton MS Nero C.X, art. 4, fol. 6; G&B 20.1:975, whose dating of this letter I adopt. In the italic hand of the nine-year-old prince. The BL catalog dates this letter 1546, but the earlier date is likelier for an English text. All of Edward's subsequent letters to KP are in Latin, except for one in French, unless this letter is a further exception. The original reads:

> Most honorable and entierly beloued mother I haue me most humbli recommended vnto youre grace with lyke thankes, both for that your grace did accepte so gentylly my simple and rude letters, and also that it pleased your grace so gentylly to vowchsaufe to directe vnto me your louing and tendre letters, which do geue me much comfort and encouragement to go forward in such thinges wherin your grace bereath me on hand, that I am alredy entered: I pray god I maie be hable in part to satisfy the good expectation of the kinges majesti my father and of your grace. Whom god have euer in his most blessed keping.
>
> Your louing sonne
> E. Prince.

38. **beareth . . . hand** beguiles me. Young Edward purports to detect the socially adept KP in a strategy frequently used by Renaissance counselors: praising a prince for qualities that it was hoped he or she would come to possess.

39. Source: BL, Cotton MS Vespasian, F.III, art 35, fol. 37r; copy of KP's Latin original in Princess Elizabeth's italic, with embellishments and a painstaking imitation of KP's signature and initials. The year is either 1545 or 1547, the two periods of known activity on the project that KP commissioned: English translations of Erasmus's paraphrases of the four Gospels and the Acts of the Apostles. Her employment of Elizabeth as amanuensis for this text in Latin suggests that KP had not yet learned to write in italic script: see Prince Edward's references to this sub-

health, which as I hope it is the best, so I very greatly desire to be made certain of it. Wherefore I send you this messenger[40] who, I judge, will be very pleasing to you both because of his skill in music, in which, I am not unaware, you as well as I delight exceedingly, and also because he, having been in service to me, can report to you with most certainty on my whole state and health. And truly, before this day it was in my mind to have made a journey to you and greeted you in person, but indeed not all things answer to my will: I hope now that, at a very early day this

---

ject in nos. 13 and 18 below. (The heading of a later seventeenth-century copy of this letter in the Bodleian Library, Smith MS 68, fol. 53, refers to "Regina Katharina dotaria" [dowager Queen Katherine], which would weigh in favor of a 1547 date, but the heading also commits the double error of asserting that the letter is in KP's hand and was written to Princess Elizabeth. I consequently dismiss its possible authority.) The Latin text reads as follows:

> Cum multa Sint Nobilissima, ac Amantissima Domina, Quae me facile Invitant hoc tempore Ad scribendum, nihil tamen Perinde me Movet, atque cura Valetudinis tuae, quam ut spero Esse optimam Ita de eadem Certiorem fieri Magnopere Cupio. Quare mitto hunc nuncium Quem judico fore tibi gratissimum, tum Propter artem illam Musicae, qua te simul mecum oppido oblectari non ignoro, tum quod a me Profectus tibi certissime referre possit de omni Statu, ac Valetudine mea. Atque sanè in animo fuit ante hunc diem Iter ad te fecisse, teque coram salutasse, verum voluntati meae non omnia Responderunt: nunc spero hac Hyeme idque Propediem Propius nos esse congressuras. Quo sanè nihil mihi erit jucundium magis, Aut magis volupe. Cum autem (ut accepi) summo, Iam manus / Imposita sit Per Maletum operi Erasmico ~~in~~ In johannem (quod ad translationem Spectat) neque quicquam nunc restet nisi ut justa quedam vigilantia, ac cura adhibeatur In eodem corrigendo Te obsecro ut opus hoc Pulcherimum, atque Utilissimum, iam Emendatum Per Malletum aut aliquem tuorum Ad me transmitti cures, Quo suo tempore Prelo Dari Possit, atque porrò significes, an sub tuo nomine in lucem felicissime Exire velis, aut potius incerto authore: cui operi mea sanè opinione injuriam facere Videberis, si tui nominis Autoritate etiam Posteris commendatum Iri recusaveris: In quo Acuratissime transferendo tantos labores summo Reipublicae Bono suscepisti: Pleures quos (ut satis notum est) susceptura, si valetudo corporis permisset. cum ergo in hac re abs te laboriose admodum sudatum fuisse nemo non intelligat, cur quam omnes Tibi merito deferant laudem reiiceas non video. Attamen ego hanc rem omnem Ita Relinquo Prudentiae tuae, Ut quamcumque velis. rationem inire eam ego maxime approbandam consuero. Pro crumena Quam ad me dono misitisti [misisti] ingenteis tibi gratias Ago. Deum optimum Maximum precor ut vera ac incontaminata felicitate perpetuo te Beare dignetur, in quo etiam diutissime valeas. Ex hanworthia 20 septembris
>
> Tuae studiosissima ac Amantissima
> Katherina Regina KP

40. **this messenger** Probably Walter Erle, groom of the queen's privy chamber, who also served her as a musician on the virginals, but possibly Robert Cooch, steward of her wine cellar, whose skill in music was commended by KP's chaplain John Parkhurst (James, *Kateryn Parr*, 127, 158).

winter, you will be visiting us. Than which truly nothing will be a greater joy or a greater pleasure.

Since, however, as I have heard, the last touch has now been put by Mallet on Erasmus's work *On John* (which he saw through translation),[41] and nothing else now remains except some due attention and care to be applied in correcting it, I pray you to send to me this very fine and very useful work, now emended by Mallet or someone of yours,[42] that it may be given to the press in its time. And further, that you signify whether you wish it to go out most happily into the light under your name, or whether rather by an unknown author. To which work really, in my opinion, you will be seen to do an injury, if you refuse the book to be transmitted to posterity on the authority of your name: for the most accurate translating of which you have undertaken so many labors for the highest good of the commonwealth; and more than these (as is well enough known) you would have undertaken, if the health of your body had permitted. Since no one does not know the amount of sweat[43] that you have laboriously put into this work, I do not see why you should reject the praise that all confer on you deservedly. However, I leave this whole matter to your prudence, so that whatever position you wish to take, I will esteem it most greatly to be approved.[44]

As for the sum of money you sent to me as a gift, I thank you exceedingly. I pray the most good and most great God that He will think it fit to bless you perpetually with true and unblemished happiness: in whom, indeed, may you fare well a very long while. From Hanworth[45] September 20

Your most devoted and most loving
Katherine the Queen KP

41. **Mallet . . . translation** When Mary fell ill, KP transferred her own chaplain, Francis Mallet, into Mary's service to help finish the translation of Erasmus's paraphrase of the Gospel of John. KP's deftness in personal relations shows not only in her success in securing Mary's participation in this evangelically oriented project but also in the solicitude for Mary's health and the cordial regard that this letter expresses. See the general introduction, pp. 16–17.

42. **someone . . . yours** KP leaves open the possibility that Mary may wish another learned person in her service to review the translation of the John paraphrase before it is published.

43. **sweat** On this metaphor for literary composition, see E. R. Curtius, *European Literature and the Latin Middle Ages*, trans. Willard Trask (Princeton, NJ: Princeton University Press 1953; rpt. 1967), 468n.

44. **whatever . . . approved** The graceful tact of this formulation is a signal feature of KP's dealings with the strong-willed Tudors.

45. **Hanworth** one of two dower houses conferred upon KP by Henry VIII, the other being Chelsea. Hanworth was located a short distance northwest of Hampton Court.

NO. 10 NICHOLAS UDALL'S LETTER TO QUEEN KATHERINE PREFACING HIS ENGLISH TRANSLATION OF ERASMUS'S PARAPHRASE UPON THE GOSPEL OF LUKE, SEPTEMBER 30, 1545[46]

To the most virtuous lady and most gracious Queen Katherine,
wife unto the most victorious and most noble Prince, Henry VIII,
King of England, France, and Ireland, etc.,
Nicholas Udall wisheth prosperous health and long continuance, with grace,
peace, and all ghostly comfort in our Lord Jesus Christ.[47]

Like as our Master, Christ, in the Gospel, most gracious Queen Katherine, when the woman that had lived wickedly, being now by His grace called from her sinful life to perfect repentance and amendment, came unto Him sitting at His repast in the house of Simon the leper, and washed his feet with the tears of her eyes, wiped the same with the hair of her head, poured forth upon His head a precious, sweet ointment, and also anointed His feet therewith, did so well allow her true devotion, her earnest zeal, and her tender compassion which she had to comfort Him, that He did not only among all the company declare her present comfort in forgiving her, even there, all her offenses and wickedness afore past, but also promised that she should not lose the condign reward of renown for her tender gentleness to Him showed, insomuch that afore all the presence[48] He openly protested that, wheresoever throughout all the world the Gospel were afterward preached, there should she in such wise at all occasions be had in mind, that the remembrance of her good heart and thankfulness towards Him should never die nor be forgotten:[49]

46. Source: *The first tome or volume of the Paraphrase of Erasmus upon the newe testament* (London: Edward Whitchurch, January 31, 1548) (STC 2854), sigs. Ci r–Cvi v (Luke section separately paginated). Nicholas Udall's reputation as a Latinist dated to his days as a student and fellow of Corpus Christi College, Oxford, where his unconcealed Lutheran leanings occasioned a ten-year delay (1524–34) in the awarding of his MA degree. His outspoken advocacy of the Reformation in this letter to Quen Katherine is the earliest dated evidence of her shift away from religious conservatism. From 1534 to 1541 Udall was headmaster of Eton College. In 1544 he resigned his appointment as vicar of Braintree to work full time on the *Paraphrases* project. Gregory D. Dodds, *Exploiting Erasmus: The Erasmian Legacy and Religious Change in Early Modern England* (Toronto: University of Toronto Press, 2009), 16–22, remarks on Udall's role in promoting Erasmus and the English *Paraphrases* through prefatory letters such as this one to KP.

47. **To . . . Christ** Udall models his salutation on the combined mode of address, greeting, and benediction used by St. Paul in his epistles to various churches; see especially the opening verses of Galatians, Ephesians, Philippians, and Colossians. This Pauline discursive mode is a common device in the writings of sixteenth-century English Reformers from William Tyndale onward.

48. **all . . . presence** all those present.

49. **Like as . . . forgotten** Jesus's encounter with the penitent woman who anoints him with precious ointment is narrated in Matthew 26:6–13 and Mark 14:3–9.

so Luke the evangelist, and Paul with the other apostles of Christ, did in their holy writings not only make mention of such men and preachers as were faithful workers or ministers in Christ's vineyard, but also by whatsoever good matrons and devout women they saw and found either that God was glorified and His honor advanced, or the Gospel preferred, the Word of God furthered, the preachers of the same maintained, the younglings in the faith cherished, the true Christians in their poverty refreshed, the need of the faithful relieved, or the unfeigned believers, in adversities comforted and succored: to such godly women they did not forget nor let pass[50] to give laud, praise, and commendation, as well for the due reward of the parties' selves, as also for the good example and encouraging of others to do the like. For this cause doth Luke in his Gospel[51] more than once make mention of Mary Magdalene, of Joanna the wife of Chuza, of Susanna, and Mary the mother of James. And in the Acts[52] he neither forgetteth nor omitteth to commend Priscilla, Tabitha, Lydia, Damaris. For this consideration Paul commendeth unto the Romans[53] Phoebe, Mary, Tryphena, Tryphosa, Persis, and others. For this respect did Jerome write a whole treatise entitled of noble and famous women,[54] whose nobility and also renown he esteemeth and measureth by none other thing but by their godliness, devotion, zeal, and endeavor to set forth Christ's holy Gospel, and by their godly conversation joined with most studious diligence in reading the Scriptures.

Wherefore, most gracious lady, although here now to renew the memory and praise of the manifold, most excellent virtues and ardent zeal of your highness towards the promoting of the knowledge of God's holy Word and Gospel be a thing more due to your most worthy deserts than easy for my rude pen to express them, and more appertaineth to my duty than it standeth with mine ability and power accordingly to set them forth: yet so to do, at this present, I have thought partly a thing needless because your excellency doth so far surmount and pass all praises which my slender utterance is able to give you that I should therein seem to do a much like thing, as if I would bring forth a smoldering, smoky firebrand in a bright,

50. **let pass** omit.

51. **Luke . . . Gospel** Mary Magdalene is mentioned in Luke 8:2 and 24:10; Joanna, wife of Chuza, in Luke 8:3 and 24:10; Susanna in Luke 8:3; and Mary, mother of James, in Luke 24:10.

52. **in . . . Acts** Priscilla is named in Acts 18:2, 18, 26; Tabitha, in Acts 9:36, 40; Lydia, in Acts 16:14, 40; Damaris, in Acts 17:34.

53. **Paul . . . Romans** Phoebe is named in Romans 16:1; Mary, in Romans 16:6; Tryphena, Tryphosa, and Persis, in Romans 16:12.

54. **Jerome . . . women** Jerome compiled *De viris illustribus* (On Illustrious Men; 393–95 C.E.), a serial account of influential early Christian authors, but he wrote no comparable treatise on illustrious Christian women. Between 383 and 385 he did, however, serve as spiritual director to a group of Roman noblewomen whom he supervised in a strict ascetic life. Several of Jerome's surviving letters are eulogies on these women, including Paula and her daughters Blesilla and Eustochium, Marcella, and Fabiola.

sunny day, of purpose to help augment the clearness of the sun:[55] and partly superfluous because that, on the one side, all men do already know your incomparable virtues and do, with one accord, magnify the same, and on the other side, for that your highness doth so much tender and seek God's glory that ye evidently declare yourself nothing less to mind or to desire than the vain praises or commendation of this world. Yet like as the shadow doth remediless follow and accompany the body in the sunlight, so glory and renown doth inevitably follow and associate[56] excellent virtue. And where the deserts of true virtue are so great and so just, it cannot be chosen[57] but that glory and renown must arise, and so much the more because your highness, as much as in you lieth, doth flee it. For glory (saith the philosophical posy) is of the nature of a crocodile which, being a beast in the flood of Nilus in Egypt, hath this property: that if one pursue him to suppress him, he fleeth and will not abide; and if ye flee, then will the crocodile follow and overtake you.[58]

And forasmuch as glory is by the philosophers defined to be a constant and perpetual praise given to any party by a common consent of good people for the excellency of virtue evidently showing itself in the same party[59] (as, indeed, virtue cannot be hidden, but will appear), how can it be possible that your renown should die, whose manifold excellent virtues do from day to day more and more increase? How can your praise decay, whose acts and monuments are consecrated to immortality, as things not builded upon the sand of ambitious seeking, nor (like bubbles

55. **a smoldering . . . sun** Tyndale's *Obedience of a Christian Man* compares Scripture to sunlight (*Doctrinal Treatises and Introductions*, ed. Walter, Parker Society 42, 317). Thomas Caius uses the figure of lighting a candle in sunlight to compare his translation with the original of Erasmus's paraphrase upon Mark; see p. 111 below.

56. **remediless . . . associate** **remediless** without other possibility. **associate** accompany, attend.

57. **chosen** acceded to, resolved upon.

58. **posy . . . you** **posy** a sententious saying and, as such, one of the "flowers" of rhetoric. **crocodile . . . you** Juan Luis Vives proposes a correlation, "Glory. Crocodile," and elaborates: "It is an animal in the Nile river in Egypt, whose conduct is of this nature: when people pursue it, it flees; when they flee it, it pursues: thus, glory flees those who seek it; it follows those who do not concern themselves with it. Sallust [said] of Cato, the less he sought glory, the more he attained it" (Animal est in Nilo amne Ægypti, cuius hanc ferunt naturam, ut persequentes fugiat, fugientes persequatur: sic gloriam quaerentes fugit, negligentes sequitur. Salustius de Catone, quo minus gloriam petebat, hoc eam magis assequebatur): Vives, *Satellitium siue symbola* (Antwerp, 1546), no. 40.

59. **glory . . . party** Lucius Annaeus Seneca develops this definition of "claritas" (renown, high estimation) in Epistle 102, secs. 8, 14: "Claritas autem ista bonorum virorum secunda opinio est. . . . Consentire in hoc plures insignes et spectabiles viri debent, ut claritas sit. . . . Dicunt claritatem esse laudem bonorum a bonis redditam" (This renown is the favorable opinion of good men. . . . To constitute renown, the agreement of many distinguished and praiseworthy men is necessary. . . . They [fellow Stoics] say that renown is praise bestowed on the good by the good). Seneca VI, *Epistles 93–124*, trans. Richard M. Gummere, Loeb Classical Library (Cambridge, MA: Harvard University Press, 2000), 172–75.

in the rainwater) puffed up with an uncertain blast of worldly vanity, but founded upon the sure rock of God's Word, from whence issueth the lively and the same, the everlasting fountain of true glory indeed? Neither may your highness, in this case, refuse any man's words of praise and commendation, forasmuch as it is a matter as laudable to acknowledge the good things which indeed are in us praiseworthy, as it is uncommendable through vain arrogancy to take upon us that we have not. And though your grace is so far from all ambition and also affection of this world's reward that ye have no eye to any mortal man's recompense, yet cannot good folks but extol and magnify the inestimable number of divine gifts of grace so plenteously heaped and couched in so noble a princess. Though ye would have your well-doings hidden and unspoken of, yet cannot the gratitude of the people hold the peace or pass it with silence. Though your gracious benignity require no thanks, yet cannot the honest hearts of the people forbear or refrain by open protestation to acknowledge by whom they daily receive incomparable benefits. Though your modesty nothing less seeketh than the fame of your good acts to be blown abroad, yet cannot our duties but burst out into words of testifying how much we think ourselves bound unto your highness: so that although the great and manifold benefits which I have privately received at your grace's hands did not now move me, yet could I not, in this most just occasion of the public gratulation, hold my peace.

For your virtuous living, even from your tender years embraced, followed, and still continued; your pregnant wittiness joined with right wonderful grace of eloquence; your studious diligence in acquiring knowledge as well of other human disciplines as also of holy Scriptures, not only to your own edifying but also to the most godly example and instruction of others; your incomparable chastity which, as a most precious jewel, ye have by avoiding all occasions of idleness and by contemning[60] provocations of all vain pastimes kept not only from all spot, but also from all suspicion of staining; your singular modesty coupled with passing[61] great integrity and innocency of all your behavior; your other manifold, unestimable gifts of grace, and among them most principally, your studious seeking to promote the glory of God and of His most holy Gospel, have been the things that have moved the most noble, the most renowned, and the most godly prince of the universal world, our most gracious sovereign lord, King Henry VIII, to judge and esteem your grace a meet spouse for his majesty and, among so many women of nobility, of honor, and of much high price[62] and worthiness, you alone to pick out to be his most dear-beloved and most lawful wife. Neither do we doubt, most gracious lady, but that as the providence of God hath formed and aptized[63] your

60. **contemning** scorning.

61. **passing** in a surpassing degree, exceedingly.

62. **price** excellence, worth.

63. **aptized** made apt. The *OED* does not record Udall's adaptation of Latin "aptare" (to fit, accommodate, adjust).

grace to be a worthy and meet spouse for such an husband, so hath it, by a special election, deputed and preserved the same to some high and notable benefit of the commonweal, and to be an instrument of His glory. The towardness and likelihood whereof, like as in men's opinions undoubted, so doth it already begin to show itself in a number of things which otherwise were not to be looked for, to proceed from any woman, much less from a woman of nobility brought up in the court of a king, where Fortune commonly nurseth, cockereth,[64] and pampereth her darlings such as, by her will, she mindeth and laboreth to corrupt with wealth, idleness, and vanity; and least of all, from a queen being set in place where, if she would become Fortune's wanton, she might without controlment swim in the delices[65] of such prosperity as might occasion her to dote on worldly felicity and to forget God.

But the Psalms and contemplative meditations[66] on which your highness, in the lieu and place of vain courtly pastimes and gaming, doth bestow your night-and-day's study, and which ye have set forth as well to the incomparable good example of all noblewomen, as also to the ghostly consolation and edifying of as many as read them, do well declare not only the thing to be true which Socrates affirmed,[67] that is to wit, that women, if they do so apply their minds, are no less apt, no less witty, no less able, no less industrious, no less active, no less fruitful and pithy in the acquiring or handling of all kinds of disciplines than men are; but also how godly ye bestow your time, how little ye set by the world, how much ye thirst[68] righteousness, how carefully ye seek the kingdom of God in the midst of a thousand occasions which otherwise might withdraw your high estate therefrom. And because ye so much tender the glory of God, that according to the lesson of Christ ye do first, of all other things and principally, seek the kingdom of heaven, therefore hath He, according to His promise in the same place contained,[69] and doth and still will, of His own provision, increase unto you all kinds of necessary comfort and consolation, in much better wise than your grace could devise, in much larger manner than your own self would wish, and in far other sort than ye could imagine to look

64. **a woman . . . cockereth a woman . . . king** Udall's intriguing allusion to KP's childhood appears to support the otherwise unverifiable possibility that she had been included in Princess Mary's nursery and schoolroom during periods when her mother, Maud Parr, was serving as a lady-in-waiting to Queen Catherine of Aragon. Without mentioning Udall, Anthony Martienssen, *Queen Katherine Parr* (New York: McGraw-Hill, 1973), 21–28, expatiates on this possibility, but James, *Kateryn Parr*, 28, dismisses it summarily. **cockereth** indulges.

65. **delices** delights, pleasures.

66. **Psalms . . . meditations** an ostensible allusion to KP as translator of Fisher's original Latin work under the title of *Psalms or Prayers*, published April 25, 1544, and a certain allusion to KP's *Prayers or Meditations*, published June 8, 1545. Not quite four months had lapsed between the appearance of the latter work in print and Udall's writing of this letter.

67. **the thing . . . affirmed** Plato *Republic* 5.455e.

68. **thirst** thirst for.

69. **promise . . . contained** Luke 12:31; Matthew 6:33.

for. These blessings hath His eternal truth and infallible promise performed unto your highness because ye seek Him more than the world, because ye more mind godly contemplation than courtly solaces, because ye more tender[70] His glory than any temporal commodities, because ye esteem the knowledge of His Word more precious than pearl, gold, or any treasures subject to corruption,[71] because ye prefer the advancing of His holy Word before and above all other things, because ye cease not with all your power, with all your diligence, and with all your industry, to set forth to all men's knowledge His holy Gospel and Testament, the only food and comfort of our souls.

And not only doth your grace with most earnest zeal, from the first hour of the day to the twelfth, labor in the vineyard of Christ, sustaining the burden of all the whole day and the parching heat of the smoldering noontide in your own person, but also, at your exceeding great costs and charges, do hire other workmen to labor in the same vineyard[72] of Christ's Gospel, to the end the same may fructify and so plenteously bring forth, that all English people may to their health and ghostly consolation be abundantly replenished with the fruit thereof. And as a good captain, partly to the encouraging of his forward soldiers, and partly to the shaming of dastards or false-hearted loiterers, leadeth and guideth his army, and goeth himself before them, so your grace, far otherwise than in the weak vessels of woman-sex is to be looked for, do show unto men a notable example of forwardness in setting pen to the book:[73] partly to the great comforting of such as fain would do good if they durst, and partly to the shame and contumely of sluggards who, having good talents, do keep them fast lapped up in their napkins, and live idly.[74] And by this means doth your highness right well delare that all your delight, all your study, and all your endeavor is by all possible means employed to the public commodity of all good English people, the King's most loving and obedient subjects, to be nuzzled[75]

70. **tender** regard, respect.

71. **more precious . . . corruption** Jesus likens the kingdom of God to a "treasure hid in the field" and "a precious pearl" (Matthew 13:44–46). He exhorts his hearers to lay up treasures for themselves in heaven, "where neither . . . rust doth corrupt, and where thieves do not . . . steal" (Matthew 6:20).

72. **hire . . . vineyard** Jesus tells the parable of the laborers in the vineyard in Matthew 20:1–16.

73. **a notable . . . book** KP set "a notable example of forwardness" as the first English woman to publish in print a work of hers under her own name. The force of the example can be seen in Princess Elizabeth's decision to translate that work, *Prayers or Meditations*, into Latin, French, and Italian as a gift for Henry VIII at New Year's 1546. She may have been working on her translation when Udall composed this letter.

74. **good . . . idly** Udall alludes to Jesus's parable in Luke 19:12–26 of a lord who entrusted various amounts of money (measured in "talents") to his servants, including one who failed to put his one talent to use but "kept [it] in a napkin."

75. **nuzzled** educated, nurtured.

and trained in the reading of God's Word and in the meditation of His most holy Gospel.

For this Gospel is that same treasure hidden under the cloddy, hard ground in the field of the letter, which your grace, after ye had found, did for joy sell all that ye had to buy the same field withal.[76] And well may such persons be said to have sold all that they had, who set less by all the world than by the Gospel, and as well for the obtaining of the knowledge to themselves as also of desire to help make the same common to others, doth not spare to spend out the treasures of their gold and substance. This is the same precious margarite that Christ speaketh of, which your grace seeking for with great desire, when ye had once found, sold all that ye had to buy,[77] and thought your treasures well bestowed if it might so fortune that ye might find means to make all Englishmen which would read or hear it, to be partakers of the same. This is the grain of mustard seed which, when it was so fine and so little that the unlearned sort of Englishmen could scarce possibly feel or see it, ye of your exceeding charity and zeal towards your country's folks did in such wise help to sow in the field of England, and did so cherish with the fat, battling earth of the Paraphrase that, where before it was in the eyes of the unlettered the least of all seeds, is now shot up and grown much larger in breadth than any other herb of the field, so that it now spreadeth the branches in such a compass, that all English readers may therein find many places where to light and to build them nests,[78] in which their souls and consciences may, to their ghostly comfort, quietly repose themselves. This is the spiritual leaven which your grace, being a ghostly housewife for the behoof of all the whole realm of England and other of the King's majesty's dominions, hath in such wise hidden in all the whole four pecks of English meal[79]—East, West, North, and South—that, by the benefit and mean of this Paraphrase, it is now all made savory and of a pleasant relish to all English people's taste.

Where the text of the Gospel afore was in some parts, though always special, good, and wholesome food, and very restorative to such as were able to brook[80] it, yet to the complexion of gross, rude, and green-stomached Englishmen, disagree-

76. **treasure . . . withal** a second allusion to Jesus's parable in Matthew 13:44.

77. **precious . . . buy** a second allusion to Jesus's parable in Matthew 13:45–46. **margarite** pearl—a borrowing from French.

78. **grain . . . nests** an allusion to Jesus's likening of the kingdom of God to a mustard seed in Luke 13:18–19, Matthew 13:31–32, and Mark 4:31–32, with echoes of the phrases in the Matthew passage describing "the least of all seeds, but when it is grown, it is the greatest among herbs, and is a tree, so that the birds of the air come and make their nests in the branches thereof." **fat** rich, nutritious. **battling** fattening or nourishing to cattle.

79. **leaven . . . meal** an allusion to Jesus's likening of the kingdom of heaven to a woman's leavening of three measures of meal with a bit of yeast in Matthew 13:33 and Luke 13:21. Udall adjusts the number of measures from three to four, to circumscribe all of England within the four points of a compass.

80. **brook** digest, retain in the stomach.

ing and hard of digestion: yet ye, by procuring the whole Paraphrase of Erasmus to be diligently translated into English, have minced it and made it every Englishman's meat, though his stomach be never so weak or tender.[81] Where afore, in some parts again, it seemed to be so light meat that the gross stomachs did no less loathe it than the children of Israel did manna in desert when they said, Our soul is qualmish over this meat, being too light, and is ready to cast it up again: your godly cure in conserving it with the Paraphrase of Erasmus in English hath made so sound and substantial meat for all complexions of people, that it may be to everybody like the abundance of quails[82] raining down in wilderness from heaven, such as best stood with everybody's stomach, appetite, and most desire to be plenteously fed withal. Where, of itself, it is a meat most pure and simple, and therefore to some dainty mouths, used to none but fine terms, to the painted colors and exornations[83] of rhetoric, it seemeth dry and unpleasant: it is now by the aigre-douce[84] sauce of the Paraphrase made more liquid, to run pleasantly in the mouth of any man which is not too much infected with indurate blindness of heart, with malicious cankeredness, and with too, too much perverse a judgment. For Erasmus, like as he doth in all his works excel and pass the most part of all other writers, so in this work of the Paraphrase upon the New Testament he passeth himself.

Therefore, most gracious lady, although your demerits[85] are so far above all praises of man that, how far soever I wade in magnifying your virtuous disposition, your devout study and endeavor to do good things, I shall be sure not to incur any suspicion of flattery: yet do I at this present, omitting all other things, only in

81. **Gospel . . . tender** Udall's image of meat minced finely for English stomachs recasts and elaborates St. Paul's image of new Christians as "babes in Christ" who must be given "milk to drink, and not meat: for ye then were not strong, neither are ye as yet. For ye are yet carnal" (1 Corinthians 3:1–3). **whole Paraphrase . . . Erasmus** Udall represents KP as intending that all of Erasmus's *Paraphrases in Novum Testamentum* be translated into English. The eventual publication of the English translations on July 31, 1548, did include the four Gospels and the Acts of the Apostles in the first volume, and the rest of the New Testament in the second volume. However, the surviving evidence of KP's commissioning activity concerns only the first volume: Luke and Acts (Udall); Mark (Thomas Caius); and John (Princess Mary, assisted by Francis Mallet, after she fell ill). See no. 9 above. Whoever translated the Matthew paraphrase had assimilated the word "hurly-burly," which was just entering English. Very rare in the mid- to late 1540s, "hurly-burly" occurs six times in the translation of the paraphrase of Matthew 24. The word is found in English works from this date by John Bale, Thomas Becon, Hugh Latimer, Thomas Paynell, and Richard Taverner, occurring most frequently in Bale and Taverner (Chadwyck-Healey database "Early English Books Online," search results pre-1547: "hurly burly"). Taverner, two of whose other translations KP used in compiling her personal prayerbook, seems the likeliest of this group to have translated the Matthew paraphrase.

82. **manna . . . quails** For God's sending of manna and quails from heaven to feed the hungry, querulous Israelites in the desert, see Exodus 16:4–17 and Numbers 11:4–9, 31–33.

83. **exornations** methods or means of rhetorical embellishment.

84. **aigre-douce** sweet-and-sour—a borrowing from French.

85. **demerits** merits, deserts.

England's behalf make one among the rest in rendering public thanks to your highness, as well for your other godly travail in furthering the knowledge of God's Word as also most specially in setting men in work to translate the Paraphrase of Erasmus upon all the New Testament. Wherein ye do, both to the young and to the old, as well to the high as to the low, and no less to the rich than to the poor, show much more bounteous liberality in dealing about and in making common unto all good English people the heavenly jewels of Christ's doctrine than if ye should open all kings' coffers of worldly treasures and deal to everyone such abundance as might make them all wealthy and rich forever in this world.[86] And as ye have herein done a deed worthy such thanks and rewards as lieth in none but only God to repay, and a deed to us, your most loving and obedient subjects, so beneficial as no heart can esteem, much less any tongue or pen express: so doubt I not but that ye have done a thing to your most regal spouse, the King's majesty, so acceptable that he will not suffer it to lie buried in silence, but will one day, when his godly wisdom shall so think expedient, cause the same Paraphrase to be published and set abroad in print, to the same use that your highness hath meant it—that is to say, to the public commodity and benefit of good English people, now a long time sore thirsting and hungering the sincere and plain knowledge of God's Word.[87]

For his most excellent majesty, being a man after the heart of the Lord, being a right David chosen to destroy Goliath,[88] the huge and cumbrous enemy of Israel, without any armor and with none other weapon but the stone of God's Word

86. **godly travail . . . world** According to John Foxe, "The Story of Queen Katherine Parr," in *Acts and Monuments* (1570 and subsequent eds.), Bishop Stephen Gardiner, leader of the religiously conservative faction of the Privy Council, sought in 1546 to discredit KP as a heretic and alienate King Henry's affections from her, charging among other things that she believed that all goods should be held in common (an especially opprobrious doctrine of the Anabaptists). Could this charge have been prompted by early access on Gardiner's part to finished portions of the translated Paraphrases and to a wilfully literal misreading of Udall's overstrained figuration of Queen KP distributing the wealth of the royal coffers to the people? See further my general introduction, pp. 22, 25n69. E. J. Devereux, "The English *Paraphrases* of Erasmus," *Bulletin of the John Rylands Library* 51:365–67, and Dodds, *Exploiting Erasmus*, 11–12, describe Gardiner's fulminations against what he considered the rampant heresies in the *Paraphrases*. Gardiner wrote from his imprisonment on heresy charges after the overtly pro-Reformation launching of Edward's rule in 1547.

87. **he will . . . Word** This expression of hope that Henry will eventually authorize the publication of the English *Paraphrases* is doubly revealing. On the one hand, Udall implies his awareness that Parliament, on the king's initiative, has placed Scripture under restrictive access, keyed to social status, in the so-called Act for the Advancement of True Religion (May 1543). This act prohibited householders under the level of yeoman, all dependents and servants, and all women except those of gentle and noble status from reading the Bible. On the other hand, such a hopeful expression regarding Henry at this juncture suggests how strongly Udall and the pro-Reformation party at court were banking on the force of KP's wifely influence.

88. **David . . . Goliath** For David's slaying of Goliath, see 2 Samuel 21:19 and 1 Chronicles 20:5. In comparing Henry to David, Udall compliments KP by alluding to the use of the same

cast out of the sling of the divine Spirit working in him and his laws made here in England; and being the elected instrument of God to pluck down the idol of the Romish Antichrist, who following the steps of his father, Lucifer, hath not only usurped a kind of supremacy and tyranny over all princes on earth, as well Christian as heathen, but also hath insurged[89] against heaven, and hath lift up and exalted himself above all thing that is called God, making void the plain commandments for the advancing of his own more than pharisaical traditions, perverting the true sense of the Holy Scriptures and wresting them to the maintenance of his abominations, being both afore God and man detestable: his highness, being our Hezekiah,[90] by the providence of God deputed and sent to be the destroyer not only of all counterfeit religious (who swarmed among us like disguised maskers and not mummers but mumblers, who under the cloak of holiness seduced the people, and devoured the houses of rich widows, and were maintainers of all superstition, idolatry, and rebellion), but also to root up all idolatry done to dead images of stone and timber as unto God, and committed to other creatures instead of the Creator, directly against the express words of the precept, "Thou shalt have no more gods but Me":[91] his most excellent Majesty, I say, from the first day that he wore the imperial crown of this realm,[92] foresaw that, to the executing of the premises, it was necessary that his people should be reduced to the sincerity of Christ's religion by knowing of God's Word; he considered that requisite it was, his subjects were nuzzled in Christ by reading the Scriptures, whose knowledge should easily induce them to the clear espying of all the sleights of the Romish juggling.[93] And therefore, as soon as might be, his highness by most wholesome and godly laws provided that it might be leeful[94] for all his most faithful, loving subjects to read the Word of

---

comparison to characterize the English army opposing the might of France in "A prayer for men to say, entering into battle," appended to *Psalms or Prayers* and to *Prayers or Meditations.*

89. **insurged** risen up.

90. **our Hezekiah** On the destruction of idols and places associated with their worship by King Hezekiah of Judah, see 2 Kings 18:1–7, 22.

91. **other creatures . . . Me other creatures . . . Creator** This is the fundamental objection of Reformers to the use of images in worship and to prayers to saints (criticized by Udall below): appeals to "other creatures" dishonor the supremacy of God (and Christ). **the precept** Exodus 20:3, the first of the Ten Commandments.

92. **imperial . . . realm** Declaring England to be "an empire" or autonomous *imperium*, governed by "one supreme head and king," the Act in Restraint of Appeals (1533) prohibited appeals by any English subject to the jurisdiction of the pope in Rome. It ordered such appeals—as, for example, Catherine of Aragon's resistance to Henry VIII's divorcing of her—to be heard by the English church courts and provided that any relating to the king would go directly to the upper house of Convocation (the ecclesiastical counterpart of Parliament). See John Guy, *Tudor England* (Oxford: Oxford University Press, 1988), 132–34.

93. **requisite . . . juggling** This is a spirited but hardly dispassionate early interpretation of the break with Rome and the ensuing Henrician Reformation.

94. **leeful** permissible, lawful.

God,[95] and the rules of Christ's discipline, which they professed. He provided that the Holy Bible should be set forth in our own vulgar language,[96] to the end that England might the better attain to the sincerity of Christ's doctrine, which they might draw out of the clear fountain and spring of the Gospel, running evermore clear without any mote or mud, rather than out of the muddy lakes and puddles purposely infected with the filthy dregs of our Philistines, the papists, who had stopped our springs to drive us to their poisoned, muddy gutters and furrows.

By this his majesty's most godly provision, it hath come to pass that the people, which long time had been led in error and blindness by blind guides, monks, friars, canons, and papistical preachers, do now so plainly see the clear light that they do willingly abhor idolatry and superstition; they do now know their duty towards God and their prince; they do now embrace the verity for verity's sale; they see where and how the leaven of the papists[97] hath, by continuance of time and for default of Scripture, soured all the whole batch of Christ's doctrine; they see how, being led by blind guides and pastors in the darkness of ignorance, they fell daily in the deep pit of manifold errors with the same guides; they see that, like as the old Pharisees in the time of Christ's being upon earth had corrupted that sincere doctrine of God's Word and the pure understanding of the Law, teaching the people to leave their poor fathers and mothers destitute, contrary to the plain commandment, rather than to let their treasury to be not enriched: which kind of offering, themselves of mere covetise[98] had invented, and did apply the same to the maintenance of themselves in gluttony and sensuality. So now had the wicked papistry devised a mean to pick the rich folks' purses, and the poor vulgar people clean to devour, under the color of going on pilgrimage to this or that stock of man's hands' making, and under pretense of seeking health of the soul and remission of sin at the hands of Peter, James, John, and Mary, which could not give it, but when such

95. **his highness . . . God** Henry ordered his vicegerent, Thomas Cromwell, to approve the circulation of an authorized English Bible (the "Great Bible") by a proclamation of November 14, 1539, and commanded this text to be placed in every church by a proclamation of May 6, 1541 (Paul L. Hughes and James F. Larkin, eds., *Tudor Royal Proclamations*, vol. 1, *The Early Tudors, 1485–1553* (New Haven, CT: Yale University Press, 1964), nos. 192, 200).

96. **He . . . language** The first edition of the Great Bible appeared from the presses of Richard Grafton and Edward Whitchurch in April 1539. The initiative behind its production has standardly been credited to Cromwell and Cranmer. But Udall's representation of the centrality of Henry's role has been strongly affirmed by G. W. Bernard, *The King's Reformation: Henry VIII and the Remaking of the English Church* (New Haven, CT: Yale University Press, 2005), 521–27.

97. **leaven . . . papists** Udall bases his identification of the Pharisees with the papists (here and above) on Jesus's warning "Beware of the leaven of the Pharisees" (Matthew 16:6, 11; Mark 8:15).

98. **the . . . commandment . . . covetise** **the . . . commandment** "Honor thy father and thy mother" (Exodus 20:12). **covetise** covetousness.

things were asked them, blushed to hear God, the only Author and Giver of all good things, to be so blasphemed.[99]

They see now that, like as the covetous Pharisees passed[100] less at the violation or breaking of God's precepts than of their traditions, and put more justice in washing the outside of their dish or their cup than in the innocency of life and purity of the conscience within; in offering of mints and rue[101] for their lucre than in performing the office of charity to the neighbor; sooner to wink at their own blasphemies against God than to remit a small trespass commited by their weak brother against the fond ceremonies which they and the lawyers had devised and added, besides the law: so the beast of Romish abomination [s]o had clean subverted the true interpretation of Christ's Gospel; and by his mere tyranny joined with most crafty delusion, [s]o had invected into[102] Christ's church and holy congregation all things that were contrary to Christ—that is to wit, instead of pure faith such as Christ requireth, a faith lapped[103] in a patched cloak of beggarly works and ceremonies of his own dressing, and setting forth, instead of religion, superstition; offerings instead of charity; building of chantries in place of relieving and maintaining the lively temple and image of God in the poor; incensing of images instead of the pure sacrifice of an innocent life; instead of trusting in God's mercies, trusting in trentals and masses of *scala coeli*;[104] instead of heaven, a purgatory consisting of material fire, and the same to be redeemed with money given to him;[105] instead of declaring our free redemption in Christ and by Christ, sealed with His most precious blood, the Antichrist of Rome seduced the simple people to put their affiance[106] for remission of sins and obtaining the joys of heaven, by his pardons contained in a piece of parchment or paper with a lump of lead hanging at it, and to be bought of him or of his generation, the monks and friars, for money; instead of the Holy Bible, *legenda*

99. **Peter . . . blasphemed** Udall's envisaged saints in heaven—three of Jesus's apostles and his mother Mary—are abashed to be asked for the salvation and forgiveness that God alone can grant.

100. **They . . . passed They** Henry VIII's English subjects. **passed** objected, stickled.

101. **mints . . . rue** "But woe unto you, Pharisees! for ye tithe mint and rue and all manner herbs, and pass over judgment and the love of God" (Luke 11:42).

102. **[s]o . . . invected [s]o, [s]o** The text reads "to," "to"—a double printer's error. **invected into** brought into, introduced.

103. **lapped** wrapped up.

104. **trentals . . . *coeli* trentals** a set of thirty requiem masses, also the payment made for these. ***scala coeli*** chapels or altars, and masses said there, to which a particular indulgence attached. This indulgence originated in a vision that St. Bernard reportedly had in a church in Rome (Scala Coeli) where he saw souls for whom he was saying mass ascending by a ladder into heaven ("scala coeli").

105. **him** a forward reference to "the Antichrist of Rome" two lines down.

106. **affiance** trust.

sanctorum, the miracles of Our Lady, and martyrologies,[107] which themselves devised and never durst set forth until the party of whom they were made had been an hundred years dead, for fear of being taken in a lie; instead of obeying our liege lord and sovereign, to be subject to foreign potentates, with other abuses so innumerable that no time or words may suffice to declare or reckon them up.

And in this blindness had England still continued, had not God of His infinite goodness and bottomless mercy raised up unto us a new Hezekiah,[108] to confound all idols, to destroy all hill-altars of superstition, to root up all counterfeit religions, and to restore (as much as in so little time may be) the true religion and worship of God, the sincere preaching of God's Word, and the book of the Law—that is to say, of Christ's holy Testament—to be read of the people in their vulgar tongue. That if, in so little time, having no more help but the mere text of the Bible, the people, through the goodness of God and the instinct of His Holy Spirit, have had the eyes of their heart and soul so opened, that they have not only espied the abuses aforementioned, and thousands more in which the Romish Babylon hath certain hundreds of years holden all Christendom captive and thrall: but also have so conformed themself to the sincere doctrine of Christ, that they do with most glad will, with most earnest zeal, and with most studious diligence embrace the truth, abhor the errors wherein they were afore drowned, detest the superstitions wherewith they were afore delighted, hunger and thirst the sincere knowledge of God's Word, by the goodness of God and the gracious provision of our most noble Hezekiah, King Henry VIII, now daily ministered unto them, how is it likely that they would profit in godly knowledge, if they had some other godly exposition or declaration of some good, sincere writer upon the New Testament, for their further edifying?

Of which sort, truly, there cannot any one man be picked out more apt and meet than Erasmus, especially in this his Paraphrase, which your highness of a most godly zeal hath thus procured to be turned into English. Whose doctrine, as it is not in any point (after my poor judgment) corrupt, so doth it without violence or extremity of words utter the doctrine, edify the conscience, declare many abuses, detecting the enemies of God's Word and supplanters of His Gospel by such

107. ***legenda* . . . martyrologies** Udall accurately categorizes major kinds of popular religious works in the later fifteenth and earlier sixteenth century. "John Myrc's *Festial*, the chief English collection of pious legends and miracles, achieved nineteen editions from 1483 to 1532. The . . . heavily fabulous *Golden Legend* by Jacob of Voragine was published in 1483 by William Caxton who, so far from pruning its luxuriance, added seventy new lives of saints." The robust popularity of the *Legenda Aurea* was attested by seven further editions between 1485 and 1527. "Books centering around the saints immensely outnumbered any other type of religious book. . . . Wynkyn de Worde published John of Tynemouth's *Sanctilogium Angliae* in 1516, while the Bridgettine monk Richard Whitford compiled the last of the great hagiographical collections, the *Martiloge*, and saw it published in 1526" (A. G. Dickens, *The English Reformation*, 2nd ed. [London: BT Batsford, 1989], 31–32).

108. **a . . . Hezekiah** See n90 above.

true and lively marks that they may be easily known: so that it cannot be doubted, but it should be incredible furtherance towards the rip[en]ing of the knowledge of God's Word, if it might or shall so stand with the pleasure of our said most gracious sovereign lord, being next and immediately under God, our Supreme Head. Which thing, verily, I would wish and pray to God, might so frame for two considerations: the one, because that the people, having the Paraphrase of Erasmus, shall have the pith of all the doctors and good writers that have anything set forth for the declaration of the Gospels, the Acts, and the Epistles, so that Erasmus may stand, one alone, in as good stead as a great number of other expositors set forth together; and the other, because my heart doth wish that the setting forth of God's glory, the destroying of idols, the confounding and defacing of all popish trumpery,[109] the publishing of the Bible and Gospel of Christ—so godly by his highness intended, so stoutly entered, and so luckily begun—might by the same our most gracious sovereign be in such wise prosecuted and brought to effect, that when heaven, no longer willing to spare him to the world, but that he must give place to nature, shall call him to receive a crown of immortality; and he, for desire thereof, shall willingly surrender and give up this imperial crown of worldly dignity to the most regal imp,[110] his son, our noble Prince Edward, he may deliver to the same a people so well framed, and framed to his hand, that the same may with all ease and prosperous success, and without any let of stumbling-blocks to be laid in his way by papistry, continue the godly trade[111] now at this day so well begun and, thanks to God, luckily proceeding. I would wish—as, indeed, I hope no less—that he might not need to be put to any further travail or cure, but well to conserve and keep things in the same stay and order that his most noble father mindeth to leave all unto him. Our David, Henry VIII, hath already so substantially cast the foundation and raised the building of the Temple, that I trust it shall be no burden for our young Solomon[112] to consummate and finish the same, when his time shall come.

But now I perceive myself, while I enter into opening the desire and prayer of my heart, to have entered into such a large field of talk, which the experience of King Henry's example concerning the trade[113] of religion, and the hope of Prince Edward to be a right follower of so right a leading father doth minister unto me, that, except I here suddenly break off, I am drawn to wade so far in their praises that I were not able in long time to find any way out again. Omitting, therefore, at this present the most worthy and most justly deserved praises of them both, I shall

109. **trumpery** fraud, trickery.

110. **imp** young shoot of a plant or tree, figuratively applied to persons.

111. **trade** practice.

112. **David . . . Solomon** The incessant warfare that prevented David from building God a temple in Jerusalem is cited by his son Solomon in 1 Kings 5:2–5. Solomon's building of the temple is recounted in 1 Kings 6.

113. **trade** course.

turn my style somewhat to treat of Luke, whom it pleased your highness to commit unto me to be translated. Which commandment, when it came first unto me in your grace's name, although I knew how little it was that I could do in this kind, yet was I glad that your commandment did so justly concur with the determination of mine own mind and purpose.

For I had long time afore, with mature deliberation and also with advised election, appointed myself to translate this Paraphrase upon Luke as soon as any such liberty might be, and to make it unto your grace a testification of my duty and thankful remembrance of your manifold benefits afore done to me, of your mere bounty; and two things there were that had moved me to take this province most specially in hand. The one, because that as Luke is the longest of all the evangelists, so is he of all men noted to have written his Gospel most exactly, as well by the relation of the apostles which were present and conversant with Christ while He lived on earth, as also by the instructions of Paul, who was most earnest and full in the justification of faith, and most pithy against the justification of works, albeit they do all, in this point of doctrine, thoroughly consent and agree. The second was, for that Erasmus, who did in this Paraphrase bestow more diligence than in most of the others, had specially dedicated the same unto our most noble King, Henry VIII. And I thought I could not devise any apter gift to present his most dear-beloved wife withal—being of the like zeal, affection, godliness, and devotion that he is—than the same work translated into English, which I certainly knew his majesty to ha[ve][114] singularly well allowed and most graciously accepted in Latin and, in perusing thereof, to be daily exceeding much delighted. And I nothing doubt, most gracious lady, but that the reading thereof should cause no less delectation of mind to you, if the thing were so well done as some man of more learning perchance could have done it. And in this behalf, none other refuge I have but to your most benign favor and pardon, well to accept mine honest heart, mine earnest zeal, and willing labors.

For, as touching the translation [it]self, though I judge and plainly confess myself to be by many degrees inferior in knowledge and faculty to all the others whom I hear that your highness hath appointed to the translating of the other parts, and though I cannot of myself promise any ableness to take such a province in hand: yet (my heart better serving me hereunto than perchance my hand hath done) when I saw that your grace's resolution and pleasure did help to minister courage to mine own heart's desire, I conceived boldness to attempt and enterprise the thing, and thought it most expedient to show mine obedience and prompt goodwill to do your commandment, trusting that though I have not been able, in all behalfs and points requisite, fully to discharge the office of a good translator, yet I have expressed the sense and meaning of the author. As for the grace of the Latin tongue, I

114. **ha[ve]** The text reads "had"—a printer's error.

think unpossible to be lively expressed as this author doth it in the Latin, by reason of sundry allusions, divers proverbs, many figures, and exornations rhetorical, with metaphors innumerable, which cannot with the like grace be rendered in any other language than in the Latin or Greek, besides that an infinite sort of words there be, whose full importing cannot, with one mere English word, equivalently be interpreted. And this imperfection I have, to my little power, so labored to redub,[115] that I trust there be not any point of pithy signification anywhere contained, which I have not in one or other place of the sentence, by some means, thoroughly touched. And forasmuch as I consider it to be a paraphrase—that is to say, a plain setting forth of the sense of the text with as many words as the circumstance thereof, for the better linking of one sentence to another, doth require—I have not so precisely bound myself to every word and syllable of the letter, but that I have taken more respect to the explanation and declaring of the sense than to the number of the Latin syllables. In translating of the very text I think it requisite to use some scrupulosity—and if the translators were not altogether so precise as they are, but had some more regard to expressing of the sense, I think, in my judgment, they should do better—but in a paraphrase, which of itself is a kind of exposition and of commentary, I think it nothing needful to be so precise in the words, so the sense be kept. And this I dare avouch: that if any interpreter should in some places be as brief in the English translation as the author is in the Latin, he should make thereof but a dark piece of work. For that is the only thing that maketh the very text [it]self so dark as it appeareth to be.

In Luke I have had somewhat the more business because that the Latin exemplaries[116] (through whose default or negligence I am uncertain) do vary and not well agree: some having more or less than others, some having another word than another copy hath, some being otherwise pointed[117] than the rest. Whereby I have in some places been driven to use mine own judgment in rendering the true sense of the book; to speak nothing of a great number of sentences which, by reason of so many members or parentheses or digressions as have come in place, are so long[118] that, unless they had been somewhat divided, they would have been too hard for an unlearned brain to conceive, much more hard, to contain and keep it still.

As touching the style—because the judgments of readers be diverse, and some love length; some desire brevity; some can well away with elegant speech; some hate all curiosity; some commend an eloquent style; some think nothing to be

115. **redub** restore, make good.

116. **exemplaries** copies of a work.

117. **pointed** punctuated.

118. **sentences . . . so long** Although he is commenting on the capacious sentence units of Erasmus's Latin, Udall's criticism applies equally to many of his own English sentences in this preface.

plain enough; some will be busy judges of other men's writings and do nothing themselves—it may please your most gracious patience to suffer me to say my poor judgment for the satisfying of them that are reasonable. First, I would not have every reader to require in every writer to be like his own wit, or conveyance, or style or phrase of speaking: but rather to consider that every man hath a vein of his own, either by imitation so confirmed, or by long use so rooted, or of desire to be plain and clear, so grown into a habit, that he cannot otherwise write than he doeth. Some writers hate brevity, and some think all long things to be tedious; and yet is neither of these two sorts to be reproved, so the matter be good, the making fine, the terms apt, and the style flowing without curiosity or affectation. For like as Cicero was so copious that nothing might be added unto him, so was Demosthenes so brief that nothing might be taken away. The same in Latin is between Cicero and Sallust. But Tully[119] would not leave till the eye, the ear, and also the mouth of the reader were full, even in every sentence; Sallust was loath to tire any of these with a whole oration. The Laconians could abide no length; the sophists of Greece could through their copiousness make an elephant of a fly, and a mountain of a molehill. And this I speak rather in commendation of eloquence, of copie,[120] of elegance of style where it is, than to claim that there is any such here. Ovid, Tully, Erasmus could have proceeded in any their invention even infinitely; some other wits could not so. Some love it when it is style-like, and some care for no more but the bare sense. But eloquence of itself, and copie—that is to say, shift[121] of terms—is a virtue in an oration; and that thing chiefly giveth to books that the Latin men call *genium*—that is, life and continuance—that every man will, an hundred years after, set store by it and esteem it worth many times reading over.

What other thing commendeth Chaucer, and causeth his works to be more set by than thousands of other fresh, hasty books hastily shooting forth like May flowers, and not withering, but utterly dying with the first reading? Nevertheless, no man of our time and in our English tongue (which none but ourselves, for our own use, do much pass on) writeth so ornately, but he that hath in sundry words and phrases some smack of his native-country phrases, that he was born in. Yet this notwithstanding, some there be which have a mind to renew terms that are now almost worn clean out of use, which I do not disallow, so it be done with judgment. Some other would ampliate[122] and enrich their native language with more

119. **Tully** an alternative English name for Cicero (Marcus Tullius Cicero), a Roman orator and philosopher.

120. **Laconians . . . copie** **Laconians** Spartans—a people better known for military prowess than for eloquence. **copie** abundance and fluency—qualities of Cicero's oratory widely admired and emulated by sixteenth-century humanist writers.

121. **shift** ingenious devising.

122. **ampliate** enlarge, amplify.

vocables,[123] which I also commend, if it be aptly and wittily assayed. So that if any other do innovate and bring up a word to me, afore not used or not heard, I would not dispraise it; and that I do attempt to bring to use, another man should not cavil at. For an easy thing it is to deprave,[124] and a small glory for one man, in matters of nothing, to labor to deface another. But forasmuch as both do our best, we ought rather thus to think, the one of the other: This man hath seen that I have not; I see no man is so barren, but he is able with some word or other to help garnish his mother tongue with other like sayings, proceeding from humanity and favor to encourage such as are studious. And what if one labor to enrich his country' language, as Tully glorieth that he did amplify the Latin tongue?[125] Is he therefore to be blamed, and not rather to be commended? Thus much I say for the defense of writers and styles in general.

As touching mine own style in this present work, if I should be so straitly examined, I am (as the Greek proverb sayeth) in like case as a man that should hold fast a wolf by both ears.[126] For if he hold him still, he hath a shrew[127] in handling, and cannot so continue ever; if he let him go, he is in jeopardy. So should I, in this

123. **vocables** names, designations.

124. **deprave** vilify, disparage.

125. **Tully . . . tongue** Cicero does not glory personally in his use of amplification to increase the eloquence of Latin; instead he greatly praises the figure for its effects, e.g., in *De oratore* 3.104: "But the highest distinction of eloquence consists in amplification by means of ornament, which can be used . . . to increase the importance of a subject and raise it to a higher level. . . . This is requisite in all the lines of argument as employed to make a speech convincing" (Summa autem laus eloquentiae est amplificare rem ornando, quod valet . . . ad augendum aliquid et tollendum altius dicendo. . . . Id desideratur omnibus eis in locis quos ad fidem orationis faciendam adhiberi). *Cicero 4: De Oratore, Book 3; De Fato, Paradoxa Stoicorum, De Partitione Oratoria,* trans. H. Rackham, Loeb Classical Library (Cambridge, MA: Harvard University Press, 1968), 82–83. Also see Cicero's praise of the linguistic resources of amplification in *De partitione oratoria* 53–54.

126. **(as . . . ears** The literary source for this proverb is Latin, not Greek—Terence's comedy *Phormio*, ll. 506-7: "I am holding the proverbial wolf by the ears. I don't know how to let go or how to hold onto her" (id quod aiunt, auribus teneo lupum / nam neque quo pacto a me amittam neque uti retineam scio). Terence, *Phormio, The Mother-in-Law, The Brothers*, ed. and trans. John Barsby, Loeb Classical Library (Cambridge, MA: Harvard University Press, 2001), 68–69. However, in his annotations on Terence's comedies the grammarian Donatus says that this proverb is of Greek origin and cites it in Greek without giving a source (*Commmenti Donatiani ad Terenti Fabulas*, ed. H. T. Karsten [Leiden: A. W. Sijthoff, 1913], 2:282). This bit of philological lore is just what might have been expected of Udall, who as headmaster of Eton published *Floures for Latine spekynge selected and gathered oute of Terence* (1533) (STC 23899), although the *Phormio* does not figure among the three Terentian texts used in his collection.

127. **a shrew** a troublesome or vexatious thing.

matter, stand in a strait brake:[128] either to incur suspicion of arrogancy if I maintain mine own, and by standing in defense thereof, to be deemed opiniative or ambitious of singularity; or else must I be driven to grant an error where perchance none is. Letting pass, therefore, all such kind of traversing, I shall remit this whole cause (as Tully doth of his book which is entitled *De officiis*[129]) to the judgment, first, of your highness, whom if my labors do satisfy, I shall the better like myself; and then of others—others, I say—in whom resteth humanity to take and interpret all things to the best. In whom is moderation, rather to pardon some faults than to condemn the thing which, though they can, they will not emend; in whom is faculty and knowledge to judge right; in whom resteth favor to wink at a little trip or stumbling in a long piece of work; in whom learning and skillfulness doth work indifferency of affection; and, finally, in whom dwelleth reasonable consideration of man's infirmity, that the best learned doth sometimes err, and no man at all times doeth all things right. For unto such an one as will be a more severe and heavy judge on another man's business than himself either would be or would have others to be on his own, I can say nothing but this: I, for my part, can do no better; if I could I would. And in case ye will either for respect of the public benefit which is meant herein, or else for love towards me, or else for any other just consideration, take your pen and emend any fault that ye shall see, I shall not only not think any wrong done to me, but also I shall, with all my heart, give you thanks for that ye so much tender either my poor honesty, or the thing [it]self, that ye would put to your helping hand, to make it well. And thus I surcease[130] with my vain talk any longer to detain your highness from the fruitful reading of Erasmus, whereof may redound such edifying and increase of knowledge to the same, as the labor of reading may be well bestowed, and the book through your grace's commendation be one day set forth, to the public utility and benefit of all the whole devout congregation of this Church of England. Given from London the last day of September, in the year of our Lord, 1545.

128. **brake** cage of iron or wooden bars; figuratively, a snare, difficulty, dilemma.

129. **Cicero . . . *De officiis*** Cicero addresses his son Marcus at the beginning and the end of *De officiis* (*On Responsibilities / On Duties*), telling him that this work of practical philosophy has been written for him as a guide to a life of moral self-awareness. Udall evidently views the Englishing of Erasmus's *Paraphrases* for the people of England in a similarly edifying light.

130. **surcease** come to an end.

NO. 11. THOMAS CAIUS'S LETTER TO QUEEN KATHERINE, PREFACING HIS ENGLISH TRANSLATION OF ERASMUS'S PARAPHRASE UPON THE GOSPEL OF MARK [CA. SEPTEMBER 30, 1545][131]

To the most excellent and virtuous princess, Queen Katherine,
wife to our most gracious sovereign lord, Henry VIII,
King of England, France, and Ireland, Defender of the Faith,
and of the Church of England and also of Ireland in earth Supreme Head,
Thomas Caius,[132] her daily orator, wisheth perpetual felicity.

Among the innumerable benefits which we have received of almighty God, most worthy and excellent Princess, there is none in mine opinion for the which we are more bounden unto His merciful goodness than for that it hath pleased Him more clearly to illumine us of this age with the knowledge of His holy Word than our forefathers and elders. For who knoweth not how long this realm hath been miserably seduced through ignorance of the Scriptures? Who, even among the uplandish,[133] perceiveth not what intolerable abuses have been, under pretense of true religion and godliness, maintained in this church of England, till such time that God, of His infinite mercy, sent us a new Josiah,[134] by whose righteous administration and godly policy, the light of God's Word that so many years before was here extinct, began to shine again, to the utter extirpation of false doctrine, the root and chief cause of all such abusions?[135]

131. Source: *The first tome or volume of the Paraphrase of Erasmus upon the newe testamente* (Edward Whitchurch, January 31, 1548), sigs. Cir–Ciir (Mark section separately paginated). I have classed this letter with Udall's preceding one because Caius expressly wrote before the death of Henry VIII on January 28, 1547 and thus during the first of the two known phases of activity on this large project. E. J. Devereux first described the project in "English *Paraphrases* of Erasmus," 348–67. Dodds, *Exploiting Erasmus*, 2–26, is a recent new treatment.

132. **Thomas Caius** a highly proficient Latinist trained at All Souls' College, appointed registrar of Oxford University in 1534, who became known to KP through his friendship with Dr. George Owen, one of Henry VIII's physicians. John Parkhurst, another friend with connections to KP, wrote Latin verses commending Caius's literary abilities: "Ad Thomam Caiam," *Ludicra siue epigrammata iuuenilia* (1573) (STC 19299), 121–22.

133. **uplandish** country folk.

134. **a new Josiah** The Old Testament Josiah, a king of Judah, acting on behalf of his people, renewed the covenant with God, to keep His commandments and statutes with all their heart and soul. Then Josiah put a violent end to idol worship in Judah, destroying images, vessels, and sacred sites, burning sacred groves and slaying the priests of the cults (2 Kings 23:1–20). Under Henry religious orders were dissolved and religious houses appropriated as crown property. See Bernard's detailed account in *King's Reformation*, 243–76, 293–319, 433–74.

135. **abusions** misuses, perversions.

This Josiah is our most redoubted sovereign lord, King Henry VIII, a prince garnished with so many excellent gifts of grace, nature, and fortune that he is, in very deed and therefore, most worthily called the perfect mirror, and pearl of all Christian princes. To wade[136] here in the praise of his princely qualities and noble acts achieved to God's honor and the public weal of this realm is not my purpose, for that I know it to be an enterprise far exceeding the compass of my simple learning and barren eloquence, but only to declare how much we are bounden, chiefly unto God and next unto his most excellent majesty, that we have the Scriptures in our mother tongue, and are cured of our old blindness by the medicine of verity. For now, having our spiritual eyes opened, and daily receiving into the same the clear light of God's Word, we begin to see and perfectly to know our only Saviour, Jesus Christ: whom to know is everlasting life and salvation. But so long as the said Scriptures were hid, and kept from the knowledge of the people, few knew Christ aright, and none less than they who appeared to be the chief professors of Christian religion.

For what else is it to know Christ, but to know and confess that, of Him only and by Him, cometh our salvation? That by Him the Father's wrath is appeased; that by Him we been franchised from the captivity and thraldom of the devil; and, to be short, that by Him we are adopted and chosen to be the children of God and inheritors of the kingdom of heaven? Who so knoweth Christ aright surely believeth to attain salvation by Him only, who sayeth: Come unto me, all ye that do travail and are charged, and I shall refresh you.[137] The very office of Christ is to save, and therefore He was called, by the high wisdom of God, "Jesu," that is as much to say as "a Saviour," because (so saith the angel in Matthew[138]) "He shall save the people from their sins." So that it appeareth hereby how greatly they are deceived that think to be saved by any other mean than by Christ, or that make themselves quarter-saviors with Him, ascribing any part of their salvation unto their own works and deservings.

Now how could Christ be known aright, that is to say, to be our only Saviour and Justifier, so long as the Scriptures were shut up and kept from the people, and *Legenda Aurea* with suchlike trumpery[139] lay open for them to pass the time withal, and read instead of the Bible? For this cause chiefly, and also for lack of good preachers to preach and teach the truth, it came to pass that He was almost

136. **wade** proceed.

137. **franchised . . . you** **franchised** made free, enfranchised. **sayeth . . . you** an allusion to Matthew 11:28.

138. **angel . . . Matthew** appearing in a dream to Joseph, espoused to Mary, and speaking thus in Matthew 1:21 of the child to be born to Mary.

139. ***Legenda* . . . trumpery** ***Legenda Aurea*** See n107. **trumpery** See n109.

clean out of knowledge in this realm, insomuch that, during the time of this great ignorance and blindness, many a thousand put more confidence of soul-health in works that were but of men's fantasizing, as in pardons, in pilgrimages, in kissing of relics, in offering to saints, in hallowed beads, in numbering of prayers, in mumbling-up of Psalms not understood, in the merits of those that called themselves religious, and in other like things, disallowed by God and His holy Word, than in Christ, the only author (as is aforesaid) of man's salvation.

But now that, by the gracious permission of our said sovereign lord, the Scriptures are open for every man to read soberly and reverently for his own edifying in virtue and godly living, it is right well known that the foresaid abusions were doctrines of Antichrist's invention, and not of God: and that all such as teach any other way or mean to attain salvation than by Him who saith "I am the way and verity"[140] are false teachers, seducers, and liars. Now do the commandments of God no longer give place, as they were wont to do, unto man's traditions. Now have we learned what is our duty to God, and what obedience we owe unto our prince, God's chief minister, and Supreme Head in earth of our church and congregation. Now is idolatry, hypocrisy, and superstition clean plucked up by roots, and true religion everywhere planted. Now is all false doctrine exiled, and God's Word truly set forth and preached. Now hath England clean forsaken Antichrist of Rome, the greatest enemy of God's holy Word, with all his most ungodly devices and devilish inventions. And all this came of the mere mercy and goodness of almighty God towards us, who, undoubtedly for the assertion of His holy Word and the deliverance of us, His people, out of captivity, ignorance, and blindness, hath raised up in our time this Christian Josiah, and joined unto the same, by most lawful matrimony, your noble grace, a lady, besides other special gifts and singular qualities, wholly given to the study of virtue and godliness.

Wherefore all England hath just occasion to rejoice at this your grace's honorable advancement, yea, rather, highly to thank God that our most gracious sovereign hath matched himself with so virtuous a lady: in whom is the very express resemblance of all his majesty's excellent virtues, but specially of that, his grace's ardent zeal and devotion in favoring and setting forth of God's Word, the mother[141] of all joyful prosperity. A manifest argument whereof, besides many other, is that your grace so much desireth to have the Paraphrases of the renowned clerk Erasmus of Rotterdam upon the New Testament—a work very fruitful and necessary for the true understanding of this part of Holy Scripture—turned into English. And, for

140. **I . . . verity** John 14:6.

141. **mother** The grammatical referent of this noun is the Scriptures, but it functions felicitously as an allusion to KP.

the exploiture[142] and speedy accomplishment of this your grace's most godly desire, hath (as is said) commanded certain well-learned persons to translate the said work, the paraphrase upon St. Mark excepted. Which the right worshipful Master Owen,[143] a man of much learning and no less honesty, and therefore worthily physician to the King's most royal person, moved me, your grace's pleasure first known, to go in hand withal, affirming that I should do a thing right acceptable unto your highness if I would diligently travail therein. The which thing, being very desirous to gratify your highness, and with my poor service and diligence to further, as much as in me lay, the godly purpose of the same, I right gladly promised him to do, trusting rather upon the benign acceptation of your gracious goodness than upon the slenderness of my wit and learning, far unable worthily to achieve so weighty an enterprise.

For the author hereof was a man of incomparable eloquence, and therefore it is not possible for a person scarcely of mean learning, as I am, to set out everything, specially in our English tongue, being very barren of words and phrases (I will not say barbarous) withal, so lively and with like grace as he wrote it first in the Latin. Wherefore I minded nothing less than to contend with him in ornate speech and eloquence, but have done my diligent endeavor so to interpret the said work, that it should be both plain and pleasant unto the reader. And not only that, but also to discharge the chiefest office of an interpreter, which is faithfully to translate, and express everything according to the true sense and meaning of the author. If I have, most virtuous Princess, anywhere failed thus to do, it hath been rather for lack of learning and better knowledge than of any goodwill and diligence. To speak here anything either in the praise of the author of this present work, or of the work itself, in mine opinion shall not be needful: for that the author is so much renowned for his excellency in learning that my praises can no more illustrate and set forth his glory than a candle (as the common proverb is) give light unto the sun;[144] and the great utility of the other cannot so well be set out by any man's praise and condemnation as it shall evidently appear unto them that will diligently read and peruse it. If this my goodwill and endeavor may be acceptable unto your highness, as the great fame of your bounty and gracious goodness putteth me in comfort it shall be, I will hereafter, God assisting me, employ my whole study and labors in such wise that the fruit thereof shall be more worthy to be presented unto your noble

142. **exploiture** achievement.

143. **Master Owen** As one of King Henry's physicians, Dr. George Owen had attended Queen Jane Seymour on her deathbed after she gave birth to Prince Edward in October 1537; in 1538 Owen was named as a physician to Edward (John Gough Nichols, ed., *Literary Remains of King Edward VI* [London, 1857], 1:xxxv).

144. **candle . . . sun** See n55 above.

grace than this rude translation, the which I am bold at this present, through the affiance[145] of your natural gentleness, to dedicate unto the same. I beseech almighty God long to preserve our said sovereign lord, your grace, and that most comfortable flower of all England, noble Prince Edward, in continual honor, joy, and prosperity.

NO. 12 JOHN PARKHURST'S TWO LATIN EPIGRAMS ON QUEEN KATHERINE PARR AND KATHERINE BRANDON, DUCHESS OF SUFFOLK [CA. LATE 1545][146]

On the incomparable women, Katherine, the English Queen, and Katherine, Duchess of Suffolk

Ennobled is England by noble Katherines;
Know thou this: one is a Queen, another a Duchess.
O blest, thrice blest is England with such jewels;
Blest thou, too, Parkhurst, in such mistresses of households.[147]

145. **affiance** See n106 above.

146. Source: John Parkhurst, *Ludicra siue Epigrammata iuuenilia*, 117. This epigram is undated; the conjectural date takes into account Udall's clear testimony to KP's advocacy of Reformation beliefs and objectives in his letter of September 30, 1545 (no. 10 above), and the equally clear advocacy of Reformation beliefs and objectives by Katherine Willoughby Brandon, Duchess of Suffolk, and her husband, Charles Brandon, Duke of Suffolk. Parkhurst served as their chaplain in 1544–45 before KP appointed him as her chaplain. Parkhurst's originals read as follows:

De faeminis incomparabilibus,
Catharina Reginae Anglicae, & Catharina Duce Suffolciae

Anglia nobilibus Catharinis nobilitatur,
Scito alteram Reginam, & alteram Ducem.
Talibus ô felix, ter felix Anglia gemmis.
Felix heris Parkhurste tuque talibus.
Terra Brittana tibi multos feliciter annos
Viuant: tibi Parkhurste viuant & diu.

De ijsdem

Si vitam spectes, non dixeris has Catharinas,
Rectius at multò dixeris has catharas.

147. **such . . . households** Parkhurst implies that he is conjointly serving in the queen's household and in the duke and duchess's household. Since the two Katherines were much in one another's company, this may well have been the case.

British earth, many years may they blessedly live on thee;
Parkhurst, for thee may they live longer still.

On the same

If you look at their life, you will not say these are Katherines;
Much more rightly you will say, these women are chaste.[148]

NO. 13 PRINCE EDWARD'S FRENCH LETTER TO QUEEN KATHERINE [LATE 1545–EARLY 1546][149]

[Addressed] To the very noble and very excellent Queen

I thank you, very noble and very excellent Queen, for your letters which you sent me lately—not only for the beauty of your letters but also for the inventiveness of the same letters. For when I saw your lovely writing and the excellence of your device that greatly surpass my own invention, I did not dare to write to you. But when I thought that your nature is so good that everything proceeding from a good spirit and will would be acceptable, I have written this letter to you. From my house of Hampton Court.

Edward

148. **Katherines . . . chaste** The Latin pun on "Catharinas" / "catharas" might be approximated in English by translating the two words as "Kates" and "chaste." But "Kates" is too familiar a name for the elegance of Parkhurst's style.

149. Source: BL, Harley MS 6986, art. 7, fol. 15; not calendared in G&B; printed in Nichols, *Literary Remains*, 1:49 (without discussion of date). In the young prince's italic hand. Assignment of the date takes account of the reference to KP's learning italic handwriting and of the likelihood that Edward gained facility in French before he gained facility in Latin. The original letter reads as follows, with square brackets enclosing letters of two words lost by fraying at the right margin of the page:

> *[Addressed]* A la tresnoble et tresexcellente Roine.
>
> Je Vous mercie tresnoble et tresexcellente Roine de voz lettres lesquelles vous menvoiastes dernierement non seulement pour la beaute de voz lettres mais aussy pour linvencion des memes lettres. Car quand ie voiois vostre belle escriture et l'excellence de vostre engin grandement precedant mon invention je nausois vous escrire: Mais quand je pensois que vostre n[ature] estoit si bonne que toute chose procedant d'un bon esprit et Vouloir se[roit] acceptable, je vous ay escrit ceste lettre cy. De ma maison de Hampton court.
>
> Edward

NO. 14 QUEEN KATHERINE'S LETTER TO THE UNIVERSITY OF CAMBRIDGE, FEBRUARY 26, [1546][150]

[Endorsed] A letter written as it see[meth][151] from the Queen in King Henry's time to the University of Cambridge.

150. Source: BL, Lansdowne MS 1236, art. 8, fol. 11; G&B 21.1:279. Draft in KP's hand, undated and lacking both salutation and subscription. I have supplied these elements, set in italic, from Corpus Christi College, Cambridge, MS 106, Art. 200, fols. 508v–509r, a copy of the letter sent by KP. KP's autograph draft reads as follows:

> your letters I haue receyved, presentyd on all your behalfes by m^{r} doctour Smythe your dyscrete and lernyd aduocate. and as they be latynly wrytten (wyche ys So sygnyfied vnto me by those that be lernyd in the latyne tonge) so I knowe you could haue vtteryd your desyres and oppynions famylierly in owre uulgare tonge aptylie for my intelligence, albeyt you seme to haue conceyvyd rather percyally then truely afauorable estimacion bothe of my ~~lernyng~~ goyng forwarde and dedycation to lernyng, wyche taduance or att the lest conserue, you by your letters move me dyverselye, Schewynge how agreable yt ys to me ‸ $^{\text{beyng in}}$ thys worldly estate, not only for myne nowne parte to be studyous, but also amayntener and cherysscher of the lernyd state, by beryng me in hande that I am indued and perfeityd with those qualytes and respectes wyche owght to be in aperson of my vocation. Truely thys your dyscrete and polytike document I as thankefully accept, as you~~r~~ desyre that I Schuld inbrace yt. and for as muche as I do well vnderstande all kynde of lernyng doth floryssche amongest you in thys age as yt dyd amongest the grekes at athenes long ago, I requyre ~~you~~ and desyre you all not So to honger for the exquysite knowlege of prophane lernyng, that yt may be thoughte the grekes vniversyte was but transposyd or nowe in england ageyne revyued, forgettyng our chrystianitye, synce theyr excellencye only dyd atteyne to morall and naturall thynges, but rather I gentyllye exhorte you to study and aplye those doctrynes as menes ‸ ^{and} apte degrees to the atteyni^{n}g and setty^{n}g forthe the better chrystes ~~most s~~ reverent and most Sacred doctryne that it may not be layd ageynst you in euydence at the trybunall seat of god how ye were aschamed of ~~thys~~ chrystes doctryne, for this latyne lesson I am taught to Say of Saynt poule, non me pudet evangelij, the Syncere Settyng forthe whereof I trust vnyversallye in all your vocations and mynysteries you woll aplie and confourme your Sondry gyftes, artes, and studies, to Such end and Sorte that ca^{m}bryge may be accompted rather an vniversite of devyne phylosophye then of naturall or morall as athenes was Vppon the confydence of wyche your acomplesschement to my expectation, zele and request, I accordyng to your desyres attempted my lord the Kynges maiestie for the staye of your possessions, in wyche not withstandyng hys maiesties propertie and intresse through the consente of the hyeghe courte of parlement, hys hyeghnis beyng Suche apatrone to good lernyng that he woll rather aduance ~~throghly~~ and erect now occasion therfore then confonde these your colleges, So that lernyng may hereafter asscrybe hys~~r~~ very oryginall, hole conformation, and Suer staye, to our Souuereyne ^{Lord} hyr only defender and worthy ornament, the prosperous estate and pryncely gouernement of whom long to preserue, I doubt not but euery of you woll ~~make~~ with dayly inuocacion cal apon hym who alone and only can dyspose all to euery creature.

151. **see[meth]** A hole in the paper has obliterated the ending of this word.

[Addition in another hand] Upon an Act that all colleges, chantries, free-chapels should be in the King's disposition.

To our right trusty, dear, and well-beloved, the chancellor and vice-chancellor of my lord the King's majesty's University of Cambridge, and to the whole said University there:

Your letters I have received, presented on all your behalfs by Mr. Doctor Smith,[152] your discreet and learned advocate. And, as they be latinly written, which is so signified unto me by those that be learned in the Latin tongue,[153] so I know you could have uttered your desires and opinions familiarly in our vulgar tongue, aptly for my intelligence, albeit you seem to have conceived, rather partially than truly, a favorable estimation both of my going forward and dedication to learning. Which, to advance or at the least conserve, you by your letters move me diversely, showing how agreeable it is to me, being in this worldly estate, not only for mine own part to be studious, but also a maintainer and cherisher of the learned state, by bearing me in hand that I am endued and perfected with those qualities and respects which ought to be in a person of my vocation. Truly, this your discreet and politic document I as thankfully accept as you desire that I should embrace it.

And, forasmuch as I do well understand all kind of learning doth flourish amongst you in this age, as it did amongst the Greeks at Athens long ago, I require and desire you all not so to hunger for the exquisite knowledge of profane learning, that it may be thought the Greeks' university was but transposed or now in England again revived, forgetting our Christianity, since their excellency only did attain to moral and natural things. But, rather, I gently exhort you to study and apply those doctrines as means and apt degrees to the attaining, and setting forth the better, Christ's reverent and most sacred doctrine, that it may not be laid against you in evidence at the tribunal seat of God, how ye were ashamed of Christ's doctrine.

152. **Mr. . . . Smith** Sir Thomas Smith began as a scholar and fellow of Queens' College, Cambridge; received degrees of doctor of civil law from the University of Padua and from Cambridge; was appointed professor of civil law in the University of Cambridge in 1544, and also served as its vice chancellor. An early advocate of the Reformation, Smith took orders and became rector of Leverington in Cambridgeshire in 1546. In that year he was also serving as clerk of Henry VIII's Privy Council. Exercising double roles as a court insider and a ranking representative of Cambridge University, Smith was ideally placed to appeal to the queen against the king's prospective confiscations.

153. **latinly . . tongue** KP's wry aside has sometimes been mistaken for an admission that she knows no Latin. This was obviously not her situation as a writer and reader of letters in Latin and a translator of Fisher's *Psalmi seu Precationes*. Rather, she remarks on the copious style and rhetoric of the Latin letters she has received from Roger Ascham and other scholars in behalf of Cambridge University and then demurely acknowledges her lack of expertise in such arts. The summary that KP proceeds to give indicates that she has read the letters and reflected on their appeals to her. None of these letters is known to survive.

For this Latin lesson I am taught to say of St. Paul, "Non me pudet evangelii":[154] the sincere setting forth whereof, I trust, universally in all your vocations and ministries you will apply, and conform your sundry gifts, arts, and studies, to such end and sort that Cambridge may be accounted rather an university of divine philosophy than of natural or moral, as Athens was.

Upon the confidence of which—your accomplishment to my expectation, zeal, and request—I according to your desires attempted my lord the King's majesty for the stay of your possessions: in which, notwithstanding his majesty's property and interest through the consent of the high court of Parliament, his highness, being such a patron to good learning that he will rather advance and erect[155] now occasion therefor than confound these your colleges, so that learning may hereafter ascribe her very original, whole conformation, and sure stay to our sovereign lord, her only defender, and worthy ornament. The prosperous estate and princely government of whom, long to preserve, I doubt not but every of you will, with daily invocation, call upon Him who, alone and only, can dispose all to every creature. *Scribbled with the hand of her that prayeth to the Lord and immortal God to send you all prosperous success in godly learning and knowledge. From my lord the King's majesty's manor of Greenwich, the twenty-sixth of February.*

NO. 15 ENGLISH VERSION OF A LOST LATIN LETTER FROM PRINCE EDWARD TO QUEEN KATHERINE, MAY 12, 1546[156]

Pardon my rude style in writing to you, most illustrious Queen and beloved mother, and receive my hearty thanks for your loving kindness to me and to my sister. Yet, dearest mother, the only true consolation is from heaven, and the only real love is the love of God. Preserve therefore, I pray you, my dear sister Mary, from all the wiles and enchantments of the evil one; and beseech her to attend no longer to foreign dances and merriments which do not become a most Christian princess. And so, putting my trust in God for you to take this exhortation in good part, I commend you to His most gracious keeping. From Hunsdon, this twelfth of May.

Edward the Prince

154. **Non . . . evangelii** "I am not ashamed of the gospel" (Romans 1:16). KP quotes Erasmus's Latin rendering of this verse in his *Annotations on Romans*, which he proposes as an emendation to the Vulgate's "Non enim erubesco evangelium" (I do not blush at the Gospel).

155. **advance . . . erect** Henry VIII founded Trinity College, Cambridge, in 1546.

156. Source: English translation in James O. Halliwell-Phillipps, ed., *Letters of the Kings of England* (London: Henry Colburn, 1848), 2:8–9, whose reference reads "Rawlinson MSS. From the Latin." Nichols, *Literary Remains of King Edward VI*, 1:2, 9, records that the librarians of the Bodleian were unable to locate the original for him.

NO. 16 PRINCE EDWARD'S LATIN LETTER TO QUEEN KATHERINE, MAY 24, 1546[157]

[Addressed] To the most illustrious Queen, my mother
[Headed] To Queen Katherine

Perhaps you will wonder at my writing to you so often, and that within so short a time, most noble Queen and dearest mother. But for the same reason you can wonder at me thus doing my duty towards you. However, I now do this the more willingly, because I have a suitable messenger, my servant,[158] and therefore I could not not write letters to you, to witness my fondness for you. May you fare very well, most noble Queen. At Hunsdon the twenty-fourth of May.

Your most obedient son
Edward the Prince

NO. 17 PRINCE EDWARD'S LATIN LETTER TO QUEEN KATHERINE, JUNE 10, 1546[159]

[Headed] To Queen Katherine

Although all of your letters have been sweet to me, yet in comparison with the others these last letters have smiled upon me, most noble Queen and most benevo-

157. Source: BL, Cotton MS Vespasian, F.III, art. 40, fol. 42a; G&B 21.2:900. This is the letter in the prince's handwriting that was actually sent to KP. An earlier, slightly shorter draft in his handwriting, dated May 2, is preserved as art. 7, fol. 3r, of BL, Harley MS 5087—a volume in which Edward entered copies of the letters he sent, each page with four wide borders ruled off in thin lines of red ink. His original reads as follows:

> *[Addressed]* Illustrissimae Reginae, matri meae.
> *[Headed]* Regine Catharine
> Fortasse miraberis me tam sepe ad te scribere, idque tam breui tempore, Regina Nobilissima et Mater charissima. Sed eadem ratione potes mirari me erga te officium facere. Hoc autem nunc facio libentius, quia est mihi idoneus nuncius seruus meus, et ideo non potui non dare ad te literas ad testificandum studium meum erga te. Optime valeas, Regina nobilissima. Hunsdoniae vigesimo quarto maii.
>
> Tibi obsequentissimus filius
> Edouardus Princeps

158. **messenger . . . servant** Probably John Fowler, a page and later a groom in Edward's household.

159. Source: BL, Harley MS 5087, art. 9, fols. 3v–4r; G&B 21.1:1036. Edward's copy, in his hand. It reads as follows:

lent mother, for which I thank you very greatly. In them I see that you have really and truly applied diligence to Roman script,[160] such that my tutor could not be persuaded but that your secretary had written them until he saw your name written equally well. I too was amazed. I also hear that your highness progresses in Latin language and in good literature,[161] wherefore I am not a little affected with joy. Literature indeed remains, but other things that seem to remain, perish. Literature also leads to good morals, but ignorance leads to bad ones. And as the sun is the light of the world, so is learning the light of the mind. All that comes from God is good; literature comes from God; thus learning is good.[162] Also Luis [Vives] said,[163] "What you see, you will not see long," meaning that riches and other goods of this life will perish. I pray the heavenly Power to keep your highness safe and sound. At Hunsdon the tenth of June in the year 1546.

Edward the Prince

[Headed] Regine Catharine

Etsi omnes literae tuae mihi dulces erant, tamen arridebant hae postreme litere pre ceteris Regina nobilissima atque mater beneuolentissima ob quus ingentes tibi gratias ego. Sane vero in his video te diligentiam adhibuisse romanis literis, ita ut non potuerit persuaderi preceptori meo quin Secretarius tuus scripserit, donec vidisset nomen tuum scriptum eque bene. Ego etiam miratus fui. Audio etiam celsitudinem tuam progredi in latina lingua et bonis literis. Quamobrem non paruo affectus sum gaudio. Literae enim manent, cetera autem que videntur pereunt. Literae etiam conducunt ad bonos mores, ignorantia autem ad malos ducit. Ac quemadmodem sol est lumen mundi, sic est doctrina lux mentis Omne quod venit ex deo, bonum est, literae ex deo veniunt, proinde doctrina est bonum. Lodouicus etiam viues ait Quod vides, non diu, significans diuitias et cetera bona huius vitae peritura. Precor numen caeleste vt seruet celsitudinem tuam incolumem. Hunsdoniae decimo Iunij anno 1546.

E. Princeps

160. **Roman script** "romanis literis"—i.e., italic handwriting. As a girl KP had been taught a mixed form of secretary hand, probably by her mother, who also used it.

161. **Latin . . . literature** Here and in the next two sentences, Edward uses Latin "litterae" (letters) in its broader sense of "literature" and specifically, it seems, in the humanist sense of literature as the study and imitation of classical authors. It is quite possible that KP's early knowledge of Latin was acquired mostly from the Vulgate and devotional works in Latin. Now she appears to be encouraging the young prince's studies by reading in Latin authors that he is assigned to read and learning, as he is, to write italic script. In this regard, see further her letter to Edward that is no. 24 below.

162. **All . . . good** Edward's formal syllogism in the so-called first figure (universal affirmative) indicates that he is learning logic as well as Latin grammar—the first two subjects of the first level of study, the trivium. The boyish self-display may suggest that his stepmother was tracking his progress in formal logic too.

163. **[Vives] said** "Quod vides, non diu. Quaecunque in uita cernis, non diu cernes: aut enim illa interitus auferet, aut te" (What you see [is] not for long. Whatever things you perceive

NO. 18 PRINCE EDWARD'S LATIN LETTER TO QUEEN KATHERINE, AUGUST 12, 1546[164]

[Headed] To Queen Katherine

I have very great thanks for you, most noble Queen and most illustrious mother, because you treated me so kindly when I was with you at Westminster. Such benign treatment suffuses the coldness[165] in me so that I love you more, although I cannot love you better. So it seems to me an age since I have seen you. I also wish to entreat your highness to overlook that I have not written[166] a letter to you for this long time. Indeed I wanted to, but daily I expected that I would be with your highness. When Fowler[167] first went, however, there was scarcely time for me to write unto your royal majesty. I further pray your highness to indicate to me, whether the admiral[168] who is coming from France knows Latin, because if he does, I want

in life, you will not perceive for long: for untimely death will carry either them or you away"): Juan Luis Vives, *Satellitium siue symbola* (1546), no. 153. Vives's collection of Latin maxims bears a dedicatory letter in Latin to "Mary, Princess of Wales, daughter of Henry VIII."

164. Source: BL, Harley MS 5087, art. 17, fol. 7; G&B 21.1:1446. Edward's copy, in his hand. It reads as follows:

> *[Headed]* Regine Catharine
>
> Ingentem tibi gratiam habeo Nobilissima Regina atque mater illustrissima quod me tam humaniter tractasti, cum tecum fui Westmonasterij. Que benigna tractatio, suffundit frigidam mihi vt te plurimum amem, quanquam te melius amare nequeo. Mihi igitur videtur seculum ex quo te vidi. Preterea exoratam celsitudinem tuam volo vt mihi, ignoscas quod hoc longo tempore ad te literas non exaraui. Volui quidem sed quotidie putaui me cum celsitudine tua futurum. Quando autem foulerus iuit primum, vix mihi fuit tempus scribendi ad regiam maiestatem. Porro celsitudinem tuam oro vt mihi significes, num Prefectus maris qui e Gallia proficiscitur calleat latine, quod si calleat vellem plus di[s]cere quod illi loquar, cum ei obuiam venero. Precor deum ut te custodiat, atque det tibi doctrinam et virtutem tutissimas diuitias. E domo Palustri, duodecimo Augusti anno 1546.
>
> E. Princeps

165. **suffuses . . . coldness** Edward's Latin phrase, "frigidam suffundere," appears to be a proverbial expression in Plautus's comedy *Cistellaria* 1.1.37, where it means "to dampen courage" or "to throw cold water" on someone (Nichols, *Literary Remains of Edward VI*, 1:22, 29). Edward, however, seems to apply the idiom to the thawing out of his own diffidence (coldness).

166. **I . . . written** Edward's "non exaraui" (I have not incised upon wax tablets) is a poeticism.

167. **Fowler** See n158 above.

168. **admiral** The French admiral Claude d'Annebaut made a visit to England as an ambassador in August 1546, after France and England had concluded a peace. The usual Latin term for "admiral" was "praefectus classis" (commander of the fleet). Edward writes "Prefectus maris" (commander of the sea).

to learn more what I should say to him when I come to meet with him. I pray God to keep you and to give you learning and virtue, the safest riches. From the Marshy House,[169] the twelfth of August in the year 1546.

Edward the Prince

NO. 19 QUEEN KATHERINE'S LETTER TO SIR EDWARD NORTH, SEPTEMBER 14, [1546][170]

[Addressed] To our right trusty and well-beloved Sir Edward North,[171] Knight
[Signed] Katherine the Queen KP

Right trusty and well-beloved, we greet you well. And forasmuch as it hath pleased almighty God to take unto His mercy our entirely beloved uncle, the late Lord Parr of Horton:[172] by occasion whereof his old clerk, this bearer,[173] is not only deprived of an especial good master, but also of all his living:

We have therefore thought good, being moved with pity of the lamentable estate of our uncle his said servant to address these our letters unto you in his favor, that the rather, at our contemplation, you will grant unto him the bailiwick of Rothwell,[174] with the accustomed fee thereunto belonging, which is now in the King's majesty's hands by the death of our said uncle. Which doing, you shall not only do a good deed in succoring the poor man's estate, but also do unto us an acceptable pleasure. Given under our signet at our manor of Hanworth[175] the fourteenth of September.

169. **Marshy House** Identified by Nichols, *Literary Remains of Edward VI*, 1:21, as "the manor of the Moor in Hertfordshire, which was then in the hands of the Crown."

170. Source: TNA, E 101/426/3, no. 21. A letter in a clerk's secretary hand, presumably dictated, with KP's sign manual in the upper left corner, with an underflourish of looped scrolls.

171. **Sir . . . North** MP for Cambridgeshire (1541), appointed chancellor of the Court of Augmentations (1545), which was established by Henry VIII to determine suits and controversies involving monastery and abbey lands; made a member of the Privy Council (1546) and named one of the executors of Henry VIII's will.

172. **late . . . Horton** William, Baron Parr, died September 10, 1546, and was buried at Horton.

173. **old . . . bearer** A faint notation in secretary hand at the bottom of the letter reads: "The contents of this letter is in the behalf of Giles Cather"—an otherwise unknown person.

174. **bailiwick . . . Rothwell** a bailiff's jurisdiction located in Northamptonshire.

175. **Hanworth** a crown manor to the northwest of Hampton Court.

NO. 20 PRINCE EDWARD'S LATIN LETTER TO QUEEN KATHERINE, SEPTEMBER 20, 1546[176]

[Headed] To Queen Katherine

When I was at court with the King, most noble Queen and dearest mother, you conferred on me so many kindnesses that I can scarcely grasp them with my mind. Which, since I cannot repay, I will nevertheless do as much as is in me, that is, I will bear you much goodwill, and I will rejoice when I hear that you are prospering in every virtue and goodness, for which things I pray the living God who governs and rules and prospers all. And now I write this letter to you, that it may be a testimony of love to you and of my study. I truly suppose that nothing will be more welcome and acceptable to you than my letters, although they are not entirely elegant. Nevertheless I hope that these will not be unpleasing to you, which I write to you by way both of love and of duty. I pray God to give you the instruction by which you will best be able to govern all of your life. Farewell, most noble Queen and dearest mother. The twentieth of September in the year 1546.

Edward the Prince

176. Source: BL, Harley MS 5087, art. 22, fol. 9r; G&B 21.1:136. Edward's copy, in his hand. It reads as follows:

> *[Headed]* Reginae Catharinae
>
> Cum essem in aula apud Regem Regina nobilissima atque mater charissima, tam multa in me contulisti beneficia, vt ea uix animo complecti possim. Que cum non possum rependere, faciam tamen quantum in me est, id est geram erga te multam beneuolentiam, et gaudebo cum audiuero te procedere in omnı vırtute et bonitate in quibus rebus precor viuentem deum qui omnia gubernat et regit vt procedas. Et iam has literas ad te scribo, vt sint testimonium amoris et studij mei erga te. Nihil enim mihi est quod opinor gratius tibi et acceptius erit literis meis que quanquam non admodum elegantes sint. tamen spero illas non iniucundas tibi futuras quas ad te scribo, tum amoris, tum officij causa. Precor deum vt det tibi doctrinam, qua optime gubernare possis totam vitam tuam Vale regina nobilissima atque mater charissima. Vigesimo Septembris anno 1546.
>
> Edouardus Princeps

NO. 21 PRINCE EDWARD'S LATIN LETTER TO QUEEN KATHERINE, NOVEMBER 7, 1546[177]

[Headed] To Queen Katherine

I owe you very great thanks, most revered mother, because you have considered my letters so much to the good that, even though they are of no importance, nevertheless you of your kindness give thanks for them to undeserving me. One truly ought to accept what is assigned as one's duty. On that account, I have settled with myself in person that these letters have both been composed inelegantly and indeed written negligently, to give to you. Hereafter if I do not perform my duty, that is, if I do not write letters to you, I will deserve very ill of you. For your highness owes me nothing at all, while all things that I do should be my best efforts. Your highness praises me, unworthy of praise. But in truth your greatness merits much larger praises that you, by your virtue, have imparted great honor to yourself. In which virtue indeed I will pray to God that you may prosper abundantly. Farewell, your highness. From Hatfield the seventh of November in the year 1546.

E. the Prince

NO. 22 SIR ANTHONY COPE'S DEDICATORY LETTER TO QUEEN KATHERINE PREFACING HIS *A GODLY MEDITATION UPON TWENTY . . . PSALMS OF THE PROPHET DAVID*, NEW YEAR'S, 1547[178]

The preface.
To the most virtuous lady and gracious princess,

177. Source: BL, Harley MS 5087, art. 27, fol. 11r; G&B 21.2:362. Edward's copy, in his hand. It reads as follows:

> *[Headed]* Reginae Catharinae
>
> Debeo tibi ingentes gratias mater venerandissima quod tam boni meas consuluisti literas, que quidem etsi nullius momenti sint tamen tua humanitas pro illis mihi gratias immerito agit. Quisque enim illud obire debet, quod officium suum postulat. Idcirco mecum ad presens constitui has literas tum ineliganter compositas, tum negligenter quidem scriptas ad te dare. Porro si non functus essem officio meo, hoc est si non ad te literas darem, pessime de de [sic] te meritus essem. Quare nihil omnino debet tua celsitudo mihi, cum omnia que facio sint partes meae. Tua sublimitas laudat me indignum laude. Verum tua amplitudo multo maiores meretur laudes que tua virtute multum consiliasti tibi honorem. In qua quidem virtute exoratum deum volo vt feliciter proficias. Valeat tua celsitudo Hatfeldie 7° Nouembris anno 1546.
>
> E. Princeps

178. Source: *A godly meditacion vpon .xx. select and chosen Psalmes of the Prophet Dauid, as wel necessary to al them that are desirous to haue the darke wordes of the Prophet declared and*

Katherine, Queen of England, France, and Ireland,
her humble servant Sir Anthony Cope, Knight,
desireth long life with health and much honor,
to the pleasure of God.

The use of giving gifts by men to their friends the first day of the New Year, most noble lady and and virtuous Queen, hath of long time continued within this realm of England, with an opinion that the lucky beginning is a good token of like prosperous success during the rest of the year. Which manner of presenting gifts, as I do right well allow, if they be given as a declaration of mutual love and hearty benevolence, so the opinion thereto annexed, I think not so commendable, which is, that the gift should be a token or presage of good fortune to come: no more than Monday's handsel[179] of a penny given to a poor beggar should be so esteemed, that the happy beginning of the week must draw to it also a fortunate end thereof.

The good intent of the giver of the penny is to relieve the poor man's necessity, not to be an augury of things that shall follow. So, in like wise, ought the New Year's gifts to be delivered, only as a testimony of the hearty service or loving minds of the givers. And, forsomuch as the most number of the givers do search to present such things as they judge should be most acceptable to the receivers thereof, I long imagined with myself what thing I might best offer unto your grace at this present, wherein I might in some part declare my loyal and obedient heart toward you, of whose heaped goodness I have so much tasted, that I can never be able to deserve the thousand part, but only with my prayer and hearty service. At the last, when I considered your gracious intent and godly purpose in the reading and study of holy Scripture, and the advancement of the true Word of God, I thought I could in nothing do your grace a more pleasant service than to make an exposition of certain Psalms of the noble prophet David, whose harmony is so sweet and pleasant that the ears of the faithful may scantly therewith be fully satisfied.

The poets feign that Orpheus[180] made so pleasant harmony on his harp that he caused the beasts and stones, dancing, to follow him. Their meaning was that his language was so pleasant, and his intent so reasonable, that he brought the people to good civility, which before were rude and beastly. But our celestial Orpheus, the prophet David,[181] hath so set forth his songs that they have strength and force to

---

made playne: as also fruitfull to suche as delyte in the contemplation of the spiritual meanyng of them. Compiled and set furth by Sir Anthony Cope knight (1547) (STC 5717), sigs. ii r–iv r.

179. **handsel** auspicious sign at the beginning of a day, year, or enterprise.

180. **Orpheus** The chief sources for the myth of Orpheus are Virgil *Georgics* 4.453–525 and Ovid *Metamorphoses* 10.1–11.84.

181. **our . . . David** Christians of late antiquity began the durable association of David, inspired by God to sing Psalms to the accompaniment of his harp, with the mythic Orpheus, inspired by the Muses to sing hymns on the world's creation and ordering, accompanied by his lyre. For a range of iconographical and textual sources, see Laurence Viellefon, *La Figure*

cause men which be carnal and beastly to become spiritual and heavenly. Whoso will learn to give to God due honor and praise may in them take a perfect pattern. Again, to give thanks for the benefits received, to call for grace, to pray for the deliverance from all enemies spiritual and temporal, to live in the heavenly meditation of God's laws, to despise the vanities of this world, to become more spiritual: may men, in them abundantly, be instructed. In conclusion, there is nothing necessary for any Christian to do, think, or say, but in them as in a mirror he may behold the perfect image thereof, beside the plain prophesying of Christ's coming our very Messiah, His nativity, passion, death, resurrection, and ascension, as lively as they were in colors set forth before our eyes, with so many tropes, figures, and allegories, that there is almost no word which lacketh an hid mystery: as the apostle Paul saith, All things happed to them in figure, and were dark and obscure.[182]

But now that the things are come whereof it was spoken, the veil is taken away from the face of Moses.[183] Now are few things left undiscussed by good holy fathers, who having a good zeal to bestow their talent of knowledge given them by God to the profit of His people, have earnestly travailed in the manifestation of such secret and hid things, being helped by the Holy Spirit of God to the achieving of their ghostly purposes. Whom I, having very small learning, but only to gratify your mind and to avoid idleness, have followed, setting forth a rude exposition (in our maternal tongue) upon twenty Psalms which I have chosen forth, reducing the same to the kind or fashion of prayers and contemplative meditations. Which I trust your grace, of your accustomed and natural goodness, will take in good part, since there wanteth in me not will, but knowledge to do better. Nevertheless I trust (conferring[184] the paraphrase to the text) ye shall have great light of the meaning of the prophet, and thereby find his diffuse, dark words made open and plain.

To move your grace and all other of the flock of Christ to the reading of Psalms, may it please you to read the chapter of the book of Kings[185] where David, by playing on his harp and singing thereto, expelled from King Saul, his father-in-law, for the season while he played, the wicked spirit which was entered into him and sore tormented him. And this thing I trust none will judge to be done by the virtue of

d'Orphée dans l'antiquité tardive—les mutations d'un mythe: Du héros païen au chantre chrétien (Paris: Du Boccard, 2003). On the later history of this association in the West, see John Block Friedman, *Orpheus in the Middle Ages* (Cambridge, MA: Harvard University Press, 1970).

182. **Paul . . . obscure** The ceremonial rites and sacrifices prescribed under Jewish law are interpreted as prefigurations of Christ's self-sacrifice for the sins of all humankind in Hebrews 9–10.

183. **veil . . . Moses** Exodus 34:29–35 narrates how Moses's face shone after God gave the Ten Commandments to him on Mount Sinai. Afterward, when he spoke to the Israelites Moses veiled his face, but he unveiled his face when he prayed to God.

184. **conferring** comparing.

185. **the chapter . . . Kings** 1 Samuel 16:15–23, in Reformed Bibles. The book of 1 Samuel is the book of 1 Kings in the Vulgate.

the sound of his harp, but through the power of the noble Psalms that he sang, playing thereon: which Psalms he undoubtedly, being inspired with the Spirit of God, had before made. Much more may we think and assuredly judge that, for our own deliverance from the power of our spiritual enemies, God will not fail to send His Holy Spirit to assist us and comfort us, expelling utterly the temptations of the wicked Serpent, if we in faith, earnestly and heartily praying and trusting to Him, read or utter the said Psalms. And I shall pray to God who is the Author and Giver of all good gifts, so to illuminate the eyes of your grace's heart, that ye may proceed in the path of His laws wherein you are already entered, according to the ardent desire which ye have hitherto had to attain to the knowledge of them, so that when ye shall leave this transitory world (whose pleasures in all your time ye never esteemed) ye may ascend to the place prepared for God's elect, there to receive joys perdurable, world without end.

NO. 23 PRINCE EDWARD'S LATIN LETTER TO QUEEN KATHERINE, JANUARY 10, 1547[186]

[Addressed] To the most noble Queen and my dearest mother

That for a long time now I have not written to you, most illustrious Queen and dearest mother, was by reason not of negligence, but of study. Truly I have not done this so that I should never write at all, but that I should write more accurately.

186. Source: BL. Cotton MS Nero, C.X, art. 6, fol. 7; G&B 21.2:686a. In Edward's hand, this is the letter he sent to KP. His own copy is BL, Harley MS 5087, art. 30, fol. 12r, dated "decimo Ianuarij anno 1546"—i.e., 1547. The sent letter reads as follows:

> *[Addressed]* Nobilissima Regina et Matri meae Charissima.
>
> Quòd non ad te iam diu scripserim Regina Illustrissima atque Mater Charissima, in causa fuit, non negligentia, sed studium. Non enim hoc feci, ut nunquam omnino scriberim, sed ut accuratius scriberem. Quare spero te futuram contentam et gauisuram quod non scripserim. Tu enim uelles me proficere in omni honestate et pietate, quod est signum insignis et diuturni tui amoris erga me. Atque hunc amorem multis beneficijs mihi declarasti, et praecipuè hac strena quam proximè ad me misisti, in qua Regiae Maiestatis, et tua effigies ad uiuum expressa continetur. Nam plurimum me delectat uestras imagines absentium contemplari, quos libentissimè uidere cupio presentes, ac quibus maximè tum natura tum officio deuinctus sum. Quamobrem maiores tibi gratias ago ob hanc strenam quam si misisses ad me preciosas uestes et aurum coelatum, aut quiduis aliud eximium. Deus tuam Celsitudinem, quam me breui uisurum spero, seruet incolumem. Hartfordiae. Decimo Januarii.
>
> Filius Celsitudini tuae Obsequentissimus
> Edouardus Princeps

Wherefore I hope you will be earnestly aware and joyful that I have not written. For you want me to progress in all goodness and piety, which is a mark of your remarkable and enduring love towards me. And you have declared this love to me by many favors, and chiefly by this New Year's gift that you recently sent to me, in which is contained the King's majesty's likeness and yours, depicted to the life. For it delights me very much to contemplate your portraits, whom, although absent, I very willingly desire to see present, and to whom I am bound most fast, both by nature and by duty. For this reason I give you greater thanks in return for this New Year's gift than if you had sent me precious garments and engraved gold, or any other exceptional thing. May God safely keep your highness, whom I hope I will see shortly. From Hartford the tenth of January.

Your Highness's most obedient son
Edward the Prince

NO. 24 QUEEN KATHERINE'S UNDATED DRAFT REPLY IN LATIN TO PRINCE EDWARD'S LATIN LETTER OF JANUARY 10, 1547[187]

That intermission of yours in writing to me until a little while ago, dearest son, I could not ascribe to excellent studies of letters or to any negligence at all, when in my soul and thought I measure how you attend with love both to me as your mother and to good literature at the same time. So that, on this side, your rever-

187. Source: BL, Cotton MS Nero, C.X, art. 8; G&B 21.2:686b; a heavily corrected text in an italic hand, presumably KP's, written on the blank lower half of the sheet containing Prince Edward's letter, which bears on its verso the address to her in his hand. The Latin original reads as follows:

> Istam ad me scribendi ~~hasce~~ [hares] aliquot dieculas intermissionem Charissime fili quomodo non praeclaris literarum studijs potiusquam ulli negligentiae ascribere possim, cum animo meo ac cogitatione metiar quanto et me matrem et bonas literas simul amore prosequaris. ^
> [Insert in left margin keyed by a caret] ut hinc te pietas in matrem hinc discendi cupiditas te prorsus veL ab omni suspitione negligentiae etiam indicta causa liberare possit.
>
> Quam [magna] autem diligentia hoc ~~dierum aliquot~~ [temporis] interuallo [Musas] excolueris, literae quas ad me dedisti iam nuperrime locupletissimi testes esse possunt quae et ~~literaru~~ [latinae orationis] puritate ac literarum eligantiori formatione reliquis omnibus à te profectis mihi longissime praenitere uidentur. Quod uero strenulam quam ad te miserim tanti facias plurimum [sanè] gaudeo, sperans fore, ~~vt cuius imaginem depictam ob semper ob oculos gestare ueLis~~ te PraecLarissima [sic] patris tui facta in omni vitam meditarum ac ad rem expressarum esse, cuius imaginem depictam ob oculos gestare tantopere placebit: ad cuius ~~singuLar~~ raras virtutes

ence to your mother, on that side, your desire to go on learning being still the cited reason, it is possible to free you from all suspicion of negligence. With how great diligence soever in this ~~few days~~ interval of time you will cultivate the Muses, the letters that you have presented to me most recently can be witnesses most fully and richly that, in the purity of Latin speech and the very elegant formation of letters and all the rest of the things in which you have made a beginning, it may be seen that you very far outshine me.

Although, in truth, that you make so much of the little token[188] I sent to you, I really rejoice, hoping perhaps ~~you will keep this depicted image for always before your eyes~~ that it has designed and expressed to the life the deeds of your most distinguished father, he of whom it will be pleasing in a great degree to keep the depicted image before your eyes. To whose ~~singular~~ rare virtues, attentively beheld and observed, as long as ~~you gaze upon them and the work~~ you direct the eyes of your mind[189] ~~and your effort soundly,~~ having accomplished a most worthy and most useful thing, you ~~will succeed~~ will distinguish both yourself and this commonwealth. Which, that you may seriously and sedulously do, may ~~he~~ God provide and perfect you with all of His heavenly gifts. From Westminster.

---

conspiciendas obseruandasque dum ~~te contu~~Lerum ^ mentis tuae oculos flexeris ~~et Laborem sanè~~ ^ ~~laborem~~ rem profecto dignissimam utilissimamque et tibi et huic Reipublicae ~~subibis~~ ^ praestabis quod ut seriò seduloque facias faxit ~~ille~~ Deus ~~q~~ te totum donis suis caelestibus exornet atque perficiatque Westmonasterii

188. **the . . . token** The double portrait of Henry VIII and KP to which Edward refers in no. 24.

189. **the eyes . . . mind** This is St. Paul's image in Galatians 1:18, rendered as "lyghten the eyes of youre myndes, that ye may knowe" in the Great Bible (1539), retaining Tyndale's (1534) phrasing verbatim.

PART 4

The Dowager Queen and Her Correspondents

February 1547 to September 1548

NO. 1 KING EDWARD VI'S LATIN LETTER TO DOWAGER QUEEN KATHERINE, FEBRUARY 7, 1547[1]

[Headed] To Queen Katherine

Many thanks to you for the last letter that you sent me, dearest mother, which certainly is a mark of your remarkable and daily love for me. Furthermore, that it has seemed good to the most great and most good God that my father and your husband, the most illustrious King, should end this life, it is a grief common to us both together. This nevertheless brings us consolation, that now he is in heaven, and that

1. Source: BL, Harley MS 5087, art. 34, fol. 14r. Edward's copy, in his hand. The text reads:

[Headed] Reginae Catharinae

Plurimas tibi gratias ago ob epistolam quam ad me postremam misisti, charissima mater, que sane est signum insignis tui, ac quotidiani amoris in me. Porro cum visum sit deo optimo maximo ut meus pater et tuus coniunx Rex illustrissimus, hanc vitam finiret, nobis ambobus communis est dolor. Hoc vero nobis consolacionem affert quod iam sit in coelo, atque quod ex has uita misera profectus sit in foelicem atque aeternam beatitudinem. Quisquis enim hic felicem agit vitam, atque rempublicam recte gubernat sicut nobilissimus meus pater fecit qui promouit omnem pietatem atque expulit omnem ignorantiam habet certissimum iter in coelum. Quamuis uero natura iubet dolere ac lachrymas effundere ob discessum eius absentis, tamen scriptura ac prudentia iubent moderari affectus istos ne videamur nullam omnino spem habere resurrectionis mortuorum et uita defunctorum. Preterea cum tua celsitudo in me tot benefitia contulit, ego debeo, quicquid commodi possem tibi affer[r]e, prestare. Opto tuae celsitudine plurimam salutem. Vale Regina Veneranda. E turri septimo Februarij anno 1546[7].

E. Rex

he has gone out of this miserable life into happiness and eternal blessedness. For whoever leads an auspicious life here and governs the commonwealth rightly, as my most noble father did, who promoted all piety and banished all ignorance, has a most certain way to heaven.

Although nature commands us, even so, to grieve and pour out tears for the departure of him who is absent, yet Scripture and prudence command us to moderate those feelings, lest we may seem to have no hope at all of the resurrection of the dead and the life of the deceased. Besides, since your highness has bestowed so many kindnesses on me, I ought to offer whatever comfort I can bring you. I wish your highness great good health. Farewell, revered Queen. From the Tower, the seventh of February in the year 154[7].

Edward the King

NO. 2 DOWAGER QUEEN KATHERINE TO LORD THOMAS SEYMOUR [CIRCA MID-FEBRUARY] 1547[2]

[Endorsed in a later hand] A letter written by Queen Katherine Parr. The Queen's letter from Chelsea to my Lord Admiral, of her former love. 1548 [sic].

2. Source: Sudeley Castle, Gloucestershire, Dent-Brocklehurst MS; in KP's hand. I have placed this letter at the head of the series exchanged by KP and Lord Thomas Seymour (hereafter "TS") because it launches a series of cross-references that loosely connect this correspondence, which unfortunately is undated for the most part. The tempo of the letter exchange accelerates: the intervals between their letters to one another reduce from the fortnight cut short by this letter to the counterproposal of every three days made in letter no. 5. See further nn6, 10, 18 below on particulars of dating. KP's reference to TS as "my lord" and the phrasing of her subscription in this letter raise the possibility that she and Seymour had by this early date exchanged vows *in praesentis*, amounting to a privately contracted marriage. (For Henry VIII and KP's vows of this kind, see no. 4 in part 1, n21.) KP's original reads as follows:

> my lord j send yow my moost humble and harty comendations beyng desyrous to knowe how ye haue done syns j sawe yow. I pray yow be not offended with me in that j send soner to yow than I sayd I wold. for my promys was but ~~such one~~ ones in [a] fourtened how be yt the tyme ys well abrevyated by what meanes I knowe not except the weakes be schorter at chelsey than in other places my lord, your brother hathe dyffered answer consernyng suche requestes as I made to hym tyll hys comyng hether wyche he sayth schalbe immediatly after the terme thys ys not hys fyrst promys I haue receyued of hys comyng and yett vnperfourmed I thynke my lady hath tawght hym that lesson for yt ys her coustome to promys many comynges to her frendes and to perfourme none I trust in greatter matters sche ys more cyrcumspect. And thus my lord I make an ende byddyng yow moost hartely farewell wyschyng yow the good I wold my self. from chelsey
> [Postscript] I wold not haue yow to thynke that thys myne onest Good Wyll towarde yow to procede of any sodayne motyon or passyon for as truly as god ys

My lord,[3]

I send you my most humble and hearty commendations, being desirous to know how ye have done since I saw you. I pray you be not offended with me in that I send sooner to you than I said I would. For my promise was but once in a fortnight. Howbeit, the time is well abbreviated: by what means I know not, except the weeks be shorter at Chelsea[4] than in other places.

My lord your brother[5] hath deferred answer concerning such requests as I made to him till his coming hither, which he saith shall be immediately after the term.[6] This is not his first promise I have received of his coming, and yet unperformed. I

---

god my mynd was fully bent the other tyme I was at lybertye [y] to marye yow before any man I knewe howbeyt god withstode my wyll theryn moost vehemently for atyme and throwgh hys grace and goodnes made that possible wyche semeth to me moost vnpossible that was made me to renownce utterly myne one wyll, and to folowe hys wyll most wyllyngly yt wer to long to wryte [all] the processe of thys mater yf I lyue I ~~trust~~ schall declare yt to yow my self I can [say] nothyng but as my lady of suffolke saith god ys amervelous man.

by her that ys yowrs to serue and obey duryng her lyf
Kateryn the Quene KP

3. **My lord** Thomas Seymour, born probably in 1508, was the handsome, ambitious, reckless younger brother of Queen Jane Seymour, mother of Edward VI. In October 1544, just after KP's regency, Henry VIII appointed TS admiral of the fleet, in command of the squadron assigned to protect the southern coast and the Channel against French attacks. Shortly before Henry's death TS was made a member of the Privy Council. Named an assistant executor in Henry's will, he was rapidly returned to the Privy Council, reappointed lord admiral, and created Baron Sudeley. Yet he aimed higher still, shirking his duties by refusing to command the fleet in the coordinated land-and-sea assault on Scotland in 1547, and instead dividing his time between London and his new manorial seat at Sudeley, Gloucestershire. In the early spring of 1547 he conducted a successful whirlwind courtship of KP, now Henry VIII's widow, having first considered (as later reported by John Fowler, a gentleman of Edward VI's chamber) the possibility of marrying Anne of Cleves, Princess Mary, or Princess Elizabeth. See the circumstantial account in G. W. Bernard, "The Downfall of Sir Thomas Seymour," in *Power and Politics in Tudor England* (Aldershot, UK: Ashgate, 2000), 134–60.

4. **Chelsea** The manor of Chelsea was Sir Thomas More's property before it reverted to the crown after More's attainder and execution for treason in 1535. In 1543 Henry VIII bestowed Chelsea on KP as one of her two dower houses.

5. **My . . . brother** Edward Seymour, Duke of Somerset, lord protector (as elder uncle) of Edward VI.

6. **the term** The royal injunctions of 1536 specified the dates of the law terms, when the Westminster courts were sitting and when official legal business could be conducted. "Hilary term," presumably the one in question here, "beginneth the twenty-third or twenty-fourth day of January, and endeth the twelfth or thirteenth day of February" (quoted in David Cressy, *Bonfires and Bells: National Memory and the Protestant Calendar in Elizabethan and Stuart England* [Berkeley: University of California Press, 1989], 10).

think my lady[7] hath taught him that lesson, for it is her custom to promise many comings to her friends, and to perform none. I trust in greater matters she is more circumspect. And thus, my lord, I make an end, bidding you most heartily farewell, wishing you the good I would myself. From Chelsea.

[Addition to body of letter]
I would not have you to think that this mine honest goodwill toward you to proceed of any sudden motion or passion. For, as truly as God is God, my mind was fully bent the other time I was at liberty, to marry you before any man I knew. Howbeit, God withstood my will therein most vehemently for a time and, through His grace and goodness, made that possible which seemeth to me most unpossible—that was, made me to renounce utterly mine own will, and to follow His will most willingly.[8] It were too long to write all the process of this matter. If I live, I shall declare it to you myself. I can say nothing but, as my lady of Suffolk[9] saith, "God is a marvelous man."

By her that is yours to serve and obey during her life,
Katherine the Queen KP

NO. 3 LORD THOMAS SEYMOUR TO DOWAGER QUEEN KATHERINE, [MARCH] 1547[10]

[Endorsed in two different hands] My Lord Admiral to the Queen. Lord Admiral to the Queen, of his waiting.

7. **my lady** Anne Seymour, Duchess of Somerset, former lady-in-waiting to KP as queen (see no. 2 in part 3) and now fast becoming her rival for precedence as the highest-ranking matron in Edward VI's court. The duchess challenged KP's precedence on the inference or knowledge of her liaison with TS, younger brother of Anne's husband, the lord protector.

8. **made . . . willingly** KP echoes phrases from her *Prayers or Meditations* (1545), sigs. Av r, Aii r: "make that possible by grace, that is to me impossible by nature," "Thy will be my will, and my will be to follow always Thy will." These phrases are, in turn, partial echoes of Matthew 19:26, Luke 1:37, 18:27, and Hebrews 11:6. On KP's sense of the providential interconnectedness of her spiritual and secular life, see my general introduction, p. 3.

9. **my . . . Suffolk** Katherine Brandon, widow of Charles Brandon, Duke of Suffolk, Henry VIII's intimate friend, was a staunch adherent of the Reformed religion and a patroness of Hugh Latimer. She became KP's closest friend besides her own sister, Anne Parr Herbert.

10. Source: TNA, State Papers Domestic, Supplementary, Edward VI, 46/1/14. In TS's loose and often nearly illegible secretary hand, signature in italic. Assignment of the date hinges on Edward Seymour's return to court after the end of Hilary term on February 13. The original letter reads as follows:

> The leke vmbell and harty Recommendashens I sende your highnes that I reseuiede / and beyng morre deseyrus to heare from your ~~high~~ then as I thowght

The like humble and hearty recommendations I send your highness that I received. And being more desirous to hear from you than, as I thought, ye desired to hear from him,[11] as yesterday in the morning I had written a letter unto your highness, upon occasion that I met with a man of my lord Marquess[12] as I came to Chelsea, whom I knew not. Who told Nicholas Throckmorton[13] that I was in Chelsea fields, with other circumstances which I defer till a more leisure. Which letter being finished, and my hand thereat, remembered your commandment to me, wherewith I

> ye dysyerde to here from ~~hem~~ hem, as yestre day in the mornyng I hade wretenn a lettre vnto your highnes, vppon occashen that I mett with a man of my lorde markes as I came to chelsey, whom I knewe nott, who tolde nycolas frogmorton that I was in chelsey ffeldes with other sercumstances whyche I deffre tyll a more laysor / whych lettre beyng fenychede and my hande thare at, remembred your commandment to me, whare with I threue it in to the ffeyer be mynddyng to kepe your requestes and dysyeres / and for that it hath plesed you to be the furst breker of your apoynttement I shull dysyr your highnes to reseue my thankes for the same, and that ye myht with as goode wyll reseue the like whom I shall sende to you, and nott to thynke that I breke ony your commandment be the same / As tochyng my lordes promes, I trost to make youe ffrendes, Assewryng you that I wayght as well onn hym as ony mann he hath to bringe in to hys ffaver, to bryng our matres well to passe
>
> my lady of Somersett tolde me on fryday nyght that she wolde to sheyn as the next day and at her retorne onn tewsday whyche ys to morow she wolde se your hyghnes but I thynke that it wylbe wensday or she com for that my lorde wylbe to morow all day in the ~~steych~~ sterchambre I pray you yf ye see your selff in good credytt with her, to desyre her grace to be my good ladey / and yf I se my selff in more faver then you I shall make the leke request for you /
>
> I ~~beshe~~ beseche your hyghnes to pout all fances out of your hede, that myght bryng you in ony on thowght, that I ~~m~~ do thynke that the godenes you haue showede me ys of ony sodenn moshenn, as at laysor your highnes shull kno to both our contentashens / and thus for lake of laysor beyng sent for to my lorde my brother, I vmbeley take my leve of your hyghnes from Sent James in hast as may apere to ~~b~~ youe be my hond
>
> fromm the body of hym whosse hart ye haue T. Seymour
>
> *[Postscript]* I neuer ouer red it after ~~I~~ it was wreten wherfor yf ony fawght be I pray you holde me exkewsede

11. **you . . . him** **you** As shown by the self-correction in the original letter, TS's attempt to scale down from a formal to a more intimate address is short lived; he soon resumes his references to "your highness." **him** TS's self-reference.

12. **my . . . Marquess** William Parr (1513–71) was KP's younger brother. He advanced himself by marrying the heiress Anne Bourchier, obtaining the title Earl of Essex, and was created first Marquess of Northampton by Henry VIII. William became a seasoned courtier in the royal service, first under Henry and later under Elizabeth. See James, *Kateryn Parr*, chaps. 3, 18–21.

13. **Nicholas Throckmorton** one of KP's cousins, whom she as queen treated generously. Episodes of his family's history were versified by a descendant in *The Legend of Sir Nicholas Throckmorton*, ed. John Gough Nichols (London: Nichols and Sons, 1874). See no. 9 in part 5.

threw it into the fire, by minding to keep your requests and desires.[14] And, for that it hath pleased you to be the first breaker of your appointment, I shall desire your highness to receive my thanks for the same. And that ye might with as goodwill receive the like whom I shall send to you, and not to think that I break any your commandment by the same.

As touching my lord's[15] promise, I trust to make you friends, assuring you that I wait as well on him as any man he hath to bring into his favor, to bring our matters well to pass. My lady of Somerset told me on Friday night that she would to Sheen[16] a[t] the next day, and at her return on Tuesday, which is tomorrow, she would see your highness. But I think that it will be Wednesday ere she come, for that my lord will be tomorrow all day in the Star Chamber.[17] I pray you, if ye see yourself in good credit with her, to desire her grace to be my good lady. And if I see myself in more favor than you, I shall make the like request for you.

I beseech your highness to put all fancies out of your head, that might bring you in any one thought, that I do think that the goodness you have showed me is of any sudden motion,[18] as at leisure your highness shall know, to both our contentations.[19] And thus, for lack of leisure, being sent for to my lord my brother, I humbly take my leave of your highness. From Saint James in haste, as may appear to you by my hand.

From the body of him whose heart ye have,
T. Seymour

[Postscript] I never over-read it[20] after it was written. Wherefore if any fault be, I pray you hold me excused.

14. **Which letter . . . desires** Evidently KP had instructed TS to burn any letters that passed between them. She soon rescinded this instruction, as the next sentence indicates. **remembered . . . me** i.e., I remembered your commandment to me. TS's omitted "I" at the head of this clause is a characteristic feature of written English at this period; see the remarks on ellipsis in *Elizabeth I: Autograph Compositions and Foreign Language Originals*, ed. Mueller and Marcus, xxiii. There are several more instances of the ellipsis of subject pronouns in TS's letters in this group.

15. **my lord's** Edward Somerset's, as further references make clear.

16. **Sheen** The former monastery, one of Edward Seymour's country estates, was located near Buxton in Staffordshire (James, *Kateryn Parr*, 306).

17. **Star Chamber** The highest court of equity in England, not bound by precedents of common law, with jurisdiction chiefly over criminal cases. It originated in the fifteenth century from judicial sttings of the King's Council, including the lord chancellor or lord keeper, the lord treasurer, the lord privy seal, and any other peers who chose to attend. The Star Chamber's sweeping prerogatives made it a potent instrument of royal supremacy.

18. **sudden motion** This echo of KP's wording in the last paragraph of no. 2 above dates the present letter to follow that one.

19. **contentations** satisfactions.

20. **it** the text of this letter.

NO. 4 DOWAGER QUEEN KATHERINE TO LORD THOMAS SEYMOUR, [CA. APRIL] 1547[21]

[Endorsed in Thomas Seymour's hand] From your highness [to your] humble servant, assured and faithful friend, and loving husband during his life.
[Endorsed in another hand] The Queen's highness' letter to the Lord Admiral.

My lord,

As I gather by your letter delivered to my brother Herbert, ye are in some fear how to frame my lord your brother to speak in your favor.[22] The denial of your request shall make his folly more manifest to the world, which will more grieve me

21. Source: Bodleian Library, Ashmole MS 1729, art. 4, fol. 5; in KP's hand, with an endorsement in TS's hand. The original reads as follows:

> My lord as I gether by your letter delyuered to my brother harbert, ye are in sum fere how to frame my lord your brother to speke in yowr fauour; the denyall of yowr request schall make hys foly more manyfest to the world, wyche ~~behold~~ [wyll] more greue me, than the want of hys spekyng. I wold not wyssche yow importune for hys good wyll, yf yt cum nott frankely at the fyrst, yt schalbe suffycyent ones to [haue] requyred yt, and after to cesse. I wold desyre ye myght obtayne the Kynges letters in yowr fauour, and also the ayde and furtherans of the moost notable ~~men~~ of the counsell, suche as ye schall thynke conuenyent, Wyche thynge obtayned schalbe no small schame to yowr brother and louyng syster, in case they do not the lyke. My lord where as ye charge me with apromys wryttin with myne one hand, to chaunge the two yeres into two monethes, I thynke ye haue no suche playne sentence wrytten with my hand, ~~w~~ I knowe not wether ye be aparaphryser or not, yf ye be ~~be~~ lerned in that syence yt ys possyble ye may of one worde make ahole sentence, and yett nott at all tymes after the true meanyng of the wryter, as yt aperyth by thys yowr exposycyon apon my wryttyng. Whan yt schalbe yowr pleasur to repayre hether ye must take sum payne to come erly in the mornyng that ye may be gone agayne by seuen aclocke and so I suppose ye may come with[out] suspect. I pray yow lett me haue knowlege ner nyght [at] what hower ye wyll come, that yowr porteresse may wayte at the gate to the feldes for yow. And thus wyth my moost humble and harty comendatyons I ~~wo~~ take my leue of yow for thys tyme gyuyng yow lyke thankes for yowr ~~beyng at~~ [comyng to] the Court whan I was there. from chelsey.
>
> I wyll kepe in store tyll I speke with yow my lordes large offer for fausterne at wyche tyme I schalbe glad to knowe your further pleasur therin
>
> By her that ys and schalbe yowr humble true and louyng wyffe duryng her lyf
>
> Kateryn the Quene KP

TS's endorsement reads: "fromm your highnis / vmbell sarvant, assewred and faythfull frende, and louyng hosbond duryng hys lyff"

22. **ye . . . favor** KP registers the seriousness of having contracted to marry TS before obtaining the lord protector's, the king's, and the Privy Council's permission. But she stands proudly on her rank as dowager queen. She will condone no subservience from TS as he attempts to find the moment to confront Edward and Anne Seymour regarding the marriage.

than the want of his speaking. I would not wish you importune for his goodwill: if it come not frankly at the first, it shall be sufficient once to have required[23] it, and after, to cease. I would desire ye might obtain the King's letters in your favor, and also the aid and furtherance of the most notable of the Council, such as ye shall think convenient: which thing obtained shall be no small shame to your brother and loving sister, in case they do not the like.

My lord, whereas ye charge me with a promise written with mine own hand, to change the two years into two months, I think ye have no such plain sentence written with my hand. I know not whether ye be a paraphraser[24] or not. If ye be learned in that science, it is possible ye may of one word make a whole sentence, and yet not at all times after the true meaning of the writer, as it appeareth by this your exposition upon my writing.

When it shall be your pleasure to repair hither, ye must take some pain to come early in the morning, that ye may be gone again by seven o'clock, and so I suppose ye may come without suspect. I pray you, let me have knowledge near night at what hour ye will come, that your porteress may wait at the gate to the fields for you.[25] And thus, with my most humble and hearty commendations, I take my leave of you for this time, giving you like thanks for your coming to the court when I was there. From Chelsea.

[Addition] I will keep in store, till I speak with you, my lord's large offer for Fausterne:[26] at which time I shall be glad to know your further pleasure therein.

By her that is and shall be your humble, true,
and loving wife during her life,
Katherine the Queen KP

23. **required** requested.

24. **a promise . . . paraphraser** Mutual playfulness is a striking feature of KP's and TS's correspondence, contrasting markedly with the extreme deference that KP always showed in writing to Henry. **no . . . hand** KP denies that she has given TS written assurance of her intention to shorten her widow's period of mourning for Henry VIII. **a paraphraser** KP's merry allusion does not merely challenge TS's tactic. It also evokes the English translation of Erasmus's *Paraphrases upon the New Testament* which she had commissioned, and probably indicates that the project is actively progressing. There must have been some reconsideration, perhaps even a delay in the project, after Gardiner and Wriostheley almost succeeded in alienating KP from Henry's favor in the summer of 1546 by representing her promotion of Reformed religion in a dangerous light. See my general introduction, pp. 22–24.

25. **your pleasure . . . for you** This passage sheds light on how this pair consummated their intended or actual marriage before it became public knowledge. **early . . . morning** that is, in the early morning hours after midnight.

26. **my lord's . . . Fausterne** Fausterne was one of the dower properties bestowed on KP by Henry VIII. Edward Seymour contracted an interest in it. KP's reference to a "large offer" is sarcastic, as becomes clear in no. 7 below.

NO. 5 LORD THOMAS SEYMOUR TO DOWAGER QUEEN KATHERINE, MAY 17, 1547[27]

[Endorsed in two hands] 17 May. The Lord Admiral to the Queen. The Lord Admiral to the Queen. Of his suit for marriage.

27. Source: TNA, State Papers 10/1/41, fols. 128r--129r. In TS's secretary hand, signature in italic. Square brackets indicate restorations of omitted or lost words near the page bottom. The original reads:

> After my vmbell commendashens vnto your highnes yester nyght I sopte at my brother harbardes of whom for your sake besydes my nowne I reseuede goode cherre, ande after the same I reseuede from your highnis be my sester harbarde your commendashens whych wurre morre welcom then they wurre sent / ande after the same she wadede fferther with me tochyng my beyng with your highnes at chelsey, whych I denyde beyng with your highnes, but that in dede I ~~was thayr~~ went be the garden, as I went to se the beshep of londenes howse, ande at this poynte stode with her for a tyme / tyll at the laste she tolde me ferther tokens whyche made me change colores, who like a ffalce wenche toke me with the maner / then rembryng what she was, and knoynge how well ye trosted her, examynede her whether thosse thynges came from your highnes or wure faynd / she answerde that they came from your highnis, and he that ~~seemd~~ knew it to be trew / for the whyche I render vnto your highnes my most vmbell and harty thankes, for be her compeney (indeffawght of youres) I shall shorten the wekes in thesse parttes, whyche heretoforre wurre iij dayes lenger in every of them then they wurre under the plummette in chelsey / besydes this commodyte I may aseuring your highnes be her how I do prosyde in my matter, (althow I shulde lake my nolde frende walter erell) /
>
> I have nott as yett atempted my sewght for that I wolde be furst thorohley in credytt er I wolde move the same / ~~besh~~ besechyng your hyghnes that I may nott so vsse ~~the same~~ my sayd sewght that they shall thynke, and hereafter cast in my teth that be theyr sewght I ataynde your goode wyll / for hither to I am owt of all theyr dangeres for any plesher that they have don for me worthey thankes, ande as I Judge youre highnes may say the lek, wherfor be myn aduyce we wyll kep vs so, nothing mystrostyng the goodnes of gode but we shalbe as abell to leve out of theyr danger, as they shall out of owers, yett I meane nott but to vsse theyr frendshep to bryng our porposse to passe as occashen shall serve
>
> yf I knewe be what meanes I might gratefey your highnes for your goodenes to me showede at our last beyng to gether it shulde nott be slakte to declare myne to you agayn / and ~~for~~ to that intent that I wylbe more bounde vnto your hyghnes I do make my request that yf it be nott paynefull to your highnes that ~~on~~ once in thre dayes I may reseve iij lynes in a letter from you, ande as many lynes and letteres mor as shall seme goode vnto your hyghnes
>
> also I shall vmbeley deseyr your highnes to geue me on of ~~mye~~ your small pictures yf you have any lefft / who with hys sylence shall geue me occashen to thynke on the frendley chere that I shall reseue whan my sewght shalbe at a nend ande thus for fere of trobelyng your hyghnes with my long and rewde letter I take my

After my humble commendations unto your highness, yesternight I supped at my brother Herbert's:[28] of whom for your sake, besides mine own, I received good cheer. And after the same, I received from your highness by my sister Herbert[29] your commendations, which were more welcome than they were sent. And after the same, she waded further with me touching my being with your highness at Chelsea. Which I denied (being with your highness), but that, indeed, I went by the garden as I went to see the Bishop of London's house. And, at this point, stood with her for a time,[30] till at the last she told me further tokens which made me change colors: who, like a false wench, took me with the manner.

Then, remembering what she was, and knowing how well ye trusted her, examined her whether those things came from your highness or were feigned. She answered that they came from your highness. And he that knew it,[31] to be true. For the which, I render unto your highness my most humble and hearty thanks. For, by her company in default of yours, I shall shorten the weeks in these parts: which heretofore were three days longer, in every of them, than they were under the plummet[32] in Chelsea. Besides this commodity I may, assuring your highness by her how I do, proceed in my matter, although I should lack mine old friend Walter Erle.[33]

I have not as yet attempted my suit, for that I would be first thoroughly in credit ere I would move the same: beseeching your highness that I may not so use my said

---

leave of your highnes, wychyng that my hap may be ones so goode that I may declare so moche be mowth at the same ower that this was writeng whych was xij of the cloke ~~at~~ in the nyght this tewsday the xvij of may at sent James

[Addition] I wrett your highnes a leyn in my last letter, that my [ ] of Somerset was going [ ] sheyne who hath ben sicke whyche [ ] the lett thereof and as I vnderstand th[ ] wyll thether as to morow

from hyme whomm ye have bounde to honour, loue, and suche in all lefull thynge obbey

T. Seymour

28. **my . . . Herbert's** William Herbert, first Earl of Pembroke, a professional soldier and gentleman in Henry VIII's service, who married Anne Parr, KP's sister, circa 1538.

29. **my . . . Herbert** KP's sister, Anne. TS's references to the Herberts as his brother and sister (in-law) likewise attest his serious intention of marrying KP, if not the actual fact of their marriage.

30. **stood . . . time** another example of TS's omission of "I" at the head of this clause. A further example occurs four lines later: "examined her."

31. **knew it** Ellipsis of a verb phrase—the sense requires that this phrase be repeated: "he [TS himself] that knew it, knew it to be true."

32. **plummet** lead weight of a clock's works. William Cecil refers to "the clock that stond so long hath now so weighty plummets . . . put on that it striketh still" in a 1579 letter written to Queen Elizabeth; see *Elizabeth I: Collected Works*, ed. Marcus, Mueller, and Rose, 240.

33. **Walter Erle** a versatile member of Queen Katherine's household, who served as a groom of her privy chamber and as a musician on the virginals. At this time he was another confidant in the amorous intrigue of KP and TS, and carried letters between them (James, *Kateryn Parr*, 158).

suit that they shall think, and hereafter cast in my teeth, that by their suit I attained your goodwill. For hitherto I am out of all their dangers, for any pleasure that they have done for me worthy thanks. And, as I judge, your highness may say the like. Wherefore, by mine advice, we will keep us so, nothing mistrusting the goodness of God. But we shall be as able to live out of their danger as they shall out of ours. Yet I mean not but to use their friendship to bring our purpose to pass, as occasion shall serve.

If I knew by what means I might gratify your highness for your goodness to me, showed at our last being together, it should not be slacked to declare mine to you again. And to that intent that I will be more bound unto your highness, I do make my request that, if it be not painful to your highness, that once in three days I may receive three lines in a letter from you—and as many lines and letters more as shall seem good unto your highness.

Also, I shall humbly desire your highness to give me one of your small pictures, if you have any left: who, with his silence,[34] shall give me occasion to think on the friendly cheer that I shall receive when my suit shall be at an end. And thus, for fear of troubling your highness with my long and rude letter, I take my leave of your highness, wishing that my hap may be once so good, that I may declare so much by mouth at the same hour that this was writing: which was twelve of the clock in the night this Tuesday, the seventeenth of May, at Saint James.

[Addition]

I wrote your highness a line in my last letter, that my [lady][35] of Somerset was going [towards] Sheen,[36] who hath been sick, which [was] the let thereof. And, as I understand, th[ey] will thither as [of] tomorrow.

From him whom ye have bound to honor, love, and such in all lawful thing obey,[37]

T. Seymour

34. **who . . . silence** TS personfies the portrait of KP as a mute companion in his separation from her.

35. **[lady]** TS inadvertently omits a noun here. The other omissions below, also signaled by square brackets, are the result of a large tear in the paper edge. I conjecturally restore these readings.

36. **Sheen** TS referred in no. 3 above to Anne Seymour's intention of visiting Sheen, which had not yet been carried out. Now she and her husband plan to travel there together.

37. **ye . . . obey** This subscription loosely echoes the wording of the question put to the bride in the "Ordo Sponsalium": "Wilt thou obey him, and serve him, love, honor, and keep him, in sickness and in health?" The mutual commitment to cohabit as a married couple is again at the fore. **ye . . . bound** i.e., ye have bound yourself—another of TS's omitted pronouns.

NO. 6 DOWAGER QUEEN KATHERINE TO LORD THOMAS SEYMOUR, [LATTER HALF OF MAY] 1547[38]

My lord,

This day at dinner I received a letter from you by the means of my sister Herbert, who sent the same unto me by one of her servants, for the which I give you my most hearty thanks. It seemed convenient unto me, at her being here upon Monday, to open the matter unto her concerning you, which I never before did: at the which, unfeignedly, she did not a little rejoice. Wherefore I pray you, at your next meeting with her, to give thanks for the same, taking the knowledge thereof at my hand.

I do well allow your advice, in that my lord your brother should not have all the thank for my goodwill in this matter. For I was fully bent, before ye wrote, so to frame mine answer to him when he should attempt the matter, as that he might well and manifestly perceive my fantasy to be more towards you for marriage than any other. Notwithstanding, I am determined to add thereto a full determination never to marry, and break it when I have done, if I live two year.[39]

I think to see the King one day this week: at which time I would be glad to see you, though I shall scarce dare ask or speak. I shall most willingly observe your commandment of writing to you once in three days, thinking myself not a little bound to you, that it hath pleased you too, so to command me. I have sent in haste to the painteress[40] for one of my little pictures, which is very perfect, by the judgment of as many as hath seen the same. The last I had myself, I bestowed it upon my lady of Suffolk. This letter had been sooner with you but for tarrying the coming of the picture, the which I am not certain to receive at this time. If I cannot perform your request at this season, I shall not fail to accomplish the same shortly.

My lord, whereas you desire to know how ye might gratify my goodness showed to you at your being here, I can require nothing for the same, more than ye say I have, which is your heart and goodwill during your life: praying you to perform

38. Source: University of Oxford, Bodleian Library, Rawlinson MS D1070, art. 2, fols. 4r–5r; a seventeenth-century copy. KP's references to TS's asking her to write every three days and to give him her picture indicate that she is responding to his letter of May 17.

39. **For . . . year** KP and TS seek an opportune moment to broach with Edward Seymour, Lord Protector, their mutual commintment to marry. His permission and that of the boy-king and the Privy Council were requisite for the marriage to take place lawfully. KP coyly declares her intent to impose conditions: she will never remarry or, if she decides to remarry, it will not be for two years. She cannot be in earnest about either condition. Had she refused or delayed remarriage with TS, she would have shown that she was not carrying a prospective heir to the throne. In fact, the marriage of KP and TS was a foregone conclusion at this point, if not a reality.

40. **the painteress** Levina (or Lavinia) Teerlinc (1515?–76), the Netherlands-born portrait miniaturist, was appointed by Henry VIII as "paintrix" to the English court in 1546 after the deaths of Hans Holbein the Younger and Lucas Horenbout, the previous court painters.

that, and I am fully satisfied. When you be at leisure, let me hear from you; I dare not desire to see you for fear of suspicion. I would the world were as well pleased with our meaning as, I am well assured, the goodness of God is. But the world is so wicked that it cannot be contented with good things. And thus, with my most humble and hearty commendations, I take my leave for this time, wishing your well-doing no less than mine own.

From Chelsea, by her that is yours to serve and obey during her life,

Katherine the Queen KP

NO. 7 DOWAGER QUEEN KATHERINE TO LORD THOMAS SEYMOUR, [LATE MAY] 1547[41]

[Endorsed] The Queen's highness' letter to my Lord Admiral.

My lord,

This shall be to advertise you that my lord your brother hath this afternoon a little made me warm. It was fortunate we were so much distant, for I suppose else

41. Source: Hatfield, Hertfordshire, Hatfield House, Cecil Papers, 133/3/248, fols. 4r-5v. In KP's hand. The original reads:

> my lord thys schalbe to aduertyssche yow that my lord your brother hathe thys after none alyttell made me Warme yt Was fortunate ~~t~~ we war so muche dystant for I suppose els I schuld haue bytten hym What cause have ~~yow~~ they to feare hauyńg suche awyff yt ys requysyte for them contynually to pray for aschort dyspatche of that hell. to morowe or els apon satterday at after none about thre a clocke I wyll se the Kynge Wher I intend to vtter all my coler to my lorde your brother yf yow schall not gyue me aduyse to the contrary for I wold be lothe to do any thyng to hynder your mater / I wyll declare vnto yow how my lord hathe vsed me consernyng fausterne and after I schall moost humbly desyre yow to dyrecte myne ~~answe~~ answer to hym in that behalf. yt lyketh hym to day to send my chancelour to me wyllyng hym to declare to me that he had bowght master longes lese and that he douted not but I wold lett him inoye the same to hys comodyte wheryn I schuld do to hys successyon no small pleasur nothyng consyderyng hys honour wyche thys mater toucheth not a lytell. for so muche as I at Sundry tymes declared vnto hym the only cause of my repayre in to those partyes was for the comodyte of that parke wyche els I wold not have done he not wythstandyng hathe so vsed the mater with gyuyng master long suche courage that he refusith to receyue such cattell as ar bowght for the prouysyon of my house, and so in the meane tyme I am forced to comytt them to fermers: my lord I beseche yow send me word with spede how I schall vse my self to my new brother. and thus I take my leue with my moost humble and harty comendatyons wysschyng yow all yowr godly desyres and so well to do as I wold myself and better. from chelsey in grett haste
>
> By your humble true and lovyng wyfe in her hart,
> Kateryn the Quene KP

I should have bitten him. What cause have they to fear [you] having such a wife?[42] It is requisite for them continually to pray for a short dispatch of that hell. Tomorrow, or else upon Saturday at afternoon about three o'clock, I will see the King:[43] where I intend to utter all my choler to my lord your brother, if you shall not give me advice to the contrary. For I would be loath to do anything to hinder your matter.

I will declare unto you how my lord hath used me concerning Fausterne,[44] and after, I shall most humbly desire you to direct mine answer to him in that behalf. It liketh him today to send my chancellor to me, willing him to declare to me that he hath bought Master Long's lease,[45] and that he doubted not but I would let him en[j]oy the same to his commodity: wherein I should do to his succession no small pleasure, nothing considering his honor, which this matter toucheth not a little. Forsomuch as I at sundry times declared unto him, the only cause of my repair into those parts was for the commodity of that park, which else I would not have done. He, notwithstanding, hath so used the matter, with giving Master Long such courage, that he refuseth to receive such cattle as are bought for the provision of my house; and so in the meantime I am forced to commit them to farmers.

My lord, I beseech you, send me word with speed how I shall use myself to my new brother.[46] And thus I take my leave with my most humble and hearty commendations, wishing you all your godly desires, and so well to do as I would myself, and better. From Chelsea in great haste.

By your humble, true, and loving wife in her heart,
Katherine the Queen KP

42. **[you] . . . wife** **[you]** As the manuscript correction shows, KP should have written "you" here to replace the "you" she struck through earlier in this sentence. **such . . . wife** The now likely fact that KP is TS's wife seems to have been communicated to Edward and Anne Seymour—the negatively reacting "them" of the next line.

43. **the King** the ten-year-old Edward, with whom KP had had little or no contact after Henry's death in late January 1547.

44. **Fausterne** See n26.

45. **chancellor . . . lease** **chancellor** a no longer current synonym for "secretary." KP's secretary was the versatile Walter Bucler, a member of the Council with the Queen during her regency. He served as Henry VIII's confidential ambassador to Duke Maurice of Saxony and the Landgrave of Hesse to explore religious and marital possibilities involving Princess Mary or Princess Elizabeth in 1544–45 (G&B 20.1:90, 91; James, *Kateryn Parr*, 187–88). **declare . . . lease** Edward Seymour has made a preemptive move against KP's proprietorship of Fausterne by undertaking to buy its lease from her current tenant, Henry Long.

46. **my . . . brother** KP's phrasing would seem to indicate that she is newly married to TS. But perhaps she refers to their marriage as news to Edward Seymour—not as a new event in itself.

NO. 8 LORD THOMAS SEYMOUR TO DOWAGER QUEEN KATHERINE, [LATE MAY] 1547[47]

[Endorsed in a later hand] The Lord Admiral to the Queen, of his suit for marriage.

After my humble recommendations, with thanks that ye have admitted me one of your counsellors, I perceive that your highness hath been warmed: whereof I am

47. Source: TNA, State Papers 10/1/43, fol. 132. In TS's hand, signed in italic. The original reads:

> After my vmbell Recommendashens with thankes, that ye haue a mettede me on of your conseleres I perseue that your highnes hath ben warmd, wharof I am glade, for that ye shulnott thynke on the ij yerres ye wrott of in your last letter be fore this / ande as tochyng myne aduyse for fastrenn your hyghnes shall declare vnto my lorde, that it hath nott ben hide fromm hyme, what was your determenashen consernyng the same for your howse; also ye haue geuen commandment to your officeres to grow to somm poynt with ~~hym~~ M long for the pattent that he hath of yow / be whom ye vnderstande that he hathe so vsed hys offes, that he hathe no entrest therein but dewryng your plesur, how be it ye do nott mynde to take it of hyme exsept ye may lawefully do the same, and yett nott with out suche recompence as he shulbe contentede with all / in the whych partes there ys soffechent pasture ~~be~~ to Fatt all your provyshen, and also my lords / and they beyng in your handes, ye wolde be loth to say my lorde nay therof or a gretter matter / and desyr hym ~~withall~~ for your sake nott to medell with all, for that ye wyll take w[a] reant at hys hande; rather thenn clayme your ryght, he meslikyng wyth all / And yf ye fynde hyme stedefast to a longe intrest, I wolde ye shulde say that yf he hath suche intrest as his lordship doth declare, then any thyng that ye shulde grant ys wel worthy of thankes, and untyll suche tyme as ye kno sertenely what intrest ye have, ye wyllnott depart with all and I mey not the same. ye wyll mack ~~my lord~~ hym suche ansour as he shall have cawse to be content
>
> I wrett your highnes a letter yester day of part of my mynd therein ~~and~~ whyche I toke to my brother harbart to be deleuerd to hys wyff, who I thynk knoth of our matters but ~~as yett~~ nott be me nor none shall but such as ye a poynt till yt be ferther forth
>
> I presome I have my lady of soffokes goode wyll toching my nown desyr of yow; who this other day talkyng ^ of me with my Frend Sir Wylliam sharyngton, wychede me to be theyr master / he demandyng of her what she ment thareby expound it, that she wolde that I warre maryd to theyer mistres / and so wolde I / and to bryng it the soner to passe I shall do my best to sett my Lorde and you at a garre, to the intent to make yow werey of your matters ~~and~~ that ye shall conuey them to me, to ansour for us both / ande thus for this tyme I take my leaue of your highnes, from sent James
>
> from hym that ys your louynge and ffaythfull hosbonde durynge hys lyff
>
> T. Seymour

glad, for that ye shall not think on the two years ye wrote of in your last letter before this.[48]

And, as touching mine advice for Fausterne,[49] your highness shall declare unto my lord that it hath not been hid from him, what was your determination concerning the same for your house. Also, ye have given commandment to your officers to grow to some point with Master Long for the patent[50] that he hath of you, by whom ye understand that he hath so used his office, that he hath no interest therein but during your pleasure. Howbeit, ye do not mind to take it of him except ye may lawfully do the same, and yet not without such recompense as he shall be contented withal. In the which parts there is sufficient pasture to fat all your provision and also my lord's: and they being in your hands, ye would be loath to say my lord nay thereof, or a greater matter. And desire him, for your sake, not to meddle withal, for that ye will take warrant at his hand[51] rather than claim your right, he misliking withal. And if ye find him steadfast to a long interest, I would ye should say that if he hath such interest as his lordship doth declare, then anything that ye should grant is well worthy of thanks. And until such time as ye know certainly what interest ye have, ye will not depart withal; and I may not the same. Ye will make him such answer as he shall have cause to be content.

I wrote your highness a letter yesterday, of part of my mind therein, which I took to my brother Herbert, to be delivered to his wife[52] who, I think, knoweth of our matters, but not by me, nor none shall, but such as ye appoint, till it be further forth.

I presume I have my lady of Suffolk's goodwill touching mine own desire of you: who, this other day, talking of me with my friend Sir William Sharington,[53] wished me to be their master. He demanding of her what she meant, [she] thereby

48. **warmed . . . this warmed** TS slyly elaborates KP's phrase "a little . . . warm" in the preceding letter, changing her sense of "angrily warmed" to "erotically warmed," and challenging her professed intent, in no. 6, of observing two years of mourning for King Henry.

49. **mine . . . Fausterne** TS proceeds to sketch the compromise solution that he wishes KP to propose to his brother: Edward Seymour will acknowledge her right of title-for-life to Fausterne; she will allow his cattle to graze with hers on the lands. The tenant, Henry Long, who is loyal to KP's interests, could have his lease terminated with fair compensation. Whoever holds the lease, the grazing rights that KP offers should accommodate Edward's interests in Fausterne, preventing him from seeking to wrest the title to the property from her.

50. **patent** a document conferring some right or privilege—in this case KP's lease to Long as tenant of Fausterne.

51. **take . . . hand** regard as an assurance from him (Henry Long).

52. **my brother . . . his wife** William Herbert and Anne (Parr) Herbert evidently acted as intermediaries for correspondence between TS and KP.

53. **William Sharington** a member of Queen Katherine's household who continued to serve her as dowager queen. From 1547 he also held an appointment as a chief officer of the king's mint. As this mention indicates, he and TS were on familiar terms. Both men would be attainted of treason and executed in March 1549.

expounded it that she would that I were married to their mistress. And so would I. And, to bring it the sooner to pass,[54] I shall do my best to set my lord and you at a jar, to the intent to make you weary of your matters: that ye shall convey them to me, to answer for us both.[55] And thus, for this time, I take my leave of your highness. From Saint James.

From him that is your loving and faithful husband during his life,

T. Seymour

NO. 9 KING EDWARD'S LATIN LETTER TO DOWAGER QUEEN KATHERINE, MAY 30, 1547[56]

[Headed] To Queen Katherine

When I was [not] far away from you and hoped daily that I would see you, it seemed best to me not to write you any letters at all. For letters are signs of remembrance and kindness between those who are far distant. But I, finally kindled by your beseeching, was not able not to send letters to you: first, so that I may do what is pleasing to you; then, indeed, so that I may answer the letter full of kindness which you sent to me from Saint James. In which, first, you set before my eyes your love

54. **were married . . . pass** TS's language regarding marriage with KP continues its playful alternations between an action already taken and a fact not yet known by others. Here the uppermost concern seems to be to "bring" public knowledge of the marriage "the sooner to pass."

55. **a jar . . . us both** TS jauntily proposes to worsen the tense relations between KP and Edward Seymour so that he can play peacemaker. He assumes what is not at all obvious: that his intervention would work to his and KP's benefit.

56. Source: BL, Harley MS 5087, art. 37, fol. 15. Edward's copy, in his own hand, with a salutation and an omitted negative supplied from Corpus Christi College, Cambridge, MS 119. KP's letter to which this replies has been lost. Edward's letter reads as follows:

> *[Headed]* Reginae Chatarinae [sic]
>
> Cum [non] procul abs te abessem et quotidie me te visurum sperarem, mihi optimum uidebatur non omnino ad te literas dare. Literae enim sunt cuiusdam memoriae et beneuolentiae longe absentium signa. Sed ego petitione tua tandem accensus, non potui non ad te literas mittere. Primum ut tibi gratum faciam, deinde uero ut tuis literis respondeam, beneuolentiae plenis, qua[s] e san[c]to Jacobo ad me misisti. In quibus primum ponis ante oculos tuum amorem erga patrem meum nobilissimae memoriae regem, deinde beneuolentiam erga me, ac postremo pietatem scientiam et doctrinam in sacris literis. Perge igitur in tuo bono incepto et prosequere patrem amore diuturno, ac exhibe mihi tanta signa beneuolentiae, que semper hactenus in te sensi, et ne desinas amare et legere sacras literas, sed semper in eis legendis perseuera. In primo enim indicas officium bonae coniugis et subiectae. In secundo ostendis laudem amicitiae tuae, et in tertio tuam pietatem erga deum. Quare cum ames patrem non possum non te

towards my father,[57] a King of most noble memory; then, your goodwill towards me; and last, your piety, wisdom, and instruction in the holy Scriptures.

Continue, therefore, in your good undertaking; and follow after my father with everlasting love; and show to me as many signs of kindness as I have ever perceived in you; and never cease to love and read the holy Scriptures, but always persevere in reading them. Truly, in the first, you show the duty of a good wife and subject. In the second, you show the glory of your friendship; and in the third, your piety towards God.

Wherefore, since you love my father, I cannot but praise you earnestly; since you love me, I can but love you in return; and since you love the Word of God, I revere and admire you from the heart. Wherefore if there is a thing in which I can be pleasing to you, in deed or in words, I will do it willingly. Farewell, the thirtieth of May.

Edward the King

NO. 10 PRINCESS MARY'S LETTER TO LORD THOMAS SEYMOUR, JUNE 4, 1547[58]

[Endorsed by two different hands] The Lady Mary to the Lord Admiral. 4th June. From the Lady Mary's grace.
[Addressed] To my Lord Admiral.

---

vehementer laudare, cum me ames non te iterum diligere et cum verbum dei ames te colam et mirabar ex animo. Quare si quid sit quo possum tibi gratum, facto uel uerbo facere, libenter prestabo. Vale xxx[mo] Maij

E. Rex

57. **your love . . . my father** Edward's rehearsal of KP's phrasing reveals his unawareness of the love intrigue between his stepmother and his younger uncle.

58. Source: BL, Lansdowne MS 1236, fol. 26. In Mary's hand, similar in kind to KP's. The original reads:

[Addressed] To my lorde admyrall

My lorde after my harty commendacions, theyse shalbe to declare to you, that accordyng to your accoustomed jentilnes I have receyued vj warrantes from you by your seruant thys berer, for the whiche I do gyue you my harty thankes, by whom also I haue receyued your lettre, wherin (as me thynketh) I parceyv strange newes concernyng a sewte you haue in hande to the quene for maryage, for the soner obtayneng wherof you seme to thynke, that my lettres myghte do you pleasure. My lorde in thys case, I truste, your wysdome doth consyder, that if it weer for my nereste kynsman and dereste frend on lyve, of all other creatures in the worlde, it standeth lest with my poore honoure to be a medler in thys matter, consyderyng whose wyef her grace was of late, and besydes that, if she be mynded to grawnt your sewte, my lettres shall do you but small pleasure, on the other syde, if the

My lord,

After my hearty commendations, these shall be to declare to you that, according to your accustomed gentleness, I have received six warrants[59] from you by your servant, this bearer: for the which, I do give you my hearty thanks. By whom also I have received your letter, wherein, as me thinketh, I perceive strange news concerning a suit you have in hand to the Queen for marriage. For the sooner obtaining whereof, you seem to think that my letters might do you pleasure.

My lord, in this case I trust your wisdom doth consider that, if it were for my nearest kinsman and dearest friend alive, of all other creatures in the world, it standeth least with my poor honor to be a meddler in this matter, considering whose wife her grace was of late. And besides that, if she be minded to grant your suit, my letters shall do you but small pleasure. On the other side, if the remembrance of the King's majesty, my father (whose soul God pardon[60]), will not suffer her to grant your suit, I am nothing able to persuade her to forget the loss of him, who is as yet very ripe in mine own remembrance.

Wherefore I shall most earnestly require you, the premises considered,[61] to think none unkindness in me, though I refuse to be a meddler any ways in this matter. Assuring you that, wooing matters set apart (wherein I, being a maid, am nothing cunning), if other ways it shall lie in my little power to do you pleasure, I shall be as glad to do it as you to require it: both for his blood's sake, that you be of,[62] and also for the gentleness which I have always found in you. As knoweth al-

---

remembrance of the kynges mayestye my father (whose soule god pardon) wyll not suffre her to grawnt your sewte, I ame nothyng able to perswade her to forget the losse of hyme, who is as yet very rype in myn owne remembrance, wherfore I shall moste earnestly requyre you (the premysses consydered) to thynke non vnkyndnes in me, thoughe I refuse to be a medler any wayes in thys matter, assuryng you, that (woweng matters set aparte, wherin I beeng a mayde am nothyng connyng) if other wayes it shall lye in my litle power to do you playser, I shalbe as gladde to do it, as you to requyre it / both for hys bloddes sake, that you be of, and also for the jentylnes, whiche I have alwayes fownde in you. As knoweth almyghty god to whose tuicyon I commytte you. from wansted thys saterday at nygh[te] beeng the iiijth of june.

your assured frend to my power /
Marye /

59. **warrants** writings conveying assurances of safeguard or protection.

60. **whose . . . pardon** Mary's pious interjection appears to allude to Henry's divorcing of her mother, Queen Catherine of Aragon.

61. **the . . . considered** A fine logical structure channels the strong emotion in Mary's dignified letter. She uses a disjunctive syllogism to prove the unaptness of TS's request: if her appeals could move KP to favor him, those appeals would be unnecessary; if her appeals could not move KP, it would be because of the still fresh loss of King Henry, which Mary herself feels at first hand.

62. **his blood's . . . of** Mary alludes to TS's nephew, Edward VI.

mighty God, to whose tuition I commit you. From Wanstead[63] this Saturday at night, being the fourth of June.

Your assured friend to my power,
Mary

NO. 11 KING EDWARD'S LETTER TO DOWAGER QUEEN KATHERINE, JUNE 25, [1547][64]

[Headed] To Queen Katherine Parr, the King's letter congratulatory, upon her marriage with the Lord Admiral

We thank you heartily, not only for your gentle acceptation of our suit[65] moved unto you, but also for your loving accomplishing of the same: wherein you have declared not only a desire to gratify us, but also moved us to declare the goodwill, likewise, that we bear to you in all your requests. Wherefore ye shall not need to fear any grief to come, or to suspect lack of aid in need: seeing that he, being mine uncle, is of so good a nature that he will not be troublesome any means unto you; and I of that mind that, for divers just causes, I must favor you.

But even as, without cause, you merely require help against[66] him whom you have put in trust with the carriage of these letters, so may I merely return the same

63. **Wanstead** a royal manor in the northeast of what is now greater London, near Woodford.

64. Source: a lost English letter of Edward's, printed by John Strype in *Ecclesiastical Memorials relating chiefly to Religion and the Reformation of it, . . . under King Henry VIII, King Edward VI, and Queen Mary I* (London, 1721; rpt. Oxford: Clarendon, 1822), 2:208–9, described in Strype's Latin marginalium as transcribed from "manuscripts in my possession." Strype's divisions of his work locate this text in the section on Edward VI's reign, as an entry for 1548. The original letter was reported by James Orchard Halliwell-Phillipps, ed., *Letters of the Kings of England* (London: H. Colburn, 1846), 2:34–35, to be "preserved among the Cottonian manuscripts" in the Bodleian Library, but its whereabouts remained unknown to John Nichols, ed., *Literary Remains of King Edward VI* (London, 1857), 1:46–47. Nichols (1:44–45) observes that "the existence of the present letter was known to the privy council at the time of the lord admiral's prosecution" for treason in January 1548. To corroborate, he transcribes this accusation against TS from the Privy Council's record book: "It is objected and laid to your charge, That you first married the queen privately, and did dissemble and keep close the same, insomuch that, a good space after you had married her, you made labour to the King's majesty, and obtained a letter of his majesty's hand, to move and require the said queen to marry with you; and likewise procured the lord protector to speak to the queen to bear you her favour towards marriage; by the which colouring . . . your evil and dissembling nature may be known."

65. **our suit** Young Edward had evidently been brought to think that the marriage of KP and TS occurred at his initiative.

66. **against** in reception of, in welcome of.

request unto you: to provide that he may live with you also without grief, which hath given him wholly unto you. And I will so provide for you both that hereafter, if any grief befall, I shall be a sufficient succor in your godly and praiseworthy enterprises. Fare ye well, with much increase of honor and virtue in Christ. From Saint James the five-and-twenty day of June.

Edward

NO. 12 KING EDWARD'S LATIN LETTER TO DOWAGER QUEEN KATHERINE, SEPTEMBER 19, 1547[67]

[Headed] To Queen Katherine

Your letters have been thoroughly enjoyable to me, most noble Queen, which you have written to me very recently. First, because I perceive your lasting love to inhere in them; then, because in their eloquence and ornate manner of expression, they very far excel other letters; lastly, because you place before my eyes and make manifest your most lovely diligence by writing to me at length. But your lasting love, so enduring, greatly stirs and incites me to return a mutual love to you. Your eloquence and diligence sound a great trumpet-call to me: that I employ all my strength and my highest power to follow by advancing at a bound, although I cannot approach your excelling virtue. May God prosper you most blessedly. From Oatlands, the nineteenth of September.

Edward the King

67. Source: BL, Harley MS 5087, art. 42, fols. 17v–18r. Edward's copy, in his own hand. The letter reads as follows:

> *[Headed]* Reginae Catherinae
>
> Periucundae fuerunt mihi tuae literae, nobilissima regina quas nouissime ad me scripsisti. Primum quia intelligo tuum veterem amorem in illis inesse. Deinde quia illae longissime eloquentia, et ornato dicendi modo aliorum literas precellebant. Postremo quia mihi ob oculos ponis et manifestas tuam sedulitatem in scribendo longe pulcherrimam. Tuus enim vetustus amor adhuc permanens me maxime prouocat incitatque, ut tibi muutuum referrem amorem, tuaque eloquentia et sedulitas maximum mihi classicum canit vti ego totis viribus, summaque potentia mea eniterer ad assequendum saltum quamquam anteuenire non possum tuam eximiam virtutem. Deus felicissime te prosperet. Otlandiae 19° septembris.
>
> E. Rex

NO. 13 ROGER ASCHAM'S LATIN LETTER TO DOWAGER QUEEN KATHERINE, APPEALING ANEW FOR HELP IN PROTECTING THE PROPERTIES OF THE COLLEGES OF THE UNIVERSITY OF CAMBRIDGE FROM CONFISCATION BY THE CROWN [NOVEMBER 1547][68]

To our most serene Queen, divine Katherine,
a Prince most distinguished in virtues, nobility, and letters.
On behalf of the University.[69]

68. Source: Roger Ascham, *Familiarium Epistolarum Libri Tres* (London: Francis Coldock, 1578) (STC 827), pt. 1, 186–88. The Latin original reads as follows:

Serenissimae Reginae nostrae divae Catarinae,
virtutis, nobilitatis, et literarum
illustrissimae Principi. Pro Academia.

Si magnam commoditatem ex beneficijs tuis in nos collatis, si maiorem voluptatem ex literis tuis proximo superiori anno ad nos scriptis percepimus, clarissima Princeps: maximam profectò culpam committeremus, si, vel tanti beneficij in adiuuando, vel eximiae voluntatis tuae in scribendo, memoriam vnquam abjiceremus. Et quanquam beneficia tua ita grata fuerint nobis, vt absqué, hijs salus Academiae nostrae contineri non queat: magnitudo tamen eorum omnium ita superata est suauitate literarum tuarum, vt istis beneficijs, quibus nunc vtimur, quàm illis literis quas olim recepimus carere maluissemus. Beneficium enim à quouis accipere, populare quiddam et quotidianum est: vti autem tantae Principis tanta beneuolentia, vt nihil est ad vsum vberius, ita profectò nec ad animi iucunditatem suauius, nec ad memoriae diuturnitatem stabilius quicquam exoptari potest. Iuua igitur nos semper, optima Princeps, et scribe ad nos saepius eruditissima Regina: hoc nomen eruditionis ne spernas prudentissima foemina: est enim laus industriae et ingenij tui maior omnibus ornamentis fortunae tuae. At fortunae quid? Hìc certè loci nihil habet, cùm tu omnia tua soli Christo accepta referas. Vehementèr sanè omnes admiramur foelicitatem tuam, foelicissima Princeps, quae plura discis in tanto negotio dignitatis tuae, quàm plurimi apud nos in tanto otio quietis nostrae: et hoc facis etiam in ea celsitatis amplitudine, vbi reliquae foeminae literas despicere velint: et in ea etiam aetate, quando doctrinam antea perceptam ex animo abijcere solent. Et hanc doctrinae laudem sic vniuersam possides, vt eam caeteris omnibus praereptam, soli tamen Diuae Elizabetae communicatam esse, cum magna mutuae societatis suauitate, libenti animo feras. Vides ergo nobilissima Regina, qua spe, et qua re commoti ad te accedimus, opem tuam imploraturi. Nam, vt opem feras nobis authoritate et iussu tuo in hoc Parlamento vehementèr petimus: qua autem ratione hoc facias, grauissimus vir, et magna eruditione ac modestia praeditus Ioannes Madew Vicecancellarius noster, tibi (si ita libet) coràm fusè declaraturus est, cui vt fidem habeas etiam atqué etiam omnes rogamus. Dominus Jesus amplitudinem tuam honore, foelicitate, doctrine, et virtute ampliorem indiès faciat.

69. **On . . . University** Ascham, writing in his capacity of public orator of the University of Cambridge, begins by acknowledging KP's prior help in securing Henry's favor, which she had reported to the university in a letter dated February 26, [1546]. This is no. 14 in part 3.

If we derived great benefit from the favors you bestowed upon us, if we derived greater pleasure from your most recent letter written to us in the past year, most illustrious Prince: we would indeed commit the greatest fault if, either of so many favors in assisting [us] or of your exceptional goodwill in writing [to us], we were to cast aside any remembrance. And yet even if your favors had been so deserving of our gratitude that, without them, the well-being of our University could not be preserved, nonetheless all their greatness was so surpassed by the agreeableness of your letter, that these favors which we now enjoy we would rather lack, than that letter that we once received. For to receive a kindness from someone is a common and everyday thing, but there is nothing more fruitful in practical use than to enjoy so many favors from a Prince. So too nothing can be hoped for that more sweetly delights the mind or more constantly preserves the memory. Therefore help us always, best of Princes, and write to us oftener, most learned Queen.

Spurn not this repute of learning, most prudent Queen, for it is a glory of your diligence and your gifts of mind, greater than all the ornaments of your state. But what of your state? It is certainly nothing here, since you attribute to Christ alone all that you have received. We all of course greatly wonder at your happiness, most happy Prince: you who learn more things in the great business of your rank than many among us in the great leisure and quietness of ours. And this you do even in the greatness of your eminence, where the rest of women would wish to look down on learning, even in that time of life when they are wont to let instruction previously grasped go out of their minds. And you so completely take possession of the universal glory of learning, carried away from all others, to be shared only with one, the divine Elizabeth, in the great sweetness of mutual company.

You see therefore, most noble Queen, with what hope and moved by what, we approach you to implore your action. For we urgently request that you set in motion for us, by your authority and command, an act in this Parliament.[70] For what

70. **you . . . Parliament** The initial focus of anxiety over the properties of the Cambridge colleges was Henry VIII's letter of commission, dated January 16, 1546, requiring an account of the foundations and possessions of the colleges, after Parliament had "freely given and granted" the king "full power of authority to order, alter, change, and reform all the colleges, hospitals, chantries, and free chapels within this our realm of England and other our dominions, or otherwise to use the same, at our pleasure, as in the act made for that purpose more at length may appear." The king's letter commands that masters and heads of colleges report how "all and every their foundations, statutes, and ordinances . . . be observed; of what values, kinds, and natures the whole possessions be, which belong to every such college, . . . and in what shires the same do lie, with the deductions upon the same; the names of the founders, and other things which your wisdoms shall think meet to be signified to us." The colleges feared that they might undergo dissolution and confiscation of their properties by the crown, as the monasteries had a decade earlier. The search for additions to the royal revenue was triggered by the sizable deficit incurred during Henry's unsuccessful military campaign (summer 1545) to recover lost English possessions in France. Anxiety over the possible dissolution of the colleges revived under the

reason, moreover, you should do this, a most reverent man endowed with great erudition and modesty, John Maddew, our vice chancellor, will come to you, if you please, to declare at length in your presence: whom we all entreat you more and more to trust. May the Lord Jesus make your greatness still greater from day to day in honor, happiness, learning, and virtue.

NO. 14 NICHOLAS UDALL'S LETTER TO DOWAGER QUEEN KATHERINE, PREFACING THE FIRST VOLUME OF ENGLISH TRANSLATIONS OF ERASMUS'S *PARAPHRASES UPON THE NEW TESTAMENT*, JANUARY 31, 1548[71]

To the most virtuous lady, Queen Katherine Dowager, late wife
to the most noble and most victorious King Henry VIII, of most famous memory,
Nicholas Udall, your most humble servant,
wisheth health, grace, and consolation in our Lord Jesus Christ everlasting.

Where your excellent highness, most gracious Queen Katherine Dowager, since the time of your first calling to the estate and dignity of espousal and marriage with the most noble prince that ever reigned, King Henry VIII, hath never ceased, by all possible means that in you might lie, to mind, to advance, and to increase the public commodity and benefit of this commonweal of England: I find on every side so great and the same so worthy matter of gratulation and thanksgiving unto God, that I cannot tell on whose part first to commence and begin the same. Whether on your own behalf, whom God of His goodness did for your singular and the same most notable virtues, without any your expectation or hope, suddenly put in King Henry's mind to choose, call, and advance to the dignity and estate of a queen; or on King Henry's part, whose good hap it was so aptly to choose such a one as should afterward be a faithful and continual coadjutrix unto him in all his most devout and godly proceedings concerning the knowledge of God and His Word to be set forth to the people; or else for England's cause, to whose public benefit and edifying in true religion, all your incessant pains and travails do finally redound.

Leaving, therefore, the prosecution of so large a matter as neither my slender wit can well contrive nor my rude pen is able to wield, I shall at this present only thank God in you, and you in God, for causing these Paraphrases of Desiderius Erasmus of Rotterdam upon the New Testament to be translated into English for

lord protector in the Parliament of November 1547, where fresh legislation to dissolve the same institutions was approved and certain exceptions were again granted (John Guy, *Tudor England* [Oxford: Oxford University Press, 1988], 205–6).

71. Source: *The first tome or volume of the Paraphrase of Erasmus upon the newe testament* (London: Edward Whitchurch, January 31, 1548) (STC 2854), sigs. C i r–C iii v (separately paginated).

the use and commodity of such people as, with an earnest zeal and with devout study, do hunger and thirst the simple and plain knowledge of God's Word. Not for contentious babbling, but for innocent living; not to be curious searchers of the high mysteries, but to be faithful executors and doers of God's biddings; not to be troublous talkers of the Bible, but sincere followers of God's precepts therein contained; not to be unreverent reasoners in Holy Scripture for vain setting-out of their painted sheath, but to be humble and lowly workers of God's glory; not to be curious disputers in the Gospel for the defense and maintenance of their inordinate lusts and carnal liberty, but to be upright walkers in holy conversation of life, in the rule of the Gospel prescribed.

Which kind of doctrine, forasmuch as no one writer hath labored in all points and behalfs more uncorruptly or more plainly to minister unto the simple reader than this author, by a perpetual discourse and continuation[72] of the text, doth: your highness undoubtedly, in procuring the same to be turned into English, hath not only after a most godly sort bestowed your charges, but also hath in the thing [it] self done unto a commonwealth a benefit by so many degrees surmounting and passing any other act of your great largesse[73] and benignity, as the soul is better than the body, as spiritual edifying is above temporal supportation,[74] as ghostly food and comfort exceedeth corporeal relief or cherishing,[75] and as heavenly treasures excel all worldly gifts or riches. And in that your highness, for the more speedy expedition of your most godly purpose to bring God's Word to the more light and to the more clear understanding, distributed this work by portions to sundry translators, to the intent it might all at once be finished, nor the devout English readers any long time defrauded of so fruitful and so profitable a work: ye have therein, most gracious lady, right well declared both how much ye tender God's honor, and also how earnestly ye mind the benefit of your country. Which (your country), what they are not able in fact with condign thanks to requite, do and ever will (as they are most bounden) supply[76] with perpetual commending your highness to God in prayer, which I think to be the only reward ye look for or desire.

As touching the translations, because they are of sundry persons' doings, though there appear in them some diversity of style and enditing,[77] yet is there in the whole work no contrariety of doctrine. Though every translator follow his own vein of turning the Latin into English, yet doth none willingly swerve or dissent from the mind and sense of his author. Albeit some go more near to the words of

72. **perpetual . . . continuation** Udall's doubling points to what he regards as the method and benefit of Erasmus's paraphrases of Scripture: speechlike or conversational conveying of thought.

73. **largesse** generosity—a borrowing from French.

74. **supportation . . . ghostly supportation** assistance. **ghostly** spiritual.

75. **cherishing** nourishing, fostering.

76. **supply** make up a whole by adding something.

77. **enditing** composing.

the letter, and some use the liberty of translating at large, not so precisely binding themselves to the strait interpretation of every word and syllable, so the sense be kept: yet do they all agree, every one as his vein serveth him, in faithfully rendering the sense of their book. So that, if any persons there be, either of such high conceit and opinion of themselves that they can like no man's doings but their own, or else of such ungentleness that they will not well interpret simple men's doings, which themselves can for the most part sooner find fault withal than amend, or else of such morosity[78] and waywardness that their stomachs cannot bear with any other man's labors, be they never so honestly intended or bestowed: such are, in this behalf, rather to be contemned[79] and left to their insolent disdainfulness than either to be pacified or answered unto.

The parts of devout readers are, with immortal thanks, to receive and take the fruition of honest and godly studies. The office of learned men is, without depraving or derogation of other men's diligence and without any arrogancy on their own behalfs, to employ their good takents to the public behoof[80] of their country, and to the furtherance of godly knowledge. The office of every studious and diligent writer is to have his eye directed to the public utility only, and then to think his upright well-doings a sufficient prize and reward of themselves, and so, without respect of any worldly reward or thank, to refer the fruit and success of his labors to God, the Motioner, the Author, and the Worker of all goodness.

As touching Erasmus and the doctrine that his books do sow, although I have before this time said as well in my preface unto your highness before the Paraphrase upon the Gospel of Luke as elsewhere, yet can I not omit thus much to say in his defense: that in case any persons be enemies to Erasmus's writing, it proceedeth more of their envy, of their unquietness of mind, and of their hatred against the light and grace of the Gospel, clearly now arising and plenteously spreading itself abroad, than of any fault or just desert in Erasmus.[81] Whoso wincheth[82] and kicketh at the Gospel, indeed cannot but spurn at Erasmus, who hath with incomparable study and travail showed himself a diligent laborer in Christ's vineyard.[83] And

78. **morosity** moroseness.

79. **contemned** treated with contempt, scorned.

80. **behoof** use, benefit, advantage.

81. **fault . . . Erasmus** Despite his adherence to the Catholic faith and his dispute with Luther, by the mid-sixteenth century Erasmus had come to be regarded as a proto- or quasi-Reformer, incurring strong condemnation from certain Catholics and varying degrees of admiration from Protestants. See Bruce Mansfield, *Phoenix of His Age: Interpretations of Erasmus c. 1550–1750* (Toronto: University of Toronto Press, 1979), 27–39, 110–14; Craig R. Thompson, *Erasmus and Tudor England* (Amsterdam: North-Holland, 1971), 50–64; and Gregory D. Dodds, *Exploiting Erasmus: The Erasmian Legacy and Religious Change in Early Modern England* (Toronto: University of Toronto Press, 2009), chaps. 1–4.

82. **wincheth** flinches, winces.

83. **Christ's vineyard** Jesus tells the parable of the vineyard in Matthew 20:1–16. Laboring in the vineyard is a figure for doing the work of the Lord.

truly, whomsoever I perceive to be an eager adversary to Erasmus's writings, I (as my poor judgment leadeth me) cannot but suppose the same to be an indurate[84] enemy to the Gospel, which Erasmus doth according to the measure and portion of his talent faithfully labor to set forth and promote.

But, like as when man is in a fever or with any other grievous infirmity distempered, the better that the drink is, the worse it tasteth in his mouth: so when the heart is corrupt with malice and hatred of God's truth, the better that the doctrine is, the more it offendeth. Some eyes cannot abide the brightness of the sun, nor a corrupt heart the clear verity of God's Word. Persons indurate are the worse for reading of Holy Scripture: neither do they of anything take more occasion of slander and offense of conscience than they do of Holy Scripture, whereby their conscience should be edified. Some there be of such malicious hardness of heart that they can abide neither book, nor teaching, nor reading nor anything else that may help or amend the ignorant people's knowledge. And such, becuse they would let and stop God's glory, deprave all good things and pronounce them to be naught. But such are, in this behoof, not to be passed on[85] nor to be heard. For as a body corrupted with ill humors or diseases, the more and better that it is nourished with good meats and drinks, the worse it is: so a cankered[86] stomach and a wicked heart, the more wholesome doctrine that is ministered unto it, the more it is indurate; the more doth it envy the public utility unto men; and the more doth it strive and wrestle again[st] the verity. Pharaoh was never more eager in persecuting the people of God than when he was, by daily plagues[87] and miracles, most of all provoked to convert. The Pharisees never more furiously swelled, insurged, or raged against Christ than when He alleged Holy Scripture unto them, or brought against them the testimony of their own law,[88] which they could not deny.

The Scripture of God is all good and godly. Yet like as the same to the good spirit is a sure port of tranquillity and peace, so is it to the wicked conscience a stumbling block and a stone of offense.[89] Out of one and the same flower the bee gathereth honey, and the spider sucketh venom:[90] so great diversity of operation

84. **indurate** hardened, obstinate.

85. **behoof . . . on behoof** obligation, duty. **passed on** attended to.

86. **cankered** venemous, spiteful, ill-tempered—frequently used in the sixteenth century.

87. **Pharaoh . . . plagues** God's sending of ten plagues upon Egypt because its pharaoh would not set the Israelites free as Moses had asked is narrated in chapters 7–10 of Exodus.

88. **Pharisees . . . law Pharisees . . . Scripture** Instances of this tactic of Jesus's are to be found in Matthew 12:38–42; 22:34-46; Mark 10:2–9; and Luke 17:20–32. **insurged** rose up. **testimony . . . law** Instances of this tactic of Jesus's are to be found in Matthew 12:1–8; 15:1–6; 19:3–8; Mark 2:23–28; 7:1–9; and Luke 6:2–5; 11:37–40; 14:1–6.

89. **a stumbling . . . offense** an allusion to Romans 14:13: "Let . . . no man put a stumbling block or an occasion to fall in his brother's way."

90. **Out . . . venom** The formulation appears proverbial. Cf. Stephen Gardiner, *A declaration of suche true articles as George Joye hath gone about to confute as false* (1546) (STC 11589), fol. lxxii: "Scripture is a sweet, pure flower, whereof spiders gather venom, and bees honey."

there is in good and evil natures. And the common fault that malignant persons do allege against the publishing of God's Word in the mother tongue, and against the setting forth of wholesome and godly expositions upon the same, is that such books cause sedition against the doctrine, and then lay their fact to the doctrine's charge.[91] This hath evermore hitherto been the practice and conveyance not only of the Romish Pharisaical sort, but also of the ancient enemies of God's truth even from the beginning. Neither have this malicious generation ever yet used any other way or color to deface the truth, to let the good proceeding of God's Word, or to stir and provoke the indignation of princes and magistrates against the publishing or against the true preachers and teachers thereof: but only by alleging that it will move sedition and teach error. Where, indeed, God's Word is, as ye would say, a perfect touchstone whereby to find out and to try such cankered stomachs as would fain rebel, and move sedition, and would gladly have it so to be. For otherwise a great wonder it were, and a very strange thing, if the Word of God, or this Paraphrase, or any other like godly exposition of the Gospel (which is, in sense, none other but the doctrine of Christ and of his apostles) should corrupt the readers, or teach error, or move sedition.

God and his most holy Word is altogether peace, unity, concord, and perfect charity. God's Word teacheth none other doctrine but peace, humility, subjection, and so much obedience to the princes and magistrates, as the Romish Babylonians[92] would not, by their goodwills, have to be put in the heads and hearts of the ignorant people. But this color have the enemies of God's Word evermore used to suppress the Gospel. So did they by all the martyrs; so have they done by the true

91. **malignant . . . charge** Udall oversimplifies the source and nature of concern about disruptive consequences when the English Bible was placed in the people's hands. This was a concern not only of Stephen Gardiner and other religiously conservative clergy but of Henry VIII himself. Having authorized the people's use of the Great Bible in 1538, Henry issued a royal proclamation for "uniformity of religion" in April 1539, deploring (in some vocabulary shared with Udall here) the "great murmur, malice, and malignity . . . risen and sprung amongst divers and sundry of his subjects by diversities of opinions. . . . Each of them dispute so earnestly against the other of their opinions . . . that there is begun and sprung among themselves slander and railing at each other as well by word as writing, one part of them calling the other papist, the other part calling the other heretic; whereby is like to follow sedition and tumult and destructions" (in Paul L. Hughes and James F. Larkin, ed., *Tudor Royal Proclamations*, 2 vols. [New Haven, CT: Yale University Press, 1964–69), 1:284–85. **malignant** ill-willed. **fact** doing of—i.e., committing—sedition.

92. **Romish Babylonians** Udall alludes to Martin Luther's *De captivitate Babylonica ecclesia praeludium* (*A Prelude concerning the Babylonian Captivity of the Church*) (1520), a treatise in Latin intended for clergy and scholars that reduced the traditional seven sacraments to the three for which Luther, in this early phase of his thinking, identified a Biblical warrant—baptism, penance, and the Lord's Supper. According to Luther, the papacy in exercising its claim to supreme religious authority had placed both the Scriptures and the conscience of individual Christians in "captivity," as Nebuchadnezzar, King of Babylon, had besieged and captured Jerusalem and led the Jews into captivity (2 Kings 24 and many other Old Testament references).

preachers; so did the old Jews by the ancient prophets of God; and so did the old Pharisees by Christ Himself: whose most grievous crimes were that He drew all the world after Him, that He taught and sowed erroneous doctrine, that He seduced the people, and that He made himself a king.[93] And the malicious Jews laid to Paul's charge that he began to be a seditious mover of rebellion against Caesar:[94] not that the thing was so indeed, but because the same was a cocksure[95] way to make all obedient people hate the Gospel, and to provoke the rulers and magistrates to suppress it.

But the Lord, who of His merciful goodness hath of late sent out the clear, radiant sunbeams of His holy Word[96] and verity to shine over all Christian regions, will, I trust, so continue the light of the same, that the simple flock shall be able to discern the spirits of men, and lively to know the ungodly maligners: which, by cavilling and depraving all good things, do wrestle and struggle, as much as in them lieth, to keep the ignorant multitude in blindness. In the meantime, all the simple English congregation is bound continually to pray for your highness, that have for their use and behoof procured the translation of this present Paraphrase upon the Gospel of Matthew and upon the residue of the New Testament, whereby they may, with a comfortable and pleasant reading in their own mother tongue, both increase from day to day in knowledge, and also continually be edified in true religion, nuzzled in right opinions, trained in sincere doctrine, and confirmed to walk in perfect innocency and integrity of a true Christian life accordingly.

NO. 15 NICHOLAS UDALL TO DOWAGER QUEEN KATHERINE, PREFACING THE PARAPHRASE ON THE GOSPEL OF JOHN, JANUARY 31, 1548[97]

To the most virtuous lady and most gracious Queen Katherine Dowager,
late wife to the most noble King Henry VIII of most famous memory, deceased,
Nicholas Udall, your highness' most humble servant,
wisheth health and all prosperity in Christ.

When I consider, most gracious Queen Katherine Dowager, the great number of noblewomen in this our time and country of England, not only given to the study

93. **drew . . . king drew . . . after Him** an allusion to John 12:32. **seduced . . . people** an allusion to Mark 11:18. **made . . . king** an allusion to Matthew 27:11, 37; Mark 15:2, 26; Luke 23:3, 38; and John 18:33–37.

94. **Paul's charge . . . Caesar** an allusion to Acts 25:7–12.

95. **cocksure** absolutely safe.

96. **sunbeams . . . Word** Udall earlier used the image of the Scriptures as sunlight (see part 3, no. 10, n55).

97. Source: *The first tome or volume of the Paraphrase of Erasmus upon the newe testament* (London: Edward Whitchurch, January 31, 1548) (STC 2854.2), sigs. C ir–C ii v (separately paginated).

of human sciences and of strange tongues, but also so thoroughly expert in Holy Scriptures that they are able to compare with the best writers, as well in enditing and penning of godly and fruitful treatises to the instruction and edifying of whole realms in the knowledge of God, as also in translating good books out of Latin or Greek into English[98] for the use and commodity of such as are rude and ignorant of the said tongues, I cannot but think and esteem the famous learned antiquity so far behind these times, that there cannot justly be made any comparison between them.

Cornelia, a noble matron of Rome, through long conversation and continuance with her learned husband, was in process of time so well learned and so eloquent that herself was the chief and principal instructress and bringer-up of her two sons, Caius Gracchus and Tiberius Gracchus, in all their learning, and made the same at length so fine, that they yet at this day remain registered in the number of the absolute and perfect orators of old time.[99] We read of one Aemelia in Rome, a woman so well spoken and so fine of tongue that, being on a time indicted and arraigned of a grievous offense, she so wittily, so pithily, and with such grace made answer for herself that all the whole bench and court then present judged her, for the mere respect of her eloquence and wit in that present peril and jeopardy there showed, worthy by their whole consents and sentences to be quit and discharged of the law for that crime.[100] Hortensia, the daughter of Quintus Hortensius, and brought up

98. **great number . . . English** By 1548 the "number of noblewomen" in England who were showing themselves capable of "enditing and penning . . . godly and fruitful treatises" and "translating good books out of Latin or Greek into English" certainly included KP herself in both categories, and in the single category of translators, the princesses Mary and Elizabeth; Jane Fitzalan, future Lady Lumley; and Margaret More Roper. Like these female translators, Lady Jane Grey and Anne Parr Herbert had been prepared by education for such literary activity. Nevertheless, Udall's hyperbolic "great number" is less a description of the present than a prognosis for the future.

99. **Cornelia . . . time** The main classical source for the domestic conduct of Cornelia (born ca. 190 BCE) is Plutarch's *Life of Tiberius Gracchus* 1.1.4–5. She is noted as having taken charge of her two sons, Tiberius and Caius, showing such discretion and scrupulous care in rearing them that although they had surpassing natural gifts, they were thought to owe their excellence more to their education than to their nature. See *Plutarch's Lives*, trans. Bernadotte Perrin, Loeb Classical Library (London: William Heinemann and Harvard University Press, 1921; rpt. 1949), 10:146–47 Valerius Maximus, *Facta et dicta memorabilia*, preface to book 4, is the source for Cornelia's widely quoted and widely admired response to a visiting noblewoman who prided herself greatly on her jewels. As Cornelia's children came in the door from school, she said to her visitor: "These are my jewels" (Valerius Maximus, *Memorable Doings and Sayings*, ed. and trans. D. R. Shackleton Bailey, Loeb Classical Library [Cambridge, MA: Harvard University Press, 2000], 1:384–85).

100. **Aemelia . . . crime** Dionysius of Halicarnassus narrates the story of Aemilia, chief vestal virgin of Rome ca. 178 BCE, who entrusted to a newly chosen vestal the tending of the sacred flame on the goddess Vesta's altar, which was always to be kept burning. Under the new vestal's tending, the flame on the altar went out. This terrible occurrence provoked a great stir in the city and an inquiry by the chief priests whether some defilement of the chief vestal had caused

continually from her cradle and tender infancy in the house and company of such a noble orator, came at length so near to the perfect eloquence of her father that she was able in public hearing to make orations, and the same of so pithy a sort: that where the noblewomen of Rome were on a time sore taxed to depart with their gold and jewels toward certain necessary charges of that commonweal, Hortensia came before the commissioners to speak in the behalf of the matrons, and with her exquisite talk, obtained a mitigation almost of the whole tax which the [a]ssessors had afore agreed upon, and appointed unto the women to contribute.[101]

These examples of eloquence in women, like as they are but very few in number, so are they things of no such high excellency to be marveled at. For what great matter of wonder is it that, among so many thousands, three or four should be found able to speak before a judge in open audience? Or what strange case is it to be reputed, if some one or two women have been found witty or learned in the Latin tongue, being their own native language which every carter and handicraftsman then spake, though not all thing so finely as the learned men and orators did? What high matter of praise and commendation is it if a few women, being either wives or daughters to excellent fine Latin men, could in continuance of a great many years speak Latin well? Yet are these women specially chronicled in histories as notable, yea, and singular examples worthy perpetual fame and memory for their wit, learning, and eloquence.

After these heathens, Jerome in his epistles[102] writeth special high praises and commendations of Eustochium, the mother; Paula, the daughter; and Blesilla, the daughter's daughter: of which, every one were passing well seen not only in Holy Scriptures, but also in Latin, Greek, and Hebrew, which tongues they learned exactly in a very short time and excelled in the same. The like testimony he giveth of Marcella, a very noble woman in Rome, whom he reporteth to have in his time

---

the flame to go out. The innocent, distraught Aemilia poured out her heart before the people in a prayer to Vesta, rehearsing her purity and faithfulness during thirty years of service, beseeching the goddess to show herself and defend her chief vestal from a miserable death. When Aemilia ended her prayer, she tore off the band of her linen garment and cast it on the long-cold ashes of the sacred fire. Instantly a great flame flared up on the altar, igniting the linen band and satisfying the high priests and city. They ceased to demand that Aemilia expiate her presumed guilt or that a new sacred flame be kindled. See 2.68. 3–5 of Dionysius of Halicarnassus, *The Roman Antiquities*, trans. Earnest Cary, Loeb Classical Library (London: Harvard University Press, 1937; rpt. 1990), 1:510–13. Udall read this work in a Latin translation, either the Paris edition of 1527 or the Basel edition of 1532. There was no edition of the original Greek text before the later sixteenth century (ibid., xli). It is noteworthy that Udall is so vague about the proceedings against Aemilia, presumably because the context is pagan religion.

101. **Hortensia . . . contribute** Udall closely paraphrases Valerius Maximus *Facta et dicta memorabilia* 8.3.3; see *Valerius Maximus: Memorable Doings and Sayings*, ed. D. R. Shackleton Bailey, Loeb Classical Library (Cambridge, MA: Harvard University Press, 2000), 2:212–13.

102. **Jerome . . . epistles** For Udall's earlier allusion to the learned ladies whose spiritual discipline and studies were personally supervised by St. Jerome, see part 3, no. 10, n54.

so well profited in the knowledge of Holy Scriptures that, after his departure from Rome, if there were any doubtful question or any point of difficulty concerning Scripture, all folks would resort to her as a judge able and also sufficient to decide any matter of controversy or ambiguity that happened among them. But this knowledge extended no further than to the private edifying of their own selves with a very few others, and the same in such places where Latin was their mother tongue and their native language.

But now in this gracious and blissful time of knowledge, in which it hath pleased almighty God to reveal and show abroad the light of His most holy Gospel, what a number is there of noblewomen, especially here in this realm of England, yea, and how many in the years of tender virginity, not only as well seen and as familarly traded[103] in the Latin and Greek tongues as in their own mother language, but also both in all kinds of profane literature and liberal arts exactly studied and exercised, and in the Holy Scriptures and theology so ripe, that they are able aptly, cunningly, and with much grace either to endite or translate into the vulgar tongue for the public instruction and edifying of the unlearned multitude. Neither is it now any strange thing to hear gentlewomen, instead of most vain communication about the moon shining in the water, to use grave and substantial talk in Greek or Latin with their husbands, of godly matters.

It is now no news in England to see young damsels in noble houses and in the courts of princes, instead of cards and other instruments of idle trifling, to have continually in their hands either Psalms, homilies, and other devout meditations, or else Paul's epistles, or some book of Holy Scripture matters, and as familiarly both to read or reason thereof in Greek, Latin, French, or Italian, as in English. It is now a common thing to see young virgins so nuzzled and trained in the study of letters, that they willingly set all other vain pastimes at nought for learning's sake. It is now no news at all to see queens and ladies of most high estate and progeny, instead of courtly dalliance, to embrace virtuous exercises of reading and writing and, with most earnest study both early and late, to apply themselves to the acquiring of knowledge as well in all other liberal arts and disciplines, as also most specially of God and His most holy Word, whereunto all Christian folks, of what estate or degree soever they be, ought to the uttermost of their possible powers most principally and most earnestly themselves to give and dedicate.

But what a great cause of public rejoicing, O Lord, may it be, that in this time of Christ's harvest—every good body most busily applying the work of his vocation towards the inning of the Lord's corn,[104] some by instructing the youth, some by teaching schools, some by preaching to their simple flocks, some by godly inducing

103. **traded** trained.

104. **Christ's . . . corn** an allusion to Jesus's representation of the spreading of the Gospel as a great harvesttime in Matthew 9:37–38 and Luke 10:1–2. **inning . . . corn** getting wheat sheaves into the barn.

of their families, some by writing good and godly treatises for the edifying of such as are willing to read, and some by translating good books out of strange tongues into our vulgar language for the help of the unlearned—the most noble women of blood and estate royal are no less diligent travailers than the best in any of the above-named offices meet for their sex, nor take any manner scorn or disdain in the labor of drawing this harvest home, to be joined as yokefellows with inferior persons of most low degree and condition. How happy art thou, O England, for whose behoof and edifying in Christ, queens and princesses spare not nor cease with all earnest endeavor and sedulity to spend their time, their wits, their substance, and also their bodies!

And in this behalf, like to your highness, most noble Queen Katherine Dowager, as well for composing and setting forth many godly Psalms and divers other contemplative meditations,[105] as also for causing these Paraphrases of the most famous clerk and most godly writer Erasmus of Rotterdam to be translated into our vulgar languge, England can never be able to render thanks sufficient: so may it never be able, as her deserts require, enough to praise and magnify the most noble, the most virtuous, the most witty, and the most studious Lady Mary's grace, daughter of the late most puissant and most victorious King Henry VIII, of most famous memory, and most dearly beloved sister to the King, our sovereign lord, that now is, may never be able (I say) enough to praise and magnify her grace for taking such great study, pain, and travail in translatig this Paraphrase of the said Erasmus upon the Gospel of John, at your highness's special contemplation, as a number of right well learned men would both have made courtesy at,[106] and also would have brought to worse frame in the doing. O how greatly may we all glory in such a peerless flower of virginity as her grace is: who in the midst of courtly delights and amidst the enticements of worldly vanities hath, by her own choice and election, so virtuously and so fruitfully passed her tender youth, yea, to the public comfort and gladful rejoicing which at her birth she brought to all England. She doth now also confer unto the same the unestimable benefit of furthering both us and our posterity in the knowledge of God's Word, and to the more clear understanding of Christ's Gospel. O royal exercise, indeed, of virginly education! O unestimable and precious fruit of maidenly studies! O noble success of princely spending the time, especially in a woman! O zeal of provoking God's glory, worthy immortality of fame and renown!

105. **Psalms . . . meditations** Udall again seems to allude to KP's *Psalms or Prayers* (1544) and *Prayers or Meditations* (1545), but not to her *Lamentation of a Sinner* (1547). See part 3, no. 10, n66, and my general introduction, p. 29.

106. **contemplation . . . at contemplation** attentive consideration (applied subjectively to describe KP's behavior toward Princess Mary). **made . . . at** expressed deprecation or apology regarding (something), in a courteous manner. Udall is prominent among early users of "courtesy" or "curtsey" in the *OED*. Here he is saying that a number of learned men would have politely declined a request that they translate one of Erasmus's Paraphrases (presumably as a task too modest for their talents).

For what could be a more manifest argument of minding the public benefit of her country; what could be a more evident proof of her will and desire to do good to all her father's most dear-beloved subjects; what could be a more plain declaration of her most constant purpose to promote God's Word and the free grace of His Gospel, than so effectually to prosecute the work of translating which she had begun? That when she had, with over-painful study and labor of writing, cast her weak body in a grievous and long sickness, yet to the intent the diligent English people should not be defrauded of the benefit intended and meant unto them, she committed the same work to Master Francis Mallet, doctor in the faculty of divinity,[107] with all celerity and expedition[108] to be finished and made complete. That, in case the King's majesty's most royal commandment by his most godly injunctions[109] expressed, declared and published—that the said Paraphrases should within certain months be set forth to the curates and people of this realm of England—had not so prevented her grace, but that she might eftsoons[110] have put her file to the polishing thereof, where it is now already very absolute and perfect, it would then, among the rude and homely doings of me and such as I am, none otherwise have glittered than cloth of gold enpowdered among patches of canvas, or pearls and diamonds among pebblestones.

But, in the meantime, to what learned man may not the sedulity[111] of such a noble princess be a spur and provocation to employ the talent of his learning and knowledge to the public use and commodity of his country? To whom may not this most notable example of so virtuous a lady be an occasion to shake off all sluggishness, and to yield unto the commonweal of England some condign fruit of his study and learning? To what idle loiterer may not this most excellent act of a King's daughter, and the same a King's sister, be a shame and reproach of negligence? To what persons, be they never so ignorant or unlearned, may not this most earnest zeal of a Princess of such high estate be an effectual provocation and encouraging to have good mind and will to read, hear, and embrace this devout and catholic[112] Paraphrase so plainly and sensibly translated, and so graciously by her offered, and (as ye would say) put in all folks' hands to be made familiar unto them? Beseech-

107. **Master . . . divinity** On Francis Mallet, see the general introduction above, pp. 13, 19, and Queen Katherine's letter to Princess Mary, no. 9 in part 3.

108. **celerity . . . expedition** Udall's doublet for "haste."

109. **King's . . . injunctions** Udall's expressions of hope in September 1545 (part 3, no. 10) that Henry VIII would command the publication of the English translations of Erasmus's Paraphrases went unrealized. Edward VI's injunctions of July 31, 1547, authorized their printing and publication, at last opening the way to the completion of KP's project.

110. **eftsoons** again, a second time.

111. **sedulity** diligence.

112. **catholic** Udall's word choice is superbly equivocal, for "catholic" can mean "Roman Catholic" (in reference to Erasmus and Princess Mary) as well as "universal" (its root sense in Greek), here referring to the royally mandated use of the Paraphrases in the Church of England.

ing, therefore, almighty God that it may in the hearts of all good English people take no less place, nor work any other effect of godly knowledge and innocent living, than your highness in procuring these translations and the said Lady Mary's grace, on her part, also have meant it, I shall semblably be a continual petitioner to His divine Majesty, long years to preserve both your estates: you, to the procuring of many such good translations for the edifying of simple people in Christ's discipline;[113] and her, to the doing of many like acts for the public utility of us all, whereby ye may, both of you, attain in this world condign fame and renown with perpetual memory among men, and after this life a crown of immortal glory and bliss in heaven, eternally there to reign with Christ and His holy angels. Amen.

NO. 16 NICHOLAS UDALL'S LETTER TO DOWAGER QUEEN KATHERINE, PREFACING THE PARAPHRASE ON ACTS, JANUARY 31, 1548[114]

To the most virtuous lady, Queen Katherine Dowager,
late wife to King Henry VIII of most famous memory, deceased,
Nicholas Udall, your grace's most humble orator and servant,
wisheth perpetual felicity and joy in Jesus Christ our Lord.

Forasmuch as nothing doth, with like speed or with better effect, either open to the world or engrave in men's hearts the knowledge of God's commandments and the rules of true Christian doctrine than devout and godly treatises for the expounding and declaring of Holy Scripture: how happy and blessed are we, and how greatly bound to thank God, that in these our times there daily come forth so many, and the same so fruitful and godly, works in our own tongue, to the ghostly comfort and edifying of all devout Christian readers in the true faith and religion. For where, in times past, the studious writers of books were enforced, with much high suit and service, to procure the favor and goodwill of princes or other estates,[115] to whom to dedicate such works as they wrote, to the intent that, under the name and protection of such noble personages, the said works might be the better abled[116] to the readers and the better accepted of people: now do kings, queens, princes, and other

113. **discipline** another equivocal keyword, which in Udall's time had a range of meanings from the general (instruction, education, formation) to the specific (military training, monastic rules of life in the Roman Catholic Church, or the theocratic regulation of civic life that was taking shape in Calvin's Geneva).

114. Source: Preface to Acts in *The first tome or volume of the Paraphrase of Erasmus upon the newe testament* (London: Edward Whitchurch, January 31, 1548), sigs. Cir–Ciiv (separately paginated).

115. **other estates** an ellipsis for "persons of other estates." **estates** degrees of rank, social status.

116. **abled** suited, adapted.

peers, especially here in England, of their own mere motions and good zeal, not only with their propense[117] favor and with their beneficial aid, comfort, and liberality, help forward the good endeavor and sedulity of studious writers minding by their godly monuments to edify the faithful congregation; but also are diligent and painful, both to put their own hands to the enditing and penning of many wholesome treatises for that purpose, yea, and further, by their example and provocation to set other in hand with writing or translating, to the fruitful exercise of the learned, to the wholesome instruction of English readers, and to the effectual edifying of the simple, ignorant multitude, if the same can be content, for their soul' health, to give ear and mind thereto.

And among this sort of public benefactors, your excellent highness, Queen Katherine Dowager, deserveth no less than next, after our sovereign lord the King's majesty, who even now already at the first entrance of this his most noble reign, and within the years of tender minority doth, with the advice and consent of the most prudent and the same his most dear uncle, Edward, Duke of Somerset, as well of his most royal person, in the time of his minority, Governor, as also of all his majesty's realms, dominions, and subjects, Protector, together with the assent and consent of the other his most honorable, most trusty, and most faithful councillors, most forwardly, most earnestly, and with all possible diligence labor day and night, as well by most wholesome laws as also by homilies of most pure doctrine, and by true preachers, to reform abuses, to sow abroad the Word of God, and to plant true religion in all parts of his realms and dominions—your highness, I say, next unto these two, deserveth no less than to be esteemed and called the chief patroness: not only for divers most godly Psalms and meditations of your own penning and setting forth,[118] but also for procuring this present work of Erasmus's Paraphrases to be thus translated to the use of the unlearned multitude, which can go no further than the understanding or reading of English.

For in this Paraphrase of Erasmus is contained, in manner, a whole library of devout and catholic expositors upon the whole New Testament, in which New Testament is contained the plenteous riches and most precious treasures of Christ's Gospel—that is, of the glad news of God's favor and mercy towards mankind. Which favor and mercy of God, whosoever doth faithfully and sincerely embrace, cannot but favor and further the setting forth of Scripture in the vulgar language, that all folks may know it, and also of any other godly treatises whereby that same general benefit of God towards mankind may the more clearly and certainly be perceived. And to this effect, forasmuch as Desiderius Erasmus of Rotterdam doth especially direct as well these his *Paraphrases upon the New Testament* as all other his right Christian writings, and that with as much indifferency as is possible to

117. **propense** well-inclined.

118. **most . . . forth** another of Udall's commendatory allusions to KP's *Psalms or Prayers* and *Prayers or Meditations*.

be: I cannot but judge that whoso are prompt and hasty condemners of Erasmus[119] or eager adversaries unto his doctrine do, under the name and color of Erasmus, rather utter their stomach and hatred against God's Word and the grace of the Gospel, which Erasmus, for his part, most diligently and most simply laboreth to bring to light.

His doctrine (will some unequal[120] judges say) is scarcely sincere. If there shall no more insincerity of doctrine appear in the writings of them that will so say than the common consent of the Christian world doth find and judge in Erasmus, I doubt not but their works shall be of all good people approved, desired, embraced, and followed. Erasmus (will some such heady persons say) doth somewhere err. It may so be, forasmuch as a man he is and so esteemeth himself, and would his works none otherwise to be read or accepted than the writings of other mortal men. But in case he should in some place say, now and then, a word too much or too little, or put a worse word for a more apt term; or if he should in some place stumble or swerve—which point of human frailty the best doctors that wrote since the apostles' time hath not escaped, nor Erasmus so standeth in his own wilful opinion, but that being found and tried [for] a fault, he would have been as ready to retract it as ever any other godly and catholic writer hath been—yet were one little trip (after my poor judgment) among so many notable good works for the interpretation of Scripture, and for the help of the simple, rather to be borne withal than so many good things to be either rejected or kept away from the hungry Christian readers. It is a cold charity that can bear with nothing; and an eager malice it is that, for a trifle or a matter of nothing, would have the ignorant multitude to lack so much good edifying as may be taken of Erasmus, as well in all his other right devout and catholic works, as also most especially in these his Paraphrases, in which he laboreth so to enlarge the process and tenor of the text, as the sense thereof may both evidently be gathered and may well hang together.

Erasmus, therefore, like as he hath by a paraphrastical discourse plainly set forth the Gospels of the four Evangelists afore, so doth he now here expound the second part of Luke's Gospel, entitled the Acts of the Apostles, which work Athanasius (at least wise if it were Athanasius indeed that wrote the little treatise entitled "Of the Books of Both the Old and the New Testament," etc.) testifieth, that Luke wrote out of Peter's mouth, and that Peter endited unto Luke what and how he should write therein, as Paul endited to the same Luke when he wrote his Gospel.[121]

119. **whoso . . . Erasmus** See n81 above.

120. **unequal** not impartial.

121. **Athanasius . . . Gospel** Udall (or his compositor) garbles the citation of two successive short passages on the authorship of the Gospels of Mark and Luke from pseudo-Athenasius, *A Synopsis of Sacred Scripture*: "The Gospel according to Mark was dictated by the apostle Peter to Mark in Rome, and published by the blessed apostle Mark"; "The Gospel according to Luke was dictated by the apostle Paul, and it was written and published by the blessed apostle Luke."

Whereof, as Erasmus in the preface to his Paraphrase upon Luke's Gospel recordeth, it is gathered and thought that the said Acts were written in Rome.

But wheresoever they were written, certes[122] the work was no less expedient and necessary to be written, nor the Paraphrase upon the same anything less requisite to be translated into English, than the rest of the New Testament. First, for that it is a plain historical narration and a piece of the very Gospel in that it declareth as well the ascension of Christ from earth up into heaven, as also His sending down of the Holy Ghost from His heavenly Father, together with the springing up of the primitive Church and the form and order of preaching that the apostles then first began with. Secondly, because it was, as Erasmus himself testifieth, the last part that he did of all the whole Paraphrases upon the Testament, and by reason thereof (as I judge) the most absolute[123] piece of work and best done of all the rest, by reason of his long exercise afore in this kind of writing. And thirdly, because this piece of the New Testament is no less profitable for the publishing and furtherance of the Gospel than Luke did devise and intend it, nor to the poor younglings[124] in Christ's discipline anything less available.

For here may we learn the beginnings of Christ's Church, by whom and by what manner persons the faith of Christ first sprung up, how it proceeded and grew, how it was persecuted, and how by persecution it waxed stronger and stronger. For as the palm tree, the more weight and burden is laid upon it, the more it ariseth and shooteth upright:[125] so the Gospel, the more persecution that was inflected unto[126]

For the original Greek of the title of this work and the sentences Udall quotes, see *Patrologia Graeca, Cursus Completus*, ed. J.-P. Migne (Paris, 1857), 28:285, 433A. **Luke wrote** "Mark wrote" is the correct reading. **unto Luke** "unto Mark" is the correct reading. **the same Luke** "Luke" is the correct reading.

122. **certes** of a truth, certainly.

123. **absolute** perfect, finished.

124. **younglings** inexperienced or ignorant persons. KP uses the term three times in her section "Weaklings mislike all things" in *The Lamentation of a Sinner* (1547); see pp. 472–73 of the text in this edition.

125. **the palm . . . upright** Udall's phrasing closely follows that of Aulus Gellius *Noctes Atticae* 3.6: "Si super palmae . . . magna pondera inponas ac tam graviter urgeas oneresque, ut magnitudo oneris sustineri non queat, non deorsum palma cedit . . . sed adversus pondus resurgit et sursum nititur" (If you place heavy weights . . . on a palm tree, and press it down so hard that the burden is too great to bear, the palm does not give way downward, . . . but it rises against the weight and struggles upward); see Aulus Gellius, *Attic Nights*, trans. John C. Rolfe, Loeb Classical Library (Cambridge, MA: Harvard University Press; London: William Heinemann Ltd., 1927; rpt. 1984), 3:254–55. If Udall did not directly consult an early sixteenth-century edition of Aulus Gellius, he could have worked from Thomas Becon's equally close translation of this passage in *A potacion or drinkynge for this hole time of lent, very comfortable for all penitent synners* (1542) (STC 1749), sig. Eviii r–v, which cites Aulus Gellius as its source.

126. **inflected unto** bent inward upon.

it, the more it grew, the more it prospered, the better it went forward, and the more it flourished. In the Acts is to be read by what means and drifts of human policy the enemies of Christ's blood and Gospel wrestled to suppress the glory of His cross, and how the more that the wisdom of the world thought to evacuate[127] the fruit of Christ's death and passion, the more did the humility of preaching the cross work in the hearts of the simple to contemn not only the pleasures and flattery of the world, but also the persecution and tyranny thereof, so that daily increased, in every place where the Gospel was preached, thousands upon thousands to augment the faithful congregation.

The Acts, therefore, were no less necessary to be translated than the rest of the Paraphrases, which Acts, I have by occasion of adding, digesting, and sorting the text with the Paraphrase thoroughly perused, and conferring the same with the Latin, I have here and there done my goodwill and diligence to make the English answerable to the Latin book, at least wise[128] in sense, as by the same occasion I did also with Matthew.[129] In John I have in manner done nothing at all, saving only placed the text and divided the paraphrase, because I knew the translators[130] thereof, with whose exquisite doings I might not, without the crime of great arrogancy and presumption, be busy to intermeddle.[131] Most humbly, therefore, beseeching your highness, most gracious lady, in good part to take my good zeal and diligence, and in case anything shall not sufficiently answer your mind or desire, the same to impute rather to the lack of faculty and knowledge than to any default of goodwill in me: I shall here, without any further circumstance of words, commend and leave this whole work to the diligent reading and following of all the devout English congregation. And with most hearty prayer beseech almighty God long years to preserve and continue the prosperous estate of your highness, to the end that, by your good help and means, the devout people that are willing and forward to learn and to live Christianly may receive many like godly works and fruitful treatises, to their continual ghostly profit, comfort, and edifying in the same our Lord Jesus Christ, to whom with the Father and with the Holy Ghost be all laud, honor, and glory, both in heaven and earth, forever and ever. Amen.

127. **evacuate** make void, deprive of validity. In English this is the original sense (and that of its Latin cognate "evacuo"), used in religious and legal contexts, but no longer current.

128. **at . . . wise** at least.

129. **the same . . . Matthew** Udall is evidently claiming that what he, as the project's general editor, did with the English translation of the Matthew paraphrase was to vet it for its closeness to Erasmus's Latin and touch up its English at certain points. By implication this translator worked independently of Udall. The remark is unfortunately of little help in identifying the translator of the Matthew paraphrase, who, I have suggested, is likeliest to have been Richard Taverner. See part 3, no. 10, n81.

130. **I knew . . . translators** Princess Mary and Francis Mallet. Udall incurred several court connections by way of KP's patronage.

131. **intermeddle** meddle with.

NO. 17 LORD ADMIRAL THOMAS SEYMOUR TO DOWAGER QUEEN KATHERINE, JUNE 9, 1548[132]

[Endorsed] 9th June. Letter [of] the Lord Admiral to the Queen's highness at Hanworth.

After my humble commendations and thanks for your letter: as I was perplexed heretofore with unkindness that I should not have justice of those that I thought would in all my causes be partial[133] (which did not a little trouble me), even so the receiving of your letter revived my spirits. Partly, for that I did perceive that ye be armed with patience, howsoever the matter will weigh; as chiefest, that I hear my little man doth shake his poll,[134] trusting if God shall give him life to live as long as

132. Source: TNA, State Papers 10/4, fols. 35r–36r. In TS's hand, loosely formed, with many signs of hasty composition. The original reads:

> after my vmbell commendashens and thanckes for your letter, as I was perplelext [sic] hereto ffore with vnkynes that I shuld nott haue Justesse of thosse, that I thowght woold in all my cawses by parshall whyche ded not a lettell trobell me, euen soo the reseyuyng of your letter reveyved my spryttes partley for that I ded perseue that ye be Armed with pashence how so euer the mater wyll way, as cheffhest that I here my lettell man doth shake his polle trostyng yf god shall geue hym lyff to leue as long as his ffather he wyll revenge suche wroonges as nether yow nor I can at this prysent. the wordell ys suche god a mend it / now to pout yow in som hopes a gean, this day a letell befforre the ryseuynge of your Letter I haue spoken with my lord, whom I ~~p I~~ haue so well handled that he ys somatt qvalyffyed, and althohe I amm in no hope therof yett I amm in no despayr I haue also brokenn with hym for your motheres geffte who makes ansour that at the ffenychyng of ~~my~~ your matter ether to have yours a gean or elce som recompense as ~~I~~ ye shalbe content with all I spake to hym of your goyng down in to the contry on weneday who was sorry therof ~~st~~ trostyng that I wold be here all to morrow to here what the ffrenchemen wyll do and onn monday euen I trost to be with yow as ffriday the ffrenchemen I haue no mistrost that they shalbe any Let of my goyng with yow this Jorney or any of my contynuance there with your ~~hyghtnes~~ highnes and thus tyll that tyme I bid your your highnes most hartley well to ffarr, and thank you for your newes whyche ware ryght hartley welcomm to me / and so I pray yow to show hym with godes blesyng and myn and ~~of~~ all good wylles and ffrenshep I do desyer your highnes to kepe the letell knaue so leanne and gantte with your good dyett and walkynge that he may be so small that he may krepe owt of a mowse holle / and thus I bed my most dere and welbeloved wyff most hartley well to fare fromm westminster this Saterday the ixth of June /
>
> Your ^ highnes most Asuerd and ffaythfull louyng hosbond
>
> T. Seymour

133. **perplexed . . . partial** TS refers to some altercation with his brother, the lord protector, in their ongoing rivalry for power and influence.

134. **little . . . poll** The negative energy that TS attributes to his unborn child's movements contrasts sharply with KP's representation, in the immediately following letter, of its stirring joyfully when she gave it its absent father's blessing. **poll** head.

his father, he will revenge such wrongs as neither you nor I can at this present. The world is such; God amend it.

Now to put you in some hopes again, this day a little before the receiving of your letter, I have spoken with my lord: whom I have so well handled that he is somewhat qualified,[135] and although I am in no hope thereof, yet I am in no despair. I have also broken with him for your mother's gift.[136] Who makes answer that, at the finishing of your matter, either to have yours again or else some recompense as ye shall be content withal. I spake to him of your going down into the country[137] on Wednesday, who was sorry thereof, trusting that I would be here all tomorrow to hear what the Frenchmen will do. And, on Monday even, I trust to be with you, as Friday the Frenchmen.[138] I have no mistrust that they shall be any let of my going with you this journey, or any of my continuance there with your highness.

And thus, till that time, I bid your highness most heartily well to fare, and thank you for your news, which were right heartily welcome to me. And so I pray you to show[er] him with God's blessing, and mine, and all goodwills and friendship. I do desire your highness to keep the little knave so lean and gaunt with your good diet and walking, that he may be so small that he may creep out of a mouse-hole.[139] And thus I bid my most dear and well-beloved wife most heartily well to fare. From Westminster this Saturday, the ninth of June.

Your highness's most assured and faithful, loving husband,
T. Seymour

135. **my lord** a possibly sarcastic reference to his brother, the lord protector. **qualified** calmed, pacified.

136. **your mother's gift** the jewels that Maud Parr had willed to KP. KP sent her jewels to the Tower for safekeeping when she assumed mourning attire upon Henry's death. Edward Seymour refused to restore KP's jewels—not just those from Henry but also those from her mother—after she had taken up with TS (James, *Kateryn Parr*, 291, 305–6).

137. **your . . . country** the plans for KP to journey to TS's estate, Sudeley Castle in Gloucestershire, for her lying-in.

138. **I would . . . the Frenchmen** An altercation at sea between English and French ships had prompted the French to send an embassy to the English court (James, *Kateryn Parr*, 328). Edward Seymour quite understandably expected TS, as lord admiral, to take part in the meeting on the incident.

139. **lean . . . mousehole** TS's husbandly and paternal anxiety about the thirty-six-year-old KP's safe delivery of her first child takes shape in a whimsical imagining that she can assure the newborn an easy passage into the world by controlling her weight (and hence the baby's weight) and taking her usual exercise.

NO. 18 DOWAGER QUEEN KATHERINE TO LORD ADMIRAL THOMAS SEYMOUR, SHORTLY AFTER JUNE 9, 1548[140]

[Endorsed] The Queen to the Lord Admiral
[Addressed] To my Lord

My lord,

This shall be to desire you to receive my humble and most hearty recommendations and thanks for your letter, which was no sooner come than welcome. I perceive ye have had no little trouble and business with your matter. I never thought

140. Source: Hatfield House, Hertfordshire, Cecil Papers 133/3, fols. 6r–7v. In KP's hand. The assignment of date hinges on TS's foregoing letter to KP dated June 9, 1548, which this letter answers. The original reads:

> *[Addressed]* To my Lord
>
> my lord thys schalbe to desyre yow to receyue my humble and moost harty recommendatyons and thankes for yowr letter Whyche Was no soner come than Welcome I perceyue ye haue had no lytell trobell and busynes with yowr mater I never thowght the contrary but ye schuld haue muche ado to brynge yt to passe as ye Wold haue yt neverthelesse I supposed my lorde protectour Wold haue vsed no delayes with his frend and naturall brother in amater wyche ys vpryght and Just as I take yt What wyll he do to other that be indyfferent to hym I juge not very Well I pray god he may dysceyue me for hys owne welthe and benyfyte more than for myne none now I haue vttered my coler I schall desyre yow good my lord with ~~my very~~ ^ all hart to not to vnquyett yowr self with any of hys vnfrindely partes but bere them for the tyme as well as ye can wyche I knowe ys muche better than ether myne aduyse or doyng can expresse I am very sory for the newes of the frenssche men; I pray god yt be not alette to our Iourney as sone as ye knowe What they wyll do good my lord I beseche yow lett me here from yow for I schall not be very qvyett tyll I knowe I gaue yowr lyttel knaue yowr blessyng Who lyke anonest man styred apase after and before for mary odell beyng abed with me had layd her hand vpon my bely to fele yt styre yt hathe styred thyse thre dayes every mornyng and evenyng so that I trust whan ye come it ^ wyll make yow sum passe tyme. And thus I end byddy^{n}g my swett hart and lovyng husband better to fare then my self. from hanworth thys saterday in the mornyng
>
> *[Addition]* my lord I thanke yow with all my hart for master hotton desyryng yow to contynewe hys good or els I fere me he schall ~~be~~ never lyve in quyet with my lord dacres to whom I pray yow make my recommendatyons asseuryng hym that I wylbe hys frend in case he use master hotton well or els hys ennemy
>
> by yowr moost lovyng
> obedyent and humble Wyf
> Kateryn the Quene KP

[Inscription on the verso of the letter, the side bearing the address, in Princess Elizabeth's hand]

Noli ~~met~~an
Nolito me tangere

the contrary, but ye should have much ado to bring it to pass as ye would have it. Nevertheless, I supposed my lord protector would have used no delay with his friend and natural brother in a matter which is upright and just, as I take it. What will he do to other that be indifferent to him, I judge not very well. I pray God he may deceive me for his own wealth and benefit more than for mine own.[141] Now I have uttered my choler. I shall desire you, good my lord, with all [my] heart not to unquiet yourself with any of his unfriendly parts, but bear them for the time as well as ye can: which I know is much better than either mine advice or doing can express.

I am very sorry for the news of the Frenchmen; I pray God it be not a let to our journey. As soon as ye know what they will do, good my lord, I beseech you let me hear from you, for I shall not be very quiet till I know. I gave your little knave your blessing, who like an honest man stirred apace after and before, for Mary Odell,[142] being abed with me, had laid her hand upon my belly to feel it stir. It hath stirred these three days every morning and evening, so that I trust when ye come it will make you some pastime. And thus I end, bidding my sweetheart and loving husband better to fare than myself. From Hanworth this Saturday in the morning.

[Addition]
My lord, I thank you with all my heart for Master Hutton,[143] desiring you to continue his good or else, I fear me, he shall never live in quiet with my lord Dacre.[144] To whom I pray you make my recommendations, assuring him that I will be his friend, in case he use Master Hutton well, or else his enemy.

By your most loving, obedient, and humble wife,
Katherine the Queen KP

141. **I . . . own** KP casts a piece of scathing sarcasm as a pious wish: May God grant that Edward Seymour at least represents his shady maneuverings as being for his self-interest and not for her benefit. **deceive** ensnare, prove false to, disappoint.

142. **Mary Odell** one of a Northumberland family of poor cousins on KP's mother's side, who served her and later became one of KP's most beloved servants and companions of the chamber (James, *Kateryn Parr*, 149).

143. **Master Hutton** Cuthbert Hutton, husband of one of KP's gentlewomen, Elizabeth Bellingham (ibid., 411n).

144. **Lord Dacre** Thomas, Lord Dacre of Gilsland, whose wife was KP's aunt. His unavailing attempt to aid Maud Parr in negotiating a first marriage for the twelve-year-old KP with his grandson, the future Lord Scrope of Bolton, had been the most notable of his varied relations with the Parrs across the years (ibid., 53–55).

[Latin inscription in Princess Elizabeth's italic hand on the reverse side of this letter, which also carried KP's address to TS][145]

~~Thou, tou[ch] me not.~~ Let him not touch me.[146]

NO. 19 PRINCESS ELIZABETH TO DOWAGER QUEEN KATHERINE, CIRCA JUNE 1548[147]

[Addressed] To the Queen's highness

Although I could not be plentiful in giving thanks for the manifold kindness receive[d] at your highness' hand at my departure, yet I am something to be borne withal, for truly I was replete with sorrow to depart from your highness, especially leaving you undoubtful[148] of health. And albeit I answered little, I weighed it more deeper when you said you would warn me of all evils that you should hear of me:

145. **Latin . . . TS** The blank side of this folded sheet is unfortunately no longer intact. Elizabeth's inscription and KP's address were cut out and mounted on another sheet of paper. The last page of KP's letter has also undergone mounting to stabilize its torn edge.

146. **~~Thou~~ . . . me** Elizabeth's double inscription in Latin begins with a quotation of John 20:17 in the Vulgate rendering of the resurrected Christ's familiar address to Mary Magdalene when she recognizes that it is He she has encountered in the garden, and not the gardener as she first supposed: "Noli me tangere" (Touch thou me not). Elizabeth strikes through this citation, recasting its familiar second-person form as a more distanced third-person form, "Nolito me tangere." This inscription raises questions on several fronts: how and when Elizabeth gained access to this addressed, thus presumably sealed letter from KP to TS, and what she meant by the inscription that she wrote. I conjecture that KP entrusted this sealed letter to Elizabeth to give to a messenger for delivery to TS, and that Elizabeth had the letter in her keeping long enough to write her admonition on its outside. This entails the not unreasonable assumption that Elizabeth was still residing in KP and TS's household in mid-June 1548, but that her departure, motivated by unwanted sexual advances from TS, was imminent. (See no. 19 and n149 below.) The allusion to Christ's words in the Vulgate comports with this range of implied meaning. There was, however, an earlier application of "Noli me tangere" in Thomas Wyatt's sonnet "Whoso list to hunt," usually read as alluding to Anne Boleyn, Elizabeth's mother, and her untouchability as Henry VIII's beloved. Could Elizabeth somehow have known Wyatt's not-yet-published sonnet? If this question seems irresistible, it is equally unanswerable.

147. Source: TNA, State Papers 10/2. fol. 84c, in Elizabeth's italic hand. Modern-spelling text and photographic reproduction of the original letter in *Elizabeth I: Collected Works*, ed. Marcus, Mueller, and Rose (Chicago: University of Chicago Press, 2000), 17–19; original-spelling text in *Elizabeth I: Autograph Compositions and Foreign Language Originals*, ed. Mueller and Marcus, 16.

148. **undoubtful . . . health** **undoubtful** i.e., doubtful—one of Elizabeth's characteristic (but rare) double negative constructions. **health** This reference and the one later in this letter ("I know you are not quiet to read") allude to KP's advanced state of pregnancy. She gave birth on August 30, 1548—hence the conjectural dating of this letter to June.

for if your grace had not a good opinion of me, you would not have offered friendship to me that way that all men judge the contrary.[149] But what may I more say than thank God for providing such friends to me, desiring God to enrich me with their long life, and me grace to be in heart no less thankful to receive it than I now am glad in writing to show it. And although I have plenty of matter, here I will stay for I know you are not quiet to read. From Cheston[150] this present Saturday.

Your highness' humble daughter,
Elizabeth

NO. 20 JOHN FOWLER TO LORD ADMIRAL THOMAS SEYMOUR, ENCLOSING KING EDWARD'S JOINT MESSAGE FOR HIM AND DOWAGER QUEEN KATHERINE, JULY 18, 1548[151]

I most humbly thank your lordship for your letter dated the fifteenth of this present, which letter, I showed it to the King's majesty. And whereas in my last letter to your lordship, I wrote unto you, if his grace could get some spare time, his grace would write a letter to the Queen's grace and to you. But his highness desires your lordship to pardon him,[152] for his grace is not half a quarter of an hour alone. But,

149. **that way . . . contrary** Elizabeth alludes to the current suspicions of TS's overfamiliar dealings with her that precipitated her departure from the household of TS and KP, probably only shortly before the writing of this letter. On the not fully consistent contemporary testimony regarding TS's advances and Elizabeth's evasions, see Janel Mueller with Linda Shenk and Carole Levin, "Elizabeth Tudor: Maidenhood in Crisis," in *Elizabeth I and the Sovereign Arts*, ed. Carole Levin, Donald Stump, and Linda Shenk (Tempe: Arizona Center for Medieval and Renaissance Studies, 2011). Also see Elizabeth's letters, no. 13 (and additional documents) and nos. 14–16, in *Elizabeth I: Collected Works*, for further sidelights on her imperilment when TS was arraigned and ultimately executed for treason in the winter of 1548–49.

150. **Cheston** one of several contemporary spellings for Cheshunt, in Hertfordshire—the site of a royal residence (no longer extant).

151. Source: TNA, State Papers 10/4, art. 31, fols. 61r, 62r. Letter in the hand of John Fowler, a groom of Edward's household, with an enclosed note in Edward's fine italic hand. The note reads:

> My lord i thanke yow and praye yow to haue me recommended to the Quene.
> From Hampton. 18 of July.
>
> Edward.

152. **his highness . . . him** Young King Edward became the main object of a tug-of-war between his two Seymour uncles. TS tries to strengthen his hold on the boy by having him correspond often. But Edward is given little opportunity to write to TS and KP, even if he had wished to. Fowler intimates the boy-king's wariness and weariness at finding himself caught in

such leisure as his grace had, his majesty has written here enclosed, his recommendations to the Queen's grace and to your lordship: willing me to signify to your lordship that he is so much bound to you, that he must need remember you always. And, as his grace may have time, you shall well perceive by such small lines of recommendations with his own hand.

News I have none to write to your lordship, but that we have good hope that Haddington shall be able to bide this great brunt.[153] The King's majesty looks every hour for good news, for, as they come, my lord's grace sends the letters to the King's majesty.

My lady of Somerset is brought to bed of a goodly boy,[154] thanks be it to God; and, I trust in almighty God, the Queen's grace shall have another. The King's majesty shall christen my lord's grace' son. I cannot tell your lordship whether his grace shall go to Sheen himself or not, for as yet the child is unchristened. I must among other news declare unto your lordship that my lord protector's grace is so good lord unto me, that his grace has given me the keeping either of the great part of Petworth or else of Woolavington. Which, I will choose; and Monday next, I intend, God willing, to go into Sussex[155] and see them. I desire your lordship, when you send me any letters, let them be delivered to myself, trusting also your lordship will provide that this shall tell no more tales after your reading. For now I wrote at length to your lordship because I am promised of a trusty messenger. And thus I commit your lordship to almighty God, who preserve your lordship with the Queen's grace and all yours, to His pleasure. Written in haste at Hampton Court this nineteenth of July.

Your lordshp's most bounden
John Fowler

[Postscript] I had forgotten to declare to your lordship concerning the manor your lordship would my friend should have. When he has need, I shall be bold to send.

a middle position. See G. W. Bernard, "The Downfall of Sir Thomas Seymour," in his *Power and Politics in Tudor England* (Aldershot, UK: Ashgate, 2000), 138–41, 147–48.

153. **Haddington . . . brunt** **Haddington** a town in east Lothian, situated between Dunbar on the east and Edinburgh on the west. Fowler alludes to yet another engagement between the English and the Scots in their ongoing border hostilities.

154. **My lady . . . boy** This newborn son was the twelfth of the Duke and Duchess of Somerset's children (James, *Kateryn Parr*, 328).

155. **Petworth . . . into Sussex** **Petworth** a medieval fortified manor house in Sussex, held by the Somerset family in the mid-sixteenth century. **Woolavington** presumably a property in or near the town of this name, which lies northeast of Bridgwater in Somerset. **into Sussex** Fowler intends to visit Petworth first, perhaps thinking it likely to be the more desirable of the two properties. He would then proceed westward to Woolavington.

[Enclosed note from King Edward]

My lord, I thank you, and pray you to have me recommended to the Queen. From Hampton [Court], eighteenth of July.

Edward

NO. 21 PRINCESS MARY TO DOWAGER QUEEN KATHERINE, AUGUST 9, 1548[156]

Madam,

Although I have troubled your highness lately with sundry letters, yet that notwithstanding, seeing my lord Marquess[157] (who hath taken the pains to come to me at this present) intends to see your grace shortly, I could not be satisfied without writing to the same, and especially because I purpose tomorrow (with the help of God) to begin my journey towards Norfolk, where I shall be further from your grace. Which journey I have intended since Whitsuntide, but lack of health hath stayed me all the while.[158] Which, although it be as yet unstable, nevertheless I am enforced to remove for a time, hoping with God's grace to return again about Michaelmas. At which time, or shortly after,[159] I trust to hear good success of your grace's great belly;[160] and, in the meantime, shall desire much to hear of your health, which I pray almighty God to continue and increase to His pleasure, as much as your own heart can desire. And thus with my most humble commendations to

156. Source: Thomas Hearne, *Sylloge Epistolarum, a variis Angliae principibus scriptarum* (A Collection of Letters Written by Various Royal Persons of England), appended to his *Titi Livii Foro-Juliensis Vita Henrici Quinti, regis Angliae* (Oxford, 1716), 151–52, referencing "small volume 47, fol. 33" in the collection of Thomas Smith of Magdalen College, Oxford. John Strype, *Ecclesiastical Memorials of the Reign of Edward VI* (London, 1721), bk. 1, chap.5, also prints this letter with an erroneous source reference: "Cotton MS Otho, C.X"; this BL manuscript compendium does not contain Mary's letter. I transcribe from Hearne and note Strype's two minor variants.

157. **my . . . Marquess** William Parr, Marquess of Northampton, KP's brother.

158. **Whitsuntide . . . the Whitsuntide** Whitsunday fell on May 20 in 1548. **the while** this while (Strype).

159. **Michaelmas . . . after** Michaelmas is September 29 in the ecclesiastical calendar. If Mary's time references are accurate, KP's baby—a daughter, to be named Mary—was born four weeks premature on August 30.

160. **your . . . belly** This is a variation on the typical close of Mary's letters to her father, assuring him that she prayed for his health and that, for example, God would shortly send him and his queen (whether her own mother or a successor) "a prince" or "issue," "which shall be gladder tidings to me than I can express in writing" (Bodleian, Smith MS 47, fols. 2a, 5a, 6a, 8a, 22, 28, 30, transcribed by Hearne, *Sylloge Epistolarum,* 124–5, 128, 129, 130, 142, 148, 149).

your highness, I take my leave of the same, desiring your grace to take the pain to make my commendations to my Lord Admiral. From Beaulieu the[161] ninth of August.

Your highness's humble and assured loving daughter,
Mary

NO. 22 LORD PROTECTOR EDWARD SEYMOUR TO LORD ADMIRAL THOMAS SEYMOUR ON THE BIRTH OF MARY SEYMOUR, SEPTEMBER 1, 1548[162]

[Addressed] To my very good sister and brother[163] Lord Admiral of England.

After our right hearty commendations, we are right glad to understand by your letters that the Queen, your bedfellow, hath had an happy hour and, escaping all danger, hath made you father of so pretty a daughter. And although (if it had so pleased God) it would have been, both to us and, as we suppose, also to you, a more joy and comfort if it had been—this, the first—a son, yet the escape of the danger, and the

161. **Beaulieu . . . the** **Beaulieu** a former abbey, then royal manor, in Hampshire. **the** this (Strype).

162. Source: TNA, State Papers 10/5/2, fol. 3r. In Edward Seymour's secretary hand with italic signature. The original reads as follows, with my conjectural restoration, in square brackets, of letters obliterated by a hole at the right page edge:

> After owr right harty comendacions we ar right glad to vnderstand by your lettres that the Quene your bedfelow hath had an happie hower and escapyng all daunger hath made yow father of so pretie a daughter / And altho (if it had so pleased god) it wold haue bene both to vs and as we suppose also to yow, a more ioie and comforte if it had benn this the furst a sonne / Yet thescape of the daunger and the Prophecie and good hansel of this to a great sort of happie sonnes, the which as you writ us trust no less then to be trew, is no small ioie and comfort to vs as we are sure it is to yow and to hir [highnes] grace also / to whom yow shall g[eue] agayn our hartie Comendacions with no litle gratulation of [her] good sucesse. Thus we bid you right hertely well / From Sion the furst of September 1548
>
> Your lovyng brother.
> E. Somerset

163. **To . . . brother** A surprisingly cordial, candid, and intimate tone characterizes this letter, written when relations between the two Seymour brothers had degenerated into bitter mutual suspicion and an increasingly grim power struggle centered on the guardianship of their nephew, King Edward. The boy as the key pawn in contention between the two men may be the subtext of the older brother's remark to the younger that it is better to have male issue than female. Or the subtext may be an implicit boast: you have a daughter, but I had a son eight weeks ago (compare no. 20, n154 above).

prophecy and good handsel[164] of this to a great sort of happy sons (the which, as you writ us, trust no less than to be true[165]), is no small joy and comfort to us. As, we are sure, it is to you and to her highness' grace also, to whom you shall g[ive] again our hearty commendations, with no little gratulation of [her] good success. Thus we bid you right heartily well. From Syon,[166] the first of September 1548.

Your loving brother,
E. Somerset

164. **handsel** See part 3, no. 22, n182.

165. **trust . . . true** i.e., I trust no less to be true. Ellipsis of a clause's subject pronoun is evidently a stylistic freedom that Edward Seymour shared with TS.

166. **Syon** the former principal monastery of the Bridgettine order, located in Twickenham Park on the Thames. At the dissolution, the buildings and land became Edward Seymour's property. He began building Syon House for himself in 1547 upon becoming lord protector, but construction was unfinished at the time of his downfall and death in 1552.

PART 5

Epilogue—Remembrances of Queen Katherine

September 1548 to post-1571

NO. 1 ELIZABETH TYRWHIT'S ACCOUNT OF DOWAGER QUEEN KATHERINE'S STATE OF MIND AND BEHAVIOR ON SEPTEMBER 3, 1548, GIVEN IN EARLY FEBRUARY 1549[1]

A two days afore the death of the Queen, at my coming to her in the morning, she asked me where I had been so long, and said unto me, she did fear such things in herself, that she was sure she could not live. Whereunto I answered, as I thought, that I saw no likelihood of death in her. She, then having my Lord Admiral by the hand, and divers other standing by, spake these words—partly, as I took it, idly: "My lady Tyrwhit, I am not well handled, for those that be about me careth not for me, but standeth laughing at my grief. And the more good I will to them, the less good they will to me."

Whereunto my Lord Admiral answered, "Why, sweetheart, I would you no hurt."

1. Source: "Elizabeth Tyrwhyt's Confession, 1548 [1549], from the Original," transcribed and published by Samuel Haynes in *A Collection of State Papers, Relating to Affairs . . . From the Year 1542 to 1570, Transcribed from Original Letters and other Authentick Memorials, Never before Publish'd, Left by William Cecill Lord Burghley, and Now remaining at Hatfield House, in the Library of the Right Honourable the present Earl of Salisbury* (London, 1740), 103–4. KP's former lady-in-waiting made this sworn deposition in early February 1549 during the investigation of TS for treason. This document is not listed in what would be its chronological place in part 1 among others relating to the investigation of TS, nor is it listed anywhere else in the Historical Manuscripts Commission's *Calendar of the Manuscripts of the Hon. The Marquis of Salisbury, K. G., Preserved at Hatfield House* (London: Eyre and Spottiswoode for HMSO, 1883). Haynes seems to be the unique source for a presumably lost original.

And she said to him again, aloud, "No, my lord, I think so." And immediately she said to him in his ear: "But, my lord, you have given me many shrewd taunts."[2] Those words I perceived she spake with good memory, and very sharply and earnestly, for her mind was unquieted.

My Lord Admiral, perceiving that I heard it, called me aside and asked me what she said; and I declared it plainly to him. Then he consulted with me, that he would lie down on the bed by her, to look if he could pacify her unquietness with gentle communication: whereunto I agreed.

And by th[e][3] time he had spoken three or four words to her, she answered him very roundly and shortly, saying: "My lord, I would have given a thousand marks to have had my full talk with Huick[4] the first day I was delivered. But I durst not, for displeasing of you."

And I, hearing that, perceived her trouble to be so great that my heart would serve me to hear no more. Such like communication she had with him the space of an hour, which they did hear that sat by her bedside.

Elizabeth Tyrwhit

NO. 2 LAST WILL AND TESTAMENT OF DOWAGER QUEEN KATHERINE PARR, SEPTEMBER 5, 1548[5]

By the lady Katherine *Queen*[6] and wife In the name of God, Amen.

Be it remembered and known that the fifth day of September, in the year of our Lord God a thousand five hundred forty and eight, and the second year of the reign of the most excellent prince Edward VI, by the grace of God King of England, France, and Ireland, Defender of the Faith, and of the Church of England and also of Ireland, in earth the Supreme Head:

The most noble and excellent princess, Dame Katherine, Queen of England, France, and Ireland; late the wife of the most excellent prince of famous memory,

2. **shrewd taunts** malicious or mischievous rejoinders.

3. **th[e]** Haynes reads "that."

4. **a thousand . . . Huick** **a thousand marks** five hundred pounds sterling; a mark was valued at 160 pence or half a pound. **Huick** Robert Huick was a trusted physician at Henry VIII's court, who attemded KP at the birth of Mary Seymour and later attended at the deathbed of Edward VI.

5. Source: Kew, Surrey, The National Archives, *Wills Proved in the Prerogative Court of Canterbury, 1383–1558,* PROB 11/32/19 Populwel (1548), fols. 142v–143r, in a clerk's secretary hand. Susan James notes that this file copy of KP's will shows signs of selective erasure and revision after its initial writing. She also notes the three-month gap between the writing of the will and its probate, remarking: "It would be of immense interest to know what the original text said" (James, *Kateryn Parr,* 332n27).

6. ***By . . . Queen*** ***By . . . lady*** "Dominae." ***Queen*** "Regine."

King Henry VIII, late King of England; and then wife to the right honorable Sir Thomas Seymour, knight of the noble Order of the Garter, Lord Seymour of Sudeley, and High Admiral of England,

Lying on her deathbed, sick in body, but of good mind, perfect memory and discretion; being persuaded, and perceiving the extremity of death to approach her; disposed and ordained by the permission, assent, and consent of her most dear, beloved husband, the Lord Seymour aforesaid, a certain disportion,[7] gift, testament, and last will of all her goods, chattels,[8] and debts, by these words or other, like in effect, being by her advisedly spoken to the intent of a testament and last will in the presence of the witness[es] and records undernamed:

That is to say, the said most noble Queen, by permission, consent, and assent aforesaid, did not only, with all her heart and desire, frankly and freely give, will, and bequeath to the said Lord Seymour, Lord High Admiral of England, her married espouse[9] and husband, all the goods, chattels, and debts that she then had, or of right ought to have in all the world, wishing them to be a thousand times more in value than they were or been; but also most liberally gave him full power, authority, and order, to dispose and prosecute the same goods, chattels, and debts at his own free will and pleasure, to his most commodity.[10]

These were witness to the premises:[11] Robert Huick, Doctor of Physic, and John Parkhurst. Given [at] the castle of Sudeley, the day and year aforesaid.

[Certification of probate]

The testament was probated[12] in the presence of the lord Archbishop of Canterbury[13] at London the sixth day of December, in the year of the Lord one thousand five hundred forty-eight. He conjointly appointed Roger Lynute procurator[14] and Thomas Seymour executor of this testament. And completion and approval were attended to with all due honors, so that we have faithfully attended to the same.

7. **disportion** Not in *OED;* the context suggests a sense like "portioning out."

8. **chattels** property, goods, money.

9. **espouse** spouse.

10. **prosecute . . . commodity** **prosecute** take advantage of. **commodity** advantage, benefit.

11. **premises** legal terminology for "matters or things stated previously."

12. **The . . . probated** **The testament** The original text is in Latin. **probated** proved—i.e., officially verified and approved—referring not only to the will itself but also to the certification of its having been proved, which was delivered to its executors.

13. **lord . . . Canterbury** Thomas Cranmer, who had issued the dispensation for Henry VIII's marriage to KP in July 1543 without any of the usual restrictions; see no. 3 in part 1.

14. **Roger . . . procurator** **Roger Lynute** Nothing seems to be known about this man but his name. **procurator** one duly authorized to act on behalf of another in any business; an agent, an attorney.

And the testament was presented in full accordance with the law, joined with an oath in the requisite form, upon the Gospels of God.

NO. 3 ANONYMOUS NARRATIVE OF DOWAGER QUEEN KATHERINE PARR'S FUNERAL AND BURIAL IN THE CHAPEL OF SUDELEY CASTLE, SEPTEMBER [7], 1548[15]

A Breviate[16] of the Interment of the lady Katherine Parr, Queen Dowager, late wife to King Henry VIII, and after, wife to Sir Thomas, Lord Seymour of Sudeley, and High Admiral of England

Item[17] On Wednesday, the fifth of September, between two and three of the clock in the morning, died the aforesaid lady, late Queen Dowager, at the castle of Sudeley in Gloucestershire, 1548, and lieth buried in the chapel of the said castle.

Item She was cered and chested in lead[18] accordingly, and so remained in her privy chamber until things were in a readiness.

Hereafter followeth the provision in the chapel.

Item It was hanged with black cloth garnished with escutcheons[19] of marriages—viz. King Henry VIII and her in pale, under the crown; her own in lozenge,[20] under the crown; also the arms of the Lord Admiral and hers in pale, without crown.

Item Rails[21] covered with black cloth for the mourners to sit in, with stools and cushions accordingly, without either hearse, majesty's valence,[22] or tapers—saving two tapers whereon were two escutcheons, which stood upon the corpse during the service.

15. Source: London, College of Arms MS RR 21/C, I ("Eye" series), vol. 15, fols. 98–99, text in a clerk's secretary hand. Although its author is unidentified, the prominent use of itemized lists to give form to this narrative suggests that it was drawn up by some official of the household, perhaps KP's secretary, Walter Bucler, or her clerk of the closet, William Harper.

16. **Breviate** a short account (from Latin "breviatum").

17. ***Item*** In this period, a frequently used formula that literally marks items (actions, objects, observations) in a series: "this," "this," "and this," etc.

18. **cered . . . lead** **cered** shut up and sealed (said of a corpse in a coffin). **chested . . . lead** put into a lead coffin.

19. **escutcheons** heraldic shields.

20. **pale . . . lozenge** **pale** a vertical strip or band in the middle of a shield. **lozenge** a diamond-shaped shield on which the arms of a widow or spinster were emblazoned.

21. **Rails** a continuous series of lengths of wood, fixed in a horizontal position for any of several purposes—here, seating for the mourners and, below, enclosure of KP's coffin.

22. **majesty's valence** Evidently an analogue of the cloth of estate, the piece of rich drapery attached lengthwise to a canopy, in front of which a monarch's throne stood on a dais. KP's sober funeral conducted in a Reformed vein, the first such for any English royalty, omits traditional trappings of honor (which might have evoked her exercise of the regency in 1544). Also omitted are a hearse and lighted tapers surrounding the body, which might have activated

The order in proceeding to the chapel.

First, two conductors in black, with black staves.[23]

Then, gentlemen and esquires.

Then, knights.

Then, officers of household, with their white staves.

Then, the gentlemen ushers.

Then, Somerset Herald in the King's coat.[24]

Then, the corpse borne by six gentlemen in black gowns, with their hoods on their heads.

Then, eleven staff torches borne on each side by yeomen about the corpse, and at each corner a knight for assistance—four, with their hoods on their heads.

Then, the Lady Jane, daughter to the lord Marquis [of] Dorset, chief mourner, led by a[n] estate,[25] her train borne up by a young lady.

Then, six other lady mourners, two and two.

Then, all ladies and gentlewomen, two and two.

Then, yeomen, three and three in a rank.[26]

Then, all other following.

The manner of the service in the church.

Item When the corpse was set within the rails, and the mourners placed, the whole choir began, and sung certain Psalms in English, and read three lessons. And after the third lesson the mourners, according to their degrees and as it is accustomed, offered into the alms-box. And when they had done, all other, as gentlemen or gentlewomen, that would.

The offering done, Doctor Coverdale,[27] the Queen's almoner, began his sermon,

beliefs rejected by the Reformation—such as the pains of purgatory and the obligation of the living to pray for the souls of the dead. Miles Coverdale's funeral sermon, described below, addresses two of these rejected beliefs.

23. **conductors . . . staves** **conductors** leaders, escorts. **staves** wooden sticks.

24. **Somerset . . . coat** In 1536 the office of Somerset Herald of Arms in Ordinary was advanced to that of an appointee in the service of the crown and a member of the royal household. His appearance here "in the King's coat" signifies his high status and his evident assignment to represent Edward VI at KP's funeral. William Harvey held this office from 1545 to 1551.

25. **lady . . . estate** **lady . . . Dorset** Lady Jane Grey, entrusted by her father, the Marquess of Dorset, to TS as a ward when he grandly promised to arrange her marriage to Edward VI. TS held Jane's wardship during 1547–48, and she resided in his household up to the end of KP's life (James, *Kateryn Parr*, 142). I infer that KP gave Jane her personal prayerbook when she knew herself to be dying. See below, pp. 489–90. **a[n] estate** a person of high standing, a dignitary.

26. **rank** row, line.

27. **Doctor Coverdale** Miles Coverdale, prominent English Reformer, who completed William Tyndale's project of Englishing the whole Bible and, like Tyndale, exiled himself to Germany and the Netherlands to pursue his translating unmolested. Coverdale's first version, *Biblia The Bible: that is: the holy Scripture, faythfully translated out of Douche and Latyn in to Englyshe* (STC 2063.3), appeared in 1535, probably at Antwerp. Henry VIII authorized publication of the hybrid Tyndale-Coverdale text in England in 1538 under the title *The byble, which is all the*

which was very good and godly. And in one place thereof, he took a[n] occasion to declare unto the people how that there should none there think, say, nor spread abroad that the offering which was there done, was done anything to profit the dead, but for the poor only. And also the lights which were carried and stood about the corpse were for the honor of the person, and for none other intent nor purpose. And so went through with his sermon, and made a godly prayer. And the whole church answered, and prayed the same with him in the end. The sermon done, the corpse was buried, during which time the choir sung *Te Deum* in English.

And this done, after dinner the mourners, and the rest that would, returned homeward again. All which aforesaid was done in a morning.

NO. 4 THE HAMMERED LEAD INSCRIPTION PLATE ON KATHERINE PARR'S COFFIN, CIRCA SEPTEMBER 1548[28]

K P
Here Lyethe quene
Kateryn Wife to Kyng
Henry the VIII And
Last the wife of Thomas
Lord of Sudeley high
Admyrall of Englond
And onkle to Kyng
Edward the VI
dyed
7 September
M.CCCCC.
XLVIII

holy scripture (STC 2066), represented to him as the work of a "Thomas Matthew." In 1539, also under royal authorization, a further revision by Coverdale appeared as *The byble in Englyshe, that is to say, the content of all the holy scrypture* (STC 2068), which became known as the "Great Bible." KP repeatedly demonstrates her familiarity with Coverdale's 1535 Bible as well as the Great Bible in her *Psalms or Prayers* and in her personal prayerbook, as notes to these texts below demonstrate. When Coverdale returned in March 1548 from his second self-exile in Germany, KP appointed him her almoner (alms-distributor). Her close friend Katherine, Duchess of Suffolk, is likely to have been have been instrumental in this appointment.

28. Source: Frederick Brooksbank Garnett, *Queen Katherine Parr and Sudeley Castle* (Kendal, Westmorland, UK: T. Wilson, 1894), 18. Garnett does not comment on the mistaken date. KP died on September 5; her funeral was held on September 7. I have made an exception to my policy in transcribing this inscription. I have reproduced its original spelling.

NO. 5 JOHN PARKHURST'S TWO LATIN EPITAPHS ON KATHERINE PARR, CIRCA SEPTEMBER 1548[29]

On the incomparable woman, Katherine, formerly Queen of England, France, and Ireland, my most gentle mistress. An epitaph. 1547.[30]

In this new sepulchre Queen Katherine sleeps,
  Flower, honor, and ornament of the female sex.
To King Henry she was a wife most faithful;
  Later, when gloomy Fate had taken him from the living,
Thomas Seymour (to whom the trident, Neptune,[31] you
  Extended) was the distinguished man she wed.
She bore a baby girl; after the birth, when the sun had run
  A seventh round, cruel Death did kill her.
For the departed, we her household flow with watery eyes;
  Damp is the British earth from moistened cheeks.

29. Source: John Parkhurst, *Ludicra sive epigrammata iuvenilia* (1573) (STC 19299), 153–54.

Incomparabilis faeminae Catharinae nuper Angliae, Franciae, & Hiberniae Reginae, Dominae meae clementissimae, Epitaphion. 1547. [1548]

Hoc Regina nouo dormit Catharina sepulchro,
  Sexus faeminei, flos, honor, atque decus.
Haec fuit Henrico coniunx fidissima regi,
  Quem postquàm è viuis parca tulisset atrox,
Thoma Seymoro (cui tu Neptune tridentem
  Porrigis) eximio nupserat illa viro.
Huic peperit natam: à partu cum septimus orbem
  Sol illustrasset, Mors truculenta necat.
Defunctam madidis famuli deflemus ocellis:
  Humectat tristes terra Britanna genas.
Nos infelices maeror consumit acerbus,
  Inter coelestes gaudet at illa choros.

Aliud eiusdem Reginae Epitaph[ion]/

Catharina in hac vrna iacet,
Regina nuper Angliae,
Decus mulierum maximum.
Pariendo perit puerpera.
Infantem enim postquàm edidit,
(Fulgente luce septima)
En illa spiritum edidit.

30. **1547** a mistake for 1548.
31. **trident . . . Neptune** an elegant allusion to TS's appointment as lord admiral in 1547.

Bitter grief consumes us, we unhappy ones;
    But she rejoices 'midst the heavenly host.

Another epitaph on the same Queen

In this urn lies Katherine:
Lately Queen of England,
Women's greatest glory.
She died in giving birth.
After bringing forth an infant girl,
Lo, at daylight's seventh shining,
She breathed her spirit forth.

NO. 6 KATHERINE, DOWAGER DUCHESS OF SUFFOLK, TO SIR WILLIAM CECIL, AUGUST 18, [1549][32]

It is said that the medicine of remedy to the sick is, first, plainly to confess and to disclose the disease. Wherefore, both for remedy, and again for that my disease is so strong that it will not be hidden, I will discover me unto you. First I will, as

32. Source: BL, Lansdowne MS 2, art. 17, fol. 39r–v. In the duchess's secretary hand. KP's closest friend at the end of her life assumed the guardianship of the orphaned Mary Seymour at TS's request before his execution for high treason in March 1549. The original letter reads:

> Hit is sayd that the ~~first sayd~~ medicin of remedie to the sicke, is first pleynly to confesse and to disclose the disease, wherfore bothe for remedie, And agayne for that my disease is so strong that hit will not be hidden I will discover me unto yow, First I will as hit were under benedicite, and in ~~fewe~~ hiegh secretes declair unto you that all the world knoweth though I goo nevre so covertly in my nette, what a vary begger I am, This sicknes as I have sayd I promise yow increaseth mightily upon me /, Amongst others for causes therof, if yow will understand not the least, the Quenes child hath layen and yet dothe lye at my howse with her companie abowte her, hooly at my chardges / I have writen to my lady Somerset at large ~~and~~ which was the let I wrote not this with myne awne hand unto yow, and amongest other thinges for the child that ther may be some pentien alotted unto her, according to my lordes grace promises, Now ~~gr~~ good Cicill help at a pinche all that yow may helpe, my lady also sent me word at whitsentide last by Bertie that my lordes grace at her suite had graunted certeyne nurserye plate shuld be delyvered with [the] child, And lest theire might [be stay] for lacke of a present bill of such plate and stuffe as was there in the nurserye I send yow one here inclosed /, of all such parcelles / as were apointed out for the childes only use, and that you may the better understand that I cry not before I am pricked I send you also mistres Eglenbies lettre unto me, who with the maydes, nourrices and others dayly call on me for their wages, whose voyces myne eares may herdly beare but my couffers muche wurse. Wherfore I cease, and committe me and my sickenes to your diligence

it were under *benedicite*[33] and in high secrets, declare unto you that, all the world knoweth, though I go never so covertly in my net,[34] what a very beggar I am. This sickness, as I have said, I promise you, increaseth mightily upon me.

Amongst others, for causes thereof, if you will understand not the least, the Queen's child hath lain and yet doth lie at my house, with her company about her, wholly at my charges. I have written to my lady Somerset[35] at large, which was the let I wrote not this with mine own hand unto you,[36] and, amongst other things for the child, that there may be some pension allotted unto her, according to my lord's grace'[37] promises. Now, good Cecil,[38] help at a pinch all that you may help.

My lady also sent me word at Whitsuntide last, by Bertie,[39] that my lord's grace at her suit had granted certain nursery plate[40] should be delivered with the child. And, lest there might be stay, for lack of a present bill of such plate and stuff as was there in the nursery, I send you one (here enclosed) of all such parcels[41] as were appointed out for the child's only use. And, that you may the better understand that I cry not before I am pricked, I send you also Mistress Aglionby's[42] letter unto me, who, with the maids, nurses, and others daily call on me for their wages: whose

---

now, with my hertie commendacions to your wief / At my Mannour of Grymesthorpe the xxviiith of August

Your asured loving frend
. k . suffoulk

33. **under *benedicite*** in accordance with a "God bless us!" ***benedicite*** Latin for "May you be blessed," used in English as an interjection ("Bless you!") or as an exclamation conveying surprise or consternation ("God bless us!").

34. **in . . . net in . . . secrets** the opposite of what the duchess is doing: plainly voicing her difficulties. **never . . . net** ever so hidden in my net—i.e., not hidden at all because she wears a weaving that can be seen through. The two inverted phrases convey the duchess's wry irony about her plight.

35. **my . . . Somerset** Anne, Duchess of Somerset, wife of the lord protector.

36. **which . . . you** The duchess's prior appeal to the lord protector's wife delayed the appeal that she is now making to Cecil.

37. **pension . . . grace pension** regular payments to maintain a certain standard of living. **my . . . grace** Edward, Duke of Somerset, Lord Protector.

38. **Cecil** Sir William Cecil was currently serving as the lord protector's chief secretary. That he and the duchess had a friendly relationship as fellow promoters of Reformed religion is indicated by their joining (together with KP's brother, William Parr, Marquess of Northampton) to induce KP to publish her *Lamentation of a Sinner* in November 1547. See the wording of the title and Cecil's letter prefacing the text of the *Lamentation* in this edition.

39. **Whitsuntide . . . Bertie Whitsuntide** Whitsunday fell on June 9 in 1549. **Bertie** Richard Bertie, the duchess's steward, whom she married after her husband's death.

40. **at . . . plate at her suit** Anne evidently interceded with her husband to provide more adequately for the infant Mary Seymour. **plate** utensils for domestic use.

41. **bill . . . parcels bill** formal written document for legal purposes—here, an inventory. **parcels** objects in a set—a use rare in current English, e.g., in auction house catalogs.

42. **Mistress Aglionby** young Mary Seymour's governess.

voices mine ears may hardly bear, but my coffers[43] much worse. Wherefore I cease, and commit me and my sickness to your diligence now, with my hearty commendations to your wife. At my manor of Grimsthorpe[44] the twenty-eighth of August,

Your assured loving friend
K. Suffolk

NO. 7 KATHERINE, DOWAGER DUCHESS OF SUFFOLK, TO SIR WILLIAM CECIL, JULY 23, [1550][45]

I have so wearied myself with the two letters that I have written at this present to my lord's grace and to my lady[46] that there is not so much as one line to be spared for Cecil. But by that time I have made you amends, you will be well pleased. For another time you shall have letters when they get none: that is to say, I will trouble you when I will not trouble them. So, I trow, you may hold you well apaid.[47]

43. **coffers** strong boxes for keeping money or valuables.

44. **Grimsthorpe** the duchess's manor house in Lincolnshire.

45. Source: TNA, State Papers Domestic 10/8/35, in the duchess's hand, with fraying and holes at the right margin; lost elements have been supplied in square brackets. C. S. Knighton, *Calendar of State Papers, Domestic Series, of the Reign of Edward VI*, rev. ed. (London: HMSO, 1992), no. 332, assigns this letter to 1549. If this is the correct year, this letter would precede no. 6 above. But since neither letter gives the year of writing, I have placed this one in 1550 because it refers to Lady Somerset's having now promised to grant the pension that the duchess besought in no. 6, for the maintenance of the orphaned baby Mary and her retinue. The original reads:

> I have so weried my selfe with the ii lettres that I have writen at this present to my lordes grace and to my Lady that ther is not so muche as one lyne to be spared for Cicill. but by that tyme I have made yow amendes yow wilbe well pleased, for A nother tyme yow shall have lettres when they get none that is to say I will trouble yow when I will not trouble them. So I trow yow may hold yow well apayed / In thiese my lettres to my lady I do put her in remembrance for the performance of her promise touching some annuall pension for the finding of the late Quenes child. for ~~hit~~ now s[he] with a dowsen persones lyethe all togither at my cha[rge] The contynuauns wherof will not bring me out of deb[te] this yere. my lord Marques Northampton to whome I should delyver her, hathe as weke a back for suche a burd[en] as I have And ~~is~~ wuld receave her, but more willengly if he might receave her with thapertenaun[ces] Thus goethe the mattier yow must helpe us beggers I pray yow [all] that yow may And then will we ~~cey~~ cease our importunitie, ~~This~~ But never avouch that yow are required by me, So farr yow hartely well with my Comendacions to your wief. At grymest[horpe] the xxiiith of July
>
> Your asured frend to my powr
> k. suffoulk
>
> good cyssel forgett not poor corneles he is uterly under withowt you spedely helpe

46. **my . . . lady** the lord protector and his wife.

47. **trow . . . apaid** **trow** believe. **apaid** a former variant of "repaid."

In these my letters to my lady, I do put her in remembrance for the performance of her promise touching some annual pension for the finding of the late Queen's child, for now s[he] with a dozen persons lieth altogether at my cha[rge], the continuance whereof will not bring me out of deb[t] this year. My lord Marquis [of] Northampton,[48] to whom I should deliver her, hath as weak a back for such a burd[en] as I have, and would receive her, but more willingly if he might receive her with the appurtenan[ces]. Thus goeth the matter.

You must help us beggars, I pray you, [all] that you may; and then will we cease our importunity. But never avouch that you are required by me.[49] So fare you heartily well, with my commendations to your wife. At Grimst[horpe] the twenty-third of July.

Your assured friend to my power,
K. Suffolk

[Postscript] Good Cecil, forget not poor Cornelius. He is utterly under, without[50] you speedily help.

NO. 8 JOHN PARKHURST'S LATIN EPITAPH ON MARY SEYMOUR, CIRCA SEPTEMBER 1550[51]

Epitaph on Mary, the much praised daughter of the same Queen

With what great travail,
And at her life's expense,
My mother, the Queen, gave birth.
A wayfarer, I, her infant girl,

48. **my . . . Northampton** Also a recipient of the Duke of Somerset's ill will, KP's brother, William Parr, was actively conspiring in the summer of 1550 with supporters of John Dudley, Earl of Warwick, to replace Somerset with Warwick as lord protector. The coup succeeded on October 14, when Somerset was imprisoned in the Tower of London, his power broken (James, *Kateryn Parr,* 353–55).

49. **never . . . me** Never declare that I have asked you—an evident sign that the duchess has become persona non grata with the lord protector and his wife.

50. **Cornelius . . . without** **Cornelius** Knighton, *Calendar of State Papers,* 438, tentatively identifies this man as Cornelius Zifridius, one of King Edward's physicians. **without** unless.

51. Source: Parkhurst, *Ludicra sive epigrammata iuvenilia,* 154. The original reads:

Inclytae puellae Mariae eiusdem Reginae filiae, Epitaphion.

Qvam cum suae dispendio
Vitae, crebrisque nixibus
Regina mater edidit,
Sub hoc viator marmore
Infans puella dormio.

Sleep beneath this marble stone.
If cruel death had given me
A longer while to live,
Those virtues of that best of mothers—
Propriety, modesty, strength,
Both heavenly and manly—
Would have lived again as my own nature.
Now, whoever you are, farewell;
And because I say no more, you
Will excuse this by my infancy.

NO. 9 RETROSPECTIVE VIGNETTES OF QUEEN KATHERINE PARR IN A POEM ON THE LIFE OF SIR NICHOLAS THROCKMORTON, ONE OF HER FIRST COUSINS, COMPOSED AFTER 1571[52]

[Queen Katherine's rescue of Throckmorton family fortunes in 1543][53]

For when the King's fifth wife[54] had lost her head,
Yet he misliked the life to live alone,

Mihi cruenta longiùs
Si Mors dedisset viuere,
Illa illa matris optimae
Virtus, pudor, modestia,
Coelestis illa et mascula
In me reuixêt indoles.
Nunc quisquis es valebis, et
Quòd plura non loquor, meae
Donabis hoc infantiae.

52. Source: *The Legend of Sir Nicholas Throckmorton,* ed. John Gough Nichols, Roxburghe Club 99 (London: Nichols and Sons, 1874), combining readings of the Parteriche MS redacted by Francis Peck, *Desiderata Curiosa* (1732, 1735), and BL, Additional MS 5841, a transcription of the Parteriche MS made by William Cole in 1762, as well as two other manuscript copies, one in the holdings of the Throckmorton family titled *The Life and Death of Sir Nicholas Throckmorton, Transcribed Anno Domini 1718,* and another, BL Harley MS 6353, headed *The Life and Death of Sir Nicholas Throckmorton, Transcribed Anno Domini* [date lacking] (preface, i, iii–vi); Nichols's spelling modernized. Written in the mode of *A Mirror for Magistrates* (1559 and later editions), this stanzaic poem opens with a dream vision in which the ghost of the courtier and diplomat Sir Nicholas Throckmorton (1515–71), appearing to a younger relative, proposes to recount the eventful story of his life and its intersections with various great powers of the realm. The anonymous poet seems to have been one of Sir Nicholas's nephews. The excerpts from the *Legend* reproduced here relate to KP as queen and dowager.

53. **1543** stanzas 26–31, 36: *Legend,* ed. Nichols, 7–8, 10.

54. **King's . . . wife** Katherine Howard, tried and executed for adultery and treason in July 1542.

And, once resolved the sixth time for to wed,
He sought outright to make his choice of one:
That choice was chance right happy for us all;
It brewed our bliss, and rid us quite from thrall.

Oh lucky looks that fawned on Katherine Parr!
A woman rare, her like but seldom seen.
To Borough first, next unto Latimer,[55]
She widow was; and then became a Queen.
My mother prayed her niece with watery eyes,
To rid both her and hers from endless cries.[56]

She, willing of herself to do us good,
Sought out the means her uncle's life to save;[57]
And, when the King was in the pleasing mood,
She humbly then her suit began to crave.
With wooing times denials disagree,
She spake, and sped: my father was set free.

And, as the ship that sticketh fast in ground
Doth rise with' th' flood, and floateth out apace,
So we, that once in deepest dumps[58] were drowned,
In court began to shew a cheerful face.

55. **Borough . . . Latimer** KP's first husband was Edward Borough, son of Thomas, third Lord Borough of Gainsborough. Her second husband was John Neville, Lord Latimer. See my general introduction, pp. 7–10.

56. **My . . . cries My mother** Catherine Vaux, half-sister of the late Sir Thomas Parr, KP's father, married Sir George Throckmorton of Coughton in Warwickshire. She bore him eighteen children, of whom the future Sir Nicholas Throckmorton was one. Unsurprisingly, such an outsized family was in frequent financial distress and appealed constantly to relatives for help (James, *Kateryn Parr,* 44).

57. **her . . . save** One of Sir George Throckmorton's brothers, Michael, incurred Henry VIII's anger by supporting Cardinal Reginald Pole's attempts to block the king's divorce from Catherine of Aragon. Michael Throckmorton was stripped of his lands and imprisoned in the Tower (*Legend,* 4–5, stanzas 12, 16–17). Conspicuous for their traditionalist Catholic sympathies, the extended Throckmorton family, including Sir George (in some way not explained here), suffered the side effects of Uncle Michael's disfavor and disgrace. KP, formerly the wife of the similarly traditionalist Lord Latimer, employed her sexual allure to reinstate Sir George and his family in Henry VIII's favor. Notably, however, all of the younger Throckmortons who subsequently prospered at court—Nicholas, Clement, George, and Kellam—broke with their parents' religion and became supporters of the English Reformation (James, *Kateryn Parr,* 44n12).

58. **dumps** heaviness of mind, dejection, low spirits. The colloquial overtones of this word postdate the sixteenth century.

This was the spring of all our budding joys
Which laughed to scorn the winter of annoys.

The frost did thaw which nipped our growth with cold;
The heat of sun did make us bud again;
The wind and waves our course which did withhold
Did drive us to the wishèd port amain.[59]
The Prince's wrath was pacified and gone;
His favor grew, which caused us spring anon.

Lo, then my brethren, Clement, George, and I,
Did seek, as youth do still, in court to be.
Each other state as base we did defy,
Compared with court, the nurse of dignity.[60]
'Tis truly said, "No fishing to the sea's;
No serving to a King's"—if you can please.
. . . .
First in the court my brother Clement served:
A fee he had to Queen her cup to bring.
And some supposed that I right well deserved,
When sewer[61] they saw me chose unto the King.
My brother George in youth, by valor rare,
A pension got, and gallant halbert bare.[62]

[Parr patronage of their Throckmorton cousins prior to Henry VIII's death in 1547][63]

Then Pembroke, and his wife, who sister was
Unto the Queen, their kinsfolk friended much;
And Parr, their brother, did them both surpass:[64]

59. **amain** with full force.

60. **defy . . . dignity** **defy** set at nought, reject. **dignity** honorable or high rank.

61. **sewer** the high-ranking household officer in charge of serving the dishes at table, and sometimes of seating.

62. **First . . . bare** Clement Throckmorton became a member of KP's household as her cup-bearer; Nicholas Throckmorton became a sewer (see preceding note) in Henry VIII's household. George Throckmorton was made a gentleman pensioner before July 1544, when Henry embarked for France. **fee** official payment. **halbert** a weapon consisting of a battle ax and a pike mounted on a six-foot-long handle, used in warfare in the fifteenth and sixteenth centuries.

63. **1547** stanzas 59, 61, 63: *Legend*, 15–16.

64. **Then . . . surpass** KP's brother-in-law and sister, the Earl and Countess of Pembroke, and her brother, William, Marquess of Northampton, emulated and extended her benevolent patronage of their Throckmorton relatives.

Who, for to pleasure us, did never grudge.
Now when these called us "cousin," at each word
The other peers would friendly speech afford.

. . . .

This was the time that we acquaintance got,
Throughout the realm, of such as bore the sway.
The beams of shining sun were very hot,
Whose warmth began, at sweating, to decay.
Which setting sudden was: Death did surprise
Our King, yea then, when most we looked to rise.

. . . .

When cruel Atropos[65] had stopped his breath:
When he interrèd lay in Windsor town:
Then was our edge abated[66] by his death,
We anchor cast; our sails were pullèd down:
We feared a storm, which vanished in the air;
The clouds consumed, the sky proved very fair.

[Nicholas Throckmorton's good fortune in the household of Katherine Parr and Thomas Seymour, 1547–48][67]

My sovereign lost, the Queen I did attend
The time that, mourning widow, she did rest;
And while she married was, unto her end
I willingly obeyed her highness' hest;[68]
Who me esteemed, and thought my service good:
Whereas in truth to small effect it stood.

Her husband (fourth) was uncle to the King;
Lord Seymour, High by office Admiral:
In praise of whom loud peals I ought to ring;
For he was hardy,[69] wise, and liberal.
His climbing high, disdainèd by his peers,
Was thought the cause he lived not out his years.

65. **Atropos** one of the three Fates who spun and cut the thread of human life—specifically, the one who did the cutting.

66. **abated** brought down, humbled, degraded.

67. **1547-48** stanzas 65-67, 71; *Legend*,17, 19.

68. **hest** behest, will.

69. **hardy** an adjective that can mean "bold" or "presumptuously bold, rashly bold." The ambiguity suits TS's character and fate.

Her house was termed "a second court" of right,
Because there flockèd still, nobility.
He spared no cost his lady to delight,
Or to maintain her princely royalty.
Elizabeth, there sojourning a time,
Gave fruitfull hope through blossoms' bloom in prime.

. . . .

Virtue, go vaunt thyself, and grant me leave
To show thee how the Queen, past middle age,
Which barren was before, did then conceive,
And bare a child; but laid her life to gage.[70]
I wish my friends, in time, they would foresee,
Lest, all too late, themselves examples be.

70. **laid . . . gage** pledged her life as a "gage"—a pawn or security to ensure the performance of some action, subject to forfeit if the action went unperformed. The metaphor is poignantly ironic. KP gives birth to a baby daughter but forfeits her life anyway—a premonition that her daughter too would not live long. Written in the tradition of *de casibus* narratives (falls of princes), *The Legend of Sir Nicholas Throckmorton* is a sustained reflection on the transitoriness of human life, reputation, and greatness.

Complete Works

OF

KATHERINE PARR

KATHERINE PARR'S

PSALMS OR PRAYERS

(1544)

INTRODUCTION TO *PSALMS OR PRAYERS* (1544)

A compact, meticulously produced, yet unattributed volume, *Psalmes or Prayers taken out of holye scripture, Anno Domini MDXLIIII*, was published by Thomas Berthelet, the king's printer, with a colophon dated April 25. For the most part, this English work is a translation of the edition of John Fisher's Latin Psalms published at Cologne around 1525.[1] With a colophon dated April 12, 1544, and likewise unattributed, Fisher's Latin Psalms had just seen their first London publication, also by Berthelet, as *Psalmi seu precationes ex variis scripturae locis collectae*.[2] This first

1. The unattributed translation is *PSALMES OR PRAYERS taken out of holy Scripture* (1544) (STC 3001.7). Its source is *Psalmi seu precationes D. Jo. Episcopi Roffensis* (Cologne: H. Alopecius, [1525?]), with a few renderings of textual variants in the 1544 London edition of this Latin text. The British Library copy of Fisher's original (shelfmark G.12149) is bound with Francesco Petrarch's seven penitential Psalms under the title *Psalmi aliquot selecti ex Davide.*

2. The 1544 reprint is STC 2994. It is self-evident why the London edition omitted Fisher's name from its title page. Fisher had been executed for treason in 1535 for refusing to take the oath affirming Henry VIII as supreme head of the Church of England. Sir Thomas More died with him and for the same reason. Despite their total political discrediting, the intrinsic spiritual value of Fisher's and More's religious writings remained in high esteem among knowledgeable contemporaries. KP included excerpts from both men's Tower meditations in her personal prayerbook, and Lady Jane Wriostheley, a member of the queen's household, likewise excerpted from More's Tower meditations in her personal prayerbook. See below, p. 495n13. The chief precedent in England for such pious subterfuge—anonymous circulation of well-regarded works by convicted traitors or heretics—was the process that led to royal authorization of the Great Bible in 1538–39. Thomas Cromwell and Thomas Cranmer led Henry VIII to understand that this English translation had been made by one "Thomas Matthew," while in fact it was largely Tyndale's work, completed by Coverdale. Betrayed by a fellow Englishman to agents of the Inquisition in Belgium, Tyndale was tried as a Lutheran heretic and burned at the

London edition of Fisher's Latin Psalms reproduces the text of the Cologne edition with infrequent minor differences and one major one: the concluding prayer for Henry VIII in the English edition is lacking in the Cologne edition.[3] John Strype, the early eighteenth-century historian of the Reformation Church of England, confidently attributed the English translation, *Psalms or Prayers*, to Queen Katherine Parr. He linked its production with the "little opinion she had of her princely state, in comparison with her . . . desire of spiritual things"—the defining features, in his judgment, of her demeanor and her household.[4] Strype's basis for identifying Queen Katherine as the translator of *Psalms or Prayers* was inferential. However, considerable circumstantial evidence exists to bolster this identification, and its soundness will be affirmed in the following discussion.[5]

On May 12, 1544, Thomas Berthelet submitted a book bill to William Harper, clerk of Queen Katherine's closet. The bill records as "delivered to my lord of Chichester"—Bishop George Day, the queen's almoner—"for the Queen's Grace" six "gorgeously bound and gilt" copies of "the Psalm prayers" and fourteen more copies of the same work "gorgeously bound and gilt on the leather" for "her Grace" herself.[6] Of these twenty copies of *Psalms or Prayers* in a print run that was probably quite limited, only two are known to survive today (and both have been de-

---

stake in 1536. Henry, who had written an *Assertio septem sacramentorum adversus Martinum Lutherum* (Affirmation of the Seven Sacraments against Martin Luther) (1521), made no move to intervene on Tyndale's behalf at this later date. Yet within three years the Great Bible containing Tyndale's translations was circulating in England at Henry's behest.

3. My notes to the English translation record the substantive variants in the Latin texts of *Psalmi seu Precationes* in the Cologne and London editions. These variants show that the English translation was produced by consulting both the Cologne and the London editions; the English follows the variants in the London text at some junctures (see, e.g., *Psalms or Prayers,* nn 14, 47, 150, 238) while preserving unique readings in the Cologne text at other junctures (see nn 495, 604, 675). The availability of both editions to the English translator is an independent indication that a highly placed person or persons had key roles in this project of making Fisher's Psalms available to an English readership. As Fisher's former student and associate, now serving as KP almoner, George Day is the likeliest person to have called her attention to Fisher's work—not only the *Psalmi seu Precationes* but also the prayer for Henry VIII that is a distinctive feature of the 1544 Latin and English editions.

4. John Strype, *Ecclesiastical Memorials, Relating Chiefly to Religion, and the Reformation of It, and the Emergencies of the Church of England* (London, 1721; rpt. Oxford: Clarendon, 1822), 2.1:204.

5. Susan James argued for identifying KP as the translator of *Psalms or Prayers;* see her *Kateryn Parr: The Making of a Queen* (Aldershot, UK: Ashgate, 1999), 200–207. Kimberly Anne Coles has broadened the argument by considering the context of the work's publishing history; see her *Religion, Reform, and Women's Writing* (Cambridge: Cambridge University Press, 2008), 47–52.

6. F. Rose-Troup, "Two Book Bills of Katherine Parr," *The Library,* 3rd ser., 2 (1911): 41, spelling modernized.

nuded of their gorgeous bindings).[7] One copy, in the library of Sir William and Lady Proby at Elton Hall, must have been Queen Katherine's gift to King Henry, for it contains two reader's jottings and an affectionate couplet addressed to her—all in Henry's handwriting.[8] Another copy, in the library of Exeter College, Oxford, must have been Queen Katherine's gift to her brother-in-law William Herbert, Earl of Pembroke, for he signed his name and title at the end of the text, following the colophon, and added "his book."[9] Further evidence linking *Psalms or Prayers* with Parr comes from its two concluding prayers: the first, "A prayer for the King," in an adaptive translation from the English edition of Fisher's *Psalmi seu Precationes*; the second, "A prayer for men to say going into battle," that may well be Parr's original composition, timed to coincide with Henry VIII's military expedition against France. Both of these prayers were first explicitly linked with Queen Katherine when they were reprinted in a volume attributed to her and published slightly more than a year later: *PRAYERS OR Medytacions . . . Collected out of holy woorkes by the most vertuous and graciouse Princesse Katherine quene of Englande, Fraunce, and Irelande. Anno domini 1545.*[10]

There is, moreover, the emphatic testimony of Nicholas Udall, to whom Queen Katherine entrusted the chief role in her commissioned project: English translations of Erasmus's Latin Paraphrases upon the Gospels and Acts. Udall knew the queen as the author-compiler of "Psalms" and "meditations"—his manner of alluding, it seems, to her *Psalms or Prayers* and her *Prayers or Meditations.* He missed no opportunity to praise his patron for these exemplary literary accomplishments, rehearsing them in each of the dedicatory letters he addressed to her. In the first, dated September 30, 1545, he hails "the Psalms and contemplative meditations . . . which ye have set forth . . . to the ghostly consolation and edifying of as many as read them." In a second letter, dated January 31, 1548, he asserts that "England can

7. The chased silver binding of KP's incomplete autograph text of her *Prayers or Meditations,* produced as a gift, may suggest the vanished splendor of the gift copies of *Psalms or Prayers.* See the introduction to *Prayers or Meditations,* p. 384 below.

8. See appendix 1, "The Elton Hall Inscriptions Relating to Katherine Parr."

9. See *Psalms or Prayers* below, p. 365. For discussion of others who were likely to have received gift copies of *Psalms or Prayers,* see Janel Mueller, "Katherine Parr and Her Circle," in *The Oxford Companion to Tudor Literature, 1485–1603,* ed. Mike Pincombe and Cathy Shrank (Oxford: Oxford University Press, 2009), 222–37.

10. In fact, three editions of this work were published in 1545, all attributed to Katherine as queen. Two of these, identical except for differently worded main titles, appeared on June 2: *Prayers stirryng the mynd vnto heauenly medytacions* (STC 4818) and *Prayers or meditacions, wherin the mynde is styrred* (STC 4818.5); both of these editions append the two prayers mentioned. Another edition, also titled *Prayers or Medytacions, wherein the mynd is stirred* (STC 4819), appeared on November 6; it is the first complete edition of this work, appending a full set of five prayers, four of them ostensibly KP's own. *Prayers or Meditations* became known as "The Queen's Prayers" in the course of its many subsequent editions.

never be able to render thanks sufficient . . . to your highness . . . for composing and setting forth many godly Psalms and divers other contemplative meditations." In his third and final letter, also dated January 31, 1548, he reiterates his admiration for her "divers most godly Psalms and meditations of your own penning and setting forth."[11] Udall knew "godly Psalms" to be one expression of Queen Katherine's literary initiative in "composing" or "penning" and "setting forth" works of devotion. Although the linkage between this phraseology and Parr's role in producing the English version of *Psalms or Prayers* remains inferential to some degree, Udall's testimony is valuable in being both firsthand and contemporary, as Strype's attribution was not.

George Day's intermediary role in Parr's *Psalms or Prayers* is likely to have begun and extended well beyond taking delivery of twenty printed copies on the queen's behalf. As the earliest of her known spiritual and literary mentors, he probably introduced her to Fisher's *Psalmi seu Precationes* in its Cologne edition and fostered her interest in translating it. Although Day accepted Henry VIII's royal supremacy over the English church, he remained a religious conservative, one of a group of fellows of St. John's College, Cambridge, whose formation had proceeded under the spiritual and intellectual influence of the university's chancellor, John Fisher.[12] Fisher's blend of Scripturalism, scholasticism, and humanism found expression in a theology centered on repentance for sin, the passion of Christ, and a dynamics of salvation that balanced the somber tonalities of late medieval devotion with certain emphases shared with English Reformers—in particular, a premium on deep familiarity with the Bible and on the soul's accountability for its own state.

Clearly recognizable as a Christian humanist exercise in sacred rhetoric, Fisher's *Psalmi seu Precationes* is a finely wrought assemblage of scores of verses excerpted or more often paraphrased from the Gallican version of the Vulgate Psalms as well as from a range of Old and New Testament books and the Apocrypha. Shorn of source references, detached from their original contexts, these frequently recast verses—or phrases and clauses from them—are recombined into fifteen new compositions titled "Psalms." As the text of *Psalms or Prayers* in the present edition documents, the artistry that produces these fifteen new Psalms requires extensive annotation to make its workings perceptible. The intricacies of the overall process

11. See, respectively, part 3, no. 10, and part 4, nos. 14 and 16, in this book's correspondence section.

12. Day had held a Fisher-sponsored fellowship from 1529 to 1534, and had also been Fisher's chaplain as well as university orator. On Fisher's influence and Day's career at Cambridge, see Brendan Bradshaw and Malcolm Underwood in *Humanism, Reform, and the Reformation: The Career of Bishop John Fisher* (Cambridge: Cambridge University Press, 1989), 2–8, 25–32, 41; and Richard Rex, *The Theology of John Fisher* (Cambridge: Cambridge University Press, 1991), 84, 87.

have been well likened to textual collage.[13] Fisher's *Psalmi seu Precationes* concludes with appended paraphrases of the Vulgate texts of Psalm 21, figured as a complaint uttered by Christ on the cross, and of Psalm 99, a general thanksgiving offered by the creation to its Creator, followed by a brief "Prayer for the King" that specifies Henry VIII as its subject.

Undertaking to translate any work entails careful, sustained attention to many specifics of theme, tone, and expression. Parr's responsiveness to Fisher's spirituality is widely demonstrated in the sensitivity with which she handles her source, and it is especially salient in *Psalms or Prayers* where key religious issues of her day come to the fore. In the fifth of the fifteen Psalms, for example, one versicle reads, "O Lord God, touch my mouth, that my iniquity may be driven away; dwell Thou in my heart, that my sins may be purged." Here Parr closely translates Fisher's paraphrase of Isaiah 6:7, "Domine Deus, tange os meum, ut recedat iniquitas mea; inhabita cor meum, ut peccata mea purgentur." The Vulgate verse, part of Isaiah's vision in which the Lord of glory sends a seraphim to hallow him as a prophet, reads "Ecce tetigit hoc labia tua, et auferetur iniquitas tua, et peccatum tuum mundabitur" (Behold, this [a coal from the heavenly altar] hath touched thy lips, and thine iniquity is taken away, and thy sin shall be made clean). Fisher's "inhabita cor meum," aptly rendered by Parr as "dwell Thou in my heart," is not a Vulgate locution. It, like Fisher's substitution of "purgentur" (is purged) for the Vulgate's "mundabitur" (shall be made clean), evokes a post-Biblical spirituality in which affective inward experience and the purging of sin, a process continuing in purgatory, figure prominently. The closeness of Parr's renderings of Fisher's additions attests the appeal that his spirituality held for her in the earliest phase of her queenship.

Further significant renderings cast light on Parr's theological positioning in *Psalms or Prayers*. Fisher has four references to "poenitentia," a term central to a Reformation-era dispute over translating it as "repentance" or as "penance." For Parr at this point, the term is unproblematic; she consistently renders it as "penance." "I have not done penance for my malice, but have increased in much vanity"; "Forgive me all my sins, O Lord God almighty, . . . for according to Thy goodness Thou hast promised forgiveness of sins ofttimes to them that do penance"; "Thou art God, gracious and merciful . . . and wouldest that no man should perish, but that all men should return to penance"; "O Lord God, . . . Thou makest as though Thou sawest not the sins of men, because they should do penance, and amend their lives."[14] Parr's rendering of "poenitentia" as "penance" aligns her with a traditional-

13. Susan M. Felch reflects on "paraphrases" and what she terms "collage psalms" in her edition of *Elizabeth Tyrwhit's Morning and Evening Prayers* (Aldershot, UK: Ashgate, 2008), 41–42.

14. These respective versicles can be located by the commentary on them in nn 25, 74, 104, and 168.

ist stance, since penance in the English context was always understood as entailing oral confession to a priest. Perhaps closest to home, this rendering signals her conformity with Henry VIII's sanctioned formulation in "The King's Book"—*A Necessary Doctrine and Erudition for any Christian Man* (1543)—that the sacrament of penance joins with faith to prepare sinners to receive God's redeeming grace.[15]

Analogously, while Fisher's text contains and Parr closely renders an unsurprisingly large number of laments for breaking God's commandments and covenant, there are also intermittent affirmations of the efficacy of moral effort, which God acknowledges and reciprocates with mercy and beneficence. "All Thy ways be mercy and truth to them that seek out Thy covenant"; "O God, eternal, just, and holy, which keepest covenant and mercy with them that love Thee, and keep Thy commandments"; "Thou art good and merciful; Thou keepest covenant and mercy with Thy servants, which walk before Thee in their whole heart"; "Thy mercy, O Lord, and Thy lovingkindness . . . endureth ever: So that we keep our promise and covenant with Thee, and so remember Thy commandments, that we do them indeed."[16]

In Lutheran (and much other Reformation) theology it is axiomatic that sinful humankind cannot keep God's commandments and covenant. While good works are the necessary fruits of salvation, they cannot earn it. But Parr's renderings in *Psalms or Prayers* concur with Fisher's repeated affirmations of a role for human cooperation in the dynamic of salvation. In this she again aligns with the Article of Good Works in "The King's Book," which concludes: "And unto all these works ought we most diligently, with all labour and care, to apply our will . . . that we may obtain everlasting life, being found fruitful in the day of judgment, where every man shall receive according to his works."[17] There is a marginal reference to the account of the Last Judgment in Matthew 25.

At only one point in *Psalms or Prayers* is Parr found moderating Fisher's ascription of efficacy to human agency in overcoming sin. One of his titles reads as follows in her translation: "The fourth Psalm is a complaint of a penitent sinner, which is sore troubled and overcome with sins." Parr here freely renders Fisher's "Psalmus .iiii. quaeritur, quod à peccatis praemitur, et superatur" (Psalm 4: it is earnestly sought that one who is oppressed by sins may surmount them). She sup-

15. See the exposition of "works of penance" in the "Article of Good Works" in *A Necessary Doctrine and Erudition for any Christian Man, Formularies of Faith Put Forth by Authority in the Reign of Henry VIII*, ed. Charles Lloyd (Oxford: Oxford University Press, 1856), 371–72. Also see G. W. Bernard's discussion in *The King's Reformation: Henry VIII and the Remaking of the English Church* (New Haven, CT: Yale University Press, 2005), 584–87. Both of Henry VIII's reader's jottings in the Elton Hall copy of *Psalms or Prayers* concern penance. See appendix 1, p. 622.

16. These respective versicles can be located by the commentary on them in nn 119, 180, 219, and 664.

17. *Necessary Doctrine and Erudition*, 375; also see Bernard, *King's Reformation*, 586–87.

presses Fisher's envisaged victory of the sinner over sin—presumably because this formulation can be read as derogating from Christ's role as the supreme victor over sin on behalf of all sinners.

The other dimension in which Parr conveys a sense of her historically specific self in *Psalms or Prayers* consists of gender consciousness that becomes legible in two areas of her translation. One such area is her marked reticence in dealing with the subject of female sexual functions and organs. Fisher's recasting of Psalm 21:10–11 reads "Te procurante prodii ex utero, et bene sperare jussisti me quum adhuc fugerem ubera matris meae. Opera tua ejectus sum è vulva, et curae tuae relictus, quum essem adhuc in utro matris meae, Deus eras mihi tu" (By Thy procuring I came out from the womb; and Thou hast commanded me to hope well when as yet I sucked my mother's breasts. By Thy work I was cast forth out of the vulva; and I was left to Thy care when as yet I was in my mother's womb; Thou wast God to me). Parr's rendering of the first clause, "By Thy procurement, O Lord, I came out of my mother's womb," mitigates as it personalizes Fisher's stark imaging of the birth process by adding "my mother's" and the direct address to the Deity in attendance. Parr goes further in refashioning the wording in Fisher's second and third clauses. Her "Thou gavest me good comfort" transforms his "bene spereare jussisti me" (Thou hast commanded me to hope well) from an exercise of authority to an act of nurturance. She declines to render Fisher's "Opera tua ejectus sum è vulva" (By Thy work I was cast forth out of the vulva), substituting a bland generality, "as soon as I was born." Such perceptible reserve regarding the private parts of the female body may evince the translator's femininity and high social status, strengthening the attribution of *Psalms or Prayers* to Queen Katherine.[18]

A second area in which Parr appears to exhibit the gender consciousness of a historically specific self (and spouse) consists of her modifications of the portrayal of Henry VIII in the "Precatio pro Rege" (Prayer for the King) that concludes *Psalms or Prayers*. The climactic petitions in this text read "Benedic illi benedictionibus dulcedinis tuae. Tribue ei longitudinem dierum. Gloriam et magnum decorem impone super eum . . . Adest illi, ut de suis ac nostris triumphet hostibus: et terrori sit omnibus inimicis sui regni" (Bless him with the blessings of Thy sweetness. Endue him with length of days. Set glory and great comeliness upon him . . . Be with him that he may triumph over his and our foes, and be of terror to all enemies of his kingdom).

Parr's retouchings accentuate the masculine regality of Henry's figure. "Endue him plentifully with heavenly gifts" replaces "Benedic illi benedictionibus dulcedinis tuae" (Bless him with the blessings of Thy sweetness), as Parr eliminates

18. These two versicles are annotated in n676. Elizabeth I's translation of Erasmus's Latin version of Plutarch's *De curiositate* contains several comparable instances of circumlocution in references to female sexuality; see *Elizabeth I: Translations, 1544–1589*, ed. Janel Mueller and Joshua Scodel (Chicago: University of Chicago Press, 2009), 16.

sweetness, even from a divine source. She also reworks the merely quantitative "Iribue ei longitudinem dierum" (Endue him with length of days) into a qualitative projection of Henry's magnificence under divine favor: "Grant him in health and wealth long to live." But it is Parr's retouchings of Fisher's last clauses that contribute most to heightening the virility of Henry's magnificence: "Set glory and great comeliness upon him" becomes "Heap glory and honor upon him." "Be with him that he may triumph over his and our foes, and be of terror to all enemies of his kingdom" becomes "So strength him, that he may vanquish and overcome all his and our foes, and be dread and feared of all the enemies of his realm." The military character of Henry's envisaged honor from God is both specified and rhetorically intensified by Parr's doublings, "vanquish and overcome," "be dread and feared." By the end of the prayer, these predicates of hers, in contrast to the Latin original, focus more emphasis on Henry's sovereign might than on God as the source of this "strength." In light, moreover, of the masculinist momentum attained in Parr's "A prayer for the King," an earlier detail in which she reworks the Latin text assumes greater significance. Where it refers to Henry in an honorific formula for a reigning monarch as "serenissimum regem nostrum" (our most serene King), Parr revises the phrasing to read "our most gracious sovereign lord." She will later use a similar ascription in her *Lamentation of a Sinner*, in referring to "my most sovereign, favorable lord and husband." Sovereignty rather than serenity is the uppermost association with Henry VIII in Queen Katherine's wifely consciousness.[19]

As an overall assemblage, Fisher's fifteen Psalms divide thematically into two nearly equal halves. An initial group of seven Psalms, dominated by the speaker's extreme self-abasement and remorse for sins committed, modulates into pleading that God will impart wisdom, hear the sinful speaker, and give order and direction for good living (Psalms 5–7). Psalm 1 powerfully intensifies the reprehension of sin with an extended meditation on the sufferings of the crucified Christ. A second group of eight Psalms, dominated by the speaker's obsessive yearnings to be delivered from enemies and persecutors, likewise modulates into professions of trust in God, patience (with an extended meditation on the patience of Christ), thanksgiving that enemies have not "gotten the overhand," praise of God's goodness in confounding enemies, and thanksgiving for God's other benefits (Psalms 11–15).

Only the advantage of hindsight across the spectrum of her eventual four works can reveal how characteristic of Katherine Parr's spirituality and writing the con-

19. It is additionally possible that both aspects of KP's gender consciousness combined with her sense of status to moderate Fisher's splicing of recast excerpts from Psalms 3:8 and 67:22. His versicle reads "Percussisti omnes adversarios meos, et virtutem eorum confregisti" (Thou hast thrust my enemies through and through; Thou hast broken their strength in pieces). Her versicle reads "Thou hast stricken all my adversaries, and hast abated their strength." A well-bred feminine sense of decorum may have operated to palliate the violence of Fisher's language, which sustains the violence of the source verses in the Vulgate. See n617.

junction of abjectly confessed sinfulness and affective meditation on Christ's passion would become. This conjunction has been proposed as a defining feature of female religious writing in England in her era.[20] At this point, near the end of Parr's first year of queenship, it can already be seen that she resists developing this crucial conjunction in the direction of mystical transport or Eucharistic adoration. True to Fisher's precedent, her conjunctions remain grounded in the phrases and images of the Biblical text, as illustrated in Parr's rendering of the following versicles from his first Psalm:

> He gave His body to be beaten, and His cheeks to be stricken; He turned not away His face from them that scorned Him, and spit upon Him.
> Through His love and mercy, He hath redeemed them that were lost, and by His blood, shed on the cross, He hath pacified all the things in heaven and earth . . .
> Look, O merciful Father, and consider, who it is that thus did suffer; and remember, I beseech Thee, for whom He hath suffered.
> For this is that innocent, whom Thou gavest to death for us, even then when we were sinners; and shall we not, being now justified by His blood, much rather be saved from wrath through Him?

With regard to Fisher's other dominant theme, the marked attraction in Katherine's spirituality to Psalm passages of anguished brooding and lamenting over one's enemies finds more obvious sources of explanation in her later experiences at the Tudor court—Stephen Gardiner and Thomas Wriothesley's nearly successful plot to discredit her with Henry and dislodge her from the throne, and her bitter competition over precedence with her former lady-in-waiting, the Duchess of Somerset, the lord protector's wife, in Edward VI's reign—than in her experiences during her first year of marriage to Henry.[21] Yet she and Lord Latimer's two chil-

20. See Christine Peters, *Patterns of Piety: Women, Gender, and Religion in Late Medieval and Reformation England* (Cambridge: Cambridge University Press, 2003), 93–94, 128, 343–47. Also see the suggestive general reflections on "the practice of piety" in Sara Mendelson and Patricia Crawford, *Women in Early Modern England, 1550–1720* (Oxford: Clarendon, 1998), 225–31.

21. KP's precarious position as wife and queen, however, can be set in parallel with the anxiety and alienation that figure so prominently in Sir Thomas Wyatt's poetry. Sensitive recent commentary on Wyatt has stressed "the claustrophobic and oppressive atmosphere within which courtiers existed in Henry's court" of the later 1530s and the 1540s—a period when the king's exaction of obedience to his will became more violent and often more difficult to construe. See Tom Bettteridge, *Literature and Politics in the English Reformation* (Manchester: Manchester University Press, 2004), 68; Greg Walker, *Writing under Tyranny: English Literature and the Henrician Reformation* (Oxford: Oxford University Press, 2005), 279–82. The threat of "enemies" that frightened KP could potentially have included Henry VIII himself.

dren had been in serious danger when rebel troops, infuriated by his maneuverings during the Pilgrimage of Grace, took him hostage on one occasion, and on another, forced their way into the Latimer residence, ransacking it and threatening violence to Katherine and the children.[22] More insidiously, hence less demonstrably, Katherine's role as Henry's sixth queen and the associations of Hampton Court with her unfortunate predecessors Anne Boleyn and Katherine Howard, whose violent ends resulted from the machinations of enemies, may have sensitized her to the special prominence of this theme—not only in Fisher's *Psalmi seu Precationes* but also, more personally appropriated, in her subsequent *Prayers or Meditations* and in the handwritten prayerbook that she would compile for herself.

As documented in the detailed annotations to her text, Parr's translations of Fisher's blendings of quotation and paraphrase in his Psalm collages are highly respectful of their source and, for the most part, closely consonant with his Latin. Mistakes or "off" choices in her translating are very rare. One example is "plagues" as a rendering of Latin "plagas" (blows, strokes).[23] It is conceivable that the sound similarity between the Latin and the English miscued Parr; if so, the effect lingered, for she also translates "plaga" as "plague" in her personal prayerbook.[24] Another "off" choice is "much grieveth" as a rendering of "gravat" (burdeneth), with the possibility that sound similarity was in play here also. "Spirit" or "soul" is clearly preferable to "mind" as a rendering of "anima" in an excerpt from Psalm 24:1, "Ad te domine deus animum meum levo," which Parr translates as "To Thee, O Lord, I lift up my mind." Likewise, her "reasons" as a rendering of "rationes"—"For men's reasons do fail in many things, and their forecasts and inventions be uncertain and unsure"—is inferior to either "reasonings" or "calculations" in translating Fisher's paraphrase of Wisdom of Solomon 9:14: "Nam rationes hominum in multis deficiunt, et parum securae adinventiones eorum" (For the reasonings of men are lacking in many things, and their inventions are not sure enough).[25] But such occasional blemishes are untypical.

On the positive side, Parr's own stamp as translator can be discerned in three prominent features of her style: her free recourse to doublings of lexical primaries (nouns, verbs, adjectives, or adverbs) for purposes of rhetorical emphasis or tonal heightening; her tendency to expand compressed or elliptical constructions in Latin into full English phrases or clauses; and her recourse to idioms or colloquialisms that reduce formality of expression to plainer, more direct utterance. Often, too, these stylistic features work effectively in combination.

Doublings abound in sixteenth-century English prose, where their effects range

22. James, *Kateryn Parr,* 78–84.

23. For a later occurrence of "plague," see my introduction to KP's personal prayerbook, p. 509.

24. See "Katherine Parr's Personal Prayerbook," p. 618.

25. These examples can be located by the respective commentary on them in nn 332, 421, and 331.

broadly from the ornamental or ceremonious to the functional.[26] Parr's doublings of single elements in Fisher often work to intensify the first-person expression in a versicle, as in "My heart desireth Thee; my soul seeketh for Thee; I tarry and look when I may behold Thy face." The doubling here, "tarry and look," undergoes further clausal expansion with Parr's addition, "when I may behold Thy face." Rendering Fisher's "faciem tuam exspecto" (I look out for Thy face), Parr's construction as a whole sequentially tracks the connotations of a state of expectancy (Latin "exspecto")—watching, waiting, looking for God to appear. In another versicle, "And although Thou wert very angry with me a little while, yet now I live through Thy mercy and goodness," the doubling of "Thy mercy and goodness" renders Fisher's technical theological term "repropitiatione tua" (Thy reconciliation), clarifying by opening up the meaning of the Latin in accessible as well as accurate English.[27]

Parr's openness of style importantly depends on her practice of phrasal or clausal expansions of compressed or elliptical Latin constructions. A typical example is provided by her versicle "Let the brightness of Thy face shine upon Thy servant, for unto Thee, O Lord God, I have fled for succor," which renders Fisher's splicing of excerpts from Psalms 118:135 and 142:9: "Illumina faciem tuam super servum tuum, quia ad te confugi domine Deus" (Shine Thy face upon Thy servant, for I have fled to Thee, O Lord God). Parr's additions, "the brightness of" and "for succor," respectively enhance the intelligibility of the versicle in English: the "brightness" of God's face makes it shine; the speaker has a motive for fleeing to God—"for succor." Another typical example is her versicle "For like as the hart, when he is chased, coveteth to the rivers of water, even so, O Lord, my soul desireth to be with Thee," which renders Fisher's slight recasting of Psalm 41:2: "Quemadmodum desiderat cervus ad fontes aquarum: ita desiderat anima mea ad te, O Deus" (As the stag desireth the springs of water, so my soul desireth Thee, O Lord). Parr's explanatory addition, "when he is chased," not only clarifies why the stag is thirsty but also intensifies the spiritual charge of the simile: the speaker likewise feels chased and hunted down, and yearns to be safely with God.[28]

The idiomatic or colloquial turns of phrase by which Parr turns Fisher's or the Vulgate's Latin into familiar English speech include "death's door," rendering as well as Christianizing "inferno" (the region below); "have the overhand of," rendering "superabit" (be exalted over), and such readily understandable though no longer current locutions as "a mocking-stock," rendering "opprobrium" (a reproach); "rablement," rendering "turba" (a disorderly crowd); and "rattle upon," rendering "subsannaverunt" ([they have] railed at). To this list may be added her characterization of the shepherd boy David as "but a little one" (Latin "parvulus") who nonetheless

26. Janel M. Mueller, *The Native Tongue and the Word: Developments in English Prose Style, 1380–1580* (Chicago: University of Chicago Press, 1984), 117, 126, 135, 147, 167, 186, 219, 230, 254.

27. To locate these two versicles, see nn 386 and 622.

28. To locate these two versicles, see nn 447 and 537.

went up against "the great, huge Goliath" in her "Prayer for men to say going into battle." While aptly used idioms and colloquialisms remain constants of Parr's English prose in her letters and in her works subsequent to *Psalms or Prayers*, to regard them merely as intrinsically appealing stylistic features may scant their interpretive potential. This is especially true of her translation, *Psalms or Prayers*. Although Parr's primary literary responsiveness is to Fisher's *Psalmi seu Precationes*, its effects in *Psalms or Prayers* are complicated and enriched by the gamut of idioms and colloquialisms that her English shares with other writers who are her contemporaries. The writers who recur across this gamut turn out to be early Reformers who produced translations of Scriptures into English—and whose influence on Queen Katherine would become more pronounced and legible with time. But even at this earlier point a suggestive conjecture can be made about the character of some of her reading prior to and concurrent with her translation of Fisher.

Thanks to the capabilities of Chadwyck-Healey's "Early English Books Online," Parr's idioms and colloquialisms can be searched for the period 1530–44. "Death's door" yields two hits—both in productions by George Joye, an English Lutheran, from the Latin of Martin Bucer and Ulrich Zwingli respectively: *The psalter of David in Englishe* (Antwerp, 1530, and London, 1534?) and *Davids psalter* (Antwerp, 1534).[29] Variations on "to have the overhand of" yield ten hits in eight contemporary works—one in the traditionalist Thomas Gascoigne's *The boke callyd the myrroure of Our Lady* (1530); one in Miles Coverdale's *Biblia, the bible* (1535); three in the Great Bible of 1539–40, another authorized publication from Thomas Berthelet; three (one each) in three works by the Reformer Thomas Becon, all from 1542; and two (one apiece) in topical tracts by Coverdale (1543) and Sir Richard Morison (1539).[30] "Mocking stock" yields ten hits in five works—one in *The manuell of the christen knight*, an anonymous English translation of Erasmus's *Enchiridion Militis Christiani* (1533); four in *The myrrour or glasse of Christes passion*, an anonymous English translation of the Latin original by Ulrich Pinder (1534); two in the conservative bishop John Longland's Good Friday sermon preached before the king at Greenwich (1536); two in Richard Taverner's *An epitome of the Psalmes*, a translation of the Latin original by a German Lutheran, Wolfgang Capito; and one in the Great Bible.[31] "Rabblement" yields three hits in three works—two in translations by Richard Taverner, one in *The confession of the fayth of the Germans* (1536), his

29. STC 2370–2371 and 2372. It must be noted, moreover, that the electronically searchable texts in the Chadwyck-Healey database are the ones that have been keyboarded to date. These constitute a subset of the titles available as page images through Early English Books Online.

30. These publications are, respectively, STC 17542 (Gascoigne), STC 20633 (Coverdale's *Biblia*), STC 2069 (Great Bible), STC 1715, 1717, 1735 (Becon), STC 17542 (Coverdale's *Christen exhortation*), and STC 18111 (Morison).

31. STC 10479 (Erasmus), STC 14553 (Pinder), STC 16795 (Longland), STC 2748 (Taverner/Capito), STC 2068, 2069 (Great Bible).

translation of Philipp Melanchthon's Latin text of the Augsburg Confession (1530), the other in *Common places of Scripture* (1538), his translation of a compilation by Erasmus Sarcerius; and a third in *Of the office of servauntes* (1543), an anonymous English translation of the Latin original by Gilbertus Cognatus, published by Berthelet.[32] "Rattle" yields one hit—in Coverdale's Bible.

Finally, "a little one" yields twelve hits in nine works which divide neatly between humanist productions and collections of Scripture in English. Among the humanist works, "a little one" occurs once in Nicholas Udall's Latin and English *Floures . . . gathered out of Terence* (1534); once in John Palsgrave's English translation of the Latin comedy for school use, *Acolastus* (1540); and twice (once each) in Sir Thomas Elyot's *Dictionary* (1538) and *Bibliotheca Eliotae* (1542). The Palsgrave and Elyot volumes were published by Berthelet. Among the collections of Scripture, "a little one" occurs twice in William Tyndale's English translation, *The Pentateuch* (1530); twice in Coverdale's Bible; once in Coverdale's *The newe testament both Latine and Englyshe* (1538); and twice in the Great Bible. To this group may be added the single occurrence of "a little one" in *The Examination of Willam Thorpe* (1530), Tyndale's redaction of the proceedings in the heresy trial of a Lollard burned in 1407.[33]

On the showing of these distributional patterns, it can plausibly be supposed that, in addition to her acquaintance since childhood with the Vulgate in devotional and liturgical contexts, Parr brought to her translating of Fisher's *Psalmi seu Precationes* a considerable familiarity with two Bibles in English: Miles Coverdale's *Biblia. the byble* (1535), which completes Tyndale's unfinished translation; and *The byble in Englyshe*—the closely similar "Great Bible," whose publication Henry VIII had authorized in 1538–39. Since, as already noted, Fisher himself gives no indication of the provenance of his source materials, the question of Parr's familiarity with Scripture inevitably arises. Do her renderings in *Psalms or Prayers* show signs that she recognized any of the Biblical source texts that Fisher excerpted, reworded, and recombined into the fifteen Latin Psalms of his own creation? It is not surprising that most of her English renderings are neutral with respect to answering this question, since the principal features they exhibit are her closeness to Fisher's Latin and her care in selectively opening up the compressions of his style.

Yet at certain points Parr's wording seems to indicate that she did not recognize Fisher's Biblical source. For example, her versicle "Yea, I am a very babe and a child, and know full little mine own life and conversation" freely renders Fisher's slight recasting of an excerpt from 3 Kings 3:7: "Etiam puer sum et parvulus, ignorans

32. STC 908, 21752.5 (Taverner's two translations), STC 5879 (*Of the office of servauntes*).

33. The humanist works are STC 23899 (Udall), STC 11470 (Palsgrave), and STC 7659 and 7659.5 (Elyot); the collections of Scripture are STC 2350 (Tyndale), 2063.3 (Coverdale's *Biblia*), STC 2816 (Coverdale's Latin-English New Testament), and STC 2069 (Great Bible). Thorpe's *Examination* in Tyndale's redaction is STC 24045.

ingressum et exitum meum" (As yet I am a child and very little, unknowing of my going-in and going-out). The Vulgate excerpt, from Solomon's prayer for wisdom, reads "ego autem sum puer parvulus, et ignorans ingressum, et introitum meum" (But I am a very little child, and unknowing of my going-in and entering). Parr's substitution of "mine own life and conversation" for Fisher's "ingressum et exitum meam" (my going-in and going-out) suggests her unawareness of the source text, for Fisher's phrasing is appreciably closer to the Vulgate's than hers is. Again, Parr's versicle "O God, make haste to deliver me; O Lord, make speed to help me" renders Fisher's recasting of Psalm 69:2: "Deus ad liberandum me; domine in auxilium meum festina" (O God, to the delivering of me, to my help, make haste, O Lord). The Vulgate verse reads "Deus in adjutorium meum intende: Domine, ad adjuvandum me festina" (God, attend to my help; Lord, make haste in helping me). Parr's doubling of "make haste . . . make speed" eases the compression of Fisher's syntax, but the near synonymity of her main verbs where the Vulgate conjoins two different verbs suggests that she did not recognize the source text.

Another sort of presumptive nonrecognition emerges in Parr's renderings of two versicles that Fisher produces by reusing the same Vulgate verse, Psalm 30:9, in close succession. Very near the end of his twelfth Psalm, Parr expansively renders his first use of an excerpt from this verse as "set my feet in a place where I may walk at liberty." Fisher reads "in spacioso loco pedes meos sistas" (set my feet in an ample place); the Vulgate reads "statuisti in loco spatioso pedes meos" (Thou hast set my feet in an ample place). The reuse occurs early in his thirteenth Psalm, where Fisher quotes nearly verbatim the whole of Psalm 30:9 as his fourth versicle: "Non conclusisti me in manibus inimicorum meorum, imo statuisti in loco spacioso pedes meos." Parr renders this as "Thou hast not closed me up in the hand of mine enemies, but Thou hast set my feet in a place both wide and broad." The Vulgate reading of the full verse is "Nec conclusisti me in manibus inimici: statuisti in loco spatioso pedes meos" (Nor hast Thou closed me up in the hands of the enemy; Thou hast set my feet in an ample place). Parr's two differently expansive renderings—"in a place where I may walk at liberty," "in a place both wide and broad"—suggest that she probably did not recognize Fisher's two uses of the same verse, or possibly that she did sense the reuse and sought to mask it through stylistic variation.[34]

There are, however, a great many more instances in *Psalms or Prayers* where Parr appears to signal her recognition of Fisher's Biblical source by conforming her English wording more closely to the Vulgate's Latin than to his Latin paraphrase. A handful of examples will illustrate; others are recorded in the notes to her text. Early in his first Psalm, Fisher composes a versicle by recasting excerpts from Daniel 2:38: "In ditione tua universa sunt posita, anima omnis viventis, et spiritus uni-

34. To locate the four versicles cited in the two preceding paragraphs, see nn 320, 395, 592, and 596.

versae humanae carnis" (Under thy dominion all things have been placed, all the breath of living things, and the spirit of all human flesh). The excerpts from Daniel, an address to King Nebuchadnezzar, read as follows in the Vulgate: "omnia, in quibus habitant filii hominum, et bestiae agri: sub ditione tua universa constituit" (all [places], where the sons of men dwell, and the beasts of the field, . . . the whole hath been placed under thy dominion). Parr's versicle reads "All things be under Thy dominion and rule, both man and beast, and all living creatures." Her explicit mention of "man and beast" brings her rendering closer to the Vulgate than Fisher's is, indicating her recognition of the source text. Again, in the midsection of his fourth Psalm, Fisher slightly recasts Psalm 142:4: "Anxius est in me spiritus meus, in me desperabundum est cor meum" (Distressed is my spirit within me; my heart within me is full of despair). The verse in the Vulgate reads "anxiatus est super me spiritus meus, in me turbatum est cor meum" (my spirit is made anxious about me; my heart within me is troubled). Parr's versicle reads "My spirit is careful and troubled within me, and desperation hath entered my heart." Her locution "troubled" has no analogue in Fisher but tallies closely with the Vulgate's "turbatus," suggesting that she recognized the Biblical source. And again, in the midsection of his twelfth Psalm, Fisher recasts Psalm 70:9: "Ne abjicias me angustiae tempore, et cum iam virtus mea deficit, tu me ne deficias" (Depart not from me in the time of difficulty; and now when my strength faileth, fail Thou me not). The corresponding text in the Vulgate reads "Ne projicias me in tempore senectutis: cum defecerit virtus mea, ne derelinquas me" (Cast me not away in the time of old age; when my strength shall fail, forsake me not). Parr's versicle reads "Cast me not away in the time of my most necessity; and now when my strength faileth me, fail not Thou me, O Lord." Her "Cast . . . away" renders the Vulgate's "projicias" exactly, as Fisher's "abjicias" (depart) does not, and her generalizing phrase "of my most necessity" deftly bridges the disjunction between Fisher's "angustiae" (of difficulty) and the Vulgate's "senectutis" (of old age). Parr thus appears to have recognized the Biblical source that Fisher was paraphrasing and accommodated her English rendering to it.[35]

In a smaller but still appreciable set of instances, Parr signals her recognition of a Biblical source by conforming key elements of her English translation to Coverdale's or the Great Bible. (These Bibles overlap extensively, with identical readings of many verses.) Again, a few examples from *Psalms or Prayers* will illustrate; others are recorded in the notes. In the midsection of his seventh Psalm, Fisher slightly recasts an excerpt from Psalm 18:15: "Sint placentes sermones oris mei, et meditatio cordis mei in conspectu tuo semper" (May the words of my mouth and the meditation of my heart be always pleasing in Thy sight). The Vulgate excerpt reads "erunt ut complaceant eloquia oris mei: et meditatio cordis mei in conspectu tuo semper" (let the fine speech of my mouth and the meditation of my heart be always pleasing in Thy sight). Parr's rendering of Fisher reads "Let the words of my mouth

35. To locate the three versicles cited in this paragraph, see nn 5, 281, and 590.

and the meditation of my heart be ever pleasant and acceptable in Thy sight." Her doubling, "pleasant and acceptable," introduces phrasing not found in the Vulgate but shared by Coverdale's Bible and the Great Bible. Her rendering produces a near echo of the Great Bible: "Let the wordes of my mouth, and the meditacion of my herte be allways acceptable in thy sight."[36] Again, late in his tenth Psalm, Fisher recasts Psalm 122:4: "Multum repleta est anima mea, et derisione me in festantium, et contemptu superborum" (My soul is greatly filled, both with the mockery of me by those in festive dress and with the contempt of the proud ones). The Vulgate verse reads "multum repleta est anima nostra: opprobrium abundantibus, et despectio superbis" (our soul is filled with scorning by the wealthy, and with despising by the proud). Parr's rendering reads "My soul is filled with the scorning and derision that mine enemies have at me, and with the despitefulness of the proud." Her last clause, in particular, is clearly indebted to the identical reading of this verse in Coverdale's and the Great Bible: "Oure soule is fylled with the scornefull reprofe of the welthy, and with the despitefulnesse of the proud."[37]

Two further examples are of interest for the evidence they yield that Parr not only recognized the Biblical source text of a versicle in Fisher but consulted the wording of that text in Coverdale and the Great Bible as a guide to her own English rendering. Late in his eleventh Psalm, Fisher recasts Psalm 49:14 from the second to the first person: "Immolabo tibi hostiam laudis: et reddam altissimo vota mea" (I will offer to Thee the sacrifice of praise, and I will render my prayers to the Most High). The Vulgate reads "Immola Deo sacrificium laudis: et redde Altissimo vota tua" (Offer the sacrifice of praise to God, and render Thy prayers to the Most High). Parr's characteristically more expansive versicle reads "I will offer up to Thee sacrifice of laud and praise; and I will render up my vows to Thee, which art the Highest). Her seemingly odd translation of "vota," which can mean "prayers" or "vows," is in fact the phrasing in Coverdale's and the Great Bible.[38] Her adoption of their alternative in rendering "vota" indicates that she both recognized the source text and consulted their precedent. Again, early in the fourteenth Psalm, Fisher slightly recasts an excerpt from Psalm 8:2: "Domine dominus noster, quam admiranda est majestas tua per universam terram" (O Lord, our Lord, how admirable is Thy majesty throughout all the earth). The Vulgate reads "Domine Dominus noster, quam admirabile est nomen tuum in universa terra" (O Lord, our Lord, how admirable is Thy name in all the earth). Parr's corresponding versicle reads "O Lord our Governor, how wonderful is Thy majesty throughout the whole world." What licenses her epithet "our Governor"? It appears in the rendering of this verse in both Cov-

36. Psalm 19:14 in *The Hexaplar Psalter, Being the Book of Psalms in Six English Versions*, ed. William Aldis Wright (Cambridge: Cambridge University Press, 1911), 40.

37. Psalm 122:4 in *Hexaplar Psalter*, 322. To locate the two versicles cited in this paragraph, see nn 433 and 528 below.

38. Psalm 50:14 in *Hexaplar Psalter*, 118.

erdale's and the Great Bible, again indicating her recognition of the Biblical source and her consultation of these English precedents. Here Parr's rendering of Fisher's Latin comes closest to the reading of Coverdale: "O Lorde our governoure: how wonderfull is thy name in all the worlde."[39]

Judged by any standard and viewed from any angle, Queen Katherine's *Psalms or Prayers* demonstrates a profound familiarity with the Bible in Latin and English—and preeminently with the Psalms. The Scripturalism that emerges in this work continues to characterize all her later compositions: *Prayers or Meditations*, *The Lamentation of a Sinner*, and her personal prayerbook. Moreover, to the considerable extent that she recognized the Biblical source texts whose wording Fisher recast, she had a firsthand exposure to the workings of paraphrase. She evidently appreciated its potential, for she went on to commission English translations of Erasmus's Latin Paraphrases of the New Testament—giving special regard to the Gospels and Acts—as her major act of patronage as queen. To the also considerable extent that she recognized how Fisher was excerpting, reordering, and freely recombining his Biblical source texts, she found a prototype for what became her own mode of composition in *Prayers or Meditations* and her personal prayerbook. As the earliest of her literary projects, *Psalms or Prayers* had a uniquely pervasive and powerful influence on Queen Katherine Parr.

39. Psalm 8:1 in *Hexaplar Psalter*, 14. To locate the two versicles cited in this paragraph, see nn 554 and 631.

English translation of *Psalmi seu Precationes*[1]

❧

PSALMS
OR PRAYERS
taken out
of holy
Scripture

ANNO DOMINI
M.D.XLIIII

1. Source: *PSALMES OR PRAYERS taken out of holy Scripture* (1544) (STC 3001.7), sigs. A8–L6, M3, Exeter College, Oxford (shelfmark MS 9M3001); this copy bears the signature of KP's brother-in-law William Herbert, Earl of Pembroke. Another copy is preserved in the library of Sir William and Lady Proby at Elton Hall; it contains jottings in Henry VIII's hand. This compact, now extremely rare volume, measuring about five by seven inches, is printed in black letter with boldface headings and intermittent Roman small capitals. It consists of an English translation of the Latin Psalms of John Fisher, first published as *PSALMI SEV PRECATIONES D. Io. Episcopi Roffensis* (Cologne: H. Alopecius, [1525?]); the British Library copy is shelfmarked G.12149. The earliest English edition of Fisher's Latin text is *PSALMI SEV PRECATIONES EX VARIIS SCRIPTURAE LOCIS COLLECTAE. ANNO 1544* (London: T. Berthelet, 1544) (STC 2994), with a colophon dated April 12, two weeks earlier than *Psalmes or Prayers*; a second edition has a colophon dated August 13, 1544 (STC 2995). The first English edition reproduces the text of the Cologne edition with infrequent minor variations; my notes give the readings of the Cologne edition and record substantive variations in the 1544 London edition. For convenience of reference to the English edition of Fisher's text electronically available on the Early English Books Online website, the letters and numbers (signatures) of the pages in *Psalmes or Prayers* are supplied in small print, enclosed in square brackets, and positioned at the head of

[Frontispiece][2]

THE FIRST PSALM, FOR THE OBTAINING REMISSION OF SINS.

[Aii r] O Lord of Lords, God almighty, great and dreadful, which by Thy word hast made heaven, earth, the sea, and all things contained in them:[3]

Nothing is able to resist Thy power; Thy mercy is over all Thy works.[4]

All things be under Thy dominion and rule, both man and beast, and all living creatures.[5]

---

the nearest full versicle. Spelling has been modernized throughout. Unless otherwise indicated, Scriptural references employ names of books and psalm and verse numbers in the Gallican version of the Vulgate.

2. ***[Frontispiece]*** Both the Elton Hall and the Exeter College copies have prominent hand-colored images of Henry VIII's royal arms on the verso of their title pages. Subsequent early editions replace the royal arms with three epigraphs: "Psalmo 101. The lorde turneth hym unto the praier of the poore destitute, and despiseth not their praier." "Colloss. 4. Continue in praier, and watche in the same with thankesgiving." "1 Thessal. 5. Rejoyce alwaie, praie continually, in all thynges be thankfull: for this is the will of God in Christe Jesu towarde us." Except for the substitution of "praier" for "desire," the first epigraph reproduces the wording in Coverdale's *Biblia* and the Great Bible. The second reproduces verbatim the wording in Tyndale's New Testament. The third epigraph varies from Tyndale's wording at three points: "alwaie" replaces "ever," "be thankfull" replaces "give thankes," and "us" replaces "you."

3. **O . . . them** KP renders Fisher's splicing of slightly recast excerpts from Exodus 34:6, Deuteronomy 10:17, and Psalm 145:6: "O Dominator Domine Deus omnipotens, magne et terribilis, qui coelum terram, mare, et omnia quae in eis sunt, verbo tuo fecisti." **O . . . God** The Exodus excerpt reads "O dominator domine deus" (O Lord of Lords, God). **almighty . . . dreadful** The Deuteronomy excerpt reads "Deus magnus, et potens, et terribilis" (God, great, powerful, and dreadful). **who . . . them** The Psalm excerpt reads "qui fecit caelum et terram, mare, et omnia, quae in eis sunt" (who made heaven and earth, the sea and all that is in them). KP does not translate Fisher's "verbo tuo" (by Thy word), perhaps recognizing that the Psalm excerpt does not contain the phrase.

4. **Nothing . . . works** KP closely renders Fisher's free paraphrase of excepts from Psalms 75:8 and 118:64: "Cuius potentia irresistibilis, et misericordia super omnia opera tua." The first excerpt reads "Tu terribilis es, et quis resistet tibi?" (Thou art fearsome, and who may resist Thee?). The second excerpt reads "Misericordia tua Domine plena est terra" (The earth is full of Thy mercy, Lord).

5. **All . . . creatures** KP freely renders Fisher's recast excerpts from Daniel 2:38: "In ditione tua universa sunt posita, anima omnis viventis, et spiritus universae humanae carnis" (Under thy dominion all things have been placed, all the breath of living things, and the spirit of all human flesh). The excerpts from Daniel, an address to King Nebuchadnezzar, read "omnia, in quibus habitant filii hominum, et bestiae agri . . . sub ditione tua universa constituit" (all [places], where the sons of men dwell, and the beasts of the field, . . . the whole has been placed under thy dominion). **dominion . . . rule** KP's doubling. **man . . . beast** KP's phrasing is closer to the Vulgate's than to Fisher's, suggesting that she recognized the source text.

Thou art merciful to whom Thou wilt, and hast compassion on whom it pleaseth Thee.[6]

[Aii v] Thy counsel shall stand for ever, and whatsoever Thou wilt shall be done.[7]

Power, dominion, and glory is Thine:[8] which art above all things, and in all things, and in us all.

Thou art Father of mercies, and God of all grace, peace, and comfort: which wilt not the death of a sinner, nor delightest in the damnation of souls.[9]

O Lord God, which art rich in mercy, and of Thine especial love towards us, even when we were Thine enemies, by sin, didst send into the world Thine only begotten Son Jesus Christ: that whosoever believeth duly in Him, shall not perish, but have everlasting life.[10]

[Aiii r] Have mercy upon me, have mercy upon me, according to Thy great mercy.

And according to the multitude of Thy mercies, put away mine offenses.

O God most holy, wash me from my wickedness, and make me clean from mine uncleanness.

For I acknowledge, O Lord, mine heinous sins, and accuse myself of mine unrighteous deeds.

6. **Thou . . . Thee** KP exchanges the main verbs in an otherwise close rendering of Fisher's recasting of an excerpt from Exodus 33:19: "miserebor cui voluero, et clemens ero in quem mihi placuerit" (I will be compassionate to whom I wish, and I will be merciful to whom it shall be pleasing to Me). The Cologne edition reads "Tu miseris" (Thou art merciful); the first English edition reads "Tu misereris" (Thou wilt be merciful). KP follows the former.

7. **Thy counsel . . . done** KP closely renders Fisher's nearly verbatim quotation of excerpts from Psalm 32:11 and Matthew 6:10: "Consilium tuum in sempiternum persistet, et omnis tua voluntas fiet." The Matthew excerpt is a clause in the Lord's Prayer.

8. **Power . . . Thine** KP closely renders Fisher's splicing of slightly recast excerpts from Jude 25: "Tua est potentia et imperium et gloria, qui es super omnia, et per omnia, et in omnibus nobis." The excerpts from Jude read "soli Deo . . . gloria et magnificentia, imperium et potestas" (to God alone . . . be glory and eminence, dominion and power).

9. **Thou . . . souls** KP closely renders Fisher's splicing of recast excerpts from 2 Corinthians 1:3, Ezekiel 33:11, and Tobias 3:22: "Pater misericordiarum et deus omnis gratiae, pacisque, ac consolationis, qui non vis mortem impii, nec delectaris in perditionibus animarum." The excerpt from 2 Corinthians reads "Pater misericordiarum, et Deus totius consolationis" (Father of mercies, and God of all consolation). The Ezekiel excerpt reads, in God's voice, "nolo mortem impii" (I do not wish the death of an impious man). The Tobias excerpt reads "Non . . . delectaris in perditionibus nostris" (Thou dost not delight in our perdition).

10. **O . . . life** KP renders Fisher's splicing of recast excerpts from Ephesians 2:4–5, 1 John 4:9, and John 3:16: "O Deus misericordia dives, qui propter nimiam charitatem tuam, qua dilexisti nos, etiam cum inimici tui essemus, unigenitum filium tuum Jesum Christum misisti in hunc mundum, ut omnis qui credit in eum, non pereat, sed habeat vitam aeternam" (O God rich in mercy, who on account of Thy great love, with which Thou hast loved us, even when we were Thy enemies, hast sent Thine only begotten Son, Jesus Christ, into this world, that all who believe in Him might not perish, but might have everlasting life). The excerpts from Ephesians

I confess against myself the wickedness of my heart, which hath been ever unfaithful, and rebelling against Thy precepts.[11]

I have been an untrue and a froward child to Thee, and have provoked Thee with my vanities.[12]

[Aiii v] O holy Father, I have offended Thy divine majesty, and am not worthy to be called Thy son.[13]

---

read "Deus . . . qui dives est in misericordiâ, propter nimium charitatem suam, quâ dilexit nos, et cum essemus mortui peccatis, convivificavit nos" (God, who is rich in mercy, on account of His very great love, with which He loved us, and when we were dead in sin, He revived us). KP's phrasing is closer to that of Ephesians than is Fisher's, suggesting that she recognized the source. The excerpt from 1 John reads "Filium suum unigenitum misit Deus in mundum" (God sent His only begotten Son into the world). The excerpt from John reads "ut omnis qui credit in ipsum non pereat, sed habeat vitam aeternam" (that all who believe in Him may not perish, but have everlasting life). **whosoever . . . life** KP's phrasing is identical with that of the Great Bible in John 3:16 except for her addition of "duly."

11. **Have mercy . . . precepts** KP renders Fisher's series of recast excerpts from Psalm 50:3–5: "Miserere mei, miserere mei secundum magnam misericordium tuam. Et secundum multitudinem miserationum tuarum dele transgressiones meas. Lava me deus sancte ab iniquitate mea, et ab immunditiis meis purga me. Scelera enim mea agnosco domine, et injusticias meas contra me pronuntio. Confiteor adversum me, impietatem cordis mei, nam erga te cor perfidum habui ac rebelle" (Have mercy on me, have mercy on me according to Thy great mercy. And according to the multitude of Thy mercies blot out my transgressions. Wash me, holy God, from my iniquity, and purge me from my uncleanness. I acknowledge my wicked acts, Lord, and I declare my injustices against myself. I confess against myself the impiety of my heart, for toward Thee I have had a faithless and rebellious heart). The Psalm excerpts read "Miserere mei Deus, secundum magnam misericordiam tuam. Et secundum multitudinem miserationum tuarum, dele iniquitatem meam . . . lave me ab iniquitate mea: et a peccata mea munda me. Quoniam iniquitatem meam ego cognosco: et peccatum meum contra me est semper" (Have mercy on me, God, according to Thy great mercy. And according to the multitude of thy mercies, expunge mine iniquity . . . Wash me from mine iniquity, and purge me from my uncleanness. For I acknowledge my evil deeds, Lord, and my sin is always before me). **most holy** KP's intensification of Fisher's "sancte" (holy). **heinous** KP's addition. **against . . . precepts** KP further expands Fisher's addition to the wording of Psalm 50:5.

12. **I . . . vanities** KP closely renders Fisher's recasting of excerpts from Deuteronomy 32:30–31: "Filius infidelis et exasperans, provocavi te in vanitatibus meus" (I, a faithless and exasperating son, have provoked Thee with my vanities). The Deuteronomy verses, spoken by God against the Israelites, read "generatio enim perversa est, et infideles filii, ipsi me provocaverunt . . . et irritaverunt in vanitatibus suis" (truly they are a perverse and faithless generation; they have provoked . . . and irritated Me with their vanities).

13. **O . . . son** KP closely renders Fisher's recasting of Luke 15:19–20: "Pater sancte peccavi in coelum et coram te, neque iam sum dignus vocari filius tuus." The verses in Luke, the prodigal son's confession to his father, read "Pater, peccavi in coelum et coram te: iam non sum dignus vocari filius tuus" (Father, I have sinned against heaven and before thee; now I am not worthy to be called thy son).

Because I provoked Thee to anger through the multitude of my sins, and have not exercised myself in Thy rightful laws.[14]

I have turned back from Thy ways, and done evil before Thee. I have done wickedly, and unjustly behaved myself, leaving Thy commandments, and murmuring against Thy correction.[15]

I have turned myself away, and not kept my promise made unto Thee; I have walked in an evil way after mine own thoughts and fantasies, choosing the things that Thou wouldst not.[16]

[Aiv r] O Lord God almighty, I have not feared Thee nor showed due reverence unto Thee: but I have been disobedient and stubborn against Thee.[17]

14. **Because . . . laws** **Because . . . sins** KP closely renders Fisher's recast excerpt from Psalm 5:11: "Quoniam irritavi iram tuam in multitudine iniquitatis meae" (Because I have provoked Thy anger with the multitude of my iniquities). The Psalm excerpt reads "secundum multitudinem impietatus eorum expelle eos, quoniam iritaverunt te Domine" (according to the multitude of their transgressions, cast them out, because they have rebelled against Thee, Lord). **have not . . . laws** KP's rendering follows the phrasing of the first English edition, Fisher's addition, "non meditatus sum in omnibus justiciis tuis" (I have not meditated on all Thy righteousness) rather than the phrasing of the Cologne edition, "mentitus sum" (I have spoken falsely about). **exercised . . . in** performed my religious duty to observe.

15. **have turned . . . correction** **have turned . . . ways** KP closely renders Fisher's "Reversus sum à viis tuis," apparently an allusive recasting of Isaiah 53:6, "unusquisque in viam suam declinavit" (everyone has turned into his own way). **done evil . . . commandments** KP closely renders Fisher's recasting of an excerpt from Daniel 9:5: "facerem malum in conspectu suo, impiè egi, et iniquè me gessi, relinquens mandata tua et detrahens correctioni tuae." The excerpt from Daniel reads "Peccavimus, iniquitatem fecimus, impie egimus, et recessimus, et declinavimus a mandatis tuis" (We have sinned, we have done evil and behaved impiously, and we have rebelled and departed from Thy commandments). **murmuring against** The participle in Fisher's added phrase is "detrahens," which primarily means "withdrawing" but can have the sense of "detracting" or "diminishing"—hence, KP's rendering.

16. **I have turned . . . not** **I have turned . . . unto Thee** KP freely renders Fisher's excerpting and recasting of Psalm 77:9–10, "Averti me, et non custodivi foedus tuum, ambulavi in via non bona" (I have turned myself away, and I have not kept Thy commandment; I have walked in a way not good). The Psalm excerpts read "conversi sunt. . . .Non custodierunt testamentum Dei. et in lege ejus noluerunt ambulare" (they turned back. . . . They did not keep the covenant of God, and they were not willing to walk in His law). **I have walked . . . fantasies** KP's phrasing is closer to Jeremiah 7:24 than is Fisher's brief, recast allusion: "ambulavi in via non bona post cogitationes meas" (I have walked in a way not good, according to my thoughts). The Vulgate reads "abierunt in voluntatibus, et in praevitate cordis sui mali" (they walked in the desires and in the perverse prompting of their evil heart). **choosing . . . not** KP closely renders Fisher's allusive recasting of the final words of Isaiah 65:12, "eligens ea quae tu noluisti." The Vulgate reads "quae nolui, elegistis" (you chose the things that I did not wish).

17. **O . . . Thee** KP closely renders Fisher's paraphrastic reacasting of Jeremiah 17:23: "Non te metui domine deus omnipotens, neque vultum tuam reveritus sum, inobediens fui, et cervicem meam induravi." The verse in Jeremiah reads "non audierunt, nec inclinaverunt aurem

As a common harlot is without shame, even so am I without shame of my sins: for, behold, I speak unto Thee, and yet I sin more and more.[18]

I have left that which is good, and gone back from Thee,[19] and I have not put my trust and hope in Thee, my Maker, but have sought for help and safeguard otherwise.

I have plowed wickedness, and reaped iniquity, and eaten the fruit of lies, because I have trusted in mine owne way.[20]

I have cast Thy laws behind my back, not regarding Thy commandments, nor leaving mine own lewd customs.[21]

[Aiv v] I have not given my heart to return to Thy paths, for I would not know Thee, but have fallen through mine iniquity.

I never unto this day turned truly unto Thee with all my heart; but as a woman

---

suam: sed induraverunt cervicem suam ne audirent me, et ne acciperent disciplinam" (they did not obey nor incline their ear, but stiffened their neck that they might not hear Me nor receive instruction).

18. **As . . . more As . . . sins** KP freely renders Fisher's recasting of an excerpt from Jeremiah 3:3 as an address of the soul to God: "Frons meretricis facta est mihi, nescio erubescere" (My forehead has become that of a whore; I do not know how to blush). The Jeremiah excerpt, God's address to faithless Israel, reads: "frons mulieris meretricis facta est tibi, noluisti erubescere" (Thy forehead became that of a whoring woman; thou didst refuse to blush). **I speak . . . more** KP closely renders Fisher's ironic inversion and recasting of Philippians 1:9, "loquor ad te, sed facio male magis ac magis." In the source St. Paul addresses a beloved congregation: "hoc oro ut charitas vestra magis et magis abundet . . . in omni sensu" (this I pray, that your love may abound more and more . . . with all feeling).

19. **I . . . Thee** KP's phrasing is closer to Jeremiah 15:6 than is Fisher's recasting, "Deservi bonum retrorsum abii" (I have left the good, I have gone backwards). The Jeremiah excerpt reads "Tu reliquisti me, dicit Dominus, retrorsum abiisti" (Thou hast left me, saith the Lord; thou hast gone backwards). **trust . . . hope** Fisher reads "spem" (hope). **help** Fisher reads "praesidium" (help, in the sense of defense). **safeguard** Fisher reads "securitatem" (safety, security).

20. **I . . . way** KP closely renders Fisher's recasting of Hosea 10:13 from the second person (God addressing an ungrateful Israel) to the first person (the soul's self-accusing): "Aravi impietatem, iniquitatem messui, comedi fructum mendacii, quia confisus sum in via mea." The Hosea excerpt reads "Arastis impietatem, iniquitatem messuistis, comedistis frugem mendacii: quia confisus es in viis tuis" (Thou hast plowed wickedness, thou hast reaped iniquity, thou hast eaten the fruit of lies, because thou didst trust in thy ways).

21. **I . . . customs I . . . back** KP closely renders Fisher's ironic recasting of phrasing in Isaiah 38:17 from the second person (the soul hailing God's forgiveness) to the first person (the soul's self-accusing before God): "Proieci legem tuam post tergum." The Isaiah excerpt reads "proiecisti post tergum tuum omnis peccata mea" (Thou hast cast all my sins behind Thy back). **not . . . commandments** KP closely renders Fisher's recasting of phrasing in Isaiah 48:18, "non adtendens mandato tuo" (not giving heed to Thy commandment). The Vulgate reads "Utinam attendisses mandata mea" (Would that thou hadst heeded My commandments). **mine . . . customs** Fisher reads "studiis meis pravis" (my perverse inclinations).

that breaketh her fidelity and promise unto her husband, even so, O Lord God, I have broken my promise unto Thee.

For I have lived abominably, and have had no remorse nor repentance for my evil deeds, but have run from sin to sin, following the lewd desires of my heart.[22]

Thou knowest all things, O Lord: how I have provoked Thee to displeasure by my lewd inventions, and none of all my sins be hid from Thee.[23]

[Av r] I hated Thy discipline and correction, and regarded not Thy words and sayings.[24]

I have not done penance for my malice, but have increased in much vanity.[25]

My heart hath been void of truth, and my hands have wrought unrighteousness.[26]

22. **I have not . . . my heart** KP quite closely renders three non-Biblical versicles composed by Fisher from vocabulary and imagery in Jeremiah 3:1, 9, 12–13, where Israel is berated as a promiscuous wife by God as her outraged husband. At several points KP heightens Fisher's phrasing: **have fallen** Fisher reads "impegi" (I have driven on). **truly** KP's addition. **that breaketh** KP omits "mendaciter" (falsely). **fidelity . . . promise** Fisher reads "fidem" (faith). **have lived** Fisher reads "feci" (have done). **have had . . . repentance** Fisher reads "nihil me poenituit" (I have repented nothing). **lewd** Fisher reads "pravas" (evil).

23. **Thou . . . Thee** KP closely renders Fisher's slight rephrasing of Psalm 68:6 to comprise the opening and closing clauses of this versicle: "Tu scis omnia domine . . . et universa mea delicta à te non sunt abscondita." The excerpt from Psalm 68 reads "Deus tu scis insipientiam meam: et delicta mea a te non sunt abscondita" (God, Thou knowest my foolishness: and my sins are not hid from Thee). **have . . . inventions** KP quite closely renders Fisher's insertion of a portion of a second verse between the two halves of the first—Psalm 105:29, recast from the third to the first person: "irritavi te in adinventionibus meis malis" (I have provoked Thee with my evil inventions). The excerpt from Psalm 105 reads "irritaverunt eum in adinventionibus suis" (they provoked Him with their inventions). **to displeasure** KP's addition.

24. **I hated . . . sayings** KP expands on Fisher's recasting of Psalm 49:17 from the second to the first person: "Exosam habui disciplinam tuam, et sermones tuos proieci retrorsum" (I hated Thy discipline exceedingly, and I cast Thy sayings behind). The Psalm verse reads "Tu vero odisti disciplinam: et proiecisti sermones meos retrorsum" (Thou hast truly hated discipline, and hast cast my sayings behind). **discipline . . . correction** KP's redoubling. **words . . . sayings** KP's redoubling.

25. **I have . . . vanity I have . . . malice** KP closely renders Fisher's recasting of vocabulary describing the boastful enemy of God in Psalm 51:3, 5: "De malitia mea poenitentiam non egi." The Psalm excerpt reads "Quid gloriaris in malitia . . . ? Dilexisti malitiam" (Why dost thou glory in malice . . . ? Thou hast loved malice). **but . . . vanity** KP renders Fisher's close paraphrase of the final clause of Psalm 51:9: "sed praevalui in vanitate multa." The Vulgate reads "et praevaluit in vanitate sua" (he was very strong in his vanity).

26. **My heart . . . unrighteousness** KP closely renders Fisher's reordering and negative recasting of phrases in Psalm 14:2–3: "In corde meo non fuit veritas, et injustitiam operatae sunt manus meae" (Truth was not in my heart, and my hands have wrought injustice). The Psalm excerpt reads "operatur justitiam: qui loquitur veritatem in corde suo" (he hath wrought justice: he who hath spoken truth in his heart).

My tongue hath spoken sinfully, and I have labored with the imagination of my heart to find out lies and deceits, and no truth hath been in my ways.[27]

I have accustomed my tongue to speake trifles and vanities, fulfilling my fleshly delights and thoughts; my purposes and inventions have been contrary to Thy will, whereby I have offended the eyes of Thy majesty.[28]

[Av v] Thou hast seen all these things, O Lord, and hast holden Thy peace; and yet they were evil in Thy sight, and displeased Thee.

In Thy anger Thou hast cast me away,[29] and art divided from me now many days.

Thou hast given me up to the desires of my heart:[30] to do the things which be not seeming.

Woe I am, that I have gone from Thee; great is my misery, that I have led my life in sin.[31]

Woe is me, that I have forsaken Thee to do my devices, not after Thy mind: to

27. **My . . . ways** KP freely renders Fisher's non-Biblical versicle by drawing on vocabulary and images from Jeremiah—the lying tongue, deceitful intent, and refusal to speak the truth (9:5, 8), especially the reiterated references to the imagination of an evil heart (3:17; 7:24; 11:8; 16:12; 18:12). Fisher's own wording is more generic and general: "Loquutus sum iniquitatem et dolos parturiui, meditatus sum cum corde meo verba mendacii, et consumpta est in viis meis veritas" (I have spoken iniquity and I have brought forth deceit; I have meditated with my heart upon lying words, and by my ways truth hath been brought to naught).

28. **I have . . . Thy majesty** KP quite closely renders Fisher's non-Biblical versicle, which employs recast excerpts from Isaiah 59:2–4. Fisher reads "Adsuefeci linguam meam loqui vanitates, perficiens voluntatem carnis et cogitationum, studia, et adinventiones meae contra te domine deus, ut provocarem [1544: et provocavi] oculos maiestatis tuae" (I have accustomed my tongue to speak vanities, fulfilling the will and thoughts of the flesh; my endeavors and imaginations have been opposed to Thee, Lord God, so that I have provoked the eyes of Thy majesty). The respective excerpts from Isaiah read "iniquitates vestrae diviserunt inter vos et Deum vestrum, et peccata vestra absconderunt faciem ejus a vobis . . . labia vestra locuta sunt mendacium, et lingua vestra iniquitatem fatur . . . confidunt in nihilo, et loquuntur vanitates: conceperunt laborem, et pepererunt iniquitatem" (your iniquities have separated between you and your God, and your sins have hid His face from you . . . your lips have spoken lies, and your tongue hath uttered iniquity . . . they [the sinners being addressed] trust in nothing at all and speak vanities: they conceive trouble and bring forth iniquity). **trifles . . . vanities** "vanitates" (Fisher, Vulgate). **Thy will** Fisher reads "te" (Thee).

29. **Thou . . . away** KP closely renders Fisher's non-Biblical versicles, which seem loosely modeled on recast excerpts from Isaiah 57:18, 11, 17: "Vidisti haec omnia Domine, et tacuisti, sed malum fuit in oculis tuis, et non placuit tibi. In indignatione tua repudiasti me." The respective excerpts from Isaiah read, in God's voice, "Vias ejus vidi . . . ego tacens, et quasi non videns. . . . Propter iniquitatem . . . ejus iratus sum, et percussi eum" (I have seen his ways . . . and I hold my peace as if I see not. . . . Because of his iniquity, I was wrathful, and I smote him).

30. **Thou . . . my heart** KP closely renders Fisher's recasting of Psalm 139:9 from a negative plea to a positive assertion: "Tradidisti me in desideria cordis mei." The Psalm verse reads "ne tradas me Domine a desiderio meo peccatori" (Give me not over, Lord, to my delight as a sinner).

31. **in sin** Fisher reads "flagitose" (shamefully).

accomplish my thoughts, which have not proceeded of Thy Spirit, but have heaped up sin upon sin.[32]

[Avi r] Mine infamy and reproach is daily before mine eyes, and for shame I dare not show my face.[33]

And now, O Lord God, why forgettest Thou me? why keepest Thou away so long Thy mercy from me?[34]

Hear now my cause graciously although Thou hast been displeased with me a great while, for Thou art merciful; be not angry always, I beseech Thee.[35]

Cast not away a contrite and a penitent person, a wretch and an abject, which humbly calleth upon Thy name.

Turn again a little toward me, O Lord God, and forgive me my mischievous deeds.[36]

[Avi v] Order me not according to my sins, nor punish me as my wickedness deserveth.[37]

32. **Woe . . . sin** KP renders Fisher's quite close recasting of Isaiah 30:1: "Vae mihi desertori, ut facerem consilia, et non ex te, et perficerem cogitationes, sed non ex spiritu tuo: propterea congregationes peccati super peccatum" (Woe is me that I have forsaken Thee to carry out intentions not proceeding from Thee, and to accomplish thoughts not proceeding from Thy spirit: in me, therefore, hordes of sins upon sins). The verse in Isaiah reads "Vae filii desertores, dicit Dominus, ut faceratis consilium et non ex me: et ordiremini telam, et non per spiritum meum, ut adderatis peccatum super peccatum" (Woe to forsaking sons, saith the Lord, that you will take counsel, but not from Me: and begin to weave a covering, but not of My Spirit, that you may add sin upon sin).

33. **infamy . . . face** **infamy . . . reproach** "ignominia" (Fisher). **for shame . . . face** Fisher reads "pudor faciem meam obtegit" (shame covers up my face).

34. **And . . . me?** KP closely renders Fisher's splicing of recast phrasing from Psalm 41:10 and Isaiah 63:15: "Et tu domine deus, quare oblivisceris mei? et tam diu contines misericordiam tuam à me?" The first verse reads "dicam Deo . . . quare oblitus mei?" (I will say unto God . . . why hast Thou forgotten me?). The second verse reads "ubi est . . . multitudo . . . miserationum tuarum? super me continuerent se?" (where is the multitude . . . of Thy mercies? are they restrained from me?).

35. **Hear . . . Thee** KP closely renders Fisher's recast excerpts from Psalm 102:8–9: "Suscipe causam meam post longam iram tuam, misericors enim es, ne irascaris obsecro imperpetuum" (Take up my cause after Thy long anger, for Thou art merciful; I pray, be not angry forever). The excerpts read "Miserator, et misericors Dominus: longanimis, et multum misericors. Non in perpetuum irascetur" (The Lord is pitying and merciful, long-suffering, and greatly merciful. He will not be angry forever).

36. **Turn . . . deeds** KP closely renders Fisher's recast excerpts from Isaiah 10:25: "Revertere aliquantulum domine deus, et exorabilis esto super sceleribus meis." The excerpts read "Adhuc enim paululum modicumque et consummabitur . . . furor meus super scelus eorum" (For yet a very little while . . . and My fury at their evildoing will cease).

37. **Order . . . deserveth** KP freely renders Fisher's recasting of Psalm 102:10: "Ne facias mihi juxta peccata mea, et secundum iniquitates meas ne reddas mihi" (Do not unto me according to my sins, nor render unto me according to my iniquities). The verse reads "Non secundum pec-

Show not forth Thy power against a poor wretch; persecute him not so sore,[38] which is without all strength.

Turn not Thy face away from my prayers,[39] but according to Thy promises take me again unto Thy favor.

For I am Thine, O righteous Father, whom Thy only dear Son hath redeemed with His precious blood.[40]

And now my soul abhorreth my old conversation; and of Thee, which art Judge of all men,[41] I ask mercy.

I do submit myself under Thy mighty hand, for after Thine anger Thou showest mercy, and in the time of tribulation Thou dost forgive sins.[42]

[Avii r] I acknowledge that I am a sinner, beseeching Thee, Lord God almighty, of Thy goodness, to do with me accordingly to Thy great mercy.

I am confounded and ashamed to lift up mine eyes unto Thee, for my sins are ascended up unto Thy sight.[43]

---

cata nostra fecit nobis: neque secundum iniquitates nostras retribuit nobis" (He hath not done with us according to our sins, nor hath He rendered unto us according to our iniquities).

38. **persecute . . . sore** KP's rendering follows Fisher's wording in the 1544 English edition, "nec eum cui nullus est virtus, tam dure persequaris" (persecute him not so hard, who has no strength), rather than that of the Cologne edition, "nec est, cui nulla est virtus, tam dure persequaris" (nor is there strength, there is none, in him that thou persecutest so hard). The Vulgate uses "persequor" (to persecute) only once in reference to an act of God, in Job 19:22.

39. **Turn . . . prayers** KP boldly recasts Fisher's blander wording: "Veniant preces meae ante vultum tuum" (Let my prayers come before Thy face).

40. **Thy . . . blood** KP closely renders Fisher's splicing of recast phrases from 1 Peter 1:18–19 and John 3:16: "precioso suo sanguine redemit unicus tibi natus" (Thine only Son, redeemed with His precious blood). The phrases from 1 Peter read "redempti estis . . . pretioso sanguine . . . Christi" (you have been redeemed . . . with the precious blood . . . of Christ). Phrasing from John 3 reads "Deus . . . Filium suum unigenitum daret" (God . . . gave His only begotten Son).

41. **my . . . men my . . . conversation** KP heightens Fisher's recasting of an excerpt from Leviticus 26:30: "abhominatur anima mea vitam meam" (my soul abhorreth my life). The Leviticus excerpt reads "abominabitur vos anima mea" (my soul shall abhor you). **Judge . . . men** KP renders Fisher's allusion to Hebrews 12:23, "judicem omnium," which reads "judicem omnium Deum" (God, Judge of all men) in the Vulgate.

42. **I . . . sins I . . . hand** KP closely renders Fisher's allusion to 1 Peter 5:6, "Humilio me sub potenti tua manu." The verse reads "Humiliamini . . . sub potenti manu Dei" (Humble yourselves under the mighty hand of God). **after . . . mercy** KP closely renders Fisher's recasting of Psalm 59:3: "cum iratus fueris, misericordiam facis." The verse reads "iratus es, et misertus es nobis" (Thou wast angry, and Thou wast compassionate to us). **in . . . sins** KP closely renders Fisher's recasting of Ecclesiasticus 2:13: "in tempore tribulationis peccata dimittis." The verse reads "Deus . . . remittet in die tribulationis peccata" (God will remit sins in the day of tribulation).

43. **I am . . . sight** KP closely renders Fisher's recasting of 1 Esdras 9:6: "Confundor et erubesco levare faciem meam ad te, quoniam delicta mea adscenderunt in conspectum tuum" (I am

Against Thee, O Father, against Thee I have sinned, and done evil before Thee;[44] Thou seest that mine iniquity is great.

Truly I have been an offender against Thee, even from my cradle; and since I sucked my mother's breasts I have not ceased to do evil.[45]

[Avii v] Behold, I was begotten in iniquity, and my mother brought me into this world defiled with sin.[46]

For the corn of an evil seed is sowed in my heart, and how much wickedness hath sprung thereof unto this day, Thou knowest, O Lord.[47]

I cannot shake off my sins and offenses,[48] but I carry still with me the infamy of my youth.

Behold, Lord, I am sold under sin, and in my flesh I find not that which is good.

For the good that I would, that do I not, but the evil that I hate, that I do.[49]

---

confounded and I am ashamed to raise my face toward Thee, for my sins have ascended into Thy sight). The verse reads "Deus meus confundor et erubesco levare faciem meum ad te: quoniam iniquitates nostrae multiplicatae sunt super caput nostrum" (My God, I am confounded and I am ashamed to raise my face toward Thee, for our multiplied iniquities are over our head).

44. **Against . . . Thee** KP's rendering is closer to the Vulgate than is Fisher's expanded and recast phrasing from Psalm 50:6: "In te, in te pater, peccavi, et quod malum est in oculis tuis admisi" (Against Thee, against Thee, Father, have I sinned, and done that which is evil in Thy sight). The Vulgate reads "Tibi soli peccavi, et malum coram te feci" (Against Thee only have I sinned, and done evil before Thee).

45. **Truly . . . evil** KP freely renders Fisher's negative recasting of locutions in Psalm 21:10–11 that are unique in the Bible: "Profectò in te praevaricatus sum ab incunabilis meis usque in hunc diem, iugiter faciens malum ab uberibus matris meae" (Truly I have been a transgressor from my cradle even to this day, from my mother's breasts continually doing evil). The unique phrases, which permit identification of the allusion, read "tu es . . . spes mea ab uberibus matris meae . . . de ventre matris meae Deus meus es tu" (Thou hast been . . . my hope from my mother's breasts . . . from my mother's womb hast Thou been my God).

46. **Behold . . . sin** KP moderates Fisher's rhetorically heightened rendering of Psalm 50:7: "En ego in iniquitate genitus sum, et peccato inquinatum enixa est me mater mea" (Behold, I was engendered in iniquity, and my exhausted mother conceived me defiled with sin). The verse reads "Ecce enim in iniquitatibus conceptus sum: et in peccatis concepit me mater mea" (Behold, I was truly conceived in iniquity, and in sin did my mother conceive me).

47. **corn . . . Lord** KP closely renders Fisher's "Granum . . . seminis mali," which he evidently invented as a negative analogue of the Vulgate's "granum sinapis" (grain of mustard seed). That grain is variously compared to the kingdom of heaven and to faith in Matthew 13:21 and 17:19; Mark 4:31; Luke 13:19 and 17:6. **Thou . . . Lord** "tu noscis domini." The Cologne edition lacks this phrase, which the first English edition appends.

48. **I . . . offenses** KP elaborates Fisher's prosaic "Transgressiones meae mecum sunt" (My transgressions are with me—i.e., remain with me).

49. **I am sold . . . I do** KP closely renders Fisher's recasting and reordering of excerpts from Romans 7:14, 15, 18: "sub peccato venundatus sum, et non invenio in carne mea bonum. Siq-

All the thoughts and imaginations of my heart have been set to do evil, ever since I was young.[50]

[Aviii r] O why do I die in my sins, Lord God, seeing Thy will is not that a sinner die, but return from his sin and live?[51]

For Thou art good and merciful, and according to Thy great mercy, savest them that be unworthy.[52]

For albeit no man is able to bear the punishment which Thou dost threaten against sinners, yet the mercy which Thou hast promised is great and unsearchable.[53]

---

uidem quod volo bonum, illud non ago: sed quod odio mihi est malum, id facio." The excerpts read "sum venundatus sub peccato . . . non enim quod volo bonum, hoc ago: sed quod odi, malum, illud facio . . . . quià non habitat . . . in carne meâ, bonum" (I am sold under sin . . . the good that I wish, that I do not do: but the evil that I hate, that I do . . . because good doth not dwell in my flesh).

50. **All . . . young** KP elaborates Fisher's recasting of Genesis 8:21: "Cuncta cogitatio cordis mei adposita est ad malum omni tempore ab adolescentia mea" (Every thought of my heart hath been set on evil, for all the time from my youth). The verse reads "sensus . . . et cogitatio humani cordis in malum prona sunt ab adolescentia sua" (the intent . . . and thought of the human heart have been prone to evil from its youth).

51. **O why . . . and live?** KP renders Fisher's recasting and reordering of phrasing in Ezekiel 33:11: "Et quare morior in peccatis meis domine deus omnipotens? quum tibi not sit voluntas ut moriatur impius, tantum ut reveratur et vivat" (And why do I die in my sins, Lord God almighty? for it is not Thy will that a sinner die, rather that he turn again and live). The excerpts from Ezekiel read "Dic ad eos . . . Dicit Dominus Deus: nolo mortem impii, sed ut convertatur impius a via sua, et vivat . . . et quare moriemini domus Israel?" (Say to them. . . . The Lord God saith, I do not wish the death of a sinner, but that the sinner be converted from his way, and live . . . and why will ye die, O house of Israel?). Similar wording, but without the final question, is found in Ezekiel 18:23.

52. **Thou . . . unworthy** KP renders Fisher's recasting of phrases from Numbers 14:18–19: "Tu etenim bonus es, et propitiabilis, qui etiam indignos salvas, iuxta magnam misericordiam tuam." The Vulgate reads "Dominus . . . auferens iniquitatem et scelera, . . . Dimitte . . . peccatum populi huius secundum magnitudinem misericordiae tuae" (Lord . . . forgiving of iniquity and transgression . . . Pardon . . . the iniquity of this people according to the greatness of Thy mercy). **merciful** propitiabilis.

53. **For . . . unsearchable** KP renders Fisher's splicing of recast excerpts from Jeremiah 10:10 and Romans 11:32–33: "Quanquam enim insustentabilis sit ira super peccatores comminationis tuae, immensa tamen et impervestigabilis misericordia promissionis tuae" (For although the wrath of Thy threatenings against sinners is unbearable, yet the mercy of Thy promises is great and unsearchable). The Jeremiah excerpt reads "ab indignatione ejus commovebitur terra: et non sustinebunt gentes comminationem ejus" (at His wrath the earth will tremble, and the nations will not be able to bear His indignation). The excerpts from Romans read "Conclusit enim Deus . . . ut omnium misereatur. O altitudo . . . quàm incomprehensibilia sunt judicia ejus" (For God hath concluded . . . that He might have mercy upon all. O the height . . . how incomprehensible are His judgments).

Thou hast showed mercy a thousand times heretofore, to make Thy name glorious[54] as it is even yet still.

The old fathers in their necessities cried unto Thee, and Thou didst deliver them; they put their trust in Thee, and they were not confounded.[55]

[Aviii v] When they were at their wits' end and wist not what to do, this was their only refuge: to lift up their eyes to Thee.[56]

Thou didst save them for Thy name's sake, to show in them Thy might and strength.[57]

Many a time they provoked Thee through their iniquities, and stirred Thy goodness to displeasure.

Yet when Thou sawest their tribulation, and their lowly submission unto Thee, Thou didst remember Thy promise, and by and by hadst pity and compassion upon them according to the multitude of Thy mercies.[58]

54. **Thou . . . glorious** **Thou . . . times** KP closely renders Fisher's recasting of an excerpt from Exodus 20:6: "Tu fecisti misericordiam in millibus." The excerpt reads "faciens misericordiam in millis"—a reference to God "showing mercy unto thousands." **glorious** KP's substitution for Fisher's "magna" (great).

55. **The old . . . confounded** KP closely renders Fisher's excerpting of Psalm 21:5–6: "Patres antiqui in angustiis suis ad te clamaverunt, et tu liberasti eos, in te speraverunt, et non sunt confusi." The excerpts read "In te speraverunt patres nostri . . . et liberasti eos. Ad te clamaverunt, . . . in te speraverunt, et non sunt confusi" (Our fathers put their trust in Thee . . .. and Thou didst deliver them. Unto Thee they cried, . . . in Thee they put their trust, and they were not confounded).

56. **When . . . Thee** KP renders Fisher's recasting of 2 Paralipomenon (2 Chronicles) 20:12: "Cum non haberent ultra quod agerent, hoc solum restabat, ut oculos suos ad te dirigerent" (When they did not know what else to do, this alone remained [to them], that they directed their eyes toward Thee). The verse reads "cum ignoremus quid agere debeamus, hoc solum habemus residui, ut oculos nostros dirigamus ad te" (when we did not know what we ought to do, this alone we had remaining [to us], that we directed our eyes toward Thee). **at their . . . do** KP's colloquial expansion of "quid agera debeamus" (what we ought to do).

57. **Thou . . . strength** KP renders Fisher's splicing of recast excerpts from Psalm 105:8 and Exodus 9:16: "Salvasti eos propter nomen tuum, ut ostenderes in eis fortitudinem tuam." The Psalm excerpt reads "salvavit eos propter nomen suum" (He saved them for His name's sake). The Exodus excerpt reads "posui te, ut ostendam in te fortitudinem meam" (I raised thee up, to show in thee My strength). **might . . . strength** KP's expansion of "fortitudinem."

58. **Yet . . . mercies** KP closely renders Fisher's excerpting and recasting of Exodus 6:5: "Et [1544: At tu] quum tribulationem eorum, et eos tibi supplices vidisses, Recordatus pacti tui, poenituit te [1544: misertus es eis] juxta multitudinem miserationum tuarum." The Exodus verse reads "Ego audivi gemitum filiorum Israel, quo Ægyptii oppresserunt eos: et recordatus pacti mei, statim misertus es eis juxta multitudinem miserationum tuarum" (I have heard the groaning of the children of Israel, how the Egyptians oppress them, and I remembered My covenant. Thou hadst mercy upon them according to the multitude of Thy mercies).

[Bi r] Have mercy upon me, O Lord God omnipotent, have mercy upon me, for I am a miserable and a wretched creature. Make me whole, I beseech Thee, whom Thou hast stricken for my sin and iniquity.[59]

My soul is troubled greatly; and how long, O Lord, wilt Thou not look towards me?[60]

How long wilt Thou reject my prayer, thus crying out unto Thee? Wilt Thou hear me at no time? How long wilt Thou turn away Thy face from me?[61]

Where be Thy old mercies, O Lord, whom[62] Thou hast stablished in Thy truth?

Wilt Thou now, O Lord God, cease to show mercy? or wilt Thou withdraw Thy goodness for displeasure?[63]

[Bi v] Hast Thou cast me away forever, that Thou wilt never hereafter be pleased with me?[64]

59. **Have . . . iniquity** KP renders Fisher's splicing of recast and elaborated phrasing from Psalm 6:3 and Isaiah 53:8: "Miserere mei, miserere mei, o domine deus omnipotens, nam miser et infelix ego sum; sana me obsecro, quem percussisti propter iniquitatem meam" (Have mercy upon me, have mercy upon me, O Lord God omnipotent, for I am poor and wretched; heal me, I pray, whom Thou hast stricken on account of my iniquity). The Psalm excerpt reads "miserere mei Domine quoniam infirmus sum: sana me" (have mercy upon me, Lord, for I am weak: heal me). The Isaiah excerpt reads "propter scelus populi mei percussi eum" (on account of the wickedness of My people have I stricken him). The verse from Isaiah has traditionally been interpreted as a prefiguration of Christ's passion. **sin . . . iniquity** KP's doubling.

60. **My . . . me** KP closely renders Fisher's splicing of recast phrases from Psalm 12:1 and John 12:27: "Anima mea vehementer turbata est, et tu domine quousque non respicies?" The first part of the Psalm verse reads "Nunc anima mea turbata est" (Now my soul is troubled); the second part reads "Usquequo Domine . . . avertis faciem tuam a me?" (How long, Lord . . . wilt Thou turn Thy face from me?). The wording in the excerpt from John is a nearly verbatim rendering of an utterance by Christ from the cross.

61. **how . . . me?** KP renders Fisher's second and closer paraphrase of Psalm 12:1: "quousque avertes faciem tuam à me?" See the preceding note for the Vulgate reading of this excerpt.

62. **Where . . . whom** **Where . . . Lord** KP closely renders Fisher's verbatim quotation of Psalm 88:50: "Ubi sunt misericordiae tuae antiquae domine?" **whom** a no longer current variant of "which."

63. **Wilt . . . displeasure** KP renders Fisher's free paraphrase of Psalm 76:10: "Num iam desines misereri deus? aut reprimes per iram bonitatem tuam?" (Wilt Thou cease, God, to be merciful? wilt Thou in anger hold back Thy goodness?). The verse reads "Aut obliviscetur misereri Deus? aut continebit in ira sua misericordias suas?" (Hath God forgotten to be merciful? hath He in His anger shut up His mercies?).

64. **Hast . . . me** KP renders Fisher's recasting of Psalm 76:8: "Num projecisti in eternum, ut nunquam posthac sis placidus?" (Wilt Thou cast off forever, that Thou wilt never be pleased hereafter?). The verse reads "Numquid in aeternum projiciet Deus: aut non apponet ut complacitior sit adhuc?" (Will God cast off forever, so that He will not be more favorable hereafter?).

Thy hand is not weakened, but it may help;[65] and Thy ears be not stopped, that they refuse to hear.

How long shall my mind be troubled with painful and heavy thoughts? How long shall sorrow torment my heart?

How long shall mine enemy have the overhand of me? Look towards me, Lord God, and hear my prayer.

Give light to my eyes, for I have slept too long in death, and my sins have prevailed against me.[66]

[Bii r] Turn again, O Lord, turn again, and deliver my soul; and save me for Thy great mercy's sake.[67]

Lo, now is the accepted time; now be the days of health and grace.[68]

In death who shall remember Thee? or in hell who shall laud or praise Thee?[69]

65. **Thy . . . help** KP closely renders Fisher's recast phrasing from Numbers 11:23: "Et manus tua non est invalida, quin juvare potest." The Vulgate excerpt is briefer: "Numquid manus Domini invalida est?" (Is the hand of the Lord weak?).

66. **How long shall my mind . . . against me?** KP closely renders Fisher's slightly recast phrasing from Psalm 12:2–4: "Quamdiu voluam cogitationes amaras cum animo meo? quanto tempore dolor cor meum torquebit? Quousque tandem superabit me inimicus meus? respice, et exaudi me o domine deus. Illumina oculos meos, diutius enim obdormivi, morte" (How long will I turn bitter thoughts in my soul? For how much time will sorrow wrench my heart? How long will my enemy rise above me? Look, and help me, O Lord God. Enlighten my eyes, lest I fall asleep in death). The Psalm passage reads "Quamdiu ponam consilia in anima mea, dolorem in corde meo per diem? Usequequo exaltabitur inimicus meus super me? Respice, et exaudi me Domine Deus meus. Illumina oculos meos ne umquam obdormiam in morte" (How long will I take counsel in my soul, having sorrow in my heart daily? How long will my enemy be exalted over me? Look, and help me, my Lord God. Enlighten my eyes, that I may never fall asleep in death). **painful . . . heavy** KP's doubling. **have . . . overhand of** KP's idiomatic rendering of "superabit" (be exalted over).

67. **Turn . . . sake** KP closely renders Fisher's slight recasting of Psalm 6:5: "Revertere, Domine, revertere, ut eripias animam meam, et salvum me facias propter magnam misericordiam tuam." The verse reads "Convertere Domine, et eripe animam meam: salvum me fac propter misericordiam tuam" (Return, O Lord, and deliver my soul: save me for Thy mercy's sake).

68. **Lo . . . grace** KP closely renders Fisher's quotation of 2 Corinthians 6:2, to which he adds a concluding doublet: "Ecce nunc tempus acceptabile, ecce nunc dies salutis et gratiae" (Behold, now is the acceptable time; now are the days of salvation and grace). The Vulgate reads identically except for omitting "et gratiae" (and grace). **of health** of spiritual well-being, of salvation; "salutis" (of salvation).

69. **In death . . . Thee?** KP renders Fisher's recasting of Psalm 6:6: "In morte quaenam erit memoria tui? aut in inferno quis confitebitur tibi?" (In death what memory shall be of Thee? or in hell who shall acknowledge Thee?). The verse reads "Quoniam non est in morte qui memor sit tui: in inferno autem quis confitebitur tibi?" (Since in death there is none who remembers Thee, who then will acknowledge Thee in hell?). **shall laud . . . praise** KP's doublet, rendering "confitebitur" (will acknowledge).

He that liveth, he that liveth, shall praise Thee, and shall make Thy mercy known.[70]

Lord, rebuke me not in Thine anger, nor punish me in Thy great displeasure.

Cast not Thy darts at me, nor lay not Thy heavy hand upon me.[71]

For I have borne Thine anger a long while, and of the cup of Thy high displeasure I have drunk very deep.[72]

[Bii v] There is no health in my flesh for fear of Thy displeasure; I have no peace nor rest when I behold my sins.

My iniquities be gone over my head, and like an heavy burden they daily press me down.

The wounds in my soul do fester and stink, even through mine own folly.

I am a wretch cast away from Thy favor and presence, and go mourning all the day long.

My soul is full of filthiness, and no part of me is whole and sound.

Wherefore my enemies do persecute me the more; the greatness of my pain maketh me to roar and cry.

[Biii r] My heart fainteth and trembleth within me, and my strength is gone away.

O Lord, Thou knowest my desire, and Thou seest my necessity.[73]

70. **He . . . known** KP closely renders Fisher's partial recasting of Isaiah 38:19: "Vivens vivens ipse te laudabit, et notam faciet misericordiam tuam" (The living, the living himself shall praise Thee, and shall make Thy mercy known). The Vulgate reads "Vivens vivens ipse confitebitur tibi . . . : pater filiis notam faciet veritatem tuam" (The living, the living shall himself acknowledge Thee . . . : the father shall make Thy truth known to his children).

71. **Lord . . . upon me** KP freely renders Fisher's partial recasting of Psalm 37:2–3: "Domine, in ira tua ne arguas me, neque in furore tuo ultionem de me sumas. Ne jacias ad me tela tua, neque adgraves super me manum tuam" (Lord, in Thy anger rebuke me not, nor lay hold of me in Thy avenging wrath. Cast not Thy darts at me, nor lay the heavy weight of Thy hand upon me). The verse reads "Domine ne in furore tuo arguas me, neque in ira tua corripias me. Quoniam sagittae tuae infixae sunt mihi: et confirmasti super me manum tuam" (Lord, rebuke me not in Thy wrath, neither seize me in Thy anger. For Thy arrows have stuck in me, and Thou hast laid Thy hand firmly upon me).

72. **For . . . deep** KP renders Fisher's recasting of imagery from Isaiah 51:17: "Iram tuam diuitius tuli, et de calice fuoris tui plus satis bibi" (I have borne Thine anger very long, and I have drunk more than enough from the cup of Thy wrath). The verse reads "Ierusalem . . . bibisti de manu Domini calicem irae ejus: usque ad fundum calicis . . . bibisti, usque ad faeces" (Jerusalem . . . you have drunk from the hand of the Lord the cup of His anger to the bottom . . . you have drunk to the dregs). **very deep** KP's rephrasing of Fisher"s "plus satis" (more than enough).

73. **There . . . necessity** KP freely renders Fisher's often paraphrastic handling of an extended sequence of verses from Psalm 37. **There . . . down** Fisher renders verses 4–5 thus: "Non est sanitas in carne à facie irae tuae, nulla mihi pax à facie peccatorum meorum. Iniquitates meae supergressae sunt caput meum, et velut pondus immane quotidie me premunt" (There is no health in my flesh in the face of Thy wrath, no peace for me in the face of my sins). The first clause reads identically in the Vulgate; the second clause reads "non est pax ossibus meis a facie

Forgive me all my sins, O Lord God almighty, for Thy own sake, and put out of Thy sight my heinous offenses; for according to Thy goodness Thou hast promised forgiveness of sins ofttimes to them that do penance.[74]

Have mercy on me, Lord, for the glory and honor of Thy name, and be no longer displeased with me; and then Thou shalt surely be known to be just and true in Thy words, and shalt overcome when Thou art judged.[75]

---

peccatorum meorum. Quoniam iniquitates meae supergressae sunt caput meum: et sicut onus grave gravatae sunt super me" (there is no peace in my bones in the face of my sins. For my iniquities are gone over my head: and like a heavy weight they weigh me down). **The wounds . . . sound** Fisher renders verses 6–8 thus: "Foetorem exhalant cicatrices meae propter stultitiam meam. Miser sum, et abiectus à facie tua, omni die merens ingredior. Anima mea plena est immunditiis, et in me toto nihil est sanum" (My wounds emit a stench on account of my folly. I am wretched, and cast away from Thy face: I go mourning all the day. My soul is full of uncleanness, and in the whole of me, nothing is sound). The Vulgate reads "Putruerunt et corruptae sunt cicatrices meae, a facie insipientiae meae. Miser factus sum, et curvatus sum usque in finem: tota die contristatus ingrediebar. Quoniam lumbi mei impleti sunt illusionibus: et non est sanitas in carne mea" (My wounds are rotted, and they stink on account of my foolishness. I am made wretched, and I am bowed toward the end; all the day I go sorrowing because my limbs are filled with deceits, and there is no health in my flesh). **favor . . . presence** KP's doublet. **Wherefore . . . away** Fisher renders verses 9–10 thus: "Hinc fit ut inimici mei crudelius me persequantur [1544: persequuntur] obrugio prae magnitudine doloris mei. Cor meum in me fluctuabundum est, et fortitudo mea à me recessit. Domine notum est tibi desiderium meum, et necessitas mea te minime latet" (Whence it is that my enemies persecute me cruelly, I roar for the greatness of my pain. My heart is vacillating within me, and my strength goeth away from me. Lord, my desire is known unto Thee, and my necessity hideth little from Thee). The Vulgate reads "Afflictus sum, et humiliatus sum nimis: rugiebam a gemitu cordis mei. Domine, ante te omne desiderium meum: et gemitus meus a te non est absconditus" (I have been afflicted, and I have been too much humbled; I have roared from the groaning in my heart. Lord, all my desire is before Thee, and my groaning is not hidden from Thee). **roar . . . cry** KP's doublet.

74. **Forgive . . . penance** KP renders Fisher's splicing of recast phrases from Psalms 24:11 and 50:3 and Luke 3:3: "Propitius esto peccatis meis propter temetipsum o domine deus omnipotens, et scelera mea coram te deleantur, nam secundum bonitatem tuam promisisti poenitentiam remissionis peccatorum" (Be propitious toward my sins for Thy name's sake, O Lord God omnipotent, and let my wickedness be effaced before Thee, for Thou hast promised, according to Thy goodness, remission of sins for penitence). **Forgive . . . sake** Psalm 24:11 reads "Propter nomen tuum Domine propitiaberis peccato meo" (For Thy name's sake, Lord, be propitious toward my sin). Psalm 50:3 reads "dele iniquitatem meam" (efface my iniquity). Luke 3: 3 describes John the Baptist's preaching: "praedicans baptismum poenitentiae in remissionem peccatorum" (preaching the baptism of penitence/ repentance for the remission of sins). KP's rendering of "poenitentia" as "penance"—not "repentance"—aligns her with a traditionalist theological outlook; see my introduction, pp. 201–2.

75. **glory . . . judged glory . . . honor** KP's doublet; Fisher reads "gloriam." **and then . . . judged** KP renders Fisher's recasting of phrasing from Psalm 50:6: "et tum vere justus agnosceris in verbis tuis, et vinces quum de te judicabitur" (and then Thou shalt be known as truly just in Thy words, and shalt prevail when judgment is passed on Thee). The Psalm phrases read "ut justificeris in sermonibus tuis, et vincas cum judicaris" (that Thou be justified in Thy sayings, and prevail when Thou judgest).

For by this, Thy great grace shall be known: that Thou takest mercy on them which have not whereof they may glory in Thy sight.

[Biii v] And all the dwellers on the earth shall learn and know Thy goodness, when Thou shalt confer and give Thy benefits to us for Thy great name's sake, and not after our evil ways[76] and wicked deeds.

Verily, Lord God, except Thou show unto us Thy manifold mercies, the world shall not have life, nor they that dwell therein.

And if Thou help us not with Thy goodness, how may they which have offended be raised up from their sins?

Have mercy on me, O good Father, have mercy on me, and for Thy glorious name, be no longer angry with me.[77]

[Biv r] Take me, sinner, unto Thy mercy, for the name of Thy holy Son Jesu, whom Thou hast sent to be the obtainer of mercy for our sins through faith in his blood.[78]

Behold, holy Father, behold Thy child, whom Thou hast chosen; behold Thy well beloved Son, in whom Thy soul delighteth, upon whom Thou hast put Thy Holy Spirit, and sent Him to preach the gospel to the poor, to heal them which for their sins be sorrowful and contrite, to preach pardon to the prisoners, and sight to the blind.[79]

76. **And . . . ways** KP renders Fisher's splicing of recast phrases from Isaiah 26:9 and Ecclesiasticus 49:11: "Et bonitatem tuam discent omnes habitatores terrae, quum benefeceris nobis propter nomen magnum tuum, et non secundum vias nostras malas" (And all the inhabitants of the earth shall learn Thy goodness, when Thou shalt confer Thy benefits for Thy great name's sake, and not according to our evil ways). The Isaiah verse reads "cum feceris judicia tua in terra, justitiam discent habitores orbis" (when Thou shalt render Thy judgments in the earth, the inhabitants of the orb shall learn justice). The Ecclesiasticus verse reads "Nam commemoratus est . . . benefacere illis, qui ostenderunt rectas vias" (For he hath remembered . . . to confer benefits on those who manifest right ways). **evil ways . . . wicked deeds** KP's doubling. **confer . . . give . . . benefits** KP's doubling.

77. **Have . . . me** KP closely renders Fisher's recasting of Psalm 102:8–9: "Miserere mei, miserere mei o pater bone, et noli diutius mecum irasci propter nomen mangnum tuum." The Vulgate reads "Miserator, et misericors Dominus . . . Non in perpetuum irascetur" (The Lord is one who hath mercy and is merciful . . . He will not always be angry).

78. **Thy . . . blood** KP closely renders Fisher's recasting of phrases from 1 John 4:10 and Romans 3:25: "nomen sancti filii tui Jesu, quem misisti propitiationem pro peccatis nostris, per fidem in sanguine suo" (the name of Thy holy Son Jesu, whom Thou hast sent as the propitiation for our sins, through faith in His blood). The first verse reads "[Deus] misit Filium suum propitiationem pro peccatis nostris" ([God] sent His Son as the propitiation for our sins); the second verse reads "quem proposuit Deus propitiationam per fidem in sanguine ipsius" (whom God hath set as a propitiation through faith in His blood). **obtainer . . . mercy** KP's less technical rendering of "propitiationem."

79. **Thy well . . . blind** **Thy well . . . Spirit** KP renders Fisher's recast phrases from Mark 1:10–11 and Luke 3:22—God's words from heaven at the baptism of Christ—and from Luke 23:35: "Ecce pater sancte, ecce puerum tuum, quem elegisti, en dilectum tibi filiolum, in quo complacitum est animae tuae, ponens spiritum tuum eum." The first two verses closely tally re-

Behold Thy little one, which was born for us; behold Thy Son, which is given to us, whom Thou hast not spared, but given to death for us all, to be a sweet offering and a sacrifice to Thee.[80]

[Biv v] Verily He took upon Him in His body our infirmities, and He bare our pains;

He was made weak for our sins, and He was wounded for our offenses.

The correction for our peace was laid upon Him; and by the strokes that He suffered, our wounds were healed.

All we went astray like sheep, every one followed his own way; and Thou, O Lord, puttest on Him our iniquities, striking Him for the offenses of Thy people.[81]

---

garding the descent of the Holy Spirit: "Spiritum . . . descendentem, et manentem in ipso" (the Spirit . . . descending and remaining on Him); "descendit Spiritus Sanctus . . . in ipsum" (the Holy Spirit descended . . . on Him). These two verses report God's voice from heaven identically: "Tu es Filius meus dilectus, in te complacui" (Thou art my well beloved Son, in Thee I am well pleased). The third verse reads "hic est Christus Dei electus" (This is Christ, the chosen of God). **sent . . . blind** KP renders Fisher's close recasting of Luke 4:18–19: "mittens eum ut evangelizaret pauperibus, ut sanaret contritos, ut consolaretur omnes lugentes, et praedicaret captivis indulgentiam, et caecis visum" (sending Him to preach the gospel to the poor, to heal the contrite, to console all who mourn, and to preach pardon to the prisoners, and sight to the blind). The Vulgate reads "evangelizare pauperibus misit me, sanare contritos corde, praedicare captivis remissionem, et caecis visum" (He sent Me to preach the gospel to the poor, to heal the contrite in heart, to preach remission to the captives, and sight to the blind).

80. **Behold . . . Thee** KP closely renders Fisher's splicing of recast phrases from Isaiah 9:6 and Hebrews 10:5: "Ecce parvulum tuum qui natus est nobis, ecce filium tuum qui datus est nobis, cui etiam non pepercisti, sed pro omnibus ad mortem tradidisti oblationem et hostiam in odorem suavitatis." The Isaiah verse reads "Parvulus . . . natus est nobis, et filius datus est nobis" (A little boy is born to us, and a son is given to us); the Hebrews verse reads "sanctificati sumus per oblationem corporis Jesus Christi semel. . . . Ideo ingrediens mundum dicit: Hostiam, et oblationem, noluisti: corpus autem aptasti mihi" (We are sanctified by the sacrifice, once, of the body of Jesus Christ. . . . When He came into the world, He said [to His Father]: Sacrifice and offering Thou dost not wish, but a body hast Thou prepared for me). **sweet** KP condenses Fisher's "in odorem suavitatis" (with a smell of sweetness).

81. **Verily . . . people** KP renders Fisher's verbatim quotation from Isaiah 53:4 and then his combined recastings and verbatim quotations from Isaiah 53:5–6: "Vere languores nostros ipse in corpore suo tulit, et dolores nostros ipse portavit. Infirmatus est propter peccata nostra, et vulneratus propter scelera nostra. Disciplina pacis nostrae irruit super eum, et livore suo vulnera nostra sanata sunt. Omnes nos quasi oves erravimus, unusquisque in viam suam declinavit, et tu domine posuisti in eo iniquitates omnium nostrum, percutiens ipsum propter scelera populi tui." Isaiah 53:5 reads as follows in the Vulgate: "Ipse autem vulneratus est propter iniquitates nostras, attritus est propter scelera nostra: disciplina pacis nostrae super eum, et livore ejus sanati sumus" (He was wounded for our iniquities, He was bruised for our wickedness: the discipline of our peace was upon Him, and with His bruising we are healed). Fisher quotes Isaiah 53:6 verbatim except for reading "te domine . . . posuisti" (Thou, Lord, . . . hast put) in place of "posuit Dominus" (the Lord hath put). **correction . . . peace** KP's felicitous ren-

[Biv v] He gave His body to be beaten, and His cheeks to be stricken; He turned not away His face from them that scorned Him, and spat upon Him.[82]

Through His love and mercy, He hath redeemed them that were lost; and by His blood shed on the cross, He hath pacified all the things in heaven and earth.[83]

He gave Himself to death, and made his prayers for them which were offenders.[84]

Look, O merciful Father, and consider who it is that thus did suffer; and remember, I beseech Thee, for whom He hath suffered.

For this is that innocent, whom Thou gavest to death for us, even then when we were sinners; and shall we not, being now justified by His blood, much rather be saved from wrath through Him?

[Bv v] If we, when we were yet enemies, were reconciled to Thee by the death of Thy Son, shall we not, being reconciled, much rather be saved by His life?[85]

---

dering of Fisher's and the Vulgate's enigmatic phrasing, "disciplina pacis nostrae" (the discipline of our peace)—i.e., the punishment that secures peace for us with God. **by . . . suffered** KP's periphrastic clarification of Fisher's "livore suo" and the Vulgate's "livore ejus" (His bruising).

82. **He . . . Him** KP closely renders Fisher's recasting of Isaiah 50:6 from first to third person: "Corpus suum dedit percutientibus, et genas vellentibus, faciem suam non avertit ab increpantibus et conspuentibus in eum."

83. **He hath redeemed . . . earth** KP renders Fisher's splicing of a recast excerpt from Luke 19:10 and a close quotation from Colossians 1:20: "perditos redemit, pacificans per sanguinem crucis suae, quae in coelis, et quae in terris sunt omnia" (He redeemed the lost, pacifying by the blood of His cross all the things that are in heaven and on earth). The first verse reads "Venit . . . Filius . . . salvum facere quod perierat" (The Son . . . comes . . . to save that which was lost). The second verse reads "omnia . . . pacificans per sanguinem crucis ejus, sive quae in terris, sive quae in coelis sunt" (pacifying all things by the blood of His cross, whether these are on earth or in heaven).

84. **He . . . offenders** KP renders Fisher's close excerpting from Isaiah 53:12: "Tradidit in mortem animam suam, et pro transgressoribus preces effudit" (He gave His soul to death, and poured out prayers for transgressors). The first clause reads identically in the Vulgate; the second reads "et pro transgressoribus rogavit" (and begged for transgressors).

85. **being . . . life?** KP adjusts the scope of comparative constructions but does not alter the sense in rendering Fisher's recasting of Romans 5:9–10. He reads "multo magis justificati nunc in sanguine ipsius salvi erimus ab ira per ipsum. Si reconciliati tibi sumus (quum adhuc inimici essemus) per mortem filii tui, an non multo magis reconciliati, salvi erimis in vita ipsius?" (much more now being justified by His blood, shall we be saved from wrath through Him. If we were reconciled to Thee (when we were yet enemies) by the death of Thy Son, shall we not much more, being reconciled, be saved by His life?). The Vulgate reads "multò . . . magis nunc justificati in sanguinae ipsius, salvi erimus ab irâ per ipsum. Si . . . cùm inimici essemus, reconciliati sumus Deo per mortem Filii ejus: multò magis reconciliati, salvi erimus in vitâ ipsius" (much more, being now justified by His blood, shall we be saved from wrath through Him. If . . . when we were enemies, we were reconciled to God by the death of His Son, much more, being reconciled, shall we be saved by His life).

Behold that pure and immaculate Lamb, which taketh away the sins of the world, by whose precious blood we are redeemed from our iniquities.[86]

Look upon that most meek innocent, which like a lamb was led to His death, and being most cruelly entreated, once opened not His mouth.[87]

Behold Thine only Son, whom, although Thou begatst of Thy almighty power, substance, and nature, yet Thou wouldst He should be partaker of my infirmity:[88] [Bvi r] Which, being God in nature, thought it no ravin to be equal with God, but made Himself low, taking upon Him the shape of a servant; and coming in the similitude of sinful flesh, condemned sin in the flesh, submitting Himself unto Thee, O Father, even to the death of the cross; and there put out the handwriting that was against us contained in the law written, and taking it out of the way, fastened it to His cross, on the which He spoiled potestates and powers, and made a show of them openly, and triumphed over them in His own person.[89]

86. **Behold . . . iniquities** KP quite closely renders Fisher's splicing of a near quotation of John 1:29 with excerpts from 1 Peter 1:18–19: "Ecce agnum immaculatum qui peccata mundi tollit, cuius precioso sanguine redempti sumus de iniquitatibus nostris." The first verse reads "Ecce Agnus Dei, ecce qui tollit peccatum mundi" (Behold the Lamb of God; behold Him who taketh away the sin of the world). The excerpts read "redempti estis . . . pretioso sanguine quasi agni immaculati Christi, et incontaminati" (you were redeemed . . . with the precious blood of Christ, as of a spotless and unblemished lamb). **Behold . . . world** Neither Fisher nor KP gives any indication of the sacramental resonances of this verse, recited by the priest celebrating the Roman mass when he elevates to the worshipers' view the wafer he has just consecrated. **pure . . . immaculate** KP produces a doubling by moving to this earlier position the attributes "immaculati" and "incontaminati" ascribed to the Lamb in 1 Peter 1:19.

87. **which. . . mouth** KP closely renders Fisher's excerpting of Isaiah 53:7, into which he inserts an allusion to Luke 18:32: "qui tanquàm ovis ad occisioné ductus, et dum male tractaretur, os suum non aperuit." The Isaiah excerpts read "sicut ovis ad occisionem ducetur, . . . et non aperiet os suum" (as a lamb he is led to his death, . . . and he opened not his mouth). The allusion to Luke derives from Jesus's prophecy of his own passion, death, and resurrection: "Tradetur . . . Gentibus, et . . . flagellabitur" (He shall be led by the Gentiles, and . . . He shall be whipped). **entreated** an earlier variant of "treated."

88. **Thy . . . infirmity** **Thy . . . nature** KP unusually expands to a tripling Fisher's singular noun phrase "omnipotente virtute tua" (Thine almighty power). **He . . . infirmity** KP renders Fisher's allusion to Matthew 8:17, itself an echo of Isaiah 53:4, read as prefiguring Christ's role as "meae . . .infirmitatis participem" (a partaker in my infirmities). Matthew 8:17 reads "Ipse infirmitates nostras accepit" (He took on our infirmities).

89. **Which . . . person** KP closely renders Fisher's splicing of a close quotation from Philippians 2:6–8 with one from Colossians 2:14–15. Fisher's excerpting of Philippians reads "Qui cum in forma dei esset, nec rapinam arbitratus esse se equalem deo, semetipsum exinanivit, formam servi accipiens: et in similitudine carnis peccati veniens, damnavit peccatum in carne: humilians semetipsum tibi pater usque ad mortem crucis" (Who, being in the form of God, thought it not robbery to equal Himself with God, but He emptied Himself, taking on the form of a servant: and came in the likeness of sinful flesh: He damned sin in the flesh, humbling Himself to Thee, O Father, even unto the death of the cross). There are a few nonsubstantive variants, but

[Bvi v] Turn the eyes of Thy majesty, O Lord God, and look upon the work of Thy ineffable goodness.

Behold Thine own sweet Son, how all His body was drawn and stretched forth[90] on the cross.

Look upon all the parts of His body, from the crown of the head unto the sole of the foot; and no pain shall be found like unto His pain.[91]

Behold, O loving Father, the blessed head of Thy dear Son, crowned with sharp thorns, and the blood running down upon His godly visage.[92]

[Bvii r] Behold His tender body, how it is scourged. His naked breast is stricken and beaten; His bloody side is thrasted through. His heart panteth; His sinews be stretched forth. His goodly eyes dazzle and lose their sight; His princely face is wan and pale. His pleasant tongue is inflamed for pain; His inward parts wax dry and stark. His arms both, blue and wan, be stiff. His bones be plucked one from another. His beautiful legs be feeble and weak;[93] and the streams of blood issuing out of His body run down apace upon His feet.

Fisher otherwise reads with the Vulgate in Philippians 2:6–8, except for one major discrepancy. His own wording "in similitudine . . . in carne" sharply disparages human nature, in contrast to the Vulgate's reading "in similitudine hominum factus, et habitu inventus ut homo" (was made in the likeness of man, and was found in the fashion of man). **ravin** robbery, rapine—cognate with Fisher's "rapinam" (robbery, rapine). **and there . . . person** Fisher's excerpting from Colossians reads "illicque chirographum quod adversum nos erat decreti, delebat [correcting the Cologne edition's "dolebat"], et tollens de medio suffixit illud cruci, in qua expolians principatus et potestates traduxit confidenter, palam triumphans eos in semetipso" (He blotted out the handwriting that was decreed against us, and taking it out of the way, He fastened it to the cross, on which He despoiled sovereigns and authorities; He made a show of it openly, triumphing by Himself over them). Except for a few nonsubstantive variants, Fisher reads with the Vulgate in Colossians 2:14–15. **contained . . . written** KP's partially redundant rendering of "erat decreti" (was decreed). **potestates** authorities. KP retains the Latin of Fisher and the Vulgate.

90. **drawn . . . forth** Fisher reads "extensum" (stretched out). Here and at several later junctures, KP inserts doublings that further heighten the rhetoric of Fisher's circumstantial evocation of Christ's sufferings.

91. **no pain . . . pain** KP renders Fisher's recasting of Lamentations 1:12: "non invenietur dolor sicut dolor illius." The Vulgate reads "attendite, et videte si est dolor sicut dolor meus" (look and see if there is sorrow like my sorrow).

92. **godly visage** Fisher reads "divinum vultum" (divine countenance).

93. **naked . . . weak** **naked . . . beaten** Fisher reads "nudum tunditur pectus" (His naked breast is stricken); the first English edition has a misprint, "nondum" (not yet). **is . . . through** is thrust through; Fisher reads "perfoditur" (is pierced through). **goodly eyes** Fisher has a poeticism, "decora lumina" (beautiful lights [of eyes]). **dazzle . . . sight** Fisher reads "languent" (are faint). **princely . . . pale** Fisher reads "regia pallent ora" (His princely face pales). **wax . . . stark** Fisher reads "arescunt" (become dry). **blue . . . wan** Fisher reads "livida" (blue or leaden-colored). **be . . . weak** Fisher reads "debilitantur" (are debilitated). KP's doublings of Fisher's closely synonymous terms heighten the rhetoric by emphasis.

Look, O my Maker, upon the humanity and gentleness of Thy dear Son, and pity the infirmity of Thy weak handiwork.

Behold, O glorious Father, the body of Thy dear Son, all to-rent and torn;[94] and remember, I beseech Thee, of how small substance I am.

[Bvii v] Look upon the pain of Him that is both God and man, and release[95] the misery of man, whom Thou hast made.

Behold the grievous suffering of the Redeemer, and forgive the sin of him that is redeemed.[96]

Keep me from all evil ways, and teach me by Thy holy Spirit to choose the way of truth.[97]

I beseech Thee, O Thou King of holiness, by Him that is most holy, by this my Redeemer, Christ, that Thou bring me again into the right way: that I may be united and made one with Him in spirit, which abhorred not to be united with me in flesh.[98]

[Bviii r] Make me to go perfectly in Thy paths, and to hate all wicked ways.[99]

Wash my heart from malice, and cleanse me from my secret sins.[100]

94. **to-rent . . . torn** Fisher reads "lacerata" (torn to pieces).

95. **release** Fisher reads "relaxa" (slacken, ease).

96. **Behold . . . redeemed** KP closely renders Fisher's bold recasting of Psalm 24:18: "Vide redemptoris supplicium, et redempti dimitte delictum." The Vulgate reads "Vide humilitatem meam, et laborem meum: et dimitte universa delicta mea" (Look upon my lowliness and my pain: and cast away all of my sins). Fisher greatly alters the sense by substituting the redeeming Christ for the abject sinner in the first clause and a redeemed sinner for an imploring sinner in the second clause.

97. **Keep . . . truth** KP renders Fisher's splicing of recast excerpts from Psalm 24:4–5,12 with his own additions: "Viam sceleratam procul à me pelle, et doce me per spiritum tuum sanctum viam veritatis eligere (Keep me far from an evil way, and teach my by Thy Holy Spirit to choose the way of truth). The Vulgate reads "Vias tuas Domine demonstra mihi . . . in veritate tua . . . doce me. . . . Quis est homo qui timet Dominum? legem statuit ei in via, quam elegit" (Show me Thy ways, Lord . . . teach me . . . in Thy truth. . . . Who is the man that feareth the Lord? him shall He teach in the way that He shall choose).

98. **Christ . . . flesh Christ** KP's insertion. **which abhorred . . . spirit** Fisher reads "qui mea non abhorruit carne vestiri" (who did not abhor to clothe Himself in flesh with me). The allusion resonates with a versicle in the ancient so-called Ambrosian hymn "Te Deum laudamus," part of the ordinary of the divine office at matins: "Tu ad liberandum suscepturus hominem, non horruist Virginis uterum" (When Thou tookest upon Thee to deliver man, Thou didst not abhor the Virgin's womb): *The Hours of the Divine Service in English and Latin* (n.p., [1963]), 83.

99. **Make . . . ways** KP closely renders Fisher's splicing of phrasing from Psalms 16:5 and 118:128: "Perfice gressus meos in semitis tuis, facque odio me habere omnes vias iniquitatis." The Vulgate reads the first clause identically and the second clause "omnem viam iniquam odio habui" (I hate every wicked way).

100. **Wash . . . sins** KP closely renders Fisher's splicing of recast phrasing from Psalms 50:11–12 and 18:13: "Ablue à malicia cor meum, et ab occultis malis munda me." The first verses read "omnes iniquitates meas dele. Cor mundum crea in me Deus" (blot out all my iniquities.

Cleanse me, O holy Father, with the blood of the new testament of Thy well-beloved Son: which hath loved us, and washed us with His blood from our sins, and hath redeemed us from all iniquity.[101]

Purify my heart by the sanctification of Thy Spirit, and the sprinkling of the blood of Thy Son from all filthiness of sin, and evil conscience.[102]

O God almighty, be merciful unto me, sinner, for Thy glorious name' sake, and remember my sins no longer.[103]

[Bviii v] For Thou art God, gracious and merciful, and patiently dost suffer us, and wouldest that no man should perish, but that all men should return to penance.[104]

Create in me a clean heart, O God); the second reads "Delicta quis intelligit? ab occultis meis munda me" (Who knoweth his sins? cleanse me from my secret ones).

101. **Cleanse . . . iniquity** KP freely renders Fisher's intricate conflation of recast excerpts from Hebrews 9:20, 14, 22 and 1 John 5:9–10: "Expia me o pater sancte, per sanguinem testamenti aeterni, filii tui dilecti, qui dilexit nos, et lavit nos à peccatis nostris in sanguine suo, et redemit ab omni iniquitate" (Atone for me, O holy Father, by the blood of the everlasting testament, Thy beloved Son, who loved us, and washed us of our sins in His blood, and redeemed [us] from all iniquity). The phrases from Hebrews 9 read "Hic sanguis testamenti, quod mandavit . . . Deus . . . sanguis Christi, qui . . . emundabit conscientiam nostram ab operibus mortuis . . . et sine sanguinis effusione non fit remissio" (This is the blood of the testament, which God . . . commanded . . . the blood of Christ, who . . . cleansed our conscience from the works of death . . . and there is no remission without shedding of blood). The phrases from 1 John 4 read "In hoc apparuit charitas Dei in nobis, quoniam Filium unigenitum misit . . . suum propitiationem pro peccatis nostris" (In this was manifested the love of God toward us, because He sent His only Son . . . as the propitiation for our sins). **washed us** KP renders the first English edition's "lavit nos" rather than the Cologne edition's "levavit nos" (raised us up). **blood . . . testament** KP's addition to the conflated phrases introduces a further echo of Matthew 26:28, Jesus's term for the wine cup at his Last Supper, as rendered in Tyndale's translation of the New Testament (1534).

102. **Purify . . . conscience** KP closely renders Fisher's splicing of recast phrases from Acts 15:8–9, 1 Peter 1:2, and Hebrews 10:22: "Purifica cor meum per sanctificationem spiritus tui, et aspersionem sanguinis filii tui ab omni immundicia peccati, et conscientia mala." The phrase from Acts reads "Deus . . . fide purificans corda eorum" (God . . . purifying their hearts by faith). The phrases from 1 Peter read "in sanctificationem Spiritùs, . . . et aspersionem sanguinis Jesu Christi (by the sanctification of the Spirit . . . and sprinkling of the blood of Jesus Christ). The phrases from Hebrews read "aspersi corda à conscientiâ malâ, et abluto corpus aquâ mundâ" (hearts sprinkled from an evil conscience, and our body washed with pure water).

103. **O . . . longer** KP closely renders Fisher's splicing of partially recast phrases from Luke 18:13, Psalm 98:3, and Jeremiah 31:34: "Deus omnipotens propitius esto mihi peccatori, propter nomen magnum tuum, et iniquitatus mearum ne memor sis amplius." The phrase from Luke reads "Deus, propitius esto mihi peccatori" (God, be merciful to me, a sinner). The Psalm phrase reads ""Confiteantur nomini tuo magno" (Let them praise Thy great name). The phrase from Jeremiah reads "iniquitati eorum . . . non memorabor amplius" (I will remember their iniquity no more).

104. **For . . . penance** KP closely renders Fisher's splicing of recast phrases from Psalm 144:8–9 and Ezekiel 18:32: "Quoniam deus es tu, bonus et misericors, ac paciens erga nos, nolens aliquos perire, sed omnes ad poenitentiam reverti." The Psalm phrases read "misericors

Make me, O Lord God, to return from my evil ways and wicked thoughts.

Remember not the sins and abominations of my youth; according to Thy mercy, be mindful of me for Thy goodness' sake, O Lord.[105]

Look not upon me with a grievous countenance, for there is no man that dare speak for me.[106]

Enter not into judgment with Thy servant; for if Thou accuse me, I shall never be quit.[107]

[Ci r] For if Thou, O Lord, mark my sins and iniquity, who shall not fall before Thee?[108]

This is certain and sure, that in Thy sight no man living shall be justified, seeing Thou hast found iniquity even in Thy angels.[109]

Dominus: patiens. . . . Suavis Dominus universis" (the Lord is merciful, patient. . . . The Lord is good to all). The phrases from Ezekiel read "nolo mortem morientis, dicit Dominus Deus, revertimini, et vivite" (I do not wish the death of a mortal, saith the Lord God; turn yourselves and live). **to penance** KP's rendering of Fisher's addition "ad poenitentiam" as "to penance" rather than "to repentance" gives it a traditionalist turn; see n74 above.

105. **Remember . . . Lord** KP closely renders Fisher's recasting of Psalm 24:7: "Peccatorum adolescentiae meae et scelerum meorum ne sis memor: secundum misericordiam tuam memor esto mei tu, propter bonitatem tuam domine." The Psalm verse reads "Delicta juventutis meae, et ignorantias meas ne memineris. Secundum misericordiam tuam memento mei tu: propter bonitatem tuam Domine" (Remember not the sins of my youth, nor my unknowing actions. According to Thy mercy remember me for Thy goodness' sake, Lord).

106. **Look . . . me** KP quite freely renders Fisher's splicing of recast phrases from Jeremiah 44:11 and Job 9:19: "Ne ponas vultum tuum adversum me in malum, quoniam nullus est, qui audet pro me testimonium dicere" (Set not Thy face against me for evil, because there is no one who dareth to testify for me). God speaks in the phrase from Jeremiah: "Ecce ego ponam faciem meam in vobis in malum" (Behold, I will set My face against you for evil). The phrase from Job reads "nemo audet pro me testimonium dicere" (no one dareth to testify for me).

107. **Enter . . . quit** KP closely renders Fisher's recasting of Psalm 142:2: "Nec ineas judicium cum servo tuo, te enim accusatore nunquam absolvar." The Psalm verse reads "non intres in judicium cum servo tuo: quia non justificabitur in conspectu tuo omnis vivens" (Enter not into judgment with Thy servant, for no living being will be justified in Thy sight). **shall . . . quit** shall be acquitted—closely rendering Fisher's "absolvar" (shall be absolved).

108. **For . . . Thee?** KP quite closely renders Fisher's recasting of Psalm 129:3: "Etenim si iniquitates adtendas domine, domine quis non cadet in conspectu tuo?" The Psalm verse reads "Si iniquitates observaveris Domine: Domine quis sustinebit?" (If Thou, Lord, wilt have observed iniquities: Lord, who shall stand?). **sins . . . iniquity** KP's doubling; Fisher reads "iniquitates" (iniquities).

109. **certain . . . justified** **certain . . . sure** KP's doubling; Fisher reads "Hoc pro certo est" (This is for certain). **in . . . justified** KP closely renders Fisher's reiteration of the second clause of Psalm 142:2 spliced with recast phrasing from Job 4:18: "coram te nemo vivens justificabitur, cum adversus angelos tuos perversi quid reperisti." For the Psalm clause, see n107 above. The phrasing in Job reads "in angelis suis reperit pravitatem" (He found perversity in His angels).

How much rather in man, which is abomination and filthiness, and dwelleth in the earthly house of this body, and drinketh iniquity as it were water?[110]

Who is clean from filthiness, when all be corrupted? Truly not one: no, though he have lived but one day on the earth, and though his months may be easily numbered.[111]

Of a truth there is no mortal man which hath not done wickedly; nor there is any righteous on earth, which doeth good and sinneth not.[112]

[Ci v] Yet because mercy is in Thy hand, O Lord, although Thou be dreadful, my hope is in Thee, in whom my soul trusteth.[113]

My soul looketh for Thee, because mercy and plentiful redemption is with Thee.[114]

110. **How . . . water?** KP renders Fisher's conflation of excerpts from Job 4:19 and 15:16: "Quanto magis in homine, qui est abhomination et foetor, et domum inhabitet luteam, et bibit sicut aquas iniquitatem?" The first verse from Job reads "quanto magis hi qui habitant domos luteas" (how much more in them who who inhabit houses of clay). **earthly . . . body** KP's expanded phrasing; Fisher and the Vulgate read "domum . . . luteam" (house of clay). The second verse from Job reads "Quanto magis abominabilis et inutilis homo, qui bibit quasi aquam iniquitatem?" (How much more abominable and unprofitable is man, who drinketh iniquity like water?).

111. **Who . . . numbered** KP closely renders Fisher's paraphrastic recasting of Job 14:4,5: "Quis purus à sorde ex iis qui omnes polluti sunt? ne unus quidem, etiamsi unius diei fuerit vita ejus super terram, et numerabiles menses illius." The verses read "Quis potest facere mundum de immundo . . . ? nonne tu qui solus es? Breves dies hominis sunt, numerus mensium ejus" (Who can make a clean thing out of an unclean one . . . ? art thou alone he? Short are the days of man, and the number of his months).

112. **there . . . not** KP closely renders Fisher's conflation of recast excerpts from Psalm 17:22 and Ecclesiastes 7:21: "nemo de genitis est, qui non impie gessit, nec quisquam iustus in terra, qui bonum facit, et non peccat" (there is no man begotten who hath not done impiously, nor anyone righteous on earth, who doeth good, and sinneth not). The Psalm excerpt reads, in a sense opposite to Fisher's, "nec impie gessi a Deo meo" (I have not done wickedly toward my God). The verse from Ecclesiastes reads "Non est enim homo justus in terra, qui faciat bonum, et non peccet" (There is no righteous man on earth, who doth good and sinneth not).

113. **Yet . . . trusteth** KP renders Fisher's conflation of recast excerpts from Psalms 128:4, 75:8, 70:5, and 76:2: "Sed quoniam tecum est, propiciatio, quum terribilis sis, spes meam te domine deus, cui fidit anima mea" (Yet because propitiation is with Thee, who art mild, my hope is in Thee, Lord God, in whom my soul trusteth). The first Psalm excerpt reads "Quia apud te propitiatio est" (For propitiation is with Thee). The second Psalm excerpt reads "Tu terribilis es" (Thou art fearsome). The third Psalm excerpt reads "Domine spes mea" (The Lord [is] my hope). The fourth Psalm excerpt reads "in te confidit anima mea" (my soul trusteth in Thee). **although . . . dreadful** KP renders the reading of the Cologne edition, "quum terribilis sis," which the first English edition radically alters to "quum mitis sis" (since Thou wilt be mild).

114. **My . . . Thee** KP closely renders Fisher's recast excerpts from Psalm 129:5, 7: "Anima mea te expectat, quoniam tecum est misericordia, et copiosa apud te redemptio." The verses read "speravit anima mea in Domino . . . Quia apud Dominum misericordia: et copiosa apud

For this I know assuredly, that Thou wilt not cast me away forever: but although Thou cast me away for my sins a while, yet Thou wilt have mercy upon me again according to the multitude of Thy mercies.[115]

For Thou, O Lord, art full of pity and mercy, and wilt not turn Thy face away from us, if we will return to Thee.[116]

[Cii r] Thou art our God, full of sweetness, verity, and patience, and disposest all things by mercy.[117]

[Cii r] The fountains of Thy goodness be ever full and flow over; Thy grace never decayeth.[118]

All Thy ways be mercy and truth to them that seek out Thy covenant and testimonies.[119]

How gentle and loving the father is to his children, so gentle and loving art Thou, O Lord, to them that fear Thee; and for the abundance of Thy mercy Thou dost pardon our infirmities.

Thou knowest Thine own handiwork; Thou rememberest what we are; Thou seest that we are flesh, and of no strength.[120]

---

eum redemptio" (my soul looketh for the Lord . . . Because mercy [is] with the Lord, and plentiful redemption with Him).

115. **Thou wilt . . . mercies** KP closely renders Fisher's recasting of Lamentations 3:31–32: "non repelles in sempiternum, sed tu ipse qui abieceris, rursum misereberis secundum multitudinem miserationum tuarum." The verses read "non repellet in sempiternum Dominus. Quia si abiecit, et miserebitur secundum multitudinem misericordiarum suarum" (the Lord will not cast off forever. For if He casteth off, He will also have mercy according to the multitude of His mercies).

116. **For . . . to Thee** KP renders Fisher's recasting of 2 Paralipomenon (2 Chronicles) 30:9: "Pius et clemens es tu domine deus, et non avertes faciem tuam à nobis, si reversi fuerimus ad te." The verse reads "pius . . . et clemens est Dominus Deus vester, et non avertet faciem suam a vobis, si reversi fueritis ad eum" (tender . . . and gentle is your Lord God, and He will not turn His face away from you, if you will return unto Him).

117. **Thou . . . mercy** KP renders Fisher's quotation of Wisdom of Solomon 15:1: "Tu enim deus noster suavis, et verus, et paciens, et in misericordia disponens omnia." The verse reads identically except for "autem" (however), where Fisher reads "enim" (truly).

118. **full . . . decayeth** **full . . . over** KP's doubling; Fisher reads "Exuberant" (They overflow). **decayeth** Fisher reads "deficit" (faileth).

119. **All . . . testimonies** KP closely renders Fisher's recasting of Psalm 24:10: "Universae viae tuae misericordia et veritas, foedus tuum, et testimonia tua exquirentibus." The verse reads "Universae viae Domini, misericordia et veritas, requirentibus testamentum ejus et testimonia ejus" (All the ways of the Lord are mercy and truth, to them that seek His testament and His testimonies).

120. **How . . . strength** KP renders Fisher's conflation of paraphrased excerpts from Psalm 102:13, 3–4,14–15: "Quam mitis est parens in pueros suos, tam mitis tu domine erga timentes te, et pro abundantia misericordiae tuae indulges infirmitatibus. Agnoscis figmentum tuum, recordaris quales sumus, memor es quod caro sumus, et nullius firmitatis" (As gentle as the

[Cii v] Thou hast not forgotten that this world is full of unrighteousness and wickedness, and that it is wholly set and bent on evil.[121]

Yet nevertheless Thou art merciful, and full of grace: and like a merciful Lord forbearest to punish sinners, when they repent themself, and return from their sins.[122]

Have mercy upon me, O Lord God my Saviour, for the glory of Thy name, and deliver me, and forgive me my sins for Thy name's sake.

O righteous Father, look not straitly upon the multitude of my sins; but look on the face of Jesu, Thy holy Son, which being without sin, bare our sins in His body on the tree of the cross.

[Ciii r] Turn away Thy face from my sins, and put out all my iniquities.

Make a clean heart in me, O God, and renew me with a right spirit.

Cast me not away from Thy presence, and take not Thy holy Spirit from me.

Give me again the comfort of Thy help, and stablish me with Thy mighty Spirit.[123]

---

father is to his sons, so gentle art Thou, Lord, to them who fear Thee, and for the abundance of Thy mercy Thou dost indulge our infirmities. Thou knowest Thy creation; Thou rememberest what we are; Thou rememberest that we are flesh, and of no strength at all). Psalm 102:13 reads "Quomodo miseretur pater filiorum, misertus est Dominus timentibus se" (As a father pitieth his children, the Lord hath pity toward those who fear Him). Excerpts from Psalm 102:3–4 read "sanat omnes infirmitates tuas . . . coronat te in misericordia et miserationibus" (He healeth all thine infirmities . . . He crowneth thee with mercy and pity). Psalm 102:14–15 read "quoniam ipse cognovit figmentum nostrum, Recordatus est quoniam pulvis sumus: homo, sicut foenim dies ejus" (For He knoweth His creation, He remembereth that we are dust: man, his days are like grass). **gentle . . . loving, gentle . . . loving** KP's reduplicated doublings; Fisher reads "mitis" (gentle) in both places.

121. **this world . . . evil** KP renders Fisher's splicing of recast excerpts from Genesis 6:11 and 1 John 5:19: "mundus hic repletur iniusticia et impietate, et totus in maligno positus est." The Genesis excerpt reads "Corrupta est . . . terra coram Deo, et repleta est iniquitate" (The earth was corrupt in the presence of God, and filled with iniquity). The excerpt from 1 John reads "mundus totus in maligno positus est" (all the world is set on wickedness). **set . . . bent** KP's doubling; Fisher and the Vulgate read "positus" (set).

122. **Yet . . . sins** Departing from her usual close rendering, KP freely substitutes for the latter part of Fisher's formulaic versicle, which reads "Attamen tu misericors es et plenus gratiae, propitius ac poenitens super maliciam hominum" (Nevertheless Thou art merciful and full of grace, propitious and sorry over the malice of men). **like . . . sinners** KP's addition. **when . . . sins** KP's substitute phrasing is close to God's declaration regarding the Jews in Jeremiah 36:3: "revertatur unusquisque a via sua pessima: et propitius ero iniquitati, et peccato eorum" (they may, every one of them, return from their very bad way, and I will be forgiving of their iniquity and their sin).

123. **Turn . . . Spirit** KP closely renders Fisher's quotation of Psalm 50:11–13: "Averte faciem tuam à peccatis meis, et omnes iniquitates meas dele. Cor mundum crea in me deus, et spiritum rectum innova intra me. Ne proiicias me à facie tua, et spiritum sanctum tuum ne auferas à me. Redde mihi leticiam de salute mea, et spiritu potentie confirma me." The Vulgate wording

Mollify my heart, O Lord God, that I may return to Thy paths, for I have wandered overlong in the way of error.[124]

Turn me to Thee, and I shall be turned; for Thou art my Maker: and I am the clay and work of Thy hands.[125]

[Ciii v] Turn not Thy face away from me, nor go not from Thy servant in Thine anger.

Be my Helper, and forsake me not; despise me not, O Lord, which art my God, and my health.[126] Amen.

THE SECOND PSALM, FOR REMISSION OF SINS.

O most mighty God of angels and of men, whose judgments be unsearchable, and whose wisdom is profound and deep:[127]

---

in these verses is identical except for reading "in visceribus meis" (in my inward parts) where Fisher reads for "intra me" (within me) and "principali" (presiding) where Fisher reads "potenti" (mighty).

124. **Mollify . . . error** KP closely renders Fisher's conflation of excerpts recast or quoted from Job 23:16, Ecclesiasticus 17:21, and Wisdom of Solomon 12:24: "Emollias cor meum domine deus, ut revertar ad semitas tuas, nam in erroris via diutius erravi." The Job excerpt reads "Deus mollivit cor meum" (God hath softened my heart); the Ecclesiasticus excerpt reads "Convertere ad Dominum, et relinque peccata tua" (Return unto the Lord, and forsake thy sins); the Wisdom excerpt reads "in erroris via diutius erraverant" (they have wandered too long in the way of error).

125. **Turn . . . hands** KP closely renders Fisher's conflation of recast excerpts from Ecclesiasticus 17:23 and 33:13: "Converte me ad te, et convertar, tu enim fictor meus es, ego vero lutum et opus manuum tuarum." The first excerpt reads "Revertere ad Dominum, et avertere ab injustitia tua" (Return unto the Lord, and turn from thy injustice); the second excerpt reads "Quasi lutum figuli in manu ipsius . . . sic homo in manu illius, qui se fecit" (Like clay in his [a potter's] hand . . . so is man in His hand, who Himself hath made him).

126. **Turn . . . health** KP closely renders Fisher's quotation of Psalm 26:9: "Ne avertas faciam tuam a me ne declines in ira à servo tuo. Adjutor esto mihi, ne deseras me, neque despicias me o domine deus meus et salus mea." The Vulgate wording is identical except for reading "derelinquas" (abandon) where Fisher reads "deseras" (forsake) and reading "salutaris" (saving, delivering) where Fisher reads "salus" (salvation, deliverance). **health** the native English equivalent for a primary sense of Latin "salus."

127. **whose . . . deep** KP renders Fisher's conflation of recast excerpts from Jeremiah 32:27 and Romans 11:33: "Fortissime Deus spirituum et universae carnis, cuius judicia inscrutabilia sunt et sapientia profunda" (O most mighty God of spirits and of all flesh, whose judgments are inscrutable, and wisdom profound). The excerpt from Jeremiah reads "Ecce ego Dominus Deus universae carnis" (Behold, I am the Lord God of all flesh); the excerpts from Romans read "O altitudo . . . sapientiae . . . Dei: quàm incomprehensibilis sunt judicia ejus, et investigabiles viae ejus" (O the depth . . . of the wisdom . . . of God: how incomprehensible are His judgments, and His ways unsearchable). **profound . . . deep** KP's doubliing.

Hear the prayers of Thy servant, and cast not away the humble suits of Thy poor creature and handiwork.[128]

[Civ r] For as long as I shall live, I will speak unto Thee; and I will not hold my peace so long as the breath is in my body.[129]

I do turn my soul unto Thee, and I set mine eyes directly upon Thee.[130]

Let Thine anger be turned away from me, I beseech Thee; and grant that I may find grace and favor in Thy sight.[131]

According to the greatness of Thy mercy, forgive me all my sins.[132]

Pluck me away from mine heinous offenses, and heal my soul, which hath offended Thee. Make me free from the guilt of my transgression, for I acknowledge my iniquity, and am sorry for my sins.[133]

128. **Hear . . . handiwork** KP renders Fisher's conflation of recast excerpts from 2 Paralipomenon (2 Chronicles) 6:19: "Exaudi preces servi tui, et ne repellas obsecrationes figmenti tui." The excerpts read "respicias orationem servi tui, et obsecrationem ejus . . . et . . . preces, quas fundit famulus tuus coram te" (Thou heedest the prayer of Thy servant, and his supplication . . . and the prayers that Thy manservant poureth out before Thee). **suits** KP's equivalent of Fisher's and the Vulgate's "obsecrationes" (supplications). **poor . . . handiwork** KP's doubling; Fisher reads "figmenti tui" (Thy handiwork).

129. **For . . . body** KP closely renders Fisher's radical recasting of Job 27:3: "Etenim donec vixero loquar ad te, et non silebo dum spiritus hos regit artus." The verse reads "donec superest halitus in me, et spiritus Dei in in naribus meis, non loquentur labia mea iniquitatem, nec lingua mea meditabitur mendacium" (as long as breath remaineth in me, and the Spirit of God in my nostrils, my lips will not speak iniquity, nor my tongue consider deceit). Fisher's adaptation focuses on addressing God, not on the uttering of righteousness only, as in the Vulgate source.

130. **I . . . Thee** KP closely renders Fisher's inversion of recast phrasing from Psalm 140:8: "Ad te animam meam converto, ad te oculos meos dirigo." The verse reads "ad te Domine, Domine oculi mei . . . non auferas animam meam" (my eyes, Lord, are toward Thee, Lord . . . do not take my soul away).

131. **Let . . . sight** KP renders Fisher's splicing of recast excerpts from Daniel 9:16 and Esther 7:3: "Avertatur obsecro ira tua à me, et da, ut inveniam gratiam coram oculis tuis." The Daniel excerpt reads "avertatur obsecro ira tua . . . a civitate tua Jerusalem" (let Thine anger be turned away, I pray, . . . from Thy city of Jerusalem); the Esther excerpt reads "dona mihi . . . gratiam in oculis tuis" (grant me . . . grace in Thy sight). **grace . . . favor** KP's doubling; Fisher and the Vulgate read "gratiam" (grace).

132. **According . . . sins** KP closely renders Fisher's recasting of Numbers 14:19: "Secundum magnitudinem misericordiae tuae remitte universa peccata mea." The verse reads "Dimitte . . . peccatum populi huius secundum magnitudinem misericordiae tuae" (Forgive . . . the sins of this people according to the greatness of Thy mercy).

133. **Pluck . . . sins** KP closely renders Fisher's conflation of recast excerpts from Psalms 58:2–3, 40:5, 30:2, 31:5, and Leviticus 5:5: "Ab omnibus sceleribus meis eripe me, et sana animam meam quae in te peccavit, liberum me fac à reatu transgressionis meae: nam iniquitatem meam agnosco, et pro peccatis meis poenitentiam ago." The excerpt from Psalm 58 reads "Eripe me de inimicis meis Deus meus: et . . . de operantibus iniquitatem" (Deliver me from my enemies, O my God, and . . . from the workers of iniquity). The excerpt from Psalm 40 reads "sana ani-

I have forsaken Thy way; and I, knowing Thy commandments, have done all things contrary to them.[134]

[Civ v] I have broken the covenant that I made with Thee, and have despised to keep Thy law.[135]

Verily I have sinned against Thee, O Lord God, and the blemish of my sin abideth still with me, even unto this day.[136]

I have forsaken Thee, O God my Maker, and gone away from Thee, my Saviour, and have rebelled against Thee like the ox that winceth and striveth when he should be yoked.[137]

I have hardened my heart against Thee, and I have lifted up my neck proudly after my sin.[138]

---

mam meam, quia peccavit tibi" (heal my soul, for it hath sinned against Thee). The excerpt from Psalm 30 reads "in justitia tua libera me" (free me by Thy justice). The excerpt from Psalm 31 reads "Confitebor adversum me injustitiam meam Domino" (Against myself I will acknowledge my wickedness to the Lord). The Leviticus excerpt reads "agat poenitentiam pro peccato" (he will be sorry for his sin). Fisher applies key verbs such as "*eripere*" (deliver) and "*libere*" (free from) to subjective release—God's rescue of the soul from sin and temptation. By contrast, in the Psalms and the Old Testament generally these verbs denote objective release—God's rescue of the speaker (or His people) from enemies and destruction.

134. **I . . . them** KP closely renders Fisher's recasting of excerpts from Judges 2:17: "Deservi viam tuam, et mandata tua intelligens, omnia feci contraria." The excerpts read "deserverunt viam . . . et audientes mandata Domini, omnia fecere contraria" (they forsook the way . . . and hearing the commandments of the Lord, they did all contrary things).

135. **I . . . law** KP closely renders Fisher's splicing of recast excerpts from Deuteronomy 31:20 and 28:45 in the Cologne edition: "Irritum feci pactum quod tecum inieram, et legem tuam servare contempsi." The 1544 London edition substitutes "nolui" (I have not wished to) for "contempsi." The first excerpt reads "detrahentque mihi, et irritum facient pactum meum" (they will withdraw from Me, and make My covenant broken). The second excerpt reads "nec servasti mandata ejus et ceremonias" (nor hast thou kept His commandments and ceremonies).

136. **Verily . . . day** KP closely renders Fisher's splicing of recast excerpts from Exodus 10:16 and Joshua 22:17: "Vere peccavi in te domine Deus, et usque in praesentem diem macula sceleris mei permanet mecum." The Exodus excerpt is spoken by the pharaoh of Egypt: "Peccavi in Dominum Deum vestrum" (I have sinned against your Lord God). The Joshua excerpt reads "et usque in praesentem diem macula huius sceleris in nobis permanet" (and to the present day the spot of this sin remaineth on us).

137. **I . . . yoked** KP renders Fisher's splicing of recast excerpts from Deuteronomy 32:15 and Ecclesiasticus 26:10: "Dereliqui te deum factorem meum, recessi à te salvatore meo, et sicut taurus recalcitrans jugo suo, rebellis sum [1544: fui] tibi." The first excerpt reads "dereliquit Deum factorem suum, et regessit a Deo salutari suo" (he forsook God his Maker, and went away from God his Saviour). The second excerpt is half of a comparison between an ox and a bad wife, both restive under the yoke: "sicut boum jugum, quod movetur, ita et mulier nequam" (as a yoked ox that is stirred up, so is a worthless woman). **winceth . . . striveth** KP's doubling; Fisher reads "recalcitrans" (disobedient). Since Fisher suppresses the reference to a bad wife, it is unclear whether KP recognized the full force of the Biblical comparison.

138. **I . . . sin** KP closely renders Fisher's splicing of recast excerpts from Exodus 4:21 and Deuteronomy 9:6–7: "Cor meum erga te induravi, et cervicem meam post peccata superbe

I have trusted in lies, and through deceit would not knowledge Thee, but I have followed the lewdness of my heart.[139]

[Cv r] My pride and arrogancy have beguiled me, and the foolish boldness of my heart hath brought me into desolate ways.[140]

Mine own counsels and advices have wrought me these things; such is the malice and rebellion that possesseth the hearts of men.[141]

My soul is put from quietness and rest, and I cannot think of any good thing.[142]

The yoke of my sins is waxed very heavy; it is lifted up and fastened about my neck.[143]

---

erexi." In the Exodus excerpt God foretells how He will deal with Pharaoh: "ego indurabo cor ejus" (I will harden his heart). In the Deuteronomy excerpt Moses confronts the Israelites with their sins against God: "cum durissimae cervicis sis populus . . . ne obliviscaris quomodo . . . semper adversum Dominum contendisti" (since thou art a very stiff-necked people . . . forget not how . . . thou hast always contended against the Lord).

139. **I . . . heart** KP closely renders Fisher's splicing of recast excerpts from Jeremiah 7:8 and 9:6 and Deuteronomy 29:19: "Confisus sum in mendacio, prae dolo te agnoscere nolui, sed sequebar pravitates cordis mei." The first excerpt reads "vos confiditis vobis in sermonibus mendacii" (you have trusted in lying words); the second reads "in dolo renuerunt scire me, dicit Dominus" (through deceit they refuse to know Me, saith the Lord). The Deuteronomy excerpt reads "ambulabo in pravitate cordis mei" (I will walk in the depravity of my heart). **lewdness** wickedness—a no longer current sense.

140. **My . . . ways** KP freely renders Fisher's recast excerpts from Jeremiah 49:16: "Arrogantia mea me decipit, et audacia cordis mei in devia me perduxit" (My arrogance hath deceived me, and the boldness of my heart hath led me out of the way). The excerpts read "Arrogantia tua decepit te, et superbia cordis tui: qui habitas in . . . altitudinem . . . inde detraham te" (Thy arrogance of heart hath deceived thee, and the pride of thy heart . . . who dwellest in . . . a high place. . . . I will bring thee down from thence). **pride . . . arrogancy** KP's doubling. **foolish boldness** Fisher reads "audacia" (boldness). **desolate ways** Fisher reads "devia" (out of the way).

141. **Mine . . . men** KP quite closely renders Fisher's splicing of recast excerpts from Ecclesiasticus 22:19 and Ecclesiastes 9:3: "Consilia et cogitationes meae fecerunt haec mihi: haec est malicia et rebellio, quae corda hominum possidet" (My counsels and thoughts have done these things to me; this is the malice and rebellion that posseseth the hearts of men). The first excerpt reads "sic et cor confirmatum in cogitatione consilii" (such is the heart established in its thought and its counsels). The second excerpt reads "corda filiorum hominum implentur malicia, et contemptu in vita sua" (the hearts of the sons of men are full of evil and contempt in their lifetimes).

142. **My . . . thing** KP freely renders Fisher's thorough recasting of Lamentations 3:17: "Depellitur à tranquillitate anima mea, et bonorum oblivio me convoluit" (My soul is driven away from quietness, and forgetfulness of good things whirleth me about). The verse reads "repulsa est a pace anima mea, oblitus sum bonorum" (My soul is driven from peace; I am forgetful of good things). **quietness . . . rest** KP's doubling. **I . . . of** KP apparently guesses at the meaning of the very rare Latin verb "convoluto" (to roll or whirl about rapidly).

143. **The . . . neck** KP closely renders Fisher's recasting of Lamentations 1:14: "Aggravatum est jugum transgressionum mearum, elevatum est et implexum collo meo." The verse reads "Vigilavit jugum iniquitatum mearum: in manu ejus convolutae sunt, et impositae collo mea"

Thou hast spoken to me, but I would not hear; Thou hast called me, but I would not answer. I believed not Thy words, nor would abide Thy counsel.[144]

[Cv v] I regarded not Thy holy Word, and I gave not my mind to Thy sayings.[145]

Thou hast stricken me, but I would not know the cause thereof; Thou hast corrected me, but I would not take Thy discipline.[146]

I did not consider in my heart, that Thou wouldest not forget my sin and malice.[147]

With my mouth and my lips I glorified Thee, but my heart was far from Thee.[148]

([The Lord] kept watch over the yoke of my sins; by His hand they are rolled about rapidly and laid upon my neck). **lifted up** KP exactly translates Fisher's "elevatum," the term he substitutes for a second occurrence of the rare "convolutae."

144. **Thou . . . counsel** KP closely renders Fisher's splicing of recast excerpts from Job 19:16 and Proverbs 1:23–25: "Tu loquutus es mihi, audire nolui: tu vocasti me, non respondi, non credidit verbis tuis, nec sustinui consilium tuum." The Job excerpt reads "Servum meum vocavi, et non respondit" (I have called My servant, and he did not answer). The excerpts from Proverbs read "ostendam vobis verba mea. Quia vocavi, et renuistis . . . et non fuit qui aspiceret. Despexistis omne consilium meum" (I will show you My words. For I have called, and you have refused . . . and there was no one who regarded. You have looked down upon My counsel).

145. **I . . . sayings** KP renders Fisher's splicing of recast excerpts from Exodus 9:21 and Proverbs 1:30: "Verbum tuum vice obprobrii fuit mihi, et non posui cor in sermonibus tuis" Thy word was as a shame to me, and I did not set my heart on Thy sayings). Her phrasing is closer to that of the first English edition, "neglexi" (I neglected), than to the Cologne edition's "vice obprobrii fuit mihi." The first English edition is closer to the Vulgate; the excerpt from Exodus reads "neglexit sermonem Domini" (he did not regard the word of the Lord). The excerpt from Proverbs reads "nec acquieverint consilio meo" (they did not give assent to My counsel).

146. **Thou . . . discipline** KP closely renders Fisher's splicing of recast excerpts from Ezekiel 7:9 and Leviticus 26:23–24: "Percussisti me, at causam agnoscere nolui; emendavisti me, sed disciplinam recipere nolui." The excerpt from Ezekiel reads "scietis quia ego sum Dominus percutiens" (you shall know that I am the Lord that strikes). The excerpts from Leviticus read "Quodsi nec sic volueritis recipere disciplinam, . . . percutiam vos . . . propter peccata vestra" (If you will not receive [My] discipline, . . . I will strike you . . . on account of your sins).

147. **I . . . malice** KP renders Fisher's splicing of recast excerpts from Isaiah 57:11 and 1 Maccabees 10:46: "Cogitavi in corde meo, quod omnis maliciae meae non esses memor." Her phrasing clearly follows that of the first English edition, "Non recordatus sum . . . quod . . . esses memor" (I did not consider . . . that . . . Thou wouldst remember), rather than the Cologne edition's "Cogitavi . . . quod . . . non esses memor" (I thought. . . . that . . . Thou wouldst not remember). The wording of the English edition is also closer to the Vulgate's. The excerpt from Isaiah reads "mei non es recordata in corde tuo" (thou didst not consider Me in thine heart). The excerpt from 1 Maccabees reads "quia recordati sunt malitiae magnae" (for great malice they remembered). **sin . . . malice** KP's doubling.

148. **With . . . Thee** KP closely renders Fisher's recasting of Matthew 15:8: "Ore meo et labiis meis glorificavi te, sed cor meum longe fuit à te." The verse reads "Populus hic labiis me honorat, cor autem eorun longè est à me" (This people honoreth Me with their lips, but their heart is far from me).

I hid my sin as Adam did: to the intent to have mine iniquity unknown.[149]

I asked not counsel of Thy mouth, and I would not follow Thy law.[150]

[Cvi r] I have sinned before Thine eyes, and therefore my soul is made unstable.

I forsook Thee, which art the fountain of continual springing waters, to the intent to dig to myself muddy pits which have no water.[151]

In all these things, I am not returned to Thee, nor I have not prayed unto Thee, that I might leave my wicked ways.[152]

See, Lord, and behold how vile I am made: all the beauty of my soul is perished and gone, insomuch that now I dare not in any wise behold and look upon Thee.[153]

149. **I . . . unknown** KP renders Fisher's recasting of Job 31:33: "Occultavi sicut Adam scelus meum, ut absconderem in occultis iniquitatem meam" (I hid my sin like Adam, that I might conceal my iniquity in hidden places). The verse reads "abscondi quasi homo peccatum meum, et celavi in sinu meo iniquitatem meam" (Like the man, I hid my sin, amd I kept my iniquity secret in my bosom). The Adamic allusion is to Genesis 3:10.

150. **I . . . law** KP renders Fisher's splicing of recast excerpts from Joshua 9:14 and 2 Maccabees 8:36: "Os tuum non interrogavi, et nolui audire de lege tua" (I did not ask Thy mouth, and I would not hear of Thy law). Her wording in the second clause is closer to that of the first English edition "nolui sequi legem tuam" (I would not follow Thy law), which in turn is closer to the phrasing in 2 Maccabees. The Cologne edition reads "nolui audire legem tuam" (I would not listen to Thy law). The excerpt from Joshua reads "os Domini non interrogaverunt" (they did not ask the mouth of the Lord [for counsel]). The excerpt from 2 Maccabees reads "sequerentur leges ab ipso constitutas" (they followed laws constituted by Him).

151. **I forsook . . . water** KP freely renders Fisher's recasting of Jeremiah 2:13: "Te enim deserui fontem aquarum perennium, ut effoderem mihi conculcatos puteos et lutosos, qui non habent aquas" (I indeed forsook Thee, the fountain of ever-living waters, so that I dug for myself contemptible and muddy wells, which have no water). The 1544 London edition, followed by KP, has "et" where the Cologne edition has "ut." "Et" is the conjunction in the Vulgate verse, which reads "Me dereliquerunt fontem aquae vivae, et foderunt sibi cisternas, cisternas dissipatas, quae continere non valent aquas" (They have forsaken Me, the fountain of living waters, and they have dug for themselves cisterns, broken cisterns, that cannot hold water).

152. **In . . . ways** KP closely renders Fisher's negative recasting of 2 Paralipomenon (2 Chronicles) 7:14–15 from the third person to the first person and from the future to the past tense: "Et in omnibus iis non sum reversus ad te, neque faciem tuam precatus sum, ut recederem à viis meis pravis." The verse reads "conversus autem populus meus, super quos invocatum est nomen meum, deprecatus me fuerit, et exquisierit faciem meam, et egerit poenitentiam a viis suis pessimis" (then My people, over whom My name is invoked, will return, and pray unto Me, and seek My face, that they might do penance for their very bad ways).

153. **See . . . Thee** KP renders Fisher's splicing of recast and reordered excerpts from Lamentations 1:11, 6 and Exodus 3:6: "Vide domine, et intuere quoniam vilis factus sum, periit à me omnis decor meus, ut te iam prorsus adspicere non possim." Her wording in the second clause does not follow the Cologne edition's "adspicere non possim" (I could not look) but rather that of the first English edition, "adspicere non ausim" (I did not dare to look), which in turn is closer to the phrasing in the Vulgate. The first excerpt reads "vide Domine et considera, quo-

And there was no cause why I should forsake Thee, and vainly follow vain things.[154]

[Cvi v] Lord, have mercy upon me, and hear my prayers; for Thou art my God, and there is no Saviour besides Thee.[155]

Turn away from me Thy heavy displeasure, and destroy me not for the sins of my youth.[156]

I humbly beseech Thee, O Lord: forgive me, forgive me for Thy exceding mercy.

O Lord God of hosts, if Thou be determined to save, who can let or resist? If Thou stretch out Thy hand, who shall turn Thee away?[157]

Thou mayest do to me as the potter doth to his pot: for, behold, I am in Thy hand, as the clay is in his.[158]

---

niam facta sum vilis" (See, O Lord, and consider, for I am made vile). The second excerpt reads "et egressus est a filia Sion omnis decor ejus" (all her beauty hath departed from the daughter of Zion [Jerusalem]). The third excerpt reads "non . . . audebat aspiceare contra Deum" (he [Moses] did not dare to look upon God). **of . . . soul** KP's addition. **perished . . . gone, behold . . . look** KP's doublings.

154. **And . . . things** KP closely renders Fisher's paraphrases of excerpts from Isaiah 30:1 and 49:4: "Et nulla fuit causa, ut te desererem, et vanus vana sectarer." The first excerpt, in God's voice, reads "Vae filii desertores" (Woe to forsaking sons). The second, in the prophet Isaiah's voice, reads "laboravi, sine causa, et vane fortitudinem meam consumpsi" (I have labored without cause, and vainly consumed my strength).

155. **Lord . . . Thee** KP closely renders Fisher's splicing of recast excerpts from Psalms 4:2 and 30:15 and Isaiah 43:11: "Domine miserere mei, et exaudi preces meas, quoniam tu es deus meus, et non est absque te salvator." The first excerpt reads "Deus . . . Miserere mei, et exaudi orationem meam" (God . . . Have mercy on me, and hear my prayer). The second excerpt reads "Deus meus es tu" (Thou art my God). The third excerpt, in the voice of God, reads "non est absque me salvator" (there is no Saviour besides Me).

156. **Turn . . . youth** KP freely renders Fisher's splicing of paraphrased excerpts from Joshua 7:26 and Job 13:26: "Avertatur furor tuus à me, nec me devastes propter peccata adolescentiae meae" (Let Thy fury be turned away from me, and do not lay me waste for the sins of my youth). The Joshua excerpt reads "aversus est furor Domini ab eis" (the fury of the Lord is turned from them). The Job excerpt reads "consumere me vis peccatis adolescentiae meae" (the strength of the sins of my youth [is made] to consume me).

157. **O . . . away?** KP closely renders Fisher's recasting of Isaiah 14:27: "Domine deus exercituum si decreveris salvare, quis poterit resistere? si extenderis manum tuam, quis te avertet?" The verse reads "Dominus . . . exercituum decrevit: et quis poterit infirmare? et manus ejus extenta: et quis avertet eam?" (The Lord of hosts hath determined, and who could annul? and His hand is stretched out, and who shall turn it back?). **let . . . resist** KP's doubling of Fisher's "resistere." **let** prevent.

158. **Thou . . . his** KP closely renders Fisher's paraphrase of excerpts from Ecclesiasticus 33:13–14: "Tu enim instar figuli potes mihi facere, ecce ego in manu tua, perinde atque lutum in manu fictoris" (For in the manner of the potter canst Thou do to me; behold, I am in Thy hand, and as the clay is in the hand of the maker). The verses read "Quasi lutum figuli in manu ipsius, . . . sic homo in manu illius, qui se fecit, et reddet illi secundum judicium suum" (As the

[Cvii r] Amend me, O Lord, but in mercy, not in Thine anger, lest Thou utterly consume me; make me to understand and know how hurtful and deadly a thing it is to forsake Thee, my Lord God, and to cast away from me the fear of Thee.[159]

There is no man that can heal me nor cure my plague; no man can deliver me but Thou, O Lord, which woundest and makest whole, which strikest and healest again.[160]

My destruction cometh of myself; my help and salvation standeth only in Thee.[161]

For none is like unto Thee; Thou art mighty, and great is the name of Thy strength.[162]

---

clay in the potter's hand, . . . so is man in His hand, who betakes Himself and renders to him according to His judgment). **to . . . pot** KP's addition.

159. **Amend . . . Thee** KP quite closely renders Fisher's splicing of recast excerpts from Jeremiah 10:24, Deuteronomy 32:29, and Joshua 24:20: "Emenda [1544: Corrige] me domine, sed in misericordia, non in ira tua, ne me in nihilum redigas, ut intelligam et cognoscam, quàm perniciosum sit atque noxium deserere te dominum deum meum et timorem tuam à me repellere." Here she follows the Cologne edition's "Emenda" rather than the first London edition's "Corrige." The excerpt from Jeremiah reads "Corripe me Domine, verumtamen in judicio: et non in furore tuo, ne fore ad nihilum redigas me" (Seize me, Lord, but in judgment and not in Thy fury, lest Thou bring me to nothing). The excerpt from Deuteronomy reads "Utinam saperent, et intelligerent, ac novissima providerent" (Would that they were wise, and understood, and considered their last end). The excerpt from Joshua reads "Si dimiseritis Dominum, . . . convertet se, et affliget vos, atque subdivertet postquam vobis praestiterit bona" (If ye will forsake the Lord, . . . He will turn, and cast you down, and bring you under after He hath given you good things).

160. **There . . . again** KP freely renders Fisher's splicing of recast excerpts from God's self-characterizations in Jeremiah 33:6 and Deuteronomy 32:39: "Nullus est qui potest sanare me, neque medicari plagae meae: nemo qui liberet me praeter te domine, qui vulnera infers, et sanas, percutis et curas" (There is no man that can heal me or cure my wounds, none who may deliver me except Thee, Lord, who causest wounds and healest, who strikest and curest). The excerpt from Jeremiah reads "Ecco ego obducam eis cicatricem et sanitatem, et curabo eos" (Behold I will close wounds and bring health, and I will cure them). The Deuteronomy excerpt reads "Videte quod ego sim solus, . . . ego occidam, et ego vivere faciam: percutiam, et ego sanabo, et non est qui de manu mea possit eruere" (See that I am [the] only [God], . . . I kill and I make alive; I strike and I will heal; nor is there any that can snatch out of My hand).

161. **My . . . Thee** KP renders Fisher's splicing of recast excerpts from 2 Peter 2:1 and Psalm 69:6: "Perditio mihi ex meipso, tantummodo in te auxilium meum et salus mea" (My perdition is from me; much more, my help and my salvation are in Thee). The excerpt from 2 Peter reads "superducentes sibi . . . perditionem" (they bring destruction upon themselves). The Psalm excerpt reads "Adjutor meus, et liberator meus es tu, Domine" (Lord, Thou art my Helper and Deliverer).

162. **For . . . strength** KP closely renders Fisher's minor recasting of Jeremiah 10:6: "Tibi enim nullus similis est, magnus es tu, et magnum est nomen fortitudinis tuae." The verse reads "Non est similis tui Domine: magnus es tu, et magnum nomen tuum in fortitudine" (There is none like unto Thee, Lord: great art Thou, and Thy name great in strength).

[Cvii v] Turn me to Thee, O Lord, and I shall be turned; take away from me this sinful heart, that Thy law may bring forth fruit in me.[163]

Remember me, Lord, for Thy goodness' sake, and for the great love that Thou bearest towards me.[164]

O Lord God, behold: Thou hast made both heaven and earth by Thy great might, and nothing is hard to Thee.[165]

Thou art that puissant and mighty, whose name is the Lord of hosts; great and marvelous in Thy counsel.[166]

As soon as Thou hast spoken the word, all things be done; as soon as Thou hast commanded, things be; and Thy word returneth not to Thee void, and without effect.[167]

163. **Turn . . . me** KP closely renders Fisher's recast quotation from Lamentations 5:21 and his recast excerpts from Baruch 1:22 and Psalm 1:2,3: "Converte me domine ad te, et convertar: auferà me cor malignum, ut faciat in me lex tua fructum." The Lamentations verse reads "Converte nos Domine ad te, et convertemur" (Turn us, Lord, toward Thee, and we shall be turned). The Baruch excerpt reads "abvimus unusquisque in sensum cordis nostri maligni" (we have gone off, every one of us, by the inclination of our ill-willling hearts). The Psalm excerpts read "qui . . . in lege Domini . . . meditabitur . . . fructum suum dabit" (He who . . . meditateth . . . on the law of the Lord . . . will bring forth his fruit).

164. **Remember . . . me** KP closely renders Fisher's paraphrase of 2 Esdras (Nehemiah) 13:22: "Memor esto mei propter bonitatem tuam domine, et amorem tuum erga me integrum." The verse reads "memento mei Deus meus, et parce mihi secundum multitudinem miserationum tuarum" (remember me, my God; and spare me according to the multitude of Thy mercies).

165. **O . . . Thee** KP renders Fisher's slightly recast excerpts from Jeremiah 32:17: "Eheu domine Deus: en tu es qui fecisti coelum et terram virtute tua magna, et brachio extento, et nihil est tibi difficile" (Ah, Lord God, behold: Thou art He who hath made heaven and earth by Thy great strength and with arm extended, and nothing is difficult for Thee). The Jeremiah excerpts read "Heu, . . . Domine Deus: ecce tu fecisti caelum et terram in fortitudine tua magna, et in brachio tuo extento: non eris tibi difficile" (Ah, . . . Lord God, behold: Thou hast made heaven and earth by Thy might; and with Thine arm extended: there is nothing difficult for Thee). KP does not translate Fisher's phrase "brachio extento" (with arm extended). This phrase is part of a formula for ascribing deliverance to God, "manu forti et brachio extento" (with His strong hand and extended arm), used in Deuteronomy 5:15, 9:29, 26:8 and in 4 Regum (2 Kings) 17:36.

166. **Thou . . . counsel** KP renders Fisher's recasting of excerpts from Jeremiah 32:18–19: "Tu es deus ille magnus et fortis, cui nomen est dominus exercituum, magnus et admirabilis in consilio tuo." The excerpts from Jeremiah read "Fortissime, magne . . . Dominus exercituum nomen tibi. Magnus consilio, et incomprehensibilis" (Mightiest, great . . . the Lord of hosts is Thy name. Great and unfathomable in counsel). **puissant . . . mighty** KP's doubling expands Fisher's "fortis" (strong) instead of translating "magne" (great), which occurs again in the latter half of this versicle. KP also does not translate Fisher's "deus" (God).

167. **As . . . effect** KP freely renders Fisher's recast excerpts from Isaiah 55:11: "Ipse enim es, qui simul atque verbum protuleris, cuncta fiunt, quum tu praeceperis, constant res, et verbum tuum non revertitur ad te vacuum" (For Thou art He, who as soon as Thou wilt speak the word, all things shall be; things accord with what Thou wilt command, and Thy word shall not

[Cviii r] Thou, O Lord God, showest mercy unto all: for Thou canst do all, and Thou makest as though Thou sawest not the sins of men, because they should do penance, and amend their lives.[168]

For Thou lovest all things that be, and hatest nothing that Thou hast made; for nothing Thou madest or hast ordained of any hatred.

Thou sparest and tenderest all men: for all things be Thine, and Thou lovest the souls of men.[169]

Thou dost minister mercy, equity, and justice in the earth, and therefore in these virtues Thou greatly delightest.[170]

Truly, O Lord, Thou art righteous and gracious, notwithstanding I have offended Thee, transgressing Thy covenant, and trespassing against Thee.[171]

---

return to Thee void). The Isaiah excerpts read "sic erit verbum meum, quod egredietur de ora meo: non revertetur ad me vacuum, sed faciet quaecumque volui, et prosperabitur in his, ad quae misi illud" (such will be My word that will go out of My mouth: it shall not return to Me void, but it will do whatever I wish, and this [word] shall prosper in the things to which I have directed it).

168. **Thou . . . lives** **Thou . . . penance** KP renders Fisher's nearly exact quotation of Wisdom of Solomon 11:24: "Domine Deus, tu misereris omnium, quia omnia potes, et dissimulas ad peccata hominum propter poenitentiam." The verse reads "misereris omnium, quia omnia potes, et dissimulas peccata hominum propter poenitentiam" (Thou hast mercy on all, because Thou canst do all, and Thou pretendest that the sins of men are not sins because of [their] repentance). KP's rendering of Fisher's and the Vulgate's "poenitentiam" as the doing of "penance" rather than as "repentance" or "penitence" explicitly aligns her with a pre-Reformation emphasis on earning salvation rather than receiving it as a gift from God; see nn74, 104, and introduction, pp. 201–2. **and . . . lives** KP's addition to Fisher's phrasing further emphasizes her focus here on the works of salvation.

169. **For Thou . . . men** KP renders Fisher's nearly exact quotations of Wisdom of Solomon 11:25, 27: "Diligis enim omnia quae sunt, et nihil eorum odisti, quae facta sunt, non enim per odium aliquid fecisti, aut constituisti. Parcis autem omnibus, quia tua sunt omnia, qui amas animas." The two verses read "Diligis enim omnia quae sunt, et nihil odisti eorum quae fecisti: nec enim odiens aliqui constituisti, aut fecisti. . . . Parcis autem omnibus: quoniam tua sunt Domine, qui amas animas" (For Thou lovest all things that are, and Thou hatest nothing of those that Thou hast made; nor indeed hast Thou constituted or made anything in hatred. . . . Thou indeed sparest all, because all are Thine, Lord, who lovest souls). **sparest . . . tenderest** KP's doubling of Fisher's and the Vulgate's "Parcis" (Sparest).

170. **Thou . . . delightest** KP closely renders Fisher's splicing of recast excerpts from Wisdom of Solomon 9:1, 3: "Tu misericordiam, equitatem, et iusticiam facis in terra, qua propter et iis unicè delectaris." The excerpts read "Domine misericordiae, qui fecisti omnia . . . ut disponat orbem terrarum in aequitate et iustitia, et in directione cordis iudicium iudicet" (Lord of mercies, who hath made all things . . . so as to establish the earth's orb in equity and justice, and to render judgment in the uprightness of Thine heart). **therefore . . . delightest** KP closely follows Fisher's deviation from the sense of God's heart in Wisdom of Solomon 9:3, where His upright judgment is foremost, not His delight in the concurrent exercise of several cardinal virtues.

171. **Truly . . . Thee** KP quite closely renders Fisher's splicing of recast excerpts from Deuteronomy 32:4 and Hosea 5:15 and 8:1: "Justus quidem et bonus tu domine, ego autem vultum tuum

[Cviii v] O Lord, Thou hast seen all my abominations: look on my cause, and consider how vile and wretched I am; see and behold my great confusion.[172]

In the time of reconciliation hear me, and in the day of salvation have mercy on me.[173]

Be merciful unto me, and have mercy on me, which have none other help but Thee: whose will nothing can resist, whensoever Thou dost purpose to save.[174]

Hear me, which am a wretch making supplication unto Thee: make me to trust in Thy name, and deliver me by Thy power.[175]

---

offendi, transgressus sum foedus tuum, in te praevaricatus sum." The Deuteronomy excerpts read "Deus . . . absque ulla iniquitate, justus et rectus" (God . . . without any evil, just and upright). The excerpt from Hosea 5, in God's voice, reads "Vadens . . . ad locum meum: donec deficiatis, et quaeratis faciem meam" (I will go . . . to My place as long as they will forsake Me, and until they will seek My face). The excerpt from Hosea 8 reads, again in God's voice, "transgressi sunt foedus meum, et legem meam praevaricati sunt" (they have transgressed My covenant and trespassed against My law). **offended Thee** KP substitutes a pronoun for Fisher's "vultum tuum offendi" (offended before Thy face).

172. **Thou . . . confusion** KP freely renders Fisher's splicing of recast excerpts from Ezekiel 8:6 and Psalm 34:23 with an expansion, by doubling, of an excerpt from Lamentations 1:11: "Vidisti domine facinora mea, inspice [1544: suscipe] causam meam, recordare quàm vilis factus sum, suscipe [1544: inspice] et contemplare obprobrium meum" (Thou hast seen, Lord, my outrages: take up my cause; be mindful how vile I have become; see and consider my disgrace). KP follows the preferable order of the two verbs in the first London edition. The Ezekiel excerpts, in which God speaks to the prophet, read "fili hominis, . . . vides tu quid isti faciunt, abominationes magnas, quas domus Israel facit hic?" (son of man, dost thou see what these people have done, the great abominations that the house of Israel doth do here?). The Psalm excerpt reads "intende judicio meo . . . Dominus meus, in causam meam" (attend unto my judgment . . . my Lord, and unto my cause). The Lamentation excerpt reads "vide Domine et considera, quoniam facta sum vilis" (see, Lord, and consider, how I have become vile). **vile . . . wretched** KP's redoubling. **great confusion** KP's approximate rendering of Fisher's "obprobrium" (disgrace, reproach).

173. **In . . . me** KP closely renders Fisher's recasting of Isaiah 49:8: "In tempore reconciliationis exaude me, et in die salutis miserere mei." The verse, in God's voice, reads "In tempore placito exaudivi te, et in die salutis auxiliatus sum tui" (In a pleasing time I have heard thee, and in a day of salvation I have helped thee).

174. **Be . . . save Be . . . on me** KP varies Fisher's verbatim repetition: "Miserere mei, miserere mei." **which . . . save** KP closely renders Fisher's recasting of excerpts from Esther 14:14 and 13:8: "nullum aliud auxilium habentis praeter te, cuius voluntati nihil resistere potest, dunmodo decreveris salvare" (having no other help besides Thee, whose will nothing can resist whenever Thou wilt decide to save). The first excerpt reads "nullum alius auxilium habentem, nisi te, Domine" (I have no other help except for Thee, Lord). The second excerpt reads "non est qui possit tuae resistere voluntati, si decreveris salvare" (there is none that may resist Thy will, if Thou wilt decide to save).

175. **make me . . . power** KP closely renders Fisher's recast excerpts from Esther 14:12, 14: "tibi supplicantem, da mihi fiduciam nominis tui, et libera me in manu tua." The first excerpt reads "Memento Domine . . . et da mihi fiduciam Domine" (Be mindful, Lord, . . . and give

[Di r] Have regard to me from heaven, O Lord; and look down from Thy holy habitation, and from the throne of Thy glory.[176]

Destroy me not because of my iniquity, but remember the sorrow and pain that I suffer.[177]

Be not still angry with me, O Lord: forget all my sins, and remember them no longer.[178]

Let my prayer ascend up unto Thee. Say unto my soul, Behold I am come to thee, Thy health and Thy salvation.[179] Amen.

THE THIRD PSALM, FOR REMISSION OF SINS.

O God, eternal, just, and holy, which keepest covenant and mercy with them that love Thee, and keep Thy commandments:[180]

---

me trust, Lord). The second excerpt reads "Nos . . . libera manu tua" (Deliver us by Thy hand). **power** KP substitutes an abstract analogue of Fisher's and the Vulgate's "manus" (hand).

176. **Have . . . glory** KP closely renders Fisher's slight recasting of Isaiah 63:15: "Adtende de coelo domine, respice de habitaculo sancto tuo, et de solio gloriae tuae." The verse reads "Attende de caelo, et vide de habitaculo sancto tuo, et gloriae tuae" (Look down from heaven, and see from Thy holy habitation and Thy glory).

177. **Destroy . . . suffer** KP freely renders Fisher's splicing of recast excerpts from Isaiah 64:7 and Exodus 3:7: "Ne allidas me in manu iniquitatis meae, nec obliviscaris doloris et adflictionis meae." The Isaiah excerpt reads, with a sense opposite to Fisher's, "allisisti nos in manu iniquitatis nostrae" (Thou hast struck us with Thy hand for our iniquities). **Destroy . . . iniquity** KP's approximate rendering of Fisher's "Ne allidas me in manu iniquitatis meae" (Do not strike me with Thy hand for my iniquity). **but . . . suffer** The Exodus excerpt is from God's expression of pity for the Israelites enslaved in Egypt: "Vidi afflictionem populi mei . . . et sciens dolorem ejus" (I have seen the affliction of My people, . . . and I know their sorrow).

178. **Be . . . longer** KP closely renders Fisher's slight recasting of Isaiah 64:9: "Ne irascaris satis domine, ne recorderis ultra omnis iniquitatis meae." The verse reads "Ne irascaris Domine satis, et ne ultra memineris iniquitatis nostrae" (Be not fully angry, Lord, and remember no longer our iniquities).

179. **Let . . . salvation** KP renders Fisher's splicing of recast excerpts from Psalms 88:2 and 34:3: "Veniat ad te oratio mea: dic animae meae, en ego salus tua iam adsum" (Let my prayer come before Thee; say unto my soul, Behold, I am now become Thy salvation). The first excerpt reads "Intret in conspectu tuo oratio mea" (Let my prayer enter Thy regard). The second excerpt reads "dic animae meae: Salus tua ego sum" (say unto my soul: I am Thy salvation). **Let . . . up** KP's variation on Fisher's "Veniat" (Let . . . come up). **health . . . salvation** KP's doubling.

180. **O . . . commandments** KP closely renders Fisher's nearly verbatim quoting of an excerpt from 2 Esdras (Nehemiah) 1:5: "Deus aeterne, juste, et sancte, qui custodis pactum et misericordiam cum iis qui te diligunt, et mandata tua servant." The excerpt reads "Domine Deus . . . fortis, magne atque terribilis, qui custodis pactum et misericordiam cum his qui te diligunt, et custodiunt mandata tua" (Lord God, . . . strong, great, and fearsome, who keepeth covenant and mercy with them who love Thee and keep Thy commandments).

[Di v] Look at me, and have mercy upon me; for I have trespassed against Thee, and done evil in Thy sight.[181]

Show forth upon me the tender affections of Thy mercy, that Thy servant may have a heart to pray unto Thee.[182]

I humbly make my prayer before Thy face, not trusting in mine own righteousness, but in Thy great mercies.[183]

For I am unclean and filthy, and all my righteousness is like a foul, bloody clout.[184]

Unto Thee, O Lord, be justice, mercy, and pity, but unto me be confusion and shame for my iniquities.[185]

181. **Look . . . sight** KP renders Fisher's splicing of slightly recast excerpts from Psalm 24:16 (identical to Psalm 85:16) and Psalm 50:6: "Respice ad me, et miserere mei, quoniam in te peccavi, et feci malum ante oculos tuos." The first excerpt reads "Respice in me, et miserere mei" (Look upon me, and have mercy upon me). The second excerpt reads "Tibi soli peccavi, et malum coram te feci" (I have sinned against Thee only, and done evil in Thy sight).

182. **Show . . . Thee** KP renders Fisher's complex splicing of recast excerpts from Ecclesiasticus 18:9, Luke 1:76, and 1 Paralipomenon (1 Chronicles) 17:25: "Effunde super me viscera misericordiae tuae, ut inveniat servus cor ad orandum te" (Pour out upon me the bowels of Thy mercy, that Thy servant may find a heart for praying unto Thee). The Ecclesiasticus excerpt reads "Deus . . . effundit super eos misericordiam suam" (God poured His mercy over them). The Luke excerpt reads "Per viscera misericordiae Dei nostri" (By the bowels of our God's mercy). The 1 Paralipomenon excerpt reads "invenit servus tuus fiduciam, ut oret coram te" (Thy servant findeth trust, that he may pray in Thy presence). **tender affections** KP's periphrasis for "viscera" (bowels, inward parts). **a . . . Thee** KP closely renders Fisher's "cor ad orandum te"—a phrase possibly originating in his own or his printer's misreading of "oret coram te" (may he pray in Thy presence). No locution of the form "cor ad orandum te" occurs in the Vulgate.

183. **I . . . mercies** KP freely renders Fisher's slightly recast excerpts from Daniel 9:18: "Non prosterno preces meas ante faciem tuam in justificationibus meis, sed in misericordiis tuis multis" (I do not strew my prayers upon the ground before Thy face for my righteousness, but for Thy many mercies). The excerpt reads "neque . . . in justificationibus nostris prosternimus preces ante faciem tuam, sed in miserationibus tuis multis" (nor do we strew prayers upon the ground before Thy face for our righteousness, but for Thy many mercies). **humbly make** KP's sensitive substitution for "prosterno" (strew upon the ground). **trusting** KP's felicitous addition to the condensed phrasing of Fisher and the Vulgate.

184. **For . . . clout** KP freely renders Fisher's slightly recast excerpt from Isaiah 64:6: "Nam ego immundus totus, et quasi pannus mulieris menstruo pollutae universae justiciae meae" (For I am wholly unclean, and all my righteousness is polluted with menstrual blood like a woman's rag). The excerpt reads "Et facti sumus ut immundus omnes nos, et quasi pannus menstruatae universae justitiae nostrae" (And all we are made unclean, and all our uprightness like the rag of a menstruating woman). **unclean . . . filthy** KP's doubling. **a . . . clout** Exhibiting feminine delicacy, KP moderates the graphic image in Fisher and the Vulgate. **clout** rag, piece of cloth.

185. **Unto . . . iniquities** KP closely renders Fisher's reordering and splicing of excerpts from Daniel 9:7, 9, 8: "Tibi domine justicia et misericordia, et propitiatio, mihi autem confusio faciei propter iniquitates meas." The excerpt from verse 7 reads "Tibi Domine justitia" (Unto Thee,

Certainly even from my beginning I have used myself proudly against Thee, doing wickedly, and ceasing not.[186]

[Dii r] O Lord, Thou hast redeemed me, and yet I have not ceased to offend Thee, and my heart hath not been straight in Thy sight.[187]

Thou hast taught and instructed me, and stablished my power; and I have been evil affected towards Thee, being like unto a deceitful bow.[188]

My pride and presumption accuse me to my face; I am overthrown in mine own wickedness. I do seek Thee, O Lord; I beseech Thee that I may find Thee. Thou art separated from me, for I have greedily followed filthiness.[189]

Lord, be justice). The excerpt from verse 9 reads "Tibi . . . Domino Deo nostro misericordia, et propitiatio" (Unto Thee, our Lord God, be mercy and pity). The excerpt from verse 8 and another from verse 7 read "Domine, nobis confusio faciei . . . propter iniquitates" (Lord, to us is confusion of face . . . on account of [our] iniquities).

186. **Certainly . . . not** KP closely renders Fisher's free recasting and splicing of excerpts from Ecclesiasticus 10:14–15 and Hosea 1:20: "Certe ab initio superbè egi contra te, faciens iniquitatem, et non cessans." The Ecclesiasticus excerpts read "initium omnis peccati est superbia . . . hominis, . . . quoniam ab Deo, qui fecit illum, recessit cor ejus" (the beginning of all sin is the pride . . . of man . . . because his heart withdrew from God who made him). The Hosea excerpt reads "fornicati sunt, et non cessaverunt" (they are fornicators, and they have not ceased). **ceasing not** The verb phrase is ambiguous in English and in Latin; in the Vulgate "cesso" can mean "to stop" or "to fail to function." Either sense fits an inveterate sinner's confession of active continuation in sin.

187. **O . . . sight** KP freely renders Fisher's splicing of recast excerpts from Psalm 30:6, Ecclesiasticus 38:15, and Psalm 77:37: "Tu redemisti me domine, sed ego adversum te mendacia dixi [1544: semper tamen deliqui], et cor meum non fuit rectum coram te" (Thou hast redeemed me, Lord, but I nevertheless have spoken untruths against Thee [have always offended Thee], and my heart was not right before Thee). Her rendering is closer to the wording of the first English edition than to that of the Cologne edition. The first Psalm excerpt reads "redemisti me Domine" (Thou hast redeemed me, Lord). The excerpt from Ecclesiasticus reads "delinquit in conspectu ejus, qui fecit eum" (he offended in the sight of Him, who made him). The second Psalm excerpt reads "cor . . . eorum non erat rectum cum eo" (their heart was not right with Him).

188. **Thou . . . bow** KP freely renders Fisher's recasting of excerpts from Hosea 7:15–16: "Tu erudisti me, et confirmasti brachium meum, et ad te [1544: coram te tantum] cogitavi malum, factus ut arcus dolosus" (Thou hast taught me, and strengthened my arm; and toward Thee I pondered [so much] evil, I acted like a deceitful bow). The excerpts, in the voice of God, read "ego erudivi eos, et confortavi brachia eorum: et in me cogitaverunt malitiam . . . facti sunt quasi arcus dolosus" (I instructed them, and strengthened their arms, but they pondered evil toward Me . . . they have acted like a deceitful bow). **taught . . . instructed** KP's doubling.

189. **My . . . filthiness** KP quite closely renders Fisher's recasting of a series of small excerpts from Hosea 5:5–6, 11: "Et respondit arrogantia in facie mea, obrutus sum in iniquitate mea, quaero te domine, obsecro ut inveniam, divisus es à me, quia cupidè post sordes abii." The excerpts, a series of predictions by God, read "Et respondebit arrogantia Israel in facie ejus: et Israel et Ephraim ruent in iniquitate sua . . . vadent ad quaerendum Dominum, et non invenient: ablatus est ab eis. . . . quoniam [Ephraim] coepit abire post sordes" (And the pride of Israel will

Yet will I accuse mine own sinful ways before Thee, O Lord, until Thou have mercy upon me, and receive me again into Thy favor.[190]

[Dii v] God forbid that ever I should depart from Thee again, and not diligently seek for Thy promises.

I will never hold my peace nor keep silence, until Thou have established that covenant with me, which Thou hast made and ordained in times past:[191]

That is to say, like as the justice of a just man shall not deliver or save him what time soever he shall offend, so the wickedness of a wicked man shall not hurt him, what time soever he shall return from his wickedness.[192]

[Diii r] In hope of this, O Lord God, I will tarry Thy pleasure, for Thou art good to them that trust in Thee, and to the soul that seeketh Thee.[193]

---

come back in their face, and Israel and Ephraim fall down in their iniquity. . . . They go to seek the Lord, and they will not find Him: He is separated from them . . . since [Ephraim] beginneth to go off after filth). **pride . . . presumption** KP's doubling.

190. **Yet . . . favor Yet . . . Lord** Adding the adjective "sinful," KP misconstrues as negative Fisher's close paraphrase of an excerpt from Job 13:15: "Veruntamen vias meas coram facie tua arguam" (Nevertheless I will declare my own ways before Thy face). She may have been misled by the possible negative senses of "arguo" (to accuse, to censure). But the full Vulgate verse makes clear the positive use of "arguo" here: "Etiam si occeiderit me, in ipso sperabo: verumtamen vias meas in conspectu ejus arguam" (Even if He shall kill me, I will trust in Him; nevertheless I will declare my ways in His sight). **receive . . . favor** KP renders Fisher's recasting of an excerpt from 2 Corinthians 6:1: "recipias me in gratiam tuam." The excerpt, a reference to the gift of salvation enabled by Christ's sacrifice of His life, reads "ne in vacuum gratiam Dei recipatis" (do not receive the grace of God in vain). KP's otherwise valid choice to render "gratia" as "favor" dulls the Christological resonance in Fisher's source text.

191. **I . . . past** KP closely renders Fisher's free recasting of excerpts from Isaiah 62:6–8: "Non tacebo, et non dabo silentium, donec confirmes mecum foedus, quod constituisti retro temporibus." The excerpts read "Qui reminiscimini Domini, ne taceatis, et ne detis silentium ei, donec stabiliat . . . Jerusalem. . . . Juravit Dominus in dextera sua, et in brachio fortitudinis suae" (You who remember the Lord, do not hold your peace, and do not keep silent toward Him, until He establish . . . Jerusalem. . . . The Lord hath sworn by His right hand, and by the arm of His strength). **hast made . . . ordained** KP's doubling of Fisher's "constituisti" (hath established).

192. **like . . . wickedness** KP closely renders Fisher's nearly verbatim quotation from Ezekiel 33:12: "sicut justitia justi non liberabit eum in quaecunque die peccaverit: ita impietas impii non nocebit ei, in quacunque die conversus fuerit ab impietate sua." The source text differs only in presenting the parallel assertions without the correlative conjunctions "sic . . . ita" (as . . . so). **shall . . . save** KP's redoubling of Fisher's and the Vulgate's "non liberabit" (shall not deliver).

193. **In . . . Thee** KP freely renders Fisher's splicing of recast excerpts from Psalm 51:11 and Lamentations 3:25: "In hoc expectabo te domine Deus: nam bonus es tu in te fidentibus, animae quaerenti te" (I will wait upon Thee, Lord God: for Thou art good to those who trust in Thee, and to the soul seeking Thee). The Psalm excerpt reads "expectabo nomen tuum, quoniam bonum est" (I will wait upon Thy name, for it is good). The excerpt from Lamentations reads "Bonus est Dominus sperantibus in ejus, animae quaerenti illum" (The Lord is good to those hoping in Him, to the soul seeking Him).

Thou keepest Thy truth for evermore, and the word which issueth forth of Thy mouth shall not be void and of none effect.[194]

Destroy me not, good Lord, for my sins, nor reserve not eternal punishment for me.[195]

Open Thine eyes and behold the greatness of my pain and affliction: for my iniquity is great in Thy sight, and my sins have brought me into this trouble.[196]

[Diii v] Destroy me not utterly, nor leave me in my sins; for Thou art [a] God of mercy and very gracious.[197]

Execute not the punishment upon me which Thou hadst purposed; do to me according to Thy name, although my defaults and sins be many.[198]

194. **Thou . . . effect** KP renders Fisher's splicing of recast excerpts from Psalm 116:2, Proverbs 12:19, and Joshua 21:43: "Tu servas veritatem tuam in aeternum, et quod egreditur de labiis tuis, non fiet irritum." The Psalm excerpt reads "veritas Domini manet in aeternum" (the truth of the Lord remaineth forever). The Proverbs excerpt reads "Labium veritatis firmum erit in perpetuum" (The lip of truth will be firm forever). The excerpt from Joshua reads "Ne unam quidem verbum, quod illis . . . promiserat, irritum fuit" (Not one word of what He . . . promised them lacked effect). **void . . . effect** KP's redoubling of Fisher's and the Vulgate's "irritum."

195. **Destroy . . . me** KP closely renders Fisher's splicing of freely recast excerpts from Psalm 25:9 and 2 Peter 2:9: "Ne perdas me domine propter iniquitates meas, neque in aeternum reserves mihi mala." The Psalm excerpt reads "Ne perdas cum impiis Deus animam meam" (O God, destroy not my soul with the sinners). The excerpt from 2 Peter reads "Novit Dominus . . . iniquos verò in diem judicii reservare cruciandos" (God knoweth how . . . to reserve the wicked unto the day of judgment to be punished).

196. **Open . . . trouble** KP freely renders Fisher's complex splicing of recast excerpts from 4 Kings (2 Kings in English Bibles) 19:16, 1 Paralipomenon (1 Chronicles) 21:15, and Isaiah 59:12: "Aperi oculos tuos, et vide magnitudinem mali mei: et multa est enim iniquitas mea in conspectu tuo, et peccata mea responderunt mihi" (Open Thine eyes, and see the magnitude of my evil; great indeed is my iniquity in Thy sight, and my sins have come back upon me). The excerpt from 4 Kings reads "aperi Domine oculos tuos et vide" (open Thine eye, Lord, and see). The excerpt from 1 Paralipomenon reads "vidit Dominus, et misertus est super magnitudine mali" (the Lord saw, and was sorry over the magnitude of evil). The excerpt from Isaiah reads "Multiplicatae sunt enim iniquitates nostrae coram te, et peccata nostra responderunt nobis" (Our iniquities are indeed multiplied before Thee, and our sins come back upon us). **pain . . . affliction** KP's doubling of "mali" (evil). **have . . . trouble** KP's idiomatic expansion of "responderunt mihi" (have come back upon me).

197. **Destroy . . . gracious Destroy . . . sins** KP renders Fisher's splicing of recast excerpts from Jeremiah 10:24 and Hebrews 13:4–5: "Ne redigas me penitus in consumptionem, ne ve deseras me in peccatis meis" (Do not bring me, a penitent, into a consumption, neither abandon me in my sins). The Jeremiah excerpt reads "Domine . . . ne forte ad nihilum redigas me" (O Lord, do not bring me, by chance, to nothing). The excerpts from Hebrews read "judicabit Deus . . . ipse enim dixit: Non te deseram" (the Lord will judge . . . He Himself indeed hath said: I will not desert Thee). **Thou . . . very gracious** KP's intensification of Fisher's "clemens es tu" (gracious art Thou).

198. **Execute . . . many** KP renders Fisher's splicing of recast excerpts from Jeremiah 26:13 and Job 13:23: "Poeniteat te mali quod [1544: punitionis, quam] in me decreveras, et secundum

O Lord, Thou art my God, and Thy name hath been put upon me; leave me not in the deepness of my troubles.[199]

Thou hast chastised and reformed many, and hast strengthed the weary hands; Thy words have set up him that staggered, and Thou hast made straight the crooked knees.[200]

[Div r] Wherefore I will seek Thee, O Lord God, which hast wrought great things, unsearchable and innumerable.[201]

Thou hast taken up the poor out of the dust, and hast exalted them which were abjects.[202]

---

nomen tuum facito, quamquàm multae sunt defectiones atque peccata" (Repent Thee of the evil [punishment] which Thou hast decreed upon me; and do according to Thy name, although my defaults and sins are many). KP's "punishment" renders "punitionis" in the first English edition although the Cologne edition's "mali" reproduces the Vulgate wording of the Jeremiah excerpt. It reads "poenitebit Dominus mali, quod locutus est adversum vos" (the Lord will repent of the evil that He hath spoken against you). The Job excerpt reads "Quantas habeo iniquitates et peccata . . . ? ostende mihi" (How many are my iniquities and sins . . . ? show me). **Execute not** KP sensitively recasts a verb that is somewhat incongruously predicated of God: "Poeniteat te" (Repent Thee).

199. **O . . . troubles** KP closely renders Fisher's recast excerpt from Jeremiah 14:9: "O domine deus meus es tu, et nomen tuum impositum est mihi, ne derelinquas me in profundo malorum meorum" (O Lord, Thou art my God, and Thy name hath been placed upon me; leave me not in the depth of my evils). The Jeremiah excerpt reads "tu . . . in nobis es Domine, et nomen tuam invocatum est super nos, ne derelinquas nos" (Thou . . . art our God, and Thy name hath been invoked over us; do not leave us).

200. **Thou . . . knees** KP renders Fisher's recasting of Job 4:3–4: "Tu erudisti multos, et manus lassas confortasti, nutantem erexerunt sermones tui, et genua incuruata direxisti" (Thou hast instructed many, and hast much strengthened the weary hands; Thy words have raised up him that tottered, and Thou hast straightened the crooked knees). The verses read "docuist multos, et manus lassas roborasti: vacillantes confirmaverunt sermones tui, et genua trementia confortasti" (Thou hast taught many, and hast strenghtened the weary hands; Thy words have upheld them that staggered, and Thou hast much strengthened the feeble knees). **chastised . . . reformed** KP's redoubling of Fisher's "erudisti" (instructed). **strengthed** strengthened—an earlier variant form of this verb.

201. **Wherefore . . . innumerable** KP closely renders Fisher's recasting of excerpts from Job 5:8–9: "Et propterea requiram te domine deus, qui fecisti magna, inperverstigabilia, et innumerabilia." The excerpts read "Quam ob rem ego deprecabor Dominum . . . qui facit magna et inscrutabilia et mirabilia absque numero" (Wherefore I will implore the Lord . . . who doth great things, unsearchable and marvelous, without number).

202. **Thou . . . abjects** KP renders Fisher's recasting of Psalm 112:7: "Suscitasti de pulvere inopes, abjectos exaltasti tuo auxilio" (Thou hast raised the poor man fron the dust, and hast exalted with Thine help them that were cast down). The verse reads "Suscitans a terra inopem, et de stercore erigens pauperem" (He lifteth the poor man up from the earth, and he raiseth the needy ones from the dunghill). KP does not translate Fisher's phrase "tuo auxilio" (with Thy help). She may have recognized it as a non-Scriptural addition. **abjects** a cognate of "abjectos" (those cast down). Besides this occurrence in *Psalms or Prayers*, singular "abject" occurs three

For Thou dost deliver the poor in his misery out of the strait and bottomless pit of tribulation, and out of the wide mouth of anguish and affliction, into rest and quietness.[203]

Thou art gracious and merciful, for that Thou showest mercy to them, which be not yet come into the world; and Thou art very merciful to them, which diligently observe and keep Thy laws; and Thou dost patiently suffer sinners, giving them time and place whereby they may be changed from their malice.[204]

[Div v] Hear me, poor wretch, making supplication unto Thee, for in Thee and in Thy name I have put my trust and affiance.[205]

---

times in KP's *Prayers or Meditations* and once in her personal prayerbook. The unusual word choice appears to add stylistic evidence to the otherwise circumstantial evidence that KP was the translator of *Psalms or Prayers*.

203. **For . . . quietness** KP renders very freely Fisher's odd recasting of excerpts from Job 36:15–16: "Tu etenim es qui liberas pauperem in miseria ab ore angustiae lato, sub quo nullum est firmamentum" (For Thou art He who dost deliver the poor man, in his misery of narrowness, from the wide mouth beneath which there is no firm support). The Job excerpts read "Eripiet de angustia sua pauperem. . . . Igitur salvabit te de ore angusto latissime, et non habente fundamentum subter se" (He pulleth the poor man out of his misery. . . . Thus He will rescue thee into a very broad place, from the narrow mouth, which has no foundation under it). **strait . . . tribulation . . . wide . . . affliction** KP copes with the obscure imagery in both Fisher and the Vulgate by creating a descriptive doublet—a very deep, narrow "pit" (a former synonym for "hole") and a "wide mouth"—to figure contrasting aspects of suffering. **into . . . quietness** KP added this phrase, probably in an attempt to lessen the obscurity of the preceding imagery.

204. **Thou . . . malice** KP closely renders Fisher's complex splicing of recast excerpts from Exodus 34:6–7; Romans 9:3, 10–11; 2 Peter 3:15; and Wisdom of Solomon 12:19–20: "Tu clemens es, et misericors, eo quod miseraberis [1544: miseraris] eis, qui non dum in saeculum venerunt, et multum misericors es illis, qui versantur in lege tua, et longanimus es erga eos, qui peccaverunt, concedens tempus et locum, per quae possunt mutari à malicia." The Exodus excerpts read "Domine Deus, misericors et clemens, patiens et multae miserationis . . . qui aufers iniquitatem . . . et peccata" (Lord God, merciful and gracious, long-suffering and of great mercies . . . who forgivest iniquity . . . and sins). The excerpts from Romans read "qui sunt Israelitae, quorum adoptio est filiorum, . . . et legislatio, et obsequium, et promissa. . . . Non enim omnes qui ex Israël sunt . . . sed . . . enim nondùm nati fuissent" (they are the Israelites, to whom is adoption as children, . . . and the law, and the service of God, and the promises . . . Not all indeed who are from Israel . . . but . . . even those who have not yet been born). The excerpt from 2 Peter reads "Domini nostri longanimitatem, salutem" (the long-suffering of our Lord is salvation). The excerpt from Wisdom of Solomon reads "quoniam judicans das locum in peccatis poenitentiae . . . dans tempus et locum, per quae possent mutari a malitia" (because Thou judgest, Thou givest sinners a place for repentance. . . . Thou givest time and a place, whereby they may be changed from their malice). **observe . . . keep** KP's doubling of Fisher's "versantur" (apply themselves to).

205. **trust . . . affiance** KP's doubling of Fisher's "fiduciam" (trust). She closely renders the formulaic language of this verse, whose separate locutions recur too frequently in the Vulgate to be precisely traced.

Take me, Thy servant, unto Thee, and make me good; and let me not be disappointed of that that I look for.[206]

Come again, O Lord God, and save my soul; destroy me not, whom Thou hast redeemed by Thy great might and power.[207]

Look not upon the hardness of my heart, nor upon my sins; but like as Thou hast many times showed mercy, so now be merciful and forgive me.[208]

[Dv r] Hear me, O Lord, and be pacified; regard my prayer, and do according to Thy great name.[209]

O Lord, I look to have help and salvation from Thee, and this is my daily meditation and exercise.[210]

For Thy mercies be great, and Thy goodness is inestimable.

206. **Take . . . for** KP freely renders Fisher's recasting of Psalm 118:116: "Suscipe servum tuum in bonum, et ne confundas me ab expectatione mea" (Raise up Thy servant to good purpose, and let me not be confounded in my expectation). The first half of the Psalm verse reads "Suscipe me secundum eloquium tuum, et vivam" (Raise me up according to Thy word, and let me live). Fisher quotes the second half of the verse exactly. **disappointed** KP is among the earliest English writers to use this adjective; its occurrence here may be stylistic evidence of her role as translator of *Psalms or Prayers*. The first *OED* citation is dated 1552.

207. **destroy . . . power** KP closely renders Fisher's recasting of excerpts from Deuteronomy 9:26: "ne disperdas me, quem redemisti in magnitudine brachii tui." The excerpts read "ne disperdas . . . hereditatem tuam, quam redemisti in magnitudine tua . . . in manu forti" (Do not destroy Thine heirs, whom Thou hast redeemed by Thy greatness . . . by Thy strong hand). **Thy . . . power** KP's doubling of abstract nouns replaces Fisher's "magnitudine brachii tui" (greatness of Thine arm).

208. **Look . . . me** KP freely renders Fisher's splicing of recast excerpts from Deuteronomy 9:27 and Isaiah 55:7: "Ne adspicias duriciam cordis et impietates meas, sed ignosce mihi in misericordiis tuis multis" (Regard not my hardness of heart and my impieties, but forgive me by Thy many mercies). The excerpt from Deuteronomy reads "ne aspicias duritiem populi huius, et impietatem" (regard not the hardness of this people, and their impiety). The excerpt from Isaiah, a description of God's mercy to sinners, reads "multus est ad ignoscendum" (there is much for Him to forgive). **be merciful . . . forgive** KP's redoubled verb phrases replace Fisher's single predicate, "ignosce . . . multis."

209. **Hear . . . name** KP closely renders Fisher's recast excerpts from Daniel 9:19: "Exaudi domine, placare domine, attende, et facias juxta magnum nomen tuum." The excerpts from Daniel read "Exaudi Domine, placare Domine: attende et fac . . . quia nomen tuum invocatum est . . . super populum tuum" (Hear, Lord; be pacified, Lord: regard and act . . . for Thy name is called upon . . . by Thy people).

210. **O . . . exercise** KP freely renders Fisher's splicing of close quotations from Genesis 22:5 and Psalm 118:97: "Expecto salutem tuam domine, omni die ipsa meditatio mea est" (I look for Thy salvation, Lord; it is my meditation all the day). Fisher quotes the Genesis excerpt verbatim. The Psalm excerpt reads "tota die meditatio mea est" (it is my meditation all the day). **help . . . salvation** KP's doubling. **daily . . . exercise** KP's redoubled nouns replace Fisher's singular predicate, "omni . . . est."

Hear me now favorably, and withhold Thy mercies no longer from me.

In the way of Thy judgments I will look after Thee; my soul desireth to magnify Thy name, and to have Thee in memory.[211]

Incline my heart to do Thy commandments, and direct my ways evermore in Thy sight.[212]

Let me never hereafter go away from Thy ways, nor leave me not now in the deepness of my troubles.

[Dv v] Turn not Thine eyes away from me, but teach me, O Lord, to do those things which are pleasant in Thy sight.[213]

Make a perpetual league and covenant with me, that Thou wilt put Thy fear into my heart, that I never swerve from Thee in all my life.[214]

Withdraw not Thy goodness from me forever, but keep Thy promise and fidelity.[215]

211. **In . . . memory** KP closely renders Fisher's recasting of Isaiah 26:8: "In via judiciorum tuorum expectabo te, erga nomen tuum, et erga memoriam tuam desiderium animae meae." The verse reads "in semita judiciorum tuorum Domine sustinuimus te: nomen tuum, et memoriale tuum in desiderio animae" (in the way of Thy judgments, Lord, we have stayed for Thee; the desire of our soul is to Thy name and to Thy remembrance).

212. **Incline . . . sight** KP closely renders Fisher's splicing of recast excerpts from Psalms 118:112 and 5:9: "Inclina cor meum ad faciendum praecepta tua, et dirige vias meas in conspectu tuo semper." The first Psalm excerpt reads "Inclinavi cor meum ad faciendas justificationes tuas in aeternum" (I have inclined my heart to do Thy commandments forever). The second Psalm excerpt reads "Domine . . . dirige in conspectu tuo viam meam" (Lord, . . . direct my way in Thy sight).

213. **Turn . . . sight** KP closely renders Fisher's splicing of recast excerpts from Job 36:7 and Deuteronomy 13:18: "Ne subducas à me oculos tuos, sed instrue me facere quae placita sunt in conspectu tuo domine." The Job excerpt reads "Non auferet a justo oculos suos" (He doth not turn His eyes from the just man). The Deuteronomy excerpt reads "quando audieris vocem Domini Dei tui . . . facias quod placitum est in conspectu Domini Dei tui" (when thou shalt hear the voice of thy Lord God . . . do what is pleasing in the sight of thy Lord God).

214. **Make . . . life** KP renders Fisher's recasting of Jeremiah 32:40: "Paciscere mecum foedus in sempiternum, quod timorem tuum daturus sis in cor meum, ut non deficiam à te omnibus diebus" (Conclude an everlasting covenant with me, that Thou wilt give fear to my heart, that I may never desert Thee in all [my] days). The verse, in God's voice, reads "Et feriam eis pactum sempiternum, et non desinam eis benefacere: et timorem meum dabo in corde eorum ut non recedant a me" (And I will make an everlasting covenant with them, and I will not fail to do them good; and I will give fear to their heart, that they depart not from Me). **league . . . covenant** KP's redoubling. **I . . . swerve** KP intensifies Fisher's "desinam" (I . . . desert).

215. **Withdraw . . . fidelity** KP renders Fisher's recasting of an excerpt from 1 Paralipomenon (1 Chronicles) 17:13: "In aeternum ne auferas à me bonitatem tuam, nec fallas mihi veritatem tuam" (Take not Thy goodness from me forever, nor cheat me of Thy truth). The excerpt reads "misericordiam meam non auferam ab eo, sicut abstuli ab eo, qui ante te fuit" (I will not take My mercy from him, as I did from him who was before thee).

Be good unto me with benevolence and favor: for Thou art merciful, and Thy displeasure continueth not forever.[216]

Remember me with favor and kindness, and visit me with Thy salvation.[217]

[Dvi r] I know, O Lord God, that Thou art gracious and merciful, patient, and of great mercifulness.[218]

Thou art good and merciful; Thou keepest covenant and mercy with Thy servants, which walk before Thee in their whole heart.[219]

There is none other god but Thou, which regardest and carest for all.[220]

For Thou hast been ever very merciful to me, delivering my soul from the deep hell.[221]

216. **Be . . . forever** KP quite freely renders Fisher's recasting of excerpts from Psalm 102:5, 8–9: "Benefac mihi in benevolentia tua, misericors enim es, nec irasceris imperpetuum" (Do good to me in Thy goodwill, for Thou art merciful, and Thou wilt not be angry forever). The excerpts, a description of God's goodness, read "Qui replet in bonis desiderium tuum . . . misericors Dominus: . . . Non in perpetuum irascetur" (Who filleth thy desire with good things . . . the Lord is merciful: . . . He will not remain angry forever). **benevolence . . . favor** KP's doubling.

217. **Remember . . . salvation** KP closely renders Fisher's minor recasting of Psalm 105:4. The verse reads "Memento nostri Domine in beneplacito populi tui: visita nos in salutari tuo" (Remember us, Lord, in Thy favor to Thy people; visit us with Thy salvation). **favor . . . kindness** KP's doubling.

218. **I . . . mercifulness** KP closely renders Fisher's recasting of Psalm 144:8: "Scio quod tu Deus clemens es et misericors, patiens ac multae miserationis." The verse reads "Miserator et misericors Dominus: patiens, et multum misericors" (The Lord is pitying and merciful, patient and greatly pitying).

219. **Thou . . . heart** KP closely renders Fisher's minor recasting of 3 Kings (1 Kings in English Bibles) 8:23: "Tu bonus ac propitius, servans pactum et misericordiam cum servis tuis, qui ambulant coram te in toto corde suo" (Thou art good and propitious, keeping covenant and mercy with Thy servants, who walk before Thee with their whole heart). The verse reads "qui custodis pactum et misericordiam servis tuis, qui ambulant coram te in toto corde suo" (who [the God of Israel] keepeth covenant and mercy with Thy servants, who walk before Thee with their whole heart).

220. **There . . . all** KP renders Fisher's splicing of recast excerpts from Judith 9:19 and 3 Kings 8:23–24: "Nec est alius praeter te, Deus, cui cura est de omnibus" (Nor is there any other besides Thee, God, whose care is of all). The excerpt from Judith reads "omnes gentes agnoscant quia tu es Deus, et non est alius praeter te" (all peoples acknowledge that Thou art God, and there is no other besides Thee). The excerpt from 3 Kings reads "non est similis tui Deus in caelo . . . et super terram . . . Qui custodisti servo tuo" (there is none like Thee, God, in heaven . . . and over the earth . . . Who hast cared for Thy servant). **regardest . . . carest** KP's doubling.

221. **For . . . hell** KP renders Fisher's recast phrasing from Psalm 85:13: "Magna siquidem semper fuit in me misericordia tua, eripiens animam meam de inferno profundo" (Great hath Thy mercy always been to me, snatching my soul from deep hell). The Psalm verse reads "misericordia tua magna est super me: et eruisti animam meam ex inferno inferiori" (above me Thy mercy is great; and Thou hast delivered my soul from the lowest of the lower depths).

Let Thy goodness, O Lord, be ever with me, for all my wealth[222] resteth only in Thee.

In the time of tribulation I call upon Thee, O Lord, for Thou art nigh unto them which call upon Thy holy name.[223]

[Dvi v] Succor me, O God, and look merrily upon me. Show me the light of Thy countenance; in Thee my soul trusteth and my heart rejoiceth.[224]

Let my prayer come unto Thy throne; bow down Thine ear unto my cry.[225]

Hear me now, being penitent, O Lord: whom Thou hast hitherto patiently suffered, to the intent I should repent and amend my life.[226]

O God, I have opened unto Thee my life; save me for Thy name' sake, for my trust is in Thee.[227]

222. **wealth** spiritual well-being—a former sense of this noun, rendering Fisher's "salus" (salvation, health).

223. **In . . . name** KP closely renders Fisher's reordering and recasting of excerpts from Psalm 144:17–18: "In tempore angustiae te invoco domine, quoniam propè iis qui invocant nomen tuum sanctum." The Psalm excerpts read "Dominus . . . sanctus in omnibus operibus suis. . . . Prope est Dominus omnibus invocantibus eum" (The Lord . . . is holy in all His works . . . The Lord is near to all those who call upon Him).

224. **Succor . . . rejoiceth** KP renders Fisher's recasting of excerpts from Psalm 66:2, 4–5: "Succurre mihi, Deus, illumina vultum tuum super me, in te confidit anima mea, de te exultat cor meum" (Succor me, God; make Thy face shine upon me; in Thee my soul trusteth; concerning Thee my soul rejoiceth). The Psalm excerpts read "Deus . . . illuminet vultum suum super nos. . . . Confeantur tibi populi Deus . . . et exultent gentes" (God will make His face shine upon us. . . . Thy people trust in Thee, God, . . . and the nations rejoice). **look . . . me** KP's addition, probably to clarify the image of God's face shining down upon the speaker.

225. **Let . . . cry** KP closely renders Fisher's splicing of recast excerpts from 2 Paralipomenon (2 Chronicles) 30:27 and Job 34:28: "Perveniat ad thronum tuum precatio mea, inclina aurem tuam clamori meo." The first excerpt reads "pervenitque oratio in habitaculum sanctum caeli" (the prayer came to the holy habitation of heaven). The excerpt from Job reads "ut pervenire facerent ad eum clamorem egeni" (that they might make the cry of the poor man come to him).

226. **Hear . . . life** KP freely renders Fisher's paraphrase of excerpts from 2 Peter 3:9: "Exaudi poenitentem domine, quem ut resipisceret cum patientia, hucusque misericorditer exspectasti" (Hear me, a penitent, Lord, whom Thou hast regarded with patience, for [the purpose] that Thou hast mercifully looked for). The excerpts read "Dominus . . . patienter agit propter vos, nolens aliquos perire, sed omnes ad poenitentium reverti" (The Lord . . . acteth patiently toward you, not willing that any should perish, but that all should turn to repentance). **I . . . life** KP's clarifying substitution for Fisher's oblique phrase "misericorditer exspectasti" comes closer than he does to the Vulgate verse, suggesting that she recognized it as source.

227. **O . . . Thee** KP closely renders Fisher's splicing of two excerpts, a quotation from Psalm 55:9 and a recasting from Psalm 142:8: "O deus, vitam meam annunciavi tibi, salvum me fac propter nomen tuum, quoniam in te speravi." The excerpt from Psalm 55 reads identically except for omitting "O." The excerpt from Psalm 142 reads "fac . . . mihi . . . misericordiam tuam: quia in te speravi" (do Thy mercy . . . to me: for I have trusted in Thee).

What care I for worldly things? This one thing only I need and desire, that I may find grace and favor in Thy sight.[228]

[Dvii r] Wherefore I beseech Thee, O Lord God, take away from me this pain and sorrow: or, at least wise, mitigate and assuage[229] it either by comfort or by counsel, or by what means soever it shall be seen good to Thee.

THE FOURTH PSALM IS A COMPLAINT OF A PENITENT SINNER, WHICH IS SORE TROUBLED AND OVERCOME WITH SINS.[230]

O Lord God, merciful and patient, and of much mercifulness and truth:[231]

Which for Thy abundant charity, and according to Thy great mercy, hast taken us out from the power of darkness, and hast saved us by the fountain of regeneration and new birth, and the renewing of the Holy Ghost, whom Thou hast shed upon us abundantly by Jesu Christ our Saviour.[232]

228. **What . . . sight** KP freely renders Fisher's splicing of excerpts from 1 Kings (1 Samuel in English Bibles) 18:8 and Genesis 33:15: "Quid mihi superest in terra? Hoc uno tantum indigeo, ut inveniam gratiam in conspectu tuo" (What remaineth to me on earth? This one thing I desire, that I find grace in Thy sight). The 1 Kings excerpt reads "Quid ei superest" (What remaineth to him). Fisher quotes the Genesis excerpt exactly. **need . . . desire** KP's doubling. **grace . . . favor** KP's doubling.

229. **pain . . . assuage pain . . . sorrow** KP's doubling of Fisher's "dolorem" (sorrow). **mitigate . . . assuage** KP's doubling of Fisher's "minue" (diminish).

230. **The . . . sins** KP freely renders Fisher's title: "Psalmus .iiii. quaeritur, quod à peccatis praemitur, et superatur" (Psalm Four: it is earnestly sought, that one who is oppressed by sins may surmount them). She omits Fisher's envisaged victory of the sinner over sin—presumably because it might seem to derogate from Christ's role as Saviour; see the introduction, pp. 202–3. **troubled . . . overcome** KP's doubling.

231. **O . . . truth** KP freely renders Fisher's verbatim quotation from Exodus 34:6: "Dominator Domine Deus misericors, et clemens, patiens, et multae miserationis ac verax" (The Lord, the Lord God, merciful and gracious, patient, and of much pity, and true). Fisher had just employed a largely similar Psalm verse; see n218.

232. **Which . . . Saviour** KP closely renders Fisher's partial recasting of phrases from Titus 3:4–6: "Qui propter nimiam [1544: maximam] charitatem tuam, et secundum misericordiam tuam magnam, eripuisti nos de potestate tenebrarum, et salvos fecisti per lavacrum regenerationis, et renovationis spiritus sancti, quem effudisti in nos abundè per Jesum Christum salvatorem nostrum." The phrases from Titus read "Cum autem benignitas . . . apparuit . . . nostri Dei . . . et . . . secundum suam misericordiam salvos nos fecit, per lavacrum regenerationis et renovationis Spiritus Sancti, quem effudit in nos abundè per Jesum Christum Salvatorem nostrum" (When the kindness of our God . . . appeared . . . and . . . He saved us according to His mercy, by the washing of regeneration and renewing of the Holy Spirit, whom He shed upon us abundantly through Jesus Christ our Saviour). **fountain** Fisher and the Vulgate read "lavacrum" (literally, bath). **regeneration . . . birth** KP's doubling of Fisher's "regenerationis."

[Dvii v] If I have found grace and favor in Thy sight, suffer me to speak a word unto Thee, and be not displeased with me.[233]

Why dost Thou ever forget me, and leavest me in the midst of my troubles and evils?[234]

Where is become Thy zeal and Thy strength? Where is the multitude of Thy tender affections and of Thy mercies?[235]

O Lord, may not he which is fallen, rise up again? or may not he which hath gone away from Thee, return to Thee again?[236]

Shall my sorrow ever endure? Shall my wound be uncurable and never healed?[237]

[Dviii r] How cometh it to pass, that I still turn away from Thee? My sin daily increaseth, and of myself I cannot return.[238]

233. **If . . . me** KP renders Fisher's splicing of recast phrases from Genesis 18:32 and 19:19: "Si inveni gratiam in conspectu tuo, permitte me loqui verbum ad te, et non irascaris mihi" (If I have found favor in Thy sight, permit me to speak a word to Thee, and be not angry with me). The first phrase, addressed by Abraham to God, is also a recurrent formula in the Old Testament: "invenit servus tuus gratiam coram te" (Thy servant hath found grace in Thy sight). The second set of phrases, in which Abraham pleads with God not to destroy the city of Sodom, reads "Obsecro . . . ne irascaris Domini, si loquar adhuc semel" (I pray . . . do not be angry, Lord, if I speak but this once). **grace . . . favor** KP's doubling.

234. **Why . . . evils?** KP renders Fisher's splicing of recast excerpts from Psalms 41:10 and 137:7: "Quare imperpetuum oblivisceris mei? et deseris me in medio malorum meorum?" (Why wilt Thou forget me forever, and desert me in the middle of my evils?). The first excerpt, a question put to God by the besieged Psalmist, reads "quare oblitus es mei?" (why hast Thou forgotten me?). The second excerpt reads "ambulavero in medio tribulationis" (I will walk in the midst of tribulation) but immediately expresses trust in God. Composing reproaches to God out of Biblical language results in strain and approximation because the initiative runs counter to prevailing tones and themes. **troubles . . . evils** KP's redoubling.

235. **Where . . . mercies?** KP closely renders Fisher's exact quotation from Isaiah 63:15: "Ubinam est zelus tuus et fortitudo tua? ubi multitudo viscerum tuorum, et miserationum tuarum?" (Where is Thy zeal and Thy strength? Where is the multitude of Thy inward feelings and of Thy mercies?). **tender affections** KP's graceful circumlocution for Fisher's and the Vulgate's "viscerum"—literally, intestines (from the Hebrew root 'mê'âh'), used to figure sympathy.

236. **O . . . again?** KP expands Fisher's close quotation of excerpts from Jeremiah 8:4: "Numquid qui cecidit domine, non resurgat? aut qui aversus, non revertatur?" The excerpts read "Numquid qui cadit, non resurget? et qui aversus est, non revertetur?" (Shall he who falleth, not arise? and he who hath turned away, not return?). **again, from Thee, again** KP's additions.

237. **Shall . . . healed?** KP closely renders Fisher's recasting of excerpts from Jeremiah 15:18: "Num dolor meus erit perpetuus? num desperabilis plaga me nunquàm curabitur?" The excerpts read "Quare factus est dolor meus perpetuus, et plaga mea desperabilis renuit curari?" (Why is my pain made perpetual, and my wound uncurable, that refuseth to be healed?).

238. **How . . . return** KP renders Fisher's splicing of recast excerpts from 3 Kings (1 Kings in English Bibles) 9:6, Exodus 9:34, and Job 15:22: "Qui fit ut avertar aversione perpetua? augescit

Inasmuch as it is not given to man to direct his own ways, neither to make perfect his own proceedings.[239]

For in Thy hand is the life of every living thing, and the spirit also of every man.[240]

Thou showest Thy mercy to whom Thou wilt, and Thou art gracious to them whom Thou favorest.[241]

Thou dost kill, and Thou dost quicken; Thou leadest down to hell gate, and bringest up again.[242]

---

mihi peccatum meum, nec [1544: per meipsum] possum reverti" (What maketh it that I turn away with perpetual aversion? my sin increaseth in me, nor can I return by myself). Her rendering follows the first London edition, which has the phrase "per meipsum" (by myself); the Cologne edition lacks it. The excerpt from 3 Kings, in God's voice, reads "Si . . . aversione aversi fueritis vos" (If you were to be turned with aversion). The excerpt from Exodus, a description of Pharaoh's stubbornness against God, reads "auxit peccatum" (he increased his sin). The Job excerpt, a description of the wicked man, reads "Non credit quod reverti possit" (He doth not believe that he could turn).

239. **Inasmuch . . . proceedings** KP renders Fisher's recasting of excerpts from Jeremiah 10:23: "Quum non sit homini datum, ut vias suas dirigat, et gressus suos perfectos reddat" (Since it is not given to man to direct his ways, nor to render his steps perfect). The excerpts read "quia non est hominis via ejus: nec viri est ut ambulet, et dirigat gressus suos" (because a man's way is not his: nor is it in a man that he walketh, and directeth his steps). **his . . . proceedings** In place of Fisher's and the Vulgate's "gressos" (steps), KP offers an abstract noun that sustains apt connotations of direction and motion.

240. **For . . . man** KP renders Fisher's inversion of phrasing from Genesis 9:2 spliced with excerpts from verse 15: "Si quidem in manu tua est anima omnis viventis, et spiritus universae humanae carnis" (Since the soul of every living thing is in Thy hand, and the spirit of all human flesh). The Genesis excerpts are a pair of promises made by God to Noah: the first that he as human will have power over all other living things, the second that no flood will ever again be sent to destroy life on earth. The first excerpt reads "cuncta animalia terrae, et . . . omnis pisces maris manui vestrae traditi sunt" (all the animals of the earth and . . . all the fish of the sea are delivered into your hand). The context of the second excerpt reads "recordabor foederis mei vobiscum, et cum omni anima vivente quae carnem vegetat: et non erunt ultra aquae diluvii ad delendum universam carnem" (I will remember my covenant with you and with every living soul that animates flesh, and there will be no more flood waters to destroy all flesh). Fisher, followed by KP, reworks the phraseology of God's promises into an ascription of God's omnipotence.

241. **Thou . . . favorest** KP closely renders Fisher's recasting of excerpts from Exodus 33:19: "Tu misericordiam tuam ostendis quibus volueris, et clemens es in quos animum habes." The excerpts, in God's voice, read "Ego . . . miserabor cui voluero, et clemens ero in quem mihi placuerit" (I . . . will be merciful to whom I will, and I will be gracious to them in whom I am pleased).

242. **Thou . . . again** KP closely renders Fisher's recasting of 1 Kings (1 Samuel) 2:6: "Tu mortificas, et vivificas, deducis ad portas inferi, et reducis." The verse reads "Dominus mortificat et vivificat, deducis ad inferos et reducit" (The Lord doth kill and doth make alive; He leadeth to the lower regions and leadeth back again).

Thy eyes behold the ways of every man, and Thou searchest the hearts of men.[243]
[Dviii v] There is no place so secret or dark, wherein sinners may hide themselves from Thee.[244]

Nor any man may so lurk and hide himself in caves, but Thou shalt see him, which dost fulfill both heaven and earth in every part.[245]

Why hast Thou cast me away from Thy presence, and takest me for Thy enemy?[246]

Why hast Thou laid upon my head the heavy weight of my sins? seeing no man is able to bear Thy displeasure.[247]

What meaneth it, that Thou showest Thy power against a wretch? Why destroyest me for the sins of my youth?[248]
[Ei r] If I have sinned, what shall I do to Thee? And if my sins be increased, what shall I do?

243. **Thy eyes . . . men** KP closely renders Fisher's splicing of recast excerpts from Jeremiah 16:17 and 17:10: "Oculi tui super vias uniuscuiusque, et corda hominum scrutaris" (Thine eyes are upon the ways of everyone, and Thou searchest the hearts of men). The first excerpt reads "oculi mei super omnes vias eorum" (My eyes are upon all their ways). The second excerpt reads "Ego Dominus scrutans cor" (I the Lord search the heart).

244. **There . . . Thee** KP freely renders Fisher's partial recasting of Job 34:22: "Non sunt tenebrae neque obscuritas, ut abscondant se illic qui faciunt iniquitatem" (There are neither shadows nor darkness where those who do iniquity may hide themselves). The verse reads "Non sunt tenebrae, et non est umbra mortis, ut abscondantur ibi qui operantur iniquitatem" (There are neither shadows nor a shade of death where those who work iniquity may hide themselves).

245. **Nor . . . part** KP renders Fisher's recasting of excerpts from Jeremiah 23:24: "Nec in latebris occultabit se quisquam, quin tu respicias eum, cum coelum ac terram undique imples" (Nor shall anyone hide himself in caves, for Thou wilt see him, since Thou dost everywhere fill heaven and earth). The excerpts, in God's voice, read "Si occultabitur vir in absconditis: et ego non videbo eum . . . ? numquid non caelum et terram ego impleo?" (If a man shall hide himself in hidden places, shall I not see him . . . ? do I not fill heaven and earth?). **lurk . . . hide** KP's doubling.

246. **Why . . . enemy?** KP closely renders Fisher's splicing of recast excerpts from Psalm 50:13 and Job 13:24: "Quare projecisti me à facie tua, et reputas me inimicum tibi?" The Psalm excerpt reads "Ne proiicias me a facie tua" (Cast me not out of Thy presence). The Job excerpt reads "Cur . . . arbitraris me inimicum tuum?" (Why . . . dost Thou consider me Thine enemy?).

247. **Why . . . displeasure** KP closely renders Fisher's splicing of recast excerpts from Psalm 37:5 and Job 9:13: "Cur nam adpendisti pondus peccatorum super caput meum, cum iram tuam nullus ferre potest?" The Psalm excerpt reads "iniquitates meae supergressae sunt caput meum: et sicut onus grave gravatae sunt super me" (my iniquities are gone over my head: and like a heavy burden they are heavy upon me). The Job excerpt reads "Deus, cuius irae nemo resistere potest" (God, whose anger none is able to bear).

248. **What . . . youth?** KP closely renders Fisher's free recasting of excerpts from Job 13:25–26: "Quid est quod contra miserum, potentiam tuam ostendis? et quid devastes me propter peccata

If I do justly, what shall I give to Thee? or what shalt Thou receive at my hand? My wickedness shall hurt myself, and my righteousness shall profit me.[249]

The life of man is a temptation upon the earth; and if I have sinned (as all men have) what may I do?[250]

Shall any man be found clean and without sin before Thee? or shall any man be without default in his deeds?[251]

How may a mortal man be pure from sin in Thy sight? or how may he which is born of a woman be righteous?[252]

---

adolescentiae meae?" The first excerpt reads "Contra folium, quod vento rapitur, ostendis potentiam tuam?" (Against a leaf, which is carried away by the wind, wilt Thou show Thy power?). The second excerpt reads "consumere me vis peccatis adolescentiae meae" (Thou willest to consume me with the sins of my youth). **a wretch** KP's native English equivalent of Fisher's "miserum," substituted for the Biblical image of the windblown leaf.

249. **If I have . . . me** KP closely renders Fisher's extended reacasting of Job 35:6–8: "Si peccaverim, quid faciam tibi? Et si multiplicatae fuerint impietates meae, quid agam tibi? Si juste egero, quid dabo tibi? aut quid tandem de manu mea accipies? Mihi impietas mea nocebit, et justicia mea mihi proderit." Job 35:6 reads "Si peccaveris, quid ei nocebis? et si multiplicatae fuerint iniquitates tuae, quid facies contra eum?" (If thou shalt sin, what will that hurt Him? or if thine iniquities were to be multiplied, what doest thou against Him?). Job 35:7 reads "Porro si juste egeris, quid donabis ei, aut quid de manu tua accipiet?" (Moreover, if thou shalt act justly, what shalt thou give Him, or what will He receive from thy hand?). Job 35:8 reads "Homini, qui similis tui est, nocebit impietas tua: et filium hominis adjuvabit justitia tua" (Thine injustice shall hurt a man like unto thee; and thy righteousness shall help a son of man). **myself, me** KP reproduces Fisher's construal of the Biblical analogies—"a man like unto thee," "a son of man"—as forms of self-reference by the speaker.

250. **The . . . do?** KP closely renders Fisher's splicing of recast excerpts from Romans 3:23 and Job 7:20: "Tentatio est vita hominis super terram: et, si (quemadmodum omnes) ego peccaverim, quid possum facere?" The excerpt from Romans reads "Omnes . . . peccaverunt" (All have sinned). The excerpt from Job reads "Peccavi, quid faciam tibi?" (I have sinned; what shall I do unto Thee?). **temptation** Instead of employing this English cognate, KP would have rendered Fisher's "tentatio" better as "trial," yielding the sense that human life on earth is a trial. Three key occurrences of "tentatio" in the sense of "trial" in the Vulgate include the characterization of Abraham as having been found faithful by God "in tentatione" (Ecclesiasticus 44:21; 1 Maccabees 2:52); the description of Satan's tempting of Jesus in the desert (Matthew 4, Mark 1, and Luke 4); and Jesus's own phrasing in the Lord's Prayer: "Ne nos inducas in tentatione" (Lead us not into temptation/trial; Matthew 6:23; Luke 11:4).

251. **Shall . . . deeds?** KP renders Fisher's splicing of recast excerpts from Job 10:14 and Tobias 10:12: "Nunquid mundus erit homo coram te? aut in operibus suis irreprehensibilis vir?" (For what man will be clean before Thee? or a man irreprehensible in his doings?). The Job excerpt reads "cur ab iniquitate mea mundum me esse non pateris?" (why wilt Thou not show me clean from my iniquity?). The Tobias excerpt stipulates the supreme gift that the guardian angel will bestow on Raguel as Tobias's wife: "et seipsam irreprehensibilem exhibere" (to show herself irreprehensible). **clean . . . sin** KP's doubling.

252. **How . . . righteous?** KP renders Fisher's recasting of Job 15:14: "Quidnam est mortalis, quod purus esset in conspectu tuo? aut quod justificaretur natus mulieris?" (What is a mortal,

[Ei v] Remember, O Lord, I beseech Thee, that Thou hast made me of the earth, and that Thou shalt bring me again into the dust of death.[253]

My days pass and vanish away like smoke; they waste daily; there is no tarrying.

My life flieth away as the wind, and considereth not that which is good.[254]

I was but lately born into this world, and shortly I shall be taken away hence by death; I never continue still in one state.

The days of my life be few and short; Thou hast appointed an end, which I shall not pass.[255]

Naked and bare I came out of my mother's womb, and naked and bare I shall return again: truly, all men living are vanity.[256]

---

that he should be pure in Thy sight? or he born of a woman, that he should be justified?). KP's rendering follows the Cologne edition although the added phrase in the first English edition, "natus ex virili feminae" (born of the strength of a woman), reproduces the Vulgate phrasing of the verse from Job: "Quid ist homo, ut immaculatus sit, et ut justus appareat natus de muliere?" (What is man, that he should be spotless? and he that is born of a woman, that he should appear righteous?). **from sin** KP's addition. **of . . . woman** KP's phrasing is closer to the Vulgate than is Fisher's "ex virili femine," suggesting that she recognized the source verse.

253. **Remember . . . death** KP closely renders Fisher's minor recasting of Job 10:9: "Memento obsecro domine, quod ex luto finxeris me, et rursus in pulverem mortis reduces me." The verse reads "Memento quaeso quod sicut lutum feceris me, et in pulverem reduces me" (Remember, I ask, that Thou hast made me as the clay, and Thou wilt bring me into dust again).

254. **My days . . . good** KP renders Fisher's splicing of recast excerpts from Job 7:6–7: "Dies mei sicut fumus evanescunt, consumuntur quotidie, nulla mora, quasi ventus vita mea fugit, nec vidit bonum" (My days vanish like smoke; they waste daily, no delay at all. Like the wind my life fleeth, nor doth it see good). The excerpts read "Dies mei velocius transierunt . . . et consumpti sunt absque ulla spe. . . . quia ventus est vita mea, et non revertetur oculus meus ut videat bona" (My days pass swiftly by . . . and are spent without any hope . . . because my life is wind, and my eye will not return to see good things).

255. **I was . . . pass** KP renders Fisher's free recasting of excerpts from Job 14:1–2, 5: "Iam pridem natus eram, moxquè morti cedam, nunquàm in eodem consisto statu. Dies vitae meae breves sunt, terminum statuisti, non transibo" (Now I was born lately, and soon I will depart in death, never do I remain in one state. The days of my life are brief; Thou hast appointed an end that I will not go beyond). The excerpts read "Homo natus . . . brevi vivens tempore. . . . Qui . . . fugit, et numquam in eodem statu permanet. . . . Breves dies hominis sunt . . . constituisti terminos ejus, qui praeterivi non poterunt" (A man who is born . . . liveth a brief time. . . . He fleeth, and never continueth in one state. . . . Brief are the days of men. . . . He hath appointed an end that they cannot go beyond). **into . . . world** KP's addition. **hence** KP's addition. **few . . . short** KP's doubling.

256. **Naked . . . vanity** KP renders Fisher's splicing of lightly recast excerpts from Job 1:21 and Psalm 38:6: "Nudus egressus sum de ventre matris meae, illucque nudus revertar, certe vanitas omnis homo vivens" (Naked have I come out of my mother's belly, and I will return there naked; certainly every living man is vanity). The Job excerpt reads "Nudus egressus sum de utero matris meae, et nudus revertar illuc" (Naked I have I come out of my mother's womb, and naked will I return there). The Psalm excerpt reads "universa vanitas, omnis homo vivens" (every living man is altogether vanity). **naked . . . bare, naked . . . bare** KP's doublings.

[Eii r] Have pity, O Lord, on them that are in misery, and despise not the works of Thy hands.[257]

Though we sin, yet are we under Thee, for we know Thy power and strength; and if we sin not, then are we sure that Thou regardest us.[258]

Cease Thy indignation, O Lord, and turn it from me, and cast all my sins behind Thy back.[259]

Take away Thy plagues from me, for Thy puishment hath made me both feeble and faint.[260]

For when Thou chastisest a man for his sins, Thou causest him by and by to consume and pine away.[261]

[Eii v] Whatsoever is delectable in him perisheth, like unto the cloth that is eaten with moths.[262]

257. **Have . . . hands** KP renders Fisher's splicing of recast excerpts from Isaiah 30:19 and Job 10:3: "Misereat te Domine miserorum, et opera manuum tuarum ne contemnas" (Let Thy pity, O Lord, be upon the miserable, and despise not the works of Thy hands). The Isaiah excerpt reads "miserans miserabitur tui, ad vocem clamoris tui" (pitying, He will have pity on thee, at the voice of thy cry). The Job excerpt reads "opprimas me opus manuum tuarum?" (dost Thou crush me, the work of Thy hands?).

258. **Though . . . us** KP freely renders Fisher's nearly verbatim quotation of Wisdom of Solomon 15:2: "Etenim si peccaverimus, tui sumus, scientes magnitudinem tuam: et si non peccaverimus, certum est, quod apud te sumus computati" (Even if we have sinned, we are Thine, knowing Thy greatness; and if we have not sinned, it is certain that we are regarded by Thee). The Vulgate reads identically except for having "scimus quoniam" (we know that) where Fisher has "certum est, quod." **power . . . strength** KP's doubling.

259. **Cease . . . back** KP renders Fisher's splicing of recast excerpts from Genesis 27:45 and Isaiah 38:17: "Domine deus, cesset à me indignatio tua, et proiice post tergum omnia peccata mea" (Lord God, let Thine indignation toward me cease, and cast all my sins behind Thy back). The Genesis excerpt refers to Esau's anger at Jacob's deceit: "cesset indignatio ejus" (let his anger cease). The Isaiah excerpt reads "proiecisti post tergum tuum omnia peccata mea" (Thou hast cast all my sins behind Thy back).

260. **Take . . . faint** KP freely renders Fisher's recast excerpts from Psalm 38:11–12: "Remove à me plagas tuas, ab exagitatione manus tuae ego defeci" (Remove Thy strokes from me; I have fainted from the flailing of Thy hand). The Psalm excerpts read "Amove a me plagas tuas; A fortitudine manus tuae ego defeci" (Take Thy strokes away from me; I have fainted from the manly strength of Thy hand). **plagues** KP stumbles, slipping into a near reiteration of Latin "plagas" (strokes), spelled "plages" in the 1544 *Psalms or Prayers*. The reading should be "strokes" or "blows"; see my introduction, p. 206. **feeble . . . faint** KP's doubling.

261. **For . . . away** KP freely renders Fisher's splicing of recast excerpts from Jeremiah 31:18–19 and Leviticus 26:39: "Etenim dum tu hominem propter iniquitates castigas, ilico tabescere eum facis" (For when Thou chastisest a man on account of iniquities, Thou makest him instantly faint). The Jeremiah excerpt reads "Castigasti me, et . . . convertar" (Thou hast chastised me, and . . . I repented). The Leviticus excerpt reads "tabescent in iniquitatibus suis" (they grew faint in their iniquities). **consume . . . away** KP's doubling.

262. **Whatsoever . . . moths** KP closely renders Fisher's drastic recasting of Job 13:28: "Perit in eo quicquid desiderabile est, sicut vestem depascit tinea" (Whatever is desirable in him per-

Would God, I had one to defend me awhile, until Thy anger were turned away, or that Thou wouldst set me a time, in the which Thou wouldst remember me.[263]

I am clean cast away from Thy presence: shall I never hereafter see Thy face again?[264]

Behold, I have opened the griefs of my soul; the days of my sorrows have taken me.[265]

The floods of tribulation compass me round about, and the streams of Thy fury run over me.[266]

And I cry unto Thee, O Lord God, but Thou hearest me not; I ask mercy, but Thou rejectest my prayers.[267]

---

ishes, as a moth eats clothing). The verse reads "quasi putredo consumendus sum, et quasi vestimentum, quod comeditur a tinea" (like a rotten thing I am consumed, and like a garment that is eaten by a moth).

263. **Would . . . me** KP quite closely renders Fisher's splicing of recast excerpts from Job 16:22 and 14:13: "Utinam esset, qui me paululum protegat, donec convertatur ira, aut tu constituas mihi tempus, in quo recorderis mei" (Would there were one who would protect me a little while, until [Thine] anger were turned away, or that Thou wouldst set me a time, in which Thou wouldst remember me). The first excerpt reads "utinam sic judicaretur vir cum Deo" (would there were a man who would plead thus with God). The second excerpt reads "donec pertranseat furor tuus, et constituas mihi tempus, in quo recorderis mei" (until Thy wrath would be passed, and Thou wouldst set me a time, in which Thou wouldst remember me).

264. **I . . . again?** KP closely renders Fisher's plaintive recasting of an excerpt from Jonah 2:5: "Abjectus sum ex oculis tuis, num nunque posthac videbo faciem tuam?" (I am cast away from Thy presence; shall I not see Thy face any more after this?). The excerpt reads "Abjectus sum a conspectu oculorum tuorum: veruntamen rursus video templum sanctum tuum" (I am cast away from the sight of Thine eyes; yet I look back again at Thy holy temple).

265. **Behold . . . me** KP freely renders Fisher's splicing of recast excerpts from Psalm 41:5 and Jeremiah 6:24: "En super me effunditur anima mea, adprehenderunt me dies doloris mei" (Behold, my soul is poured out over me; the days of my grief have laid hold on me). The Psalm excerpt reads "effudi in me animam meam" (I have poured out my soul within me). The Jeremiah excerpt reads "tribulatio apprehendit nos, dolores" (tribulation has laid hold on us, griefs). **I . . . opened** KP's active rendering of Fisher's passive "effunditur" (is poured out) suggests the primary sense of "open"—to admit passage to someone or something.

266. **The . . . me** KP renders Fisher's splicing of recast excerpts from Psalm 123:5 and Jonah 2:4: "Torrentes tribulationis involvunt me, et gurgites furoris tui super me pertranseunt" (Torrents of tribulation surround me, and the streams of Thy fury have gone over me). The Psalm excerpt reads "Torrentem pertransivit anima nostra" (Our soul passed through the torrent). The Jonah excerpt reads "omnes gurgites tui . . . super me transierunt" (all Thy streams . . . went over me).

267. **And . . . prayers** KP closely renders Fisher's complex splicing of recast phrases from Job 30:20, Baruch 2:19, and Lamentations 3:8: "Et clamo ad te domine deus, at non exaudis: misericordiam peto, sed preces meas excludis." The Job excerpt reads "Clamo a te, et non exaudis me" (I cry unto Thee, and Thou dost not hear me). The Baruch excerpt reads "petimus misericordiam ante conspectum tuum" (we shall ask for mercy before Thy face). The Lamentations

[Eiii r] Why thrustest Thou down a poor wretch from Thy presence? or why forsakest me so long time?[268]

Why takest not away my iniquity? and why puttest Thou not away the wickedness of my heart?[269]

Arise and tarry no longer, O Lord; arise, and reject me not forever.[270]

Have me in remembrance, I beseech Thee, for I thoroughly tremble and shake for fear.[271]

Yet I will not hold my tongue, but cry still unto Thee with a mourning and a heavy heart.[272]

Turn away the stroke of Thy vengeance from me; bring my mind out of troubles into rest.[273]

---

excerpt reads "cum clamavero, et rogavero, exclusit orationem meam" (when I would have cried and would have asked, He rejected my prayer).

268. **Why . . . time?** KP closely renders Fisher's splicing of rhetorically reworked excerpts from Psalm 26:9: "Quare miserum à facie tua detrudis? cur deseris tanto tempore?" The excerpts read "Ne avertas faciem tuam a me: . . . ne derelinquas me" (Turn not Thy face from me: . . . forsake me not).

269. **Why . . . heart?** KP closely renders Fisher's inversion and close recasting of the two halves of Job 7:21: "Quare non aufers iniquitatem meam, et tollis impietatem cordis mei?" The verse reads "Cur non tollis peccatum meum, et quare non aufers iniquitatem meam?" (Why dost Thou not take away my iniquity, and why dost Thou not bear away my impiety?).

270. **Arise . . . forever** KP closely renders Fisher's recast excerpts from Psalm 43:23: "Consurge, ne cessa diutius domine, excitate, ne depellas perpetuo." The verse reads "Exurge, quare obdormis Domine? exurge, et ne repellas in finem" (Arise, why dost Thou fall asleep, Lord? arise, and drive us not away forever).

271. **Have . . . fear** KP renders Fisher's splicing of recast excerpts from Tobias 3:3 and Job 4:14: "Memorare mei obsecro, nam pavor occupat me et tremor, totusque in me exterritus sum" (Remember me, I pray, for fear taketh hold of me, and trembling, and I am wholly frightened within myself). The Tobias excerpt reads "nunc Domine memor esto me" (Be mindful of me now, Lord). The Job excerpt reads "pavor tenuit me, et tremor, et omnia ossa mea perterrita sunt" (fear held me, and trembling, and all my bones were shaken). **tremble . . . fear** KP recasts Fisher's loosely conjoined phrasing into a characteristic doubling.

272. **Yet . . . heart** KP renders Fisher's recasting of an excerpt from Job 7:11: "Veruntamen non prohibebo os meum, quin ad te loquar in merore spiritus mei" (Yet I shall not stop my mouth, but I shall speak to Thee in the grief of my spirit). The excerpt reads "ego non parcam ori meo, loquar in tribulatione spiritus mei" (I will not refrain my mouth; I will speak in the affliction of my spirit). **a mourning . . . a heavy** KP's doubling.

273. **Turn . . . rest** KP renders with unusual freedom what is perhaps a wholly original versicle by Fisher: "Deflecte à me ultionem, et animum meum parumper à molestiis abducas" (Turn vengeance away from me, and lead my soul out of troubles for a little while). Only one passage in the Vulgate even conceives the possibility of God mitigating His vengeance (ultio). This is Isaiah 35:4, traditionally read as a prophecy of Christ's coming: "ecce Deus vester ultionem adducet retributionis: Deus ipse veniet, et salvabit vos" (behold, your God will bring a vengeance of recompense: God Himself will come, and He will save you). Fisher's versicle has some thematic affinities with the Isaiah text, which KP's free rendering sustains.

[Eiii v] I am here, no longer continuer, but a pilgrim and a stranger, as all other mortal men be.[274]

And what is man, that Thou shouldst be angry with him? or what is mankind, that Thou shouldst be so heavy, Lord, unto us?[275]

What, wilt Thou bring sorrow upon sorrow? I pant for pain and find no rest.[276]

My sorrow grieveth me when I should eat, and sudden sighs overwhelm my heart.[277]

I am as if my bones were all to-broken, when I hear mine enemies rail upon me, and say to me day by day, Where is thy God?[278]

Why turnest Thou Thy face away from these things, O Lord? why hast Thou no regard of my trouble?[279]

274. **I . . . be** KP also renders with unusual freedom Fisher's recasting of excerpts from Psalm 38:13: "Peregrinum hic ago, sicut omnes alii mortales" (Here I go as a pilgrim, like all other mortals). The excerpted verse reads "advena ego sum apud te, et peregrinus, sicut omnes patres mei" (I am a stranger before Thee, and a pilgrim, like all my fathers). **continuer** one who remains, one who stays. **a pilgrim . . . a stranger** KP's rendering is closer to the verse than is Fisher's, indicating that she recognized this source. Coverdale's Bible (1535) reads "a straunger and pilgrymme."

275. **And . . . us?** KP renders with unusual freedom Fisher's negative recasting of Psalm 8:5: "Et quid est homo, ut ei indigneris? aut genus corruptibile, ut ita amarus sis erga ipsum" (And what is man, that Thou regardest him as unworthy? and what is this corruptible species, that Thou art thus bitter toward him?). The verse reads "Quid est homo, quod memor es eius? aut filius hominis, quoniam visitas eum? (What is man, that Thou art mindful of him? or the son of man, since Thou visitest him?).

276. **What . . . rest** KP renders Fisher's recasting of an excerpt from Jeremiah 45:3: "Nunquid addes dolori dolorem? anhelans laboro, et requiem non inveni" (Wilt Thou add further sorrow to sorrow? Panting, I suffer, and I find no rest). The excerpt reads "addidit Dominus dolorem dolori meo: Laboravi in gemitu meo, et requiem non inveni" (the Lord hath added sorrow to my sorrow: I have suffered in my groaning, and I have not found rest).

277. **My . . . heart** KP freely renders Fisher's recasting of Job 3:24: "Ante cibum dolor meus me cruciat, et adoriuntur in me sicut aquae, suspiria" (Before a meal my sorrow afflicts me, and sighs are poured out in me like water). The verse reads "Antequam comedam suspiro: et tamquam inundantes aquae, sic rugitus meus" (Before I eat, I sigh: and like flooding waters, such is my groaning).

278. **I . . . God?** KP renders Fisher's recasting of Psalm 41:10: "Tanquam ossa mea confringerentur est mihi, cum probris adficiunt me inimici mei, dicentes ad me omni die, ubinam est Deus tuus?" (My bones are as if they were broken when my enemies inflict shame on me, saying to me all the day, Where now is thy God?). The verse reads "Dum confringuntur ossa mea, exprobraverunt mihi qui tribulant me inimici mei: dum dicunt mihi per singulos dies: Ubi est Deus tuus?" (My bones will break in pieces, when my enemies, who press me, will reproach me while they say to me day after day, Where is thy God?).

279. **Why . . . trouble?** KP closely renders Fisher's splicing of a recast excerpt from Job 13:24 and an inverted excerpt from Genesis 16:11: "Quare ad haec faciem tuam abscondis domine? nullam habens adflictionis meae rationem?" The Job excerpt reads "Cur faciem tuam abscon-

I earnestly make my prayers daily in Thy sight: and the heaviness of my heart I do show unto Thee.[280]

My spirit is careful and troubled within me, and desperation hath entered into my heart.[281]

Is it Thy pleasure, O Lord God, to cast away Thine own handiwork?[282]

Deliver my soul from corruption, and my life from everlasting darkness.[283]

What availeth it me, that ever I was born, if Thou cast me straight into damnation? seeing that the dead shall not praise Thee, nor any of them which go down to hell.[284]

---

dis?" (Why dost Thou hide Thy face?). The Genesis excerpt reads "audierit Dominus afflictionem tuam" (the Lord will have heard thine affliction).

280. **I . . . Thee** KP renders Fisher's close recasting of Psalm 141:3: "Effundo quotidie preces meas in conspectu tuo, et merorem meum coram te pronuncio" (Daily I pour out my prayers in Thy sight, and I declare my grief in Thy presence). The verse reads "Effundo in conspectu ejus orationem meam, et tribulationem meam ante ipsum pronuncio" (I pour out my prayer in His sight, and I declare my affliction before Him).

281. **My . . . heart** KP renders Fisher's slight recasting of Psalm 142:4: "Anxius est in me spiritus meus, in me desperabundum est cor meum" (Distressed is my spirit within me; my heart within me is full of despair). The verse reads "anxiatus est super me spiritus meus, in me turbatum est cor meum" (my spirit is made anxious about me; my heart within me is troubled). **careful . . . troubled** KP's doubling. Her choice of "troubled" is close to the Vulgate's "turbatus" and has no analogue in Fisher, again suggesting that she recognized the Biblical source.

282. **Is . . . handiwork?** KP renders another versicle that Fisher produces by negating Scriptural phraseology: "Placet ne tibi Deus, ut reprobes laborem manuum tuarum?" (Doth it please Thee, Lord, to cast away the work of Thy hands?). The phrase "the work of His hands" consistently has positive associations with God in Scripture—for example, Psalm 142:5: "meditatus sum in omnibus operibus tuis: in factis manuum tuarum meditabar" (I have meditated on all Thy works; I will meditate on the works of Thy hands). Fisher's "placet ne" may indicate that Job's words after God had permitted him to fall from high to low estate prompted the negative formulation here. The relevant excerpt from Job 1:21 reads "Dominus dedit, Dominus abstulit: sicut Domino placuit, ita factum est" (The Lord giveth, the Lord taketh away: as it pleaseth the Lord, so is it done).

283. **Deliver . . . darkness** KP freely renders Fisher's complex splicing of recast excerpts from Job 33:28 and Jonah 2:7: "Libera animam meam, nec abeat in corruptionem, et vita mea non videat lumen" (Deliver my soul, lest it go down in corruption, and my life, lest it not see the light). Thr first excerpt reads "liberavit animam suam ne pergeret in interitum, sed vivens lucem videret" (He delivered his soul, that it not go on into destruction, but that, living, it might see the light). The second excerpt reads "sublevabis de corruptione vitam meam, Domine Deus meus" (Thou hast raised up my life from corruption, Lord my God).

284. **What . . . hell** KP closely renders Fisher's splicing of recast excerpts from Psalms 29:10 and 113:17: "Quid proderit, quod unquam natus fuerim, si mox demandes in perditionem aeternam? quum non mortui laudabunt te, neque omnes, qui descendunt in infernum." The first excerpt reads "Quae utilitas in sanguine meo, dum descendo in corruptionem?" (What use is there in my blood, when I descend into corruption?). The second excerpt reads "Non mortui laudabunt te Domine: neque omnes, qui descendunt in infernum" (The dead will not praise Thee, Lord, nor will all who go down into the lower depths).

[Eiv v] I have sinned, what shall I do to Thee? why hast Thou put me to be contrary to Thee? I am weary of mine own self.[285]

Why searchest Thou out my sins so narrowly, when there is no man that can take out of Thy hand?[286]

If I would say that I were righteous and without sin, then Thou mightest worthily condemn me to the fire prepared for the devil and his angels.[287]

But I confess that I am a sinner, and I do humble my heart in Thy sight.[288]

Surely if any man would stand with Thee in judgment, he shall not be able to answer one word to a thousand things wherewith Thou mightest charge him.[289]

This maketh me to fear all my deeds, knowing that Thou sparest not him that offendeth.[290]

285. **I . . . self** KP renders Fisher's nearly verbatim excerpting of Job 8:20: "Peccavi, quid faciam tibi: quare posuisti me contrarium tibi, et factus sum mihimetipsi molestus?" The excerpt reads "Peccavi, quid faciam tibi . . . ? quare posuisti me contrarium tibi, et factus sum mihimetipsi gravis? (I have sinned; what shall I do to Thee . . . ? why hast Thou set me contrary to Thee? I am made burdensome to myself). **weary** While Fisher reads "molestus" (troublesome), KP's substititution for Fisher's "molestus" (troublesome).

286. **Why . . . hand?** KP closely renders Fisher's nearly verbatim excerpting of Job 10:6–7: "Quid tam exacte iniquitatem meam quaeris? Quum nemo sit qui de manu tuae possit eripere." The excerpts read "quaeras iniquitatem meam . . . cum sit nemo qui de manu tua possit eruere" (Thou searchest out my iniquity . . . when there is no one who could snatch out of Thy hand). **so narrowly** with such close attention, rendering Fisher's "tam exacte" (so exactly).

287. **If . . . angels** KP renders with unusual freedom Fisher's splicing of recast excerpts from Job 34:5 and 9:20, and Matthew 25:41: "Si justum me dixerim, meritò me condemnares ad ignem paratum" (If I would pronounce myself righteous, Thou shouldst condemn me deservedly to the fire prepared). The first excerpt reads "dixit Job: Justus sum" (Job said, I am righteous). The second excerpt reads "Si justificare me voluero, os meum condemnabit me" (If I shall wish to call myself righteous, my mouth will condemn me). The third excerpt reads, in the voice of God at the Last Judgment: "Discedite à me, maledicti, in ignem aeternum, qui paratus est diabolo, et angelis ejus" (Go from me, ye cursed ones, into the everlasting fire, which is prepared for the devil and his angels). **righteous . . . sin** KP's doubling. **for . . . angels** KP's addition to Fisher indicates that she recognized the source text, Matthew 25:41, which is merely an allusion in Fisher: "ignem paratum" (the fire prepared).

288. **But . . . sight** KP closely renders Fisher's splicing of recast excerpts from Psalm 31:5 and James 4:10: "Sed ego peccatorem me confiteor, et humilio cor meum in conspectu tuo." The first excerpt reads "Confitebor adversum me injustitiam meam" (I will confess mine unrighteousness against myself). The second excerpt reads "Humiliamini in conspectu Domini" (Let us humble ourselves in the sight of the Lord).

289. **Surely . . . him** KP renders Fisher's recasting of Job 9:3: "Certe si cui placuerit contendere tecum in judicio, non respondebit unum pro mille" (Surely if it should please someone to contend with Thee in judgment, he will not answer one [charge] in a thousand). The verse reads "Si voluerit contendere cum eo, non poterit ei respondere unum pro mille" (If one wilt contend with Him, he shall not be able to answer Him one in a thousand). **wherewith . . . him** KP's clarifying expansion of Fisher's and the Vulgate's terse phrasing.

290. **This . . . offendeth** KP closely renders Fisher's recasting of Job 9:28: "Hinc fit ut verear omnia opera mea, sciens quod delinquenti non parces." The verse reads "Verebar omnia opera

[Ev r] If I look upon Thy power, O how mighty and strong Thou art; if I shall call for judgment, who shall defend my matter, or speak for me?[291]

To Thee, O Lord, I call and cry; to Thee, my God, I make mine humble suit.[292]

Turn away Thine anger from me, that I may know that Thou art more merciful unto me than my sins deserve.[293]

What is my strength, that I may endure? or what is the end of my trouble, that my soul may patiently abide it?

My strength is not a stony strength, and my flesh is not made of brass.

There is no help in myself, and my strength fleeth away from me.[294]

---

mea, sciens quod non parceres delinquenti" (I fear all my works, knowing that Thou wilt not spare him who has offended).

291. **If . . . me?** KP renders Fisher's recasting of Job 9:19: "Si ad potentiam tuam respexero, o quam robustus es: si ad judiciam provocavero, quis pro me causam dicet?" (If I will look upon Thy power, O how mighty Thou art; if I shall call for judgment, who will speak for my cause?). The verse reads "Si fortitudo quaeritur, robustissimus est: si acquitas judicii, nemo audet pro me testimonium dicere" (If strength is sought, He is most mighty; if I rest judgment, no one will dare to give testimony on my behalf). **mighty . . . strong** KP's doubling. **who . . . me?** KP heightens the pathos by redoubling Fisher's final verb phrase, which is also singular in the Vulgate.

292. **To . . . suit** KP renders Fisher's recasting of Job 19:7 from a cry of desperation to a cry of hope: "Ad te Domine vociferor, tibi supplico o mi Deus" (To Thee, O Lord, I cry; I supplicate Thee, O my God). The verse reads "Ecce clamabo . . . et nemo audiet: vociberabor, et non est qui judicet" (Behold, I will cry . . . and no one will hear; I will cry aloud, and there is no one who will judge). **call . . . cry** KP's doubling. **make . . . suit** KP's expansion of Fisher's "supplico" suggests that she recognized the source text with its allusion to pleading one's case before a judge.

293. **Turn . . . deserve** KP freely renders a versicle that Fisher seems to have crafted out of recast excerpts from Psalm 84:7: "Quiescat à me ira tua, ut intelligam quod sis mihi magis propitius, quam peccata mea ferant" (Let Thine anger against me rest, that I may know that Thou hast more mercy than my sins bring me). The relevant Vulgate excerpts read "Mitigasti omnem iram tuam: . . . Numquid in aeternum irasceris nobis? . . .Ostende nobis Domine misericordiam tuam, et salutare tuum da nobis" (Assuage all Thine anger: . . . Wilt Thou be angry with us forever? . . . Show us Thy mercy, Lord, and grant us Thy salvation). The comparative construction makes for curious theology: a God "more merciful" than the speaker's sins "bring" (Fisher) or "deserve" (KP). What mercy do sins "bring" or "deserve"?

294. **What . . . from me What . . . it?** KP expansively renders Fisher's slight recasting of Job 6:11: "Quae est fortitudo mea, ut perdurem? aut quis finis, ut patiens sit anima mea?" (What is my strength, that I may endure? Or what [is my] end, that my soul may be patient?). The verse reads "Quae est enim fortitudo mea ut sustineam? aut quis finis meus, ut patienter agam?" (For what is my strength, that I may bear up? or what [is] my end, that I may carry on patiently?). **of . . . trouble** KP's clarifying addition. **My . . . brass** KP closely renders Fisher's slight recasting of Job 6:12: "Virtus mea, non est virtus lapidea, nec aenea est caro mea." The verse reads "Nec fortitudo lapidum fortitudo mea, nec caro mea aenea est" (My strength is not a stony strength, nor is my flesh [the strength of] brass). **There . . . me** KP renders as a declarative Fisher's re-

[Ev v] Although Thou hide these things in Thy heart, yet I know that Thou wilt remember me at length.[295]

For Thou art true and just, O Lord God; Thou dost not condemn unjustly, which rewardest man according to his deserts.[296]

All this is come unto me because I have forgotten Thee, and not used myself truly in Thy testament.[297]

My heart hath turned backward, and I have followed the desires of my flesh.[298]

---

casting of Job 6:13 into a rhetorical question: "Nonne potius nullum in me auxilium, et robur meum à me fugit?" (Is not there no more help in me, and doth not my strength flee from me?). The verse reads "Ecce, non est auxilium mihi in me, et necessarii quoque mei recesserunt a me" (Behold, there is no help in me, and my necessities [of life] depart from me). KP's declarative, reproducing the Vulgate's declarative, suggests that she recognized the source verse.

295. **Although . . . length** KP renders Fisher's recasting of excerpts from Job 14:13: "Et licet abscondas haec in corde tuo, novi tamen quod tandem recordaberis mei" (And it may be that Thou hidest these things in Thine heart, nevertheless I know that later Thou wilt remember me). Fisher's recasting and KP's rendering substantially alter the meaning of the verse in the Vulgate. Its relevant phrases read "Quis mihi hoc tribuat, ut . . . abscondas me, donec pertranseat furor tuus, et constituas mihi tempus, in quo recordaris mei" (O that one would bestow this on me, that . . . Thou wouldst hide me until Thy wrath were past, and that Thou wouldst set me a time, when Thou wilt remember me).

296. **For . . . deserts** KP closely renders Fisher's splicing of paraphrased excerpts from Psalm 18:10, Job 34:12, and Psalm 27:4: "Verus enim et justus tu domine Deus, non injuste condemnas, qui opus suum homini rependis." The first excerpt reads "judicia Domini vera, justificata" (the judgments of the Lord are true and justified). The Job excerpt reads "Deus non condemnabit frustra, nec Omnipotens subvertet judicium" (God will not condemn vainly, nor will the Almighty subvert judgment). The third excerpt reads "Secundum opera manuum eorum . . . redde retributionem eorum ipsis" (According to the works of their hands . . . give them their retribution).

297. **All . . . testament** KP renders Fisher's recasting of excerpts from either of two closely similar verses, Deuteronomy 4:23 or 4 Kings (2 Chronicles) 17:38: "Totum hoc accidit mihi, quod oblitus sum tui, et perfidè me habui in testamento tuo" (All this befalleth me because I have forgotten Thee, and have used myself faithlessly toward Thy covenant). Both Vulgate verses warn the Israelites against relapsing into idol worship. The Deuteronomy excerpts read "Cave ne quando obliviscaris pacti Domini Dei tui . . . et facias . . . quae fieri Dominus prohibuit" (Beware that thou never forgettest the covenant of the Lord thy God . . . and make . . . what God hath forbidden thee to make). The excerpts from 4 Kings read "Et pactum, quod percussit vobiscum, nolite oblivisci: nec colatis deos alienos, sed Dominum Deum vestrun timete" (And forget not the covenant that He struck with you, and do not worship strange gods, but fear the Lord your God).

298. **My . . . flesh** KP closely renders Fisher's splicing of recast excerpts from Psalm 43:19 and Ephesians 2:4: "Deflexit retro cor meum, et secutus sum desideria carnis meae." Fisher converts the Psalm excerpt from negative to positive; it reads:"non recessit retro cor nostrum" (our heart did not go backward). The excerpt from Ephesians reads "nos omnes aliquando conversati sumus in desideriis carnis nostrae" (we all once had our conversation in the desires of our flesh).

And Thou hast surely known this thing, which knowest the secrets of the heart.[299]

Lay not against me, O Lord, the sins of my youth, nor have in remembrance mine old injuries done against Thee.[300]

[Evi r] Daily, sorrow overcometh me, and sadness possesseth my heart.[301]

I look after peace, but I cannot have it; I look for a time of health, but my grief continueth still.[302]

When the time of Thine anger is past, let mercy come, yet am I unhappy more and more.[303]

Woe and alas, that ever I sinned: my heart therefore mourneth and is sad; all mirth and joy be banished from me.[304]

299. **And . . . heart** KP renders Fisher's recasting of Psalm 43:22: "Et tu exploratum hoc habuisti, qui noveris recondita cordis" (And Thou hast had this discovery, who wilt know the secrets of the heart). The verse reads "nonne Deus requiret ista? ipse . . . novit abscondita cordis" (shall God not search these things out? He . . . knoweth the secrets of the heart).

300. **Lay . . . Thee** KP closely renders Fisher's recast excerpt from Psalm 24:7: "Ne imputes mihi domine peccata adolescentiae meae, nec veterem injuriam in memoria teneas." The verse reads "Delicta juventutis meae, et ignorantias meas ne memineris" (Remember not the sins of my youth, nor my lack of knowledge). **done . . . Thee** KP's addition.

301. **Daily . . . heart** KP closely renders Fisher's rhetorical redoubling of the second clause of Psalm 13:2: "Obruit me quotidianus dolor, et moesticia cor meum occupat." The verse in full reads "Quamdiu ponam consilia in anima mea, dolorem in corde meo per diem?" (How long shall I take counsel in my soul, with sorrow daily in my heart?).

302. **I . . . still** KP freely renders Fisher's recast excerpt from Jeremiah 14:19: "Expecto pacem, at res nihilo meliores se habent: tempus sanitatis, sed ecce tumor" (I look for peace, but no better things at all are to be had; a time of health, but, behold, a swelling). The excerpt reads "expectavimus pacem, et non est bonum; et tempus curationis, et ecce turbido" (we have looked for peace, and there is no good; and for the time of healing and, behold, trouble). **I can . . . it, my grief . . . still** KP's phrasal expansions may indicate that she had difficulty with Fisher's modulation from singular "res" to plural "meliores" and with his metaphorical use of "tumor" (swelling).

303. **When . . . more** KP closely renders Fisher's splicing of recast excerpts from Psalm 77:38 and Romans 7:24: "Et [1544: Cum] praeteriit tempus irae tuae veniat misercordia, ego adhuc infelix sum magis ac magis." The first excerpts read "Ipse . . . est misericors, et . . . averteret iram suam: et non accendit omnem iram suam" (He is merciful, and . . . will turn His anger away, and not kindle all His anger). The second excerpt reads "Infelix ego homo" (An unhappy man [am] I).

304. **my . . . me** KP renders Fisher's splicing of recast excerpts from Lamentations 5:16 and Proverbs 15:13: "Heu mihi quod peccavi, idcirco moeret cor meum, et desiit gaudium meum" (Woe is me, that I have sinned: therefore my heart mourneth, and my joy ceaseth). The Lamentation excerpt reads "vae nobis, quia peccavimus" (woe unto us, for we have sinned). The excerpts from Proverbs read "Cor gaudiens exhilarat . . . in moerore . . . dejicitur spiritus" (A joyful heart cheers . . . in mourning . . . the spirit is cast down). **Woe . . . alas, mourneth . . . sad, mirth . . . joy** KP's doublings.

How am I wasted, how miserably am I confounded, because I have forsaken and cast away Thy law.[305]

Death hath ascended up by the windows, piercing the inward parts of my heart.[306]

When I daily one while muse secretly with myself, another while with loud voice cry out and complain, the meantime my life draweth near to the pit.[307]

[Evi v] Who shall give me a place to rest in from all my griefs and troubles? and I will forsake all men and get me away from them.[308]

Who shall give me water to my head, and a fountain of tears to mine eyes? that I may bewail my sins both night and day.[309]

And I will look for Him which may save me, and deliver me from the wrath to come.[310]

305. **How . . . law** KP renders Fisher's splicing of recast excerpts from Jeremiah 9:19, 13: "Quomodo vastatus sum? quo miserè confusus? quoniam dereliqui legem tuam" (How I am wasted, how miserably I am confounded, because I have forsaken Thy law). The excerpts from verse 19 read "Quomodo vastati sumus et confusi vehementer? quia dereliquimus terram" (How we have been wasted, how vehemently confounded, because we have forsaken the land). The excerpts from verse 13, in God's voice, read "Quia derelinquerunt legem meam" (Because they have forsaken My law). **forsaken . . . away** KP's doubling.

306. **Death . . . heart** KP closely renders Fisher's splicing of recast excerpts from Jeremiah 9:21 and Proverbs 7:27: "Ascendit mors per fenestras penetrans ad interiora cordis mei." The Jeremiah excerpt reads "ascendit mors per fenestras nostras" (death hath ascended by the windows). The Proverbs excerpt reads "viae inferi . . . penetrantes in interiora mortis" (the ways to hell . . . leading through the inner places of death).

307. **When . . . pit** KP freely renders Fisher's bold splicing of recast excerpts from Luke 5:22, John 11:33, and Psalm 87:4: "Dum quotidie nunc tacitus mecum cogito, nunc voce infremo, vita mea inferno propinquat" (While daily I ponder with myself, now silently, now with a groaning voice, my life draweth nearer to hell). In the Luke excerpt, Jesus reproaches the Pharisees for conceiving evil of Him: "Quid cogitatis in cordibus vestris?" (What are you pondering in your hearts?). In the excerpt from John, Jesus joins in grieving for the dead Lazarus: "infremuit spiritu" (He groaned in His spirit). The Psalm excerpt reads "vita mea inferno appropinquavit" (my life hath approached hell). **cry . . . complain** KP's doubling.

308. **Who . . . them** KP renders Fisher's recasting of Jeremiah 9:2: "Quis dabit mihi diversorium à molestiis, et deseram homines, atque ab eis recedam?" (Who will give me a small lodging place from troubles? and I will forsake men, also I will draw back from them). The verse reads "Quis dabit me in solitudine diversorium viatorum, et derelinquam populum meum, et recedam ab eis?" (Who will give me a small lodging for wayfarers, in solitude? and I will forsake my people, and draw back from them). **to rest . . . troubles** KP's clarifying addition, incorporating a characteristic doubling.

309. **Who . . . day** KP closely renders Fisher's minor recasting of Jeremiah 9:1: "Quis dabit aquam capiti meo, et oculis meis fontem lachrimarum, ut noctu diuque peccata mea defleam?" The verse reads "Quis dabit capiti meo aquam, et oculis meis fontem lacrymarum? et plorabo die ac nocte interfectos filiae populi mei" (Who will give me water for my head, and a fountain of tears for my eyes? and I will bewail day and night the slain of the daughter of my people).

310. **And . . . come** KP closely renders Fisher's splicing of excerpts from Psalm 54:9, 17, 19 and Matthew 3:7 (or Luke 3:7): "Et expectabo eum, qui me salvare potest, et eripere ab ira ven-

I have no trust neither in life nor death, but I fear Thy judgment, O Lord, and the pains prepared for wicked sinners.

The fear of my sin maketh me careful, and the burden of my conscience oppresseth me sore.[311]

[Evii r] O God, which tenderly lovest mankind, and art most rightful Judge: spare me now, I beseech Thee, and show me some favor while time is.

Forgive that which I fear; put away that which I dread, before I depart hence and shall not return again.[312]

My sins do vex and trouble me sore; they be so great that none can be greater.

Alas my fall, alas my misery, alas the grief of my plague and stroke: certainly my sin is the cause of all this, and so I will take it and suffer it.[313]

---

tura." The excerpts from Psalm 54 read "Expectabam eum, qui salvum me fecit. . . . Dominus salvabit me. . . . Redimet . . . animam meam" (I will look for Him, who will make me safe. . . . The Lord will save me. . . . He will deliver . . . my soul). In the identically worded excerpt from Matthew or Luke, Jesus refers to God's final judgment on the earth as "ventura ira" (the wrath to come).

311. **I . . . sore** KP renders two consecutive versicles that appear to be original compositions by Fisher: "Non est mihi vivendi neque moriendi fiducia, judicium tuum vereor, O Deus, et poenas paratas impiis. Pavor peccati sollicitat me, et pondus conscientiae meae me premit" (Trust is not mine, neither in living nor in dying; I fear Thy judgment, O God, and the pains prepared for the ungodly. Fear of sin fills me with anxiety, and the weight of my conscience presses on me). Vulgate concordances show no prototypes for several formulations expressed here: the absence of trust in living or dying, the pains (or punishments) prepared for the ungodly, a state of fear and anxiety about one's sins, and the pressing weight of conscience. A general analogue is provided by Psalm 9:16–17: "Cognoscetur Dominus judicia faciens: in operibus manuum suarum comprehensus est peccator. Convertantur peccatores in infernum" (The Lord is known by the judgment He maketh: the sinner is ensnared by the works of his own hands. Sinners shall be turned into hell). But the Psalm excerpt lacks the brooding intensity and foreboding of these versicles, which evoke a late medieval consciousness of sinfulness and impending damnation.

312. **O . . . again** KP quite freely renders a second pair of versicles that appear mainly to be Fisher's original compositions: "Amator hominum Deus et judex aequissime, parce mihi obsecro modo dum tempus est. Remitte quod timeo, dele quod vereor priusquam abeam, et posthac non subsistam" (O God, Lover of men and most favorable Judge, spare me, I pray, now while there is time. Forgive what I fear, put away what I dread, before I shall go away, and shall not abide thereafter). **show . . . favor** KP's addition. **Forgive . . . again** Fisher incorporates excerpts from Psalm 38:14, which read "Remitte mihi . . . prius quam abeam, et amplius non ero" (Forgive me . . . before I shall go away, and shall be no longer).

313. **My . . . it** KP quite freely renders a third pair of versicles that appear to be the last of Fisher's mostly original compositions in his Psalm 4: "Peccata mea me supra modum cruciant, quibus maiora esse quae possunt? Eheu contricionem meam, et dolorem plagae meae: certe haec iniquitas mea est, et reputabo et feram" (My sins torment me above measure; could there be ones greater than these? Alas for my grief and the pain of my strokes: certainly this is my iniquity, and I will account it thus and will bear it). **vex . . . trouble** KP's doubling. **Alas . . . fall** KP's addition. **alas my misery . . . it** Fisher incorporates recast excerpts from Jeremiah

[Evii v]

THE FIFTH PSALM, FOR THE OBTAINING OF GODLY WISDOM.

O Lord God of mercy, which by Thy word hast made all things, and by Thy wisdom hast created man:[314]

O God eternal, to whom all things be known, be they never so secret; which knowest all things before they be done:[315]

Open my lips and my mouth, that I may speak and show forth the glory and praise of Thy name.[316]

Give me a new heart and a right spirit, and take from me all wicked and sinful desires.[317]

O Lord, I am foolish, ignorant, and blind, when I am destitute of Thy knowledge.[318]

10:19: "Vae mihi super contritione mea, pessima plaga mea . . . Plane haec infirmitas mea est, et portabo illam" (Woe is me over my grief, my worst strokes . . . Plainly this is my infirmity, and I will bear it). **plague . . . stroke** KP's doubling. **plague** See n260.

314. **O . . . man** KP closely renders Fisher's near verbatim quotation of Wisdom of Solomon 9:1–2: "Domine, Deus misericordiae, qui omnia verbo tuo fecisti, et sapientia tua constituisti hominem." The verses read "Deus . . . Domine misericordiae, qui fecisti omnia verbo tuo, et sapientia tua constituisti hominem" (God . . . Lord of mercy, who hast made all things by Thy word, and by Thy wisdom hast constituted man).

315. **O . . . done** KP renders Fisher's near verbatim quotation of an excerpt from Daniel 13:42: "Deus aeterne et absconditorum cognitor, qui omnia noveris priusquàm fiunt" (Eternal God and Knower of hidden things, who will know all things before they be done). The verse excerpt reads "Deus aeterne, qui absconditorum es cognitor, qui nosti omnia antequam fiant" (Eternal God, who art the Knower of hidden things, who knoweth all things before they are done). **be . . . secret** KP's clarifying expansion of "absconditorum" (of hidden things).

316. **Open . . . name** KP renders Fisher's slight recasting of Psalm 50:17: "Aperi labia mea et os meum, ut nunciem laudes nominis tui" (Open my lips and my mouth, that I may declare praises of Thy name). The verse reads "Domine, labia mea aperies: et os meum annunciabit laudem tuam" (Lord, open my lips: and my mouth will make known Thy praise). KP's "may . . . show forth" is closer to the Vulgate's "annunciabit" than is Fisher's "nunciem" (may declare); she may have recognized the source text. **lips . . . mouth, may speak . . . forth** KP's doublings.

317. **Give . . . desires** KP renders Fisher's splicing of paraphrased excerpts from Psalms 50:12 and 139:9: "Cor novum et spiritum rectum intra me pone, omneque desiderium pravum procul à me repelle" (Put a new heart and a right spirit within me, and drive every wicked desire far from me). The first excerpt reads "Cor mundum crea in me Deus: et spiritum rectum innova in visceribus meis" (Create in me, God, a clean heart, and renew a right spirit in my inward parts). The second excerpt reads "ne tradas me Domine a desiderio meo peccatori" (do not consign me, O Lord, to my desire, [that] of a sinner). **wicked . . . sinful** KP's doubling.

318. **O . . . knowledge** KP freely renders Fisher's strenuous recasting of Psalm 72:22–23: "Stultus sum ego Domine, et rerum ignarus, et [1544: cum] scientia tua non est [1544: sit] mecum" (Foolish am I, Lord, and ignorant of things, when Thy wisdom is not with me). KP's "when" follows the first English edition where the Cologne edition reads "and." The Vulgate

[Eviii r] I am ignorant and without intelligence; my dulness is so great that my eyes cannot see, nor my heart perceive.[319]

Yea, I am a very babe and a child, and know full little mine own life and conversation.[320]

My lips be defiled and unclean; my time is short, and I am not able to understand Thy law.[321]

Give Thy servant, I beseech Thee, a heart apt to take learning: that I may know what thing is acceptable in Thy sight at all times.[322]

---

verses read "ego ad nihilum redactus sum, et nescivi. Ut jumentum factus sum apud te: et ego semper tecum" (I have been reduced to nothing, and I knew nothing. I have been made as a beast of burden before Thee: and I [was] ever with Thee). **and blind** KP's addition.

319. **I . . . perceive** KP renders Fisher's splicing of recast excerpts from Psalm 81:5, Ecclesiastes 10:10, and Isaiah 6:10: "Nescio ego nec intelligo, quoniam hebetudo tanta, ut non videant oculi mei, et cor meum non cognoscat" (I do not know nor do I understand, because such [is my] dullness that my eyes may not see, and my heart may not know). The Psalm excerpt reads "Nescierunt, neque intellexerunt" (They have not known, neither have they understood). The excerpt from Ecclesiastes, a description of an iron tool, reads "si retusum fuerit . . . et hebetatum fuerit" (if it shall be made blunt . . . and shall be made dull). This is the only recorded instance of any form of "hebeto" (to make dull) in the Vulgate, and Fisher's "hebetudo" (dullness) derives from this verb. The excerpt from Isaiah reads "ne forte videat oculis suis . . . et corde suo intelligat" (lest he see with his eyes . . . and understand with his heart). **am . . . intelligence** KP's expansive rendering of "nec intelligo" (nor do I understand).

320. **Yea . . . conversation** KP freely renders Fisher's close recasting of an excerpt from 3 Kings (1 Chronicles) 3:7: "Etiam puer sum et parvulus, ignorans ingressum et exitum meum" (I am as yet a child and very little, unknowing of my going in and going out). The excerpt, from Solomon's prayer for wisdom, reads "ego autem sum puer parvulus, et ignorans ingressum, et introitum meum" (But I am a very little child, and unknowing of my going in and entering). **mine . . . conversation** KP's substitution for Fisher's "ingressum et exitum meum" indicates that she did not recognize the source text here. See the introduction, pp. 209–10.

321. **My . . . law** KP renders Fisher's splicing of closely quoted excerpts from Isaiah 6:5 and Wisdom of Solomon 9:5: "Vir pollutis labiis ego, exiguique temporis, et minor ad intellectum legis tuae" (I am a man of unclean lips, and of little time, and less for understanding of Thy law). The first excerpt reads "vir pollutus labiis ego sum" (I am a man polluted in my lips). The second excerpt reads "homo . . . exigui temporis, et minor ad intellectum judicii et legum" (a man . . . of little time, and less for understanding of Thy judgments and laws). **My, my, I** KP's degendering of the speaker's gendered self-references in Fisher and the Vulgate may well be deliberate. Degendering to create a generic first-person speaking voice becomes a major stylistic tactic in KP's *Prayers or Meditations*, first published in June 1545, one year after this translation of *Psalms or Prayers*.

322. **Give . . . times** KP renders Fisher's splicing of closely quoted excerpts from 3 Kings (1 Chronicles) 3:9 and Wisdom of Solomon 9:10: "Da obsecro, cor docile servo tuo, ut sciam quid acceptum sit coram te omni tempore" (Give, I pray, a teachable heart to Thy servant, that I may know what may be agreeable in Thy sight every time). The first excerpt, again taken from Solomon's prayer for wisdom, reads "Dabis . . . servo tuo cor docile" (Give . . . Thy servant a teachable heart). The second excerpt, also from Solomon's prayer for wisdom, reads "ut sciam

Send down from heaven the spirit of Thy wisdom, and replenish my heart with knowledge thereof.[323]

Thy wisdom giveth true knowledge, and out of Thy mouth proceedeth both counsel and intelligence.[324]

[Eviii v] Thy wisdom openeth the mouth of the dumb, and maketh the tongue of infants eloquent.[325]

If any seem to be perfect among men, yet if Thy wisdom forsake him, he shall be reckoned nothing worth.[326]

Thy wisdom is to men a treasure that faileth not: which whoso use, they are joined to God in love and amity.[327]

How well it is with that man which is witty in this behalf, and hath his soul indued with Thy wisdom.[328]

---

quid acceptum sit apud te" (that I may know what may be acceptable before Thee). **apt . . . learning** KP's clarifying expansion of "docile" (teachable).

323. **Send . . . thereof** KP closely renders Fisher's splicing of recast excerpts from Wisdom of Solomon 9:10 and Proverbs 2:9–10: "Mitte de coelo spiritum sapientiae tuae, et sensu illius cor meum imple." The first excerpt, again from Solomon's prayer, reads "Mitte illam [sapientia tua] de caelis sanctis tuis" (Send it [Thy wisdom] down from Thine holy heavens). The excerpts from Proverbs read "Tunc intelliges . . . Si intraverit sapientia cor tuum" (Then shalt thou understand . . . If wisdom will come into thy heart).

324. **Thy . . . intelligence** KP closely renders Fisher's recasting of Proverbs 2:6: "Sapientia tua dat veram scientiam, et ex ore tuo consilium et intelligentia." The verse reads "Dominus dat sapientiam: et ex ore ejus prudentia, et scientia" (The Lord giveth wisdom, and out of His mouth [proceed] prudence and understanding).

325. **Thy . . . eloquent** KP closely renders Fisher's minor recasting of Wisdom of Solomon 10:21: "Sapientia tua os mutorum aperit, et linguas infantium eloquentes reddit." The verse reads "sapientia aperuit os mutorum, et linguas infantium fecit disertas" (wisdom hath opened the mouth of the dumb, and hath made fluent the tongues of infants).

326. **If . . . worth** KP closely renders Fisher's minor recasting of Wisdom of Solomon 9:6: "Si quis videtur perfectus inter filios mortalitum, si tamen effugerit ab illo sapientia tua, in nihilum computabitur." The verse reads "si quis erit consummatus inter filios hominum, si ab illo abfuerit sapientia tua, in nihilum computabitur" (if any man shall be consummate among the sons of men, if Thy wisdom shall forsake him, he shall be reckoned as nothing).

327. **Thy . . . amity** KP renders Fisher's near verbatim quotation of Wisdom of Solomon 7:14: "Hominibus thesaurus indeficiens est sapientia tua, qua qui usi sunt, participes facti sunt amicitiae dei" (An unfailing treasure to mankind is Thy wisdom, which whosoever [they be] who use it, are made partakers of the amity of God). The verse opening reads "Infinitus enim thesaurus est hominibus" (An infinite treasure it is to mankind). The rest of the verse reads identically with Fisher's wording above. **love . . . amity** KP's doubling.

328. **How . . . wisdom** KP renders Fisher's elaboration of Wisdom of Solomon 8:19: "Quam bene se habet homo ille qui ingeniosus est, et qui animam sortitus est sapientia praeditam" (How well within himself is the man who is superior of mind, and who hath been allotted a soul endowed with wisdom). The verse reads "Puer autem eram ingeniosus, et sortitus sum animam bonam" (I have been a boy superior of mind, and have been allotted a good soul). **witty** hav-

What man in all the world knoweth Thy counsel, or who can compass in his mind what Thy will is?[329]

[Fi r] Who can comprehend Thy purpose and mind, except Thou give him wisdom, and instruct him with Thy Holy Spirit?[330]

For men's reasons do fail in many things, and their forecasts and inventions be uncertain and unsure.[331]

For the mortal and corruptible body much grieveth the soul, and the earthly house of the body holdeth down the mind musing upon many things.[332]

Counsel and good success cometh from above, where also wisdom is, and virtue.[333]

---

ing good judgment or discernment—an apt rendering of "ingeniosus" although this sense of "witty" is no longer current. **in . . . behalf** KP's circumlocution for Fisher's reflexive construction "se habet" (he possesses in himself).

329. **What . . . is?** KP renders Fisher's minor recasting of Wisdom of Solomon 9:13: "Quisnam inter homines consilium tuum noscit? aut quis poterit cogitare quid velis tu?" (Who is he among men [that] may know Thy counsel, or who could ponder what Thou wouldst will?). The verse reads "Quis . . . hominum poterit scire consilium Dei? aut quis poterit cogitare quid velit Deus?" (Who . . . among men would be able to know the counsel of God, or who could ponder what God would will?). **in . . . world** KP's idiomatic rendering of Fisher's "inter homines" (among men). **compass . . . mind** another idiomatic rendering of Fisher's and the Vulgate's "cogitare" (ponder).

330. **Who . . . Spirit?** KP renders Fisher's minor recasting of Wisdom of Solomon 9:17: "Sensum tuum quis intelligat, nisi tu dederis sapientiam illi, et instruos eum per spiritum tuum sanctum?" The verse reads "Sensum . . . tuum quis sciet, nisi tu dederis sapientiam, et miseris spiritum sanctum tuum?" (Who may comprehend Thy frame of mind, unless Thou shalt give him wisdom, and shalt send Thy Holy Spirit?).

331. **For . . . unsure** KP renders Fisher's drastic recasting of Wisdom of Solomon 9:14: "Nam rationes hominum in multis deficiunt, et parum securae adinventiones eorum" (For the reasonings of men are lacking in many things, and their inventions are not sure enough). The verse reads "Cogitationes . . . mortalium timidae, et incertae providentiae nostrae" (The reasonings . . . of mortals are faint-hearted, and our foresight is uncertain). **reasons** KP's less than optimal choice among possible renderings of "rationes," where "reasonings" or "calculations" would better fit the context; see the introduction, p. 206. **forecasts . . . inventions** KP's doubling. Her "forecasts" is closer to the Vulgate's "providentiae" than is Fisher's "adinventiones" (inventions) and may indicate that she recognized the source text. **uncertain . . . unsure** KP's doubling.

332. **For . . . things** KP renders Fisher's close recasting of Wisdom of Solomon 9:15: "Corruptibile enim corpus animum gravat, et terrenum domicilium retardat mentem multa cogitantem" (For the corruptible body burdeneth the soul, and the earthly house hindereth the mind pondering many things). The verse reads "Corpus enim, quod corrumpitur, aggravat animam, et terrena inhabitatio deprimit sensum multa cogitantem" (For the body, which is wasting away, maketh the soul heavier, and the earthly habitation weigheth down the mind pondering many things). **mortal . . . corruptible** KP's doubling. **much grieveth** KP's less than optimal choice for rendering "gravat" (burdeneth); see the introduction, p. 206.

333. **Counsel . . . virtue** KP closely renders the recast phrasing and the shift from heavenly to earthly perspective that Fisher imposes on an excerpt from Wisdom of Solomon 8:7:

With Thee, O Lord, is riches, glory, and righteousness, which be treasures incorruptible.[334]

He that hath found out Thee, hath found life; and he that loveth not Thee, loveth death.[335]

[Fi v] O Lord God, touch my mouth, that my iniquity may be driven away; dwell Thou in my heart, that my sins may be purged.[336]

Wisdom doth not enter into a malicious soul, nor will abide in a body which is subject to sin.[337]

Teach me, O Lord God, lest my ignorance increase, and my sins wax more and more.[338]

"Superne consilium et successus, et illic prudentia ac etiam virtus." The excerpt reads "sobrietatem . . . et prudentiam . . . et justitiam, et virtutem, quibus utilius nihil est in vita hominibus" (reasonableness . . . and prudence . . . and justice, and virtue, among which nothing is more useful to men in life).

334. **With . . . incorruptible** KP closely renders Fisher's recasting of Psalm 111:3: "Tecum sunt divitiae et gloria, opes incorruptibiles et justicia." The verse reads "Gloria, et divitiae in domo ejus: et justitia ejus manet in saeculum saeculi" (Glory and riches [are] in His house, and His justice endureth from age to age).

335. **He . . . death** KP closely renders Fisher's recast excerpts from Proverbs 8:35–36: "Qui te invenerit, invenit vitam: et te qui non amat, diligit mortem." The excerpts, which detail the last of Wisdom's self-ascribed benefits, read: "Qui me invenerit, inveniet vitam. . . . Omnes, qui me oderunt, diligunt mortem" (Who shall have found me, shall find life. . . . All they that hate me, love death).

336. **O . . . purged** KP closely renders Fisher's elaboration of Isaiah 6:7: "Domine Deus, tange os meum, ut recedat iniquitas mea; inhabita cor meum, ut peccata mea purgentur." The verse, part of Isaiah's vision in which the Lord of glory sends a seraphim to ordain him a prophet, reads "Ecce tetigit hoc labia tua, et auferetur iniquitas tua, et peccatum tuum mundabitur" (Behold, this [a coal from the heavenly altar] hath touched thy lips, and thine iniquity is taken away, and thy sin shall be made clean). **dwell . . . heart** Fisher's addition, "inhabita cor meum," aptly rendered by KP, is not a Vulgate locution. It, like Fisher's substitution of "purgentur" (is purged) for the Vulgate's "mundabitur" (shall be made clean), evokes a post-Biblical spirituality in which affective inward experience and the purging of sin, a process continuing in purgatory, figure prominently. KP's close renderings demonstrate her attraction to these aspects of Fisher's spirituality.

337. **Wisdom . . . sin** KP closely renders Fisher's minor recasting of Wisdom of Solomon 1:4: "In malevolam animam sapientia non intrat, nec manebit in corpore quod peccatis subditur." The verse reads "in malevolam animam non introibit sapientia, nec habitabit in corpore subdito peccatis" (into an ill-willed soul wisdom shall not enter, neither shall it inhabit a body subjected to sins).

338. **Teach . . . more** KP closely renders Fisher's splicing of excerpts from Psalm 118:12 and Ecclesiasticus 23:3: "Doce me domine Deus, ne augescat ignorantia mea, et delicta mea multiplicentur." The Psalm excerpt reads "Domine: doce me" (Lord, teach me). The excerpt from Ecclesiasticus reads "ne adincrescant ignorantiae meae, et multiplicentur delicta mea" (lest my ignorance increase, and my sins be multiplied). **wax . . . and more** a characteristically idiomatic rendering of Fisher's and the Vulgate's "multiplicentur."

Let Thy Spirit teach me the things that be pleasant unto Thee, that I may be led into the straight way, out of error wherein I have wandered overlong.[339]

Let Thy wisdom be stablished in my spirit, and write Thy law in my heart.[340] [Fii r] Thy wisdom is to me more precious than all riches; and I desire more to have it than all other things, be they never so fair and goodly.[341]

O Lord, Thou knowest how sore I am inflamed with the love of Thy wisdom, which is my only study and meditation.[342]

O how pleasant and sweet Thy words be to my heart: truly much more than honey is to my mouth.

Thy word is a bright candle to my feet, and a light to my ways.

Thy wisdom pleaseth me more than thousands of gold or of silver can do.[343]

339. **Let . . . overlong** KP renders Fisher's assemblage of a set of frequent and conventional moral images in the Old Testament, by way of excerpts from 2 Esdras (Nehemiah) 9:20, 3 Kings (1 Chronicles) 14:8, Psalm 106:7, and Wisdom of Solomon 12:24: "Spiritus me doceat, quae tibi placita sunt, et ducat in viam rectam, nam in erroris via diutius erravi" (Let the Spirit teach me what things are pleasing to Thee, and let it lead [me] into the straight way, for I have wandered too long in the way of error). The excerpt from 2 Esdras reads "Et spiritum tuum bonum dedisti qui doceret eos" (And Thou gavest Thy good Spirit, that it might teach them). The excerpt from 3 Kings, God's praise of King David, reads "faciens quod placitum esset in conspectu meo" ([a man] doing what was pleasing in My sight). The Psalm excerpt reads "deduxit eos in viam rectam" (He led them in the straight way). The excerpt from Wisdom of Solomon reads "in erroris via diutius erraverant" (they have wandered too long in the way of error).

340. **Let . . . heart** KP closely renders Fisher's recasting of excerpts from Jeremiah 31:33: "Firmetur sapientia in animo meo, et legem tuam in corde meo scribe." These excerpts, part of God's renewed covenant with Israel, read "Dabo legem meam in visceribus eorum, et in corde eorum scribam eam" (I shall put My law in their inward parts, and I shall write it in their heart).

341. **Thy . . . goodly** KP renders Fisher's splicing of excerpts from Ecclesiasticus 25:7 and Wisdom of Solomon 7:7–8: "Super omnia quae speciosa sunt et pulchra, sapientiam desidero: in comparatione illius divitias non aestimo" (More than all things that are splendid and beautiful, I will desire wisdom; in comparison with that, I do not esteem riches). The Ecclesiasticus excerpt reads "Quam speciosa . . . sapientia" (How splendid . . . [is] wisdom). The Wisdom of Solomon excerpts read "venit in me spiritus sapientiae . . . et divitias nihil esse duxi in comparatione illius" (the spirit of wisdom came into me . . . and I have reckoned riches to be nothing in comparison with it). **be . . . goodly** KP's characteristic expansion of phrasing.

342. **O . . . meditation** KP renders with unusual freedom Fisher's paraphrase of Psalm 118:97: "Quàm amo sapientiam tuam, domine, quae unica meditatio mea est" (How I love Thy wisdom, Lord, which is my only meditation). The Psalm verse reads "Quomodo dilexi legem tuam Domine: tota die meditatio mea est" (How I love Thy law, Lord; it is my meditation all the day). **study . . . meditation** KP's doubling.

343. **O how . . . do** KP renders Fisher's close quotation of excerpts from Psalm 118:103, 105, 72: "Quam dulcia cordi meo eloquia tua? multo magis quàm mel ori meo. Verbum tuum pedibus meis lucerna est, et viis meis lumen. Magis mihi placet sapientia tua, quàm milia auri vel argenti" (How sweet are Thy fine words to my heart: much more than honey in my mouth. Thy word is a lamp to my feet, and a light to my ways. Thy wisdom pleaseth me much more than thousands in gold or silver). The verses read "Quam dulcia faucibus meis eloquia tua, super

I have more pleasure and delectation in the way of Thy wisdom than in great abundance of treasure.

[Fii v] Would God my ways may be so ordered, that I may learn Thy wisdom and Thy words.

Thy word giveth heat and inflameth: wherefore I greatly desire it.[344]

O happy is he, Lord, whom Thou instructest, and makest learned in Thy law.[345]

His soul shall always study wisdom, and his tongue shall speak judgment.[346]

The law of God shall be written in his heart, and he shall not be overthrown as he goeth.[347]

O Lord, which art my God and my Saviour: hear my prayer, and my tongue shall ever speak and set out Thy mercies.[348]

---

mel ori meo. Lucerna pedibus meis verbum tuum, et lumen semitis meis. Bonum mihi lex oris tui, super millia auri, et argenti" (How sweet in my throat are Thy fine words, beyond honey in my mouth. Thy word is a lamp to my feet, and a light to my paths. To me the law of Thy mouth is good, above thousands in gold and silver). **pleasant . . . sweet** KP's doubling. **bright candle** KP's image.

344. **I have . . . it** KP renders Fisher's recast and reordered excerpts from Psalm 118:14, 5, 140: "In via sapientiae tuae delector magis, quàm ingenti divitiarum copia. Utinam dirigantur viae meae, ut sapientiam tuam et sermones tuos discam. Eloquium tuum ignitum est, hinc fit ut vehementer illud cupiam" (In the way of Thy wisdom I delight more than in abundance of riches. Would that my ways were so directed that I might learn Thy wisdom and Thy words. Thy fine speech hath kindled [in me]; hence it maketh me vehemently desire it). The verses read "In via testimoniorum tuorum delectatus sum, sicut in omnibus divitiis. Utinam dirigantur viae meae, ad custodiendas justificationes tuas. Ignitum eloquium tuum vehementer: et servus tuus dilexit illud" (In the way of Thy testimonies I have been delighted, as in all riches. Would that my ways were directed to the keeping of Thy due proceedings. Thy fine speech [hath] kindled vehemently, and Thy servant hath loved it). **pleasure . . . delectation, giveth heat . . . inflameth** KP's doublings.

345. **O . . . law** KP closely renders Fisher's minor recasting of Psalm 93:12: "O beatum illum, quem tu instruis domine, et in lege tua doctum facis." The verse reads "Beatus homo, quem tu erudieris Domine: et de lege tua docueris eum" (Blessed is the man whom Thou shalt instruct, Lord, and shalt teach him concerning Thy law). **Lord** KP's direct address is not in Fisher but is in the Vulgate. She may have recognized the source text.

346. **His . . . judgment** KP closely renders Fisher's expansive recasting of Psalm 34:28: "Anima ejus sapientiam meditabitur, et lingua ejus loquetur judicium." The verse reads "Et lingua mea meditabitur justitiam tuam, tota die laudem tuam" (And my tongue shall meditate on Thy righteousness and Thy praise all the day). **always** KP's addition to Fisher renders the Vulgate's "tota die," suggesting that she recognized the source text.

347. **The . . . goeth** KP closely renders Fisher's minor recasting of Psalm 36:31: "Lex dei in corde suo scribetur, et non supplantabuntur gressus ejus." The verse reads "Lex Dei ejus in corde ipsius: et non supplantabuntur gressus ejus" (The law of God [is] in his heart; and his steps shall not be tripped up). **shall . . . goeth** a characteristically colloquial expansion of phrasing.

348. **O . . . mercies** KP freely renders Fisher's splicing of recast excerpts from Psalms 64:6 and 50:16: "O domine deus salutis meae, exaudi precem meam, et lingua mea misericordias tuas semper loquetur" (O Lord God of my salvation, hear my prayer, and my tongue shall ever speak Thy praises). The first excerpt reads "Exaudi nos Deus salutaris noster" (Hear us, God of our

[Fiii r] Give me wisdom, which is assistant to Thy throne: that I may discern between good and evil, and may know Thy holy mysteries.[349]

Open mine eyes, that I may perceive and behold the wonderful things which be in Thy law.[350]

Remember Thy word, now I call upon Thee; for I have put my hope in it. Make me to know the way of Thy wisdom, and hide not Thy knowledge from me.[351]

Order me according to Thy mercy, and disappoint me not of that I look for.

Teach me right wisdom and intelligence, for Thy wisdom is all that I desire.[352]

---

salvation). The second excerpt reads "et exultabit lingua mea justitiam tuam" (and my tongue shall exalt Thy righteousness). **God . . . Saviour, speak . . . set out** KP's doublings.

349. **Give . . . mysteries** KP renders Fisher's splicing of excerpts from Wisdom of Solomon 9:4, 3 Kings (1 Chronicles) 3:9, and Psalm 50:8: "Da sedium tuarum adsistricem sapientiam, ut bonum et malum discernere possim, et occulta tua cognoscam" (Give wisdom, the assistant of Thy throne, that I may be able to discern good and evil, and may know Thy hidden things). The first excerpt reads "Da mihi sedium tuarum assistricem sapientiam" (Give me wisdom, the assistant of Thy throne). The second excerpt, from King Solomon's prayer for wisdom, reads "ut . . . possit . . . discernere inter bonum et malum" (that he may be able . . . to discern between good and evil). The third excerpt reads "et occulta sapientiae tuae manifestasti mihi" (and the hidden things of Thy wisdom hast Thou manifested to me). **between . . . evil** KP's phrasing is identical to the Vulgate's, as Fisher's is not. She may have recognized the source text. **holy** KP's addition.

350. **Open . . . law** KP renders Fisher's minor recasting of Psalm 118:18: "Revela oculos meos, ut admiranda perspiciam, quae in lege tua sunt" (Open mine eyes, that I may perceive the wonderful things that are in Thy law). The first English edition has a misprint, "oculos tuos" (Thine eyes). The Vulgate verse reads "Revela oculos meos: et considerabo mirabilia de lege tua" (Open mine eyes, and I shall consder the wonderful things of Thy law). **perceive . . . behold** KP's doubling.

351. **Remember . . . me** KP closely renders Fisher's splicing of recast excerpts from Psalms 118:49, 142:8, and 118:19: "Memor esto verbi tui te invocanti, nam in illo spem meam posui. Viam sapientiae notam fac mihi, et scientiam tuam ne celes à me." The first excerpt reads "Memor esto verbi tui servo tuo, in quo mihi spem dedisti" (Remember Thy word to Thy servant, in which I have put my hope). The second excerpt reads "Notam fac mihi viam, in qua ambulem" (Make known to me the way in which I shall walk). The third excerpt reads "non abscondas a me mandata tua" (hide not Thy commandments from me).

352. **Order . . . desire** KP renders Fisher's splicing of recast and reordered excerpts from Psalms 118:124, 116, 66 and 37:10: "Fac mecum juxta misericordiam tuam, et ne confundas me ab expectatione mea. Recte sapere et intelligere doceto me, nam sapientia tua, totum quod volo" (Do with me according to Thy mercy, and do not confound me in my expectation. Teach me to know rightly and understand, for all that I wish [is] Thy wisdom). The first excerpt reads "Fac cum servo tuo secundum misericordiam tuam" (Do with Thy servant according to Thy mercy). The second excerpt reads "non confundas me ab expectatione mea" (confound me not in my expectation). The third excerpt reads "Bonitatem, et disciplinam, et scientiam doce me" (Teach me goodness, and learning, and knowledge). The fourth excerpt reads "ante te omne desiderium meum" (all my desire is before Thee). **Order me** Deal with me—a no longer current sense of the verb, but an apt rendering of "Fac me" (Do with me). **intelligence** the fact of

Put Thy word in my mouth, and fasten Thy wisdom in my heart.[353]

[Fiii v] Let Thy wisdom rule and guide my thoughts, that they may always please Thee.[354]

Thy words be wonderful and marvelous: wherefore my soul delighteth in them.[355]

Thy wisdom is perfect, and Thy knowledge is clear, and giveth light to the eyes.

It is more amiable than gold and precious stones; it is far sweeter than the honeycomb.

Thy wisdom is pure and undefiled, and maketh souls strong; Thy words be certain and true, and give understanding unto the simple.[356]

---

mentally apprehending something—a no longer current sense of the noun, but a contextually apt cognate of "intelligere" (to understand).

353. **Put . . . heart** KP closely renders Fisher's splicing of recast excerpts from Exodus 4:18 and Ecclesiasticus 23:2: "Da verbum tuum in ore meo, et in corde meo sapientiam tuam fige." The first excerpt, God's charge to Moses to rally the Israelites enslaved in Egypt, reads "Loquere . . . et pone verba mea in ore . . . tuo . . . et ego ero in ore" (Speak . . . and put My words in . . . thy mouth . . . and I will be in [thy] mouth). The second excerpt, a reference to God, reads "Quis superponet . . . in corde meo doctrinam sapientiae" (Who hath imposed . . . on my heart the doctrine of wisdom).

354. **Let . . . Thee** KP quite closely renders Fisher's splicing of recast excerpts from Wisdom of Solomon 8:17 and 9:9: "Sapientia tua cogitationes meas regat, ut placeant coram oculis tuis semper." The first excerpts, from Solomon's reflections on becoming king, read "Haec cogitans apud me . . . immortalitas est in cognitione sapientiae" (Thinking this within me . . . there is imperishability in the thought of wisdom). The second excerpt reads "sapientia tua . . . sciebat quid esset placitum oculis tuis, et quid directum" (Thy wisdom . . . will know what would be pleasing and what would be straightforward in Thine eyes). **rule . . . guide** KP's doubling may register her recognition of the second source text with its "esse . . . directum" (be . . . straightforward) locution. Fisher has no corresponding term.

355. **Thy . . . them** KP renders Fisher's recasting of Psalm 118:129: "Mirabilia sunt eloquia tua, quapropter delectantur in eis anima mea" (Wonderful are Thy fine words, on which account my soul delighteth in them). The verse reads "Mirabilia testimonia tua: ideo scrutata est ea anima mea" (Wonderful [are] Thy testimonies; therefore hath my soul examined them closely). **wonderful . . . marvelous** KP's doubling.

356. **Thy . . . simple** KP renders Fisher's splicing of recast and reordered excerpts from Psalm 18:9, 11, 8: "Sapientia tua perfecta est, scientia tua lucida, et oculos illuminans. Amabiliora super aurum et gemmas, et dulciora quàm mel de favo. Sapientia tua immaculata, animas confortans, eloquium tuum verax, intellectum docens parvulos" (Thy wisdom is perfect; Thy knowledge is clear, enlightening the eyes. It is lovelier than gold and gems, and sweeter than honey from the honeycomb. Thy wisdom is pure, comforting the soul; Thy fine words are true, instructing the mind [of] little ones). The excerpts from verse 9 read "Justitiae Domini rectae . . . praeceptum Domini lucidum, illuminans oculos" (The judgments of the Lord are right . . . the precept of the Lord is clear, enlightening the eyes). The excerpts from verse 11 read "Desiderabilia super aurum et lapidem pretiosum multum: et dulciora super mel et favum" (More desirable [are they] than gold and many precious stones, and sweeter than honey and the honeycomb). The excerpts from verse 8 read "Lex Domini immaculata convertens animas,

When shall he that erreth in his spirit, have knowledge? And when shall he that is ignorant, have learning?
[Fiv r] When wilt Thou send down Thy Holy Spirit from above? When shall the blind heart be lightened with knowlege? When shall the tongue that stammereth be made eloquent?[357]

I am like a babe without wisdom and discretion; let Thy strong hand, O Lord, be my help.[358]

I know that Thou canst do all things, and nothing is hard to Thee.[359]

---

testimonium Domini fidele, sapientiam praestans parvulis" (The law of the Lord [is] pure, redirecting souls; the testimony of the Lord is faithful, outstanding [as] wisdom for little ones). **pure . . . undefiled, certain . . . true** KP's doublings.

357. **When shall . . . eloquent?** KP quite closely renders a series of five questions that Fisher composes around various Vulgate excerpts: "Quando sciet errans spiritu intelligentiam? et ignorans doctrinam discet? Quando effundetur de excelso spiritus tuus, quando cor insipiens scientiam callebit, quando lingua balbutiens diserta erit?" (When will he, erring in his spirit, know the power of discerning? and he, ignorant, become acquainted with learning? When will Thy Spirit be poured down from on high? When will the foolish heart understand knowledge? When will the stammering tongue be fluent?). Perceiving the allusive thrust of each question depends on identifying the source text. The first question appears to allude to Wisdom of Solomon 12:24: "in erroris via diutius erraverunt, deos aestimantes haec, quae in animalibus sunt supervacua" (they have erred in the way of error for a long time, valuing those things as gods, which are useless to beasts). The second question appears to allude to Proverbs 19:27: "Non cesses fili audire doctrinam, nec ignores sermones scientiae" (Do not cease, son, to hear learning, nor be ignorant of words of knowledge). The third question alludes to Isaiah 32:15, part of a prophecy traditionally interpreted as prefiguring the coming of Christ's kingdom to inaugurate a reign of righteousness and peace: "donec effundatur super nos spiritus de excelso" (at the time when the Spirit is poured out over us from on high). The fourth question alludes to Psalm 52:1: "Dixit insipiens in corde suo: Non est Deus" (The fool hath said in his heart: There is no God). The fifth question alludes to Isaiah 32:4, another part of the prophecy of the coming of Christ's kingdom and its beneficent effects: "lingua balborum velociter loquetur et plane" (the stammerers' tongue will speak quickly and plainly).

358. **I . . . help** KP renders Fisher's splicing of excerpts from 3 Kings (1 Chronicles) 3:7 and Exodus 13:9: "Parvulus et insipiens sum domine, auxilio sit mihi manus tua fortis" (I am a little one, Lord, and foolish; let Thy strong hand be my help). The excerpt from 3 Kings derives from Solomon's prayer for wisdom: "ego . . . sum puer parvulus, et ignorans" (I . . . am a little boy, and unkowing); see n320 for a previous use of this verse. The Exodus excerpt is from God's commands to Moses to establish Passover as a memorial celebration: "Et erit quasi signum . . . in manu enim forti eduxit te Dominus de Aegypto" (And it will be as a sign . . . truly with His strong hand the Lord hath brought thee out of Egypt). **without . . . discretion** KP's circumlocution rendering "insipiens" (foolish).

359. **I . . . Thee** KP closely renders Fisher's splicing of recast excerpts from Job 42:2 and Genesis 18:14: "Novi, quod omnia potes, et nihil est tibi difficile." The first excerpt, in which Job addresses God, reads "Scio quia omnia potes" (I know that Thou canst do all things). The second excerpt, God's question about Abraham and Sarah's doubts that a son could be born to them in their old age, reads "Numquid Deo quidquam est difficile?" (Is anything difficult for God?).

Thou art great, O Lord, and canst not be known, and Thy wisdom is infinite.[360]

I have declared my cause before Thee; do with Thy servant according to Thy great mercy.[361]

[Fiv v] Look toward me and have mercy upon me: that I may bring to pass that, which I believe and think, may be done by Thee.[362]

Make the way of Thy wisdom known unto me, and replenish my heart with the knowledge thereof.[363]

Hear my voice, O Lord, according to Thy mercy; entreat me according to judgment.[364]

Give glory unto Thy name, O Lord, for Thou only art good and wise, and there is none other Saviour beside Thee.[365]

360. **Thou . . . infinite** KP closely renders Fisher's recasting of Job 5:9: "Tu magnus es, incognoscibilis, et sapientiae tuae nullus est numerus." The verse reads "qui facit magna et inscrutabilia et mirabilia absque numero" ([God] who doth great and inscrutable things, and marvelous without number).

361. **I . . . mercy** KP closely renders Fisher's splicing of recast excerpts from 3 Kings (1 Chronicles) 8:59 and 3:6: "Annunciavi coram te causam meam, fac cum servo tuo juxta magnam misericordiam tuam." Both excerpts are utterances of King Solomon. The first reads "deprecatus sum coram Domino . . . ut faciat judicium servo suo" (I have interceded before the Lord . . . that He may render judgment for His servant). The second is an appeal to God: "Tu fecisti cum servo tuo David patre meo misericordiam magnam" (Thou hast done great mercy in connection with Thy servant David, my father).

362. **Look . . . Thee** KP closely renders Fisher's recasting of excerpts from Judith 13:7: "Respice ad me, et miserere mei, ut hoc quod credens per te posse fieri cogito, perficiam." The excerpts, from Judith's prayer just before she kills Holofernes, read "Confirma me Domine Deus Israel, et respice . . . ut . . . hoc quod credens per te posse fieri cogitavi, perficiam" (Strengthen me, Lord God of Israel, and look upon me . . . that . . . I may bring to pass this that I, believing, have thought I could accomplish through Thee).

363. **Make . . . thereof** KP closely renders Fisher's splicing of recast excerpts from Psalms 142:8 and 31:8: "Viam sapientiae tuae notam fac mihi, et intellectum illius cor meum imple." The first excerpt reads "Notam fac mihi viam, in qua ambulem" (Make known to me the way in which I should walk). The second excerpt reads "Intellectum tibi dabo, et instruam te in via" (I will give thee knowledge, and instruct thee in the way).

364. **Hear . . . judgment** KP closely renders Fisher's near verbatim quotation of Psalm 118:149: "Vocem meam audi secundum misericordiam tuam domine, secundum judicium mecum agito." The verse reads identically, except for ending with "secundum judicium tuum vivifica me" (enliven me according to Thy judgment). **entreat** deal with, treat—no longer current senses of this verb, applied to give a more general cast to Fisher's "agito" (impel, arouse). KP clearly did not recognize the source text here.

365. **Give . . . Thee** KP closely renders Fisher's splicing of recast excerpts from Psalm 28:1, Romans 16:27, and Isaiah 45:21: "Da gloriam nomini tuo domine, tu enim solus es bonus et sapiens, et non est alius praeter te salvator." The Psalm excerpt reads "afferte Domino gloriam nomini ejus" (Give the Lord the glory of His name). The Romans excerpt reads "soli sapienti Deo" (to the only wise God). The Isaiah excerpt reads "Deus justus, et salvans non est praeter me" ([I am] a just God, and there is no one who saveth besides Me).

Hear me, O Lord, for Thy name' sake, and withhold not Thy mercy from me.[366]

My lips shall speak and set forth Thy laud and praise when Thou hast taught me Thy wisdom,[367]

[Fv r] Then I will declare Thy marvels: that other also may be converted unto Thee,[368]

And may bless Thy name forever, world without end. Amen.[369]

THE SIXT[H] P[S]ALM.
A CHRISTIAN MAN PRAYETH THAT HE MAY BE HEARD OF GOD.[370]

O Lord, hear my prayers, and let my cry come to Thee.
Turn not away Thy face from me in the day of my tribulation.
What day soever I shall call upon Thee, hear me, O Lord God.[371]
For Thou art great and workest wonders; Thou only art God.[372]
Also Thy works be great; Thy thoughts be very profound and deep.[373]

366. **Hear . . . me** KP closely renders Fisher's splicing of two formulaic Vulgate phrases with an excerpt from Psalm 76:10 rephrased as an entreaty: "Exaudi me domine propter nomen tuum, et ne contineas à me misericordiam tuam." The Psalm excerpt that Fisher rephrases is a question: "Deus . . . continebit in ira sua misericordias suas?" (Will God . . . withhold His mercies in His anger?).

367. **My . . . wisdom** KP renders Fisher's near verbatim quotation of Psalm 118:171: "Eructabunt labia mea laudem, cum docueris me sapientiam tuam." The Vulgate verse reads identically except for ending with "justificationes tuas" (Thy due proceedings) where Fisher reads "sapientam tuam" (Thy wisdom). **laud . . . praise** KP's doubling.

368. **Then . . . Thee** KP closely renders Fisher's splicing of recast excerpts from Psalms 25:7 and 21:28: "Tum enarrabo mirabilia tua, ut alii etiam ad te convertantur." The first excerpt reads "ut . . . enarrem universa mirabilia tua" (that I may declare all Thy wonders). The second excerpt reads "convertentur ad Dominum universi fines terrae" (all the ends of the earth shall be converted unto the Lord).

369. **And . . . Amen** KP closely renders Fisher's recast excerpt from Psalm 88:53: "Et benedicant nomen tuum in sempiternum, et in saeculum saeculi. Amen." The excerpt reads "Benedictus Dominus in aeternum" (Blessed be the Lord forever).

370. **A . . . God** KP expands the descriptive portion of Fisher's title, which reads "ut exaudiatur à Deo" (that he may be heard by God).

371. **O Lord . . . God** KP closely renders Fisher's near verbatim quotation of Psalm 101:2–3: "Domine, exaudi preces meas, et clamor meus ad te perveniat. Ne avertas faciem tuam à me in die tribulationis meae. In quacumque die invocavero te, exaudi me O domine Deus." The verses read "Domine exaudi orationem meam: et clamor meus ad te veniat. Non avertas faciem tuam a me: in quacumque die tribulor, inclina ad me aurem tuam" (Lord, hear my prayer, and may my cry come to Thee. Turn not Thy face from me; in whatsoever day I shall be afflicted, incline Thine ear unto me).

372. **For . . . God** KP closely renders Fisher's minor recasting of Psalm 85:10: "Magnus enim es tu, et admiranda faciens, tu es deus solus." The verse reads "Quoniam magnus es tu, et faciens mirabilia: tu es Deus solus" (Since Thou art great, working wonders: Thou only art God).

373. **Also . . . deep** KP quite closely renders Fisher's minor recasting of Psalm 91:6: "Magna etiam sunt opera tua, nimis profundae cogitationes tuae." The verse reads "Quam magnificata

[Fv v] Bow down Thine ear unto me and hear me, for I am poor and without help.[374]

Have mercy upon me, O Lord, for when trouble cometh, I flee unto Thee for succor.[375]

Make glad the soul of Thy servant, for I have lifted up my heart unto Thee.[376]

O Lord, Thou art good and merciful, and of much mercy to all them that call upon Thee.[377]

Hear my request and petition, and graciously accept my prayers.

O Lord God, in Thee I trust; let me not be confounded, I beseech Thee; deliver me in Thy righteousness.[378]

Hearken unto the voice of my cry, O my King and my God, for I make my humble suit unto Thee.[379]

[Fvi r] Hear my voice, with which I call upon Thee; have mercy upon me, and save me.[380]

My prayers be ever unto Thee, O Lord God, if that the time of Thy gracious

---

sunt opera tua Domine! nimis profundae sunt cogitationes tuae" (How exalted are Thy works, Lord! Thy thoughts are deep beyond measure). **profound . . . deep** KP's doubling.

374. **Bow . . . help** KP closely renders Fisher's near verbatim quotation of Psalm 85:1: "Inclina ad me aurem tuam, et exaudi me, inops enim et pauper ego sum." The verse reads "Inclina Domine aurem tuam, et exaudi me: quoniam inops, et pauper sum ego" (Incline Thine ear, Lord, and hear me: since I am helpless and poor).

375. **Have . . . succor** KP freely renders Fisher's splicing of a formulaic Vulgate phrase with recast excerpts from Psalm 142:9 and Proverbs 11:8: "Miserere mei domine, ad te enim, cum angustia mihi imminet, confugio" (Have mercy on me, Lord; for unto Thee do I flee when trouble hangeth over me). The Psalm excerpt reads "Domine, ad te confugi" (Lord, unto Thee have I fled). The Proverbs excerpt reads "Justus de angustia liberatus est" (The just man is delivered from trouble).

376. **Make . . . Thee** KP closely renders Fisher's exact quotation of Psalm 85:4: "Laetifica animam servi tui, quoniam ad te animam meam levavi."

377. **O . . . Thee** KP closely renders Fisher's elaboration and recasting of an excerpt from 2 Paralipomenon (2 Chronicles) 30:18: "Tu domine bonus es et propitiabilis, ac multae misericordiae omnibus te invocantibus." The excerpt reads "Dominus bonus propitiabitur cunctis qui . . . requirunt Dominum Deum" (The Lord is good and will be merciful to all who . . . call upon the Lord God).

378. **O . . . righteousness** KP closely renders Fisher's recasting of excerpts from Psalm 70:1–2: "Exaudi orationem meam, et preces meas clementer suscipe." The excerpts read "In te Domine speravi, non confundar . . . in justitia tua . . . eripe me" (In Thee, Lord, have I trusted, let me not be confounded . . . in Thy justice . . . deliver me).

379. **Hearken . . . Thee** KP freely renders Fisher's splicing of recast excerpts from Psalm 5:2–4: "Intende voci clamoris mei o rex meus et deus meus, quoniam tibi supplico" (Attend to the voice of my cry, O my King and my God, for I supplicate Thee). The excerpts read "Domine, intellige clamorem meum. Intende voci orationis meae, rex meus et Deus meus. Quoniam ad te orabo" (Lord, listen to my cry. Attend to the voice of my prayer, my King and my God, for to Thee I will pray). **make . . . suit** a characteristic phrasal expansion by KP, aptly rendering "supplico" (supplicate, pray humbly to).

380. **Hear . . . me** KP closely renders Fisher's recasting of Psalm 26:7: "Audi vocem meam, qua te invoco, miserere mei, et salva me." The verse reads "Exaudi . . . vocem meam, qua cla-

pleasure shall come, when that according to the multitude of Thy mercy Thou wilt hear me in the truth of Thy health.[381]

Have regard unto me, O Lord, for Thy mercy is sweet; according to the multitude of Thy mercies, look upon me.[382]

Go not far away from me, O my God, but make haste to help me.[383]

Let my words be pleasant unto Thee: and make that the thoughts and meditation of my heart may be acceptable afore Thee.[384]

[Fvi v] Turn not away Thy face from Thy servant, for trouble riseth up against me on every side: wherefore now succor me.[385]

My heart desireth Thee; my soul seeketh for Thee; I tarry and look when I may behold Thy face.[386]

Turn not away Thy face from me; cast not away Thy servant in a displeasure.

---

mavi ad te: miserere mei, et exaudi me" (Hear . . . my voice, with which I have called unto Thee; have mercy upon me, and hear me).

381. **My . . . health** KP renders Fisher's close recasting of Psalm 68:14: "Preces meae semper ad te domine, siquando venerit tempus beneplaciti tui Deus in multitudine misericordiae tuae, ut exaudias me in veritate salutis tuae" (My prayers [are] ever to Thee, Lord, if ever the time well-pleasing to Thee will come, O God, in the multitude of Thy mercies, that Thou wilt hear me in the truth of Thy salvation). The verse reads "Ego vero orationem meam ad te Domine: tempus beneplaciti Deus. In multitudine misericordiae tuae exaudi me, in veritate salutis tuae" (As for me, my prayer [is] ever to Thee, Lord, in a time well-pleasing to [Thee], O God. In the multitude of Thy mercies, hear me, in the truth of Thy salvation). **health** salvation.

382. **Have . . . me** KP closely renders Fisher's splicing of recast excerpts from Psalm 108:21, 26: "Adtende mihi domine, quoniam suavis est misericordia tua, secundum multitudinem miserationum tuarum respice me." The verse excerpts read "Domine, . . . suavis est misericordia tua . . . Adjuva me . . . salvum me fac secundum misericordiam tuam" (Lord, . . . sweet is Thy mercy . . . Help me . . . save me according to Thy mercy).

383. **Go . . . me** KP closely renders Fisher's splicing and minor recasting of excerpts from Psalms 70:12 and 69:2: "Ne longe abeas à me, o mi Deus, in auxilium meum festina." The first excerpt reads "Deus ne elongeris a me" (God, go not far from me). The second excerpt reads "ad adjuvandum me festina" (make haste in helping me).

384. **Let . . . Thee** KP closely renders Fisher's recasting of Psalm 18:15: "Verba mea grata tibi sint, accepta sit coram te meditatio cordis mei." The verse reads "erunt ut complaceant eloquia oris mei: et meditatio cordis mei in conspectu tuo" (Let the fine words of my mouth and the meditation of my heart be well-pleasing in Thy sight). **thoughts . . . meditation** KP's doubling.

385. **Turn . . . me** KP renders Fisher's recasting of Psalm 68:18: "Et ne avertas faciem tuam à servo tuo, tribulatio undique mihi imminet, adjuva me" (And turn not Thy face away from Thy servant, for affliction presseth upon me from every side; help me). The verse reads "Et ne avertas faciem tuam a puero tuo: quoniam tribulor, velociter exaudi me" (And turn not Thy face from Thy child: since I am afflicted, help me speedily).

386. **My . . . face** KP renders Fisher's splicing of recast excerpts from Psalms 118:10, 68:33, and 41:3: "Te desiderat cor meum, quaerit te anima mea, faciem tuam exspecto" (My heart desireth Thee; my soul seeketh Thee; I look for Thy face). The first excerpt reads "In toto corde meo exquisivi te" (With my whole heart have I sought Thee). The second excerpt reads "quaerite Deum, et vivet anima vestra" (seek God, and your soul shall live). The third excerpt reads "quando . . . apparebo ante faciem Dei?" (when . . . shall I appear before the face of God?).

Thou hast always helped me before this time; forsake me not now in my most need, O my Lord and my God.[387]

To Thee I cry daily; go not away from me, and turn not the deaf ear unto me.

Cause my prayer to enter into Thy presence, and let my cry come unto Thee.[388]

[Fvii r] Hear me, O Lord, for I lift up my mind unto Thy holy temple.[389]

Help now in time of trouble, for vain is the help of man.[390]

I look after Thy help, O Lord, and to Thy judgments my will is conformable.[391]

---

tarry . . . look KP's doubling, aptly rendering "exspecto" (look out for); see the introduction, p. 207. **when . . . behold** KP's addition.

387. **Turn . . . God** KP freely renders Fisher's recasting of Psalm 26:9: "Ne avertas vultum à me, ne rejicias per iram servum tuum, auxilio mihi fuisti semper, ne deseras me iam in angustiis meis o domine mi Deus" (Turn not Thy face from me, cast not Thy servant away in anger; Thou hast always been a help to me; forsake me not now in my trouble, O Lord my God). The verse reads "Ne avertas faciem tuam a me: ne declines in ira a servo tuo. Adjutor meus esto: ne derelinquas me, . . . Deus salutaris meus" (Turn not Thy face from me; nor turn away in anger from Thy servant. Be my Helper; do not forsake me, . . . God of my salvation). **before . . . time** KP's addition. **most** KP's addition.

388. **To . . . Thee** KP closely renders Fisher's splicing of recast and reordered excerpts from Psalms 85:3, 2; 38:14; and 101:2: "Ad te quotidie clamo, ne desilias a me, ne obsurdescas mihi. Ingrediatur coram te precatio mea, clamor meus ante te veniat." The excerpts from Psalm 85 read " ad te clamavi tota die: . . . Custodi animam meam" (to Thee I have cried all the day: . . . Keep watch over my soul). Fisher reworks the excerpt from Psalm 38:14, a self-description by the Psalmist, into a plea that God will listen: "Ego . . . tamquam surdus non audiebam" (I, . . . as though deaf, did not hear). Psalm 101:2, a verse previously utilized by Fisher, reads "Domine exaudi orationem meam: et clamor meus ad te veniat" (Lord, hear my prayer; and let my cry come unto Thee). See n371.

389. **Hear . . . temple** KP closely renders Fisher's minor recasting of Psalm 27:2: "Exaudi me domine, animum enim meum extollo ad templum sanctum tuum." The verse reads "Exaudi Domine vocem deprecationis meae . . . dum extollo manus meas ad templum sanctum tuum" (Hear, O Lord, the voice of my supplications . . . when I lift up my hands toward Thy holy temple).

390. **Help . . . man** KP closely renders Fisher's near verbatim quotation of Psalm 59:13: "Da auxilium in tribulatione, quia vana est salus ab homine." The first clause of the verse reads identically in the Vulgate; the second varies slightly: "quia vana salus hominis" (for vain is man's help). **help . . . man** KP's rendering blurs the distinction between a subjective genitive (help given to man) and an objective genitive (help given by man); the latter is in play here. In contrast, Fisher's "salus ab homine" is unambiguous: "help [or salvation] from—i.e., given by—man."

391. **I . . . conformable** KP renders Fisher's splicing of recast excerpts from Psalm 39:2, 9: "Exspecto adjutorium tuum domine, et judicia tua voluntas mea" (I look for Thy help, Lord, and Thy judgments [are] my will). The excerpts read "Exspectans exspectavi Dominum, . . . ut facerem voluntatem tuam, Deus meus volui" (Looking, I have looked out for the Lord. . . . I have wished that I might do Thy will, my God). **to . . . conformable** a characteristically expanded rendering by KP, to clarify Fisher's compressed "judicia tua voluntas mea" (Thy judgments [are] my will).

Look unto me, and take pity upon me, for I am poor and left alone.[392]

O Lord God of hosts, if Thou wilt, Thou mayest help me; nothing can overcome Thy strength.[393]

My God, my God, leave me not in these grievous tribulations, for Thy great name's sake.[394]

O God, make haste to deliver me; O Lord, make speed to help me.[395]

Be contented to deliver me, for in Thee I trust, O Lord God.[396]

392. **Look . . . alone** KP closely renders Fisher's near verbatim quotation of Psalm 24:16: "Respice ad me, et miserere mei, quia solus et pauper sum ego." The first half of the verse reads identically in the Vulgate; the second half has "unicus" (one and no more) where Fisher has "solus" (alone). **left alone** KP's intensification may indicate her recognition of the source verse and its occurrence of "unicus."

393. **O . . . strength** KP closely renders Fisher's splicing of recast excerpts from Isaiah 51:15 and 41:10 and Judith 16:16: "Domine Deus exercituum, si velis potes me juvare, fortitudinem tuam nihil superare potest." The first Isaiah excerpt reads "Ego . . . sum Dominus Deus tuus, . . . Dominus exercituum nomen meum" (I am the Lord thy God, . . . the Lord of hosts [is] My name." The second Isaiah excerpt reads "ego Deus tuus: . . . auxiliatus sum tibi" (I am thy God: . . . I have been a Helper to thee). The Judith excerpt reads "Domine . . . es . . . praeclarus in virtute tua, et quem superare nemo potest" (O Lord . . . Thou art . . . outstanding in Thy strength, which no one is able to overcome).

394. **My . . . sake My . . . tribulations** KP closely renders Fisher's recasting and elaboration of Christ's outcry on the cross in Matthew 27:46 and Mark 15:34: "Eli, Eli, ne deseras me in angustiis meis propter nomen magnum tuum." The outcry reads almost identically in both sources. Matthew has "Eli, Eli, lamma sabacthani? hoc est: Deus meus, Deus meus, ut quid dereliquisti me?" ([the question in transliterated Aramaic] that is: My God, my God, why hast Thou forsaken me?). Mark reads "quod est interpretatum" (which is to be translated) in place of "hoc est." The New Testament occurrences are a long-recognized echo of Psalm 21:2: "Deus Deus meus . . . quare me dereliquisti?" (God, my God . . . why hast Thou forsaken me?). **in . . . tribulations** KP intensifies Fisher's "in angustiis meis" (in my difficulties). **for . . . sake** KP closely renders Fisher's splicing of a formulaic phrase applied to God in a number of places in Scripture, where it functions to heighten ascriptions of honor and power to Him. Its addition here increases the pathos of Christ's appeal to His Father.

395. **O . . . me** KP renders Fisher's recasting of Psalm 69:2: "Deus ad liberandum me; domine in auxilium meum festina" (O God, to the delivering of me, to my help, make haste, O Lord). The verse reads "Deus in adjutorium meum intende: Domine, ad adjuvandum me festina" (O God, attend to helping me; O Lord, make haste to help me). **make haste . . . make speed** KP's doubling eases the compression of Fisher's syntax, but her synonymous main verbs where the Vulgate conjoins two different verbs suggests that she did not recognize the source text; see the introduction, p. 210.

396. **Be . . . God** KP closely renders Fisher's splicing of recast excerpts from Psalms 90:15 and 24:2: "Placeat tibi ut eripias me, quia in te confido domine Deus." The first excerpt, in God's voice, reads "Clamabit ad me, et ego exaudiam eum . . . eripiam eum" (He called upon Me, and I heard him . . . I will deliver him). The second excerpt reads "Deus meus in te confido" (My God, I trust in Thee). **Be contented** KP's close but awkward rendering of Fisher's "Placeat tibi"

[Fvii v] Behold, I have no help in myself; there is no man that regardeth my necessity.[397]

I am poor, and in misery and great calamity; and my strength is gone from me.[398]

Arise up, O Lord, and declare Thy glory unto Thy servant.[399]

Let salvation and health come to me from Thee: that all my enemies may be ashamed.[400]

Thine arm is mighty and strong; and when Thou wilt, all things be obedient unto Thee.[401]

Heaven is Thine, yea, and the earth is Thine; Thou madest the world, and all that is therein.[402]

(May it please Thee) perhaps reflects the absence of any analogous phrasing in Psalm 90:15, the likeliest source text in its explicit declaration by God of His willingness to deliver.

397. **Behold . . . necessity** KP closely renders Fisher's splicing of a verbatim quotation from Job 6:13 with recast excerpts from Job 30:20–21: "Ecce non est auxilium mihi in me, nec est qui respicit ad necessitatem meam." The recast excerpts read "non respicis me. Mutatus es mihi in crudelem" (Thou regardest me not. Thou hast become cruel to me).

398. **I . . . me** KP closely renders Fisher's splicing of recast excerpts from Psalm 68:30, Job 6:2–3, and Psalm 37:11: "Pauper sum ego, et in miseriis, ac calamitate multa, et robur meum à me recessit." The first excerpt reads "Ego sum pauper et dolens" (I am poor and grieving). The second set of excerpts reads "calamitas, quam patior . . . gravior appareret: unde et verba mea dolore sunt plena" (the calamity which I suffer . . . would be heavier: therefore my words are full of grief). The third excerpt reads "dereliquit me virtus mea" (my strength leaveth me).

399. **Arise . . . servant** KP closely renders Fisher's recasting of excerpts from Isaiah 60:1: "Excita me [1544: te] domine, et manifestetur servo tuo gloria tua." The excerpts, a summons not to God but to Jerusalem, read "Surge illuminare Ierusalem . . . et gloria Domini super te orta est" (Rise, shine, Jerusalem . . . and the glory of the Lord is risen upon thee). KP concurs with the first English edition in correcting the misprint "me" instead of "te" in the Cologne edition.

400. **Let . . . ashamed** KP quite closely renders Fisher's recasting of excerpts from Psalm 69:1, 3–4: "Veniat ad me salus tua, ut pudesiant omnes inimici mei." The excerpts read "Psalmus David . . . salvum fecerit eum Dominus . . . Confundantur . . . et erubescant, qui volunt mihi mala" (A Psalm of David . . . the Lord shall make him safe . . . Let them be confounded . . . and let them blush, who wish me evil). **salvation . . . health** KP's doubling.

401. **Thine . . . Thee** KP renders Fisher's splicing of recast excerpts from Jeremiah 32:17 and Wisdom of Solomon 12:18: "Tuum brachium potens est, et cum volueris, omnia tibi subsunt" (Thine arm is mighty, and when Thou wilt, all things are under Thee). The first excerpt reads "tu fecisti . . . in fortitudine tua magna, et in brachio tuo extento" (Thou hast wrought . . . with Thy great strength, and with Thy extended arm). The second excerpt reads "Tu . . . dominator . . . subest enim tibi, cum volueris" (Thou [art] . . . the Lord . . . for when Thou wilt, it [everything] is subject unto Thee). **mighty . . . strong** KP's doubling.

402. **Heaven . . . therein** KP closely renders Fisher's recasting of excerpts from Psalm 23:1–2: "Tui sunt coeli, etiam tua est terra, orbem et plenitudinem ejus tu fundasti." The excerpts read "Domini est terra, et plenitudo ejus: . . . et universi, qui habitant in eo. Quia ipse . . . fundavit eum, et . . . praeparavit eum" (The earth is the Lord's, and its fullness . . . and all that dwell therein. For He . . . hath founded it, and . . . furnished it).

Let Thy mercy comfort me, which surely I desire more than this life.[403]

[Fviii r] I stick to Thy testimonies, O Lord; let me not be confounded.[404]

Out of the deep I have called unto Thee, O Lord; Lord, hear my voice.

O let Thine ears mark well the voice of my complaint.

O Lord, if Thou impute my sins unto me, how may I look for Thy grace and pardon?[405]

But Thy mercy exceedeth all things, and Thy truth passeth the heavens.[406]

Wherefore my soul hath looked to Thee, and to Thee maketh humble prayers.[407]

O God, be not still, keep not silence, but for Thine own sake see that Thy holy name be not dishonored.[408]

403. **Let . . . life** KP renders Fisher's splicing of a quotation from Psalm 118:76 and an elaborated excerpt from Psalm 62:4: "Fiat misericordia tua, ut me consoletur, certe optabiliorem hac vita longe eam duco" (Let Thy mercy be done, that it may comfort me; surely this is more to be hoped than that I lead a long life). The Psalm quotation reads "Fiat misericordia tua ut consoletur me." The Psalm excerpt reads "melior est misericordia tua super vitas" (Thy mercy is better than life).

404. **I . . . confounded** KP closely renders Fisher's near verbatim quotation of Psalm 118:31: "Adhaereo testimoniis tuis domine, noli me confundere." The verse reads "Adhaesi testimoniis tuis Domine: noli me confundere" (I have adhered to Thy testimonies, Lord; let me not be confounded).

405. **Out . . . pardon** KP renders Fisher's increasingly bold recasting of Psalm 129:1–3: "De profundis te invoco domine, domine exaudi vocem meam. Aures tuae adtentae sint in vocem precationis meae. Commissa mea si imputes domine, quomodo possum gratiam tuam exspectare?" (From the depths I cry unto Thee, Lord; Lord, hear my voice. Let Thine ears be attentive to the voice of my prayers. If Thou imputest [to me], Lord, my committed [sins], how can I look for Thy grace?). The verses read "De profundis clamavi ad te Domine: Domine exaudi vocem meam: fiant aures tuae intendentes, in vocem deprecationis meae. Si iniquitates observaveris Domine: Domine quis sustinebit?" (From the depths have I cried unto Thee, Lord; Lord, hear my voice: let Thine ears be attentive to the voice of my prayers for pardon. If Thou shouldst observe iniquities, Lord: Lord, who shall stand upright?).

406. **But . . . heavens** KP closely renders Fisher's recasting of Psalm 56:11: "Sed misericordia tua omnia excellit, et veritas coelos superat." The Vulgate verse reads "magnificata est usque ad caelos misericordia tua, et usque ad nubes veritas tua" (Thy mercy is magnified as far as the heavens, and Thy truth as far as the clouds).

407. **Wherefore . . . prayers** KP renders Fisher's splicing of recast excerpts from Psalm 85:4 and Baruch 2:19: "Et idcirco anima mea ad te respicit, et preces tibi suppliciter fundit" (And therefore my soul hath looked to Thee, and humbly poureth out prayers to Thee). The Psalm excerpt reads "ad te Domine animam meam levavi" (to Thee, Lord, have I lifted up my soul). The excerpt from Baruch reads "fundimus preces, et petimus misericordiam ante conspectum tuum" (we pour out prayers and we beg mercy before Thy face).

408. **O . . . dishonored** KP closely renders Fisher's splicing of recast excerpts from Psalm 82:2 and Ezekiel 39:7: "Deus, ne taceas, ne sileas, propter temetipsum facito, ut non polluatur nomen tuum sanctum." The first excerpt reads "Deus, . . . ne taceas, neque compescaris" (God, be not silent nor hold [Thyself] in check). The second excerpt reads "nomen sanctum meum

[Fviii v] Extend out Thy mercy to them that call upon Thee, and Thy righteousness to them that seek Thee.[409]

I have cast my burden upon Thee; bear me up, and let me not always be in wavering, seeing that I have put my trust in Thee.[410]

My soul cleaveth unto Thee; make Thy right hand to strength me aganst the power of mine enemies.[411]

Hear me, O Lord, and deliver me; incline Thine ears unto my prayers, and save me, for I am poor; O Lord, have regard unto me.[412]

Thou, O Lord God, art my help and my Saviour.[413]

[Gi r] O God, Thy way is holy and rightful; what god is so great as Thou, our God, art?

---

notum faciam . . . et non polluam nomen sanctum meum amplius" (I shall make My holy name known . . . and I will not [allow them to] pollute My holy name any more).

409. **Extend . . . Thee** KP closely renders Fisher's partial recasting of Psalm 35:11: "Protrahe misericordiam tuam te invocantibus, et justiciam tuam iis qui te quaerunt." The verse reads "Praetende misericordiam tuam scientibus te, et justitiam tuam his, qui recto sunt corde" (Hold out Thy mercy to them who know Thee, and Thy righteousness to them who are upright in heart).

410. **I . . . Thee** KP renders Fisher's recasting of excerpts from Psalm 54:23–24: "Projeci super te onus meum, sustenta me, ne des in aeternum fluctuationem in te confidenti" (I have cast my burden upon Thee; uphold me; give me not over to wavering forever; I have put my trust in Thee). The verse excerpts read "Jacta super Dominum curam tuam, et ipse te enutriet: non dabit in aeternum fluctuationem justo . . . sperabo in te Domine" (Cast thy care upon the Lord, and He will support Thee: He will not give the just man over to wavering forever . . . I will hope in Thee, Lord).

411. **My . . . enemies** KP closely renders Fisher's splicing of recast excerpts from Psalm 62:9: "Adhaeret anima mea post te, corroboret me dextera tua contra potentiam inimicorum meorum." The verse excerpts read "Adhaesit anima mea post te: me suscepit dextera tua. . . . in vanum quaesierunt animam meam introibunt in inferiora terrae" (My soul cleaveth unto Thee; Thy right hand beareth me up. . . . they that would hunt my soul into nothingness shall go into the lower parts of the earth). **strength** an earlier variant of "strengthen."

412. **Hear . . . me** KP renders Fisher's interspersing of formulaic phrases repeated in various Psalms with other excerpts from Psalms 60:2 and 108:22: "Exaudi me domine, et eripe me, inclina aurem tuam ad preces meas, et salva me. Quoniam egenus sum ego, domine curam habe me" (Hear me, Lord, and deliver me, incline Thine ear unto my prayers, and save me. Since I am weak, Lord, have a care of me). The excerpts from Psalm 60 read "Exaudi Deus . . . intende orationi meae" (Hear, Lord, . . . attend unto my prayer). The excerpts from Psalm 108 read "Libera me quia egenus, et pauper ero sum" (Deliver me, for I am weak and poor). **have . . . me** KP renders Fisher's "curam habe me" (have a care of me), a locution that the Vulgate does not employ regarding God until the New Testament, and rarely there (1 Corinthians 9:9; 1 Peter 5:7). As Fisher's very next versicle suggests, the proleptic resonance of his language is likely to be deliberate, and KP's rendering makes explicit the connection with the New Testament Saviour.

413. **Thou . . . Saviour** KP closely renders Fisher's quotation from Psalm 61:7: "Auxiliam meum et salvator meus tu es domine Deus." The verse excerpt reads "ipse Deus meus, et salvator meus: adjutor meus" (He is my God and my Saviour, my Helper).

Thou dost marvelous things; Thy name is, The Lord; Thou only art the highest upon all the earth.[414]

Be now pacified toward Thy servant, and hide Thy face from me no longer.[415]

Be good unto me, Lord, as Thou art full of goodness Thyself, that I may glory in Thee all the days of my life.[416]

My lips rejoice to sing praise unto Thee, and even so doth my soul, which Thou hast redeemed.[417]

My heart shall always study Thy righteousness, when they shall be confounded, which seek to do me harm.[418]

[Gi v] I will run all the way of Thy commandment, when Thou shalt dilate and enlarge my heart. Amen.[419]

414. **O . . . earth** KP closely renders Fisher's splicing of recast excerpts from Psalms 76:14–15 and 82:19: "O Deus, sancta et justa est via tua, quis deus magnus sicut tu deus noster? Tu es qui facis mirabilia, nomen tuum est dominus, tu solus altissimus super omnem terram." The excerpts from Psalm 76 read "Deus in sancto via tua: quia deus magnus sicut Deus noster? Tu es Deus qui facis mirabilia" (God, Thy way [leadeth] into the holy [place]: for who is a great god like our God? Thou art a God who doest wonderful things). The excerpts from Psalm 82 read "nomen tibi Dominus: tu solus Altissimus in omni terra" (the Lord is Thy name; Thou alone art the Most High in all the earth).

415. **Be . . . longer** KP closely renders Fisher's recasting and inverting of the two clauses of Psalm 26:9: "Placatus sis erga servum tuum, et ne faciem tuam diutius à me abscondas." The Vulgate verse reads "Ne avertas faciem tuam a me: ne declines in ira a servo tuo" (Hide not Thy face from me: turn not aside from Thy servant in anger).

416. **Be . . . life** KP freely renders Fisher's recasting and inverting of excerpts from Psalm 5:12–13: "Benefac mihi in bonitate tua, ut glorier de te omnibus diebus vitae meae" (Do good unto me in Thy goodness, that I may glory in Thee all the days of my life). The excerpts from verse 13 read "tu benedices justo Domine . . . bonae voluntatis tuae" (Thou wilt bless the righteous man, Lord, with Thy goodwill). The excerpts from verse 12 read "Et laetentur omnes . . . in aeternum . . . et gloriabuntur in te" (And let them all rejoice . . . forever . . . and they will glory in Thee). **as . . . Thyself** KP adds a reflexive reference to God's goodness which is not in Fisher or the Vulgate.

417. **My . . . redeemed** KP renders Fisher's minor recasting of Psalm 70:23: "Gestiunt labia mea, ut tibi canam, aeque et anima mea quam redemisti" (My lips rejoice that I may sing unto Thee, and equally my soul, which Thou hast redeemed). The verse reads "Exultabunt labia mea cum cantavero tibi: et anima mea, quam redemisti" (My lips will exult when I shall have sung unto Thee, and my soul, which Thou hast redeemed). **to . . . praise** KP's addition.

418. **My . . . harm** KP closely renders Fisher's splicing of recast excerpts from Psalms 118:117 and 34:4: "Cor meum omni tempore meditabitur justitiam tuam, cum confusi sint, qui malum mihi quaerunt." The first excerpt reads "meditabor in justificationibus tuis semper" (I shall always meditate upon Thy righteousness). The second excerpt reads "confundantur . . . quaerentes . . . mala mihi" (they shall be confounded . . . who seek . . . evils for me).

419. **I . . . Amen** KP quite closely renders Fisher's recasting of Psalm 118:32: "Et viam mandatorum tuorum percurram, quum dilataveris cor meum" (And I shall run through the way of Thy commandments, when Thou shalt enlarge my heart). The verse reads "Viam mandatorum

THE SEVENTH PSALM, FOR AN ORDER AND DIRECTION OF GOOD LIVING.[420]

To Thee, O Lord, I lift up my mind.

In Thee I trust, O Lord God, let me not be confounded, lest my enemies make me their jesting-stock, and a matter to laugh at.[421]

O Lord, make Thy ways known unto me, and trade me in Thy paths.

Direct me in Thy truth, and instruct me: for Thou art God my Saviour. I look after Thee every day.[422]

[Gii r] O Lord, Thou art sweet and rightful, and bringest again into Thy way, them that went out.

Thou leadest straight in Thy judgment, them that be mild and tractable, and teachest them that be meek, Thy words and testimonies.[423]

---

tuorum cucurri, cum dilatasti cor meum" (I shall run the way of Thy commandments, when Thou hast enlarged my heart). **all** KP's addition. **dilate . . . enlarge** KP's doubling. **Amen** The reading of the Cologne edition, omitted in the first English edition.

420. **For . . . living** KP renders Fisher's "Pro recte vivendi directione," inserting a characteristic doubling.

421. **To . . . at** KP expansively renders Fisher's recasting of excerpts from Psalm 24:1–3: "Ad te Domine deus, animum meum levo. In te confido domine Deus, ne confundar, ne letentur de me inimici mei" (To Thee, Lord God, I lift up my soul. In Thee I trust, Lord God; let me not be confounded, and let not my enemies rejoice concerning me). The verse excerpts read "Ad te Domine levavi animam meam: Deus meus in te confido, non . . . irrideant me inimici mei" (To Thee, Lord, have I lifted up my soul: My God, in Thee do I trust: let not . . . my enemies ridicule me). **mind** KPs rendering of "animam" is possible, but "soul" is preferable here; see introduction, p. 206. **their . . . at** a characteristically idiomatic expansion of phrasing.

422. **O Lord . . . day** KP closely renders Fisher's minor recasting of Psalm 24:4–5: "Vias tuas domine notas fac mihi, semitis tuis assue facito me. Dirige me in veritate tua, et instrue me, quia tu es deus salvator meus, te exspecto omni die." The verses read "Vias tuas Domine demonstra mihi: et semitas tuas edoce me. Dirige me in veritate tua, et doce me: quia tu es Deus salvator meus, et te sustinui tota die" (Show me Thy ways, Lord, and teach me Thy paths. Direct me in Thy truth, and teach me: for Thou art God my Saviour, and I have maintained Thee all the day). **trade me** train me, rendering "edoce me" (teach me). **look after** KP employs "after" in a no longer current sense of "over at" or "along the course of," aptly rendering Fisher's "exspecto" (expect, look for).

423. **O . . . testimonies** KP closely renders Fisher's minor recasting of Psalm 24:8–9: "Dulcis et rectus tu domine, et propterea reducis errantes in viam tuam. Dirigis mansuetos in judicio tuo, doces mites testimonia tua." The verses read "Dulcis et rectus Dominus propter hoc legem dabit delinquentibus in via. Diriget mansuetos in judicio: docebit mites vias suas" (Sweet and upright [is] the Lord; therefore He will give a rule for the way to those that have transgressed. He will guide the mild in judgment, and He will teach the meek His ways). **rightful** upright, just. **mild . . . tractable, words . . . testimonies** KP's doublings.

Thou healest them that be contrite in heart, and assuagest their pains and griefs.[424]

Thou holdest up all them, which else should fall; and all that are fallen, Thou liftest up again.

Thou givest sight to the blind, and loosest them that be bounden.

[Gii v] Thou art nigh unto all them that call upon Thee, so that they call upon Thee faithfully and heartily.

Thou fulfillest the desire of them that fear Thee, and hearest their prayer, and savest them.[425]

Have mercy upon me, O God. have mercy upon me: for in Thee my soul trusteth.[426]

Verily my soul hath a special respect unto Thee, for my health, my glory, and all my strength cometh from Thee.[427]

424. **Thou . . . griefs** KP closely renders Fisher's minor recasting of Psalm 146:3: "Tu sanas contritos corde, et dolores eorum mitigas." The verse reads "Qui sanat contritos corde, et alligat contritiones eorum" (Who healeth the contrite in heart, and bindeth up their griefs). **pains . . . griefs** KP's doubling.

425. **Thou holdest . . . them** KP closely renders Fisher's splicing and reordering of recast excerpts from Psalms 144:14; 145:8, 7; and 144:18–19: "Sustentas omnes qui casuri sunt, et omnes collapsos erigis. Tu das visum caecis, et solvis vinctos. Prope es omnibus qui te invocant, dummodo te invocant in veritate. Voluntatem timentium te facis, et preces eorum exaudis, eosque salvas." The excerpts read "Allevat Dominus omnes, qui corruunt: et erigit omnes elisos. Dominus illuminat caecos . . . Dominus solvit compeditos . . . Prope est Dominus omnibus invocantibus eum: omnibus invocantibus eum in veritate. Voluntatem timentium se faciet, et deprecationem eorum exaudiet: et salvos faciet eos" (The Lord upholdeth all that fall down, and raiseth up all the broken-down. The Lord lighteneth the blind. . . . The Lord looseth the shackled . . . The Lord is near unto all those who call upon Him, unto all those who call upon Him in truth. He shall fulfill the desire of them who fear Him, and He will hear their supplication, and will make them safe). **faithfully . . . heartily** KP's doubling, loosely rendering Fisher's and the Vulgate's "in veritate" (in truth).

426. **Have . . . trusteth** KP closely renders Fisher's near verbatim quotation of Psalm 56:2: "Miserere mei deus, miserere mei, quia in te confidit anima mea." The Vulgate verse reads identically except for having "quoniam" where Fisher has "quia"—alternative expressions of "for," "because."

427. **Verily . . . Thee** KP freely renders Fisher's recasting and splicing of excerpts from Psalm 61:6, 8: "Certe ad te respicit anima mea, à te enim salutare meum, gloria mea, et robur fortitudinis meae" (Surely my soul looketh to Thee, from Thee indeed [are] my salvation, my glory, and the abundance of my strength). Verse 6 reads "Verumtamen Deo subjecta esto anima mea: quoniam ab ipso patientia mea" (Nevertheless, my soul, be subject to God, because my endurance [is] from Him). The excerpts from verse 8 read "In Deo salutare meum, et gloria mea" (In God is my salvation and my glory). **hath . . . Thee** KP renders Fisher's literal "ad te respicit" (looketh to Thee) in a figurative sense, with "hath respect" replacing "looketh." **all . . . strength** KP tones down Fisher's "robur fortitudinis meae" (the abundance of my strength), itself a rhetorical heightening of the Vulgate's "patientia mea" (my endurance).

For Thine own sake, O Lord God, lay not my sins to my charge.[428]

I understand not all mine errors: innumerable troubles close me round about; my sins have taken hold upon me, and I am not able to look up.[429]

[Giii r] Put to Thy hand to help me, and lead me right in all my works.[430]

Make me to walk perfectly in Thy ways, that no kind of sin overcome me.[431]

Set a watch before my mouth, and keep the door of my lips.[432]

Let the words of my mouth and the meditation of my heart be ever pleasant and acceptable in Thy sight.[433]

428. **For . . . charge** KP closely renders Fisher's splicing of recast excerpts from Psalms 30:4 and 31:2: "Propter temetipsum domine Deus, ne imputes mihi peccata mea." The first excerpt reads "propter nomen tuum" (for Thy name's sake). The second excerpt reads "cui non imputavit Dominus peccatum" (to whom the Lord hath not imputed [his] sin).

429. **I . . . up** KP closely renders Fisher's splicing of recast excerpts from Psalms 18:13 and 39:13: "Errores omnes non intelligo, circumvolvunt me mala, quorum non est numerus, adpraehenderunt me iniquitates meae, et videre non possum." The first excerpt reads "Delictis quis intelligit?" (Who understandeth [his] failings?). The second excerpt reads "circumdederunt me mala, quorum non est numerus: comprehenderunt me iniquitates meae, et non potui ut viderem" (evils that are numberless have compassed me about; my iniquities have taken hold upon me, and I cannot look up).

430. **Put . . . works** KP freely renders Fisher's unusually free recasting of Psalm 89:17: "Sit manus tua mihi in auxilium, et dirigat me in omnibus operibus meis" (Let Thy hand be a help to me, and let it direct me in all my works). She follows the Cologne edition; the first London edition has a misprint, "operibus tuis" (Thy works). The verse reads "sit splendor Domine . . . super nos, et opera manuum nostrarum dirige super nos: et opus manuum nostrarum dirige" (let the splendor of the Lord be . . . over us, and [being] over us, let it direct the works of our hands, and let it direct the work of our hands). Fisher evidently took the liberty of attributing to God one of the two sets of hands in the redoubled clauses of the Hebrew text, which the Vulgate replicates. KP extends Fisher's "manus tua" (Thy—i.e., God's—hand) further into an idiomatic appeal: "Put to Thy hand to help me"—i.e., "Lend a hand to help me." This versicle, moreover, serves as a pivot for the turn into the explicit subject of the seventh Psalm: "the order and direction of life."

431. **Make . . . me** KP renders Fisher's splicing of recast excerpts from Psalms 16:5 and 118:133: "Perfice gressus meos in viis tuis, ut non dominetur mihi [1544: mei] omnis iniquitas" (Make perfect my steps in Thy ways, that every iniquity may not overcome me). The first excerpt reads "Perfice gressos meos in semitis tuis" (Make perfect my steps in Thy paths). The second excerpt reads "et non dominetur mei omnis injustitia" (and let not every injustice overcome me).

432. **Set . . . lips** KP closely renders Fisher's near verbatim quotation of Psalm 140:3: "Pone custodiam ori meo, et serva ostium labiorum meorum." The verse reads "Pone Domine custodiam ori mea: et . . . circumstantiae labiis meis" (Set a guardian, O Lord, before my mouth; and . . . stationing around my lips).

433. **Let . . . sight** KP renders Fisher's slight recasting of an excerpt from Psalm 18:15: "Sint placentes sermones oris mei, et meditatio cordis mei in conspectu tuo semper" (May the sayings of my mouth and the meditation of my heart be always pleasing in Thy sight). The verse excerpt reads "erunt ut complaceant eloquia oris mei: et meditatio cordis mei in conspectu tuo semper" (let the fine words of my mouth and the meditation of my heart be always pleasing

Let the word of truth never go away from my mouth, and suffer no malice to dwell in my heart.[434]

O Lord, deliver my soul from lying lips, and save me from the deceitful tongue.[435]

Put into my mouth Thy true and holy word, and take clean from me all idle and unfruitful speech.[436]

[Giii v] Deliver me from false surmises and accusations of men; rule me even as Thou thinkest good, after Thy will and pleasure.[437]

---

in Thy sight). **pleasant . . . acceptable** KP's doubling introduces "acceptable"—the analogue of "complaceant" (be pleasing) in Coverdale's Bible and the Great Bible—suggesting that she recognized the source text.

434. **Let . . . heart** KP closely renders Fisher's splicing of recast excerpts from Isaiah 59:21 and Psalm 140:4: "Ne recedat de ore meo sermo veritatis, et cor meum malicia non inhabitet." The Isaiah excerpt, in the voice of God renewing His covenant with Israel, reads "Spiritus meus . . . et verba mea . . . non recedent de ore tuo" (Let not My Spirit . . . and My words . . . depart from thy mouth). The Psalm excerpt reads "Non declines cor meum in verba malitiae" (Let not my heart incline toward words of malice).

435. **O . . . tongue** KP closely renders Fisher's minor recasting of Psalm 119:2: "Domine erue animam meam à labiis mendatii, et a lingua dolosa libera me." The verse reads "Domine libera animam meam a labiis iniquis, et a lingua dolosa" (O Lord, deliver my soul from wicked lips, and from a deceitful tongue).

436. **Put . . . speech** KP quite closely renders what is evidently an original composition in which Fisher conjoins and adapts excerpts from the Vulgate: "Verbum verum et sanctum insere in os meum, et ociosos sermones longe à me removeas" (Put the true and holy word into my mouth, and remove idle words far from me). The nonoccurrence of the phrase "verbum sanctum" (holy word) in the Vulgate is the first clue to what Fisher does here. There is one analogue of "verbum verum" (true word), in Psalm 118:160: "Principium verborum tuorum, veritas" (Truth is the origin of Thy words). There is one instance only of God's being called "sanctus, et verus" (holy and true), in Revelation 6:10, where the martyrs implore Him to proceed in judgment upon the wicked. Finally, there is only one analogue of the phrase "ociosos sermones," in Matthew 12:36, where Jesus warns against the danger of speaking idly about His message: "Dico autem vobis, quoniam omne verbum otiosum, quod locuti fuerint homines, reddent rationem de eo in die judicii" (I say unto you, that every idle word that men will have spoken, they will give an account of it in the day of judgment). Fisher's versicle thus centers on the imperative of speaking about Holy Scripture with respect and reverence, and KP's rendering sustains his focus. **idle . . . unfruitful** KP emphatically doubles the keyword in the latter half of the versicle.

437. **Deliver . . . pleasure** KP renders Fisher's splicing of an exact quotation and a recast excerpt from Psalm 118:134,156: "Redime me à calumniis hominum, secundum judicium tuum moderare me" (Deliver me from the cunning devices of men; restrain me according to Thy judgment). The excerpt from verse 156 reads "secundum judicium tuum vivifica me" (according to Thy judgment enliven me). **false surmises . . . accusations, will . . . pleasure** KP's redoublings respectively substitute specific expressions for more general Latin terms, "calumniis" and "judicium."

Turn away mine eyes, that they behold no vain thing; fasten them in Thy way.[438]

Take from me fornication and all uncleanness, and let not the love of the flesh beguile me.[439]

Yea, deliver my soul from pride, that it reign not in me; and then shall I be clean from the greatest sin.[440]

Stay and keep my feet from every ill way, lest my steps swerve from Thy paths.[441]

[Giv r] My eyes look ever up unto Thee, O Lord, because Thou art nigh at hand; and all Thy ways be the truth.[442]

Thy mercies be great and many, O Lord: blessed is he, whosoever trusteth in Thee.[443]

438. **Turn . . . way** KP closely renders Fisher's minor recasting of Psalm 118:37: "Averte oculos, ne vana videant, in via tua illos fige." The verse reads "Averte oculos meos ne videant vanitatem: in via tua vivifica me" (Turn my eyes away lest they see vanity: enliven me in Thy way). Fisher adapts the verb "vivifica" (enliven) differently in the preceding versicle: see n437.

439. **Take . . . me** KP closely renders Fisher's splicing of recast excerpts from Ephesians 5:3 and 2:3: "Fornicationem et immunditiam omnem aufer à me, et amor carnis non me decipiat." The first excerpt reads "Fornicationem . . . et omnis immunditia . . . nec nominetur in vobis, sicut decet sanctos" (Let not fornication . . . and all uncleanliness . . . be named by you, as befitteth saints). The second excerpt reads "conversati sumus in desideriis carnis nostrae" (we have dwelt in the desires of our flesh). The intensity of the revulsion against the body and sexuality expressed in this versicle goes beyond its Biblical sources.

440. **Yea . . . sin** KP renders Fisher's splicing of an excerpt from Job 33:17 with recast excerpts from Psalms 118:133 and 14:2, plus a final phrase of his own composition: "Etiam à superbia libera animam meam, ne dominetur in me, et tunc immaculatus ero à peccato maximo" (Yet deliver my soul from pride, that it may not have dominion in me, and then I shall be spotless from the greatest sin). The Job excerpt reads "ut . . . liberet eum de superbia" (that . . . he [the man] may be delivered from pride). The two Psalm excerpts read "non dominetur me omnis injustitia" (may no injustice have dominion in me) and "qui ingreditur sine macula" (he who walketh spotless). Fisher's own contribution to this versicle can be recognized by its reference to pride as "the greatest sin" ("peccato maximo"). The taxonomy of seven deadly sins headed by pride postdates the Bible.

441. **Stay . . . paths** KP quite closely renders Fisher's recasting of Psalm 16:5: "Ab omni via mala prohibe pedes meos, ne deflectant vestigia à semitis tuis." The verse reads "Perfice gressus meos in semitis tuis: ut non moveantur vestigia meos" (Perfect my steps in Thy paths, that my footprints do not swerve). **Stay . . . keep** KP's doubling.

442. **My . . . truth** KP closely renders Fisher's splicing of near verbatim quotations from Psalms 24:15 and 118:151: "Oculi mei ad te domine, quoniam propè es, et omnes viae tuae veritas." The first excerpt reads "Oculi mei semper ad Dominum" (My eyes are ever toward the Lord). The second excerpt reads "Prope es tu Domine: et omnes viae tuae veritas" (Thou art near, Lord, and all Thy ways are truth).

443. **Thy . . . Thee** KP quite closely renders Fisher's splicing of an exact quotation from Psalm 118:156 with a recast excerpt from Psalm 56:2: "Misericordiae tuae multae domine, beatus ille quisquis in te confidit." The excerpt from Psalm 56 reads "in te confidit anima mea" (in Thee my soul trusteth). **great . . . many** KP's doubling.

For when I said unto Thee, my feet be slipped: Thy mercy, O Lord, by and by did hold me up.[444]

Teach me to do Thy will, and lead me by Thy pathway, for Thou art my God.[445]

O Lord, save my soul, and deliver me from the power of darkness.[446]

Let the brightness of Thy face shine upon Thy servant, for unto Thee, O Lord God, I have fled for succor.[447]

[Giv v] Look unto me, and have mercy upon me, for I am desolate and poor.

Keep my soul, and deliver me, that I be not confounded, for I have trusted in Thee.[448]

O Lord God, forsake me not, although I have done no good in Thy sight.[449]

444. **For . . . up** KP closely renders Fisher's recasting of Psalm 93:18: "Ego enim quum dicerem tibi, moti sunt pedes mei, misericordia tua domine statim sustentavit me." The verse reads "Si dicebam: Motus est pes meus: misericordia tua Domine adjuvabat me" (If I said [to Thee,] My foot hath slipped: Thy mercy, Lord, helped me).

445. **Teach . . . God** KP closely renders Fisher's splicing and reordering of a quotation from Psalm 142:10 and a recast excerpt from Psalm 85:11: "Doce me facere voluntatem tuam, et deduc me per semitam rectam, quia Deus meus es tu." The quotation reads "Doce me facere voluntatem tuam, quia Deus meus es tu" (Teach me to do Thy will, for Thou art my God). The excerpt reads "Deduc me Domine in via tua" (Lead me, Lord, in Thy way).

446. **O . . . darkness** KP closely renders Fisher's splicing of recast excerpts from Psalm 30:8 and Colossians 1:13: "O domine salva animam meam, et de potestate tenebrarum redime me." The Psalm excerpt reads "Salvasti . . . animam meam" (Thou hast saved . . . my soul). The Colossians excerpt, a thanksgiving to God, reads "qui eripuit nos de potestate tenebrarum" (who delivered us from the power of darkness).

447. **Let . . . succor** KP freely renders Fisher's splicing of excerpts from Psalms 118:135 and 142:9: "Illumina faciem tuam super servum tuum, quia ad te confugi domine Deus" (Make Thy face to shine upon Thy servant, for I have fled to Thee, O Lord God). The first excerpt reads "Faciem tuam illumina super servum tuum" (Shine Thy face upon Thy servant). The second excerpt reads "Domine, ad te confugi" (I have fled to Thee, Lord). **the brightness of, for succor** KP's clarifying expansions of phrasing.

448. **Look . . . Thee** KP closely renders Fisher's near verbatim quotation of Psalm 24:16, 20: "Respice ad me, et miserere mei, quia solus et pauper sum ego. Custodi animam meam, et eripe me, ne confundar, quoniam speravi in te." The first verse reads "Respice in me, et miserere mei: quia unicus et pauper sum ego" (Look on me, and have mercy on me: for I am solitary and poor). The second verse reads "Custodi animam meam, et erue me: non erubescam quoniam speravi in te" (Keep my soul, and rescue me; I will not be ashamed because I have trusted in Thee).

449. **O . . . sight** KP closely renders Fisher's splicing of a quoted excerpt from Psalm 37:22 with an allusion to 4 Kings (2 Chronicles) 20:3: "Domine Deus ne derelinquas me, quanquàm nihil boni fecerim coram te." The Psalm excerpt reads "Ne derelinquas me Domine Deus" (Forsake me not, Lord God). The allusion to 4 Kings ironically echoes King Hezekiah's prayer for longer life, in which he pleads his record of exemplary conduct before God: "quod placitum est coram te, fecerim" (I have done what is pleasing in Thy sight). Fisher's speaker asserts the opposite: he has done nothing good in God's sight, yet prays God not to forsake him.

For Thy goodness grant me, that at the least wise I may begin to live well. Amen.[450]

THE EIGHTH PSALM.
A CHRISTIAN MAN PRAYETH,[451]
THAT HE MAY BE DEFENDED FROM HIS ENEMIES.

O God almighty, save me from mine enemies, and by Thy strong power defend and keep me.[452]

[Gv r] Preserve my soul, for Thou art holy; save Thy servant, which trusteth in Thee.[453]

For strangers do assault me daily, and seek my soul to destroy it.[454]

O God, help Thou me; O Lord, deliver me from them that rise up against me.[455]

450. **For . . . Amen** KP renders Fisher's splicing of an allusion to 1 Timothy 6:17–18 with a final clause of original composition: "Praesta mihi pro bonitate tua, saltem modo assumere initia bene vivendi. Amen" (Grant me, for Thy goodness' sake, that I may at least take to myself the beginnings of right living. Amen). The 1 Timothy allusion concerns St. Paul's explanation of God's purpose in giving Christians good things: "qui praestat nobis omnia abundè ad fruendum: benè agere, divites fieri in bonus operibus" ([God] who granteth us all things to enjoy abundantly: to do good, to be rich in good works). Fisher's own phrasing applies God's purpose to the speaker's self: as KP renders it, "that . . . I may begin to live well." **at . . . wise** at least, anyhow, rendering "saltem modo" (leastways, at least).

451. **A . . . prayeth** KP's addition; Fisher's subtitle simply reads "ut protegatur ab inimicis" (that he may be protected from enemies).

452. **O . . . me** KP renders Fisher's splicing of recast excerpts from Psalm 58:2, 17: "Deus omnipotens, serva me ab inimicis meis, et in virtute fortitudinis tuae protege me" (God almighty, preserve me from my enemies, and protect me with the power of Thy strength). The first excerpt reads "Eripe me de inimicis meis Deus meus" (Deliver me from my enemies, my God). The second excerpt reads "Ego . . . cantabo fortitudinem tuam. . . . Quia factus es susceptor meus, et refugium meum" (I . . . will sing Thy strength. . . . For Thou art made my Protector and my refuge). **defend . . . keep** KP's doubling.

453. **Preserve . . . Thee** KP closely renders Fisher's recasting of Psalm 85:2: "Custodi animam meam, quoniam sanctus es tu, salvum fac servum tuum, qui in te confidit." The verse reads "Custodi animam meam, quoniam sanctus sum: salvum fac servum tuum, Deus meus, sperantem in te" (Protect my soul, for I am holy; my God, save Thy servant who trusteth in Thee).

454. **For . . . it** KP closely renders Fisher's recasting of Psalm 53:5: "Alieni enim quotidie me obpugnant, et animam meam quaerunt, ut perdant eam." The verse reads "alieni insurrexerunt adversum me, et . . . quaesierunt animam meam" (strangers have risen up against me, and . . . they have sought my soul).

455. **O . . . against me** KP closely renders Fisher's splicing of slightly recast excerpts from Psalms 108:26 and 58:2: "Deus, adjuva me, domine ab insurgentibus in me libera me." The first excerpt reads "Adjuva me, Domine Deus meus" (Help me, Lord, my God). The second excerpt reads "Deus meus: . . . ab insurgentibus in me libera me" (My God, . . . free me from those rising against me).

Be ready, O God, to succor me; make haste to help me, O Lord.[456]

Be Thou my Protector and a place of strength, wherein I may safely be.[457]

For Thou art my strength and my refuge; for Thy name's sake lead and guide me.[458]

Take me, O God, out of the hands of mine enemies, and cast me not away in the time of tribulation, when all my might is decayed and gone.[459]

[Gv v] Help me, O Lord God, and save me for Thy mercy's sake.[460]

Have mercy upon me, O Lord, the God of my health; and in Thy righteousness deliver me,

From the vexation of them that persecute me, from the assault of mine enemies, which compass me about on every side.[461]

Let them be confounded and brought to naught, which be adversaries unto my soul; let them be covered with shame and rebuke, which seek my hurt.

456. **Be . . . Lord** KP renders Fisher's near verbatim quotation of Psalm 69:2: "Deus in adjutorium meum intende, domine ut me juves festina" (God, attend to my help; Lord, make haste that Thou mayest help me). The first half of the verse reads identically in the Vulgate; the second reads "Dominus ad adjuvandum me festina" (Lord, make haste to help me). KP's rendering is closer to the Vulgate than Fisher's; she may have recognized the source verse.

457. **Be . . . be** KP freely renders Fisher's splicing of recast excerpts from Psalm 90:1–3: "Esto mihi in protectionem, et in locum munitum, ut salvum me facias" (Be to me a protection and a fortified place, that Thou mayest save me). The excerpts read "Qui habitat . . . in protectione Dei . . . Dicet Domino: Susceptor meus es tu, et refugium meum . . . Quoniam ipse liberavit me" (He who liveth . . . in God's protection . . . Will say to the Lord: Thou art my Protector and my refuge . . . Because He hath delivered me).

458. **For . . . me** KP closely renders Fisher's near verbatim quotation of Psalm 30:4: "Quoniam fortitudo mea et refugium meum es tu, propter nomen tuum deduc me et dirige me." The verse reads "Quoniam fortitudo mea, et refugium meum es tu: et propter nomen tuum deduces me, et enutries me" (For Thou art my strength and my refuge; and for Thy name's sake Thou leadest me and nourishest me).

459. **Take . . . gone** KP renders Fisher's splicing of recast excerpts from Psalms 30:16 and 70:9: "Mi Deus eripe me de manibus inimicorum meorum, nec projicias me in tempore tribulationis, cum defecit me omnis mea virtus" (My God, deliver me from the hands of mine enemies, and cast me not away in the time of tribulation, when all my strength faileth me). The first excerpt reads "Eripe me de manu inimicorum meorum" (Deliver me from the hand of mine enemies). The second excerpt reads "Ne projicias me in tempore senectutis: cum defecerit virtus mea" (Throw me not down in the time of old age, when my strength will have failed). **is decayed . . . gone** KP's doubling.

460. **Help . . . sake** KP closely renders Fisher's near verbatim quotation of Psalm 108:26: "Adjuva me domine Deus, et salva me propter misericordiam tuam." The verse reads "Adjuva me Domine Deus meus: salvum me fac secundum misericordiam tuam" (Help me, Lord my God: make me safe according to Thy mercy).

461. **Have . . . side** KP closely renders Fisher's splicing of recast excerpts from Psalms 85:7, 70:2, and 16:9: "Miserere mei o domine deus salutis meae, et in tua justicia eripe me. "Ab infestatione me persequentium, ab hostili cursu, qui me undique obcingunt." The first excerpt reads "Domine misericordiam . . . salutare tuum da nobis" (God of mercy, . . . give us Thy sal-

Let them turn back with rebuke and shame, which say, God hath forsaken him; let us set on him and take him, for there is none that shall deliver him.[462]

[Gvi r] Conjoin Thyself, O God, unto my soul; make it strong, and deliver me from mine enemies.

Destroy them by Thy power, and bring to naught all their strength,[463]

That they rejoice not and say among themselves: We have overcome him, and utterly cast him down.[464]

Save me, O Lord God, for in Thee have I trusted; say to my soul, Be not afraid, for I am with Thee.[465]

---

vation). The second excerpt reads "in justitia tua . . . eripe me" (in Thy justice . . . deliver me). The third excerpt reads "a facie impiorum qui me afflixerunt; inimici mei animam meam circumdederunt" (from the face of the wicked that have oppressed me; my enemies have surrounded my soul).

462. **Let them be . . . him** KP renders Fisher's splicing of recast excerpts from Psalms 70:13, 55:10, and 70:10: "Confundantur et deficiant, qui animae meae adversantur, operiantur obprobrio et confusione, qui malum mihi quaerunt. Revertantur cum ignominia multa, illi qui dicunt, Deus deseruit eum, persequamur et compraehendamus, nam non est qui eum eripiet" (Let them be confounded and fail, who are hostile to my soul; let them be covered with disgrace and confusion, who seek evil for me. Let them turn back with much ignominy, they who say, God hath forsaken him; let us persecute him and take him, for there is none who will deliver him). The first excerpt reads "Confundantur, et deficiant detrahentes animae meae: operiantur confusione, et pudore qui quaerunt mala mihi" (Let the detractors of my soul be confounded and fail; let them be covered with confusion and shame, who seek evil for me). The second excerpt reads "tunc convertentur inimici mei retrorsum" (then my enemies shall turn back). The third excerpt reads "dicentes: Deus dereliquit eum, persequimini, et comprehendite eum: quia non est qui eripiat" (saying, God hath forsaken him; let us persecute him, and take him, for there is none who will deliver [him]). **rebuke . . . shame** KP's doubling.

463. **Conjoin . . . strength** KP closely renders Fisher's recasting and splicing of excerpts from Psalms 53:6, 142:9, 53:7, and 67:22: "O Deus adjunge te animae meae, conforta eam, ab inimicis meis eripe me. Disperde illos in virtute tua, et fortitudinem illorum confringe." The first excerpt reads "Deus adjuvat me: et Dominus susceptor est animae meae" (God hath helped me, and the Lord is the Supporter of my soul). The second excerpt reads "Eripe me de inimicis meis" (Deliver me from my enemies). The third excerpt reads "in veritate tua disperde illos" (destroy them with Thy truth). The fourth excerpt reads "Deus confringet capita inimicorum suorum" (God shall break in pieces the heads of His enemies).

464. **That . . . down** KP renders Fisher's recasting and splicing of excerpts from Psalms 12:5 and 34:25: "Nec dicant inter se, hunc superavimus, et omnino dejecimus" (Let them not say among themselves, We have overcome this man, and we have altogether cast him down). The first excerpt reads "ne . . . dicat inimicus meus: Praevalui adversus eum" (let not my enemy say: I have prevailed against him). The second excerpt reads "nec dicant: Devoravimus eum" (let them not say: We have devoured him).

465. **Save . . . Thee** KP closely renders Fisher's splicing of recast excerpts from Psalms 15:1 and 22:4: "Salvum me fac domine deus, in te enim speravi, dic animae meae, ne metuas, quia ego tecum sum." The first excerpt reads "Conserva me Domine, quoniam speravi in te" (Save me, O Lord, for I have trusted in Thee). The second excerpt reads "non timebo mala: quoniam tu mecum es" (I shall not fear evils, for Thou art with me).

It is in Thy hand, what shall come of me; deliver me from mine enemies, for yet they cease not.[466]

Their cruelty increaseth daily more and more, and companies of tyrants violently come on me, and they have not Thee before their eyes.[467]

[Gvi v] But Thou, O Lord, art gracious and merciful, and sufferest long; and Thy mercy and truth be great.[468]

Look unto me, and have mercy upon me; endue Thy servant with some of Thy strength, for I call upon Thee, and earnestly make my prayers in Thy sight.[469]

My enemies rejoice that I am fallen, and that my heart hath turned out of Thy way.

But I trust in Thy mercy, and my heart is comforted in hope to have help and salvation from Thee.[470]

466. **It . . . not** KP closely renders Fisher's splicing of recast excerpts from Psalm 30:15 and Job 3:17: " In manu tua sors mea, libera me ab inimicis meis, quoniam adhuc non cessant." The first excerpt reads "in manibus tuis sortes mea. Eripe me de manu inimicorum meorum" (in Thy hands [is] my lot. Deliver me from the hand of my enemies). The second excerpt, part of Job's description of the realm of death, reads "Ibi impii cessaverunt a tumultu" (There the wicked will have ceased from troubling).

467. **Their . . . eyes** KP freely renders Fisher's splicing of recast excerpts from Psalms 55:2, 58:4, and 85:14: "Indies augescit sevitia eorum, et coetus robustorum irrunt in me, et non ponunt te in conspectu suo" (From day to day their ferocity increaseth, and a company of very strong men rush upon me, and they do not set Thee before their eyes). The first excerpt reads "tota die impugnans tribulavit me" (daily he, fighting, oppresseth me). The second excerpt reads "irruerunt in me fortes" (the strong men have rushed upon me). The third excerpt reads "Deus, iniqui insurrexerunt super me, et synagoga potentium . . . et non proposuerunt te in conspectu suo" (God, evil men have risen up over me, and a company of powerful men . . . and they have not placed Thee before their eyes). **companies . . . tyrants** KP's odd rendering of Fisher's "coetus robustorum" (company of very strong men) perhaps indicates that she recognized the source text and was puzzled by its even odder phrase "synagoga potentium" (company—literally, synagogue—of powerful men). Her translation of this Latin phrase recurs in the Ninth Psalm below.

468. **But . . . great** KP closely renders Fisher's near verbatim quotation of Psalm 85:15: "Sed tu Domine Deus miserator et misericors, patiens, et multae misericordiae, et verax." The Vulgate verse reads "Et," not "Sed." Psalm 144:8, which reads very similarly, was used earlier; see n218.

469. **Look . . . sight** KP renders Fisher's splicing of slightly recast excerpts from Psalms 85:16 and 141:3: "Respice ad me, et miserere mei, da fortitudinem tuam servo tuo, quoniam te invoco, et effundo preces meas in conspectu tuo" (Look upon me, and have mercy upon me; give Thy strength to Thy servant, for I call upon Thee, and I pour out my prayers in Thy sight). The first excerpt reads identically with Fisher except for its last clause: "da imperium tuum puero tuo" (give Thy direction to Thy child). The second excerpt reads "ad Dominum clamavi: effundo in conspectu ejus orationem meam" (I have called unto the Lord; I pour out my prayer in His sight).

470. **My . . . Thee** KP renders Fisher's splicing of recast excerpts from Psalms 12:5, 43:18, and 12:6: "Hostes mei exultant eo quòd lapsus sum, et deflexit cor meum à via tua. Sed ego in misericordia tua confido, de salute tua cor mihi gaudet" (My enemies exult at it, that I have fallen,

For Thou art good and gracious; Thy mercy endureth ever, and Thy truth continueth from one generation to another.[471]

[Gvii r] Let all them rejoice in Thee, and be glad, which seek Thee; and let them which love to have salvation of Thee, say, Magnified be the Lord forever. Amen.[472]

THE NINTH PSALM, AGAINST ENEMIES.

See, Lord, and behold, how many they be which trouble me: how many, which make rebellion against me.

They say among themselves, of my soul: There is no help of God for it to trust upon.[473]

O Lord God, in Thee I have put my hope and trust; save me from them, which do persecute me, and deliver me,

[Gvii v] Lest peradventure at one time or another they take my life from me, and there be none to deliver me from them.[474]

---

and my heart hath turned from Thy way). The first excerpt reads "Qui tribulant me, exultabunt si motus fuero" (They who trouble me rejoice that I have been disturbed). The second excerpt, omitting its negative particle that yields the opposite sense, reads "declinasti semitas nostras a via tua" (our paths have declined from Thy way). The third excerpt reads "ego . . . in misericordia tua speravi. Exultabit cor meum in salutari tuo" (I . . . have hoped in Thy mercy, and my heart will rejoice in Thy salvation). **is . . . have** KP's expansive rendering of Fisher's "gaudet" (rejoiceth). **help . . . salvation** KP's doubling.

471. **For . . . another** KP closely renders Fisher's slight recasting of Psalm 99:5: "Quoniam bonus tu es, in aeternum misericordia tua, et usque in generationem et generationem veritas tua." The verse reads "quoniam suavis est Dominus, in aeternum misericordia ejus, et usque in generationem et generationem veritas ejus" (for the Lord is sweet, His mercy [is] everlasting, and His truth [is] from generation to generation). **good . . . gracious** KP's doubling.

472. **Let . . . Amen** KP closely renders Fisher's slight recasting of Psalm 39:17: "Exultent et laetentur in te omnes qui te quaerunt, et dicant semper, magnificetur dominus, qui diligunt salutem tuam." The verse reads "Exultent et laetentur super te omnes quaerentes te: et dicant semper: Magnificetur Dominus: qui diligunt salutare tuum" (Let all them who seek Thee exult and be glad in Thee; and let them who love Thy salvation ever say: Let the Lord be magnified). **Amen** KP's addition.

473. **See . . . upon** KP renders Fisher's recasting of Psalm 3:1–2: "Domine, ecce quàm multi sunt, qui me tribulant, quàm multi qui contra me insurgunt. Dicunt inter sese de anima mea, quod à deo non est ei salus speranda" (Lord, look how many they are who trouble me, how many who rise against me. Of my soul they say among themselves, that there is no help from God that it may hope for). The verses read "Domine quid multiplicati sunt qui tribulant me: multi insurgunt adversum me. Multi dicunt animae: Non est salus ipsi in Deo ejus" (Lord, how numerous they are who trouble me; many rise against me. Many say of my soul: There is no help for him from his God). **See . . . behold** KP's doubling. **for . . . upon** KP felicitously fills out the elliptical phrasing in Fisher and the Vulgate.

474. **O . . . them** KP closely renders Fisher's recasting of excerpts from Psalm 7:2–3: "Domine Deus in te spem meam posui, salva me ab iis qui me persequuntur, et eripe me: Ne forte

Have pity upon me, O Lord; look upon the affliction which I suffer of my enemies.

Forget not Thy poor servant; suffer not them which be oppressed to look for help always in vain.[475]

Put them to flight; disappont them of their purposes. Cast them down headlong as their wickedness hath deserved, for they are traitors and rebels against Thee.[476]

Let their power be brought to naught, and their wickedness light upon their own heads.[477]

Let the wicked sinners return into hell, and let them fall and be taken in the pit which they have digged.[478]

---

aliquando rapiant animam meam, et nullus sit qui eripiat." The verses read "Domine Deus meus in te speravi: salvum me fac ex omnibus persequentibus me, et libera me. Nequando rapiat . . . animam meam, dum non est qui redimat" (Lord, my God, in Thee have I hoped; save me from all who persecute me, and deliver me, Lest one seize . . . my soul, when there is no one to redeem [it]). **hope . . . trust** KP's doubling. **from them** KP again fills out the elliptical phrasing in her sources.

475. **Have . . . vain** KP renders Fisher's splicing of recast excerpts from Psalm 9:14, 19: "Mei te misereat domine, respice adflictionem quam patior ab inimicis meis. Ne tradas in oblivionem pauperem tuum, expectatio oppressorum ne pereat in aeternum" (Take Thou pity on me, Lord; look on the affliction that I suffer from my enemies. Lead not Thy poor one into oblivion; let not the hope of the oppressed perish forever). The first excerpt reads "Miserere mei Domine: vide humilitatem meam de inimicis meis" (Have pity on me, Lord; see my abasing by my enemies). The second excerpt reads "Quoniam non in finem oblivio erit pauperis: patientia pauperum non peribit in finem" (For oblivion shall not finally be to the poor man; the patience of the poor shall not finally perish).

476. **Put . . . Thee** KP renders Fisher's splicing of recast excerpts from Psalms 88:24 and 5:11: "In fugam converte eos, decidant à consiliis suis, juxta nequitiam suam praecipita eos, nam rebelles tibi sunt" (Turn them to flight; let them put an end to their purposes; cast down them and their worthlessness alike, for they are rebels to Thee). The first excerpt reads "et odientes eum in fugam convertam" (And I will put to flight those who hate him). The second excerpt reads "Decidant a cogitationibus suis, secundum multitudinem impietatum eorum expelle eos, quoniam irritaverunt te Domine" (Let them put an end to their thoughts; drive them out according to the multitude of their sins, for they have mocked Thee, Lord). **disappoint** As in her use of the past participle "disappointed" (see n206), KP's use of the transitive verb "disappoint" in the sense of "frustrate the expectations of" is one of the earliest recorded in the *OED*. **traitors . . . rebels** KP's doubling.

477. **Let . . . heads** KP closely renders Fisher's splicing of recast excerpts from Psalms 17:38 and 7:17: "Consumantur vires eorum, et perversitas ipsorum in caput suum descendat." The first excerpt reads "persequar inimicos meos . . . et non convertar donec deficiant" (I have pursued mine enemies . . . and I did not turn until they wore out). The second excerpt reads "in caput ejus . . . iniquitas ejus descendet" (his wickedness shall come down . . . upon his own head).

478. **Let . . . digged** KP closely renders Fisher's splicing of recast excerpts from Psalms 9:18 and 7:16: "Revertantur impii ad infernum, capiantur in fovea quam perfoderunt." The first excerpt reads "Convertantur peccatores in infernum" (Let the sinners return into hell). The second excerpt reads "incidit [peccator] in foveam, quam fecit" (he [the sinner] hath fallen into the

[Gviii r] I will trust in Thee, O Lord, which savest them that in Thee put their confidence.[479]

They say that Thou forgettest Thy servants, and that Thou hidest Thy face, because Thou wilt not see their trouble.[480]

Their pride is to us much grief and vexation, and they glory and triumph in our trouble and adversity.[481]

How long, O Lord, wilt Thou stand afar off, and hide Thyself in the time of tribulation?

How long shall the wicked despise Thee, and say in their heart, that Thou regardest nothing?[482]

Rise up, O Lord, stretch out Thy hand: forget not them, which be oppressed.[483]

---

pit that he made). **sinners** KP's rendering is closer to the Vulgate "peccatores" than is Fisher's "impii," suggesting that she may have recognized the source verse.

479. **I . . . confidence** KP renders Fisher's splicing of recast excerpts from Psalm 17:3–4: "Ego autem in te sperabo, qui salvos facis in te confidentes" (But I will hope in Thee, who savest those who trust in Thee). The excerpts read "sperabo in eum . . . cornu salutis meae . . . et salvus ero" (I will hope in Him . . . the horn of my salvation . . . and I shall be saved).

480. **They . . . trouble** KP closely renders Fisher's recasting of Psalm 9:32: "Illi dicunt, quòd tu tuorum oblivisceris, abscondis faciem tuam, ut non videas afflictionem eorum." The verse reads "Dixit [peccator] enim in corde suo: oblitus est Deus, avertit faciem suam ne videat in finem" (He [the sinner] hath said in his heart: God hath forgotten; He hath turned His face away, so that He may never see).

481. **Their . . . adversity** KP freely renders Fisher's splicing of recast excerpts from Psalm 93:2–5: "In superbia illorum persecutionem patimur, et in malo nostro vehementer gloriantur" (We suffer persecution from their pride; in our trouble they glory vehemently). The excerpts read "redde retributionem superbis. . . . usquequo peccatores gloriabuntur . . . qui operantur injustitiam. . . . Populum tuam Domine humiliaverunt: et . . . vexaverunt" (give retribution to the proud. . . . how long shall sinners glory . . . who work injustice? . . . They have abased Thy people, Lord, . . . and troubled them). **grief . . . vexation, glory . . . triumph, trouble . . . adversity** KP's repeated doublings heighten the rhetorical urgency of the versicle.

482. **How . . . O Lord . . . nothing** KP closely renders Fisher's splicing of recast excerpts from Psalm 9:22, 34: "Quousque domine persistes à longe? et te abscondes in angustiae tempore? Quousque tandem contemnent te impii, et in corde suo dicent, quod nihil cures?" The first excerpt reads "quid Domine recessisti longe, despicis in opportunitatibus, in tribulatione? (why, Lord, hast Thou withdrawn afar off, [and] lookest away in good times [and] in tribulation?). The second excerpt reads "Propter quid irritavit impius Deum? dixit enim in corde suo: Non requiret" (Wherefore hath the wicked man provoked God [and] said in his heart: He [God] will not require [it]?). **regardest** lookest to, hast a care of—senses that aptly render Fisher's "cures" (hast a care of).

483. **Rise . . . oppressed** KP closely renders Fisher's splicing of recast excerpts from Psalms 9:20, 54:21, and 73:19: "Surge domine, extende manum tuam, et ne obliviscaris eorum, qui oppressi sunt." The first excerpt reads "Exurge Domine" (Rise up, Lord). The second excerpt reads "extendit manum suam in retribuendo" (He hath extended His hand in retribution). The third excerpt reads "animas pauperum tuorum ne obliviscaris" (forget not the souls of Thy poor people).

[Gviii v] Bring down the power of the wicked, that they may perish together with their wickedness.[484]

Let Thy zeal suddenly come upon them; the fiery thunderbolts and the spirit of the whirlwind be portion of their part.[485]

Prevent me in the day of my tribulation, and deliver me out of my distresses.[486]

Have mercy upon me, for I am troubled on every side; and my strength is decayed through mine iniquity.

Mine enemies speak of me much shame and rebuke, and they are wholly bent to take my life from me.[487]

The pains of death compass me round about, and the floods of my sins trouble me sore.[488]

484. **Bring . . . wickedness** KP closely renders Fisher's thorough recasting of Psalm 9:36: "Contere fortitudinem malignantium, ut simul cum impietate sua pereant." The verse reads "Contere brachium peccatoris et maligni: quaeretur peccatum illius, et non invenietur" (Break in pieces the arm of the sinner and the evil man: let his sin be sought out [until] it will not be found [any longer]).

485. **Let . . . part** KP closely renders Fisher's splicing of recast excerpts from 4 Kings (2 Chronicles) 19:31 and Psalm 10:7: "Irruat in eos zelus tuus, ardentia fulmina, et spiritus turbinis portio partis eorum." The first excerpt reads "zelus Domini exercituum faciet hoc" (the zeal of the Lord of hosts shall do this). The second excerpt reads "Pluet super peccatores . . . ignis, et sulphur, et spiritus procellarum pars calicis eorum" (He shall rain upon siners . . . fire, and sulphur, and the spirit of tempests [shall be] a portion of their cup). **Let . . . upon** KP's expansive rendering of **t** Fisher's "Irruat in" (Let . . . rush in upon).

486. **Prevent . . . distresses** KP closely renders Fisher's splicing of recast excerpts from Psalm 17:19 and Job 36:15: "Praeveni me in die afflictionis meae, et de angustiis meis eripe me." The first excerpt reads "praevenerunt me in die afflictionis meae" (They have come upon me too soon in the day of my tribulation). The second excerpt reads "Eripiet de angustia sua pauperem" (He shall deliver the poor man from his distress). **Prevent** Come before—i.e., come more quickly than. KP's cognate renders "Praeveni," which Fisher predicates of God. The subject of this verb in the Psalm verse is "they" (enemies).

487. **Have . . . me** KP closely renders Fisher's splicing of recast excerpts from Psalm 31:10–12, 14: "Miserere mei, quoniam undique premor, et virtus mea in iniquitate mea diminuitur. Apud inimicos meos obprobrium sum factus, ut perdant animam meam toti incumbunt." The excerpts read "Miserere mei Domine quoniam tribulor . . . Infirmata est in paupertate virtus mea. . . . Super omnes inimicos meos factus sum opprobrium. . . . audivi vituperationem multorum. . . . convenirent simul adversum me, accipere animam meam consiliati sunt" (Have mercy upon me, O Lord, for I am oppressed: . . . My strength hath been weakened by want. . . . Among all mine enemies I have been made a reproach. . . . I have heard the slander of many. . . . They came against me at the same time; they have consulted to take away my life). **shame . . . rebuke** KP's doubling.

488. **The . . . sore** KP closely renders Fisher's minor recasting of Psalm 17:5: "Circumdant me dolores mortis, et torrentes iniquitatis me conturbant." The verse reads "Circumdederunt me dolores mortis: et torrentes iniquitatis conturbaverunt me" (The sorrows of death have encompassed me; and the torrents of wickedness have disturbed me).

[Hi r] The ropes of hell be tied round about me, and I am wrapped in the snares of death; and which way soever I go, I find stumbling-blocks to overthrow me.[489]

Stand up, O Lord, and punish this naughty people, and deliver me from my deceitful enemies.[490]

Hear me in the day of my tribulation; let Thy mighty name defend me.[491]

For Thou art my fortress and my glory, and bearest up my weakness and infirmity.[492]

Save me, Lord, I beseech Thee, that mine enemies prevail not against me.[493]

[Hi v] Pour out Thy indignation upon them, and let the wrath of Thy fury vex and trouble them.[494]

489. **The . . . me** KP closely renders Fisher's splicing of recast excerpts from Psalm 17:6 and Isaiah 57:14: "Funes inferni cingunt me, et implicant me laquei mortis, et qua parte iter agendum est, offendicula invenio." The Psalm excerpt reads "Dolores inferni circumdederunt me: praeoccupaverunt me laquei mortis" (The sorrows of hell have encompassed me; the snares of death have taken possession of me). The Isaiah excerpt reads, in the voice of God, "auferte offendicula de via populi mei" (take away the stumbling-blocks from the way of My people). **ropes** KP closely renders Fisher's image "funes" (ropes, cords), which has no Vulgate counterpart.

490. **Stand . . . enemies** KP closely renders Fisher's splicing of recast excerpts from Psalms 93:1–3 and 42:1: "Eleva te Deus, supplicium sume de gente perversa, ab inimicis fraudeulentis eripe me." The excerpts from Psalm 93 read "Deus ultionum Dominus . . . Exaltare . . . redde retributionem. . . . usequequo peccatores gloriabuntur?" (O Lord God of vengeance, . . . Lift Thyself up . . . render retribution. . . . how long shall the sinners triumph?). The excerpt from Psalm 42 reads "ab homine . . . doloso erue me" (from the man . . . [who is] deceitful, deliver me).

491. **Hear . . . me** KP closely renders Fisher's recasting of Psalm 19:2: "Exaudi me in die tribulationis meae, protegat me nomen magnum tuum." The verse reads "Exaudiat te Dominus in die tribulationis: protegat te nomen Dei Jacob" (May the Lord hear thee in the day of trouble; may the name of the God of Jacob protect thee).

492. **For . . . infirmity** KP renders Fisher's recasting of excerpts from Psalm 3:3: "Quoniam tu es propugnator meus, et gloria mea, et sustentans infirmitatem meam" (For Thou art my Defender, and my glory, supporting my weakness). The excerpts read "Tu . . . domine susceptor meus es, gloria mea, et exaltans caput meum" (Thou . . . Lord, art my Guardian, my glory, lifting up my head). **fortress** KP's image fits the overall sense, but it is unusual for her to substitute an impersonal noun for Fisher's personification—"propugnator" (defender, one who fights for me)—as well as the Vulgate's "susceptor" (guandian). **weakness . . . infirmity** KP's doubling.

493. **Save . . . me** KP closely renders Fisher's recasting of excerpts from 2 Paralipomenon (2 Chronicles) 14:11: "Obsecro domine, salva me, ut non praevaleant adversum me inimici mei." The excerpts read "invocavit Dominum Deum, et ait . . . adjuva nos Domine Deus noster . . . non praevaleat contra te homo" (he [King Asa] prayed to the Lord God, and said . . . help us, Lord our God, . . . that man may not prevail against Thee).

494. **Pour . . . them** KP closely renders Fisher's minor recasting of Psalm 68:25: "Effunde super eos indignationem tuam, et ira furoris tui eos conturbet." The verse reads "Effunde super eos iram tuam: et furor irae tuae comprehendat eos" (Pour out Thy wrath upon them, and let the fury of Thy wrath encompass them).

Let them be confounded forever: yea, let them tremble and perish together.[495]

Let them fall into the deep pit, and never be able to rise up again.

That they may know Thy name to be the Lord of hosts, only mighty and high, world without end. Amen.[496]

THE TENTH PSALM, WHEN THE ENEMIES BE SO CRUEL THAT HE CANNOT SUFFER THEM.[497]

Have mercy upon me, O God, for mine enemy treadeth me under his feet; he ceaseth not to assault me, and to do me much grief.[498]

[Hii r] He always coveteth to swallow me up, and many they be that proudly brag and crake against me.[499]

495. **Let . . . together** KP closely renders Fisher's recasting of excerpts from Psalm 82:18: "Confundantur usque in aeternum, contremiscant et pereant simul." KP's "perish together" follows the Cologne edition; the first London edition lacks "simul" (together) as does the Vulgate verse. It reads "Erusbescant, et conturbentur in saeculum saeculi: et confundantur, et pereant" (Let them be ashamed, and troubled from age to age; and let them be confounded, and perish).

496. **Let . . . Amen** KP closely renders Fisher's splicing of recast excerpts from Psalms 54:24 and 82:18–19: "Cadant in puteum profundum, et non apponant ut resurgeant. Ut cognoscant quod nomen tibi dominus exercituum, solus potens et excelsus in secula seculorum. Amen." The first excerpt reads "Tu . . . Deus deduces eos, in puteum interitus" (Thou . . . Lord, shalt lead them down into the pit of destruction). The second pair of excerpts, the conclusion of a Psalm that catalogues God's enemies and the punishments destined for them, reads "et confundantur, et pereant. Et cognoscant quia nomen tibi Dominus: tu solus Altissimus in omni terra" (and let them be confounded, and perish. And let [the people] know that Thy name is the Lord: Thou alone art Most High in all the earth). **Lord . . . hosts** a very frequent appellation for the God of the Old Testament, although not found in the Vulgate versions of these particular source texts. **mighty . . . high** KP's doubling.

497. **When . . . them** KP idiomatically renders Fisher's subtitle, "Quum usque adeo inimici seviant, ut ferre non potest" (When the enemies are cruel for so long a time, that he cannot bear [it]).

498. **Have . . . grief** KP renders Fisher's recasting of Psalm 55:1: "Miserere mei Deus, quoniam conculcat me inimicus, sine intermissione obpugnans coarctat me" (Have mercy upon me, God, for mine enemy treadeth me down; attacking without interruption, he presseth upon me). The verse reads "Miserere mei Deus, quoniam conculcavit me homo: tota die impugnans tribulavit me" (Have mercy upon me, God, for the man hath trodden me down: fighting all the day, he hath oppressed me). **under . . . feet, to . . . grief** two of KP's characteristically idiomatic expansions for clarity or emphasis.

499. **He . . . me** KP renders Fisher's splicing of recast excerpts from Psalms 57:10 and 30:19: "Absorbere me cupit omni tempore, et multi sunt qui superbè mihi insultant" (He craveth to swallow me at all times, and many they are who taunt me proudly). The first excerpt, part of a description of the wicked man's excess, reads "Priusquam intelligerent . . . in ira absorbet eos"

They gather themselves together in corners; they watch my steps, that they may take my soul in a trap.[500]

They be like unto a lion that is greedy of his prey, and like a young lion they privily lie in wait for me.[501]

They do beset my ways, that I should not escape; they look and stare upon me, to take me in their snare.[502]

They have prepared a net for my feet; they have digged a deep pit, that my soul might fall therein.[503]

Make me strong, O Lord God, by Thy might and power; make my way perfect before Thee.[504]

[Hii v] Keep my steps continually in right paths, lest perchance my feet begin to slip.[505]

(Before they feel . . . he swalloweth them up in his anger). The second excerpt reads "loquuntur adversus justum iniquitatem, in superbia, et in abusione" (they speak evil against the just man, proudly and abusively). **brag . . . crake** KP's doubling. **crake** boast, brag.

500. **They . . . trap** KP freely renders Fisher's thorough recasting of excerpts from Psalms 55:7 and 58:4: "Cogunt se pariter et abstrudunt, latenter vestigia mea observant, quomodo animam meam capiant" (They assemble and conceal themselves as well; they watch my steps secretly, how they may seize my soul). The first excerpt, part of what came to be treated as a description of King Saul's devious strategies for capturing David, reads "Inhabitabunt et abscondent: ipsi calcaneum meum observabunt" (They install themselves and hide; they attend to my heel). The second excerpt reads "ecce ceperunt animam meam" (behold, they lie in wait for my soul).

501. **They . . . me** KP closely renders Fisher's recasting of Psalm 16:12: "Similes sunt leoni praedae avido, et sicut catulus leonis ex occulto insidiantur." The verse reads "Susceperunt me sicut leo paratus ad praedam: et sicut catulus leonis habitans in abditis" (They catch me up like a lion prepared for its prey, and like a young lion living in secret places).

502. **They . . . snare** KP freely renders Fisher's recasting and reordering of excerpts from Psalm 9:9 (in the Vulgate's second numbered set of verses of this Psalm): "Itinera mea obsident, et oculos suos in miserum obverunt" (They beset my ways, and they turn their eyes on the poor man). The excerpt reads "Oculi ejus in pauperem respiciunt . . . Insidiatur ut rapiat pauperem . . . In laqueo suo" (His eyes are set against the poor man . . . he lieth in wait to catch the poor man . . . in his snare). **that . . . escape** a characteristic phrasal expansion by KP, for emphasis or clarity. **look . . . stare** KP's doubling.

503. **They . . . therein** KP closely renders Fisher's recasting of an excerpt from Psalm 56:7: "Rete paraverunt pedibus meis, ad incurvandum animam meam profundam foderunt foveam." The excerpt reads "Laqueum paraverunt pedibus meis: et incurvaverunt animam meam. Foderunt ante faciem meam foveam" (They have prepared a snare for my feet: and my soul is bowed down. They have digged a pit before my face).

504. **Make . . . Thee** KP renders Fisher's recasting of Psalm 17:33: "Deus corrobora me virtute tua, pone perfectam coram te viam meam" (God, strengthen me with Thy strength; set me in a perfect way before Thee). The verse reads "Deus qui praecinxit me virtute: et posuit immaculatam viam meam" (God, who hath surrounded me with strength, and hath made my way spotless). **might . . . power** KP's doubling.

505. **Keep . . . slip** KP closely renders Fisher's recasting of Psalm 16:5: "Sustenta gressus meos in semitis rectis, ne forte labascant pedes mei." The verse reads "Perfice gressus meos

I am so vexed that I am utterly weary; help me against them that lie in wait for me.[506]

Make Thy mercy to be marvelous in me; and deliver my soul out of their hands.[507]

Hide me from the company of the wicked, and from the rage of them that work iniquity.[508]

According to Thy great mercy quicken me, that now in my sorrow I be not brought under the power of mine enemy, which rageth against me.[509]

Send forth Thy light and Thy truth, and they shall lead me unto Thy holy hill, and into Thy tabernacles.[510]

[Hiii r] Instruct and teach my hands to battle; make my arms strong like a bow of steel.

Gird me with strength to battle; overthrow them that arise against me.[511]

---

in semitis tuis: ut non moveantur vestigia mea" (Make my steps perfect in Thy paths, that my footsteps slip not).

506. **I . . . me** KP closely renders Fisher's splicing of extensively reworked excerpts from Psalms 6:3–4 and 69:1–2: "Afflictus sum usque ad saturitatem, adjuva me propter insidiatores meos." The first set of excerpts reads "infirmus sum . . . conturbata sunt ossa mea. Et anima mea turbata est valde" (I am weak . . . my bones are vexed. And my soul is greatly vexed). The second set of excerpts reads "Domine ad adjuvandum me festina. Confundantur . . . qui quaerunt animam meam" (Lord, hasten to help me. Let them be confounded . . . who seek after my soul).

507. **Make . . . hands** KP closely renders Fisher's recasting of excerpts from Psalm 16:7, 13: "Mirabilem fac in me misericordiam tuam, et eripe animam meam de manibus eorum." The first excerpt reads "Mirifica misericordias tuas" (Wonderful are Thy mercies). The second excerpt reads "eripe animam meam ab impio" (deliver my soul from the wicked one).

508. **Hide . . . iniquity** KP closely renders Fisher's recasting of Psalm 63:3: "Abscondi me à conventu malignantium, à tumultu operantium iniquitatem." The verse reads "Protexisti me a conventu malignantium: a multitudine operantium iniquitatem" (Thou hast protected me from the company of the wicked, from the multitude of the workers of iniquity).

509. **According . . . me** KP quite freely renders Fisher's splicing of an exact quotation from Psalm 118:88 with a recast excerpt from Psalm 13:4: "Secundum misericordiam tuam vivifica me, ne tristis dejiciae, sevienti [1544: seviente] in me inimico meo" (According to Thy mercy revivify me, lest I, sorrowing, be thrown down by my enemy raging against me). The excerpt from Psalm 13 reads "ne . . . dicat inimicus meus: Praevalui adversus eum" (lest . . . my enemy say, I have prevailed against him).

510. **Send . . . tabernacles** KP closely renders Fisher's near verbatim quotation of Psalm 42:3: "Mitte lucem tuam, et veritatem tuam, ipsa me ducent ad montem sanctum tuam, et in tabernacula tua." The Vulgate verse reads identically except for "Emitte" (Send forth) in place of "Mitte" (Send), and two perfect-tense verbs in place of a single future-tense one—"deduxerunt et adduxerunt" (have led and have brought) in place of "ducent" (shall lead).

511. **Instruct . . . against me** KP closely renders Fisher's recasting and splicing of Psalm 17:35, 40: "Instrue manus meas ad bellum, compone quasi arcum aerum brachia mea. Accinge me fortitudine ad praelium, prosterne insurgentes in me sub[t]us me." The first verse reads "Qui docet manus meas ad praelium: et posuisti, ut arcum aereum, brachia mea" (Who instructeth my hands for battle so that Thou hast made my arms as a bow of bronze). The second

Instruct me in the way wherein I may walk; provide for me by Thy oversight.[512] Cast down mine enemies before my face, and destroy them that hate me: Lest mine enemies overcome me, and the companies of tyrants overwhelm me:[513] Make my feet to be steadfast, and my paths straight.[514]

They rejoice and be glad of my fall and declination; they be assembled together against me; they strike to kill me in the way, before I may be ware of them.[515] [Hiii v] They curse and ban my words every day; and all their thoughts be set to do me harm.[516]

My life is as it were in the midst of fierce lions, whose teeth be like unto spears, and their tongue like a sharp sword.[517]

---

verse reads "praecinxisti me virtute ad bellum: et supplantasti insurgentes in me subtus me" (Thou hast girded me with strength for war, and Thou hast thrown down under me those rising against me). **Instruct . . . teach** KP's doubling.

512. **Instruct me . . . oversight** KP closely renders Fisher's reordering and recasting of Psalm 31:8: "Instrue me in via qua ambulem, consule super me oculo tuo." The verse reads "Intellectum tibi dabo, et instruam te in via hac, qua gradieris" (I will give thee understanding, and I will instruct thee in that way in which thou shalt walk).

513. **Cast . . . me** KP closely renders Fisher's recasting and splicing of excerpts from Psalms 88:24 and 37:17, 20: "Concide ante faciem meam hostes meos, et odio me habentes disperde. Ne superent me inimici mei, et coetus robustorum non obruant me." The first verse reads "Et concidam a facie ipsius inimicos ejus: et odientes eum in fugam convertam" (I will cut his enemies to pieces before his face, and I will put to flight those who hate him). The excerpts from Psalm 37 read "Nequando supergaudeant mihi inimici mei . . . Inimici autem mei . . . confirmati sunt super me" (Lest my enemies rejoice over me . . . But my enemies . . . are strong over me).

514. **Make . . . straight** KP closely renders Fisher's recasting of excerpts from Psalm 26:11: "Pone stabiles pedes meos, et rectas facito semitas meas." The excerpts read "pone mihi Domine in via tua: et dirige me in semitam rectam" (put me, Lord, in Thy way, and lead me in a right path). A subsequent reference to "inimicos meos" (my enemies) in this particular verse strengthens its identification as the source here.

515. **They rejoice . . . them** KP expands in rendering Fisher's recasting of Psalm 34:15: "In defectione mea letantur, collecti sunt adversum me, percutiunt, et non noverim ut interficiant in via" (They rejoiced in my failing; they have assembled against me; they struck, and I did not know that they might kill [me] in the way). The verse reads "Et adversum me laetati sunt, et convenerunt: congregata sunt super me flagella, et ignoravi" (They have rejoiced against me, and they have assembled; whips have been gathered above me, and I did not know [it]). **rejoice . . . be glad, fall . . . declination** KP's doublings. **before . . . them** KP's felicitous clarification of Fisher's elliptical "et non noverim," rendering the equally elliptical Vulgate phrase "et ignoravi"—both with the sense of "and I did not know."

516. **They . . . harm** KP closely renders Fisher's minor recasting of Psalm 55:6: "Omni die verba mea execrantur, contra me universae cogitationes eorum in malum." The verse reads "Tota die verba mea execrabantur: adversum me omnes cogitationes eorum, in malum" (All the day long they cursed my words: all their thoughts [were] against me for evil). **curse . . . ban** KP doubles synonyms; one sixteenth-century sense of "ban" was "curse."

517. **My . . . sword** KP closely renders Fisher's recasting of excerpts from Psalm 56:5: "Anima mea quasi in medio leonum ferocientium, quorum dentes velut lanceae, et lingua ut acutus

And who shall stand with me against all these? or who shall overcome these worke[r]s of iniquity?[518]

They shall flee and run away, O Lord, as soon as Thou rebukest them; from the voice of Thy thunder they shall run headlong,

Which lookest upon the earth, and it wholly quaketh: which touchest the hills, and they smoke.[519]

Judgment proceedeth from Thy face; Thine eyes do approve equity.

[Hiv r] Keep me, O Lord, from mine adversaries; and under the shadow of Thy wings defend me.[520]

Judge them that hurt me; fight against them that fight with me.

Let them go backward and have ill luck, which persecute me; put them to shame that will my hurt.

Make them to be as dust in the wind, and let Thy angel vex and disquiet them.[521]

---

gladius." The verse excerpts read "eripuit animam meam de medio catulorum leonum . . . Filii hominum dentes eorum arma et sagittae: et lingua eorum gladius acutus" (He hath delivered my soul from the midst of lion cubs: . . .The sons of men, whose teeth [are] weapons and arrows, and whose tongue [is] a sharp sword).

518. **And . . . iniquity?** KP closely renders Fisher's recasting and reordering of Psalm 93:16: "Et quis stabit pro me adversus omnes istos? aut quis expugnabit operantes iniquitatem?" The verse reads "Quis consurget mihi adversus malignantes? aut quis stabit mecum adversus operantes iniquitatem?" (Who will rise up for me against the evildoers? or who will stand with me against the workers of iniquity?). **worke[r]s** The 1544 *Psalms or Prayers* reads "workes"—identifiably a misprint because the corresponding Latin is "operantes" (workers). Coverdale's Bible and the Great Bible read "the wicked."

519. **They . . . smoke** KP renders Fisher's minor recasting of Psalm 103:7, 32: "Ab increpatione tua domine fugient, à voce tonitrui tui praecipites ruent. Qui respicis terram, et tremit tota, tangis montes, et fumant" (From Thy rebuke, Lord, they fled; at the voice of Thy thunder they rushed headlong. [Thou] who lookest on the earth, and all trembleth; who touchest the mountains, and they smoke). Verse 7 reads identically in the Vulgate except for omitting "domine" (Lord) and having "formidabunt" (they feared) in place of "praecipites ruent" (they rushed headlong). Verse 32 reads "qui respicit terram, et facit eam tremere: qui tangit montes, et fumigant" (He looketh upon the earth, and maketh it tremble; He toucheth the mountains, and they smoke). **flee . . . run away** KP's doubling. **as soon . . . them** KP's characteristic clausal expansion of Fisher's "Ab increpatione tua" (From Thy rebuke).

520. **Judgment . . . me** KP closely renders Fisher's recasting of Psalm 16:2, 8: "A facie tua judicium prodit, oculi tui aequitatem probant. Custodi me domine ab inimicis meis, sub umbra alarum tuarum protege me." Verse 2 reads "De vultu tuo judicium meum prodeat: oculi tui videant aequitates" (Let my judgment proceed from before Thy face; let Thine eyes see righteousness). The relevant portions of verse 8 read "A resistentibus dexterae tuae custodi me . . . Sub umbra alarum tuarum protege me" (From them who resist Thy right hand, keep me . . . Cover me with the shadow of Thy wings).

521. **Judge . . . them** KP renders with varying degrees of freedom Fisher's recasting of Psalm 34:1, 4–5: "Judica mihi nocentes, pugna contra obpugnatores meos. Abeant retrorsum, qui me persequuntur, obprobrium ferant, qui malum mihi volunt. Sint sicut pulvis ante faciem venti, et angelus tuus eos exagitet." **Judge . . . me** The Vulgate's verse 1, which KP closely renders in

Let them vanish away like smoke; and as wax melteth with the heat of the fire, so let them perish, O Lord, from Thy sight and presence.[522]

Beat them down, that they be not able to stand; never give over, until Thou have utterly destroyed them.[523]

[Hiv v] Make their ways dark and slippy; and let Thine angel fiercely go upon them.[524]

And Thou, O Lord God, have mercy upon me; send me help, and then I shall be able to resist them.[525]

For I am weak and in sorrow; give Thou me health and salvation.[526]

Fisher's slight recasting, reads "Judica Domine nocentes me, expugna impugnantes me" (Judge, Lord, them who hurt me; blot them out who fight against me). **Let . . . hurt** Excerpts from the Vulgate's verse 4, reordered and recast by Fisher and more freely rendered by KP, read "quaerentes animam meam . . . Avertantur retrorsum, et confundantur cogitantes mihi mala" (they who seek my soul . . . Let them be turned back, and let them be confounded who devise evil things for me). **and . . . luck** KP's colloquial addition. **Make . . . them** Verse 5, which KP freely renders in Fisher's slight recasting, reads "Fiant tamquam pulvis ante faciem venti: et angelus Domini coarctans eos" (Let them be made as dust before the face of the wind: the angel of the Lord pressing them down). **vex . . . disquiet** KP's doubling of Fisher's "exagitet" (let him [the angel] disturb).

522. **Let . . . presence** KP closely renders Fisher's recasting of Psalm 67:3: "Sicut propellitur fumus, evanescant, sicut liquescit cera à calore ignis, sic pereant illi à facie tua domine." Verse 3 reads "Sicut deficit fumus, deficiant: sicut fluit cera a facie ignis, sic pereant peccatores a facie Dei" (As smoke goeth away, let them go away; as wax floweth in the presence of fire, so let sinners perish in the presence of God). **sight . . . presence** KP's felicitous doubling of Fisher's and the Vulgate's "facie" (presence—elsewhere frequently with the sense of "face").

523. **Beat . . . them** KP somewhat freely renders Fisher's recasting and reordering of excerpts from Psalm 17:39, 38: "Confringe eos, ut non possunt consistere, ne cesses donec eos deleveris" (Wound them, so that they be unable to stand; cease not until Thou wilt have destroyed them). The relevant Vulgate excerpts read "Confringam illos, nec poterunt stare . . . et non convertar donec deficiant" (I have wounded them, nor are they able to stand . . . nor did I turn again until they expired). **never, utterly** KP's intensifying additions.

524. **Make . . . them** KP closely renders Fisher's recasting of Psalm 34:6: "Sint viae eorum obscurae ac lubricae, et angelus tuus eos urgeat." The verse reads "Fiat via illorum tenebrae et lubricum: et angelos Domini persequens eos" (Let their way be dark and slippery, with the angel of the Lord chasing them). **slippy** a variant of "slippery," also used by Udall in translating chapter 14 of the Gospel of Luke in Erasmus's Latin paraphrase. **fiercely** KP's addition.

525. **And . . . them** KP somewhat freely renders Fisher's recasting of Psalm 40:11: "Et tu domine Deus miserere mei, opem mihi ferto [1544: ferro], et resistam eis" (And Thou, O Lord God, have mercy upon me, [give] me help by the force of arms, and I will oppose them.) The verse reads "Tu autem Domine miserere mei, et resuscita me: et retribuam eis" (But Thou, Lord, have mercy upon me, and revive me: and I shall requite them).

526. **For . . . salvation** KP freely renders Fisher's near verbatim quotation of Psalm 68:30: "Ego enim infirmus sum, et dolens, salus tua me suscipiat" (But I am weak and grieving; let Thy salvation raise me up). The verse reads "Ego sum pauper et dolens: salus tua, Deus, suscepit me" (I am poor and grieving: Thy salvation, God, shall raise me up). **health . . . salvation** KP doubles two senses of Latin "salus."

Let Thy hand correct and chastise me, but deliver me not unto mine enemies.[527]

My soul is filled with the scorning and derision that mine enemies have at me, and with the despitefulness of the proud.[528]

[Hv r] My soul is clean discouraged within me; it groaneth and fretteth in itself against me. Yet will I trust in Thee, for that I shall eftsoons give Thee thanks again for the help and salvation that Thou sendest me.[529]

For Thy very truth, now help, O Thou which art my health, and the hope and comfort of all regions of the earth, and of the main sea.[530]

Which by Thy power rulest from the beginning; Thine eyes behold all things.[531]

527. **Let . . . enemies** KP closely renders Fisher's recasting of excerpts from Psalm 117:16, 18: "Corrigat et castiget me dextera tua, inimicis autem meis ne me tradas." The excerpts read "Dextera Domini . . . castigans castigavit me . . . et morti non tradidit me" (The right hand of the Lord . . . chastising, hath chastised me . . . but He hath not delivered me unto death).

528. **My . . . proud** KP freely renders Fisher's recasting of Psalm 122:4: "Multum repleta est anima mea, et derisione me in festantium, et contemptu superborum" (My soul is greatly filled, both with the mockery of me by those in festive dress and with the contempt of the proud ones). The verse reads "multum repleta est anima nostra: opprobrium abundantibus, et despectio superbis" (our soul is greatly filled with scorning by the wealthy and with despising by the proud). **scorning . . . at me** KP combines two characteristic devices of her style: a doubling and a clausal expansion of a Latin participial construction: "that . . . at me" in place of "in festantium" (those in festive dress). **the despitefulness . . . proud** KP's wording is identical to that of Coverdale's Bible and the Great Bible in Psalm 123:4, suggesting that she recognized the source text; see the introduction, p. 212.

529. **My . . . me** KP freely renders Fisher's thorough recasting of Psalm 41:12: "Dejecta est in me anima mea, adversum me fremit, sed ego sperabo in te, quoniam iterum pro salute reddita, gratias agam tibi" (My soul is cast down within me; it murmureth against me, but I shall hope in Thee, since I shall thank Thee for the salvation likewise given [to me]). The verse reads "Quare tristis es anima mea? et quare conturbas me? Spera in Deo, quoniam adhuc confitebor illi: salutare vultus mei, et Deus meus" (Why art thou sad, my soul? and why dost thou trouble me? Hope in God, for I shall confess Him thus far [to be] the health of my countenance, and my God). **clean, groaneth . . . fretteth, in itself** KP's various additions intensify the evocation of a disturbed soul. **eftsoons** soon afterward. **again, help . . . salvation, that . . . me** KP's various expansions emphasize the gratitude of a saved soul.

530. **For . . . sea** KP expansively renders Fisher's splicing and recasting of excerpts from Psalms 44:5 and 64:6: "Propter veritatem tuam adjuva me, o salus mea, spesque omnium finium terrae, et maris immensi" (For the sake of Thy truth, help me, O my salvation, and the hope of all the ends of the earth, and of the boundless regions of the sea). The first excerpt supplies the phrase "Propter veritatem." The second excerpt reads "Exaudi nos Deus salutaris noster, spes omnium finium terrae, et in mari longe" (Hear us, God of our health / salvation, the hope of all the ends of the earth, and [of them] far off upon the sea). **very, and comfort** KP's additions. **main sea** a former synonym for "high seas."

531. **Which . . . things** KP closely renders Fisher's recasting of Psalm 65:7: "Qui virtute tua ab aeterno imperas, oculi tui omnia contemplantur." The verse reads "Qui dominatur in virtute sua in aeternum, oculi ejus super gentes respiciunt" (Who ruleth in His power forever; His eyes look upon the nations).

What god is there but Thou? who is so strong as Thou our God?[532]
In Thy protection I will trust, until iniquity be past and gone.[533]
In Thee I shall be strong and sure for evermore.[534]

[Hv v]

THE ELEVENTH PSALM.
OF CONFIDENCE AND TRUST IN GOD.[535]

O Lord, which art my light and my health: of whom shall I be afraid?

O Lord, Thou art the strength of my life; in Thee I will ever trust.[536]

For like as the hart, when he is chased, coveteth to the rivers of water, even so, O Lord, my soul desireth to be with Thee.

My soul thirsteth to be with Thee, for with Thee is the fountain of life, and recreation in adversity.[537]

532. **What . . . God?** KP closely renders Fisher's recasting of excerpts from Psalm 17:32–33: "Quis deus praeter te? quis fortis sicut tu, Deus noster?" These verses read "quis Deus praeter Dominum? aut quis Deus praeter Deum nostrum? Deus qui praecinxit me virtute" (who [is] God besides the Lord? or who [is] God besides our God? God, who hath girded me with strength).

533. **In . . . gone** KP freely renders Fisher's nearly verbatim quotation of Psalm 56:2: "In umbra alarum tuarum sperabo, donec praetereat malicia" (In the shadow of Thy wings will I hope, until ill will be past). The verse reads "Et in umbra alarum tuarum sperabo, donec transeat iniquitas" (In the shadow of Thy wings will I hope until iniquity be passed by). **iniquity . . . gone** KP's wording is closer to the Vulgate than is Fisher's, suggesting that she recognized the Biblical source.

534. **In . . . evermore** KP briefly renders a versicle that seems to be Fisher's own composition: "In te fortis ero, et securus in sempiternum et in saeculum saeculi" (In Thee I shall be strong and secure for evermore and from age to age). The closest Biblical analogue is Psalm 70:3: "Esto mihi in Deum protectorem, et in locum munitum . . . quoniam . . . refugium meum es tu" (Be to me as a protector God, and as a fortified place . . . for . . . Thou art my refuge). The conjunction of the synonymous time expressions, "in sempiternum et in saeculum saeculi," has no Vulgate analogue; it seems to be Fisher's rhetorical flourish to conclude this Psalm.

535. **Of . . . God** Fisher reads "De fiducia in Deum." **confidence . . . trust** KP's doubling.

536. **O Lord, which . . . trust** KP closely renders Fisher's recasting of Psalm 26:1: "Domine lux mea, et salus mea tu [1544: cum sis], à quonam metuam? Domine fortitudo vitae meae tu, in quo semper sperabo." KP's "which art" reflects the clausal expansion in the first English edition, "cum sis" (when Thou shalt be). The Cologne edition retains the Vulgate wording of the verse: "Dominus illuminatio mea, et salus mea, quem timebo? Dominus protector vitae meae, a quo trepidabo?" (The Lord [is] my illumination, and my health/salvation, whom shall I fear? The Lord [is] the Protector of my life, at whom shall I tremble?).

537. **For . . . adversity** KP somewhat freely renders Fisher's slight recasting and splicing of Psalms 41:2–3, 35:10, and 31:7: "Quemadmodum desiderat cervus ad fontes aquarum: ita desiderat anima mea ad te, O Deus. Sitit ad te anima mea, quoniam apud te est fons vitae et refrigerium in tribulatione" (As the stag desireth the springs of water, so my soul desireth Thee, O God. My soul thirsteth after Thee, for with Thee is the fountain of life and consolation of

Here in this world is labor and pain, calamity and misery.[538]

[Hvi r] We have battle daily with enemies; we have no rest here so long as we live.[539]

But whensoever we put our trust in Thy help, then we shall be sure by Thy protection, saying unto Thee: Thou art our Defender, our refuge, and our God; and in Thee we trust.

Thou shalt deliver me from the snares of the hunters, and from the perils of my persecutors.

Thou shalt make a shadow for me under Thy shoulders; and under Thy wings I shall be harmless.

Thy truth shall be my shield and buckler; and no evil shall approach near unto me.[540]

---

trouble). The first excerpt reads identically to Fisher, except for "Deus" in place of "O Deus" and "Sitivit" (hath thirsted) in place of "Sitit" (thirsteth). The second and third excerpts read "Quoniam apud te est fons vitae, et . . . Tu es refugium meum a tribulatione" (For with Thee is the fountain of life, and . . . Thou art my refuge in trouble). **(when . . . chased)** KP's clarifying explanation why the stag is thirsty also intensifies the simile; see the introduction, p. 207. **hart** a male deer. **recreation** comfort, consolation—no longer current senses of this noun, which aptly renders Fisher's "refrigerium," substituted for the Vulgate's "refugium." KP's following of Fisher in this case suggests that she did not recognize the Biblical source.

538. **Here . . . misery** KP expands Fisher's splicing of phrases from Psalm 89:10 and Job 30:3: "Hic [1544: Nam hic] labor atque dolor, calamitas atque miseria" (Here [are] labor and pain, calamity and misery). The first phrase reads "labor et dolor" (labor and pain). The second reads "calamitate et miseria" (in calamity and misery).

539. **We . . . live** KP closely renders a sententious formulation that appears to be Fisher's original composition: "Quotidie bellum cum inimicis, nulla requies, nec pax in vita nostra." The closest Biblical analogue is an excerpt from 2 Corinthians 7:5: "nullam requiem habuit caro nostra, sed omnem tribulationem passi sumus: foris pugnae, intùs timores" (our flesh had no rest, but we have suffered every trouble: fights without, fears within).

540. **But . . . me** KP closely renders Fisher's recasting of an extended sequence of excerpts from Psalm 90:1–5, 7. She follows the first English edition for the wording of the first two verses: "Sed cum in adjutorio tuo fiduciam nostram ponamus, securi protectione tuae in aeternum erimus, dicentes, susceptor noster, et refugium nostrum es tu, Deus noster in te speramus." The Cologne edition's somewhat garbled reading of these verses is cast in the singular throughout: "Sed quisquis in adjutorio tuam fiduciam posuit, securus protectione tua in aeternum consistet. Is tibi dicet, susceptor meus es tu et refugium meum, deus meus, in te sperabo" (But whoever relieth on Thy trust for help, he shall be placed secure in Thy protection forever. He shall say, Thou art my Defender and my refuge; my God, in Thee will I hope). Except for one difference in grammatical person, the remaining verses read identically in the two editions: "Tu liberabis me de laqueo venantium et à periculis me persequentium. Sub scapulis tuis umbram mihi facies, et sub alis tuis illaesus ero. Scuto circundabit me veritas tua, et malum ad eum [1544: me] non adpropinquabit." The Vulgate sequence, also cast in the singular, reads "Qui habitat in adjutorio Altissimi, in protectione Dei caeli commorabitur. Dicet Domino: Susceptor meus es tu, et refugium meum: Deus meus sperabo in eum. Quoniam ipse liberavit me de laqueo venantium, et a morbo aspero. Scapulis suis obumbrabit tibi: et sub pennis ejus sperabis. Scuto circumdabit te veritas ejus . . . ad te [malum] non appropinquabit" (He who dwelleth in the help of the Most High shall abide in the protection of the God of heaven. He shall say to the Lord: Thou art my

[Hvi v] And therefore if my enemies shall war against me, that they may devour me wholly, yet I will not flee nor turn my back.

Although never so strong enemies shall pitch their tents against me, my heart shall not be afraid; if death suddenly come upon me, in Thee will I rest without fear.

Thou shalt hide me in Thy tabernacle in the time of adversity; Thou shalt hide me in some secret place of Thy tent; Thou shalt set me upon a sure rock.

Thou shalt lift me up above my enemies besieging me round about, and Thou shalt deliver me out of their hands.[541]

[Hvii r] If I shall walk in the midst of tribulation, Thou shalt keep me, and shalt stretch forth Thy hand against mine enemies; and Thy right hand shall save me.

O Lord, Thou shalt do and bring to pass all things for me; Thy mercy endureth ever; Thou wilt not despise Thy own handiwork.[542]

Protector, and my refuge; my God, I will trust in Thee. Since He hath delivered me from the snare of the hunters, and from severe sickness, He will shadow thee with His shoulders, and beneath His wings thou shalt put thy trust. His truth shall be set around thee for a shield . . . [evil] shall not approach thee). **shield . . . buckler** KP's doubling, rendering Fisher's and the Vulgate's "scuto" (for a shield), demonstrates that she recognized the Biblical source text and knew the translation "shield and buckler" in Coverdale's Bible and the Great Bible. **buckler** a leather-covered shield.

541. **And . . . hands** KP closely renders Fisher's next recasting of a sustained sequence of excerpts from Psalms 26:2–3, 5–6 and 30:16: "Et propterea si inimici mei adversum me praelientur, ut me totum devorent, terga minime vertam. Si steterint adversum me castra potentium, non timebit cor meum, si ingruat mihi mors, in te securus ero. Tu abscondes me in tabernaculo tuo, in die malorum abscondes me in secreto tentorii tui, super petram me constitues. Levabis me supra inimicos meos me circumvallantes, et de manibus eorum me eripies." The Vulgate sequence from Psalm 26 reads "Dum appropiant super me nocentes, ut edant carnes meas: qui tribulant me inimici mei, ipsi infirmati sunt et ceciderunt. Si consistant adversum me castra, non timebit cor meum. Si exurgat adversum me praelium, in hoc ego sperabo. . . . Quoniam abscondit me in tabernaculo suo: in die malorum protexit me in abscondito tabernaculi sui. In petra exaltavit me: et nunc exaltavit caput meum super inimicos suos" (When the harmful ones came upon me to eat my flesh, and my enemies who troubled me, they were weak and they fell. If they set up an encampment against me, my heart shall not fear. If war rise up against me, in this I shall hope. . . . Because He hath hid me in His tabernacle; in the day of the wicked He hath protected me in the hidden place of His tabernacle; He hath exalted me upon a rock. And now he hath exalted my head above mine enemies). The excerpt from Psalm 30 reads "Eripe me de manu inimicorum meorum" (Deliver me from the hand of my enemies). **flee nor** KP's addition. **sure** KP's addition.

542. **If . . . handiwork** KP quite closely renders Fisher's recasting of Psalm 137:7–8: "Si ambulavero in medio tribulationis, me custodies; adversus inimicos tuos manum tuam extendes, et dextera tua me salvabis. Domine tu omnia pro me perficies, O Deus in eternum misericordia tua, opus manuum tuarum non despicies." The verses read "Si ambulavero in medio tribulationis, vivificabis me: et super iram inimicorum meorum extendisti manum tuam, et salvum me fecit dextera tua. Dominus retribuet pro me: Domine misericordia tua in saeculum: opera manuum tuarum ne despicias" (If I shall walk in the midst of tribulation, Thou shalt revive me: and Thou hast stretched forth Thy hand against the wrath of my enemies, and Thy right hand shall save me. The Lord shall restore [things] for me; Thy mercy, Lord, [endureth] for ages;

Thou shalt lead me out of the net which mine enemies have spread abroad to catch me in; Thou shalt take me out of their pit.[543]

O how great be the good things which Thou layest up in store for them that fear Thee: which also Thou showest to them that trust in Thee, even in the sight of the children of men.

[Hvii v] Thou hidest them in the secret place of Thy countenance, from trouble of enemies, and from their contentions.[544]

O Lord, what a precious treasure is Thy goodness, and men shall trust in Thy protection.

They shall be filled with the plentifulness of Thy house, and Thou shalt make them drink of Thy river of dainties.

They shall drink with Thee of the fountain of life, and in Thy light they shall see light.

Thy righteousness is as the highest mountains, and Thy judgments be like unto the deep, bottomless waters.

Thy mercy stretcheth up to the heavens: and Thy truth ascendeth up to the same.[545]

---

forsake not the works of Thine hands). **shalt do . . . pass** KP's doubling renders Fisher's "perficies" ([Thou] shalt accomplish), substituted for the Vulgate's "retribuet" ([He] shall restore). **for me** KP does not translate Fisher's "O Deus" (O God), which follows at this point.

543. **Thou . . . pit** KP closely renders Fisher's splicing of recast excerpts from Psalms 30:5 and 56:7: "Educes me de reti, quod panderunt pro me inimici mei, et de fovea eorum me subduces." The first excerpt reads "Educes me de laqueo hoc, quem absconderunt mihi" (Thou shalt pull me out of this snare that they concealed from me). The second set of excerpts reads "Laqueum paraverunt pedibus meis . . . Foderunt ante faciem meam foveam" (They have prepared a snare for my steps . . . They have digged a pit before my face).

544. **O how . . . contentions** KP expansively renders Fisher's further recasting of verses from Psalm 30:20–21: "Quanta sunt bona quae reponis iis, qui te timent, quae ostendis etiam confidentibus in te coram filiis hominum? Occultas eos in occulto vultus tui à conturbatione hostium, et à contentionibus eorum" (How many are the good things that Thou layest up for them who fear Thee, that Thou also showest to those who trust in Thee before the sons of men! Thou hidest them in the hidden place of Thy presence, from the confounding of enemies and from their contentions). The verses read "Quam magna multitudo dulcedinis tuae Domine, quam abscondisti timentibus te. Perfecisti eis, qui sperant in te, in conspectu filiorum hominum. Abscondes eos in abscondito faciei tuae a conturbatione hominum. Proteges eos in tabernaculo tuo a contradictione linguarum" (How great is the multitude of Thy sweetness, Lord, that Thou hast hidden for them who fear Thee. [This] Thou hast accomplished for them who hope in Thee, in the sight of the sons of men. Thou shalt hide them in the hidden place of Thy countenance, from the confounding of men. Thou shalt cover them in Thy tabernacle from the strife of tongues).

545. **O Lord . . . same** KP renders with varying degrees of closeness Fisher's reordering and recasting of Psalm 35:8–10, 7, 6: "Quam preciosa est bonitas tua domine, et filii hominum in umbra alarum tuarum sperabunt. Saturabuntur ab ubertate domus tuae, et torrente deliciarum eos potabis. De fonte vitae tecum bibent, et in tuo lumine lumen videbunt. Justicia tua sicut montes altissimi, et judicia tua abissus multa. Coelos pertingit misericordia tua, et usque ad

[Hviii r] O Lord God, Thou hast ever from age to age been our refuge and succor.

Before the foundations of the earth were laid, without beginning and ending, Thou art God.[546]

O my God, Thou hast helped me ever from my youth; and until my old age and last days, forsake me not.

I will acknowlege that I have all my strength of Thee, for Thou art my protection, my God, and my Saviour.[547]

And therefore, what time soever I shall be afraid, I will trust in Thee.

What time soever I shall call upon Thee, I know that Thou art my God.[548]

---

coelos veritas tua" (How precious is Thy goodness, Lord; and the sons of men shall hope in the shadow of Thy wings. They shall be abundantly satisfied with the plenty of Thy house, and Thou shalt make them drink from the stream of Thy pleasures. They shall drink from the fountain of life with Thee, and in Thy light shall they see light. Thy righteousness [is] like the highest mountains, and Thy many judgments [are like] the abyss. Thy mercy reacheth the heavens, and Thy truth unto the heavens). The Vulgate verses read "quemadmodum multiplicasti misericordiam tuam Deus. Filii autem hominum, in tegmine alarum tuarum sperabunt. Inebriabuntur ab ubertate domus tuae: et torrente voluptatis tuae potabis eos. Quoniam apud te est fons vitae: et in lumine tuo videbimus lumen. Praetende misericordiam tuam scientibus te, et justitiam tuam his . . . Justitia tua sicut montes Dei: judicia tua abyssus multa . . . Domine in caelo misericordia tua: et veritas tua usque ad nubes" (how hast Thou multiplied Thy mercy, God. Yet the sons of men shall hope in the cover of Thy wings. They shall be drunk from the plenty of Thy house, and Thou shalt make them drink from the stream of Thy pleasures. Since with Thee is the fountain of life, and in Thy light we shall see light . . . Thy righteousness [is] like the mountains of God; Thy many judgments [are like] the abyss . . . Lord, Thy mercy [reacheth] unto the heavens, and Thy truth unto the clouds).

546. **O . . . God** KP renders Fisher's recasting of Psalm 89:1–2: "Deus tu refugium fuisti nobis à generatione in generationem. Priusquàm fundamenta terrae jacerentur à saeculo et usque in saeculum tu es deus" (O God, Thou hast been a refuge for us from generation to generation. Before the foundations of the earth were laid, from age to age Thou art God). The verses read "Domine, refugium factus es nobis, a generatione in generationem. Priusquam montes fierent, aut formaretur terra et orbis: a saeculo et usque in saeculum tu es Deus" (O Lord, Thou art made a refuge for us from generation to generation. Before the mountains were, or the earth and world was formed, from age to age Thou art God).

547. **O my . . . Saviour** KP closely renders Fisher's recasting and reordering of excerpts from Psalm 70:17–18, 3: "Deus meus tu opem mihi tulisti à juventute mea, et usque ad [1544: in] senectam et canos ne derelinquas me. Fortitudinem meam adscribam tibi, quoniam tu es protectio mea, Deus meus, et salvator meus." The excerpts read "Deus docuisti me a juventute mea: et usque nunc pronunciabo mirabilia tua. Et usque in senectam et senium: Deus ne derelinquas me. . . . Esto mihi in Deum protectorem . . . ut salvum me facias, quoniam firmamentum meum, et refugium meum es tu" (God, Thou hast taught me from my youth, and now will I declare Thy wonders. And now in old age, God, do not forsake me. . . . Be to me as a protector God, . . . that thou mayest save me, for Thou art my rock and my refuge).

548. **And . . . God** KP closely renders Fisher's splicing of excerpts from a Vulgate gloss to Psalm 55:4 and from verse 10: "Et ideo quacunque die territus fuero, ego in te confidam. In quaqunque die te invocavero, scio quod Deus meus es tu." The gloss reads "Quacumque die territus fuero, ego in te confidam" (In whatever day I shall be frightened, I shall trust in Thee).

[Hviii v] Keep Thy mercy for me always; and the covenant that Thou hast made with me, let it be surely performed.

And if I have swerved from Thy law, and not walked in Thy judgments,

If I have broken Thy statutes, and transgressed Thy commandments:

Then with Thy rod visit mine offenses, and with stripes correct my trespasses.

But take not Thy mercy away from me, nor let not Thy promise be void and of none effect.

Break not the covenant that Thou hast made with me, and change not that which hath issued out of Thy mouth.[549]

[Ii r] For in Thee, O God, our health and glory doth consist; Thou art our Helper, in whom we do ever trust.

And this is certain, that all they which trust in Thee shall not be confounded.

For who is he that hath trusted in Thee, and is confounded? or who hath called upon Thee, and Thou hast despised him?[550]

The excerpt from verse 10 reads "in quacumque die invocavero te: ecce . . . Deus meus es" (In whatever day I shall call upon Thee, behold. . . . Thou art my God). **time . . . time** KP's colloquial substitution for the Latin "dies" (day).

549. **Keep . . . mouth** KP fairly closely renders Fisher's recasting of a series of verses and excerpts from Psalm 88:29, 31–35: "In aeternum custodi mihi misericordiam tuam, et foedus tuum fidele mecum perstet. Et si deseruerim legem tuam, et in judiciis tuis non ambulaverim, Si statua tua prophanaverim, et praecepta tua contempserim: Iam virga tua visita praevaricationes meas, et verberibus tuis scelera mea. At misericordiam tuam à me ne tollas, neque fidem tuam irritam reddas. Ne scindas foedus, quod nobiscum iniisti, et quod egressum est de labiis, ne immutes." The Vulgate series is cast in the first person, with God as speaker: "In aeternum servabo illi misericordiam meam: et testamentum meum fidele ipsi. . . . Si autem dereliquerint filii ejus legem meam: et in judiciis meis non ambulaverint: si justitias meas profanaverint, et mandata mea non custodierint: visitabo in virga iniquitates eorum: et in verberibus peccata eorum. Misericordiam autem meam non dispergam ab eo: neque nocebo in veritate mea: neque profanabo testamentum meum: et quae procedunt de labiis meis non faciam irrita" (My mercy will I keep for him forever, and My covenant faithfully for the same. . . . But if his sons shall forsake My law, and shall not walk in My judgments; if they shall pollute My righteousness, and shall not keep My commandments, then will I visit their iniquities with the rod, and their sins with whips. But I will not take My mercy away from him, nor will I do harm to My truth, nor will I violate My covenant; and I will not stir up the things that have proceeded from My lips). **covenant . . . performed** KP idiomatically expands Fisher's elliptical "foedus tuum fidele mecum perstet" (may Thy covenant with me stand faithfully). **I have broken . . . transgressed** KP gives a general turn to Fisher's more specific "prophanaverim" (I shall have violated) and "contempserim" (I shall have disdained). **offenses** KP again gives a general turn to Fisher's more specific "praevaricationes" (derelictions of duty). Her Latin vocabulary may not have extended to these items in question, but her guesses are educated ones. **stripes** lashes.

550. **For . . . him?** KP closely renders Fisher's thorough recasting and splicing of Psalm 61:8 with excerpts from Psalm 21:5–6: "In te enim salus et gloria nostra consistit deus, adjutor nobis, in quo speramus semper. Et hoc certum est, quòd omnes, qui in te confidunt, non confundentur. Quis enim speravit in te, et confusus est? aut quis invocavit te, et despexisti illum?" The

For Thy name' sake, O Lord, Thou forgivest our sins, although they be many and grievous.

Thou art a sure stay to them that dread Thee, and showest them Thy testament.[551]

And unto Thee I cry, O Lord, and I believe that Thou wilt save me for Thy great mercy's sake.[552]

Thou shalt redeem my soul in peace, from the wrath which is to come in the last day.[553]

[Ii v] I will offer up to Thee sacrifice of laud and praise; and I will render up my vows to Thee, which art the Highest.[554]

---

first verse reads "In Deo salutare meum, et gloria mea: Deus auxilii mei, et spes mea in Deo est" (In God [is] my health / salvation and my glory; God [is] of help to me, and my hope is in God). The excerpted verses read "In te speraverunt patres nostri . . . et non sunt confusi. . . . Ad te clamaverunt, et salvi facti sunt" (In Thee our fathers have trusted, and they have not been confounded. . . . To Thee they called, and they have been saved). Fisher recasts the last verse as a rhetorical question that anticipates a negative answer, substituting "despexisti illum?" (hast Thou despised them?) for "salvi facti sunt" (they have been made safe).

551. **For . . . testament** KP closely renders Fisher's recasting and splicing of Psalm 24:11, 14: "Propter nomen tuum domine remittis [1544: remitte] peccata nostra, licet multa sint et grandia. Tu firmamentum es timentibus te, et testamentum tuum illis ostendis." KP follows the Cologne edition with its indicative verb, "remittis" (Thou remittest) rather than the petitionary verb, "remitte" (remit Thou), in the first English edition. In the Vulgate the first verse reads "Propter nomen tuum Domine propitiaberis peccato meo: multum est enim" (For Thy name's sake, Lord, Thou wilt be gracious toward my sin; truly it is great). The second verse reads "Firmamentum est Dominus timentibus eum: et testamentum ipsius ut manifestetur illis" (The Lord is a support to them that fear Him, so that His covenant also will be manifested to them).

552. **And . . . sake** KP closely renders a mixed composition by Fisher assembled mainly from formulaic Psalm and credal utterances spliced with an excerpt from Psalm 6:5: "Et ego ad te clamo domine, et credo quod salvabis me propter magnam misericordiam tuam." "Ego ad te clamo" (I cry unto Thee) occurs several times in the Psalms, in the past or future tense: e.g., Psalms 27:1; 29:3, 9; 56:3; 85:3. The expression "credo quod" (I believe that) is formulaic in the Apostles' Creed. The Psalm excerpt reads "salvum me fac propter misericordiam tuam" (save me for Thy mercy's sake).

553. **Thou . . . day** KP closely renders Fisher's recasting and splicing of excerpts from Psalm 54:19 and 1 Thessalonians 1:10: "Redimes in pace animam meam ab ira quae ventura est in extremo die." The first excerpt reads "Redimet in pace animam meam" (He shall redeem my soul in peace). The second excerpt reads "Jesum, qui eripuit nos ab irâ venturâ" (Jesus, who delivered us from the wrath to come).

554. **I . . . Highest** KP expansively renders Fisher's slight recasting of Psalm 49:14: "Immolabo tibi hostiam laudis: et reddam altissimo vota mea" (I will offer to Thee the sacrifice of praise, and I will render my prayers to the Most High), The verse reads "Immola Deo sacrificium laudis: et redde Altissimo vota tua" (Offer the sacrifice of praise to God, and render Thy prayers to the Most High). **laud . . . praise** KP's doubling. **vows** This seemingly odd translation of "vota," which can mean "prayers" or "vows," is in fact the phrasing of this verse in all English Bibles beginning with Coverdale's. KP's adoption of this usage indicates that she recognized the source text. See the introduction, p. 212.

The wicked watch and look to destroy me, but I trust in Thy mercy.[555]

Thou art my Protector and my buckler: my God, my strength, my refuge, and Deliverer.[556]

I tarry and look for help from Thee, O Lord; blessed is the man that trusteth in Thee.[557]

O Lord, what great pleasures Thou hast prepared for me in heaven, that I should delight in no earthly thing but in Thee.

[Iii r] My most pleasure is to cleave fast unto Thee, and in Thee to set my hope and trust.[558]

I commit my spirit into Thy hands; deliver me from the powers of darkness of this world. Amen.[559]

555. **The . . . mercy** KP closely renders Fisher's splicing of near quotations from Psalms 118:95 and 12:6: "Me expectant impii, ut perdant me, sed ego in misericordia tua confido." The first excerpt reads "Me expectaverunt peccatores ut perderent me" (Sinners have waited for me, so that they might destroy me). The second excerpt reads "ego autem in misericordia tua speravi" (but I have trusted in Thy mercy). **watch . . . look** KP's doubling.

556. **Thou . . . Deliverer** KP closely renders Fisher's splicing of epithets for God drawn mainly from Psalm 17:2–3 but also from two others: "Protector meus, et scutum meum es tu Deus meus, fortitudo mea, et refugium meum, et liberator meus." Excerpts from Psalm 83:10 read "Domine fortitudo mea . . . et refugium meum, et liberator meus" (Lord, my strength . . . and my refuge, and my Deliverer). **Protector** A phrase in Psalm 83:10 reads "Protector noster." **buckler** A clause in Psalm 90:6 reads "Scuto circumdabit te veritas ejus" (He will gird thee with the buckler of His truth).

557. **I . . . Thee** KP closely renders Fisher's splicing of nearly verbatim excerpts from Psalms 118:166 and 83:13: "Exxpecto salutem tuam domine, beatus homo qui in te confidit." The first excerpt reads "Exxpectabam salutare tuum Domine" (I shall look for Thy salvation, Lord). The second excerpt reads "beatus homo, qui sperat in te" (blessed is the man, who trusteth in Thee). **tarry . . . look for** KP's doubling.

558. **O . . . trust** KP expansively renders Fisher's splicing of recast excerpts from Psalm 72:25, 28: "Quanta mihi in coelis domine, ut nihil praeter te placeat in terra! Tibi adhaerere per optime mihi placet, et te in fiduciam meam collocare" (How many things [will there be] for me in heaven, Lord, so that nothing but Thee should be pleasing on earth. To cleave to Thee pleaseth me best, and to place my trust in Thee). The first excerpt reads "Quid enim mihi est in caelo? et a te quid volui super terram?" (But what is mine in heaven, and what have I desired from Thee on earth?). The second excerpt reads "Mihi autem adhaerere Deo bonum est: ponere in Domino Deo spem meam" (It is good for me to cleave unto God, to place my hope in the Lord God). **hope . . . trust** KP's doubling.

559. **I . . . Amen** KP closely renders Fisher's splicing of an excerpt from Psalm 30:6 with phrasing based on Ephesians 6:12: "In manus tuas spiritum meum committo, redime me de potestatibus tenebrarum saeculi huis. Amen." The Psalm excerpt reads "In manus tuas commendo spiritum meum: redemisti me Domine" (Into Thy hands I commend my spirit; Thou hast redeemed me, Lord). This excerpt is echoed in Jesus's last words on the cross in Luke 23:46. The relevant phrasing from Ephesians reads "est nobis colluctio adversus . . . potestates . . . tenebrarum" (our struggle is against . . . powers . . . of darkness). **powers . . . darkness** The exact phrase "potestates tenebrarum" (powers of darkness) is late patristic in origin, occurring in Cassiodorus, Bernard of Clairvaux, and Rabanus Maurus, among other authors.

THE TWELFTH PSALM.
IF GOD DEFER TO HELP LONG TIME.[560]

O my God, my God, why forsakest Thou me? Why lookest not upon my necessity?[561]

Shall Thy mercy fail forever? Wilt Thou never be pleased more?[562]

How long wilt Thou be miscontented with me, O Lord? Wilt Thou kindle Thine anger thoroughly, as it were fire?[563]

When wilt Thou have any regard to deliver my soul, to deliver my life from destruction of enemies?[564]

[Iii v] How long shall I cry, and Thou wilt not hear? How long shall I make exclamation for very pain, and Thou wilt not save me?[565]

O Lord God of hosts, how long wilt Thou be angry with the prayers of Thy servant?[566]

Come again unto me, O God, my Saviour, and take away Thine indignation against me.

560. **If . . . time** KP revises and intensifies Fisher's heading: "Si Deus paulo diutius auxilium suum differat" (If God deferreth His help for a little longer).

561. **O . . . necessity?** KP closely renders Fisher's recasting of an excerpt from Psalm 21:2: "Deus meus, Deus meus, ecquare me derelinquis? cur non respicis ad necessitatem meam?" The excerpt reads "Deus Deus meus respice in me: quare me dereliquisti?" (God, my God, look upon me; why hast Thou forsaken me?). It is echoed in Jesus's words on the cross in Matthew 27:46 and Mark 15:34.

562. **Shall . . . more?** KP closely renders Fisher's recasting and reordering of excerpts from Psalm 76:9, 8: "Nunquid deficiet in aeternum misericordia tua? num nunque placidus eris ultra?" The excerpts read "Numquid in aeternum . . . misericordiam suam abscindet? . . . aut non apponet ut complacitior sit adhuc?" (Is His mercy . . . cut off forever? . . . will He no longer be more favorable?).

563. **How . . . fire?** KP closely renders Fisher's recasting of Psalm 78:5: "Quousque indignaberis mihi domine? an ne penitus accendes velut ignem iram tuam?" The verse reads "Usquequo Domine irasceris in finem: accendetur velut ignis zelus tuus?" (How long, Lord: wilt Thou be angry forever? shall Thy zeal burn like fire?).

564. **When . . . enemies?** KP freely renders Fisher's recasting of Psalm 34:17: "Quando tandem respicies, ut eripias animam meam? à devastatione inimicorum unicam meam?" (When, at last, wilt Thou look, that Thou mayest deliver my soul, [and] my one and only from enemies' devastation?). The verse reads "Domine quando respicies? restitue animam meam a malignitate eorum, a leonibus unicam meam" (Lord, how long wilt Thou look on? rescue my soul from their malice, my one and only from the lions).

565. **How . . . me?** KP closely renders Fisher's quotation of Habakkuk 1:2: "Usquequo clamabo, et non exaudies? vociferabor ad te vim patiens, et non salvabis?" The Vulgate verse differs only in having a vocative of address, "Domine" (Lord), following "Usquequo."

566. **O Lord . . . servant?** KP clsely renders Fisher's minor recasting of Psalm 79:5: "Domine Deus exercituum, quousque irasceris super precibus servi tui?" The Vulgate verse reads identically except for having "virtutum" (of powers) in place of "exercituum" (of hosts), and "orationem" (the prayer) in place of "precibus" (the prayers).

When Thou art turned, O Lord, Thou shalt restore all things again; and he that was in sadness before, shall take joy and comfort of Thee.[567]

Let Thy hand be to help man which is Thy handiwork, whom Thou hast exalted and magnified to set forth Thy glory.[568]

[Iiii r] Mine enemies live wealthily and are strong; and they which hate me, increase and go forward daily.[569]

They dispraise and set at naught my counsel, because I take God for my hope and comfort.

They say to me daily, Thou trustest in God: let Him deliver thee and save thee, if so be that He bear love and favor towards Thee.[570]

They leap at me as it were so many dogs; the companies of the wicked bark at me; they beset my hands and feet round about.

O Lord, go not far away from me; Thou art my strength, make speed to help me.

567. **Come . . . Thee** KP quite closely renders Fisher's expansive recasting and splicing of Psalm 84:5, 7: "Redi ad me, O Deus salvator meus, et solve tuam erga me indignationem. Deus tu conversus omnia restitues, et qui prius moestus erat, de te leticiam capiet." KP's rendering of "omnia" (all things) follows the Cologne edition; the first English edition lacks "omnia." In the Vulgate the verses read "Converte nos Deus salutaris noster: et averte iram tuam a nobis. . . . Deus tu conversus vivificabis nos: et plebs tua laetabitur in te" (Turn us, our God of salvation, and turn away Thine anger from us. . . . Thou, God, when turned, shalt revive us: and Thy people shall rejoice in Thee). **joy . . . comfort** KP's doubling.

568. **Let . . . glory** KP freely renders Fisher's elaboration of an excerpt from Psalm 107:7: "Adsit manus tua figmento dexterae tuae, filio hominis quem tibi magnificasti" (Let Thy hand be with the creation of Thy right hand, the son of man whom Thou hast magnified with Thyself). The verse reads "ut liberentur dilecti tui, Salvum fac dextera tua" (make him safe with Thy right hand, that Thy beloved may be delivered). **exalted . . . magnified** KP's doubling. **to set . . . glory** KP's addition looks like an allusion to the preceding verse, Psalm 107:6, which reads "Exaltare super caelos Deus, et super omnem terram gloria tua" (Be exalted, God, above the heavens, and Thy glory above all the earth). She thus seems to have recognized the Vulgate source.

569. **Mine . . . daily** KP renders Fisher's recasting of Psalm 37:20: "Inimici mei prospere vivunt, et fortes sunt, augescunt quotidie, qui me odio habent" (My enemies live prosperously, and are strong; they increase daily, who have me in hatred). The verse reads "Inimici autem mei vivunt, et confirmati sunt super me: et multiplicati sunt qui oderunt me inique" (But my enemies live, and they are strong over me; and they have multiplied, who wrongly hate me). **increase . . . go forward** KP's doubling.

570. **They . . . Thee** KP renders quite closely, but with several doublings, Fisher's recasting and reordering of excerpts from Psalm 21:10, 8–9: "Consilium meum vituperant, eo quod deum spem mihi constitui. Dicunt mihi indies, tu sperasti in domino, is te eripiat, salvum te faciat, siquidem complacentiam habet in te." The excerpts read "Quoniam tu es . . . spes mea . . . Omnes . . . deriserunt me: . . . Speravit in Domino, eripiat eum: salvum faciat eum, quoniam vult eum" (Because Thou art . . . my hope . . . All men . . . scorn me, . . . [saying]: He hoped in the Lord, that He would deliver him; let Him save him, because He favors him). These Psalm verses are partially echoed in Job 12:4 and Matthew 27:39, 43. **dispraise . . . naught, hope . . . comfort, love . . . favor** KP's doublings.

Deliver my soul from death; turn my way from the rage of dogs.[571]

[Iiii v] Keep me out of the mouth of lions, and save me from the deep lake.[572]

Thou art both holy and strong, and no man is able to resist Thee when Thy anger is great and fervent.[573]

Who shall not fear Thee, O Lord? or which of all princes shall not obey Thee?

The earth trembleth and quaketh for fear of Thine anger; and the people shall not be able to abide Thy threatening.[574]

571. **They . . . dogs** KP closely renders Fisher's continued recasting of excerpts from Psalm 21:17, 20–22: "Insiliunt in me tanquam canes, coetus iniquorum me oblatrant, manus ac pedes meos obsident. O domine ne longe abeas à me, fortitudo mea in auxilium meum festina. Erue de interitu animam meam, et de rabie canum declina viam meam." The verses read "Quoniam circumdederunt me canes multi: concilium malignantium obsedit me. Foderunt manus meas et pedes meos . . . Tu autem Domine ne elongaveris auxilium tuum a me: ad defensionem meam conspice. Erue a framea Deus animam meam: et de manu canis unicam meam" (For many dogs have encircled me; the council of the malignant hath beset me. They have pierced my hands and my feet: . . . But Thou, Lord, shalt not distance Thy help from me; see to my defense. God, deliver my soul from the spear, and my one and only from the dog's paw). **so many** KP's addition to Fisher brings the wording closer to the Vulgate's "multi canes" (many dogs), suggesting that she recognized the source text.

572. **Keep . . . lake** KP closely renders Fisher's recasting of excerpts from Daniel 6:20, 27: "Salva me ex ore leonum, et de profundo lacu libera me." The first excerpt, a taunt to Daniel, reads "Deus tuus, . . . putasne valuit te liberare a leonibus?" (Thy God, . . . dost thou think He hath the strength to deliver thee from the lions?). The second excerpt states the narrative ending: "Ipse liberator, atque salvator . . . qui liberavit Danielem de lacu leonum" (He is the Deliverer, and Saviour . . . who delivered Daniel from the den of lions). **lake** a late medieval and early modern cognate of Latin "lacus," one meaning of which is "a den for lions." See n151 to KP's personal prayerbook for another instance of this rendering.

573. **Thou . . . fervent** KP quite closely renders Fisher's splicing of epithets for God in Psalms 98:9 and 23:8 with a recasting of Psalm 75:8: "Tu sanctus es et fortis, et nullus resistet tibi, ex quo servescit ira tua." The first excerpt reads "sanctus Dominus Deus noster" (the Lord our God [is] holy). The second excerpt reads "Dominus fortis et potens" (the Lord strong and mighty). The verse from Psalm 75 reads "Tu terribilis es, et quis resistet tibi, ex tunc ira tua?" (Thou art fearsome, and who may resist Thee then. after Thine anger?). **great . . . fervent** KP's doubling.

574. **Who . . . threatening** KP closely renders Fisher's splicing of recast excerpts from Jeremiah 10:7, 10: "Quis non timebit te domine? aut ex principibus tibi non morem geret? Ab indignatione tua contremiscit terra, et non ferent gentes comminationem tuam." The excerpts read "Quis non timebit te o rex gentium? tuum est enim decus inter cunctos sapientes gentium, et in universis regnis eorum. . . . Dominus autem Deus verus est . . . ab indignatione ejus commovebitur terra: et non sustinebunt gentes comminationem ejus" (Who will not fear Thee, O King of the nations? for honor is Thine among all the wise men of the nations, and in all their kingdoms. . . . For the Lord is the true God . . . at His wrath the earth shall tremble, and the nations shall not be able to abide His indignation). **obey** KP aptly renders Fisher's "morem geret," literally, "do the will of." **abide** endure, bear.

Help me, O Lord God, my Saviour: and for the glory of Thy name deliver me, and forgive my trespasses.[575]

[Iiv r] For I do utter and express mine iniquity unto Thee, and my sin grieveth me very sore.[576]

Arise up, O Lord, and help me; and deliver me for Thy mercy's sake.[577]

O God, my refuge and my strength, which hast been ever a great help in tribulation:[578]

Thou didst receive me into Thy tuition when I came out of my mother's womb, and Thou wast my Helper when I sucked my mother's breasts.

I was left to Thee as soon as I was born: even from my mother's womb Thou art my God.

Withdraw not Thyself far away from me, for tribulation is near at hand, and there is none that can help me.[579]

575. **Help . . . trespasses** KP closely renders Fisher's recasting of Psalm 78:9: "Adjuva me Deus, salvator meus, et p[r]opter gloriam nominis tui libera me, et placare super sceleribus meis." The verse reads "Adjuva nos Deus salutaris noster: et propter gloriam nominis tui Domine libera nos: et propitius esto peccatis nostris" (Help us, God of our salvation; and for the glory of Thy name, deliver us: and be gracious toward our sins).

576. **For . . . sore** KP closely renders Fisher's recasting of Psalm 37:19: "Quoniam iniquitatem meam annuncio tibi, et peccatum meum vehementer me vexar." The verse reads "Quoniam iniquitatem meam annunciabo: et cogitabo pro peccato meo" (For I will declare my iniquity to Thee, and I will meditate on my sin). **utter . . . express** KP's doubling.

577. **Arise . . . sake** KP closely renders Fisher's recasting of Psalm 6:4: "Surge domine in auxilium meum, et redime me propter misericordiam tuam." The verse reads "Converte Domine, et eripe animam meam: salvum me fac propter misericordiam tuam" (Turn, Lord, and deliver my soul; save me for Thy mercy's sake).

578. **O . . . tribulation** KP expansively renders Fisher's recasting of Psalm 45:2: "O deus refugium meum, et robur, auxilium in tribulatione inventus semper validum" (O God, my refuge and strength, a Helper in tribulation, always found [to be] powerful). The verse reads "Deus noster refugium, et virtus: adjutor in tribulationibus, quae invenerunt nos nimis" (God, our refuge and strength, [is] a Helper in tribulations, which too often find us out).

579. **Thou . . . me** KP effectively expands Fisher's recasting of an elliptical sequence from Psalm 21:10–12: "Tu excepisti me de ventre prodeuntem, et auxilium mihi fuisti ad ubera matris meae. In te conjectus sum à partu, ab utero matris meae Deus meus es tu. Ne subtrahas te longe à me, quoniam tribulatio iam appropinquat, et nullus est, qui opem mihi ferat" (Thou hast taken me up when I was coming forth from the belly, and Thou hast been my help from my mother's breasts. I have been cast upon Thee from birth; from my mother's womb Thou art my God. Withdraw not Thyself far from me, for tribulation now approacheth, and there is none who will help me out). The verses read as follows in the Vulgate: "Quoniam tu es, qui extraxisti me de ventre: spes mea ab uberibus matris meae. In te projectus sum ex utero: de ventre matris meae Deus meus es tu. Ne discesseris a me: quoniam tribulatio proxima est: quoniam non es qui adjuvet" (For Thou art [the one] who hath taken me out from the womb, my hope from [when I was at] my mother's breasts. I was cast upon Thee from the womb; from [when I was in] my mother's belly Thou art my God. Depart not from me, for tribulation is near, for there is none who will help). **into . . . tuition, when . . . sucked, at hand** KP's additions. **tuition** care, safekeeping.

[Iiv v] Mine enemies compass me round about; my persecutors besiege me on every side.[580]

And I am feeble and weak and sore broken; the pain of my heart maketh me to groan and sigh.[581]

I am as the water that is cast forth; my strength is gone and utterly dried up, as it were a tilestone.[582]

Have mercy upon me, O Lord, have mercy upon me; and impute not my sins unto me, which I have done by folly.[583]

Remember not my sins past; let Thy mercies prevent them, for I am in a marvelous wretched case.[584]

[Iv r] I am weakened and clean outworn, and go mourning every day.[585]

580. **Mine . . . side** KP closely renders Fisher's recasting of excerpts from Psalm 16:9, 11: "Circundant me inimici mei, infestatores mei undique me cingunt." The excerpts read "Inimici mei animam meam circumdederunt. . . . Projicientes me nunc circumdederunt me" (My enemies have surrounded my soul. . . . They who are thrusting at me have surrounded me now).

581. **And . . . sigh** KP expansively renders Fisher's recasting of excerpts from Psalm 6:3, 7: "Et ego infirmus sum, et comminutus vehementer, ejulatum exprimit mihi dolor cordis mei" (I am weak, and exceedingly impaired; the grief of my heart forceth lamentation from me). The Vulgate excerpts read "infirmus sum . . . conturbata sunt ossa mea; . . . Laboravi in gemitu meo" (I am weak . . . my bones are afflicted; . . . I have suffered in my groaning). **feeble . . . weak, groan . . . sigh** KP's doublings. **sore** very.

582. **I . . . tilestone** KP expansively renders Fisher's recasting of excerpts from Psalm 21:15–16: "Sicut aqua proiectus sum, separata est fortitudo mea, et instar teste exaruit tota" (I am cast out like water; my strength is disjoined, and it is all dried up like a clay pot). The excerpts read "Sicut aqua effusus sum. . . . Aruit tamquam testa virtus mea" (I am poured out like water. . . . My strength is dried up like a clay pot). **gone . . . dried up** KP's doubling. **tilestone** a brick, or the dried clay from which bricks are made.

583. **Have . . . folly** KP expansively renders Fisher's splicing of reiterated phrasing from the Psalms with a recast excerpt from David's prayer in 2 Kings (2 Samuel) 24:20: "Miserere mei, Deus, miserere me, nec imputes mihi peccata, quae stultè commisi" (Have mercy on me, God, have mercy on me; do not impute to me sins that I have foolishly committed). The excerpt from 2 Kings reads "precor Domine, ut transferas iniquitatem servi tui, quia stulte egi nimis" (I pray, Lord, that Thou put aside the iniquity of Thy servant, for I have acted very foolishly).

584. **Remember . . . case** KP expansively renders Fisher's splicing of recast excerpts from Psalm 24:7, 16–17: "Noli meminisse meorum retro peccatorum, antevertant ea misericordiae tuae, quia miser sum nimis" (Remember not my sins in the past; let Thy mercies come before them, for I am very wretched). The excerpts read "Delicta juventutis meae, et ignorantias meas ne memineris. Secundum misericordiam tuam memento me tu:. . . quia unicus et pauper sum ego" (Remember Thou not the sins of my youth and my transgressions. According to Thy mercy remember Thou me . . . for I am alone and feeble). **marvelous** astonishingly. KP makes memorable use of the adjective in a postscript to a letter written to Thomas Seymour in early 1547, recalling her earlier attraction to him at the time that Henry VIII decided to make her his wife: "God is a marvelous man" (see no. 2 in part 4 of the correspondence section).

585. **I . . . day** KP closely renders Fisher's recasting of Psalm 37:7: "Debilitatus et attritus sum valde, merens ingredior omni die." The verse reads "Miser factus sum, et curvatus sum usque

And now, O Lord, what look I after? Verily, my soul looketh to Thee for help.[586]

Show now and declare Thy goodness to me, and withhold not Thy help from me.[587]

My soul is replenished with troubles and adversities, and draweth near unto death's door.[588]

I am in great poverty and need, and my heart is sore troubled within me.[589]

Cast me not away in the time of my most necessity; and now when my strength faileth me, fail not Thou me, O Lord.[590]

Deliver me from mine enemies, and make me not a mocking-stock to them, that jest and rattle upon me.

---

in finem: tota die contristatus ingrediebar" (I am made poor, and I am bowed to the utmost; I walk about mourning all the day long).

586. **And . . . help** KP expansively renders Fisher's recasting of exceerpts from Psalm 24:1–2: "Et nunc quid exspecto domine? certe anima mea ad te respicit" (And now what do I look for, Lord? surely my soul looks to Thee). The excerpts read "Ad te Domine levavi animam meam: Deus meus in te confido" (To Thee, Lord, have I lifted my soul: my God, I trust in Thee).

587. **Show . . . me** KP freely renders Fisher's recasting of Psalm 39:12: "Ostende mihi bonitatem tuam, et salutare tuum à me ne contineas" (Show me Thy goodness, and withhold not Thy salvation from me). The verse reads "Tu autem Domine ne longe facias miserationes tuas a me: misericordia tua et veritas tua semper susceperunt me" (Do not, Lord, withhold Thy lovingkindness from me: let Thy mercy and Thy truth ever preserve me). **Show . . . declare** KP's doubling.

588. **My . . . door** KP expansively renders Fisher's near verbatim quotation of Psalm 87:4: "Satiatur malis anima mea, et inferno appropinquavit" (My soul is overfilled with evils, and hath approached the region below). The verse reads "repleta est malis anima mea: et vita mea inferno appropinquavit" (my soul is filled with evils, and my life hath approached the region below). **is replenished** KP's verb is closer to the Vulgate's "repleta est" than is Fisher's "Satiatur," suggesting that she recognized the source text. **troubles . . . adversities** KP's doubling. **death's door** KP's rendering of "inferno" aptly Christianizes the "region below" while introducing an idiomatic English turn of phrase; see the introduction, p. 207.

589. **I . . . me** KP expansively renders Fisher's near verbatim quotation of an excerpt from Psalm 108:22: "Egenus et pauper ego sum, et cor meum conturbatur intra me" (I am needy and poor, and my heart is confused within me). The Vulgate excerpt reads identically except for having a compound passive verb, "conturbatum est," in place of "conturbatur." **in . . . need** KP's phrasal expansion of the predicate adjectives "egenus et pauper" (needy and poor). **sore** very—KP's intensification.

590. **Cast . . . Lord** KP expansively renders Fisher's recasting of Psalm 70:9: "Ne abjicias me angustiae tempore, et cum iam virtus mea deficit, tu me ne deficias" (Depart not from me in the time of difficulty; and now when my strength faileth, fail Thou me not). The verse reads "Ne projicias me in tempore senectutis: cum defecerit virtus mea, ne derelinquas me" (Cast me not away in the time of old age; when my strength shall fail, forsake me not). **Cast . . . away** KP's phrasing renders the Vulgate's "projicias" exactly, as Fisher's "abjicias" does not. She seems to have recognized the source verse. **most** KP's intensification. See n459 on Psalm 70:9.

[Iv v] Save me from these roaring lions ready to devour, and from the hands of them that would have my life from me.[591]

I do cry to Thee, O Lord; for Thou art my hope, and my portion in the land of livers.

Bring my soul out of prison, and set my feet in a place where I may walk at liberty.[592]

Turn not Thy face away from me, lest I be made like unto them that descend into the pit.

Give ear unto my prayers, for I am punished and brought very low.

Deliver me from my persecutors, for they be much stronger than I.

[Ivi r] O Lord, hear me speedily, lest my spirit fail within me.

Deliver my soul out of trouble, and in Thy mercy destroy all mine enemies.

And make them to perish, which would destroy me, for I am Thy servant. Amen.[593]

591. **Deliver . . . from me** KP freely renders Fisher's splicing of recast excerpts from Psalms 30:16 and 34:15–17: "Ab inimicis meis eripe me, opprobrium mihi insultantibus ne me ponas. Libera me de rugientibus ad escam paratis, de manibus quaetentium animam meam" (Deliver me from my enemies; make me not a reproach among those who insult me. Save me from the roaring beasts ready to eat me, from the hands of those who are seeking my soul). The first excerpt reads "Eripe me de manu inimicorum meorum" (Deliver me from the hand of my enemies). The excerpts that follow read "Et adversum me laetati sunt . . . subsannaverunt me subsannatione. . . . Domine, . . . restitue animam meam a malignitate eorum, a leonibus" (They have been joyful against me . . . they have insulted me with mockery. . . . Lord . . . rescue my soul from their malice, from the lions). **mocking-stock** a synonym for "laughing-stock," noted by the *OED* as occurring frequently in the sixteenth and seventeenth centuries. **jest . . . rattle** KP's doubling. **rattle** rail at, rendering "subsannaverunt" (insulted). **would . . . life** KP's aptly idiomatic rendering of "quaerentium animam meam" (are seeking my soul).

592. **I . . . liberty** KP quite closely renders Fisher's splicing of recast excerpts from Psalms 146:6, 8 and 30:9: "Clamo ad te domine, quoniam tu es spes mea, et portio mea in terra viventium. Educ de carcere animam meam, et in spacioso loco pedes meos sistas." The first set of excerpts reads "Clamavi ad te Domine. . . . Tu es spes mea, portio mea in terra viventium. . . . Educ de custodia animam meum" (I have cried unto Thee, Lord. . . . Thou art my hope, my portion in the land of the living. . . . Lead my soul out of confinement). The final excerpt reads "statuisti in loco spatioso pedes meos" (Thou hast set my feet in an ample place). **may . . . liberty** KP's effective expansion of Fisher's and the Vulgate's "in spacioso loco" (in an ample place).

593. **Turn . . . Amen** KP closely renders Fisher's splicing and reordering of recast excerpts from Psalms 142:7, 12 and 141:7–8: "Ne avertas faciem tuam à me, ne similis fiam descendentibus in lacum. Intende ad preces meas, quia humiliatus et contristatus sum. Libera me à persequentibus me, quia robusti sunt supra me. Velociter exaudi me domine, ne deficiat in me spiritus meus. Educ de tribulatione animam meam, et in misericordia tua disperde omnes inimicos meos. Et perde eos qui me perdere volunt, quoniam ego servus tuus sum. Amen." The reordered halves of Psalm 142:7 read "Non avertas faciem tuam a me: et similis ero descendentibus in lacum. . . . Velociter exaudi me Domine: defecit spiritus meus" (Turn not Thy face from me, lest I be like them that go down into the pit. . . . Hear me speedily, Lord; my spirit

THE THIRTEENTH PSALM, IN WHICH HE GIVETH THANKS TO GOD THAT HIS ENEMIES HAVE NOT GOTTEN THE OVERHAND OF HIM.[594]

I will magnify and praise Thee, O Lord God, for Thou hast exalted me and set me up; and my enemies have not gotten the overhand of me.

O Lord of hosts, I have cried unto Thee, and Thou hast saved me.

[Ivi v] Thou hast brought my soul out of hell; Thou hast holden me up from falling into the deep lake, from whence no man returneth.[595]

Thou hast not closed me up in the hand of mine enemies, but Thou hast set my feet in a place both wide and broad.[596]

---

faileth). The excerpts from Psalm 141 read "Intende ad deprecationem meam: quia humiliatus sum nimis. Libera me a persequentibus me: quia confortati sunt super me. Educ de custodia animam meam" (Attend unto my prayer: for I am brought very low. Deliver me from them who persecute me, for they are stronger than I. Lead my soul out of confinement). Psalm 142:12 reads "et in misericordia tua disperdes inimicos meos. Et perdes omnes, qui tribulant animam meam: quoniam ego servus tuus sum" (and in Thy mercy, destroy my enemies. And let them perish, who oppress my soul, for I am Thy servant).

594. **In . . . him** KP closely renders Fisher's "In quo gratias agit deo, quod non praevaluerunt hostes."

595. **I will . . . returneth** KP freely renders Fisher's recasting of Psalm 29:2–4: "Laudibus te celebrabo domine Deus, quoniam exaltasti me, et non praevaluerunt inimici mei super me. Domine exercituum ad te clamavi, et tu salvasti me. Extraxisti ab inferis animam meam, tenuisti me ne ruerem in profundum lacum, unde nullus reditus" (With praises I will celebrate Thee, Lord God, for Thou hast exalted me; and my enemies have not prevailed over me. Lord of hosts, I have called unto Thee, and Thou hast saved me. Thou hast drawn my soul out from the depths; Thou hast held me lest I fall into the deep pit, from which no one returneth). The verses read "Exaltabo te Domine quoniam suscepisti me: nec delectasti inimicos super me. Domine Deus meus clamavi ad te, et sanasti me. Domine eduxisti ab inferno animam meam: salvasti me a descendentibus in lacum" (I will exalt Thee, Lord, for Thou hast raised me up; nor hast Thou made my enemies pleased over me. Lord, my God, I have cried unto Thee, and Thou hast healed me. Lord, Thou hast brought my soul up from hell; Thou hast saved me from among those that go down into the pit). **exalted . . . up** KP's doubling. **gotten . . . overhand** a characteristically idiomatic phrasal exapansion of Fisher's "praevaluerunt" (prevailed). **lake** KP again employs (cf. n572) a cognate of "lacus" (pit, den).

596. **Thou hast . . . broad** KP quite closely renders Fisher's reuse of Psalm 30:9 (see n592), which he here quotes nearly verbatim and in its entirety: "Non conclusisti me in manibus inimicorum meorum, imo statuisti in loco spacioso pedes meos." The verse reads "Nec conclusisti me in manibus inimici: statuisti in loco spacioso pedes meos" (Thou hast not shut me up in the hands of my enemy; Thou hast set my feet in a spacious place). **a place . . . broad** KP's doubling may indicate that she did not recognize Fisher's reuse of this verse, because she translated his first use of this phrase periphrastically, as "a place where I may walk at liberty." Alternatively, she may have recognized the reuse and sought to offset it with stylistic variation; see the introduction, p. 210.

I have sought Thee, and Thou hast heard me; Thou hast brought me into liberty out of great distress.[597]

Thou hast turned my sorrow into gladness; Thou hast ceased my mourning, and compassed me round about with mirth.[598]

Thou hast declared Thy great magnificence in helping Thy servant.

Thou hast done mercifully with me in my miseries.[599]

[Ivii r] Thou hast regarded the pain of the poor; Thou hast not turned away Thy face from me.[600]

I will ever be singing and speaking of Thy mercies, and I will publish to other Thy fidelity and truth so long as I shall live.[601]

My mouth shall never cease to speak of Thy righteousness and of Thy benefits, which be so many that I cannot number them.[602]

597. **I have . . . distress** KP quite closely renders Fisher's recasting of Psalm 33:4: "Quaesivi te, et exaudisti me, et de angustiis meis liberum me fecisti." The verse reads "Exquisivi Dominum, et exaudivit me: et ex omnibus tribulationibus meis eripuit me" (I have sought out the Lord, and He heard me; and He delivered me from all my tribulations). **brought . . . distress** KP's clarifying phrasal expansion of Fisher's "de angustiis meis liberum me fecisti" (made me free from my difficulties).

598. **Thou . . . mirth** KP closely renders Fisher's recasting of Psalm 29:12: "Convertisti dolorem in gaudium mihi, dissoluisti luctum meum, et circundedisti me laetitia." The verse reads "Convertisti planctum meum in gaudium mihi: conscidisti saccum meum, et circumdedisti me laetitia" (Thou hast turned my mourning into joy for me; Thou hast torn my sackcloth in pieces, and hast surrounded me with joy).

599. **Thou . . . miseries** KP closely renders Fisher's expansive recasting of Psalm 17:51: "Magnificasti salutem tuam servo tuo, fecisti misericordiam mecum in miseriis meis." In the Vulgate, where the subject is King David, not a servant, the verse reads "magnificans salutes regis ejus, et faciens misericordiam christo suo, David" (magnifying the deliverance of His king, and doing mercy to His anointed, David).

600. **Thou hast . . . me** KP quite closely renders Fisher's recasting of an excerpt from Psalm 21:25: "Non contempsisti afflictionem pauperis, nec avertisti à me faciem tuam." The excerpt reads "neque despexit deprecationem pauperis: nec avertit faciem suam a me" (He hath not despised the prayer of the poor man: nor hath He turned His face from me). **Thou . . . regarded** KP gives a positive rendering of Fisher's "Non contempsisti" (Thou hast not disdained).

601. **I . . . live** KP expansively renders Fisher's splicing of recast excerpts from Psalms 100:1 and 142:2: "Misericordias tuas in aeternum cantabo, notam faciam veritatem tuam in vita mea" (I will sing Thy mercies forever; I will make known Thy truth during my life). The first excerpt reads "Misericordiam, et judicium cantabo tibi Domine" (I will sing of mercy and judgment to Thee, Lord). The second excerpt reads "laudabo Dominum in vita mea" (I will praise the Lord during my life). **will . . . be singing . . . speaking of, fidelity . . . truth** KP's intensifying doublings.

602. **My . . . them** KP expansively renders Fisher's condensed recasting of Psalm 70:15: "Os meum narrabit justitiam tuam, omne tempore beneficia tua, certe non novi numerum" (My mouth shall tell of Thy righteousness [and] at all times of Thy benefits; surely I have not known

But I will give Thee thanks till death take me away; I will sing in the praise of Thee so long as I shall continue.[603]

I will triumph and rejoice in Thy mercy, for that Thou hast looked upon my necessities and regarded my soul in my great distress.[604]

Thou hast been my sure refuge, and the strength of my trust and hope.[605]

[Ivii v] I thank Thee, Lord, for Thy goodness always, and for Thy exceeding mercy.[606]

Thou hast been my comfort in the time of my trouble; Thou hast been merciful unto me, O Lord, and hast revenged the wrongs that mine enemies have done to me.[607]

[their] number). The verse reads "Os meum annunciabit justitiam tuam: tota die salutare tuum. Quoniam non cognovi litteraturam" (My mouth shall declare Thy justice [and] Thy salvation all the day. For I have not learned their recorded [amount]). **which . . . them** KP's idiomatic clarification of Fisher's "non novi numerum" (I have not known [their] number).

603. **But . . . continue** KP closely renders Fisher's splicing of recast excerpts from Psalms 6:6 and 103:33: "Sed gratias agam donec mors me rapiat, tibi psallam quàmdiu fuero." The first excerpt reads "in morte . . . quis confitebitur tibi?" (in death . . . who shall acknowledge Thee?). The second excerpt reads "psallam Deo meo quamdiu sum" (I will sing praise to my God as long as I am [alive]).

604. **I . . . distress** KP closely renders Fisher's near verbatim quotation of Psalm 30:8: "Exultabo et letabor in misericordia tua, quoniam respexisti necessitates meas, et cognovisti [1544: consolatus es] in angustiis animam meam." KP's "Thou hast looked upon" renders "cognovisti" in the Cologne edition rather than the "consolatus es" (Thou hast comforted) in the first London edition. In the Vulgate the verse reads "exultabo et laetabor in misericordia tua. Quoniam respexisti humilitatem meam, salvasti de necessitatibus animam meam" (I will exult and rejoice in Thy mercy, for Thou hast looked upon my lowness; Thou hast saved my soul from inevitable [things]).

605. **Thou . . . hope** KP closely renders Fisher's splicing of recast excerpts from Psalm 17:2–3: "Fuisti mihi in firmum refugium, et in fortitudinem fiduciae meae." The excerpts read "Dominus firmamentum meum, et refugium meum . . . et sperabo in eum" (The Lord [is] my support, and my refuge . . . and I will hope in Him). **trust . . . hope** KP's doubling. Her addition of "hope" brings her phrasing closer to the Vulgate's "sperabo" (I will hope) than Fisher's is, indicating that she may have recognized the source text.

606. **I . . . mercy** KP closely renders what appears to be a generic and general versicle of Fisher's own composing: "Gratulor tibi domine pro sempiterna bonitate tua, et misericordia tua immensa."

607. **Thou . . . me** KP expansively renders Fisher's splicing of recast excerpts from Psalms 118:50 and 98:8: "Tu consolatus es me in tempore malo; Deus tu propitius mihi fuisti, et ultus es injuriam inimicorum meorum" (Thou hast been a consolation to me in a bad time; God, Thou hast been favorable to me, and hast revenged the injury of my enemies). The first excerpt reads "Haec me consolata est in humilitate mea" (This [hope in God] has consoled me in my abasement). The second excerpt reads "Deus tu propitius fuisti eis, et ulciscens in omnes adinventiones eorum" (God, Thou hast been gracious to them, while taking vengeance on all their inventions).

According to the multitude of the heavy thoughts that I had in my mind, Thy comforts have cheered and lightened my heart.[608]

Thou hast sent me now joy for the days wherein I was in sorrow, and for the years in whom I suffered many a painful storm.[609]

Thou hast called to remembrance the rebuke that Thy servant hath been put to, and how furiously mine enemies have persecuted me.

[lviii r] O Lord God of hosts, who may be compared unto Thee? Thou art great, and greatly to be praised.[610]

Thou art high upon all the earth; Thou art exalted far above all gods.[611]

Glory and honor before Thy face, holiness and magnificence in Thy sanctuary:[612]

608. **According . . . heart** KP closely renders Fisher's recasting of Psalm 93:19: "Pro multitudine cogitationum mearum intra me, consolationes tuae laetificaverunt animam meam." The verse reads "Secundum multitudinem dolorum meorum in corde meo: consolationes tuae laetificaverunt animam meam" (According to the multitude of my sorrows within me, Thy consolations have cheered my soul). **have . . . lightened** KP's doubling for rhetorical highlighting. **my heart** KP's idiomatic substitution for a literal rendering of "animam meam" (my soul).

609. **Thou . . . storm** KP expamsively renders Fisher's recasting of Psalm 89:15: "Gaudium mihi dedisti pro diebus quibus adflictus fui, pro annis quibus mala tuli multa" (Thou hast given me joy for the days in which I was afflicted, for the years in which I have borne many evils). The verse reads "Laetati sumus pro diebus, quibus nos humiliasti: annis, quibus vidimus mala" (We have been glad for the days in which Thou hast brought us low, for the years in which we have seen evils). **in . . . storm** KP's addition. **whom** a former variant of "which."

610. **Thou . . . praised** KP expansively renders Fisher's splicing of recast and reordered excerpts from Psalms 88:51–52, 9 and 95:4: "Recordatus es obprobrii servi tui, et in furore quomodo persequebantur me inimici mei. Domine Deus exercituum, quis similis tibi? fortissime Deus magnus es tu, et laudabilis multum" (Thou hast remembered the reproaches of Thy servant, and with what kind of fury my enemies have persecuted me. Lord God of hosts, who is like unto Thee? most mighty God, great art Thou, and much to be praised). The excerpts from Psalm 88 read "Memor esto Domine opprobrii servorum tuorum . . . Quod exprobraverunt inimici tui Domine. . . . Domine Deus virtutum, quis similis tibi? potens es Domine" (Remember, Lord, the reproach of Thy servants . . . With which Thy enemies have upbraided [them], Lord. . . . Lord God of hosts, who is like unto Thee? Thou art mighty, Lord). The excerpt from Psalm 95 reads "magnus Dominus, et laudabilis nimis" (the Lord is great, and beyond measure to be praised).

611. **Thou . . . gods** KP closely renders Fisher's near verbatim quotation of Psalm 96:9: "Tu excelsus es super omnem terram, nimis exaltatus es super omnes deos." The verse reads "tu Dominus altissimus super omnem terram: nimis exaltatus es super omnes deos" (Thou, Lord, art most high above all the earth; above all gods Thou art to be exalted beyond measure).

612. **Glory . . . sanctuary** KP quite closely renders Fisher's free recasting of excerpts from Psalm 28:2: "Gloria et decor ante vultum tuum, sanctitas et magnificentia in sanctuario tuo" (Glory and seemliness before Thy face, holiness and magnificence in Thy sanctuary). The excerpts read "afferte Domino gloriam et honorem, . . . adorate Dominum in atrio sancto ejus" (give glory and honor to the Lord, . . . worship the Lord in His holy dwelling). **honor** KP does not translate Fisher's "decor" (seemliness) but rather the Vulgate's "honorem," indicating that she recognized this source text.

With justice and judgment Thy royal throne is stablished; mercy and truth go before Thy face.[613]

Blessed art Thou, O Lord, which hast not holden back Thy mercy from Thy servant.[614]

After that I had long looked for Thee, O Lord, at the last Thou didst attend unto me, and heardst my cry.

[Iviii v] Thou hast taken me out of the lake of misery, and set my feet upon a rock, and made my steps sure.[615]

Thou hast given me my desire; I have seen Thy joyful countenance.[616]

Thou hast stricken all my adversaries, and hast abated their strength.[617]

Thou hast rebuked the rabblement of them that vexed me, and hast plucked me forth of their hands.[618]

613. **With . . . face** KP quite closely renders Fisher's near verbatim quotation of Psalm 88:15: "Justitia et judicium firmamentum throni tui, misericordia et veritas faciem tuam praecedunt." The verse reads "Justitia et judicium praeparatio sedis tuae. Misericordia et veritas praecedent faciem tuam" (Justice and judgment are the preparation of Thy throne. Mercy and truth shall go before Thy face). **royal** KP's addition.

614. **Blessed . . . servant** KP closely renders Fisher's recasting of excerpts from Psalm 65:20: "Benedictus es domine, qui non retinuisti misericordiam tuam à servo tuo." The excerpts read "Benedictus Deus, qui non amovit . . . misericordiam suam a me" (Blessed be God, who hath not withdrawn . . . His mercy from me).

615. **After . . . sure** KP freely renders Fisher's recasting of Psalm 39:2–3: "Quum diu exspectavissem te domine, tandem adtendisti mihi, et clamorem meum audisti. Eduxisti me de lacu miseriae, et de luto limi, statuisti supra petram pedes meos, et gressus meos solidasti" (As long as I shall have awaited Thee, Lord, so long hast Thou attended to me, and hast heard my cry. Thou hast brought me up from the pit of misery and the muddy clay; Thou hast set my feet upon a rock and hast established my steps). The verses read "Exspectans exspectavi Dominum, et intendit mihi. Et exaudivit preces meas: et eduxit me de lacu miseriae, et de luto faecis. Et statuit super petram pedes meos: et direxit gressus meos" (Expectant, I have looked for the Lord, and He hath attended to me. He hath heard my prayers, and hath brought me up from the pit of misery and the filthy clay. And He hath set my feet upon a rock, and He hath made my steps straight).

616. **Thou . . . countenance** KP closely renders Fisher's reordering of recast excerpts from Psalm 4:7: "Desiderium meum mihi dedisti, vidi laetitiam vultus tui." The excerpts read "dedisti laetitiam in corde meo. . . . Signatum est . . . lumen vultus tui Domine" (Thou hast given joy in my heart. . . . Manifest is . . . the light of Thy countenance, Lord).

617. **Thou . . . strength** KP moderates as she renders Fisher's splicing of recast excerpts from Psalms 3:8 and 67:22: "Percussisti omnes adversarios meos, et virtutem eorum confregisti" (Thou hast thrust my enemies through and through; Thou hast broken their strength in pieces). The Vulgate excerpts read "tu percussisti omnes adversantes mihi" (Thou hast thrust all my adversaries through and through); "Deus confringet capita inimicorum suorum" (God shall break in pieces the heads of His enemies). On possible evidence of a feminine sense of decorum in KP's stylistic choices, see the introduction, n19.

618. **Thou . . . hands** KP expansively renders Fisher's splicing of recast excerpts from Psalms 9:6 and 17:1: "Increpasti turbam infestantium, et evulsisti me de manibus eorum" (Thou hast

Thou hast cast them headlong into their own pit; their feet be wrapped in the net which they laid privily for me.[619]

Mine enemies are recoiled back; they are fallen down and destroyed from Thy sight.[620]

[Ki r] Thou hast been the poor man's defense, and his helper in tribulation, when most need was.

Thou hast done judgment for me; Thou hast defended my cause against my accusers.[621]

And although Thou were very angry with me a little while, yet now I live through Thy mercy and goodness.[622]

Verily I supposed with myself, that I was clean cast away out of Thy favor.

But Thou hast heard my prayers, and according to Thy great mercy hast taken me again into Thy favor.[623]

---

rebuked the disorderly crowd of troublemakers, and Thou hast plucked me out of their hands). The first excerpt reads "Increpasti Gentes" (Thou hast rebuked the Gentiles, i.e., alien peoples). The second excerpt reads "David . . . in die, qua erupuit eum Dominus de manu omnium inimicorum ejus" (David . . . on the day in which the Lord plucked him out of the hand of all his enemies). **rabblement** mob, rendering "turba" (a disorderly crowd).

619. **Thou . . . for me** KP closely renders Fisher's recasting and reordering of excerpts from Psalm 56:7: "Precipitasti eos in foveam suam, in reti quod pro me abscondiderunt, pedes eorum illaqueantur." The excerpts read "Laqueum paraverunt pedibus meis . . . Foderunt ante faciem meam foveam: et inciderunt in eam" (They have prepared a snare for my feet . . . They have digged a pit before my face, and they have fallen into it).

620. **Mine . . . sight** KP freely renders Fisher's recasting of Psalm 9:4: "Reversi sunt inimici mei retrorsum, corruerunt, et perierunt à facie tua" (My enemies have been turned back; they will fall and will come to nothing before Thy face). The verse reads "in convertendo inimicum meum retrorsum: infirmabuntur, et peribunt a facie tua" (in the turning back of my enemies, they shall weaken amd shall perish before Thy face). **are recoiled** have retreated.

621. **Thou hast been . . . accusers** KP closely renders Fisher's splicing of recast excerpts from Psalm 9:10, 5: "Fuisti munimentum inopi, adjutor in op[p]ortunitatibus in tribulatione. Fecisti judidium pro me, et egisti causam meam contra accusatores meos." The excerpts read "Et factus est Dominus refugium pauperi: adjutor in opportunitatibus, in tribulatione. . . . Quoniam fecisti judicium meum et causam meam" (And the Lord has been made a refuge for the poor man, a helper in good times, [and] in tribulation . . . For Thou hast settled my case and my cause). **when . . . was** KP's apt phrasal expansion of "in opportunitatibus" (in good times).

622. **And . . . goodness** KP closely renders Fisher's strenuous recasting of excerpts from Psalm 88:47, 50: "Et licet ad momentum exardebat ira tua, tamen vita iam in repropitiatione tua." The corresponding Vulgate excerpts are anguished questions, not affirmations as in Fisher: "Domine avertis in finem: exardescet sicut ignis ira tua? . . . Ubi sunt misericordiae tuae antiquae Domine?" (Lord, wilt Thou finally turn? Will Thy anger burn like fire? . . . Where are Thy former mercies, Lord?). **mercy . . . goodness** KP's doubling, aptly clarifying Fisher's "repropitiatione" (reconciliation).

623. **Verily . . . into Thy favor** KP expansively renders Fisher's splicing of excerpts from Psalms 30:23 and 68:17: "Putabam equidem, quòd penitus abjectus essem à conspectu tuo. Sed

[Ki v] O Lord, of Thine own mind and will Thou hast given strength unto my soul; but when Thou hiddest Thy face from me, O Lord, how greatly was I astonished.[624]

When I was in adversity, then I cried unto Thee, and Thou didst answer me; when my soule was in great anguish and trouble, then, O Lord, I did remember Thee.[625]

I have tasted and seen how sweet Thou art; truly blessed is that man that trusteth in Thee.[626]

According to Thy name, so is Thy commendation and praise; but Thy counsels touching us be without example, and greater than can with words be expressed.[627]

---

tu preces meas audisti, et pro abundantia misericordiae tuae recepisti me in gratiam tuam" (Truly I thought inwardly that I had been cast away from Thy sight. But Thou hast heard my prayers, and in the abundance of Thy mercy hast Thou received me into Thy favor/grace). The excerpt from Psalm 30 reads "Ego autem dixi in excessu mentis meae: Projectus sum a facie oculorum tuorum. Ideo exaudisti vocem orationis meae" (For I said in the aberration of my mind: I have been cast from the sight of Thine eyes. Therefore Thou hast heard the voice of my prayer). The excerpt from Psalm 68 reads "benigna est misericordia tua . . . secundum multitudinem miserationum tuarum respice in me" (Thy mercy is kind . . . according to the multitude of Thy lovingkindness look upon me). **out . . . favor** The first occurrence of "favor" in this versicle appears to be KP's penslip or the printer's eyeskip. The corresponding phrase in Fisher is "à conspectu tuo" (from Thy sight). The second occurrence of "favor" in this versicle accurately renders Fisher"s "gratia" (favor, grace).

624. **O . . . astonished** KP closely renders Fisher's recasting of Psalm 29:8: "Domine in voluntate tua robur animae meae dedisti, cum absconderis faciem tuam, quam turbatus eram." The verse reads "Domine in voluntate tua, praestitisti decori meo virtutem. Avertisti faciem tuam a me, et factus sum conturbatus" (Lord, by Thy will Thou hast maintained strength fitting for me. Thou hast turned Thy face from me, and I have been confounded). **mind . . . will** KP's doubling to heighten the antithesis expressed in the versicle.

625. **When . . . Thee** KP expansively renders Fisher's splicing and reordering of recast excerpts from Psalm 76:2–4: "Ad te clamavi de tribulatione mea, et respondisti mihi, cum angustiaretur in me anima mea, tui Domine recordabar" (I have cried unto Thee from my tribulation, and Thou hast answered me; when my soul was anguished within me, I did remember Thee, Lord). The Vulgate excerpts read "ad Dominum clamavi . . . in die tribulationis meae . . . et intendit mihi. . . . Renuit consolari anima mea, memor fui Dei" (I have cried unto the Lord . . . in the day of my tribulation . . . and He heard me. . . . My soul refused to be comforted; I remembered God). **When . . . adversity** KP expands Fisher's adverbial phrase "de tribulatione mea" (from my tribulation) into an idiomatic English clause. **great . . . trouble** KP's doubling for rhetorical emphasis.

626. **I . . . Thee** KP closely renders Fisher's slight recasting of Psalm 33:9: "Degustavi, et vidi quàm suavis es tu, certe felix est quisquis in te sperat." The verse reads "Gustate, et videte quoniam suavis est Dominus: beatus vir, qui sperat in eo" (Taste and see how sweet the Lord is; blessed is the man who trusteth in Him).

627. **According . . . expressed** KP expansively renders Fisher's splicing of a quotation from Psalm 47:11 with a near quotation from Psalm 39:5: "Secundum nomen tuum sic est laus tua, sed consilia tua erga nos, exemplo carent [1544: non carent] et maiora sunt, quàm manifestari possint" (According to Thy name, so is Thy praise, but Thy counsels regarding us [do not] lack for

[Kii r] Dominion, power, and glory be Thine, for Thou hast made all things; and because Thy will is so, they do still continue.[628]

Thy name be blessed, praised, and magnified, both now and ever, and world without end. Amen.[629]

THE FOURTEEN[TH] PSALM, IN WHICH THE GOODNESS OF GOD IS PRAISED.[630]

O Lord our Governor, how wonderful is Thy majesty throughout the whole world, which hast set Thy glory above all the heavens.

What is man that Thou magnifiest him so greatly? or the son of man that Thou dost visit him?[631]

---

a precedent, and they are greater than they may be shown to be). KP's amelioration of the mistaken reading, "carent" (lack), in the Cologne edition accords with "non carent" (do not lack) in the first English edition, but may have been made independently. The first Vulgate excerpt reads identically with Fisher except for inserting a vocative, "Deus" (God). The second excerpt reads "Beatus vir, cuius est nomen Domini spes ejus" (Blessed is the man, whose hope is the name of the Lord). **commendation . . . praise** KP's doubling.

628. **Dominion . . . continue** KP closely renders Fisher's splicing of a recast excerpt from Jude 25 with one from Psalm 134:6 and with a phrase evidently of his own composition: "Tuum est imperium et potentia, et gloria, quia tu fecisti omnia et propter voluntatem tuam adhuc consistunt." The Jude excerpt reads " soli Deo . . . gloria et . . . imperium et potestas" (to God alone . . . be glory and . . . dominion and power). The Psalm excerpt reads "Omnia quaecumque voluit, Deus fecit" (God hath made all things, whatsoever He willeth). **because . . . continue** KP slightly expands Fisher's addition, "propter voluntatem tuam adhuc consistunt" (on account of Thy will, they [all things] remain such).

629. **Thy . . . Amen** KP expansively renders Fisher's near verbatim quotation of Psalm 112:2: "Sit nomen tuum benedictum, ex hoc nunc et usque in sempiternum" (Thy name be blessed, from this time forth and for evermore). The verse reads "Sit nomen Domini benedictum, ex hoc nunc, et usque in saeculum" (Let the name of the Lord be blessed, from this time forth and continually for ages).

630. **In . . . praised** KP renders Fisher's subtitle, "In quo divina laudatur bonitas" (In which divine goodness is praised).

631. **O . . . him?** KP expansively renders Fisher's splicing of slightly recast excerpts from Psalm 8:2,5: "Domine dominus noster, quam admiranda est majestas tua per universam terram? qui dedisti laudem tuam super omnes coelos. Quid est homo quod usque adeo eum magnificas? aut filius hominis quoniam visitas eum?" (Lord, our Lord, how admirable is Thy majesty throughout all the earth, who hast bestowed Thy glory above the heavens. What is man, that Thou magnifiest him so greatly? or the son of man, that Thou visitest him?). The Vulgate excerpts read "Domine Dominus noster, quam admirabile est nomen tuum in universa terra. . . . Quid est homo, quod memor es ejus? aut filius hominis, quoniam visitas eum?" (Lord, our Lord, how admirable is Thy name in the whole earth. . . . What is man, that Thou art mindful of him? or the son of man, since Thou visitest him?). **our Governor** This, rather than the literal rendering "our Lord," is the wording of this verse in Coverdale's and the Great Bible, indicating that KP recognized the source text.

O Lord, Thou art great, and much to be praised in Thy holy hill.[632]

[Kii v] Praise be unto Thee, O Lord God: let our vows made to Thee, be always performed.[633]

Confession and magnificence are Thy work, and Thy righteousness continueth for evermore.[634]

Thou hast done many things, O Lord God, both marvelous and great; and there is none that can be like unto Thee in Thy works.[635]

Thy ways be just and true; who will not fear and dread Thee, and magnify Thy name?[636]

I thank Thee, O Lord God, with all my heart, and I will hallow Thy name forever.[637]

632. **O . . . hill** KP closely renders Fisher's recasting of excerpts from Psalm 47:2: "Magnus es domine, et multum laudandus in monte sanctitatis tuae." The excerpts read "Magnus Dominus, et laudabilis nimis . . . in monte sancto ejus" (Great is the Lord, and very greatly to be praised . . . in His holy mountain). **holy hill** This, rather than the literal rendering "holy mountain," is the wording of this verse in Coverdale's and the Great Bible, again indicating that KP recognized the source text.

633. **Praise . . . performed** KP closely renders Fisher's recasting of excerpts from Psalm 60:9: "Tibi hymnus Deus, tibi vota nostra in omni tempore solvantur." The excerpts read "psalmum dicam nomini tuo . . . ut reddam vota mea de die in diem" (I will recite a psalm to Thy name . . . that I may perform my vows from day to day).

634. **Confession . . . evermore** KP closely renders Fisher's minor recasting of Psalm 110:3: "Confessio et magnificentia opus tuum, et justitia tua in aeternum permanet." The verse reads "Confessio et magnificentia opus ejus: et justitia ejus manet in saeculum saeculi" (Acknowledgment and eminence [are] His work, and His righteousness endureth from age to age). **Confession** acknowledgment that a person or thing has a certain character. Translators employ paraphrase to render this elusive Vulgate term.

635. **Thou . . . works** KP closely renders Fisher's splicing of recast excerpts from Psalms 39:6 and 85:8: "Multa fecisti tu domine Deus miranda et magna, et in operibus tuis non est qui similis est tibi." The first excerpt reads "Multa fecisti tu Domine Deus meus mirabilia tua" (Lord my God, many are the wonders that Thou hast done). The second excerpt reads "Non est similis tui . . . Domine . . . secundum opera tua" (There is none like Thee . . . Lord, . . . in Thy works).

636. **Thy . . . name?** KP quite closely renders Fisher's splicing of recast excerpts from Psalms 144:17, 24:12, and 33:4: "Justae et verae sunt viae tuae, quis non timebit te, et nomen tuum magnificabit?" The excerpts read "Justus Dominus in omnibus viis suis" (The Lord [is] just in all His ways); "Quis est homo qui timet Dominum?" (Who is the man that feareth the Lord?); "Magnificate Dominum mecum et . . . nomen ejus" (Magnify with me the Lord . . . and His name). **fear . . . dread** KP's doubling for rhetorical emphasis.

637. **I . . . ever** KP closely renders Fisher's splicing of recast excerpts from Psalm 9:2 and the Lord's Prayer in Matthew 6:9 and Luke 11:2: "Gratias ago tibi, Domine Deus, ex toto corde meo, et nomen tuum in aeternum sanctificabo." The Psalm excerpt reads "Confitebor tibi Domine in toto corde meo" (I will acknowledge Thee, Lord, with my whole heart). The Lord's Prayer excerpt reads "sanctificetur nomen tuum" (hallowed be Thy name).

O Lord, Thou art my strength and my praise; Thou hast brought down mine enemies, which art a Judge even from the beginning.[638]

[Kiii r] Thy right hand is exceeding strong; Thy right hand worketh many great acts.

Thine arm is mighty and strong; and because it hath pleased Thee, Thou hast strengthened mine infirmity.[639]

I will praise Thy great and dreadful name, for it is holy.[640]

Although I have fallen, yet I am not crushed in pieces; for Thou hast sustained my hand.

I have opened and showed my way unto Thee, and in Thee I have trusted; and Thou at length hast accomplished my desires.[641]

[Kiii v] Thou hast broken the heads of mine enemies, and hast made them to stoop, which walked proudly in their sins.[642]

638. **O . . . beginning** KP closely renders Fisher's splicing of an excerpt quoted verbatim from Psalm 117:14 with recast excerpts from Psalms 49:6 and 88:11: "Fortitudo mea, et laus mea Domine, qui humilasti inimicos meos, qui judex es ab initio." The recast excerpt from Psalm 49 reads "Deus judex est" (God is a Judge). The recast excerpt from Psalm 88 reads "Tu humiliasti . . . inimicos tuos" (Thou hast brought low . . . Thine enemies).

639. **Thy . . . infirmity** KP expansively renders Fisher's splicing of recast excerpts from Psalm 88:14, 22: "Dextera tua fortissima, dextera tua multas operatur virtutes. Tuum brachium cum potentia, et in voluntate tua infirmitatem meam roborasti" (Thy right hand is very strong; Thy right hand exerciseth many strengths. With power Thine arm, and with Thy will Thou hast strengthened my infirmity). The excerpts read "Firmetur manus tua, et exaltetur dextera tua . . . tuum brachium cum potentia . . . brachium meum confortabit eum" (Thy hand is strong, and Thy right hand is raised up . . . with power Thine arm . . . My arm will strengthen him). The last excerpt is in God's voice and refers to David. **because . . . Thee** KP aptly expands Fisher's condensed phrase "in voluntate tua" (by Thy will) into a full clause.

640. **I . . . holy** KP closely renders Fisher's near verbatim quotation of Psalm 98:3: "Confitebor nomini tuo magno et terribili, quoniam sanctum est." The verse reads "Confiteantur nomini tuo magno: quoniam terribile, et sanctum est" (Let them praise Thy great name, for it is fearsome and holy).

641. **Although . . . desires** KP freely renders Fisher's splicing of recast excerpts from Psalm 36:24, 5: "Quanquam ceciderim, non sum allisus, nam tu manum meam sustentasti. Revelavi tibi viam meam, et in te speravi, et tandem optata fecisti" (Although I will have fallen, I have not been bruised; for Thou hast steadied my hand. I have disclosed my way unto Thee, and I have trusted in Thee, and at length Thou hast done the things hoped for). The excerpts read "Cum ceciderit, non collidetur: quia Dominus supponit manum suam" (Although he will have fallen, he hath not been bruised, for the Lord putteth His hand under [him]); "Revela Domino viam tuam, et spera in eo: et ipse faciet" (Disclose thy way unto God, and hope in Him; and He will bring [it] to pass).

642. **Thou . . . sins** KP somewhat freely renders Fisher's recasting of Psalm 67:22: "Fregisti capita inimicorum meorum, et verticem eorum qui superbè incedebant, in delictis suis humiliasti" (Thou hast wounded the heads of my enemies, and Thou hast brought low the scalp of them who go along proudly in their transgressions). The verse reads "Deus confringet capita

Thou hast dominion over their power; and when they be exalted and set aloft in their ways, Thou abatest their courage, and destroyest them with Thy mighty arm.[643]

In Thy name I will ever rejoice, and in Thy mercy is all my glory.[644]

Thou lovest righteousness and judgment; the earth is replenished with Thy mercy.

Thy eye looketh favorably upon them that dread Thee, and trust in Thy mercy.[645]

There shall no good thing be lacking to them that seek Thee, and they that fear Thee shall not be helpless.[646]

[Kiv r] For Thou dost order their ways, and hearest them when they cry unto Thee:[647]

---

inimicorum suorum: verticem capilli perambulantium in delictis suis" (God shall wound the heads of His enemies, the scalp of hair of one who walketh about in his transgressions). **hast . . . stoop** KP's image aptly intensifies "humiliasti" (hast brought low).

643. **Thou . . . arm** KP quite closely renders Fisher's recasting of excerpts from Psalm 88:10–11: "Tu dominaris potestati eorum, et dum elevantur in viis suis, tu compescis eos, et in brachio fortitudinis tuae illos disperdis. In nomine tuo exultabo semper, et in misericordia omnis mea gloria." The excerpts read "Tu dominaris potestati. . . . Tu humiliasti . . . superbum: in brachio virtutis tuae dispersisti inimicos tuos" (Thou hast dominion over powers. . . . Thou hast brought low . . . the proud man: with the strength of Thine arm hast Thou dispersed Thine enemies). **exalted . . . aloft** KP's doubling. **abatest . . . courage** KP offers an apt phrasal rendering of "compescis eos" (repressest them). "Abate" no longer has the senses of "beat back, blunt" that were available to her. **destroyest** an imprecise rendering of "disperdis," a verb with primary senses of "disperse, scatter."

644. **In . . . glory** KP closely renders Fisher's recasting of excerpts from Psalm 85:12–13: "In nomine tuo exultabo semper, et in misericordia tua omnis mea gloria." The excerpts read "glorificabo nomen tuum in aeternum . . . misericordia tua magna est super me" (I will glorify Thy name forever . . . Thy great mercy is above me).

645. **Thou . . . mercy** KP closely renders Fisher's reordering of recast excerpts from Psalm 32:5, 18: "Diligis justitiam et judicium, misericordia tua impleta est terra. Oculus tuus timentes te respicit, et eos qui in misericordia tua confidunt." The first excerpt reads "Diligit misericordiam et judicium: misericordia Domini plena est terra" (He loveth mercy and judgment; the earth is filled with the mercy of the Lord). The second excerpt reads "oculi Domini super metuentes eum: et in eis, qui sperant super misericordia ejus" (the eyes of the Lord [are] upon them who fear Him, and on those who trust in His mercy).

646. **There . . . helpless** KP closely renders Fisher's minor recasting of an excerpt from Psalm 33:11 and a variant reading from the Gallican Vulgate apparatus: "Quaerentibus te non deerit omne bonum, et nulla erit inopia iis, qui te timent." The excerpt reads "non est inopia timentibus eum" (there is no lack for them that fear Him). The variant reads "quaerentibus autem dominum non deerit omne bonum" (but to those that seek the Lord, no good thing shall be wanting). **helpless** destitute of (something)—a former sense that aptly renders "inopia" (lack, scarcity).

647. **For . . . Thee** KP closely renders Fisher's splicing and reordering of recast excerpts from Psalm 5:9, 2: "Tu enim dirigis vias eorum, et aurem prebes ad clamorem eorum." The first excerpt reads "Domine . . . dirige tu conspectu tuo viam meam" (Lord, . . . direct Thou my way

That Thou mayest deliver their souls from death, and assuage their pains when they be grieved.[648]

For Thou helpest them whose hearts be broken with sorrow, and bearest up with Thy hand them that be contrite in spirit.[649]

Thou savest the souls of Thy servants, and all they that trust in Thee shall not be destroyed.

Wherefore my tongue shall sing Thy praise, O Lord God; I will always magnify Thee.[650]

I will love Thee, O Lord, which art my strength, my stay, my might, my Saviour, and my refuge.

[Kiv v] My God, my Defender, and my buckler, the strength of my salvation, and my Supporter.

After that I had called upon Thee with due laud and praise, Thou hast saved me from mine enemies.

When I was in trouble I called upon Thee; Thou hast heard my voice out of Thy holy temple, and my cry hath entered up into Thine ears.

Thou hast saved me from mine adversaries that rose up ageinst me; Thou hast delivered me from wicked enemies.[651]

---

in Thy sight). The second excerpt reads "auribus percipe Domine . . . clamorem meam" (with [Thine] ears, Lord, hear . . . my cry).

648. **That . . . grieved** KP closely renders Fisher's recasting of an excerpt from Psalm 114:8: "Ut eripias à morte animas eorum, et in pressura lenias dolores eorum." The excerpt reads "Quia eripuit animam meam de morte: oculos meos a lacrymis" (For He hath delivered my soul from death, [and] my eyes from tears). **when . . . grieved** KP's apt clausal expansion of Fisher's phrase, "in pressura" (under pressures).

649. **For . . . spirit** KP closely renders Fisher's splicing of recast excerpts from Psalms 146:3 and 36:24: "Ades enim confractis corde, et spiritu contritos manu tua sustentas." The first excerpt reads "Qui sanat contritos corde: et alligat contritiones eorum" (Who healeth the brokenhearted, and bindeth their brokenness). The second excerpt, reused here (see n641), reads "Dominus supponit manum suam" (The Lord putteth His hand under [him]).

650. **Thou . . . magnify Thee** KP closely renders Fisher's splicing of recast and reordered excerpts from Psalm 33:23, 2: "Redimis animas servorum tuorum, et non devastabuntur omnes qui sperant in te. Et propterea canet lingua mea laudem tuam, domine Deus in aeternum confitebor tibi." Verse 23 reads "Redimet Dominus animas servorum suorum: et non delinquent omnes qui sperant in eo" (The Lord will save the souls of His servants, and all who trust in Him shall not be lacking). Verse 2 reads "Benedicam Dominum in omni tempore: semper laus ejus in ore meo" (I will bless the Lord at all times; His praise [shall be] ever in my mouth).

651. **I . . . enemies** KP closely renders Fisher's mostly verbatim quotation of a sequence of excerpts from Psalm 17:2–4, 7, 49: "Diligam te domine, fortitudo mea, domine firmamentum meum es tu, et robur meum, salvator meus, et refugium meum. Deus meus et propugnator meus, scutum meum, cornu salutis meae, et susceptor meus. Postquam cum laude te invocaverim, ab inimicis meis me salvasti. Cum tribularer invocavi te, exaudisti me de templo sancto tuo vocem meam, et clamor meus introivit coram te in aures tuas. Servasti me ab inimicis meis,

Thou hast taken me from the company of evil men, and mine eye hath seen upon mine enemies the things that I desired.[652]

[Kv r] And therefore if it should fortune me to pass through the dark vale of death, I will go without fear, for Thou wilt be with me; Thy rod and Thy staff shall comfort me.[653]

Thou shalt deliver me from tribulation; Thou shalt keep me from them which seek to destroy me.[654]

Mine eyes be upon Thee, O Lord, for Thou shalt bring my feet forth of the snare.[655]

---

qui insurrexerunt adversum me, ab hostibus iniquis eripuisti me." The excerpts from verses 2–4 read "Diligam te Domine, fortitudo mea . . . firmamentum meum, et refugium meum, et liberator meus. Deus meus adjutor meus . . . Protector meus, et cornu salutis meae, et susceptor meus . . . invocabo Dominum: et ab inimicis meis salvus ero" (I will love Thee, Lord, my strength . . . my support, and my refuge, and my Saviour. My God [is] my Helper . . . my Protector, and the horn of my salvation, and my Supporter . . . I will call upon the Lord, and I will be saved from my enemies). The excerpts from verse 7 read "In tribulatione mea invocavi Dominum . . . et exaudivit de templo sancto suo vocem meam: et clamor meus . . . introivit in aures ejus" (In my trouble I have called upon the Lord, . . . and He hath heard my voice from His holy temple, and my cry . . . hath entered into His ears). Verse 49 reads "[Deus est] liberator meus de inimicis meis iracundis. Et ab insurgentibus in me exaltabis me: a viro iniquo eripies me" ([God is] my Saviour from my wrathful enemies. And Thou hast lifted me up above those that are risen up against me; Thou hast delivered me from the wicked man). **due . . . praise** KP's doubling.

652. **Thou . . . desired** KP closely renders Fisher's recasting of Psalm 53:9: "Ex coetu malignantium rapuisti me, et super inimicos meos optata vidit oculus meus." The verse reads "ex omni tribulatione eripuisti me: et super inimicos meos despexit oculus meus" (Thou hast delivered me out of all trouble, and mine eye hath looked with contempt upon mine enemies). **the things . . . desired** KP expands into a clause Fisher's participle "optata" (things hoped for), which has no Vulgate counterpart.

653. **And . . . me** KP closely renders Fisher's recasting of Psalm 22:4, which incorporates a variant reading from the Gallican Vulgate apparatus: "Et propterea cum fortassis transeundum est mihi per vallem umbrae mortis, impavidus incedam, nam tu mecum eris, virga tua et baculus tuus ipsa me consolabuntur." The verse and its variant (in square brackets) read "Nam, et si ambulavero in medio [valle] umbrae mortis, non timebo mala: quoniam tu mecum es. Virga tua, et baculus tuus: ipsa me consolata sunt" (For if I walk in the midst [the valley] of the shadow of death, I will not fear evils, for Thou art with me. Thy rod and Thy staff, these have comforted me).

654. **Thou . . . me** KP quite closely renders Fisher's splicing of recast excerpts from Psalms 31:7 and 118:95: "Tu mihi refugium eris à tribulatione, custodies me, ab iis qui me perdere quaerunt." The first excerpt reads "Tu es refugium meum a tribulatione . . . erue me" (Thou art my refuge from trouble . . . deliver me). The second excerpt reads "Me expectaverunt peccatores ut perderent me" (Sinners have waited for me, that they might destroy me).

655. **Mine . . . snare** KP closely renders Fisher's slight recasting of Psalm 24:15: "Oculi mei ad te domine, quoniam tu educes de laqueo pedes meos" (My eyes [are] toward Thee, Lord, for Thou shalt lead my feet from the snare). The verse reads "Oculi mei semper ad Dominum: quo-

Unto Thee, O Lord God, I will perform my vows; I will give Thee thanks both now and evermore, and world without end. Amen.[656]

[Kv v] **THE FIFTEENTH PSALM,**

OF THE BENEFITS OF GOD, WITH THANKS FOR THE SAME.[657]

My soul praiseth Thee, O Lord, and all that is within me praiseth Thy holy name.

My soul giveth Thee humble thanks, and Thy benefits I will never forget:

Which forgivest all my sins, and healest all my infirmities.

Which hast saved my life from destruction, and showed in me Thy grace and mercy.

Which hast satisfied my desire with good things, and shalt once restore my youth again.[658]

Thou hast entreated me mercifully at all times, and hast revenged me of mine enemies.

---

niam ipse eveliet de laqueo pedes meos" (My eyes [are] ever toward the Lord, for He will pull my feet away from the snare).

656. **Unto . . . Amen** KP closely renders Fisher's recasting of Psalm 60:9: "Ad te, O Deus, sunt vota mea, reddam tibi gratiarum actiones et nunc, et in secula seculorum. Amen." The verse, used earlier (see n633), reads "Sic psalmum dicam nomini tuo in saeculum saeculi: ut reddam vota mea de die in diem" (Thus I will recite a psalm to Thy name from age to age, that I may perform my vows from day to day).

657. **Of . . . same** KP expansively renders Fisher's subtitle, "De beneficiis dei cum gratiarum actione" (Of the benefits of God, with thanksgiving).

658. **My soul praiseth . . . again** KP closely renders Fisher's minor recasting of Psalm 102:1–5: "Collaudat te anima mea, O Deus, et omnia quae intra me sunt, nomen tuum sanctum. Gratias tibi agit anima mea, et nunque tradam oblivioni universa tua beneficia. Qui propiciaris omnibus meis deliciis, et sanas omnes infirmitates meas. Qui redemisti de morte vitam mem, ostendens in me gratiam et misericordiam tuam. Qui satias bonis desiderium meum, et olim restitues juventutem meam." The Vulgate sequence of verses reads "Benedic anima mea Domino: et omnia, quae intra me sunt, nomini sancto ejus. Benedic anima mea Domino: et noli oblivisci omnes retributiones ejus: qui propitiatur omnibus iniquitatibus tuis: qui sanat omnes infirmitates tuas. Qui redimit de interitu vitam tuam: qui coronat te in misericordia et miserationibus. Qui replet in bonis desiderium tuum: renovabitur ut aquilae juventus tua" (My soul, bless the Lord; and all [powers] that are within me, [bless] His holy name. My soul, bless the Lord; and forget not all His recompenses: who is gracious toward all thine iniquities, who healeth all thine infirmities. Who redeemeth thy life from destruction, who crowneth thee with mercy and lovingkindness. Who filleth thy desire with good things, so that thy youth is renewed like the eagle's). **humble** KP's addition. **from destruction** KP's phrasing is closer to the Vulgate's "de interitu" (from destruction) than to Fisher's "de morte" (from death), indicating her recognition of the source text. Coverdale's and the Great Bible also read "from destruction." **once** at a particular time.

[Kvi r] Thou hast been a defense to me, O Lord, and a sure foundation of my wealth.[659]

Thou hast guided me with Thy counsel, and taken me to Thee through Thy mercy.[660]

Thou hast many ways declared in me Thy great might and power; and after Thine anger hath been past, Thou hast turned again and comforted me.

Thou hast sent me many grievous troubles, but at the length Thou hast brought me out of the bottomless deepness.[661]

Thou hast made me privy to Thy ways, and hast not hid Thy counsels from me.[662]

Thou art full of mercy and grace, O Lord: slow to wrath, and ready to goodness. [Kvi v] Thy displeasure lasteth not always, and Thou keepest not back Thy mercies in Thine anger forever.

Thou rewardest us not according to our sins, nor punishest us according to our deserts.

Look how high the heaven is, in comparison of the earth: so great is Thy mercy towards us;

How far as the East is distant from the West: so far, O Lord, remove our sins from us.

659. **Thou . . . wealth** KP renders in general terms Fisher's splicing of recast excerpts from Psalms 58:17 and 61:3: "Fuisti mihi o domine in munimentum, et in petram securam salutis meae" (Thou, O Lord, hast been a fortification to me, and a safe rock of my health / salvation). The first excerpt reads "factus es . . . refugium meum" (Thou art made . . . my refuge). The second excerpt reads "ipse Deus meus, et salutaris meus" (He [is] my God and my salvation). **wealth** See n222.

660. **Thou . . . mercy** KP closely renders Fisher's splicing and reordering of recast excerpts from Psalm 77:72, 52: "In consilio tuo dux mihi fuisti, et in misericordia tua assumpsisti me." The first excerpt reads "in intellectibus . . . deduxit eos" (with understanding . . . He hath led them). The second excerpt reads "Et abstulit . . . populum suum" (And He took up . . . His people). This Psalm celebrates God's leading of the Israelites out of Egypt, although they would later prove unfaithful to Him.

661. **Thou hast many . . . deepness** KP expansively renders Fisher's near verbatim quotation and reordering of Psalm 70:21, 20: "Multiplicasti in me magnitudinem tuam, et post iram tuam conversus consolatus est me. Ostendisti mihi tribulationes multas et malas, sed tandem de profundis abyssis eduxisti me" (Thou hast multiplied Thy greatness upon me; and after Thine anger, Thou hast turned and comforted me. Thou hast shown me many and bad troubles, but at last Thou hast led me out of the deep abyss). Verse 21 reads "multiplicasti magnificentiam tuam: et conversus consolatus es me" (Thou hast multiplied Thy magnanimity: and Thou hast turned and comforted me). Verse 20 reads "ostendisti mihi tribulationes multas, et malas . . . de abyssis terrae iterum reduxisti me" (Thou hast shown me many and bad troubles . . . from an abyss in the earth Thou hast led me out again).

662. **Thou . . . me** KP closely renders Fisher's recasting of Psalm 102:7: "Notas mihi fecisti vias tuas, non abscondisti a me consilia tua." The verse reads "Notas fecit vias suas Moysi, filiis Israel voluntates suas" (He made known His ways unto Moses, His wishes unto the sons of Israel).

Like as a natural father hath pity upon his children: even so, O Lord God, Thou hast had compassion upon us.[663]

Thou hast not forgotten Thy creature; Thou rememberest that we are flesh—yea, all men living.

[Kvii r] And that the age of men is like unto grass, and may be compared to the flowers in the field:

Which, as soon as the sharp wind hath blown upon them with his blasts, wither away and die, so that no man can tell where they did grow.

But Thy mercy, O Lord, and Thy lovingkindness is always upon them that fear Thee; and Thy righteousness endureth ever:

So that we keep our promise and covenant with Thee, and so remember Thy commandments, that we do them indeed.

O Lord, Thou hast stablished Thy throne in heaven, and Thou governest all things by Thine imperial power.[664]

663. **Thou art full . . . us** KP renders, for the most part closely, Fisher's minor recasting of a sequence of twelve verses from Psalm 102:8–19. The first half of Fisher's sequence reads "Misericors et plenus es gratia domine Deus, tardus ad iram, et propensus ad bonitatem. Non irasceris imperpetuum, neque in aeternum retines in ira miserationes tuas. Non reddis nobis juxta peccata nostra, nec punis nos juxta iniquitates nostras. Quantum coelum excelsus est quàm terra, tantum misericordia tua praevaluit erga nos. Quantum distat oriens ab occidente, tam longe semovisti [1544: tam longe domine semoveas] à nobis transgressiones nostras. Sicut miseretur pater suis liberis, ita super nos misertus es tu domine Deus noster." The first half (verses 8–13) of the Vulgate sequence reads "Miserator, et misericors Dominus: longanimis, et multum misericors. Non in perpetuum irascetur: neque in aeternum comminabitur. Non secundum peccata nostra fecit nobis: neque secundum iniquitates nostras retribuit nobis. Quoniam secundum altitudinem caeli a terra: corroboravit misericordiam suam super timentes se. Quantum distat Ortus ab Occidente: longe fecit a nobis iniquitates nostras. Quomodo miseratur pater filiorum, misertus est Dominus timentibus se" (Pitying and merciful [is] the Lord, patient and greatly merciful. He will not be angry forever, nor will He forever be threatening. He hath not dealt with us according to our sins, nor hath He repaid us according to our iniquities. For as the height of the heaven above the earth, [so far] hath He strengthened His mercy toward them that fear Him. As far as the East is from the West, [so] far hath He removed our iniquities from us. As a father pitieth his children, the Lord is pitying toward them that fear Him). **deserts** KP's free rendering of "iniquitates" (iniquities) is appropriate in its context. **Look, in comparison of** KP's idiomatic expansions of Fisher's compressed Latin phrasing. **natural** KP's addition.

664. **Thou hast . . . power** KP renders, again for the most part closely, the second half of Fisher's recast sequence from Psalm 102: "Non oblitus plasmatis tui, recordaris quod caro sumus omnis homo vivens. Quodque aetas mortalium tanquam foenum est, ac instar florum agri se habet. Quos protinus ut austerior ventus flabris suis vexaverit nulli sunt, neque loci eorum ultra inveniuntur. Misericordia autem tua domine perpetua est super timentes te, et justicia tua semper perseverat. Dummodo servemus foedus tuum, et mandatorum tuorum memores sumus, ut ea faciamus. Domine in coelis thronum tuum firmasti, et imperio tuo universa regis." The second half (verses 14–19) of the Vulgate sequence reads "Quoniam ipse cognovit figmentum, recordatus est quoniam pulvis sumus: homo, sicut faenum dies ejus, tamquam flos agri sic ef-

[Kvii v] I will magnify Thee, O God, and praise Thy name world without end.

I will give Thee thanks always, and make Thy name glorious forever.

O Lord, Thou art puissant and great, and Thy magnificence is unsearchable.

One generation shall show to another Thy works, and they shall declare Thine ancient noble acts.

They shall ever praise the magnificence of the glory of Thy holiness, and the memory of Thy great goodness.

For Thou art good and gracious to all men, and Thy mercy exceedeth all Thy works.[665]

---

florebit. Quoniam spiritus pertransibit in illo, et non subsistet: et non cognoscet amplius locum suum. Misercordia autem Domini ab aeterno, et usque in aeternum super timentes eum. Et justitia illius in filios filiorum, his qui servant testamentum ejus: et memores sunt mandatorum ipsius, ad faciendum ea. Dominus in caelo paravit sedem suam: et regnum ipsius omnibus dominabitur" (For He hath understood [our] formation, He hath remembered we are dust: man, his day is like hay, as a flower of the field so will he flourish. For a breeze will pass by it, and it will not remain standing, and will not know its place any more. But the mercy of the Lord [is] from everlasting to everlasting unto them that fear Him. And His righteousness unto the sons of sons, to such as keep His covenant, and are mindful of His commandments, for doing them. The Lord hath prepared His seat in heaven, and His reign will have dominion over all). **yea** KP's colloquial addition for emphasis. **wither . . . die** KP expands Fisher's "nulli sunt" (are nothing), heightening the pathos of human mortality. **mercy . . . lovingkindness, promise . . . covenant** KP's doublings.

665. **I will magnify . . . works** KP renders, for the most part quite closely, a sequence of eleven versicles assembled by Fisher out of selected and recast excerpts from Psalm 144:1–5, 9, 15–17, 20–21. The first half of Fisher's sequence reads "Exultabo te O Deus, et nomen tuum in aeternum laudabo, et in seculum seculi. Omni tempore gratias tibi agam, et nomen tuum illustre reddam imperpetuum, et siquid ultra est. Magnus es tu domine, et supra omnem laudem, et magnitudinis tuae nulla est pervestigario. Generatio ad generationem opera tua dicent, et virtutes tuas antiquas enunciabunt. Magnificentiam gloriae sanctitatis tuae, et memoriam multae bonitatis tuae semper laudabunt. Quoniam omnibus bonus es tu, et misericordia tua super universa opera tua." Verses 1–5 and 9 read as follows in the Vulgate: "Exaltabo te Deus . . . benedicam tibi: et laudabo nomen tuum . . . in saeculum saeculi. Magnus Dominus et laudabilis nimis: et magnitudinis ejus non est finis. Generatio et generatio laudabit opera tua: et potentiam tuam pronunciabunt. Magnificentiam gloriae sanctitatis tuae loquentur: et mirabilia tua narrabunt. . . . Suavis Dominus universus: et miserationes ejus super omnia opera ejus" (I will exalt Thee, O God, . . . I will bless Thee: and I will praise Thy name . . . from age to age. Great is the Lord and very greatly to be praised; and of His greatness there is no end. One generation shall praise Thy works to another, and shall declare Thy power. They shall speak of the magnificence of Thy glory and holiness, and they shall tell of Thy wonderful acts. . . . Pleasant is the Lord to all, and His tender mercies are over all His works). **world . . . end** KP freely renders Fisher's "in aeternum . . . et in seculum seculi" (forever . . . and from age to age). **forever** KP tones down Fisher's "imperpetuum, et siquid ultra est" (for eternity, and beyond, if so there be). **puissant . . . great** KP doubles "Magnus" (Great) but does not translate Fisher's next phrase, "et supra omnem laudem" (and above all praise). **good . . . gracious** KP's doubling of "bonus" (good).

[Kviii r] The eyes of all men behold and wait upon Thee: that Thou shouldst give them their sustenance in time convenient.

Thou openest Thine hand, and fillest every living creature with food necessary.

O Lord, Thou art rightful in all Thy ways, and holy in all Thy deeds. Thou keepest all them that love Thee, and the torment of malice shall not touch them.

My mouth shall speak Thy glory and praise, and all living creatures shall honor Thy holy name forever.[666]

Praise the Lord, O ye His angels, mighty in power, which do His commandments, and obey the voice of His word.

[Kviii v] Praise ye all together God, O ye, all His hosts, you His ministers, that do His will and pleasure.[667]

Praise the Lord, as I do, and let us magnify His name together.

Praise the Lord, O ye, all His saints; for His name is glorious, and His praise goeth above both heaven and earth.[668]

666. **The eyes . . . forever** KP continues to render quite closely the second half of Fisher's sequence of recast excerpts from Psalm 144: "Oculi omnium te exspectant, ut des eis cibum suum in tempore. Aperis manum tuam, et imples omne quod vivit, refectione. Justus es domine in omnibus viis tuis, et sanctus in omnibus operibus tuis. Custodis omnes te diligentes, et non tanget eos tormentum maliciae. Laudem tui loquetur os meum, et omne vivens celebret nomen tuam sanctum imperpetuum et semper." Verses 15–17 and 20–21 read as follows in the Vulgate: "Oculi omnium in te sperant Domine: et tu das escam illorum in tempore opportune. Aperis tu manum tuam: et imples omne animal benedictione. Justus Dominius in omnibus viis suis: et sanctus in omnibus operibus suis. . . . Custodit Dominus omnes diligentes se: et omnes peccatores disperdet. Laudationem Domini loquetur os meum: et benedicat omnis caro nomini sancto ejus in saeculum, et in saeculum saeculi" (The eyes of all hope in Thee, Lord; and Thou givest food to them in a seasonable time. Thou openest Thy hand, and fillest every living thing with blessing. Righteous is the Lord in all His ways, and holy in all His works. . . . The Lord watcheth over all those who love Him, and destroyeth all sinners. My mouth shall speak the praise of the Lord; and let all flesh bless His holy name for an age, and from age to age). **behold . . . upon** KP's doubling of "exspectant." **necessary** KP's clarifying addition. **the torment . . . them** KP closely renders Fisher's odd substitution for the Vulgate's "omnes peccatores disperdet" (destroyeth all sinners). **glory . . . praise** KP's doubling of "laudem" (praise). **forever** KP undoes Fisher's doubling, "imperpetuum et semper" (eternally and always).

667. **Praise the . . . pleasure** KP closely renders Fisher's minor recasting of Psalm 102:20–21: "Laudate Dominum o vos angeli ejus, potentes virtute, facientes jussus ejus, obedientes voci verbi illius. Collaudate Deum universi exercitus ejus, ministri ejus, qui facitis voluntatem ejus." The verses read "Benedicite Domino omnes angeli ejus: potentes virtute, facientes verbum illius, ad audiendam vocem sermonum ejus. Benedicite Domino omnes virtutes ejus: ministri ejus, qui facitis voluntatem ejus" (Bless the Lord, all His angels, mighty in power, who do His word, hearkening unto the voice of His speech. Bless the Lord, all His powers, His ministers, who do His will). **will . . . pleasure** KP's doubling.

668. **Praise . . . earth** KP freely renders Fisher's splicing of an exact quotation from Psalm 33:4 with recast excerpts from Psalm 148:7, 13–14: "Magnificate dominum mecum, et exaltemus nomen ejus in idipsum. Laudate dominum omnes sancti ejus, cuius solius nomen sublime est,

Praise the Lord together, O ye, all his works, everything that liveth, praise the Lord. Amen.[669]

Finis. XV. Psalmorum.[670]

[Li r]

THE TWENTY-FIRST PSALM OF DAVID. THE COMPLAINT OF CHRIST ON THE CROSS.[671]

My God, my God, why hast Thou forsaken me? It seemeth that I shall not obtain deliverance, though I seek for it with loud cries.

My God, I will cry all the day long, but Thou wilt not answer; and all the night long, without taking any rest.[672]

---

cuius laus coelos ac terram superat" (Magnify the Lord with me, and let us exalt His name together. Praise the Lord, all His saints, the name of whose throne is lofty, whose praise is above heaven and earth). The excerpts from Psalm 148 read "Laudate Dominum . . . quia exaltatum est nomen ejus solius . . . Confessio ejus super caelum et terram . . . Hymnus omnibus sanctis ejus" (Praise the Lord . . . for the name of His throne is lofty . . . His acknowledgment is above heaven and earth . . . The praise from all His saints).

669. **Praise . . . Amen** KP freely renders Fisher's splicing of recast excerpts from Psalms 102:22 and 116:1: "Collaudate dominum universa opera ejus in omni loco imperii ejus. Omne quod vivit laudet te domine. Amen" (Praise the Lord together, all His works, in every place of His empire. Let all that liveth praise Thee, Lord). The first excerpt reads "Benedicite Domino omnia opera ejus: in omni loco dominationis ejus" (Bless the Lord, all His works, in every place of His dominion). The second excerpt reads "Laudate Dominum omnes gentes: laudate eum omnes populi" (Praise the Lord, all you nations; praise Him, all you peoples). **works** KP's uncharacteristic omission of Fisher's "in omni loco imperii ejus" (in every place of His empire) in her rendering may be the result of fatigue or hurry as she neared the end of translating his fifteen substantial Psalm assemblages.

670. **Finis . . . Psalmorum** "The End of the Fifteen Psalms"—a subheading taken over from the English edition of *Psalmi seu Precationes,* and derived from the subheading in the Cologne edition, which reads "Finis quindecim psalmorum D. Iohan. Episcopi Roffensis" (The end of the fifteen Psalms of the divine, John, Bishop of Rochester).

671. **The . . . cross twenty-first Psalm** In both the Cologne and the first London editions, this heading reads "PSALMVS DAVID. 22," reproducing the numbering of this Psalm in Coverdale and the Great Bible. In marked contrast to the fifteen Psalms preceding, the versicles that follow are at once selective and expansive paraphrases of the sequence of thirty-one verses constituting the Vulgate text of Psalm 21. While they fill out the collection of Fisher's fifteen Psalms, the paraphrases of this and the following Psalm are unindentified; they may or may not be Fisher's work. KP usually renders these recastings quite closely, continuing her practice with Fisher's fifteen Psalms. **The complaint . . . cross** This title highlights the traditional typological interpretation of Psalm 21, cued significantly by three echoes of its verses in the New Testament narratives of the Passion—verse 1 (Matthew 27:46; Mark 15:34), verses 7–8 (Matthew 27:39, 43; Luke 23:35), and verse 18 (Mark 15:23; Luke 23:34).

672. **My God, my God . . . rest** KP closely renders this recasting of excerpts from Psalm 21:2–3: "Deus meus, Deus meus, cur deseruisti me, videor non impetraturus, quamvis id magnis agam clamoribus liberationem. Mi deus clamabo per diem, sed non respondebis [1544:

The meantime Thou, most holiest, seemest to sit still, not caring for the things that I suffer: which so oft hast helped me heretofore, and hast given to Thy people Israel sufficient argument and matter to praise Thee with songs, wherewith they have given thanks to Thee for Thy benefits.[673]

[Li v] Our forefathers were wont to put Their trust in Thee; and as often as they did so, Thou didst deliver them.

As oft as they cried for help to Thee, they were delivered; as oft as they committed themself to Thee, they were not put to any shame.[674]

But, as for me, I seem rather to be a worm than a man, the dunghill of Adam, the outcast of the vulgar people.

As many as have seen me have laughed me to scorn and reviled me, and shaking their heads in derision at me, have cast me in the teeth, saying:

[Lii r] He is wont to boast and glory that he is in great favor with God; wherefore let God now deliver him, if He love him so well.[675]

---

respondes], et per noctem, absque ulla intermissione." Her phrasing, "Thou wilt not answer," renders "non respondebis" in the Cologne edition, not the variant "non respondes" in the first English edition, "Thou dost not answer." The corresponding excerpts read "Deus Deus meus . . . quare me dereliquisti? . . . Deus meus, clamabo per diem, et non exaudies: et nocte, et non ad insipientiam mihi" (God, my God . . . why hast Thou forsaken me? . . . My God, I cry by day, and Thou hearest not; and in the night I am not [given over] to senselessness).

673. **The . . . benefits** KP further expands this verbose recasting of Psalm 21:4: "Interim tuò sanctissime, veluti securus horum quae patior, desidere videris, qui succurristi toties, et materia fuisti carminum ipsi Israeli, quibus gratias tibi pro beneficiis agebant" (Meanwhile Thou most holy, art as if unconcerned for the things that I suffer; Thou shalt see [my] desire, who hast hastened to help many times, and hast been matter of songs for Israel itself, with which they have given thanks to Thee for Thy benefits). The corresponding verse reads "Tu autem in sancto habitas, Laus Israel" (But Thou dwellest in holiness, the praise of Israel). **sufficient . . . matter** KP's expansion.

674. **Our . . . shame** KP quite closely renders this expansive recasting of Psalm 21:5–6: "Spem suam ponere in te solebant patres nostri, et quoties id faciebant, tu liberabas eos. Quoties ad te clamaverunt, liberati sunt, quoties sese tibi crediderunt, pudore non sunt suffusi." The corresponding verses read "In te speraverunt patres nostri: speraverunt, et liberasti eos. Ad te clamaverunt, et salvi facti sunt: in te speraverunt, et non sunt confusi" (In Thee our fathers have trusted, and Thou hast delivered them. To Thee they have cried, and they have been made safe; in Thee they have trusted, and were not confounded). **not put . . . shame** KP gives a general cast to the more specific "pudore non sunt suffusi" (were not suffused with shame).

675. **But . . . well** KP freely renders this excerpting and recasting of Psalm 21:7–9: "Ego vero vermis esse videor magis quam vir, sterquilinium Adae, et infimae plebis f[a]ex. Quotquot videbant me, subsannabant me, conviciabantur, et moto capite irridentes insultabant mihi. Gloriari solet hic inquientes charum se esse domino, liberet ergo nunc eum si tantopere amat eum" (Truly I seem to be a worm more than a man, the dungpit of Adam, and the dregs of the people. As many as have seen me have scorned me; they have reviled me, and shaking the head, jeering, they have insulted me: "This man, when disquieted, used to glory in being dear to the Lord; let us then see now if He loveth him so greatly"). The corresponding verses read "Ego autem sum vermis, et non homo: opprobrium hominum, et abjecto plebis. Omnes vi-

By Thy procurement, O Lord, I came out of my mother's womb; and Thou gavest me good comfort even whan I sucked my mother's breasts.

Through Thy means I came into this world; and as soon as I was born, I was left to Thy tuition—yea, Thou wast my God when I was yet in my mother's womb.[676]

Wherefore go not far away from me: for danger is even now at hand, and I see no man that will help me.

[Lii v] Many bulls have closed me in, both strong and fat; they have compassed me round about.

They have opened their mouth against me, like unto a lion that gapeth upon his prey and roareth for hunger.[677]

I am poured out like water, and all my limbs loosed one from the other; and my heart is melted within me, as it were wax.

All my strength is gone, and dried up like unto a tilestone; my tongue cleaveth

---

dentes me, deriserunt me: locuti sunt labiis, et moverunt caput. Speravit in Domino, eripiat eum: salvum faciat eum, quoniam vult eum" (But I am a worm, and not a man: the reproach of men, and the outcast of the people. All who see me mock me; they say with their lips and shake the head: "He hath trusted in the Lord, that He would deliver him; let Him save him, because He is willing [to save] him"). **dunghill . . . Adam** KP renders the wording "sterquilinium Adae" in the Cologne edition; the first London edition lacks this phrase. **laughed . . . scorn, cast . . . teeth** KP's phrasal expansions of "subsannabant" (scorned) and "insultabant" (insulted). **boast . . . glory** KP's doubling.

676. **By . . . womb** KP adaptatively renders this recasting of Psalm 21:10–11: "Te procurante prodii ex utero, et bene sperare jussisti me quum adhuc fugerem ubera matris meae. Opera tua ejectus sum è vulva, et curae tuae relictus, quum essem adhuc in utero matris meae, Deus eras mihi tu." The corresponding verses read "Quoniam tu es, qui extraxisti me de ventre: spes mea ab uberibus matris meae. In te projectus sum ex utero: de ventre matris meae Deus meus es tu" (For it is Thou who hast taken me out of the belly: [Thou hast been] my hope from [when I sucked] my mother's breasts. By Thee I was cast forth from the womb; Thou art my God from [when I was in] my mother's belly). **procurement** means or doing, rendering the participle "procurante" (taking care, looking after). **came . . . world** KP notably substitutes a general locution in place of a literal rendering of "ejectus sum è vulva" (I was cast forth out of the vulva). Such reticence regarding the female body may well imply that the translator was female, bolstering the ascription of this work to KP; see the introduction, p. 203. **tuition** See n579.

677. **Wherefore . . . hunger** KP quite closely renders this expansive recasting of Psalm 21:12–14: "Ne procul igitur abscesseris à me, quia periculum praesentissimum est, nec quemquam video qui auxilio futurus sit. Cinxerunt me tauri multi, fortes, et velut saginati in Basan circundederunt me. Aperuerunt adversum me os suam, non aliter quam leo inhians praedae, et prae fame rugiens." The corresponding verses read "ne discesseris a me: quoniam tribulatio proxima est: quoniam non est qui adjuvet. Circumdederunt me vituli multi: tauri pingues obsederunt me. Aperuerunt super me os suum, sicut leo rapiens et rugiens" (be not distant from me, for trouble is near: for there is none who will help. Many bulls have closed in around me; fat bulls have besieged me. They have opened their mouth over me, like a ravishing and roaring lion). **strong . . . fat** KP's rendering is closer to the Vulgate's "pingues" (fat, rich) than is Fisher's "fortes, et velut saginati in Basan" (strong, and like [ones] fattened in Bashan).

to the roof of my mouth; and at the last I shall be buried in the earth as the dead be wont.

[Liii r] For dogs have compassed me round about, and the most wicked have conspired against me; they have made holes through my hands and my feet.[678]

I was so ungently entreated of them, that I might easily number all my bones; and after all the pain and torment that they did to me, with grievous countenance they stared and looked upon me.

They divided my clothes among them, and cast lot[s] for my coat.[679]

Wherefore, Lord, I beseech Thee, go not far from me; but forasmuch as Thou art my power and my strength, make haste to help me.

Deliver my soul from danger of the sword, and keep my life, destitute of all man's help, from the violence of the dog.

[Liii v] Save me from the mouth of the lion, and take me from the horns of the unicorns.[680]

678. **I am . . . feet** KP quite closely renders this expansive recasting of Psalm 21:15–17: "Tanquam aqua fluidus factus sum, et soluta sunt omnia membra mea, cor meum veluti cera diffluxit intra praecordia mea. Exaruit tanquam testa omne robur meum, et lingua mea agglutinata est palato meo, et tandem in pulvere, quemadmodum mortui solent, sepelies me. Circu[m]dederunt na[m]que me canes, conspiraverunt adversum me pessimi, quique foderunt manus meas et pedes meos." The corresponding verses read "Sicut aqua effusus sum: et dispersa sunt omnia ossa mea. Factum est cor meum tamquam cera liquescens in medio ventris mei. Aruit tanquam testa virtus mea, et lingua mea adhaesit faucibus meis: et in pulverem mortis deduxisti me. Quoniam circumdederunt me canes multi: concilium malignantium obsedit me. Foderunt manus meas et pedes meos" (I have been poured out like water: and all my bones have been scattered. My heart has been made like wax melting in the middle of my belly. My strength is dried up like a brick, and my tongue sticks in my throat; and Thou hast led me into the dust of death. For many dogs have surrounded me; the assembly of malicious [ones] hath besieged me. They have pierced my hands and my feet). **within me** KP gives a general rendering of "intra praecordia me" (within my midriff); she may not have known the anatomical Latin term. **is gone . . . up** KP's doubling of "Exaruit" (is dried up).

679. **I was . . . coat** KP quite closely renders this expansive recasting of Psalm 21:18–19: "Tractatus sum ab eis tam inhumaniter, ut numerare potuerim facile omnia ossa mea, ipsi adhuc post omnem cruciatum torve aspiciebant, et contemplabantur me. Partiebantur vestes meas, et de tunica mea sortiebantur." The corresponding verses read "Dinumeraverunt omnia ossa mea. Ipsi vero consideraverunt et inspexerunt me: diverserunt sibi vestimenta mea, et super vestem meam miserunt sortem" (They have numbered all my bones. Truly they have looked at me closely and have examined me; they have divided my clothes among themselves, and they have cast lots for my coat). **I was . . . easily** KP elaborates on the addition "Tractatus . . . facile" (I was treated so inhumanely by them that I might easily have). **pain . . . to me** KP again elaborates on the addition "ipsi . . . torve" (thus far, after the whole tormenting, they beheld [me] fiercely).

680. **Wherefore . . . unicorns** KP quite closely renders this recasting of Psalm 21:20–22: "Quare tu quaeso domine, ne longe abscesseris hinc, quin potium (quam sis fortitudo mea) ferre mihi suppetias festina. Eripe à gladio animam meam, et à violentia canis unicam meam

I will show unto my brethren the majesty of Thy name; and when the people is most assembled together, I will praise and set forth Thy most worthy acts and deeds.

All that worship the Lord, praise Him; all the posterity of Jacob, magnify Him; all ye that be of the stock of Israel, with reverence serve and honor him.

For He hath not despised and set at naught the poor man because of his misery, nor He hath not disdainfully turned away his face from Him; but rather as soon as the poor man cried unto Him for help, He hath heard by and by.[681]

[Liv r] I will praise Thee with my songs openly in a multitude of people, and I will perform my vows in the sight of them that honor Thee.

The poor shall eat and be satisfied; they shall praise the Lord, that study to please Him; and as many of you as continue still such, your hearts shall live.

All the ends of the world shall consider these things, and be turned to the Lord; and all heathen nations shall submit themself, and do homage unto Thee.

[Liv v] For the Lord hath a power royal, and an imperial dominion over the heathen.[682]

---

omni humano auxilio destitutam. Salva me ab ore leonis, et à cornibus unicornium eripe me." The corresponding verses read "Tu autem Domine ne elongaveris auxilium tuum a me: ad defensionem meam conspice. Erua a framea Deus animam meam: et de manu canis unicam meam. Salva me ex ore leonis: et a cornibus unicornium humilitatem meam" (But Thou, O Lord, do not distance Thy help from me; see to my defense. Deliver Thou my soul, God, from the spear, and my one and only [soul] from the dog's paw. Save me from the lion's mouth, my lowness from the unicorns' horns). **power . . . strength** KP's doubling of "fortitudo" (strength). **danger of** KP's expansion of "à gladio" (from the sword).

681. **I will . . . by** KP quite closely renders this expansive recasting of Psalm 21:23–25: "Commemorabo majestatem nominis tui fratribus meis, in frequentissima populi turba laudes tuas praedicabo. Quotquot estis cultores domini laudate eum, universi posteri Jacob magnificate eum, et reverenter colite illum omnes posteri Israelis. Quia non despexit, neque vilipendit ob miseriam, pauperem, neque avertit contemptim faciem suam ab eo, quin potius quum pauper clamaret ad illum, diligenter auscultavit." The corresponding verses read "Narrabo nomen tuum fratribus meis: in medio ecclesiae laudabo te. Qui timetis Dominum laudate eum: universum semen Jacob glorificate eum: timeat eum omne semen Israel: quoniam non sprevit, neque despexit deprecationem pauperis: non avertit faciem suam a me: et cum clamarem ad eum exaudivit me" (I will tell my brothers Thy name; in the midst of the congregation I will praise Thee. You who fear the Lord, praise Him; all the seed of Jacob, glorify Him; let all the seed of Israel fear Him. For He hath not spurned nor hath He despised the averting prayer of the poor man; He hath not turned His face from me, and when I have cried unto Him, He hath delivered me). **when . . . together** KP expands the phrase "in frequentissima populi turba" (in the thickest crowd of people) into a full clause. **will praise . . . forth, serve . . . honor** KP doubles "praedicabo" (I will proclaim) and "colite" (worship ye). **most . . . deeds** KP Fisher's "laudes tuas" (Thy praises). **magnify** KP misreads "magnifacite" (make much of) as "magnificate" (praise, glorify). **by . . . by** within a certain period of time: KP's substitution for "diligenter" (attentively).

682. **I will praise . . . heathen** KP quite closely renders this recasting of Psalm 21:26–29: "Te laudabo carminibus meis publicè in frequentia populi, et quae novi persoluam videntibus

The most mighty and greatest of all them that dwell on the earth have eaten, and after that they have tasted the spiritual gifts of the Lord, they have submitted themself, and made humble suit unto Him—yea, and all the dead which are buried in the earth shall kneel and make reverence in His honor, because He hath not disdained to spend His own life for them.

They that shall come after us, shall honor and serve Him; these things shall be written of the Lord, that our posterity may know and understand them.

[Lv r] That they also may come and show these things to the people that shall be born of them: that the Lord hath done these things, which be so marvelous.[683]

illis, qui reverentur te. Comedent pauperes et saturabuntur, laudabunt dominum, quicunque student placere illi, vivent corda vestra, quotquot estis tales perpetuò. Considerabunt haec et [1544: cum] convertentur ad dominum cuncti [1544: omnes] fines terrae, et supplices fient tibi domine universae nationes gentium. Domini enim est potestas regia, et imperium habet etiam in gentes." The corresponding verses read "Apud te laus mea in ecclesia magna: vota mea reddam in conspectu timentium eum. Edent pauperes, et saturabuntur: et laudabunt Dominum qui requirunt eum: vivent corda eorum in saeculum saeculi. Reminiscentur et convertentur ad Dominum universi fines terrae: et adorabunt in conspectu ejus universae familiae gentium. Quoniam Domini est regnum: et ipse dominabitur gentium" (Of Thee [shall be] my praise in the great congregation; I will perform my vows [or: render my prayers] in the presence of them that fear Him. The poor shall eat and be satisfied, and they that seek Him shall praise the Lord; their hearts shall live from age to age. All the ends of the earth shall call to mind and shall turn to the Lord, and all the households of the nations shall worship in His presence. For the kingdom is the Lord's, and He shall have dominion over the nations). **The poor . . . live** a further instance in which KP leaves unaltered a verse that emphasizes the efficacy of moral effort in cooperation with divine blessing. See the introduction, p. 202. **shall submit . . . homage unto** KP's emphatic doubling of "supplices fient" (they shall be supplicants).

683. **The most . . . marvelous** KP elaborates further on this expansive recasting of Psalm 21:30–32: "Comederunt, et quum gustassent spiritualia domini dona, supplices facti sunt potentissimi quique eorum, qui terram inhabitant, et in venerationem illius genua flectent, etiam mortui omnes in terra supulti: quia propriam vitam non est dedignatus impendere pro illis. Posteri nostri colent eum, scribentur haec de domino, ut posteri intelligant. Ut et illi veni[en]t, et annuncient populo qui ab ipsis nascetur, quod haec fecerit tam stupenda dominus." The corresponding verses read "Manducaverunt et adoraverunt omnes pingues terrae: in conspectu ejus cadent omnes qui descendunt in terram. Et anima mea illi vivet: et semen meum serviet ipsi. Annuntiabitur Domino generatio ventura: et annunciabunt caeli justitiam ejus populo qui nascetur, quem fecit Dominus" (All the well-off of the earth shall have eaten and worshiped; all they that descend into the earth shall fall down before His presence. And my soul shall live by Him, and my seed shall serve Him. A future generation shall be proclaimed for the Lord, and the heavens shall declare His righteousness to the people that shall be born, what the Lord hath done). **have submitted . . . suit unto** KP's doubling of Fisher's "supplices facti sunt" (they have been made supplicants). **in . . . honor** KP's addition. **shall honor . . . serve** KP's doubling of "colent" (shall worship). **may know . . . understand** KP's doubling of "intelligant" (may understand). **which . . . marvelous** KP expands "tam stupenda" (so marvelous) into a full clause.

A PSALM OF THANKSGIVING. JUBILATE DEO OMNIS TERRA.[684]

Rejoice and sing in the honor of the Lord, all ye that live on earth.

Worship and serve the Lord with gladness; come into His sight and presence with joy and mirth.

Acknowledge you and confess, that the Lord is that God which hath created and made us, for truly we made not ourself, but we be his people and his flock, which He nourisheth and feedeth continually.[685]

[Lv v] Go ye through His gates to give Him thanks for the innumerable benefits which ye have received of Him, and to sing through His courts His worthy acts and deeds; praise Him, and highly comciomend His name.

For the Lord is both good and gracious, and His mercy is infinite; He is most constant in keeping of His promises, not to one generation only, but even to all.[686]

684. **A . . . terra** KP quotes the first phrase of the Latin Psalm but omits its number, which both the Cologne and the first English edition give in Arabic numerals as "100." In Vulgate numbering, however, this is Psalm 99.

685. **Rejoice . . . continually** KP systematically elaborates on this expansive recasting of Psalm 99:2–3: "Jubilate Deo omnis terra, jubilate in honorem Domini, quotquot in terra versamini. Colite Dominum cum laetitia, venite in conspectum ipsius cum exultatione. Agnoscite Dominum esse illum Deum, qui fecit nos, neque etiam ipsi fecimus nos, sed populus ejus sumus, et grex quem ipse pascit assiduè" (Rejoice in the Lord, all the earth; rejoice in the honor of the Lord, howsoever many dwell upon the earth. Worship the Lord with joy, come into His presence with exultation. Know that the Lord, He is God, who hath made us, nor yet have we made ourselves, but we are His people, and the sheep whom He feedeth continually). **Rejoice . . . sing** KP's doubling of "Jubilate." **Worship . . . serve** KP's doubling of "Colite." **sight . . . presence** KP's doubling of "conspectum." **joy . . . mirth** KP's doubling of "laetitia." **Acknowledge . . . confess** KP's doubling of "Agnoscite." **created . . . made** KP's doubling of "fecit." **nourisheth . . . feedeth** KP's doubling of "pascit."

686. **Go . . . all** KP continues to elaborate on this expansive recasting of Psalm 99:4–5: "Intra te per portas illius gratias acturi pro acceptis ab eo innumeris beneficiis, et per atria cantaturi laudes illius, laudate illum et celebrate laudibus nomen illius. Benignus est enim dominus, et infinitae misericordiae, et in servandis promissis constantissimus, non uni generationi tantum sed omnibus" (Enter through His gates, giving thanks for the innumerable benefits received from Him; and let His praises be sung throughout His courts; praise Him and fill His name with praises. Truly the Lord is kind and of infinite mercy, and most steadfast in keeping promises, not just to one generation but to all). The Cologne edition's sequence of assemblages of Psalm excerpts and recastings ends at this point, followed by a centered heading "FINIS" (The End). **acts . . . deeds** KP's doubling of "laudes" (praises). **highly** KP's intensifier. **both . . . gracious** KP's doubling of "Benignus."

[Lvi r] **A PRAYER FOR THE KING**[687]

O Lord Jesu Christ, most high, most mighty, King of Kings, Lord of Lords, the only Ruler of princes, the very Son of God, on whose right hand sitting, dost from Thy throne behold all the dwellers upon earth: with most lowly hearts we beseech Thee, vouchsafe with favorable regard to behold our most gracious sovereign lord, King Henry the eight[h], and so replenish him with the grace of Thy Holy Spirit, that he alway incline to Thy will and walk in Thy way.[688] Keep him far off from ignorance, but through Th[y] gift, let prudence and knowledge alway abound in his royal heart.
[Lvi v] So instruct him, O Lord Jesu, reigning upon us in earth, that his human majesty always obey Thy divine majesty in fear and dread.[689] Endue him plentifully with heavenly gifts. Grant him in health and wealth long to live. Heap glory and honor upon him. Glad him with the joy of Thy countenance. So strength him, that

687. **A . . . King** an exact rendering of the heading, "Precatio pro Rege," in the first English edition of Fisher's *Psalmi seu Precationes*. Since the Cologne edition does not contain this prayer, it must derive from another source of Fisher's compositions, most likely one available to George Day, Fisher's former chaplain and KP's almoner. While the date of composition cannot be ascertained from the generalities of its Latin phrasing, its phraseology seems to predate all the parliamentary and royal acts that withdrew England from papal jurisdiction from 1533 onward. The prayer invocates a plenitude of divine protection, guidance, and favor upon Henry VIII as the monarch of England.

688. **O . . . way** KP recasts portions of the opening sentence: "Domine Jesu Christe, qui es altissimus, omnipotens, rex regum, dominus dominorum, monarcha monarchum, verus filius Dei, ad cuius sedens dexteram, de throno prospicis super universos habitatores orbis terrarum: tibi submissis animis supplicamus, ut serenissimum regem nostrum Henricum octavum, placato vultu respicias, simulque illum tui sancti spiritus afflatu adimpleas, virtute cuius eò feratur, quò illum voluntas tua vocat." **only . . . princes** KP expands and varies Fisher's wording, "monarcha monarchum" (Monarch of Monarchs). **upon earth** KP condenses Fisher's "orbis terrarum" (on the globe of the earth). **our most . . . lord** KP works a variation on "serenissimum regem nostrum" (our most serene king). She will use a closely similar ascription in her *Lamentation of a Sinner*, where she refers to Henry as "my most sovereign, favorable lord and husband" (p. 468). **the grace of** KP recasts Fisher's "afflatu" (the breath of). **that he . . . way** KP recasts "virtute . . . vocat" (that he may be moved by its [the Spirit's] power, by which Thy will urgeth him) to place the burden of emphasis on Henry's initiative.

689. **Keep . . . dread** KP quite closely renders the next pair of petitions: "Procul ab illo sit ignorantia, sed te largiente, prudentia et scientia semper abundent in regio suo corde. Sic illum erudi Domine Jesu, super nos regnantem in terris, ut tuae divinae majestati, semper serviat sua humana majestas in timore et tremore." **through . . . gift** KP recasts Fisher's participial construction "te largiente" (Thou bestowing). **Th[y]** The 1544 text of *Psalms or Prayers* reads "the"—a misprint.

he may vanquish and overcome all his and our foes, and be dread and feared of all the enemies of his realm. Amen.[690]

[Mi r] A PRAYER FOR MEN TO SAY ENTERING INTO BATTTLE[691]

O almighty King and Lord of hosts, which, by Thy angels thereunto appointed, dost minister both war and peace; and which didst give unto David both courage and strength, being but a little one, unarmed and unexpert in feats of war, with his sling to set upon and overthrow the great, huge Goliath:[692] Our cause now being just, and being enforced to enter into war and battle, we most humbly beseech Thee, O Lord of hosts, so to turn the hearts of our enemies to the desire of peace, that no Christian blood be spilt.

[Mi v] Or else grant, O Lord, that with small effusion of blood, and to the little hurt and damage of innocents, we may, to Thy glory, obtain victory. And that the wars being soon ended, we may all, with one heart and mind, knit together in concord and unity, laud and praise Thee: which livest and reignest, world without end. Amen.

690. **Endue . . . Amen** KP freely renders the final set of petitions: "Benedic illi benedictionibus dulcedinis tuae. Tribue ei longitudinem dierum. Gloriam et magnum decorem impone super eum. Laetifica illum gaudio vultus tui. Adest illi, ut de suis ac nostris triumphet hostibus: et terrori sit omnibus inimicis sui regni. Amen" (Bless him with the blessings of Thy sweetness. Bestow on him length of days. Set glory and great comeliness upon him. Gladden him with the joy of Thy countenance. Be with him, that he may triumph over his and our foes, and be of terror to all enemies of his kingdom. Amen). **plentifully . . . gifts** KP replaces the evocation "dulcidinis tuae" (of Thy sweetness) with a more general positive formulation. **health . . . wealth** KP's addition. **honor** KP replaces "decorum" (comeliness, beauty) with a more masculine attribute. **vanquish . . . overcome** KP's doubling of "triumphet." **dread . . . feared** KP's doubling of "terrori." **Amen** This is the final word of the translated material. In the English edition of *Psalmi seu precationes* the Latin colophon follows on the overleaf: "Londini. In officina Thomae Bertheleti regii impressoris typis excusum. Anno. M.D.XLIIII duodevigesimo die mensis Aprilis. Cum privilegio ad imprimendum solum." (At London. Type set in the workshop of Thomas Berthelet, the King's printer. In the year 1544, on the eighteenth day of the month of April. With the privilege of sole printing.)

691. **A . . . battle** This prayer was quite possibly composed by KP with a view to the military campaign in France that Henry was preparing to conduct in July-September 1544. She reprinted this prayer and her translation of the preceding prayer for the king at the end of the first and subsequent editions of her *Prayers or Meditations*, published under her name slightly more than a year later (June 2–November 6, 1545). The style of the text, especially the prominent doublings of lexical primaries in balanced phrases, fits well with KP's authorship.

692. **David . . . Goliath** The killing of the Philistine giant Goliath of Gath by the shepherd boy David, armed only with his slingshot and his trust in God, is narrated in 1 Samuel 17:20–54.

[Colophon]

[Mii r]

Imprinted at London in Fleet Street
by Thomas Berthelet, printer to
the King's highness, the twenty-
fifth day of April, the year of
our Lord. M.D.X.LIIII.
Cum privilegio ad imprimendum solum.[693]

[Inscription in William Herbert's secretary hand]
Mr William H the Elder Pem[b]roke his booke

693. **Cum . . . solum** With the privilege of sole printing—a predecessor of copyright.

KATHERINE PARR'S

PRAYERS OR MEDITATIONS

(1545)

INTRODUCTION TO
PRAYERS OR MEDITATIONS (1545)

The first edition of Queen Katherine Parr's *Prayers or Meditations* appeared on June 2, 1545, under the title *Prayers stirryng the mynd vnto heauenlye medytacions.* This volume reprinted the two non-Biblical prayers—one for King Henry, the other for men to say going into battle—that concluded her translation *Psalms or Prayers*, published a year earlier. A second edition with the same contents, bearing the same date, carried the title *Prayers or meditacions, wherin the mynde is styrred paciently to suffre all afflictions here.* The definitive version (the third edition) appeared on November 6, 1545, under the title *PRAYERS OR Medytacions, wherein the mynd is stirred, paciently to suffre all afflictions here, to set at nought the vayne prosperitee of this worlde, and alwaie to longe for the everlastynge felicitee: Collected out of holy wookes by the most vertuous and graciouse Princesse Katherine quene of Englande, Fraunce, and Irelande.*[1] This volume concluded with four prayers that may well be Queen Katherine's compositions, the latter of the two just mentioned and three others that gradate from a public to a private perspective: "A devout prayer to be daily said," "Another prayer," and "A devout prayer." The first two editions, identical except for their titles, and the third, definitive one rapidly gained popularity with English readers, who often knew the work as "The Queen's Prayers." Thirteen editions appeared before the end of the sixteenth century.

My general introduction proposes a dual rationale for Parr's publishing of *Prayers or Meditations*, her own work under her own name, the earliest such oc-

1. *Prayers stirryng the mynd vnto heauenlye medytacions* (two prayers appended) is STC 4818; *Prayers or meditacions wherin the mynde is styred* (two prayers appended) is STC 4818.5; the definitive edition, *PRAYERS OR Meditacions, wherein the mynd is stirred* (five prayers appended) is STC 4819.

currence for a woman author in England.[2] One motive is evidently a self-certifying gesture, signaling Queen Katherine's recently attained membership in the exalted circle of English royalty. Yet to reduce Parr's motive merely to an affirmation of her status fails to engage and explore the pertinence of Elaine Beilin's generalization regarding the intersection of gender and literary production in early modern England: "The Reformation, with its emphasis on individual salvation and the reading of Scripture, was . . . the single most important influence on women writers."[3] In fact, dualities of origin and motive are widely if delicately inscribed in the text of *Prayers or Meditations.* On the one hand Queen Katherine's efforts eventuate and speak from a private, personal sphere where, if anywhere, women have conventionally found room for expression. It does not seem mere coincidence that an incomplete text of *Prayers or Meditations* surviving in Queen Katherine's own hand and in miniature format, beautifully illuminated, was a gift from her, at an unknown date, to one of the ladies of the court.[4] On the other hand, for this queen to circulate her work in print, she surely needed to obtain the permission of her famously autocratic consort. Thus, in her case, considerations of gender figured crucially twice over—not just in undertaking authorship but also in aspiring to official Tudor legitimation in a personal voice.

Queen Katherine's *Prayers or Meditations* registers as an ambitious, even an autonomous attempt to provide English readers—first among them, it seems, King Henry—with a private counterpart to the English *Litany* that Archbishop Thomas Cranmer published in 1544.[5] The *Litany* was the first royally authorized vernacular manual for public devotion in the Church of England. An earlier gesture by Queen Katherine in this direction was her anonymous translation of Bishop John Fisher's assemblage of frequently reworked excerpts from the Gallican version of the Vulgate Bible under the title *Psalms or Prayers,* also published in 1544. One year later, she had completed her own selection and assemblage of another vernacular text for use in personal devotion, her *Prayers or Meditations,* and must surely have obtained Henry's approval before being identified in print as the originator of the work.

As remarked above regarding the number of sixteenth-century editions, *Prayers or Meditations* compiled a strong record of success with an English readership. There is evidence of its immediate positive reception as well. Princess Elizabeth made a trilingual—Latin, French, and Italian—translation of *Prayers or Medita-*

2. A prior discussion is Janel Mueller, "Devotion as Difference: Intertextuality in Queen Katherine Parr's *Prayers or Meditations* (1545)," *Huntington Library Quarterly* 53.3 (1990): 171–97.

3. Elaine V. Beilin, *Redeeming Eve: Women Writers of the English Renaissance* (Princeton, NJ: Princeton University Press, 1987), xxi.

4. This incomplete text in KP's hand, "The Kendal Autograph Fragment," is printed in the present edition preceding the modern-spelling version of *Prayers or Meditations.*

5. The full title of Cranmer's compilation was *An exhortation vnto prayer . . . to be read in euery church afore processyons. Also a letanie with suffrages* (T. Berthelet, 1544) (STC 10620–10621.5). See my general introduction, p. 14.

tions as a New Year's gift for King Henry in 1546, extolling it in her prefatory letter to her father as a "pious work . . . by the pious exertion and great diligence of a most illustrious queen . . . assembled in English, and on that account . . . more desired by all, and held in greater value by your majesty." Elizabeth urges on King Henry the complexly intimate propriety of her translation of an exemplary work that Queen Katherine had compiled and offered to him: "it was thought by me a most suitable thing that this work, . . . an assemblage by a queen as subject matter for her king, be translated into other languages by me, your daughter, who by this means would be indebted to you not only as an imitator of your virtues but also as an inheritor of them."[6]

For Queen Katherine's project to win approval from the monitoring king and archbishop for general release and use, it was strategically advisable for its first-person voice to assume the generic human tonalities of a pious Christian soul. Such a voice had a rich, well-established history tracing ultimately to the Hebrew Psalms, the perennially favored model for devotion. Its keynotes mingle universalized affirmations of sin, frailty, and vital dependence upon God with an equally inclusive assurance of the preciousness of the speaker's soul to God. Degendering tendencies are observable in this generic voice of devotion—a soul in need, yearning for the divine—as one ground on which its inclusiveness is staked. Yet where the grammar of so-called natural language forces a specification of gender, the generic voice predictably becomes a "he," exposing the masculine norm implicit in linguistic as in other cultural universals. However Queen Katherine might otherwise gauge the cultural limits on her self-expression, completely feminizing the voice of her *Prayers or Meditations* would have been a tactical impossibility. Her pursuit of this project at this date required an authorial orientation that would now be termed male-identified—that is, accommodated to the existing power relations of her society—since she would have had no prospect of officially authorized publication without working with and through the all-male hierarchy of the English church and crown.[7]

Once the necessary quotient of male identification in Parr's enterprise is ac-

6. *Elizabeth I: Translations, 1544–1589*, ed. Janel Mueller and Joshua Scodel (Chicago: University of Chicago Press, 2009), 136 (editors' translation). See the original Latin of Elizabeth's letter on 138–39. Elizabeth was the most prestigious and precocious translator of *Prayers or Meditations*, but not the only one. The British Library manuscript Royal 7.D.9, fols. 1–29, stitched together and bound in limp parchment, is the young John Radcliffe's undated Latin translation of *Prayers or Meditations*, written in his own hand, with a prefatory letter, also in Latin, addressed to his father as "tua dominatione" (your lordship). Although the *Oxford Dictionary of National Biography* does not list a John among his three sons, the fatherly recipient was probably Henry Radcliffe, second Earl of Sussex (1506?–57).

7. On the contemporary appeal of KP's transitional spirituality in *Prayers or Meditations*, see Kimberly Anne Coles, *Religion, Reform, and Women's Writing* (Cambridge: Cambridge University Press, 2008), 52–62.

knowledged, the compositional challenge that she took upon herself comes more clearly into view. For Parr in her *Prayers or Meditations* this challenge seems to have lain primarily in working toward a genuine inclusiveness for the affective range of a generic human voice by preventing its full-scale assimilation to masculine norms for literary expression. Despite its obligatory strategic accommodations, an individuated authorial design stamps Parr's creation—what C. Fenno Hoffman identified and described in 1959 as a "60-page abridgment" of the 177-page third book of Thomas à Kempis's *De Imitatione Christi* in the English translation of the whole work published by Richard Whitford, a Bridgettine monk of Syon monastery, under the title *The Following of Christ* (1531?).[8] When carefully examined, the "abridgment" that is Parr's *Prayers or Meditations* takes shape and substance as a determined, sustained act of intertextual appropriation that constitutes a genuine claim to authorship. As her controlling design, she aims to foster Reformed devotion among the literate laity of the late Henrician church of England by performing a generic reorientation on the masterpiece of late medieval Catholic spirituality in northern Europe. Circumstantial information, moreover, permits Queen Katherine to be followed as she claims her place in a program of vernacular religious publication spearheaded by Archbishop Cranmer.

After her marriage to Henry VIII in July 1543, Parr so quickly secured his trust that she found herself appointed regent of the realm from July to late September 1544, while the king in person conducted military actions in France. Before leaving for France, Henry commanded Cranmer to revive the traditional custom of holding public processions to pray for "the miserable state of Christendom." The king made a major concession to his reformist archbishop: the litany and prayers chanted publicly in procession would be "in our native English tongue," and some new occasional prayers would be composed. During the summer of 1544, while Katherine exercised the sovereignty of the realm in Henry's stead, Cranmer was carrying out another of Henry's directives—that he, as a designated member of her regency council, attend daily on the queen. The inception of Katherine's pro-Reformation alignment, which became more overt and explicit with time, is most plausibly dated to her contact with Cranmer that summer. John Strype's *Ecclesiastical Memorials* records a report that Parr intended "A prayer for the King" and "A prayer for men to say entering into battle" to be included in Cranmer's issue of an English *Litany with Suffrages to be said or sung* that went through two editions in 1544.[9] While both these editions and subsequent ones from Henry's reign intro-

8. C. Fenno Hoffman Jr., "Catherine Parr as a Woman of Letters," *Huntington Library Quarterly* 23 (1959): 354.

9. John Strype, *Ecclesiastical Memorials, Relating Chiefly to Religion, and the Reformation of It, and the Emergencies of the Church of England* (Oxford: Clarendon, 1822), 2.1:205–6. The earliest edition of Cranmer's *Litany* that is available electronically through Early English Books Online is STC 10621 (May 27, 1544).

duce bidding prayers for the king, Queen Katherine, and Prince Edward, none in fact includes these two prayers. They found their separate way into print at the end of her *Psalms or Prayers* and thereafter at the end of *Prayers or Meditations.*

Closely conjoined in date, Cranmer's and Parr's two works also manifest a close complementarity in their motives, direction, and norms for expression. The basic principles are spelled out in "An exhortation unto prayer, thought meet by the King's majesty, and his clergy, to be read to the people in every church afore processions" prefaced to Cranmer's Reformed version of the *Litany.* Because prayer offered to God must be heartfelt and intelligible, English is the language for English speakers to use. Any "true use of prayer" must also be "grounded upon the sure foundation of God's holy and blessed Word, which cannot deceive us." While the litany and biddings instruct how "to make our common prayer to our heavenly Father," Cranmer exhorts that prayer be made individually as well: "It is very convenient, and much acceptable to God, that you should use your private prayer in your mother tongue, that you understanding what you ask of God, may more earnestly and fervently desire the same, . . . ever having . . . an earnest request and desire of those godly benefits which are appointed in God's Word."[10] Cranmer, however, gives no instruction in the personal mode of Biblically grounded, vernacular prayer. This is where Parr's *Prayers or Meditations* enters as a culturally available project for a trustworthy, educated gentlewoman who, besides being the king's consort, had recently been judged capable of the exercise of the powers of the king himself in council. Cranmer's is the work for souls in public, Parr's the work for souls in private. Both attained the status of royally sanctioned productions of an English church that was making its first moves from traditionalist to Reformed formulation in handbooks for worship offered to its literate membership at large.

In a study of European women authors who wrote histories between 1400 and 1820, Natalie Zemon Davis has emphasized two "especially important" psychological factors: a deep personal sense of connection and involvement with the areas of public life considered appropriate for the writing in question, and sufficient assurance that the work would find an audience to take its author seriously.[11] A crucial catalyst for Queen Katherine's foray into authorship must have been the revisionary influence exerted by Cranmer on her religious alignment and beliefs, at the very point when her autocratic husband had bolstered her self-confidence by entrusting her with the rule of the realm. The text of Parr's *Prayers or Meditations* readily submits to analysis as a sensitive and discerning contribution to a late Henrician liter-

10. [Thomas Cranmer,] *An Exhortation unto Prayer . . . Also a Litany with Suffrages,* sigs. Aii v, Bi v, Bii r.

11. Natalie Zemon Davis, "Gender and Genre: Women as Historical Writers, 1400–1820," in *Beyond Their Sex: Learned Women of the European Past,* ed. Patricia LaBalme (New York: New York University Press, 1980), 154.

ary program on popularizing pro-Reformation lines. Its most prominent thematic and textual features will be addressed in the disussion that follows.

Degendering from explicit masculinist norms in the direction of a fresh universalizing of the Christian gospel appears to be the chief design and effect of the *Prayers or Meditations*, produced by selecting, reworking, and reordering passages from book 3 of *The Following of Christ*, Whitford's English version of à Kempis's Latin original. Entirely dismantling the monastic framework and its affiliated terms of reference in à Kempis and Whitford, Parr does away with dialogue between a gender-marked pair of intimates who are identified as "Jesu," "Lord," "sir," or "sire," on the one hand, and invariably as "my son" on the other. Elimination of this dialogue also dispenses with a dynamic in which the monk of the source text is brought, by instruction and exhortation, through stages of moral and spiritual proficiency to the privilege of mystical rapture in a relation of ever closer male bonding. Parr replaces dialogue with monologue—the "I," "me," and "my" of a needy, erring human speaker whose psychology is characterized solely in terms of a generic heart, mind, and will. Her text consists of the soul's personal addresses to Christ, yearning for grace in various guises—consolation, patience, strength—so as to follow and be united with Him. From the densely Scriptural weave of the *Imitatio* as sustained in Whitford's *Following*, she consistently selects lyric and affective verses couched in the first person or restyles them in this form. The result is to center her abridgment of Whitford's version in a generically human speaker who yields self to God in a posture of total dependency and in utterances drawn from God's own Word. The defining characteristics of Parr's speaker reflect a notable theme of the earlier English Reformation: the yet unprobed and unproblematic presumption of the spiritual equality of all persons before God.[12]

In Whitford's translation as in à Kempis's original, devotional method is cast as a dynamic of spiritual progress displaying important affinities with St. Bonaventure's "threefold way" ("triplici via"). Book 1 embodies the outlook of the active life of moral self-regulation that weans the soul from the world (the purgative way). Book 2 fosters the turning to an inward life that refers all experience to the suffering and love manifest in the crucified Christ (the illuminative way). Book 3 posits a contemplative merger with Christ, so that Christ speaks to the soul from within the soul (the unitive way). While allowance is made throughout the three books

12. Hugh Latimer was the most outspoken among ranking midcentury churchmen on the subject of spiritual equality, explicitly traced to its Pauline source: see *Selected Sermons of Hugh Latimer*, ed. Allan G. Chester (Charlottesville: University of Virginia Press for the Folger Shakespeare Library, 1968), which restores passages suppressed in earlier printings; and John N. King, *English Reformation Literature: The Tudor Origins of the Protestant Tradition* (Princeton, NJ: Princeton University Press, 1982), 175–76. For an overview of the complications in period thinking about "spiritual equality," see Margaret R. Sommerville, *Sex and Subjection: Attitudes to Women in Early-Modern Society* (London: Arnold, 1995), 43–51.

for extreme oscillations of feeling, the sequencing of the *Imitatio*, reproduced in the *Following*, clearly models the respective stages of progress in the spiritual life as methodized in medieval Catholicsm: the levels of the beginner, the proficient, and the so-called perfect.[13]

Parr takes no account whatever of this dynamic of spiritual progress. To launch her *Prayers or Meditations*, she plunges into the central section of the long third book in Whitford's translation. Cued by à Kempis's "incipit," "Audiam quid loquatur in me Dominus Deus" (I listen to what the Lord God speaks within me), this section of the text is conventionally known as the "Book of Internal Consolation," the acme of spiritual rapture in the work. Parr's redaction, however, deals very sparingly in the ecstatic intimacies that make the third book distinctive. She omits altogether the famous pair of chapters, 5 and 6, "Of the marvelous effect of the love of God" and "Of the proof of a true lover of God," and she sorts some passages of aspiration and longing from more highly charged expressions of transport as she selects from chapter 39, "How our Lord God savoreth to his lover sweetly above all things and in all things." As becomes obvious in a recasting like *Prayers or Meditations* that shortens its source text by two-thirds, Parr's most potent compositional strategy is excision—in effect, silencing.[14]

From the standpoint of Catholic method, this *in medias res* entry into book 3 is an illegitimate trespass on a sacred preserve: the disclosures, experiences, and formulations attained only by contemplatives long practiced in arduous spiritual techniques. But Parr's reworking shows her to be acting deliberately and to know what she is after. In violating her source text in this fashion, she repudiates the implied

13. For fuller discussion, see Sr. M. Augustine Scheele, *Educational Aspects of Spiritual Writings* (Milwaukee, WI: St. Joseph, 1940), 76–95.

14. Silencing some themes and tonalities intensifies the remainder, as an early reader saw fit to note in KP's margin. The handwriting is evidently that of Anne Dyson, who signed the copies of *Prayers or Meditations* (STC 4819) and Cranmer's *Litany* (the second edition of 1544; STC 10621) held by Cambridge University Library, which are electronically available through Chadwyck-Healey's Early English Books Online under these STC numbers. Anne's marginal note appears next to this passage in KP: "O Jesu, the joy and comfort of all Christian people, . . . my heart crieth to Thee by still desires, and my silence speaketh unto Thee, and saith: How long tarrieth my Lord God to come to me?" The note, the only writing besides emphasis marks in the whole volume, is legible except for its last word. It reads simply, "the faithful dooe servisse to god with theyr soul." This appreciative jotting by a sixteenth-century woman reader is a poignant response to emphasis laid by a woman writer, her contemporary, on the expressive capacities in the soul's silence—a condition identified as a historically feminine one. See Suzanne W. Hull, *Chaste, Silent, and Obedient: English Books for Women, 1475–1640* (San Marino, CA: Huntington Library, 1982), and Gary Waller, "Struggling into Discourse: The Emergence of Renaissance Women's Writing," in *Silent But for the Word: Tudor Women as Patrons, Translators, and Writers of Religious Works*, ed. Margaret P. Hannay (Kent, OH: Kent State University Press, 1985), 238–56.

constraints on its scope. Her speaker, not one of "the perfect" or even an adept, but an undifferentiated human "I" or "me," displays a quite standard psychology for the period. What singles out this speaking soul is not some rarefied spiritual effort but the advent of saving grace that it perceives and heralds. On this grace depends not only true devotion but any relation whatever of the soul to Christ. Parr's text opens at just this point of recognition, and it is directly sharpened through deployment of her two other major authorial techniques besides excision—insistent, minute rewording on the one hand and interpolation of sentence-length new material on the other.[15]

"Most benign Lord Jesu, grant me Thy grace," begins Parr in words taken from Whitford's translation of the opening of book 3, chapter 17. "That it may," he continues, "work with me," but she substitutes "work in me" (*Following*, fol. 82v; *Prayers*, sig. Aii r). A sentence without a counterpart in Whitford soon spells out her identification of such grace with the unmerited gift of salvation: "O what thanks ought I to give unto Thee, which hast suffered the grievous death of the cross, to deliver me from my sins, and to obtain everlasting life for me?" (*Prayers*, sig. Aiii v). This gift of saving grace registers on the speaking soul as desire for a oneness of will with its Lord; this desire, itself enabled by grace, sustains the entire lyric movement of *Prayers or Meditations*. Parr now backtracks from chapter 17 in Whitford to excerpt from chapter 16. She reinforces the origin of the soul's desire in the gift of grace by inserting another new sentence. Its effect is to merge the two—the gift, the desire—in the onset of regeneration that for her functionally defines grace: "Lord Jesu, I pray Thee grant me grace, that I never set my heart on the things of this world, but that all worldly and carnal affections may utterly die and be mortified in me" (*Prayers*, sig. Aii v).

Next excerpting from chapter 18 and then from chapter 19, Parr pointedly deflates the self-confidence of the contemplative soul in her source, who offers: "Lord, I will gladly suffer for Thee whatsoever Thou wilt shall fall upon me . . . indifferently will I take of Thy hand good and bad" (*Following*, fol. 74v). Instead Parr's soul declares anew its utter reliance on grace: "Lord, give me grace gladly to suffer, whatsoever Thou wilt shall fall upon me, and patiently to take at Thy hand good and bad" (*Prayers*, sig. Aiii v). Such dislocation of the order of chapters in the process of excerpting from her source is unusual compositional practice for Parr. She departs from sequence only twice in her *Prayers or Meditations*, both times at its extremities. At the beginning she skips backwards and forwards from chapter 17, as just noted, before proceeding selectively in order. Again, at the close of her work she makes an enormous jump from midway in chapter 56 back to the opening of chapter 4. Such strenuous interventions in her source text collapse its arpeggios of

15. KP learned these techniques at first hand in the process of translating Fisher's *Psalmi seu Precationes*; see the introduction to *Psalms or Prayers*, p. 213.

mystical transport into a deep chord of basic dependence on divinity, so that Parr's soul leaves off speaking where that of her source virtually begins in book 3—with a prayer, significantly, "to obtain the grace of devotion" (*Prayers*, sig, Cviii v; *Following*, fol. 64r-v).

Through Parr's systematic selections and alterations, the connotations of spirituality are wrenched from a perceptibly traditional to an emergently Reformist cast. Book 3 of the *Following* recurrently limits the term "grace" to the preferential divine favor accorded the contemplative, as illustrated by Whitford's phrasing in chapter 23: "Give me, Lord Jesu, this special grace, for to rest me in Thee above all creatures" (*Following*, fol. 89r). Parr reworks the sentence toward greater inclusiveness of both subject and object: "Lord Jesu, I pray Thee, give me the grace to rest in Thee above all things" (*Prayers*, sig. Avi v). Whitford renders and glosses the ecstatic longing in chapter 36 as follows: "'Lord, I have great need of Thy grace . . . that of Thy great singular grace . . . I may fly freely to Thee.' He coveted to fly without let that said thus" (*Following*, fol. 104r). Parr pares down as follows, cutting the gloss altogether and renewing emphasis on grace with phrases spliced in from chapter 39: "Lord, grant me Thy singular grace that I may . . . freely ascend to Thee . . . O Lord, . . . it must be through help of Thy grace" (*Prayers*, sig. Bv r).

Grace in Parr shifts away from associations with divine favor understood as preferential dispensations and functions of the spirit. Her *Prayers or Meditations* figures grace as the vital empowerment by which God opens in the sin-marred human soul the only conduit to a positive relation between the two. Parr adopts the Reformation sense that the term first acquires in Luther.[16] Her reworking of a notable apposition in Whitford highlights their disparate apprehensions. "Gather my wits and powers of my soul together in Thee," implores the soul in Whitford's chapter 54; "grant me to cast away and wholly to despise all fantasies of sin" (*Following*, fol. 126r-v). The soul in Parr's text explicitly refers its hope for psychic wholeness and moral strength to the workings of grace: "Gather, O Lord, my wits and the powers of my soul together in Thee, and make me . . . by Thy grace strongly to resist and overcome all motions and occasions of sin" (*Prayers*, sig. Cii v).

Because the theology and psychology of spiritual effort remain fundamental to the *Imitatio Christi*, Whitford's translation insistently inscribes a harsh late medieval dualism regarding life and the self. Heaven is to be embraced, this world renounced. The body and all earthly concerns are to be shunned as evils together with the world; only the spirit freed of the flesh can achieve and experience goodness. Parr's recasting just as insistently parts company with the enforcement of such

16. See Heinrich Bornkamm's exposition of what he terms "the fundamental axioms of evangelical belief"—"by faith alone," "by grace alone," "Christ alone," "Scripture alone"—in *The Heart of Reformation Faith*, trans. John W. Doberstein (New York: Harper and Row, 1965), 16–44. For fuller discussion, see Brian A. Gerrish, *Grace and Reason: A Study in the Theology of Luther* (Oxford: Clarendon, 1962).

dualisms, and especially with implications that privilege the cloistered recluse as the true "religious." Thus, where Whitford's text proposes to "witness the apostles" as chief examples of Christ's elect, they figure as "princes of all the world which nevertheless were conversant among the people without complaining" (*Following*, fol. 92r-v). Parr reworks this representation along discernibly Cranmerian lines to model a clergy busy among the people in preaching and visitation: "Witness be Thy blessed apostles, whom Thou madest chief pastors and spiritual governors of Thy flock" (*Prayers*, sig. Bi v).

Divergences in theological and psychological outlook widen as Parr excerpts and reworks her source. The *Following* invokes a calculus of meritorious motives by which the soul can gauge its progress from worldliness to otherworldliness: "I would be above all temporal things, but whether I will or not, I am compelled . . . to be subject unto my flesh" (*Following*, fol. 125v). Recasting this passage, Parr turns it outside in, implying her rejection of any possible calculus of the soul's progress. In her text neat dualisms are replaced by evocations of constant inward struggle: "I would subdue all evil affections, but they daily rebel and rise against me, and will not be subject unto my spirit" (*Prayers*, sig. Cii v). The persistence of a calculus of progress and of concern with what Luther decried as works-righteousness climaxes in the prudential balancing of the reflections on justification offered in Whitford:

> I ought alway to meeken myself and patiently to suffer all things in charity after Thy pleasure. Forgive me, Lord, as oft as I have not so done. . . . Thy mercy is [a] more profitable and more sure way for me to the getting of pardon and forgiveness of my sins than a trust in mine own works. . . . And though I dread not my conscience, yet . . . Thy mercy removed and taken away, no man may be justified nor appear righteous in Thy sight. (*Following*, fols. 127v–128r)

Parr reduces the foregoing to a brief, direct appeal for justification in Reformation terms as the righteousness that inheres nowhere in the soul but is imputed to it by its "Lord God": "To Thy mercy I do appeal, seeing no man may be justified nor appear righteous in Thy sight, if Thou examine him after Thy justice" (*Prayers*, sig. Bviii r).

If the presence interchangeably called "Lord" or "Christ" does not converse with the soul in Parr's pages as it does, so familiarly and lengthily, in the *Following*, it is not because the divine voice is absent from *Prayers or Meditations*. In fact this voice sounds copiously, but it does so through Biblical echoes within human utterance. This consistent and conspicuous feature of Parr's text implements, in a personal register, the program for grounding all prayer in God's Word that Cranmer announced in his "Exhortation unto Prayer" prefacing his *Litany*. Where, for example, the Lord in Whitford characteristically exhorts the soul to "learn to have patience with Me, and not to disdain to bear the miseries and the wretchedness of this life as I have done for thee . . . unto My death upon the cross" (*Following*, fols. 84v–85r), in Parr the soul just as characteristically replaces such discourse with reminiscences of relevant Scripture—here, Philippians 2:8—that it quotes back to its Lord: "Thou gavest us most perfect example of patience: fulfilling and obeying the will of Thy Father even unto the death" (*Prayers*, sig. Aiv r). Parr's excision of all mystical impartings that are not phrased as echoes of Scripture—in other words, her identification of all communication between God and the soul with the text of the Bible—makes for some of her most radical differences from Whitford and opens a rich further dimension of intertextuality in her work.[17]

The deliberate design of Parr's Scripturalism can be illustrated by her characteristic handling of an oblique echo of Matthew 6:21 in Whitford: "Wherefore Thou that art everlasting truth sayest openly, There as thy treasure is, there is thy heart" (*Following*, fol. 126r). Parr's rephrasing makes the Biblical echo more audible: "Accordingly, as Thou doest say in the Gospel, Where as a man's treasure is, there is his heart" (*Prayers*, sig. Civ r). Her Scripturalist norms and design emerge, however, most insistently in a multitude of tiny departures that take Whitford's phrasings toward ever greater heightening of sense parallelisms and Psalm-like cadencing in the already densely woven, allusive texture of à Kempis's original. Typography too plays a part in this overall difference, for Whitford's text is set in block format throughout while Parr's is disposed in versicles like the Psalter—and Cranmer's *Litany*.

The intertextuality that Parr practices with Scripture in her *Prayers or Meditations* contrasts markedly with the free hand she exercises in dealing with non-Scriptural material in Whitford's translation. She is so highly respectful of the authoritative status of the Bible that she preserves its wording verbatim within hers. The effect is particularly striking when the soul in Parr assumes an explicitly masculine gender to conform with the reading of one or more Biblical texts. Thus, within a comparatively brief stretch of text, an echo of Psalm 8:4—"O Lord, what is man, that Thou vouchsafest to have mind of him"—compounds with an allusion to the "perfect man" of Psalm 37:37 who finds his peace in God and with the further echoes of Psalms 24:4 and 19:14 in "Blessed is that man that, for the love of Thee, . . . in a clean and pure conscience . . . may offer his prayers to Thee." The sequence climaxes in a close echo of phrasing from Romans 6:6: "But alas, mine old man, that is my carnal affections, live still in me and are not crucified" (*Prayers*, sigs. Bii r, Bv v, Civ r-v). There are even instances in Parr where the normative force of masculine gender in Scripture operates as a trace element, although nei-

17. The *Imitatio Christi* is itself replete with Biblical echoes and allusions, a feature inadequately annotated in the many English-language editions that have appeared. KP thus further intensifies an already prominent strain in her original source. For remarks on the quotient of Scripture in à Kempis's text, see J. E. G. de Montmorency, *Thomas à Kempis, His Age and Book*, 2nd ed. (London: Methuen, 1907), 174–80.

ther she nor Whitford is quoting or alluding to Scripture at these particular points. One such instance, a passage beginning "Where man is oftentimes defiled with sin, encumbered with affliction, unquieted with troubles, wrapped in cares," may be more clearly generic than clearly gendered (*Prayers*, sig. Ci r, adapting *Following*, fol. 120r). But four other instances are gendered masculine despite the absence of precedent from a Biblical source. "O Lord, all gifts and virtues that any man hath in body or soul, . . . be Thy gifts, and come of Thee, and not of ourself," Parr reads in one such passage; and shortly thereafter, "Lord, I know that no man ought to be abashed or miscontent, that he is in a low estate in this world" (*Prayers*, sig. Bi r-v, a free handling of *Following*, fols. 91v, 92r). A third such passage reads "This is Thy grace, O Lord, to Thy friend, to suffer him to be troubled in this world for Thy love" (*Prayers*, sig. Cvi r-v; cf. *Following*, fol. 130v). A fourth invokes "Thou, Lord God, . . . which . . . bringest a man nigh unto death, and after restorest him to life again, that he may thereby learn to know his own weakness" (*Prayers*, sig. Cv r; cf. *Following*, fol. 131r).

Such masculinist assimilation might remain unremarkable in a sixteenth-century devotional text except for a considerably larger group of readings that show Parr at pains to demasculinize the soul of her text where opportunities arise for doing so.[18] Her authorial decision to revamp the dialogue of the *Following*'s third book as monologue appears in a fresh light with the realization that in the process she excised literally dozens of masculine forms of address in Whitford. Parr leaves herself with her "I," "my," and "me," largely sufficient for personal reference except in contexts where her soul figures itself to itself in mindfulness of its relation to its ever-present Lord. Here her authorial practice, unaffected by a Scriptural prototype, proves revealing. In what looks simply like a universalizing move in some of these contexts, Parr degenders the masculine locutions in her source. For example, she refers to "Thy secret and terrible judgments, which scourge the righteous with the sinner," where Whitford reads "the righteous man with the sinner" (*Prayers*, sig. Cvii r; *Following*, fol. 130v). And she revises where Whitford expands first-person pronouns into third-person masculine references—"if Thou withdraw Thyself from me . . . then may not Thy servant run the way of Thy commandments as he did first . . . for it is not with him as it was before"—so that her text sustains ungendered first-person pronouns throughout the passage: "if Thou

18. For discussion of manipulations of French, a language far richer than English in grammatical gender markings, by a sixteenth-century woman poet, see François Rigolot, "Gender vs. Sex Difference in Louise Labé's Grammar of Love," in *Rewriting the Renaissance: The Discourses of Sexual Differences in Early Modern Europe*, ed. Margaret W. Ferguson, Maureen Quilligan, and Nancy J. Vickers (Chicago: University of Chicago Press, 1986), 287–98. The substance of Rigolot's analysis is unaffected by recent claims that "Louise Labé" was the pseudonym of one or more male poets; see Mireille Huchon, *Louise Labé: Une créature de papier* (Geneva: Droz, 2006).

withdraw Thyself from me . . . then may not Thy servant run the way of Thy commandments, as I did before. For it is not with me as it was" (*Prayers*, sig. Cv v; *Following*, fol. 130r).

But can universalizing fully account for what Parr does when she recasts the figurations of the speaking soul in her *Prayers or Meditations?* Evidently it cannot, for two reasons. One is a stylistic tendency that goes far beyond the explicit degenderings in Parr's text: she works at a number of points to heighten the connotations of deference and dependency in her vocabulary of self-reference. Where, for example, the soul in Whitford's version upbraids itself as a "wretched man" and laments, "I am but vanity, and naught before Thee, a[n] unconstant man," the soul in Parr substitutes "wretched creature" and intensifies self-deprecation before the Lord: "I am nothing else of myself, but vanity before Thee, an unconstant creature" (*Following*, fols. 125v, 119v; *Prayers*, sigs. Cii v, Bvi v). For Parr's soul, daring to speak at all—not, as in Whitford, the manner of speaking—is in question before a Lord whose creature the soul is.

Reformation thought does not seem a likely source for the insistent dependency and submissiveness expressed by the soul in *Prayers or Meditations.* More likely these traits were ingrained in Parr as a feminine obligation—and reinforced by her experience as Henry's wife. A near analogue to the lyric posture adopted by the soul of *Prayers or Meditations* appears in a letter written by Queen Katherine to King Henry in France during the summer of her regency: "I make like account with your majesty as I do with God for His benefits and gifts. . . . Zeal and affection forceth me to be best content with that which is your will and pleasure. Thus love maketh me in all things to set apart mine own convenience and pleasure, and to embrace most joyfully his will and pleasure whom I love." Who is the "he" of "his will and pleasure"—Henry or God? The ambiguity appears irresolvable in light of Parr's declaration that God's and Henry's benefits and demands have been all of a piece in her experience.[19]

One augmentation of the Lord's lordship and the soul's submissiveness appears particularly suggestive among Parr's reworkings of Whitford. It offers a self-contained vignette of the relationship that becomes a structuring principle for the text of *Prayers or Meditations.* Whitford's phrasing runs: "Comfort and glad Thy lover . . . to be so well contented and pleased that he would as gladly be holden least as other would be holden most" (*Following*, fol. 92v). As she rewords in her genderless first person, Parr additionally recasts the soul from a lover to a servant: "O Lord, grant that I, Thy servant, may be as well content to be taken as the least, as other be to be greatest" (*Prayers*, sigs. Bi v-Bii r). Very visible here, such local ten-

19. For the full text of this letter of KP to Henry, see no. 11 in part 2 of the correspondence. My general introduction treats this passage as paradigmatic of KP's existential outlook, pp. 3–4.

dencies in self-reference to style the soul as the creation and the utter dependent of the Lord emerge as the comprehensive means by which Parr makes the larger whole of her *Prayers or Meditations* return full circle upon itself.[20] A comparison of its beginning and ending reveals the exactness of the thematic and tonal reprise that gives shape to Parr's text. Its opening petitions read "Most benign Lord Jesu, grant me . . . that I may ever desire and will that, which is most p[l]easant, and most acceptable to Thee. . . . Lord, Thou knowest what thing is most profitable, and most expedient for me" (*Prayers*, sig. Aii r-v). The prayer that closes out Parr's use of material from Whitford reprises these petitions: "Teach me, Lord, to fulfill Thy will, to live meekly . . . before Thee, for Thou art . . . He that knowest me as I am" (*Prayers*, sig. Di r-v; *Following*, fol. 64v).

The stylistic and structural dominance that Parr accords in her *Prayers or Meditations* to a lyrical posture of subjection, the forfeiting of personal will to an all-powerful and all-knowing Lord, again proves traceable to an experiential source through the turns of phrasing in another of her private letters. Henry chose Katherine for his queen, and there was no resisting this, although at the time, in 1543, she had hoped to marry Thomas Seymour. When this mutual attraction rekindled after Henry's death in January 1547, Katherine explained to Thomas how she came to accept her marriage with Henry. The echoes of *Prayers or Meditations* are telling and unmistakable: "As truly as God is God, my mind was fully bent, the other time I was at liberty, to marry you before any man I knew. Howbeit, God withstood my will therein most vehemently for a time, and, through His grace and goodness, made that possible which seemed to me most impossible—that was, made me to renounce utterly mine own will, and to follow His will most willingly."[21] Such intensifications in the intertextuality linking *Prayers or Meditations* with Parr's letters to Henry VIII and Thomas Seymour work to confirm that addresses of love and submission from a soul that deliberately styles itself "creature" and "servant" rather than "man" do not only universalize but also personalize the speaker in feminine terms.[22]

Nor do the ramifications of intertextuality stop here. As will presently be described in more detail, a unique tiny volume in Katherine Parr's handwriting con-

20. It must also be noted that Marguerite de Navarre's *Le Miroir de l'âme pécheresse* offers a conspicuous precedent for styling the self as God's creation and utter dependent, as conceived by a woman poet of royal status. Princess Elizabeth translated this work into English prose as a 1545 New Year's gift for KP. For examples of Marguerite's abject self-presentation, see *Elizabeth I: Translations, 1544–1589*, ed. Mueller and Scodel, 54–55, 59–61, 66–68.

21. See no. 2 in part 4, p. 131.

22. For discussion of a precedent in English, a century earlier, for using "creature" and "servant" to inscribe the first-person subject of feminine devotion, see Janel Mueller, "Autobiography of a New 'Creatur': Female Spirituality, Selfhood, and Authorship in *The Book of Margery Kempe*," in *Women in the Middle Ages and in the Renaissance: Literary and Historical Perspectives*, ed. Mary Beth Rose (Syracuse, NY: Syracuse University Press, 1986), 155–72.

tains a version of *Prayers or Meditations* that is two-thirds the length of the printed text. An inscription records that Parr presented this miniature book to a Mistress Tuke, one of three daughters of Sir Brian Tuke, a secretary to Henry VIII.[23] In this redaction prepared by hand in a single copy for another woman, Queen Katherine could have produced a text potentially quite different from that of her publicly printed version. There are some substantive differences. Generic masculine references dwindle to a residue of two—one being the Psalmic echo "perfect man"—while the figuration of the lyrical soul, the "I," as a loving dependent and subordinate is retained and even sharpened by the shortening and reordering of the text. The most notable feature of Mistress Tuke's version, however, is its ending. Parr works a major variant on the structural circularity of her published *Prayers or Meditations*. Beginning, like the longer version, "Most benign Lord Jesu, grant me . . . that I may ever desire and will that which is most acceptable to Thee," the short text concludes with the soul's longing to be united with Christ. In this new ending, significantly, Parr takes care to avoid the rapture of a solitary contemplative by excerpting from Whitford a tissue of Biblical echoes—Romans 8:21, Psalm 9:2, 1 Corinthians 4:28, Matthew 25:34—that clearly situate this union in a heavenly afterlife and extend it to all chosen souls. "When shall I be clearly delivered from the bondage of sin?" her ending asks. "When shall I, Lord, have only mind on Thee and fully be glad and merry in Thee? When shalt Thou be All in all, and when shall I be with Thee in Thy kingdom that Thou hast ordained for Thine elect people from the beginning?" (*Prayers*, sig. Cii r).

It is tempting at first to infer that the spousal climax given to the soul's creaturely dependency in this shortened text of *Prayers or Meditations* was shaped by Parr for Mistress Tuke as a devotional reinforcement of her feminine social identity. A corrective emerges, however, from Queen Katherine's previously quoted letter to King Henry to belie any easy stereotypic inference about gendering. She concludes this letter by "committing" her royal consort "to the governance of the Lord . . . and after this life to enjoy the kingdom of His elect"—a benediction tonally but not substantively modified in the concluding cadence of Mistress Tuke's version: "when shall I be with Thee in Thy kingdom that Thou hast ordained for Thine elect?" As Parr configures the condition and attitude of the soul—the "I"—in her *Prayers or Meditations*, her language works delicately and ceaselessly to mediate between universalizing and gendering tendencies. Significantly, this mediation operates as surely in the longer text published with royal authorization as it does in the shortened, private version made by Parr for another woman.

Keith Thomas has remarked on how mysterious many aspects of the ener-

23. See "Tuke, Sir Brian (d. 1545)," in the online *Oxford Dictionary of National Biography*. Both the circumstances of presentation and the relationship between Queen Katherine and Sir Brian's daughter are unknown.

gizing force of the Reformation in the lives and personalities of sixteenth- and seventeenth-century Englishwomen still remain.[24] The situation for readers is more favorable, however, in the case of Katherine Parr. With sidelights from her personal letters, she can be observed in both versions of her *Prayers or Meditations* as she conjointly authors a paradigm for private devotion in the late Henrician Church of England and a chapter of her spiritual and human autobiography.

The unique, incomplete autograph text of Katherine Parr's *Prayers or Meditations* displayed in the Mayor's Parlor, Kendal, Cumbria (formerly Westmorland), is an object of local pride. This tiny book, measuring four centimeters in width, six centimeters in length, and one and one-half centimeters in thickness, contains sixty-six leaves of text and ten blank leaves at the end. There are no contemporary identifying marks: no title page, no presentational inscription, no signature. A modern note in pencil on the front flyleaf records that Katherine Parr made this volume as a gift for Mistress Tuke, a daughter of Sir Brian Tuke, one of King Henry VIII's secretaries, and that it was acquired by Thomas Lawrence in 1669. Offered at auction in London in 1936, it was purchased with public funds raised in Kendal, claimed by some at that time to be Katherine Parr's birthplace.[25]

Except for its crudely pasted-in endpapers, a later addition, the volume is in a superb state of preservation. Queen Katherine wrote out her text on vellum—soft, pliable, now manila-hued, with a slippery surface permitting easy turning of the tiny leaves, which have held their inks and gilding well. The solid silver binding has hinged front and back covers; the spine is decorated with a stamped Tudor rose and crown and with raised bands simulating a leather binding.

The presentation of the text is equally beautiful. Each page has a hand-ruled rectangular border in gold, indented about half a centimeter from its edges. Within these borders, the text is set out in versicles, each beginning at the left margin. The

24. Keith Thomas, "Women and the Civil War Sects," *Past and Present* 13 (1958): 42–62. Fortunately our knowledge regarding early modern English women writers has been greatly extended in recent years. For primary source materials, there is the indispensable Ashgate series The Early Modern Englishwoman in Print, edited by Anne Lake Prescott and Betty Travitsky. Among a number of studies and critical editions, the following may be signaled: *The Examinations of Anne Askew*, ed. Elaine V. Beilin (New York: Oxford University Press, 1996); Beilin, *Redeeming Eve*, chaps. 3–5, 9; Kimberly Anne Coles, *Religion, Reform, and Women's Writing in Early Modern England* (New York: Cambridge University Press, 2008); *The Polemics and Poems of Rachel Speght*, ed. Barbara K. Lewalski (New York: Oxford University Press, 1996); Christine Peters, *Patterns of Piety: Women, Gender, and Religion in Late Medieval and Reformation England* (Cambridge: Cambridge University Press, 2003).

25. Susan E. James, *Kateryn Parr: The Making of a Queen* (Aldershot, UK: Ashgate, 1998), 14–15, argues that KP's birthplace was much more likely to have been the Blackfriars district in London or, alternatively, Rye House in Hertfordshire.

versicles are lettered in black ink, interspersed with a muted color scheme in four tones of wash: deep blue and medium blue, crimson and scarlet. The capital letter that begins each versicle is traced in gold on the background of a square wash in one color, and the space between the end of the text of each versicle and the facing line border in gold is filled by a similar rectangular wash in another color. On each of these terminal rectangles, one of several simple, curvilinear motifs suggesting vines and leaves is thinly traced in gold.

Any opening of the volume displays, across a pair of pages, the visual patterning of small intermittent blocks of color overlaid with gold tracery and framed within a gold rule. But the graceful written text remains in clear ascendancy throughout, both because it occupies the largest amount of page space and because its black characters contrast more with the vellum than the reds, blues, and golds do. As a material object, this tiny volume figures as a transitional item in the history of the book. Its origins clearly lie in manuscript production, specifically late medieval Catholic primers for private devotion, but its restrained decoration and its premium on readability bespeak the norms for textual preeminence that governed humanist and Reformation print culture.

Queen Katherine's handwriting is instantly recognizable. All of her autograph letters in English are in a legible "bastard"—or hybrid—hand composed of mixed, predominantly secretary forms that quite closely resembles the hand of Mary Tudor, two years her junior, as well as the hand of Maud Parr, Katherine's mother. Since Maud Parr was a longtime lady-in-waiting and intimate of Mary's mother, Queen Catherine of Aragon, their daughters may have been taught to write by a similar (or even the same) method.[26] The absence of information regarding the nature and extent of Mary and Katherine's relationship before Henry VIII married Katherine in July 1543 is regrettable, as is the lack of information about the date and auspices of Katherine's sumptuously embellished, scripted excerpt of her *Prayers or Meditations*.

It is, furthermore, unclear whether the state of the incomplete text and the ten leaves left blank at its end harbor clues regarding the order in which the two texts were produced. It is conceivable that the Kendal autograph represents a state of Queen Katherine's text prior to any print. The blank leaves would have sufficed to contain the rest of the material adapted from Whitford's translation of à Kempis's *De Imitatione Christi* in composing her *Prayers or Meditations*. But there would have been no space for the additional prayers—first two, later five—appended in the printed editions of 1545 and thereafter. However, the very close textual correspondence of the incomplete Kendal autograph and the printed editions of *Prayers*

26. W. J. Hardy, *The Handwriting of Kings and Queens of England* (London: Religious Tract Society, 1893), reproduces specimens that illustrate the similarities in Mary Tudor's and Katherine Parr's handwriting.

or Meditations precludes any secure inference regarding their chronological relationship.[27] The only available conclusion seems to be that *Prayers or Meditations* was a highly stable text from the moment it began to circulate, whether in print or in this unique autograph, and that this stability resulted from the special care with which its authorial copyist and its successive printers treated the text.

27. Three slight, repeated divergences between the text of the Kendal autograph and that of *Prayers or Meditations* (November 5, 1545) may at first appear significant in suggesting the priority of the incomplete text. At two points the Kendal autograph retains the "Therefore" of Whitford's translation where the 1545 printed editions of *Prayers or Meditations* revise to "Wherefore" (see nn 46, 49 of the modern-spelling version). At a third point the autograph text reads "Therefore" and the printed editions "Wherefore," but here "Wherefore" is also Whitford's reading (see n10 of the original-spelling version). The variants themselves show no consistent pattern, suggesting that they are probably best explained by KP's penchant for stylistic variation, observable even in minimal differences of wording—as here.

The Kendal Autograph Fragment of *Prayers or Meditations*[1]

Most beninge lorde Jesu, graunt me thy grace, that it may alway worke in me, and persever with me unto the ende.

Graunt me, that I maye ever desyre and will that which is moste acceptable[2] to the.

Thy will be my will, and my will be to follow alway thy wille.

Let there be alwaye in me one will, and one desire with the, and that I have no desire to will or not to will, but as thowe wilte.

Lorde, thou knowest what thinge is most profitable and most expedient for me.

Geve therfore what thow wilte, asmuche as thou willte, and whan thou wilte.

Dooe with me what thou wilte, as it shall please the, and as shalbe moste to thyne honour.

Put me where thou wilte, and freely do withe me in all thinges after thy will.

Thy creature I am, and in thy handes, leade and tourne me where thou wilte.

1. Source: Kendal, Cumbria, The Mayor's Parlor, an incomplete text of *Prayers or Meditations*, in KP's hand with embellishments in colored inks and gilt, as described in the introduction. Page divisions—always left unnumbered by KP—have not been indicated because they occur with obtrusive frequency in a volume as tiny as this one. Capital letters in boldface indicate where KP has used gilt tracery on deep red and blue fields to set off these initials as ornamental features of her text. Unfortunately there is no feasible way to indicate typographically the rectangular blocks of deep reds or blues overlaid with vine tracery that fill in the blank spaces between the endings of versicles and the righthand margin of the text. The notes here record the minor infrequent variants between this autograph text and the third, definitive printed version of *Prayers or Meditations*—hereafter, *P or M*.

2. **most acceptable** most pleasant and most acceptable (*P or M*).

Lo, I am thy servaunt ready to all thinges that thou commaundest: for I desyre not to lyve to my selfe but to the.

Lorde Jesu, I pray the graunte me grace, that I never set my herte on the thynges of thys worlde, but that all worldly and carnall affections may utterly dye and be mortified in me.

Graunt me above all thinges, that I may rest in the, and fully quiet and pacifye my herte in the.

For thou lorde, arte the verye true peace of herte and the perfecte reste of the soule: and, with oute the, all thinges be grevous and unquiet:

My lorde Jesu, I beseche the, bee with me in every place, and at all tymes, and lette it be to me a speciall solace, gladly for thy love to lacke all worldly solace.

And if thou with drawe thy comforte from me at any tyme keepe me, O lorde, from desperacion, and make me paciently to abide thy will and ordinaunce.

O lorde Jesu, thy jugementes bee rightuouse, and thy provydence is muche better for me than all that I can imagine or devyse.

Wherfore do with me in all thinges as it shall please the: for it maye not be but well, all that thou doest.

If thou wilte that I be in light, be thou blessed: If thou wilte that I be in darknes, be thou also blessed.

If thou vouche safe to comforte me, be thou highly blessed: If thou wilte I lyve in trouble, and without comforte, be thou likewyse ever blessed.

Lorde, geve me grace gladly to suffer what so ever thou wilte shall falle upon me, and paciently to take at thy hande good and badde, bitter and swete: joye and sorowe: and for all thinges that shall befalle unto me, hertely to thanke the.

Keepe me lorde from synne, and I shall than neither dreade death nor helle.

O what thankes ought I to geve unto the, which hast suffred the grevous deathe of the crosse, to delyver me from my sinne[3] and to obteine everlastinge liffe for me.

Thou gavest us most perfecte example of pacience, fulfillinge and obeinge the will of thy father even unto the deathe.

Make me wretched synner, obediently to use my selfe after thy wil in all thinges and paciently to beare the burden of this corruptible life.

For though this life be tedious, and as an hevy burdeyne to my soule: yet nevertheless through thy grace, and by example of the, it is nowe made muche more easy and comfortable than it was before thy incarnacion and passion.

Thy holy lyfe is our waye to the, and by folowinge of the, we walke to the, that art our head and savyour: And yet excepte thou haddest gone before, and shewed us the way to everlastynge lyfe, who wolde endevor hymselfe to folowe the seing we be yet so slow and dull, having the light of thy blessed example and holy doctrine to leade and directe us.

3. **sinne** sins (*P or M*).

O lorde Jesu, make that possible by grace that is impossible to me by nature.

Thou knowest welle, that I maie litle suffre and that I am anone cast downe and overthrowne with a litle adversitie: wherfore I beseche the O lorde, to strengthen me with thy spirite that I maye wyllinglye suffre for thy sake all maner of trouble and affliction.

Lorde, I still[4] knowelege unto the all myne unrightuousnes, and I will confesse to the all the unstablenesse of my herte.

Oftentymes a varieble[5] thynge troubleth me sore, and maketh me dull and slow to serve the

And somtyme I purpose to stand strongly, but whan a litle trouble cometh it is to me great anguishe and greffe, and of a right litle thinge riseth a greveouse temptacion to me.

Yea, whan I thinke my selfe to be sure and stronge and that (as it seemeth) I have the upper hande: sodeinly I feele my selfe ready to falle with a litle blaste of temptacion.

Beholde therfore good lorde my weakenes, and consydre my fraylnesse best knowen to the.

Have mercy on me, and delyver me from all iniquitie and synne, that I be not intangled therwith.

Oftentymes it greveth me sore, and in maner confoundeth me, that I am so unstable, so weke, and so fraile in resisting synfull mocions.

Whiche although they drawe me not alwaye to consent, yet never thelesse their assaltes be veraie grevous unto me.

And it is tedious to me to live in suche bataile, all be it I perceyve that suche battaile is not unprofitable unto me, for therby I knowe the better my selfe and myne owne infirmytes and that I must seke helpe only at thy hand.[6]

O lorde god of Israel the lover of all faithfull soules, vouchesafe to beholde the laboure and sorowe of me thy poore creature.

Assist me in all thinges withe thy grace, and so strength me with hevenly strength that nother my cruelle enemye the fende neither my wretched fleshe whiche is not yet subjecte to the spirite, have victorie or dominion over me.

O what a life maie this be called, where no trouble nor miserie lacketh: where every place is full of snares of mortall enemyes.

For one trouble or temptacion overpassed an other cometh by and by and the first conflicte yet duringe a new battaile sodeinly ariseth.

Wherfore, lorde Jesu, I praye the, geve me the grace to reste in the above all thinges and to quiet me in the above all creatures, above all glorie and honour above all dignitie and power, above all connynge and polecie above all health, and beautie,

4. **still** will (*P or M*).
5. **varieble** very little (*P or M*).
6. **hand** hands (*P or M*).

above all riches and treasure above all joy and pleasure above all fame and praise: above all mirthe and consolacion that mans herte maie take or feele besides the.

For thou lorde god, arte best, moste wise, moste high, moste myghtie, most sufficient, and moste full of all goodnes, most swete, and moste comfortable moste faire, most lovynge, moste noble moste glorious, in whome all goodnes most parfitly is.

And therfore what soever I have beside the it is nothinge to me: For my herte maye not rest, ne fully be pacified but only in the.

O lorde Jesu most lovinge spouse, who shall geve me wynges of perfecte love, that I maie flie up from these worldly myseries and reste in the.

O whan shalle I assende to the, and see, and feele how swete thou art.

Whan shalle I wholy gather my selfe in the so perfectely, that I shall not for thy love feele my selfe, but the only above my selfe, and above all worldely thinges that thou maiste vouchesafe to visite me in suche wise as thou doest visite thy moste faithfull lovers.

Nowe I often mourne and complayne of the myseries of this life, and with sorowe and greate heavynesse suffre theym.

For many thinges happen dayly to me, whiche oftentymes trouble me, make me heavy, and darken my understandinge.

They hynder me greatly, and put my mynde from the, and so encumbre me many waies that I can not freely and clerely desire the, ne have thy swete consolacions whiche with thy blessed sayntes be alwaie present.

I beseche the lorde Jesu, that the sighinges and inwarde desires of my herte may move and inclyne the to heare me.

O Jesu, kynge of everlastinge glory the joye and comfort of all christen people that are wandringe as pilgrymes in the wyldernesse of this worlde: my hert cryeth to the by stille desires, and my silence speaketh unto the, and saieth: howe longe tarieth my lorde god to come to me.

Come, O Lorde, and visite me, for without the I have no true joye, without the, my soule is heavy and sadde.

I am in prison and bounde with fetters of sorowe till thou O lorde, with thy gracious presence, vouchesafe to visit me, and bringe me agayne to lybertie and joye of spirite, and to shewe thy favorable countenaunce upon me.

Open my herte lorde, that I may beholde thy lawes and teache me to walke in thy commaundementes.

Make me to know and folowe thy will, and to have alwaies in my remembraunce thy manyfolde benefites, that I maye yelde due thankes to the for theym.

But I knowlage and confesse for trouthe that I am not able to gyve the condyne thankes for the least benefit that thou hast gyven me.

O lorde, all giftes and vertues that any man hathe in bodye or soule, naturall or supernaturall, bee thy giftes and come of the and not of our self and thei declare the great riches of thy mercie and goodnes unto us.

And thoughe some haive mo giftes then other, yet they all procede from the and without the, the least can not be had.

O lorde, I accompte it for a greate benefit not to have many worldelye giftes, wherby the laude and praise of men myght blynde my soule and deceave me.

Lorde, I knowe that no man ought to be abashed or miscontent, that he is in a lowe estat in this worlde, and lackethe the pleasures of this life: but rather to bee glade and rejoyse therat.

For so muche as thou haste chosen the poore and meke persones and suche as ar dispised in the worlde, to be thy servantes and famylier frendes

Witnesse by[7] thy blessed Apostles, whom thou madeste chiefe pastures and spirituall governours of thy flocke, which departed frome the counsaile of the Jewes, rejoysinge that they weare counted worthy to suffre rebuke for thy name.

Even so, O lorde, graunt, that I thy servaunt maie be as well contente to be taken as the leaste, as other bee to bee greatest, and that I bee as well pleased to bee in the lowest place, as in the highest, and as glade to be of noo reputacion in the worlde for thy sake, as other are to be noble and famous.

Lorde, it is the worke of a perfeite man, never to sequester his mynde from the, and amonge many worldly cares to go withoute care: not after the maner of an ydle or a dissolute person but by the prerogatyve of a free mynde, alwaie myndinge heavenly thinges, and not clevynge by inordinat affection to any creature.

I beseche the therfore my lorde Jesu, kepe me from the superfluous cares of thies worlde, that I be not inquieted[8] with bodely necessities, ne that I be not taken with the voluptuouse pleasures of the worlde, ne of the flesshe.

Preserve me from all thinges, which hyndereth my soule[9] health, that I be not overthrown with theym.

O lorde god, which art swetenesse unspekable, turn in to bitternesse to me all worldly and fleshlye delytes, whiche mought drawe me from the love of eternall thinges, to the love of shorte and vile pleasures.

Let not fleshe and bloude overcome me, ne yet the worlde with his vayne glorye deceyve me, nor the feend with hys manyfold craftes suplante me: but geve me gostely strength in resistinge theym pacience in sufferinge theym, and constance in perseveringe to the ende.

Geve me for all worldly delectacions, the moste swete consolacion of thy holy spirite, and for all fleshely love indue my soule with fervente love of the.

Make me stronge inwardly in my soule, and cast out therof all unprofitable cares of this worlde, that I bee not ledde by unstable desyres of earthely thinges but that I maye repute all thinges in this worlde (as they bee) transitorie, and soone vanishing awaye, and my selfe also with theim, drawynge towarde myne ende.

7. **by** be (*P or M*).
8. **inquieted** unquieted (*P or M*).
9. **hyndereth my soule** hinder my soules (*P or M*).

For nothinge under the sonne may longe abide, but all is vanitee and affliction of spirite

Geve me lorde, therfore heavenly wysedom, that I maye learne to seke and fynde the and above all thinges to love the.

Geve me grace to withdrawe me from theym that flatter me, and paciently to suffre theym that unjustly greve me.

Lorde whan temptacion or tribulacion comethe, vouchesafe to succure me, that all maye turne to my gostly comforte, and paciently to suffre, and alwaye to saye Thy name be blessed

Lorde, trouble is nowe at hande I am not well, but I am greatly vexed with this present affliction. O most glorious father, what shall I do anguyshe and trouble are on every side, helpe now I beseche the in this houre, thou shalte be lauded and praised whan I am perfectly made meke before the, and whan I am clerely delyverde by the.

May it therfore please the to deliver me, for whate maie I moste synfull wretche do or whither maie I goo for succoure but to the.

Geve me pacience now at this tyme in all my troubles, helpe me lorde God, and I shall not feare ne dreade, what troubles so ever fall upon me.

And now whate shall I say, but that thy will be done in me: I have deserved to be troubled and greved: and therfore it behoveth, that I suffre as longe as it pleaseth the.

But wolde to god, that I myght suffre gladlye till the furious tempestes were overpassed, and that quietnesse of herte might come agayne.

Thy mightye hande Lorde, is strong inough to take this trouble frome me and to asswage the cruelle assaultes therof, that I be not overcome with them as thou hast oftentymes done before this tyme, that whan I am clereli delyvered by the I maye with gladnes saie,

The right hande of him that is highest, hathe made this chaunge.

Lorde graunte me thy singuler grace, that I maie come thyther, where no creature shall lett me, ne kepe me from the perfite beholdinge of the.

For as longe as any traunsitory thinge kepeth me backe or hath rule in me, I maie not freely ascende to the.

O lorde, without the, nothing maie longe delite or please: For if any thinge shulde be liking and savory, it must be through helpe of thy grace, seasonede with the spice of thy wisedom.

O everlastinge light farre passinge all thinges, sende downe the beames of thy bryghtnesse from above, and purifie and lighten the inwarde partes of my herte.

Quycken my soule, and all the powers there of, that it maie cleave fast, and be joyned to the in joyfull gladnes of gostely ravyshinges.

O when shall that blessed houre com that thou shalte visite me, and glad me with thy blessed presence, when thou shalt be to me all in al, verely until that tyme come, there can be no perfecte joye in me.

But alas, myne olde man, that is my carnall affections lyve still in me, and are not crucified nor perfitly deade.

For yet stryveth the fleshe agaynst the spirite, and movethe greate battaile inwardli agaynste me, and suffereth not thy kyngedome of my soule to lyve in peace.

But thou, good lorde, that haste the lordeshippe over all, and power of the sea, to asswage the rages and surges of the same, aryse and helpe me, destroie the power of myne enemyes, which alwaies make battaile agaynste me, shewe forthe the greatnesse of thy goodnesse, and let the power of thy right hande be glorified in me. For there is to me none other hope nor refuge, but in the only my lorde, my god: to the be honour and glorie everlastyng.

O lorde, graunte me, that I maie wholy resigne my selfe to the, and in all thinges to forsake my selfe, and paciently to beare my crosse, and to followe the

O lorde, what is man, that thou vouchesaveste to have mynde of hym: and to visit hym.

Thou arte alwaye one alwaye good, alwaye rightouse and holy, justly and blessedly disposinge all thinges after thy wisedom.

But I am a wretche, and of my selfe alway redy and prone to evell, and dooe never abide in one state, but many tymes dooe varie and chaung.

Neverthelesse it shall be better with me, whan it shall please the: for thou O lorde, onely arte he, that maiste helpe me, and thou maiste so confirme, and stablishe me, that my herte shall not be chaunged from the, but bee surely fixed and fynally rest and be quieted in the.

I am nothinge elles of myselfe but vanytie before the, an unconstant creature and a feeble; and therfore, wherof maie I rightfully glorie or why shulde I looke to be magnified.

Who so pleasethe hymselfe withoute the, displeasethe the and he that deliteth in menes praysinges, loseth the true prayse before the.

The true praise is to be praised of the: And the true joye is, to rejoyce in the.

Therefore[10] thy name (O lorde) be praysed, and not myne.

Thy workes bee magnified and not myne, and thy goodnesse bee alwayes lauded and blessed.

Thou arte my glorye, and the joye of my herte, in the, shall I glorye and rejoyce, and not in my selfe nor in any wordely[11] honoure or dignitee, which to thy eternall glorie compared, is but a shadowe and a veraye vanytie.

O lorde, we lyve here in great darkenesse, and are sone deceived with the vanities of this worlde, and are sone greved with a litle trouble: yet if I coulde beholde my selfe well, I shulde playnely see, that what trouble so ever I have suffered, it

10. **Therefore** Wherefore (*P or M*). "Therefore" is the reading in Whitford's *Following of Christ,* KP's source.

11. **wordely** worldly—KP's penslip.

hathe justely comen upon me, because I have often synned, and greveously offended the.

To me therefore confusyon and despyte is due but to the laude, honour and glory.

Lorde, sende me helpe in my troubles, for mannes healpe is lytle worth.

How often have I ben disapoynted where I thought I shulde have found frendeship:

And howe often have I founde it wher as I least thought.

Therefore[12] it is a vayne thinge, to truste in man, For the true truste and health of man, is onely in the.

Blessed be thou lorde therefore in all thinges, that happenethe unto us: For we be weake and unstable, soone deceyved, and soone chaunged from one thinge to an other.

O lorde god most rightuous judge, stronge and pacient, whiche knowest the frailtee and malice of man, be thou my whole strength and comfort in all necessities for myne owne conscience (Lorde) Suffiseth not.

Therfore[13] to thy marcie I do appeale, seinge no man maye be justified ne appere rightuous in thy sight, if thou examyne hym after thy justice.

O blessed mansion of thy heavenly citee, O moste clerest daie of eternitee, whom the nyghte maie never darken.

This is the daie alwaye clere and mery, alwaie sure, and never chaungynge his state.

Wolde to god this daye myght shortely appeere and shyne upon us, and that this worldely fantasies were at an ende.

This daie shyneth clerely to thy sayntes in heaven with everlastinge brightnes, but to us pilgrims in earth, it shyneth obscurelye, and as throughe a myrour or glasse.

The heavenlye sytezins knowe, howe joyous this daye is: but we outlawes, the children of Eve weepe and waile the bitter tediousenes of our daie, that is of this present liffe, shorte and evill, full of sorowe and anguishe.

Where man is often tymes defiled with synne, encombred wythe affliccion, inquieted[14] with troubles wrapped in cares, busied with vanities, blynded with errours, overcharged with laboures, vexed withe temptacions, overcome with vayne delites and pleasures of the worlde and greveously tourmented with penury and nede.

O when shall the ende come of all these miseries.

When shall I bee clerely delyvered from the bondag of synne.

12. **Therefore** Wherefore (*P or M*). "Therefore" is the reading in Whitford's *Following of Christ,* KP's source.

13. **Therfore** Wherefore (*P or M*). Whitford's *Following* also reads "Wherefore."

14. **inquieted** unquieted (*P or M*).

Whan shall I (lorde) have only mynde on the, and fully be glade and mery in the.

Whan shall I be free without lettinge, and be in perfite libertie without griefe of bodie and soule.

When shall I have peace without trouble: peace within and without: and on every side stedfast and sure.

O lorde Jesu whan shall I stande and beholde the and have full sight and contemplacion of thy glory.

When shalte thou be to me all in all, and whan shall I be with the in thy kyngdome that thou hast ordeyned for thyne electe people from the begynnynge.

I am lefte here poore, and as an outlawe, in the lande of myne enemyes,

Where daily be battayles and greate mysfortunes.

[280] Comfort myne exile aswage my sorowe for all my desire is to be with the.

It is to me an unplesaunt bourdayne, what plea[15] soever the worlde offereth me here.

I desyre to have inwarde fruycion in the, but I can not atteyne therto.

I coveyte to cleve faste to heavenly thinges, but worldely affeccions plucke me downward.

I wolde subdue all ivelle affections, but they daily rebell and rise against me and will not be subjecte unto my spirite.[16]

[The last line of text is filled out with a scarlet block overlaid with a gold leaf design; two-fifths of the last page remain blank. Ten blank, gold-bordered leaves follow, to complete the tiny volume.]

15. **plea** KP's writing runs into the page edge, leaving unfinished the word "pleasure" (the reading of *P or M*).

16. **I wolde . . . spirite** This versicle seems to be KP's original composition. It does not appear anywhere in the printed versions of *Prayers or Meditations.* Nor does it appear in Whitford's chapter 53, which KP is recasting in this section of the text. It is noteworthy in this connection that Fisher's original compositions in *Psalmi seu Precationes* tend to occur at the ends of the "collages" of Biblical excerpts that are his "Psalms": see nn 311–13, 436, 450, 539 to *Psalms or Prayers.* The connection may constitute more circumstantial evidence that KP was the translator of Fisher's work.

The Printed Text of *Prayers or Meditations*[1]

[Title]

[Ai r] Prayers or Meditations, wherein the mind is stirred, patiently to suffer all afflictions here, to set at naught the vain prosperity of this world, and always to long for the everlasting felicity: Collected out of holy works by the most vertuous and gracious Princess Katherine, Queen of England, France, and Ireland. Anno Domini 1545.

1. Source: *PRAYERS OR Medytacions, wherein the mynd is stirred* (Thomas Berthelet, 6 November 1545) (STC 4819), sigs. Ai–Dviii. The following text is a modern-spelling version of the Magdalene College, Cambridge, copy of STC 4819 (shelfmark A.9.29), the earliest edition to contain all five of the prayers eventually appended to the main body of this text. To facilitate reference to this source, signature numbers have been inserted in square brackets in front of the versicle or paragraph in which the page break occurs. All Biblical citations are from the Great Bible (spelling modernized). As recognized by Hoffman in "Catherine Parr as a Woman of Letters," 354, KP authored her *Prayers or Meditations* by redacting excerpts from book 3 of Thomas à Kempis's *De Imitatione Christi* in the English translation of Richard Whitford, a Bridgettine monk and former fellow of Queens' College, Cambridge. Corroborating the phenomenal popularity of à Kempis's work among its late fifteenth- and early sixteenth-century readership, three editions of Whitford's translation appeared in close conjunction circa 1531–35. Robert Wyer published *A boke newely translated out of Laten in to Englysshe, called the folowynge of Cryste* (STC 23961); Thomas Godfray published *The folowyng of Christ. Lately translated out of latyn in to Englisshe, and newly examyned* (STC 23963); and Robert Redman published *A boke ne[we]ly translated out of Latyn [in] to Englisshe, called the folowynge of Christ* (STC 23964). Redman's edition disqualifies itself as KP's source with its cluster of early readings that diverge in small and greater degrees from Godfray's and Wyer's editions, but thereafter settles into quite considerable consonance with them. By contrast, Godfray's and Wyer's editions of Whitford's English translation display remarkably close textual correspondences throughout. Their high degree of correspondence attests to the care with which these editions were prepared, but it also

[Epigraph]

[Ai v] Colossians 3. If ye be risen again with Christ, seek the things which are above, where Christ sitteth on the right hand of God. Set your affection on things that are above, and not on things which are on the earth.

[Aii r] Most benign Lord Jesu, grant me Thy grace, that it may always work in me, and persevere with me unto the end.

Grant me that I may ever desire and will that which is most pleasant and most acceptable to Thee.

Thy will be my will, and my will be to follow always Thy will.

Let there be always in me one will and one desire with Thee, and that I have no desire to will or not to will, but as Thou wilt.[2]

Lord, Thou knowest what thing is most profitable and most expedient for me.[3]

[Aii v] Give, therefore, what Thou wilt, as much as Thou wilt, and when Thou wilt.

Do with me what Thou wilt, as it shall please Thee, and as shall be most to Thine honor.

Put me where Thou wilt, and freely do with me in all things after Thy will.

Thy creature I am, and in Thy hands; lead and turn me where Thou wilt.

Lo, I am Thy servant, ready to all things that Thou commandest; for I desire not to live to myself, but to Thee.[4]

Lord Jesu, I pray Thee, grant me grace, that I never set my heart on the things of this world, but that all worldly and carnal affections may utterly die, and be mortified in me.[5]

---

confounds any secure identification of the source that KP employed in crafting her *Prayers or Meditations*. Difficulties are further compounded by the multitude of minute (but often substantive) changes that KP made in Whitford's wording, thus generating a host of her own deviations from the wording in all three of the earliest English editions of his translation. On balance, the often equivocal evidence slightly favors Wyer's edition as her source.

2. **Most benign . . . wilt** KP excerpts nearly verbatim from book 3, chap. 17, of Whitford's translation of the *Folowing* (Godfray, fol. 77r; Redman, fol. 81v; Wyer, fol. 82v). All subsequent references to chapter numbers are to chapters from book 3 of the *Following of Christ*. **grace, that** Redman and Wyer add "it maye be alwaye with me." **work in** "worke with." **Grant . . . that** Redman and Wyer read "And that" **will . . . Thy will** Redman and Wyer read "wyll alway to folowe thy wyll and beste accorde therwith." **Let . . . always** Redman and Wyer read "Be there alway." **no desire** Redman and Wyer read "no power." **I have . . . wilt** an echo of Matthew 26:39: "not as I will, but as Thou wilt." **Thou wilt** Redman and Wyer add "or wyll nat."

3. **Lord, Thou . . . for me** KP recasts an excerpt from chap. 19: "I knowe what is best and most expedient to the" (Godfray, fol. 78v; Redman, fol. 83r; Wyer, fol. 84r).

4. **Give . . . to Thee** KP excerpts nearly verbatim from chap. 16 (Godfray, fols. 76v–77r; Redman, fol. 81r; Wyer fol. 82r). **Give, therefore** "Gyve me." **what . . . wilt** Redman and Wyer read "as thou knowest best to be done." **I am . . . servant** an echo of Psalm 116:16: "O Lord, truly I am Thy servant, I am Thy servant."

5. **Lord Jesu . . . in me** KP's own composition.

[Aiii r] Grant me, above all things, that I may rest in Thee, and fully quiet and pacify my heart in Thee.

For Thou, Lord, art the very true peace of heart, and the perfect rest of the soul; and without Thee, all things be grievous and unquiet.[6]

My Lord Jesu, I beseech Thee, be with me in every place, and at all times; and let it be to me a special solace, gladly for Thy love to lack all worldly solace.[7]

And if Thou withdraw Thy comfort from me at any time, keep me, O Lord, from desperation; and make me patiently to abide Thy will and ordinance.[8]

[Aiii v] O Lord Jesu, Thy judgments be righteous; and Thy providence is much better for me than all that I can imagine or devise.[9]

Wherefore, do with me in all things as it shall please Thee; for it may not be but well, all that Thou doest.

If Thou wilt that I be in light, be Thou blessed; if Thou wilt that I be in darkness, be Thou also blessed.

If Thou vouchsafe to comfort me, be Thou highly blessed; if Thou wilt I live in trouble and without comfort, be Thou likewise ever blessed.[10]

[A iiii r] Lord, give me grace gladly to suffer whatsoever Thou wilt shall fall upon me, and patiently to take at Thy hand good and bad, bitter and sweet, joy and sorrow; and for all things that shall befall unto me, heartily to thank Thee.

Keep me, Lord, from sin, and I shall then neither dread death nor hell.[11]

6. **Grant me . . . and unquiet** KP excerpts nearly verbatim from chap. 17 (Godfray, fol. 77v; Redman, fol. 81v; Wyer, fol. 82v). **me, above** "me also above." **things . . . I** "things that can be desyred that." **fully . . . Thee** "fully in the to pacifye my hert." **of . . . soul** "and of soule."

7. **My Lord . . . solace** KP excerpts nearly verbatim from chap. 18 (Godfray, fol. 78v; Redman, fol. 82v; Wyer, fol. 83v). **Thee, be** "the that thou be." **at all** "in every." **let** "that." **lack . . . worldly** Redman and Wyer read "wante all mannes."

8. **And if . . . ordinance** KP's own composition.

9. **O Lord . . . devise** KP reworks an excerpt from chap. 19 (Godfray, fol. 78v; Redman, fol. 83r; Wyer, fol. 84r): "O lorde it is true al that thou sayest, thy prouydence is much more better for me, than al that I can do or saye for my selfe." **O Lord . . . me** an allusion to Psalm 119:76: "I know, O Lord, that Thy judgments are right, and that Thou of very faithfulness hast caused me to be troubled."

10. **Wherefore, do . . . ever blessed** KP excerpts from chap. 19, with a sizable excision (Godfray, fol. 79r; Redman, fol. 83r-v; Wyer, fol. 84r-v). **Wherefore, do** KP excises Whitford's phrasing between these two words: "it may wel be sayd and verified that he standeth very casually that setteth nat all his trust in the, therefore lorde whyle my wit abydeth stedfast and stable." **likewise ever** "also" (Godfray, Wyer); "in lyke moche" (Redman). These particular variants shed no light on which edition of the *Following* served KP as a source, since she has chosen to revise the phrasing.

11. **Lord, give . . . nor hell** KP continues to excerpt from chap. 19. **Lord, give . . . thank Thee** KP reworks a sizable portion of this excerpt, which reads identically in Godfray, Redman, and Wyer: "Lorde I wyll gladly suffre for the what so euer thou wylt shall fall upon me, indifferently wyll I take of thy hande good and bad, bytter and swete, gladnesse and sorowe, and for all thynges that shal befall to me, hertely wyll I thanke the."

O what thanks ought I to give unto Thee, which hast suffered the grievous death of the cross, to deliver me from my sins, and to obtain everlasting life for me?

Thou gavest us most perfect example of patience: fulfilling and obeying the will of Thy Father even unto the death.[12]

Make me, wretched sinner, obediently to use myself after Thy will in all things, and patiently to bear the burden of this corruptible life.

[A iii v] For though this life be tedious and as an heavy burden to my soul, yet, nevertheless, through Thy grace and by example of Thee, it is now made much more easy and comfortable than it was before Thy incarnation and passion.[13]

Thy holy life is our way to Thee, and by following of Thee, we walk to Thee that art our Head and Saviour. And yet, except Thou hadst gone before, and showed us the way to everlasting life, who would endeavor himself to follow Thee?—seeing we be yet so slow and dull, having the light of Thy blessed example and holy doctrine, to lead and direct us.[14]

O Lord Jesu, make that possible by grace, that is to me impossible by nature.[15]

[Av r] Thou knowest well that I may little suffer, and that I am anon cast down and overthrown with a little adversity: wherefore I beseech Thee, O Lord, to strengthen

12. **O what . . . the death** KP's own composition, incorporating a reworked clause from chap. 20 (Godfray, fol. 80r; Redman, fol. 84v; Wyer, fol. 85v): "O what thankes am I bounde therfore to yelde to the."

13. **Make me . . . and passion** KP excerpts and reworks a passage from chap. 20 to sharpen a Reformation emphasis on Christ as the sole agent of redemption, independent of any human works (Godfray, fols. 79v–80r; Redman, fol. 84r-v; Wyer, fol. 85r-v): "it is fyttynge that I moste wretched sinner bere me paciently after thy wyll in all thinges, and as longe as thou wylte that I for myne owne helthe bere the burden of this corruptyble lyfe. For thoughe this lyfe be tedious, and as an hevy burden to the soule, yet neverthelesse, it is nowe through thy grace made verye meritorious, and by example of the and of thy holy payntes it is nowe made to weyke persones more sufferable, and more clerer, and also moche more comfortable than it was in the olde lawe: whan the gates of heven were shitte [shut], and the way thyderwarde was darke, and that so fewe dyde covet to seke it. And yet they that were than rightwyse and were ordayned to be saved before thy blessed passion and dethe myght never have come thider."

14. **Thy holy . . . direct us** KP continues her excerpting and reworking of a passage that immediately follows in chap. 20 (Godfray, fol. 80r; Redman, fol. 84v; Wyer, fol. 85v): "Thy holy lyfe is our waye, and by thy pacience we walke to the that art our heed and governour. And but thou lorde haddest gone before and shewed us the way, who wolde have endevoured hym to have folowed. O how many shulde have taried behynde, if they had nat sene thy blessed examples goynge before: we be yet slowe and dulle nowe we have sene and herde thy signes and doctryns. What shuld we than have ben if we had seene no suche light goyng before us." **except . . . the way** an allusion to John 14:5–6: "Thomas saith unto him: Lord, we know not whither thou goest. And how is it possible for us to know the way? Jesus saith unto him: I am the way . . . No man cometh unto the Father but by me."

15. **O Lord . . . nature** a paraphrase of Mark 14:36: "And He said, . . . Father, all things are possible unto Thee . . . Nevertheless not that I will, but that Thou wilt, be done."

me with Thy Spirit, that I may willingly suffer, for Thy sake, all manner of trouble and affliction.[16]

Lord, I will knowledge unto Thee all mine unrighteousness, and I will confess to Thee all the unstableness of my heart.

Oftentimes a very little thing troubleth me sore, and maketh me dull and slow to serve Thee.

[Av v] And sometime I purpose to stand strongly; but when a little trouble cometh, it is to me great anguish and grief, and, of a right little thing, riseth a grievous temptation to me.[17]

Yea, when I think myself to be sure and strong, and that (as it seemeth) I have the upper hand, suddenly I feel myself ready to fall with a little blast of temptation.

Behold, therefore, good Lord, my weakness; and consider my frailness, best known to Thee.

Have mercy on me, and deliver me from all iniquity and sin, that I be not entangled therewith.[18]

Oftentimes it grieveth me sore, and in manner confoundeth me, that I am so unstable, so weak, and so frail in resisting sinful motions.

[Avi r] Which, although they draw me not always to consent, yet nevertheless their assaults be very grievous unto me.

And it is tedious to me to live in such battle, albeit I perceive that such battle is not unprofitable unto me. For thereby I know the better myself and mine own infirmities, and that I must seek help only at Thy hands.[19]

16. **O Lord . . . affliction** KP reworks a passage from chap. 21, strengthening the emphasis on the role of grace in moral endeavor (Godfray, fol. 81v; Redman, fol. 86r; Wyer, fol. 87r): "O lord Jesu, make it possyble to me by grace, that is impossyble to me by nature. Thou knowest well that I maye lytell suffre and that I am anone cast downe with a lytel adversite, wherfore I besech the, that trouble and adversitie may herafter for thy name be beloved and desyred of me, for truly to suffer and to be vexed for the, is very good and profitable for the helth of my soule."

17. **Lord, I . . . to me** KP embarks upon a series of minute local reworkings in an extended passage from chap. 22 (Godfray, fols. 81v–82r; Redman, fol. 86r-v; Wyer, fol. 87r-v). The following compose the first group. **will . . . Thee** "shall knowlege agaynste me." **will . . . Thee** "shall confesse to the lorde." **a very . . . sore** "it is but a lytell thynge that casteth me downe." **serve Thee** "all good workes." **trouble** "temptacion." **and, of** "and somtyme of." **I . . . heart** an allusion to Psalm 32:5: "I will acknowledge my sin unto Thee, and mine unrighteousness have I not hid."

18. **Yea . . . therewith** The following constitute the second group of KP's minute reworkings of an extended passage from chap. 22 that continues to read identically in Godfray, fol. 82r; Redman, fol. 86v; and Wyer, fol. 87v. **Yea** "and." **sure . . . strong** "somwhat syker [more sure]." **upper** "higher." **ready . . . temptation** "nere hande [close to being] overcome by a lyght temptacion." **all . . . therewith** "the filthy dregges of synne, that my fete be never fixed in them."

19. **Oftentimes . . . hands** The following constitute the third group of KP's minute reworkings of the same passage that continues to read identically in Godfray, Redman, and Wyer.

O Lord God of Israel, the lover of all faithful souls, vouchsafe to behold the labor and sorrow of me, Thy poor creature.

[Avi v] Assist me in all things with Thy grace, and so strength me with heavenly strength, that neither my cruel enemy the fiend, neither my wretched flesh, which is not yet subject to the spirit, have victory or dominion over me.

O what a life may this be called? where no trouble nor misery lacketh, where every place is full of snares of mortal enemies.

For, one trouble or temptation overpassed, another cometh by and by; and the first conflict yet during, a new battle suddenly ariseth.[20]

[Avii r] Wherefore, Lord Jesu, I pray Thee, give me the grace to rest in Thee above all things, and to quiet me in Thee above all creatures, above all glory and honor, above all dignity and power, above all cunning and policy, above all health and beauty, above all riches and treasure, above all joy and pleasure, above all fame and praise, above all mirth and consolation that man's heart may take or feel, besides Thee.

For Thou, Lord God, art best, most wise, most high, most mighty, most sufficient, and most full of all goodness, most sweet, and most comfortable, most fair, most loving, most noble, most glorious, in whom all goodness most perfectly is.[21]

Oftentimes . . . grieveth "But this is it that ofte grudgeth." **me, that** "me before the, that." **in resisting . . . motions** "to resist my passions."

20. **O Lord . . . ariseth** KP skips over fourteen lines of text and resumes her minute reworkings with a later passage from chap. 22 that also reads identically in Godfray (fol. 82r-v), Redman (fol. 87r), and Wyer (fols. 87v–88r). **O Lord . . . Israel** "But wolde to god that thou most strongest god of Israel." Exodus 5:1 is the first instance of the recurrent Old Testament appellation "Lord God of Israel." **vouchsafe** "woldest vouchsafe." **poore creature** "poorest servaunt." **with . . . grace** "that I have to do." KP's insertion of a reference to grace is noteworthy. **my cruel** "the olde." **yet subject** "yet fully subjecte." **strength** (verb) an earlier variant of "strengthen." **victory . . . dominion** "power ne lordship." **over me** Whitford adds "agaynst whom I must fight continually whyle I shall lyve in this miserable lyfe." **O . . . called** "But alas what lyfe is this." **lacketh** "wanteth." **overpassed** "goyng away." **during** an earlier variant of "enduring." **a new . . . ariseth** "many other sodaynly ryse, mo than can be thought."

21. **Wherefore . . . is** KP skips over thirty-six lines of text and resumes her minute reworkings with a passage from the beginning of chap. 23, titled "Howe a man shulde rest in god above all thyng" (Godfray, fol. 83v; Redman, fol. 88r; Wyer, fol. 89r-v). **Wherefore . . . grace** "Above all thynges and in all thynges reste thou my soule in thy lorde God, for he is the eternal rest of all aungels and sayntes. Gyve me lorde Jesu this speciall grace." **to rest . . . creatures** "to rest me in the above all creatures, above all helthe and fairenesse." **health . . . besides Thee** "riches and craftes, above all gladnesse of body and of soule, above all fame and praysing, above all swetnesse and consolation, above all hope and repromyssion [promise given in return], above all merite and desire, above all giftes and rewardes that thou mayst gyve or sende beside thy self; and above all joye and mirthe that mannes hert or mynde may take or fele; and also above all angels and archaungels, and above all the company of hevenly spirites, above all thynges visyble and invysible, and above all thynges [Redman and Wyer: thynge] that is nat thy selfe." **best** "moste beste." **most mighty** "most mightiest." **most sufficient . . . perfectly is** The close of

And, therefore, whatsoever I have beside Thee, it is nothing to me; for my heart may not rest, nor fully be pacified, but only in Thee.

O Lord Jesu, most loving Spouse, who shall give me wings of perfect love, that I may fly up from these worldly miseries, and rest in Thee?

[Aviii r] O when shall I ascend to Thee, and see and feel how sweet Thou art?

When shall I wholly gather myself in Thee so perfectly, that I shall not for Thy love feel myself, but Thee only above myself, and above all worldly things?—that Thou mayest vouchsafe to visit me in such wise as Thou dost visit Thy most faithful lovers.

Now I often mourn and complain of the miseries of this life, and with sorrow and great heaviness suffer them.

For many things happen daily to me, which oftentimes trouble me, make me heavy, and darken mine understanding.[22]

[Aviii r] They hinder me greatly, and put my mind from Thee, and so encumber me many ways, that I cannot freely and clearly desire Thee, nor have Thy sweet consolations, which with Thy blessed saints be always present.

I beseech Thee, Lord Jesu, that the sighings and inward desires of my heart may move and incline Thee, to hear me.

O Jesu, King of everlasting glory, the joy and comfort of all Christian people that are wandering as pilgrims in the wilderness of this world, my heart crieth to Thee by still desires, and my silence speaketh unto Thee, and sayeth: How long tarrieth my Lord God to come to me?[23]

---

this sentence in à Kempis's *Imitatio* alludes to Augustine *Confessions* 13.8: "satis ostendis, quam magnam rationalem creaturam feceris, cui nullo modo sufficit ad beatam requiem quidquid te minus est" (Thou dost sufficiently show how great is the reasonable creature whom Thou hast made: unto whom in no way will anything suffice for blessed rest that is inferior to Thyself). **glorious . . . perfectly is** "glorious above all thyng, in whom all goodnesse is together perfitely and fully, hath bene and shal be."

22. **And therefore . . . understanding** KP continues her minute reworkings of this passage from chap. 23 (Godfray, fols. 83v–84r; Redman, fol. 88r-v; Wyer, fol. 89v). **I have . . . to me** "thou gyve [Redman: gyvest; Wyer: gyves] me besyde thy [Redman: me] selfe, it is lytell and insufficient to me." **only** KP's insertion. **in Thee** KP omits Whitford's rendering of the mystical yearning that concludes this sentence: "so that it assende above all gyftes, and also above all maner of thinges that be create." **Spouse, who** KP omits the phrases intervening between these two words: "spouse, most purest lover, and governoure of every creature, who." **Spouse** an allusion to a term of endearment in Song of Solomon 4:8–12 and 5:1, traditionally construed as figuring the love of Christ and the soul (or the church). **love** "lyberty." **who shall . . . in Thee?** an allusion to Psalm 55:6: "O that I had wings like a dove, for then would I fly away and be at rest." **ascend to** "fully tente to" (give heed to). **see . . . sweet** an allusion to Psalm 34: "O . . . see that the Lord is good." **worldly** "bodily." **mayest vouchsafe to** KP's addition. **great . . . them** "wo, bere them with right great hevynesse." **many . . . to me** "many yvell thynges happen dayly in this lyfe." **me heavy** "me very hevy." **darken** "gretly darken."

23. **They hinder . . . to me?** KP continues her minute reworkings of this passage from chap. 23 (Godfray, fol. 84r-v; Redman, fol. 89r). Except for one variant, Wyer (fol. 90r) reads identi-

[Aviii v] Come, O Lord, and visit me; for, without Thee, I have no true joy; without Thee, my soul is heavy and sad.

I am in prison, and bound with fetters of sorrow, till Thou, O Lord, with Thy gracious presence vouchsafe to visit me, and to bring me again to liberty and joy of spirit, and to show Thy favorable countenance unto me.[24]

Open my heart, Lord, that I may behold Thy laws, and teach me to walk in Thy commandments.

Make me to know and follow Thy will, and to have always in my remembrance Thy manifold benefits, that I may yield due thanks to Thee for them.

[Bi r] But I knowledge and confess for truth, that I am not able to give Thee condign thanks for the least benefit that Thou hast given me.[25]

O Lord, all gifts and virtues that any man hath, in body or soul, natural or supernatural, be Thy gifts, and come of Thee, and not of ourself; and they declare the great riches of Thy mercy and goodness unto us.

And though some have more gifts than other, yet they all proceed from Thee; and without Thee, the least cannot be had.[26]

---

cally with Godfray and Redman. **freely . . . desire Thee** "have free mynde and clene desire to the." **consolations** "embrasynges." KP moderates the sexualized spirituality of à Kempis's original and Whitford's rendering. **Lord Jesu** "lord Christ Jesu." **heart may** KP excises the phrasing between these two words: "with my manyfolde desolacions." **move** "somwhat move." **King** "the light and brightnes." Hebrews 1:3 alludes to the brightness of glory; Psalm 24:9–10 alludes to the Lord as the "King of glory." KP's revised wording shifts the allusion. **wandering** "walkynge and laborynge" (Wyer). **How long . . . Lord God** an allusion to Revelation 6:10: "How long tarriest Thou, Lord?"

24. **Come . . . unto me** KP continues her minute reworkings of this passage from chap. 23. Wyer has one variant but otherwise reads identically with Godfray and Redman. **and visit me** Omitted in Wyer. **no true . . . sad** KP condenses Whitford's phrasing: "no glad day ne houre, for thou arte al my joy and gladnes: and without the my soule is barayne and voyde." **I am . . . prison** KP condenses Whitford's phrasing: "I am a wretche and in maner in pryson." **visit me** KP omits the next phrase, "and to refresshe me." **and joy** KP's addition. **favorable** KP omits the next phrase, "and lovely."

25. **Open . . . given me** KP skips over thirty-one lines of text and resumes her minute reworkings with a passage from the beginning of chap. 24, titled "Of remembring of the great and manyfolde benefytes of god" (Godfray, fol. 85v; Redman, fol. 90r-v; Wyer, fol. 91r-v). **Open . . . commandments** KP recasts Whitford's awkward sentence: "Open myne herte lorde, in to the beholdyng of thy lawes: and in thy commaundementes teche me to walke." The allusion is to Psalm 119:32: "I will run the way of Thy commandments." **Make . . . follow** "Gyve me grace to knowe and to understande." **and to . . . remembrance** "and with great reverence and dilygent consideration to remembre." **knowledge** "knowe." **give** "yelde to." **thanks** "thankynges."

26. **O Lord . . . had** KP skips over four lines of text before beginning to recast thoroughly a subsequent passage from chap. 24 (Godfray, fols. 85v–86r; Redman, fol. 90v; Wyer, fol. 90v). The passage reads: "O lorde, all that we have in body and in soule, withinforthe and withoutforthe, naturally or supernaturally, they be thy [Redman: they—a misprint] benefites, and show the openly to be a blessed and a good benefactour, of whom we have receyved suche gyftes: and though one hath receyved more and another lesse, yet they all be thy gyftes, and without

O Lord, I account it for a great benefit, not to have many worldly gifts, whereby the laud and praise of men might blind my soul and deceive me.

[Bi v] Lord, I know that no man ought to be abashed or miscontent that he is in a low estate in this world, and lacketh the pleasures of this life, but rather to be glad and rejoice thereat:[27]

Forsomuch as Thou hast chosen the poor and meek persons, and such as are despised in the world, to be Thy servants and familiar friends.

Witness be Thy blessed apostles, whom Thou madest chief pastors and spiritual governors of Thy flock, which departed from the counsel of the Jews, rejoicing that they were counted worthy to suffer rebuke for Thy name.[28]

[Bii r] Even so, O Lord, grant that I, Thy servant, may be as well content to be taken as the least, as other be to be greatest; and that I be as well pleased to be in the lowest place, as in the highest; and as glad to be of no reputation in the world for Thy sake, as other are to be noble and famous.[29]

Lord, it is the work of a perfect man, never to sequester his mind from Thee, and among many worldly cares, to go without care: not after the manner of an idle or a dissolute person, but by the prerogative of a free mind, always minding heavenly things, and not cleaving by inordinate affection to any creature.

---

the the lest can nat be had, and he that hath more receyved, may nat rightfully glorifye hym self therin."

27. **O Lord . . . thereat** **O Lord . . . me** KP skips over twenty-eight lines of text before so thoroughly recasting two successive sentences later in chap. 24 that they emerge as largely original compositions (Godfray, fol. 86v; Redman, fol. 91r; Wyer, fol. 92r). The first sentence reads "wherfore lorde I accompt it for a great benefit nat to have many [Godfray: my—a misprint] giftes wherby outwardlye and after mannes jugement, laude and praysinge shulde folowe." **Lord . . . thereat** The second sentence reads "And over that, as me semeth, although a man consydre and beholde his owne povertie, and the vylenesse of his owne persone, he aught nat therfore take grefe, [Redman and Wyer: or] hevynesse, nor [Redman and Wyer: or] dejection, but rather to conceyve therby gret gladnesse of soule."

28. **Forsomuch . . . name** KP continues her thorough recasting of this passage from chap. 24. **Forsomuch . . . friends** **Forsomuch** "For." **hast chosen** KP omits the following phrase, "and dayly doste choose." **Thy . . . friends** "thy famylier and housholde servauntes." KP's revision introduces an allusion to Jesus's words in John 15:15: "Henceforth call I you not servants. . . . but you have I called friends." **Witness . . . name** **Witness be** "wytnes." **chief . . . name** "prynces of all the worlde which neuerthelesse were conversaunt among the people without complaynynge [Redman and Wyer add: or myssaynge], so meke and simple, without al malyce and deceyte that they joyed to suffre reprofes for thy name."

29. **Even . . . famous** KP skips over five lines of text and then thoroughly recasts more of Whitford's phrasing from the end of chap. 24 (Godfray, fols. 86v–87r; Redman. fol. 91v; Wyer, fol. 92v). Whitford reads: "there ought nothynge so moche to comforte and glad thy lover . . . as that . . . he ought to be so wel contented and pleased, that he wolde as gladly be holden lest, as other wolde be holden moste: and . . . as well pleased in the lowest place as in the hyghest, and as glad to be dispised and abject and of no name ne reputacyon in the worlde, as other to be nobler or greater."

[Bii v] I beseech Thee therefore, my Lord Jesu: keep me from the superfluous cares of this world, that I be not unquieted with bodily necessities, nor that I be not taken with the voluptuous pleasures of the world, nor of the flesh.

Preserve me from all things which hinder my soul's health, that I be not overthrown with them.[30]

O Lord God, which art sweetness unspeakable, turn into bitterness to me all worldly and fleshly delights, which might draw me from the love of eternal things, to the love of short and vile pleasures.

[Biii r] Let not flesh and blood overcome me; nor yet the world, with his vainglory, deceive me; nor the fiend, with his manifold crafts, supplant me. But give me ghostly strength in resisting them, patience in suffering them, and constancy in persevering to the end.

Give me, for all worldly delectations, the most sweet consolation of Thy Holy Spirit; and, for all fleshly love, endue my soul with fervent love of Thee.[31]

[Biii v] Make me strong inwardly in my soul, and cast out thereof all unprofitable cares of this world, that I be not led by unstable desires of earthly things, but that I may repute all things in this world (as they be) transitory, and soon vanishing away; and myself also with them, drawing toward mine end.[32]

30. **Lord . . . them** KP skips over five chapters of the text and resumes excerpting and reworking Whitford's phrasing with the beginning of chap. 30, titled "Of the lybertye, excellencie, and worthynes of a fre mynde" (Godfray, fol. 91r; Redman, fols. 95v–96r; Wyer, fol. 98r-v). **from Thee** "fro [Redman and Wyer: from] the beholdynge of hevenly thynges." **many . . . care** "many cures to go as he were without cure." KP's "care" can pertain to the condition of any Christian. The English word "cure" is Whitford's term, probably chosen for its connotations of the priestly office (cure of souls). **prerogative** "specyal prerogatyve." **minding . . . things** "busy in goddes servyce." **Lord Jesu** KP omits the immediately following phrase, "moste meke and mercyfull." **superfluous cares** "busynes and cures." **bodily necessities** "necessytyes of the bodyly kynde." **things . . . health** "hynderaunce of the soule." **overthrown . . . them** "broken with over moche hevynes, sorowe, nor worldeley drede."

31. **O Lord . . . Thee** KP skips over nine lines of text and resumes her reworking with three successive sentences of Whitford's near the middle of chap. 30 (Godfray, fol. 91v; Redman, fol. 96r-v; Wyer, fol. 98v). **worldly and** KP's addition. **might** "wolde." **short . . . pleasures** "a shorte and a vyle delectable pleasure." **flesh** "the fleshe." **yet** KP's addition. **vainglory** "shorte glorie." **manifold** "thousandefolde." **to . . . end** KP's addition. **Give me** "Gyve me also." **delectations** "consolacions." **Thy . . . Spirit** "the holy goost." **endue . . . Thee** "sende in to my soule the love of thy holy name."

32. **Make . . . end** KP skips to the beginning of chap. 32 (misnumbered "33" in Godfray, Redman, and Wyer), which is titled "A prayer for the purgyng of mannes soule, and for hevenly wysedome and the grace of god, to be optayned and had." She resumes her excerpting while adhering more closely to Whitford's wording (Godfray, fol. 93r; Redman, fol. 98r-v; Wyer, fol. 100r). **Make me** "gyve me grace to be." **cares . . . world** "busynes of the worlde and of the flesshe." **but . . . repute** "And that I may beholde." **soon . . . away** "of shorte abidyng." **myself** "me." **drawing . . . end** KP's addition.

For nothing under the sun may long abide, but all is vanity and affliction of spirit.[33]

Give me, Lord, therefore, heavenly wisdom, that I may learn to seek, and find Thee, and above all things, to love Thee.

Give me grace to withdraw me from them that flatter me, and patiently to suffer them that unjustly grieve me.[34]

Lord, when temptation or tribulation cometh, vouchsafe to succor me, that all may turn to my ghostly comfort; and patiently to suffer, and always to say: Thy name be blessed.[35]

[Biiii r] Lord, trouble is now at hand; I am not well, but I am greatly vexed with this present affliction. O most glorious Father, what shall I do? Anguish and trouble are on every side: help now, I beseech Thee, in this hour. Thou shalt be lauded and praised when I am perfectly made meek before Thee, and when I am clearly delivered by Thee.[36]

May it, therefore, please Thee to deliver me: for what may I, most sinful wretch, do? or whither may I go for succor, but to Thee?

Give me patience now, at this time, in all my troubles; help me, Lord God, and I shall not fear nor dread, what troubles soever fall upon me.

[Biiii v] And now, what shall I say, but that Thy will be done in me. I have deserved to be troubled and grieved; and therefore it behooveth that I suffer as long as it pleaseth Thee.[37]

33. **For . . . spirit** The allusions "under the sun" and "vanity and affliction of spirit" are to recurring phrases in Ecclesiastes 1:3, 14 and 2:17, 26.

34. **grace . . . me grace to** "grace also wisely to." **unjustly** KP's addition.

35. **Lord . . . blessed** KP skips to the opening of chap. 34, titled "Howe almighty god is to be inwardly called unto, in tyme of tribulation," where she thoroughly recasts excerpts from several of Whitford's sentences and makes original additions (Godfray, fol. 94r; Redman, fol. 99r; Wyer, fol. 101r). **Lord . . . cometh** "Lord thy name be blessed for ever that thou woldest this temptation and tribulacion shuld fall upon me." **vouchsafe . . . comfort** "I am driven to fle to the that thou vouchsafe to helpe me, and to turne all in to my goostly profyte." **patiently . . . suffer** KP's addition. **alway . . . blessed** Slightly adjusting Whitford's phrasing—"Lord thy name be blessed for ever"—KP here inserts the allusion to Psalm 113:2, "Blessed be the name of the Lord," that she had not previously used from the opening of chap. 34.

36. **Lord, trouble . . . by Thee** KP thoroughly recasts a series of Whitford's sentences from near the opening of chap. 34 (Godfray, fol. 94r-v; Redman, fol. 99r-v; Wyer, fol. 101v): "O lorde, I am nowe in trouble, and it is nat well with me, for I am greatly vexed with this present passyon. And nowe moost best beloved father, what shall I say? I am now taken with anguysshes and troubles on every syde: save me in this hour. But I trust that I am come in to this houre that thou shalte be lauded and praysed whan I am perfitely made meke before the, and that I am clerely delyvered by the."

37. **May . . . pleaseth Thee** KP adheres much more closely to Whitford's phrasing from the latter half of chap. 34 (Godfray, fol. 94v; Redman, fol. 99v; Wyer, fols. 101v–102r). **May . . . Thee** "be it therfore plesaunt to the," an allusion to Psalm 40:13: "O Lord, let it be Thy pleasure

But would to God that I might suffer gladly, till the furious tempests were overpassed, and that quietness of heart might come again.

Thy mighty hand, Lord, is strong enough to take this trouble from me, and to assuage the cruel assaults thereof, that I be not overcome with them, as Thou hast oftentimes done before this time: that when I am clearly delivered by Thee, I may with gladness say,

The right hand of Him that is highest, hath made this change.[38]

[Bv r] Lord, grant me Thy singular grace: that I may come thither, where no creature shall let me, nor keep me from the perfect beholding of Thee.

For, as long as any transitory thing keepeth me back, or hath rule in me, I may not freely ascend to Thee.[39]

O Lord, without Thee nothing may long delight or please. For if anything should be liking and savory, it must be through help of Thy grace, seasoned with the spice of Thy wisdom.[40]

O everlasting Light, far passing all things, send down the beams of Thy brightness from above, and purify and lighten the inward parts of my heart.

[Bv v] Quicken my soul and all the powers thereof, that it may cleave fast, and be joined to Thee in joyful gladness of ghostly ravishings.

O when shall that blessed hour come, that Thou shalt visit me and glad me with Thy blessed presence, when Thou shalt be to me All in all? Verily, until that time come, there can be no perfect joy in me.[41]

---

to deliver me." **for succor** KP's addition. **Lord God** "my lord god." **Thy . . . done** an allusion to Jesus's words in Matthew 6:10, repeated in Matthew 26:42. **pleaseth Thee** "shall please the."

38. **But would . . . change** KP continues to adhere quite closely to Whitford's phrasing at the end of chap. 34. **I . . . overcome** KP tempers a reference to moral effort: "I do not utterly fayle." **The right . . . change** "This is the chaungynge of the right hande of him that is highest, that is the blessyd Trinitie." An allusion is to the reading of Psalm 76:11 in the Vulgate text and numbering: "Dixi . . . haec mutatio dexterae Excelsi" (I said . . . "This change [has been made] by the right hand of the Most High").

39. **Lord, grant . . . to Thee** KP skips over chap. 35 and resumes her close adherence to Whitford's phrasing at the beginning of chap. 36, titled "Howe we shulde forgete all creatures that we myght fynde our creatour" (Godfray, fol. 97r; Redman, fol. 102r; Wyer, fol. 104r). **let** prevent. **freely . . . Thee** "flye [Redman: fle] freely to the." KP omits the immediately following gloss: "he coveyted to flye [Redman: fle] without let, that sayd thus."

40. **O Lord . . . wisdom** KP skips from the beginning of chap. 36 to the midpoint of chap. 39, sustaining her close adherence to Whitford's phrasing (Godfray, fol. 101r; Redman, [fol. 106r]; Wyer, fol. 108v). **may . . . please** "maye be longe lykynge ne pleasaunt." The sense is close to that of an earlier allusion to a passage in Augustine; see n21. **seasoned . . . spice** "tempered with the spicery."

41. **O everlasting . . . in me** KP skips over twenty-one lines of text, resuming her quite close adherence to Whitford's phrasing in the latter half of chap. 39 (Godfray, fol. 101r-v; Redman, fols. 106v–107r; Wyer, fols. 108v–109r). **all things** "all thinges that are made." **purify . . . lighten** "purifie, glade [gladden] and clarifie in me all." **soul and** "spirite with." **All in all** an

But, alas, mine old man (that is my carnal affections) live still in me, and are not crucified nor perfectly dead.

For yet striveth the flesh against the spirit, and moveth great battle inwardly against me, and suffereth not Thy kingdom of my soul to live in peace.

[Bvi r] But Thou, good Lord, that hast the lordship over all, and power of the sea, to assuage the rages and surges of the same: arise and help me. Destroy the power of mine enemies, which always make battle against me. Show forth the greatness of Thy goodness; and let the power of Thy right hand be glorified in me. For there is to me none other hope nor refuge, but in Thee only. My Lord, my God, to Thee be honor and glory everlasting.[42]

O Lord, grant me that I may wholly resign myself to Thee: and in all things to forsake myself, and patiently to bear my cross, and to follow Thee.[43]

[Bvi v] O Lord, what is man, that Thou vouchsafest to have mind of him, and to visit him?[44]

Thou art always one, always good, always righteous and holy, justly and blessedly disposing all things after Thy wisdom.

But I am a wretch, and of myself always ready and prone to evil: and do never abide in one state, but many times do vary and change.

---

allusion to 1 Corinthians 15:28: "When all things are subdued unto Him, then shall the Son also Himself be subject unto Him . . . , so that God may be all in all." **verily . . . in me** "As longe as that gifte is nat gyven to me, that thou be to me all in all, there shalbe no ful joy in me."

42. **But alas . . . everlasting** KP sustains a fairly close adherence to Whitford's phrasing up to the end of chap. 39 (Godfray, fols. 101v–102r; Redman, fol. 107r-v; Wyer, fol. 109r-v). **alas** "alas for sorowe." **carnal . . . still** "flesshly lyking yet lyveth." **mine . . . man** an allusion to Romans 7:22–23. **are not . . . dead** "is nat yet fully crucifyed nor perfitely deed in me." **against** "strongly agaynst." The strife of flesh and spirit alludes to Galatians 5:17. **great . . . inwardly** "great inwarde batayle." **Thy kingdom** "the kyngdome." **the lordship . . . enemies** an allusion to the description of God's cosmic power in Psalm 89:8–10. **to assuage . . . the same** "and doste aswage the stremes of his flowynges." **Destroy** "Breake downe." **make . . . against** "move this batayle in." **Show forth** "shewe." **to Thee** "to whom."

43. **O Lord . . . Thee** KP skips over two chapters and resumes her recasting of Whitford's text near the beginning of chap. 42, titled "Of a pure and an hole forsakynge of our selfe and of our owne wyll, that we myght gete the fredome of spirite and folowe the wyl of god" (Godfray, fol. 104r; Redman, fol. 109v; Wyer, fol. 112v). **O Lord . . . myself** "O lorde, howe ofte shal I resigne me to the, and in what thynges shal I forsake my [Redman: me] selfe." **and patiently . . . Thee** KP's addition, introducing an allusion to Jesus's words in Matthew 16:24: "If any man will follow Me, let him . . . take up his cross and follow Me."

44. **O Lord . . . him?** KP skips from near the beginning of chap. 42 to the opening sentence of chap. 45, titled "That a man hath no goodnes of hym selfe, and that he may nat rightfully glorifie hym selfe in any thinge" (Godfray, fol. 107r; Redman, fol. 112v; Wyer, fol. 114r). **of him?** "on hym? Or what hath he done for the." KP suppresses this reference to meritorious works. **to visit him?** "that thou wylt visite hym with thy grace." KP's two excisions sharpen the allusion to Psalm 8:4: "What is man, that Thou art mindful of him, and . . . visitest him?"

[Bvii r] Nevertheless, it shall be better with me when it shall please Thee. For Thou, O Lord, only art He that mayest help me; and Thou mayest so confirm and stablish me, that my heart shall not be changed from Thee, but be surely fixed, and finally rest and be quieted in Thee.[45]

I am nothing else, of myself, but vanity before Thee, an unconstant creature, and a feeble: and, therefore, whereof may I rightfully glory? or why should I look to be magnified?

Whoso pleaseth himself without Thee, displeaseth Thee; and he that delighteth in men's praisings, loseth the true praise before Thee.

The true praise is to be praised of Thee; and the true joy is to rejoice in Thee.

Wherefore Thy name, O Lord, be praised, and not mine.

Thy works be magnified, and not mine; and Thy goodness be always lauded and blessed.

[Bvii v] Thou art my glory and the joy of my heart. In Thee shall I glory and rejoice, and not in myself, nor in any worldly honor or dignity: which, to Thy eternal glory compared, is but a shadow and very vanity.[46]

O Lord, we live here in great darkness, and are soon deceived with the vanities of this world, and are soon grieved with a little trouble. Yet, if I could behold myself well, I should plainly see, that what trouble soever I have suffered, it hath justly come upon me, because I have often sinned, and grievously offended Thee.

45. **Thou art . . . in Thee** KP skips over ten lines of text, resuming her reworking of Whitford's phrasing with a series of sentences later in chap. 45 (Godfray, fol. 107r-v; Redman, fol. 113r; Wyer, fol. 114r-v). **Thou art** "O lord thou art." **alway one** KP omits the added phrase "and ever shalte be one." **justly** "well rightwysely." **But . . . change** "but I wretche that alwaye am more redy and more prone to yvell than to good, am nat alway abydynge in one, for .vii. tymes be chaunged upon me." **please Thee** KP omits the immediately following phrase, "whan it shall please the to put to thy helpynge hande." **not . . . changed** "nat so lyghtly be chaunged." **but . . . Thee** "but that it maye be [w]holly fixed in the and finally to rest in the." The allusion is to Psalm 37:7: "Hold thee still in the Lord, and abide patiently upon Him."

46. **I am . . . vanity** KP skips over eleven lines of text, resuming her reworking of Whitford with six sentences selected from the latter part of chap. 45 (Godfray, fols. 107v–108r; Redman, fol. 113v; Wyer, fol. 114v–115r). **I am . . . glory?** "I am but vanytye and nought before the, a unconstaunt man and a feble, and therfore wherof maye I ryghtwysely gloryfye my selfe." **Whoso . . . before Thee** Omitting six lines of text that denounce vainglory, KP condenses this and the following sentence: "For whan a man pleaseth hym selfe he dyspleaseth the, and whan he delyteth in mannes praysynges, he is deprived fro the trewe vertues." **The true . . . in Thee** "For the trewe stedfast joye and gladnes is to joye in the and not in hym selfe, in thy name and nat in his owne vertue ne in any creature." **Wherefore** "Therfore." **lauded . . . blessed** "blessed"; KP introduces one of her characteristic doublings. **I glory . . . vanity** "I be glorified and alway shal I joy in thee, and in my selfe nothynge, but in my infirmities . . . for all mannes glory, al temporall honour, and al worldely hyghnes, to thy eternall glorye compared, is but as folysshnes and a great vanitie." **Thy . . . glory compared** an allusion to Psalm 62:7, 9: "In God is . . . my glory . . . the children of men . . . are altogether lighter than vanity."

To me, therefore, confusion and despite is due; but to Thee, laud, honor, and glory.[47]

[Bviii r] Lord, send me help in my troubles, for man's help is little worth.[48]

How often have I been disappointed, where I thought I should have found friendship? And how often have I found it, where as I least thought?

Wherefore it is a vain thing to trust in man: for the true trust and health of man, is only in Thee.

Blessed be Thou, Lord, therefore, in all things that happeneth unto us. For we be weak and unstable, soon deceived, and soon changed from one thing to another.[49]

[Bviii v] O Lord God, most righteous Judge, strong and patient, which knowest the frailty and malice of man: be Thou my whole strength and comfort in all necessities. For mine own conscience, Lord, sufficeth not.

Wherefore, to Thy mercy I do appeal, seeing no man may be justified, nor appear righteous in Thy sight, if Thou examine him after Thy justice.[50]

47. **O Lord . . . glory O Lord . . . Thee** KP skips over ten lines of text, resuming her reworking of Whitford with the second sentence of chap. 46, titled "Howe all temporall honour is to be dispised" (Godfray, fol. 108v; Redman, fol. 114r; Wyer, fol. 115v). **live** "be." **soon deceived . . . trouble** KP elaborates Whitford's "soone are we deceyved with vanities." **yet . . . behold** "but veryly if I behelde." **plainly** "openly." **what trouble . . . Thee** KP condenses "there was never wronge done to me by any creature, ne . . . I have nothing wherof I may rightwysly complayne. But for as moche as I have ofte synned, and ryght grevously offended agaynste the, therfore all creatures be armed agaynst me." **confusion . . . due** "is dewe confusyon and dyspite." **but** KP's addition.

48. **Lord, send . . . worth** KP skips from near the end of chap. 46 to the opening sentence of chap. 50, titled "That men be nat alway to be byleved, for that they so lyghtly offende in wordes" (Godfray, fols. 111v-112r; Redman, fol. 117v; Wyer, fol. 119r-v). **send . . . worth** an allusion to Psalm 60:11: "O be Thou our help in trouble, for vain is the help of man."

49. **How often . . . another** KP continues to rework Whitford's phrasing from the beginning of chap. 50. **have I . . . disappointed** "have I nat founde frendshyp." **disappointed** KP's adjectival usage is earlier than the first occurrence (1552) recorded in the *OED*. **friendship** "it." **where as . . . thought** "where I leest presumed to have founde it." **Wherefore** "therfore." **the true . . . health** Godfray reads "trewely the helthe." Redman and Wyer read "the true and sothfast truste and helth." KP's phrasing here is closer to Wyer and Redman than to Godfray, yet not identical to any one source. What these variants indicate most clearly is her characteristic fondness for doublings.

50. **O Lord . . . justice** KP skips to the closing section of chap. 51, selecting its initial and final sentences (Godfray, fol. 115r-v; Redman, fol. 121r; Wyer, fol. 122v). **O Lord . . . sufficeth not** KP reproduces verbatim Whitford's wording in all three editions but omits his final clause: "for thou knowest in me that I knowe nat." The attributes of God allude to Psalm 7:12: "God is a righteous Judge, strong and patient." **Wherefore . . . justice** The opening and closing clauses of this sentence are KP's original compositions, enclosing a quotation from Whitford that ends chap. 51: "no man may be justyfyed ne appere rightwyse in thy sight."

O blessed mansion of Thy heavenly city; O most clearest day of eternity, whom the night may never darken.[51]

This is the day always clear and merry, always sure, and never changing his state.

Would to God this day might shortly appear and shine upon us, and that these worldly fantasies were at an end!

[Ci r] This day shineth clearly to Thy saints in heaven with everlasting brightness; but to us pilgrims in earth, it shineth obscurely, and as through a mirror or glass.[52]

The heavenly citizens know how joyous this day is. But we outlaws, the children of Eve, weep and wail the bitter tediousness of our day, that is, of this present life, short and evil, full of sorrow and anguish:

[Ci v] Where man is oftentimes defiled with sin, encumbered with affliction, unquieted with troubles, wrapped in cares, busied with vanities, blinded with errors, overcharged with labors, vexed with temptations, overcome with vain delights and pleasures of the world, and grievously tormented with penury and need.[53]

O when shall the end come, of all these miseries?

When shall I be clearly delivered from the bondage of sin?

When shall I, Lord, have only mind on Thee, and fully be glad and merry in Thee?

When shall I be free without letting, and be in perfect liberty without grief of body and soul?

When shall I have peace without trouble, peace within and without, and on every side steadfast and sure?

O Lord Jesu, when shall I stand and behold Thee, and have full sight and contemplation of Thy glory?

51. **O . . . darken** KP skips over chap. 52 and resumes her reworking of sentences from Whitford with an extended sequence at the beginning of chap. 53, titled "Of the day of eternitie and of the myseries of this life" (Godfray, fols. 116v–117r; Redman, fols. 122v–123r; Wyer, fols. 124v–125r). **Thy heavenly** "the hevenly."

52. **This . . . glass** KP continues her reworking of Whitford at the beginning of chap. 53. **This is** KP's addition. **clear . . . merry** "mery"; KP's doubling. **sure** "seker"—an earlier variant of "secure." **shortly** "ones." **worldly fantasies** "temporal things." KP's revision moderates the contempt of the world emphasized in Whitford and à Kempis. **This day . . . glass** KP condenses: "This blessid day shineth to sayntes in heven with everlastynge bryghtnes and cleretye, but to us pylgrymes in erthe it shyneth nat but a farre of, as throughe a morrour [mirror] or glasse."

53. **The heavenly . . . need** KP continues by quoting nearly verbatim Whitford's next sentences from the beginning of chap. 53. **know** "knowe wel." **bitter tediousness** "bytternes and tedyousnes." **sorrow . . . anguish** "sorowes and anguysshes"; Redman reads "sorowes amguysshes." **defiled** "defouled"—an error for "befouled" in Godfray, Redman, and Wyer. **afflictions** "passyons." **troubles** "dredes." **wrapped . . . cares** "bounden with charges." **vain** KP's addition, qualifying the contempt of the world expressed in Whitford and à Kempis. **tormented** "tourmented somtyme."

[Cii r] When shalt Thou be to me All in all? And when shall I be with Thee in Thy kingdom, that Thou hast ordained for Thine elect people from the beginning?

I am left here poor, and as an outlaw, in the land of mine enemies, where daily be battles and great misfortunes.

Comfort mine exile, assuage my sorrow; for all my desire is to be with Thee.

It is to me an unpleasant burden, what pleasure soever the world offereth me here.

I desire to have inward fruition in Thee, but I cannot attain thereto.[54]

[Cii v] I covet to cleave fast to heavenly things, but worldly affections pluck my mind downward.[55]

Thus I, wretched creature, fight in myself, and am grievous to myself: while my spirit desireth to be upward, and, contrary, my flesh draweth me downward.

O what suffer I inwardly? I go about to mind heavenly things; and, straight, a great rabble of worldly thoughts rush into my soul.

Therefore, Lord, be not long away, nor depart not, in Thy wrath, from me.

[Ciii r] Send me the light of Thy grace; destroy in me all carnal desires.

Send forth the hot flames of Thy love, to burn and consume the cloudy fantasies of my mind.[56]

Gather, O Lord, my wits and the powers of my soul together in Thee; and make

54. **O when . . . thereto** KP continues at uncharacteristic length to quote nearly verbatim from Whitford's phrasing in chap. 53 (Godfray, fol. 117r-v; Redman, fol. 123r-v; Wyer, fol. 125r-v). **I, Lord . . fully be** "I only, Lord, have mynde on the and fully be made." **peace** "sad peace." **sure** "seker"—an earlier synonym of "sure." **When** "And whan." **All in all** See n41. **Thy kingdom . . . beginning** an allusion to Jesus's words to the redeemed at the Last Judgment in Matthew 25:34: "Come, ye blessed of my Father, inherit the kingdom prepared for you from the beginning of the world." **is to . . . with** "cryeth to." **unpleasant** "grevous." **here** "here to my solace."

55. **downward** The correspondences between the Kendal autograph and the 1545 printed editions of KP's *Prayers or Meditations* end at this point. See the different close of the original-spelling text, p. 395.

56. **I covet . . . my mind** KP mitigates some of the stark negative dualism attached to the world and the flesh in Whitford's wording as she continues to excerpt from chap. 53 (Godfray, fols. 117v–118 [misnumbered 117] r; Redman, fols. 123v–124r; Wyer, fols. 125v–126r). **worldly . . . downward** "temporall thynges and passions unmortyfied pull me alway downwarde." **wretched creature** KP degenders Whitford's phrase "moost wretched man." **am grievous** "am made grevous." **while . . . me downward** "whiles my spirite desireth to be upwarde and my flesh downwarde." **I go . . . soul** "whan in my mynde I beholde hevenly thinges, and anone [Redman omits: anone] a great multytude of carnall thoughtes entre in to my soule." **straight** immediately. **away** "away fro me." **from me** "fro me thy servaunt." **Send me . . . light** "Sende to me thy lightes" (Godfray); "sende to me the lyghtnes" (Redman, Wyer). **destroy** "breake downe." **carnal** Redman mistakenly reads "eternall." **desires** "thoughtes." **hot flames** "dartes." **burn . . . my mind** "breke therwith all fantasies of the enemy." **burn . . . consume** KP's doubling.

me to despise all worldly things, and by Thy grace strongly to resist and overcome all motions and occasions of sin.

Help me, Thou everlasting Truth, that no worldly guile nor vanity hereafter have power to deceive me.

Come also, Thou heavenly sweetness, and let all bitterness of sin flee far from me. [Ciii v] Pardon me and forgive me, as oft as in my prayer my mind is not surely fixed on Thee.[57]

For many times I am not there, where I stand or sit; but rather there, whither my thoughts carry me.

For there I am, where my thought is; and there, as customably is my thought, there is that that I love.

And that oftentimes cometh into my mind, that by custom pleaseth me best, and that delighteth me most to think upon.

Accordingly, as Thou dost say in Thy Gospel: Where as a man's treasure is, there is his heart.[58]

[Ciiir] Wherefore, if I love heaven, I speak gladly thereof, and of such things as be of God, and of that that appertaineth to His honor, and to the glorifying of His holy name.

And if I love the world, I love to talk of worldly things; and I joy anon in worldly felicity, and sorrow and lament soon for worldly adversity.

If I love the flesh, I imagine oftentimes that that pleaseth the flesh.

If I love my soul, I delight much to speak and to hear of things that be for my soul's health.

And whatsoever I love, of that I gladly hear and speak, and bear the images of them still in my mind.

[Ciiii v] Blessed is that man that, for the love of Thee, Lord, setteth not by the pleasures of this world, and learneth truly to overcome himself. And, with the fervor of spirit, crucifieth his flesh, so that in a clean and a pure conscience he may offer his

57. **Gather . . . on Thee** KP continues to rework specifics of Whitford's phrasing in citing from chap. 53. **O Lord** KP's addition. **despise** "forgete." KP moves a verb in Whitford from the subsequent clause to this earlier position. **by Thy . . . sin** KP significantly adds divine grace to Whitford's formulation of spiritual effort: "graunt me to cast away and [w]holly to dispise all fantasies of sin." **resist . . . overcome, motions . . . occasions** KP's doublings. **worldly . . . vanity** "worldly vanitie." **power . . . deceive** "power in." **forgive . . . on Thee** "mercifully forgyve me whan I thinke in my prayer of any thyng but of the."

58. **For many . . . heart** KP continues to rework specifics of phrasing from chap. 53 (Godfray, fol. 118 [misnumbered 117] r-v; Redman, fol. 124 r-v; Wyer, fol. 126 r-v). **rather there** "rather I am there." **carry** "lede." **as . . . thought** "as my thought is accustomed to be." **is that** "is it." **Accordingly . . . Gospel** KP rewords to signal that Whitford's allusion is a Scriptural citation: "wherfore thou that arte everlastyng trouthe sayth openly." **Where . . . heart** Matthew 6:21: "Where your treasure is, there will your heart be also."

prayers to Thee, and be accepted to have company of Thy blessed angels, all earthly things excluded from his heart.[59]

Lord and holy Father, be Thou blessed, now and ever. For, as Thou wilt, so is it done; and that Thou doest, is always best.[60]

Let me, thy humble and unworthy servant, joy only in Thee, and not in myself, nor in anything else besides Thee.

For Thou, Lord, art my gladness, my hope, my crown, and all mine honor.

[Cv r] What hath Thy servant, but that he hath of Thee, and that without his desert?

All things be Thine; Thou hast created and made them.

I am poor, and have been in trouble and pain ever from my youth. And my soul hath been in great heaviness through manifold passions that come of the world and of the flesh:

Wherefore, Lord, I desire that I may have of Thee the joy of inward peace.[61]

I ask of Thee to come to that rest, which is ordained for Thy chosen children that be fed and nourished with the light of heavenly comforts: for, without Thy help, I cannot come to Thee.

[Cv v] Lord, give me peace, give me inward joy; and then my soul shall be full of heavenly melody, and be devout and fervent in Thy lauds and praisings.

But if Thou withdraw Thyself from me (as Thou hast sometime done), then may not Thy servant run the way of Thy commandments, as I did before.

For it is not with me as it was, when the lantern of Thy ghostly presence did

59. **Wherefore . . . heart** This is the last section of KP's excerpting and reworking of material from chap. 53. **thereof** "of hevenly thynges." **I love . . . things** "I speke gladly of hevenly thynges." **that . . . appertaineth** "that pertayne most." **glorifying** "glorifyeng [Redman: of] and worshippyng." **holy** KP's addition. **I love to . . . adversity** "I joye anone at worldely felycitie, and sorowe anon at his adversyte." **still** "ofte." **the love of** KP's addition. **setteth . . . world** "forgetteth all creatures." **accepted** "worthy." KP's revision signals a Reformation emphasis on unearned merit imputed by God. **his heart** "hym and [Redman and Wyer add: fully] set aparte."

60. **Lord . . . best** KP skips over the extensive chap. 54, titled "Of the desire of everlastyng lyfe, and of the great rewarde that is promysed to them that strongly fight agaynst sinne," and resumes her excerpting of Whitford at the beginning of chap. 55, titled "Howe a man that is desolate ought to offre hym selfe [w]holly to god" (Godfray, fol. 111v; Redman, fol. 127v; Wyer, fol. 129v). **best** "well."

61. **Let me . . . peace** KP continues to rework specifics of Whitford's phrasing in citing from chap. 55. **humble . . . servant** "porest servaunt and most unworthy." **only** KP's addition. **my hope** "thou art my hope." **What . . . Thee** an allusion to Paul's words in 1 Corinthians 4:7: "What hast thou, that thou hast not received?" **Thou . . . them** "that thou hast gyven and made." An allusion to God's words in Isaiah 66:12: "For all those things hath Mine hand made." **I am . . . youth** In à Kempis's Latin, this is a quotation of Psalm 87:16 in the Vulgate reading: "Pauper sum ego, et in laboribus à juventute mea" (I am poor and [have been] in troubles from my youth). **I am** "And I am." **pain** "in payne." **heaviness through** KP omits phrasing that intervenes between these two words in Whitford: "with wepynge and teares, and somtyme it hath ben troubled in it selfe."

shine upon my head, and I was defended under the shadow of Thy wings from all perils and dangers.[62]

[Cvi r] O merciful Lord Jesu, ever to be praised: the time is come, that Thou wilt prove Thy servant. And rightful is it, that I shall now suffer somewhat for Thee.

Now is the hour come, that Thou hast known from the beginning: that Thy servant for a time should outwardly be set at naught, and inwardly to lean to Thee.

And that he should be despised in the sight of the world, and be broken with affliction: that he may, after, arise with Thee in a new light, and be clarified and made glorious in Thy kingdom of heaven.[63]

O holy Father, Thou hast ordained it so to be; and it is done as Thou hast commanded.

[Cvi v] This is Thy grace, O Lord, to Thy friend: to suffer him to be troubled in this world for Thy love, how often soever it be, and of what person soever it be, and in what manner soever Thou wilt suffer it to fall unto him. For, without Thy will or sufferance, what thing is done upon earth?

It is good to me, O Lord, that Thou hast meekened me: that I may thereby learn to know Thy righteous judgments; and to put from me all manner of presumption and stateliness of heart.[64]

62. **I ask . . . dangers** KP continues to rework phrasing in citing from chap. 55 (Godfray, fol. 112r; Redman, fol. 128r; Wyer, fol. 130r). **ask . . . children** KP's phrasing sharpens Whitford's muted reference to God's elect: "aske the rest of thy chosen chyldren." **with** "of the in." **for** "but." **to Thee** "thereto." **Lord, give . . . then** "If thou lord gyve peace, or if thou gyve inwarde joy." **be full** "be anone full." **I did, with me, my head, I was** KP substitutes genderless first-person pronouns for Whitford's third-person masculine singular pronouns: "he dyd . . . with hym . . . his hed . . . he was." **shadow . . . wings** "shadowe of thy mercy." KP's revised wording introduces an allusion to Psalms 17:8, 36:7, 57:1, and 63:7 (in the numbering of English Bibles), where God's protection is called "the shadow of Thy wings."

63. **O merciful . . . heaven** KP continues to rework phrasing in citing from chap. 55. **merciful . . . Jesu** "rightwyse father." KP's transfer of focus from God the Father to His Son is characteristic of the Christocentric piety of this period. **Thou . . . servant** "thou wylte thy servaunt be proved." **rightful . . . it** "rightwysely is it done." **Now . . . heaven** KP's phrasing activates a generalized allusion to Jesus's appeal to God from the cross in John 17:1, 4–5: "Father, the hour is come. . . . I have finished the work which Thou gavest me to do. And now glorify Thou me, . . . Father, with . . . the glory, which I had with Thee, ere the world was." There are passing secondary allusions to Isaiah 53:3, "He was despised and rejected of men," and to Isaiah 63:9, "In their affliction he was afflicted"—verses traditionally interpreted as prophecies of Christ—as well as to Ephesians 5:14: "Stand up from death, and Christ shall give thee light." **affliction** "passyons and sykenes." KP's revision of Whitford's phrasing strengthens the Scriptural allusion.

64. **O holy . . . heart** KP begins to cite more closely from chap. 55, while reworking selected phrases (Godfray, fol. 112v; Redman, fol. 128v; Wyer, fol. 130v). **O Lord** KP's addition. **without . . . earth?** "without thy counsayle and provydence, ne without cause, nothynge is done." Redman and Wyer add "upon erthe." The allusion is to Job 5:6 in the Vulgate rendering: "Nihil

It is very profitable for me, that confusion hath covered my face: that I may learn thereby, rather to seek to Thee for help and succor, than to man.

[Cvii r] I have thereby learned to dread Thy secret and terrible judgments: which scourgest the righteous with the sinner, but not without equity and justice.

Lord, I yield thanks to Thee, that Thou hast not spared my sins: but hast punished me with scourges of love, and hast sent me affliction and anguishes within and without.

No creature under heaven may comfort me but Thou, Lord God, the heavenly Leech of man's soul. Which strikest and healest, which bringest a man nigh unto death, and after restorest him to life again: that he may thereby learn to know his own weakness and imbecility, and the more fully to trust in Thee, Lord.[65]

[Cvii v] Thy discipline is laid upon me, and Thy rod of correction hath taught me; and under that rod I wholly submit me.

Strike my back and my bones, as it shall please Thee; and make me to bow my crooked will unto Thy will.

Make me a meek and an humble disciple, as Thou hast sometime done with me: that I may walk after Thy will.

To Thee I commit myself to be corrected; for it is better to be corrected by Thee here, than in time to come.[66]

Thou knowest all things; and nothing is hid from Thee, that is in man's conscience.

[Cviii r] Thou knowest all things to come, before they fall. And it is not needful that any man teach Thee, or warn Thee of anything that is done upon the earth.

Thou knowest what is profitable for me, and how much tribulations help to purge away the rust of sin in me.

---

in terra sine causa fit" (Nothing may be done in the world without cause). **It . . . Lord** "O it is good to me lorde." **stateliness** "highnes"—an earlier variant of "height."

65. **It is . . . Lord** KP continues to cite closely from chap. 55, while reworking selected phrases. **It is** "and it is." **for me** "to me." **I have** "And I have." **the righteous** KP degenders Whitford's "the rightwyse man." **Lord** KP's addition. **affliction** "sorowe." **No . . . may** "There is no creature under heven that maye." **Leech** healer, physician. **Which . . . again** an allusion to God's self-description in Deuteronomy 32:38: "There is no god with Me: I kill, and I make alive: I wound, and I heal." **unto death** "unto bodyly dethe." **life** "helthe." **his own . . . imbecillity** "the lytelnesse of his owne power." KP rewords with a characteristic doublet. **Thee, Lord** "the."

66. **Thy discipline . . . come** KP continues to cite closely from chap. 55, while reworking selected phrases (Godfray, fol. 113 [misnumbered 123] r; Redman, fol. 129r; Wyer, fol. 13 r). **Thy discipline . . . taught me** The allusions in à Kempis's Latin are to Psalm 17:36 in the Vulgate reading, "Disciplina tua correxit me . . . et disciplina tua ipsa me docebit" (Thy discipline hath corrected me . . . and this Thy discipline will teach me), and to the "virga disciplinae" (rod of correction) in Proverbs 22:15. **laid** "fallen." **walk after** "walke all after." **commit myself** "commyt my selfe and all myne."

Do with me after Thy pleasure. I am a sinful wretch, to none so well known as to Thee.

Grant me, Lord, that to know, that is necessary to be known; that to love, that is to be loved; that to desire, that pleaseth Thee; that to regard, that is precious in Thy sight; and that to refuse, that is vile before Thee.

[Cviii v] Suffer me not to judge Thy mysteries after my outward senses, nor to give sentence after the hearing of the ignorant; but, by true judgment, to discern things spiritual, and, above all things, always to search and follow Thy will and pleasure.[67]

O Lord Jesu, Thou art all my riches; and all that I have, I have it of Thee.[68]

But what am I, Lord, that I dare speak to Thee? I am Thy poor creature, and a worm most abject.

Behold, Lord, I have naught; and of myself, I am naught worth. Thou art only God, righteous and holy. Thou orderest all things; Thou givest all things; and Thou fulfillest all things with goodness.

[Di r] I am a sinner, barren and void of godly virtue.[69]

Remember Thy mercies, and fill my heart with plenty of Thy grace: for Thou wilt not that Thy works in me should be made in vain.

How may I bear the misery of this life, except Thy grace and mercy do comfort me?

67. **Thou knowest . . . pleasure** KP continues to cite closely from chap. 55, while reworking selected phrases (Godfray, fol. 1[1]3r-v; Redman, fol. 129v; Wyer, fol. 131v). **all . . . come** KP adds "all" to what is otherwise Redman's and Wyer's phrasing, "thynges to come." Godfray reads "thynges that are to come." **profitable** "spedeful" (profitable, advantageous). **purge away** "pourge." **I . . . wretch** KP's addition. Whitford reads "and dysdayne nat my synfull lyfe." **desire . . . pleaseth** "prayse that highly pleseth." **is precious** "appereth precious." **judge . . . senses** "juge after my outward wyttes." **of . . . ignorant** "of unconnyng [unknowing] men." **but, by** "but in a." **spiritual** "visible and unvisible."

68. **O Lord . . . Thee** Here KP makes her giant flip backward in Whitford's translation, from the end of chap. 55 to the beginning of chap. 4, titled "A prayer to optayne the grace of devotion" (Godfray, fol. 58v; Redman, fol. 63 [misnumbered 64] r-v; Wyer, fol. 64r). She quotes the first sentence verbatim.

69. **But what . . . virtue** KP reworks some local wording as she continues to quote from chap. 4 (Godfray, fol. 59r; Redman, fol. 63v; Wyer, fol. 64v). **dare speak** "dare thus speke." **poor creature** "poorest servaunt." **a worm** an allusion to Psalm 32:6: "I am a worm and no man." **most abject** Whitford adds "more pore and more dispisable than I can or dare say." **Behold, Lord** KP omits Whitford's immediately following clause, "that I am nought, that." **art . . . God** This is the reading in Redman and Wyer; Godfray reads "art onely good." **orderest . . . things, givest . . . things, with goodness** Wyer reads "orderest . . . thing," "givest . . . thing," "with thy goodnes." **I am . . . virtue** KP thoroughly recasts Whitford's immediately following phrase, "levynge onely the wretched synner bareyne and voyde of hevenly comforte." She thus suppresses what in her work would be a late reference to divine retribution, instead relocating the emphasis on sinful human nature.

Turn not Thy face from me; defer not Thy visiting of me; nor withdraw not Thy comforts, lest haply my soul be made as dry earth without the water of grace.

Teach me, Lord, to fulfill Thy will, to live meekly and worthily before Thee. For Thou art all my wisdom and cunning; Thou art He that knowest me as I am, that knewest me before the world was made, and before I was born, or brought into this life.[70] To Thee, O Lod, be honor, glory, and praise for ever and ever. Amen.

[Di v] Laudes Deum in aeternum. Amen.[71]

A PRAYER FOR THE KING

[Dii r] O Lord Jesu Christ, most high, most mighty, King of Kings, Lord of Lords, the only Ruler of princes, the very Son of God, on whose right hand sitting, dost from Thy throne behold all the dwellers upon earth: With most lowly hearts we beseech Thee, vouchsafe with favorable regard to behold our most gracious sovereign lord, King Henry the Eight[h]; and so replenish him with the grace of Thy Holy Spirit, that he always incline to Thy will, and walk in Thy way. Keep him far off from ignorance; but through Thy gift let prudence and knowledge always abound in his royal heart. So instruct him, O Lord Jesu, reigning upon us in earth, that his human majesty always obey Thy divine majesty in fear and dread. Endue him plentifully with heavenly gifts. Grant him in health and wealth long to live. Heap glory and honor upon him. Glad him with the joy of Thy countenance. So strength him, that he may vanquish and overcome all his and our foes, and be dread and feared of all the enemies of his realm. Amen.

[Dii v] A PRAYER FOR MEN TO SAY, ENTERING INTO BATTLE[72]

[Diii r] O almighty King and Lord of hosts, which, by Thy angels thereunto appointed, dost minister both war and peace; and which didst give unto David both

70. **Remember . . . life** KP continues to rework some local wording as she quotes from the remainder of chap. 4 (Godfray, fol. 59r-v; Redman, fol. 63v; Wyer, fols. 64r-v). **plenty . . . grace** "thy manyfold graces." **should be** "be." **except** "but." **comfort me** "comforte me therin." **comforts** "comfortes fro me." **to live** "and to live." **cunning** "connynge, and." **life** This is the last word of chap. 4 in Whitford's rendering.

71. **To Thee . . . Amen** KP's additions furnish her recasting of selected portions of Whitford's translation, *The Following of Christ*, with an appropriate conclusion. **Laudes . . . aeternum** Praises be to God forever.

72. **A . . . battle** This and the three following prayers may well be KP's original compositions. They exhibit some textual correspondences with her known work; these are footnoted below. Fisher's tendency to place his original versicles toward the close of his compositional units in *Psalmi seu Precationes* may have furnished KP with a precedent for appending these four prayers to *Prayers or Meditations*; see n16 to her original-spelling text (the Kendal autograph fragment).

courage and strength, being but a little one, unarmed and unexpert in feats of war, with his sling to set upon and overthrow the great, huge Goliath:[73] Our cause now being just, and being enforced to enter into war and battle, we most humbly beseech Thee, O Lord God of hosts, so to turn the hearts of our enemies to the desire of peace, that no Christian blood be spilt. Or else grant, O Lord, that with small effusion of blood, and to the little hurt and damage of innocents, we may, to Thy glory, obtain victory. And that, the wars being soon ended, we may all, with one heart and mind, knit together in concord and unity, laud and praise Thee: which livest and reignest, world without end. Amen.

[Diii v] **A DEVOUT PRAYER, TO BE DAILY SAID**[74]

O almighty and eternal God, which vouchsafest that we, as it were heavenly children, should every one of us call Thee our heavenly Father: Grant that among us, by pureness and example of innocent life, Thy most holy name may be sanctified, that all other nations, beholding our goodness and virtuous deeds that Thou workest in us, may be stirred to hallow and glorify Thee.

[Div r] Grant, O Lord, that the kingdom of Thy grace and mercy may reign continually in our hearts, so that we may be worthy to be partakers of the realm of glory and majesty. Grant that, unto the very death, we refuse not to follow Thy divine will; and that we (according to the example of the celestial citizens,[75] agreeing together quietly), united in spirit, all controversy in opinions laid apart, the lusts of the flesh being subdued, and the flattering assaults of the world and the devil overcome, never wrestle against Thy most holy will, but obey it in all things.

[Div v] Grant, O Lord, for our body, needful sustenance, that we may the more freely serve Thee. Give us, we beseech Thee, O merciful Father, that heavenly bread, the body of Thy Son, Jesu Christ, the very food and health of our souls. Give us the bread of Thy divine precepts, that we may truly walk and live after them. Give us the bread of Thy heavenly Word, which is the strong buttress and sure defense of our souls, that we, being well fed and filled with this food, may worthily come to the celestial feast, where as is no hunger.

[Dv r] Grant, O Lord, that we be not utterly led into temptation, that thereby we should be lost. But, in all perils of temptation and in the midst of the stormy tem-

73. **David . . . Goliath** The killing of the Philistine giant Goliath of Gath by the shepherd boy David, armed only with his slingshot and his trust in God, is narrated in 1 Samuel 17:20–54.

74. **A . . . said** The composition of this prayer perceptibly tracks, in overall content and expansive rephrasings, the petitions of the Lord's Prayer (Matthew 6:9–15, Luke 11:2–4). KP's personal prayerbook incorporates paraphrases of the sixth and seventh petitions, "Lead us not into temptation, but deliver us from evil," from William Marshall's *A goodly prymer in Englyshe* (1535); see n152 to that text.

75. **celestial citizens** a partial echo of "heavenly citizens" in the main text of *Prayers or Meditations*; see p. 411 above.

pests of tribulations, let us, Thy children, perceive and feel Thy fatherly succor, ready to help us: lest that we, overcome with the naughty crafts and deceits of the tempter, should be drawn into everlasting destruction. But, when we be well assayed, approved, and purged with the fire of temptation, then let us finish our course; and so well and valiantly fight, that we may for evermore live with Thee, in that heavenly city, where, and against the which, no manner temptation can prevail.

[Dv v] Finally grant, most merciful Father, that we, through Thy benign goodness, may be delivered from all evils present and to come, both of body and soul: and that, at the last, the yoke of the foul fiend being shaken off, we may possess the heritage of the heavenly kingdom, which Thy Son, with His precious blood, bought for us, Thy children. And there, forever, to have the fruition of celestial delectations, accompanied with angels and blessed saints, through the help, benignity, and grace of our Saviour, Jesu Christ: To whom, and to Thee, our Father, and to the Holy Ghost, be glory and honor, now and ever. Amen.

ANOTHER PRAYER

[Dvi r] O heavenly Father, God almighty, I pray and beseech Thy mercy, benignly to behold me, Thy unworthy servant, that I may, by gift of Thy Holy Spirit, fervently desire Thy kingdom: that I may know Thy will, and work thereafter. Give me, O Lord, wisdom;[76] make me constant, patient, and strong in Thee. Keep me, Lord, from the sleighty[77] invasion of the old, wily serpent. Defend me from the counsels and cursings of evil tongues. Let Thy mighty arm be my shield against all the malignity of this wicked world. Remember not, Lord, mine offenses; instruct, prepare me to repent, to be sorry for my sins. Make me to love justice and hate wrong, to do good, and abstain from all evils: that I may be worthy to be called Thy child.[78] To Thee be honor and glory forever and ever. Amen.

[Dvi v]

A DEVOUT PRAYER

Lord, hearken to my words, consider the thought of mine heart; behold, how loud I cry unto Thee. Let my just prayer enter into Thine ears, which unfeignedly cometh from mine heart. Hear me, Lord, for I am poor, and destitute of man's help. Take care for my soul: save me, Thy servant, which wholly trust in Thee. Have mercy

76. **Give . . . wisdom** an echo of Widsom of Solomon 9:4—a verse that had figured in "The fifth Psalm, for the obtaining of godly wisdom" in *Psalms or Prayers*; see n349 to that text.

77. **sleighty** sly, cunning, subtle.

78. **I . . . child** a positive recasting of the prodigal son's self-accusation in Luke 15:19: "I . . . am no more worthy to be called thy son." This verse had been incorporated in the first Psalm of *Psalms or Prayers*; see n13 to that text.

upon me, O Lord: for I will never cease crying to Thee for help. For Thou art mild and more merciful than my tongue can express.

[Dvii r] As often as adversity assaileth me, I will cry and call for help unto Thee. I will call upon Thee in the daytime; and in the night my cry shall not be hid from Thee.[79] O Thou, God of the heavens, the Maker of the waters, and Lord of all creatures: hear me, a poor sinner, calling upon Thee, and putting my whole trust in Thy mercy. Have mercy upon me, O Lord God, have mercy upon me. For Thy manifold mercies' sake, forgive all mine offenses. Amen.

Finis.

[Colophon]

[Dvii v]

Imprinted at London in Fleet Street
by Thomas Berthelet, printer to
the King's highness, the sixt[h]
of November, the year of
our Lord. M.DXLV.
Cum privilegio ad imprimendum solum.[80]

79. **I . . . Thee** an expansively recast excerpt from Psalm 88:1: "O Lord God of my salvation, I have cried day and night before Thee."

80. With the privilege of sole printing—a predecessor of copyright.

KATHERINE PARR'S

THE LAMENTATION OF A SINNER

(1547)

INTRODUCTION TO *THE LAMENTATION OF A SINNER*[1]

Katherine Parr's *Lamentation of a Sinner* was first published on November 5, 1547, slightly more than nine months after Henry VIII's death in late January. Her text, however, evokes Henry as both alive and active: "my most sov[er]eign, favorable lord and husband," "our . . . most godly, wise governor and King" (*Lamentation*, sig. Dvi r). These references point to a date of composition for the *Lamentation* in the autumn of 1546 at the latest, before the king's fatal decline toward the end of that year.

Another suggestive turn of phrase comports well with a compositional date in the latter part of 1546. The title of the *Lamentation* declares that the work has been "set forth and put in print at the instant desire" of two of the queen's intimates—her brother William Parr, Marquess of Northampton, and her closest friend Katherine Brandon, Duchess of Suffolk. John Bale had used the phrase "at the instant desire of certain faithful men and women" to characterize his motive for editing and publishing the *First* and *Latter Examinations* written by Anne Askew, an outspoken adherent of Reformed religion, as her own account of the two interrogations that she underwent for heresy in spring 1545 and early summer 1546. The phrasal echo does not seem merely fortuitous.[2] Askew's second interrogation involved her illegitimate

1. *The lamentacion of a sinner, made by the most vertuous Ladie, Quene Caterin* (Edward Whitchurch, November 5, 1547) (STC 4827), sigs. Ai–Gv.

2. Bale published Askew's *First Examination* (STC 748) at "Wesel" (Marburg) in Germany in November 1546, and her *Latter Examination* (STC 750) on January 16, 1547, at the same place. The revised STC suggests that a combined edition of the *Examinations* that also bears the date January 16, 1547, and a "Wesel" designation (STC 751) may be a clandestine London production. The relative closeness in date of the published texts of the *Examinations* and the *Lamentation*—

torture at the hands of two members of the Privy Council who were seeking information on suspected heretical leanings in Queen Katherine's inner circle of ladies and their possible support of Askew. While Askew steadfastly denied any contact with the queen or her ladies, the new audacity of her witness—a forthright denial of transubstantiation—ensured that she would be burned at the stake for heresy, and she was, in mid-July 1546.

In spring and summer 1546 the same two members of the Privy Council, Lord Chancellor Thomas Wriostheley and Sir Richard Rich, abetted a third, Bishop Stephen Gardiner, the ranking English religious conservative, in a separate plot to bring down Queen Katherine Parr by discrediting her with King Henry as a heretic. My general biographical introduction considers in some detail (pp. 21–25) this crucial episode—in the category of "what might well have happened but did not"—as narrated by John Foxe, starting with the 1570 edition of *Acts and Monuments*. Foxe represents Queen Katherine as saving her own life by prevaricating about her intentions and beliefs in urging King Henry to further reforms of the English church. Attention is again directed to this episode here to stress its uniquely plausible connection with Queen Katherine's decision to compose her *Lamentation of a Sinner*—and, in particular, to employ as its springboard a first-person confession of such extreme self-condemnation that Sir William Cecil, a sympathetic privy councillor, devotes his prefatory letter to an apologia for the queen's public abasement of herself.[3] He appeals to English readers to be charitable and understanding toward the harshly negative example the queen makes of herself to impress on her fellow Christians their own personal need for Christ's forgiveness, redemption, and redirection in a new life.

---

all within the compass of a single year—bolsters the possibility that "at the instant desire of" served as an intertextual prompt to link the self-accountings of Askew and KP, two prominent women witnesses to explicitly Reformist convictions. Askew's two texts have been sensitively edited by Elaine V. Beilin: *The Examinations of Anne Askew* (New York: Oxford University Press, 1996).

3. It is understandable that Cecil considered his apologia necessary. By late 1547 English readers had been exposed to nothing resembling such abjection in print from so exalted a personage. In the very next year, however, John Bale's publication of Princess Elizabeth's translation (for Queen Katherine) of Marguerite de Navarre's *Miroir de l'âme pécheresse* under the title *A godly medytacyon of the christen sowle* (STC 17320) would make a model for this aspect of the *Lamentation* available in English. For Elizabeth's text, see *Elizabeth I: Translations, 1544–1589*, ed. Janel Mueller and Joshua Scodel (Chicago: University of Chicago Press, 2009), 25–125. While evidence of a wider English familiarity with *Le Miroir* at this date seems to be lacking, the English court had long recognized Marguerite as a person of strategic importance. On the attentions she attracted from English emissaries as the French king's sister, a queen in her own right, and a bellwether for possible rapprochements between England and France, see Anne Lake Prescott, "'And Then She Fell on a Great Laughter': Tudor Diplomats Read Marguerite de Navarre," in *Culture and Change: Attending to Early Modern Women*, ed. Margaret Mikesell and Adele Seeff (Newark: University of Delaware Press / London: Associated University Presses, 2003), 41–65.

The Lamentation of a Sinner attained markedly less circulation among English readers than *Psalms or Prayers* and *Prayers or Meditations* did.[4] Yet the *Lamentation* made an unusual bid for a complex role as the production of a woman author in earlier sixteenth-century England.[5] The *Lamentation* is the most free-standing of Parr's works in its preponderance of original composition and its often only allusive connections with other authors' works. The *Lamentation* is also the most free-standing of Parr's works in the range and originality that it attains through generic hybridity. Through its structuring and apportioning of material, this prose tract situates its first section in the private sphere and its final section in the public sphere. The central section groups the speaker and her readers as fellow Christians with shared spiritual needs and desires. This section serves as a transition between the opening focus of the *Lamentation* on devotional self-examination and its concluding focus, where reflection and exhortation combine to address the present state of the body politic and ecclesiastic in England.

The opening section of the *Lamentation* is penitential and confessional. Parr acknowledges her sins, her wilfulness, her blindness, and her ignorance; she also heralds the onset of salvation through justifying faith. This she variously terms "lively faith" and "feeling faith"—tantamount to an inward knowing that Christ is her Saviour and Redeemer—as contrasted to a "dead, human, historical faith and knowledge" consisting in belief that Jesus lived in such and such a historical place and time and said and did the things reported of Him (sig. Biv r-v). To judge from affinities of vocabulary and phrasing signaled in the notes to the *Lamentation*, Queen Katherine became acquainted with the experiential correlates of Martin Lu-

4. If the quality of a reader's response can be given precedence over quantity, KP's *Lamentation* makes a strong showing in a contemporary translation into rhymed French decasyllabics. It survives in a manuscript draft (Hatfield House, Cecil Papers, vol. 314) and in a fair copy (BL, Royal MS 16.E.28). James Kelsey McConica called attention to this poem while expressing uncertainty whether it was KP's own work or that of a translator: see his *English Humanists and Reformation Politics under Henry VIII and Edward VI* (Oxford: Clarendon, 1965), 229–30. The linguistic and metrical facility exhibited throughout the poem indicates that the poet's native language was French. Moreover, the graceful italic handwriting in both manuscripts is identical—and, I infer with McConica, the translator's own. Judging from the handwriting and the facility in French, the highly probable creator of this anonymous verse translation of the *Lamentation* was Jean Belmain, tutor in French to Princess Elizabeth and Prince Edward. Before seeking religious asylum in England, probably in 1540, Belmain had associated with John Calvin in France. See Gordon Kipling, "Belmaine, Jean (fl. 1546–1559)," in *Oxford Dictionary of National Biography* (2004), available at http://www.oxford.dnb.com/view/article/2041. For a specimen of Belmain's handwriting, see figure 1 in *Elizabeth I: Autograph Compositions and Foreign Language Originals*, ed. Janel Mueller and Leah S. Marcus (Chicago: University of Chicago Press, 2003), xv.

5. A prior discussion is Janel Mueller, "A Tudor Queen Finds Voice: Katherine Parr's *Lamentation of a Sinner*," in *The Historical Renaissance: New Essays on Tudor and Stuart Literature and Culture*, ed. Heather Dubrow and Richard Strier (Chicago: University of Chicago Press, 1988), 15–47.

ther's "justification by faith" through sources available in English—particularly, it appears, William Tyndale and Thomas Cranmer.[6] There are also certain analogues in Marguerite de Navarre, made easily accessible in Princess Elizabeth's translation of the *Miroir*.

Within the framework provided by foundational studies of the discovery and construction of subjectivities in early modern England,[7] the *Lamentation* emerges as a significantly early "depth" text in its degree of articulation—speaking from within one's own mind, emotions, and body. As she differentiates her faculties, Parr renders herself accountable to God for them: her "obstinate, stony, and intractable heart," her will, "despising that which was good, holy, pleasant, and acceptable in His sight, and choosing that which was delicious, pleasant, and acceptable in my sight," her "vain, foolish imaginations" by which she "called superstition godly meaning, and true holiness, error," and her "carnal and human reasons" that preferred "rotten ignorance" to "ripe and seasonable knowledge" (sigs. Ai r, Aii v, Avi v). Parr repeatedly registers her sense of disjunction between her outward and inward selves, and the distorted or false perceptions that result. The following passage will illustrate:

> I could not think but I walked in the perfect and right way: having more regard to the number of the walkers than to the order of the walking, believing also most surely with company to have walked to heaven, whereas I am most sure they would have brought me down to hell. I forsook the spiritual honoring of the true, living God, and worshiped visible idols and images made of men's hands, believing by them to have gotten heaven. Yea, to say the truth, I made a great idol of myself: for I loved myself better than God. (sig. Aiv r)

Certain specifics of Parr's vocabulary—her self-characterization as "a dunghill of wickedness" and as "mire," "ignorant, blind, weak, and feeble," entangled in "a maze of iniquity" that is equally "a maze of death" (sigs. Bi r-v)—tally with

6. See Brian Cummings, *The Literary Culture of the Reformation: Grammar and Grace* (Oxford: Oxford University Press, 2002), chap. 2; and Peter Marshall, "Evangelical Conversion," in his *Religious Identities in Henry VIII's England* (Aldershot, UK/ Burlington, VT: Ashgate, 2006), 19–42.

7. See, variously, Catherine Belsey, *The Subject of Tragedy: Identity and Difference in Renaissance Drama* (London: Methuen, 1985); Anne Ferry, *The "Inward" Language: Sonnets of Wyatt, Sidney, Shakespeare, Donne* (Chicago: University of Chicago Press, 1983); Katherine Eisaman Maus, *Inwardness and Theater in the English Renaissance* (Chicago: University of Chicago Press, 1995); and Michael Schoenfeldt, *Bodies and Selves in Early Modern England: Physiology and Inwardness in Spenser, Shakespeare, Herbert, and Milton* (Cambridge: Cambridge University Press, 1999).

the English vocabulary employed by Princess Elizabeth to translate Marguerite de Navarre's *Le Miroir de l'âme pécheresse* as a gift for Queen Katherine at New Year's 1545.[8] Beyond shared expressions of extreme self-denigration and emotional lability, the spectacle in the mind's eye of the reader tallies as well. Two queens (the Queen of Navarre, elder sister to François I, King of France, and the Queen of England, wife of King Henry VIII) humble themselves publicly, declaring themselves of no worth or merit as they apprehend Christ's redeeming love and grace as a personal gift from their Lord and Saviour. In both texts devotional "mood swings" observably aim at breaking down and dissolving self-possession and psychological composure, leaving the speaker open to—or better, incapable of resisting—the new self that is coming into being through divine love and direction.

Convergences between the *Miroir* and the *Lamentation* mainly inhere in the extravagant rhetoric of negation used to characterize the speaker's self. Marguerite gives her *Miroir* a passionately mystical turn, brooding on her roles as Christ's sister, daughter, wife, and mother, and yearning for an immediate sense of union with her divine love object, even and especially if this requires her to die out of this life and world. When Parr crafted her *Prayers or Meditations* from recast and rearranged excerpts from book 3 of *The Following of Christ* (Whitford's translation of à Kempis's *De Imitatione Christi*), she had broached some themes and tonalities similar to Marguerite's while sustaining reliance on the Psalms as her expressive model. Marguerite, for all of her Scripturalism, sets herself no such confines. Even where the *Miroir*, like the *Lamentation*, records what appears as an experience of justifying faith, a wholly unmerited sense of salvation as Christ's free, loving gift, the experience registers quite differently because the two works are so differently pitched. The *Miroir*—as shows clearly in Elizabeth's close translation—is allegorical, analogical, unliteral, subjective; it has no this-world setting or context.[9] Parr's

8. See the phrasing in Elizabeth's translation of Marguerite: "I do confess that, as for me, I am much less than nothing: before my birth, mire; and after, a dunghill" (lines 45–48); "I knowledge myself to be but mire and muck" (line 1426): *Elizabeth I: Translations, 1544–1589*, ed. Mueller and Scodel, 49, 125. Also see Anne Lake Prescott's pioneering discussion "The Pearl of the Valois and Elizabeth I: Marguerite de Navarre's *Miroir* and Tudor England," in *Silent but for the Word: Tudor Women as Patrons, Translators, and Writers of Religious Works*, ed. Margaret P. Hannay (Kent, OH: Kent State University Press, 1985), 61–76.

9. To illustrate: Marguerite's onset of what appears to be justifying faith occurs within the context of her mystical sense of her soul's becoming Christ's mother (with a significant pun on "conceive"): "Suddenly Thou vouchsafest to draw my soul in such highness that she . . . , poor, ignorant, and lame, doth find herself with Thee rich, wise, and strong, because Thou hast written in her heart . . . Thy Spirit and Holy Word, giving her true faith to receive it: which thing made her to conceive Thy Son, believing Him to be God, man, Saviour, and also the true remitter of all sins" (*Elizabeth I: Translations, 1544–1589*, 57). The marginal references accompanying this passage are exclusively Pauline—to Philippians, 2 Corinthians, and Romans (twice)—strengthening the connections with Luther's justification by faith.

Lamentation, by contrast, presents a life-changing conversion experience in the mode of personal history, of spiritual autobiography, set in this world. Its this-world setting assumes definitive prominence in the work's final section, where earlier conventional images of a "loving father" and recalcitrant "child" or a "worldly prince or magistrate" (sigs. Av r, Avi r, Bii v) take on concrete social and political identities as the monarch of England, Henry VIII, the estates of his realm, and his subjects in their respective vocations and behaviors (sigs. Dv v–Dvii r).

The generic originality attained by the *Lamentation* as it gradates along a continuum from a private, inward domain to a public, outward one is importantly the result of Parr's eclectic adaptation of major themes and key vocabulary employed by ranking male authors of her day. Yet she consistently maintains a measure of authorial difference in how she handles these materials. One device Parr uses for local structuring in the *Lamentation* is the pairing of spiritually charged topics with certain images. These topic-image pairings may recur at irregular intervals in combination with other topics, to form new thought complexes. For example, envisaging one's relation to God as that of a loving child, not that of a bondservant working for wages, appears first as a sheer impossibility for an unregenerate soul, next as a possibility glimpsed for herself, then as the focus of a prayer Parr makes for all Christians, and finally as a sustaining element in the faith with which the godly confront the world (sigs. Avi r, Biii v, Div v, Fv v). Likewise, stonyheartedness is the condition that Parr first reprehends in herself, later pinpoints as the source of the world's disregard of Christ, and still later absorbs into a prayer that the Gospel may bear fruit in the hearts of English men and women (sigs. Ai r, Avi r, Bv r, Eii r, Fii r).

The single most striking of Parr's topic-image pairings is her representation of the saving knowledge of God in Christ as reading in the "book of the crucifix"—an image adapted and recast from a Lenten sermon delivered circa 1531–34 by John Fisher, Bishop of Rochester.[10] Parr's earlier attraction to the strongly Scripturalist bent of Fisher's spirituality had prompted her first publication, a translation of his *Psalmi seu Precationes* as *Psalms or Prayers*. At this later juncture the conjoint object of Fisher's and Parr's affective apprehension is the figure—or figuration—of salvation presented by the crucified Christ.[11] But the Reformation emphases that

10. The earliest edition now extant is John Fisher, *A sermon . . . very aptely applyed unto the passion of Christ*, appended to his *A spirituall consolation* (1578?) (STC 10899). The text to which KP had access seems not to have survived. Considered in its broader medieval context, the book of the crucifix had the status of a commonplace for certain writers. See Beryl Smalley, *The Study of the Bible in the Middle Ages*, 3rd ed., rev. (Oxford: Basil Blackwell, 1983), 283–84; Margaret Aston, *Lollards and Reformers: Images of Literacy in Late Medieval Religion* (London: Hambledon, 1984), 104–5.

11. Christine Peters contends that a centering on Christ as crucified Saviour is the principal shared element in traditionalist and Reformed devotion of the late medieval and early modern eras: see her *Patterns of Piety: Women, Gender, and Religion in Late Medieval and Reformation*

now inflect her Scripturalism take Parr on a course that diverges from Fisher's in developing the image.[12]

Fisher's "book of the crucifix" is a graphic image of the distended, bleeding, suffering body of Christ on the cross, metaphorically transmuted into a manuscript where the devoutly penitent soul apprehends the truths of sacrifice, mercy, love, and salvation. Its parchment is Christ's stretched and fastened skin; its illuminated capitals are His wounds; the blue lines of its message are the bruises inflicted by His tormenters. There is no "reading" as a textual activity here: rather, a visceral apprehension of divine suffering and benefaction. In contrast, although Parr's "book of the crucifix" begins as Fisher's does with inward meditation, the image rapidly takes focus as what becomes a book of the crucifixion[13]—a printed Bible in which the reader apprehends the truths of sacrifice, mercy, love, and salvation as the inspired Word of God, pointedly keyed by the marginal references to St. Paul's epistles:

> Inwardly to behold Christ crucified upon the cross is the best and godliest meditation that can be. . . . Then we shall see our own cruelty, when we feel His mercy, our own unrighteousness and iniquity, when we see His righteousness and holiness. Therefore, to learn to know truly our own sins is to study in the book of the crucifix by continual conversation in faith.
>
> . . . This crucifix is the book, wherein God hath included all things, and hath most compendiously written therein all truth profitable and necessary for our salvation [mg. 1 Corinthians 2]. . . . And that this is true, is evident and clear, because the very true Christian is a Christian by Christ. And the true Christian feeleth inwardly by Christ [mg. 2 Corinthians 4.] . . . The true Christian, by Christ, is disburdened from the servitude of the law, having the law of grace (graven by the Spirit) inhabiting his heart [mg. Romans 7]. (sigs. Bviii v, Cii v, Di v)

England (Cambridge: Cambridge University Press, 2003), 94–96, 128. Also see Ellen M. Ross, *The Grief of God: Images of the Suffering Jesus in Late Medieval England* (New York: Oxford University Press, 1997).

12. See further Janel Mueller, "Complications of Intertextuality: John Fisher, Katherine Parr, and the Book of the Crucifix," in *Representing Women in Renaissance England,* ed. Claude J. Summers and Ted-Larry Pebworth (Columbia: University of Missouri Press, 1997), or in *Texts and Cultural Change in Early Modern England,* ed. Cedric Brown and Arthur Marotti (London: Macmillan, 1997), 15–36.

13. One early reader, however, did not find Parr's Reformist recasting of this key image sufficiently precise and revised her phrasing at three points; see the text of the *Lamentation,* p. 461, n62. The incident sheds a revealing sidelight on the transitional state of religion and religious vocabulary in England at this date.

Parr's tendency in structuring her *Lamentation* across longer stretches is to introduce a major theme and then return to it at irregular intervals. One prominent example is the theme of spiritual warfare made newly familiar to English readers by the popularity of Desiderius Erasmus's *Enchiridion Militis Christiani* in the successive editions of the translation ascribed to William Tyndale under the title *The Manual of the Christian Knight*, and the abridgment published by Miles Coverdale.[14] Erasmus's point of departure in the *Enchiridion* is St. Paul's allegory of the "whole armor of God" in Ephesians 6:11–15, which he characterizes in chapter 3 as an array of weaponry that every Christian can deploy at will. Just as a soldier dons greaves, sandals, breastplate, helmet, and shield in a prescribed order, so Erasmus lays out his *Enchiridion* for his reader in a sequence of thirty-nine chapters, twenty-two of which are numbered "rules" for progress in the Christian life.

Although the *Lamentation* has explicit passages on "Spiritual Armor. Ephesians 6," on "David and Christ compared in fight," and on Christ's victories over sin, death, and the world culminating in "A conclusion of the victories" (sigs. Ciii v–Civ r, Cvi r, Cviii r), Parr's handling of form is very different. Her text unfolds through discrete reflections on topics and Bible verses, keyed for the reader by marginal headings.[15] In one typical run the headings go as follows: "Two yokefellows, blindness and hardness of heart," "Profession in baptism," "Christ innocent," "Man sinful," "Christ obedient," "Man stubborn," "Christ humble," "Man proud," Christ heavenly," "Man worldly," "Christ poor," "Man rich," Many Christians know not their patron," "Ignorant wisdom" (sigs. Avi v–Avii v). While antithetical patterning is discernible, the larger progression from topic to topic—from blindness and hardness of heart to baptism, or from Christ as poor to Christ as patron—remains unpredictable.

Parr's recourse to antitheses to provide local structure in some passages may have been suggested by their striking use in a sermon "De Christo" (On Christ) by the self-exiled Italian Reformer Bernardino Ochino, which was in print by 1543, and which Princess Elizabeth translated from Italian to Latin for Prince Edward circa 1547–48. Ochino's extended run of antitheses between Moses and Christ personifies the Law-Gospel dichotomy with an immediacy that Parr would have found literarily and theologically suggestive if she read this sermon with her royal stepdaughter or stepson, in whose education she took such a demonstrable interest.[16]

14. There were eight editions of Tyndale's translation (STC 10479–85) by the time the *Lamentation* appeared in 1547; four more followed by 1576. Coverdale's abridgment (STC 10488) appeared in 1545.

15. In this as in other printed works of the period, the origin(s) of the marginal headings can only be conjectured, for there is no explicit assignment of responsibility. Although the headings cannot be shown to be authorial, whoever else may have inserted them (Cecil while drafting his preface? the compositor in the course of setting type?) was a reader who attended closely to the themes and dynamics of KP's prose.

16. See *Elizabeth I: Translations, 1544–1589,* ed. Mueller and Scodel, 298, 312–14.

Except for a few topic-image pairings, scattered local antitheses, and the gradual replacement of private concerns by more public and general ones, the overall sense of structure conveyed by the *Lamentation* is that of serialism. One thing simply follows another. In comparison with the orderly progression of Erasmus's *Enchiridion*, the *Lamentation* may seem uncontrolled, rhetorically inept. Yet if Barbara Lewalski's account of the defining features of "Protestant emblematics" is projected back a century, Katherine Parr emerges as a formative writer of the Reformation period both in the handling of such topic-image pairings as that of the stony heart and in the larger assemblage of her work. In Protestant representations of the heart, "the special feature," says Lewalski, "is that God acts powerfully *upon* the heart—not located within it . . . and not in conjunction" with the efforts of the human subject. "The implication is (in accordance with Protestant doctrine) that the renovation of the heart is entirely the work of grace and not a cooperative venture." Lewalski further notes that Protestant revisions of Catholic gradations of spirituality work "in the direction of randomness" to chart the Christian life "as an irregular, episodic sequence of graces and temptations, successes and failures, rather than an ordered progress by set stages to spiritual perfection."[17]

Among possible prototypes for the overall form of Parr's *Lamentation* in the works of eminent English Reformers, the degree of resemblance to be found in William Tyndale's *Obedience of a Christian Man* (1528) is historically as well as literarily suggestive. This was the one work of Tyndale's that reportedly "delighted" Henry VIII when he read it at Anne Boleyn's prompting.[18] The *Obedience* opens with a long, personal, urgently affective preface in which Tyndale exhorts his readers to be steadfast and ready to suffer for free access to the Word of life, the promises of the Gospel, in their own tongue. A much briefer prologue then modulates between personal and social concerns by reflecting that God turns the abuse of temporal power to His own ends, trying the constancy of true believers and exposing hypocrites. The extended body of the work follows. Deploying the categories of the Pauline epistles—rulers and people, clergy and laity, husbands and wives, parents and children, masters and servants—across the spectrum of Tudor society, Tyndale proposes to develop a full account of Christian social obligation.[19] The

17. Barbara Kiefer Lewalski, *Protestant Poetics and the Seventeenth-Century Lyric* (Princeton, NJ: Princeton University Press, 1979), 195–96. The motif of the stony heart also emerges as a staple in the prose of William Tyndale, Hugh Latimer, and Thomas Becon; see the Chadwyck-Healey Early English Books Online database for this entry pre-1547. In a Lewalskian vein, Kimberly Anne Coles has recently argued that KP's *Lamentation of a Sinner* is modeled on Luther's *Preface to the Romans* in the Latin translation by Justus Jonas (1524). See Coles, *Religion, Reform, and Women's Writing* (Cambridge: Cambridge University Press, 2008), 62–74.

18. John Strype transcribed and published this account from John Foxe's manuscripts in *Ecclesiastical Memorials . . . under King Henry VIII* (Oxford: Clarendon, 1822), 1.1:172–73.

19. Tyndale is likely to have been familiar with Luther's reflections on the degrees and relations that structured society as a system of reciprocity and duties. See Paul Althaus, *Die Ethik*

account becomes all the fuller as polemical and theological digressions swell the main discussion.

While Parr differentiates the genre of her prose and the gender of her authorship by avoiding all such forays into polemics or theology, she joins with Tyndale in her concern with the domain of communal Christian behavior and daily social life. Both writers reflect the social optimism that characterizes early English Reformers until the accession of Mary Tudor: the polity itself is sound in its order, but occupants of specific positions within it stand in need of moral renewal, a livelier sense of responsibility for the welfare of their own and their fellow subjects' souls. Two categories of persons come in for Parr's reprehension, but she significantly leaves their social positions unspecified; they are denominated only in terms common to Tyndale (and other early English Reformers influenced by Lutheranism)[20] as "weaklings" and "vain gospellers"—timid or misguided souls who hinder the establishment of true Reformation in the realm. By contrast, those whom she commends are "children," "servants," "husbands," and "wives" who enact Pauline prescriptions for godliness as they attend to their respective callings. The final section of the *Lamentation* concludes with a summons to general amendment of life, reinforced with a sobering, heavily Scriptural evocation of the Second Coming.

The affinities displayed in the overall tripartite structure of Tyndale's *Obedience* and Parr's *Lamentation* are reinforced by others at the local level of composition. The largely unpredictable serialism of both works marks them with the distinctively Protestant irregularity of design that Lewalski has identified for a later period. To organize smaller units of discourse within this open design, Parr employs strategies that Tyndale adapted from earlier scholastic methods for disputation and Biblical exposition. Among the welter of Biblical citations and the runs of miscellaneous headings in the margins of both works, a class of rubrics serves to point up discursive tactics and sectarian implications from time to time. Examples from Tyndale include "An apt similitude," "Contrary preaching, contrary doctors," "A compendious rehearsal of that which goeth before."[21] Comparable headings in Parr read "A similitude," "Application of the similitude," "Good Latinists and evil divines," "A conclusion with an answer to objections" (sigs. Cv r-v, Fiv r, Giii r).

Martin Luthers (Gutersloh, Germany: Verlagshaus Gerd Mohn, 1965), 88–158; and William Henry Lazareth, *Luther on the Christian Home: An Application of the Social Ethics of the Reformation* (Philadelphia: Muhlenberg, 1960), 102–65.

20. These early English Reformers include Thomas Becon, Miles Coverdale, and Richard Taverner in their capacities as Bible translators as well as prose writers. See the Chadwyck-Healey Early English Books Online database results for "weaklings" and for "gospellers" preceded by a negative qualifier.

21. William Tyndale, *The Obedience of a Christian Man,* in *Doctrinal Treatises and Introductions,* ed. Henry Walter, Parker Society 43 (Cambridge: Cambridge University Press, 1848), 149, 174, 351.

While considerably more pertinent than Erasmus's *Enchiridion*, Tyndale's *Obedience* proves a far from exhaustive model of composition for Parr. Time and time again her *Lamentation* takes leave of Tyndalian disputation and Biblical exposition to range into doctrinal articulation, prayer, self-reprehension, hopeful expectation, and social and moral concern. Parr's polyphony makes her voice much more varied than Tyndale's. If certain twentieth-century feminist theorists are correct, the best achievements of women writers will assume the form of "antiphonal, many-voiced works" that resist both the demure silence and the male-dominant norms of expression to which female gender and authorship have historically been assimilated.[22] Yet Parr's case also resists easy accommodation either to this latter-day feminist outlook or to Harold Bloom's influential theory of literary history since the Renaissance as a (male) succession in which predecessors and models repeatedly trigger among later writers "the anxiety of influence" and a conflictual stance.[23] In the late Henrician court where the *Lamentation* emerges as a unique production by a female author, the current queen, such polyphony as Parr achieved seems to have been fostered rather than hindered by acquaintance with the Reformed convictions of two authoritative and authoring males—Thomas Cranmer and Hugh Latimer. It is known that Cranmer, on King Henry's instructions, consulted daily with the queen during her regency in the summer of 1545. No personal contact is known to have occurred between Queen Katherine and Latimer, although the Duchess of Suffolk, the close friend who insisted that Parr publish her *Lamentation*, was his principal patron. In the present context, however, personal contact is not at issue. Any voicings consonant with Cranmer or Latimer are textual in character; they bear the relation of analogue—stylistic and thematic affinities between Parr's *Lamentation* and their works—rather than of source. Significant traces of an analogical relation can be found in both cases.

The most notable textual analogue between Parr and Cranmer emerges in her excursus on justifying faith, a passage that resembles Cranmer in thought and style alike. The following is an excerpt from his "Homily of Salvation," first published in July 1547:

> This sentence, that we be justified by faith only, is not so meant . . . that we should or might . . . be justified without our good works, that we should do no good works at all. . . . Truth it is, that our own

22. Rachel Blau DuPlessis and Members of Workshop 9, "For the Etruscans: Sexual Difference and Artistic Production—The Debate over a Female Aesthetic," in *The Future of Difference*, ed. Hester Eisenstein and Alice Jardine (Boston: G. K. Hall, 1980), 131. Also see Hélène Cixous's 1975 essay "The Laugh of the Medusa," in *New French Feminisms*, ed. Elaine Marks and Isabelle de Courtivron (New York: Schocken Books, 1981), 245–64.

23. Harold Bloom, *The Anxiety of Influence: A Theory of Poetry* (New York: Oxford University Press, 1973).

> works do not justify us, to speak properly of our justification. . . . Nevertheless, because faith doth directly send us to Christ for remission of our sins, and that by faith given us of God we embrace the promise of God's mercy and of the remission of our sins (which thing none other of our virtues or works properly doth): therefore Scripture useth to say, that faith doth justify. . . . But that we be justified by faith only, freely and without works, is spoken for to take away clearly all merit of our works, . . . and thereby wholly to ascribe the merit and deserving of our justification unto Christ only, and His most precious blood-shedding.[24]

As Cranmer's thought threads its way through antitheses laden with predicate complements ("not so meant . . . that we should or might . . . be justified without our good works," "do not justify us, to speak properly of our justification," "But that . . . is spoken for to take away clearly all merit of our works"), he locates the domain of justifying faith between two extremes: antinomianism, with its disdain for good works, and the works-religion that Reformers decried in Catholic doctrine and practice. Cranmer's procedure, moreover, is meticulously analytic—that is, definitional—with respect to basic terms: "faith," "justification," "remission," "merit."

When Parr in her *Lamentation* likewise undertakes to articulate justifying faith, her predicates also evince antithetical weighting as they thread their way between the same extremes of antinomianism and works-religion ("is no derogation . . . for out of this faith springeth . . . Yet we may not impute . . . but ascribe and give"). Her technical vocabulary and her penchant for doublings ("ascribe and give," "refer and attribute," "knowledge and perceiving," "very true, only property") apply Cranmer's own characteristic means for achieving exact and exhaustive expression. Like his, Parr's prose echoes with balanced sonorities of phrasing:

> This dignity of faith is no derogation to good works, for out of this faith springeth all good works. Yet we may not impute to the worthiness of faith or works our justification before God; but ascribe and give the worthiness of it, wholly, to the merits of Christ's passion; and refer and attribute the knowledge and perceiving thereof, only to faith. Whose very true, only property is to take, apprehend, and hold fast the promises of God's mercy, the which maketh us righteous. (sig. Biv r-v)

24. [Thomas Cranmer,] "An homelie of the salvacion of mankynde, by onely Christe our sauior," in *Certayne sermons, or homiliess appoynted . . . to be declared and read . . . in . . . Churches* (London, 1547) (STC 13639), sigs. Ei v–Eii r, Eiv r; modern-spelling version in *Miscellaneous Writings and Letters of Thomas Cranmer,* ed. John Edmund Cox, Parker Society 16 (Cambridge: Cambridge University Press, 1846), 131–32.

Apart from this notable excursus, however, Parr's voicings in the *Lamentation* owe more to the liturgical than the doctrinal Cranmer. The collectlike prayers inserted at intervals in her text evoke Cranmer's mastery in this form.[25] Parr works surehandedly in assembling the various elements—a vocative or "naming" noun phrase, followed by verb phrases of petition or thanksgiving with their associated complements, and then by a final ascription or "renaming"—that fill the subject and predicate positions of a collect sentence. She also proves responsive to the chief syntactic devices used by Cranmer to spread and endow with nuance the capacious single sentence that constitutes a collect. Thus, in the example below, she emulates Cranmer's characteristic circularity of form and reference ("I shall pray to the Lord . . . that we may serve the Lord"). At the same time Parr's "that" clauses sustain the rich ambiguities between purpose and result on which Cranmer often plays to evoke the conformity of human will and action with the divine:

> I shall pray to the Lord to take all contention and strife away, and that the sowers of sedition may have mind to cease their labor, or to sow it amongst the stones; and to have grace to sow gracious virtues, where they may both root and bring forth fruit: with sending also a godly unity and concord amongst all Christians, that we may serve the Lord in true holiness of life. (sig. Dv r)

If Queen Katherine saw Cranmer as a model for certain formulary dimensions—both doctrinal and liturgical—in this work of hers, she found something different but equally essential to her authorial purposes in the homiletics of Hugh Latimer. As a public figure who commanded respect while remaining provocative, he offered a contemporary vocal precedent for the strains of introspection and social commentary that mingle in the *Lamentation*. Parr's authorship appears to draw a stimulus from the self-referential mode so conspicuous in Latimer's preaching. Consciously universalizing in its terms and appeal, the Latimerian strategy projects the speaker's identity as a Reformer through avowals of personal failings and personal commitments that are figured, in turn, as responses to the impact of Scripture on experience. Here, for example, are excerpts from the reflections on his chosen text that open Latimer's sermon preached before the convocation of the clergy in 1536:

> Ye be come together to entreat of things that most appertain to this commonwealth. . . . Ye look, I am assured, to hear of me, . . . albeit I am unlearned, and far unworthy such things as shall be

25. On the stylistic and thematic achievement of Cranmer's collects in the Book of Common Prayer, see Janel Mueller, *The Native Tongue and the Word: Syntax and Style in English Prose, 1380–1580* (Chicago: University of Chicago Press, 1984), 226–43.

> much meet for this your assembly. I, therefore . . . as plainly as I can, will speak of . . . that notable sentence in which our Lord was not afraid to pronounce "the children of this world to be much more prudent and politic than the children of light in their generation." . . . Which sentence would God it lay in my poor tongue to explicate with such light of words . . . that you might rather seem to see the thing, than to hear it. But I confess plainly this thing to be far above my power. Therefore this being only left to me, I wish for that I have not, and am sorry that that is not in me which I would so gladly have, that is, power so to handle the thing that I have in hand, that all that I say may turn to the glory of God, your souls' health, and the edifying of Christ's body. Wherefore I pray you all to pray with me unto God.[26]

Latimer's penchant for disparaging himself before reprehending others finds a continuing analogue in Parr's *Lamentation.* This self-effacing path to authorship, while ultimately Pauline, allowed for contemporary access by a woman as well as a man, when both, in "feeling faith" rather than "historical faith," knew themselves as sinners personally accountable to God. In her opening section Parr's efforts to establish her subject and herself as the speaker of her text move toward expression through self-reprehension. Before that point is reached, a suggestive grammatical detail intervenes. Parr's access to self-reference and self-representation, the "I" of her text, opens by way of some generic "he" who sets an example for her. "Who is he," she asks, "that is not forced to confess . . . if he consider what he hath received of God, and doth daily receive?" She then continues: "Truly I am constrained and forced to speak and write thereof, to mine own confusion and shame, but to the great glory and praise of God." "I had a blind guide called Ignorance, who dimmed so mine eyes, that I could never perfectly get any sight of the fair, goodly, straight and right ways of His doctrine" (sig. Aiii v).

This vocabulary of incapacity and ignorance suggests the influence of Latimer on Parr's setting of her course in her *Lamentation.* Yet limitations on the viability of a Latimerian model soon begin to emerge in Parr's text, and these can be traced to social and gender differences. Certain of Latimer's most characteristic strains—his indulgence in autobiographical reminiscences, his frank delight in his reputation for earthy utterance, his topical innuendos regarding the mighty of the realm,

26. *THE SERMON THAT THE Reuerende father in Christ, Hugh Latimer . . . made to the clergie, in the convocation, before the Parlyament began the .9. day of June, the .28. yere of the reigne of our Souerayne lorde kynge Henry viii, now translated out of latyn into englysshe, to the intent, that thingis well said to a fewe, may be vnderstande of many* (1536) (STC 15286), sigs. Aii r–Aiii r, Biv r-v; modern-spelling version in *Sermons by Hugh Latimer,* ed. George Elwes Corrie, Parker Society 27 (Cambridge: Cambridge University Press, 1844), 33–34, 39–40.

his sharp assertions of his pastoral authority[27]—have no analogue in Parr's voice. Largely because of his outspokenness in the plainest English about Gospel imperatives for England in the here and now, Latimer became the most famous preacher of his age. For him it was feasible if intermittently risky to be a *succès de scandale*. By contrast, when she undertook to compose her *Lamentation* Queen Katherine held a position so much more contingent and precarious that the question of how she was able to find and sustain her voice acquires new force.[28]

At no point in her life or authorship, least of all after the double plot against Anne Askew and herself in the spring and summer of 1546, were the prerogatives of a ranking male cleric open to Parr. Her *Lamentation* pervasively if tacitly acknowledges that authorial constraint. It also significantly gestures toward and comments on another constraint within female gender. In testing her authorial voice, Katherine, the compliant woman, implicitly distinguishes herself from Anne, the defiant woman—and the fatally silenced author. What is plausibly taken as an allusion to Askew begins in sympathy for those who are "most cruelly persecuted" when they set themselves "contrary" to "pastors . . . so blinded with the love of themselves and the world, that they extol men's inventions and doctrines, before the doctrine of the Gospel" although "they be not able to maintain their own inventions and doctrine with any jot of the Scripture." "Is not this miserable state," asks Parr, "much to be lamented of all good Christians?"

She proceeds, however, to distance herself from the sly, derisive exposure of error that Askew records herself as practicing in her *Examinations*. "Yet I cannot allow, neither praise, all kind of lamentation," says Parr, "but such as may stand with Christian charity" (sig. Eii r). It was notorious that Anne Askew had left her husband and children in Lincolnshire to exercise her Bible knowledge in London. Parr draws a further distinction from Askew in voicing her conception of her primary "vocation" as queen—that of "women married"—in terms as conformably Pauline in content as in style: "Not being accusers, or detractors, . . . they teach honest things, to make the young women sober-minded, to love their husbands, to love their children, to be discreet, chaste, housewifely, good, obedient unto their husbands, that the Word of God be not evil spoken of." And Parr characteristically ends this reflection by generalizing her concern, appropriate to her royal status, for social and religious concord throughout the realm of England: "Verily, if all sorts of people would look to their own vocation, and ordain the same according

27. On these traits as consciously cultivated aspects of Latimer's public persona, see Robert L. Kelly, "Hugh Latimer as Piers Plowman," *Studies in English Literature* 17 (1977): 13–26.

28. For reflections on how KP's "gender inflects [her] assertions regarding theology and faith practices, especially vernacular Bible reading," see Edith Snook, *Women, Reading, and the Cultural Politics of Early Modern England* (Aldershot, UK: Ashgate, 2005), 31, 45–50. Also see Andrew Hiscock, "'A Supernal Lively Fayth': Katherine Parr and the Authoring of Devotion," *Women's Writing* 9 (2002): 188.

to Christ's doctrine, we should not have so many eyes and ears to other men's faults as we have" (sig. Gii v).

As she pursues and develops her distinction between an unwarranted and a warranted "kind of lamentation . . . such as may stand with Christian charity," Parr's concluding self-reflections explicitly reveal how the rightness of her lamentation and the writing of her *Lamentation* came to seem inseparable. While she as a woman can neither legislate nor preach reform, she can make an example of herself as a regenerate sinner through her authorship. By this means, in turn, her voice can and does entreat a serious hearing from others:

> God knoweth of what intent and mind I have lamented mine own sins and faults to the world. I trust nobody will judge I have done it for praise or thank of any creature, since rather I might be ashamed than rejoice in rehearsal thereof. For if they know how little I esteem and weigh the praise of the world, that opinion were soon removed and taken away. For . . . I seek not the praises of the same, neither to satisfy it none other wise, than I am taught by Christ to do, according to Christian charity.
>
> If any man shall be offended at this my lamenting the faults of men, which be in the world, fantasying with themselves that I do it either of hatred or malice to any sort or kind of people: verily, in so doing, they shall do me great wrong. For I thank God, by His grace, I hate no creature; yea, I would say more, to give witness of my conscience, that neither life, honor, riches, neither whatsoever I possess here, which appertaineth unto mine own private commodity, be it never so dearly beloved of me, but most willingly and gladly I would leave it, to win any man to Christ, of what degree or sort soever he were. And yet is this nothing in comparison to the charity that God hath showed me, in sending Christ to die for me. . . . God knoweth of what intent and mind I have lamented mine own sins and faults to the world. (sigs. Giii r–Giv r)

Multiple implications regarding social, religious, and literary dimensions of the earlier English Reformation arise from the play of contraries in Parr's self-representation and self-realization as an author. On the one hand, her passing reference to her relation to Henry VIII and her Pauline excursus on wifehood mark her gender and position as conformably feminine. On the other hand, the process of composing the *Lamentation* bespeaks a gradually intensifying sense of spiritual authority, however much Parr hedges this in with disclaimers. Thus a sentence may begin modestly enough: "Truly, in my simple and unlearned judgment . . ." But it continues in ringing tones that cast self-effacement behind: "no man's doctrine is to be esteemed, or is preferred like unto Christ's and the Apostles,' nor to be taught as a perfect and true doctrine, but even as it doth accord and agree with the doctrine of the Gospel" (sig. Ei r). As the work approaches its close, Parr's increased self-assurance conveys her intuition of the power to be wielded in the larger religious and social domains of her age, specifically through authorship. Particularly in her final exhortations to her readers to embrace her vision of England as an inclusive Christian community bound together by willing adherence to "God's precepts and ordinances" (sig. Giv v), Queen Katherine broaches the themes of the "commonwealth" men of midcentury—notably Robert Crowley, Hugh Latimer, Wiliam Turner, and the Strassburg émigré Martin Bucer—who anticipated key concerns of the subsequent Puritan movement in England.[29]

Yet Parr herself insists that any spiritual authority attaching to her words has no further design or objectification than the work she has in hand. "I have, certainly," she says, "no curious learning to defend this matter withal, but a simple zeal and earnest love to the truth, inspired of God, who promiseth to pour His Spirit upon all flesh: which I have, by the grace of God, whom I most humbly honor, felt in myself to be true" (sig. Bvii v). Here the egalitarian tendencies of the earlier Reformation, a strain arising from its Scripturalism ("the truth, inspired of God, who promiseth to pour His Spirit upon all flesh"), clearly register their contribution to Queen Katherine's authorship as an effect of God's Spirit—"felt in myself to be true."[30] No less clearly, however, she is careful to refer her authorship to a realm where the single, ultimate relation of the soul to God transcends and sets at naught both gender and every other mark of human difference. Overlaying its subtly feminine tones with a prevailing generality and near-anonymity of expression, Parr's *Lamentation* does nothing to impede the program of defusing the radical social potentialities of the Reformation, which was gaining momentum in the England of her day.

However muted the femininity of Parr's voice through long stretches of the *Lamentation*, her gender operates authorially nonetheless. In the Henrician court as in the later Jacobean one, a low voice was ever an excellent thing in woman.[31] It was surely requisite for keeping one's head as the last of Henry VIII's queens. Femininity as an authorial effect circumscribes the public domain within Parr's discourse, screening topicality, polemic, and personality from her text. Gender,

29. For discussion see W. R. D. Jones, *The Tudor Commonwealth, 1529–1559* (London: Athlone, 1970); G. R. Elton, "Reform and the 'Commonwealth-Men' of Edward VI's Reign," in *The English Commonsealth, 1547–1640*, ed. Peter Clark, Alan G. R. Smith, and Nicholas Tyacke (New York: Barnes and Noble, 1979), 23–38; and Henning Graf Reventlow, *The Authority of the Bible and the Rise of the Modern World* (Philadelphia: Fortress, 1985), 73–86.

30. On the most conspicuous instance in England of female empowerment afforded by the egalitarian strain that periodically surfaces in Protestant spirituality, see Keith Thomas, "Women and the Civil War Sects," *Past and Present* 13 (1958): 44–47, 50.

31. Shakespeare, *King Lear,* 5.3.273–74: "Her voice was ever soft, / Gentle, and low, an excellent thing in woman."

activated in Parr's writing as an experienced fact and a lived factor, consistently produces a measure of literary distance between her voice and the various partial models afforded her by ranking English Reformers of her day. If both its shared and its individuating features are accorded due attention, Queen Katherine Parr's *Lamentation of a Sinner* will emerge as one of the rarer literary achievements of the earlier Reformation in England. The rarity of the work, however, does not consist only in the gender of its author. As suggested in some of the textual notes that follow, it consists as well in Parr's prophetic anticipation of the premiums that would attach to conversion as a personal experience and to the earthly realization of a true Christian commonwealth in the literary productions of the later Reformation in England.

The Lamentation of a Sinner[1]

[Title]

The Lamentation of a Sinner, made by the most virtuous lady Queen Katherine, bewailing the ignorance of her blind life: set forth and put in print at the instant desire of[2] the right gracious lady Katherine, Duchess of Suffolk, and the earnest request of the right honorable lord William Parr, Marquess of Northampton.

[Prefatory letter]

[1r] William Cecil, having taken much profit by the reading of this treatise following, wisheth unto every Christian, by the reading thereof, like profit with increase from God.

1. Source: *The lamentacion of a sinner, made by the most vertuous Ladie, Quene Caterin* (November 5, 1547) (STC 4827), six unnumbered (r-v) leaves + sigs. Ai–Gv; Pembroke College, Cambridge, copy—shelfmark LCI.42(2). Except for a number of imprecise marginal references to Scripture, which could be due to the compositor and not the author, this imprint is remarkable for its careful preparation. Infrequent minor corrections made in the 1548 and 1563 editions are recorded in the notes. To facilitate reference to the source text without disrupting the discursive flow of the prose, page numbers in square brackets have been added to the prefatory letter, and the signature notations used in the body of the text have been inserted in square brackets in front of the sentence unit or major clause that is closest to a given page break.

2. **at . . . of** This phrase echoes John Bale's in his prefatory letter to his edition of the *Examinations of Anne Askew* (Wesel [Marburg], 1546): "Here hast thou (gentle reader) the two examinations of Anne Askew, which she wrote with her own hand at the instant desire of certain faithful men and women" (*Select Works of Bishop John Bale*, ed. Henry Christmas, Parker Society 1 [Cambridge: Cambridge University Press, 1847], 147, also reproduced in John Foxe's

Most gentle and Christian reader, if matters should be rather confirmed by their reporters than the reports warranted by the matters, I might justly bewail our time, wherein evil deeds be well worded, and good acts evil cleped.[3] But since truth is, that things be not good for their praises, but praised for their goodness, I do not move thee to like this Christian treatise because I have mind to praise it. [1v] But I exhort thee to mind it, and, for the goodness, thou shalt allow it. For whose liking I labor not to obtain, only moved by my example; their judgment I regard chiefly confirmed by[4] the matter. Truly our time is so disposed to grant good names to evil fruits, and excellent terms to mean works, that neither can good deeds enjoy their due names, being defrauded by the evil; neither excellent works can possess their worthy terms, being forestalled by the mean. Insomuch that men seek rather how much they can than how much they ought to say, inclining more to their pleasure than to their judgment, and to show themselves rather eloquent than the matter good: so that neither the goodness of the cause can move them to say more, neither the evilness less.

[2r] For if the excellency of this Christian contemplation, either for the goodness herein to marvel appearing, either for the profit hereupon to the reader ensuing, should be with due commendation followed, I of necessity should either travail to find out new words, the old being anticipated by evil matters, or wish that the common speech of praising were spared until convenient matters were found to spend it. Such is the plenty of praising, and scarceness of deserving. Wherefore, lacking the manner in words, and not the matter indeed of high commendation, I am compelled to keep in my judgment with silence, trusting whom my report could not have moved to like this present treatise, the worthiness of the matter shall compel to give it honor.

[2v] Any earthly man would soon be stirred to see some mystery of magic, or practice of alchemy, or perchance some enchantment of elements. But thou, which art christened, hast here a wonderful mystery of the mercy of God, a heavenly practice of regeneration, a spiritual enchantment of the grace of God. If joy and triumphs be showed when a king's child is born to the world, what joy is sufficient when God's child is regenerated from heaven? The one is flesh, which is born of flesh; the other is spirit, which is born of spirit. [3r] The one also shall wither like the grass of the earth[5] in short time; the other shall live in heaven beyond all time. If the finding of one lost sheep be more joyful than the having of ninety and nine,

account of Askew in *Acts and Monuments,* ed. Stephen R. Cattley [London, 1838], 6:537). Beilin reproduces only Foxe's phrasing in her edition, *Examinations of Anne Askew,* 165. On the probably deliberate associative linking of KP and Askew, see the introduction, p. 425.

3. **cleped** termed, named.

4. **by** The reading from 1548 onward; the 1547 edition reads "by by."

5. **wither . . . earth** See Psalm 103:13–15 (in the numbering of sixteenth-century English Bibles) for this simile depicting the brevity of human life.

what joy is it to consider the return of a stray child of almighty God, whose return teacheth the ninety and nine to come to their fold?[6] Even such cause of joy is this, that the angels in heaven take comfort herein. Be thou, therefore, joyful where a noble child is newly born. Show thyself glad where the lost sheep hath won the whole flock. Be thou not sad, wherein angels rejoice.

[3v] Here mayst thou see one (if the kind may move thee) a woman, (if degree may provoke thee) a woman of high estate: by birth made noble, by marriage most noble, by wisdom godly; by a mighty King, an excellent Queen; by a famous Henry, a renowned Katherine. A wife to him that was a King to realms: refusing the world wherein she was lost, to obtain heaven, wherein she may be saved; abhorring sin, which made her bound, to receive grace, whereby she may be free; despising flesh, the cause of corruption, to put on the Spirit, the cause of sanctification; forsaking ignorance, wherein she was blind, to come to knowledge,[7] whereby she may see; removing superstition, wherewith she was smothered, to embrace true religion, wherewith she may revive.

The fruit of this treatise, good reader, is thy amendment; this only had, the writer is satisfied. [4r] This good lady thought no shame to detect her sin, to obtain remission, no vileness, to become nothing, to be a member of Him, which is all things in all;[8] no folly to forget the wisdom of the world, to learn the simplicity of the Gospel; at the last, no displeasantness to submit herself to the school of the cross, the learning of the crucifix, the book of our redemption, the very absolute[9] library of God's mercy and wisdom. This way thought she her honor increased, and her state permanent: to make her earthly honor heavenly, and neglect the transitory for the everlasting. Of this, I would thee warned,[10] that the profit may ensue.

[4v] These great mysteries and graces be not well perceived, except they be surely studied; neither be they perfectly studied, except they be diligently practiced; neither profitably practiced, without amendment. See and learn hereby what she hath done: then mayst thou practice, and amend that thou canst do. So shalt thou practice with ease, having a guide; and amend with profit, having a zeal. It is easier to see these than to learn. Begin at the easiest, to come to the harder. See thou her confession, that thou mayst learn her repentance; practice her perseverance, that thou mayst have like amendment; displease thyself in eschewing vice, that thou mayst please God in asking grace. Let not shame hinder thy confession, which hindered not the offense. [5r] Be thou sure, if we knowledge our sins, God is faithful to forgive us, and to cleanse us from all unrighteousness. Obey the prophet's

6. **If . . . fold?** See Matthew 18:12–14 and Luke 15:3–7 for Jesus's parable of the lost sheep.
7. **knowledge** an earlier variant of "acknowledge."
8. **i[n] all** The reading from 1548 onward; the 1547 edition reads "is all."
9. **absolute** complete, consummate.
10. **warned** informed, notified.

saying: "Declare thy ways to the Lord."[11] Thus far, thou mayst learn to know thyself; next this, be thou as diligent to relieve thyself in God's mercy as thou hast been to reveal thyself in thine own repentance.

For God hath concluded all things under sin, because He would have mercy upon all. Who hath also borne our sins in His body, upon the tree, that we should be delivered from sin, and should live unto righteousness: by whose stripe[s] we be healed.[12] [5v] Here is our anchor; here is our Shepherd; here we be made whole. Here is our life, our redemption, our salvation, and our bliss.

Let us, therefore, now feed by this gracious Queen's example; and be not ashamed to become in confession publicans, since this noble lady will be no Pharisee.[13] And to all ladies of estate I wish as earnest mind to follow our Queen in virtue as in honor: that they might once appear to prefer God before the world, and be honorable in religion, which now be honorable in vanities. So shall they (as in some virtuous ladies of right high estate it is with great comfort seen) taste of this freedom of remission, of this everlasting bliss which exceedeth all thoughts and understandings, and is prepared for the holy in spirit. [6r] For the which, let us, with our intercession in holiness and pureness of life, offer ourselves to the heavenly Father an undefiled host:[14] to whom be eternal praise and glory, through all the earth, without end. Amen.

11. **if we . . . Lord if we . . . unrighteousness** Cecil quotes 1 John 1:9. **Obey . . . Lord** The prophet is David. The allusion is to Psalm 119:26, which reads as follows in *Biblia; that is, the Bible,* ed. and trans. Miles Coverdale (Antwerp, 1535) (STC 2063), fol. xxxiii r: "I knowledged my wayes, and thou herdest me, O teach me then thy statutes." Subsequent references to this edition are cited as "Coverdale 1535." *The most sacred Bible, Whiche is the holy scripture,* ed. Richard Taverner (London, 1539) (STC 2067), fol. xlvi r, reads identically. Subsequent references are cited as "Taverner 1539." The first Great Bible to contain Archbishop Thomas Cranmer's preface, *The Byble in Englyshe, that is to saye the content of al the holy scrypture* (London, 1540) (STC 2070), fol. lxxxvii r, also reads identically. Subsequent references are cited as "Great Bible 1540." No English Bible before the Geneva Bible (1560) contains verse numbers. For convenience these have been inserted to follow chapter numbers in the marginal citations of the *Lamentation.*

12. **Who . . . healed** Cecil closely paraphrases 1 Peter 2:24, which itself alludes to Isaiah 53:5, part of a passage traditionally interpreted as foretelling the redemptive sufferings of Jesus. **stripe[s]** The reading from 1548 onward; the 1547 edition reads "stripe." This plural noun means "strokes or lashes with a whip or scourge."

13. **publican . . . Pharisee** See Luke 18:9–14 for Jesus's contrast between the self-abnegating publican and the self-righteous Pharisee in their respective modes of prayer.

14. **offer . . . host** Cecil seems to adumbrate Cranmer's decisive contribution to the theology of the Eucharist—a recasting of the ritual act of sacrifice that constituted the holiest moment of the sacrament. For Roman Catholics, the priest officiating at the mass reenacts the crucifixion of Jesus by elevating the consecrated bread and saying the prayer of oblation, rededicating Jesus as a sacrifice for the sins of the world. For the Church of England in the Book of Common Prayer (1549) (STC 16267) compiled by Cranmer, the corresponding sacramental action

❧

[Title] [Ai v] A Lamentation or Complaint of a Sinner.

When I consider, in the bethinking of mine evil and wretched former life, mine obstinate, stony, and untractable heart to have so much exceeded in evilness that hath not only neglected, yea, contemned and despised God's holy precepts and commandments, but also embraced,[15] received, and esteemed vain, foolish, and feigned trifles: I am, partly by the hate I owe to sin, who hath reigned in me, partly by the love I owe to all Christians, [Ai v] whom I am content to edify, even with the example of mine own shame, forced and constrained with my heart and words to confess and declare to the world, how ingrate,[16] negligent, unkind, and stubborn I have been to God my Creator; and how beneficial, merciful, and gentle He hath been always to me, His creature, being such a miserable and wretched[17] sinner.

By knowledge of sin cometh confession.

Charity is not abashed.

became the communicants' self-sacrifice—an offering up of their sinful wills and selves to God for direction and inspiration. In Cranmer's prayer of oblation in Holy Communion, the officiating minister "without any eleuacion, or shewing the Sacrament to the people," speaks on the worshipers' behalf: "And here we offre and present unto thee (O Lorde) oure selfe, oure soules, and bodies, to be a reasonable, holy, and lively sacrifice unto thee: . . . And although we be unworthy (through our manyfolde synnes) to offre unto thee any Sacryfice: Yet we beseche thee to accepte thys our bounden duetie and seruice, . . . not waiyng our merites, but pardonyng our offences" ("The Supper of the Lorde, and Holy Communion," in *The First and Second Prayer Bookes of Edward VI,* intro. E. C. S. Gibson [London: Dent, 1910], 223). See further Peter N. Brooks, *Thomas Cranmer's Doctrine of the Eucharist: An Essay in Historical Development* (London: Macmillan, 1965).

15. **embraced** The reading from 1548 onward; the 1547 edition reads "enbraced."

16. **ingrate** ungrateful.

17. **miserable . . . wretched** The reading from 1548 onward; the 1547 edition reads "miserable, wretched."

The argument of the book. *The author's sins.* *Psalm 12.* *The goodness of God.* *Luke 19.* *God in goodness marvelous. Man in evilness wondrous.*

Truly, I have taken no little, small thing[18] upon me: first, to set forth my whole stubbornness and contempt in words, the which is incomprehensible in thought, as it is in the Psalm: Who understandeth his faults?[19] [Aii r] Next this, to declare the excellent beneficence, mercy, and goodness of God, which is infinite, unmeasurable; neither can all the words of angels and men make relation thereof, as appertaineth to His most high goodness. Who is he that is not forced to confess the same, if he consider what he hath received of God, and doth daily receive? Yea, if men would not acknowledge and confess the same, the stones would cry it out.[20] Truly I am constrained and forced to speak and write thereof, to mine own confusion and shame, but to the great glory and praise of God. For He, as a loving Father, of most abundant and high goodness, hath heaped upon me innumerable benefits; and I, contrary, have heaped manifold sins, despising that which was good, holy, pleasant, and acceptable in His sight,[21] and choosing that which was delicious, pleasant, and acceptable in my sight.

John 3. *The judgment of man is corrupt in all things.* *Every man's sin accuseth himself.*

[Aii v] And no marvel it was that I so did. For I would not learn to know the Lord and His ways, but loved darkness better than light:[22] yea, darkness seemed to me, light. I embraced ignorance as perfect knowledge; and knowledge seemed to me superfluous and vain. I regarded little God's Word, but gave myself to vanities and shadows of the world. I forsook Him, in whom is all truth, and followed the vain, foolish imaginations of my heart. I would have covered my sins with the pretense of holiness. I called superstition godly meaning, and true holiness, error. [Aiii r] The Lord did speak many pleasant and sweet words unto me, and I would not hear; He called me diversely, but through frowardness I would not answer. Mine evils and miseries be so many and so great, they accuse me even to my face. Oh, how miserably and wretchedly am I confounded when, for the multitude and greatness of my

18. **little . . . thing** This particular pleonastic doubling is one of KP's most characteristic turns of phrase. Later instances in the *Lamentation* include "no small nor little gift" (p. 455) and "no little or small benefit" (p. 467). Pleonastic or "empty" phrasing can be a marker of feminine speech; see Robin Lakoff, *Language and Woman's Place* (New York: Harper and Row, 1975, rpt. 1989), 53.

19. **Psalm . . . faults? Psalm 12** The marginal reference from 1548 onward; the 1547 edition reads "Psalm iix." **Who . . . faults?** an allusion to Psalm 19:12.

20. **Yea . . . out** In Luke 19:39 Jesus counters the Pharisees' demand that He silence His disciples: "If these should hold their peace, the stones would cry out." The image further alludes to Habbakuk 2:11.

21. **acceptable . . . sight** an allusion to St. Paul's phrasing in 1 Timothy 2:3.

22. **loved . . . light** KP's wording is closest to the Great Bible's in John 3:20: "Thys is the condemnacion, that lyght is come into the world, and men loved darcknes more then light: because their dedes were euyll" (Great Bible 1540, fol. xxxvii v). Minor variants—e.g., definite articles preceding "darkness" and "light"—differentiate the readings of Coverdale 1535, fol. xli v, and Taverner 1539, fol. xxxiv r.

sins, I am compelled to accuse myself![23] Was it not a marvelous unkindness, when God did speak to me and also call me, that I would not answer Him? What man, so called, would not have heard?[24] Or what man, hearing, would not have answered? If an earthly prince had spoken or called him, I suppose there be none but would willingly have done both. [Aiii v] Now, therefore, what a wretch and caitiff am I: that when the Prince of Princes, the King of Kings, did speak many pleasant and gentle words unto me, and also called me so many and sundry times that they cannot be numbered; and yet, notwithstanding these great signs and tokens of love, I would not come unto Him; but hid myself out of His sight, seeking many crooked and by-ways, wherein I walked so long that I had clean lost His sight.

A blind guide for a blind way.

The number of people may not be followed, but the goodness.

A fleshly man regardeth not spiritual things.

Mark a number of idols.[26]

And no marvel or wonder: for I had a blind guide called Ignorance,[25] who dimmed so mine eyes, that I could never perfectly get any sight of the fair, goodly, straight, and right ways of His doctrine, but continually traveled uncomfortably in the foul, wicked, crooked, and perverse ways. [Aiv r] Yea, and because they were so much haunted of many, I could not think but I walked in the perfect and right way: having more regard to the number of the walkers than to the order of the walking, believing also most surely with company to have walked to heaven, whereas I am most sure they would have brought me down to hell. I forsook the spiritual honoring of the true, living God, and worshiped visible idols and images made of men's hands, believing by them to have gotten heaven. Yea, to say the truth, I made a great idol of myself; for I loved myself better than God. And certainly, look: how

23. **for . . . myself!** KP's self-accusation resembles the dynamic in chap. 2, verse 15, of Martin Luther's *Lectures on Romans* (written 1515–16), where the heart's severe deploring of its sin and its unfeelingness toward Christ's love directly precedes the onset of justifying faith with its attendant trust, assurance, and release. In Luther's words, "If the heart of a believer in Christ accuses him and reprimands him and witnesses against him that he has done evil, he will immediately turn away from evil and will take his refuge in Christ and say, 'Christ has . . . has died for me. He has made His righteousness my righteousness, and my sin His sin. . . . The Defender is greater than the accuser, immeasurably greater. It is God who is my Defender. It is my heart that accuses me'" (*Lectures on Romans,* ed. and trans. Hilton C. Oswald, vol. 25 of *Luther's Works,* gen. ed. Jaroslav Pelikan [St. Louis: Concordia Publishing House, 1972], 188).

24. **have heard** The reading from 1548 onward; the 1547 edition reads "heave harde."

25. **blind . . . Ignorance** KP's phrasing tallies generically with that of the English Lutheran William Marshall at the opening of the Dirige section of his *A goodly prymer in englyshe* (1535) (STC 15988), sig. Hiv r: "Amongest all other workes of . . . deep ignoraunce, . . . we have blyndly wandred, folowynge a sorte of blynde guydes." The ultimate source of this image is Matthew 15:14.

26. **Mark . . . idols** KP sounds identifiably Reformed notes in her sharp denunciation of her idolatry and in her equation of "idolatry" both with Catholic image-worship and with her own self-love. On the peculiarly Reformation detestation of idolatry thus construed, see Nicholas Udall's polemic in his dedicatory letter to KP (1545) prefacing the English Paraphrase on Luke that she had commissioned: "The people which long time had been led in error and blindness

The sin against the first commandment. Deuteronomy 6.

The blood of Christ. The Word of God is only the doctrine of salvation. Bishop of Rome is an evil usurper of Christ's power.

The Father is honored in His Son. Hebrews 10.

The most horrible sin. The honor of God abounded upon the cross. Hebrews 1.

many things are loved or preferred in our hearts before God, so many are taken and esteemed for idols and false gods. [Aiv v] Alas, how have I violated this holy, pure, and most high precept and commandment of the love of God, which precept bindeth me to love Him with my whole heart, mind, force, strength, and understanding.[27] And I, like unto an evil, wicked, disobedient child, have given my will, power, and senses to the contrary, making almost of every earthly and carnal thing, a God. Furthermore, the blood of Christ was not reputed by me sufficient for to wash me from the filth of my sins, neither such ways as He hath appointed by His Word. But I sought for such riffraff as the Bishop of Rome[28] hath planted in his tyranny and kingdom, trusting with great confidence, by the virtue and holiness of them, to receive full remission of my sins. [Av r] And so I did as much as was in me to obfuscate and darken the great benefit of Christ's passion: than the which no thought can conceive anything of more value. There cannot be done so great an injury and displeasure to almighty God our Father, as to tread underfoot Christ, His only-begotten and well-beloved Son.[29] All other sins in the world, gathered together in one, be not so heinous and detestable in the sight of God. And no wonder, for in Christ crucified, God doth show Himself most noble and glorious, even an almighty God, and most loving Father, in His only dear and chosen blessed Son. [Av v] And therefore I count myself one of the most wicked and miserable sinners, because I have been so much contrary to Christ my Saviour.

1 Corinthians 2. To know Christ crucified is the cunningest lesson in divinity. Philippians 3. Luke 18. Man of his own proud nature is easily made a Pharisee.

Saint Paul desired to know nothing but Christ crucified,[30] after he had been rapt into the third heaven, where he heard such secrets as were not convenient and meet to utter to men,[31] but counted all his works and doings as nothing, to win Christ. And I, most presumptuously thinking nothing of Christ crucified, went about to set forth mine own righteousness, saying with the proud Pharisee: Good Lord, I thank Thee, I am not like other men; I am none adulterer nor fornicator,

---

by blind guides, monks, friars, canons, and papistical preachers, do now so plainly see the clear light, that they do willingly abhor idolatry and superstition" (part 3, no. 10 above, p. 99). The ultimate source of this reprehension of image worship is Romans 1:23.

27. **which . . . understanding** Deuteronomy 6:5: "Thou shalt love the LORDE thy God with all thy hart, with all thy soule, and with all thy mighte" (Coverdale 1535, fol. lxxvii v). Taverner 1539, fol. lxiv v, and Great Bible 1540, fol. lxxii v, read identically.

28. **Bishop . . . Rome** in England, the obligatory form of reference to the pope after Parliament's passage of the Act in Restraint of Appeals (April 1533). This act prohibited any English subject from appealing to papal jurisdiction any cause that lay within the jurisdiction of the English monarch.

29. **There . . . Son** KP's wording is closest to the Great Bible's in Hebrews 10:29: "how much sorer (suppose ye) shall he be ponished which tredeth under fote the sonne of God . . . ?" (Great Bible 1540, fol. lxxix r). Minor variants—e.g., the plural in "under feet"—distinguish the shared readings in Coverdale 1535, fol. ciii r, and Taverner 1539, fol. xcii v.

30. **Saint . . . crucified** an allusion to 1 Corinthians 2:2.

31. **third . . . men** an allusion to St. Paul's elliptical description of a "certain man's" mystical experience in 2 Corinthians 12:2–4.

and so forth:[32] with suchlike words of vainglory, extolling myself and despising others, working as an hired servant for wages or else for reward;[33] [Avi r] and not as a loving child, only for very love without respect of wages or reward, as I ought to have done. Neither did I consider how beneficial a Father I had, who did show me His charity and mercy of His own mere grace and goodness, that when I was most His enemy, He sent His only begotten and well-beloved Son into this world of wretchedness and misery, to suffer most cruel and sharp death for my redemption. But my heart was so stony and hard, that this great benefit was never truly and lively printed in my heart,[34] although with my words it was often rehearsed, thinking myself to be sufficiently instructed in the same, and being indeed in blind ignorance. And yet I stood so well in mine own judgment and opinion, that I thought it vain to seek the increase of my knowledge therein. [Avi v] Paul calleth Christ the wisdom of God, and even the same Christ was to me foolishness; my pride and

Children, learn to be thankful to your father.
Romans 5.
Hard hearts receive no print.

1 Corinthians [1].
Two yokefellows, blindness and hardness of heart.

32. **saying . . . forth** KP's wording is closest to Coverdale's in Luke 18:11: "The Pharisee . . . prayed by himself after this maner: I thanke the God, that I am not as other men, robbers, unrighteous, advouters [adulterers], as this publican" (Coverdale 1535, fol. xxxvi r). Minor variants respectively distinguish the readings of Taverner 1539, fol. xxix v, and Great Bible 1540, fol. xxxii v.

33. **working . . . reward** KP reworks the contrast drawn by the prodigal son in Jesus's parable (Luke 15:11–32) in wording closest to Coverdale's. The prodigal assumes that he has forfeited his sonship by squandering his inheritance from his father. Destitute and famished, he decides to return home, confess his wrongdoing, and beg for a position that will at least allow him to eat. "Father, I haue synned agaynst heauen and before the, and am no more worthy to be called thy sonne, make me as one of thy hyred seruantes" (Coverdale 1535, fol. xxxiv v, [verses 18–19]). Taverner and the Great Bible omit the mention of hired servants, reading simply: "father, I haue synned agaynst heuen, and in thy sight, and am no more worthy to be called thy sonne" (Taverner 1539, fol. xxviii v; Great Bible 1540, fol. xxxi v).

34. **But . . . heart** KP's understanding of human psychology, the affective language of Scripture, and the imperative that it be imprinted in the heart anticipates the description of the model preacher in Hugh Latimer's "Sermon on the Plowers," delivered January 18, 1548, little more than two months after the *Lamentation* appeared in print. The "busy work" of Latimer's preacher is "to bring his flock to a right faith and then to confirm them in the same faith; now casting them down with the law and with threatenings of God for sin; now ridging them up again with the gospel and with the promises of God's favor; . . . now clotting them by breaking their stony hearts and by making them supplehearted and making them to have hearts of flesh, that is, soft hearts and apt for doctrine to enter in; now teaching to know God rightly and to know their duty to God and their neighbors" (*Selected Sermons of Hugh Latimer,* ed. Allan G. Chester [Charlottesville: University of Virginia Press for Folger Shakespeare Library, 1967], 31.) **heart . . . hard** God uses this image in Ezekiel 11:19 to renew His covenant with Israel: "And I wil geue you one herte. . . . That stony herte wil I take out of youre body, and geue you a fleshy

blindness deceived me, and the hardness of my heart withstood the growing of truth within it. Such were the fruits of my carnal and human reasons, to have rotten ignorance in price,[35] for ripe and seasonable knowledge. Such also is the malice and wickedness that possesseth the hearts of men; such is the wisdom and pleasing of the flesh.

Profession in baptism. I professed Christ in my baptism when I began to live, but I swerved from Him after baptism, in continuance of my living, even as the heathen which never had begun. [Avii r] Christ was innocent and void of all sin; and I[36] wallowed in filthy sin, and was free from no sin. Christ was obedient unto His Father, even to the death of the cross;[37] and I disobedient and most stubborn, even to the confusion of truth.Christ innocent. Christ was meek and humble in heart; and I most proud and vainglorious. Christ despised the world with all the vanities thereof; and I made it my God, because of the vanities. Christ came to serve His brethren; and I coveted to rule over them. Christ despised worldly honor; and I much delighted to at-

Christ innocent. Isaiah 53. Man sinful. Philippians 2. Christ obedient. Man stubborn. Matthew 10.[38] *Christ humble. Man proud. John 8. Matthew 4.*

---

herte: that ye maye walke in my commaundementes, and kepe myne ordinaunces, and do them: that ye maye be my people, and I youre God" (Coverdale 1535, fols. lviii v–lix r). Taverner 1539, fol. li r, and Great Bible 1540, fol. xci v, read identically. **truly . . . heart** KP's imagery of imprinting the heart with Scripture closely resembles Cranmer's in the first part of the homily "Of the Knowledge of Holy Scripture" (1547), ascribed to him: "This Word whosoever is diligent to read, and in his heart to print that he readeth, the great affection to the transitory things of this world shall be minished in him. . . . For that thing, which (by continual use of reading of holy Scripture, and diligent searching of the same) is deeply printed and graven in the heart, at length turneth almost into nature. And moreover, the effect and virtue of God's Word is to illuminate the ignorant, and to give more light unto them that faithfully and diligently read it" (*Certain Sermons and Homilies, Appointed to Be Read in Churches* [Oxford: Oxford University Press, 1840], 3–4).

35. **have . . . in price** value or esteem highly.

36. **Christ was . . . and I** KP's serial antitheses resemble those of Bernardino Ochino, in a sermon "De Christo" (On Christ) translated from Italian to Latin by Princess Elizabeth circa 1547–48. See the introduction, p. 432.

37. **Christ . . . cross** a nearly verbatim quotation from Philippians 2:8, which reads identically in Coverdale 1535, fol. lxxxvi v; Taverner 1539, fol. lxxvii v; and Great Bible 1540, fol. lxxix r.

38. **Matthew 10** The correct reference from 1548 onward; the 1547 edition reads "Math. ix."

tain the same. Christ loved the base and simple things of the world; and I esteemed the most fair and pleasant things. Christ loved poverty; and I, wealth. Christ was gentle and merciful to the poor; and I, hardhearted and ungentle. [Avii v] Christ prayed for His enemies; and I hated mine. Christ rejoiced in the conversion of sinners; and I was not grieved to see their reversion to sin. By this declaration, all creatures may perceive how far I was from Christ, and without Christ: yea, how contrary to Christ, although I bore the name of a Christian. Insomuch that, if any man had said I had been without Christ, I would have stiffly withstood the same. And yet I neither knew Christ, nor wherefore He came. As concerning the effect and purpose of His coming, I had a certain vain, blind knowledge, both cold and dead, which may be had with all sin: as doth plainly appear, by this my confession and open declaration.

Christ heavenly. Man worldly.[39] *John 13, 6. Matthew 18, 7. 2 Corinthians 8. Christ poor. Man rich. Luke 14. John 8. Matthew 9. Many Christians know not their patron. Ignorant wisdom. Without the cause, nothing is rightly known. Romans 2. Lamentation.*[40]

What cause now have I to lament, mourn, sigh, and weep for my life, and time so evil spent! [Aviii r] With how much humility and lowliness ought I to come and knowledge my sins to God, giving Him thanks, that it hath pleased Him, of His abundant goodness, to give me time of repentance: for I know my sins, in the consideration of them, to be so grievous, and in the number, so exceeding, that I have deserved very often, eternal damnation. And, for the deserving of God's wrath, so manifoldly due, I must uncessantly give thanks to the mercy of God, beseeching also that the same delay of punishment cause not His plague to be the sorer, since mine own conscience condemneth my former doings. But His mercy exceedeth all iniquity. And, if I should not thus hope: alas, what[41] should I seek for refuge and comfort? [Aviii v] No mortal man is of power to help me; and, for the multitude of my sins, I dare not lift up mine eyes to heaven, where the seat of judgment is: I have so much offended God. What, shall I fall in desperation? Nay, I will call upon Christ, the Light of the world, the fountain of life, the relief of all care-full, and the peacemaker between God and man, and the only health and comfort of all true re-

God showeth goodness in deferring His wrath. Psalm 103. Psalm 108. Luke 18.

Christ draweth man from desperation. 1 John 1. John 4. 1 John 2. John 3. Matthew 18.[42]

39. **worldly** The reading from 1548 onward; the 1547 edition reads "wordly."

40. **Lamentation** The "lamentation" that begins here is reprised and intensified beginning on p. 466 below, facing the marginal heading "A Christian complaint." Thematic and tonal development by way of successive surges of deepening feeling and insight characterizes this work of KP's and, more generally, the mode of devotion in Thomas à Kempis's *De imitatione Christi.* KP had recast as her own *Prayers or Meditations* (1545) excerpts from book 3 of à Kempis's work in the English translation by Richard Whitford.

41. **alas, what** The reading of the 1547 and 1548 editions; the 1563 edition reads "alas where."

42. **Matthew 18** The correct reference from 1548 onward; the 1547 edition reads "Math. xxiii."

The power and will of God. John 3. No Saviour but one. Luke 19. Matthew [9].

pentant sinners. He can, by His almighty power, save me and deliver me out of this miserable state; and hath will, by His mercy, to save even the whole sin of the world. I have no hope nor confidence in any creature, neither in heaven nor earth, but in Christ, my whole and only Saviour. [Bi r] He came into the world to save sinners, and to heal them that are sick; for He saith, "The whole have no need of a physician."[43] Behold, Lord, how I come to Thee: a sinner, sick and grievously wounded.

Man's humility. Matthew 15.

I ask not bread, but the crumbs that fall from the children's table.[44] Cast me not out of Thy sight, although I have deserved to be cast into hell fire. If I should look upon my sins, and not upon Thy mercy, I should despair. For in myself I find nothing to save me, but a dunghill[45] of wickedness to condemn me. If I should hope, by

A maze of sin.

mine own strength and power, to come out of this maze of iniquity and wickedness wherein I have walked so long, I should be deceived. [Bi v] For I am so ignorant, blind, weak, and feeble that I cannot bring myself out of this entangled and wayward maze. But the more I seek means and ways to wind myself out, the more I am wrapped and tangled therein. So that I perceive my striving therein to be hindrance, my travail to be labor spent in going back.

Psalm 18. Philippians 2. 2 Corinthians 3. God beginneth with man. Matthew 16. 1 Corinthians 12. Romans 8.

It is the hand of the Lord. that can and will bring me out of this endless maze of death; for, without I be prevented by the grace[46] of the Lord, I cannot ask forgiveness, nor be repentant or sorry for them. There is no man can avow that Christ is the only Saviour of the world, but by the Holy Ghost: yea, as Saint Paul saith, "No man can say 'The Lord Jesus' but by the Holy Ghost."[47] The Spirit helpeth our in-

43. **Matthew [9] . . . physician"** **Matthew [9]** The correct reference, not given in any edition; the 1547 and 1548 editions read "Math. ii." **"The . . . physician"** A nearly verbatim quotation from Matthew 9:12, which reads identically in Coverdale 1535, fol. v r, and Taverner 1539, fol. iv v. By contrast the Great Bible 1540, fol. v r, reads "They that be stronge, nede not the phisicyon."

44. **I . . . table** an allusion to Jesus's exchange in Matthew 15:22–28 with a woman of Canaan who begs Him to cure her daughter vexed by a devil. Jesus initially rebuffs her, saying it is improper to cast the children's bread to dogs. The woman acknowledges this but counters that dogs eat crumbs that fall from their master's table. Jesus in turn responds: the woman's faith is great, and her daughter is cured.

45. **a dunghill** On this phraseology from Marguerite de Navarre, see the introduction, n8.

46. **prevented . . . grace** Preventing or "prevenient" grace is the illumination or inspiration from the Holy Spirit that enables a sinner to respond positively to subsequent grace. Scripture cited in support of its existence includes Psalm 59:10 (Vulgate), Romans 8:30, and 2 Timothy 1:9. St. Augustine prominently invoked "gratia praeveniens" in various writings: see *De gratia et libero arbitrio* (On Grace and Free Will), in *Patrologia Latina,* ed. J.-P. Migne (Paris, 1841), 44. col. 904; *De predestinatione sanctorum* (On the Predestination of the Saints), PL 44, cols. 959, 964; and *Epistolae* (Letters), PL 33: cols. 989, 1003, 1004.

47. **"No . . . Ghost"** a nearly verbatim quotation from 1 Corinthians 12:3, which reads identically in Coverdale 1535, fol. lxxvi r, and Taverner 1539, fol. lxix r. By contrast, the Great Bible 1540, fol. lxix v, reads "no man can saye that Jesus is the Lorde, but by the holy ghost."

firmities, and maketh continual intercession for us, with such sorrowful groanings as cannot be expressed. [Bii r] Therefore, I will first require and pray the Lord to give me His Holy Spirit: to teach me to avow that Christ is the Saviour of the world, and to utter these words, "The Lord Jesus," and finally, to help mine infirmities, and to intercede for me. For I am most certain and sure, that no creature in heaven nor earth is of power, or can by any mean help me, but God, who is omnipotent, almighty, beneficial, and merciful, well-willing, and loving to all those that call, and put their whole confidence and trust in Him. And therefore I will seek none other means nor advocate, but Christ's Holy Spirit, who is only the Advocate and Mediator between God and man, to help and relieve me. [Bii v] But, now, what maketh me so bold and hardy, to presume to come to the Lord with such audacity and boldness, being so great a sinner? Truly, nothing but His own Word: for He saith, Come to me all ye that labor, and are burdened, and I shall refresh you. What gentle, merciful, and comfortable words are these, to all sinners! What a most gracious, comfortable, and gentle saying was this, with such pleasant and sweet words to allure His enemies to come unto Him! Is there any worldly prince or magistrate that would show such clemency and mercy to their disobedient and rebelllious subjects, having offended them? [Biii r] I suppose they would not with such words allure them, except it were to call them whom they cannot take, and punish them, being taken. But even as Christ is Prince of Princes and Lord of Lords, so His charity and mercy surmounteth all others.

The teaching of the Holy Spirit.
Jesus. Acts 4.
God is only the Helper. 1 John 2.
Christ is the only mean between God and man.

Objection: What maketh man bold?
Solution: The promise of Christ.[48]
Matthew 11.

Apocalypse 17.

Christ saith, If carnal fathers do give good gifts to their children when they ask them, how much more shall your heavenly Father, being in substance all holy and most highly good, give good gifts to all them that ask Him? It is no small nor little gift that I require, neither think I myself worthy to receive such a noble gift, being so ingrate, unkind, and wicked a child. [Biii v] But when I behold the benignity, liberality, mercy, and goodness of the Lord, I[49] am encouraged, boldened, and stirred to ask such a noble gift. The Lord is so bountiful and liberal that He will not

Matthew 7.
The giver.
The gift.
The taker.

The goodness of God boldeneth His chosen.
Zechariah 10.
John 16.

48. **promise . . . Christ** KP signals her awareness of "promise" as a key term for the heart of the Gospel message—Christ's freely offered assurance of salvation from sin and damnation to those who believe and trust him—and hence a term that complements "justification by faith" (a marginal heading on p. 456 below). The chief English exponent of the "promises" was William Tyndale, who declared in his *Parable of the Wicked Mammon* (1527): "See therefore thou have God's promises in thine heart, and that thou believe them without wavering. . . . The promises, when they are believed, are they that justify; for they bring the Spirit, which looseth the heart, giveth lust to the law, and certfieth us of the goodwill of God unto usward. . . . Christ . . . hath made amends or satisfaction to Godward for all the sin which they that repent (consenting to the law and believing the promises) do, have done, or shall do" (Tyndale, *Doctrinal Treatises and Introductions,* 48, 52). KP's *Lamentation* echoes the vocabulary of *Wicked Mammon* at several points.

49. **I** The reading from 1548 onward; the 1547 edition reads "I" twice, before and after a page break.

Faith is ever necessary. Romans 13, 3. 1 John 4. Learn what true faith doth in man. Hosea 3. Ephesians 2. Romans 5. Galatians 3.

have us satisfied and contented with one gift, neither to ask simple and small gifts. And therefore he promiseth, and bindeth Himself by His Word, to give good and beneficial gifts to all them that ask Him with true faith: without which, nothing can be done acceptable or pleasing to God. For faith is the foundation and ground of all other gifts, virtues, and graces; and therefore I will say: Lord, increase my faith. For this is the life everlasting, Lord, that I must believe Thee to be the true God, and whom Thou didst send, Jesus Christ. [Biv r] By this faith I am assured; and by this assurance, I feel the remission of my sins. This is it that maketh me bold; this is it that comforteth me; this is it that quencheth all despair.[50] I know, O my Lord, Thy eyes look upon my faith.

Justification by a Christian faith.[52] *Romans 5.*

Saint Paul saith we be justified by the faith in Christ, and not by the deeds of the law. For if righteousness come by the law, then Christ died in vain. Saint Paul meaneth not, here, a dead, human, historical faith,[51] gotten by human industry, but a supernal, lively faith which worketh by charity, as he himself plainly expresseth.

50. **For faith . . . despair** KP's successive formulations on the primacy of faith over "all other gifts, virtues, and graces," on the effects of justifying faith in bringing assurance of salvation and the remission of one's sin, and on the proper ascription of justifying faith to Christ's agency alone evince her informed theological comprehension of her subject, her own conversion to a Lutheran strain of Christianity. **Lord . . . faith** a nearly verbatim quotation from Luke 17:5, which reads identically in Coverdale 1535, fol. xxxv v; Taverner 1539, fol. xxix r; and Great Bible 1540, fol. xxxii r: "Lorde: increase oure fayth." **For . . . Christ** an expatiating paraphrase of an excerpt from John 6:40.

51. **historical faith** KP invokes terminology introduced to English readers in the Reformation by Tyndale in his *Answer to More* (1532). There Tyndale distinguishes between "historical" faith—i.e., believing that such a person as Jesus actually lived—and "feeling" faith, an assurance "written in thine heart . . . because the Spirit of God so preacheth and so testifieth unto thy soul . . . that thou shalt be saved through Christ" (*An Answer to Sir Thomas More's Dialogue,* ed Henry Walter, Parker Society 45 [Cambridge: Cambridge University Press, 1850], 50–52, 55–56). Tyndale's earlier, less developed formulation in *Parable of the Wicked Mammon* emphasizes the link between "feeling" and direct personal experience: "He that hath not the Spirit hath no feeling, . . . neither hath any more certainty of the promises of God, than I have of a tale of Robin Hood, or of some gest that a man telleth me was done at Rome. Another man may lightly make me doubt, or believe the contrary, seeing I have no experience thereof myself: so it is of them that feel not the working of the Spirit" (*Doctrinal Treatises and Introductions,* ed. Walter, Parker Society 43, 80). See further Mueller, *Native Tongue and the Word,* 191–92.

52. **Justification . . . faith** In embracing Luther's formulation, to which she had probably been introduced by Cranmer or by a reading of Tyndale's *Parable of the Wicked Mammon,* KP parts company with Erasmian Christianity; see William P. Haugaard, "Katherine Parr: The Religious Convictions of a Renaissance Queen," *Renaissance Quarterly* 22 (1969): 346–59. This distinctively Reformed concept attributed salvation solely to Christ, without any cooperating act or affection on the part of sinful humans. Justifying faith was a personal assurance that Christ had saved one's soul freely and unilaterally—that is, a faith that made such justification a truth to and for that soul. Luther elaborates in chapter 3, verses 22–26, of his *Lectures on Ro-*

This dignity of faith is no derogation to good works, for out of this faith springeth all good works. [Biv v] Yet we may not impute to the worthiness of faith or works our justification before God; but ascribe and give the worthiness of it, wholly, to the merits of Christ's passion; and refer and attribute the knowledge and perceiving thereof, only to faith. Whose very true, only property is to take, apprehend, and hold fast the promises of God's mercy, the which maketh us righteous; and to cause me continually to hope for the same mercy; and, in love, to work all manner of ways allowed in the Scripture, that I may be thankful for the same. Thus I feel myself to come, as it were, in a new garment before God; and now, by His mercy, to be taken just and righteous: which of late, without His mercy, was sinful and wicked; and by faith to obtain his mercy, the which the unfaithful cannot enjoy. [Bv r] And although Saint John extolleth charity in his epistle, saying that God is charity, and He that dwelleth in charity dwelleth in God: truly, charity maketh men live like angels; and of the most furious, unbridled, carnal men maketh meek lambs.

Dignity of faith hurteth no works.[53] *Mark diligently without offense. Romans 3; 5.*

[1] John [4].[54] *Objection. 1 John 2. Solution.*

Yea, with how fervent a spirit ought I to call, cry, and pray to the Lord, to make His great charity to burn and flame in my heart, being so stony and evil affected, that it never would conceive nor regard the great, inestimable charity and love of God, in sending His only-begotten and dear beloved Son into this vale of misery, to suffer the most cruel and sharp death of the cross for my redemption? [Bv v] Yet I never had this unspeakable and most high charity and abundant love of God printed and fixed in my heart duly, till it pleased God, of His mere grace, mercy, and pity, to open mine eyes, making me to see and behold with the eye of lively

Charity knoweth not Christ, but by report of faith.

---

mans: "Since all have sinned, have been made and declared to be sinners before God, and fall short of, that is, lack, are empty of, the glory of God, . . . they are justified as a gift, that is, all, as many as are justified, are not justified except freely, by His, God's, grace, without merits or works. This grace is not given except through the redemption which is in Christ Jesus. By this grace He Himself alone has redeemed those who were 'sold under sin,' making satisfaction for us and freeing us. . . . On what principle? On the principle of works? No, this principle actually . . . makes people proud. No, but on the principle of faith, because this humbles a man and makes him confess that he is a sinner before God. For . . . we conclude from what is said that a man is justified, reckoned righteous before God, . . . by faith apart from works of the Law, without the help and necessity of the works of the Law" (*Lectures on Romans,* ed. and trans. Oswald, in *Luther's Works,* 25:31–33).

53. **Dignity . . . works** KP rehearses one of Cranmer's fundamental claims in the first part of "A Short Declaration of the True, Lively, and Christian Faith" in the *Book of Homilies* (July 1547): "This faith . . . is lively and fruitful in bringing forth good works. . . . Without it can no good works be done, that shall be acceptable and pleasant to God. . . . Such is the true faith . . . when it seeth and considereth what God hath done for us, is also moved, through continual assistance of the Spirit of God, to serve and please Him, . . . to continue His obedient children, showing thankfulness again by observing His commandments, and that freely, for true love chiefly, . . . considering how clearly, without our deservings, we have received His mercy and pardon freely" (*Certain Sermons or Homilies,* 31, 32).

54. **[1] John [4]** The correct reference; all editions read "John iii."

faith, Christ crucified to be mine only Saviour and Redeemer. For then I began (and not before) to perceive and see mine own ignorance and blindness; the cause thereof was that I would not learn to know Christ, my Saviour and Redeemer. But when God, of His mere goodness, had thus opened mine eyes, and made me see and behold Christ, the wisdom of God, the Light of the world, with a supernatural sight of faith: all pleasures, vanities, honor, riches, wealth, and aids of the world began to wax bitter unto me. [Bvi r] Then I knew it was no illusion of the devil, nor false nor human doctrine I had received, when such success came thereof: that I had in detestation and horror, that which I erst[55] so much loved and esteemed, being of God forbidden, that we should love the world or the vain pleasures and shadows in the same. Then began I to perceive that Christ was my only Saviour and Redeemer, and the same doctrine to be all divine, holy, and heavenly, infused by grace into the hearts of the faithful. Which never can be attained by human doctrine, wit, nor reason,[56] although they should travail and labor for the same to the end of the world. [Bvi v] Then began I to dwell in God by charity, knowing by the loving charity of God, in the remission of my sins, that God is charity, as Saint John saith.[57]

1 Corinthians 1.

John 1.

1 John 2.

John 14.

Charity immediately followeth lively faith.

So that, of my faith (whereby I came to know God, and whereby it pleased God, even because I trusted in Him to justify me) I think no less, but many will wonder and marvel at this my saying, that I never knew Christ for my Saviour and Redeemer until this time. For many have this opinion, saying, Who knoweth not there is a Christ? Who, being a Christian, doth not confess Him his Saviour? And, thus believing their dead, human, historical faith and knowledge (which they have learned in their scholastical books) to be the true, infused faith and knowledge of Christ, which may be had (as I said before) with all sin: [Bvii r] they use to say by their own experience of themselves, that their faith doth not justify them. And true

Secret objection.

55. **erst** formerly.

56. **the same . . . reason** This theme had been a key emphasis in the letter KP wrote on February 26, 1546 to the University of Cambridge after its heads of colleges appealed to her to use her influence with King Henry to prevent the confiscation of college lands (as a policy extension of what was being done with monastery lands). KP forthrightly stated the condition on which she would intercede with the king: "I require and desire you all not so to hunger for the exquisite knowledge of profane learning that it may be thought the Greeks' university was but transposed, or now in England again revived, forgetting our Christianity, since their excellency only did attain to moral and natural things. But rather I gently exhort you to study and apply those doctrines as means and apt degrees to the attaining and setting forth the better Christ's reverent and most sacred doctrine" (part 3, no. 14 of correspondence, p. 115). Tyndale had affirmed similar priorities in his *Parable of the Wicked Mammon* (*Doctrinal Treatises and Introductions,* 107).

57. **God . . . saith** an allusion to 1 John 4:8, 16—two occurrences of the assertion "God is love," the rendering in sixteenth-century English Bibles. **charity** KP's resort to the English cognate of the Vulgate Latin "caritas" is a traditionalist, not a Reformed, move. Judging from the facing marginal rubric, "Charity immediately followeth lively faith," her word choice seems to

it is, except they have this faith, the which I have declared here before, they shall never be justified. And, yet, it is not false that, by faith only, I am sure to be justified: even this is the case, that so many impugn this office and duty of true faith because so many lack the true faith. And, even as the faithful are forced to allow true faith, so the unfaithful can in no wise probably intreat[58] thereof: the one, feeling in himself that he saith; the other, having not in him for to say. [Bvii v] I have, certainly, no curious learning to defend this matter withal, but a simple zeal and earnest love to the truth, inspired of God, who promiseth to pour His Spirit upon all flesh:[59] which I have, by the grace of God, whom I most humbly honor, felt in myself to be true.

A mild and true solution.

Let us therefore, now, I pray you, by faith, behold and consider the great goodness of God, in sending His Son to suffer death for our redemption when we were His mortal enemies; and after what sort and manner He sent Him. First it is to be considered, yea, to be undoubtedly with a perfect faith believed, that God sent Him to us freely: for He did give Him, and sold Him not. A more noble and rich gift He could not have given. [Bviii r] He sent not a servant, or a friend, but His only Son, so dearly beloved: not in delights, riches, and honors, but in crosses, poverties, and slanders; not as a lord, but as a servant. Yea, in most vile and painful passions, to wash us: not with water, but with His own precious blood; not from mire, but from the puddle and filth[60] of our iniquities. He hath given Him, not to make us poor, but to enrich us with His divine virtues, merits, and graces: yea, and in Him He hath given us all good things, and, finally, Himself, and that with such great charity as cannot be expressed. [Bviii v] Was it not a most high and abundant charity of God, to send Christ to shed His blood, to lose honor, life, and all, for His enemies? Even in the time when we had done Him most injury, He first showed His char-

How God sent His Son.
John 3.

Philippians 2.
1 John 1.

Romans 8.

The charity of God toward man.
Romans 5.

---

have been guided by a resolve to emphasize that justifying faith produces not merely feelings of love and gratitude toward God but indeed full-scale moral renewal. Cranmer also makes this emphasis in the first part of "A Short Declaration of the True, Lively, and Christian Faith": "The first coming unto God, good Christian people, is through faith, whereby . . . we be justified before God." This faith "*worketh by charity,* (as Saint Paul declareth [Galatians 5:6]), which . . . may . . . be called a quick or lively faith" (*Certain Sermons or Homilies,* 29, 30). Also see KP's reflections facing the marginal headings "Christian liberty" and "Charity," pp. 470–71 below.

58. **intreat** an earlier variant of "treat."

59. **God . . . flesh** an allusion to the comprehensive promise in Joel 2:28–29, repeated in Acts 2:17–18. God declares that He will pour out His Spirit upon "your sons and your daughters," "your old men," "your young men," "and also upon the servants and upon the handmaids." The divine validation of every soul's capacity to receive inspiration, regardless of age, gender, or status, makes this a key Scriptural text for Reformation evangelicals—particularly for a devout, enterprising queen like KP.

60. **mire . . . filth** On KP's employment of Marguerite de Navarre's rhetoric of self-abasement, see the introduction, pp. 426, 428–29.

ity to us, with such flames of love, that greater could not be showed. God in Christ hath opened unto us (although we be weak and blind of ourselves) that we may behold, in this miserable state, the great wisdom, goodness, and truth, with all the other godly perfections, which be in Christ. Therefore, inwardly to behold Christ crucified upon the cross is the best and godliest meditation that can be. We may see also, in Christ crucified, the beauty of the soul, better than in all the books of the world. [Ci r] For who that, with lively faith, seeth and feeleth in spirit that Christ, the Son of God, is dead for the satisfying and the purifying of the soul, shall see that his soul is appointed for the very tabernacle and mansion of the inestimable and incomprehensible majesty and honor of God. We see also, in Christ crucified, how vain and foolish the world is; and how that Christ, being most wise, despised the same. We see also how blind it is; because the same knoweth not Christ, but persecuteth Him. We see also how unkind the world is, by the killing of Christ, in the time He did show it most favor. How hard and obstinate was it, that would not be mollified with so many tears, such sweat, and so much bloodshed of the Son of God, suffering with so great and high charity? [Ci v] Therefore, he is now very blind that seeth not how vain, foolish, false, ingrate, cruel, hard, wicked, and evil the world is.

A godly meditation.

The beauty of the soul.

John 14.

The world vain.

Blind.

Unkind.

Sin.

We may also, in Christ crucified, weigh our sins as in a divine balance: how grievous and how weighty they be, seeing they have crucified Christ; for they would never have been counterpoised, but with the great and precious weight of the blood of the Son of God. And therefore God, of His high goodness, determined that His blessed Son should rather suffer bloodshed than our sins should have condemned us. [Cii r] We shall never know our own misery and wretchedness, but with the light of Christ crucified. Then we shall see our own cruelty, when we feel His mercy; our own unrighteousness and iniquity, when we see His righteousness and holiness. Therefore, to learn to know truly our own sins is to study in the book of the crucifix,[61] by continual conversation in faith; and to have perfect and plentiful charity is to learn first, by faith, the charity that is in God, towards us. We may see also, in Christ upon the cross, how great the pains of hell and how blessed the joys of heaven be; and what a sharp, painful thing it shall be to them that, from

A Christian man's book.

Lessons of the crucifix.

Pain of hell.

61. **the book . . . crucifix** KP's striking metaphor conflates disparate domains in Christian symbolics: the book as Holy Scripture, the acme of verbal truth; and the crucifix as the simulacrum of Jesus's crucified body, the most sacred object, the acme of nonverbal truth. KP's ostensible source was a Good Friday sermon preached circa 1531–34 by John Fisher, Bishop of Rochester. Fisher images the distended, bruised, and bleeding body of Christ as an illuminated manuscript treating the theme of lamentation and transmuting its truths in the stigmata of Francis of Assisi (*A Sermon verie fruitfull, godly and learned* in *The English Works of John Fisher*, pt. 1, ed. John E. B. Mayor, Early English Text Society, extra series 27 [London: N. Trübner, 1876], 388–92). KP's book of the crucifix is really a book of the crucifixion, her metaphor for the heart of Scripture, the promises of the Gospel apprehended in Tyndalian fashion as the felt truth of one's personal salvation, made available to all who can read God's Word.

that sweet, happy and glorious joy, Christ, shall be deprived. There this crucifix is the book,[62] wherein God hath included all things, and hath most compendiously written therein, all truth profitable and necessary for our salvation. [Cii v] Therefore let us endeavor ourselves to study this book, that we, being lightened with the Spirit of God, may give Him thanks for so great a benefit. If we look further in this book, we shall see Christ's great victory upon the cross: which was so noble and mighty, that there never was, neither shall be such. If the victory and glory of worldly princes were great, because they did overcome great hosts of men, how much more was Christ's greater? Which vanquished not only the prince of the world,[63] but all the enemies of God: triumphing over persecution, injuries, villainies, slanders, yea, death, the world, sin, and the devil; and brought to confusion, all carnal prudence. [Ciii r] The princes of the world never did fight without the strength of the world. Christ, contrarily,[64] went to war, even against all the strength of the world. He would fight, as David did with Goliath, unarmed of all human wisdom and policy, and without all worldly power and strength. Nevertheless, He was fully replenished and armed with the whole armor of the Spirit.[65] And in this one battle, he overcame, forever, all His enemies. There was never so glorious a spoil, neither a more rich and noble, than Christ was upon the cross: which delivered all His elect from such a sharp, miserable captivity. He had, in this battle, many stripes, yea, and lost His life; but His victory was so much the greater. [Ciii v] Therefore, when I look upon the Son of God with a supernatural faith and light, so unarmed, naked, given up, and alone; with humility, patience, liberality, modesty, gentleness, and with other His divine virtues; beating[66] down to the ground all God's enemies, and making the soul of man so fair and beautiful: I am forced to say that His victory and triumph was marvelous. And therefore Christ deserved to have this noble title: "Jesus of Nazareth, King of the Jews."[68]

Joy of heaven.

1 Corinthians 2.

Christ's victory.

Colossians 2.

Wisdom of Solomon 17.

David and Christ compared in fight.

Spiritual armor.

Ephesians [6].[67]

Matthew 27.

Jesus' style.

62. **this crucifix . . . book** An early reader of the Pembroke College, Cambridge, copy of the first edition of the *Lamentation* contested KP's phrasing at three points, striking it through and carefully lettering in alternative readings as follows: "study in the book of the [bible] ~~crucifix~~," "this [bible] ~~crucifix~~ is the boke," "Lessons of the [bible] ~~Crucifix~~."

63. **the prince . . . world** the devil—nomenclature used in John 12:31, 14:30, and 16:11.

64. **contrarily** The reading from 1548 onward; 1547 reads "contrary."

65. **the whole . . . Spirit** See Ephesians 6:13–17 for the extended allegory of the "whole armor of God" including the "breastplate of righteousness," the "shield of faith," "the helmet of salvation," and the "sword of the Spirit."

66. **beating** The reading from 1548 onward; 1547 reads "bearing."

67. **Ephesians [6]** The correct reference; all editions read "Ephe. v."

68. **"Jesus . . . Jews"** According to Matthew 27:37, the "cause of his death in wrytinge" nailed to the cross above Jesus's head (Coverdale 1535, fol. xiv v). Taverner 1539, fol. xii v, and the Great Bible 1540, fol. xiv r, read "the cause of his deathe, wrytten." The epithet "Jesus of Nazareth, King of the Jews" would acquire crucial poetic and devotional resonances in another work by an Englishwoman, the title poem of Aemilia Lanyer's *Salve Deus Rex Judaeorum* (1611). See *The Poems of Aemilia Lanyer,* ed. Susanne Woods (Oxford: Oxford University Press, 1993).

Victory over sin. *Colossians 1.* *Acts 7.* *Romans 6; 7.* *Colossians 2.* *Sin hurteth not the elect.* *Concupiscence the original sin.* *Romans 8.* *Objection.* *Solution.* *A similitude.*

[Civ r] But if we will particularly unfold and see His great victories, let us first behold how He overcame sin with His innocency, and confounded pride with His humility, quenched all worldly love with His charity, appeased the wrath of His Father with His meekness, turned hatred into love with His so many benefits and godly zeal. Christ hath not only overcome sin, but rather He hath killed the same: inasmuch as He hath satisfied for it Himself, with the most holy sacrifice and oblation of His precious body,[69] in suffering most bitter and cruel death. Also, after another sort: that is, He giveth to all those that love Him, so much spirit, grace, virtue, and strength, that they may resist, impugn, and overcome sin, and not consent, neither suffer it to reign in them. [Civ r] He hath also vanquished sin, because He hath taken away the force of the same: that is, He hath cancelled the law, which was, in evil men, the occasion of sin. Therefore sin hath no power against them, that are with the Holy Ghost united to Christ; in them there is nothing worthy of damnation. And although the dregs of Adam do remain, that is, our concupiscences, which indeed be sins: nevertheless they be not imputed for sins, if we be truly planted in Christ.[70] It is true that Christ might have taken away all our immoderate affections, but He hath left them for the greater glory of His Father, and for His own greater triumph.[71] As for an example: When a prince, fighting with his enemies which sometime had the sovereignty over his people, and subduing them, may kill them if he will, yet he preserveth and saveth them. [Cv r] And whereas they were lords over his people, he maketh them after to serve, whom they before had ruled. Now, in such a case, the prince doth show himself a greater conqueror, in that he hath made them, which were rulers, to obey; and the subjects to be lords over them, to whom they served, than if he had utterly destroyed them upon the conquest. For, now, he leaveth continual victory to them whom he redeemed: whereas, otherwise, the occasion of victory was taken away, where none were left

69. **the most . . . body** KP's theologically precise wording in a devotional register anticipates Cranmer's formulation for public worship in "The Supper of the Lorde and Holy Communion" in the Book of Common Prayer (1549): "Christ [did] suffre death . . . [and] made . . . (by his one oblacion once offered) a full, perfect, and sufficient sacrifyce, oblacion, and satysfaccyon, for the sinnes of the whole worlde" (*First and Second Prayer Books of Edward VI,* 222).

70. **concupiscences . . . Christ** **concupiscences** The English rendering of St. Paul's term "epithumia"—desire for things of the flesh or things of the world (Romans 7:8; Colossians 3:5; 1 Thessalonians 4:5). **planted . . . Christ** St. Paul's image in Romans 6:5 for the death and resurrection that the baptized will undergo "in the likeness" of Christ's death and resurrection.

71. **Christ . . . triumph** KP's rationale for free will is theologically rather than humanistically oriented, as is John Milton's in *Areopagitica* (1644) a century later: "Many there be that complain of divin Providence for suffering *Adam* to transgresse, foolish tongues! when God gave him reason, he gave him freedom to choose. . . . Wherefore did he creat passions within us, pleasures round about us, but that these rightly temper'd are the very ingredients of virtu? They are not skilfull considerers of human things, who imagin to remove sin by removing the matter of sin" (*Areopagitica,* ed. Ernest Sirluck, in *Complete Prose Works of John Milton* [New Haven, CT: Yale University Press, 1959], 2:527).

to be the subjects. Even so, in like case, Christ hath left in us these concupiscences, to the intent they should serve us to the exercise of our virtues, [Cv v] where first they did reign over us, to the exercise of our sin. And it may be plainly seen that, whereas first they were such impediments to us, that we could not move ourselves towards God: now by Christ we have so much strength that, notwithstanding the force of them, we may assuredly walk to heaven. And although the children of God sometime do fall by frailty into some sin, yet that falling maketh them to humble themselves, and to reknowledge[72] the goodness of God, and to come to Him for refuge and help.

Application of the similitude.

Likewise Christ, with His death, hath overcome the prince of devils with all his host, and hath destroyed them all. For, as Paul saith: This is verified, that Christ should break the serpent's head, prophesied by God.[73] [Cvi r] And although the devil tempt us, yet if by faith we be planted in Christ, we shall not perish; but rather, by his temptation, take great force and might. So it is evident that the triumph, victory, and glory of Christ is the greater, having in such sort subdued the devil that, whereas he was prince and lord of the world, holding all creatures in captivity, now Christ useth him as an instrument to punish the wicked, and to exercise and make strong the elect of God in Christian warfare. Christ likewise hath overcome death in a more glorious manner (if it be possible), because He hath not taken it away. But leaving universally all subject to the same, [Cvi v] He hath given so much virtue and spirit that, whereas afore we passed thereto with great fear, now we be bold, through the Spirit, for the sure hope of resurrection, that we receive it with joy. It is now no more bitter, but sweet; no more feared, but desired. It is no death, but life. And, also, it hath pleased God that the infirmities and adversities do remain to the sight of the world; but the children of God are, by Christ, made so strong, righteous, whole and sound, that the troubles of the world be comforts of the spirit; the passions of the flesh are medicines of the soul. For all manner things worketh to their commodity and profit; for they in spirit feel that God, their Father, doth govern them, and disposeth all things for their benefit; therefore, they feel themselves sure. [Cvii r] In persecution, they are quiet and peaceful; in time of trouble, they are without weariness, fears, anxieties, suspicions, miseries; and finally, all the good and evil of the world worketh to their commodity.

Victory over the devil.

Colossians 2.

Genesis 3.

Victory over death.

Philippians 4.

2 Corinthians 1.

All things profit the chosen.

Romans 8.

Moreover, they see that the triumph of Christ hath been so great, that not only He hath subdued and vanquished all our enemies and the power of them, but He hath overthrown and vanquished them after such a sort, that all things serve to

72. **reknowledge** a variant form of *acknowledge,* common in the sixteenth century. "Reknowledge" occurs in Tyndale's *Answer to Sir Thomas More's Dialogue,* 22.

73. **This . . . God** a glancing allusion to St. Paul's prophecy in 1 Corinthians 15:24–28 that Christ at the end of time shall put all His enemies under His feet, including death, and then subject Himself to God His Father.

our health. He might and could have taken them all away, but where, then, should have been our victory, palm, and crown?[74] For we daily have fights in the flesh, and, by the succor of grace, have continual victories over sin: [Cvi v] whereby we have cause to glorify God that, by His Son, hath weakened our enemy the devil and, by His Spirit, giveth us strength to vanquish his offsprings. So do we knowledge daily the great triumph of our Saviour, and rejoice in our own sights: the which we can nowise impute to any wisdom of this world, seeing sin to increase by it. And where worldly wisdom most governeth, there most sin ruleth: For as the world is enemy to God, so also the wisdom thereof is adverse to God. And therefore Christ hath declared and discovered the same for foolishness.[75] And although He could have taken away all worldly wisdom, yet He hath left it for His greater glory, and triumph of His chosen vessels. [Cviii r] For before, whereas it was our ruler against God, now, by Christ, we are served of it for God, as of a slave in worldly things; albeit, in supernatural things, the same is not to be understand.[76] And, further, if any time men would impugn and gainsay us with the wisdom of the world, yet we have, by Christ, so much supernatural light of the truth, that we make a mock of all those that repugn[77] the truth. Christ, also, upon the cross, hath triumphed over the world. First, because He hath discovered the same to be naught: that whereas it was covered with the veil of hypocrisy and the vesture of moral virtues, Christ hath showed that, in God's sight, the righteousness of the world is wickedness; [Cviii v] and He hath yielded witness that the works of men, not regenerated by Him in faith, are evil. And so Christ hath judged and condemned the world for naught. Furthermore, He hath given, to all His, so much light and spirit, that they know it, and dispraise the same: yea, and tread it under their feet, with all vain honors, dignities, and pleasures, not taking the fair promises, neither the offers, which it doth present. Nay, they rather make a scorn of them. And, as for the threatenings and force of the world, they nothing fear. Now, therefore, we may see how great the victory and triumph of Christ is, who hath delivered all those the Father gave Him from the power of the devil, cancelling, upon the cross, the writing of our debts. [Di r] For He hath delivered us from the condemnation of sin, from the bondage of the law, from the fear of death, from the danger of the world,

The wisdom of the world.
1 Corinthians 2, 3.

Victory over the world.
John 14.

John 3.
Romans 14.
How Christians regard[78] the world.

A conclusion of the victories.
John 17.
Colossians 2.

74. **where . . . crown?** KP again anticipates Milton's *Areopagitica,* this time more closely: "I cannot praise a . . . vertue, unexercis'd and unbreath'd, that never sallies out and sees her adversary, but slinks out of the race, where that immortall garland is to be run for" (*Complete Prose Works of John Milton,* 2:515). Both authors implicitly draw on the imagery in 2 Timothy 4:7–8.

75. **For . . . foolishness** The vocabulary of the "foolishness" of the wisdom of the world is St. Paul's, but what exposes the world's wisdom as foolishness is the redemption brought to humankind by Christ crucified. See 1 Corinthians 1:20–25; 2:14; 3:18–19.

76. **understand** a former variant of the past participle "understood." On KP's conception of the relation of reason to "supernatural things," see n56.

77. **repugn** oppose, contradict.

78. **regard** The reading from 1548 onward; the 1547 edition reads "regardeth."

and from all evils in this life, and in the other to come. And He hath enriched us, made us noble and most highly happy, after such a glorious and triumphant way, as cannot with tongue be expressed. And therefore we are forced to say: His triumph is marvelous.[79] It is also seen and known, that Christ is the true Messiah, for He hath delivered man from all evils; and by Him, man hath all goodness, so that He is the true Messiah. Therefore all other helpers be but vain and counterfeited saviors, seeing that, by this our Messiah, Christ, wholly and only, we be delivered from all evils and, by Him, we have all goodness.

Christ is Messiah.

[Di v] And, that this is true, it is evident and clear, because the very true Christian is a Christian by Christ. And the true Christian feeleth inwardly, by Christ,[80] so much goodness of God, that even troublous life and death be sweet unto him, and miseries happy. The true Christian, by Christ, is disburdened: from the servitude of the law, having the law of grace (graven by the Spirit) inhabiting his heart, and from sin that reigned in him, from the power of the infernal spirits, from damnation, and from every evil; and is made a son of God, a brother of Christ, heir of heaven, and lord of the world. So that in Christ, and by Christ, he possesseth all good things. [Dii r] But, let us know, that Christ yet fighteth in spirit in His elect vessels, and shall fight even to the day of judgment. At which day shall the great enemy, death, be wholly destroyed, and shall be no more. Then shall the children of God rejoice on him, saying: O death, where is thy victory and sting?[81] There shall be, then, no more trouble nor sin, nay, rather none evil: but heaven for the good, and hell for the wicked. Then shall wholly be discovered the victory and triumph of Christ: who (after Paul) shall present unto His Father the kingdom, together with His chosen, saved by Him. It was no little favor towards His children, that Christ was chosen of God to save us, His elect, so highly, by the way of the cross. Paul cal-

2 Corinthians 4.

Romans 7.

The title of a Christian.

Romans 8.

Hosea 13.

1 Corinthians 15.

Salvation by the cross.

Romans 4.

79. **His . . . marvelous** an allusion to God's exaltation of Jesus as the supreme agent of His divine purpose in Matthew 21:42 and Mark 12:11. These New Testament verses allude in turn to Psalm 118:23, which reads identically in Coverdale 1535, fol. xxxii v; Taverner 1539, fol. ccix v; and Great Bible 1540, fol. xxiii r: "This was the Lordes doinge, and it is marvelous in our eyes." **marvelous** KP's theme of the marvelous spiritual victory won by Christ for all Christians' benefit will attain equal prominence in another woman's work, Aemilia Lanyer's *Salve Deus Rex Judaeorum* (*Poems of Lanyer*, 121–22).

80. **the true . . . Christ** KP strikes the resonant notes of early English Reformed affectivity. Compare Tyndale in *Parable of the Wicked Mammon*: "God's gift and grace, purchased through Christ . . . reneweth a man, . . . and turneth him altogether into a new nature and conversation; so that a man feeleth his heart altogether altered and changed, and far otherwise disposed than before; and . . . delighteth in that which before he abhorred; and hateth that which before he could not but love. And it setteth the soul at liberty, and maketh her free to follow the will of God" (*Doctrinal Treatises and Introductions*, 53–54). Compare Thomas Bilney on his feeling sense of being redeemed by Christ after reading a verse from St. Paul's first epistle to Timothy (quoted in Mueller, *Native Tongue and the Word*, 185).

81. **O . . . victory** 1 Corinthians 15:55: "Deth where is thy stynge? Hell where is thy victory?" (Taverner 1539, fol. lxx r; Great Bible 1540, fol. lxx v).

leth it a grace, and a most singular grace. [Dii v] We may well think that He, having been to the world so valiant a captain of God, was full of light, grace, virtue, and spirit. Therefore He might justly say: "Consummatum est."[82] We, seeing then that the triumph and victory of our captain Christ is so marvelous, glorious, and noble, to the which war we be appointed: let us force ourselves to follow Him, with bearing of our cross, that we may have fellowship with Him in His kingdom.

John 19.

Romans 8.

The book of the crucifix.

Truly, it may be most justly verified that to behold Christ crucified, in spirit, is the best meditation that can be. I certainly never knew my own miseries and wretchedness so well, by book, admonition, or learning, as I have done by looking into the spiritual book of the crucifix.[83] [Diii r] I lament much I have passed so many years not regarding that divine book, but I judged and thought myself to be well instructed in the same: whereas now I am of this opinion, that if God would suffer me to live here a thousand years, and [I] should study continually in the same divine book, I should not be filled with the contemplation thereof. Neither hold I myself contented, but always have a great desire to learn and study more therein. I never knew my own wickedness, neither lamented for my sins truly, until the time God inspired me with His grace, that I looked in this book. Then I began to see perfectly, that mine own power and strength could not help me, and that I was in the Lord's hand: [Diii v] [even as the clay is in the potter's hand.[84] Then I began to cry, and say: Alas, Lord, that ever I have so wickedly offended Thee, being to me from the beginning so gracious and so good a Father, and most specially, now hast declared and showed Thy goodness unto me when, in the time I have done Thee most injury, to call me, and also to make me know and take Thee for my Saviour and Redeemer. Such be the wonderful works of God, to call sinners to repentance, and to make them to take Christ, His well-beloved Son, for their Saviour. This is the gift of God, and of all Christians to be required and desired. For, except this great benefit of Christ crucified be felt, and fixed surely in man's heart, there can be no good work done, acceptable before God. [Div r] For in Christ is all fullness of the Godhead, and in Him are hid all the treasures of wisdom and knowledge. Even He is the water of life, whereof whosoever shall drink, shall nevermore thirst; but it shall be in him a well of water, springing up into everlasting life. Saint Paul saith there is no damnation to them that are in Christ, which walk not after the flesh, but after the spirit. Moreover, he saith: "If when we were enemies, we were reconciled to God by the death of His Son, much more, seeing we are reconciled, we shall be

A presumptuous truant.

A man is never glut with knowledge.

The first lesson in the book.

Jeremiah 18.

A Christian complaint.

Matthew 9.

Romans 6.

John 15.

Christ is the fullness of the Godhead.

Colossians 2.

John 4.

Romans 8.

Paul's argument.

82. **"Consummatum est"** "It is finished"—Jesus's last words from the cross in the Vulgate text of John 19:30.

83. **the spiritual . . . crucifix** See n61.

84. **I . . . hand** KP personalizes the reference in Jeremiah 18:6: "O ye house of Israel, sayth the Lorde: . . . ye are in my hand, euen as the claye in the Potters hande" (Taverner 1539, fol. xxvii v; Great Bible 1540, fol. lxix v).

preserved by His death."[85] It is no little or small benefit we have received by Christ, if we consider what He hath done for us, as I have perfectly declared heretofore. *Romans 5.*

[Div v] Wherefore I pray the Lord that this great benefit of Christ crucified may be steadfastly fixed and printed in all Christian hearts, that they may be true lovers of God, and work as children, for love, and not as servants, compelled with threatenings or provoked with hire. The sincere and pure lovers of God do embrace Christ with such fervency of spirit, that they rejoice in hope, be bold in danger, suffer in adversity, continue in prayer, bless their persecutors; further, they be not wise in their own opinion, neither high-minded in their prosperity, neither abashed in their adversity, but humble and gentle, always, to all men. For they know by their faith they are members all of one body, and that they have possessed, all, one God, one faith, one baptism, one joy, and one salvation. [Dv r] If these pure and sincere lovers of God were thick sown, there should not be so much contention and strife growing on the fields of our religion, as there is. Well, I shall pray to the Lord to take all contention and strife away, and that the sowers of sedition may have mind to cease their labor, or to sow it amongst the stones; and to have grace to sow gracious virtues, where they may both root and bring forth fruit: with sending also a godly unity and concord amongst all Christians, that we may serve the Lord in true holiness of life. *Christian prayer.* *1 Peter 1.* *True Christians.* *Romans 12.* *1 Corinthians 12.* *Ephesians 4.* *Prayer.* *Luke 1.*

The example of good living is required of all Christians, but especially in the ecclesiastical pastors, and shepherds: for they be called in Scripture, [Dv v] workmen with God, disbursers of God's secrets, the light of the world, the salt of the earth,[86] at whose hands all other should take comfort, in working knowledge of God's will, and sight, to become children of the light, and taste of seasonable wisdom. They have, or should have, the Holy Spirit abundantly, to pronounce and set forth the Word of God, in verity and truth. If ignorance and blindness reign among us, they should, with the truth of God's Word, instruct and set us in the truth, and direct us in the way of the Lord. But thanks be given unto the Lord, that hath now sent us such a godly and learned King,[87] in these latter days, to reign over us: that, with the virtue and force of God's Word, hath taken away the veils and mists of errors, and *The clergy.* *1 Corinthians 3, 4.* *Matthew 5.* *Preaching.* *2 Timothy 4.* *King Henry VIII.* *Moses.*

85. **If . . . death** KP reworks the last clause in this nearly verbatim quotation from Romans 5[:10] in Coverdale 1535, fol. lxviii r. Taverner and the Great Bible read "yf when we were ennemyes, we were reconcyled to God by the dethe of his sonne: moche more seyng we are reconcyled, we shall be preserved by his lyfe" (Taverner 1539, fol. lxii r; Great Bible 1540, fol. lxii r).

86. **workmen . . . earth** KP adduces a succession of Scriptural phrases for God's ministers and prophets. **workmen . . . God** 2 Timothy 2:15. **disbursers . . . secrets** Amos 3:7. **light . . . world** Matthew 5:14. **salt . . . earth** Matthew 5:13.

87. **Lord . . . King** KP's phrasing implies that Henry VIII is living and ruling—hence, that the composition of the *Lamentation*, for which there is otherwise no explicit information, preceded Henry's death on January 28, 1547. For a circumstantial argument that KP's *Lamentation* was composed in the aftermath of the abortive plot by members of the Privy Council to discredit her with Henry in the summer of 1546, see my general introduction, pp. 24–25.

brought us to the knowledge of the truth by the light of God's Word, [Dvi r] which was so long hidden and kept under, that the people were nigh famished and hungered for lack of spiritual food. Such was the charity of the spiritual curates, and shepherds. But our Moses, and most godly, wise governor and King hath delivered us out of the captivity and bondage of Pharaoh.[88] I mean by this Moses, King Henry the eight[h], my most sovereign, favorable lord and husband:[89] one (if Moses had figured any more than Christ), through the excellent grace of God, meet to be another expressed verity of Moses's conquest over Pharaoh. And I mean by this Pharaoh the Bishop of Rome,[90] who hath been and is a greater persecutor of all true Christians than ever was Pharaoh, of the children of Israel. [Dvi v] For he is a persecutor of the Gospel and grace, a setter-forth of all superstition and counterfeit holiness, bringing many souls to hell with his alchemy and counterfeit money, deceiving the poor souls under the pretense of holiness; but so much the greater shall be his damnation, because he deceiveth and robbeth under Christ's mantle. The Lord keep and defend all men from his jugglings and sleights, but specially the poor, simple, unlearned souls. And this lesson I would all men had of him, that when they begin to mislike his doing, then only begin they to like God, and certainly not before. As for the spiritual pastors, and shepherds, I think they will cleave and stick fast to the Word of God, even to the death, to vanquish all God's enemies. [Dvii r] If need shall require, all respects of honor, dignity, riches, wealth, and their private commodities laid apart, following also the examples of Christ and

Judge Christianly.

Bishop of Rome. Pharaoh.

A godly wish.

A sure lesson.

Good preachers.

88. **Moses . . . Pharaoh** Moses's leading of the Israelites out of bondage in Egypt under Pharaoh is narrated in Exodus 3–15. **Judge Christianly** The marginal rubric admonishes the reader not to take offense at an analogy between Moses and Henry VIII—an analogy usually drawn between Moses and Christ, as KP goes on to note parenthetically. Who inserted the rubric? KP herself? Cecil? the compositor?

89. **I . . . husband** This is KP's sole self-identifying reference and her only allusion to her gender in this text. Although the "Judge Christianly" rubric seems to imply some sense of indecorum in this wifely public tribute, elsewhere in this period excess goes uncurbed when a monarch is the subject of praise. See, for example, Cranmer in the third part of the homily "Of Good Works": "Honour be to God, who did put light in the heart of His faithful and true minister of most famous memory, King Henry the eighth, and gave him the knowledge of His Word, an an earnest affection to seek His glory, and to put away all such superstitious and pharsaical sects, by Antichrist invented, and set up against the true Word of God, and glory of His most blessed name" (*Certain Sermons and Homilies*, 52). For fulsome tributes to King Henry and Queen Katherine elsewhere in the present volume, see Goldsmith's and Udall's several letters in part 3, nos. 1, 10 and part 4, no. 15 of the correspondence. **sovereign** The reading from 1548 onward; the 1547 edition has the misprint "soraigne."

90. **the Bishop . . . Rome** The obligatory form of reference to the pope after 1533 in England. At Hampton Court there was a grisaille painting called *The Four Evangelists Stoning the Pope*, executed for Henry VIII by Girolamo da Treviso the Younger. The painting hung outside the king's bedchamber in his long gallery, through which he normally passed twice daily. As queen, KP would also have seen this painting often.

His chosen apostles, in preaching and teaching sincere, pure, and wholesome doctrine, and such things as make for peace, with godly lessons, wherewith they may edify others: that every man may walk after his vocation, in holiness of life, in unity and concord, which unity is to be desired of all true Christians.

1 Timothy 2.

It is much to be lamented: the schisms, varieties, contentions, and disputations that have been, and are, in the world about Christian religion; and no agreement nor concord of the same, amongst the learned men. [Dvii v] Truly, the devil hath been the sower of sedition,[91] and shall be the maintainer of it, even till God's will be fulfilled. There is no war so cruel and evil as this: for the war with the sword killeth but the bodies, and this slayeth many souls. For the poor, unlearned persons remain confused, and almost everyone believeth and worketh after his own way. And yet there is but one truth of God's Word, by the which we shall be saved. Happy be they that receive it; and most unhappy are they which neglect and persecute the same. For it shall be more easy for Sodom and Gomorrah at the day of judgment, than for them.[93] And not without just cause, if we consider the benevolence, goodness, and mercy of God: who hath declared His charity towards us, greater and more estimable, than ever He did to the Hebrews. [Dviii r] For they lived under shadows and figures, and were bound to the law. And Christ (we being His greatest

Contentions in religion.
The devil.
War in religion.[92]
2 Corinthians 3.
One truth.
Psalm 1.
Persecutors of the Word.
Matthew 10.
Hebrews 10.
Galatians 4.[94]

91. **the devil . . . sedition** KP's metaphor predates Hugh Latimer's notable near-analogue by at least a year: "There is one that passeth all the other and is the most diligent prelate and preacher in all England. And will ye know who it is? I will tell you; it is the devil. . . . Oh, that our prelates would be as diligent to sow the corn of good doctrine as Satan is to sow cockle and darnel! . . . Who is able to tell his diligent preaching, which every day and every hour laboreth to sow cockle and darnel, that he may bring out of form and out of estimation and room the institution of the Lord's Supper and Christ's cross?" ("Sermon on the Plowers," in *Selected Sermons of Hugh Latimer*, ed. Chester, 41, 42–43).

92. **War . . . religion** Although England and Europe would see considerable warfare after 1547, by this date there had been bloody clashes in Germany, notably the Peasants' Revolt of 1525–26, in which Anabaptists sought to institute community of property by force of arms; this uprising turned Luther into a political conservative. Also significant was the Anabaptist uprising led by Thomas Münster in 1535. Recent examination by ultraviolet rays has revealed that a painting at Hampton Court, dated circa 1565–67, is largely an overpainting. Underneath is Pieter Breughel the Elder's *The Slaughter of the Innocents*, a Scriptural subject (Matthew 2:1–18) that was often read in this period as an allegory of religious warfare. KP may have known this painting in its original state. For discussion of Erasmus's antipathy to religious war, which is likely to have influenced KP's outlook, see Robert P. Adams, *The Better Part of Valor: More, Erasmus, Colet, and Vives, on Humanism, War, and Peace, 1496–1535* (Seattle: University of Washington Press, 1962), 96–111.

93. **it . . . them** a near verbatim quotation of Jesus's words in Mark 6:12 in the wording of the Great Bible: "it shalbe easier for Zodom and Gomor in the daye of judgement than for that cytye." **Sodom . . . Gomorrah** The eventual destruction of the two cities of Sodom and Gomorrah, despite Abraham's attempts to save them from God's wrath upon their evildoing, is narrated in Genesis 18:20–19:25.

94. **Galatians 4.** The reading after 1548; the 1547 edition reads "Ga. liiii."

Matthew 11. enemies) hath delivered us from the bondage of the law, and hath fulfilled all that was figured in their law, and also in their prophecies: shedding His own precious
2 Corinthians 3. blood to make us the children of His Father, and His brethren; and hath made us
Christian liberty. free, setting us in a godly liberty. I mean not license to sin, as many be glad to interpret the same, when Christian liberty is godly entreated of. Truly, it is no good spirit, that moveth men to find fault at everything; [Dviii v] and when things may be well taken, to pervert them into an evil sense and meaning. There be, in the
Holy works. Few know the holiness. world, many speakers of holiness and good works; but very rare and seldom is declared, which be the good and holy works. The works of the Spirit be never, almost, spoken of. And therefore very few know what they be. I am truly able to justify the ignorance of the people to be great: not in this matter alone, but in many other which were most necessary for Christians to know. Because I have had just proof of the same, it maketh me thus much to say, with no little sorrow and grief in my
Matthew 12. heart, for such a miserable ignorance and blindness amongst the people. I doubt
Matthew 15. not, but we can say, all: Lord, Lord. [Ei v] But I fear God may say unto us: "This people honoreth me with their lips, but their hearts be far from me."[95] God desireth
John 4. nothing but the heart, and saith He will be worshipped in spirit and truth.[96] Christ condemned all hypocrisy and feigned holiness, and taught sincere, pure, and true
Traditions of men. godliness. But we, worse than frantic or blind, will not follow Christ's doctrine, but
Matthew 15. trust to men's doctrines, judgments, and sayings, which dimmeth our eyes: and so the blind leadeth the blind, and both fall into the ditch.

The Word of God the only sure doctrine. Truly, in my simple and unlearned judgment, no man's doctrine is to be esteemed, or is preferred like unto Christ's and the Apostles', nor to be taught as a perfect and true doctrine, [Ei v] but even as it doth accord and agree with the
The cause of the estimation of traditions. doctrine of the Gospel. But yet those that be called spiritual pastors, although they be most carnal, as it doth very evidently and plainly appear by their fruits, are so blinded with the love of themselves and the world, that they extol men's inventions and doctrines, before the doctrine of the Gospel. And when they be not able to maintain their own inventions and doctrine with any jot of the Scripture, then they most cruelly persecute them that be contrary to the same. Be such, the lovers of Christ? Nay, nay: they be the lovers of the wicked Mammon,[97] neither regarding

95. **"This . . . me"** a nearly verbatim quotation from Matthew 15:8 in Coverdale 1535, fol. viii r, and Taverner 1539, fol. vii r. Additional variants distinguish the reading of the Great Bible 1540, fol. viii r.

96. **He . . . truth** KP's wording is closest to Taverner's in John 4:24: "God is a sprete and they that worshyp him, must worshyppe hym in sprete and trouthe" (Taverner 1539, fol. xxxiv v). The Great Bible's "and in the treuth" (fol. xxxviii r) sets its reading at a further remove.

97. **the lovers . . . Mammon** The connotations of KP's phrase resemble Tyndale's in *Parable of the Wicked Mammon*. Tyndale's and KP's wicked Mammonists disparage Bible reading, trust to their good works to earn their way to heaven, and fail to experience the faith that justifies. However, the identification of the Mammonists with ranking Catholic clerics is all but explicit in Tyndale, at most inferential in KP. Her comparative authorial restraint may be a mark of her gender.

God nor His honor. For filthy lucre hath made them almost mad; but frantic they be, doubtless. [Eii r] Is not this miserable state of spiritual men in the world, much to be lamented of all good Christians?

But yet I cannot allow, neither praise, all kind of lamentation, but such as may stand with Christian charity. Charity suffereth long, and is gentle; envieth not, upbraideth no man, casteth frowardly no faults in men's teeth, but referreth all things to God: being angry without sin, reforming others without their slanders, carrying ever a storehouse of mild words to pierce the stonyhearted men. I would all Christians, that like as they have professed Christ, would so endeavor themselves to follow Him in godly living. For we have not put on Christ to live any more to ourselves, in the vanities, delights, and pleasures of the world and the flesh, [Eii v] suffering the concupiscence and carnality of the flesh to have his full swing. For we must walk after the spirit, and not after the flesh. For the spirit is spiritual, and coveteth spiritual things, and the flesh carnal, and desireth carnal things. The men regenerate by Christ despise the world, and all the vanities and pleasures thereof. They be no lovers of themselves, for they feel how evil and infirm they be, not being able to do any good thing without the help of God, from whom they knowledge all goodness to proceed. [Eiii r] They flatter not themselves, with thinking everything which shineth to the world to be so good and holy, for they know all extern and outworks,[99] be they never so glorious and fair to the world, may be done of the evil as well as of the good. And therefore they have in very little estimation the outward show of holiness, because they be all spiritual, casting up their eyes upon heavenly things, neither looking nor regarding the earthly things, for they be to them vile and abject. They have also the simplicity of the dove, and the policy of the serpent:[100] for, by simplicity, they have a desire to do good to all men and to hurt no man, no, though they have occasion given. And by policy, they give not, nor minister, any just cause to any man, whereby their doctrine might be reproved. They be not also as a reed shaken with every wind,[101] [Eiii v] when they be blasted with tempests and storms of the world, then remain they most firm,

1 Corinthians 13.
Charity.
Ephesians 4.
A godly wish.
Ephesians 4.
Galatians 5.
Romans 8.
Christian[98] *men.*
Self-love.
James 1.
World's love.
Simple wisdom in men.
Matthew 10.
Christian constantness.

98. **Christian** The reading from 1548 onward; the 1547 edition reads "Christened."

99. **extern . . . outworks** One of KP's characteristic doublings. **extern** a variant form of "external." **outworks** works performed out of doors or outwardly.

100. **They have . . . serpent** an allusion to Jesus's figurative language in Matthew 10:16. KP's elaboration of the figure suggests familiarity with Tyndale's preface to the reader in *The Obedience of a Christian Man* (1528): "Let us . . . look diligently whereunto we are called. . . . 'Be harmless as doves,' saith Christ, 'and wise as serpents.' The doves imagine no defence, nor seek to avenge themselves. The serpent's wisdom is, to keep his head, and those parts wherein his life resteth. Christ is our Head; and God's Word is that wherein our life resteth. To cleave, therefore, fast unto Christ, and unto those promises which God hath made us for His sake, is our wisdom" (*Doctrinal Treatises and Introductions*, 137).

101. **a reed . . . wind** an allusion to Jesus's sardonic questions in Matthew 11:7, put to the curious crowds who followed John the Baptist: "What went ye out into the wilderness to see? A reed that is shaken with the wind?"

Matthew 11. *2 Corinthians 4.* *1 Peter 2.*

stable, and quiet, feeling in spirit that God, as their best Father, doth send and suffer all things for their benefit and commodity. Christ is to them a rule, a line, an example of Christian life. They be never offended at anything, although occasion be ministered unto them.

The works of God offend not the Christian.

For like as Christ, when Peter would have withdrawn Him from death, answered, and said, "Go back from me, Satan, for thou offendest me":[102] that is, As much as lieth in thee, thou givest me occasion with thy words to make me withdraw myself from death, although I yielded not thereto. For this thy procurement cannot extingish the burning desire I have to shed My blood for My chosen. [Eiv r] Even so, the perfect men are never offended at anything. For although the world were full of sin, they would not withdraw themselves from doing of good, nor wax cold in the love of the Lord. And much less they would be moved to be evil; yea, the rather they be so much the more moved to do good. The regenerated by Christ are never offended at the works of God, because they know by faith that God doeth all things well, and that He cannot err, neither for want of power, nor by ignorance, nor malice. For they know Him to be almighty, and that He seeth all things, and is most abundantly good. [Eiv v] They see and feel in spirit that, of that will most highly perfect, cannot but proceed most perfect works. Likewise they be not offended at the works of men: for, if they be good, they are moved by them to take occasion to follow them, and to reknowledge the goodness of God, with giving of thanks and praising His name, daily the more. But if they be indifferent, and such as may be done with good and evil intents, they judge the best part, thinking they may be done to a good purpose, and so they be edified. But if they be so evil that they cannot be taken in good part by any means, yet they be not offended although occasion be given. Nay, rather they be edified, inasmuch as they take occasion to be better, although the contrary be ministered unto them. [Ev r] Then begin they to think and say thus: If God had not preserved me with His grace, I should have committed this sin, and worse. O how much am I bound to confess and knowledge the goodness of God! They go also thinking and saying further: He that hath sinned may be one of God's elect; peradventure the Lord hath suffered him to fall, to the intent he may the better know himself. I know he is one of them that Christ hath shed His blood for, and one of my Christian brethren. Truly I will admonish and rebuke him; and in case I find him desperate, I will comfort him and show him the great goodness and mercy of God, in Christ; and with godly consolations I will see if I can lift him up. [Ev v] And thus ye may see how the men regenerated by Christ, of everything win and receive fruits.

Hebrews 4. *The works of men offend not the Christian.* *Matthew 7.* *Ephesians 5.* *The Christian profiteth by sin.* *Psalm 145.*[103]

Weaklings mislike all things.

And, contrary, the younglings[104] and unperfect are offended at small trifles, tak-

102. **"Go . . . me"** an allusion to Jesus's reproach to Peter in Matthew 16:23.

103. **Psalm 145** The correct reference, from 1548 onward; the 1547 edition reads "Ps. cxiv."

104. **younglings** inexperienced or ignorant persons. Udall refers to "younglings" in his letter to KP prefacing the Paraphrase of Acts; see part 4, no. 16, in the correspondence.

ing everything in evil part, grudging and murmuring against their neighbor; and, so much the more, as they show themselves fervent in their so doing, they are judged of the blind world, and of themselves, great zeal-bearers to God. If this were the greatest evil of these younglings, it were not the most evil. But I fear they be so blind and ignorant that they are offended also at good things, and judge nothing good but such as they embrace and esteem to be good, with murmuring against all such as follow not their ways. [Evi r] If there be any of this sort, the Lord give them the light of His truth, that they may increase and grow in godly strength. I suppose if such younglings and unperfect had seen Christ and His disciples eat meat with unwashed hands, or not to have fasted with the Pharisees, they would have been offended, seeing Him a breaker of men's traditions. Their affections dispose their eyes to see through other men, and they see nothing in themselves: where charity (although it be most fullest[105] of eyes to see the faults of others, whom it coveteth to amend) thinketh none evil, but discreetly and rightly interpreteth all things, by the which, more justly and truly, everything is taken. Now these superstitious weaklings, if they had been conversant with Christ, and seen Him lead His life, [Evi v] sometime with women, sometime with Samaritans, with publicans, sinners, and with the Pharisees, they would have murmured at Him. Also, if they had seen Mary pour upon Christ the precious ointment, they would have said with Judas: "This ointment might have been sold, and given to the poor."[106] If they also had seen Christ with whips drive out of the Temple those that bought and sold, they would forthwith have judged Christ to have been troubled and moved with anger, and not by zeal of charity. How would they have been offended, if they had seen Him, going[107] to the Jews' feast, heal a sick man upon the Sabbath day, practice with the woman of Samaria, yea, and show her of His most divine doctrine and life? [Evii r] They would have taken occasion to have hated and persecuted Him, as the scribes and Pharisees did. And, even so, should Christ, the Saviour of the world, have been to them an offense and ruin.

Acts 13.
Godly.
Matthew 15.
Matthew 9.
1 Corinthians 13.
Matthew 26.
John 7.
Matthew 12.
John 4.
Romans 9.

There be another kind of little ones unperfect, which are offended after this sort and manner: as when they see one that is reputed and esteemed holy, to commit sin, forthwith they learn to do that, and worse, and wax cold in doing of good, and confirm themselves in evil. And then they excuse their wicked life, publishing the same, with the slander of their neighbor. If any man reprove them, they say: Such a man did this, and worse. So, it is evident that such persons would deny Christ, if they saw other men do the same. [Evii v] If they went to Rome and saw

A second sort of weaklings.

105. **most fullest** Subsequent editions read "most full."

106. **"This . . . poor"** a nearly verbatim quotation from Matthew 26[:9], which reads identically in Coverdale 1535, fol. xiii v; Taverner 1539, fol. xi v, and Great Bible 1540, fol. xiii r: "This oyntment myght haue bene well solde, and geuen to the poore."

107. **going** Subsequent editions read "go."

the enormities of the prelates, which is said to reign there among them,[108] I doubt not if they saw one of them sin, which were reputed and taken for holy, their faith should be lost: but not the faith of Christ, which they never possessed. But they should lose that human opinion which they had of the goodness of prelates. For if they had the faith of Christ, the Holy Ghost should be a witness unto them, which should be mighty in them: that in case all the world would deny Christ, they would remain firm and stable in the true faith. The Pharisees also took occasion of the evil of others to wax haughty and proud, [Eviii r] taking themselves to be men of greater perfection than any other because of their virtue, even as the Pharisee did when he saw the publican's submission. And so they be offended with every little thing, judging evil, murmuring against their neighbor; and, for the same, they are of many reputed and taken for the more holy and good, whereas, indeed, they be the more wicked. The most wicked persons are offended even at themselves; for, at their little stability in goodness, and of their detestable and evil life, they take occasion to despair.[109] Where they ought the more to commit themselves to God, asking mercy for their offenses, and forthwith to give thanks, that it hath pleased Him of His goodness to suffer them so long a time. [Eviii v] But, what needeth it any more to say? The evil men are offended even at the works of God. They see God suffer sinners. Therefore, think they, sin displeaseth Him not. And because they see not the good rewarded with riches, oftentimes they imagine that God loveth them not. It seemeth to them[110] God is partial, because He hath elected some, and some reproved. And therefore they say, That the elected be sure of salvation: taking by that, occasion to do evil enough, saying, Whatsoever God hath determined, shall be performed.[111] If also they see the good men oppressed, and the evil men exalted, they judge God unjust, taking occasion to live evilly, saying: Inasmuch as God favoreth

Ephesians 1.

Pharisees.

Luke 17.

Wicked men mislike good things.

Psalm 27.

Offense of God's election.

Romans 9.

Romans 11.

Psalm 27.

Romans 3.

108. **If . . . them** Roger Ascham's tirade against the immorality practiced and countenanced by clerics at Rome was published posthumously in his *The Schoolmaster (1570)*, ed. Lawrence V. Ryan (Charlottesville: University of Virginia Press for Folger Shakespeare Library, 1967), 72–73. KP's and Ascham's censures are, however, close in date, KP's being the earlier of the two. Ascham's eyewitness experience in Rome occurred in the early 1550s, when he was in the service of Sir Richard Morison, the English ambassador to the Hapsburg court. Again, KP's authorial restraint contrasts with Ascham's rhetorical excess and may be a mark of her gender and high status. **among** The reading from 1548 onward; the 1547 edition reads "emonges."

109. **The most . . . despair** The psychological acuteness of KP's remark is one sign of how attention in earlier religious writing to having and recognizing complex feelings contributed to literary developments later in the century. Doctor Faustus experiences such self-revulsion as his tragedy of damnation deepens. See especially his exchange with the old man in 5.1.36–65 and his tortured final soliloquy in 5.2.61–116 of the "A-Text" (1604) in Christopher Marlowe, *Doctor Faustus*, ed. David Scott Kastan (New York: W. W. Norton, 2005), 47–48, 52–53.

110. **them** The reading from 1548 onward; the 1547 edition reads "then."

111. **God . . . performed God** The reading from 1548 onward; the 1547 edition reads "good." **It seemeth . . . performed** KP links what would shortly become the even more problematic doctrine of double predestination—to salvation, to damnation—with the antinomian ratio-

the naughty men, let us do evil enough, to the intent He do us good. [Fi r] If, then, the wicked be offended even at God, it is no wonder if they be offended at those that follow and walk in His paths and ways.

Now I will speak, with great dolor and heaviness in my heart, of a sort of people which be in the world, that be called "professors of the Gospel,"[112] and by their words do declare and show, they be much affected to the same. But, I am afraid, some of them do build upon the sand, as Simon Magus did, making a weak foundation.[113] I mean, they make not Christ their chiefest foundation, professing His doctrine of a sincere, pure, and zealous mind. But either for because they would be called "gospellers" to procure some credit and good opinions of the true and very savorers of Christ's doctrine, [Fi v] either to find out some carnal liberty, either to be contentious disputers, finders, or rebukers of other men's faults, or else, finally, to please and flatter the world: such gospellers are an offense and a slander to the Word of God, and make the wicked to rejoice and laugh at them, saying: Behold, I pray you, their fair fruits. What charity, what discretion, what godliness, holiness, or purity of life is amongst them? Be they not great avengers, foul gluttons, slanderers, backbiters, adulterers,[114] fornicators, swearers, and blasphemers? Yea, and wallow and tumble in all sins; these be the fruits of their doctrine. [Fii r] And thus it may be seen how the Word of God is evil spoken of, through licentious and evil living.[115] And yet the Word of God is all holy, pure, sincere, and godly, being the

Vain gospellers.

Acts 13.

Galatians 5.

Romans 2.

Evil living slandereth the best profession.

Psalm 12.

nales offered by German Anabaptists for their lawlessness. This linkage, rather than a Calvinist emphasis on the assurance to be derived from double predestination, attests the comparatively early date of the *Lamentation* as a Reformation text. In a longer historical timeline, it is well worth noting that Augustine and Thomas Aquinas had articulated double predestination as a fundamental Biblical (Pauline) doctrine. See Augustine *De spiritu et littera* (On the Spirit and the Letter) 412; Aquinas *Summa Theologica* 1a.23.5.

112. **"professors of the Gospel"** KP's critique closely anticipates Latimer's in his "Sermon on the Plowers" (1548), itself with prototypes in late medieval preaching: "I fear me some be rather mock gospellers than faithful plowmen. I know many myself that profess the Gospel and live nothing thereafter. . . . I know them, and—I speak it with an heavy heart—there is as little charity and good living in them as in any other, according to that which Christ said in the Gospel to the great number of people that followed Him" (*Selected Sermons*, 37).

113. **build . . . foundation** an allusion to Jesus's parable in Matthew 7:24–27 of the respective fortunes of the wise man who built his house on a rock and the foolish man who built his house on sand. **Simon Magus** The story of this Samaritan sorcerer is narrated in Acts 8:9–24. When Simon perceives the miraculous power of the apostles Peter and Philip to be far superior to his own, he offers to pay money for "this power, that on whomsoever I lay hands, he may receive the Holy Ghost" (v. 19). Peter sternly admonishes Simon to repent for thinking that he could purchase the gift of God. Simon in return asks Peter to pray for him, that no evil befall him.

114. **adulterers** The reading from 1563 onward; the 1547 and 1548 editions have the earlier form "advouterers."

115. **And thus . . . living** KP's concern that those who profess Scripture live in accordance with it tallies with Anne Askew's sturdy self-assertion during interrogation by the Bishop of

doctrine and occasion of all holy and pure living. It is the wicked that perverteth all good things into evil, for an evil tree cannot bring forth good fruit.[116] And when good seed is sown in a barren and evil ground, it yieldeth no good corn, and so it fareth by the Word of God. For when it is heard and known of of wicked men, it bringeth forth no good fruit; but when it is sown in good ground, I mean the hearts of good people, it bringeth forth good ruit abundantly: so that the want and fault is in men, and not in the Word of God. [Fii v] I pray God all men and women may have grace to become meet tillage for the fruits of the Gospel, and to leave only the jangling[117] of it. For only speaking of the Gospel maketh not men good Christians, but good talkers, except their facts and works agree with the same. So, then, their speech is good, because their hearts be good.

A similitude. *Matthew 13.* *Application.* *Prayer.* *John 1.* *Matthew 12.*

And even as much talk of the Word of God, without practicing the same in our living, is evil and detestable in the sight of God, so it is a lamentable thing to hear how there be many in the world that do not well digest the reading of Scripture, and do commend and praise ignorance, and say that much knowledge of God's Word is the original of all dissension, schisms, and contention, [Fiii r] and maketh men haughty, proud, and presumptuous by reading of the same.[118] This manner of saying is no less than a plain blasphemy against the Holy Ghost. For the Spirit of God is the author of His Word, and so the Holy Ghost is made the author of evil: which is a most great blasphemy and, as the Scripture saith, a sin that shall not be forgiven in this world, neither in the other to come.[119] It were all our parts and duties, to procure and seek all the ways and means possible, to have more knowledge of God's Word[120] set forth abroad in this world. And not allow ignorance, and discommend knowledge of God's Word, stopping the mouths of the unlearned with subtle and crafty persuasions of philosophy and sophistry, [Fiii v] whereof

Psalm 50. *Reading of the Scripture.* *The Word of God.* *John 16.* *Matthew 12.* *Knowledge wished against ignorance.*

London in 1545: "Then sayd my lorde, There are manye that reade and knowe the scripture, and yet do not folow it, nor live thereafter. I sayd agayne, My lorde, I wolde wyshe, that all men knew my conversacyon and lyvynge in all poyntes, for I am so sure of my selfe thys houre, that there are non able to prove anye dyshonestie by me. If yow knowe anye that can do it, I praye yow brynge them fourth" (Askew, *Examinations*, 57–58).

116. **evil tree . . . good fruit** KP's image from Jesus's parable is prominent in Tyndale's *Parable of the Wicked Mammon* (*Doctrinal Treatises and Introductions*, 50) and in the Third Part of Cranmer's "Sermon of Faith" (*Certain Sermons or Homilies*, 39–40).

117. **jangling** noisy altercation, wrangling.

118. **much . . . same** For a critique of vernacular Bible reading in England from the 1520s to the 1540s, alleging its pernicious effects on readers' minds and conduct, see James Simpson, *Burning to Read: English Fundamentalism and Its Reformation Opponents* (Cambridge, MA: Belknap Press of Harvard University Press, 2007), 47–48, 52–58.

119. **not . . . come** a nearly verbatim quotation from Matthew 12[:32] in Coverdale 1535, fol. vii r; Taverner 1539, fol. vi r; and Great Bible 1540, fol. vi v, which reads "whosoeuer speaketh agaynst the holy gost, it shall not be forgeuen him, nether in this worlde, nether in the worlde to come."

120. **Word** The reading from 1548 onward; the 1547 edition reads "wordes."

cometh no fruit, but a great perturbation of the mind to the simple and ignorant, not knowing which way to turn them. For, how is it not extreme wickedness to charge the holy, sanctified Word of God with the offenses of men, to allege the Scriptures to be perilous learning because certain readers thereof fall into heresies? These men might be forced, by this kind of argument, to forsake the use of fire because fire burned their neighbor's house, or to abstain from meat or drink because they see many surfeit. O blind hate! They slander God for man's offense, and excuse the man whom they see offend, and blame the Scripture, which they cannot improve. [Fiv r] Yea, I have heard of some that have very well understand the Latin tongue that, when they have heard learned men persuade to the credit and belief of certain "unwritten verities,"[121] as they call them, which be not in Scripture expressed, and yet taught as doctrine apostolic and necessary to be believed, they have been of this opinion: That the learned men have more "epistles" written by the apostles[122] of Christ than we have abroad in the canon of the Old and New Testament, or known of any, but only to them of the clergy. Which belief I did not a little lament in my heart, to hear that any creature should have such a blind, ignorant opinion. [Fiv v] Some kind of simplicity is to be praised, but this simplicity without the verity, I can neither praise nor allow. And thus it may be seen how we that be unlettered remain confused, without God, of His grace, lighten our hearts[123] with a heavenly light and knowledge of His will, for we be given, of ourselves, to believe men better than God. I pray God send all learned men the Spirit of God abundantly, that their doctrine may bring forth the fruits thereof.

Like reason, like conclusion.

Good Latinists and evil divines.

Forged writings.

The unlearned be taught by grace.

I suppose there was never more need of good doctrine to be set forth in the world than now, in this age: for the carnal children of Adam be so wise in their generation that, if it were possible, they would deceive the children of light.[124] [Fv r] The

This age requireth learning.

Worldly children.

121. **"unwritten verities"** KP articulates a fundamental opposition that ranged Catholics against Reformers. Catholics, who held the authority of the church paramount, maintained that Jesus had orally transmitted to his apostles certain "unwritten verities" that laid the basis for papal supremacy and continuous apostolic succession of a hierarchy of bishops, cardinals, etc. Reformers, who held the authority of the Bible paramount, maintained that the church received what authority it possessed through the recorded New Testament testimony to its earliest workings, in the Acts of the Apostles, and in St. Paul's and St. Peter's epistles. Tyndale and More led off in contending over "unwritten verities" in their polemical exchanges of 1532–33, but the issue remained divisive long afterward. Cranmer wrote his *A Confutation of Unwritten Verities* circa 1547; see *Miscellaneous Writings and Letters of Thomas Cranmer*, ed. John Edmund Cox, Parker Society 16 (Cambridge: Cambridge University Press, 1846, 1–67). For discussion, see Georges H. Tavard, *Holy Writ or Holy Church: The Crisis of the Protestant Reformation* (London: Burns and Oates, 1959), and Marshall, *Religious Identities in Henry VIII's England*, 81–99.

122. **apostles** The reading from 1548 onward; the 1547 edition has the misprint "appostes."

123. **without . . . hearts** **without** except. **hearts** The 1548 edition reads "hartes and mindes."

124. **the carnal . . . light** KP alludes to Hugh Latimer's two-part convocation sermon of 1536 on a portion of Luke 16:8: "The children of darkness are wiser in their generation than

Matthew 24. world loveth his own, and therefore their facts and doings be highly esteemed of *John 17.* the world. But the children of God are hated because they be not of the world. For *God's children.* their habitation is in heaven, and they do despise the world as a most vile slave. *2 Corinthians 5.* The fleshly children of Adam be so politic, subtle, crafty, and wise in their kind that the elect should be illuded,[125] if it were possible. For they are clothed with Christ's garment in utter appearance, with a fair show of all godliness and holiness in their words. But they have so shorn, nopped,[126] and turned Christ's garment and so disguised themselves, that the children of light, beholding them with a spiritual eye, *Like garment, like man.* account and take[127] them for men which have sold their Master's garment, and have stolen a piece of every man's garment. [Fv v] Yet, by their subtle art and crafty *Crafty tailors.* wits, they have so set those patches and pieces together that they do make the blind *God's children be wise.* world and carnal men to believe it is Christ's very mantle. But the children of light know the contrary. For they are led by the Spirit of God to the knowledge of the truth; and therefore they discern and judge all things right, and know from whence *Bishop of Rome.*[128] they come: even from the bishop of Rome and his members, the head-spring[129] of all pride, vainglory, ambition, hypocrisy, and feigned holiness.

The children of God be not abashed, although the world hate them. [Fvi r] They believe they are in the grace and favor of God,[130] and that He, as a best Father, doth govern them in all things, putting away from them all vain confidence, and trust in *Romans 7.* their own doings. For they know they can do nothing but sin, of themselves. They

---

the children of light." See *Sermons by Hugh Latimer*, ed. George E. Corrie, Parker Society 27 (Cambridge: Cambridge University Press, 1844), 33–59, and the discussion in Mueller, "A Tudor Queen Finds Voice," 39–40.

125. **illuded** a variant of "deluded."

126. **nopped** a variant of "napped" or "knapped"—referring to a process for trimming cloth by shearing its nap.

127. **take** The reading from 1548 onward; the 1547 edition reads "toke."

128. **Bishop . . . Rome** See n108 above.

129. **head-spring** chief source, origin.

130. **the grace . . . God** KP activates a crucial distinction in the religious vocabulary of the period. For Catholics "grace" meant the infusion of divine power that enabled humans to overcome the damages inflicted by sin on their reason and will. For Reformers "grace" meant the unmerited favor of an all-good God toward all-sinful humans, thereby drawing the key term "grace"—like the key term "the promises"—into near synonymity with "justification by faith." Thus Tyndale defends his decision regarding the translation of "charis" in New Testament Greek: "With like reasons rageth he [Thomas More], because I turn *charis* into *favor*, and not into *grace*: saying that 'every favour is not grace, and that in some favor there is but little grace.' I can say also, 'in some grace there is little goodness'; and when we say 'he standeth well in my lady's grace,' we understand no great godly favor .. . . In which all he [More] cannot prove that I give not the right English unto the Greek word. . . . They [the Catholics] have lost their juggling terms. For the doctors and preachers were wont to make many divisions, distinctions, and sorts of grace: *gratis data, gratum faciens, praeveniens*, and *subsequens*" [grace freely given, making acceptable, going before, and following thereafter] (Tyndale, *Answer to Sir Thomas More's Dialogue*, 22).

be not so foolish and childish, not to give God thanks for their election, which was before the beginning of the world. For they believe most surely, they be of the chosen: for the Holy Ghost doth witness to their spirit that they be the children of God, and therefore they believe God better than man. They say with Saint Paul: "Who shall separate us from the love of God? Shall tribulation, anguish, persecution, hunger, nakedness, peril, or sword? As it is written: For Thy sake are we killed all day long, and are counted as sheep appointed to be slain. [Fvi v] Nevertheless, in all these things, we overcome through Him that loveth us. For I am sure that neither death, neither life, neither angels, nor rule, neither power, neither things present, neither things to come, neither quantity or quality, neither any creature, shall be able to depart us from the love of God, which is in Christ Jesu our Lord."[131] They are not by this godly faith presumptuously inflamed, nor by the same become they loose,[132] idle, or slow in doing of godly works, as carnal men dream of them: so much the more fervent they be in doing most holy and pure works, which God hath commanded them to walk in. [Fvii r] They wander not in men's traditions and inventions, leaving the most holy and pure precepts of God undone, which they know they be bound to observe and keep. Also they work not like hirelings for meed, wages, or reward, but as loving children, without respect of lucre, gain, or hire. They be in such liberty of spirit, and joy so much in God, that their inward consolation cannot be expressed with tongue. All fear of damnation is gone from them, for they have put their whole hope of salvation in His hands, that will and can perform it. Neither have they any post or pillar to lean to, but God and His smooth and unwrinkled Church.[133] For He is to them All in all things, and to Him they lean, as a most sure, square pillar, in prosperity and adversity, [Fvii v] nothing doubting of His promises and covenants, for they believe most surely they shall be fulfilled. Also the children of God be not curious in searching the high mysteries of God, which be not meet for them to know. Neither do go about with human and carnal reasons to interpret Scripture, persuading men, by their subtle wits and carnal doctrine, that much knowledge of Scripture maketh men heretics, without they temper it with human doctrine, philosophy, and logic: wherewith to be seduced according to the traditions of men, after the ordinances of the world, and not after Christ.[134] Saint Paul doth most diligently admonish us, which arts are not convenient and meet to be made checkmate[135] with Scripture: [Fviii r] for the Scriptures

Ephesians 1.
Sure faith.
Romans 8.

Of godly faith no evil cometh.

Matthew 15.
1 Peter 1.

God's secrets.
Ecclesiastes 3.

Colossians 2.
1 Timothy 6.
Prerogative of the Scripture.

131. **"Who . . . Lord"** a nearly verbatim quotation of Romans 8:35–39, which reads identically in Coverdale 1535, fol. lxix v; Taverner 1539, fol. lxiii v; and Great Bible 1540, fol. lxiii r.

132. **loose** free of obligation or attachment.

133. **smooth . . . Church** an allusion to Ephesians 5:27.

134. **the traditions . . . Christ** a nearly verbatim quotation from Colossians 2:8 in Coverdale 1535, fol. lxxxviii r, and Great Bible 1540, fol. lxxx r. Several variants further distinguish the reading in Taverner 1539, fol. lxxix r.

135. **checkmate** equal in a contest, rival.

A similitude. Application. be so pure and holy that no perfection can be added unto them. For even as fine gold doth excel all other metals, so doth the Word of God, all men's doctrines.

I beseech the Lord to send the learned and unlearned such abundance of His Holy Spirit, that they may obey and observe the most sincere and holy Word of God. And show the fruits thereof, which consisteth chiefly in charity and godly unity: that, as we have professed one God, one faith, and one baptism,[136] so we may be all of one mind and one accord, putting away all biting and gnawing; for, in backbiting, slandering, and misreporting our Christian brethren, we show not *Christ is our example.* ourselves the disciples of Christ, whom we profess. [Fviii v] In Him was most high charity, humility, and patience, suffering most patiently all ignominy, rebukes, and *Prayer.* slanders, praying to His eternal Father for His enemies with most fervent charity: *Matthew [26.]*[137] and in all things did remit His will to His Father's, as the Scripture doth witness, when He prayed in the Mount. A goodly example and lesson for us to follow at all *Psalm 37.* times and seasons, as well in prosperity as in adversity: to have no will but God's will, committing and leaving to Him all our cares and griefs, and to abandon all our policies and inventions, for they be most vain and foolish, and, indeed, very shadows and dreams. [Gi r] But we be yet so carnal and fleshly that we come head- *The love of God.* long, like unbridled colts, without snaffle or bit.[138] If we had the love of God printed in our hearts, it would keep us back from running astray. And until such time as it please God to send us this bit to hold us in, we shall never run the right way, although we speak and talk never so much of God and His Word.

Every man attend to his vocation. The true followers of Christ's doctrine hath always a respect and an eye to their vocation.[139] If they be called to the ministry of God's Word, they preach and teach *Preachers.* it sincerely, to the edifying of others, and show themselves, in their living, follow- *2 Corinthians 4.* ers of the same. If they be married men,[140] having children and family, they nour-

136. **one God . . . baptism** an allusion to Ephesians 4:5–6.

137. **Matthew [26.]** The correct reference; all editions read "Math."

138. **we come . . . bit** KP's vocabulary of "snaffle" and "bit" recurs in the draft of a letter addressed by Queen Elizabeth to the House of Commons in January 1567, after its members took it upon themselves to urge her to marry and to specify the line of succession (*Elizabeth I: Collected Works*, ed. Leah S. Marcus, Janel Mueller, and Mary Beth Rose [Chicago: University of Chicago Press, 2000], 93). **come** Subsequent editions read "runne."

139. **look . . . vocation** KP's is a notably early instance of the Reformed emphasis on having a vocation in this world (countering the Catholic sense of vocation as a calling to take vows as a nun, priest, or monk). However, as the distinction drawn in the following two "if" clauses indicates ("If they be called to the ministry," "If they be married men"), KP retained a traditionalist conception of the clergy as unmarried. Her stepdaughter Elizabeth would also retain this conception throughout her long reign.

140. **married men** The content of KP's prescriptions for the conduct of "married men" as husbands, fathers, and householders tallies closely with three successive sections in Tyndale's *Obedience of a Christian Man*: "The Office of a Father / Husband / Master, and how he should rule" (*Doctrinal Treatises and Introductions*, 199–201). On the origins of this topic in Luther and

ish and bring them up, without all bitterness and fierceness, in the doctrine of the Lord; [Gi v] in all godliness and virtue, committing the instruction of others, which appertaineth not to their charge, to the reformation of God and His ministers, which chiefly be kings and princes, bearing the sword even for that purpose, to punish evildoers. If they be children, they honor their father and mother, knowing it to be God's commandment, and that He hath thereto annexed a promise of long life. If they be servants, they obey and serve their masters with all fear and reverence, even for the Lord's sake, neither with murmuring nor grudging, but with a free heart and mind. If they be husbands, they love their wives as their own bodies, after the example as Christ loved the congregation,[141] and gave Himself for it, [Gii r] to make it to Him a spouse, without spot or wrinkle. If they be women married, they learn of Saint Paul, to be obedient to their husbands, and to keep silence in the congregation, and to learn of their husbands, at home.[142] Also they wear such apparel as becometh holiness and comely usage, with soberness: not being accusers or detractors, not given to much eating of delicate meats and drinking of

Laymen.
Ephesians 6.
Romans 13.
Children.
Deuteronomy 5.
Servants.
Ephesians 6.
Husbands.
Ephesians 5.
Wives' obedience.
1 Timothy 2.
Silence.
Apparel.
2 Timothy 2.

its incorporation under the rubric "The office of all estates" in various primers published by English Lutheran printers, see Charles C. Butterworth, *The English Primers (1529–1545): Their Publication and Connection with the English Bible and the Reformation in England* (Philadelphia: University of Pennsylvania Press, 1953), 108–9, 123, 144, 184, 185–86.

141. **the congregation** KP's use of "congregation" rather than "church" to render Greek *ekklēsia* aligns her with Tyndale's practice in translating the New Testament (1525; rev. 1534). The choice was no mere stylistic option. As More protested against Tyndale, replacing "church" with "congregation" had the effect of weakening the authority of the Catholic clergy at many junctures. Tyndale explains his practice as follows: "Wherefore, inasmuch as the clergy . . . had appropriate unto themselves the term that of right is common unto all the whole congregation of them that believe in Christ; and . . . had beguiled and mocked the people, and brought them into the ignorance of the word, making them understand by this word *church* nothing but the shaven flock of them that shore the whole world; therefore in the translation of the New Testament, where I found this word *ecclesia*, I interpreted it by this word *congregation*. Even therefore I did it, and not of any mischievous mind or purpose to stablish heresy, as Master More untruly reporteth of me in his dialogue, where he raileth on the translation of the New Testament" (*Answer to More's Dialogue*, 13–14, where More's attack is also reproduced).

142. **to keep . . . home** KP alludes to St. Paul's injunctions to women in 1 Corinthians 14:34–35 and 1 Timothy 2:11–14, probably recalling how she had endangered herself in the spring and summer of 1546 by her outspoken discussions with King Henry about further reforming the Church of England. Juan Luis Vives attests the normative cultural force of these Pauline injunctions in his *Institutio Feminae Christianae* (1523), a work written for Queen Catherine of Aragon to guide the education of her daughter, Princess Mary. Richard Hyrde's translation, *A very frutefull and pleasant boke called the instruction of a christen woman* (STC 24856) appeared circa 1529. Citing St. Paul, Vives adds his own pronouncement: "I gyue no licence to a woman to be a teacher nor to haue authoritie of the man but to be in silence" (Valerie Wayne, "'Some Sad Sentence': Vives's *Institution of a Christian Woman*," in *Silent but for the Word*, ed. Hannay, 19). There were eight editions of Vives's work in England before 1600 (Gloria Kaufman, "Juan Luis Vives on the Education of Women," *Signs* 3, no. 4 [1978]: 893 n7).

1 Peter 1, 3.

wine.[143] But they teach honest things, to make the young women sober-minded, to love their husbands,[144] to love their children, to be discreet, chaste, housewifely, good, obedient unto their husbands, that the Word of God be not evil spoken of. Verily, if all sorts of people would look to their own vocation, [Gii v] and ordain the same according to Christ's doctrine, we should not have so many eyes and ears to other men's faults as we have. For we be so busy and glad to find and espy[145] out other men's doings, that we forget and can have no time to weigh and ponder our own: which, after the Word of God, we ought first to reform, and then we shall the better help another with the straw out of his eyes.[146] But, alas, we be so much given to love and to flatter ourselves, and so blinded with carnal affections, that we can see and perceive no fault in ourselves. And therefore it is a thing very requisite and necessary for us, to pray all with one heart and mind to God, to give us an heavenly light and knowledge of our[147] own miseries and calamities, [Giii r] that we may see them and acknowledge them truly before Him.

Overmuch eyesight.

Matthew 7.

Self-love.

A conclusion with an answer to objections.

If any man shall be offended at this my lamenting the faults of men which be in the world, fantasying with themselves that I do it either of hatred or malice to any sort or kind of people: verily, in so doing, they shall do me great wrong. For I thank God, by His grace, I hate no creature; yea, I would say more, to give witness of my conscience,[148] that neither life, honor, riches, neither whatsoever I possess here, which appertaineth unto mine own private commodity, be it never so dearly beloved of me, but most willingly and gladly I would leave it, to win any man to

143. **not given . . . wine** KP's phrases aptly characterize an intermittent resident in her household in 1547–48, Princess Elizabeth, and what would become her lifelong practices in eating and drinking. As Anne Somerset notes, "Elizabeth . . . was a frugal eater: she habitually eschewed rich food and watered her wine" (*Elizabeth I* [New York: St. Martin's, 1991], 350).

144. **to love . . . husbands** This phrase is curiously omitted in the 1548 and 1563 editions.

145. **espy** observe, perceive.

146. **we ought . . . eyes** KP alludes to Jesus's image in Matthew 7:4, figuring the failure to perceive one's own great fault while perceiving another's lesser fault: "Why seest thou a mote in thy brothers eye, but consydrest not the beame that is in thyne owne eye?" (Great Bible 1540, fol. iv r). **straw** an earlier specific sense of "mote." "Mote" is now usually glossed with its more general sense, "a minute particle."

147. **our** The reading from 1548 onward; the 1547 edition has the misprint "our our."

148. **I would . . . conscience** Much is made of having a conscience in the last two decades of Henry VIII's reign, starting with the king himself, who cites this as his paramount motive for divorcing Catherine of Aragon, appealing to the prohibition in Leviticus 20:21 against marrying a brother's wife. Edward Hall's chronicle history of Henry VIII's reign after 1528 in *The Union of the Two Noble and Illustre Families of Lancaster and York* (1548) reports several instances of the king's tender conscience regarding his divorce (Hall, *The Triumphant Reign of King Henry the Eighth*, ed. Charles Whibley [London: E. C. Jack, 1904], 143–47, 151, 172, 209–10). There is, however, no Reformed monopoly on appeals to conscience. Thomas More went to the executioner's block protesting his conscience for refusing to swear the Oath of Supremacy acknowledging Henry VIII as supreme head of the English Church.

Christ,[149] of what degree or sort soever he were. [Giii v] And yet is this nothing in comparison to the charity that God hath showed me, in sending Christ to die for me: no, if I had all the charity of angels and apostles, it should be but like a spark of fire compared to a great heap of burning coals. God knoweth of what intent and mind I have lamented mine own sins and faults to the world.[150] I trust nobody will judge I have done it for praise or thank of any creature, since rather I might be ashamed than rejoice in rehearsal thereof. For if they know how little I esteem and weigh the praise of the world, that opinion were soon removed and taken away. For I thank God, by His grace, I know the world to be a blind judge, and the praises thereof vain and of little moment, [Giv r] and therefore I seek not the praises of the same, neither to satisfy it none other wise, than I am taught by Christ to do, according to Christian charity.

It is lawful to boast in God.

I would to God we would all,[151] when occasion doth serve, confess our faults to the world, all respects to our own commodity laid apart. But, alas, self-love doth so

Godly wish.

149. **whatsoever . . . Christ** KP carries to potentially controversial lengths her conviction that the true Christian should apply all worldly means in enacting Christ's love to others. Compare Tyndale in *Parable of the Wicked Mammon*: "Christ is Lord over all; and every Christian is heir annexed with Christ, and therefore lord over all; and every one lord of whatsoever another hath. If thy brother or neighbour therefore need, and thou have to help him, and yet . . . withdrawest thy hands from him, then robbest thou him of his own, and art a thief" (*Doctrinal Treatises and Introductions*, 97). This passage yielded one of the heresies that John Foxe reports Thomas More as charging against Tyndale: "Every man is lord of another man's goods." Foxe replies on Tyndale's behalf: "This place giveth to none any propriety of another man's goods, but only by way of Christian communion" (John Foxe, *Acts and Monuments*, ed. Stephen Reed Cattley [London: R. B. Seeley and W. Burnside, 1837], 5:574). In "The Story of Queen Katherine Parr," Foxe reports (6:556) that Stephen Gardiner accused KP to Henry of believing in the commonality of all goods—one of the most opprobrious tenets of the Anabaptists. If his motive was not simple malice, Gardiner may have seized on the connection between KP's opinion and Tyndale's *Wicked Mammon* as a pretext for his accusation. See my general introduction, pp. 22, 25.

150. **God . . . world** KP makes a late, single reference to the possible public scandal of her *Lamentation of a Sinner*, which offers the spiritual and rhetorical spectacle of an English queen in open self-abjection, accusing herself in the medium of print, before God and her readership, of perverse wilfulness and blind ignorance of true religion. While this major aspect of the *Lamentation* found no English imitators, it had, as variously noted above, a crucial precedent in the abject self-presentation of Marguerite, Queen of Navarre, in *Le Miroir de l'ame pécheresse* (1533). For a survey of the earliest accounts of Reformist conversion in England, see Marshall, *Religious Identities in Henry VIII's England*, 19–22.

151. **we . . . all** KP's "I" references change to "we's" as she exhorts her readers to join in her vision of England as an inclusive, truly Christian community bound together by willing adherence to "God's precepts and ordinances." Her themes and tonalities are those of the "commonwealth" men of midcentury—notably Robert Crowley, Hugh Latimer, William Turner, and the Edwardine émigré Martin Bucer—but they equally anticipate the English Puritanism that would signal its advent with John Hooper and the "vestiarian" controversy (objections to

much reign amongst us that, as I have said before, we cannot espy our own faults. And although sometime we find our own guilt, either we be favorable to interpret it no sin, or else we be ashamed to confess ourselves thereof. Yea, and we be sore offended and grieved to hear our faults charitably and godly told us of other, putting no difference between charitable warning and malicious accusing. [Giv v] Truly, if we sought God's glory, as we should do in all things, we should not be ashamed to confess ourselves to digress from God's precepts and ordinances, when it is manifest we have done, and daily do. I pray God our own faults and deeds condemn us not, at the last day, when every man shall be rewarded according to his doings. Truly, if we do not redress and amend our living, according to the doctrine of the Gospel, we shall receive a terrible sentence of Christ, the Son of God, when He shall come to judge and condemn all transgressors and breakers of His precepts and commandments, and to reward all His obedient and loving children. [Gv r] We shall have no man of law[152] to make our plea for us, neither can we have the day deferred; neither will the just Judge be corrupted with affection, bribes, or reward; neither will He hear any excuse or delay; neither shall this saint or that martyr help us, be they never so holy; neither shall our ignorance save us from damnation. But, yet, wilful blindness and obstinate ignorance shall receive greater punishment, and not without just cause. Then shall it be known who hath walked in the dark, for all things shall appear manifest before him. No man's deeds shall be hidden, no, neither words nor thoughts. The poor and simple observers of God's commandments shall be rewarded with everlasting life, as obedient children to the heavenly Father. [Gv v] And the transgressors, adders and diminishers of the law of God, shall receive eternal damnation for their just reward. I beseech God we may escape this fearful sentence, and be found such faithful servants and loving children, that we may hear the happy, comfortable, and most joyful sentence, ordained for the children of God, which is: "Come hither, ye blessed of my Father, and receive the

Shame hindereth confession.

1 Corinthians 6.

Matthew 25.

A true threatening.

Doomsday compared to a law day.[153]

Wilful sin is the greatest.

Apocalypse 22.

Reward of sinners.

Prayer.

Matthew 25.

---

clerical vestments and other ceremonial practices) in the 1560s. The salient difference between commonwealth and early Puritan writing is John Calvin's influence as a major authority in the latter.

152. **man of law** lawyer.

153. **Doomsday . . . law day** KP's equation of Doomsday with a "law day" activates a former sense of this term: a day appointed for the discharge of a bond, after which the debtor could not be relieved from forfeiture under English common law. As the ultimate sanction for her moral exhortations, KP issues a highly traditional warning of Christ's Second Coming and Last Judgment at which all human actions will be given their just reckoning. She had similarly warned the heads of colleges in the University of Cambridge in her February 1546 letter "that it may not be laid against you in evidence at the tribunal seat of God, how ye were ashamed of Christ's doctrine" (part 3, no. 14, correspondence section).

kingdom of heaven, prepared for you before the beginning of the world."[154] Unto the Father, the Son, and the Holy Ghost, be all honor and glory, world without end. Amen.

Finis.

[Colophon]

Imprinted at London, in Fleet Street, at the sign of the Sun,
over against the Conduit, by Edward Whitchurch,
the fifth day of November, in the year of our Lord, 1547.

Cum privilegio ad imprimendum solum.[155]

154. **"Come . . . world"** a nearly verbatim quotation from Matthew 25:34 in Coverdale 1535, fol. xiii r. Variant readings in Taverner 1539, fol. xi v, and Great Bible 1540, fol. xii v, place their renderings at a further remove.

155. **Cum . . . solum** With the privilege of sole—i.e., exclusive—printing. This royal privilege, accorded to a specified printer by way of this formula, was a forerunner of copyright.

KATHERINE PARR'S

PERSONAL PRAYERBOOK

(ca. 1544 to 1548)

INTRODUCTION TO *KATHERINE PARR'S PERSONAL PRAYERBOOK*

British Library MS Harley 2342 has been known as "Lady Jane Grey's Prayerbook" because of its demonstrable associations with her.[1] When she was beheaded for usurping Queen Mary's right to the throne in 1553, she took it with her to the scaffold and there entrusted it to the keeping of Sir John Bridges, lieutenant of the Tower of London. Inside the tiny prayerbook, across the bottoms of four pages, is a brief exchange of messages of comfort in the handwritings of Guildford Dudley and Jane Grey, husband and wife, awaiting their deaths in separate cells, and a message to Bridges in Jane's handwriting, referring to his having instructed her "to write in so worthy a book."[2] The implicit drama is not difficult to piece together. The compassionate Bridges evidently helped Jane and Guildford convey their farewells to Jane's father, the Duke of Suffolk, before the executions of all three, by carrying the prayerbook with its messages from the one to the other, allaying any possible suspicions with his show of piety. At this juncture, the prayerbook unquestionably belonged to Jane.

Its earlier history, however, lies entirely with Queen Katherine Parr. I have identified the handwriting on all 143 vellum leaves of Harley 2342 as hers. I believe

1. A substantially similar account is Janel Mueller, "Prospecting for Common Ground in Devotion: Queen Katherine Parr's Personal Prayerbook," in *English Women, Religion, and Textual Production, 1500–1625*, ed. Micheline White (Farnham, UK: Ashgate, 2011).

2. See the anonymous contemporary account *The Chronicle of Queen Jane, and of Two Years of Queen Mary*, ed. John Gough Nichols, Publications of the Camden Society 48 (London, 1849), 56, 55; and nn 18 and 22 of the original-spelling version below for a transcription of these messages, found on fols. 78r–80r. Here and hereafter, spelling has been modernized in quotations from Harley 2342 and other sources.

that Jane was given this tiny prayerbook in early September 1548, when Katherine lay dying of puerperal fever after the birth of her only child, a daughter, Mary, on August 30. Jane was residing in the household, her presence due to the intrigues of Katherine's husband, Lord Thomas Seymour, who aimed at arranging a marriage between Jane and his nephew, the boy king Edward VI. Jane was the chief mourner at Katherine's funeral, held in the chapel of the manor house at Sudeley in Gloucestershire, where Katherine had gone for her lying-in. She evidently retained possession of Harley 2342 until close to her end, for her otherwise controlled and distinct handwriting becomes wobbly, oversized, and faint on the last five leaves, and textual embellishment of any kind ceases.

Unusually for this date, "Katherine Parr's Personal Prayerbook" offers access to the spirituality of one strongly motivated, highly placed, and deeply studied woman in England's swirling climate of religious and political contestation and transition during the mid to late 1540s. This is the likely period for the compilation of the prayerbook, since all of Parr's other known literary activity dates to and after her marriage to Henry VIII in July 1543—seemingly as the direct consequence of the incentives and opportunities that came with her queenship. Her handwriting in her prayerbook, moreover, closely resembles that in her letters from 1544 to 1548. Beyond this evidence, the versicles and prayers inscribed on the prayerbook's miniature vellum leaves (measuring approximately three by four inches) are ornamented with gold-retraced capital letters on red and blue fields, and with red and blue rectangles, some with vinelike gold tracery, inserted in blank spaces at line ends. This is exactly the decorative program used by Parr in her incomplete manuscript of *Prayers or Meditations* (the Kendal autograph), reportedly made as a gift for a Mistress Tuke, an attendant at the Henrician court, presumably in or after 1545.[3]

As her own creation, Harley 2342 should be known as "Katherine Parr's Personal Prayerbook"—"personal" because Parr seems not to have intended its contents for publication, as she so clearly did intend with *Psalms or Prayers* (1544), *Prayers or Meditations* (1545), and *The Lamentation of a Sinner* (1547).[4] Harley 2342, however, deserves circulation and critical attention as much as her three published works do. Parr's personal prayerbook exemplifies her textual procedures and interests as clearly as the other composition in which we know her to have excerpted, recast, and rearranged a prior source—her production of *Prayers or Meditations* out of the materials of book 3 of Thomas à Kempis's *De Imitatione Christi* in the English translation made by Richard Whitford and published as *The Following of*

3. See figures 1 and 2 on p. x, above. A color image of an opening of Harley 2342 can be accessed at http://www.bl.uk/onlinegallery/onlineex/histtexts/ladyjane/large17632.html.

4. For discussion of the respective circumstances of publication of these three works, see Susan E. James, *Kateryn Parr: The Making of a Queen* (Aldershot, UK: Ashgate, 1999), 200–207, 214–19, 234–49.

Christ. Parr's sensitive and systematic interventions in Whitford's text result in a radically refashioned devotional work that makes personal access to Christ available to any reader, without the gender and status markings of Whitford's (and à Kempis's) original. On this basis she can justly be regarded as an author, not merely an adapter, in *Prayers or Meditations*.[5]

A similar but more intricate line of reasoning can be advanced with regard to Parr's personal prayerbook. Generically, this compilation conforms to the widely popular type of prayerbook for lay devotion known as the book of hours—or, in English nomenclature, the primer.[6] English primers variously manifested a traditionalist or Reformed orientation in scores of separate editions from many publishers. The orientation would emerge through the choice of language (Latin, Latin and English, English only); through the inclusion or exclusion of prayers to the Virgin Mary and the saints, prayers for the souls of the departed, and formulaic prescriptions of penance that remitted time in purgatory; and through the emphases shaping their instructional materials, whether geared, in a traditionalist fashion, more to the priestly office and the sacramental system or, in Reformed fashion, more to individual accountability and the exemplary precedents of Biblical heroes and heroines. Yet whatever its overall orientation, every primer would display an intense, introspective turning away from the world and an attendant placing of primary focus on Christ as the sole Saviour of sinful humankind.[7] This inward turn and this Christocentrism constituted a notable common denominator in the devotionalism fostered by primers.[8] On the evidence of Parr's personal prayerbook, she recognized this common denominator and applied herself to exploring its possibilities.

The prayerbook's generic interest is twofold. There is, first, the question of which sources (overwhelmingly, primers and Psalters) figured in its compilation; second, there is the question of what Parr achieved in fashioning a book of devotion from the multiple sources that she excerpted, arranged, and combined into a new, personalized whole. In broader terms, the historically specific, pathbreaking trajectory

5. See the introduction to *Prayers or Meditations*, pp. 372–79.

6. For an excellent overview, see Susan M. Felch, "A Brief History of English Private Prayer Books," prefacing her edition of *Elizabeth Tyrwhit's Morning and Evening Prayers* (Aldershot, UK: Ashgate, 2008), 19–32.

7. Two classic studies of the sixteenth-century English primers remain useful: Helen C. White, *Tudor Books of Private Devotion* (Madison: University of Wisconsin Press, 1951); and Charles C. Butterworth, *The English Primers (1529–1545): Their Publication and Connection with the English Bible and the Reformation in England* (Philadelphia: University of Pennsylvania Press, 1953). The pioneering treatment of the subject, mostly in the form of an enumerative bibliography (now superseded by the *Short-Title Catalogue*), is Edgar Hoskins, *Horae Beatae Mariae Virginis or Sarum and York Primers with Kindred Books and Primers of the Reformed and Roman Use* (London: Longman, Green, 1901).

8. Christine Peters, *Patterns of Piety: Women, Gender, and Religion in Late Medieval and Reformation England* (Cambridge: Cambridge University Press, 2003), 345–49.

of Katherine Parr's literary activity, as the first woman in England to publish work of her own in English under her own name, reveals how her intense piety generated and directed this activity, while her status as Queen of England empowered her to range across a spectrum of roles as translator, adapter, author, and patron that found public expression and recognition in print. The notable exception, her personal prayerbook, could take on certain functions that a diary or privately kept journal might serve in our own day. Parr could assemble a set of contents that expressed her own priorities and preferences in devotional utterance without being constrained by institutional or confessional norms, and she could give free expression to the tonalities and vocabulary that resonated most compellingly with her. Yet at certain points noted in the following discussion, a complementary relation emerges between Parr's personal prayerbook and her published prose.

In contrast to the narrow time frame of 1544–48 postulated for its composition, Parr's personal prayerbook employs sources (of which I have identified more than 90 percent) ranging in date from 1530 to 1540; there is no evidence of more recent material. Conspicuous time lags between the date of a published source and the date when Parr employed it are characteristic of her other works also. John Fisher's *Psalmi seu Precationes*, first published circa 1525, is the text she translates in *Psalms or Prayers* (1544); and Whitford's *Following of Christ*, published circa 1531, is the text she redacts in *Prayers or Meditations* (1545). There is no obvious reason—only, perhaps, a penchant for retrospection in devotion—to account for the time lags in the case of these two works. But there does appear to be an explanation of considerable interest for the time lag between the sources and the contents of Parr's personal prayerbook.

By means of these earlier sources, and a compilation destined not to be published, Parr evidently undertook to position herself reflectively with regard not primarily to the widening divide but to the extent of common ground to be found in Catholic and Reformed strains of lay devotion.[9] For such an undertaking, she required publications in English that made pertinent developments traceable. The primers and Psalters of the 1530s and her other sources from this decade did just that, enabling her project of exploration and integration. To be sure, any such incentive to explore alternative modes of Christian devotion could not be neutral from the 1530s onward in England, for conservative Catholics—notably Cuthbert

9. KP was by no means the first or the only searcher for possible common ground between Catholics and Reformers as religious differences came to the fore and multiplied in the earlier sixteenth century. Prominent northern European figures engaged in this enterprise included Desiderius Erasmus, Martin Bucer, and Philipp Melanchthon. While the grounds on which they sought for commonality lay principally in doctrinal agreement and shared understandings of Scripture, the devotional thrust of KP's search was likely to have been impelled by her recognition of the considerable overlaps (as well as key differences) in early sixteenth-century primer texts, whether issued by a traditionalist or a Reformed compiler or printer.

Tunstall, Bishop of London, and his designated vernacular polemicist, Lord Chancellor Thomas More, as well as John Stokesley, Tunstall's successor—sharply decried as heresy all Reformation charges of abuses and proposals for change, especially the proposal to grant worshipers access to the Bible and devotional materials in English rather than Latin. Moreover, after authorizing the publication and circulation of the Great Bible in English in 1538–39, Henry VIII largely returned the laity of his realm to their *status quo ante* by curtailing reading of the Bible in English with the dubiously titled Act for the Advancement of True Religion (1543).[10] In inquiring for herself into the spirituality of the old religion and the new in her day while including lavish recourse to Scripture in English, Parr exhibits her receptivity to the advent of the English Reformation as she sustains the Christ-centered, inward turn found conjointly in traditional and more recent modes of lay devotion.

Parr's personal prayerbook begins in a conventional fashion with a summary narrative (source unidentified) focused on the passion and crucifixion of Jesus as the culmination of His life and ministry, and the demonstration that He is the Saviour of humankind. This type of narrative, usually in the form of a far lengthier "harmony" or parallel rehearsal of the events leading to the crucifixion as recorded in the four Gospels, is one among several standard beginnings for the text of a primer, whether Catholic or Lutheran, whether in Latin or in English. Yet the passion narratives in primers remain just that: accounts of Jesus's last days, doings, and sayings lifted verbatim from the Gospels, whatever the language. No sooner is Parr's very brief narrative launched, however, than it breaks with primer convention by modulating into a fluid mixture of self-examination, prayer, and nonnarrative quotation of Scripture, as this excerpt will illustrate:

> . . . being so cruelly consumed, He offered Himself a sacrifice to God His Father for us all. Who am I, then, that I should [dispute?] and suffer with an unpatient mind if any trouble do chance unto me, if I suffer any incommodity, if any persecution of envious persons cumber me, specially seeing no evil can be done unto me which my sins hath not deserved? Therefore I will not suffer grievously that thing which is bestowed righteously, but I shall pray my Lord God to grant me patience in all things. And, in that patience, purging and forgiveness of mine ungraciousness, that He, which vouchsafed to make me partaker of His pains, may also make me

10. This act permitted only licensed clergy to read publicly from the Bible. Nobles and gentry could read it aloud only within their own households; merchants, noblewomen, and gentlemen could read it only privately. The remainder of the population was prohibited from reading the English Bible at all, although the king could suspend this clause if he wished to do so. *Statutes of the Realm*, 895–96 (34–35 Henry VIII, chap. 1), cited in John Guy, *Tudor England* (Oxford: Oxford University Press, 1988), 194.

> partaker of His glory, according to the Apostle's saying, "As ye be fellows of His passions, so shall ye be of His comfort."[11]

Once this modulation occurs, the initial conventionality of Parr's personal prayerbook yields to its more distinctive course. All of its subsequent contents sustain and intensify the turns of self-examination and redirection that Parr conducts through prayer and nonnarrative Scriptural citation, predominantly verses from the Psalms. While English primers serve her repeatedly as sources of prayers and Scriptural citations, her appropriations carry no trace of the primers' prominent internal structure. This might take the traditional form of the canonical hours of the day appointed for prayers and devotions in the medieval church, followed by intercessions for the souls of the dead. Or this structure might take a newer form: adaptations of praying and devotion to an everyday routine of arising, taking meals, going about one's activities, encountering temptation, giving praise for a blessing received, and retiring to rest. In the absence of either of these standard coordinates for devotion pegged to a daily round (however conceived and specified), a profound sense of interiority, of charged subjectivity, emerges from Parr's stark sequencing of prayers and extensive runs of verses from the Psalms.

The idea that Queen Katherine's personal prayerbook serves as her proving ground for alternative modes and common expressions of Christian devotion in her day arose as I worked at identifying her sources. Parr's opening sequence is headed by three English prayers from Thomas More's Tower meditations, written while he was awaiting execution for treason in July 1535 after refusing to swear the Oath of Supremacy declaring Henry VIII (rather than the pope) the supreme head of the Church of England. More's three prayers include a lengthy, impassioned one beginning "O holy Trinity—the Father, the Son, the Holy Ghost—three equal, coeternal Persons and one God almighty, have mercy upon me, vile, abject, abominable, sinful wretch," followed by the short text of "A prayer for our enemies," beginning "Almighty God, have mercy on me, and all them that bear me evil will and would me harm," and then by a still shorter prayer of self-resignation into God's hands, beginning "Lord, give me patience in tribulation, grace in everything, to conform my will to Thine."[12]

Parr displays respect and empathy in mostly verbatim transcriptions of More's prayers, but she is not uncritical. She consistently renders his Latin quotations of Scripture into English, and she makes two key excisions, signaled in italics below. One is the reference to purgatory in More's "not for the avoiding of the calamities of this wretched world, *nor so much for the avoiding of the pains of purgatory,* nor of

11. British Library, Harley MS 2342 ("Queen Katherine Parr's Personal Prayerbook"), fols. 3v–4v; hereafter cited as "PP." Square brackets enclose my conjectural restoration of an illegible word. The freely handled quotation is from St. Paul in 2 Corinthians 1:5.

12. "PP," fols. 9r–16r. Throughout this introduction, italics signal wording excised by KP from her sources.

the pains of hell neither." The other is Parr's curt substitution of the single pronoun "Thee" in place of More's fervent salutation to Christ's Real Presence in the consecrated host of the mass: "*Thine holy sacraments, and specially . . . the presence of Thy very blessed Body, sweet Saviour Christ, in the holy Sacrament of the Altar: . . . duly to thank Thee for Thy gracious visitation therewith, and at that high memorial, with tender compassion, to remember and consider Thy most bitter passion.*"[13]

Immediately following the three prayers by More, Parr transcribes, virtually verbatim, two prayers—compositions by Nicholas Shaxton—from the verso of the title page of Miles Coverdale's *Biblia. The Byble* (1535). The two prayers from the Coverdale Bible title page are "O Lord God almighty, which long ago saidst by the mouth of James, Thine apostle," a petition for efficacy in prayer and for godly wisdom, and a briefer petition, "Lead me, O Lord, in Thy way, and let me walk in Thy truth."[14] In inscribing these prayers in her personal prayerbook, Parr omits the identifying rubric that prefaces the first of the pair in the Coverdale Bible: "*Because that when thou goest to study in Holy Scripture, thou shouldst do it with reverence, therefore for thy instruction and loving admonition thereto, the reverend Father in God, Nicholas [Shaxton], Bishop of Salisbury, hath prescribed thee the prayer following, taken out of the same.*"[15] Shaxton, a sympathizer with the Reformation, was appointed by Henry VIII to the see of Salisbury in 1535, but he resigned it on refusing to subscribe to the religiously conservative Six Articles (1539). Queen Katherine gives Shaxton a voice in her prayerbook as an advocate of vernacular Scripture and Scripture-based prayer who, in the first instance, had been judged worthy by Coverdale, an associate of Luther's and a self-exile in Germany, to supply two prayers as epigraphs on the title page of the first English Bible. (This Bible, significantly, had appeared without Henry VIII's authorization.)

Thesis and antithesis—More's prayers, then Shaxton's—but what comes next is

13. More's texts are printed in *The Yale Edition of the Complete Works of St. Thomas More*, vol. 13, *Treatise on the Passion, Treatise on the Blessed Body, Instructions and Prayers*, ed. Garry E. Haupt (New Haven, CT: Yale University Press, 1976), 228–31. How Parr gained access to these prayers of More's is unknown, but there is contemporary evidence that they circulated informally. Transcriptions of More's Tower prayers are to be found in the Bodleian Library manuscript Laud Misc. 1, fols. 52r–59r. This is the prayerbook of Lady Jane Wriostheley, an attendant of KP and wife of Sir Thomas Wriostheley, lord chancellor in the 1540s. KP wrote a letter of condolence to Lady Jane: see no. 3 in part 3 of the correspondence section. The Wriostheleys were committed Catholics; he joined with Bishop Stephen Gardiner and Sir Richard Rich in attempting to discredit KP with the king in 1546.

14. "PP," fols. 16r–17v.

15. Miles Coverdale, *Biblia the byble: that is: the holy Scripture, faythfully translated in to Englyshe. M.D.XXXV* (Southwark: J. Nicholson, 1535) (STC 2063.3), unnumbered, first folio sheet. Shaxton and Coverdale had noteworthy subsequent histories. Shaxton realigned as a traditionalist after recanting his Reformed beliefs under prosecution in 1546. Coverdale returned from exile in Germany in 1548, encouraged by the vigorous embrace of the Reformation in Edward VI's reign. KP, now Lord Thomas Seymour's wife, appointed Coverdale as one of her chaplains. He officiated at her funeral in September 1548.

less synthesis than common ground. Parr follows Shaxton's prayers with an English version of a prayer that is a staple item in primers of the period, whether Roman or Reformed, known by its opening phrase in Latin, "Conditor celi et terre" (O Maker of heaven and earth). The traditional instruction for the use of this prayer is as the first of the suffrages (petitionary prayers) under the rubric "Oratio ad imaginem corporis Christi" (Prayer to the image of the body of Christ), directing the user to prepare for confession by praying to a crucifix.[16] True to her habitual practice in her prayerbook, Parr omits the rubric, thus excising the reference to praying to a crucifix; but she also, for no obvious reason, excises the ascriptive opening clauses of this prayer: *"O Maker of heaven and earth, King of Kings and Lord of Lords, which of nothing didst make me to Thy image and likeness, and didst redeem me with Thine own blood: whom . . ."* Parr instead begins her text after the *whom*, with "I, a sinner, am not worthy to name, or call upon, nor think on in my heart."[17] The effect upon this prayer, a prolonged confession of sin and unworthiness and a plea for God's mercy and forgiveness, is to intensify its humility and self-abasement by eliminating its opening salutation to a mighty and glorious Lord Christ.

Parr's source for "Conditor celi et terre" is the version in *A Primer in English, with Divers Prayers* (1535), issued by Thomas Godfray, an English Lutheran printer and publisher based in London.[18] Little else is known about him except that he derived his text from the first primer in English, *Ortulus animae: The Garden of the Soul* (1530), an adaptative translation of a traditionalist Latin original made by George Joye, another English Lutheran working in exile in Germany.[19] Godfray was also an associate of the outspokenly Lutheran William Marshall, who was publishing primers of his own in London in the same period.[20] As will be evident in due course, at one point or another Parr's personal prayerbook utilizes all of these English Lutheran sources (and more), beginning with Godfray's primer.

While continually revising its phrasing, Parr hews closely to the sense of Godfray's version of "Conditor celi" with its profuse allusions to Biblical sinners. She smoothes out many awkward turns in the style (this awkwardness stems from Joye and is one of the chronic features of his prose).[21] Parr also heightens the emotional and moral cogency of this traditional prayer with a free hand, as this example will illustrate. One of the catalogs of sins in Godfray runs headlong into anacoluthon: *"in tasting, in touching, in thinking, in sleeping, in working, and in all*

16. White, *Tudor Books of Private Devotion*, 74.

17. "PP," fols. 18r–21r.

18. Thomas Godfray, *A primer in Englysshe, with dyuers prayers* (1535?) (STC 15988a), sigs. Ciii v–Ciiii v.

19. Joye's *Ortulus anime; The garden of the soule* is STC 13828.4, described as "a Protestant version in English" of *Hortulus anime ad vsum insignis ecclesie Sarum* (STC 13828.2), a traditionalist Latin compilation published in Antwerp and London ca. 1524 by the printer F. Byrckman.

20. Butterworth, *English Primers*, 73–78.

21. Ibid., 41–43.

ways in which I, a frail man and most wretched sinner, might sin: my default, my most grievous default." Parr recasts this catalog in surer-footed syntax while also notably eliminating its gender-specific locution and universalizing the potential frame of reference: "in tasting, in feeling, in speaking, in thinking, in working, and in all manner ways wherein I, an unstable and frail creature, might offend my Maker by any fault or trespass."[22]

After honing her compositional skills on Godfray's uneven prose, Parr proceeds to the most literarily interesting and ambitious undertaking in all of her personal prayerbook. This is her elaboration on a sequence of sentence prayers from *A Spiritual Consolation, Written by John Fisher, Bishop of Rochester, to His Sister Elizabeth*, the other famous Tower meditation from the other eminent English Catholic who refused to swear the Oath of Supremacy and died as a traitor in 1535.[23] This sequence of sentence prayers, one for each day of the week but none assigned to a particular day, concludes Fisher's reflections on "the ways to perfect religion." Again typically dispensing with a heading, Parr launches into the text of the comprehensive single prayer that she crafts by hinging her serial expressions of devotion to Jesus on Fisher's seven brief sentences.[24]

For Parr, Fisher's sentence prayers become sweeping gestures of invitation to engage with the prime subject of late medieval Catholic and early Reformed—especially Lutheran—devotion: the sufferings and self-sacrifice of Jesus on the cross, dying to save humankind in obedience to God the Father's will. The affinity in Fisher's and Parr's temperaments shows elsewhere in the prominent yet divergent treatment that they give to "the book of the crucifix," the legibility of salvation in the passion of Christ.[25] Here, in her personal prayerbook, Parr demonstrates the heights of lyrical responsiveness to which she is moved, taking up the lead of Fisher's Christocentric intensity, to meditate on the crucified Jesus. Her successive effusions are anchored fore and aft by Fisher's sentences (set in boldface in the following quotation). Even so, Parr does not stickle at giving his wording a Reformed turn that denies human nature any role in the divine work of redemption, as seen in her substitution of "continual" for Fisher's "natural" in the first clause below:

22. "PP," fols. 19v–20r.

23. As with More's Tower prayers, there is the question of how KP obtained Fisher's last writings, which were first published more than forty years after his death as *A spirituall consolation, written by John Fyssher* [W. Carter, 1578?] (STC 10899). Here the question of access finds a plausible answer in the person of George Day, Fisher's former student and chaplain, who was appointed KP's almoner when she became queen in 1543. As her spiritual adviser, Day evidently encouraged her to translate Fisher's *Psalmi seu Precationes* as her *Psalms or Prayers*, for orders for multiple finely bound presentation copies of both works were billed to him in May 1544. See my introduction to *Psalms or Prayers*, pp. 198, 200.

24. *The English Works of John Fisher*, ed. John E. B. Mayor, pt. 1 1, Early English Text Society, extra series, 27 (London: N. Trübner, 1876), 387; spelling modernized.

25. See my introduction to *The Lamentation of a Sinner*, pp. 430–31.

> **O sweet Jesu, give me** continual **remembrance of Thy passion.** . . . Whereas Thou wert rich, for our sakes Thou becamest full poor; Thou tookest great labor to ease us, Thou sufferest many pains to relieve us. Where we were bound, Thou madest us free. We were condemned by justice of the painful prison of hell, and Thou by Thy mercies madest us inheritors to the joyful kingdom of heaven. Thou wert unkindly betrayed. Thou wert traitorously taken, and cruelly bound with hard ropes. Thou wert mocked and scorned and spitted upon. Thou wert beaten and bobbed, and crowned with sharp thorns. Thou wert drawn and stretched and through-pierced into Thy heart. Thy sinews and veins were broken, and Thy skin and flesh was torn. Thy hands and feet nailed to the cross, Thou sheddest all Thy blood, and yielded up Thy ghost. All this and much more Thou diddest and sufferest for sinful man's sake. Moist my dry heart, blessed Jesu, with Thy sweet drops of Thy grace, and **give me** continual **remembrance of** this **Thy** painful **passion. O sweet Jesu, possess my heart, and keep it only to Thee.**[26]

While the shared sense of the centrality of Christ's passion to faith and devotion forges connections across the confessional gap between traditionalists and Reformers, there are nonetheless differences to be found. Aspects of Parr's Reformed orientation in this prayer include her careful situating of Christ's death on the cross within a continuum of actions and initiatives that scripturally certify His role as Saviour; her reiterated, slightly heightened closing petition for "continual remembrance of this Thy painful passion" rather than for participation in the sacramental reenactment of it that is the Catholic Mass; and her restrained use of affective metaphor ("Moist my dry heart").

The emotional intensity of Parr's prayer does not approach the extremes of graphic detail or of physical union with the Saviour imagined in the "Fifteen Oes," a set of lyrical ejaculations on the names of Jesus that is regularly included in traditionalist primers of the period.[27] One of the briefer ejaculations in the "Oes" runs as follows in English: "O blessed Jesu, deepness of endless mercy, I beseech Thee for the deepness of Thy wounds that went through Thy tender flesh, Thy bowels,

26. "PP," fols. 24v–25v. Compare KP's rendering of a similar contemplative passage from Fisher on the sufferings of the crucified Saviour in *Psalms or Prayers*, pp. 235–36.

27. The "Fifteen Oes," so called because each prayer in the original Latin began "O Jesu, O Rex" or "O Domine Jesu Christe," have standardly been ascribed to St. Brigitta of Sweden (1303–73). Eamon Duffy, however, asserts that "they are English in origin," composed either in the devotional line "of Richard Rolle and his disciples or in the circle of the English Bri[d]gettines" (*The Stripping of the Altars: Traditional Religion in England, c. 1400–c. 1580* [New Haven, CT: Yale University Press, 1992], 249).

and The marr[ow] of Thy bones, that it shall please Thee to draw me out of sin, and hide me ever after in the holes of Thy wounds, from the face of Thy wrath, unt[il] time, Lord, that Thy dreadful doom be passed. Amen."[28]

Parr's tonality and sensibility are closer to the prayers interspersed in Miles Coverdale's *Fruitful Lessons upon the Passion*. The dynamic of Coverdale's prayer on the passion proceeds, like Parr's, from a dual contemplation of Christ's actions and their benefits to humankind, although here without Parr's serial specificity—which is, however, conspicuous in Coverdale's preceding prayers on the agony in the garden, the flagellation, and the crowning with thorns. His prayer, also like Parr's, does not end in imagined physical union but contents itself with tender proximity to the Saviour, invoking His sustaining love and its elevating inward effects in time-sanctioned imagery of flying "unto Thee under the protection of Thy holy cross" and being drawn "*up on high, O Lord* Jesu, from all worldly things."[29] A Reformed orientation discernibly predominates in the materials on Christ's passion that Parr adapts in her personal prayerbook.

Parr's next set of entries confirms that Scripture and the emotions stirred by reading and reflecting on it are basic to her own devotion. The set consists of prayers by prominent men and women of the Bible, each introduced by an identifying rubric: "The prayer of Queen Esther for help against her enemies" (Esther 13); "The prayer of Sarah, the daughter of Raguel, when she was slandered" (Tobias 3); "The prayer of Judith for the victory of Holofernes" (Judith 9); "The prayer of Jesus, the son of Sirach" (Ecclesiasticus 51); "The prayer of the three children that were delivered from the hot, burning fire" (apocryphal addition to Daniel 3 in the Vulgate); and "The prayer of Manasses, sixth king of Judah" (1 Paralipomenon 36).[30] Several observations regarding this set of prayers are germane to the matter of the old religion and the new in Parr's day.

The sources of all of these prayers are the Apocrypha or additions from it to canonical books of the Old Testament, with the one ostensible exception of the prayer of Sarah, daughter of Raguel.[31] The "Bible" in question here is common ground—

28. "The Fifteen Oes in English," in *Hore beatissime virginis Marie ad legitimum Sarisburiensis Ecclesis ritum* (Paris: François Regnault, 1536) (STC 15987), fol. clix r. Square brackets enclose emendations of typographical errors.

29. Miles Coverdale, *Fruitfull Lessons upon the Passion, Bvriall, Resvrrection, Ascension, and of the Sending of the holy Ghost* (T. Scarlet, 1593) (STC 5891), sig. R1 r-v. Regarding the comparative lateness of this English edition, the *STC* notes that Thomas Tanner's *Bibliotheca Britannico-Hibernica* (1748), 203, mentions printings of the *Fruitful Lessons* at Marburg in 1540 and 1547—dates contemporaneous with KP's literary activity.

30. "PP," fols. 27v–37v.

31. "PP," fols. 28v–29r. KP's source seems to be François Regnault's edition of *Hore beatissime virginis Marie* (1536) (STC 15987), sig. Mi v, a traditionalist Latin primer from which she translates selected portions in her only discernible departure from Lutheran sources in this section. A Lutheran source for the prayer of Sarah may yet come to light.

the canon of the Latin Vulgate—used by vernacular translators with Lutheran affiliations as their source for the versions of these prayers that Parr handles in varying ways. Her closely reproduced source for the prayers of Jesus the son of Sirach and of the three "children" in the fiery furnace is Coverdale's 1535 Bible; beyond the near verbatim correspondences of the two texts, the case for this particular source is strengthened by the location of the two prayers on successive folio pages.

Common ground remains conspicuous, moreover, with regard to the prayers of Jesus the son of Sirach and of Manasses, sixth king of Judah. Not only do these two prayers regularly figure among the suffrages in the Hours of the Blessed Virgin Mary in Latin primers according to Salisbury use.[32] They also are staples of the several English Lutheran compilations titled "Prayers of the Bible" that derive, with their sometimes convergent, sometimes discrepant renderings, from the Latin original *Precationes Biblicae* (1531), assembled from the Vulgate by Otto Brunfels, one of Luther's associates. The English Lutheran compilations that contain these two prayers (and various others) include Robert Redman's *Prayers of the Bible* (1535?), Miles Coverdale's *Psalter and Certain Other Devout Prayers Taken Out of the Bible* (after 1535), Richard Grafton's *Prayers of Holy Fathers, Patriarchs, Prophets* (1540?), and Richard Taverner's *An Epitome of the Psalms . . . With Divers Other Prayers* (1539).[33] What makes these compilations of prayers by men and women of the Bible "Lutheran" is the acted-upon commitment to reproducing and highlighting extracts of Scripture in English, before the authorization to do so was granted by Henry VIII in 1538–39. Otherwise, the extracted prayers engage with none of the differences in belief and practice that were opening a rift between Catholics and Reformers in this period.

Parr handles the first overtly Scriptural material in her personal prayerbook with confidence and freedom. It is a noteworthy aspect of her embrace of the equality of all souls before God that she accords equal place to prayers by men and women, three of each. She likewise maintains her premium on devotional expression that can be lifted above and beyond its circumstantial setting and promptings—one contributory reason for not identifying More's, Shaxton's, and Fisher's prayers in earlier sections. Now Parr excises from Queen Esther's prayer a lengthy deploring of the Persians' idolatry and oppression of the Jews, which God has allowed because of the Jews' sins. The residue retained by Parr distills Esther's predicament into a yearning appeal to God to help the Jews and to help her in particular: "Think upon us, O Lord, and show Thyself in the time of our distress and of our trouble. Strength me, O Thou, King of gods and Lord of all power; deliver us with Thy hand, and help me, desolate woman, which have no defense nor helper, but only Thee. Lord, Thou knowest all things. Thou knowest and wotest my neces-

32. See, e.g., STC 15984, 15985, and 15987.

33. For full titles of these compilations and other bibliographical information, see the *Short-Title Catalogue* entries for Redman (STC 20200.3), Coverdale (STC 2379), Grafton (STC 20200), and Taverner (STC 2748).

sity."[34] Likewise, Judith's prayer is stripped almost entirely of contextual reference to her daring and ultimately successful plot to behead the enemy giant Holofernes; there is a single allusion to "this device." What Parr wanted of Judith's words in her personal prayerbook were precisely and only these: "O Thou, God of the heavens, Thou, Maker of the waters and Lord of all creatures, hear me, poor woman, calling upon Thee, and putting my trust in Thy mercy. Remember Thy covenant, O Lord, and minister words in my mouth, and stablish this device in my heart. Thou art God, and there is none other but Thou. Amen."[35]

Parr's prominent endorsement of vernacular Scripturalism in the six prayers of identified men and women is followed in her prayerbook by a sequence of prayers taken alternately from traditionalist and Reformed primers. Her traditionalist primer yields Latin texts that she translates and redacts. Parr's Reformed source is William Marshall's *A goodly prymer in englyshe* (1535), which contains an "Instruction how we ought to pray." The proper use of prayer, modeled for us by Christ's example in the Lord's Prayer, reduces to three essential points: "to know thyself a sinner; of whom to take remedy; and how thou shalt obtain it, truly, by prayer."[36] The alternations of the ensuing sequence, from traditionalist to Reformed prayers and back again, heighten the sense that Parr is prospecting for common ground by collocating and comparing the texts she chooses, both in style and in substance. The net effect of her alternating sequence is a remarkable demonstration of the extent to which adherents of the old religion and the new could pray together in the same words.

A reflexive turn—a prayer about the nature of prayer—characterizes the initial item in this sequence, taken almost verbatim from the last prayer of the ninth canonical hour, just before Evensong, in Marshall's *A goodly prymer*: "Our merciful Father, which in teaching us to pray by Thy Son, Christ, hast commanded us to call Thee Father, and to believe that we are Thy well-beloved children; which stirrest up none of Thine to pray, but to the intent Thou wouldest hear them."[37] Identifying rubrics for the individual prayers are, again, mainly lacking in this alternating se-

34. "PP," fols. 27v–28r. Parr's sources are Grafton's *Prayers of Holy Fathers*, fols. 22v–23v, and ultimately Coverdale's translation of the book of Esther.

35. "PP," fol. 29r-v. Parr's sources are Grafton's *Prayers of Holy Fathers*, fol. 21r-v, and ultimately Coverdale's translation of the book of Judith. Among the prayers of male figures, Parr excises references to the Persians' idolatry and to animal sacrifices in "The prayer of the three children," "PP," fols. 32v–35v, but otherwise leaves intact the body of the text, from Coverdale's translation of Ecclesiasticus 51. The lengthy prayers of Jesus son of Sirach and Manasses, King of Judah, remain alogether intact.

36. William Marshall, *A goodly prymer in englyshe, newly corrected and prented, With certeyne godly meditations and prayers added to the same* (J. Byddell for W. Marshall, 1535) (STC 15998), sigs. Bi v–Biv v. Marshall's material on the Lord's Prayer derives, in turn, from Luther's *Kurze Form der Zehen Gebote, des Glaubens und des Vater Unsers* (Short Form of the Ten Commandments, the Creed, and the Our Father) (1520); see Butterworth, *English Primers*, 280, 285.

37. Marshall, *A goodly prymer*, sigs. Hiv v–Ii r.

quence. Next follow three markedly traditionalist prayers: the first (source unidentified) a petition to be enabled to cooperate with divine grace in the sacrament of penance and in works of mercy: "Grant me, O Lord my God: in my heart, repentance; in my spirit, contrition; in my eyes, a fountain of tears; out of my hands, liberality of alms."[38] The second of this trio of traditionalist prayers is Parr's translation of "De sanctissima trinitate" (Of the most holy Trinity), which immediately follows the section "In elevatione corporis Christi" (At the elevation of the Body of Christ) in a 1534 Latin primer commissioned for sale by a London bookseller, John Growte. A large woodcut image of the Trinity precedes this Latin prayer in Growte's edition. Parr effectively sustains the incantatory energies of its repeated petitions to the Persons of the Godhead, together and severally:

> O the true and unfeigned Trinity, the great and incomparable goodness, the everlasting and sweet cleanness, and the inseparate majesty of the Father, the Son, and the Holy Ghost, have mercy on me. O good Father, and meek Son, O Holy Ghost, O Light that cannot be put out; O Thee, only Father of heaven, have mercy on me. Thee, good Lord do I call upon; to Thee I do make my intercession and prayer.[39]

The third of these traditionalist prayers follows in close proximity to "De sanctissima trinitate" in Growte's primer. With this prayer Parr selects for translation and inclusion in her prayerbook a Latin text that could indisputably find a place in a Lutheran primer. She thereby signals and stakes common ground. This prayer is another serial petition for mercy that proceeds on the strength of Biblical examples of deliverance—"Daniel from the lake of the lions . . . the three children, Shadrach, Mesach, Abednego, from the hot, burning fire . . . Thy beloved disciple Peter, being in great jeopardy of drowning"—to entreat a "merciful God" to "save and deliver me from all tribulation and enemies. . . . For I am ignorant . . . to whom I should flee, or seek for help or comfort, but only to Thee, which art my Maker and Redeemer."[40]

From this rapprochement on common ground Parr next proceeds to transcribe, closely for the most part but sometimes selectively, the devotional commentary on the sixth petition, "And lead us not into temptation," and on the seventh, "But deliver us from evil," in "The Prayer of Our Lord" section in Marshall's *A goodly*

38. "PP," fol. 39r.

39. *Thys prymer of salysbury vse* (Paris: Y. Bonhomme, widow of T. Kerner, at the expenses of J. Groute, 1534) (STC 15985), fol. lxxxviii r-v.

40. *This prymer of salysbury vse*, fols. lxxxviii v–lxxxix r. Another closely similar prayer (source unidentified) that proceeds by instancing Biblical figures whom God delivered occurs later in this section of "PP," fols. 59v–62v.

prymer. The expanded phrasing of both clauses in this Reformed source emits its own incantatory energy, evoking the serialism of a vernacular litany: "Keep us that we fall not into the sin of hate and envy, what occasion soever be given to us. Keep us that we doubt not in the faith, neither fall in desperation now, nor in the point of death." "Keep us from hunger and dearth. Keep us from war and manslaughter. Keep us from Thy most grievous strokes: the pestilence, French pox, falling sickness, and such other diseases. Keep us from all evils and perils of the body."[41] Such an evocation of a litany in the vernacular may have been premature, or only just on the way to realization, as Parr copied these clauses into her personal prayerbook. Not until May 1544 would Henry VIII grant Archbishop Thomas Cranmer permission to issue a litany in English for public worship. It is possible that these litanylike prayerbook selections of Queen Katherine's, made in private, proceeded in tandem with the official promulgation of *A Litany* in the Church of England.[42]

Whether influenced by the authorization of Cranmer's English litany or not, this section of Parr's prayerbook documents a sustained attraction to prayers structured by runs of parallel, sometimes slightly varied phrasing, and with responses that likewise take parallel form. After Marshall's elaboration of two clauses of the Lord's Prayer, the unusual appearance of a rubric signals Parr's reversion to the passion of Christ, the central object and subject of primer devotion: "Here followeth a devout prayer to Christ, the second Person in Trinity, our only Redeemer, God and man." This gracefully styled prayer, the longest in her personal prayerbook, proceeds through serial affirmations, ordered associatively rather than chronologically, of belief in the truth of the Gospel narrative of the final events in Christ's life. The recurring form of the affirmations displays felicitous minor variations:

> Lord Jesus Christ, King of mercy and of pity, I believe and knowledge that Thou sufferest in Thy blessed feet, to be nailed grievously on the cross for our sins and offenses . . .
> Also, Lord Jesus, King of glory, I believe and knowledge that when Thou wert yet hanging on the cross, Thou Lord, openest Thy most holy mouth, and prayed for Thine enemies . . .

The litanylike structure of the enclosing prayer is rounded out by the responses to each of the affirmations of belief, also in a recurring form—pleas for mercy and forgiveness that recast the cruelty and injustice done to Christ in His passion as effects of the speaker's own sins committed and now confessed:

> I pray Thee, Lord Jesus, . . . for the painful wounds that Thou, Lord, sufferest there in Thy feet, that Thou, Lord, forgive me clean all

41. Marshall, *A goodly prymer*, sigs. Ciii r–Ciiii r.
42. See my general introduction, p. 14.

> my sin that I have done, in going, in working, idleness, and vanities . . .
>
> I pray Thee, Lord Jesus, . . . for the merciful words that proceeded out of Thy holy mouth, forgive me utterly all the sins, the which I have done in my vile speaking, and give me grace that, all the days of my life, I speak no leasings, backbitings, nor harm of any person. . . .[43]

Parr's source for this passion prayer is the compilation titled "Here followeth devout meditations and prayers with contemplations called The Paradise of the Soul" and appended to John Gough's composite primer—English, with parallel Latin text in the margins—published in 1536.[44] By the late 1520s, Gough was active as a translator, redactor, and compiler of works by such early adherents of the Reformation as John Frith in England and Patrick Hamilton in Scotland. Although recurrently questioned by the ecclesiastical authorities in London, Gough managed to sustain his publishing ventures and, in particular, to circulate his curiously inclusive composite primer, with its ample supply of pre-Reformation as well as Reformation materials.[45] Parr closely reproduces Gough's translation of this prayer to Christ, making only one substantive alteration in its lengthy text. In what is now a recognizable Reformed move, she deletes a clause following the opening reference to Christ's "painful death"—*"which body is daily offered in the sacrament of the altar, where . . ."*

Yet the proceeding and tonality of this section overall are anything but partisan or adversarial. The original of Gough's English "Paradise of the Soul" is a pre-Reformation Latin compilation, of which the earliest printing is thought to be *Orationale Paradisus Anime Nuncupatum* (A Manual of Prayers Named the Paradise of the Soul), published at Basel in 1498.[46] What Parr indelibly registers in copying this lengthy passion prayer is the nearly complete compatibility of her own devotion with this traditionalist expression of devotion to the crucified, redeeming Christ, as well as her gravitation to this particular Catholic prayer, plucked out of the matrix of a Lutheran primer for inclusion in her own compilation. Reaching its midpoint, Parr's personal prayerbook documents a significant extent of common ground for prayer in the old religion and the new, particularly when its substance is given utterance in litanylike responses for participatory worship by a lay Christian such as herself.

43. "PP," fols. 51r–54v.

44. John Gough, *This prymer of Salysbery vse, bothe in Englyshe and in Laten* ([Antwerp: widow of C. Ruremond for] J. Gough, 1536) (STC 15992), fols. clxviii v–clxxi r. In Gough, the text of this prayer is prefaced by a half-length woodcut of Jesus, crowned with thorns and dripping blood from His lacerations.

45. Butterworth, *English Primers*, 120–28.

46. Ibid., 62n.

The midpoint of Parr's prayerbook is also recognizable, in hindsight, as a pivot that sections her compilation into two halves. The discrete prayers thus far discussed constitute the first half; the second half consists predominantly of large assemblages of Biblical verses, mostly from the Psalms, in English translations from various Lutheran sources. Parr's impetus simply to copy a preexisting assemblage into her prayerbook was probably aroused by a staple item in many primers, both traditionalist and Reformed: the 189 versicles of what had come to be known as "Saint Jerome's Devotion out of David's Psalter." Parr includes 130 of these versicles, in a sequence broken just once; and she again uses as her closely followed source Gough's English-Latin primer.[47] Revered as the translator of the Latin Vulgate as well as the self-revising retranslator of the Psalms after he had learned Hebrew, St. Jerome could be considered the patron saint—certainly a major forerunner—of Parr's intense and rigorous immersion in the text of Scripture, especially the Psalter.

Another lengthy stretch of copied-out material is the Lord's Prayer followed by an assortment of 172 verses from the Old Testament, Apocrypha, and New Testament, for which Parr's source, again closely followed, is another compilation issued by Thomas Godfray, *The Fountain or Well of Life* (ca. 1534).[48] A shorter run of Biblical material is composed of Psalms 86, 13, 18:1–6, and 54, copied almost verbatim from Coverdale's English translation of Johan van den Campen's Latin paraphrase of the Hebrew Psalms.[49] Parr's interest not only in Coverdale's textual labors but also in those of van den Campen, lecturer in Hebrew in the University of Louvain, evinces her inexhaustible appetite for multiple renderings of the language of Scripture and the deepened understanding and appreciation that such multiple renderings could offer.

There are, additionally, repercussions of Parr's public literary activity in the latter half of her personal prayerbook. Her own initial venture had been to translate, as *Psalms or Prayers*, the Latin compositions that John Fisher had created by selecting, recasting, and splicing excerpts from the Gallican version of the Vulgate Psalter into new wholes, which he himself styled his "Psalmi" (Psalms). Among the materials that Parr copied into her prayerbook, "St. Jerome's Devotion out of David's Psalter" and Godfray's rangy assemblage in *Fountain or Well of Life* were produced by the same process of selection and recombination. So were her *Prayers*

47. "PP," fols. 77v–96r, reproducing Gough, *This prymer of Salysbery vse*, fols. cxxvi r–cxxxvii v.

48. "PP," fols. 109v–136v, reproducing *The Fountayne or well of lyfe / out of whiche doth springe most swete consolations / right necessary for troubled consciences / to thentent that they shall nat despeyre in adversitie and trouble. Translated out of latyn into Englysshe* (T. Godfray, [1534?]) (STC 11211), sigs. Cii v–Dv v. If not Godfray himself, the compiler and translator of this series of verses is unknown.

49. "PP," fols. 97v–105r, reproducing the specified Psalms from Coverdale, *A Paraphrasis vpon all the Psalmes of Dauid, made by Johannes Campensis, reader of the Hebrue lecture in the vniuersite of Louane, and translated out of Latine into Englyshe* (Thomas Gibson, 1539) (STC 2372.6), itself a translation of *Psalmorum omnium: iuxta Hebraicam veritatem paraphrastica interpretatio authore Joanne Campensi* (1534) (STC 23540).

or Meditations, in which Parr authored a new text by transformatively redacting excerpts from à Kempis's *De Imitatione Christi* in Whitford's translation.

In her personal prayerbook Parr again applies this process, choosing and arranging excerpts from George Joye's *The Psalter of David in English* (1530) to create a new sequence of eighty-three versicles.[50] Joye's subtitle announces that his English text is "purely and faithfully translated after the text of Feline." "Aretius Felinus" was a pseudonym used by the Strassburg Reformer Martin Bucer, the most prominent figure of the 1530s and 1540s in attempts to maintain peace and amity between Swiss and German Protestants, and between Protestants and Catholics. Parr's responsiveness to Bucer's Psalter in Joye's rendering, which she quarries to create psalms of her own in her personal prayerbook, is as suggestive of affinities in outlook and spirit as was her earlier responsiveness to Fisher in the prayer she composed on Christ's passion.[51] The difference, however, in her authorial responses to Fisher and to Bucer is her complete immersion in the phrases and tonalities of the Psalter in the latter case. Parr's piety attains a Scriptural abundance that approaches repletion in the latter half of her prayerbook. Scores of its tiny pages give broad devotional implementation to a central Lutheran tenet: *sola scriptura* (Scripture alone).

It would, however, be misleading to imply that prayers like those in the first half of Parr's personal prayerbook are simply replaced by lengthy sequences of lyric and meditative portions of Scripture in the prayerbook's latter half. Individual prayers do make their appearance, although in modest proportions. What is striking about them is their clear character as a group: these are texts marked in form and content as prayers originating in public worship, taken over here into a private context. So-called "collects" make up the largest category of Parr's prayers in the latter half of her prayerbook. These are prayers generally in the form of a single capacious sentence, whose origins in early Christian worship trace to Latin *collectio*, a summation offered by an officiating minister to draw together the various inward responses of the people to the biddings enjoined on them in the liturgy, or to Latin *collecta*, short for *oratio ad collectam*, a prayer said over the gathered people, and hence one that speaks for them all as a group. Either etymology conveys the vital associations of the collect with collective or congregational utterance in worship, the difference being a more subjective emphasis in the *collectio* and a slightly more institutional one in the *collecta*.[52]

50. "PP," fols. 62r–73r, selectively using Joye, *The psalter of Dauid in Englishe purely and faithfully translated aftir the texte of Feline* (Argentine: F. Foxe [i.e., Antwerp: Martin de Keyser], 1530) (STC 2370).

51. A discussion of Parr's redacting of Bucer's Psalter in Joye's rendering would require an essay in itself. As a preliminary measure, annotations to the text of her personal prayerbook in this edition supply Psalm and verse references for each of these excerpts from Joye.

52. On collect form, see Janel M. Mueller, *The Native Tongue and the Word: Developments in English Prose Style, 1380–1580* (Chicago: University of Chicago Press, 1984), 227. The gradation

The source of Parr's first three collects—"A prayer to the Father," "A prayer to the Holy Ghost," and "A prayer to the Trinity"—is a sequence in the service of Matins that reads identically in Marshall's *A Prymer in Englyshe* and its revision, *A goodly prymer*; a fourth collect, "A prayer to Jesus Christ," concludes the introductory passion narrative in Joye's *Ortulus anime.*[53] While the subjects of these prayers are familiar as recurrences from the first half of the prayerbook, the stateliness and sonority of collect form lend a previously unregistered gravity of utterance to the treatment of these subjects. Parr's transcription of Marshall's "A prayer to the Father" will illustrate:

> O God almighty, our merciful Father, which hast so exceedingly loved us, Thy chosen children, that Thou wouldest vouchsafe to give us Thy only and well-beloved Son, Jesus Christ, our Saviour, to suffer death for our sins, so that all that thus believe in Him might not perish, but have life everlasting: we beseech Thee, for Thy abundant mercy and for that inestimable love which Thou barest to Thy Son, Christ, our Saviour, give us, of Thy grace and power, Thy favor into our hearts, that we may believe, feel, and know perfectly, that Thou only art our God, our Father, and to us an almighty Helper, Deliverer, and a Saviour from sin, from all the devilish power of hell, of this world, and from death: and that by Thy Son, our Lord, Jesus Christ. Amen.

Parr's introduction of collects into her personal prayerbook expands the sense of common ground identified and attained that was evoked by the litanylike petitions of the later prayers in the prayerbook's first half. Now, in the second half, she broadens the frame of self-reference from first-person singular to first-person plural, and ushers into corresponding prominence a number of shared Christian concerns. In Marshall's collect some of these concerns are given a Reformation bent, including the petition for God's grace (equated in Lutheran fashion with God's "favor") and the premium placed on personalized faith (faith *in* God and Christ as agents of redemption) rather than objective faith (faith *that* God can hear prayer, *that* Christ is the Son of God), a distinction emphatically pointed by the tripled verb conjunction "believe, feel, and know perfectly."[54] The echo of John 3:15—"that all that thus believe in Him shall not perish, but have life everlasting"—also en-

from individual and personal expression to collective and communal expression in KP's prayerbook reprises an analogous development in her *Lamentation of a Sinner.*

53. "PP," fols. 106r–109v, closely following Marshall, *A Primer in English*, sig. Mvii r-v, or *A goodly prymer*, sig. Gii r-v; and George Joye, *Ortulus anime. The garden of the soule* (Argentine: F. Foxe [Antwerp: M. de Keyser,] 1530–31) (STC 13828.4), sig. Gviii r-v.

54. On grace as divine favor and on "feeling faith" as contrasted with "historical faith," see *The Lamentation of a Sinner*, nn 51, 130.

hances with the universalism of the Gospel the sense of inclusiveness elicited by the form and substance of this type of collective prayer.

That Parr gravitates toward prayers more focused on the church than on the individual in the latter half of her prayerbook is further confirmed by her selection and inclusion of the majestic prayer-hymn to the God of all creation "Te Deum laudamus," under the title "The song of Austin [Augustine] and Ambrose," which is also its title in her source, Marshall's *A goodly prymer*. Likewise, Parr includes the introit, the first part of the traditional "proper" of Matins, beginning with Psalm 51:15 (in the numbering of English Bibles), "O Lord, open Thou our lips, and our mouths shall show forth Thy praise," and ending with the doxology, "Glory be to the Father, to the Son, and to the Holy Ghost"—a sequence for which Marshall or Gough, reading identically, is her source.[55] This devotional turn toward collective concerns of Christians, conceived as the body of Christ in the church, reconceptualizes the body of Christ as conceived in the earlier passion prayers of Parr's prayerbook. Equally, this devotional turn toward collective Christian concerns finds counterparts both in her universalizing evocation of the relations of Christ and the soul in her *Prayers or Meditations* and in her vision of the godly potential of England as a commonwealth of persons of all estates that concludes her *Lamentation of a Sinner*.

If Parr's personal prayerbook had ended with the text that she embellished with retraced gold capitals and vinelike tracery on rectangular fields of deep red and deep blue, then the foregoing account of the dynamic of this work would be complete at this point. The prayerbook would stand as Parr's proving ground, the site of her intense and sustained personal engagement with devotional crosscurrents and continuities in the early phases of the English Reformation. But the text of the prayerbook does not end with its embellished portion; it continues across five leaves on which Parr's handwriting loosens and eventually trails off altogether. These final tiny leaves seemingly inscribe the poignant record of her soul's struggles in the late stages of her only known pregnancy and the onset of the fever that caused her death at the age of thirty-six. The five leaves contain five prayers—"A prayer in trouble," "For the lightening of the Holy Ghost," "In adversity and grievous distress," "For strength of mind to bear the cross," and "A prayer of the faithful in adversity"—with the text of the last one left incomplete. Parr's source for these final prayers is another work by an English Lutheran, Richard Taverner's *An Epitome of the Psalms* (1539), which she follows quite closely but does not transcribe verbatim.

With Parr's appropriation of Taverner's Psalm paraphrases, first-person singular locutions resume, and with them the charged interiority of the prayers in the first half of her prayerbook. While registering heights and depths, the subjectivity expressed in these last prayers selected from Taverner is repeatedly steadied by a

55. "PP," fols. 74v–76v; 136v-137r, closely reproducing Marshall, *A goodly prymer*, sigs. Fi r–Fii r, Ei r.

sense of equipoise that is recognized as God's gift. To illustrate, the prayer adapting Psalm 60, "For strength of mind to bear the cross," pleads, "Stop my wounds, for I am all too plagued and beaten. Yet, Lord, this notwithstanding, I abide patiently, . . . continually waiting for relief at Thy hand." The speaker then proceeds to identify—using some Lutheran keywords, "favor," "promise"—the wellspring of inward patience: "I have received a token of Thy favor and grace. I mean Thy word of promise concerning Christ, who for me was offered upon the cross, for a ransom, a sacrifice, and satisfaction for my sins. Wherefore, . . . be Thou my stay in perils, for all human stays are but vain."[56] Likewise, the speaker of "A prayer in trouble" acknowledges a God-granted balance that steadies the soul in its vicissitudes. Uniquely in this group of prayers, this one adapts collect form to personal expression before appending a petitionary cry at its close:

> Lord, hear my petition, and have compassion upon me; turn my sorrow into joy: strip me once of this grievance, and so clothe me with joy, to the end my tongue may blaze Thy name, and give praises unto Thee without stop. Ah, Lord my God, deliver me out of these straits, and to Thee I will sing praises everlastingly. Amen.[57]

Parr's faltering transcriptions from Taverner's epitomes of selected Psalms draw the massively eclectic compilation of materials in her prayerbook to a circular close. The work's movement encompasses a historically specific circuit of devotional common ground for Christians at the advent of the English Reformation. Such a deliberately created assemblage as Parr's, moreover, was a harbinger of developments to come in English devotion. While the authorization of Cranmer's Book of Common Prayer in 1549 for public worship in the Church of England was the single most decisive factor in the decline of primers, they were replaced by a gamut of publications that approached devotion as personal exercise and cultivation, as Parr had done.[58] Her prayerbook's prevailing tendencies in tracing devotional common

56. "PP," fols. 140r–141v, following *An epitome of the psalmes, or briefe meditacions upon the same, with diuerse other moste christian prayers*, trans. Richard Taverner (London, 1539) (STC 2748), sig. Giiii r-v. Taverner's original is a Latin work by Wolfgang Capito, an associate of Luther and later of Bucer. On an earlier occurrence of "plague" as KP's mistaken cognate for Latin *plaga* (blow, stroke), see my introduction to her *Psalms or Prayers*, p. 206.

57. "PP," fol. 137r-v, transcribing the last three sentences only of Psalm 30 in Taverner, *Epitome*, sig. Diii r.

58. Butterworth (*English Primers*, 274–75) emphasizes the "end of an era" with the advent of the Book of Common Prayer. White (*Tudor Books of Private Devotion*, chaps. 9–12) acknowledges the decline in "official Primers" but argues persuasively for the diffusion of the type into such genres as "Scripture for private devotion," "guides to the devout life," "general prayerbooks," and "adaptation of traditional materials" in the later course of the sixteenth and seventeenth centuries.

ground for Christians would prove a no less predictive development. As traces of her own choices and direction, its combination of traditionalist and Reformed sources subjected to many minute restylings sets the syncretic stamp of the English Reformation on the remarkable register of spiritual process and progression that is "Katherine Parr's Personal Prayerbook."

The Autograph Text of the Personal Prayerbook[1]

[1r-v is a badly damaged leaf. The recto side begins with an outsized, illuminated capital W on a red ground, but is otherwise illegible. The vellum of the left half of the verso side is discolored, shrunken together, and illegible. The legible portions of its right half read as follows.]

[1v] . . . of this present aduersites seinge my lorde god . . . as . . . in erth . . . hyd . . . a . . . but in . . . desiered any plesure . . . but tribulacyones . . . hated of wicked folk and the moste bitter and spitefull deth of the crosse he, albeit that he was god toke vpon hym the nature of man to saue me which was loste and after he was [2r] made man he neuer rested goinge on Judie galleie and samaryae to instructe the ingnorant[2] to hele the sike to raise the dede & to worke many meruayles elles incredible. And although he was full in al thing / he dyd those pouerties for hym selfe he susteyned his life by thexpence of other folk he was harbored by other he was hungered neither [2v] we haue often redde of his wepinge / but neuer of his laughing / When he was but achilde he was sought to haue byn dystroyed / afterwarde whan he grew to more adge he alweis suffered the hates of wicked folkes / he was solde and betrayed of his owne dissiple: taken and ponisshed of the Iues and he which dyd no sinne beten downe compased [3r] aboute with fals witnes spitte vpon beatyn

1. **The . . . Prayerbook** Numbering for the 143 vellum leaves of this text has been provided in smaller type, enclosed in square brackets, within the following transcription of BL, Harley MS 2342, and the recto side (r) or verso (v) side of each leaf has been specified. Titles and letters in boldface indicate where KP has used gilt tracery on deep red and blue fields to set off these elements as ornamental features of her text.

2. **ingnorant** ignorant—an idiosyncratic spelling of KP's.

with blowes mocked Cursed crowned with thornes beten with Reeds scordged naked ge[ten?][3] to the crosse naked suffereth wundes of nayles in his handes and fete ·[4] of aspect reu[ilide?][5] and is all powred ouer with bloode springynge oute of sondry wondis: when at his dethe he was athriste they made drinke eysell and gaulle [3v] and beinge so cruelli consomid he offered hym selfe a sacrifice to god his father for vs all. who am I then that I shulde dis[pute?][6] and suffer with an unpacient minde yf any trouble do chaunce vnto me yf I suffer any incommoditie: yf any persecution of enuyous persones comber me / spetially seinge non euyll can be don vnto me which [4r] my synnes hath not deserued Therfor I will not suffer greuously that thinge which ys bestowed rightuously· but I shal pray my lord gode to graunt me pasience in all thinges. And in that pacience pourgynge and forgeuenes of myne vngraciousnes that he which vouchesaued to make me partaker of his paynes may also make me partaker of his glorie accordinge to thapposteles [4v] sayinge, as ye be felowes of his passions so shal ye be of his compforte. And agayne and we die with hym saith he: we shal all lyue with hym; And yf we suffer with hym / we shal also raigne with hym / therfore whether we be prouoked with priuate envy: or elles ani vyolente power take away our ryches or haue cruell silence / or oftyn deth of oure dere frend or any other aduersite [4a r][7] chaunce vnto vs / we muste gyue thankes for all thing: confesse and say: lorde: thow art Juste and thie Judgement ys true: Reproue not the rebukinge of our lorde. For he wondeth and gyueth medysynes / he smyteth and his handes shall hele / Paule and Scilas beinge betyn with roddes in macidone put in preson and laide in fetters sange prayses to our lorde· and our [4a v] lorde hymselfe whan he toke the challes: gave thankes to tech vs: to gyue thankes to god as oftyn as we be greued and ponisshed with any aduersitie: for by the Challys ye vnderstonde the tribulations of this worlde / accordinge to that sayenge Lette this Challes passe from me: therefore lette thankes be gyuen vnto hym for all thinges: by whose prouidence all thinges [5r] do chaunc to thyntente by that we may be proued both to pacience in aduersitie: and not vnkynde in prosperite. amen.

3. **ge[ten?]** Severe local discoloration renders the word ending illegible here and at two later points. My restoration is necessarily conjectural since KP's source for this passage has not been identified.

4. Here and elsewhere, in accordance with KP's occasional practice, I reproduce her raised-dot punctuation mark, which had the approximate value of a modern colon. See M. B. Parkes, *Pause and Effect: An Introduction to the History of Punctuation in the West* (Berkeley: University of California Press, 1993), 42, 45, 52.

5. **reu[ilede?]** another conjectural restoration.

6. **dis[pute?]** a final conjectural restoration.

7. **[4a r]** The accidental repetition of fol. 4 in the penciled numbering of the leaves of the manuscript is notated as 4a r-v to preserve the possibility of consulting the original or digitized images of Harley 2342.

A PRAYER CONSERNYNGE THE LOUE OF MY NEIGHBOUR

Moste swete lorde Jhesu Criste which hatiste no thynge that ys well done yf for a good will and be gentile intent of a man which hath done [5v] no hurte. But lorde it ys amoch gretter thinge and liker to thie moste highe benignite yf I loue myn enymy and alweis will good and do it yf I can to hym which hath done me hurte / this procedeth of thie grace and goodnes / nothing is liker to the in nature then that man which is gentill and peaseble to his yll willers and enymyes that [6r] hurte hym: For he that loueth his enemyes foloweth the: which dideste loue vs / and not only didest loue vs / but also woldeste then die for vs: the moste shamfull deth: and dideste pray for thie crusifiers / Also thow haste commaunded vs to loue our enymyes as it ys wrettyn / Loue your enymys / and do good to them which hate you / and the rewarde that thow promiseste foloweth· [6v] to thintent ye may be [the] children of your fader which ys yn heuyn: for our lorde Jhesu Criste / whose propertie ys to haue mercy and to forgyue. The only and hole profe of loue ys: yf we loue hym which is ageynste vs and letteth our welth / Also loue ys wonte to be proued by the only contr[a]rietie of hate / Wherfore as man ys ouercom with wordely [7r] prosperyte: so ys the deuyll ouercom with loue of our enymy. O lorde Jhesu Christe moste mercifull in loue / and most louynge in mercy,· I knowe that seperattinge from the ys deth of the sowle: and contrywise knyttynge to the by loue ys lyfe· Therfore as euery man naturally loueth his bodyly helth / and ferethe deth· So likewise he ought to loue trew[lye] and eschew [7v] hate. For he that hathe not that loue remayneth in deth of synne and dettour of eternal deth. O moste merciful lord Jhesu Christe· from whom loue cannot be banesh[ed]: although those thynges be not hyd from the / Which I moste wicked synner haue commytted / yf I confesse with my harte and mouth that I haue lyued vngraciously· and by the reason of my malice and [8r] iniquitie I haue lacked [the] trew loue besides other thinges lorde / which I haue euill conceaued and done I haue hated myne enymy. And although I knewe by thy commaundement that I ought to loue hym yet I haue dispised and sette lytill by thy commaundement: I haue conceaued hatefull dyspleasure ageynste many: and after the conceauinge thereof: I haue [8v] fulfilled the fa[ntas]es[8] of my harte and mynde: And although at sum tyme I performed it not in dede / yet I purposed to bacbitinge and sclaundringe. Therfore moste petifull lorde Jhesu Christe helpe me through thy blessed and mercifull loue: grauntinge me forgyuenes And that I maye amend my myserable life / and so loue the and all other for thie sake. That loue may [9r] neuer faile But contynewe into life euerlastynge. Amen

8. **fa[ntas]es** a conjectural reconstruction of this word's illegible midsection.

O holy trynite the father the sonne the holy goste Thre eagall coeternall persons and one god almyghty: haue mercy vpon me / vyle abiecte: abomynable synfull wretche: Mekely knowledgynge befor [9v] thy hye maieste my longe contynued synfull life / euen fro my childhed hetherto / thow good gratious lorde as thow gyueste me thy grace to knoweledge them / so gyue me thie grace not in only woorde but in harte also with sorowful contrition to repente them and vtterly to forsake them / Forgyf me those synnes also in which by myn owne defaulte throwe euyl affections [10r] and euel custumes my reson is with sensualite so blynded that I cannot disserne them for syn And illumen good lord myn harte and gyue me grace to knowlege them. And forgyue me my synnes necligently forgotten / And bringe them to my mynde with grace to be puerly confessed of them: Gloryous god / gyue me from hens forthe thie grace with litell respecte [10v] vnto the worlde so to sette and fixe fermely my harte vpon the that I may say with the blessed Apostell saincte Paule the worlde ys crusified to me and I to the worlde Criste is to me life / and to dye ys my gayne and adv[a]ntage: I desire to be lewsed and to be with Christe / Lorde gyue me thi grace to amende my lyfe / and to haue an eye to myn ende withoute anye grudge or fere of deth which [11r] to them that die in the good lord ys the gate of a welthye lyfe / Almyghty god tech me to do thy will: Take my right hand and lede me into the tru mercy for myn enymys. Drawe me after the bynd my mouth with asnafel and bridell when I wyl not drawe vnto the. O gracius god al synful fere / al synfull sorowe and pensiuenesse / all synful hope / all synfull myrth and [11v] gladnes euite fro me / on the other side / concernynge such fere / such hevynes / suche comfort consolacion and gladnes / as shalbe profitable to my sowle / do with me according to thie greate goodnesse / Good lorde gyue me grace in all my fere and agony to haue recourse to that great fere and wonderfull agony that thowe my Swete Sauyour haddest at the mounte of olyuet / before thi [12r] moste bitter passion / and in the meditation thereof to conceaue gostely comforte and consolacion profitable for my soule: Almyghty god take fro me al veyneglorious myndes: all apetit of myne owne prayse: al enuy: couetusnes [glotony] slewth:[9] and lechery: all wrathfull affections: all apetite of reuengynge: all desire or delite of other fokes harme: all pleasure in prouokynge any parson to wrath and anger: all delite of [12v] tauntinge or mockynge any parson: in their affliction or trouble: And gyue me good lord an humble lowly / quiet / pesable pacient / cheritable / kynd / tendre and petyfull mynde: in all my walkes / all my wordes / and all my thoughtes / to haue a taste of thye holye blessed sprite / Gyue me good Lord a full feithe / a ferme hope / a feruent Cherytye / and loue to the Good lorde / incomperable [13r] aboue the loue of my selfe / and that I loue no thinge to thie displeasure / but euery thinge in a dewe order to the: Gyue me good lorde a longynge to be with

9. **slewth** sloth. This northern form of the word was perhaps acquired by KP during one or the other of her two marriages to northerners: Sir Edward Borough and John Neville, Lord Latimer.

the not for the aduoydinge of the aduercyties of this wretched worlde: nor somuch for the aduoidynge of the paynes of helle / nother so muche for the attteynynge of the Joyes of heuyn in the respecte of myne owene commoditie / as [13v] euyn for a very loue to the: And bere me, goode lorde thie loue and fauour which thinge my loue to thewarde / ware it neuer so grete / could not but of thie greate goodnes disserve. And pardon me good lorde that I am so bolde to aske the so hye peticions beinge so vyle a synfull wretche and so vnworthy to atteyne the loweste. but yet goode lorde suche they be as I am bounden to desire and wisshe: and shulde be [14r] euer the affectall desire of the yf my manyfolde synnes were not the lette. From which O glorious trynytie vouchesaue of thie goodnes to wasshe me with that blessed blood that thow O swete sauyour Christe sheddest oute of thy body in the dyuers tormentes of thye moste bitter passyon. Take fro me good lorde this luke warme fassion or rather cay colde maner of medytation and this dulnes [14v] In prayinge vnto the: and geue me warme delyte and quietnes in thinkinge vpon the and gyue me thye grace to longe for the and make vs all lyuely members (o sauyour Christe) of thy holy mysticall body the catholike Churche: Vouchsaue lorde to kepe vs this day withoute synne haue mercy on vs lorde haue mercy on vs: lette thy mercy be showed vpon vs as we haue trysted in the. [15r] O lord in the haue I trysted / Lette me neuer be confunded eternally. Amen

A PRAYER FOR OUR ENYMIES

Allmyghty god, haue mercy on me and all them that bere me euyll wyll and woulde me harme: And ther faultes and myne to gether: by suche easy / tender mercifull / mercynesse as thyne Infynyte [15v] Wysdom and petyousnes / so vouchesafe to amend and redres and make vs sauyd soules in heuyn to gether where we may euer lyue and loue together with the and thy blessed sainctes, O glorius trinite for this bytter passion of oure swete sauyour Criste. Amen

Lorde geue me pacyens in tribulation / grace in euerythinge [16r] to conforme my will to thyn that I may truly saye thye wille be fulfilled / in erth as it ys in hevyn. The thinges good lorde that I pray for, gyue me grace to labour for. Amen

O lorde god almighti which longe ago saidest by the mouth of James thyn Appostle: If any of you lacke [wisdom] Let hym aske it of [God which geueth it] plenteously to all [men, and casteth][10] [16v] no man in the tethe, and it shalbe gyuen hym. Hyre my peticion for this thi promes sake. Lette my pr[a]yer ascende lukely into thi sight

10. **[wisdom], [God . . . it], [men . . . casteth]** Illegible words in KP's manuscript have been restored by reference to her source, Shaxton's prayer.

like incense. Let thyn eare be attent vnto my depe desyre. Geue me wisdom which is euer assistent aboute thi seate. And putte me not out from among thi children for I am thi seruant and the sonn of thi handmaid Oh send her (I mene thi godli wisdom) oute of thyn holi heauens and from the trone of thi majesti, that she may be with me and labour with me· that I may knowe [17r] what is acceptable in thi sight Oh lern me goodnes nurtour and knowlege, for I beleue thi commandementes. Thow art good and gr^a^cious, instruct me in thyn ordinances. Let myn herti besichyng ascend into thi presens. Geue me vnderstonding according to thi worde. O geue me vnderstonding: I shall kepe thi Lawe, yee I shall kepe it with all myn harte. Shewe me thie weie o Lorde, and teche me thy patthes. Led me into thi trueth [17v] and lerne me, for thow art the god of my helth and on the do I depend alwei. Here now my voice O lord with which I haue cryed vnto the / haue merci vpon me and graciously here me for Jesvs Cristes sake o Lorde whiche lyueth and reigneth with the hye father and the holy gooste worlde withoute ende. Amen

[Squeezed addition at the foot of fol. 17v:]
Leade me o lorde in thy way & lette me walke in thi trewth. O lette my harte delyte in fearing thi name. Ordre my goinge after thi worde that no wyckednes raigne in me / Kepe my stepes within thi pathes· lesst my fete turne awaye an contaryrye way /

[18r] I myserable synner am not worthie to name or caule vpon nor thynke on in my harte / I humbly besyche the good lorde mercyfulli to looke on me thyne vnkynde seruaunte and haue petie on me lyke as thow haddeste petye and dydeste forgeue the woman of Chanane, Mary magdaleyne, the Publican, and the thefe hangyng on the crosse. I confesse vnto the moste mercyfull father all my synnes whiche yf I wolde, I can [18v] not hide frome the / Forgeue me my lorde Jhesu chryste, where as I wretched synner haue offended the, in pride, in couetousenes, in slouthe, in wrathe, in envye, in glotenye, in lechery, in vayne glorye, in adulterie, in thefte, in lying / in blasphemynge, in wanton gestes and sportes, in heringe, in seinge, in tastinge, in felynge, in spekinge, in thinkinge, in workinge, and in all manner waies wherein I (an unstable [19r] and frayle creature) myghte offende my maker by anny faute or trespas. Therefore I besyche thie mercys and goodnesse which cam downe frome heuen to erthe for my soule helth (whiche also reysed vp kynge Davyd from the faule of syn) to forgeue me / Forgeue me good lorde whiche forgaueste Peter that denyed and forsoke the Thow arte my maiker / my helper / my redemer / my gouernour [19v] my father, my lorde, my king, my god thow arte my hope my truste / my gouernaunce / my helpe my comforte my strength / my defence my delyueraunce / my lyfe my helth my resurrection

Thow arte my staye and my Refuge my lighte my desire and my socoure good Lorde I besich the helpe me and I shalbe saffe, gouerne me and defende me. Comforte me and confirme [20r] me in gladnes Geue me light and viset me / Reuyve me that am dede in synne / Despise me nat good Lorde for I am the worke of thi handes / thi seruaunt I am though I be euell / though I be a synner and vnworthie, yet howsoeuer I be good lorde I am thyne. To whom than shoulde I fle good lorde, but onelie to the. If thow caste me oute who will receyve me, If thow despise me who will regarde me? Therefore good lorde though I be [20v] vnworthie, vyle and uncleane, yet knowlege me returnyng agayne vnto the For yf I be vyle and filthie, thow mayste make me cleane / If I be blynde thow maist make me se agayne / If I be seke thow mayste make me hole / If I be dede and buried in synne thowe mayste reuyve me / For thi mercye is gretter than myne Inyquyte / that maiste forgeue more than I can offende / Therefore good Lorde consydre not the nomber of my fautes [21r] but according to the aboundauns of thie petye, haue mercye on me and be gracious vnto me moste myserable synnar

O Good lorde which saidest, I will not that a synner shoulde dye, but rather that he shoulde lyue and be conuerted to goodness. Say now vnto my soule / I am thie helth, turne me (good lorde) towarde the, and be not despleased with me.

O moste mercyfull lorde and [21v] father / I besiche the for thie Inestymable mercye and goodnesse brynge me vnto a good ende Amen

O blessed Jhesu make me to loue the intierlye O moste mercyfull sauyour make thow me to loue the, for withoute the, blyssed Jhesu, I cannot loue the Wherefore I besiche the moste louyng lorde make thow me to loue the intierlye with all my [22r] harte with all my mynde and withe all my power and strength. O moste blissed Jhesu, I wolde fayne loue the, but I cannot withoute thie helpe. O moste swete Jhesu my comforte and solace fayne woulde I loue the but without thie helpe I can do nothinge. my great enemyes, the worlde, the flesshe, and the feende, be right fearce and cruell and euermore Redye to lette me frome thi loue. helpe me therefore good lorde [22v] and strength me with thie grace so that I may euer loue the as thie will is. O blyssed Jhesu lett me depelye considre the contentes of thie loue towardes me. O my lorde god almyghtie thow arte my maker, thow arte my redemer, thow arte my sauyour, thow good lorde haste made me not a stone withoute lyfe, not of a tre withoute sencyble parceyuyng, not a beeste withoute resonne, but thow haste made me a perfite [23r] creature hauyng lyfe sencyble parceyuyng and reasonable vnderstanding. Also thow haste Redemed me not with corruptible golde and siluer, but with thie moste precyous bloode, wherby thow haste made me partaker of thie grete glorye and Joye in heuen. Moreouer thow haste preserued me frome myche yll, and yet daylie thow doeste preserue me and norysshe [me] both bodely and gostely. Graunte me myne [23v] owne good lorde depely to plante within my breste, the remembraunce of this thie greate loue towards me. O blyssed

Jhesu geue me grace, hartely to thanke the for thi benefites. O moste gracious lorde I am full of fraylte and feble as thow knowest beste and utterly Insufficyent of my selffe to rendre thankes vnto thie goodnesse for my creacion, for my redemcion and conseruacion. Thow therefore blyssed Lorde Jhesu [24r] Receyue me after thy will and geue me grace hartely to thank the for this and other of thye manyfolde benefettes. O blyssed Jhesu geue me good will to serve the and suffer for the. O moste good and lyberall lorde thow arte the very gyuer of all good thinges, geue me good lorde a good will to loue the, to dread the, and to suffre / my dewtye good lorde is gret and my power ys but smalle. I oughte to loue the above all creatures [24v] and my neyghbour as my selffe / I aught to fle synne for thye sake and onely to folow the / I aught to be content with all my trybulacion, and gladlye to suffre theym for the loue of the, but in nowyse I canne do this by myne owne power and strength / Helpe me therefore blyssed Jhesu with thy specyall grace, and geue me good wille thus to serve the obediently, and pacyently to suffre. O swete Jhesu geue me contynuall [25r] remembraunce of thy passyon. O moste benyng Jhesu / myne hole helthe and welthe / I confesse me and lowly submytte my selffe vnto thi greate mercy and goodness, for I haue lytle remembred the, and lesse I haue thanked the for thi great kyndnes shewed vnto me and al mankynde. Where as thow werte ryche, for our sakes thow becamest full poore, thow tokest great labour to ease us, thou suffreste many paynes to Releve [25v] us. Where we were bounde thu madest vs fre, We were condemned by Justice of the paynefull pryson of hell And thow by thi mercys madest vs inheritours to the Joyfull kingdome of hevyn. Thow werte vnkyndely betraied. Thow werte traiterousely taken and cruelly bounde with harde ropes. Thow werte mocked and scorned and spitted upon. Thow werte beaten and bobbed, and crowned with sharpe thornes. Thow [26r] werte drawen and stretched and through perced into thy harte / thi senewes and vaynes were broken, and thy skynne and flessh was torne, thie handes and feete nayled to the crosse. thowe shedeste all thi bloode and yelded vp thi goste. All this and mych more thow dideste and suffrest for synfull mannes sake. Moyste my drye harte blyssed Jhesu with thie swete droppes of thi grace, and geue me contynuall [26v] remembraunce of this thie paynefull passyon O swete Jhesu possesse my harte and kepe it onely to the. O moste noble and myghtye prynce lorde of all lordes and kynge of all kynges thow madeste heuen and erth and all the creatures in theym. Now than like as I am thyn by creacion, so make thow me euer thyne by possession: make thow me mekely to confesse myne owne dedes, words [27r] and thoughtes, and to put my hole truste and confidence in thi grace / Make me utterly to despyse this wretched worlde and all the unlawfull pleasures and desyres of the same, make thow me meke pacyent and petyfull, and geue me parfecte faythe, hope and charyte Make thow my harte also O moste swete Jhesu a pleasaunte Palles for thie high magestye and possesse it holde it and kepe it onelye to [27v] the good lorde Amen

THE PRAIER OF QUENE ESTER FOR HELP AGAYN HER ENYMYES

O Thow Lorde, thow onely arte our kynge / helpe me desolate woman which haue no helper but the / for my mysery and destruction ys harde at my hande. Thinke apon vs O lorde and shew thi selffe in the tyme of oure destres and of our trouble / Strength me O thow kynge of godes and lorde of all [28r] power delyuer vs with thye hand and helpe me desolate woman whiche haue no defence nor helper, but onely the. Lorde thow knoweste all thinges. thou knoweste and woteste my necessite. O lorde thow god [of] habraham O thow myghtye god aboue all / here the voyce of theym that haue none other hope and delyyuer vs oute of the handes of the wicked and delyuer me oute of my fere Amen

[28v] THE PRAER OF SARA THE DOUGHTER OF RACHIELL WHAN SHE WAS SLAUNDRED

Blyssed be thie name O god of oure fathers whiche whan thow arte wroth shewest marcye and in the tyme of trouble thow forgeueste the synnes of theym that call apon the / Vnto the lorde turne I my face / vnto the lyfte I vpp myne eyes / I besyche the O lorde loose me oute of the bondes of this rebuke After a storme thow makest the [29r] wether quyet and still / After wepinge and heuynes thow geuest greate Joye / Thy name O god of Israhell be praysed for euer. Amen

THE PRAIER OF JUDITH FOR THE VICTORIE OF OLYFFERNES.

O Thow god of the heuens, thow maker of the waters, and lorde of all creatures, here me poore woman calling apon the and putting my truste in thie [29v] mercy. Remembre thie conuenaunt[11] O lorde and mynystre wordes in my mouth and stablysshe this devyse in my harte / thow arte god and ther ys none other but thowe Amen

THE PRAIER OF JESSVS THE SONNE OF SIRAKE.

I Thanke the O Lorde and kynge, and prayse the O god my sauyour We yelde preyse vnto thi name for thow arte my defendre and [30r] helper and haste preserued my bodye frome destruction, frome the snare of traitorous tonges and from the lyppes that are occupied with lyes / Thow haste bene my helper frome suche as stood vppe agaynste me and haste delyuered [me] after the multitude of thie mercy

11. **conuenaunt** KP's consistently idiosyncratic spelling of "covenant" is also found in the girlhood translations made by her stepdaughter Elizabeth in the mid-1540s; see *Elizabeth I: Translations, 1544–1589*, ed. Janel Mueller and Joshua Scodel (Chicago: University of Chicago Press, 2009), 52n42, 258n42.

and for thi holy nameis sake Thow haste delyuered me frome the roring of theym that prepared them selffes to deuoure me / ~~After~~ out of the handes of [30v] suche as soughte after my lyfe Frome the multytude of theym that troubled me and went aboute to sette fier apon me on euery syde so that I am not burned in the myddes of the fyer / From the depe of Helle From an vncleane tonge From lying wordes From an vnryghtuous tonge. my soule shall prayse the, lorde vnto deth, for my lyfe drew nye vnto hell / They [31r] compassed me rounde aboute on euery syde and there was no man to helpe me / I loked aboute me yf there were any man that wolde socoure me but there was none. Then thought I apon thye mercye O lord, and apon thye actes, that thow haste done euer of olde namely thow delyuerest suche as put ~~no~~ theire truste in the, and reddeste them oute of the handes of theire enemyes [31v] Thus lyfted I vp my prayer frome the erth, and prayed for delyueraunce frome my enemyes. I cauled apon the, lorde my father that he wolde not leve me withoute helpe in the day of my trouble and in the tyme of the proude I praysed thye name contynuallye yelding honor and thankes vnto the. And so my prayer was harde / thow saueste me frome destruction and delyuereste [32 r] me frome the vnryghtwyse tyme. Therefore will I acknowledge and prayse the and magnyfye the name of the lorde. Amen

THE PRAIER OF THE III CHILDREN THAT WERE DELYUERED FROM THE HOTE BURNYNG FYRE

Blissed be thow O lord god of oure Fathers Righte worthie to be praysed and honoured ys that Name of thyne for euermore. For thow arte Rightwise in [32v] all those thinges that thow haste doone to vs / yea faythfull are all thye woorkes / thye wayes are righte and thye Judgementes trew / yea accordinge to righte and equyte haste thow broughte these thinges apon vs bycause of oure synnes / for whye we haue offended and doone wickedlye / deparetinge from the / in all thinges haue we trespassed and not obeied thye [33r] commaundementes / nor kepte theym neyther done as thow haste beden us, that we myghte prospere / Wherefore all that thu haste broughte apon vs and euery thinge that thow haste done to us, thow haste done theym in trew Judgment as in delyuerynge vs into the handes of oure enemyes, yet for thy names sake we besych the geue vs not vppe foreuer / breke not thy convenaunte [33v] and take not away thi mercye frome vs for thy beloued Abrahames sake for thi seruaunte Isaacis sake and for thi holy Israelis sake to whom thow haste spoken and promysed that thow woldest multyplye theire sede as the starres of heuen and as the sande that lyeth apon the se syde / for we O lorde are become lesse then any people / and be kept undre this day in all the worlde [34r] bycause of oure synnes / neuerthelesse in a contryte harte and an humble spyrytte / let vs be receyued that we may optayn thi mercy / for ther is no confusion vnto them that put theyre trust in the / and now we folowe the with all our harte / we fere the and seke thy face / Put vs not to shame but deale with vs after thy louyng kyndnes and according to the multytude of thy mercyes delyuer vs by thy [34v] myracles O lorde and gette thy name an honour / that all they whiche do thy seruauntes euyll may be confounded. Let them be asshamed through thy almyghty power and let their strength be broken that they may know how that thou onely arte the lorde god / and honour worthy throughoute all the worlde / Blyssed be the holy name of thy glory for it is worthy to be praysed and magnyfied [35r] in all worldes. Blyssed be thow in the holy temple of thi glory / for aboue all thinges, thow arte to be prased, yea and more worthye to be magnyfied for euer. Blyssed be thow in the trone of thi kyngedome / for above all thow arte worthye to be well spoken of and to be more then magnyfied foreuer / Blyssed be thow that lokeste through the depe and sitteste apon the Cherubyn [35v] for thow arte worthy to be praysed and above all to be magnyfied foreuer / Blyssed be thow in the firmament of heuen for thow arte prayse and honor worthye foreuer Amen

THE PRAIER OF MANASSES, 6TH KINGE OF JUDA.

O lorde almyghty, god of our fathers, Abrah^{a}m Isaac and Jacob, and of the ryghtwys sede of them: whiche haste made heuen and earth with [36r] all the ornamentes thereof / which haste ordened the see by the word of thy commaundement: which haste shut vp the depe / and haste sealed it for thy fearefull and laudable name / whiche all men feare / they tremble before the face of thy presence / and for the angre of thy thretnyng / the whiche is unportable to synners. But the mercy of thy promes ys great and unsearcheable: for thow arte the lorde [36v] god moste high above all therth / longe suffringe and exceding mercyfull and repentaunt for the malice of men / Thow lorde after thy goodnes haste promysed repentance of the remyssion of synnes: and thow that arte the god of the ryghtwes hast not put repentaunce to the ryghtwes Abraham Isaac and Jacob / vnto them that haue not synned agaynste the. But bicause I haue synned above the nomber [37r] of the sandes of the see and that myne Inyquytees are multyplyed. I am humbled with many bands of Iron, and there ys in me no breathinge. I haue prouoked thyne angre and haue done euyll before the / in commyttyng abhomynacions and multyplying offences / and now / I bow the knees of my harte requyring goodnes of the O lorde / I haue synned lord I haue synned and know my [37v] Inyquyte. I desyre the by prayer O lorde: forgeue me, forgeue me and destroy me not with myn Inyquyties, neyther do thow alwayes remembre myne euylls to punysshe them / but saue me (whiche am unworthy) after thi great mercye / and I will preys the euerlastyngly all the dayes of my lyfe for all ^{the} vertu of heuen prayseth the and vnto the belongeth Glory worlde withoute ende Amen

[38r] **Oure** mercyfull father whiche in teachinge vs to pray by thie sonne Chryste haste commaunded vs to caull the father and to beleue that we are thye welbelovyd

children / whiche sterreste vppe none of thyne to pray but to thentente thow woldest heare them / geuyng vs also all thinges more effectuouslye and plentyously than we can eyther aske or thinke / we besich [38v] the for thy sonnes sake geue vs grace to beleue and to knowe stedfastely that thi sonne oure sauyour Chryste ys geuen of the vnto vs to be vnto vs our sauyour / oure ryghtwysnes / our wysdom / our holynes / our redempcion and our satisfaction / And suffre not vs to truste in any other saluacion but in thy sonne and by thi sonne onely our sauyoure Amen

[39r] **O Lorde** god geue, that my harte maye desyre the / In desiringe, seke the In sekinge, to fynde the In fyneding to loue the / in luuyng the, to fynde remedye of my euylls / and remedye had, that I may abide stille in the. Graunte me O lorde my god in my harte, repentaunce / in my Spiritte contrition / in my eyes, a fountayn of teares / oute of my handes, lyberalite of almes / my kyng [39v] quenche in me the desires and lustes of the flesshe and kyndle in me, the fier of thye loue / My redemer put oute of me the spiritte of Pride and graunte me Of thye mercy the treasure of thye mekenes and humylite / My sauyour expell from me fumysshnes and wrathe and geue me for thye Petye sake, the buckeler of pacience. My creature[12] pull oute of me the rancoure Of mynde and [40r] graunte thow me that arte so mercyfull a louyng harte. Geue me O moste tendre and pytefull father, sure faythe / lyke hope / and charyte contynuall. My gouernour put frome me all vanyte, inconstancye of mynde, wauering of the harte, Jestyng, or raylyng of my mouthe, proude lokyng / Gloteny of the bellye, uncharytable rebukyng of myne neyghbours / the loue or desyre of worldely [40v] Ryches, the desyre of vayne glory / the myschefe of hypocrysye, the poyson of flattery, the dysdayne of the nedye, the oppressyon of the poore and feable, the ruste of enuye, the death of blasphemy. Cut away from me (O my maker) unryghtfull rasshnes, Sturdynes, unquyetnes, Idlenes, Slouthfulnes, Dulnes of the wytte, Blyndenes of the harte, Obstynacye of the mynde, Crewelnes of behaviour [41r] Dysobedience of that ys good / Resystence agaynste good councell, unrulynes of my tonge / Pollinge of poore people, vyolente dealynge with the Impotent, Slaundring of Innocentes Crabbednes agaynste those that be with me in howseholde, vnkyndnes towardes my freendes and famylyer acquayntaunce, Rygoure or extreme dealynge with my neyghboures. O my god, my mercy, I pray the for [41v] the loue of thy sonne make me to do deades of marcy, to exercyse petye, to haue compassyon on those that be in afflyctyon or trouble. To geue concell to those that be oute of the ryght way. To socoure those that be in mysery. To releue the oppressed. To comforte theym that be in heuynes. To refresh the poore. To chere theym that wepe. To forgeue theym that trespas agaynste me. To loue [42r] those that hate me, To recompence good for euyll. To despyse none but to honour

12. **creature** Creator. KP's spelling is a variant of the older form "creatur" which came into English from Old French.

all men. To folow the good. To eschew the euyll. To enbrace vertewes, and to refuse vyces. In aduersyte, pacyence, In prosperyte, moderatyon and kepyng of my tonge and to holde close my lipes warely To despyse thinges earthly and to thirste after thinges heuenly Amen

[42v] **Moste** soueraygne and holye Trenyte, the father, the Sonne and the holy goste thre parsons and one god haue mercy on me. O blyssed and gloryous Trenyte haue mercy on me. O the moste holye mercyfull and euerlastynge Trenyte haue mercy on me. O the trew and unfeyned Trenyte the greate and incomperable goodnes, the euerlastyng and swete clennes, [43r] and the inseperate magestye of the Father, the son and the holye goste, haue mercy on me. O good father and meke sonne, O holy goste, O lighte that cannot be put oute. O the onely father of heuen haue mercye on me. The good lorde do I call upon. To the I do make my intercessyon and prayer. The do I laude and prayse now and is[13] euer in mynde so to contynew which [43v] arte the onely begynner of all vertew and goodnes, and the fynall ender of all good workes. O holy god, O stronge god, O euerlastinge god, haue mercy on me, and remember me with thye manyfeste goodnes that I unworthye seruaunt and handewoorke / for my greate Inyquyte and synne be not withoute thy mercy loste and dampned, for thow arte my maker and redemer my [44r] onely Joye and comfort and my onely hope and health of whom I haue all thinges necessary to my lyuynge wherefore I thancke the now and euer Amen

O marcifull God whiche through thye infynyte mercye did saue harmelesse Susanne from deathe to the whiche she wrongfully was accused and condempned [44v] and did delyuer thye seruante Danyell frome the lake of the lyons, and did delyuer the thre Childrenne Sydrack Mysaac Abdenago,[14] from the hote burnynge fier and didde retche oute thy hande to thye welbelovyd dissiple Peter beynge in great Jeobardye of drownynge, I desire the that thow whyche in so many thinges did shew and manyfeste thy infynyte mercy [45r] wolde saue and delyuer me frome all trybulacion and enymyes / and from all the power of all myne enemyes and frome all theym that consent to my destructyon and pardicion, for I am Ingnoraunt[15] (mercyfull lorde) to whom I shoulde fle or seke for helpe or comforte / but onely to the which arte my maker and redemer and I do knowe none other [45v] that will helpe and defende me agaynste this worlde and deceytfull temptacion but thow

13. **is** i.e., am—KP's penslip.

14. **Sydrack . . . Abdenago** The normalized spellings of these names are Shadrach, Mesach, Abednego.

15. **Ingnorant** ignorant—another occurrence of KP's idiosyncratic spelling. See n2.

onely my god which doest raygne and shall raygne thre parsons in one god, the father, the sonne and the holy goste withoute ende Amen

We are assaulted with thre manners of temptacions, The flesshe, the worlde and the deuyll, Therefore we desyre [46r] the, moste dere father, endew vs so wyth thy grace, that we may withstande the desyres of the flessh Make that we resyste and fyght agaynste thys superfluyte of meats, dryncke, slepe, slouthe and Idlenes, Make that we may bryng the flesshe into bondage and fastninge wyth fastyng, temperate dyete, convenyent clothynge, slepe, rest, watche, and laboure, so that yt may be thine and a perfete good [46v] workes.[16] Kepe vs from the grete synnes of covetousnes, and desire of worldly Ryches. Geue vs grace that we seke not the rule and honor of thys worlde or consent to suche desyres. Kepe vs that the falce subtylte of thys worlde, the conterfet bryghtnes and entyesement of the same parswade vs not to folow yt. Kepe vs that we [be] not drawen by the euylles and aduersytees of this worlde, to Inueyesnes[17] [47r] avendgement, wrathe, or such other vyces. Geue vs grace that we may despyse the lyes of the world, coloures, decytes, promyses and falsehoode. And to be shorte, that we may esteme of lytle reputatyon all that belongeth to hym, good and euyll, as we haue promysed in baptysme, and that we may contynew in thye purpose, going forwarde daylye more and more. Kepe vs fro the entyesmentes of the deuyll, that [47v] we consente not to pryde, which wolde cause vs to sette myche by oure selffes, and despyse other for ryches, kyn, power, fauuer, learnyng, beautye, or anny other gyftes, or goodes. Kepe vs that we falle not into the synne of hate, and envye, what occasyon soeuer be geuen to us. Kepe vs that we doubte not in the faithe, neyther falle in desperacion, nowe nor in the poynte of death. Put [48r] thy helping hande, oure best heuenly father to theym that fighte and labour agaynste thys harde and manyfolde temptacion. Comforte them that now do stande, and lyfte theym vp that are fallen and be ouercom. Fynally, fulfyll vs all with thy grace, that in thys myserable, and perlous lyffe (whyche ys compassed with so many contynuall enemyes, that neuer cese) [48v] we may fyghte boldely wyth stable and noble fayth, and obteyne the euerlastynge crowne Amen

THYS PETYCION PRAYETH FOR ALL THE EUYLLES OF PAYNES & PUNYSHMENTES

O Father delyuer vs from thy euerlastyng wrathe and punysshementes of helle. Delyuer vs from thy streyt Judgement in death and at [49r] the laste daye of dome. Delyuer vs frome sodayne death. Kepe vs frome the vyolence of water and fyre, from thondre lyghtnyng and haile. Kepe vs frome hungre and derth / kepe vs frome

16. **workes** work—KP's penslip.
17. **Inueyesnes** enviousness—KP's sound spelling.

warre and manslaughter. Kepe vs from thy moste greuous strokes, the pestylence, Frenche pocks, Falling sikenes / and such other deseases. Kepe vs from all euells, and parelles of the [49v] bodye. Prouyded alway, that in all these thinges, be the glory of thy name, encreace of thy kyngdome and fulfilling of thy wylle. Amen

HERE FOLOWETH A DEUOUTE PRAYER TO CRISTE THE SECONDE PERSON IN TRYNYTE OUR ONELY REDEMER GOD AND MAN

O lorde Jesu thow arte the very lambe of god: and very god and man, moste meke and kynde: which [50r] waste offred in the aulter of the crosse and there suffredest paynfull death. I worshyppe and honour the and magnyfye the, besyching the that my soule may escape the daunger of euerlastyng paynes of death: sithen thow lorde haste boought me with thye precyous bloode Lorde kynge of glorye, and of m^{e}rcye and petye. I do beleue and knowledge that thow suffrest thy moste holy handes to be [50v] drawen abrode and nayled paynefully on the crosse. Therfore I besyche the mercyfull lorde, for thy infynyte petye and goodnes: and for that petyfull woundes and paynes that thow suffrest in thy blyssed armes, geue thow me grace lorde that all the dayes of my lyfe I do not stretche furth my armes or handes to do anye wickednes or harme to my Crysten brother or neyghbour [51r] but onely to do good warkes to thy honor and worship, and proffette of my euen cristen about me, or elles where

Also lorde Jesu criste kynge of mercye and of petye. I beleue and knowledge that thu suffreste in thy blyssed fete to be nayled greuously on the crosse for our synnes and offences. I p^{a}y[18] the lorde Jesu for thy endelesse mercy and petye. I humebly besyche the for that paynefull [51v] woundes that thow lorde suffreste there in thy feete, that thu lorde forgeue me cleane all my synne that I haue doone in going, in working, Idlenes and vanytees. and geue me grace that all the dayes of my lyffe I go not aboute foly and Idle vanytees, but to conuerte my steppes to good works pleasante in thy syghte, that it may be pleasante to the and proffitable to all about me

[52r] **Also lorde** Jesu kynge of Glorye I beleue and I knowledge that whan thow saweste the Cetye of Jierusalem geuen to horryble synnes, for which it shoulde be destroied: thowe wepeste full tenderly for other mennes synnes. I pray the Jesu Criste and kynge of mercye, for thyne endeles mercy and pety whiche shedde so pyteous teares for our synfulnes oute of thy glorious eyes, that thow lorde forgeue [52v] me all my synnes whiche I haue done in myspendinge, in the sighte of myne eyes and geue me grace that all the dayes of my lyfe I may no more offend thy goodnes in vayne and synfull sightes, but onelye lorde to looke on thy creatures, and stirre me to thy loue and dreade, and that I may perceyue to do good workes profitable to my soule to thye pleasure and wille

18. **p^{a}y** pray—KP's penslip.

Also lorde Jesu I beleue and [53r] knoweledge that whan thowe hongeste nailed on the crosse, thow hardest thy enemyes reporte and speke of the myche falcenesse and sclaundre agaynste thy moste endeles mercye and pacyence, for all the paynes that thow suffrest in thy hering, that thow lorde please to forgeue me all my synnes that I haue offended, in heringe of euell tailes and reaporte agaynste my cristen brother. Geue [53v] me grace lorde that I spende no more my tyme in hering of lesinges, backe bytinge, or reioysing in suche lyke thinges but onely to heare thy trew and moste holye woordes of the gospell preached or taughte, and to kepe it in my mynde, and to doo thereafter to the honour worshype of my lorde god, and to the proffette of my neighbour and so to further theym to my power in worde and dede.

[54r] **Also lorde** Jesu kynge of glorye I beleue and knowledge that whan thow were yet hanginge on the crosse thow lorde openeste thy moste holye mouthe and praied for thyne enemyes and exorting the vnlerned and conforted theym that were conforteles. I pray the lorde Jesu for thyne endeles mercye and goodnes, and for the mercyfull woordes that proceded oute of thie holye [54v] mouthe, Forgeue me utterly all the synnes the whiche I haue done in my vile speking and geue me grace that all the dayes of my lyfe, I speke no lesinges, Backe bytinges nor harme of any parson and also that I sow no dyscorde amonge cristen people but only lorde that I speke the treuth, and flattre not for fauour nor lucre and that I may speke nothing but [55r] fruytefull and vertuous wordes to concorde and se at unyte, peace and charite those that be at discorde, that they and I may loue the and dred the Lorde

Also lorde Jesu kynge of Glorie. I beleue and knoweledge that thow thirsted full sore on the crosse and saideste I thurste: then thow lorde thu tasteste of the bitter easell and galle with myrre as the holye [55v] Gospell witnesseth. I pray the lorde Jesu for thyne endelesse petye and mercye and for the bitternesse of that drynke that thow tasteteste of, that thow lorde please to forgeue me all my synnes doone agaynste the, whiche I haue offended in tasttynge and in relysinge[19] of meates and drinckes and in superfluous tastetyng thereof. Geue me grace Lorde that all the dayes of my lyffe, I no [56r] more offende the lorde in Gloteny, in etyng and dringkinge: but that I may tempre my mouthe in eatinge and dryncking and to fede the poore that lacke that I haue to myche Lorde

Also lorde Jesu kynge of Glorye and Omnypotente. I beleue and knowledge that thu lorde waste crowned with a sharp Garlande of thornes: I pray the lorde for thy endelesse mercye and petye, mekenes and pacience [56v] that thow lorde clerely forgeue me all the synnes that I haue doone in Pride, Boste and in vayne glorie: and Geue me grace while I doe lyue, that I doe use no Pride, but to use mekenesse and geue ensample thereof to all men where I vse companye with.

Also lorde Jesu kynge of mercy and petye I stedfastely beleue and knowledge that thow lorde suffreste thy blissed sydes to be beten, rente and torne [57r] with

19. **relysinge** relishing; KP's spelling reproduces that of Gough, her source.

scourges, and thie tendre bodie strayned, insomyche all the Joyntes of thie precious bodie myghte haue been nombred and tolde, as the prophet David saieth Dinumerauerunt omnia ossa mea. I humbly pray the my Lorde god of thie endelesse fauoure and pety for all the pytefull woundes that thow suffreste in thy moste tendre and pitefull bodie to forgeue me all the filthie [57v] synfulnes of my bodie as in Lecherie and in all other synfull operacions that I haue wroughte in synne of anye parte of my bodie. Geue me grace lorde foreuer to despice all woorkes of synfull lecheri whiche violeth[20] the temple of god: whiche is my soule whan it is oute of dedely synne Frome the whiche filthie synne Geue me grace vtterly to expell frome all partes [58r] of my bodie, and so kepe cleane my saule whiche is the holy temple as Saynte Paule witnesseth.

Also swete Jesu I do knowledge and beleue, that whille thow were yet hanging on the crosse, thow suffreste thie moste blissed side to be persed and thie glorious harte

Also with[21] a sharpe spere that bothe bloode and water felle oute thereof. I hartely besich [58v] the lorde to forgeue me clene all my crewell synnes which hathe proceded from my vnclene harte, by thoughte or dede in vayne glorie, or in dedly synne, In Imagynynge or delytinge, that I hensefurth whiles I lyue spende no more my tyme in suche daunger of synne and vanyte of this worlde, nor in Idle thoughtes but to vse deuoute exortacions and to haue communycacions [59r] feruente praiers and holy desires, that may be vnto thie pleasure and wille, and that all my hartes desire may alwaye Joy in the my father eternall: so that I may through thie precious bloode and paynes escape the Immortall daunger of helle and paynes Intollerable and so surely come to the eternall fruycion and heritage, which thow lorde haste prepared [59v] for all that hartely loue the and do thie wille and pleasour in this troublous lyffe. Amen

A PETICION & PRAIER TO OURE LORDE

Delyuer me from my enemyes (oh god) the god of my helthe, and my tonge shall triumphe in thie rightwisenes. I crye vnto the, lorde, lorde harken vnto my voice. Tary not for [60r] I am euen at the poynte of death. Helpe me lorde, least I perishe. Oh god, whiche gouerneste all thinges, which onely canste delyure me, in whose handes is the sprite of life, Rydde and pourge me frome myne enemyes, delyuer me frome theym Oh god, thauctour of my health. God, in whom onely consisteth my saluacion, delyuer me lorde as thow delyuerest [60v] Noe from the waters of the Floode. Delyuer me as thow delyuereste[22] Lothe from the fier of Sodome. Delyuer

20. **violeth** an earlier variant of "violateth."

21. **Also with** KP reproduces Gough's midsentence paragraph break.

22. **Tary not for . . . delyuereste** Across the foot of the opening made by fols. 59v–60r, Guildford Dudley bids a last farewell to his father-in-law, Henry Grey, Duke of Suffolk, with

me as thow delyuereste the Children of Israell from the deapthe of the Reede See. Delyuer me as thow delyuereste Jonas from the bellye of the whall. Delyuer me as thow delyuereste the thre Children from the Furnace of brennynge fire [61r] Delyuer me as thow delyuereste Peter frome the perell of the see. Delyuer me as thu delyuerest Paule from the deape of the See. Delyuer me as thow delyuereste infinyte synners from the power of death and frome the gates of helle, and than my tonge shall tryumphe apon thie Rightwisnes, for thie rightwisnes as thappostle saiethe commeth by the [61v] Faithe of Jesvs criste vnto all and apon all theym that beleue in hym. than shall my tonge tryumphe in praysing this thie rightwisnes commendinge thie fauoure, Magnyfiyng thie petie, knowledging my synnes that thie mercye may be declared in me which wolde vouchesaffe to Justyfie suche a great synnar and that all men maye [62r] know that thow saueste them whiche truste in the, delyuerest them frome extreme anguysshe and aduersite oh Lorde God. Amen

My God my god. Lo, wherefore forsakeste thowe me, how farre is thie helpe frome my oute cryinge.

My god, shall I thus crye and [62v] call apon the all day, and yet wilte thow not heare / Shalte I crie all nyghte and neuer cease?

But yet thow arte he which leadeste me oute of my mothers wombe / myne owne refuge euen frome my mothers teates.

As soone as I cam into this worlde, I was laide in thy lappe. thow arte my god euen from my mothers [63r] wombe.

Go thow not farre from me, for my trouble draweth nyghe, neither is there any man wille helpe.

The lorde is my rocke of stone, my buckeler, my delyuerer, my god, my defender, vnto whose faithfulnes I betake my selffe, my shelde, my sauyng power, my refuge

Thow haste defended me with thie sauynge shelde and buckler, and thie righte hande [63v] staied me, thie fauorable gentlenes made me to haue the upper hande of myne enemyes.

Wherefore I shall magnyfie the Oh lorde with highe prayse amonge the nacions and shall singe with thanckesgyuyng vnto thie name

More worthie to be desired than Golde or precious stones. sweter than the honye Combe whan it droppethe

To thie mercy shall I cleue [64r] Lorde whiche arte my strength.

---

this note in hybrid hand and italic signature: "youre louyng and obedyent son wischethe vnto youre grace long lyfe In this woorld, with as muche Joy and comforte as euere I wyshte to my selfe, and in the world to come ioy euerlastyng your most humble son tel his dethe G Duddeley R." The *R*, short for "Rex" (King), that Dudley appends to his name conveys his pride in having coreigned during his wife Jane's nine-day queenship.

Let the speches of my mouthe and the thoughtes of my hartes be pleasant and accepte[23] vnto the, lorde my defender and my Redemer
Let not the proude men falle vpon me, neither lette the vngodly move me.
Verely I haue been yong and olde and yet sawe I neu^er the rightwis forsaken
[64v] In tyme of aduersite they shall not be shamed, in tyme of hongre, they shalbe well filled.
Helthe shall com vnto the rightwis men from the lorde, he is theire strength in tyme of tribulacion.
The lorde for a surety will helpe theym and wille delyuer them from the vngodly and he wolle saue theym by cause they haue trusted in hym.
[65r] God ys for vs a defence and Strength. he is oure moste presente helper, whan aduarsite thrusteth vs downe.
With p^raise shall I remember the worde of god, With praise shall I remember the promis of the lorde.
In God shall I truste, and so shall I not feare what soeuer man may do to me.
I Shall make my vowes vnto the Oh god. Vnto the shall [65v] I geue praises.
For thow wilte delyuer my soule frome death, and my fete surely frome slyding that I myghte walke before the, in the lyuely lighte.
Looke vppe vnto god, O my verey stille soule, for vpon hym dependeth my abiding.
He is verely my defender and my sauyoure, he is also my strong Castell, leste I be moued and falle.
[66r] OF god dependeth my helth and glorie. it is the power of god, whereby I am defended & holpen[24]
This mercie of the lorde shall I praise in my song perpetually, and this faithfulnes shall I declare with my mouthe into all ages
LOrde the god of hostes· who is lyke the in power. Oh lorde, all thinges aboute the are faithfulnes.
[66v] And it is thow lorde, whiche haste the verey mercye, whiche geueste vnto euery man after his dealing.
Blissed is the man whome thow O lorde teacheste and chasteneste and instructeste hym in thie lawe.
I shall surely magnyfie the with all my harte in the concell of the rightwis, and in the congregacion.
I loue the lorde, for he hath [67r] harde me, he hathe harde the depe desires of my harte.
He bowed downe his eares vnto me, wherefore while I lyue, I shall call vpon hym.
Excepte the lorde had helpt me / my soule had shortelye dwelte in the place of silence

23. **hartes . . . accepte** **hartes** heart—KP's penslip. **accepte** a cognate of Latin "acceptus" and an earlier form of the deverbal adjective "acceptable."

24. **holpen** helped—the earlier, "strong" form of this past participle.

But whan I thoughte, now my foote is sliden away, then thie mercie Oh lorde helde me vppe

Theise manyfolde and carefull [67v] thoughtes brente[25] me not within so sore, but thie consolacions Refresshed agayne my soule myche more.

The lorde shalbe a castle afore me, in whiche I may be saffe, and my god is my rocke of stone in whome I may be defended.

Prayse thow the lorde O my soule, and all that are within me prayse his holie name.

Praise thow the lorde O my [68r] Soule and forgette not his benefettes.

Whiche forgeueth the all thi Inyquites and healeth all thy deseases.

The lorde is prone vnto mercie and bente vnto fauor, he is slowe vnto wrathe, and plenteous in goodnes.

O how excellente are thie woorkes, O lorde, all thinges wiselye haste thow made, therth swymmeth in thie goodnes.

[68v] I shall singe vnto the lorde while I lyue. I shall singe vnto my God as longe as I shall haue any being.

Remember me O lorde accordinge to thie good wille promysed to thye people, visette with thie sauynge helpe, whiche thow haste promysed.

For thie goodnes is so grete that it passeth the heuens / and thie faithfulnes also, that it lifteth vppe it selffe vnto the clowdes.

[69r] God in whom I reioyse & Glorie, holde not thie selffe from me.

Helpe me lorde my god, [ ][26] me for thie marcies sake.

Not vnto vs lorde, not vnto us, but vnto thie name geue the glorie and preyse, for thie mercy and for thie treuthes sake

Vnto the shall I make the sacrifices of preyse, and the name of the lorde shall I call vpon.

[69v] Let my aduersaries be weried with shame, and couered with confusion, like as with a cloke.

Let theym cursse, but blisse thow, Let theym rise agaynste me but to theire owne confusion, but yet lette thie saruantes rejoyce.

I shall magnyfie the lorde diligently with my mouthe, I shall praise hym among manye.

For he wille stonde at the poore mannes righte hand, to [70r] kepe his soule from Tyrauntes in auctorite

The lorde kepeth the poore simple ons, I was full poore and full of care, and he saued me.

Wherefore vnto the O lorde ~~Lorde~~ God, myne eyes are lifted vp whan in the I put my truste / poure thow not oute my soule

25. **brente** burned—another "strong" verb form.

26. [ ] KP scraped away whatever word she first wrote but failed to insert another; see n207 of the modern-spelling version.

For thow haste delyuered my soule frome deathe, myne eyes frome teares, and my [70v] fete frome sliding.

What shall I geue agayne to the lorde, for all the benyfittes whiche he hathe geuen me.

It is thow that arte my god, and I shall exalte the.

My helpe commeth frome the lorde, the maiker of heuen and erthe.

Lorde sette a keper to my mouthe, and kepe thow diligently the dores of my lippes.

Vnto the lorde I cried, before [71r] the lorde I felle downe, and made my praier.

Before hym I powred furth my heauy meditacion, before hym I laide my streyte angwisshe.

I cried vnto the O lorde and I saied thow arte my helpe, thow arte my portion amonge the lyuyng men.

Attende vnto my cryinge For I am in a greuous and wretched state, delyuer me fro [71v] my persuers, for they haue preuailed agaynste me.

But yet the name of the lord I cauled upon, I besiche the lorde delyuer my soule.

The lorde oure rightwis God is prone vnto fauoure / he is redie and bente vnto mercye

Vnto the Oh lorde haue I lifted vppe my mynde, my god I truste in the. lette me not be shamed, leste myne enemyes Reioyse apon me.

[72r] ARise lorde, Oh god, lifte vp thie hande despise not the poore afflicte.

ARise, awake for my defence in Judgement to affirm my cause my god and my lorde.

Gyue sentence with me for thi rightwisnes sake, lorde my god, leaste they reioyse apon me.

Let theym be shamed and also confounded together that thus reioyse apon my trouble. [72v] let theym be clothed with shame and Ignomynye that thus swelle agaynste me.

Let theym be gladde and reioyse that fauour my rightwisnes, and make theym to say, the lorde moughte euer be magnyfied, whom it hath thus pleased to sette his seruaunte at reste

And my tonge also shall speke of thie rightwisnes daylye shewing furthe thi praise.

[73r] My eyes shalbe euer apon the lorde, for he wille drawe my fete oute of the nette.

Beholde me and haue mercy apon me, for I am alone forsaken, full of affliction.

The sorowfull sighes of my harte encrease more and more: leade me oute of my angwisshe.

Beholde my poore state and my heuenes, forgeue me all my synnes.

[73v] Kepe my soule and delyuer me leaste I be shamed, for I haue put my truste in the.

Defende me that I may lyue rightlye, hurting no man for of the doo I depende.

For I am but a halting criple, redie euer to fall, my sorow neuer goeth from me.

Spede the to helpe me lorde my sauyng helthe.

Shew me lorde I besiche the what myne ende shalbe, or [74r] what shalbe the measure of my life. let me knowe I besiche the, how shorte is my tyme.
The lorde will bring all thinges to passe for me. O lorde thie mercy standeth forth foreuer, thow shalte not forsake the woork of thi handes.
The lorde of Israel be praised from worldes into worldes, and that all people moughte say Amen.

[74v] **THE SONGE OF AUSTEYN AND AMBROSE**

WE praise the O god we knowlege the to be the lorde.
All therthe moughte[27] worship the, whiche arte the father euerlasting.
TO the crie furthe all aungells, the heauens, and all the powers therin
TO the thus crieth Cherubyn and Seraphyn continually.
[75r] Holy[28] arte thow Holy arte thow Holy arte thow
Thow arte the lorde god of hostes
Heauen and earthe are fulfilled with the glorie of thi magestye
The glorious company of the appostells praise the
The godly felowshippe of the prophetes worship the
The faire felowshippe of marters praise the.
The holy congregacion of [75v] faithfull throughoute all the worlde magnyfie the.
They knowledge the, to be the Father of an Infynyte majestie
They knowledge thie honorable and verie onely sonne.
They knowledge the holy goste to be a conforter
Thow arte the kinge of glorie O Christe.
Thow arte the euerlasting sonne of the father
[76r] Thow whan thow shouldest take apon the oure nature to delyuer man didste not abhore the virgens wombe
Thow haste opened the kingdome of heauen to the beleuers Deathes darte ouercom
Thow sitteste on the right hande of god in the glorie of the father.
Thow arte beleued to com oure Judge

27. **moughte** a former "strong" variant of "may."

28. **continually . . . Holy** Across the bottom of the successive openings of fols. 74v–75r, 75v–76r, and 76v–77r, Lady Jane wrote a message to Sir John Bridges, Lord Lieutenant of the Tower of London, in her embellished italic hand: "Forasmutche as you haue desired so simple a woman to wrighte in so worthye a booke goode Mayster Leaftenaunte therefore I shall as a frende desyre you and as a christian require you to call uppon god to encline youre harte to his lawes to quicken you in his waye and not / to take the worde of trewethe vtterlye oute of youre mouthe lyue styll to dye that by deathe you may purchase eternall life and remembre how the ende of Mathusael [or Methuselah] whoe as we reade in the scriptures was the longeste liuer that was of a manne died at the laste for as the / precher sayethe there is a tyme to be borne and a tyme to dye, and the daye of deathe is better than the daye of oure birthe youres as the lorde knoweth, a frende Jane Duddeley."

Therefore we pray the help [76v] thie seruauntes whome thow thow[29] haste redemed with thi precious bloode.
Make them to be nombred with thie sayntes in Joye euer lasting.
O lorde saue thie people and blisse thyne heritage
Gouerne and also lifte them vppe foreuer
We praise the euerie day
And we worship thy name euer worlde without ende.
[77r] **O** Lorde, let it be thie pleasour to kepe vs this day without syn.
O Lorde haue mercy vpon us: haue mercy vpon us.
O Lorde, let thie mercye lighten vpon us, euen as we trust in the.
O Lorde I truste in the, let me neuer be confounded
Criste is deade for our sinnes.
And is Risen agayne for oure Rightwisnes

[77v] SAYNT JEROMS DEVOCION OUTE OF DAUYD SAULTER

Lysten vnto my wordes lorde, and considre my lowde complaynte.
Gyue eare vnto my cryinge my gouernoure and my god: for before the do I power furthe my praier.
Oh lorde, rebuke me not in thie wrathe, neither chasten me in thyne anger
[78r] **But** deale fauorably with me (oh lorde) for full sore broken am I: heale me lorde for my bones are [all] to shaken
My soule trembleth sore: but lorde how longe?
Turne the (lorde) and Delyvere my soule: saue me for thie mercies sake
Beholde and aunswere me lorde my god: keape me wakinge, leaste the slomber of deathe com vpon me
[78v] **Make** faste my steppes I pr[a]ye the in thie pathes: leaste my fete slide.
Vpon the I call, for thowe arte wonte to heare me, o god lay thyne eare to me to heare my speche
Declare thie excellente mercy whiche are wonte to saue men trusting in the, for they rise agaynste thie right hande
Kepe me, as the apple of thyn [79r] eye, and hide me as though I were vnder the shadowe of thy wynges
Who may perceyue and considre what thinge is synne? pourge me from secret euels.
But thow Oh lorde be not farre: O my strength, haste the to com and helppe me.
Delyuer my lyfe frome the deathe stroke: and my deare soule from the woodnesse of these dogges
[79v] **Saue** me frome the mouthes of these Lyons: and defende my poore symplenes frome the hornes of these vnycornes

29. **thow thow** KP's repetition.

I shall sprede thie name amonge my bretherne, in the myddes of the congregacion I shall praise the.
O shew me thi waies lorde, and enstruct me to thy pathes
LOrde remember thie mercy and thie gracious fauoure: for in these thinges thow excellest [80r] euen from the begynninge.
But[30] the synnes of my youth with my vngodlynes also, remember thow not: Remember me accordinge to thye goodnes and for thie mercies sake oh lorde.
For thie names sake (oh Lorde) forgeue me my wickednes: for it is verie mych.
Beholde my poore state and my heauenes: forgeue me [80v] all my synnes.
Take not away my soule with the vngodly: neither yet my lyffe with these bloudy men.
Lorde heare my voice, I call apon the: haue mercy vpon me and aunswere me.
Turne not thie face from me, suffre not thie seruant to slide in thie wrathe. hetherto haste thow beene my helper. caste me not now away, neither forsake me (o god) my [81r] sauyoure.
Lorde teach me thie way and lede me furth in the righte pathe from them that laye awaite for me.
Let them not take theire plesure vpon me whiche are my troublous enemyes: lyinge wittenesses stoode together stiffe agaynste me.
Vpon the (lorde) doo I call which arte my stronge defence: despise me not, neither forsake [81v] thow me, oneles I be like men lette downe into their graues.
Heare my praier, whiles I crie vnto the and lifte vppe my handes vnto thie holy temple.
Plucke me not into vengeance with the vngodly, with those which studye for shrewdenes, speaking peasably with theire neighboures whiles they norisshe euyll in theire hartes.
Saue thie people, do good to thyne heritage, Fede and gouerne [82r] them and lifte them vppe for euermore.
Bow downe thyne eare vnto me spede the to delyuer me: be thow my stonye rocke wherapon I mighte sitte faste Be thow my stronge defensed Castell wherin thow maiste preserue me.
Betake my sprite into thie handes, for thow haste redemed me (lorde my god) which keapeste trew promys at all [82v] tymes.

30. **begynninge. But** Starting at the foot of fol. 78r and continuing across the bottoms of fols.78v–79r and 79v–80r, Lady Jane wrote this message to her father, Henry Grey, Duke of Suffolk, who was also awaiting death on the scaffold: "the Lorde comforte youre grace and that in his worde wherein all creatures onlye are to be comforted and thoughe / it hathe pleased god to take awaye ii of youre children yet thincke not I most humblye beseche youre grace / that you haue loste them but truste that we by leasinge thys mortall life haue wunne an immortal Life and I for / my parte as I haue honoured youre grace in thys life wyll praye for you in another life. youre gracys humble daughter Jane Duddley."

Delyuer me from the hande of myne enemyes, euen from theym whiche persecute me.
Let thie presence shyne vpon thy seruauntes, saue me for thie mercie sake.
Thy mercy lighten vpon vs (Oh lorde) euen as we depende and truste apon the
I shall praise and magnyfie the lorde at all tymes: [83r] his prayse shalbe in my mouthe contynuallye
In the Lorde my soule shall Glorie: the meke spreted shall heare and be gladde.
Mangnyfie[31] ye the lorde with me: and lette vs extolle his name all together.
Lorde sette agaynste my aduersaries, smyte downe them that fighte agaynste me.
Take anon vnto the shilde and buckeler: and rise vppe spedely [83v] to helpe me.
Ye thow haste sene (lorde): cese thow (lorde) no longer, be not farre absente.
Arise, awake for my defence in Judgemente: to affirme my cause, my god and my lorde.
Stretche furthe thie mercy to theym that knowe the, and thie righwisnes to the vprighte in harte.
Let not the prowde men fall apon me, neither lette the vngodlye [84r] move me.
Lorde heare my praier, geue eare vnto my cryinge: cease not whilles I wepe.
For I am geuen vnto the here, but a waifaringe straunger as were all my fathers.
Spare me, that I myghte breathe alitell: before I cease and go out of this worlde.
Neither thow (lorde) also haste holden thie gracious mercies from me: thie gentle fauour [84v] and thie treuthe preserue me perpetuallye.
For I was ouerwhelmed with Innumerable troubles, my synnes combred me so that I myghte not se them all.
They were farre mo than the heares of my hede: for the whiche thinge my harte failed me.
Let it please the (Lorde) to delyuer me, Lorde haste the to helpe me.
[85r] I was in affliction and pouerte, but the lorde loked to me, thow arte my helpe and my delyuerer (my God) thow shalte not tarrye.
I verely saide (lorde) haue mercy apon me: heale my soule for I am a synner agaynste the.
Awake wherefore slepest? (Oh lorde) arise uppe. Wherfore forsakest thow vs for euer?
[85v] Wherefore hideste thie face hauyng no respecte to our adfliction and oppression
Arise and helpe us: redeme and loose vs for thi mercies sake.
Haue mercie apon me god for thie gentlenesse sake: for thie great mercies sake wipe awaye my synnes.
And yet agayne washe me more from my [86r] wickednes and make me cleane frome my vngodlynes.
For my greuous synnes doo I knowledge: and my vngodlynes is euer before myne eyes.

31. **Mangnyfie** Magnify—KP's penslip or idiosyncratic spelling.

Agaynste the agaynste the onely haue I synned, and that it sore offendeth the haue I doone: wherefore verie Juste shalte thow be knowne in thy wordes and pure [86v] whan it shalbe Judged of the.

Lo I was fashoned in wickednes: and my mother conceyued me polluted with syn.

But lo, thow woldeste treuth to occupie and rule in my inwarde partes: thow sheweste me wisdome which thow woldeste to sitte in the secretes of my harte.

Sprynckle me with Isope and so shall I be cleane: thow shalte wasshe me and than [87r] shall I be whiter then snow.

Poure vpon me Joye and gladnes: make my bones to reioyse which thow hast smyten.

Turne thie face from my synnes: and wipe away all my wickednes.

A pure harte create in me (Oh lorde) and a stedfast righte spiritte make anew within me

Caste me not away: and [87v] thie holy goste take not from me.

Make me agayne to reioyse while thow bringest me my sauynge healthe and let thy chiefe gouernyng spirit strengthen and lede me.

Lorde open thow my lipes and then my mouthe shall shew furthe thy praise.

Oh god saue me for thye names sake: delyuer me by thy power.

[88r] Oh god heare my praier: lysten to the wordes of my mouthe.

For straunge men are risen agaynste me: and strong Tirauntes pursew my soule they haue not god before their eies

Oh God, listen to my praier: and hide not thie selffe frome my depe desire.

I remembre[32] the promys of god with preyse and trusted [88v] in god: wherefore I feared not what soeuer mortall man coulde doo to me.

I shall make my vowes to the (oh god) vnto the shall I give praises.

For thow wilte delyuer my soule frome death and my fete surely from slydinge: that I myghte walke before the in the lyvely light.

Haue mercy vpon me (oh god) haue mercy vpon me [89r] ~~**Haue** mercye vpon me (oh God) haue mercye~~: for my soule hath commytted her selffe vnto thye protection. I crepe vnder thie wynges to be defended vntill this violente blaste be ouer blowen.

Delyuer me frome these men whiche are all geuen vnto myschieffe saue me frome these bloudesheders.

For lo, they laye awaite [89v] for my lyffe: they are come together agaynste me strong and boistous[33] men.

But I (lorde) in the meane tyme made my praier to the whan tyme was offered me (Oh god) for thy infinite mercye and trouthe heare me: for the whiche thow wert wonte to healpe.

32. **remembre** remembered—KP's penslip.

33. **boistous** an earlier variant of "boisterous."

Delyuer me frome this toughe claye and suffre me not to be drowned: let me [90r] be delyuered frome these odious persuers, euen from these depe waters.
Let not the streame cary me awaye, neither the deapthe swalowe me in / nor the pitte shute her mouthe ouer me.
Aunswere me (oh lorde) for full gentle is thye mercye looke vpon me after thie greate humanyte.
Joyne the to my soule and [90v] redeme it lose me frome my enemyes.
Oh God spede the to delyuer me: oh lorde haste the to helpe me.
I am a carefull poore afflicte,[34] spede the vnto me thow arte my helper and delyuerer / se thow tarie not.
In the (lorde) haue I trusted, suffre me not at anye tyme to be shamed.
Delyuer me for thie rightwisnes [91r] and take me uppe: bowe downe thyne eare vnto me and saue me.
Be thow vnto me a rocke of stone in the whiche I myghte kepe me and to the which I myghte euer flee.
My God delyuer me from the hande of the vngodlie man: delyuer me from the fiste of the myscheuous and violent man.
My mouthe shalbe yet fulfilled [91v] with praises, lette it daylie extolle thie clere maiestye.
Caste me not away in myn olde age: forsake me not whan my strength shall faile me.
God be thow not farre from me: my god spede the to helpe me.
But I shall tarye for thie help and shall excede all men in thye praise.
Let not the lyfe of the turtell [92r] com into the companye of these aduersaries: the company of the poore afflicte forgette not foreuer.
Looke vpon thy promys: for amonge these blynde wretches of therthe all are full of violence and trouble.
Be present with vs (God) saue vs for thie glorious name and delyuer us, pardonne our synnes for thye names sake.
Oh God restore us, make thy [92v] face to shyne vpon vs and we shalbe saued.
Oh lorde whiche arte the god of hostes, how longe wilte thu be angrie with the praier of thi people
Restore vs God our Sauyour: quenche thy indignacion agaynste us.
Wylte thow be angrye with vs alwaies / wilte thow stretche furthe thy wrathe into the worldes ende.
[93r] Thow verely arte euen he whiche bringeste thye selffe agayne to vs / thow wilte quycken vs / in the shall thy people yet reioyse.
Lay furthe for vs (lorde) thye mercyfull goodnes and give vs thy sauynge helpe.
Bowe downe thyne eare (Oh lorde) and aunswere me me:[35] for I am full poore and full of trouble.

34. **afflicte** See n294 of the modern-spelling version.
35. **me me** KP's uncaught repetition.

Kepe my lyffe for I studye [93v] to be good: saue thow thye seruaunte (my God) for he trusteth in the withoute anye doute.
Haue mercye apon me (lorde) for I calle vnto the daylye. Make gladde the mynde of thy seruaunte, for vnto the (Oh lorde) lyfte I vppe my harte.
But yet thow (lorde) arte prone vnto mercye: thow arte redye to fauoure and [94r] to forgeue / slowe vnto wrathe / Swymmynge in Mercye and Faythfullnes.
Beholde me and haue mercy vpon me: Gyue thy strength vnto thy seruaunte / and preserue that sonne of thy handmaiden.
Do Good vnto me openly that they that hate me, myghte be asshamed to se that thu (lorde) helpeste and confortest me.
[94v] Oh lorde god thautor of my healthe, I haue cried vnto the by day and by nyghte also before the.
Let my praier com before the, bow downe thyne eare to my cryinge.
Where are those thie mercys shewed of old tyme ~~haste~~: Oh lorde whiche thow sworeste vnto David of thi Faithe
Remember the rebukses whiche are laied vpon thye [95r] seruauntes (Oh lorde) I receaued into myne owne bosome all the rebukes of myche people.
Turne the lorde, how long wilte be ere thow be pleased? sette thy harte at reste with thy seruaunt.
The glorious maiestye of the lorde oure god be ouer vs and make thow to prosper / what soeuer we go aboute, what soeuer we begynne [95v] make it to succeede luckelye
Lorde heare my praier and suffre my depe desire to comm vnto the.
Hyde not thy face from me in tyme of my tribulation: bowe downe thyne eare vnto me in the daye.
Whan I call vpon the, spede the to Graunte me.

[Note inserted in the outer margin, in a sixteenth- or earlier seventeenth-century hand]
Fauete quidpiam deest.

[ ][36] say my god take me not awaye in the myddes of my dayes; for thy yeres endure.
[96r] My sprite is sore troubled within me: and my harte waxeth colde in my breste.
But at laste I remembred the daies paste: I considered all thy woorkes and pondred in mynde the dedes of thy handes.
I stretched furthe my hand vnto the my soule desirously panted and breathed for the

36. **Fauete . . . [ ]** **Fauete . . . deest** "Be kind; somewhat is missing"—a jotting by an early reader of KP's prayerbook. [ ] On this unfilled blank and on the block of source material omitted after this versicle, see n316 of the modern-spelling version.

I gaped for the like thirstye erthe.
Haste the to graunte me [96v] (Oh lorde) for my sprite faynteth: hide not thye face frome me, onelesse I be like men going downe into their Graves.
Make me shortely to here of thye mercyable goodnes for in the do I truste.
Shew me the way wherein I may goo: for vnto the haue I lyfted vppe my soule.
Delyuer me from myne enemyes (Oh lorde my god) [97r] for at the doo I hide my selfe.
Teache me to do thy pleasures for thow arte my god, thy good sprite moughte lede me into the righte waye.
Ye and for thye mercis sake also destroy my enemye and shake awaye all that trouble my soule, for I am thye seruaunte.

Amen

[97v] **Inclyne** thyne eare and agre to my desire (O lorde) for I am poore and destytute of all mans helpe
Take care for my soule / for I am of an vnfayned harte towarde the / saue thye seruaunt (o my God) thy seruaunte I saye whiche hangeth hole vpon the.
Haue mercy vpon me (Oh Lorde) for I call contynually and will calle for thi helpe.
[98r] Refresshe thy seruauntes mynde (O lorde) for I will laboure with my harte to comm euen vnto thee, though thow dwellest neuer so high.
For thow (oh lorde) arte louynge and Jentle, and more mercyfull than can be expressed vnto all theym that call for thye helpe.
Gyue eare (Lorde) vnto my peticion / lette it not greue the to herken vnto my clamorous [98v] praiers.
As ofte as anye aduersite happeneth vnto me / I shall call for thye helpe, trusting in tyme to come that thowe wilte graunte me the thing which thowe shalte thyncke moste for my proffet.
There is not one of theym that wicked men take for goddes / to be compared vnto the O lorde, neither can anye of theym do suche thinges as [99r] thow doeste.
Therefore the tyme wilbe that straunge nations whom thow haste created shall comm and submytte theym selves vnto the, yea and earnestlye feare the maiesty of thy name.
For thow arte greate and doeste wonderfull thynges, thow arte god alone.
Lorde teache me the way which leadeth vnto the, that I may boldely walke in it not doubtynge [99v] but that thow wilte faithfully kepe me company in my Journey / wake thow my harte vppe that it maye specyally feare the maiesty of thy name.
I will prayse the (O god my lorde) with my hole harte, and wille magnyfie thy name with contynuall praises.
For there are to shew at hande right many tokens of thy louynge kyndenesse [100r] towarde me: for why as ofte as I was in great perelles thow haste delyuered me and cauled my soule agayne, euen in a manner frome dethe vnto lyffe.

Proude personnes are rysen agaynste me (O god) and a greate multitude of myghtye men hauynge no regard of the laboure sore for this intente, that they maye take my lyfe from me.

[100v] But thow O lorde god arte mercyfull and good, slowe vnto wrathe but meruelous prone vnto kyndenesse and kepinge of thy promysses.

Beholde me and haue mercy apon me, geue strengthe vnto thy seruaunte, and preserue the sonne of thye handmaiden.

Shew som token of thy loue towarde me that my enemyes may se and be [101r] asshamed / that they (I say) may se that it was thow whiche helped me and auenged the wronge that they did vnto me.

LOrde how long wilte thow forget me, foreuer? how longe turneste thow thye face from me as thow wert angrie.

How longe shall I vexe [101v] my soule with taking of sorows in vayne which gendre no thinge but contynuall heuynes: how longe wilte thu suffre myne enemye to exalte hym selffe agaynste me.

Considre my calamyte and heare me parfitely (lorde my god) lighten myne eyes, least paraduenture, the slepe of deathe com stelinge vpon me.

Leaste myne enemye [102r] takinge courage, saye: I haue ouercom hym and my enemyes reioise if I myscarie.

As for me I haue put all my truste in thye goodnes / wherefore I doubte not but the tyme shall com, that my harte shall reioyse for the healthe that thow haste brought me and that I shall haue occasion to singe the prayses of the lorde when he shall haue auenged the wronge that [102v] myne enemyes haue doon me

I wille loue the (O lorde) as thow arte worthye, for thow arte my strength.

The lorde hath been to me euer lyke a rocke and like a tower, my sauyoure, my guide, and my strength, wherefore I shall sette all my hope in hym whiche was to me in stede of a shilde, he hathe [103r] beene euer the horne of my healthe, and my trew defens.

I wille call apon the lorde moste worthye of all honor / and I shalbe fre from myne enemyes.

I was sette in the moste present parells of deathe, bounde as it were with deadely cheynes / for the riuers of the deuyll put me in feare.

The ropes of helle compassed me aboute / mortall nettes [103v] helde me in the snare.

As ofte as I was troubled I cauled apon the lorde, and I cried to my god / whiche bothe harde my voice frome his kinglye palace and my caulinge came into his presence / yea euen to his eares

Saue me (O god) for the mageste of thi names sake / and seing thu haste myghte ynough / auenge this wronge that is done [104r] vnto me.
Heare my praier (O god) enclyne thyne eares to the woordes of my mouthe.
For straungers also ar risen vp agaynste me / and cruell men laboure sore to destroye me / hauynge no regard of the (O god)
But bicause god is my helpe / and the lorde is one of the nomber of theym that defende my soule
[104v] Therefore the euell that ~~the~~ they ordeyne for me / he shall bringe ageynste theymselfes whiche doo me wronge / wherefore I besike [the] for thy good faithfulnes in kepinge thy promysses / destroy theym.
I shall offre thye sacrifyces willingly I shall magnyfie thy name (O lorde) with praises for it is a good and louynge name.
For he hathe delyuered me [105r] frome all trouble / and thorowe his goodnes myne eie hath sene as myche as anye man wolde desire to see in his deadlye enemyes.

Hayle Jesu Christe kinge of mercye / oure lyfe our Swetnes and oure hope / we salute the: vnto the we crie whiche art the bannysshed children of Eve: vnto the we sighe: sobbinge [105v] and wepinge in this vaile of wretchednes / haste the therefore our medyatoure: turne vnto vs those thy mercyfull eyes. O Jesu all prayse worthy shew vs the presence of the father after this outelawrye. O gentle, O mercyfull / O swete Jesu Christe / In all our trouble and hevynes O Jesu our healthe and glorie socoure us. Amen

[106r]

A PRAIER TO THE FATHER

O God almyghtye / oure mercyefull Father which haste so excedingly loued vs thy chosen children: that thu woldeste wouchsafe[37] to geue vs thie onely and welbeloued sonne Jesu Christe our sauyoure to suffre deathe for our synnes: so that all that thus beleue in hym / myghte not perisshe / but haue lyfe [106v] euerlastinge: We besiche the for thye aboundaunte mercye / and for that inestymable loue whiche thow bareste to thy sonne Christe oure sauyoure, Geue vs of thye grace / and power thy fauoure into our hartes, that we may beleue, feale and knowe parfitely that thow onelye arte our god, our father and to vs an almyghtye helper, delyuerer, and a sauyour from [107r] synne / frome all the deuelish power of helle, of this worlde and from deathe, and that by thye sonne our lorde Jesu Christ. Amen

A PRAIER TO THE HOLY GOSTE

COme holie spirit Replenyshe the hartes of thy faithfull: and kyndle in theym thye brennynge loue. Sende furthe thye spiritte and men shalbe created a new. For so re-

37. **wouchsafe** an early modern variant spelling of *vouchsafe*.

neweste thu the soule of man [107v] **the praier** O God whiche haste instructed the hartes of faithfull men with the lyghtnyng of thye holye goste: graunt vs to sauyoure a lighte in the same spiritte: and to rejoise euermore of his holye consolacion, whiche lyveste and raigneste in the same spiritte euer amen

A PRAIER TO THE TRENYTE

[108 r] **Delyuer** us, saue us: and Justyfie vs O blissed Trenyte **vers** The name of god be blissed foreuer From age to age euerlastinge
O almyghtie euerlastinge god whiche haste geuen vs thie seruauntes to knowledge the glorie of the euerlastinge Trenyte with a faithfull knowledge: and to worship one god in thy almyghty magestye: we besiche the that thorowe the [108v] stedfastnes of this faithe: we moughte be defended frome all aduersitees: which lyuest and raigneste one god in the Trenyte of parsones worlde withoute ende Amen

A PRAIER TO JESU CHRISTE.

O Lorde Jesu Christ the sonne of the lyuyng God: put thy passion, Crosse, and thye death, bytwene thye Judgemente and our sowles [109r] now and in the owre of deathe and graunte vs whilles we lyue mercye and grace / to them that departe forgeuenes and Reste: vnto thy holy churche geue peace and concorde and to vs that are synners lyfe and euerlastinge glorie whiche lyueste and reigneste with the father and with the holye goste euer
The Glorious Passion of our lorde Jesu Christe / delyuer vs frome sorowfull heuynes and [109v] brynge vs to the Joyes of Paradyse Amen

Oure father that arte in heuen hallowed be thye name Let thie kingdome comm to us. Thye wille be fulfilled aswell in erthe, as it is in heuen. Geue vs this daye oure daily brede and forgeue vs our offences, like as we doo forgeue them that offende us. Lede vs not into temptation, [110r] but delyuer vs frome euyll. For it is thye kingdom and power and glorie foreuermore
Blyssed arte thowe lorde god of Israhell our father euerlastyngly / For it is thy magnyficence (O lorde) and thye power and glorie and victorye and prayse to the.
O Gouernoure (lorde god) petyfull and benynge / pacyent of of[38] greate mercye which [110v] doeste extende thy mercye vnto thowsandes / whiche takest away

38. **of of** KP's repetition.

wickednes / myschefe and synne / and none of hym selffe is innocente before the. I besiche the that thow wilte take away our wickednes and synne.

I besiche the lorde god of heuen / stronge / myghty and terrible / whiche kepeste conuenaunte and mercie with suche as loue the and observe thye commaundementes. Let thyn [111r] eares be harkenynge / and thi eyes open that thow mayste here the prayer of thye seruant.

O lorde whiche arte pacient and of greate mercie and takeste away our Inyquyte and myschiefe, forgeue (I besiche the) the synne of this thy people after the gretnes of thye mercy.

Lorde god, do not destroye thi people / and thyne enheritance whiche thow haste boughte through thye power.

[111v] Thow haste beene guyde in thy mercye to the people which thow haste redemed.

Forgeue thow thy people / though they be synneres, for thu arte my god. Let thyne eyes (I besiche the) be open and thyne eares intentyffe vnto the prayer that is made in this place.

O lorde thow arte our father and we are but claye / thow arte our creatoure and all we but the worke of thyne handes (O lorde) [112r] be not ouermyche angrie and be nomore myndefull of oure Inyquyte / beholde haue respecte, all we are thye people.

Lorde thy mercye is euerlastinge do not despise the worke of thyne handes.

O thow lorde whiche arte our Father / our redemer / thye name hathe been euermore.

For we not presente oure praiers before thye face in Justyfieinge oure selffes, but [112v] in truste of the greate mercye / herken lorde / be pleased / O lorde attende / and doo / be not slakke (my god) for thyne owne sake / for thi name hathe been cauled vpon this Cetye and vpon the people.

Lorde god here the clamoure of this people and open vnto them thie treasure / the well of the water of lyfe.

Let all that knowe thye namm lorde truste in the for thow haste not forsaken them that seke the.

[113r] Thow verely: whiche arte a god mercyfull meke and petyfull / paciente and of highe compassion / haste not forsaken them.

Arise (lorde) helpe vs and redeme vs / for thye names sake.

Do not remember our olde iniquytees / but let thye mercye preuente vs quyckelye / for we are made verie poore helpe vs (oure lorde god) and for the glorie of thi name lorde. delyuer vs / and be [113v] mercyfull vnto our synnes for thye names sake.

I shall doo sacryfice vnto the with good wille / and shall confes thye name / for it is good.

Forasmyche lorde as thowe arte swete and gentle and of plenteous mercye vnto suche as call apon the

Lorde heare our praiers and our peticions and delyuer vs out for thye sake

Heare (O lorde) and haue mercy for thu arte a mercyfull god and haue mercy[39] [114r] on vs for we haue synned agaynste the.
We haue synned with oure fathers / we haue done unjustlye / We haue commytted wickednes: thow that arte holye, haue mercye on us.
Whan thow arte angrie remember mercye.
Be not myndefull of the wickednes of oure fathers / but be in mynde of thye power and thye name at this tyme / for [114v] thow arte oure lorde god.
Let albe gladde that truste in the / they shall reioyse euermore and thow shalte dwell in them / and all that loue thi name shall glorie in the
Thow arte rightwis (O lord) and all thye Jugementes are trew and all thye waies mercy treuthe and Jugemente.
Blyssed is thye name (O god of our fathers) whiche in thye wrathe doeste shew mercye and [115r] in tyme of trouble doeste forgeue synnes to them that call on the
All that serue and honor the be certeyne and sure that his lyffe (if it haue beene tried and proued) shall receyue the crowne of victorye and yf it be in trouble it shalbe delyuered, and yf it be in corruptyon and synne / he may com vnto thye mercye.
For thow arte not delited [115v] in destroying vs / for after tempeste / thow maketh all thinges quyete and after wepinge and moornynge thow causeste gladnes / blyssed be thye name therefore (O god) of Israhell euermore.
God is at hande vnto all that call on hym / to suche as call on hym in treuthe
When I did call / thy good and rightwisnes did here me in my tribulacion / thow [116r] haste sette me at large.
O lorde let me not be confounded / for I haue cauled on the.
I haue cauled on the lorde oute of tribulacion / and the lorde hathe harde me abrode.
In my tribulacion I will caull on the lorde / and I wil crye vnto my god / and he will here my voice oute of his holye temple and my crye shall com vnto hys [116v] eares.
Thy good spirit shall brynge me into a right grounde for thy names sake (lorde) thow shalte make me alyue in thyne equyte / thow shalte bringe my soule out of trouble / and in thy mercye thow shalte destroy all myn enemyes.
We will crie vnto the in our tribulacions / and thow shalte here vs / and make vs saffe
[117r] Whan we be ingnoraunte what we oughte to doo / we haue onely this remedye / for to dyrecte our eyes vnto the.
Geue vs helpe in our trouble / for the helpe of man is vanyte.
Lorde thow arte my refuge my strength / my fortres / in the tyme of trouble.
I truly shall singe of thye strength and shall exalte thy mercye betymes.

39. **for thu . . . mercy** This line is squeezed into the bottom margin of the leaf.

For thow arte made my [117v] suretye and my socoure in the tyme of my tribulacion
O God that arte my helper / I wille singe vnto the / thow arte my socoure / my god / thy mercye be vnto me.
So let thye mercye be done that it may conforte me / and accordinge vnto thye promes made to thye seruaunt
Let thy mercies comm vnto me / and I shall lyue / for thy loue is my meditacion.
[118r] **Geue vs** helpe oute of our troble / for the helpe of man is vayne / let vs worke vertue in god / and he shall bringe vnto nought all that trouble us.
In the tyme of my trouble I soughte oute god with my handes and I was not deceaued
I wille looke vnto the lorde / I wille tary vpon god my sauyoure: my god wille here me.
Lorde haue mercye on vs for we haue looked after the [118v] be our defence betymes and our healthe in tyme of tribulacion.
No eye hath seen (O god) without the / the thinges that thow haste prepared to suche as looke after the.
I haue remembred thy mercy lorde and of thye woorkes that be euerlastinge / for thow delyuereste suche as suffre the and doeste take the oute of the handes of the people.
For thow arte as a defender [119r] vnto the poore / a defence vnto the nedye in his trouble / a saue garde frome wynde / a shadow frome the hete.
For there is none other god eyther in heuen or in erthe that is able to doo the woorkes and to be compared vnto thi strength.
The lorde is made my strength and my prayse and he is a saluacion vnto me.
I do blisse the lorde god of Israell / for thow haste chastysed [119v] me / and thow haste saued me.
Lorde I wille confesse vnto the bicause thow haste bene angry / thy furoure is turned / and thu haste conforted me / beholde God my sauyoure / I will doo boldelye, and will not be aferde / for the lorde is my fortres / and my prais / and he is a sauyour vnto me.
Lorde all that forsake the shal be confounded / they that depart from the shalbe graven in [120r] the erthe / bicause they haue left the lorde the vayne of waters of lyffe.
Heale me lorde and I shalbe healed / saue me / and than I shalbe saued.
And let thye mercye com apon me lorde / the salvation according to thye promes.
Shew vnto vs Lorde thy mercy and geue vs thye sauegarde.
O lorde of all vertu blissed is the man that trusteth in the.
Be myndefull of thye petye (O [120v] lorde) and of thy mercy whiche is euerlasting.
Do not remember the defautes of my youthe and myne ignoraunce
Accordinge to thy mercy remember me (thow good lorde) of thye goodnes
For thye names sake lorde forgeue my synne / for it is mych.

Haue mercye on me (O lorde) accordinge to thi grete mercy: and according to the gretnes of thy pety take away myne Inyquyte /

[121r] Turne away thy face frome myne offences / and put away all my wickednes.

Create in me a pure harte (O god) and renew a righte spiritte within me.

Do not caste me away frome thy face and do not take frome me thyne holie spirit.

O Lorde do not withdraw thy compassion from me / thy mercye and thi treuth haue euer defended me.

In the aboundaunce of thye [121v] mercy here me in treuthe of thie salvacion here me Lorde / for thie mercye is moche / after the plenteousnes of thy compassions regarde me / and do not turne awaie thie face from thie seruaunte / for I am troubled / here me hastely.

And thow lorde god arte petuous / and mercyfull / pacient and of excedinge mercye and trewe.

For I do knowe that thow [122r] arte a good[40] gentle and mercyfull paciente and of moche compassion and not vengeable vpon malice.

Haue mercie on me Lorde for I am weake heale me lord / for all my bones be troubled and my soule is greatlye troubled / but yet O Lorde be converted / and delyuer my soule / saue me for thie mercys sake.

And thow Lorde do with me for [122v] thie names sake / for thie mercy is swete· delyuer me for I am poore and nedye and my hart is troubled within me.

Healpe me lorde god / saue me for thie grete mercye.

Deale with thie seruaunte accordinge to thy mercye and teache me thye Justificacions.

Who will not feare the lorde and magnyfie thie name: for thow alone arte holye.

Vnto the lorde be Justice and [123r] vnto vs shamefastnes of face / vnto the truly our Lorde god be mercy ande forgevenes.

Not vnto vs Lorde god, not vnto vs / but vnto thie name give glorie.

Oure helpe is in the name of the lorde, whiche hathe created heuen and earthe.

Thow arte worthie (O lorde our god) to take glorie and honour and vertue / for thow haste created all thinges and for thie [123v] pleasure they were and be created.

O lorde god the creatoure of all thinges / terrible and stronge / rightwis and mercifull which onelye arte good / onely thexcellent kinge / onely Juste almyghtye / and eternall / whiche delyuered Israell from all evell.

For he that was conuerted was not made hole by anye thinge visible / but by the sauyoure of all.

[124r] Thereby truly / thow haste declared vnto thyne enemyes / that thow arte he whiche delyuerest from all evell.

For neither erbe[41] ne plaister hath made hym hole / but thye worke lorde that healeth all thinges.

40. **good** KP's penslip for "God."

41. **erbe** herb—KP's sound spelling.

Lo thow haste created heuen and erthe in thye greate strength and in thye stretched oute arme. No worde shalbe difficill vnto the / for thow doeste mercye [124v] vnto thowsandes.
Is there anye thing difficill vnto god?
Is the ende of the lorde feble
I know that thow arte able to do all thinges / and no thoughte is preuye to the.
It is in thy power to do all thinges at thye pleasure.
Thow arte he Lorde that haste power of lyfe and death and doest lede into the gates of death and lede oute.
[125r] For and if I shoulde walke in the myddes of the shadowe of deth / I woulde fere no harme / bicause thow arte with me.
And thye mercye shall folow me / all the daies of my lyfe.
Thow haste mercye on all bicause thow mayste do all and pretendeste to be ignoraunte of the synnes of me bicause of repentaunce for thow louest the thinges that be / and thow haste not hated that that thow haste [125v] made nor thow haste not ordeyned or made anythinge with hate.
Thow doeste spare all thinges bicause they are thyne owne O Lorde that loueste soules.
Bycause thow arte swete and good lorde thy spirit is in all thinges.
Howe greate is the haboundaunce of thye swetenes (O lorde) whiche thow haste hidde from theym that feare the.
[126r] Thow truly whiche arte our god / arte swete trew and pacyente and disposinge all thinges in mercye
For to know the is parfite Justice and to knowe thy Justice and vertu, is the roote of Immortalite
For there is none other god but thow / whiche haste cure of all thinges.
Lorde god of Israell / there is no god like vnto the / neither [126v] in heuen nor earthe whiche kepeste conuenaunte / and mercy with thye seruauntes goinge before the with all theire harte.
What god is like vnto the that takeste away wickednes and carieste away the synne of suche as are lefte to their inheritaunce.
For thy mercy is magnyfied vnto the heuens and thy trouthe vnto the cloudes.
Spare lorde / spare the people [127r] and do not geue thy inheritance in reproffe.
Haue mercy on me O god haue mercie on me / for my soule trusteth in the / and I shall truste in the shadowe of thye wynges / until sickenesse be passed.
Be thow not dredefull vnto me my comforte in the daye of affliction.
Make meruelous thie mercies Lorde, whiche doeste saue all that [127v] truste in the.
The lorde is my helper and my defender / and my harte hathe trusted in hym / and I was holpen.
Verely the children of men shall truste in the coueringe of thye winges.
In God is my comforte and my glorie / the god of my helpe and my truste is in god.
Ye and though he kill me I will truste in him / neuerthelesse [128r] I will reprove my waies in the sighte of hym.

Lorde I haue trusted in the / Let me neuer be confounded.
For suche as withdrawe theym selffes from the / shall perish / thowe haste destroied all that fornycate from the.
Truly for to cleue vnto god is verie good vnto me and to put my truste in the Lorde god.
Preserue me Lorde for I haue trusted in the / I haue saide [128v] vnto the Lorde thow arte my god / and thow haste no nede of my goodnes.
I will loue the Lorde my defence / Lorde / my fortres and my refuge / and my redemer my god / I wille truste in hym / my protectoure and horne of my health and my surete /
The lorde ruleth me / and I shall wante nothinge.
Lorde I haue lyfte vppe my mynde vnto the / I do truste [129r] in the Let me not be shamed.
For there is no confusion to theym that truste in the.
The lorde god is my helper and therefore I was not rebuked.
The lorde is my helper / I will not feare what that man [can] do vnto me.
The lorde is my helper and I shall despise myn enemyes.
The lorde is made a refuge vnto me / and my god is a [129v] conforte vnto my hope.
Verely I am poore and nedie helpe me god.
Truly I am a begger and poore and the lorde hathe care of me· thow arte my helper and my defender / O my god be not slow.
Be vnto me as a defending god and as a howse of socor that thow maiste make me safe / for thow arte my fortres and my refuge and [130r] for thye names sake / thowe shalte brynge me furthe and maynteyne me.
Thow Lorde arte my surety my glorie / and doest exalte my hede.
Verely I shall reioyse in the Lorde / and shalbe gladde in god my sauyoure / my god my fortres.
My mercy and my refuge / my surety and my redemer.
Thow haste remembred [130v] me (O god) and thow haste not forsaken theym that loue the.
Lede me lorde in thie waye and I will go in thie treuth / my harte may be gladde for to dred thye name.
They that loue the / shall shyne / like as doeth the sonne in his risinge.
For thy mercye is above all lyfe / my lippes shall praise the.
Delyuer me from clay / Leste [131r] I sticke in it / delyuer me from theym that hate me / and from the depenes of waters.
I haue saide lorde haue mercy on me / heale my soule for I haue offended the.
I haue saide / I wille knowledge my wickednes vnto the lorde agaynste my selffe / and thow haste forgeuen the Impiete of my synne.
Thow haste delyuered my soule bicause it shoulde not perisshe / [131v] thow haste caste behynd thye backe all my synnes.

I haue trusted in God / I wille not feare / what flesshe may do vnto me.
I haue trusted in the lorde I wilbe gladde and Joifull in thy mercye.
Throwgh the / I shalbe delyuered from temptacion / and through my god I wille pas ouer the stone wall.
I am inferioure to thie manyfold [132r] myserationes / and to thi treuthe that thow haste accomplisshed vnto thy seruantes.
Haue mercye on vs (O god of all creatures) and beholde vs and shew vnto vs the light of thy petie.
O God converte vs / shewe thy face / and we shalbe saued.
Shew vnto vs / how thowe doste not forsake theym that presume of the / and suche as presume of theymselves / gloreing [132v] in theire owne vertu thow doest bringe lowe.
Remember Lorde / and shew thye selfe vnto vs in tyme of our tribulacion / and geue me comforte / O lorde kinge of godes and of unyversall power.
In the manyfolde mercies thow haste not created them vnto consumption neither haste thow forsaken theym / for thow arte a god pitefull and mercyfull.
[133r] Lorde thy mercies are manyfolde accordinge to thye judgemente reuyue me.
Verely thow arte amongest vs lorde and thie holie name hath bene cauled vpon by vs / do not forsake us.
Haue mercy on vs lorde / haue mercye on vs / for we are gretely fulfilled with despite.
Whan my soule was vexed within me lorde: I remembred that my praier myghte com vnto [133v] the euen vnto thye holy temple.
Troubles do oppresse me on euery parte but it is better for me to falle into the handes of the lorde (for his petye is greate) then into the handes of men.
The lorde wille do that / that semeth good in his sighte.
The sorowes of death haue compassed me and the perelles of hell haue founde me oute.
I haue founde oute tribulacion and sorowe / and I will calle vpon [134r] the name of the lorde.
O lorde delyuer my soule / oure mercyfull lorde and rightwis god is pitefull.
Lorde all my desire is before the: and my moornynge is not hidde from the.
The mercy of thy promes is greate and unsearcheable / for thow arte the higheste lorde god ouer all the erthe / Longe sufferynge and passing mercifull and sorye for the malice of men.
[134v] Thow arte worthy lorde for to open the booke and to lose the seales of it / for thow waste slayn and haste redemed vs (O god) in thye bloode.
And thow lorde god haste delyuered[42] vs accordinge to all thy goodnes and accordinge to all thie great petie.
Thow arte Christe the sonne of the lyuynge god.

42. **delyuered** KP's copying error; Godfray reads "delte with."

I haue beleued that thow arte Christe the sonne of the lyuyng [135r] god whiche cam into the worlde
For thow arte our god thow haste delyuered vs from our wickednes and haste geuen health vnto vs
God be mercifull to me that ame a synner.
Father I haue offended agaynste heuen / and before the / now I am not worthye to be cauled thye sonne / let me be as one of thye hired seruauntes.
We are unproffitable seruantes [135v] we haue done but our deutye
Increase faith in us.
Haue mercy on vs sonne of davyd.
For in the is the well of life / and by thye lighte we shall se light.
Lyke as a harte longeth after welles of water / so my soule longeth after the (O god).
My soule hath thristed[43] after God the lyuyng well / whan shall I comm and appere before the face of the lorde?
[136r] My soule hathe desired the in the nyghte / but in my spirit and in my harte shall wake for the betyme.
I bow the knees of my harte prayinge vnto thy goodnesse Lorde / I haue synned lorde I haue synned / and I knowledge my wickednes. I aske prayinge the Lorde to forgeue me
[136v] forgeue me do not destroye me all together with my synnes / do not reserve myne offences for euer / for thow shalte saue me unworthie accordinge to thie greate mercye. I shall prayse the euer all the daies of my lyfe / for all the vertu of heuen prayseth the. And to the is all glorie foreuermore. Amen.

O Lorde open thow my lippes: and than shall my mouthe shew furthe thie prayse.
O God bende thye selffe into [137r] my helpe: lorde haste the to helpe me.
Glorie be to the Father / to the sonne and to the holye ghoste.
As it was in the begynnynge: as it is now and euer shalbe. So be it.

A PRAYER IN TROBIL

Lord heare my peticion and haue compassion vpon me, turne my sorow into Joye. Strippe me ons [137v] of this greuaunce, and so clothe me with Joye, to thend my tonge may blase thy name, and gyue prayses vnto the without stoppe. Ah lorde my god deliver me out of theys strayghtes, and to the I wyll synge praysis euerlastyngly. amen.

43. **thristed** thirsted. KP replicates the spelling in Godfray, her source.

[138r] **FOR THE LYGHTENYNG OF THE HOLYE GHOSTE**

Heare me whan I crye in pain for succour to the (O christ) which art myne innocency / and in aduersitye solace me with the Joye of thy spirit, infownd[44] thy grace and graunte me my peticions / lyfte vp ouer me the lyght of thy cowntenaunce (O lorde) and thy fauour, that throwgh thy spirit I may [138v] accknoweledge the, and with it be hertely cherful for euermore. Make (O lord almyghty) peace, fyrme hope, affiaunce in the euermore to endure. amen.

[138v] **IN ADUERSITE AND GREUOUS DISTRESSE**

In thys my tribulacion lorde heare me, for thy names sake helpe me, and [139r] sende me succours from thyn holy place. Strengtthen and comfort me O lorde, [be] myndful of my prayers and long awaytyng, that I may doo sacrifice vnto the, and in my sacrifice doinge rejoyse. Or rather call to remembrance thou my god that selfe sacrifice whiche Jesvs christ thy welbeloued soone made vnto [139r] the his most louyng father for me vpon the crosse, who prayed for me in the dayes of his lyfe, and for his humilite and reuerence was herd. / For his sake, I saye, be merciful vnto me, and helpe me. Out of thy heauenly towre graunt that I ones annoynted with thy soden and perpetual Joye, may [140r] plenteously displey[45] abrod thy moste excellent ~~n~~ name. amen.

FOR STRENGTHE OF MYNDE TO BEARE THE CROSSE.

How haste thou (o Lord) humbled and pluckt me downe? I dare now unnethes make my prayers vnto the. for thow art angry [140v] with me, but nat without my deseruyng. Certenly I haue synned lorde, I confesse yt, I wyll nat denye yt. O my god pardone my trespas, release my debtes, rendre now agayne thy grace vnto me, stoppe my woundes for I am all to plaged and beten, yet lord this natwithstandyng I abyde paciently, and gyue [140a r][46] myne attendance vpon the, contynually waytyng for relyef at thy hande, and that nat without skill for I haue receaued a token of thy fauour and grace towerdes me. I mene thy worde of promise concernyng christ, who for me was offerd vpon the cross, for a rawnsom a sacrifice, and satisfaction for my synnes. Wherfore [140a v] acordyng to that thy promys, defende me lorde by thy right hande, and gyue a gracious ere to my requestes, be thow my steye in perelles, for all humane stayes are but vayne. Beate downe therfore myne enemyes thyne awen selfe with thy power, Which art myne only aydour and protectour O lord [141r] god almighty. So be it.

44. **infownd** infund (pour in).
45. **displey** KP replicates the spelling in Taverner, her source.
46. **[140a r]** This is a second instance of a repeated page number in pencil. See n7.

A PRAYER OF THE FAYTHFUL IN ADUERSITE.

A Praer. All myne hope and hole affiance most pityfull lorde haue I cast on the / let me be no more [I praye] the shaken of, for [that] were sore to my rebuke [and] shame amonges [my] enemyes. Delyuer [and] succour me of thi [justice][47]. . .

47. **[I praye] . . . [justice]** The last manuscript leaf is severely stained and darkened, rendering several faintly written words illegible. They have been supplied, in square brackets, from Taverner's text.

Modernized Text of the Personal Prayerbook[1]

[The severely discolored first leaf of this tiny manuscript begins to be legible on the right half of its verso side]

. . . of these present adversities,[2] seeing my Lord God . . . as . . . in earth . . . hid . . . a . . . but in . . . desired any pleasure . . . but tribulations . . . hated of wicked folk,

1. Source: BL, MS Harley 2342, 143 unnumbered vellum leaves measuring approximately three inches by four inches, bound within five modern leaves at front and back. The severe discoloration and wrinkling of the initial leaves appear to be effects of water damage. The whole text is written in KP's "bastard" or hybrid hand, and its presentation exhibits the same ornamental features as those of her incomplete Kendal autograph text of *Prayers or Meditations*. See figs. 1 and 2 on p. x.

2. **of . . . adversities** KP's source for this capsule narrative of Christ's ministry and death has not been identified to date. Books of devotion belonging to the prolific genre of books of hours, known in England as primers, typically open with a narrative of Christ's last acts, culminating in the crucifixion, distilled from the four Evangelists or from the Gospel of John alone. Here the more inclusive focus and the brevity of KP's narrative are unusual features. Likewise unusual is the final modulation into first-person expressions of penitence and discipleship. There is a general analogue in Miles Coverdale's serial modulations from "doctrine" into "fruit" in *Fruitfull Lessons vpon the Passion, Buriall, Resurrection, Ascension, and of the Sending of the holy Ghost* (1593) (STC 5891)—for example, "O Lord Iesus Christ, graunt vs, so to consider thy holy passion, that it bring fruite in vs: make vs pacient, when hurt and displeasure is done vnto vs: teach vs after thine owne liuing example, not to feare the rayling wordes and persecution of wicked people, neither to be discouraged for any wrongfull accusation that happeneth vpon vs" (sig. Oi v). Coverdale's *Fruitfull Lessons*, reportedly first published at Marburg in Germany between 1540 and 1547, is a thorough recasting of Ulrich Zwingli's *Breuis commemoratio mortis Christi* (Brief Commemoration of the Death of Christ).

and the most bitter and spiteful death of the cross, He, albeit that He was God, took upon Him the nature of man, to save me which was lost.

And after He was made man, He never rested, going on Judea, Galilee, and Samaria to instruct the ignorant, to heal the sick, to raise the dead, and to work many marvels else incredible. And although He was full in all thing, He did those poverties for Himself. He sustained His life by the expense of other folk; He was harbored by other; He was hungered neither. We have often read of His weeping,[3] but never of His laughing. When He was but a child, He was sought to have been destroyed. Afterward, when He grew to more age, He always suffered the hates of wicked folks. He was sold and betrayed of His own disciple, taken and punished of the Jews, and He, which did no sin, beaten down, compassed about with false witness, spit upon, beaten with blows, mocked, cursed, crowned with thorns, beaten with reeds, scourged naked, go[tten] to the cross naked, suffereth wounds of nails in His hands and feet, of aspect rev[iled],[4] and is all poured over with blood springing out of sundry wounds. When at His death He was athirst, they made drink, eisell and gall;[5] and being so cruelly consumed, He offered Himself a sacrifice to God His Father for us all.

Who am I, then, that I should dis[pute] and suffer with an unpatient mind, if any trouble do chance unto me, if I suffer any incommodity, if any persecution of envious persons cumber me, specially seeing no evil can be done unto me which my sins hath not deserved? Therefore I will not suffer grievously that thing which is bestowed righteously, but I shall pray my Lord God to grant me patience in all things. And, in that patience, purging and forgiveness of mine ungraciousness, that He, which vouchsafed to make me partaker of His pains, may also make me partaker of His glory, according to the Apostle's saying: "As ye be fellows of His passions, so shall ye be of His comfort."[6] And again, "And we die with Him," saith he, "we shall all live with Him; and if we suffer with Him, we shall also reign with Him."[7] Therefore, whether we be provoked with private envy, or else any violent power take away our riches, or have cruel silence, or often death of our dear friend,

3. **His weeping** e.g., in Luke 19:41; John 11:35.

4. **go[tten] . . . rev[iled]** **gotten** taken, brought; see *Middle English Dictionary*, ed. Sherman M. Kuhn and John Reidy (Ann Arbor: University of Michigan Press, 1963), 4:98. **reviled** abused, debased.

5. **eisell . . . gall** vinegar and bile—astringents to counter thirst; see Matthew 27:34, 48; Mark 15:36; Luke 23:36; John 19:29, 30. **eisell** The foregoing references in Reformed English Bibles read "vinegar." There are two occurrences of the traditionalist phrasing of KP's text in *The Manuall of prayers, or the prymer in Englyshe* (1539) (STC 16010), compiled by John Hilsey, Bishop of Rochester: "with eysel and gall to be gyven drynke vnto" (sig. Kiii v); "the aysell & gall that thou tasted" (sig. Riv r). See n178 for another occurrence in KP's prayerbook.

6. **Apostle's . . . comfort** Paul, in 2 Corinthians 1:5.

7. **"And . . . Him"** Paul, in 2 Timothy 2:11–12. **And** If. Conjunctive "and" or "an'" with the conditional sense of "if" is a colloquialism peculiar to early modern English.

or any other adversity chance unto us, we must give thanks for all thing, confess and say, "Lord, Thou art just, and Thy judgment is true."[8] Reprove not the rebuking of our Lord. For He woundeth, and giveth medicines; He smiteth, and His hands shall heal.[9]

Paul and Silas, being beaten with rods in Macedonia, put in prison, and laid in fetters, sang praises to our Lord.[10] And our Lord Himself, when He took the chalice, gave thanks, to teach us to give thanks to God, as often as we be grieved and punished with any adversity; for by the chalice ye understand the tribulations of this world, according to that saying, "Let this chalice pass from me."[11] Therefore, let thanks be given unto Him for all things, by whose providence all things do chance, to the intent, by that, we may be proved[12] both to patience in adversity, and not unkind in prosperity. Amen.

A PRAYER CONCERNING THE LOVE OF MY NEIGHBOR[13]

Most sweet Lord Jesus Christ, which hatest nothing that is well done, if for a good will and by gentle intent of a man which hath done no hurt: but, Lord, it is a much greater thing, and liker to Thy most high benignity, if I love mine enemy, and always will good and do it, if I can, to him which hath done me hurt. This proceedeth of Thy grace and goodness. Nothing is liker to Thee in nature than that man which is gentle and peaceable to his ill-willers and enemies that hurt him. For he that loveth his enemies followeth Thee, which didst love us: and not only didst love us, but also wouldst then die, for us, the most shameful death, and didst pray for Thy crucifiers.[14] Also, Thou hast commanded us to love our enemies, as it is written, "Love your enemies, and do good to them which hate you"—and the reward that Thou

8. **"Lord . . . true"** a paraphrase of Psalm 19:9.

9. **He woundeth . . . heal** a paraphrase of Job 5:18.

10. **Paul . . . Lord** an allusion to Acts 16:29.

11. **"Let . . . me"** Matthew 26:39, 42; Mark 14:39; Luke 22:42. **chalice** The wording of Jesus's appeal indicates that KP's source contained a close English rendering of the Vulgate reading, "calix." English Bibles from Tyndale's 1534 New Testament onward read "cup."

12. **proved** made trial of, tested.

13. **A . . . neighbor** The source of this prayer has not been identified to date. A suggestive general analogue is Anselm of Canterbury's Oratio 24, "Ad Christum. Pro inimicis" (Prayer 24, To Christ, for [my] enemies). The speaker first begs forgiveness for his stubborn failure to love his enemies as Christ has commanded. He then implores Christ to empower him with His own love, so that he may love his enemies as well as his friends, and that all, friends and enemies alike, may do Christ's will and be saved by His mercy (*Patrologia Latina*, ed. J.-P. Migne [Paris, 1863], 158, cols. 908–10). Anselm's *Orationes* circulated in two devotional collections that went through several editions in the earlier sixteenth century: *Opusculum multarum bonarum rerum refertum* (Venice, 1502, 1512, 1516, 1520) and *Diui Bernardi Abbatis Meditationes deuotissimae . . . & aliorum pia opuscula* (Venice, 1537, 1538, 1543).

14. **die . . . crucifiers** an allusion to Luke 23:33–34.

promisest followeth—"to the intent ye may be the children of your Father, which is in heaven."[15] For our Lord Jesus Christ, whose property is to have mercy[16] and to forgive, the only and whole proof of love is, if we love him which is against us and letteth our wealth.[17] Also, love is wont to be proved by the only contrariety of hate: wherefore, as man is overcome with worldly prosperity, so is the devil overcome with love of our enemy.

O Lord Jesu Christ, most merciful in love and most loving in mercy, I know that separating from Thee is death of the soul and, contrariwise, knitting to Thee by love is life. Therefore, as every man naturally loveth his bodily health and feareth death, so likewise he ought to love truly, and eschew hate. For he that hath not that love, remaineth in death of sin, and debtor of eternal death. O most merciful Lord Jesus Christ, from whom love cannot be banished: although those things be not hid from Thee which I, most wicked sinner, have committed, if I confess with my heart and mouth that I have lived ungraciously and, by the reason of my malice and iniquity, I have lacked the true love (besides other things, Lord, which I have evil conceived and done); I have hated mine enemy. And although I knew by Thy commandment that I ought to love him, yet I have despised and set little by Thy commandment. I have conceived hateful displeasure against many, and, after the conceiving thereof, I have fulfilled the fa[ntas]ies of my heart and mind. And although at some time I performed it not in deed, yet I purposed to backbiting and slandering. Therefore, most pitiful Lord Jesus Christ, help me through Thy blessed and merciful love, granting me forgiveness, and that I may amend my miserable life, and so love Thee and all other for Thy sake: that love may never fail,[18] but continue into life everlasting. Amen.

O holy Trinity[19]—the Father, the Son, the Holy Ghost—three equal, coeternal Persons and one God almighty, have mercy upon me, vile, abject, abominable, sin-

15. **"Love . . . heaven"** Matthew 5:44–45 reads, in Tyndale and the Great Bible: "Love youre enymyes. . . . Do good to them that hate you . . . that ye maye be the children of youre father which is in heaven."

16. **Lord . . . mercy** "Lord Jesus Christ, whose property is to be merciful" is the opening of a prayer for the Sixth Hour (noon) in the royally authorized compilation *The primer set foorth by the kynges maiestie and his clergie, to be taught, lerned, & read* (Richard Grafton, [May 29,] 1545) (STC 16034), sig. Fi r. Diarmaid MacCulloch, *Thomas Cranmer: A Life* (New Haven, CT: Yale University Press, 1996), 335, asserts: "There can be no doubt of Cranmer's close involvement with its compilation."

17. **wealth** well-being.

18. **love . . . fail** an allusion to 1 Corinthians 13:8.

19. **O . . . Trinity** KP's source is "A deuoute prayer, made by sir Thomas More knight, after he was condempned to die, and before he was put to deth who was condemned the thursdaye the first daye of Iuly in the yere of our lord god .1535. and in the .xxvii. yere of the raigne of king Henry the eight, and was behedded at the tower hill at London, the tewesday folowing." KP's

ful wretch, meekly knowledging before Thy high majesty my long-continued sinful life, even from my childhood hitherto.[20] Thou,[21] good, gracious Lord, as Thou givest me Thy grace to knowledge them, so give me Thy grace not in only word, but in heart also, with sorrowful contrition[22] to repent them, and utterly to forsake them. Forgive me those sins, also, in which by mine own default, through evil affections and evil customs,[23] my reason is with sensuality so blinded that I cannot discern them for sin. And illumine, good Lord, mine heart, and give me grace to knowledge[24] them; and forgive me my sins negligently forgotten, and bring them to my mind, with grace to be purely confessed of them. Glorious God, give me from henceforth Thy grace, with little respect unto the world so to set and fix firmly my heart upon Thee, that I may say with the blessed apostle Saint Paul: "The world is crucified to me, and I to the world. Christ is to me life, and to die is my gain and advantage. I desire to be loosed and to be with Christ."[25]

---

text here has been collated with that in the *Yale Edition*, 228–31. How KP gained access to this and the following prayers of More's is unknown. They were first printed in *The workes of Sir T. More . . . wrytten by him in the Englysh tonge*, ed. William Rastell (London, 1557) (STC 18076), a volume that appeared nine years after KP's death. There is circumstantial evidence, however, that More's devotional writings circulated among Queen Katherine and her ladies. Excerpts from his Tower prayers are found in the private prayerbook of Lady Jane Wriostheley, one of KP's ladies of the chamber; see the introduction, n13. Elizabeth Tyrwhit, another of KP's ladies of the chamber, probably became acquainted with More's prayer to the Trinity while attending on the queen. Her adaptation of this prayer was printed in the 1574 and 1582 editions of her devotional compilation: see *Elizabeth Tyrwhit's Morning and Evening Prayers*, ed. Felch, 83–84, 138–39.

20. **God . . . hitherto** **God almighty** More reads "almightye God." **upon** More reads "on." **Thy** More reads "thyne." **childhood** More reads "very childhed." **hitherto** KP omits More's rubrics for filling out the confession: "In my childehed in this poynte, and that poynte, &c. After my childehed in thys pointe, and that point, &c. and so foorth by euery age."

21. **Thou** More reads ""Now."

22. **Thy grace . . . contrition** The conjoining of divine grace and human sorrow for sin implies human cooperation in salvation, rejected by Luther in affirming "justification by faith alone," for which he claimed the authority of Paul in Romans 3–7, Galatians 2:16, and Ephesians 2:8–9. **sorrowful contrition** "very sorowful contricion" (More). **contrition** the efficacious element of human emotion in the penance enacted by a confessing sinner before an officiating priest. In the first phase of the Reformation, the seven sacraments were reduced only to those that Christ had instituted. Following Luther's view at the time, the Church of England under Henry VIII affirmed three sacraments—baptism, the Eucharist, and penance. See the official formularies of doctrine known as *The Bishops' Book* (1537) and *The King's Book (Necessary Doctrine and Erudition for Any Christian Man)* (1543); also see MacCulloch, *Thomas Cranmer*, 189, 212, 278.

23. **customs** More reads "custome."

24. **grace . . . knowledge** **grace** More reads "thy grace." **knowledge** More reads "know."

25. **Thy . . . Christ"** **Thy** More reads "the." **"The world . . . Christ"** More cites these verses in Latin: "Gala. 6. Mundus mihi crucifixus est, et ego mundo. Phil. 1. Mihi viuere Christus est. et mori lucrum. Cupio dissolui et esse cum Christo." The two excerpts, Galatians 6:14 and Philippians 1:21, 23, read respectively in the Great Bible: "the crosse of oure Lorde Jesus Christ,

Lord, give me Thy grace to amend my life, and to have an eye to mine end without any grudge or fear[26] of death, which, to them that die in Thee, good Lord, is the gate of a wealthy life.[27] Almighty God, teach me to do Thy will. Take my right hand, and lead me into the true mercy for mine enemies. Draw me after Thee; bind my mouth with a snaffle and bridle when I will not draw unto Thee.[28] O gracious God, all sinful fear, all sinful sorrow and pensiveness, all sinful hope, all sinful mirth and gladness, evite[29] from me; on the other side, concerning such fear, such heaviness, such comfort, consolation, and gladness as shall be profitable to my soul, do with me according to Thy great goodness.[30] Good Lord, give me grace in all my fear and agony to have recourse to that great fear and wonderful agony that Thou, my sweet Saviour, hadst at the mount of Olivet before Thy most bitter passion; and in the meditation thereof to conceive ghostly comfort and consolation profitable for my soul.

Almighty God, take from me all vainglorious minds, all appetite[31] of mine own praise, all envy, covetousness, gluttony, sloth, and lechery, all wrathful affections, all appetite of revenging, all desire or delight of other folks' harm, all pleasure in provoking any person to wrath and anger, all delight of taunting or mocking any person in their affliction or trouble.[32] And give me, good Lord, a humble, lowly, quiet, peaceable, patient, charitable, kind, tender, and pitiful mind: in all my walks,[33] all

---

wherby the worlde is crucified vnto me, and I vnto the worlde"; "Christ is to me lyfe, and deeth is to me auauntage"; "I desyre to be loosed: and to be with Christ."

26. **Lord . . . fear** **Lord** KP's addition. **Thy** More reads "the." **without . . . fear** More reads "wythoute grudge."

27. **them . . . life** More alludes to Apocalypse (Revelation) 14:13, which reads, in the Great Bible: "I hearde a voyce from heauen saying vnto me, wryte: Blessed are the deed, which hereafter dye in the Lorde, euen so sayth the sprete [Spirit]: that they rest from their laboures, but their workes folowe them." Roman Catholics interpreted the heavenly dictum as implying that good works count toward salvation. **wealthy** happy.

28. **teach . . . Thee** KP selectively translates the Latin to which More shifts at this point: "Doce me facere voluntatem tuam. Fac me currere in odore vnguentorum tuorum. Apprehende manum meam dexteram, et deduc me in via recta propter inimicos meos. Trahe me post te. In chamo et freno maxillas meas constringe, quum non approximo ad te." She omits the second sentence: "Make me to run in the fragrance of Thy ointments." She also reads "true mercy" for More's "via recta" (right way).

29. **gracious . . . evite** **gracious** "glorious" (More). **evite** avoid, shun—here in a transitive sense of "shunt away." More reads "take."

30. **such fear . . . goodness** **such fear** KP omits More's next phrase, "such sorow." **do . . . goodness** KP translates More's "Fac mecum secundum magnam bonitatem tuam, Domine"—an unsignaled quotation from the Magnificat (Luke 1:38).

31. **minds . . . appetite** More reads "mindes . . . appetites." **minds** states of thinking.

32. **taunting . . . trouble** **taunting . . . mocking** More reads "exprobracion, or insultacion against." **or trouble** More reads "and calamitie."

33. **in . . . walks** More reads "with all my workes and."

my words, and all my thoughts to have a taste of Thy holy, blessed Spirit. Give me, good Lord, a full faith, a firm hope, a fervent charity, and love to Thee, good Lord, incomparable[34] above the love of myself; and that I love nothing to Thy displeasure, but everything in a due order[35] to Thee. Give me, good Lord, a longing to be with Thee: not for the avoiding of the adversities of this wretched world, nor so much for the avoiding of the pains of hell,[36] neither so much for the attaining of the joys of heaven in the respect of mine own commodity, as even for a very love to Thee. And bear me, good Lord, Thy love and favor, which thing my love to Thee-ward, were it never so great, could not, but of Thy great goodness, deserve. And pardon me, good Lord, that I am so bold to ask Thee so high petitions, being so vile a sinful wretch, and so unworthy to attain[37] the lowest. But yet, good Lord, such they be as I am bounden to desire and wish, and should be ever[38] the effectual desire of Thee, if my manifold sins were not the let.[39]

From which, O glorious Trinity, vouchsafe of Thy goodness to wash me with that blessed blood that Thou, O sweet Saviour Christ, sheddest out of Thy body[40] in the divers torments of Thy most bitter passion. Take from me, good Lord, this lukewarm fashion or, rather, kay-cold[41] manner of meditation and this dullness in praying unto Thee. And give me warm delight and quietness in thinking upon Thee, and give me Thy grace to long for Thee;[42] and make us all lively members, O[43]

34. **a fervent . . . love** More reads "and a feruent charity, a loue." **incomparable** More reads "incomparably."

35. **a . . . order** More reads "an order."

36. **nor . . . hell** KP condenses More's "nor so much for the auoiding of the paines of purgatory nor of the paines of hel neither," signaling her Reformed perspective by excising the mention of purgatory.

37. **Thee . . . attain** **Thee** KP's addition. **attain** More reads "obtaine."

38. **bounden . . . ever** **bounden . . . wish** More reads "bounden to wyshe." **ever** More reads "nerer"—i.e., nearer.

39. **let** hindrance.

40. **that Thou . . . body** More reads "that issued out of thy tender bodie (O swete sauiour Christ."

41. **kay-cold** More reads "key colde." This compound adjective, unattested in the *OED*, seems to mean "contrary and unresponsive." **kay** an obsolete adjective with the sense of "left" (as opposed to "right"). The *OED* ascribes connotations of "the reverse effect" and "the weaker side" to *left*.

42. **warm . . . Thee** **warm . . . quietness** More reads "warmeth, delight and quicknes." **Thee** KP substitutes this pronoun for More's fuller phrasing: "thine holy sacramentes, and specially to reioise in the presence of thy very blessed body (sweete sauiour christe, in the holy sacrament of the altare): and duelye to thanke the for thye gracious visitacion therewith, and at that high memorial, with tender compassion, to remember and consider thy most bitter passion."

43. **all . . . O** **all** KP omits More's fuller phrasing: "good lorde virtually participaunt of that holye sacrament thys day, and euery daey make vs all." **O** More reads "swete."

Saviour Christ, of Thy holy mystical Body, the Catholic church. Vouchsafe, Lord, to keep us this day without sin. Have mercy on us, Lord; have mercy on us. Let Thy mercy be showed upon us, as we have trusted in Thee. O Lord, in Thee have I trusted. Let me never be confounded eternally.[44] Amen.

A PRAYER FOR OUR ENEMIES[45]

Almighty God, have mercy on me,[46] and all them that bear me evil will and would me harm: And their faults and mine together, by such easy, tender, merciful merciness[47] as Thine infinite wisdom and piteousness so[48] vouchsafe, to amend and redress and make us saved souls in heaven together, where we may ever live and love together, with Thee and Thy blessed saints, O glorious Trinity, for this bitter passion of our sweet Saviour Christ. Amen.

Lord, give me patience in tribulation, grace in everything, to conform my will to Thine, that I may truly say, "Thy will be fulfilled in earth, as it is in heaven."[49] The things, good Lord, that I pray for, give me grace to labor for. Amen.

O Lord God almighty,[50] which long ago saidst by the mouth of James, Thine apostle: "If any of you lack [wisdom], let him ask it of [God, which giveth it] plenteously

44. **Vouchsafe . . . eternally** KP translates the Latin to which More shifts at this point, a quotation of the concluding versicles of the traditional hymn "Te Deum laudamus" and three Psalm verses: "Dignare domine die isto sine peccato nos custodire. Psal. 122. Miserere nostrî domine, miserere nostrî. Psal. 39. Fiat misericordia tua, Domine, super nos, quemadmodum sperauimus in te. Psal. 30. In te, Domine, speraui, non confundar in aeternum." KP does not translate the Latin sentence that More appends at the end: "Ora pro nobis sancta dei genitrix. Vt digni efficiamur promissionibus Christi" (Pray for us, holy Mother of God, that we may be made worthy of the promises of Christ).

45. **A . . . enemies** KP's source for this prayer and the one following are two of the next items in More's sequence of English prayers (*Works*, 13:231). KP's heading translates More's "Pro inimicis" (For [our] enemies).

46. **me** "N & N. &c." (More). More provides for naming specific enemies at this point; KP turns the phrasing to self-reference.

47. **merciness** More reads "mercifull meanes." KP's ostensible variant of "mercifulness" is unattested in the *OED*.

48. **and . . . so** More reads "best can deuise."

49. **"Thy . . . heaven"** KP translates More's "Fiat voluntas tua, sicut in celo et in terra," closely echoing the second petition of the Lord's Prayer in Luke 11:2 as translated by Tyndale: "Thy will be fulfilled, even in earth as it is in heaven."

50. **O . . . almighty** KP's all but verbatim sources for this and the next prayer are the two printed on the verso of the title page of Coverdale's *Biblia The Bible: that is: the holy Scripture,*

to all [men, and casteth] no man in the teeth, and it shall be given him."[51] Hear my petition, for this Thy promise' sake. Let my prayer ascend luckily into Thy sight like incense. Let Thine ear be attent unto my deep desire.[52]

Give me wisdom, which is ever assistant about Thy seat. And put me not out from among Thy children, for I am Thy servant, and the son of Thy handmaid. O send her (I mean Thy godly wisdom) out of Thine holy heavens and from the throne of Thy majesty, that she may be with me, and labor with me, that I may know what is acceptable in Thy sight. O learn me goodness, nurture, and knowledge, for I believe Thy commandments. Thou art good and gracious; instruct me in Thine ordinances.[53] Let mine hearty beseeching ascend into Thy presence. Give me understanding according to Thy Word. O give me understanding: I[54] shall keep Thy law, yea, I shall keep it with all mine heart.[55] Show me Thy way, O Lord, and teach me Thy paths. Lead me into Thy truth and learn me, for Thou art the God of my health, and on Thee do I depend alway.[56] Hear now my voice, O Lord, with which I have cried unto Thee. Have mercy upon me and graciously hear me, for Jesus Christ's sake, O Lord, which liveth and reigneth with Thee, high Father, and Thee, Holy Ghost,[57] world without end. Amen.

---

faythfully translated in to Englyshe. M.D.XXXV (1535) (STC 2063.3), unnumbered folio sheet. The first prayer bears this heading: "Because that whan thou goest to study in holy scripture, thou shuldest do it with reuerence, therfore for thy instruction and louynge admonicion therto, the Reuerend father in god, Nicolas [Shaxton], Bishoppe of Salisbury hath prescribed the this prayer folowynge, taken out of the same." Shaxton, named to the see of Salisbury in 1535, resigned it when he declined to subscribe to the Six Articles. This formulary of the essentials of the faith—including transubstantiation, Communion by the laity in one kind (bread only), auricular confession of sin to an absolving priest, clerical celibacy, and monastic vows—was compiled by conservatives under the leadership of Stephen Gardiner, Bishop of Winchester, and authorized by Henry VIII in 1539.

51. **If . . . him** The marginal reference reads "Jacob. 1." This is a near verbatim quotation of Tyndale's translation of James 1:5, as printed in Coverdale's *Biblia*: "If ony of you lacke wysdome, let hym axe [ask] of God, whiche geueth to all men indifferently, and casteth noman in the teth, and it shalbe geuen hym." **[wisdom]**, **[which . . . it]**, **[men . . . casteth]** See n10 to the original-spelling version.

52. **Let my . . . desire** Marginal references read "Psal. 140. Psal. 129. Gen. 9." **attent** attentive—an adjective derived from the Latin past participle *attentus*.

53. **Thou . . . ordinances** The marginal reference reads "Psal. 118."

54. **I** Shaxton reads "and I."

55. **Give . . . heart** The marginal reference reads "Psal. 24."

56. **Show . . . alway** The marginal reference reads "Psal. 26." **way** Shaxton reads "wayes."

57. **high . . . Ghost** Shaxton reads "his father and the holy ghost."

[Squeezed addition at the foot of the page]
Lead me, O Lord,[58] in Thy way, and let me walk in Thy truth. O let my heart delight in fearing Thy name. Order my going[59] after Thy Word, that no wickedness reign in me. Keep my steps within Thy paths, lest my feet turn away, a contrary way.

I, miserable sinner,[60] am not worthy to name, or call upon, nor think on in my heart.[61] I humbly beseech Thee, good Lord, mercifully to look on me, Thine unkind servant, and have pity on me, like as Thou hadst pity and didst forgive[62] the woman of Canaan, Mary Magdalene, the publican, and the thief hanging on the cross.[63] I confess unto Thee, most merciful Father, all my sins,[64] which, if I would, I cannot hide from Thee. Forgive me, my Lord Jesus Christ, whereas I, wretched sinner, have offended[65] Thee in pride, in covetousness, in sloth, in wrath, in envy,[66] in gluttony, in lechery, in vainglory, in adultery, in theft, in lying, in blaspheming, in wanton jests and sports,[67] in hearing, in seeing, in tasting, in feeling, in speaking, in think-

58. **Lead . . . Lord** Shaxton's second prayer, KP's source here, bears this heading: "After the ende of any Chapter (yf thou wylt) thou mayest saye these verses folowynge." The marginal reference reads "Psal. 118."

59. **going** Shaxton reads "goynges."

60. **I . . . synner** The next four paragraphs (18r–21v) minutely rework, in a manner characteristic of KP, the traditional prayer known as "Conditor celi et terre" that became a staple in Latin and English primers of Salisbury use. KP's source is the version of this prayer in Thomas Godfray's *A primer in Englysshe, with dyuers prayers* (1535?) (STC 15988a), sigs. Ciii v–Ciiii v. The Latin version of this prayer is often the first of the petitionary prayers to follow a rubric instructing the user to prepare for confession by praying to a crucifix; see White, *Tudor Books of Private Devotion*, 74. Equally often this prayer immediately precedes the "Fifteen Oes," a tonally intense meditation on the stages of Christ's passion. **I** The first word of the second clause of the prayer. KP omits the opening address and ascriptions: "Oh maker of heuen / and erthe / kymge of kynges / and lorde of lordes / whiche of nothyng dydest make me to thy ymage and likelines, and dydest redeme me with thyne owne bloude / whom . . ." **miserable sinner** Godfray reads "a synner."

61. **or . . . heart** Godfray reads "neyther to call vpon / neyther with my herte to thynke vpon."

62. **I humbly . . . forgive** Godfray reads "humbly I desyre the / and mekely pray the / that gently thou behold me thy wycked seruaunt, And haue mercy on me / whiche haddest mercy on."

63. **woman . . . cross** Allusions are, respectively, to Matthew 15:22–28 (the woman of Canaan); Luke 8:2 (Mary Magdalene); Matthew 9:10–13 (the publican); and Luke 23:42–43 (the thief on the cross).

64. **I . . . sins** Godfray reads "Unto the I confesse / oh moste mekest father / my synnes."

65. **Forgive . . . offended** Godfray reads "Haue mercy on me Christ / for I a wretche / haue sore offended."

66. **in sloth . . . envy** KP's additions.

67. **in blaspheming . . . sports** Godfray reads "in backebytynge \in sportynge \in dissolute wanton laughynge \in ydell wordes."

ing, in working, and in all manner ways wherein I, an unstable and frail creature, might offend my Maker by any fault or trespass.[68] Therefore I beseech Thy mercies and goodness, which came down from heaven to earth for my soul' health (which also raised up King David from the fall of sin), to forgive me. Forgive me, good Lord, which forgavest Peter, that denied and forsook Thee.[69]

Thou art my Maker, my Helper,[70] my Redeemer, my Governor, my Father, my Lord, my King, my God.[71] Thou art my hope, my trust, my governance, my help, my comfort, my strength, my defense, my deliverance,[72] my life, my health, my resurrection.

Thou art my stay and my refuge, my light, my desire, and my succor. Good Lord. I beseech Thee, help me, and I shall be safe; govern me and defend me. Comfort me, and confirm me in gladness. Give me light, and visit me. Revive me that am dead in sin. Despise me not, good Lord, for I am the work of Thy hands.[73] Thy servant I am, though I be evil, though I be a sinner and unworthy; yet howsoever I be, good Lord, I am Thine.[74] To whom, then, should I flee, good Lord, but only to Thee.[75] If Thou cast me out, who will receive me? If Thou despise me, who will regard me?[76] Therefore, good Lord, though I be unworthy, vile, and unclean, yet knowledge me returning again unto Thee. For if I be vile and filthy, Thou mayest make me clean. If I be blind, Thou mayest make me see again. If I be sick, Thou mayest make me whole. If I be dead and buried in sin, Thou mayest revive me.[77] For Thy mercy is

68. **in seeing . . . default** Godfray reads "in tastyng \in touchynge \in thynkynge \in slepynge \in workyng \and in all wayes \in which I a freyle man and moste wretched synner \myghte synne : My defaulte \my mooste greuous defaulte."

69. **I beseech . . . Thee** Godfray reads "I mooste humbly praye and beseche thy gentlenes \whiche (for my helthe) descended from heuen \whiche dyd holde vp Dauid \that he shulde not fall in to synne."

70. **Thou . . . Helper** Godfray reads "Thou art my creator \and my helper \my maker and."

71. **my King . . . God** Godfray reads "my god \my kinge."

72. **my governance . . . deliverance** Godfray reads "my gouernour . . . my redemption."

73. **Thou . . . hands** Godfray reads "Thou arte my stedfastnes \my refuge or succour \my light \and my helpe, I moste humbly and hertely desyre and pray the help me \defende me \make me stronge \and comfort me \make me stedfast \make me mery \gyue me lyghte and visite me \reuiue me agayne \whiche am deade. For I am thy makymge and thy worke \oh lorde \despise me not."

74. **Thy . . . thine** Godfray reads "I am thy seruaunt thy bondman although euyll \although vnworthy \and a synner. But whatsoeuer I am wether I be good \or badde, I am euer thyne."

75. **but . . . Thee** Godfray reads "except I flee vnto the?"

76. **despise . . . me?** Godfray reads "despise me \and turne thy face from me \who shall loke vpon me? And recognise and knowlage me (although vnworthy) commyng to the \although I be vile \and vnclene."

77. **Therefore . . . me** Godfray reads "For yf I be vyle and vnclene \thou canste make me clene. If I be sycke \thou canste heale me. If I be deade and buryed \thou canste reuiue me."

greater[78] than mine iniquity; that mayest forgive more than I can offend. Therefore, good Lord, consider not the number of my faults, but according to the abundance of Thy pity, have mercy on me, and be gracious unto me, most miserable sinner.[79]

O good Lord, which saidst, "I will not that a sinner should die, but rather that he should live and be converted to goodness," say now unto my soul: "I am Thy health."[80] Turn me, good Lord, toward Thee, and be not displeased with me. O most merciful Lord and Father, I beseech Thee, for Thy inestimable mercy and goodness, bring me unto a good end.[81] Amen.

O blessed Jesu,[82] make me to love Thee entirely, O most merciful Saviour, make Thou me to love Thee; for without Thee, blessed Jesu, I cannot love Thee. Wherefore I beseech Thee, most loving Lord, make Thou me to love Thee entirely, with all

78. **greater** Godfray reads "moche more."

79. **Therefore . . . sinner** Godfray reads "Therfore oh lorde \do not consydre \nor haue respecte to the nombre of my synnes \but accordyng to the greatnes of thy mercy forgiue me; and haue mercy on me most wretched sinner."

80. **O . . . health"** Godfray reads "Say vnto my soule \I am thy helthe \whiche saydest \I wyll not the death of a synner \but rather that he lyue and be conuerted." **"I . . . goodness"** an allusion to Ezekiel 33:11, which reads as follows in the Great Bible and Coverdale: "As truly as I lyue, saieth the Lord God, I haue no pleasure in the death of the wycked, but moche rather that the wycked turne from his waye and lyue." **"I . . . health"** an allusion to a verse that reads nearly identically in Psalm 42:11 and Psalm 43:5 in the Great Bible and in Coverdale: "Put thy trust in God: for I will yet thanke him / geue him thankes, which is the helpe of my countenaunce, and my God."

81. **Turn . . . end** Godfray reads "Turne me \oh lorde \to the \and be not angry with me. I pray the moste meke father\and for thy great mercy \I most humbly beseche the that thou brynge me to the blysse \that neuer shall ceasse." **bring . . . end** Godfray reveals his Reformed bias in truncating this prayer at this point. The Latin original closes as follows: "perducas me ad bonum finem: ad veram penitentiam, puram confessionem, et dignam satisfactionem omnium peccatorum meorum. Amen" (bring me to a good end: to true penance, pure confession, and worthy satisfaction of all of my sins. Amen).

82. **O . . . Jesu** The capsule source of KP's elaborated prayer is the series of sentence prayers following "the finall conclusion of all" in "The wayes to perfe[c]t Religion made by Iohn Fysshér, Byshop of Rochester, being Prysoner in the Tower of London" (1535), one of the texts in *A spirituall consolation, written by John Fyssher Bishoppe of Rochester, to hys sister Elizabeth* [1578?] (STC 10899), sig. Cii r. (This is the earliest recorded extant text.) Fisher offers as an "effectuall prayer, earnestly calling for helpe and succour vpon the most sweete Jesu, . . . these short prayers following, for euerie day in the weeke one. . . . O blessed Jesu make me to loue thee intierlie. O blessed Jesu I would fayne, but without thy helpe I can not. O blessed Jesu let me deeply consider the greatnesse of thy loue towards mee. O blessed Jesu giue vnto mee grace hartilie to thanke thee for thy benifites. O blessed Jesu giue me good will to serue thee, and to suffer. O sweete Jesu giue me a natural remembraunce of thy passion. O sweet Jesu possesse my hart, holde and keepe it onelie to thee." As indicated above, these sentence prayers were first

my heart, with all my mind, and with all my power and strength. O most blessed Jesu, I would fain love Thee, but I cannot without Thy help.[83] O most sweet Jesu, my comfort and solace, fain would I love Thee, but without Thy help I can do nothing. My great enemies—the world, the flesh, and the Fiend—be right fierce and cruel, and evermore ready to let[84] me from Thy love. Help me, therefore, good Lord, and strength me with Thy grace, so that I may ever love Thee as Thy will is.

O blessed Jesu, let me deeply consider the contents of Thy love towards me.[85] O my Lord God almighty, Thou art my Maker, Thou art my Redeemer, Thou art my Saviour. Thou, good Lord, hast made me not a stone without life, not of a tree without sensible perceiving, not a beast without reason; but Thou hast made me a perfect creature, having life, sensible perceiving, and reasonable understanding. Also, Thou hast redeemed me not with corruptible gold and silver, but with Thy most precious blood, whereby Thou hast made me partaker of Thy great glory and joy in heaven. Moreover, Thou hast preserved me from much ill, and yet daily Thou dost preserve me and nourish me, both bodily and ghostly. Grant me, mine own good Lord, deeply to plant within my breast the remembrance of this Thy great love towards me. O blessed Jesu, give me grace, heartily to thank Thee for Thy benefits.[86]

O most gracious Lord, I am full of frailty and feeble, as Thou knowest best, and utterly insufficient of myself to render thanks unto Thy goodness for my creation, for my redemption and conservation. Thou, therefore, blessed Lord Jesu, receive me after Thy will, and give me grace heartily to thank Thee for this and other of Thy manifold benefits. O blessed Jesu, give me good will to serve Thee and suffer for Thee.[87] O most good and liberal Lord, Thou art the very Giver of all good things; give me, good Lord, a good will to love Thee, to dread Thee, and to suffer. My duty, good Lord, is great, and my power is but small. I ought to love Thee above all creatures and my neighbor as myself. I ought to flee sin for Thy sake, and only to follow

---

published thirty years after KP's death. Her access to a manuscript of Fisher's last composition before he was executed for treason in July 1535 is most plausibly explained by positing her almoner, George Day, as an intermediary. See my introduction to *Psalms or Prayers*, pp. 198, 200, and introduction to this text, pp. 497–98.

83. **O . . . help** KP expands Fisher's second sentence prayer, "O blessed Jesu I would fayne, but without thy helpe I can not."

84. **let** keep.

85. **O . . . me** Preparing the way for elaboration, KP substitutes "contents" for "greatness" in Fisher's third sentence prayer: "O blessed Jesu let me deeply consider the greatnesse of thy loue towards mee."

86. **O . . . benefits** KP employs Fisher's fourth sentence prayer to conclude her serial consideration of God's loving care for her and to pivot into her loving response to God: "O blessed Jesu giue vnto mee grace hartilie to thanke thee for thy benifites."

87. **O . . . Thee** KP slightly expands and renders more emphatic Fisher's fifth sentence prayer to introduce her serial elaboration of her desire to become like Christ in service and suffering: "O blessed Jesu giue me good will to serue thee, and to suffer."

Thee. I ought to be content with all my tribulation, and gladly to suffer them for the love of Thee; but in no wise I can do this by mine own power and strength. Help me, therefore, blessed Jesu, with Thy special grace, and give me good will thus to serve Thee obediently, and patiently to suffer.

O sweet Jesu, give me continual remembrance of Thy passion.[88] O most benign Jesu, mine whole health and wealth, I confess me, and lowly submit myself unto Thy great mercy and goodness; for I have little remembered Thee, and less I have thanked Thee for Thy great kindness showed unto me and all mankind. Whereas Thou wert rich, for our sakes Thou becamest full poor; Thou tookest great labor to ease us, Thou sufferest many pains to relieve us. Where we were bound, Thou madest us free. We were condemned by justice of the painful prison of hell, and Thou by Thy mercies madest us inheritors to the joyful kingdom of heaven. Thou wert unkindly betrayed. Thou wert traitorously taken, and cruelly bound with hard ropes. Thou wert mocked and scorned and spitted upon. Thou wert beaten and bobbed, and crowned with sharp thorns. Thou wert drawn and stretched and through-pierced into Thy heart. Thy sinews and veins were broken, and Thy skin and flesh was torn. Thy hands and feet nailed to the cross,[89] Thou sheddest all Thy blood, and yielded up Thy ghost. All this and much more Thou diddest and sufferest for sinful man's sake.

Moist my dry heart, blessed Jesu, with Thy sweet drops of Thy grace, and give me continual remembrance of this Thy painful passion. O sweet Jesu, possess my heart, and keep it only to Thee.[90] O most noble and mighty Prince, Lord of all lords, and King of all kings, Thou madest heaven and earth, and all the creatures in them. Now, then, like as I am Thine by creation, so make Thou me ever Thine by possession. Make Thou me meekly to confess mine own deeds, words, and thoughts, and to put my whole trust and confidence in Thy grace. Make me utterly to despise this wretched world and all the unlawful pleasures and desires of the same. Make Thou me meek, patient, and pitiful, and give me perfect faith, hope, and charity. Make

88. **O . . . passion** KP embarks upon what her *Lamentation of a Sinner* signals as her central subject of devotion by way of Fisher's sixth sentence prayer: "O sweete Jesu giue me a naturall remembraunce of thy passion." **continual** KP intensifies Fisher's "a naturall."

89. **Whereas Thou wert . . . cruelly bound . . . nailed to the cross Whereas Thou wert . . . poor** an allusion to 2 Corinthians 8:9. **Thou wert . . . cruelly bound . . . nailed to the cross** In tone and specifics, KP's graphic detailing of the crucifixion is a close, literal analogue of an extended depiction of the scene as an illuminated manuscript book in "A sermon verie fruitfull, godlie, and learned . . . very aptely applyed vnto the passion of Christ: Preached vpon a good Friday, by the same Iohn Fisher, Bishop of Rochester," which is printed immediately following *A spirituall consolation*, sigs. Eviii r–Fi r. See my introduction to *The Lamentation of a Sinner*, pp. 430–31.

90. **O . . . Thee** KP employs Fisher's seventh sentence prayer to draw her own elaborated composition toward a close by expressing desire for union with Christ in mutual love: "O sweet Jesu possesse my hart, holde and keepe it onelie to thee."

Thou my heart also, O most sweet Jesu, a pleasant palace for Thy high majesty, and possess it, hold it, and keep it only to Thee, good Lord. Amen.

THE PRAYER OF QUEEN ESTHER FOR HELP AGAINST HER ENEMIES[91]

O Thou,[92] Lord, Thou only art our King. Help me, desolate woman, which have no helper but Thee, for my misery and destruction is hard at my hand.[93] Think upon us, O Lord, and show Thyself in the time of our distress and of our trouble.[94] Strength me, O Thou, King of gods and Lord of all power;[95] deliver us with Thy hand, and help me, desolate woman, which have no defense nor helper,[96] but only Thee. Lord, Thou knowest all things. Thou knowest and wotest[97] my necessity. O Lord, Thou, God of Abraham, O Thou, mighty God above all, hear the voice of

91. **The prayer . . . enemies** KP crafts this prayer by stringent excerpting and then near-verbatim quoting of snippets from her source, "The prayer of quene Hester for her selfe and all her countrye menne. Hester 13," in the "Prayers of the Bible" section of Richard Grafton's publication *Praiers of Holi Fathers, Patryarches, Prophetes, Judges, Kynges, and renowmed men and wemen of eyther testaments* (1540?) (STC 20200), fols 22v–23v. *Precationes Biblicae* (1528), compiled by Otto Brunfels, an associate of Luther, is the Latin precursor of the English Prayers of the Bible sections appended to English primers with overt Lutheran leanings (Butterworth, *English Primers (1529–1545)*, 37–38). The ultimate source of the English wording of this prayer is Coverdale's translation of the book of Esther.

92. **Thou** "my" (Grafton).

93. **desolate . . . hand** **desolate** Grafton reads "a desolate." **hand** KP omits the rest of the following first half of the prayer, which reads: "Of a chyld, I learned of my father, that thou tokest vp Israel out of all peoples, and oure fathers out of all theyr progenitours: that they shuld bee thy perpetuall enheritaunce: and loke, what thou dyddest promyse theim thou hast made it good vnto them. Now Lorde wee haue synned before thee: therfore hast thou geuen vs into the handes of our enemyes, because wee worshypped theyr goddes: Lorde thou art ryghteous, neuerthelesse, they are not satisfied that they oppresse vs with most heuy thraldome, but also imputing the strength of theyr handes vnto the power of their ydols, they wyll chaunge thy promises: and destroye thyne enherytaunce and stoppe the mouthes of theim that prayse thee, and quenche the glorie of thyne house: and thyne aulter, to open the mouthes of the heathen: that they may prayse the power of ydols, and magnifie the fleshly kyng for euer. Lorde geue not thy scepter vnto theim that bee nothyng worthy: least they laugh at our fall, but tourne theyr devyce vpon theimselues, and punyshe hym that hath begoon to rage vpon vs."

94. **and . . . trouble** KP's addition.

95. **Strength . . . power** **Strength** Grafton reads "Strengthen." **and** Grafton reads "thou." **power** KP omits the remainder of this sentence: "geue me pleasaunt speche in my mouth before the Lyon"—Esther's allusion to her husband, the fearsome Ahasuerus, King of Persia.

96. **help . . . helper** **help . . . woman** Grafton reads "helpe the forsaken woman." **helper** Grafton reads "help."

97. **all things . . . wotest** **all things** Grafton reads "all." KP omits the remainder of this sentence: "Thou wotest I loue not the glory of the unrighteous, and hate the bed of the uncircumcysed and of all heathen." **and wotest** KP's doubling of "knowest."

them that have none other hope, and deliver us out of the hands of the wicked, and deliver me out of my fear. Amen.

THE PRAYER OF SARAH, THE DAUGHTER OF RAGUEL, WHEN SHE WAS SLANDERED[98]

Blessed be Thy name, O God of our fathers, which, when Thou art wroth, showest mercy, and in the time of trouble, Thou forgivest the sins of them that call upon Thee. Unto Thee, Lord, turn I my face; unto Thee lift I up mine eyes. I beseech Thee, O Lord, loose me out of the bonds of this rebuke. After a storm, Thou makest the weather quiet and still; after weeping and heaviness, Thou givest great joy. Thy name, O God of Israel, be praised forever. Amen.[99]

THE PRAYER OF JUDITH FOR THE VICTORY OF HOLOFERNES[100]

O Thou, God of the heavens, Thou, Maker of the[101] waters and Lord of all creatures, hear me, poor woman, calling upon Thee, and putting my trust in Thy mercy. Remember Thy covenant, O Lord, and minister words in my mouth, and stablish this device in my heart. Thou[102] art God, and there is none other but Thou. Amen.

98. **The . . . slandered** KP's source for her highly selective translation of this prayer is a section of suffrages (petitionary prayers) taken from the Vulgate Bible and captioned in English in *Horae beatissime virginis Marie ad Legitimum Sarisburiensis ecclesie ritum* (Paris: F. Regnault, 1536) (STC 15987), sig. Mi v. Her source gives a reference to Tobias 3.

99. **Blessed . . . Amen** KP translates excerpts of three early sentences and the last two clauses of the fifth sentence of her source; she then paraphrases its final clause. The omitted material bewails the distress of being slandered and suffering the loss of one's good name, then affirms God's responsiveness to prayers for deliverance. The relevant Latin excerpts read "Benedictum sit nomen tuum deus patrum nostrorum / qui cum iratus fueris misericordiam facis: et in tempore tribulationis peccata dimittis his qui inuocant te. Igitur ad te domine faciem meam conuerto: et ad te oculos meos conuerto. Peto domine vt a vinculo improperij huius absolutas me. . . . post tempestatem tranquillum facis: et post lachrymationem et fletum exultationem infundis . . . vt laudem et glorificem te in secula seculorum. Amen" (Blessed be Thy name, O God of our fathers, who, when Thou wert angry, haddest mercy, and in time of tribulation dost remit the sins of those who call upon Thee. Thus I turn my face to Thee, Lord; and I turn mine eyes to Thee. I beseech Thee, Lord, to loose me from the bond of this rebuke. . . . After a storm, Thou makest stillness; and after tears and weeping, Thou infusest exultation. . . . that I may laud and glorify Thee from age to age. Amen).

100. **The . . . Holofernes** KP excerpts only the final petitions of her lengthy source, "The prayer of Judith for the delyeraunce of her countrey from the tyraunt. Judith, chap. 9," in the version in Grafton's *Prayers of Holi Fathers*, fol. 21 r-v.

101. **the heavens . . . the waters** Grafton reads "heavens," "waters."

102. **heart. Thou** KP excises the two clauses that intervene between "heart" and "Thou" in Grafton's text: "that thy house may contynue styll in holinesse, and that al the heathen may knowe and vnderstand that . . ."

THE PRAYER OF JESUS, THE SON OF SIRACH[103]

I thank Thee, O Lord and King, and praise Thee, O God, my Saviour; we yield praise[104] unto Thy name. For Thou art my Defender and Helper, and hast preserved my body from destruction, from the snare of traitorous tongues, and from the lips[105] that are occupied with lies. Thou hast been my Helper from such as stood up[106] against me, and hast delivered me after the multitude of Thy[107] mercy, and for Thy holy name's sake. Thou hast delivered me from the roaring of them that prepared themselves to devour me, out of the[108] hands of such as sought after my life, from the multitude of them that troubled me, and went about to set fire upon me on every side, so that I am not burned in the midst of the fire, from the deep of hell, from an unclean tongue, from lying words, from an unrighteous tongue.[109] My soul shall praise Thee, Lord, unto death, for my life drew nigh unto hell. They compassed me round about on every side, and there was no man to help me. I looked about me, if there were any man that would succor me, but there was none. Then thought I upon Thy mercy, O Lord, and upon Thy acts that Thou hast done ever, of old—namely, Thou deliverest such as put their trust in Thee, and riddest them out of the hands of their enemies.[110] Thus lifted I up my prayer from the earth, and

103. **The . . . Sirach** KP's closely followed source is the first half of "A prayer of Jesus the sonne of Sirac," which concludes Ecclesiasticus 51 in Coverdale's *Biblia* (1535), fol. lvi r-v (separately foliated); a second edition, printed in England, followed in 1537. This prayer circulated widely: it was reprinted in Coverdale's *Psalter and Certain other devout prayers taken out of the Bible* (STC 2379), fol. 148, and in a nearly identical version in Grafton's *Prayers of Holy Fathers*, fols. 47 r–48 r. Another closely related version is found in Taverner's *Epitome of the Psalms*, sigs. Ei v–Eii v. The variants recorded in the following notes indicate that KP's source was Coverdale's Bible (1535 or 1537). Additional confirmation comes from the fact that the next prayer to be copied by KP is found on the next folio page in Coverdale's Bible. Taverner's version of this prayer was reprinted in the royally authorized English primer (1545); see *Three Primers Put Forth in the Reign of Henry VIII*, 2nd ed. (Oxford: Oxford University Press, 1848), 508–10. The original source, the "Oratio Jesus filii Syrak," regularly figures among the suffrages in the Hours of the Blessed Virgin Mary in Latin primers according to Salisbury use (see, e.g., STC 15984, 15985, 15987).

104. **we . . . praise** we "I will" (Coverdale, Grafton, Taverner). **praise** "praises" (Grafton, Taverner).

105. **and hast . . . lips** **and hast . . . destruction** omitted in Taverner. **traitorous** "traitours" (Grafton); "traitorours" (Taverner). **the lips** "them" (Grafton, Taverner).

106. **stood up** "rose" (Taverner).

107. **after . . . Thy** "according to Thy great" (Taverner).

108. **the** "thy" (Grafton).

109. **am . . . tongue** **am . . . burned** "was not brent" (Grafton, Taverner). **hell** Taverner adds at this point: "Thou deliveredst me." **an unclean . . . tongue** "the unclean tongue," "the vnrighteous tongue" (Taverner). **from . . . tongue** "and from an vnrighteous tongue" (Coverdale); "from vnrighteouse toungue" (Grafton).

110. **riddest . . . their enemies** **riddest** deliverest. **their enemies** "the Heathen" (Grafton); "the false panims"—i.e., pagans (Taverner).

prayed for deliverance from my enemies.[111] I called upon the Lord my Father, that He would not leave me without help in the day of my trouble, and in the time of the proud. I praised Thy name continually, yielding honor and thanks unto Thee.[112] And so my prayer was heard: Thou savedst me from destruction, and deliveredst me from the unrighteous time. Therefore will I acknowledge and praise Thee, and magnify[113] the name of the Lord. Amen.

THE PRAYER OF THE THREE CHILDREN THAT WERE DELIVERED FROM THE HOT, BURNING FIRE

Blessed be Thou,[114] O Lord God of our fathers, right worthy to be praised and honored is that name of Thine for evermore. For Thou art righteous in all those[115] things that Thou hast done to us; yea, faithful are all Thy works. Thy ways are right and Thy judgments true;[116] yea, according to right and equity hast Thou brought these things upon us because of our sins. For why[117] we have offended and done wickedly, departing from Thee; in all things have we trespassed and not obeyed Thy commandments, nor kept them, neither done as Thou hast bidden us, that we might prosper. Wherefore all that Thou hast brought upon us, and everything that Thou hast done to us, Thou hast done them in true judgment, as in delivering us into the hands of our enemies.[118] Yet, for Thy name's sake, we beseech Thee, give us not up forever. Break not Thy covenant, and take not away Thy mercy from us, for Thy beloved Abraham's sake, for Thy servant Isaac's sake, and for Thy holy Israel's sake, to whom Thou hast spoken and promised that Thou wouldest multiply their seed as the stars of heaven, and as the sand that lieth upon the seaside.[119] For we, O Lord, are become less than any people, and be kept under this day in all the world

111. **lifted . . . enemies** **lifted** "lift" (Coverdale). **my enemies** "deathe" (Coverdale, Grafton, Taverner).

112. **Thee** "it" (Grafton, Taverner).

113. **praise . . . magnify** "praise Thee and advance" (Taverner).

114. **Blessed . . . Thou** KP's selectively utilized source is "The prayer of Azarias and the songe of the thre children after Theodotions translacion: which wordes are wrytten in the thirde chapter of Daniel after the olde text in Latyn," which immediately follows Ecclesiasticus 51 in the Apocrypha section of Coverdale's *Biblia*, fols. lvi v–lvii r (separately foliated).

115. **those** Coverdale reads "the."

116. **true** KP omits the immediately following sentence: "In all the thinges that thou hast brought vpon vs, and vpon the holy cite of our fathers (euen Jerusalem) thou hast executed true iudgment."

117. **For why** Because.

118. **enemies** KP omits the immediately following passage: "among vngodly and wicked abhominacions, and to an vnrighteous kinge, yee the most frowarde vpon earth. And now we maye nat open our mouthes, we are become a shame and reprofe vnto thy seruauntes, and to them that worship the."

119. **seaside** Coverdale reads "sea shore."

because of our sins.[120] Nevertheless, in a contrite heart and an humble spirit, let us be received, that we may obtain Thy mercy.[121] For there is no confusion unto them that put their trust in Thee, and now we follow Thee with all our heart; we fear Thee and seek Thy face. Put us not to shame, but deal with us after Thy lovingkindness; and according to the multitude of Thy mercies. Deliver us by Thy miracles, O Lord, and get Thy name an honor, that all they which do Thy servants evil may be confounded. Let them be ashamed through Thy almighty power, and let their strength be broken, that they may know how that Thou only art the Lord God, and honor-worthy throughout all the world.[122] Blessed be the holy name of Thy glory, for it is worthy to be praised and magnified in all worlds. Blessed be Thou in the holy temple of Thy glory, for, above all things, Thou art to be praised, yea, and more worthy to be magnified forever. Blessed be Thou in the throne of Thy kingdom, for, above all, Thou art worthy to be well spoken of, and to be more than magnified forever. Blessed be Thou that lookest through the deep, and sittest upon the cherubim,[123] for Thou art worthy to be praised and, above all, to be magnified forever. Blessed be Thou in the firmament of heaven, for Thou art praise- and honor-worthy forever. Amen.

THE PRAYER OF MANASSES, SIXTH KING OF JUDAH[124]

O Lord almighty, God of our fathers Abraham, Isaac, and Jacob, and of the righteous seed of them: which hast made heaven and earth with all the ornaments thereof, which hast ordained the sea by the word of Thy commandment, which

120. **sins** KP omits the next clause: "So that now we haue nether prynce, duke, prophet, burnt offerynge, sacrifice, oblacion, incense, nor Sanctuary before the."

121. **mercy** KP omits the next sentence: "Like as in the burnt offerynge of rammes, and bullockes, and like as in thousandes of fat lambes: so let our offrynge be in thy sight this daye, that it maye please the."

122. **world** This is the last word of Azarias's prayer. The song he sings with his two companions in the fiery furnace commences with the following sentence, which KP omits: "Blessed be thou, o Lorde God of oure fathers: for thou art prayse and honoure worthy, yee and to be magnified for evermore." She begins with the song's second sentence, but excerpts "thou art praise and honor worthy" to use below in concluding this prayer.

123. **cherubim** Coverdale reads "Cherubyns."

124. **The . . . Judah** KP's quite closely followed source is "The prayer of Manasses kyng of Juda, when he was in pryson, for remission of synnes, and for Goddes fauoure, and deliverance, I Paralipomenon 36," in Grafton's *Prayers of Holy Fathers*, fols. 18v–19v. A substantially similar version is found in the "Prayers of the Byble" section of Richard Taverner's *An epitome of the psalmes. or briefe meditacions with diuerse other prayers* (1539) (STC 2748), sig. Bviii r-v, but Taverner cannot be KP's source because he omits several lines that she and Grafton include. Substantive variants are recorded in the notes below. This prayer also occurs in the royally authorized English primer (1545), reprinted in *Three Primers*, 506–7, but that version is even more distant from KP's.

hast shut up the deep and hast sealed it for Thy fearful and laudable name, which all men fear; they tremble before the face of Thy presence, and for the anger of Thy threatening, the which is unportable to sinners.[125] But the mercy of Thy promise is great and unsearchable, for Thou art the Lord God, most high above all the earth, long-suffering and exceeding merciful, and repentant[126] for the malice of men. Thou, Lord, after Thy goodness, hast promised repentance of the remission of sins; and Thou, that art the God of the righteous, hast not put repentance to the righteous Abraham, Isaac, and Jacob, unto them that have not sinned against Thee. But because I have sinned above the number of the sands of the sea, and that mine iniquities are multiplied, I am humbled with many bands of iron, and there is in me no breathing.[127] I have provoked Thine anger, and have done evil before Thee in committing abominations and multiplying offenses. And now I bow the knees of my heart, requiring goodness of Thee, O Lord.[128] I have sinned, Lord, I have sinned, and know my iniquity. I desire Thee by prayer, O Lord: forgive me, forgive me,[129] and destroy me not with mine iniquities; neither do Thou always remember mine evils, to punish them. But save me (which am unworthy) after Thy great mercy, and I will praise Thee everlastingly all the days of my life. For all the virtue of heaven praiseth Thee, and unto Thee belongeth glory, world without end. Amen.

Our merciful Father,[130] which in teaching us to pray by Thy Son, Christ, hast commanded us to call Thee Father, and to believe that we are Thy well-beloved children; which stirrest up none of Thine to pray, but to the intent[131] Thou wouldest hear them, giving us also all things more effectuously and plenteously than we can

125. **which all . . . sinners** "dread of all men, and honorable before the face of thy vertue, the fearce anger of thy thretenyng is importunate [troublesomely] heuy to synners" (Grafton). Taverner reads identically except for substituting "aboue measure" for "importunate." **unportable** unbearable.

126. **repentant** "sory" (Taverner). KP evidently understands "repentant" to mean "sorrowful," not necessarily with connotations of culpability or guilt.

127. **Thou, Lord . . . breathing** Taverner omits these two sentences.

128. **of . . . Lord** "of the lord" (Grafton).

129. **forgive . . . me** "forgeue me" (Grafton). The repeated "forgive me" is KP's addition.

130. **Our . . . Father** KP's closely followed source is the last prayer of the ninth canonical hour—that is, it comes just before Evensong—in William Marshall's *A Prymer in Englyshe, with certeyn prayers and godly meditations, very necessary for all people that vnderstonde not the Latyne tongue* [1534] (STC 15986), sigs. Nvii v–Nviii r, or in Marshall's revision, *A goodly prymer in Englyshe, newly corrected and printed with certeyne godly meditations and prayers added to the same, very necessarie and profitable for all them that ryghte assuredly vnderstande not the latine and greke tongues* (1535) (STC 15988), sigs. Hiv v–Hv r. The texts of this prayer read identically in both. Another identical version (except for one nonsensical misprint) is found in Godfray's compilation *A primer in Englysshe*, sigs. Miiii v–Mv r.

131. **intent** "entente that" (Marshall 1534, 1535).

either ask or think: we beseech Thee, for Thy Son's sake, give us grace to believe and to know steadfastly that Thy Son, our Saviour Christ, is given of Thee unto us, to be unto us[132] our Saviour, our righteousness, our wisdom, our holiness, our redemption, and our satisfaction. And suffer us not to trust in any other salvation, but in Thy Son and by Thy Son only, our Saviour. Amen.

O Lord God: give, that my heart may desire Thee;[133] in desiring, seek Thee; in seeking, to find Thee; in finding, to love Thee; in loving Thee, to find remedy of my evils, and remedy had, that I may abide still in Thee.[134] Grant me, O Lord my God: in my heart, repentance; in my spirit, contrition; in my eyes, a fountain of tears; out of my hands, liberality of alms. My King, quench in me the desires and lusts of the flesh,[135] and kindle in me the fire of Thy love. My Redeemer, put out of me the spirit of pride; and grant me, of Thy mercy, the treasure of Thy meekness and humility.[136] My Saviour, expel from me fumishness and wrath;[137] and give me, for Thy pity' sake, the buckler of patience. My Creator, pull out of me the rancor of mind; and grant Thou me, that art so merciful, a loving heart.[138] Give me, O most tender and pitiful Father,[139] sure faith, like hope, and charity continual. My Governor, put

132. **unto us** KP's repetition.

133. **O . . . Thee** KP's source is the opening prayer (bk. 1, chap. 1) in the compilation traditionally known as St. Augustine's *Meditations* (or *Prayers*) but no longer attributed to him; for the Latin original, see *Patrologia Latina, Cursus Completus*, ed. J.-P. Migne (Paris, 1887), 40:902. No fewer than three English translations of these *Meditations* were published under various titles from 1570 onward (STC 924, 933, 944; cf. STC 950); of these, Thomas Rogers's translation circulated by far the most widely. Queen Elizabeth excerpted from it in a note on Augustine that she inscribed in her Geneva New Testament ca. 1581; see *Elizabeth I: Translations, 1544–1589*, 404. All three of these English translations appeared too late to be KP's source; her version, moreover, bears only a family resemblance to them. Rogers's title, *A right Christian Treatise, entituled S. Augustines Praiers: Published in more ample sort than yet it hath bin in the English tong; purged from diuers superstitious points; and adorned with manifold places of the S. Scriptures* (1581) (STC 950), casts disapproval on an earlier English translation, which his dedicatory letter critiques in further detail. Rogers says he does not know who made this translation. This earlier English version, possibly KP's source, has not proved traceable thus far. Since, alternatively, she could have translated from the original Latin of this medieval work, the notes below record substantive variants between its opening prayer and her English version.

134. **to find . . . Thee** "mala mea redimere redempta non iterare" (to make amends for my wrongs, and not repeat those that have been amended). KP replaces the speaker's moral activism with dependence on God for relief.

135. **desires . . . flesh** "desideria carnis" (desires of the flesh). Here and repeatedly below, KP adds emphasis with a doublet.

136. **treasure . . . humility** "thesaurum humilitatis tuae" (treasure of Thy humility).

137. **fumishness . . . wrath** "furorem irae" (fury of wrath), recast as a doublet. **fumishness** hot-temperedness.

138. **loving heart** "mentis dulcedinem" (sweetness of disposition).

139. **most . . . Father** "clementissime Pater" (most gentle Father). **pitiful** merciful.

from me all vanity, inconstancy of mind, wavering of the heart, jesting or railing of my mouth,[140] proud looking, gluttony of the belly, uncharitable rebuking of mine neighbors, the love or desire of worldly riches,[141] the desire of vainglory,[142] the mischief of hypocrisy, the poison[143] of flattery, the disdain of the needy, the oppression of the poor and feeble, the rust of envy, the death of blasphemy. Cut away from me, O my Maker, unrightful rashness, sturdiness, unquietness, idleness, slothfulness, dullness of the wit, blindness of the heart, obstinacy of the mind, cruelness of behavior, disobedience of that [which] is good, resistance against good counsel, unruliness of my tongue, polling of poor people, violent dealing with the impotent, slandering of innocents, crabbedness[144] against those that be with me in household, unkindness towards my friends and familiar acquaintance, rigor or extreme dealing[145] with my neighbors. O my God, my mercy, I pray Thee, for the love of Thy Son, make me to do deeds of mercy;[146] to exercise pity; to have compassion on those that be in affliction or trouble;[147] to give counsel to those that be out of the right way; to succor those that be in misery; to relieve the oppressed; to comfort them that be in heaviness; to refresh the poor; to cheer them that weep; to forgive them that trespass against me; to love those that hate me; to recompense good for evil; to despise none, but to honor all men; to follow the good, to eschew the evil, to embrace virtues, and to refuse vices. In adversity, patience; in prosperity, moderation, and keeping of my tongue, and to hold close my lips warily; to despise things earthly, and to thirst after things heavenly. Amen.[148]

Most sovereign and holy Trinity,[149] the Father, the Son, and the Holy Ghost, three Persons and one God, have mercy on me. O blessed and glorious Trinity, have

140. **jesting . . . mouth** "oris scurrilitatem" (scurrility of the mouth).

141. **uncharitable . . . riches** **uncharitable . . . neighbors** The next two phrases are omitted by KP: "scelera detractionum, curiositatis pruriginem" (the vices of slander, the itching of curiosity). **love . . . riches** "divitiarum cupiditatem" (greed for riches).

142. **desire . . . vainglory** "potentatuum rapinam inanis gloriae" (seizure of political powers and vainglory). **vainglory** empty ostentation.

143. **poison** "naevum" (blemish, fault).

144. **crabbedness** "severitatem" (harshness). KP omits the preceding phrase: "subditorum negligentiam" (neglect of subordinates).

145. **rigor . . . dealing** "duritiam" (rigor).

146. **make . . . mercy** "da mihi misericordiae opera" (grant me the works of mercy). Reversing the relation between translated and original phrasing registered in n134, here KP's text stresses moral effort; the Latin, God's grant.

147. **to have . . . trouble** a conflation of three phrases: "compati afflictis, subveniri egenis, succurrere miseris" (to have compassion on the afflicted, to assist the needy, to hasten to help the unfortunate).

148. **Amen** an addition to the Latin original.

149. **Most . . . Trinity** The source for KP's moderately elaborated translation is the first prayer in the section "De sanctissima trinitate" immediately following the section "In eleua-

mercy on me. O the most holy, merciful, and everlasting Trinity, have mercy on me. O the true and unfeigned Trinity, the great and incomparable goodness, the everlasting and sweet cleanness, and the inseparate majesty of the Father, the Son, and the Holy Ghost, have mercy on me. O good Father, and meek Son, O Holy Ghost, O Light that cannot be put out; O the only Father of heaven, have mercy on me. Thee, good Lord, do I call upon; to Thee I do make my intercession and prayer. Thee do I laud and praise now, and [am] ever in mind so to continue, which art the only Beginner of all virtue and goodness, and the final Ender of all good works. O holy God, O strong God, O everlasting God, have mercy on me, and remember me with Thy manifest goodness, that I, unworthy servant and handiwork, for my great iniquity and sin, be not without Thy mercy, lost and damned. For Thou art my Maker and Redeemer, my only joy and comfort, and my only hope and health, of whom I have all things necessary to my living: wherefore I thank Thee, now and ever. Amen.

O merciful God,[150] which through Thy infinite mercy did save harmless Susannah from death, to the which she wrongfully was accused and condemned; and did deliver Thy servant Daniel from the lake of the lions, and did deliver the three chil-

tione corporis christi" in *This primer of Salisbury use* (Paris: Yvonne Bonhomme for J. Grout, bookseller in London, 1534) (STC 15985), fol. lxxxviii r-v. A large woodcut image of the Trinity precedes this prayer, which reads in its entirety as follows: "Sancta trinitas vnus deus: miserere nobis. O beata et gloriosa trinitas: miserere nobis. O sacra et summa et sempiterna trinitas: miserere nobis. O vera et gloriosa et ineffabilis trinitas et vna deitissima et incomparabilis bonitas: eterna et suauissima claritas: trium personarum indiuisa maiestas: o pater bone: o fili pie: o spiritus paraclite: o lumen indeficiens: vnus deus: cuius opus vita: cuius amor gratia: cuius contemplatio gratia est omnium sanctorum: te Domine inuoco: te adoro: totò cordis affectu nunc: et in seculum vndico. Alpha et oo: agyos: emanuel: sancte deus: sancte fortis: sancte et immortalis: miserere nobis. Memento mei deus meus in bonum: et do propicius veniam ne pereat opus manuum tuarum. Tu es creator meus: tu es spes mea: tu es salutare meum domine: ex quo omnia: perquem omnia: tu quo omnia: tibi honor et gloria. Amen" (Holy Trinity, one God, have mercy on us. O blessed and glorious Trinity, have mercy on us. O sacred, and most high, and everlasting Trinity, have mercy on us. O true and glorious and ineffable Trinity, and the one most divine and incomparable goodness, the everlasting and sweetest clearness, the undivided majesty of three Persons: O good Father, O meek Son, O accompanying Spirit. O unfailing light, one God, whose work is life, whose love is grace, whose contemplation is the grace of all saints: I call upon Thee, Lord; I adore Thee with the whole affection of my heart, now and evermore. Alpha and Omega, Holy One; Emmanuel, holy God, holy and strong, holy and immortal, have mercy on us. Remember me, my God, with goodness, and be propitious regarding my sin, that the work of Thy hands may not perish. Thou art my Maker; Thou art my hope; Thou art my salvation: from whom and by whom [I have] all things. Thou, by whom all things [are done], to Thee be honor and glory. Amen).

150. **O . . . God** The source for KP's moderately elaborating translation is the third prayer in the section "De sanctissima trinitate" in *This primer of Salisbury use* (STC 15985), fols. lxxxviii v–lxxxix r. The prayer in its entirety reads as follows: "Deus qui liberasti susannan de falso cri-

dren, Shadrach, Mesach, Abednego, from the hot, burning fire;[151] and did reach out Thy hand to Thy well-beloved disciple Peter, being in great jeopardy of drowning: I desire Thee, that Thou which, in so many things, did show and manifest Thy infinite mercy, would save and deliver me from all tribulation and enemies, and from all the power of all mine enemies, and from all them that consent to my destruction and perdition. For I am ignorant, merciful Lord, to whom I should flee, or seek for help or comfort, but only to Thee, which art my Maker and Redeemer. And I do know none other that will help and defend me against this world and deceitful temptation, but Thou only, my God, which dost reign and shall reign, three Persons in one God, the Father, the Son, and the Holy Ghost, without end. Amen.

We are assaulted with three manners of temptations,[152] the flesh, the world, and the devil. Therefore we desire Thee, most dear Father, endue[153] us so with Thy grace, that we may withstand the desires of the flesh. Make that we resist and fight against this superfluity of meats,[154] drink, sleep, sloth, and idleness. Make that we may

---

mine: et danielem de lacu leonum: et tres pueros de camino ignis ardentis: petro mergenti dexteram porrexisti: tu me liberare digneris de hac et omni tribulatione et angustia: ac de potestate omnium inimicorum meorum: et de omnibus qui consentiunt eis: quia nescio vbi fugiam nisi ad te deum: quia non est alius qui me adiuuet nisi tu solus deus qui in trinitate perfecta viuis et regnas deus: Per omnia secula seculorum. Amen" (God, Thou who didst free Susannah from false accusation, and Daniel from the den of the lions, and the three children from the furnace of burning fire; Thou who didst reach out Thy right hand to the drowning Peter: deliver Thou me, who am worthy of this and all tribulation and hardship, from the power of all of my enemies, and from all they who consent with them. For I do not know where I may flee, unless to Thee, God, because there is none other who will help me, except Thou only, O God, who liveth and reigneth, one God in perfect Trinity, from age to age forever. Amen).

151. **Daniel . . . Abednego** The allusion is to chapters 3 and 6 of Daniel, and the respective punishments visited on the young Jews at the Persian court for refusing to worship idols: Daniel was thrown into the lions' den, while earlier the three others had been thrown into a fiery furnace. After they survived their ordeals, the Persian king acknowledged God's deliverance of His faithful. **lake** a late medieval and early modern cognate of Latin *lacus*, one meaning of which is "a den for lions." See n572 to *Psalms or Prayers* for another instance of this rendering.

152. **We . . . temptations** KP's generally closely followed, sometimes selectively employed sources for the next two prayers are the sections "The syxte peticion. And lede vs not into temptation" and "The seuenth petition. But delyuer vs from euyll," of the devotional commentary on "The prayer of the lorde" in William Marshall's 1535 revision, *A goodly prymer in Englyshe*, sigs. Ciii r–Ciiii r. The ultimate source of this commentary is either Otto Brunfels's *Precationes Biblicae* (1531) or Luther's *Betbüchlein* (Little Prayerbook) (1522) (Butterworth, *English Primers*, 283). The readings "adversities" and "esteem" (nn 159, 160) indicate that KP did not use Marshall's 1534 primer. **temptations** "temptation" (Marshall 1534).

153. **Thee . . . endue** **Thee, most** "the more," (Marshall 1534). **endue** "to endowe" (Marshall 1534).

154. **meats** "meate" (Marshall 1534, 1535).

bring the flesh into bondage and fastening[155] with fasting, temperate diet, convenient clothing, sleep, rest, watch, and labor, so that it may be Thine, and a perfect good work.[156] Keep us from the great sins of covetousness and desire of[157] worldly riches. Give us grace that we seek not the rule and honor of this world, or consent to such desires. Keep us that the false subtlety of this world, the counterfeit brightness and enticement[158] of the same persuade us not to follow it. Keep us that we be not drawn by the evils and adversities of this world, to enviousness, avengement, wrath, or such other[159] vices. Give us grace that we may despise the lies of the world: colors, deceits, promises, and falsehood. And, to be short, that we may esteem of little reputation all that belongeth to him,[160] good and evil, as we have promised in baptism, and that we may continue in Thy[161] purpose, going forward daily more and more. Keep us from the enticements of the devil, that we consent not to pride, which would cause us to set much by ourselves and despise other for riches, kin, power, favor, learning, beauty, or any other gifts or goods.[162] Keep us that we fall not into the sin of hate and envy, what occasion soever be given to us. Keep us that we doubt not in the[163] faith, neither fall in desperation now, nor in the point of death. Put Thy helping hand, our best heavenly Father, to them that fight and labor against this hard and manifold temptation. Comfort them that now do stand, and lift them up that are fallen and be overcome. Finally, fulfill us all with Thy grace, that in this miserable and perilous life (which is compassed with so many continual enemies

155. **the flesh . . . fastening** **the flesh** it" (Marshall 1534). **fastening** "subjection" (Marshall 1534, 1535).

156. **may . . . work** "may be mete and apte to good works" (Marshall 1534, 1535). **works** KP omits several sentences that follow immediately in Marshall: "Make that with Christe we may fasten on the crosse [and mortyfy (1534)] his [the flesh's (1534)] euyll desyres to lechery, with [with (omitted 1534)] all his affections and instigations: that we neuer consent, or folowe any of his temptations. Make, that yf (by chaunce) we loke on a well made or a [a (omitted 1534)] fayre man or womman: or any other beautifull ymage or creature, that they be not to vs a cause of temptation. But that the rather of them we may take occasyon to loue chastite, and to prayse thee in thy creatures. Make that when we heare any gladde or pleasaunt armonie: or melodie [thyng (1534)], or fele any swete sente or odours [thyng (1534)], that we seeke not therin our delyte and pleasure, but thy prayse and glorie."

157. **the great . . . of** **the** "this" (Marshall 1534). **sins . . . of** "synne" (Marshall 1534, 1535). **of** "to" (Marshall 1534).

158. **subtlety . . . enticement** **subtlety** "subtleties" (Marshall 1535). **enticement** "entisementes" (Marshall 1534, 1535).

159. **adversities . . . other** **adversities** "mynysters" (Marshall 1534). **enviousness** "impatience" (Marshall 1534, 1535). **such other** "to other suche" (Marshall 1534).

160. **esteem . . . him** **esteem** "forsake" (Marshall 1534). **him** the world.

161. **thy** "this" (Marshall 1534, 1535).

162. **favor . . . goods** **favor** "scyence" (Marshall 1534, 1535). **goods** "goodnes" (Marshall 1534, 1535).

163. **the** "thy" (Marshall 1534).

that never cease) we may fight boldly with stable and noble faith, and obtain the everlasting crown. Amen.[164]

THIS PETITION PRAYETH FOR ALL THE EVILS OF PAINS AND PUNISHMENTS[165]

O Father, deliver us from Thy everlasting wrath, and punishments of hell. Deliver us from Thy strait judgment in death, and at the last day of doom. Deliver us from sudden death. Keep us from the violence of water and fire, from thunder, lightning, and hail. Keep us from hunger and dearth. Keep us from war and manslaughter. Keep us from Thy most grievous strokes: the pestilence, French pox,[166] falling sickness, and such other diseases. Keep us from all evils and perils of the body. Provided alway, that in all these things, be the glory of Thy name, increase of Thy kingdom, and fulfilling of Thy will. Amen.[167]

HERE FOLLOWETH A DEVOUT PRAYER TO CHRIST, THE SECOND PERSON IN TRINITY, OUR ONLY REDEEMER, GOD AND MAN[168]

O Lord Jesu, Thou art the very Lamb of God, and very God and man, most meek and kind: which wast offered in the altar of the cross, and there sufferedst painful death.[169] I worship and honor Thee, and magnify Thee, beseeching Thee that my soul may escape the danger of everlasting pains of death, since Thou, Lord, hast bought me with Thy precious blood. Lord, King of glory, and of mercy and pity, I do believe and knowledge that Thou suffere[d]st Thy most holy hands to be drawn abroad and nailed painfully on the cross. Therefore I beseech Thee, merciful Lord, for Thy infinite pity and goodness, and for that pitiful wounds and pains that Thou suffere[d]st in Thy blessed arms, give Thou me grace, Lord, that all the days of my life I do not stretch forth my arms or hands to do any wickedness or harm to my

164. **Amen** KP's addition. She also adds "Amen" at the end of the prayer that follows.

165. **punishments** KP omits Marshall's concluding phrase (1534, 1535): "as doth the Churche in the Letany."

166. **French pox** syphilis.

167. **Amen** "So be it" (Marshall 1535).

168. **Here . . . man** KP's closely followed source for the following extended prayer bears this title in the section "Here foloweth deuote meditations and prayers with contemplacions called the paradyse of the soule," appended to John Gough's *This prymer of Salysbery vse, bothe in Englyshe and in Laten* (1536) (STC 15992), fols. clxviii v–clxxi r. Substantive variants are recorded in the notes.

169. **death** KP omits the following clause: "whych body is dayly offred in the sacrament of the alter: wher . . ."

Christian brother or neighbor, but only to do good works to Thy honor and worship, and profit of my even-Christian,[170] about me or elsewhere.

Also, Lord Jesu Christ, King of mercy and of pity, I believe and knowledge that Thou suffere[d]st in Thy blessed feet, to be nailed grievously on the cross for our sins and offenses. I pray Thee, Lord Jesu, for Thy endless mercy and pity; I humbly beseech Thee, for that painful wounds that Thou, Lord, suffere[d]st there in Thy feet, that Thou, Lord, forgive me clean all my sin that I have done, in going, in working, idleness, and vanities. And give me grace that, all the days of my life, I go not about folly and idle vanities, but to convert my steps to good works pleasant in Thy sight, that it may be pleasant to Thee, and profitable to all about me.

Also, Lord Jesu, King of glory, I believe and I knowledge that when Thou sawest the city of Jerusalem given to horrible sins, for which it should be destroyed, Thou wepst full tenderly for other men's sins. I pray Thee, Jesu Christ and King of mercy, for Thine endless mercy and pity, which shed so piteous tears for our sinfulness out of Thy glorious eyes, that Thou, Lord, forgive me all my sins, which I have done in misspending,[171] in the sight of mine eyes. And give me grace that, all the days of my life, I may no more offend Thy goodness in vain and sinful sights; but only, Lord, to look on Thy creatures, and stir me to Thy love and dread, and that I may perceive[172] to do good works profitable to my soul, to Thy pleasure and will.

Also, Lord Jesu, I believe and knowledge that when Thou hungst nailed on the cross, Thou heardst Thy enemies report and speak of Thee much falseness and slander against Thy most endless mercy and patience: for all the pains that Thou suffere[d]st in Thy hearing, that Thou, Lord, please to forgive me all my[173] sins that I have offended, in hearing of evil tales and report against my Christian brother. Give me grace, Lord, that I spend no more my time in hearing of leasings,[174] backbiting, or rejoicing in suchlike things, but only to hear Thy true and most holy words of the Gospel preached or taught, and to keep it in my[175] mind, and to do thereafter to the honor, worship of my Lord God, and to the profit of my neighbor, and so to further them to my power, in word and deed.

Also, Lord Jesu, King of glory, I believe and knowledge that when Thou wert yet hanging on the cross, Thou, Lord, opene[d]st Thy most holy mouth, and prayed for Thine enemies, and exhorting the unlearned, and comforted them that were comfortless. I pray Thee, Lord Jesu, for Thine endless mercy and goodness, and for the merciful words that proceeded out of Thy holy mouth, forgive me utterly all the sins, the which I have done in my vile speaking, and give me grace that, all

170. **even-Christian** fellow Christian.
171. **misspending** misusing.
172. **perceive** recognize.
173. **my** Gough reads "the."
174. **leasings** lies, falsehoods.
175. **my** KP's addition.

the days of my life, I speak no leasings, backbitings, nor harm of any[176] person. And also that I sow no discord among Christian people, but only, Lord, that I speak the truth, and flatter not for favor nor lucre; and that I may speak nothing but fruitful and virtuous words, to concord[177] and see at unity, peace, and charity, those that be at discord, that they and I may love Thee and dread Thee, Lord.

Also, Lord Jesu, King of glory, I believe and knowledge that Thou thirsted full sore on the cross, and saidest, "I thirst"; then Thou, Lord, Thou taste[d]st of the bitter eisell and gall, with myrrh, as the holy Gospel witnesseth.[178] I pray Thee, Lord Jesu, for Thine endless pity and mercy, and for the bitterness of that drink that Thou tastedst of, that Thou, Lord, please to forgive me all my sins[179] done against Thee, which I have offended in tasting and in relishing of meats and drinks, and in superfluous tasting thereof. Give me grace, Lord, that, all the days of my life, I no more offend Thee, Lord, in gluttony, in eating and drinking, but that I may temper my mouth in eating and drinking, and to feed the poor that lack that I have—too much, Lord.

Also, Lord Jesu, King of glory, and omnipotent: I believe and knowledge that Thou, Lord, wast crowned with a sharp garland of thorns: I pray Thee, Lord, for Thy endless mercy and pity, meekness and patience, that Thou, Lord, clearly forgive me all the sins that I have done in pride, boast, and in vainglory. And give me grace, while I do live, that I do use no pride; but to use meekness and give example thereof to all men, where I use[180] company with.

Also, Lord Jesu, King of mercy and pity, I steadfastly believe and knowledge that Thou, Lord, suffere[d]st Thy blessed sides[181] to be beaten, rent, and torn with scourges, and Thy tender body strained, insomuch all the joints of Thy precious body might have been numbered and told, as the prophet David saith: "Dinumeraverunt omnia ossa mea."[182] I humbly pray Thee, my Lord God, of Thy endless favor and pity, for all the pitiful wounds that Thou suffere[d]st in Thy most tender and pitiful body, to forgive me all the filthy sinfulness of my body, as in lechery and in all other sinful operations that I have wrought, in sin of any part of my body. Give me grace, Lord, forever to despise all works of sinful lechery, which violateth the temple of God: which is my soul, when it is out of deadly sin. From the which filthy sin, give me grace utterly to expel, from all parts of my body, and so keep clean my soul, which is the holy temple, as Saint Paul witnesseth.[183]

176. **any** Gough reads "no."

177. **concord** to arrange by concord or by agreement.

178. **"I . . . witnesseth "I thirst"** John 19:28. **eisell . . . witnesseth** See n5 above.

179. **sins** Gough reads "synful offencys."

180. **use** pass time in.

181. **sides** Gough reads "body."

182. **Dinumeraverunt . . . mea** "They [the assembly of the wicked] have numbered all my bones," Psalm 21:18 (Vulgate).

183. **the . . . witnesseth the** Gough reads "thy." **as . . . witnesseth** "Know ye not that ye are the temple of God, and how that the spirit of God dwelleth in you? If any man defile the temple

Also, sweet Jesu, I do knowledge and believe, that while Thou were yet hanging on the cross, Thou suffere[d]st Thy most blessed side to be pierced, and Thy glorious heart also, with a sharp spear, that both blood and water fell out thereof. I heartily beseech[184] Thee, Lord, to forgive me clean all my cruel sins which hath proceeded from my unclean heart, by thought or deed, in vainglory or in deadly sin, in imagining or delighting, that I henceforth, while I live, spend no more my time in such danger of sin and vanity of this world, nor in idle thoughts; but to use devout exhortations and to have communications, fervent prayers, and holy desires that may be unto Thy pleasure and will, and that all my heart's desire may alway joy in Thee, my Father eternal: so that I may, through Thy precious blood and pains, escape the immortal danger of hell and pains intolerable, and so surely come to the eternal fruition and heritage which Thou, Lord, hast prepared for all that heartily[185] love Thee, and do Thy will and pleasure in this troublous life. Amen.

A PETITION AND PRAYER TO OUR LORD

Deliver me from my enemies, O God, the God of my health; and my tongue shall triumph in Thy righteousness.[186] I cry unto Thee, Lord; Lord, hearken unto my voice. Tarry not, for I am even at the point[187] of death. Help me, Lord, lest I perish.[188] O God, which governest all things, which only canst deliver me, in whose hands is the spirit of life:[189] rid and purge me from mine enemies; deliver me from them,[190] O God, the Author of my health, God, in whom only consisteth my salva-

of God, him shall God destroy. For the temple of God is holy, which temple ye are," 1 Corinthians 3:16–17 (Great Bible).

184. **heartily beseech** Gough reads "cordially sypply." "Supply"—French "supplie"—means "I beg," "I implore."

185. **hartely** Gough reads "cordyally."

186. **Deliver . . . righteousness** KP's slightly excerpted, closely followed source for this prayer is a passage in an English translation of Girolamo Savonarola's "An exposition after the maner of a contemplation vpon the li. psalme, called Miserere mei Deus," appended to Marshall's 1535 *A goodly prymer*, sigs. Q ii v–Q iii v. The text reads almost identically in Marshall's 1534 *Prymer*, sigs. C vii r–C viii r (separately paginated), but variant readings in nn 187, 189, and 198 indicate that KP's source was Marshall's 1535 text. The first sentence is a translation of Psalm 51:14 in the Vulgate (52:14 in English Bibles). **my enemies** "bloude" (Marshall 1535); "bloudes" (Marshall 1534)—a literal rendering of *dâm* in Hebrew (what, when shed, causes the death of a human or animal). Transliterations from Hebrew, here and hereafter, are those of James Strong, *A Concise Dictionary of the Words in the Hebrew Bible*, appended to his *The Exhaustive Concordance of the Bible* (New York, 1894; 21st printing, 1970).

187. **not . . . point not** "not lorde" (Marshall 1535, 1534). **the point** "the verye poynte" (Marshall 1534).

188. **perish** KP omits five sentences that follow in both Marshall editions at this point; in them Savonarola figuratively expounds "bloudes" as "the lyfe of a synner in his synne."

189. **life** "al lyfe" (Marshall 1534),

190. **mine enemies . . . them** "these bloudes . . . bloudes" (Marshall 1535, 1534).

tion. Deliver me, Lord, as Thou delivere[d]st Noah from the waters of the flood.[191] Deliver me, as Thou delivere[d]st Lot from the fire of Sodom.[192] Deliver me, as Thou delivere[d]st the children of Israel from the depth of the Red Sea.[193] Deliver me, as Thou delivere[d]st Jonah from the belly of the whale.[194] Deliver me, as Thou delivere[d]st the three children from the furnace of burning fire.[195] Deliver me, as Thou delivere[d]st Peter from the peril of the sea.[196] Deliver me, as Thou delivere[d]st Paul from the deep of the sea.[197] Deliver me, as Thou deliverest infinite sinners from the power of death and from the gates of hell. And then my tongue shall triumph upon Thy righteousness;[198] for Thy righteousness, as the Apostle saith,[199] cometh by the faith of Jesus Christ, unto all and upon all them that believe in Him. Then shall my tongue triumph in praising this Thy righteousness, commending Thy favor, magnifying Thy pity, knowledging my sins: that Thy mercy may be declared in me, which would vouchsafe to justify such a great sinner. And that all men may know that Thou savest them which trust in Thee, deliverest them from extreme anguish and adversity, O Lord God. Amen.

My God,[200] my God: lo, wherefore forsakest Thou me? How far is Thy help from my outcrying?

191. **Noah . . . flood** Genesis 8:1–3.
192. **Lot . . . Sodom** Genesis 18:29.
193. **children . . . Sea** Exodus 14:22, 29.
194. **Jonah . . . whale** Jonah 2:10.
195. **three . . . fire** Daniel 3:22–28.
196. **Peter . . . sea** Matthew 14:28–32.
197. **Paul . . . sea** Acts 27:41–44.
198. **then . . . shall** "then shall my tongue triumphe vpon thy ryghtwysnes" (Marshall 1535); "then shall my tongue triumphe thy ryghtwysnes" (Marshall 1534). KP omits the gloss that follows: "that is, for thy ryghtwysnes whiche I shall feale an[d] perceyue in me through thy gracyous fauoure."
199. **the . . . saith** KP omits a reference that follows at this point in both Marshall editions, signaling the allusion to Christ in Romans 3:25–26: "whom God hath set forth . . . to shew at thys tyme hys ryghtewesnes, that he myght be counted . . . the iustyfyar of hym whych beleueth" (Great Bible).
200. **My God** KP's selectively utilized source for the following assemblage of eighty-three versicles is George Joye's *The psalter of Dauid in Englishe purely and faithfully translated aftir the texte of Feline* (1530) (STC 2370). "Aretius Felinus" was a pseudonym of Martin Bucer. John Stokesley, Bishop of London, denounced Joye's translation of Bucer's Latin Psalter as a prohibited book in December 1531 (Butterworth, *English Primers*, 16). As John Fisher had done in his *Psalmi seu Precationes* (Cologne, ca. 1525), KP here adopts the eclectic practice of recombining Psalm verses as translated by Joye from Bucer's renderings to form new clusters and sequences—in effect, creating new devotional compositions from recycled materials. Susan M. Felch refers to such compositions as "psalm collages" (*Elizabeth Tyrwhit's Morning and Evening Prayers*, 41). References inserted in the text and enclosed in square brackets are editiorial additions. The English numbering of the Psalms is used here because KP's source is in English.

My God, shall I thus cry, and call upon Thee all day, and yet wilt Thou not hear? Shall I cry all night, and never cease?[201] [Psalm 22:1–2]
But yet Thou art He which leadest me out of my mother's womb, mine own refuge even from my mother's teats.
As soon as I came into this world, I was laid in Thy lap. Thou art my God, even from my mother's womb.
Go Thou not far from me, for my trouble draweth nigh; neither is there any man will help. [Psalm 22:9–11]
The Lord is my rock of stone,[202] my buckler, my Deliverer, my God, my Defender, unto whose faithfulness I betake myself, my shield, my saving Power, my refuge. [Psalm 18:2]
Thou hast defended me with Thy saving shield and buckler, and Thy right hand stayed me. Thy favorable gentleness made me to have the upper hand of mine enemies. [Psalm 18:35]
Wherefore[203] I shall magnify Thee, O Lord, with high praise among the nations, and shall sing with thanksgiving unto Thy name. [Psalm 108:3]
More worthy to be desired than gold or precious stones, sweeter than the honeycomb when it droppeth. [Psalm 19:10]
To Thy mercy shall I cleave, Lord, which art my strength. [Psalm 18:1]
Let the speeches of my mouth and the thoughts of my heart be pleasant and accept[able] unto Thee, Lord, my Defender and my Redeemer. [Psalm 19:14]
Let not the proud men fall upon me; neither let the ungodly move me. [Psalm 36:11]
Verily, I have been young and old, and yet saw I never the righteous forsaken:
In time of adversity, they shall not be shamed; in time of hunger, they shall be well filled.[204] [Psalm 37:25, 19]
Health shall come unto the righteous men from the Lord; He is their strength in time of tribulation.
The Lord, for a surety, will help them, and will deliver them from the ungodly; and He will save them, because they have trusted in Him. [Psalm 37:39–40]
God is for us a defense and strength; He is our most present Helper,[205] when adversity thrusteth us down. [Psalm 46:1]
With praise shall I remember the word of God; with praise shall I remember the promise of the Lord.
In God shall I trust, and so shall I not fear whatsoever man may do to me.
I shall make my vows unto Thee, O God; unto Thee shall I give praises.

201. **How far . . . cease?** In the Vulgate, and in Jerome's later revision of his translation of the Hebrew Psalter, these questions are statements.

202. **rock . . . stone** Joye's phrasing may have influenced the Great Bible reading, "stonye rock."

203. **Wherefore** KP's addition.

204. **filled** Joye reads "satisfied."

205. **a defense . . . Helper** **a defense** Joye reads "defense." **Helper** Joye reads "helpe."

For Thou wilt deliver my soul from death, and my feet surely from sliding, that I might walk before Thee in the lively light. [Psalm 56:10–13]

Look up unto God, O my very still soul, for upon Him dependeth my abiding.

He is verily my Defender and my Saviour; He is also my strong castle, lest I be moved and fall.

Of God dependeth my health and glory; it is the power of God, whereby I am defended and helped. [Psalm 62:6–7]

This mercy of the Lord shall I praise in my song perpetually; and this faithfulness shall I declare with my mouth into all ages.

Lord, the God of hosts, who is like Thee in power? O Lord, all things about Thee are faithfulness. [Psalm 89:1, 8]

And it is Thou, Lord, which hast the very[206] mercy, which givest unto every man after his dealing. [Psalm 62:12]

Blessed is the man whom Thou, O Lord, teachest and chastenest, and instructest him in Thy law. [Psalm 94:12]

I shall surely magnify Thee with all my heart in the council of the righteous, and in the congregation. [Psalm 111:1]

I love the Lord, for He hath heard me; He hath heard the deep desires of my heart.

He bowed down His ears unto me: wherefore while I live, I shall call upon Him. [Psalm 116:1–2]

Except the Lord had helped me, my soul had shortly dwelt in the place of silence.

But when I thought, now my foot is slidden away, then Thy mercy, O Lord, held me up.

These manifold and careful thoughts burned me not within so sore, but Thy consolations refreshed again my soul, much more.

The Lord shall be a castle before me, in which I may be safe; and my God is my rock of stone, in whom I may be defended. [Psalm 94:17–19, 21]

Praise Thou the Lord, O my soul, and all that are within me praise His holy name.

Praise Thou the Lord, O my soul, and forget not His benefits,

Which forgiveth thee all thy iniquities, and healeth all thy diseases.

The Lord is prone unto mercy, and bent unto favor; He is slow unto wrath, and plenteous in goodness. [Psalm 103:1–3, 8]

O how excellent are Thy works, O Lord: all things wisely hast Thou made; the earth swimmeth in Thy goodness.

I shall sing unto the Lord while I live; I shall sing unto my God as long as I shall have any being. [Psalm 104:24, 33]

Remember me, O Lord, according to Thy goodwill promised to Thy people; visit with Thy saving help, which Thou hast promised. [Psalm 106:4]

For Thy goodness is so great that it passeth the heavens; and Thy faithfulness also, that it lifteth up itself unto the clouds. [Psalm 108:4]

206. **very** true.

God, in whom I rejoice and glory, hold not Thyself from me.
Help me, Lord my God; [keep][207] me for Thy mercy's sake. [Psalm 109:1, 26]
Not unto us, Lord; not unto[208] us; but unto Thy name give the glory and praise, for Thy mercy and for Thy truth's sake. [Psalm 115:1]
Unto Thee shall I make the sacrifices of praise, and the name of the Lord shall I call upon. [Psalm 116:17]
Let my adversaries be wearied[209] with shame, and covered with confusion, like as with a cloak.
Let them curse, but bless Thou; let them rise against me, but to their own confusion; but yet let Thy servants rejoice.
I shall magnify the Lord diligently with my mouth; I shall praise Him among many.
For He will stand at the poor man's right hand, to keep his soul from tyrants in authority. [Psalm 109:29, 28, 30–31]
The Lord keepeth the poor, simple ones; I was full poor and full of care, and He saved me. [Psalm 116:6]
Wherefore unto Thee, O Lord God,[210] mine eyes are lifted up, when in Thee I put my trust; pour Thou not out my soul. [Psalm 141:8]
For Thou hast delivered my soul from death, mine eyes from tears, and my feet from sliding.
What shall I give again to the Lord, for all the benefits which He hath given me? [Psalm 116:8, 12]
It is Thou that art my God, and I shall exalt Thee.[211] [Psalm 118:28]
My help cometh from the Lord, the Maker of heaven[212] and earth. [Psalm 121:2]
Lord, set a keeper to my mouth, and keep Thou diligently the doors[213] of my lips. [Psalm 141:3]
Unto the Lord I cried; before the Lord I fell down and made my prayer.
Before Him I poured forth my heavy meditation; before Him I laid my strait anguish.
I cried unto Thee, O Lord, and I said: Thou art my help; Thou art my portion among the living men.

207. **[keep]** Identification of Joye as KP's source makes it possible to rectify the correction that she left incomplete. See n26 of the original-spelling version.

208. **unto . . . unto** Joye reads "to . . . to."

209. **wearied** KP's verb choice is probably a puzzled guess in reaction to Joye's reading, "laced yn" (laced in), which the printer ran together as "lacedyn." The Hebrew word here, "*lâbash,*" means "to wrap around," "to clothe" (oneself or another).

210. **Wherefore . . . God** Joye reads "Wherfore vnto the o lorde / lorde."

211. **It . . . Thee** KP condenses Joye's versicle, which reads in full: "It is thou that arte my god / and I shall magnyfye the: thou arte my god and I shall exalte the."

212. **heaven** Joye reads "heavens."

213. **doors** Joye reads "door." KP's plural is not necessarily an error. While Joye's Latin source has the singular "ostium" (door), a pair of lips could be imagined as a double door.

Attend unto my crying, for I am in a grievous and wretched state; deliver me from my pursuers, for they have prevailed against me. [Psalm 142:1–2, 5–7]
But yet the name of the Lord I called upon; I beseech Thee, Lord, deliver my soul.
The Lord, our righteous God, is prone unto favor; He is ready and bent unto mercy. [Psalm 116:4–5]
Unto Thee, O Lord, have I lifted up[214] my mind; my God, I trust in Thee. Let me not be shamed, lest mine enemies rejoice upon me. [Psalm 25:1–2]
Arise, Lord; O God, lift up Thy hand; despise not the poor afflicte[d].[215] [Psalm 10:13]
Arise, awake for my defense in judgment, to affirm my cause, my God and my Lord.
Give sentence with me, for Thy righteousness' sake, Lord my God, lest they rejoice upon me.
Let them be shamed, and also confounded together, that thus rejoice upon my trouble.
Let them be clothed with shame and ignominy, that thus swell against me.
Let them be glad and rejoice, that favor my righteousness; and make them to say, the Lord may ever be magnified, whom it hath thus pleased to set His servant at rest.
And my tongue also shall speak of Thy righteousness, daily showing forth Thy praise. [Psalm 35:23–24, 26–28]
My eyes shall be ever upon the Lord, for He will draw my feet out of the net.
Behold me, and have mercy upon me; for I am alone, forsaken, full of affliction.
The sorrowful sighs of my heart increase more and more; lead me out of my anguish.
Behold my poor state and my heaviness; forgive me all my sins.
Keep my soul, and deliver me, lest I be shamed; for I have put my trust in Thee.
Defend me, that I may[216] live rightly, hurting no man; for of Thee do I depend. [Psalm 25:15–18, 20–21]
For I am but a halting cripple, ready ever to fall; my sorrow never goeth from me.
Speed Thee to help me, Lord, my saving health. [Psalm 38:17, 22]
Show me, Lord, I beseech Thee, what mine end shall be, or what shall be the measure of my life. Let me know, I beseech Thee: how short is my time? [Psalm 39:5]
The Lord will bring all things to pass for me. O Lord, Thy mercy standeth forth forever; Thou shalt not forsake the work of Thy hands. [Psalm 138:9]

214. **have . . . up** Joye reads "I lyft vp."

215. **affllicte[d]** KP reproduces Joye's "afflicte." "Afflict" is a rare earlier form of the past participle of the verb "afflict," cognate with the Latin deverbal adjective "afflictus." It could function as a noun meaning "an afflicted person."

216. **may** Joye reads "moughte"—an earlier variant form of "may."

The Lord of Israel be praised from worlds into worlds; and that all people may say Amen.[217] [Psalm 108:48]

THE SONG OF AUGUSTINE AND AMBROSE[218]

We praise Thee, O God,[219] we knowledge Thee to be the Lord.
All the earth may[220] worship Thee, which art the Father everlasting.
To Thee cry forth all angels, the heavens, and all the powers therein;
To Thee thus crieth cherubim and seraphim continually.
Holy art Thou; holy art Thou; holy art Thou;[221]
Thou art the Lord God of hosts;[222]
Heaven and earth are fulfilled with the glory of Thy majesty.
The glorious company of the apostles[223] praise Thee;
The godly[224] fellowship of the prophets worship Thee;
The fair fellowship of martyrs praise[225] Thee.
The holy congregation of faithful throughout all the world magnify Thee.
They knowledge Thee to be the Father of an infinite majesty;[226]
They knowledge Thy honorable and very, only Son;
They knowledge the[227] Holy Ghost to be a Comforter.
Thou art the King of glory, O Christ;

217. **from worlds . . . Amen** **from worlds** "from worlds and" (Joye). **Amen** KP moderates Joye's exuberant reading, in black-letter capitals: "AMEN PRAISE YE THE LORDE."

218. **The . . . Ambrose** The Latin hymn "Te Deum laudamus" (We praise thee, O God) is mentioned as early as the sixth century in monastic rules; by the ninth century it had been mistakenly ascribed to St. Ambrose (337–97) or St. Augustine (354–410). The final petitionary verses are an early addition. KP's source for this text is the version of "Te Deum laudamus" that appears under the title "The songe of Austen and Ambrose" in Marshall's 1535 *A goodly prymer*, sigs. Fi r–Fii r. The identically worded titles in Marshall and KP point to Marshall's revised primer as her source, and the variant reading recorded in n228 confirms that she did not use his first primer of 1534. Closely similar versions include the untitled text in George Joye's *Ortulus anime*, sigs. M1v–M3r; "The songe of Austen and Ambrose" in Thomas Godfray's *A primer in Englysshe*, sig. S viii r-v; and "The blessyng and prayses of sainte Ambrose and Augustyne. Te Deum laudamus," in Richard Grafton's *Prayers of the Bible*, fols. 43v–44v. The notes recording the few substantive variants suggest the extent to which this hymn was common property in Christian devotion.

219. **God** "god" (Marshall, Godfray, Joye); "Lorde" (Grafton).

220. **may** "doth" (Godfray).

221. **Holy . . . Thou** "Holy. Holy. Holy" (Godfray).

222. **Thou . . . hosts** "Lorde god of Sabaothe" (Godfray).

223. **apostles** Godfray reads "prophets"—a manifest eyeskip—and lacks the next line.

224. **godly** "goodly" (Marshall, Joye, Grafton).

225. **fair . . . praise** "noble armye of martyres do prayse" (Godfray).

226. **They . . . majesty** Marshall, Godfray, and Joye have this versicle; Grafton omits it.

227. **the** "thy" (Marshall 1534, Godfray, Joye).

Thou art the everlasting Son of the Father.
Thou, when Thou shouldest take upon Thee our nature, to deliver man, didst not abhor the Virgin's womb.[228]
Thou hast opened the kingdom of heaven to the believers, death's dart overcome.[229]
Thou sittest on the right hand of God, in[230] the glory of the Father.
Thou art believed to[231] come our Judge;
Therefore,[232] we pray Thee, help Thy servants, whom Thou hast redeemed with Thy precious blood;
Make them to be numbered with Thy saints in joy everlasting.
O Lord, save Thy people, and bless Thine heritage;
Govern, and also lift them up forever.[233]
We praise Thee every day,
And we worship Thy name ever, world without end.
O Lord, let it be Thy pleasure to keep us this day without sin.
O Lord, have mercy upon us; have mercy upon us.
O Lord, let Thy mercy lighten upon us, even as we trust in Thee.
O Lord, I trust in Thee; let me never be confounded.

Christ is dead for our sins,
And is risen again for our righteousness.[234]

SAINT JEROME'S DEVOTION OUT OF DAVID'S PSALTER[235]

Listen unto my words, Lord; and consder my loud complaint.
Give ear unto my crying, my Governor and my God; for before Thee do I pour forth my prayer. [Psalm 5:2–3]

228. **womb** "bodye" (Marshall 1534, Godfray, Joye).

229. **Thou . . . overcome** "Whan thou hadest ouercomen the sharpenes of deth thou openedest the kingedome of heuens to them that beleued in the" (Godfray, Grafton).

230. **in** "in" (Marshall, Grafton); "into" (Godfray, Joye).

231. **Thou . . . to** "Wee beleue that thou shalt" (Godfray, Grafton).

232. **Therefore** "Wherefore" (Marshall, Godfray, Joye, Grafton).

233. **forever** "into blesse euerlastyng" (Grafton).

234. **Christ . . . righteousness** These two versicles are not part of the "Te Deum laudamus." Marshall 1535 and Joye read "The versicle. Christe is deade for our synnes. Thaunswere. And is rysen agayne for ower rightwisnes. Ro[mans] iiii." Grafton reads: "In thee O lorde dooe I trust, let me not bee confounded for eure Amen." Marshall 1534 and Godfray have both endings, first "O lord I trust in the \ let me neuer be confounded," and then the versicle and response as in Marshall 1535 and Joye.

235. **Saint . . . Psalter** KP's closely followed source is the section titled "Here folowyth the Psaulter of saynt Hierom" in John Gough's *This prymer of Salysbery vse, bothe in Englyshe and in Laten* (1536) (STC 15992), fols. cxxvi r–cxxxvii v. Variants are recorded in the notes. This English

O[236] Lord, rebuke me not in Thy wrath; neither chasten me in Thine anger.
But deal favorably with me, O Lord, for full sore, broken am I;[237] heal me, Lord, for my bones are all to-shaken.
My soul trembleth sore: but, Lord, how long?
Turn Thee, Lord, and deliver my soul; save me for Thy mercy's sake. [Psalm 6:2–5]
Behold and answer me, Lord, my God; keep me waking,[238] lest the slumber of death come upon me. [Psalm 12:4]
Make fast my steps, I pray Thee, in Thy paths, lest my feet slide.
Upon Thee I call, for Thou art wont to hear me; O God, lay Thine ear to me, to[239] hear my speech.
Declare Thy excellent mercy: which are wont to save men trusting in Thee, for they rise against Thy right hand.[240]
Keep me as[241] the apple of Thine eye; and hide me as though I were under the shadow of Thy wings. [Psalm 16:5–9]
Who may perceive and consider, what thing is sin? Purge me[242] from secret evils. [Psalm 18:13]
But Thou, O Lord, be not far; O my strength, haste Thee to come and help[243] me.
Deliver my life from the death-stroke, and my dear soul from the woodness of these[244] dogs.
Save me from the mouths of these lions; and defend my poor simpleness from the horns of these unicorns.

---

text is one of several versions that translate the "Psalterium beati Hieronymi," a time-honored abridgment of the Psalter that is a staple in primers of Salisbury use. In Gough, the Latin of either the Vulgate or the so-called *Versio Hebraica Hieronymi* (Jerome's Hebrew Version), a revision of the Vulgate Psalms, is printed in smaller type in the margins, next to the corresponding English text. References to the verses of the Psalms in the numbering of modern Vulgate editions have been inserted in square brackets in the text.

236. **O** Gough reads "Ah."

237. **deal . . . I** **deal favorably** The Vulgate text in Gough's margin reads "Miserere" (have mercy). **full . . . I** The Vulgate text in the margin reads "infirmus sum" (I am weak).

238. **keep . . . waking** The Vulgate text in Gough's margin reads "Illumina oculos meos" (Illumine my eyes).

239. **to** Gough reads "and," rendering the Vulgate's "et."

240. **are . . . hand** **are** Gough reads "arte." **for . . . hand** "A resistentibus dexterae tuae"—the initial phrase of Psalm 16:8 in *Versio Hebraica Hieronymi*, omitted by Gough in both his Latin and his English texts. KP evidently consulted another Psalter containing the *Versio Hebraica* to supply the phrase.

241. **as** Gough reads "euen as."

242. **me** KP reproduces Gough. The marginal reading in the *Versio Hebraica* is "servum tuum" (Thy servant).

243. **come . . . help** KP reproduces Gough's doubling. The *Versio Hebraica* reads "in auxilium meum festina" (hasten to my help); the Vulgate reads "ad defensionem meam conspice" (look to my defense).

244. **woodness . . . these** **woodness** madness. **these** "theyr" (Gough).

I shall spread Thy name among my brethren; in the midst of the congregation I shall praise Thee. [Psalm 21:20–22]
O[245] show me Thy ways, Lord; and instruct me to Thy paths.
Lord, remember Thy mercy and Thy gracious favor, for in these things Thou excellest even from the beginning.[246]
But the sins of my youth, with my ungodliness also, remember Thou not; remember me according to Thy goodness, and for Thy mercy's sake,[247] O Lord. [Psalm 24:4, 6–7]
For Thy name's sake, O Lord, forgive me my wickedness, for it is very much.
Behold my poor state and my heaviness; forgive[248] me all my sins. [Psalm 24:11, 18]
Take not away my soul with the ungodly, neither yet my life with these bloody men. [Psalm 25:9]
Lord, hear my voice; I call upon Thee: have mercy upon me, and answer me.
Turn not Thy face from me; suffer not Thy servant to slide in Thy wrath.[249] Hitherto hast Thou been my Helper: cast me not now away, neither forsake me, O God, my Saviour.
Lord, teach me Thy way, and lead me forth in the right path from them that lay await for me.
Let them not take their pleasure upon me, which are my troublous enemies:[250] lying witnesses stood together stiff against me. [Psalm 26:7, 9, 11–12]
Upon Thee, Lord, do I call, which art my strong defense.[251] Despise me not, neither forsake Thou me, unless I be like men let down into their graves.[252]

245. **O** KP's addition.

246. **for . . . beginning** The Vulgate reading in Gough's margin is "quae a saeculo sunt" (which have been for an age).

247. **ungodliness . . . sake** **ungodliness** The Vulgate reading in Gough's margin is "ignorantias" (want of knowlege). **for . . . sake** Gough's reading; the Vulgate reading in his margin is "propter veritatem tuam" (on account of Thy truth).

248. **state . . . forgive** **state** Gough reads "estat." **forgive** Gough reads "and forgyue."

249. **suffer . . . wrath** Gough's mistranslation; the *Versio Hebraica* text in his margin reads "ne declines in ira a seruo tuo" (turn not away in anger from Thy servant).

250. **Let . . . enemies** Gough's free rendering of the Vulgate text in his margin, "Ne tradideris me in animas tribulantium me" (Deliver me not to the wills of them who trouble me).

251. **which . . . defense** Gough renders the unique reading of the *Versio Hebraica*, "fortis meus," although the Vulgate text in his margin lacks this phrase.

252. **Despise . . . graves** **Despise . . . like** KP follows Gough's rendering of the Latin in his margin, "ne sileas a me ne vnque discedas a me et ero similis" (be not silent to me, neither forsake me lest I be like). This wording only partially corresponds to the Vulgate, "ne sileas a me: ne quando taceas a me, et assimilabor" (be not silent to me, lest if Thou speak not to me, I resemble), and it is even further from the *Versio Hebraica*,"ne obsurdescas mihi: ne fortè tacente te me, comparer" (be not deaf to me, lest, perhaps, Thou being silent to me, I be comparable to). **into . . . graves** "in lacum" (into the pit), the shared reading of the Vulgate and the *Versio Hebraica* in Gough's margin.

Hear my prayer, while I cry unto Thee, and lift up my hands unto Thy holy temple.[253]
Pluck me not into vengeance with the ungodly, with those which study for shrewdness, speaking peaceably with their neighbors while they nourish evil in their hearts.
Save Thy people; do good to Thine heritage; feed and govern them; and lift them up for evermore.[254] [Psalm 27:1–3, 9]
Bow down Thine ear unto me; speed Thee to deliver me. Be Thou my stony rock, whereupon I might sit fast; be Thou my strong-defensed castle, wherein Thou mayest preserve me.[255] [Psalm 30:3–4]
Betake my spirit into Thy hands, for Thou hast redeemed me, Lord, my God, which keepest true promise at all times.[256]
Deliver me from the hand[257] of mine enemies, even from them which persecute me.
Let Thy presence shine upon Thy servants;[258] save me for Thy mercy' sake. [Psalm 30:6, 16, 18]
Thy mercy lighten upon us, O Lord, even as we depend and trust upon Thee.[259] [Psalm 32:22]
I shall praise and magnify the Lord at all times; His praise shall be in my mouth continually.
In the Lord my soul shall glory; the meek-spirited[260] shall hear, and be glad.

253. **unto Thy . . . temple** KP follows Gough's rendering of the the Vulgate in his margin, "ad templum sanctum tuum."

254. **feed . . . evermore** **feed . . . govern** Gough conflates the *Versio Hebraica* reading, "pasce eos" (feed them), and the Vulgate reading, "rege eos" (govern them). **evermore** KP omits the following versicle in Gough: "In the (oh lorde) do I trust let me neuer I beseche be shamed / but for thy mercys sake delyuer me."

255. **Be Thou . . . me** KP expands into full clausal parallelism Gough's succinct phrasing, "Be my stronge rocke / and well defence house: wherin thou wilt saue me," rendering the Vulgate text in his margin: "Esto mihi in Deum protectorem: et in domum refugii, ut salvum me facias" (Be to me as a protector God, and as a house of refuge, that Thou mayest save me).

256. **Betake . . . times** **Betake . . . God** KP reworks Gough's "Into thy handes I commende my spirite: redeme me / lorde god." In the present context of Psalm excerpts with the focus on David as speaker, she may have wished to mute the echo of Jesus's dying words (Luke 23:46, quoting Psalm 30:6). **Lord . . . times** a paraphrastic rendering of the shared Vulgate and *Versio Hebraica* reading, "Domine Deus veritatis" (Lord God of truth), not reproduced in Gough's margin.

257. **hand** KP's singular form tallies with the Vulgate and *Versio Hebraica*; Gough reads "handes."

258. **servants** Gough reads "servaunt"; the Vulgate and *Versio Hebraica* also have singular forms.

259. **Thy . . . Thee** KP reproduces Gough's free rendering of the Vulgate text in his margin, "Fiat misericordia tua, Domine, super nos: quemadmodum speravimus in te" (Let Thy mercy, Lord, be upon us, accordingly as we have trusted in Thee).

260. **meek-spirited** KP's animate plural noun tallies with the Vulgate's "mansueti" (the meek-spirited) in Gough's margin; Gough has an objective singular construction, "meke spirite."

Magnify ye the Lord with me; and let us extol His name all together. [Psalm 33:2–4]
Lord, set against my adversaries; smite down[261] them that fight against me.
Take anon unto Thee shield and buckler; and rise up speedily to help me. [Psalm 34:1–2]
Yea, Thou hast seen, Lord; cease Thou, Lord, no longer; be not far absent.
Arise, awake for my defense in judgment: to affirm my cause, my God and my Lord. [Psalm 34:22–23]
Stretch forth Thy mercy to them that know Thee,[262] and Thy righteousness to the upright in heart.
Let not the proud men fall upon me; neither let the ungodly[263] move me. [Psalm 35:11–12]
Lord, hear my prayer; give ear unto my crying; cease not[264] while I weep.
For I am given[265] unto Thee here but a wayfaring stranger, as were all my fathers.
Spare me, that I might breathe[266] a little, before I cease, and go out of this world. [Psalm 38:13–14]
Neither Thou, Lord, also hast holden[267] Thy gracious mercies from me; Thy gentle favor and Thy truth perserve me perpetually.
For I was overwhelmed with innumerable troubles; my sins cumbered me so that I might not see them all.[268]
They were far more than the hairs of my head: for the which thing, my heart failed me.
Let it please Thee, Lord, to deliver me; Lord, haste Thee to help me.
I was in affliction and poverty,[269] but the Lord looked to me. Thou art my help and my Deliverer; my God, Thou shalt not tarry. [Psalm 39:12–14, 18]
I verily said, Lord, have mercy upon me; heal my soul, for I am a sinner[270] against Thee. [Psalm 40:5]

261. **set against . . . smite down** **set against** condemn; Gough's margin has the Vulgate's "Judica" (Condemn). **smite down** Gough's margin has the Vulgate "expugna" (subdue).

262. **knowe Thee** Gough reads "knoweth."

263. **proud men . . . ungodly** KP reproduces Gough's rendering, which eliminates two figures of speech in the shared reading of the Vulgate and *Versio Hebraica* in his margin: "pes superbiae" (the foot of pride) and "manus impiorum" (the hand of the ungodly).

264. **cease not** Gough's margin reads with the Vulgate, "ne sileas" (be not silent).

265. **I . . . given** Gough's margin reads with both Latin versions, "aduena ego sum" (I have come).

266. **that I . . . breathe** Gough's margin reads with the Vulgate "vt refrigerer" (that I may be refreshed).

267. **Neither . . . holden** KP reproduces Gough's incorrect rendering of the mood of the Vulgate verb in his margin, "Tu autem, Domine, ne longe facias" (But Thou, Lord, withhold not).

268. **that I . . . all** KP follows Gough in adding "all" to the Vulgate reading in his margin, "non potui vt viderem" (I could not see).

269. **in affliction . . . poverty** The *Versio Hebraica* in Gough's margin reads "egenus et pauper" (needy and poor).

270. **a sinner** Gough reads "synner."

Awake: wherefore sleepest, O Lord? Arise up: wherefore forsakest Thou us[271] forever?
Wherefore hidest[272] Thy face, having no respect to our affliction and oppression?
Arise and help us; redeem and loose us for Thy mercy's sake.[273] [Psalm 43:23–26]
Have mercy upon me, God, for Thy gentleness' sake; for Thy great mercies' sake,[274] wipe away my sins.
And, yet again, wash me more from my wickedness; and make me clean from my ungodliness. [275]
For my grievous sins do I knowledge; and my ungodliness[276] is ever before mine eyes.
Against Thee, against Thee only, have I sinned; and that (it sore offendeth Thee) have I done: wherefore very just shalt Thou be known in Thy words, and pure when it shall be judged of Thee.[277]
Lo, I was fashioned in wickedness; and my mother conceived me polluted with sin. [Psalm 50:3–7]
But, lo, Thou wouldest truth to occupy and rule in my inward parts; Thou showest me wisdom, which Thou wouldest to sit in the secrets of my heart.[278]

271. **sleepest . . . us** **sleepest** KP's error of omission; Gough reads "slepest thou." **Wherefore . . . us** KP reproduces Gough's transformation of the Vulgate reading in his margin from a declarative, "ne repellas" (Thou dost not spurn), to a question.

272. **hidest** Gough reads "hydest thou."

273. **for . . . sake** Although his margin has the Vulgate reading "propter nomen tuum" (for Thy name's sake), Gough renders the *Versio Hebraica*, "propter misericordiam tuam," which KP reproduces.

274. **for . . . sake** Gough's margin has the Vulgate phrases, "secundum magnam misericordiam . . . secundum multitudinem miserationum" (according to Thy great mercy . . . according to the multitude of Thy lovingkindnesses).

275. **more . . . ungodliness** **more** Gough's margin has the *Versio Hebraica* reading, "multum" (much). **from . . . wickedness, from . . . ungodliness** Gough's margin has the readings "ab iniquitate mea" (from my iniquity), "a peccato meo" (from my sin).

276. **my grievous . . . ungodliness** **my . . . sins** "iniquitates meas" (my iniquities). **my ungodliness** "peccatum meum" (my sin). The annotations in this and the preceding note expose Gough's inconsistency in rendering the vocabulary of misdoing in the Latin Psalter.

277. **and that . . . Thee** **and that . . . done** Gough reads "and that the sore offendeth the haue I done." His first "the" should read "that": "and that that sore offendeth Thee, have I done." KP recognizes a mistake in Gough's first "the," but the "it" with which she replaces it does not clarify the sense. The Vulgate text in Gough's margin reads simply "et malum coram te feci" (and I have done evil in Thy sight). **and pure . . . Thee** KP reproduces Gough's garbled phrasing. "And pure" seems to be a misprint for "and prevail"; the Vulgate reading in the margin is "et vincas." The construction "when it shall be judged of Thee" is ambiguous: is God being judged or doing the judging? The verb is unambiguous in the Vulgate reading in his margin, identical with that of the *Versio Hebraica* except for a difference in tense: "cum judicaris / judicaveris" (when Thou judgest / when Thou shalt judge).

278. **Thou wouldest . . . heart** Gough's paraphrastic rendering of the Vulgate reading in his margin: "veritatem dilexisti incerta et occulta sapientiae tuae manifestasti mihi" (Thou hast de-

Sprinkle me with hyssop, and so shall I be clean; Thou shalt wash me, and then shall I be whiter than snow.
Pour upon me joy and gladness; make my bones to rejoice, which Thou hast smitten.[279]
Turn Thy face from my sins, and wipe away all my wickedness.
A pure heart create in me, O Lord; and a steadfast, right spirit make anew within me.
Cast me not away, and Thy Holy Ghost take not from me.
Make me again to rejoice, while Thou bringest me my saving health; and let Thy chief, governing[280] Spirit strengthen and lead me.
Lord, open Thou my lips; and then my mouth shall show forth Thy praise. [Psalm 50:8–17]
O God, save me for Thy name's sake; deliver[281] me by Thy power.
O God, hear my prayer; listen to the words of my mouth.
For strange men are risen against me, and strong tyrants[282] pursue my soul. They have not God before their eyes. [Psalm 53:3–5]
O God, listen to my prayer; and hide not Thyself from my deep desire.[283] [Psalm 54:2]
I remembere[d] the promise of God with praise, and trusted in God: wherefore I feared not[284] whatsoever mortal man could do to me.
I shall make my vows to Thee, O God; unto Thee shall I give praises.
For Thou wilt deliver my soul from death, and my feet surely from sliding: that I might walk before Thee in the lively light.[285] [Psalm 55:11–13]

---

sired truth in the inward [not clearly visible] parts; Thou shalt make me know wisdom in the hidden parts).

279. **Pour . . . smitten** Gough's free rendering of the Vulgate reading in his margin, "Auditui meo dabis gaudium et laetitiam: et exsultabunt ossa humiliata" (Thou shalt make me hear of joy and gladness, and my humbled bones shall rejoice).

280. **Make . . . governing** **Make . . . health** KP reproduces Gough's expansive rendering of the Vulgate reading in his margin: "Redde mihi leticiam salutaris tui" (Give to me again the joy of Thy salvation). **chief, governing** KP omits "free," the third and final adjective in Gough's series. The Vulgate simply reads "principali" (governing).

281. **deliver** The Vulgate reading in Gough's margin is "judica" (judge).

282. **strong tyrants** The Vulgate and *Versio Hebraica* read "fortes" (strong men).

283. **hide . . . desire** Gough's imprecise rendering of the Vulgate and *Versio Hebraica* reading in his margin, "ne despexeris deprecationem meam" (Thou wilt not despise my supplication).

284. **I remembered . . . not** **I remembered . . . praise** KP reproduces Gough's puzzling rendering, which corresponds to nothing in the Vulgate or the *Versio Hebraica* reading in his margin, "In Deo laudabo verbum" (In God will I praise His word). **I . . . not** "non timebo" (I will not fear).

285. **wilt deliver . . . light** **wilt deliver** The Vulgate reading in Gough's margin is "eripuisti" (Thou hast delivered). **in . . . light** The Vulgate reading is "in lumine viventium"; the *Versio Hebraica* reading is "in luce viventium," both meaning "in the light of the living [ones]." **lively** living, having life—senses glossed by the *OED* as "various applications of Latin *vivus*." Gough's marginal reference has a misprint, "in terra viuentium" (in the land of the living).

Have mercy upon me, O God; have mercy upon me: for my soul hath committed herself unto Thy protection. I creep under Thy wings to be defended, until this violent blast be overblown.[286] [Psalm 56:2]
Deliver me from these men, which are all given unto mischief; save me from these bloodshedders.[287]
For, lo, they lay a-wait for my life; they are come together against me, strong and boisterous men.[288] [Psalm 58:3–4]
But I, Lord, in the meantime made my prayer to Thee, when time was offered me. O God, for Thy infinite mercy and truth, hear me: for the which Thou wert wont to help.[289]
Deliver me from this tough clay, and suffer me not to be drowned; let me be delivered from these odious pursuers,[290] even from these deep waters.
Let not the stream carry me away;[291] neither the depth swallow me in; nor the pit shut her mouth over me.
Answer me, O Lord, for full gentle is Thy mercy; look upon me, after Thy great humanity.[292]
Join Thee to my soul, and redeem it; loose me from my enemies. [Psalm 68:14–17, 19]
O God, speed Thee[293] to deliver me; O Lord, haste Thee to help me.

286. **hath . . . overblown** **hath . . . protection** The Vulgate reading in Gough's margin is "confidit" (hath confided). **until . . . overblown** The Vulgate reading in the margin is "donec transeat iniquitas" (until this evil be past).

287. **from . . . bloodshedders** **from . . . mischief** The Vulgate reading in Gough's margin is "de operantibus iniquitatem" (from the workers of iniquity). **from . . . bloodshedders** The Vulgate reading in the margin is "de viris sanguinum" (from bloody men).

288. **strong . . . men** The Vulgate reading in the margin is "fortissimi" (very strong men). **boisterous** "boytuous" (Gough).

289. **when time . . . help** **when time . . . me** The Vulgate reading in Gough's margin is "tempus beneplaciti" (in a time well-pleasing [to God]). **for Thy . . . help** KP reproduces Gough's free rendering of the Vulgate reading in his margin, "In multitudine misericordiae tuae exaudi me, in veritate salutis tuae" (In the multitude of Thy mercy, hear me, in the truth of Thy salvation).

290. **from this . . . pursuers** **from this . . . clay** The Vulgate reading in Gough's margin is "a luto" (from the mire). **from . . . pursuers** The reading in the margin is "ex odientibus me" (from those who hate me). This is the sense but not the wording in the Vulgate and *Versio Hebraica*, "ab iis, qui oderunt me" (from those who hate me).

291. **Let . . . away** KP reproduces Gough's free rendering of the Vulgate reading in his margin: "Non me demergat tempestas" (Let not the tempest submerge me).

292. **Answer . . . humanity** The Vulgate reading in Gough's margin is "Exaudi me, Domine, quoniam benigna est misericordia tua: secundum multitudinem miserationum tuarum respice in me" (Hear me, Lord, for Thy mercy is kind; look upon me according to the multitude of Thy lovingkindnesses). As in renderings of negatively charged nouns (nn282–83), so too in renderings of positively charged nouns, Gough makes no attempt at consistency but is content with conveying a generally concordant sense (see also n280).

293. **Join Thee . . . speed Thee** In both cases the Vulgate reading in Gough's margin is "Intende" (Attend Thou).

I am a careful, poor afflict: speed Thee[294] unto me. Thou art my Helper and Deliverer; see Thou tarry not. [Psalm 69:2, 6]
In Thee, Lord, have I trusted; suffer me not at any time to be shamed.
Deliver me for Thy righteousness, and take me up; bow down Thine ear unto me, and save me.
Be Thou unto me a rock of stone:[295] in the which I might keep me, and to the which I might ever flee.
My God, deliver me from the hand of the ungodly man; deliver me from the fist of the mischievous and violent man.[296]
My mouth shall be yet fulfilled with praises; let it daily extol Thy clear majesty.[297]
Cast me not away in mine old age; forsake me not when my strength shall fail me.
God, be Thou not far from me; my God, speed Thee to help me.
But I shall tarry for Thy help, and shall exceed all men in Thy praise. [Psalm 70:1–4, 8–9, 12, 14]
Let not the life of the turtle come into the company of these adversaries; the company of the poor afflict, forget not forever.[298]
Look upon Thy promise: for among these blind wretches of the earth, all are full of violence and trouble.[299] [Psalm 73:19–20]
Be present with us, God: save us[300] for Thy glorious name, and deliver us; pardon our sins for Thy name's sake. [Psalm 78:9]
O God, restore us:[301] make Thy face to shine upon us, and we shall be saved.

294. **afflict . . . Thee** **afflict** afflicted person; for "afflict" in another of KP's sources, George Joye, see n215 above. **speed Thee** The Vulgate reading in Gough's margin is "adjuva me" (help me).

295. **a . . . stone** The Vulgate in Gough's margin reads "in protectorem Deum" (as a protector God). See n255.

296. **from . . . man** The Vulgate in Gough's margin reads "de manu contra legem agentis et iniqui" (from the hand of him who acts against the law, and is hurtful).

297. **My . . . majesty** The Vulgate in Gough's margin reads "Repleatur os meum laude, ut cantem gloriam tuam: tota die magnitudinem tuam" (Let my mouth be filled with Thy praise, that I may sing of Thy glory and Thy greatness all day long). **praises** Gough reads "thy prayse."

298. **Let . . . forever** The Vulgate in Gough's margin reads "Ne tradas bestiis animas confitentes tibi, et animas pauperum tuorum ne obliviscaris in finem" (Deliver not the souls of them who trust in Thee to the beasts, and forget not the souls of Thy poor ones forever). **the turtle** KP's variation on Gough's "thy turtle douve." Setting a continuing precedent in English translations, Coverdale's Bible and the Great Bible read "thy turtle dove," rendering Hebrew *"tôr"* (ring-dove), used figuratively as a term of endearment.

299. **Thy . . . trouble** **Thy promise** KP sustains Gough's Reformed inflection in rendering the Vulgate's "testamentum tuum" (Thy covenant). **among . . . trouble** Gough misconstrues the Vulgate's place references as references to persons: "repleti sunt, qui obscurati sunt terrae domibus iniquitatum" (the dark places of the earth are filled with the habitations of the unjust).

300. **Be . . . us** KP reproduces Gough's free rendering of the Vulgate reading in his margin: "Adjuva nos, Deus, salutaris noster" (Help us, our God of salvation).

301. **restore us** KP reproduces Gough's free rendering of the Vulgate text in his margin, "converte nos" (turn us again).

O Lord, which art the God of hosts, how long wilt Thou be angry with the prayer of Thy people? [Psalm 79:3–4]
Restore us, God, our Saviour;[302] quench Thy indignation against us.
Wilt Thou be angry with us always? Wilt Thou stretch forth Thy wrath into the world's end?
Thou verily art even He which bringest Thyself again to us. Thou wilt quicken us; in Thee[303] shall Thy people yet rejoice.
Lay forth for us, Lord, Thy merciful goodness; and give us Thy saving help. [Psalm 84:5–8]
Bow down Thine ear, O Lord, and answer me; for I am full poor, and full of trouble.[304]
Keep my life, for I study to be good. Save Thou Thy servant, my God, for he trusteth in Thee without any doubt.[305]
Have mercy upon me, Lord, for I call unto Thee daily. Make glad the mind of Thy servant, for unto Thee, O Lord, lift I up my heart.[306] [Psalm 85:1–4]
But yet Thou, Lord, art prone unto mercy; Thou art ready to favor and to forgive, slow unto wrath, swimming in mercy and faithfulness.[307]
Behold me, and have mercy upon me; give Thy strength unto Thy servant, and preserve that son of Thy handmaiden.
Do good unto me openly,[308] that they that hate me might be ashamed to see that Thou, Lord, helpest and comfortest me. [Psalm 85:15–17]
O Lord God, the Author of my health,[309] I have cried unto Thee by day, and by night also before Thee.
Let my prayer come before Thee; bow down Thine ear to my crying. [Psalm 87:2–3]

302. **Restore . . . Saviour** KP reproduces Gough's free rendering of the Vulgate in his margin: "Converte nos, Deus, salutaris noster" (Turn us again, our God of salvation).

303. **Thou verily . . . Thee** **Thou . . . us** KP reproduces Gough's free rendering of the Vulgate in his margin: "Deus, tu conversus vivicabis nos" (God, when Thou hast turned again, Thou wilt revive us). **in Thee** "in that" (Gough).

304. **Bow . . . trouble** **Bow** "Inclyne" (Gough). **full . . . trouble** KP emends Gough's misrendering,"full of trouth"; the Vulgate in his margin reads "egenus" (needy).

305. **for . . . doubt** **for . . . good** KP reproduces Gough's recasting of the Vulgate text in his margin: "quoniam sanctum sum" (for I am holy). **without . . . doubt** Gough's addition to the Vulgate.

306. **mind . . . heart** At both points, the Vulgate in Gough's margin reads "animam" (soul). See n292.

307. **But . . . faithfulness** KP reproduces Gough's expansive recasting of the Vulgate text in his margin: "Et tu, Domine Deus, miserator et misericors, patiens, et multae misericordiae, et verax" (And Thou, Lord, art compassionate and merciful, God, patient, and of great mercies, and true).

308. **Do . . . openly** The Vulgate text in Gough's margin reads "Fac mecum signum in bonum" (Show upon me a token for good).

309. **O . . . health** The Vulgate text in Gough's margin reads "Domine Deus salutis meae" (Lord, the God of my salvation).

Where are those Thy mercies showed of old time, O Lord, which Thou sworest unto David, of Thy faith?
Remember the rebukes which are laid upon[310] Thy servants, O Lord; I received into mine own bosom all the rebukes of much people. [Psalm 88:50–51]
Turn Thee, Lord: how long wilt be ere Thou be pleased? Set Thy heart at rest with Thy servant.[311]
The glorious majesty of the Lord our God be over us. And make Thou to prosper whatsoever we go about; whatsoever we begin,[312] make it to succeed luckily. [Psalm 89:13, 17]
Lord, hear my prayer, and suffer my deep desire[313] to come unto Thee.
Hide not Thy face from me in time of my tribulation. Bow down Thine ear unto me in the[314] day when I call upon Thee; speed Thee to grant me.[315]
[I] say, my God, take me not away in the midst of my days, for Thy years endure.[316] [Psalm 101:2–3, 25]
My spirit is sore troubled within me; and my heart waxeth cold[317] in my breast.
But, at last, I remembered[318] the days past; I considered all Thy works, and pondered in mind the deeds of Thy hands.
I stretched forth my hand unto Thee; my soul desirously panted and breathed for Thee. I gaped[319] for Thee like thirsty earth.

310. **rebukes . . . upon** **rebukes** The Vulgate text reads "opprobrii" (reproaches). **upon** "unto" (Gough).

311. **how . . . servant?** **how . . . pleased** "howe longe? be pleasyd" (Gough). **Set . . . servant** The Vulgate text reads "deprecabilis esto super servos tuos" (be Thou receptive to entreaty concerning Thy servants). **servant** Gough reads "servauntes."

312. **whatsoever . . . about; whatsoever . . . begin** The Vulgate in Gough's margin has two occurrences of "opus manuum nostrarum" (the work of our hands).

313. **my . . . desire** The Vulgate in Gough's margin reads "clamor meus" (my cry).

314. **the** Gough reads "thy."

315. **speed . . . me** The Vulgate in Gough's margin reads "velociter exaudi me" (hear me speedily).

316. **[I] . . . endure** **[I]** KP's text has an unfilled blank for an illuminated *I*; Gough reads "I." **endure** "endure thorow al agis" (Gough). At this point KP omits the next fifty-eight verses in the sequence before she resumes copying. The facing margin has a pointed comment in Latin: "Fauete quidpiam deest" (Be kind; somewhat is missing). An early reader recognized both that Gough is KP's source and that she has omitted a large amount of material at this point, not just an *I*. See n36 to the original-spelling version. KP's omission here involves a large jump—from Psalm 89 to Psalm 110—similar to the one she makes near the end of *Prayers or Meditations*; see the introduction to that text, p. 376. The omitted material occupies the verso and recto sides of three leaves in Gough (fols. cxxxiii v–cxxxvi v).

317. **waxeth cold** The Vulgate in Gough's margin reads "turbatum est" (is troubled).

318. **I remembered** KP emends Gough's "I remember"; the Vulgate in his margin reads "Memor fui" (I remembered).

319. **stretched, panted, breathed, gaped** all present-tense verbs in the Vulgate. **hand** "handes" (Gough).

Haste Thee to grant me, O Lord, for my spirit fainteth.[320] Hide not Thy face from me, unless I be like men going down into their graves. [Psalm 142:3–7]
Make me shortly to hear of Thy merciable goodness;[321] for in Thee do I trust.
Show me the way wherein I may go; for unto Thee have I lifted up my soul.
Deliver me from mine enemies, O Lord, my God; for at Thee[322] do I hide myself.
Teach me to do Thy pleasures, for Thou art my God; Thy good Spirit may lead me into the right way.[323]
Yea, and for Thy mercies' sake, also destroy my enemy; and shake away[324] all that trouble my soul, for I am Thy servant. [Psalm 142:8–10, 12]

Amen.[325]

Incline Thine ear,[326] and agree to my desire, O Lord; for I am poor, and destitute of all man's help.
Take care for my soul, for I am of an unfeigned heart toward Thee. Save Thy servant, O my God—Thy servant, I say—which hangeth wholly upon Thee.
Have mercy upon me, O Lord; for I call continually, and will call for Thy help.
Refresh Thy servant's mind, O Lord; for I will labor with my heart to come even unto Thee, though Thou dwellest never so high.
For Thou, O Lord, art loving and gentle, and more merciful than can be expressed, unto all them that call for Thy help.

320. **Haste . . . fainteth** **Haste . . . me** The Vulgate repeats "velociter exaudi me"; see n243. **fainteth** "fayneth"—a misprint in Gough.

321. **Thy . . . goodness** KP reproduces Gough's elaboration of the Vulgate phrase, "misericordiam tuam" (Thy mercy). **merciable** merciful, compassionate.

322. **at Thee** KP reproduces Gough's overliteral rendering of the Vulgate's "ad te"—here meaning "in Thee."

323. **Thy pleasures . . . way** **Thy pleasures** The Vulgate reads "voluntatem tuam" (Thy will). **into . . . way** The Vulgate reads "in terram rectam" (into the right land).

324. **enemy . . . away** **enemy** Gough reads "enemyes." **shake away** The Vulgate reads "perde" (waste, ruin).

325. **Amen** KP's insertion, ending this selection from Gough. He continues with a prayer beginning "Graunt / I beseche the lord god / that by the holy melody of this heuenly Psaulter my soule may be refreshed" (fol. cxxxvii v).

326. **Incline . . . ear** KP's closely followed source for extensive poritions of this and the next three Psalms is Miles Coverdale's *A paraphrasis, vpon all the psalmes of Dauid, . . . made by Johannes Campensis, reader of the Hebrue lecture in the vniuersite of Louane, and translated out of Latine into Englyshe* (1535) (STC 2372.2), which had another edition in 1539 (STC 2372.6). The first text is a paraphrase of Psalm 86 (in English numbering), sigs. Miiii r–Mv v. Significant variants are recorded in the notes. The word omitted in the second edition, recorded in n327, suggests that KP's source was Coverdale's first edition. The Latin original translated by Coverdale is *Psalmorum omnium: iuxta Hebraicam veritatem paraphrastica interpretatio authore Joanne Campensi* (1534) (STC 2354).

Give ear, Lord, unto my petition; let it not grieve Thee to hearken unto my clamorous prayers.
As oft as any adversity happeneth unto me, I shall call for Thy help: trusting in time to come, that Thou wilt grant me the thing which Thou shalt think most for my profit.
There is not one of them, that wicked men take for gods, to be compared unto Thee, O Lord; neither can any of them do such things as Thou doest.
Therefore the time will be that strange nations whom Thou hast created shall come[327] and submit themselves unto Thee, yea, and earnestly fear the majesty of Thy name.
For Thou art great, and doest wonderful[328] things; Thou art God alone.
Lord, teach me the way which leadeth unto Thee, that I may boldly walk in it, not doubting but that Thou wilt faithfully keep me company in my journey. Wake Thou my heart up, that it may specially fear the majesty of Thy name.
I will praise Thee, O God, my Lord,[329] with my whole heart, and will magnify Thy name with continual praises.
For there are to show, at hand, right many tokens of Thy lovingkindness toward me: for why,[330] as oft as I was in great perils, Thou hast delivered me and called my soul again, even, in a manner, from death unto life.
Proud persons are risen against me, O God, and a great multitude of mighty men, having no regard of Thee, labor sore for this intent, that they may take my life from me.
But Thou, O Lord God,[331] art merciful and good, slow unto wrath, but marvelous prone unto kindness and keeping of Thy promises.
Behold me, and have mercy upon me; give strength unto Thy servant, and preserve the son of Thy handmaiden.[332]
Show some token of Thy love toward me, that my enemies may see and be ashamed: that they, I say, may see that it was Thou which helped me and avenged the wrong that they did unto me.

Lord, how long wilt Thou forget me—forever?[333] How long turnest Thou Thy face from me, as Thou wert angry?

327. **Therefore . . . come** **Therefore** Coverdale reads "Wherefore." **come** Omitted in Coverdale 1539.

328. **wonderful** Coverdale reads "wonderous."

329. **O . . . Lord** Coverdale reads "O Lorde my God."

330. **for why** because.

331. **O . . . God** Coverdale reads "O Lorde."

332. **handmaiden** Coverdale reads "handmayed."

333. **Lord . . . forever?** These are the opening words of the paraphrase of Psalm 13 (in English numbering) in Coverdale, *A paraphrasis*, sig. Biiii r-v.

How long shall I vex my soul with taking of sorrows in vain, which [en]gender nothing but continual heaviness? How long wilt Thou suffer mine enemy to exalt himself against me?
Consider my calamity, and hear me perfectly, Lord my God; lighten mine eyes lest, peradventure, the sleep of death come stealing upon me.
Lest mine enemy, taking courage, say: I have overcome him; and my enemies rejoice if I miscarry.
As for me, I have put[334] all my trust in Thy goodness: wherefore I doubt not, but the time shall come, that my heart shall rejoice for the health that Thou hast brought me; and that I shall have occasion to sing the praises of the Lord, when He shall have avenged the wrong that mine enemies have done me.

I will love Thee,[335] O Lord, as Thou art worthy; for Thou art my strength.
The Lord hath been to me ever like a rock and like a tower, my Saviour, my Guide, and my strength, wherefore I shall set all my hope in Him, which was to me in stead of a shield; He hath been ever the horn of my health, and my true defense.
I will call upon Thee, Lord, most worthy of all honor; and I shall be free from mine enemies.
I was set in the most present perils of death, bound as it were with deadly chains; for the rivers of the devil put me in fear.
The ropes of hell compassed me about; mortal nets held me in the snare.
As oft as I was troubled, I called upon the Lord; and I cried to my God, which both heard my voice from His kingly palace, and my calling came into His presence, yea, even to His ears.

Save me, O God,[336] for the majesty of Thy name's sake; and, seeing Thou hast might enough, avenge this wrong that is done unto me.
Hear my prayer, O God; incline Thine ears to the words of my mouth.
For strangers also are risen up against me; and cruel men labor sore to destroy me, having no regard of Thee, O God.[337]

334. **me . . . put** **me** Coverdale adds "verely." **put** Coverdale reads "set."

335. **I . . . Thee** These are the opening words of the paraphrase of Psalm 18:1–6 (in English numbering) in Coverdale, *A paraphrasis*, sig. Bviii r. There this Psalm is introduced by a title which KP omits: "A thankes geuynge of Dauid the seruaunt of the Lorde, whiche songe this dytye vnto the Lordes honour what tyme as the Lorde deluered hym from the tyrannye of all his enemyes, and from the persecution of Saul, wherfore he sayed . . ."

336. **Save . . . God** These are the opening words of the paraphrase of Psalm 54 (in English numbering) in Coverdale, *A paraphrasis*, sigs. Gvi v–Gvii r.

337. **God** KP omits Coverdale's addition, "It is euen so."

But because God is my help, and the Lord is one of the number of them that defend my soul:
Therefore the evil that they ordain for me, He shall bring against themselves which do me wrong: wherefore, I beseech Thee, for Thy good faithfulness in keeping Thy promises, destroy them.
I shall offer Thy[338] sacrifices willingly; I shall magnify Thy name, O Lord, with praises, for it is a good and loving name.
For He hath delivered me from all trouble; and, through His goodness, mine eye hath seen as much as any man would desire to see in his deadly enemies.

Hail, Jesu Christ, King of mercy,[339] our life, our sweetness, and our hope: we salute Thee; unto Thee we cry, which art the banished children of Eve; unto Thee we sigh, sobbing and weeping in this vale of wretchedness. Haste Thee, therefore, our Mediator; turn unto us those Thy merciful eyes. O Jesu, all praiseworthy, show us the presence of the Father after this outlawry.[340] O gentle, O merciful, O sweet Jesu Christ: in all our trouble and heaviness, O Jesu, our health and glory, succor us. Amen.

A PRAYER TO THE FATHER[341]

O God almighty, our merciful Father, which hast so exceedingly loved us, Thy chosen children, that Thou wouldst vouchsafe to give us Thy only and well-beloved Son, Jesu Christ. our Saviour, to suffer death for our sins, so that all that thus believe in Him might not perish, but have life everlasting: we beseech Thee, for Thy abundant mercy and for that inestimable love which Thou barest to Thy Son, Christ, our Saviour, give us, of Thy grace and power, Thy favor into our hearts, that we may believe, feel, and know perfectly, that Thou only art our God, our Father, and to us an almighty Helper, Deliverer, and a Saviour from sin, from all the devilish power of hell, of this world, and from death: and that, by Thy Son, our Lord, Jesus Christ. Amen.

338. **Thy** Coverdale reads "the." "Thy" has been retained, since the sense of Coverdale's "the" in this context is somewhat ambiguous between "Thee" and "the."

339. **Hail . . . mercy** KP's exactly followed source for this prayer is Joye's *Ortulus anime*, sig. D3r-v.

340. **outlawry** state of being put outside the protection of the law; exile, banishment—reversed by Christ's salvation of sinners.

341. **A . . . Father** KP's closely followed source for this and the three following prayers is a sequence beginning with a collect and continuing with brief versicles, responses, and prayers in the Matins section immediately preceding the service for the canonical hour of Prime, which reads identically in Marshall's *A Prymer in Englyshe* (1534), sig. Mvii r-v, and in his *A goodly prymer* (1535), sig. Gii r-v. The readings "Amen" in place of "So be it" suggest but do not suffice to prove that Marshall's 1534 primer was KP's source.

A PRAYER TO THE HOLY GHOST

Come, Holy Spirit, replenish the hearts of Thy faithful; and kindle in them Thy burning love. Send forth Thy Spirit, and men shall be created anew. For so renewest Thou the soul of man.[342]

THE PRAYER

O God, which hast instructed the hearts of faithful men with the lightening of Thy Holy Ghost, grant us to savor a light in the same Spirit, and to rejoice evermore of His holy consolation, which livest and reignest in the same Spirit ever. Amen.[343]

A PRAYER TO THE TRINITY

Deliver us, save us, and justify us, O blessed Trinity.

VERSE

The name of God be blessed forever, from age to age everlasting.[344]

O almighty, everlasting God, which hast given us, Thy servants, to knowledge the glory of the everlasting Trinity with a faithful knowledge, and to worship one God[345] in Thy almighty majesty: we beseech Thee that, through the steadfastness of this faith, we might be defended from all adversities: which livest and reignest one God in the Trinity of Persons, world without end. Amen.[346]

A PRAYER TO JESU CHRIST

O Lord Jesu Christ,[347] the Son of the living God, put Thy passion, cross, and Thy death between Thy judgment and our souls, now and in the hour of[348] death: And

342. **Send . . . man** KP combines what Marshall separates liturgically as "The versicle. Sende furth thy spirite, and men shalbe created a newe. Thaunswere. For so renewest thou the soule of man."

343. **of faithful . . . Amen** **of faithful** "of the faithful" (Marshall 1534, 1535). **of Thy** "of the" (Marshall 1534, 1535). **Amen** "So be it" (Marshall 1535).

344. **The . . . everlasting** KP again treats as one sentence what in Marshall 1535 are a separate versicle and response: "The versycle. The name of god be blessed. The aunswere. From age to age euerlastynge. So be it."

345. **one God** "the one God" (Marshall 1534), with the sense of "Thee, one God."

346. **Amen** "So be it" (Marshall 1535).

347. **O . . . Christ** KP's closely followed source for this prayer's wording is the prayer and appended benediction that conclude the initial "Passion of oure savioure Christe" section in Joye's *Ortulus anime*, sig. Gviii r-v.

348. **of** "of ower" (Joye).

grant us, while we live, mercy and grace; to them that depart, forgiveness and rest; unto Thy holy Church give peace and concord; and to us, that are sinners, life and everlasting glory:[349] which livest and reignest with the Father and with the Holy Ghost, ever.
The glorious passion of our Lord Jesus Christ deliver us from sorrowful heaviness and bring us to the joys of paradise. Amen.[350]

Our Father,[351] that art in heaven, Hallowed be Thy name. Let Thy kingdom come to us; Thy will be fulfilled, as well in earth as it is in heaven. Give us this day our daily bread; and forgive us our offenses, like as we do forgive them that offend us. Lead us not into temptation, but deliver us from evil. For it is Thy kingdom, and power, and glory for evermore.[352] [Matthew 6:9–13]
Blessed art Thou, Lord God of Israel, our Father everlastingly;[353] for it is Thy magnificence, O Lord, and Thy power and glory and victory, and praise to Thee. [1 Paralipomenon (1 Chronicles) 29:11]
O Governor, Lord God, pitiful and benign, patient, [and] of[354] great mercy, which dost extend Thy mercy unto thousands, which takest away wickedness, mischief,

349. **everlastinge glorie** Joye reads "glorye everlastinge."

350. **The . . . Amen** In Joye this sentence is separated and set off by a title: "Gloriosa Passio."

351. **Our Father** KP's closely followed source for the wording of the Lord's Prayer and for the 172 Biblical verses following is *The Fountayne or well of lyfe / out of whiche doth springe most swete consolations / right necessary for troubled consciences / to thentent that they shall nat despeyre in adversitie and trouble. Translated out of latyn into Englysshe* (London: T. Godfray, [1534?]) (STC 11211), sigs. Cii v–Dv v. Thomas Godfray was an English Lutheran printer and publisher. If not Godfray himself, the compiler and translaor of this series of verses is unknown. The section that so extensively serves here as KP's source is prefaced by this heading: "The Pater noster with other lytell prayers of the Byble / beyng gathered togyther into a compendyous ordre / in the commendation or prayse of the excedyng and incomparable mercy of god / and for the behofe of the deuout reder / that prayeth nat in waggynge of his lyppes / but with the feruent desyre of herte." Substantive variants are recorded in the notes. Square brackets enclose the marginal source references given for each versicle in Godfray's edition, which KP omits. Verse numbers have been added silently to chapter references, and erroneous source references corrected.

352. **for evermore** This version of the Lord's Prayer is also found in a later compilation, *Thys primer in Englyshe and Latine* (1538) (STC 16008.3), a religiously conservative text, where it is followed by the Ave Maria. Such crossover phenomena are frequent, documenting the transitional character of Catholic and Reformed devotion in the 1530s and 1540s.

353. **everlastingly** The Vulgate reads "ab aeterno in aeternum" (from everlasting age to everlasting age).

354. **[and] of** Godfray reads "and of."

and sin; and none of himself is innocent before Thee: I beseech Thee, that Thou wilt take away our wickedness and sin.[355] [Exodus 34:6–8]
I beseech Thee, Lord God of heaven, strong, mighty, and terrible, which keepest covenant and mercy with such as love Thee and observe Thy commandments: let Thine ears be hearkening, and Thy eyes open, that Thou mayest hear the prayer of Thy servant. [Nehemiah 1:5–6]
O Lord, which art patient, and of great mercy, and takest away our iniquity and mischief: forgive, I beseech Thee, the sin of this Thy people, after the greatness of Thy mercy.[356] [Numbers 14:18–19]
Lord God, do not destroy Thy people and Thine inheritance, which Thou hast bought through Thy power.[357] [Deuteronomy 9:26]
Thou hast been Guide, in Thy mercy, to the people which Thou hast redeemed. [Exodus 15:16]
Forgive Thou[358] Thy people, though they be sinners, for Thou art my God. Let Thine eyes, I beseech Thee, be open, and Thine ears intentive[359] unto the prayer that is made in this place. [2 Paralipomenon (2 Chronicles) 6:39–40]
O Lord, Thou art our Father, and we are but clay; Thou art our Creator, and all we but the work of Thine hands. O Lord, be not overmuch angry, and be no more mindful of our iniquity. Behold, have respect;[360] all we are Thy people. [Isaiah 64:8–9]
Lord, Thy mercy is everlasting; do not despise the work of Thine hands. [Psalm 137:8]
O Thou, Lord, which art our Father, our Redeemer: Thy name hath been evermore. [Isaiah 63:16]
For we not present our prayers before Thy face in justifying ourselves, but in trust of the[361] great mercy. Hearken, Lord, be pleased; O Lord, attend, and do. Be not slack, my God, for Thine own sake; for Thy name hath been called upon this city and upon the people. [Daniel 9:18–19]
Lord God, hear the clamor of this people, and open unto them Thy treasure: the well of the water of life.[362] [Numbers 20:5, 8, 11–12; Apocalypse (Revelation) 21:6]

355. **O . . . sin** KP reproduces Godfray's combination of excerpts from three verses, closely rendering the Vulgate.

356. **O . . . mercy** KP reproduces Godfray's splicing of the first halves of two verses, closely rendering the Vulgate.

357. **which . . . power** The Vulgate reads "quam redemisti in magnitudine tua" (which Thou hast redeeemed through Thy greatness).

358. **Thou** KP's addition.

359. **intentive** attentive.

360. **have respect** The Vulgate reads "respice" (regard, look upon [us]).

361. **we . . . the** **we . . . present** Godfray reads "we do not prostrate." **the** KP reproduces Godfray; the likelier reading is "Thy."

362. **Lord . . . life** KP reproduces Godfray's pastiche of Biblical phrases conjoining the cry of the Israelites to Moses and Aaron for water to drink in the desert; God's instructions to Moses

Let all that know Thy name, Lord, trust in Thee.[363] For Thou hast not forsaken them that seek Thee. [Psalm 9:11]
Thou, verily, which art a God merciful, meek, and pitiful, patient, and of high compassion,[364] hast not forsaken them. [Nehemiah 9:17]
Arise, Lord, help us; and redeem us, for Thy name's sake. [Psalm 43:26]
Do not remember our old iniquities, but let Thy mercy prevent us quickly; for we are made very poor. Help us, our Lord God;[365] and for the glory of Thy name, Lord, deliver us. And be merciful unto our sins, for Thy name's sake. [Psalm 78:8–9]
I shall do sacrifice unto Thee with good will,[366] and shall confess Thy name, for it is good. [Psalm 53:8]
Forasmuch, Lord, as Thou art sweet and gentle, and of plenteous mercy unto such as call upon Thee,
Lord, hear our prayers and our petitions, and deliver us out, for Thy sake.[367] [Psalm 85:5–6, 13]
Hear, O Lord, and have mercy, for Thou art a merciful God. And have mercy on us, for we have sinned against Thee. [Baruch 3:2]
We have sinned with our fathers; we have done unjustly. We have committed wickedness; Thou that art holy, have mercy on us. [Judith 7:19–20]
When Thou art angry, remember mercy. [Habbakuk 3:2]
Be not mindful of the wickedness of our fathers. But be in mind of Thy power and Thy name at this time, for Thou art our Lord God. [Baruch 3:5–6]
Let all be glad that trust in Thee. They shall rejoice evermore, and Thou shalt dwell in them, and all that love Thy name shall glory in Thee. [Psalm 5:12]
Thou art righteous, O Lord, and all Thy judgments are true,[368] and all Thy ways mercy, truth, and judgment. [Tobias 3:2]

---

to command water to come from a rock; Moses's impatient striking of the rock, which then flowed abundantly with water; and one of St. John's visions—God's promise to give drink freely to the thirsty from the fountain of the water of life.

363. **Let . . . Thee** Instead of the two imperatives in Godfray and KP, the sequence of verbs in the Vulgate has a future followed by a perfect indicative: "Et sperent in te qui noverunt nomen tuum" (They will trust in Thee, who have known Thy name).

364. **merciful . . . compassion** a partial variation on the series of God's attributes in the Vulgate: "propitius, clemens, et misericors, longanimis, et multae miserationis" (favorably inclined, mild, and merciful, long-suffering, and of great compassion).

365. **our . . . God** Godfray reads "our god." The Vulgate reads "Deus salutaris noster" (our God of salvation).

366. **with good will** The Vulgate reads "voluntarie" (of [my] own accord).

367. **hear . . . sake** **hear . . . petitions** The Vulgate reads "Auribus percipe Domine orationem meam: et intende voci deprecationis meae" (Receive my prayer, Lord, with Thy ears; and attend to the voice of my supplications). **deliver . . . sake** KP reproduces Godfray's free recasting of the Vulgate reading in verse 13, "eruisti animam meam ex inferno inferiori" (Thou hast delivered my soul from the lower depths of the earth).

368. **true** The Vulgate reads "justa" (righteous).

Blessed is Thy name, O God of our fathers, which in Thy wrath dost show mercy, and in time of trouble dost forgive sins to them that call on Thee. [Tobias 3:13]
All that serve and honor Thee be certain and sure that his life (if it have been tried and proved) shall receive the crown of victory;[369] and if it be in trouble, it shall be delivered; and if it be in corruption and sin, he may come unto Thy mercy. [Tobias 3:21]
For Thou art not delighted in destroying us; for, after tempest, Thou maketh all things quiet; and, after weeping and mourning, Thou causest gladness. Blessed be Thy name, therefore, O God of Israel, evermore. [Tobias 3:22–23]
God is at hand unto all that call on Him: to such[370] as call on Him in truth. [Psalm 144:18]
When I did call, [the God of][371] righteousness did hear me in my tribulation; Thou hast set me at large. [Psalm 4:2]
O Lord, let me not be confounded, for I have called on Thee. [Psalm 30:18]
I have called on the Lord out of tribulation; and the Lord hath heard me abroad. [Psalm 117:5]
In my tribulation I will call on the Lord, and I will cry unto my God; and He will hear my voice out of His holy temple, and my cry shall come unto His ears. [2 Kings (2 Samuel) 22:7]
Thy good Spirit shall bring me into a right ground; for Thy name's sake, Lord, Thou shalt make me alive in Thine equity. Thou shalt bring my soul out of trouble; and in Thy mercy Thou shalt destroy all mine enemies. [Psalm 142:11–12]
We will cry unto Thee in our tribulations, and Thou shalt hear us and make us safe. When we be ignorant what we ought to do, we have only this remedy: for to direct our eyes unto Thee.[372] [2 Paralipomenon (2 Chronicles) 20: 9, 12]
Give us help in our trouble, for the help of man is vanity.[373] [Psalm 107:12]
Lord, Thou art my refuge, my strength, my fortress[374] in the time of trouble. [Jeremiah 16:19]
I truly shall sing of Thy strength, and shall exalt Thy mercy betimes. For Thou art made my surety, and my succor in the time of my tribulation. O God, that art my

369. **(if . . . victory** The Vulgate reads "si in probatione fuerit, coronabitur" (if it has been put to the proof, it will be crowned with a crown).

370. **to such** The Vulgate repeats "omnibus" (to all).

371. **[the God of]** KP reproduces Godfray's nonsensical "thy good and." The reading in the Vulgate, "Deus justitiae" (God of righteousness), restores the sense. The Vulgate also shifts here from third-person to second-person reference.

372. **We . . . Thee** KP reproduces Godfray's conflation of the halves of two nonsequential verses in the Vulgate, which are quoted exactly.

373. **for . . . vanity** The Vulgate reads "quia vana salus hominis" (for vain is the deliverance of man).

374. **my refuge . . . fortress** The Vulgate sequences God's attributes as follows: "fortitudo mea, et robur meum, et refugium meum" (my strength, and my firmness, and my refuge).

Helper, I will sing unto Thee; Thou art my succor, my God; Thy mercy be unto me.[375] [Psalm 58:17–18]
So let Thy mercy be done, that it may comfort me, and[376] according unto Thy promise made to Thy servant.
Let Thy mercies come unto me, and I shall live; for Thy love[377] is my meditation. [Psalm 118:77]
Give us help out of our trouble; for the help of man is vain. Let us work virtue in God, and He shall bring unto naught all that trouble us.[378] [Psalm 107:12–13]
In the time of my trouble, I sought out God with my hands,[379] and I was not deceived. [Psalm 76:3]
I will look unto the Lord; I will tarry upon God, my Saviour. My God will hear me. [Micah 7:7]
Lord, have mercy on us; for we have looked after Thee. Be our defense betimes,[380] and our health in time of tribulation. [Isaiah 33:2]
No eye hath seen, O God, without Thee, the things that Thou hast prepared to such as look after Thee. [Isaiah 64:4]
I have remembered Thy mercy, Lord, and of Thy works that be everlasting; for Thou deliverest such as suffer Thee, and dost take the[m] out[381] of the hands of the people. [Ecclesiasticus 51:11–12]
For Thou art as a Defender unto the poor, a defense unto the needy in his trouble, a safeguard from wind,[382] a shadow from the heat. [Isaiah 25:4]
For there is none other God, either in heaven or in earth, that is able to do Th[y][383] works, and to be compared unto Thy strength. [Deuteronomy 3:24]

375. **my God . . . me** The Vulgate merely has two ascriptive phrases: "Deus meus misericordia mea" (my God, my mercy).

376. **and** KP's addition.

377. **love** KP follows Godfray in error; the Vulgate reads "lex" (law).

378. **for . . . us for . . . vain** The first half of this versicle repeats Psalm 107:12 and offers a better rendering of the Vulgate than the one in n373. **all . . . us** Vulgate: "inimicos nostros" (our enemies).

379. **with . . . hands** KP follows Godfray in truncating the Vulgate phrase evoking the search for God in nocturnal prayer: "manibus meis nocte contra eum" (with my hands [lifted] toward Him in the night).

380. **our . . . betimes** a literalizing of the Vulgate image, "brachium nostrum in mane" (our arm in the morning).

381. **such . . . out such . . . Thee** The Vulgate reads "sustinentes te" (those who uphold Thee). **suffer** This verb seems to be adapted from Latin "sufferre" (to uphold). **dost . . . out** The Vulgate reads "libera eos" (dost free them from). **the[m]** KP reproduces Godfray's mistaken reading, "the."

382. **Defender . . . wind Defender, defense** KP follows Godfray in reading variants of "defense" twice; the Vulgate reads "fortitudo" (strength) twice. **safeguard . . . wind** The Vulgate reads "spes ab turbine" (hope [of protection] from the whirlwind).

383. **Th[y]** KP reproduces Godfray's mistaken reading, "the." The Vulgate reads "tua" (Thy).

The Lord is made my strength and my praise; and He is a salvation unto me. [Exodus 15:2]
I do bless Thee, Lord God of Israel: for Thou hast chastised me; and Thou hast saved me. [Tobias 1:17]
Lord, I will confess unto Thee, because Thou hast been angry; Thy furor is turned, and Thou hast comforted me. Behold, God my Saviour, I will do boldly, and will not be afeared. For the Lord is my fortress,[384] and my praise; and He is a Saviour unto me. [Isaiah 12:1–2]
Lord, all that forsake Thee shall be confounded; they that depart from Thee shall be graven in the earth, because they have left Thee, Lord, the vein of waters of life. Heal me, Lord, and I shall be healed; save me, and then I shall be saved. [Jeremiah 17:13–14]
And let Thy mercy come upon me, Lord: the salvation according to Thy promise.[385] [Psalm 118:41]
Show unto us, Lord, thy mercy; and give us Thy safeguard.[386] [Psalm 84:8]
O Lord of all virtue, blessed is the man that trusteth in Thee. [Psalm 83:13]
Be mindful of Thy pity, O Lord; and of Thy mercy, which is everlasting.
Do not remember the defaults of my youth and mine ignorance.
According to Thy mercy, remember me, Thou, good Lord, of Thy goodness.
For Thy name's sake, Lord, forgive my sin; for it is much. [Psalm 24:6–7, 11]
Have mercy on me, O Lord, according to Thy great mercy; and according to the greatness of Thy pity, take away mine iniquity.
Turn away Thy face from mine offenses; and put away all my wickedness.
Create in me a pure heart, O God; and renew a right spirit within me.[387]
Do not cast me away from Thy face, and do not take from me Thine holy Spirit. [Psalm 50:2–3, 11–13]
O Lord, do not withdraw Thy compassion from me; Thy mercy and Thy truth have ever defended me. [Psalm 39:12]
In the abundance of Thy mercy, hear me; in truth of Thy salvation, hear me, Lord; for Thy mercy is much. After the plenteousness of Thy compassions, regard me; and do not turn away Thy face from Thy servant;[388] for I am troubled. Hear me hastily. [Psalm 68:14, 17–18]

384. **boldly . . . fortress boldly** The Vulgate reads "fiducialiter" (confidently). **fortress** The Vulgate reads "fortitudo" (strength).

385. **promise** The Vulgate reads "eloquium" (speech, utterance).

386. **safeguard** The Vulgate reads "salutare" (salvation).

387. **take away . . . me take away, put away** The Vulgate has two occurrences of "dele" (blot out, efface). **within me** The Vulgate reads "in visceribus meis" (in my inward parts).

388. **much . . . servant much** The Vulgate reads "benigna" (liberal, generous). **Thy servant** The Vulgate reads "puero tuo" (Thy son).

And Thou, Lord God, art piteous and merciful; patient, and of exceeding mercy, and true. [Psalm 85:15]
For I do know that Thou art a [God][389] gentle and merciful; patient and of much compassion; and not vengeable upon malice.[390] [Jonah 4:2]
Have mercy on me, Lord, for I am weak; heal me, Lord, for all my bones be troubled, and my soul is greatly troubled. But yet, O Lord, be converted, and deliver my soul; save me for Thy mercy's sake.[391] [Psalm 6:3–5]
And Thou, Lord, do with me for Thy name's sake; for Thy mercy is sweet. Deliver me, for I am poor and needy; and my heart is troubled within me.
Help me, Lord God; save me for[392] Thy great mercy. [Psalm 108:21–22, 26]
Deal with Thy servant according to Thy mercy, and teach me Thy justifications. [Psalm 118: 24]
Who will not fear Thee, Lord, and magnify Thy name? For Thou alone art holy. [Apocalypse (Revelation) 15:4]
Unto Thee, Lord, be justice; and unto us, shamefastness of face. Unto Thee, truly, our Lord God, be mercy and forgiveness.[393] [Daniel 9:7, 9]
Not unto us, Lord God, not unto us, but unto Thy name, give glory.[394] [Psalm 113:1 (in the second sequence of numbered verses in the Vulgate)]
Our help is in the name of the Lord, which hath created heaven and earth. [Psalm 123:8]
Thou art worthy, O Lord our God, to take glory and honor and virtue. For Thou hast created all things, and for Thy pleasure they were and be created. [Apocalypse (Revelation) 4:11]
O Lord God, the Creator of all things, terrible and strong, righteous and merciful: which only art good; only the excellent King; only just, almighty, and eternal; which delivered Israel from all evil. [2 Maccabees 1:24–25]
For he that was converted was not made whole by anything visible, but by the Saviour of all.

389. **[God]** KP's "good" is a penslip. Godfray reads "god"; the Vulgate reads "Deus."

390. **not . . . malice** The Vulgate reads "ignoscens super malitia" (forgiving of wickedness).

391. **be converted . . . sake** **be converted** The Vulgate reads "convertere" (turn back). **for . . . sake** Godfray reads "for thy great mercy"; the Vulgate reads "propter misericordiam tuam." KP's superior rendering seems accidental, for there is no evidence that she independently consulted the Vulgate, and (as this series of notes demonstrates) she reproduces Godfray's mistaken readings at several points.

392. **sweet . . . for** **sweet** The Vulgate reads "suavis" (pleasant). **for** The Vulgate reads "secundum" (according to).

393. **shamefastness . . . forgiveness** **shamefastness** ashamedness. The Vulgate reads "confusio" (consternation, embarrassment). **forgiveness** The Vulgate reads "propitiatio" (propitiation, atonement). God's justice elicits shame from sinners; God's mercy shields them from the punishment their sin deserves.

394. **Not . . . glory** The Psalmist imagines the song of the Israelites after they were delivered from captivity in Egypt.

Thereby, truly, Thou hast declared unto Thine enemies, that Thou art He which deliverest from all evil.
For neither herb nor plaster hath made him whole, but Thy work,[395] Lord, that healeth all things. [Wisdom of Solomon 16:7–8, 12]
Lo, Thou hast created heaven and earth in Thy great strength, and in Thy stretched-out arm. No word shall be difficile[396] unto Thee, for Thou doest mercy unto thousands. [Jeremiah 32:17]
Is there anything difficile unto God?[397] [Genesis 18:14]
Is the [hand][398] of the Lord feeble? [Numbers 11:23]
I know that Thou art able to do all things; and no thought is privy to Thee.[399] [Job 42:2]
It is in Thy power to do all things at Thy pleasure. [Wisdom of Solomon 12:18]
Thou art He, Lord, that hast power of life and death, and dost lead into the gates of death, and lead out. [Wisdom of Solomon 16:13]
For, and if I should walk in the midst of the shadow of death, I would fear no harm, because Thou art with me.
And Thy mercy shall follow me all the days of my life. [Psalm 22:4, 6]
Thou hast mercy on all, because Thou mayest do all; and pretendest to be ignorant of the sins of me[n],[400] because of repentance. For Thou lovest the things that be; and Thou hast not hated that, that Thou hast made; nor Thou hast not ordained or made anything with hate.
Thou dost spare all things, because they are Thine own, O Lord, that lovest souls. [Wisdom of Solomon 11:24–25, 27]
Because Thou art sweet, and good, Lord, Thy Spirit is in all things. [Wisdom of Solomon 12:1]
How great is the abundance of Thy sweetness, O Lord, which Thou hast hid[401] from them that fear Thee. [Psalm 30:20]

395. **plaster . . . work him** Godfray reads "them," rendering Vulgate "eos." **plaster** The Vulgate reads "malagma" (ointment or poultice). **work** KP reproduces Godfray's mistaken reading, "worke." The Vulgate reads "sermo" (word).

396. **difficile** an early modern variant form of "difficult," probably prompted by occurrences of Latin "difficile" (troublesome) in this and the next versicle in the Vulgate.

397. **Is . . . God?** God's own question, asked of Abraham, after Abraham's aged wife, Sarah, had laughed at God's promise to give them a son.

398. **the [hand]** KP reproduces Godfray's mistaken reading, "the ende." The Vulgate reads "manus" (the hand).

399. **no . . . Thee** KP reproduces Godfray's mistaken reading, which yields a sense contrary to the Vulgate's "nulla te latet cogitatio" (no thought lieth hidden from Thee).

400. **of me[n]** KP reproduces Godfray's mistaken reading, "of me," which may involve a letter dropped by the typesetter. The Vulgate reads "hominum" (of men).

401. **Thou . . . hid** KP reproduces Godfray's rendering of the difficult reading of the main Vulgate text, "abscondisti" (Thou hast hid); a textual variant reads "perfecisti" (Thou hast brought about [for]).

Thou, truly, which art our God, art sweet, true, and patient, and disposing all things in mercy.
For to know Thee is perfect justice; and to know Thy justice and virtue is the root of immortality. [Wisdom of Solomon 15:1, 3]
For there is none other God but Thou, which hast cure[402] of all things. [Wisdom of Solomon 12:13]
Lord God of Israel, there is no God like unto Thee, neither in heaven nor earth: which keepest covenant and mercy with Thy servants, going before Thee with all their heart. [2 Paralipomenon (2 Chronicles) 6:14]
What God is like unto Thee, that takest away wickedness, and carriest away the sin of such as are left to Th[y][403] inheritance? [Micah 7:18]
For Thy mercy is magnified unto the heavens, and Thy truth unto the clouds. [Psalm 56:11]
Spare, Lord, spare the people; and do not give Thy inheritance in reproof. [Joel 2:17]
Have mercy on me, O God; have mercy on me. For my soul trusteth in Thee, and I shall trust in the shadow of Thy wings until sickness[404] be passed. [Psalm 56:2]
Be Thou not dreadful unto me, my comfort[405] in the day of affliction. [Jeremiah 17:17]
Make marvelous Thy mercies, Lord: which dost save all that trust in Thee. [Psalm 16:7]
The Lord is my Helper and my Defender; and my heart hath trusted in Him; and I was helped. [Psalm 27:7]
Verily, the children of men shall trust in the covering of Thy wings. [Psalm 35:8]
In God is my comfort[406] and my glory; the God of my help, and my trust is in God. [Psalm 61:8]
Yea, and though He kill me, I will trust in Him. Nevertheless, I will reprove my ways in the sight of Him. [Job 13:16]
Lord, I have trusted in Thee; let me never be confounded. [Psalm 70:1]
For such as withdraw themselves from Thee shall perish. Thou hast destroyed all that fornicate from Thee.
Truly, for to cleave unto God is very good unto me, and to put my trust in the Lord God. [Psalm 72:27–28]
Preserve me, Lord, for I have trusted in Thee. I have said unto the Lord: Thou art my God; and Thou hast no need of my goodness.[407] [Psalm 15:1–2]

402. **cure** care. KP reproduces Godfray's borrowing of Latin "cura," the Vulgate reading here.

403. **Th[y]** KP reproduces Godfray's mistaken reading, "their." The Vulgate reads "tuae" (Thy).

404. **sickness** The Vulgate reads "iniquitas" (adversity).

405. **Thou . . . comfort** **Thou not** Godfray reads "nat thou." **comfort** The Vulgate reads "spes" (hope).

406. **comfort** The Vulgate reads "salutare" (salvation).

407. **of . . . goodness** KP's rendering is superior in sense to Godfray's "of my goods," a literal construal of the Vulgate's "bonorum meorum."

I will love the Lord, my defense; Lord, my fortress[408] and my refuge, and my Redeemer, my God. I will trust in Him, my Protector, and horn of my health, and my surety. [Psalm 17:1–3]
The Lord ruleth me; and I shall want nothing. [Psalm 22:1]
Lord, I have lift up my mind unto Thee; I do trust in Thee. Let me not be shamed. [Psalm 24:2]
For there is no confusion to them that trust in Thee. [Daniel 3:40]
The Lord God is my Helper, and therefore I was not rebuked. [Isaiah 50:7]
The Lord is my Helper; I will not fear what that man can do unto me.
The Lord is my Helper; and I shall despise mine enemies. [Psalm 117:6–7]
The Lord is made a refuge unto me; and my God is a comfort unto my hope.[409] [Psalm 62: 8–9]
Verily, I am poor and needy; help me, God. Truly, I am a beggar, and poor; and the Lord hath care of me. Thou art my Helper and my Defender; O my God, be not slow. [Psalms 69:6; 39:18]
Be unto me as a defending God; and as a house of succor, that Thou mayest make me safe. For Thou art my fortress[410] and my refuge; and, for Thy name's sake, Thou shalt bring me forth, and maintain me. [Psalm 30:3–4]
Thou, Lord, art my surety, my glory; and dost exalt my head. [Psalm 3:4]
Verily, I shall rejoice in the Lord; and shall be glad in God my Saviour, my God, my fortress; [Habbakuk 3:18–19]
My mercy and my refuge, my surety and my Redeemer. [Psalm 143: 2]
Thou hast remembered me, O God; and Thou hast not forsaken them that love Thee. [Daniel 14:37]
Lead me, Lord, in Thy way, and I will go in Thy truth; my heart may be glad for to dread Thy name. [Psalm 85:11]
They that love Thee shall shine,[411] like as doth the sun in his rising. [Judges 5:31]
For Thy mercy is above all life; my lips shall praise Thee. [Psalm 62:4]
Deliver me from clay, lest I stick in it; deliver me from them that hate me, and from the deepness of waters. [Psalm 68:15]
I have said: Lord, have mercy on me; heal my soul, for I have offended Thee. [Psalm 40:5]

408. **my defense . . . fortress** The Vulgate reads "fortitudo mea . . . firmamentum meum" (my strength . . . my support).

409. **The . . . hope** KP reproduces Godfray's paraphrase of excerpts from two Vulgate verses. The excerpts read: "Ipse Deus meus, . . . fortitudo mea et salus mea . . . Deus auxilii mei, et spes mea in Deo est" (He is my God, . . . my strength and my salvation . . . God of my help, and my hope is in God). **comfort** Again, Godfray's wording varies: this noun renders "spes" (hope) at one earlier point and "salutare" (salvation) at another: see nn405, 406.

410. **fortress** The Vulgate reads "fortitudo" (strength).

411. **They . . . shine** KP reproduces Godfray's substitution of a declarative for the Vulgate's subjunctive: "qui autem diligunt te . . . rutilant" (Let those that love Thee . . . shine).

I have said: I will knowledge my wickedness unto the Lord, against myself. And Thou hast forgiven the impiety of my sin. [Psalm 31:5]
Thou hast delivered my soul because it should not perish;[412] Thou hast cast behind Thy back all my sins. [Isaiah 38:17]
I have trusted in God; I will not fear what flesh[413] may do unto me. [Psalm 55:11]
I have trusted in Thee, Lord; I will be glad and joyful in Thy mercy. [Psalm 30:78]
Through Thee I shall be delivered from temptation; and through my God I will pass over the stone wall. [Psalm 17:30]
I am inferior to Thy manifold miserations, and to Thy truth that Thou hast accomplished unto Thy servants.[414] [Genesis 32:10]
Have mercy on us, O God of all creatures;[415] and behold us, and show unto us the light of Thy pity. [Ecclesiasticus 36:1]
O God, convert us; show Thy face, and we shall be saved.[416] [Psalm 84:5, 7]
Show unto us how Thou dost not forsake them that presume of Thee; and such as presume of themselves, glorying in their own virtue, Thou dost bring low. [Judith 6:15]
Remember, Lord: and show Thyself unto us in time of our tribulation. And give me comfort, O Lord, King of gods, and of universal power. [Esther 14:12]
In Th[y] manifold mercies, Thou hast not created them unto consumption; neither hast Thou forsaken them. For Thou art a God pitiful and merciful.[417] [2 Esdras 9:17, 19]
Lord, Thy mercies are manifold; according to Thy judgment, revive me. [Psalm 118:156]
Verily Thou art amongst us, Lord; and Thy holy name hath been called upon by us. Do not forsake us. [Jeremiah 14:9]

412. **because . . . perish** The Vulgate reads "ut non periret" (so that it would not perish).

413. **flesh** The Vulgate reads "homo" (man).

414. **I . . . servants** KP reproduces Godfray's overliteral rendering of the Vulgate's "minor sum cunctis miserationibus tuis, et veritate tua quam explevisti servo" (I am unworthy of the least of Thy mercies, and of Thy truth which Thou hast showed unto Thy servant). **servants** The noun is singular in the Vulgate verse—a prayer of Jacob in distress, pursued by his brother Esau.

415. **O . . . creatures** The Vulgate reads "Deus omnium" (O God of all [of us]).

416. **O . . . saved** KP reproduces Godfray's free rendering of the Vulgate's "Converte nos Deus . . . ; Ostende nobis . . . misericordiam tuam: et salutare tuum da nobis" (Turn us, God . . . ; show us . . . Thy mercy, and grant us Thy salvation).

417. **In . . . merciful In Th[y]** KP reproduces Godfray's mistaken reading, "In the." The Vulgate reads "tuorum" (in Thy). She also reproduces his reordering and recasting of a sequence of phrases: "Tu autem Deus . . . clemens, et misericors, . . . et multae miserationis non dereliquisti eos. . . . Tu autem in misericordiis tuis multis non dimisisti eos in deserto" (For Thou art a God . . . mild and merciful; . . . and in many pityings Thou hast not forsaken them. . . . For Thou, in Thy many mercies, hast not sent them away into the desert).

Have mercy on us, Lord; have mercy on us. For we are greatly fulfilled with despite.[418] [Psalm 122:3]
When my soul was vexed within me, Lord, I remembered that my prayer might come unto Thee, even unto Thy holy temple. [Jonah 2:8]
Troubles do oppress me on every part. But it is better for me to fall into the hands of the Lord (for His pity is great) than into the hands of men. [1 Paralipomenon (1 Chronicles) 21:13]
The Lord will do that, that seemeth good in His sight. [1 Paralipomenon (1 Chronicles) 19:13]
The sorrows of death have compassed me; and the perils of hell have found me out. I have found out tribulation and sorrow; and I will call upon the name of the Lord. O Lord, deliver my soul. Our merciful Lord and righteous God is pitiful. [Psalm 114:3–5]
Lord, all my desire is before Thee; and my mourning is not hid from Thee. [Psalm 37:10]
The mercy of Thy promise is great and unsearchable; for Thou art the highest Lord God over all the earth: long-suffering, and passing merciful, and sorry for the malice of men.[419] [Job 5:8–9; Psalm 96:9; Joel 2:13]
Thou art worthy, Lord, for to open the book, and to loose the seals of it; for Thou wast slain, and hast redeemed us, O God,[420] in Thy blood. [Apocalypse (Revelation) 5:9]
And Thou, Lord God, hast [dealt with][421] us, according to all Thy goodness, and according to all Thy great pity. [Baruch 2:27]
Thou art Christ, the Son of the living God.[422] [Matthew 16:16]
I have believed that Thou art Christ, the Son of the living God, which came into the world.[423] [John 6:69, 14]

418. **despite** contempt.

419. **The . . . men** KP reproduces Godfray's composite assemblage of three Vulgate passages: Job 5: 8–9, "ad Deum ponam eloquium meum: qui facit magna et inscrutabilia" (I will direct my utterance to the Lord, who doth great and unsearchable things); Psalm 96:9, "tu Dominus altissimus super omnem terram" (Thou art the highest Lord God above all the earth); Joel 2:13, "patiens et multae misericordiae et praestabilis super malitia" (long-suffering, and of much mercy, and sorry for the malice [of men]).

420. **O God** The Vulgate reads "Deo" (to God)—alluding to Christ's reconciliation of sinful humans to God.

421. **[dealt with]** KP miscopied Godfray; see n42 of the original-spelling version. The Vulgate verse reads "fecisti in nobis Domine Deus" (Thou, Lord God, hast dealt with us).

422. **Thou . . . God** Simon Peter's response to Jesus's question: "Whom say ye that I am?"

423. **I . . . world** KP reproduces Godfray's reordering and splicing of excerpts of two verses from the same chapter: one, Simon Peter's response on the disciples' behalf; the other, a response of those who had witnessed Jesus' miraculous feeding of the five thousand. The Vulgate reads "Et nos credidimus . . . quia tu es Christus Filius Dei"; "Hic est verò Propheta, qui ven-

For Thou art our God: Thou hast delivered us from our wickedness, and hast given health unto us. [1 Esdras 9:13]
God, be merciful to me, that am a sinner.[424] [Luke 18:13]
Father, I have offended against heaven and before thee. Now I am not worthy to be called thy son. Let me be as one of thy hired servants.[425] [Luke 15:18–19]
We are unprofitable servants; we have done but our duty.[426] [Luke 17:10]
Increase faith in us.[427] [Luke 17:5]
Have mercy on us, Son of David.[428] [Matthew 9:27; 20:30–31]
For in Thee is the well of life; and by Thy light we shall see light. [Psalm 35:10]
Like as a hart longeth after wells of water, so my soul longeth after Thee, O God. My soul hath thirsted after God, the living well.[429] When shall I come and appear before the face of the Lord? [Psalm 41:2–3]
My soul hath desired Thee in the night, but in my spirit and in my heart shall wake for Thee betime.[430] [Isaiah 26:9]
I bow the knees of my heart, praying unto Thy goodness, Lord. I have sinned, Lord, I have sinned; and I knowledge my wickedness. I ask praying Thee, Lord, to forgive me. Forgive me: do not destroy me altogether with my sins; do not reserve mine offenses forever. For Thou shalt save me, unworthy, according to Thy great mercy. I shall praise Thee ever, all the days of my life. For all the virtue of heaven praiseth Thee; and to Thee is all glory for evermore. Amen.[431] [2 Paralipomenon (2 Chronicles) 6:19, 21, 41, 37, 39, 14; 7:3]

---

turus est in mundum" (We have believed . . . that Thou art Christ, the Son of God; this is truly that Prophet who was to have come into the world).

424. **God . . . sinner** The prayer of the penitent publican, contrasted with that of the self-righteous Pharisee, in one of Jesus' parables.

425. **Father . . . servants** The prodigal son's appeal to his father upon returning home, in one of Jesus's parables.

426. **We . . . duty** Jesus warns His disciples what they will end up saying if they overestimate their lives of faith and service to Him.

427. **Increase . . . us** The disciples' appeal to Jesus.

428. **Have . . . David** The cry of two pairs of blind men, whose sight Jesus restored.

429. **God . . . well** KP reproduces Godfray's misreading of the Vulgate phrase "Deum fortem vivum" (strong, living God) as "Deum fontem vivum."

430. **betime** in good time, early.

431. **I bow . . . Amen** KP reproduces Godfray's composite of excerpted (or recast) and reordered phrases from King Solomon's prayer at the consecration of the Temple he built for the worship of God at Jerusalem. The prayer culminates in the descent of God's glory upon the Temple, whereupon the people fall on their knees and praise God. Key phrases include "Domine Deus meus, . . . audias preces, quas fundit famulus tuus coram te . . . et exaudias preces . . . populi tui Israel . . . laetentur in bonis. . . . Peccavimus, inique fecimus, iniuste egimus . . . propitiare peccato populi tui Israel . . . et facias iudicium, et dimittas populo tuo, quamvis peccatori. . . . Sacerdotes tui Domine Deus induantur salutem . . . qui custodis pactum et misericordiam cum servis tuis. . . . Sed et omnes filii Israel videbant . . . gloriam Domini super

O Lord, open Thou my lips;[432] and then shall my mouth show forth Thy praise.
O God, bend Thyself into my help; Lord, haste Thee to help me.
Glory be to the Father, to the Son, and to the Holy Ghost.
As it was in the beginning, as it is now, and ever shall be. So be it.[433]

A PRAYER IN TROUBLE[434]

Lord, hear my petition, and have compassion upon me; turn my sorrow into joy. Strip me once[435] of this grievance, and so clothe me with joy, to the end my tongue may blaze Thy name, and give praises unto Thee without stop. Ah, Lord my God, deliver me out of these straits, and to Thee I will sing praises everlastingly. Amen.

FOR THE LIGHTENING OF THE HOLY GHOST[436]

Hear me, when I cry in pain, for succor to Thee, O Christ, which art mine innocency;[437] and in adversity solace me with the joy of Thy Spirit. Infund[438] Thy grace, and grant me my petitions. Lift up over me the light of Thy countenance, O Lord,

---

domum: . . . adoraverunt, et laudaverunt Dominum: Quoniam bonus, quoniam in saeculum misericordia eius" (O Lord, my God, . . . hear the prayers which Thy servant poureth out before Thee. . . . And hear the prayers . . . of thy people, Israel . . . let them rejoice in goodness. . . . We have sinned; we have done wrong; we have dealt unjustly . . . be lenient toward the sin of Thy people Israel . . . and render judgment, and send Thy people forth, although they are sinners. . . . Let Thy priests, O Lord God, be clothed with salvation . . . Who keepest covenant and mercy unto Thy servants. . . . But when all the children of Israel saw . . . the glory of the Lord upon the house, they bowed themselves in worship, and praised the Lord, [saying] For He is good, for His mercy [endureth] for an age). This is the end of the section in Godfray that KP reproduces.

432. **O . . . lips** KP's exactly reproduced source is Psalm 51:15 (Psalm 50:17 in Vulgate numbering), functioning as an introit to Matins in three texts that read identically at this point: Marshall's *A goodly prymer*, sig. Ei r; his earlier *A Prymer in Englyshe*, sig. Liii v; and Gough's Latin-English *Primer*, sig. Eiii v.

433. **So . . . it** KP's handwriting becomes larger, fainter, and more loosely formed from this point onward through the end of the text (137r–141r). The illuminated capitals and the ornamental rectangles that fill out line ends also cease.

434. **A . . . trouble Ghost** KP's source for this and the four following prayers is *An Epitome of the Psalmes, or briefe meditacions upon the same, with diuerse other moste christian prayers*, trans. Richard Taverner (1539) (STC 2748). Significant variants are recorded in the notes. Taverner's original is a Latin work by Wolfgang Capito, an associate of Luther. The specific source for this prayer is the final three sentences of "In great tribulacions. Psalm 30," sig. Diii r.

435. **once** Taverner reads "out."

436. **For . . . Ghost** KP's source for this prayer is "For the lyghtenyng of the holy ghoste. Psalm 4," in Taverner, *Epitome*, sig. Avii r-v.

437. **in pain . . . innocency** **in pain** KP's addition. **mine innocency** Taverner reads "my righteousnes and innocency."

438. **Infund** KP's Latinate verb replaces Taverner's more ordinary locution, "Poure vpon me."

and Thy favor, that through Thy Spirit I may acknowledge Thee, and with It[439] be heartily cheerful for evermore.[440] Make, O Lord almighty, peace, firm hope, affiance in Thee,[441] evermore to endure. Amen.

IN ADVERSITY AND GRIEVOUS DISTRESS[442]

In this my tribulation, Lord, hear me; for Thy name's sake, help me, and send me succors from Thine holy place. Strengthen and comfort me, O Lord; be mindful[443] of my prayers and long awaiting, that I may do sacrifice unto Thee, and in my sacrifice-doing, rejoice. Or, rather, call to remembrance, Thou, my God, that self-sacrifice[444] which Jesus Christ, Thy well-beloved Son, made unto Thee, His most loving Father, for me, upon the cross; who prayed for me in the days of His life, and for His humility and reverence was heard. For His sake, I say, be merciful unto me, and help me. Out of Thy heavenly tower, grant that I, once anointed with Thy sudden and perpetual joy, may plenteously display abroad Thy most excellent name. Amen.

FOR STRENGTH OF MIND TO BEAR THE CROSS[445]

How hast Thou, O Lord, humbled and plucked me down? I dare now uneaths[446] make my prayers unto Thee. For Thou art angry with me, but not without my deserving. Certainly I have sinned, Lord; I confess it; I will not deny it. O my God, pardon my trespass; release my debts; render now again Thy grace[447] unto me. Stop my wounds, for I am all too plagued and beaten. Yet, Lord, this notwithstanding, I abide patiently, and give mine attendance upon Thee, continually waiting for relief at Thy hand. And that, not without skill, for I have received a token of Thy favor and grace towards me. I mean Thy word of promise concerning Christ, who for me

439. **acknoweledge . . . It** **acknowledge** Taverner reads "knoweledge." **It** Taverner reads "the same."

440. **for evermore** Taverner reads "for ever."

441. **Make . . . Thee** **Make** Taverner reads "Graue within me." **firm . . . Thee** Taverner reads "fast hope brennyng loue, and fayth vnfeyned."

442. **In . . . distresse** KP's closely followed source is Taverner's "In aduersitie and greuous distresse. Psalm 20," *Epitome*, sig. Ci r-v.

443. **be mindful** Taverner reads "mindful."

444. **self-sacrifice** "selfe same sacrifice" (Taverner).

445. **For . . . cross** KP's source is Taverner's "For strength of mynde to beare the crosse. Psalm 60," sig. Giiii r-v.

446. **uneaths** hardly, scarcely.

447. **O . . . grace** **O** Taverner reads "But oh." **trespass** Taverner reads "trespasses." **again . . . grace** Taverner reads "thy grace again."

was offered upon the cross, for a ransom, a sacrifice, and satisfaction[448] for my sins. Wherefore, according to that Thy promise, defend me, Lord, by Thy right hand, and give a gracious ear to my requests. Be Thou my stay in perils, for all human[449] stays are but vain. Beat down, therefore, mine enemies Thine own self, with Thy power, which art mine only Aider and Protector, O Lord God almighty. So be it.[450]

A PRAYER OF THE FAITHFUL IN ADVERSITY[451]

A PRAYER

All mine hope and whole affiance, most pitiful Lord, have I cast on Thee. Let me be no more, [I pray] Thee, shaken off, for [that] were sore to my rebuke [and] shame amongst [my] enemies. Deliver [and] succor me of Thy [justice] . . .[452]

448. **satisfaction** Again, KP substitutes a more elevated term; Taverner reads "penyworth."

449. **human** Taverner reads "mans."

450. **So . . . it** Taverner reads "Amen."

451. **A . . . adversity** KP's source for this fragmentary prayer is Taverner's "A prayer of the faythfull in aduersitye. Psalm 71," *Epitome*, sig. Hiiii r–Hv r.

452. **[justice]** Signaling the final descent of KP's personal prayerbook into silence, the text breaks off here at the bottom of 141 r; 141 v is blank. This is the last of the original vellum leaves in the binding.

APPENDIX 1

The Elton Hall Inscriptions Relating to Katherine Parr

At Elton Hall, Elton, near Peterborough, the seat of Sir William and Lady Proby, the library preserves a very fine hand-embellished copy of *Psalmes or Prayers taken out of holye scripture* (London: Thomas Berthelet, April 25, 1544). As argued above in my introduction to this text, this translation of Bishop John Fisher's *Psalmi seu Precationes ex variis scripturae locis collectae*, 1st ed. (Cologne, 1525), and 2nd ed. (London: Thomas Berthelet, 1544) (STC 2994), is convincingly ascribed to Queen Katherine Parr. The copy at Elton Hall was evidently Queen Katherine's gift to King Henry VIII, for he made a pair of reader's jottings in its margins and inscribed an affectionate rhymed message to her at the bottom of one of its pages.

Yet the interest of the Elton Hall copy of *Psalms or Prayers* does not end with its evidence that Katherine presented it to Henry and that he made the book his own by writing in it. After Henry died in late January 1547, the Elton Hall copy of *Psalms or Prayers* likely found its way into a library that was accessible to other members of the royal household—a possibility that is strongly suggested by an additional three inscriptions in Princess Elizabeth's hand.

Nor does the trail of historical interest end there. The Elton Hall *Psalms or Prayers* accrues further significance from its rebinding (in red plush covers) at a later date, together with a copy of another publication by the king's printer, also from spring 1544: Archbishop Thomas Cranmer's *An exhortation vnto prayer . . . to be read in euery church afore processyons. Also a letanie with suffrages to be said or song in the tyme of the said processyons* (London: Thomas Berthelet, May 27, 1544) (STC 10620). On the evidence of an inscription in the hand of Princess Mary, the Elton Hall copy of Cranmer's English *Litany* belonged to Queen Katherine Parr, whom Mary addresses.

A likely motive for the later binding together of these two copies—the one, of

Psalms or Prayers, the other, of *An Exhortation . . . Also a Litany*—is the shared association with Queen Katherine Parr made explicit in the inscriptions they contain. The Elton Hall inscriptions are, moreover, remarkable for their personal, even confidential character. This description applies equally to a separately written message in Henry VIII's hand that was pasted inside the back cover of the conjointly bound works. As a group, the Elton Hall inscriptions afford intimate insights into thoughts and concerns of Henry VIII and Princesses Mary and Elizabeth, the first ones probably entered shortly after the publication of both volumes in spring 1544, the last probably in or around spring 1549. It is fortunate as well as fortuitous that the two works underwent rebinding into one volume, for this enhanced the impact and the interest of the resulting series of inscriptions.

What follows here is a serial transcription, first of the inscriptions in the Elton Hall copy of *Psalms or Prayers*, then of the single one in the Elton Hall copy of *An Exhortation . . . Also a Litany*, and finally of the pasted-in inscription at the back of the conjointly bound volume. For each inscription, the context within the printed text is indicated where this appears relevant, and the wording is reproduced either in original and modern spellings or in Latin and in English translation.

HENRY VIII'S JOTTINGS AS A READER OF *PSALMS OR PRAYERS*

[In loosely formed letters, in the right margin of sig. A v recto, opposite the printed phrase "I haue not done penance"]

> trewe re pentens is the beste penence (True repentance is the best penance).

[In loosely formed letters in the right margin of sig. B iii recto, opposite the printed phrase "promysed forgevenes oftimes to them that do penance"]

> remember beste penence (Remember best penance).

HENRY VIII'S VERSE INSCRIPTION IN *PSALMS OR PRAYERS*

[Below a handcolored drawing of Henry VIII's coat of arms borne up by two rampant lions and censed by a pair of floating angels, on the verso of the title-page (A i), carefully lettered in the king's blocky inscriptional hand]

remember thys writghter wen yow doo praye for he ys yours noon can say naye	(Remember this writer When you do pray: For he is yours. None can say nay.)

Henry *[followed by his insignia of an H and an R (R for "Rex"), superimposed]*

This message, a blend of piety and a lover's profession of loyalty, must have been addressed to Queen Katherine Parr. The inscription was probably entered in 1544, shortly after the volume was published (and presented to the king as a gift), during the royal couple's first year of marriage.

PRINCESS ELIZABETH'S INSCRIPTIONS IN *PSALMS OR PRAYERS*

[Across the bottom of sig. Civ verso, in Elizabeth's fine italic hand]

Mors est ingressus quidam immortalis future, quae tamen est maximè horribilis carnè	(Death is a certain entry into becoming immortal, which nevertheless is exceedingly horrible to the flesh.
Catharina Regina R *[signature and insignia underscored* *with a linked horizontal series of loops]*	Katherine the Queen R[egina])

In this inscription Elizabeth adopts the persona of Queen Katherine to offer a comment without a perceptible connection to the adjacent printed text (where the subject is vehement self-castigation for sin and faithlessness). Elizabeth's subject may be the puerperal fever that took the dowager queen's life in early September 1548, days after she had given birth to her only child, a daughter, Mary. The intensity of the mixed thoughts ascribed to Queen Katherine demonstrates Elizabeth's poignantly imaginative identification with her stepmother, who served as a maternal substitute and role model during the princess's impressionable girlhood years.

Elizabeth's hand here resembles that of a letter in Latin for which she served Queen Katherine as a copyist or scribe. This letter, addressed to Princess Mary, is dated September 20, the year unspecified.[1] Since its contents concern Queen Katherine's commissioning of English translations of Erasmus's Latin Paraphrases on the four Gospels and Acts, the year is either 1545 or 1547—the two years of documented activity on this project. The likelier date is 1545.

[Across the bottom of the page opening formed by sigs. C viii verso–D i recto, beneath phrases in the printed text "O lord . . . Be mercifull unto me . . . whiche have none other healpe but the," in Elizabeth's fine italic hand:]

Debemus longissimè abesse a sententia eorum qui metiuntur felicitatem commodis huius uite. Salus optanda est non quam Mundus det sed quam Christe suis largitur.	(We ought to be very far removed from the opinion of those who measure happiness by the good things of this life. The salvation to be hoped for is not what the world may give, but what is bestowed upon His own by Christ.

1. For the text of this letter, see no. 9 in part 3 of the correspondence section.

Catherina Regina R *[signature and insignia underscored with a linked horizontal series of loops]*	Katherine the Queen R[egina])

In this inscription Elizabeth again adopts the persona of Queen Katherine, this time to offer a distillation of the devotional outlook and priorities expressed in the printed texts of *Psalms or Prayers* (1544) and *Prayers or Meditations* (1545). The generality of Elizabeth's comment gives no clue to the date of this inscription, unless it is to be read as continuous with the one that follows on the overleaf, and as providing a starkly dramatic contrast to it.

[At the bottom of sig. D i verso, immediately below phrasing in the printed text from the third Psalm, "Certaynly euen from my begynnynge I haue vsed my selfe proudely," in Elizabeth's fine italic hand:]

Vanitas vanitatum et summa vanitatis	(Vanity of vanities, and the height of vanity
T. Seymour *[followed by an insignia of a superimposed T and R, the* R *for "Rex"]*	T. Seymour [insignia])

In this inscription Elizabeth adopts the persona of Lord Thomas Seymour, younger brother of Lord Protector Edward Seymour and younger uncle of King Edward VI. Dowager Queen Katherine Parr secretly married Thomas Seymour sometime in the spring of 1547, a scant few months after Henry VIII's death. A deadly struggle for influence over the boy king poisoned the relationship between the two Seymour brothers. After the dowager queen's death in September 1548, Thomas Seymour intensified his plotting to replace the lord protector as the power behind the throne, not scrupling to endanger Princess Elizabeth by covertly probing his prospects of marriage with her.[2]

Thomas Seymour's machinations eventually brought upon himself arraignment on charges of treason. He was beheaded in March 1549. Elizabeth's inscription evidently alludes to Seymour's end. Speaking in his persona, she voices the self-reproach he expressed before his execution by way of a near quotation of Ecclesiastes 1:2 in the Vulgate wording. Hugely compounding the implications of negative judgment, Elizabeth endows Thomas Seymour with an insignia on the model of her father's, suggesting that he aspired illegitimately to the kingship that had been

2. See Janel Mueller with Carole Levin and Linda Shenk, "Elizabeth Tudor: Maidenhood in Crisis," in *Elizabeth I and the Sovereign Arts*, ed. Carole Levin, Donald Stump, and Linda Shenk (Tempe: Arizona Center for Medieval and Renaissance Studies, 2011).

Henry VIII's by right. She thus demonstrates a thorough lack of sympathy for Seymour and his fate.

PRINCESS MARY'S INSCRIPTION IN *AN EXHORTATION . . . ALSO A LITANY*

[At the end of A letanie, *across the bottom of the page opening formed by sigs. C iii verso–C iv recto, below the printed line "We beseche the O lorde to shew vpon vs thyne exceding great mercy," written in Mary's hybrid hand:]*

Madame I shall desyer your grace
moste humblye to accepte thys rude
hande and vnworthy whose harte
and seruyce vnfaynedly you shall be
sure of duryng my lyf contynually

Your most humble dowghter
and seruant
Marye

(Madame, I shall desire your grace
most humbly to accept this rude
hand and unworthy, whose heart
and service unfeignedly you shall be
sure of, during my life continually.

Your most humble daughter
and servant,
Mary)

This graceful message of deference, with its self-characterization as "daughter and servant," must have been addressed to Queen Katherine Parr close to the date of this volume's publication, when the queen had been married to Henry VIII for ten months. The inscription is significant in its expression of loyal affection bespeaking a prior association between Katherine and Mary that had its probable origins in their girlhoods (Maud Parr's longstanding position as lady-in-waiting to Queen Catherine of Aragon). The inscription is additionally significant in its implication that Princess Mary is writing in Queen Katherine's own copy of Cranmer's *Litany*—a custom among eminent court ladies of the day, as illustrated by the various inscriptions by associates and family members in Lady Jane Wriostheley's closely contemporary *Manuale Pretium*, including a signed inscription by Queen Katherine herself.[3] Mary's handwriting in this inscription is similar to hers in a 1544 letter that she and Queen Katherine Parr wrote in tandem to Anne Seymour, Edward Seymour's wife and a member of the queen's retinue.[4]

3. This volume, preserved as Bodleian, MS Laud Misc. 1, is a manuscript compilation containing signed inscriptions in the hands of Queen Katherine Parr, Mary Tudor, Margaret Douglas (Henry VIII's niece), and others. Lady Wriostheley was a member of Queen Katherine Parr's circle of ladies, receiving a handwritten letter of condolence from the queen on the death of a young son, probably in the summer of 1544. This letter is no. 3 in part 3 of the correspondence.

4. For the text of this conjoint letter, see no. 2 in part 3 of the correspondence.

HENRY VIII'S PERSONAL ENTREATY TO ONE OF HIS DAUGHTERS

[On a separate piece of paper about one inch square, pasted inside the back cover of the conjoint rebinding of Psalms or Prayers *and* An Exhortation . . . Also a Litany, *lettered in the king's blocky, here unusually diminutive hand]*

myne awne good daugther	(Mine own good daughter,
I pray yow remember me	I pray you, remember me
most hertely wen yow in	most heartily when you in
your prayers do pray for	your prayers do pray for
grace to be attayned assuredly	grace to be attained assuredly
to yor lovyng fader	to your loving father.
henry	Henry)
[followed by his insignia of an H and an R, for "Rex," superimposed]	

The original context of this message, which could have been written to Princess Mary (born 1514) or to Princess Elizabeth (born 1533), has been lost and can only be conjectured. Its theological resonances are likewise equivocal: does Henry refer to prayer for assurance of grace to be attained while he is still alive or by his soul after death? On balance, the king's traditionalist emphasis on prayer as a means for attaining assurance of grace (rather than the Lutheran emphasis on justification by faith as imputing saving grace to a believing soul, which he never accepted) suggests the greater probability that Henry wrote this message to Mary, perhaps during his terminal illness in late 1546–early 1547. The addition of this inscription as a paste-in at the back of the conjoint rebinding of the Elton Hall copies of *Psalms or Prayers* and *An Exhortation . . . Also a Litany*, fittingly accords the volume's last words to the king whose agency brought the Church of England into being and Katherine Parr into her queenship.

APPENDIX 2

The Inventory of Katherine Parr's Personal Effects[1]

[Headed] The inventory of all such jewels and other parcels found in a square coffer covered with fustian of Naples, within a great standard[2] belonging to the late Queen. The keys of which standard were sent by Sir John Thynne,[3] knight, the 16th of November, the third year of King Edward VI, to the Lord St. John,[4] lord great master of the King's household, and by his Lordship delivered to the hands of Sir Walter Mildmay,[5] knight, James Ruffworth, and Nicholas Bristol, with command-

1. Source: BL, Additional MS 46348, fols. 205–9. The interlineated commentary reproduced in a smaller font records what disposition (if any) was made of a given item or items belonging to KP. This inventory was compiled when the deceased KP's personal effects were confiscated by the crown and removed from Sudeley Castle subsequent to the attainder and execution of Thomas Seymour for treason in March 1549.

2. **fustian . . . standard** **fustian** cotton velvet. **standard** a large case or chest.

3. **Sir John Thynne** (1512/13–80) served first as steward, then as secretary to Edward Seymour between 1536 and 1552. He is also known for rebuilding and enlarging the magnificent manor house of Longleat, a former Carthusian monastery.

4. **Lord St. John** Sir William Paulet (1474/5?–1572) held many offices of trust under Henry VIII and subsequent Tudors, including master of the Court of Wards (1526), treasurer of the royal household (1537), great master of the royal household and lord president of the Privy Council (1545), and lord treasurer (1550). He was created Baron St. John in 1539, in a ceremony that also elevated KP's brother William to a barony; Earl of Wiltshire in 1539 after Thomas Boleyn, Anne's father, died without surviving issue; and Marquess of Winchester in 1551. Together with Thomas Wriostheley and Stephen Gardiner, Paulet exerted considerable influence on policy in the latter years of Henry VIII's reign, remaining a prominent figure in inner court circles during the reigns of Edward VI and Mary, and the initial years of Elizabeth's reign.

5. **Sir Walter Mildmay** (1520/21–89) became a leading financial expert at court in the mid- and later sixteenth century, gaining experience as clerk and auditor for the Court of Augmen-

ment to them to open the said standard and coffer, and to make perfect inventory of all such things as they found in the same. Which standard was found by them sealed with the seals of Sir John Thynne and John Bonham,[6] esquire, the parcels whereof hereafter ensue.

Parcel of the Queen's jewels and other stuff, which come from the late Admiral's house of Sudeley, in the county of Gloucestershire

In the uppermost room or place of the said coffer:

First, nine rings of gold set with nine diamonds of divers sizes, whereof seven are table[7] diamonds and two are lozenges.
One ring set with a fair table diamond was given by the King's majesty to the Scottish queen[8] at her being here, as appeareth by his Highness's warrant to the Lord Treasurer,[9] dated 24 March, the seventh year of King Edward VI.
One ring set with a long diamond cut full of squares was given to the lady Elizabeth, daughter of France,[10] ~~at the christening of the French queen's son,~~ as appeareth by the warrant to the Lord Treasurer, dated 24 March, the seventh year of King Edward VI.

Item: two rings of gold set with an emerald.
One emerald was delivered 20 November 1549 by commandment of the Council to Sir William Herbert as his own, being sent to the Queen[11] for a token, and not of the excise goods[12] of the Queen.

Item: five rings of gold, set with rubies, whereof three are tabletted, two rocks, and one pointed,[13] part of the pointed ring being broken.

---

tations (1545–47), which he was instrumental in reorganizing as a source of royal revenue and a mechanism for administering royal lands. Having overseen the massive inventory of Henry VIII's goods in September 1547, Mildmay was designated to receive the coffer and standard containing KP's personal effects so that it would be properly inventoried. Late in life, he founded Emmanuel College, Cambridge, with Elizabeth's permission (1584).

6. **James Ruffworth . . . Nicholas Bristol . . . John Bonham** lesser court functionaries about whom nothing further appears to be known.

7. **table** flat and smooth.

8. **Scottish queen** Mary of Guise, Dowager Queen of Scotland, mother of Mary, Queen of Scots, visited the English court in July 1551 (the fifth and not, as stated, the seventh year of Edward VI's reign).

9. **Lord Treasurer** Here and hereafter Sir William Paulet, under one of his several titles.

10. **Elizabeth . . . France** Elisabeth de France (1545–68), daughter of Henri II and Catherine de Médicis.

11. **Sir . . . Queen** **Sir William Herbert** KP's brother-in-law. **the Queen** Here, KP.

12. **excise goods** goods on which the payment of some toll or tax was levied.

13. **tabletted . . . pointed** reference to three kinds of finishing given to precious stones for use in jewelry: **tabletted** (cut flat and smooth), **rocks** (quarried but not cut further), **pointed** (cut in acute facets).

One table ruby delivered the said day and year by like commandment to the lord Marquess of Northampton[14] as his own, upon like cause.
Delivered to the Queen's highness[15] by warrant dated 20 August, six rings with table diamonds and one ring with a lozenge[16] diamond, one ring with an emerald, and five rings with rubies, whereof two table, two rock, and one pointed, part of the ring being broken.

Item: six little hoops of gold, whereof five are enameled and one plain.
Delivered to the Queen's highness by the said warrant of 20 August 1553.

Item: a little piece of a broken ring of gold.
Item: a pearl, being round.
These two parcels are discharged by the Queen's warrant dated 20 September 1553.

Item: two turquoises set in gold.
Item: a case covered with crimson velvet, garnished with silver and gilt, having in the same a whetstone tipped at the end with silver and gilt.
Delivered to the Queen by the said warrant, 20 August 1553.

Item: eleven buttons of gold, enameled black, whereof one is round.
Item: five buttons of gold, enameled blue.
Item: a clasp of gold, enameled, set with a little sapphire.
Item: a clasp of gold set with a little emerald and four very little pearls.
Item: six buttons of gold, made like Catherine wheels.[17]
Item: seventeen little buttons of gold garnished with small pearls, some lacking pearls.
Item: a brooch of gold, enameled black upon the border, with a table diamond, a table ruby, and a very small rock ruby.
Item: a purse of green silk, gold and silver.
All these parcels were delivered to the Queen's highness by the said warrant of the 20th day of August, 1553.

14. **Marquess of Northampton** KP's brother, William.

15. **Queen's highness** Here and hereafter Queen Mary Tudor, who acceded to the English throne on Edward VI's death in July 1553. A number of the records entered on this inventory indicate that Mary, upon becoming queen, issued warrants appropriating the residue of KP's personal effects. Delivery was evidently made in two lots, one in August and one in September 1553.

16. **lozenge** so-called diamond shape—composed of four equal lines or sides, with two acute and two obtuse angles.

17. **Catherine wheels** symbols of the martyrdom of St. Catherine of Alexandria, KP's name saint. See part 1, no. 1, n4, in the correspondence section.

Item: fifty-and-three pair and one odd aglets[18] of gold, enameled white.
Item: an agate[19] garnished with gold, with the nativity of Christ.
Item: a little tassel of crimson silk and gold, garnished with little blue stones and pearls.
Item: a book of gold, enameled black, garnished with eight-and-twenty small table rubies, and one rock ruby upon the clasp, and on each side of the book, a table diamond.

Item: a book of prayers, covered with purple velvet and garnished with gold.
Item: a little hamper, of wire silver.
These two parcels are discharged by the Queen's warrant dated 20 September 1553.

Item: a little box of silver and gilt, book-fashion, with diverse small garnishing pearls and beadstones of gold and two pearls pierre-fashion.[20]
Delivered to the Queen by the said warrant 20 August 1553.

Item: a book of Psalms covered with crimson velvet and garnished with gold.
Item: a little book covered with green velvet, with stories and letters finely cut.
Item: a muffler of black velvet garnished with twenty rubies, coarse, and fully furnished with pearls, with a small chain hanging at it, of gold and pearl.
Item: two dogs' collars of crimson velvet, embroidered with damask gold, tirettes[21] gilt silver.
Item: one habillement[22] of gold, enameled black, containing forty-one pieces.
Item: one other habillement of gold, containing thirty-nine pieces.
Item: one other habillement of gold, containing thirty-five pieces.
Item: one other habillement of gold, containing of thirty-four pieces.
Item: three broken pieces of gold, of an habillement.
Item: a pair of shears in a case of crimson velvet garnished with silver and gilt.
All these parcels delivered to the Queen's highness by the said warrant of 20 August 1553.

Item: a white ostrich feather.

Item: an old box with diverse coarse stones and pearls.
Item: a piece of an unicorn's horn.
Item: a box of silver and gilt, with two bundles of cramp rings,[23] white.
These three parcels delivered to the Queen by the said warrant of 20 August 1553.

18. **aglets** ornamental metal tags of laces to be strung through eyelet-holes in clothing.

19. **agate** a precious stone belonging to the chalcedony group, having colors disposed in parallel bands or blended in clouds.

20. **pierre-fashion** in a cluster. **pierre** alternatively, perrie—a borrowing of French "pierre" (stone).

21. **tirettes** rings on a dog's collar to which leashes were attached.

22. **habillement** array or set of jewelry.

23. **cramp rings** rings believed effective at this period in warding off cramps and other abdominal disorders.

Item: a purse of leather with eighteen pieces of silver, of sundry strange coins.
Item: twelve crowns, and ditto of the Rose.[24]
Item: three French crowns, whereof one broken.
Item: a guilder[25] of gold.
Item: four old halfpence of silver.
Item: eight little halfpence, and farthings of latten.[26]
Twenty-five pieces of silver, parcel of the within-written stores, are delivered to the Queen's highness 20 August 1553. And all the rest are delivered 20 September 1553.

Item: a little hamper of white silver wire, wherein is a pair of bracelets of gold enameled black.
Delivered to the Queen's highness by the said warrant of 20 August 1553.

Item: three hoops of gold.
Two hoops delivered to the Queen by the said warrant, and one delivered by warrant of 20 September 1553.

Item: four rings of gold, lacking stones.
Item: one ring with a turquoise.
Item: one ring with a sapphire.
Item: one ring with an amethyst.
Delivered to the Queen's highness by the said warrant of 20 August 1553.

Item: three rings with seals.
Item: two little hoop rings.
Two of these rings delivered to the Queen, and two hoop rings by the said warrant, and the third ring with a seal is discharged by warrant of 20 September 1553.

Item: a collet[27] of gold.
Item: one aglet or a piece of an habillement of gold.
Item: a purse of black silk and gold, wherein is two crowns of the Rose.
Item: four patterns for testoons[28] of silver.

24. **crowns . . . Rose crowns** various coins bearing the imprint of a crown. **Rose** the stamp of the Tudor rose, an emblem derived from the conjoining of the Lancastrian and the Yorkist roses ("the white and red") with the accession of the Tudor dynasty at the end of the Wars of the Roses (1485).

25. **guilder** a species of coin current in the Netherlands and parts of Germany.

26. **farthings . . . latten farthings** coins with the value of a quarter of a penny. **latten** a mixed metal of yellowish color, either identical with or closely resembling brass.

27. **collet** in general, an encompassing band or ring, collar; also the term for a setting for a precious stone in a piece of jewelry.

28. **testoons** alternatively, "testons"—a French term for various silver coins bearing a ruler's portrait. In England the term was applied to the shillings issued by Henry VIII and to early issues by Edward VI.

Item: sixteen pence, two farthings, and two halfpence.
Item: a ring of gold, with a pointed diamond.
All these parcels are discharged by warrant of the 20th of September 1553.

Item: a broken ring of gold, with a spark of a ruby.
Delivered to the Queen by warrant, 20 August 1553.

Item: a pair of twitchers[29] of silver.
Declared discharged by the Queen's warrant, 20 September 1553.

Item: a tablet of gold, on each side a table diamond.
Delivered to the Queen by the said warrant, 20 August 1553.

Item: ten pieces of broken silver, in a paper.
Discharged by the said warrant, 20 September 1553.

Item: a purse of cloth of gold, containing a ring of gold with a great stone graven.
Delivered to the Queen by the said warrant, 20 August 1553.

Item: a ring of gold, with a death's head.
Discharged by the said warrant, 20 September 1553.

Item: a very small chain of gold.
Item: two rings of gold, whereof one hath a small emerald and the other a small ruby.
Delivered to the Queen's highness by warrant, 20 August 1553.

Item: twelve cramp rings of gold.
Delivered to the Queen by the said warrant, 20 August 1553.

Item: two little hoops of gold, enameled black.
Item: two pieces of unicorn's horn.
Item: three little pieces of gold, in paper.
20 November 1549. One piece taken by the Earl of Arundel,[30] being at the opening of the chest and writing of these parcels.
Discharged by warrant, 20 September 1553.

In the second room or till in the said coffer:

Item: a girdle of gold, enameled blue and white, containing twenty-eight pieces, with a knop[31] of gold and little tassels of gold hanging, weighing 10 oz.

29. **twitchers** tweezers (for shaping eyebrows).

30. **Earl of Arundel** Henry Fitzalan (1511?–80), the twelfth earl, appointed lord chamberlain at the accession of Edward VI in 1547.

31. **knop** an ornamented stud or button (knob) used to fasten clothing.

Item: a girdle of gold, enameled, with a knop of gold and a tassel with small pearls and little garnets, weighing together 14 oz.
Item: a girdle of gold, enameled, with a broken knop, weighing together 12¼ oz.
These girdles are delivered to the Queen by the said warrant of 20 August 1553.

Item: a girdle of gold with Bowster knots,[32] with knops, weighing together 10¼ oz.
Item: a girdle of gold with wreaths without enamel, weighing 11¼ oz.
Discharged by warrant of 20 September 1553.

Item: a girdle of gold garnished with small diamonds and red stones, wanting some of them, poids[33] together 7¼ oz.
Item: a knop of a girdle with tassels of gold, weighing together 1¼ oz.
Item: a pair of beads of blue stones, garnished with gold and small pearls, with a tassel of Venice gold, poids together 10 oz.
Item: another pair of beads of blue stones, garnished with gold, weighing together 6¼ oz.
Item: one pair of beads of blue stones, with white stones like potes,[34] all garnished with gold, with a tassel of Venice gold, all weighing together 9¼ oz.
These five parcels are delivered to the Queen 20 August 1553, by warrant.

Item: a pair of beads of cameos[35] garnished with gold, with a tassel of Venice gold and silk, weighing together 9 oz.
Item: a pair of beads of pearl, contining forty-eight pearls and beadstones of gold, weighing together 5 oz.

In the third room or till in the said coffer, downwards:

Item: a remnant of crimson satin, containing 1 yard.
Item: a remnant of white satin, containing 1¾ yards.
Item: a remnant of purple velvet, single jean,[36] containing ditto yards.
Item: a broken remnant of purple velvet, containing by estimation ¼ of a yard.

32. **Bowster knots** perhaps "Bourchier's knots," a heraldic device consisting of two half-hitches tied in the same direction. Such knots were used as decorative motifs in jewelry of this period. There ia a possible further connection with Lady Anne Bourchier, William Parr's first wife; the girdle may have been a gift from her.

33. **poids** weight—a borrowing of French *poids* (weight).

34. **potes** rods.

35. **cameos** precious stones containing two layers of different colors, the lower layer serving as the backdrop or ground for the carving of a figure into the upper layer. Susan E. James (*Kateryn Parr: The Making of a Queen* [Aldershot, UK: Ashgate, 1999], 440n) suggests that this item may be the girdle of cameos worn by KP in the magnificent full-length portrait of her in the National Portrait Gallery, London (NPG 4451). The suggestion is compelling. James overturned the standing identification of this portrait in her revisionary article "Lady Jane Grey or Queen Kateryn Parr?" *Burlington Magazine* 138 (January 1996): 20–24.

36. **jean** a twilled cotton cloth; a kind of fustian; see n2 above.

Item: a remnant of taffeta, containing ¾ [of a yard], 3 nails.[37]
Item: a looking-glass garnished with two blue sapphires, two rock rubies, and twenty-six pearls great and small, and an agate with a cover, and a small pointed diamond in the top, weighing altogether 21 oz.
Item: a fan or a screen for to hold in the hand, of black ostrich feathers set in gold, garnished with six counterfeit stones and some pearls.
All these parcels are delivered to the Queen by the said warrant of 20 August 1553.

Item: a cap of black velvet garnished with a brooch of gold, having therein one table diamond, and twenty-one pair of aglets, and fourteen small buttons of gold.
Item: a cap of black velvet with a brooch, having a cameo in the same, and thirty-six pair of small aglets, and thirty-six small buttons of gold.
These two caps with their furniture were delivered to the Queen by the said warrant of 20 August 1553, except the two brooches, which are discharged by warrant of 20 September 1553.

Item: one cap of black velvet, garnished with twenty-two pair of aglets of gold, and eleven buttons of gold, enameled black.
Delivered the Queen by the said warrant of 20 August 1553.

Item: a cap of velvet garnished with twenty-two long buttons of gold, enameled white, and fourteen buttons of gold, enameled green and black.
Item: a cap of velvet garnished with forty-five buttons of gold, and small pearls, and forty-eight small buttons of gold.
Delivered to the Queen the 20th of August 1553 by the said warrant.

Item: a book of parchment written in Italian,[38] covered with blue.
Delivered by the said warrant of the 20th of September 1553.

Item: a New Testament in French,[39] covered with black velvet.
Delivered to the Queen the 20th of August 1553 by warrant.

Item: a Testament of Mr. Neville's,[40] under the Bishop's seal.

In the fourth room or till in the said coffer, downward:

37. **3 nails** 6¾ inches. A "nail" was the sixteenth part of a yard: 2¼ inches.

38. **book . . . Italian** a further piece of presumptive evidence that KP knew this language. Elizabeth's earliest surviving letter, written in Italian to KP, is no. 4 in part 3 of the correspondence section.

39. **in French** presumptive evidence that KP knew this language. James P. Carley (*The Books of King Henry VIII and His Wives* [London: British Library, 2004], 140) notes that KP owned a copy of Robert Estienne's *Les mots françois selon l'ordre des lettres, ainsi que les fault escrire* (Paris, 1544), inscribed with her name on the flyleaf. This book is now in the holdings of the British Library (shelfmark C.28.f.3).

40. **Testament . . . Neville's** KP's memento of her second husband, John Neville, Lord Latimer.

Item: a little square box of silver and gilt, with lozenges in it.
Item: a box of crimson satin embroidered with Venice and damask gold, having therein upon a vrouw's paste[41] forty-six round pearls.
Delivered to the Queen by the said warrant of 20 August 1553.

Item: twenty-eight crippins[42] of gold and silver.
Item: a book of the New Testament in English, covered with purple velvet, garnished with silver and gilt.[43]
Delivered to the Queen by the said warrant of 20 August 1553.

Item: a primer in English, convered with crimson velvet, garnished with silver and gilt.
Discharged by warrant of 20 September 1553.

Item: a New Testament in French, covered with purple velvet, garnished with silver and gilt.
Delivered to the Queen by the said warrant of 20 August 1553.

Item: a little book of prayers, covered with purple velvet, and garnished with gold.
Item: two books covered with black velvet.
Discharged by warrant of 20 September 1553.

Item: two books covered with blue velvet.

Item: two books covered with crimson velvet.
Item: a book covered with printed leather.
Delivered to the Queen 20 August 1553, per warrant.

In the fifth room of the said coffer:

Item: a little square coffer covered with needlework, having in the same two sables' skins with heads of gold, being a clock: in each eye, a rock ruby; about the collar, three small table rubies and three small table diamonds; with four feet of gold.
Delivered to the Queen by warrant of 20 August 1553.

Item: a little square box of gold and silver, with a pair of shears and diverse shreds of satin in the same.
Item: in a white paper, a little pearl of damask gold.
Discharged by warrant of 20 September 1553.

41. **vrouw's paste** **vrouw's** lady's—a borrowing of the Dutch for "lady." **paste** a hard vitreous composite material used to make imitations of precious stones for jewelry.

42. **crippins** alternatively "crespines"—decorative hairnets.

43. **a book . . . gilt** Carley has identified this New Testament as being formerly in the possession of Katherine Howard, KP's ill-fated predecessor as queen (*Books of King Henry VIII and His Wives*, 138). Carley also comments (141–42) on Mary's appropriation of KP's books upon becoming queen.

Item: a standish[44] of silver and parcel gilt.
Item: a looking-glass, covered with crimson velvet, and garnished with silver.
Delivered to the Queen by warrant, 20 August 1553.

Item: a pair of knives in a case of black silk.
Item: two books covered with leather.
Discharged by warrant, 20 September 1553.

Item: a written book of certain of the late Queen's apparel.
~~Delivered to the Queen by warrant, 20 August 1553~~.
Rem[inder].[45]

Item: a book containing jewels of the late Queen's.
Rem[inder].

Item: a little box, covered with crimson satin, having therein two clusters of grapes garnished with gold.
Discharged by warrant, 20 September 1553.

Memorandum: the 20th day of April, the fourth year of King Edward VI, the said coffer with all the parcels before written were, by commandment of the Earl of Wiltshire,[46] Lord High Treasurer of England, put and delivered into the King's secret jewel house in the Tower, under his lordship's keeping.

44. **standish** either an inkpot or inkwell or a stand holding pens, ink, and other materials for writing.

45. **Rem[inder]** Here and after the next entry, the manuscript has the enigmatic abbreviation "rem:" with a line drawn above the three letters. I conjecture that these are "reminders" to get information on the whereabouts of the two books, which were of clear further significance regarding KP's personal effects.

46. **Earl of Wiltshire** Sir William Paulet, by another of his several titles; see n4 above.

INDEX